RATTINER'S REVIEW FOR THE CFP® CERTIFICATION EXAMINATION

RATTINER'S REVIEW FOR THE CFP® CERTIFICATION EXAMINATION

FAST TRACK STUDY GUIDE

Jeffery H. Rattiner

WILEY

John Wiley & Sons, Inc.

Published by John Wiley & Sons, Inc., Hoboken, New Jersey.

Published simultaneously in Canada

For general information on our other products and services, or technical support, please contact our Customer Care Department within the United States at 800-762-2974, outside the United States at 317-572-3993 or fax 317-572-4002.

Wiley also publishes its books in a variety of electronic formats. Some content that appears in print may not be available in electronic books.

For more information about Wiley products, visit our Web site at *www.wiley.com*.

Library of Congress Cataloging-in-Publication Data:

Rattiner, Jeffrey H., 1960-
    Rattiner's review for the CFP certification examination : fast track
study guide / Jeffrey H. Rattiner.
        p. cm.
Includes bibliographical references and index.
    ISBN 0-471-27265-5 (pbk.)
    1.   Certified Financial Planner Examination—United States—Study
guides. 2.   Financial planners—United States—Examinations—Study
guides. I. Title: CFP certification examination. II. Title: Review for
the CFP certification examination. III. Title: Fast track study guide.
IV. Title.
    HG179.5.R38 2003
    332.024—dc21

                                                2003001695

Printed in the United States of America

10 9 8 7 6 5 4 3 2 1

CONTENTS

DEDICATION

This book is dedicated to the many aspiring CFP® Certificants who wish to achieve the highest level of success within our industry—the right to hold the marks and practice as a CERTIFIED FINANCIAL PLANNER™ (CFP®) Certificant.

PREFACE

As the originator of the Metropolitan State College of Denver Financial Planning Fast Track (FPFT) program that satisfies the Certified Financial Planner (CFP) Board's educational requirements to sit for the CFP® Certification Examination, and instructing students through all parts of FPFT for the last 14 years at the Metropolitan State College of Denver, New York University, and the College for Financial Planning, I have been actively looking for a short-and-sweet set of reference materials that can be used as a guide to bridge the gap between the many financial planning textbooks in the marketplace and the CFP Board's 101 topic curriculum, something that would tie into the contents of the exam itself. Many financial planning textbooks do a fine job of teaching the subject matter, but few do an adequate job of tying specifically to the CFP Board's master list for examination inclusion. We saw this unfulfilled need as an opportunity to satisfy the missing piece of the puzzle and thus entered the journey to formalize the process to benefit students wishing to sit for the CFP® Certification Examination.

When John Wiley & Sons approached me about making inroads into the CFP® educational marketplace, in much the same manner as this publisher has been dominating the CPA Examination Review marketplace for the last 30 years, I mentioned the need to have a guide in place to tie the many financial planning texts to the CFP Board's educational curriculum. My aim was to ensure that students were being exposed to the many facets of the CFP Board's development of the financial planning curriculum as defined through its Job Analysis. The Job Analysis is a listing of the specific duties and responsibilities CFP® Certificants encounter in practice, and as such, the CFP Board incorporates these tasks and responsibilities into its examination.

This book is a synopsis of my notes from FPFT. These notes are part of my classroom educational process, in addition to the Keir Educational Resources and American College books we use to supplement our program.

HOW THE GUIDE IS ORGANIZED

This guide is organized according to the six categories of financial planning tested as determined by the CFP Board, in topic order (from Topic 1 to Topic 101). All 101 CFP Board topics are covered individually. You can expect to see the following percentages of each category represented on the CFP® Certification Examination.

Financial Planning	13%
Insurance Planning and Risk Management	10%
Employee Benefit Planning	8%
Investment Planning	19%
Income Tax Planning	17%
Retirement Planning	18%
Estate Planning	15%

ABOUT THE CFP® Certification Examination

The CFP® Certification Examination is offered on the third Friday and Saturday of November, March, and July at various sites across the country. The Friday afternoon session is four hours, and on Saturday a morning and afternoon session are three hours each. This 10-hour exam consists of approximately 285 multiple-choice questions in total, including mainly stand-alone multiple-choice items and three comprehensive case studies given during each session of the examination. Each case study tests a variety of topics and contains 12 to 20 multiple-choice questions. The stand-alone multiple-choice questions are worth two points each, and the case study multiple-choice questions are worth three points each, with no partial credit allowed. Each multiple-choice question is designed to test a single area; however, the questions can integrate more than one topic. For example, life insurance and taxation or investments in retirement plans can be integrated into a single question.

With 10 hours (or 600 minutes) and approximately 285 multiple-choice questions, the student should be ready for an average question response of about two minutes. However, you may want to pace yourself with 1.5 minutes per question and provide ample time to review open items and transfer your answers.

Pass rates have ranged from as low as 42 percent to as high as 66 percent. Generally, pass rates are somewhere in the 50 percent range. You cannot pass the exam in sections—this is an all-or-nothing proposition.

The CFP® Certification Examination, although difficult, is a passable exam. Even though a little more than half of all test-takers pass, it is certainly achievable. The key issue is not to study as if knowledge of the topics is too difficult, but, rather, to approach the test from a sheer volume perspective. Six major areas encompassing 101 topics is quite a bit of information for anyone to master. Therefore, the only proven way to study for this exam is to understand this concept up front and pace yourself for a long journey. Be prepared to spend whatever time is necessary to ensure success. There is nothing better than developing a comprehensive study plan and following that plan through the duration of your studies.

HOW TO USE THIS GUIDE

The purpose of this guide is to supplement all the existing financial planning texts that instructors, students, educators, and practitioners use as part of the local college or university CFP Board registered educational program. It should be purchased at the very beginning of the program and used as the singular reference guide during each of the remaining classes.

You should develop your own spreadsheet to accompany this guide as a study reference. Organize it per line as follows:

- CFP Board Topic No.
- Identify the topic
- Identify the exposure or risk to the client
- Identify solutions to address the exposure

Use this format for all 101 topics. When writing your synopsis, follow each topic number with a one- or two-sentence description. If you can summarize each of the 101 topics in this clear and concise format, then you truly do understand the topic and you are well on your way to being prepared and successful when taking the CFP® Certification Examination. After you have reviewed each topic with the instructor during class, then proceed to complete this spreadsheet for all your classes.

ABOUT THE METROPOLITAN STATE COLLEGE OF DENVER FINANCIAL PLANNING FAST TRACK (FPFT) PROGRAM

The Metropolitan State Financial Planning Fast Track (FPFT) program is an intensive six-part educational program that covers the required 101 topics tested by the CFP Board on the CFP® Certification Examination. FPFT offers five consecutive four-day sessions every six weeks. Sessions begin Thursday and end on Sunday. Testing is performed daily, and group study assignments are given in the evenings. The sixth class is a five-day comprehensive review of all 101 topics just prior to the exam. FPFT is designed to take a comprehensive and focused approach to the subject of financial planning so that you can gain the knowledge you need to pass the exam and to succeed in practice.

How Do You Satisfy the Educational Requirement Offered through FPFT?

To satisfy this requirement, you must attend FPFT sessions 1 through 5. Classroom attendance is mandatory for each and every session. If you cannot attend a session, you must satisfy the classroom requirements by either attending a later training session in Denver or completing the session through one of the CFP Board's other Registered Programs at your own cost.

To satisfy the education requirement, you must successfully pass each class with a grade of 70 percent or better. If you fail any one class, you must make up that class, in its entirety, to receive credit. Once all classes have been successfully completed, you will then receive a certificate of completion from the Metropolitan State College of Denver.

Are There Other Requirements for Becoming a CFP® Certificant?

Yes. Besides successfully completing an educational program at a CFP Board Registered Program, you must also satisfy three other requirements:

1. *Examination.* Successfully complete the two-day exam.

2. *Experience.* Demonstrate three to five years of work experience.

3. *Ethics.* Sign ethics documents provided by the CFP Board.

If you want further detail on becoming a CFP® Certificant, contact the CFP Board at (800) 487-1497 or *initialcert@CFP-Board.org*, or visit the CFP Board Web site at *www.CFP-Board.org*.

What Has Been Our Pass Rate?

We are pleased that our pass rate has been consistently above the national average. Visit our Web site *(www.financialplanningfasttrack.com)* for more information.

Who Should Sit for This Program?

Only serious applicants need apply. This rigorous program is designed to condense two years of training into approximately seven months (including a review class). Sufficient prep time is necessary to ensure success. For additional information about FPFT, call (720) 529-1888, e-mail me at *jeff@jrfinancialgroup.com*, or visit our Web site at *www.financialplanningfasttrack.com*.

ACKNOWLEDGMENTS

I am extremely grateful for the extraordinary staff that works with me at JR Financial Group, Inc., in Englewood, Colorado, and Scottsdale, Arizona. In particular, Richard Yasenchak, Director of Investments, was the guiding force behind this project and set the tone for what needed to be included and the degree of information that should be covered. He has spent countless hours ensuring that the materials included in this manuscript are first-rate and that they cover each topic thoroughly. I thank Jake Koebrich, Director of Financial Planning, who provided his expertise and guidance to make sure that the materials also had a real-world approach and that they tied into academia and the model established by the CFP Board, and Rochele Rattiner, Office Manager, who oversees the administrative side of the Financial Planning Fast Track program and makes sure that things are done in a timely manner. Finally, I wish to thank my children, Brandon, Keri, and Matthew, for putting up with me through yet another authored book.

I am grateful to Louis Garday, CEO of the CFP Board, who has taken time from his demanding schedule to address the students in many of the Fast Track classes held in Denver, as well as to Katherine K. Ioannides, Director of Education and Examinations, and Cynthia Coyle, Coordinator of Registered Programs, who have been integral in the development and monitoring of the Metropolitan State College of Denver Financial Planning Fast Track program and have shared in the success. I would also like to acknowledge Dr. Kenneth Huggins, CFP®, chairman of the finance department of the Metropolitan State College of Denver, and Maria Carillo, Financial Planning Coordinator, for their undying belief in the Fast Track format as an alternative educational approach for those students for whom the traditional educational distribution system does not work.

Finally, I am grateful for the many great instructors we are lucky enough to have nationwide, including, but not limited to, Gregory Fong, John Phillips, Gary Sidder, and others, who participate in teaching the FPFT program.

JEFFREY H. RATTINER
CPA, CFP®, MBA, RFC

January 10, 2003

Chapter 1

GENERAL PRINCIPLES OF FINANCIAL PLANNING

TOPIC 1: THE FINANCIAL PLANNING PROCESS

1. Purpose, benefits, and components

   A. The purpose of financial planning is to provide sound, coordinated financial advice to individuals and their families.

   B. The benefits of financial planning include a coordinated approach to the multiple facets of the daily and lifetime financial needs of clients who are too busy to learn what they need to know. Further, clients benefit from having one person in their corner who can work with the various experts required to put together a comprehensive financial plan and who can help them understand the language of those experts.

   C. Financial planning consists of five major components: insurance, investments, income tax planning, retirement planning, and estate planning.

2. Steps

   A. Establishing client-planner relationships sets the expectations of the parties and lays the groundwork for developing the trust required for successful financial planning.

      (1) Identifying the service(s) to be provided

      (2) Disclosing the financial planning practitioner's compensation arrangement(s)

      (3) Determining the client's and the financial planning practitioner's responsibilities

      (4) Establishing the duration of the engagement

      (5) Providing any additional information necessary to define or limit the scope of the process

   B. Gathering client data and determining goals and expectations. A financial plan is only as good as the data collected and assumptions on which the data is based. Quantitative and qualitative data is used to establish a client's goals and objectives.

      (1) Quantitative versus qualitative

         (a) *Quantitative* data tells you where the client is and what it will take to get the client to a specific financial goal. Quantitative data is found using a *fact-finding questionnaire*.

         (b) *Qualitative* data tells you why the client wants to reach the goal, what will make him or her work toward it, and what the client is not likely to do. Qualitative data is obtained by conducting a *goals and objectives interview*.

      (2) Goals versus objectives

         (a) *Goals* are broad-based projections of a client's aspirations. *Example*: A client's goal may be to retire rich.

         (b) *Objectives* are quantifiable ways of achieving goals over a specified time period. *Example*: Saving $5 million by age 65 is an objective, whereas retiring rich is the goal.

   C. Determining the client's financial status by analyzing and evaluating general financial status, special needs, insurance and risk management, investments, taxation, employee benefits, retirement, and/or estate planning

      (1) Identify strengths and weaknesses of client.

      (2) Revise goals if necessary.

   D. Developing and presenting the financial plan

      (1) Design strategies tailored to the client's objectives and goals.

      (2) Seek approval from the client.

E. Implementing the financial plan

(1) Motivate the client.
(2) Draw on outside experts as needed.

F. Monitoring the financial plan

(1) Evaluate the performance.
(2) Review changes in client's circumstances and tax laws.
(3) Revisit other steps as necessary.

3. Responsibilities

A. Financial planner, client, other advisers

(1) *Financial planner.* Evaluate client needs, explain financial planning concepts and clarify client goals, analyze client circumstances and prepare financial plans, and implement and monitor financial plans.
(2) *Client.* Express concerns, hopes, and goals; do not procrastinate; be honest with your answers to questions; live within your current income and do not live up to or beyond it; be open to formulating a financial plan and identifying strategies to reach goals and objectives.
(3) *Other advisers.* The planner may seek out the help of others when implementing the financial plan. Their responsibilities fall within the realm of their expertise.

TOPIC 2: CFP BOARD'S CODE OF ETHICS AND PROFESSIONAL RESPONSIBILITY AND DISCIPLINARY RULES AND PROCEDURES

The following contains wording from both the *Code of Ethics and Professional Responsibility* and *Disciplinary Rules and Procedures* (© 2002 by Certified Financial Planner Board of Standards, Inc.). It is strongly suggested by this author that all candidates for the CFP® examination read their own copies of the original *Code of Ethics and Professional Responsibility* and *Disciplinary Rules and Procedures*. These materials can be obtained from the CFP Board's Web site.

1. Code of ethics and professional responsibility

A. Preamble and applicability

(1) The *Code of Ethics and Professional Responsibility (Code of Ethics)* has been adopted by the Certified Financial Planner Board of Standards, Inc. (CFP Board) to provide principles and rules to all persons whom it has recognized and certified to use the CFP certification mark and the marks CFP® and CERTIFIED FINANCIAL PLANNER™.
(2) This *Code of Ethics* also applies to candidates for the CFP® certification who are registered as such with CFP Board.

B. Composition and scope

(1) The *Code of Ethics* consists of two parts: Part I, "Principles," and Part II, "Rules."

(a) The Principles are statements expressing in general terms the ethical and professional ideals that CFP Board designees are expected to display in their professional activities. As such, the Principles are intended to provide a source of guidance for CFP Board designees.
(b) The Rules describe the standards of ethical and professionally responsible conduct expected of CFP Board designees in particular situations.

(2) Because of the nature of a CFP Board designee's particular field of endeavor, certain Rules may not be applicable to that CFP Board designee's activities.

C. Compliance—The CFP Board requires adherence to this *Code of Ethics* by all CFP Board designees.

D. Terminology

(1) *Client* denotes a person, persons, or entity who engages a practitioner and for whom professional services are rendered.

(2) *CFP Board designee* denotes current certificants, candidates for certification, and individuals who have any entitlement, direct or indirect, to the CFP certification marks.

(3) *Commission* denotes the compensation received by an agent or broker when the same is calculated as a percentage on the amount of his or her sales or purchase transactions.

(4) Compensation is any economic benefit a CFP Board designee or related party receives from performing his or her professional duties.

(5) Conflicts of interest exist when a CFP Board designee's financial, business, property, and/or personal interests, relationships, or circumstances reasonably may impair his or her ability to offer objective advice, recommendations, or services.

(6) *Fee-only* denotes a method of compensation in which compensation is received solely from a client with neither the personal financial planning practitioner nor any related party receiving compensation that is contingent upon the purchase or sale of any financial product.

(7) Financial planning engagement exists when a client, based on the relevant facts and circumstances, reasonably relies upon information or services provided by a CFP Board designee using the financial planning process.

(8) *Personal financial planning* or *financial planning* denotes the process of determining whether and how an individual can meet his or her life goals through the proper management of financial resources.

(9) *Personal financial planning process* or *financial planning process* denotes a process that typically includes, but is not limited to, these six elements: establishing and defining the client-planner relationship; gathering client data, including goals; analyzing and evaluating the client's financial status; developing and presenting financial planning recommendations and/or alternatives; implementing the financial planning recommendations; and monitoring the financial planning recommendations.

(10) *Personal financial planning subject areas* or *financial planning subject areas* denotes the basic subject fields covered in the financial planning process, which typically include, but are not limited to, financial statement preparation and analysis (including cash flow analysis/planning and budgeting), investment planning (including portfolio design, i.e., asset allocation and portfolio management), income tax planning, education planning, risk management, retirement planning, and estate planning.

(11) *Personal financial planning professional* or *financial planning professional* denotes a person who is capable and qualified to offer objective, integrated, and comprehensive financial advice to or for the benefit of individuals to help them achieve their financial objectives.

E. *Principles—Part I.* The *Code of Ethics* Principles apply to all CFP Board designees and provide guidance to them in the performance of their professional services.

> *Principle 1   Integrity*
> *Principle 2   Objectivity*
> *Principle 3   Competence*
> *Principle 4   Fairness*
> *Principle 5   Confidentiality*
> *Principle 6   Professionalism*
> *Principle 7   Diligence*

F. *Rules—Part II.* As stated in Part I, the Principles apply to all CFP Board designees. However, certain rules may not be applicable to a CFP Board designee's activities. The universe of activities engaged in by a CFP Board designee is indeed diverse. When considering the Rules, a CFP Board designee must first recognize the specific services he or she is rendering and then determine whether a specific Rule is applicable to those services. The *Code of Ethics* includes definitions to help a CFP Board designee determine which services he or she provides and which Rules are applicable to those services.

(1) Rules that relate to the Principle of Integrity

    (a) *Rule 101.* Do not solicit clients through false or misleading communications or advertisements.

    (b) *Rule 102.* Do not engage in conduct involving dishonesty, fraud, deceit, or misrepresentation.

    (c) *Rule 103.* This rule lists the specific responsibilities a Board designee has to his or her clients.

        i. Act in accordance with the authority set forth in the governing legal instrument (e.g., special power of attorney, trust, letters testamentary, etc.).

        ii. Identify and keep complete records of all funds or other property of a client.

        iii. Deliver any funds or other property that the client or third party is entitled to receive, and render a full accounting regarding such funds or other property.

        iv. Do not commingle client funds or other property with the CFP Board designee's personal funds or property. Two or more clients' funds or other property may be commingled, subject to compliance with applicable legal requirements and maintenance of accurate records.

        v. Show the care required of a fiduciary.

(2) Rules that relate to the Principle of Objectivity

    (a) *Rule 201.* Exercise reasonable and prudent professional judgment.

    (b) *Rule 202.* Act in the interest of the client.

(3) Rules that relate to the Principle of Competence

    (a) *Rule 301.* Keep informed of developments in the field of financial planning and participate in continuing education.

    (b) *Rule 302.* Offer advice only in those areas in which the CFP Board designee has competence. In areas where the CFP Board designee is not professionally competent, the CFP Board designee shall seek the counsel of qualified individuals and/or refer clients to such parties.

(4) Rules that relate to the Principle of Fairness

    (a) *Rule 401.* Disclose to the client:

        i. Material information, such as conflict(s) of interest(s), changes in business affiliation, address, telephone number, credentials, qualifications, licenses, compensation structure, and any agency relationships

        ii. The information required by all laws applicable to the relationship in a manner complying with such laws

    (b) *Rule 402.* A financial planning practitioner shall make timely written disclosure of all material information relative to the professional relationship. In all circumstances such disclosure shall include conflict(s) of interest(s) and sources of compensation. Written disclosures that include the following information are considered to be in compliance with this rule:

> i. The basic philosophy of the CFP Board designee (or firm) in working with clients
> ii. Resumes of individuals who are expected to provide financial planning services to the client and a description of those services
> iii. Source of compensation and referral fees
> iv. A statement indicating whether the CFP Board designee's compensation arrangements involve fee only, commission only, or fee and commission. A CFP Board designee cannot hold out as a fee-only financial planning practitioner if he or she receives commissions or other forms of economic benefit from related parties.
> v. Any material agency or employment relationships with third parties and the fees or commissions resulting from such relationships
> vi. A statement identifying conflict(s) of interest(s)

(c) *Rule 403.* Disclose in writing, prior to establishing a client relationship, relationships that may reasonably compromise the CFP Board designee's objectivity or independence.

(d) *Rule 404.* Should conflict(s) of interest(s) develop after a professional relationship has been commenced, but before the services contemplated by that relationship have been completed, a CFP Board designee shall promptly disclose the conflict(s) of interest(s) to the client or other necessary persons.

(e) *Rule 405.* Disclosure of compensation must be made annually to ongoing clients. The annual requirement is satisfied by offering to provide clients a current copy of Securities and Exchange Commission (SEC) Form ADV, Part II, or the disclosure called for by Rule 402.

(f) *Rule 406.* Compensation shall be fair and reasonable.

(g) *Rule 407.* References may be provided that include recommendations from present and/or former clients.

(h) *Rule 408.* Ensure that the scope of authority is clearly defined and properly documented.

(i) *Rule 409.* All CFP Board designees shall adhere to the same standards of disclosure and service.

(j) *Rule 410.* Perform professional services with dedication to the lawful objectives of the employer and in accordance with this *Code of Ethics.*

(k) *Rule 411.* A CFP Board designee shall

> i. Advise an employer of outside affiliations that may reasonably compromise service to an employer
> ii. Provide timely notice to the employer and clients, unless precluded by contractual obligation, in the event of change of employment or CFP Board certification status

(l) *Rule 412.* A CFP Board designee must act in good faith with partners.

(m) *Rule 413.* A CFP Board designee must disclose to partners all relevant and material information regarding credentials, competence, experience, licensing and/or legal status, and financial stability.

(n) *Rule 414.* A CFP Board designee who is a partner or co-owner of a financial services firm must withdraw in compliance with any applicable agreement and in a fair and equitable manner.

(o) *Rule 415.* A CFP Board designee must disclose to an employer any compensation or other benefit arrangements in connection with his or her services to clients that are in addition to compensation from the employer.

(p) *Rule 416.* If a CFP Board designee enters into a business transaction with a client, the transaction shall be on terms that are fair and reasonable to the client.

(5) Rules that relate to the Principle of Confidentiality

(a) *Rule 501.* Do not reveal, without the client's consent, any personally identifiable information relating to the client relationship, except when use is reasonably necessary:

    i. To establish an advisory or brokerage account, to effect a transaction for the client, or as otherwise impliedly authorized in order to carry out the client engagement

    ii. To comply with legal requirements or legal process

    iii. To defend the CFP Board designee against charges of wrongdoing

    iv. In connection with a civil dispute between the CFP Board designee and the client

(b) *Rule 502.* Maintain the same standards of confidentiality to employers as to clients.

(c) *Rule 503.* Adhere to reasonable expectations of confidentiality while in business and thereafter.

(6) Rules that relate to the Principle of Professionalism

(a) *Rule 601.* Use the marks in compliance with the rules and regulations of CFP Board (see Topic 2, Section 1.A.(1)).

(b) *Rule 602.* Show respect for other financial planning professionals and related occupational groups by engaging in fair and honorable competitive practices.

(c) *Rule 603.* Inform the CFP Board when another CFP Board designee has committed a violation of the *Code of Ethics* and there is no substantial doubt.

(d) *Rule 604.* Inform the appropriate regulatory and/or professional disciplinary body when there is unprofessional, fraudulent, or illegal conduct by another CFP Board designee or other financial professional and there is no substantial doubt.

(e) *Rule 605.* Disclose illegal conduct to the immediate supervisor and/or partners if illegal conduct is suspected. If appropriate measures are not taken to remedy the situation, alert the appropriate regulatory authorities, including the CFP Board, in a timely manner.

(f) *Rule 606.* In all professional activities, a CFP Board designee shall perform services in accordance with

    i. Applicable laws, rules, and regulations of governmental agencies and other applicable authorities

    ii. Applicable rules, regulations, and other established policies of the CFP Board

(g) *Rule 607.* Do not engage in any conduct that reflects adversely on the profession.

(h) *Rule 608.* Disclose to clients the firm's status as registered investment advisers. It is proper to use the term *registered investment adviser* if the CFP Board designee is registered individually. If the CFP Board designee is registered through his or her firm, then the firm is the registered investment adviser.

(i) *Rule 609.* A CFP Board designee must not practice any other profession or offer to provide such services unless the CFP Board designee is qualified to practice in those fields and is licensed as required by state law.

       (j) *Rule 610.* Return the client's original records in a timely manner upon request of the client.

       (k) *Rule 611.* Do not bring or threaten to bring a disciplinary proceeding under this *Code of Ethics* or report or threaten to report information to CFP Board pursuant to Rules 603 and/or 604 for no substantial purpose other than to harass, embarrass, and/or unfairly burden another CFP Board designee.

       (l) *Rule 612.* Comply with all applicable renewal requirements established by CFP Board.

  (7) Rules that relate to the Principle of Diligence

       (a) *Rule 701.* Provide services diligently.

       (b) *Rule 702.* Enter into an engagement only after securing sufficient information to satisfy the CFP Board designee that

          i. The relationship is warranted by the individual's needs and objectives.

          ii. The CFP Board designee has the ability to either provide requisite competent services or to involve other professionals who can provide such services.

       (c) *Rule 703.* Implement only recommendations that are suitable for the client.

       (d) *Rule 704.* Make a reasonable investigation regarding the financial products recommended to clients.

       (e) *Rule 705.* Supervise subordinates with regard to their delivery of financial planning services.

2. Disciplinary Rules and Procedures

  A. Board of Professional Review

    (1) Is charged with the duty of investigating, reviewing, and taking appropriate action with respect to alleged violations of the *Code of Ethics* and alleged noncompliance with the *Financial Planning Practice Standards*

    (2) Can divide the Board into two panels consisting of an Inquiry Panel and a Hearing Panel and designate a chair for each panel. No member of an Inquiry Panel shall act as a member of a Hearing Panel on the same matter

  B. Inquiry Panel

    (1) Investigates alleged grounds for discipline, with appropriate assistance from members of CFP Board staff

    (2) Can dismiss allegations as being without merit, dismiss allegations with a letter of caution recommending remedial action and entering other appropriate orders, or refer the matter to CFP Board for preparation and processing of a complaint against the CFP Board designee

    (3) All answers to complaints shall be in writing. The answers shall be submitted within 20 calendar days from the date of service of the complaint upon the CFP Board designee.

    (4) If the CFP Board designee fails to file an answer within the period provided, such CFP Board designee shall be deemed to be in default and the allegations set forth in the complaint shall be deemed admitted.

  C. Hearing Panel

    (1) Conducts all hearings on complaints seeking disciplinary action against a CFP Board designee

    (2) Reports its findings and recommendations to the Board for final decision

    (3) Appeals must be made within 30 calendar days after notice of the order is sent to the CFP Board designee, or such order shall be final.

D. Staff counsel—maintains a central office for the filing of requests for the investigation of CFP Board designee conduct, for the coordination of such investigations, for the administration of all disciplinary enforcement proceedings carried out pursuant to these procedures, for the prosecution of charges of wrongdoing against CFP Board designees pursuant to these procedures, and for the performance of such other duties as are designated by the Board or the Chief Executive Officer of CFP Board

E. Grounds for discipline

    (1) Any act or omission that violates the provisions of the *Code of Ethics*

    (2) Any act or omission that fails to comply with the *Practice Standards*

    (3) Any act or omission that violates the criminal laws of any state or of the United States or of any province, territory, or jurisdiction of any other country

    (4) Any act that is the proper basis for professional suspension

    (5) Failure to respond to a request by the Board, without good cause shown

    (6) Any false or misleading statement made to CFP Board

F. Forms of discipline

    (1) *No action.* In cases where no grounds for discipline have been established, the Board may dismiss the matter either as being without merit or with a cautionary letter.

    (2) *Continuing education.* The Board has the right to require CFP Board designees to complete additional continuing education or other remedial work.

    (3) *Private censure.* The Board may order private censure of a CFP Board designee (i.e., an unpublished written reproach mailed by the Board to a censured CFP Board designee).

    (4) *Public Letter of Admonition.* The Board may order that a Letter of Admonition be issued against a CFP Board designee (i.e., a publishable written reproach of the CFP Board designee's behavior).

    (5) *Suspension.* The Board may order suspension for a specified period of time, not to exceed five years, for those individuals it deems can be rehabilitated. CFP Board designees receiving a suspension may qualify for reinstatement to use the marks.

    (6) *Revocation.* The Board may order permanent revocation of a CFP Board designee's right to use the marks. Revocation is permanent.

G. Investigation—The CFP Board designee shall have 20 calendar days from the date of notice of the investigation to file a written response to the allegations with the Board.

    (1) *No response.* The matter shall be referred to the Hearing Panel.

    (2) *Response.* A report is submitted to the Inquiry Panel.

TOPIC 3: CFP BOARD'S FINANCIAL PLANNING PRACTICE STANDARDS

The following contains wording from the *Financial Planning Practice Standards* (© 2002 by Certified Financial Planner Board of Standards, Inc.). It is strongly suggested by this author that all candidates for the CFP® examination read their own copies of the original *Financial Planning Practice Standards*. This material can be obtained from the CFP Board's Web site.)

1. Purpose and applicability
    A. The *Financial Planning Practice Standards* (*Practice Standards*) establish the level of professional practice that is expected of a CFP® Certificant engaged in personal financial planning. The *Practice Standards* are intended to (1) ensure that the practice of financial planning by CERTIFIED FINANCIAL PLANNER™ professionals is based on established norms of practice, (2) advance professionalism in financial planning, and (3) enhance the value of the financial planning process.
    B. Similarly, standards help practitioners to focus on what to provide as part of the six-step financial planning process and to base services on what clients need.
    C. The Board of Practice Standards drafted 10 standards, with one or more standards for each of the six steps in the financial planning process.
    D. Compliance with Practice Standards is covered in Rule 606(b) in the *Code of Ethics and Professional Responsibility.*
    E. The Practice Standards do not require practitioners to provide comprehensive planning for clients.

2. Content of each series
    A. Establishing and defining the relationship with the client

    100-1. Defining the scope of the engagement before any financial planning service is provided

    B. Gathering client data
        (1) *200-1*. Determining a client's personal and financial goals, needs, and priorities before any recommendation is made and/or implemented
        (2) *200-2*. Obtaining quantitative information and documents before any recommendation is made and/or implemented. If not obtained, restrict the scope of the engagement or terminate the engagement.

    C. Analyzing and evaluating the client's financial status

    300-1. Analyzing to gain an understanding of the client's financial situation and evaluating to what extent the client's goals, needs, and priorities can be met by the client's resources and current course of action

    D. Developing and presenting the financial planning recommendation(s)
        (1) The 400 Series represents the very heart of the financial planning process. It is at this point that the financial planning practitioner, using both science and art, formulates the recommendations designed to achieve the client's goals, needs, and priorities.
        (2) *400-1*. Identifying and evaluating financial planning alternative(s) to reasonably meet the client's goals, needs, and priorities
        (3) *400-2*. Developing the financial planning recommendation(s) from among the selected alternatives
        (4) *400-3*. Presenting the financial planning recommendation(s) to the client

    E. Implementing the financial planning recommendation(s)
        (1) *500-1*. Agreeing on implementation responsibilities
        (2) *500-2*. Selecting products and services for implementation

    F. Monitoring

    600-1. Mutually defining monitoring responsibilities

3. Enforcing through disciplinary rules and procedures

   A. The practice of financial planning consistent with these Practice Standards is required for CFP Board designees.

   B. Enforcement is based on the disciplinary rules and procedures established by CFP Board and administered by CFP Board's Board of Professional Review and Board of Appeals.

TOPIC 4: PERSONAL FINANCIAL STATEMENTS

1. Balance sheet (statement of financial position)

   A. It is a financial snapshot of the individual's wealth at a moment in time.

   B. It contains three categories: (1) assets, (2) liabilities, and (3) net worth.

   C. Net worth measures the client's wealth or equity at a specified period of time (i.e., net worth *equals* total assets *minus* total liabilities).

     (1) Net worth increases from the following:

        (a) Appreciation in the value of assets

        (b) Increase in assets from retaining income

        (c) Increase in assets from gifts or inheritances

        (d) Decrease in liabilities through forgiveness

     (2) Net worth is unchanged by the following:

        (a) Paying off debt

        (b) Buying an asset with cash

   D. Assets and liabilities are indicated at fair market value (FMV), footnotes are used to describe details of assets and liabilities, and property is identified by type of ownership.

   E. Assets are categorized as (1) cash and cash equivalents (checking and savings account, money markets), (2) invested assets (stocks, bonds, mutual funds), and (3) use assets (home, furnishings, cars).

   F. Liabilities are categorized as (1) current liabilities (credit card balances) and (2) long-term liabilities (auto loans, real estate mortgages, life insurance loans).

2. Cash flow statement

   A. Must indicate the period of coverage, usually a calendar year

   B. *Step 1.* Estimate the family's annual income.

   C. *Step 2.* Develop estimates for both fixed and discretionary expenses.

   D. *Step 3.* Determine the excess of shortfall of income within the budget period. Net cash flow *equals* total income *minus* total expenses. If net income is positive, the client can increase discretionary expenses.

   E. *Step 4.* Consider available methods of increasing income or decreasing expenses.

   F. *Step 5.* Calculate income and expenses as a percentage of the total to determine a better allocation of resources.

3. Pro forma statements

   A. Forecasting future balance sheets and cash flow statements

   B. It may make sense to include three different cash flow statements: (1) worst-case budget, based on lowest income and highest expenditures expected, (2) average-case budget, based on reasonable expectations of income and expenses, and (3) best-case budget, based on highest income and lowest expenditures.

TOPIC 5: BUDGETING

1. Discretionary versus nondiscretionary

   A. *Discretionary expenses* are flexible and can be prevented or timed.
   B. *Nondiscretionary* or fixed expenses can be changed, but must be paid.
   C. Various strategies are used to maximize income and minimize expenses:

      (1) *Debt restructuring.* The process of paying off all outstanding credit cards by consolidating debt into one low personal line of credit
      (2) *Asset reallocation.* This process involves the change in assets from underperforming assets to more productive investment assets to improve return and income.
      (3) *Expenditure control.* The process of reducing consumption expenditures by emphasizing the savings element
      (4) *Income tax planning.* Process of benefiting from proper tax planning
      (5) *Incorporating children's assets.* The process of saving for a child in a custodial account or trust to benefit from the lower tax rate of the child
      (6) *Qualified plan vehicles.* The process of utilizing a qualified plan to benefit from saving programs and deductibility

2. Financing strategies

   A. Consolidating credit card debt and student loan debt
   B. Taking a *cash-out refinance.* A cash-out refinance will give a new first mortgage by paying off the current first mortgage and provide additional cash. If current mortgage rates are lower than that of the existing first mortgage, a new first mortgage will allow the borrower to save on the current debt. The combined loan to value of 80 percent is recommended to avoid mortgage insurance. Interest is tax deductible, as with all home mortgages.
   C. Taking out a home equity loan or a home equity line of credit
   D. Using the cash value of a life insurance policy for a loan. Interest rate charges are generally less than for personal or credit card loans.
   E. Tapping into a company savings plan
   F. Using after-tax money from a Roth IRA. Tap into money that can be taken out without penalty or tax consequences.

3. Savings strategies

   A. *Goal setting.* Goals should be realistic and agreed upon by the family.
   B. *Self-rewarding plan.* If a family exceeds the savings goal, they should spend the extra savings on themselves.
   C. *Savings-first approach.* Save first and pay cash to avoid high interest charges on loans and to earn interest by investing the savings.
   D. *Automatic savings plan.* Deduct directly from a paycheck and invest the funds in savings. This includes dollar cost averaging into mutual funds and contributions to company retirement plans.

TOPIC 6: EMERGENCY FUND PLANNING

1. Adequacy of reserves—Three to six months of monthly expenses is typically a reasonable range. For one-income families, a six-month level may be more appropriate. For two-income families, a three-month level may be adequate.
2. Liquidity versus marketability

   A. *Marketability.* The ease with which an asset may be bought or sold
   B. *Liquidity.* The ease with which assets can be converted into cash with little risk of loss of principal

C. Real estate is considered illiquid because it may take a while to sell and the asking price may be lowered. However, real estate is marketable because it is relatively easy to sell a house if priced below market value.

3. Liquidity substitutes—Checking and savings accounts, money market accounts, U.S. Treasury bills, certificates of deposit (CDs), cash value of a life insurance policy, company savings plan, and home equity loans

TOPIC 7: CREDIT AND DEBT MANAGEMENT

1. Ratios

   A. The client should have sufficient liquid assets for an emergency fund (generally three to six months of fixed and variable outflows).

   B. *Rule of thumb*. Consumer debt, such as credit cards, auto loans, and the like, should not exceed 20 percent of net income (gross income – taxes).

   C. *Rule of thumb*. Monthly payments on a home (including principal, interest, taxes, and insurance) should be no more than 28 percent of the owner's gross income. This is known as the *housing payment ratio*.

   D. *Rule of thumb*. Total monthly payment on all debts should be no more than 36 to 38 percent of gross monthly income (principal interest taxes insurance (PITI), credit payments, alimony, child support, and maintenance). This is known as the *total payment ratio*.

   E. Renter's expenses divided by gross income ≤ 30 percent.

   F. Preferably more than one source of income. If there is only one source of income, greater planning is required. Having many sources of income creates greater financial stability.

   G. Savings and investments of at least 5 to 10 percent of gross income, not including reinvested dividends and income

2. Consumer debt

   A. Types of consumer debt

      (1) Thirty-day or regular charge accounts

      (2) Revolving and optional charge accounts

      (3) Installment purchases or time-payment plans. Involves two methods: (1) buying on time from the seller or (2) borrowing money from credit institution, usually in the form of credit cards.

   B. Sources of consumer credit—commercial banks, consumer finance companies, credit unions, savings and loan associations, life insurance companies (cash value), brokerage companies (margin), and auto dealers (auto financing)

3. Home equity loan and home equity line of credit

   A. A *home equity loan* is cash that is given up front (interest charged from start) at a fixed interest rate. In contrast, a *home equity credit line* allows the individual to use the money only when needed (no interest charged until used), but at a variable rate that is usually tied to the prime rate.

   B. Keep the current first mortgage and get a second loan for the necessary cash amount.

   C. If current mortgage rates are higher than that of the existing first mortgage, a home equity will allow the borrower to keep the current low first mortgage rate.

   D. Interest is fully tax deductible on home equity loans up to $100,000.

4. Secured versus unsecured debt

    A. *Secured loans*. Collateral is used to protect the lender from a loan defaulting. The borrower may lose the asset if payment is not made to the lender.

    B. *Unsecured loans*. No collateral is used; interest rates are higher to the borrower.

5. Bankruptcy

    A. Bankruptcy Code

        (1) Article I, Section 8, of the United States Constitution authorizes Congress to enact "uniform Laws on the subject of Bankruptcies." Under this grant of authority, Congress enacted the "Bankruptcy Code" in 1978. The Code, which is codified as Title 11 of the United States Code, has been amended several times since its enactment.

        (2) Title 11 of the United States Code governs bankruptcy proceedings.

        (3) Bankruptcy is a matter of federal law and is, with the exception of exemptions, the same in every state.

        (4) There is a bankruptcy court for each judicial district in the country. Each state has one or more districts. There are 90 bankruptcy districts across the country.

    B. Chapter 7 bankruptcy

        (1) Chapter 7 of the United States Bankruptcy Code is the Bankruptcy Code's "liquidation" chapter.

        (2) To qualify for relief under chapter 7 of the Bankruptcy Code, the debtor must be an individual, a partnership, or a corporation.

        (3) The individual debtor is permitted to retain certain "exempt" property. The debtor's remaining assets are liquidated by a trustee.

        (4) Accordingly, potential debtors should realize that the filing of a petition under chapter 7 may result in the loss of property.

        (5) The discharge has the effect of extinguishing the debtor's personal liability on dischargeable debts. A discharge is available to individual debtors only, not to partnerships or corporations.

    C. Chapter 11 bankruptcy

        (1) Reorganizations of persons, firms, and corporations, especially those whose debts exceed the limits of chapter 13

        (2) The court ultimately approves (confirms) or disapproves the plan of reorganization.

        (3) The debtor usually remains in possession of his or her assets and continues to operate any business, subject to the oversight of the court and the creditors' committee.

    D. Chapter 13 bankruptcy

        (1) Repayment plan for individuals, even if self-employed or operating an unincorporated business, with regular income and unsecured debt less than $290,525 and secured debt less than $871,550

        (2) The debtor keeps his or her property and makes regular payments to the chapter 13 trustee out of future income to pay creditors over time (three to five years).

        (3) An individual debtor faced with a threatened foreclosure of the mortgage on his or her principal residence can prevent an immediate foreclosure by filing a chapter 13 petition.

        (4) Certain debts that cannot be discharged in chapter 7 can be discharged in chapter 13.

        (5) Chapter 13 is often preferable to chapter 7 because it enables the debtor to keep a valuable asset, such as a house.

E. Property of the estate

    (1) Property that is not exempt

    (2) Property of the estate is usually sold by the trustee, and the claims of creditors are paid from the proceeds.

F. Qualified retirement plans

    (1) The Supreme Court held that retirement plans that have a legally enforceable *anti-alienation clause* (a provision preventing creditors from attacking the retirement funds of a debtor) are not property of the estate and thus are not subject to the jurisdiction of the bankruptcy court and cannot be accessed to pay creditors. Nearly all pensions and 401(k) savings plans that are qualified under Employee Retirement Income Security Act (ERISA), the federal pension savings act, have an anti-alienation clause that excludes them from the bankruptcy estate.

    (2) An exception to this rule is retirement plans that have only one participant, such as single employee corporate plans, and some other plans originating in self-employment.

G. Tax-advantaged saving plans

    (1) When retirement savings are property of the estate, because they are not ERISA qualified or because they are held in an IRA, they may be exempted from the estate under the available exemption statutes.

    (2) Property that is exempt is removed from the estate and is not liable for the payment of creditor claims.

    (3) The exact scope of the exemption and how much value can be exempted depends on the language of the exemption selected under state law.

H. Exemptions

    (1) Exemptions are the lists of the kinds and values of property that is legally beyond the reach of creditors or the bankruptcy trustee.

    (2) Exemptions constitute the one area in which bankruptcy law varies from state to state. Congress created a set of exemptions in the Bankruptcy Code but allowed each state to opt out of those exemptions in favor of the state exemptions.

    (3) Sixteen states allow debtors to elect the Bankruptcy Code exemptions. In those states, debtors have a choice between the federal exemptions and those in the law of their state.

    (4) For the rest of the states, only the state exemptions can be selected.

I. Dischargeable versus nondischargeable

    (1) A discharge releases the debtor from personal liability for discharged debts and prevents the creditors owed those debts from taking any action against the debtor or his or her property to collect the debts.

    (2) Most unsecured debt is dischargeable.

    (3) Most secured debt (liens and mortgages) survives bankruptcy as a charge on the property to which it attaches unless a court order modifies the lien.

    (4) The following debts cannot be discharged in either chapter 7 or chapter 13. If you file for chapter 7, you will still be responsible for repaying these debts after your discharge. If you file for chapter 13, these debts will have to be paid in full in your plan. If they are not, the balance will remain at the end of your case:

        (a) Debts you forget to list in your bankruptcy papers, unless the creditor learns of your bankruptcy case

        (b) Child support

       (c) Alimony

       (d) Debts for personal injury or death caused by driving while intoxicated

       (e) Student loans, unless it would be an undue hardship for you to repay

       (f) Fines and penalties for violating the law, including traffic tickets and criminal restitution

       (g) Recent income tax debts (past three years) and all other tax debts

       (h) Certain long-term obligations (such as a home mortgage)

    (5) The following debts may be declared nondischargeable by a bankruptcy judge in chapter 7 if the creditor challenges your request to discharge them:

       (a) Debts you incurred on the basis of fraud

       (b) Credit purchases of $1,150 or more for luxury goods or services made within 60 days of filing

       (c) Loans or cash advances of $1,150 or more taken within 60 days of filing

       (d) Debts resulting from willful or malicious injury to another person or another person's property

       (e) Debts arising from embezzlement, larceny, or breach of trust

       (f) Debts you owe under a divorce decree or settlement, unless after bankruptcy you would still not be able to afford to pay them or the benefit you would receive by the discharge outweighs any detriment to your ex-spouse (who would have to pay them if you discharge them in bankruptcy)

  J. Alternatives—debt consolidation, debt negotiation, and home equity loans or line of credit

6. Consumer protection laws

  A. Federal Trade Commission (FTC)

    (1) The Commission has enforcement and administrative responsibilities under 46 laws.

    (2) Statutes relate to competition and consumer protection missions.

  B. Consumer protection mission of the FTC

    (1) Truth in Lending Act

       (a) Title I of the Consumer Credit Protection Act

       (b) Requires all creditors who deal with consumers to make certain written disclosures concerning all finance charges and related aspects of credit transactions (including disclosing finance charges expressed as an annual percentage rate)

    (2) Fair Credit Billing Act

       (a) Amendment to the Truth in Lending Act

       (b) Protects the borrower in the event a credit card is lost or stolen to a maximum loss of $50 per card or until the card has been reported as missing if less

       (c) Prohibits creditors from taking actions that adversely affect the consumer's credit standing until an investigation is completed

    (3) Equal Credit Opportunity Act

       (a) Title VII of the Consumer Credit Protection Act

       (b) The Act prohibits discrimination on the basis of race, color, religion, national origin, sex, marital status, age, receipt of public assistance, or good faith exercise of any rights under the Consumer Credit Protection Act.

       (c) The Act also requires creditors to provide applicants, upon request, with the reasons underlying decisions to deny credit.

(4) The Fair Debt Collection Practices Act

    (a) Title VIII of the Consumer Credit Protection Act

    (b) The Act prohibits a debt collector from communicating with a consumer in connection with the collection of any debt at the consumer's place of employment.

    (c) The convenient time for communicating with a consumer is after 8:00 A.M. and before 9:00 P.M. local time at the consumer's location.

    (d) A debt collector may not communicate with any person other than a consumer, his or her attorney, and a consumer-reporting agency.

    (e) If a consumer notifies a debt collector in writing that the consumer refuses to pay a debt or that the consumer wishes the debt collector to cease further communication with the consumer, the debt collector shall not communicate further with the consumer except to notify that the debt collector or creditor may invoke specified remedies that are ordinarily invoked by such debt collector or creditor.

(5) Fair Credit Reporting Act

    (a) The Act gives the consumer the right to see his or her file and request corrections.

    (b) Information in a consumer report cannot be provided to anyone who does not have a purpose specified in the Act.

    (c) Government cannot see the file unless it is considering employing the individual, granting a license of some kind, considering him or her for security clearance, or if back taxes are owed.

    (d) IRS must have a legitimate case to receive a report.

    (e) Obsolete information: 7 years for adverse information and 10 years for bankruptcies

TOPIC 8: BUYING VERSUS LEASING

1. Calculation

  A. Buying or leasing an automobile

    (1) To buy:

      (a) For business use, taxpayers who own an auto can choose the standard mileage rate in the first year and switch to actual expense method in a later year if it becomes more favorable. Taxpayers who lease an auto can choose the standard mileage rate in the first year, but must use it for the life of the auto.

      (b) Consumer intends to keep the auto for more than four years.

      (c) Auto is driven for more than 15,000 miles per year. Lease contracts generally have a 15,000 limit and charge for excess miles.

      (d) Consumer has cash for the purchase or down payment.

    (2) To lease:

      (a) Lower monthly payments with little or no down payment. This leaves more cash to invest elsewhere, such as business or investments.

      (b) Leasing is suited for individuals who desire a new car every two or three years and who would borrow to pay for a new car. The trade-in value would be less than the loan value, resulting in a loss.

      (c) Service, convenience, and flexibility

      (d) Taxpayer needs or desires a high-priced vehicle for business use. Tax advantages of leasing over buying increase with a car's value and percentage of business use.

      (e) Off-balance-sheet financing for business

      (f) For business use, taxpayers who trade in autos every three years or less usually end up with a realized loss that cannot be deducted. The taxpayer's basis (after limited depreciation deductions) exceeds the trade-in value, but the loss is not recognized, because of Section 1031 like-kind exchange rules.

      (g) For business use, the cost of interest is included in the lease payments (the entire payment is 100 percent deductible). Interest is not deductible for employees who purchase their vehicles.

  B. Buying a house or leasing (renting)

    (1) The most common reason for renting instead of buying is the lack of funds for a down payment.

    (2) Buying a home offers many advantages:

      (a) There are tax advantages with home ownership.

      (b) Creditors look more favorably on homeowners.

      (c) A residence may be an appreciating asset.

      (d) Monthly housing costs tend to be more stable than the cost of renting.

    (3) Renting may make sense if the stay is short term.

2. Adjustable and fixed rate loans

  A. Fixed rate loans have a stated interest rate that lasts for the term of the loan and are more appropriate for clients with a low tolerance for risk.

  B. Adjustable rate loans have provisions that permit the lender to change the interest rate periodically.

  C. If the time expected to be in a house is short term, an adjustable rate mortgage (ARM) may be preferred to a fixed rate mortgage because of lower initial interest rates resulting in the lowest current payment. This assumes the client has a higher risk tolerance for a variable rate.

  D. An ARM with a 2/6 cap indicates a 2 percent maximum interest rate increase per year, 6 percent life of loan.

  E. In a low or increasing interest rate environment, a client is best served using a fixed rate loan. In contrast, in a high or decreasing interest rate environment, the client may be best served with a variable rate loan.

3. Effect on financial statements

  A. Balance sheet effect:

    (1) Leased or rented assets have no entry except to the extent that a lump sum may have been taken from one of the listed assets as an initial payment to secure the leased asset. An initial payment results in a cash decrease and a decrease in net worth. There is no debt, so there is no asset.

    (2) Purchased assets with 100 percent cash—reduce cash but add in the asset by the same amount—result in no change to net worth.

    (3) Purchased assets with loan—result in a reduction of cash or other liquid asset that was used for the purchase or down payment. If there is a loan that was secured in order to purchase the asset, it will show up as a liability. This results in no change to net worth. For example, assume $5,000 cash is used as a down payment to purchase a car valued at $10,000, and the remaining $5,000 is financed through an auto loan. The effect is a $5,000 increase in assets ($10,000 market value of car *minus* $5,000 decrease in cash) and a $5,000 increase in liabilities (loan amount).

B. Cash flow statement effect—The purchase of an asset or lease payment is shown as an outflow of cash.

TOPIC 9: FUNCTION, PURPOSE, AND REGULATION OF FINANCIAL INSTITUTIONS

1. Banks

    A. Primary depository for checking accounts and short-term financing for corporations
    B. Insured by the Federal Deposit Insurance Corporation (FDIC)

2. Credit unions

    A. Primary depository for checking accounts and short-term financing for corporations
    B. Nonprofit, cooperative financial institutions owned and run by members
    C. Members pool their funds to make loans to one another. The volunteer board that runs each credit union is elected by the members.
    D. Depositors benefit from earnings—in the form of dividends—after operating expenses are paid and reserve requirements are satisfied.
    E. Organized to serve people in a particular community, group or groups of employees, military, or members of an organization or association
    F. Insured by the National Credit Union Administration (NCUA), an agency of the United States government, for losses up $100,000

3. Brokerage companies

    A. Primary depositories of investment accounts for trading stocks and bonds
    B. The distinction between brokerage firms and banks has become blurred; however, the Glass-Steagall Act of 1933 forbids banks from underwriting corporate securities.
    C. Insured by the Securities Investor Protection Corporation (SIPC)

4. Insurance companies

    A. Primary places for obtaining life, health, property, and disability insurance
    B. In the McCarran-Ferguson Act, Congress reaffirmed the right of the federal government to regulate insurance, but agreed it would not exercise this right as long as the industry was adequately regulated by the states. In effect, the law explicitly grants the states the power to regulate the insurance business.
    C. The National Association of Insurance Commissioners (NAIC) is composed of the commissioners of insurance from all states. It has no legal power over insurance regulation, but the Commissioner of Insurance in each state is charged with the administration of the state's insurance laws and operations and recommends legislation.

5. Mutual fund companies

    A. Primarily start open-end and closed-end mutual funds and sell these to the investing public, but some offer other services like the sale of stocks and bonds
    B. Insured by the SIPC

6. Other

    A. Savings and loans

        (1) Primarily a source for mortgage loans
        (2) Insured by the FDIC

    B. Federal Deposit Insurance Corporation (FDIC)

        (1) Reimburses the depositor for any losses up to $100,000

(2) A depositor does not have to be a U.S. citizen, or even a resident of the United States. Protects deposits that are payable in the United States. Deposits payable only overseas are not protected.

(3) All types of deposits received by a financial institution in its usual course of business are insured.

(4) FDIC does not insure Treasury securities.

(5) Deposits in different institutions are insured separately. If an individual deposits at the main office and at one or more branch offices of the same institution, the deposits are added together in calculating deposit insurance coverage.

(6) Deposits maintained in different categories of legal ownership are separately insured. A depositor can have more than $100,000 insurance coverage in a single institution. Joint accounts are insured separately from single-ownership accounts.

(7) IRA and Keogh funds are separately insured from any nonretirement funds the depositor may have at an institution. If a depositor has both a Roth IRA and a traditional IRA at an insured depository institution, the funds in those accounts would be added together.

C. Securities Investor Protection Corporation (SIPC)

(1) SIPC protects customers of broker-dealers as long as the broker-dealer is an SIPC member.

(2) If an SIPC member's registration with the U.S. Securities and Exchange Commission is terminated, the broker-dealer's SIPC membership is also automatically terminated.

(3) The cost of insurance is paid by brokerage firms that are members of the SIPC.

(4) Customers of a failed brokerage firm get back all securities (such as stocks and bonds) that already are registered in their names or are in the process of being registered.

(5) If sufficient funds are not available in the firm's customer accounts to satisfy claims within these limits, the reserve funds of SIPC are used to supplement the distribution, up to a ceiling of $500,000 per customer, including a maximum of $100,000 for cash claims.

(6) Among the investments that are ineligible for SIPC protection are commodity futures contracts and currency, as well as investment contracts (such as limited partnerships) that are not registered with the U.S. Securities and Exchange Commission under the Securities Act of 1933.

TOPIC 10: CLIENT ATTITUDES AND BEHAVIORAL CHARACTERISTICS

1. Cultural

A. Culture comprises the values and beliefs that exist within a group of people.

B. A culture may include easy-to-identify aspects, such as race and language, as well as more difficult-to-recognize/subtle aspects, such as expressions.

C. Gaining a better understanding of a culture can lead to deeper business relationships with contacts.

D. One way to establish relationships with diverse people is to expand activities beyond normal boundaries.

2. Family

A. Planning for children's college education, having a cash reserve or emergency fund to meet unexpected contingencies, and making sure the family is properly insured to protect against financial disasters

   B. Risk tolerance is affected by an individual's family situation (e.g., marital status and the number and ages of children).

3. Emotional

   A. There is a *cost* to letting emotions drive investment decisions.

   B. Most people invest emotionally instead of objectively.

   C. When emotions run high, investors are easily swayed by "noise" from the media.

   D. Investors have an aversion to losses, mixed with a tendency to hang onto losing stocks. They often do not acknowledge making a mistake, resulting in their selling winners instead of losers.

   E. Investors wrestle with sell decisions based on how much they have invested—but the amount invested should not matter. The price paid is a sunk cost and should have no influence on the decision to buy more, sell, or hold.

   F. Proper diversification is an alternative to emotional investing.

4. Life cycle and age

   A. There are four life cycle phases:

     (1) Accumulation phase

       (a) Early to middle years (approximately before 40 years old)

       (b) Protecting the family from a potential financial disaster resulting from death or disability

       (c) Building cash reserves and emergency funds to meet unexpected situations and saving for home, car, retirement, and children's education

       (d) Individuals are accepting of high-risk investments for above-average returns.

     (2) Consolidation phase

       (a) Past midpoint of their careers (approximately 40 to 60 years old)

       (b) Paid off most or all outstanding loans and have children's education funded, but continue saving for retirement

       (c) Individuals are accepting of moderate-risk investments.

     (3) Spending phase

       (a) Begins when an individual retires

       (b) Individuals seek greater capital preservation.

       (c) Individuals are accepting of low-risk investments, but they still need to have some risky investments for inflation protection.

     (4) Gifting phase

       (a) Similar to and may mirror the spending phase

       (b) Estate planning is critical in this phase.

5. Level of knowledge, experience, and expertise

   A. Risk tolerance often rises with an increase in knowledge and experience, but declines as a client approaches retirement.

   B. Planners should identify their clients' knowledge level before investing in instruments their clients do not understand.

6. Risk tolerance

   A. In certain cases, measuring risk tolerance can be objective, but generally it is a subjective measure of the emotional and financial ability of an investor to withstand financial loss.

B. A careful analysis of the client's risk tolerance should precede any discussion of return objectives.

C. In a simplistic sense, investors are classified as high, moderate, and low risk takers.

TOPIC 11: EDUCATIONAL FUNDING

1. Needs analysis

   A. The goal is to establish a saving schedule for the client, which requires the following:

      (1) The age of the child

      (2) The age at which the child will attend college

      (3) The after-tax earnings rate of the parents

      (4) The inflation-adjusted interest rate

      (5) The current cost of tuition and the rate of increase—the rate of increase is generally the rate of inflation but can differ.

   B. *Example*: John Harris wants to plan for his son's education. His son was born today and will attend a private university for four years beginning at age 18. Tuition is currently $20,000 a year and increases annually at 7 percent, whereas inflation increases only at 3 percent per year. John expects to earn an after-tax return of 10 percent from investments. How much must John save at the end of each year if he would like to make his last payment at the beginning of his son's first year of college?

   C. *Solution*: Requires three steps:

      (1) Inflate the current cost of tuition by the tuition inflation rate for the number of years until the child begins college. Calculator → 20,000 [PV]; 18 [N]; 7 [I]; 0 [PMT] = −67,598 [FV]

      (2) Calculate the present value of an annuity due for the number of years the child will attend college. Use the inflation-adjusted discount rate for this step. Calculator → begin mode; 67,598 [PMT]; 0 [FV]; 4 [N]; 1.10 [ENTER] 1.07 [÷] 1 [−] 100 [×][I] = −259,530 [PV]

      (3) Determine the periodic payment that must be made to reach the account balance in step 2. Calculator → end mode; 259,530 [FV]; 18 [N]; 10 [I]; 0 [PV] = 5,691 [PMT]

2. Tax credits and deductions

   A. Hope Credit

      (1) Available only for first two years of undergraduate work

      (2) Qualified expenses include tuition (books and supplies are included as qualified tuition only if the fees must be paid to the institution as a condition of enrollment).

      (3) Expenses that do not qualify include room and board and, generally, books and supplies.

      (4) The amount of credit is 100 percent of the first $1,000 of qualified tuition you paid for each eligible student and 50 percent of the next $1,000.

      (5) The maximum amount is $1,500 times the number of eligible students.

   B. Lifetime Learning Credit

      (1) Available for all years of undergraduate and graduate work

      (2) Qualified expenses include tuition (books and supplies are included as qualified tuition only if the fees must be paid to the institution as a condition of enrollment).

      (3) Expenses that do not qualify include room and board and, generally, books and supplies.

(4) The amount of the credit is 20 percent of the first $10,000 of qualified tuition paid for all eligible students.

(5) The maximum amount per family is $2,000 and is calculated as 20 percent × $10,000.

C. Student loan interest

(1) Taxpayers can deduct up to $2,500 of interest on qualified education loans for college expenses as an adjustment to income.

(2) The deduction phases out when modified adjusted gross income (AGI) exceeds certain limits.

(3) Voluntary payments of interest are also deductible.

(4) Deductible amounts must be reduced by any nontaxable education benefits received, such as employer-provided assistance and nontaxable distributions from a Coverdell education savings account (ESA).

D. Deduction for higher education expenses

(1) For tax years 2002 through 2005, taxpayers will be allowed to claim a deduction for qualified higher education expenses as an adjustment to income. The deduction expires for tax years after 2005.

(2) The allowable deduction is based on the tax year and the taxpayer's modified AGI. In 2003, if AGI does not exceed $65,000 if single or $130,000 if married filing jointly (MFJ), then the deduction limit is $3,000.

(3) There is no phase-out range—a married taxpayer with $3,000 in qualified educational expenses and modified AGI of $130,000 would be entitled to deduct the full $3,000. The same taxpayer with just $1 more in modified AGI would not be entitled to a deduction.

(4) Cannot be claimed in a year in which a Hope or Lifetime Learning Credit has been claimed for the same student

3. Qualified tuition plans (QTP or 529 plans)

A. Every state's program must meet the regulations of Section 529 of the Internal Revenue Code defining qualified tuition plans (QTP).

B. It is a state-sponsored, taxed advantage plan used for undergraduate- and graduate-level expenses; extends tax-exempt status to qualified tuition programs funded by private institutions, starting in 2004.

C. Account owner selects beneficiary.

(1) Contributor stays in total control and can reclaim funds at any time.

(2) If beneficiary does not attend college, the contributor is allowed to replace the current designated beneficiary with a new beneficiary who is a member of the family.

D. Can be established by anyone to pay for qualified education expenses

E. Tax-free growth of earnings if withdrawn for qualified educational expenses. Penalty-free withdrawals include tuition, room and board, and books and supplies.

F. The funding is treated as a gift of a present interest qualifying for the annual $11,000/$22,000 tax exclusion. Contributor may elect to treat the gift as occurring ratably over a five-year period, so that the $11,000/$22,000 exclusion can be leveraged to as much as $55,000/$110,000 in one year.

G. Contributions are treated as a completed gift for estate and gift tax purposes. This rule applies despite the fact that the owner retains ownership rights, which would normally be treated as his or her estate.

(1) Varies by state, but generally no age restriction for beneficiary

(2) Contributions can be made to a Coverdell (education) IRA and a 529 College Savings Plan in the same year for the same beneficiary without penalty.

(3) Contributions may be deductible for state income tax (depending on state plan).

H. Contribution limits vary by state, but some plans allow an annual contribution up to $265,000.

I. Investment choices—vary by type of plan:

(1) *Prepaid tuition plan.* Guarantees money saved today matches the growth in tuition inflation at state-run colleges

(2) *College savings plan.* Managed by state treasurer or outside investment adviser—invests in stocks, bonds, and cash

J. Impact of financial aid—varies by type of plan:

(1) *Prepaid tuition plan.* Every dollar used for tuition takes a dollar away from the student's eligibility for aid.

(2) *College savings plan.* If plan is in parent's name, the college will count no more than 5.6 percent of the money each year. If the plan is in the child's name, each year the school may want 25 or 30 percent of the money.

K. *Coordination with Hope and Lifetime Learning Credits.* Can claim the Hope and Lifetime Learning Credit in the same year of receiving a tax-free distribution, provided the distribution is not used for the same expenses for which the credit is claimed.

L. Major drawbacks:

(1) This is a long-term plan that should be started when the child is 10 years old or younger.

(2) Withdrawals are treated as income to the child and could hurt financial aid.

(3) Typically provide very few investment choices

(4) Difficult to transfer to another program

(5) Earnings taxed as ordinary income and a 10 percent penalty tax on nonqualified distributions

(6) The 2001 tax law sunsets on January 1, 2011—on that day Congress could make withdrawals from these accounts taxable.

4. Education IRAs (also called Coverdell ESAs)

A. An education savings plan used for undergraduate- and graduate-level expenses

B. Account owner selects beneficiary.

(1) Parent or guardian establishes the account and can elect to maintain control over the account for educational purposes (the institution where you establish the Coverdell ESA will have policies determining the decision-making authority for the account).

(2) Any withdrawals from the Coverdell ESA are paid to the beneficiary and are not refunded to the parent or other person who establishes the account.

(3) If beneficiary does not attend college, the beneficiary can be changed to a member of the beneficiary's family if under the age of 30.

C. To establish the account, beneficiary must be under age 18 unless the individual is designated as a special needs beneficiary.

D. Tax-free growth of earnings occurs if withdrawn for qualified educational expenses before the child is age 30.

E. Withdrawals are tax free if they are not more than the beneficiary's qualified education expenses for the tax year.

F. Contributions

    (1) Can be made only after the beneficiary reaches age 18 if the beneficiary is a special needs beneficiary

    (2) Can be made to one or several Coverdell ESAs for the same designated beneficiary, provided that the total contributions are not more than the contribution limit

    (3) Can be made to a Coverdell ESA and a 529 College Savings Plan in the same year for the same beneficiary without penalty

    (4) Are nondeductible from taxes

G. Penalty-free withdrawals are tuition, room and board, and books and supplies.

H. Earnings are taxed as ordinary income and subject to 10 percent penalty for nonqualified use.

I. Investment choices are managed by parent or guardian, and there is a broad choice of investment vehicles, including stocks and bonds.

J. May impact financial aid

K. *Coordination with Hope and Lifetime Learning Credits.* Can claim the Hope and Lifetime Learning Credit in the same year of receiving a tax-free distribution from a Coverdell ESA or 529 Plan, provided the distribution is not used for the same expenses for which the credit is claimed.

L. The contribution is phased out if AGI exceeds limits (unlike a 529 Plan).

5. Savings bonds or CDs

A. Savings bonds

    (1) Sold at a discount and pay no annual interest

    (2) Interest earned is not taxable at the state and local levels, but is taxable at the federal level.

    (3) Interest is excluded from federal income tax if used for higher education expenses in the same calendar year the bonds are redeemed. The following criteria must also be satisfied:

        (a) A person has to be at least 24 years old at time of issuance.

        (b) Registered in name of purchaser or child if intended for child's education

        (c) Only savings bonds issued after December 21, 1989

    (4) Qualified educational expenses include tuition and fees.

    (5) The cost of books and room and board are not qualified expenses.

    (6) The exclusion is phased out with high AGI.

    (7) The exclusion is not available for married taxpayers filing separately.

B. CollegeSure CD

    (1) Sold in whole units and fractional units and is purchased from College Savings Bank

    (2) Do not have to buy CollegeSure CDs in one lump sum

    (3) Calculates the annual interest on a CD on the basis of the Independent College 500 Index

    (4) There is no limit on how much a CD can earn—the CD is guaranteed to keep up with college costs. The CD is guaranteed to earn a minimum of 4 percent even if college costs do not increase in a given year.

    (5) Insured by FDIC for up to $100,000, and investors pay no fees or commissions.

    (6) If student earns a scholarship, the parents get back all the money they have invested plus the accumulated interest.

6. Government grants and loans

   A. Grants and scholarships

      (1) Pell Grants

         (a) Distributed on the basis of financial need—maximum amount is up to $3,750 per year.

         (b) Available to undergraduate students only, both part-time and full-time (reduced grants for part-time students)

      (2) Federal Supplemental Education Opportunity Grants (FSEOGs)

         (a) Distributed on the basis of financial need—maximum amount is up to $4,000 per year.

         (b) Available to undergraduate students only, both part-time and full-time (reduced grants for part-time students)

         (c) Students receiving Pell Grants are given highest priority.

   B. Student loans

      (1) Perkins Loan

         (a) Funded by the federal government, but administered by the individual schools

         (b) Distributed on the basis of financial need—maximum amount is $4,000 per year for undergraduate students and $6,000 per year for graduate students.

         (c) Available to graduate and undergraduate students, both part-time and full-time

         (d) Five percent interest, and allows for a grace period of nine months after graduation before loan payments are due

         (e) Repayment usually 10 years

      (2) Stafford Loans

         (a) Available to graduates and undergraduates, both part-time and full-time

         (b) Based on financial need, with limits applying as to the amount of funds that may be received, both in any one year and cumulatively

         (c) Interest rate fluctuates with the 91-day T-bill plus 3.1 percent, capped at 9 percent for the first four years of repayment.

         (d) *Subsidized loans (needs based).* Students will not be charged any interest before they begin repayment or during authorized periods of deferment.

         (e) *Unsubsidized loans.* Repayment begins at loan inception.

      (3) Parent Loans to Undergraduate Students (PLUS) and Supplemental Loans to Students (SLS)

         (a) PLUS is available to parents of undergraduate students, allowing them to borrow up to 100 percent of the cost of college less the amount the student receives from Stafford and Perkins Loans and other aid sources.

         (b) SLS is available to students themselves who have applied for both a Pell Grant and Stafford Loan for graduate and undergraduate studies.

         (c) PLUS/SLS are not needs-based loans, and neither is available to part-time students.

         (d) Loans are made by private lenders.

      (4) College work study

         (a) Funded by the federal government and administered by individual schools

         (b) Eligibility is based on financial need.

         (c) Available to graduate and undergraduates, both part-time and full-time

       (d) Eligible students are provided employment to earn maximum amounts stated by the federal government while attending school.

7. Other sources

  A. Uniform Gifts to Minors Act (UGMA) and Uniform Transfer to Minors Act (UTMA)

     (1) Two vehicles designed to set up custodial accounts in a child's name for the benefit of the child

     (2) Simple and inexpensive method of making a gift to a child without the expense of a trust

     (3) Parents often transfer assets to children to reduce the income taxes on the earnings (taxed to the child's bracket).

     (4) Money transferred to a custodial account is considered an irrevocable gift. Once the child reaches the age stipulated by law—usually 18 or 21—the money is the child's to do as he or she pleases. No guarantee is required that the child will use the money for college.

     (5) Ownership of assets has implications for college financial aid. In calculating estimated family contributions toward college costs, the standard federal aid formula requires children to pay 35 percent of savings held in their names. In contrast, parents contribute only 5.6 percent of their assets.

  B. Section 2503(c) Minor's Trust

     (1) Allows the transferred trust property to be treated as a gift of a present interest to the child and so qualifies for the annual gift tax exclusion

     (2) The trust is used when (1) the grantor's income tax bracket is high and the recipient's tax bracket is low and (2) the grantor does not want an appreciating asset included in the gross estate.

     (3) If income of the trust is distributed each year, it is taxable to the recipient (who is usually at a lower tax bracket); if income is accumulated, it is taxed to the trust.

     (4) All of the trust property and accumulated income must be payable to the child at his or her age 21.

  C. Zero coupon bonds

     (1) Promise no interest during the life of the bonds but only the payment of the principal at maturity—the bonds are sold at a discount.

     (2) A tax feature reduces the attractiveness of zero coupon bonds. The IRS taxes the accrued interest even though the investor does not receive the funds until a bond matures.

8. Ownership of assets

  A. Affects financial aid

  B. When determining how much a family can afford to pay, the processing firm uses the federal methodology formula known as the *expected family contribution*.

  C. To pay for college, parents can use as much as 47 percent of after-tax income, but no more than 5.6 percent of assets—capital gains are treated as income.

  D. The amount of total contribution expected from a family is reduced by

     (1) Saving money in the parent's name and not the child's name—the formula calls on students to contribute 35 percent of their assets to college costs.

     (2) Investing in a 401(k) or other tax-sheltered retirement plans is excluded in calculating total value of assets owned by parents.

TOPIC 12: FINANCIAL PLANNING FOR SPECIAL CIRCUMSTANCES

1. Divorce

   A. Property valuation and settlement

      (1) It is important to understand that "equitable" does not mean "equal"; it only means "fair."

      (2) Property settlements—Section 1041—no gain or loss on divorce transactions

   B. Career assets

      (1) Sometimes one spouse has significant assets tied to his or her career. *For example*: A wife quits her job so her husband can move and advance his career.

      (2) Career assets include life, health, disability, and long-term care insurance; vacation and sick pay; Social Security; stock options; and pension and retirement plans.

      (3) Career assets are assumed to be jointly owned by both spouses.

   C. *Family business and house*. Three options when deciding how to divide a business and/or house:

      (1) One spouse keeps the business/home by buying out the other's interest.

      (2) Both spouses continue to own business/home.

      (3) The business/home is sold and proceeds are divided.

   D. *Retirement plans*. Two methods for dividing:

      (1) *Buy-out or cash-out method*. Nonemployee spouse gets a lump sum settlement—or marital asset of equal value—at the time of divorce in return for the employee's right to keep the retirement plan.

      (2) *Deferred division or future value method*. No present value is determined—each spouse gets an equal share of the benefits when they are paid.

   E. Alimony

      (1) A series of payments from one spouse to another, or to a third party on behalf of the receiving spouse

      (2) Taxable income to the recipient and, generally, tax-deductible expense to the payer

   F. Child support

      (1) Established by the courts and based on the ratio of each parent's income, the percentage of time the child spends with each parent, and the amount of alimony payments made to the custodial parent

      (2) Cannot be deductible by the payor and not includible in the income of the recipient

      (3) The child can be counted as an exemption by only one parent but the exemption can be traded back and forth each year.

      (4) Only the custodial parent is entitled to claim both the child and the dependent care credit.

2. Disabilities

   A. The chance of becoming disabled prior to retirement is greater than the chance of death. Purchasing a disability income policy satisfies full protection.

   B. Workers' compensation handles work-related injuries.

   C. Company sickness and accident plans have waiting periods and are limited to years of coverage.

3. Terminal illness

   A. *Long-term care insurance*. Insurance policy used to provide funding for long-term care, such as stays in nursing homes, not covered under Medicare or other medical expense policies

   B. *Viatical agreements*. Terminally ill individuals may be able to sell their life insurance policies to a viatical company.

4. Nontraditional families

   A. Proper estate planning through wills and trust is essential—there is no unlimited marital deduction for unmarried couples.

   B. Planning is necessary for single parents, as well as ensuring necessary amounts of insurance inasmuch as there is only one wage earner.

5. Job change and job loss, including severance packages

   A. Emergency fund covering three to six months of expenses

   B. State unemployment insurance programs exist in all states and are designed to provide protection against involuntary unemployment when the individual is available for work but is temporarily unemployed.

      (1) Protection is limited in amount and duration.
      (2) Payable through state unemployment offices
      (3) Unemployment compensation is taxable and reported by a taxpayer on Form 1099-G.

6. Dependents with special needs

   A. The special needs are typically those that help support and educate a child with serious physical, emotional, and/or cognitive problems.

   B. Special needs trusts can preserve state-provided benefits that would be prohibitively expensive otherwise.

TOPIC 13: ECONOMIC CONCEPTS

1. Supply and demand

   A. Demand curve

      (1) The *law of demand* states that higher prices reduce the demand for an item and lower prices increase the demand for an item.
      (2) Consumers buy less of a product as prices increase primarily because of the availability of substitutes.

         (a) A *substitute* is an item that performs functions similar to those of an item it has replaced.
         (b) Consumers are more responsive to price when more viable substitutes are available.

      (3) The demand curve slopes down to the right, indicating that as price drops, the quantity demanded will increase—indirect relationship.
      (4) *Price elasticity* is manifested when a small price change causes a rather large change in the amount purchased.

         (a) This is common with goods that have many substitutes. For example, if the price of Pepsi rises, consumers will purchase Coke.
         (b) Perfect elasticity results in a horizontal demand curve.

(c) Time has the greatest effect on elasticity; when the price of a product increases, consumers will reduce their consumption more in the long run than in the short run—called the *second law of demand.*

(5) *Price inelasticity* is manifested when a large price change does not cause much change in the quantity demanded.

   (a) Inelastic goods have few substitutes. An example of an inelastic good is gasoline. Even as the price rises, people still need to buy gasoline.
   (b) Perfect inelasticity is represented by a demand curve that is vertical.

(6) Movement along the demand curve represents a *change in quantity demanded* resulting from a change in price. However, some factors will cause a *shift in demand*. A shift in demand is caused by

   (a) Changes in consumer income
   (b) Changes in the price of related goods (substitutes and complements). If two goods go together, they are *complements*—for example, ice cream and hot fudge. A price rise in one good will cause a drop in demand for its complement.
   (c) Changes in consumer expectations
   (d) Changes in the number of consumers in the market
   (e) Demographic changes
   (f) Changes in consumer tastes and preferences

B. Supply curve

(1) The *law of supply* indicates that a higher price will increase the supply of a good.
(2) There is a direct relationship between the price of a good and the amount supplied in the marketplace.
(3) The supply curve is elastic when a price change leads to a large change in quantity supplied. This happens when resources are added inexpensively. The supply curve is inelastic when a price change leads to a small change in supply.
(4) *Change in quantity supplied* is identified as movement along the supply curve. It is the willingness of producers to offer a good at different prices. A shift in the entire supply curve is referred to as a *change in supply*.
(5) Factors that increase the opportunity cost of producing a good will discourage production and shift the supply curve inward to the left; the reverse is also true. Such factors include the following:

   (a) *Changes in resource prices.* Higher resource prices (and opportunity costs) will reduce the supply of a good, causing a shift to the left in the supply curve.
   (b) *Changes in technology.* Lower cost techniques will increase production and decrease the opportunity cost of a good, causing the supply curve to shift outward to the right.
   (c) *Natural disasters and political disruptions*

C. Income elasticity is the sensitivity of demand to change in consumer income.

(1) An *inferior good* has negative income elasticity. This means that when income increases, the quantity demanded decreases; when income decreases, the quantity demanded increases. An example of an inferior good is margarine.
(2) A *normal good* has positive income elasticity. When income increases (decreases), the quantity demanded also increases (decreases). An example of a normal good is butter.

2. Fiscal policy

 A. Fiscal policy refers to the government's ability to influence the economy by raising or lowering government spending and taxes.

 B. If the government wants to stimulate the economy, it can implement expansionary fiscal policy by increasing spending or reducing taxes. This generally results in increased gross domestic product (GDP) and higher price levels.

 C. The government can use restrictive fiscal policy to slow the economy by decreasing spending and increasing taxes.

3. Monetary policy

 A. Monetary policy is used by the Federal Reserve System (Fed) to influence the money supply.

 B. The Federal Reserve controls the money supply with three policy tools:

   (1) *The required reserve ratio.* Required reserves are the minimum reserves banks must hold as required by law. These funds do not earn interest and cannot be lent to customers. When the required reserve ratio falls, the money stock rises. However, the money supply increases only if member banks are willing to lend and their customers are willing to borrow. This is an uncommon choice by the Fed.

   (2) *Open market operations.* This is the Fed's most powerful tool for controlling the money supply. If the Fed sells government securities, it receives money in return, which reduces the money supply. If the Fed buys government securities, it adds reserves into the banking system and the money supply grows.

   (3) *Discount rate.* The discount rate is the rate charged to member banks when they borrow from the Fed. If the discount rate drops, member banks can borrow at a lower cost to meet reserve requirements. Therefore, banks are more willing to provide loans to consumers because they can borrow from the Fed at a lower rate in case of emergency. The result is an increase in the money supply when the discount rate drops. However, this is overestimated in the public's eyes because most of the borrowing and lending of reserves takes place in the federal funds market, rather than through direct borrowing from the Fed. The federal funds market is where banks borrow reserves from other banks. The rate of interest charged is called the *federal funds rate.* As a result, the discount rate has little impact on the money supply.

 C. The Fed can participate in expansionary or restrictive policy.

   (1) Expansionary policy is manifested when the Fed increases the money supply by lowering the required reserve ratio, buying government securities, or lowering the discount rate.

   (2) Restrictive policy is manifested in a reduction in the growth rate of the money supply caused by raising the required reserve ratio, selling government securities, or raising the discount rate.

 D. In the short run, an *unanticipated* increase in the supply of money will increase aggregate demand.

 E. If the increase in money supply is *anticipated,* there will be little or no impact on aggregate demand or real interest rates. In addition, an anticipated change in the money supply has the same effects as *long-run implications* of monetary policy.

 F. Supply of money

   (1) M-1, the simplest definition of the supply of money, includes currency in circulation (coins and paper), checkable deposits, and traveler's checks.

    (2) M-2, a broader definition, equals M-1 plus savings deposits and time deposits less than $100,000 plus money market mutual fund shares.

    (3) If individuals shift from savings accounts to checking accounts, the money supply is increased under the narrow definition (M-1) but is unaffected under the broader definition (M-2).

G. The impact of monetary policy of stock prices

    (1) The effects of monetary policy are shown via the dividend-discount model:

        (a) $V = D_0(1 + g)/k - g$

        (b) Where V is the value of the stock, D_0 is the dividend that is currently being paid, k is the investor's required rate of return, and g is the growth rate in the firm's dividend.

        (c) Any factor that affects any variable of the model then must have an impact on the valuation of the stock.

    (2) When the Federal Reserve tightens credit and drains the money out of the system, interest rates rise.

        (a) Higher interest rates increase the required rate of return *(k)* and suggest that the value of the stock should decline.

        (b) Higher interest rates may also reduce the firm's earnings, hurting its ability to grow and pay dividends; the D_0 or g is reduced, causing the value of the stock to decline.

    (3) The easing of credit has the opposite effect.

        (a) Lower interest rates may increase the value of a stock by increasing earnings.

        (b) This leads to higher dividends or increased growth, and a lower required rate of return *(k)*.

    (4) The anticipation of higher interest rates suggests that investors should avoid (1) fixed income investments, (2) firms whose cost of funds is sensitive to changes in interest rates and unable to pass on the increased cost, and (3) firms in cyclical industries whose product demand is affected by changes in interest rates.

4. Economic indicators

A. Investors who invest on the basis of relationships between security prices and economic activity want to know the direction of economic change before it happens. An emphasis is placed on leading economic indicators of economic activity.

B. The National Bureau of Economic Research (NBER) tabulates a series of economic indicators. The 10 leading indicators are

    (1) Stock prices (S&P 500 index)

    (2) Average weekly work hours

    (3) Average unemployment claims

    (4) Manufacturers' new consumer goods orders

    (5) Manufacturers' new orders for nondefense capital goods

    (6) Vendor performance (companies receiving slower deliveries)

    (7) New building permits

    (8) Interest rate spread (difference between 10-year Treasury bond and federal funds rate)

    (9) Inflation-adjusted M-2

    (10) Consumer expectations from the University of Michigan Research Center

C. Measures of inflation can have an important impact on investor behavior.

    (1) Inflation is a general rise in prices and is measured by an index.

(2) Two commonly used indexes are the Consumer Price Index (CPI) and the Producer Price Index (PPI).

    (a) CPI is calculated by the Bureau of Labor Statistics and measures the cost of a basket of goods and services over time.

    (b) PPI is calculated by the U.S. Department of Labor and measures wholesale cost of goods over a period of time.

5. Business cycle

  A. The term *business cycle* refers to a pattern of changing economic output and growth. The business cycle starts at an initial period of growth and rises as the economy expands until it reaches a peak. The economy then declines, reaching a trough, and subsequently starts to rebound to repeat the process.

  B. The peak is generally accompanied by an increased rate of inflation. This results in a period of rising unemployment and declining national output, called a recession.

  C. A *recession* is a period when Real GDP declines for two or more successive quarters; a *depression* is a prolonged and very severe recession.

  D. Gross domestic product (GDP) is the most common means of measuring economic activity.

    (1) GDP is the total value of all final goods and services newly produced within a country by domestic factors of production.

    (2) Trucks made in the United States by Honda are included in GDP, whereas IBM computers made in Europe are not.

  E. The key variables used for determining the phase of the business cycle are Real GDP and the unemployment rate. Real GDP is nominal GDP that has been adjusted to remove the impact of inflation.

6. Inflation, deflation, disinflation, and recession

  A. Definitions

    (1) Inflation is manifested when prices are rising, when it costs more one year to buy the same goods and services as it did the year before.

    (2) Deflation is manifested when prices are falling.

    (3) Disinflation is manifested when the rate of inflation decreases; prices are still rising, but at a slower pace.

    (4) Recession is a period of rising unemployment (which may or may not be accompanied by deflation)—Real GDP declines for two or more successive quarters.

  B. Inflation

    (1) In a period of inflation, investors should avoid interest-sensitive securities and long-term debt instruments that pay fixed amounts of interest.

    (2) They should acquire short-term instruments (U.S. Treasury bills) whose yields will increase with the rate of inflation.

    (3) The expectations of an inflationary environment suggest that investors should stress common stocks of firms whose asset bases will be enhanced by increased asset values (oil, metal, and land companies). Investors should avoid stocks of firms lacking assets that would rise with inflation.

  C. Deflation

    (1) In periods of deflation, prices of tangible assets (real estate, collectibles, and precious metals) will decline.

    (2) The anticipation of deflation strongly suggests that investors should acquire those financial assets whose values will not fall.

    (3) The safest strategy is to acquire short-term liquid assets, such as bank deposits, because deflation will increase the purchasing power of money.

    (4) Deflation makes long-term debt obligations good investments, but an investor should purchase only bonds of excellent quality, because deflation may be accompanied by bankruptcies as firms are unable to meet their financial obligations.

    (5) The same stress on quality applies to common stocks. Because many firms will experience falling demand and declining profit margins, quality should be stressed in purchasing stocks.

  D. Recession and economic stagnation

    (1) During a recession, the Federal Reserve will put money into circulation and expand the supply of credit. This expansion will at least initially decrease interest rates until the stimulus increases the level of economic activity.

    (2) The federal government will adopt an expansionary fiscal policy. Lower taxes and increased government expenditures will increase aggregate demand for goods and services. This increased demand is designed to stimulate economic activity, which reduces the level of unemployment.

    (3) To take advantage of the economic stimulus, the investor will seek to move out of short-term money market instruments into common stocks of firms that will benefit from the expansionary monetary and fiscal policy.

    (4) Once the investor identifies the firms most likely to benefit from the expansionary monetary and fiscal policy, he or she may adopt any of a number of individual strategies:

        (a) A conservative strategy may include the purchase of convertible securities (i.e., convertible bonds and preferred stock) and common stocks of firms with low beta coefficients. Fixed-income securities may be purchased in anticipation of lower interest rates. But the investor must be willing to move rapidly out of fixed-income securities, because they do not benefit from economic expansion and may be hurt if the expansion leads to higher interest rates.

        (b) An aggressive strategy designed to take advantage of expansionary fiscal policy will stress less current income (i.e., no fixed-income securities) and more potential for capital gains. The investor will then primarily purchase common stocks of firms with low payout ratios that retain earnings to finance expansion.

7. Yield curve

  A. A graph showing the relationship between *term to maturity* and *yield to maturity* is known as a yield curve.

  B. The yield curve shows the relationship between interest rates and time, typically relating to government Treasury securities.

  C. The yield curve is important to investors because as rates change, they usually do not change by the same amount of basis points across maturities.

  D. *Yield curve risk* is the risk that yields for different maturities may not change by the same amount in the presence of an interest rate change.

    (1) The risk is measured with the help of *duration*—a measure of bond price sensitivity to interest rates.

(2) If long-term rates are low, the present value of future cash flows into the future are high, causing a higher bond price. The bond's price will rapidly drop if interest rates increase because of the compounding effect of distant cash flows.

(3) If the bond has a shorter maturity and interest rates rise, its price will not drop as much as the bond with a longer-term maturity.

(4) The reason is that short- and intermediate-term rates are lower in an upward-sloping yield curve.

TOPIC 14: TIME VALUE OF MONEY CONCEPTS AND CALCULATIONS

1. Present value (PV)

   A. Present value is determined by taking the future value of a sum of money and calculating what it is worth today, using a discount rate. The formula is $PV = FV/(1 + I)^N$.

      (1) *Example*: Calculate the present value of $10,000 to be received in five years, using an annual interest rate of 10 percent.

      (2) *Solution*: 10,000 FV, 10 I, 5 N, calculate PV → $6,209.21 (ignore the sign).

   B. The more frequent the compounding, the smaller the present value.

2. Future value (FV) is the future amount of a sum invested today that will grow over time when it is compounding interest. The formula for finding the future value of a single cash flow is $FV = PV(1 + I)^N$.

   A. *Example*: Calculate the future value of $10,000 invested for five years, using an annual interest rate of 10 percent.

   B. *Solution*: −10,000 PV, 10 I, 5 N, calculate FV → $16,105.10

3. Ordinary annuity and annuity due

   A. An annuity is a series of equal cash flows that occur at equal intervals over a period of time. For example, the receipt of $1,000 at the end of each year for the next 10 years is an annuity.

      (1) An ordinary annuity is one in which cash flows begin at the end of each year.

      (2) An annuity due is one in which cash flows begin on the same day as the initial investment.

   B. *Example 1*: Finding the future value of an ordinary annuity

      (1) Calculate the future value of an ordinary annuity that will pay $1,000 per year for each of the next 10 years while earning a 12 percent rate of return.

      (2) *Solution*: 10 N, 12 I, 1,000 PMT, compute (CPT) FV → $17,548.73.

   C. *Example 2*: Finding the present value of an annuity due

      (1) Calculate the present value of an annuity of $2,000 received annually, beginning today and continuing for 15 years, earning a 10 percent rate of return.

      (2) First, put your calculator in the *begin* mode.

      (3) *Solution*: 15 N, 10 I, 2,000 payment (PMT), CPT PV → $16,733.38.

   D. *Example 3*: Finding the annual payment in an ordinary annuity

      (1) Calculate the annual payments required to fund your retirement plan in order to have $25,000 at the end of 10 years while earning a 12 percent rate of return.

      (2) *Solution*: 10 N, 12 I, FV 25,000, CPT PMT → $1,424.61.

   E. *Example 4*: Finding the monthly payment in an annuity due

      (1) Calculate the annual payments received at the beginning of each month for 10 years from an investment of $50,000 earning an annual return of 7 percent, compounded monthly.

      (2) First, put your calculator in the *begin* mode.

      (3) *Solution*: 120 N (10 × 12), .5833 (7/12) I, −50,000 PV, CPT PMT → $577.17.

4. Net present value (NPV)

   A. Net present value is the amount of cash flow (in present value terms) that a project generates after repaying the invested capital and required rate of return on that capital.

   B. If the project generates a positive NPV, then shareholder wealth increases. In contrast, a negative NPV will decrease shareholder wealth.

   C. NPV is considered better than internal rate of return (IRR) because it measures profitability in dollars added to shareholder value. In contrast, IRR measures profitability as a rate of return.

   D. NPV assumes that the reinvestment rate of cash flows is the cost of capital, whereas IRR assumes that the reinvestment rate is the IRR.

   E. When the IRR is equal to the cost of capital, the NPV will be zero. If the IRR is less than the cost of capital, the result is a negative NPV.

   F. *Example*: Calculate the NPV of a project with an initial cost of $2,000 that produces the following cash flows (CF): year (1) +1,000; year (2) +500; year (3) +700; year (4) −500; year (5) +300. The cost of capital is 5 percent.

      Solution: −2,000[CF_0]; 1,000 CF_j; 500 CF_j; 700 [CF_j]; −500 [CF_j]; 300 [CF_j]; 5 [I]; [NPV] → −$165.71.

5. Internal rate of return (IRR)

   A. The IRR calculates the rate of return at which the present value of a series of cash inflows will equal the present value of the project's cost.

   B. It is also defined as the rate of return in which the net present value of a project is zero. It assumes that all cash flows are reinvested at the IRR.

   C. The IRR is equivalent to the yield to maturity (YTM), the geometric average return, and the compounded average rate of return.

   D. If IRR is less than the cost of capital, reject the project. If IRR is greater than the cost of capital, accept the project.

   E. *Example*: Calculate the IRR of a project that has an initial outflow of 5,000 and will generate the following cash flows: year (1) 3,000; year (2) −500; year (3) 2,500; year (4) 500; year (5) 1,500.

      Solution: −5,000[CF_0]; 3,000 CF_j; −500 CF_j; 2,500 [CF_j]; 500 [CF_j]; 1,500 [CF_j]; [IRR] → 14.09 percent.

6. Irregular cash flow

   A. It is common for the stream of cash flows to change from year to year for projects or investments, so it is not an annuity. The uneven cash flow is simply just a stream of (annual) single cash flows.

   B. To determine the FV/PV of irregular cash flows, you need to find the FV/PV of each cash flow and then add them up. The PV of an uneven cash flow stream is also calculated using the NPV function on your calculator.

   C. *Example 1*: Calculate the present value of an uneven cash flow series using a 10 percent discount rate and PV_1 though PV_5. Assume cash flows are:

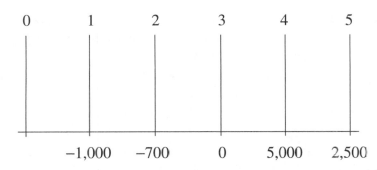

PV$_1$: enter FV = −1,000; I/Y = 10; N = 1; CPT → PV$_1$ = −909.09
PV$_2$: enter FV =   −700; I/Y = 10; N = 2; CPT → PV$_2$ = −578.51
PV$_3$: enter FV =   0; I/Y = 10; N = 3; CPT → PV$_3$ =   0.00
PV$_4$: enter FV =   5,000; I/Y = 10; N = 4; CPT → PV$_4$ = 3,415.07
PV$_5$: enter FV =   2,500; I/Y = 10; N = 5; CPT → PV$_5$ = 1,552.30
                 Add up the PVs   3,479.77

    D. Regarding *Example 2*, what you are really doing is finding the NPV of a series of cash flows:

    Solution: 0[CF$_0$]; −1,000 CF$_j$; −700 CF$_j$; 0 [CF$_j$]; 5,000 [CF$_j$]; 2,500 [CF$_j$]; 10 [I]; [NPV] → $3,479.77.

7. Inflation-adjusted earnings rate

    A. Nominal rate of return investors require is: nominal risk-free rate = (1 − real risk-free rate) × (1 + inflation rate) − 1.
    B. Real risk-free rate = [(1 + nominal risk-free rate)/(1 + inflation rate)] − 1.
    C. Calculate the nominal risk-free rate if the real rate is 5 percent and the expected inflation rate is 3 percent: (1.05) × (1.03) − 1 = 8.15 percent.

8. Serial payments

    A. A serial payment is a payment that increases at some constant rate on an annual basis; the constant rate is usually inflation.
    B. The last serial payment will have the same purchasing power as the initial serial payment.
    C. Serial payments are not fixed payments like annuities; the first serial payment will be less than an annuity payment, but the last serial payment will be more than an annuity payment.
    D. *Example 1*: Assume Jeff wants to start a business in five years. He needs to have $250,000 (today's dollars) in five years to finance his business. Inflation is expected to average 3 percent, and Jeff can earn an 8 percent annual compounded rate on his investments. What serial payment should Jeff invest at the end of the first year?

    Solution: 250,000 FV; 5 N; 0 PV; [(1.08/1.03 − 1)] × 100[I]; [PMT] 1.03 [×] → $46,736.78.

    E. *Example 2*: What is Jeff's payment in the second year?

    Solution: $46,736.78 [×] 1.03 → $48,138.88.

TOPIC 15: CHARACTERISTICS AND CONSEQUENCES OF TYPES OF ENTITIES

1. Sole proprietorship

    A. A sole proprietorship is the most common form of business ownership. This is due to its relative administrative simplicity.

B. A sole proprietorship is not a legal entity separate and apart from its owner. Thus, the owner's personal assets are exposed without limitation to any and all liabilities related to the business.

C. Sole proprietorships are easy to establish and require no special forms. Sole proprietors file just a Schedule C in addition to their personal tax forms.

D. A sole proprietor can use that business structure to employ and shift income to other family members, which can result in lower taxes.

E. There is no flexible ownership, continuity of life, or capital structure, because there is only one owner. The business cannot be transferred, although its assets may be sold.

2. Partnerships

A. General partnership

(1) A general partnership consists of two or more owners doing business together with the intent to divide the income and profits.

(2) The legal aspects of general partnerships are governed by state partnership statutes, most of which are in conformity with the Federal Uniform Partnership Act and the Revised Uniform Limited Partnership Act.

(3) Authority and responsibility of a general partnership:

(a) As to authority, a partner can bind other partners to a contract made in the ordinary course of business.

(b) As to responsibilities, each partner has duties to every other partner, which include fiduciary duties, duty to act in good faith, and so forth.

(c) Notice to one partner is viewed as notice to all partners.

(4) General partners can be liable for actions of other partners.

(a) For torts, the partners are *jointly and severally liable*. *Joint liability* means that all partners must be sued together. *Several liability* means that a party may sue any partner for the full amount of the claim. Thus, a partner who commits a tort in the ordinary course of partnership business has a personal liability and has created a liability for all other partners.

(b) Each partner is *jointly liable* with all other partners for the contracts of the partnership.

(5) General partners are co-owners of the business.

(a) Each partner is entitled to share in the profits and surplus of the partnership.

(b) Partners are not entitled to salaries. There is no inherent right to a salary, only to a pro rata share of profits. A partnership agreement can specify the specific method by which profits (and losses) are to be allocated.

(c) All partners have the right to participate in the management of the business. All partners must agree before a change can be made to this right.

(d) Each partner has the right to use specific partnership property for partnership business.

(e) A new partner cannot be admitted without the unanimous consent of all partners.

(f) An incoming partner is liable only for future debts of the partnership, not for existing debts.

(6) A general partnership can dissolve for any of several reasons.

(a) Dissolution of the partnership occurs automatically and without notice because of any of the following events:

        i. Death of a partner

        ii. Bankruptcy of a partner

        iii. Termination as specified under the partnership agreement

  (b) Actual business may be continued, but only as a new partnership.

  (c) If the business is not continued, the assets of the business must be distributed according to set guidelines.

(7) Unlike corporations, partnerships offer no continuity of life, centralized management, or ownership transfer.

(8) Form 1065 is required to be filed for the organization. Schedule K-1 is the tax form on which owner's compensation is reported.

B. Limited partnership

(1) There must be one or more general partners and one or more limited partners.

(2) Limited partners have limited liability.

(3) A limited partner is an investor only:

  (a) Cannot participate in managing the business

  (b) Has no authority to bind the business

  (c) Cannot use last name (surname) in the name of the partnership

(4) A number of events can lead to the termination of a limited partnership:

  (a) A judicial order

  (b) Withdrawal, death, insolvency, or insanity of a general partner

  (c) Termination does not result from the withdrawal, death, insolvency, or insanity of a limited partner.

  (d) Termination does not result from the transfer of a limited partner's interest to another party.

(5) Form 1065 is required to be filed for the organization. Schedule K-1 is the tax form on which owner's compensation is reported.

C. Limited liability partnership (LLP)

(1) Formed and operated pursuant to state LLP statutes—requires at least two owners, but no maximum

(2) If a general partnership organizes or converts to an LLP, it can retain its normal operating characteristics, with the added advantage of limited liability for the owners.

(3) All partners have limited liability.

  (a) An LLP partner may be personally liable for his or her own tort-related acts and his or her own professional errors, omissions, and negligence.

  (b) An LLP partner may also be personally liable for the professional errors, omissions, and negligence of others who are under the partner's direct supervision or who should have been.

  (c) LLP partners generally are not liable for any debts, obligations, or liabilities of the partnership.

D. Limited liability companies (LLC)

(1) Offers limited liability protection to all of its owners (called members) but is still treated as a partnership under federal income tax rules—some states allow a one-member LLC.

(2) Differences between an LLC and an LLP:

(a) One of the principal differences between an LLC and an LLP is the level of limited liability protection for the owners and the entity. Each LLP partner remains liable for the malpractice of people he or she directly controls or supervises, whereas members of an LLC are not.

(b) An LLP, in some states, has to reregister as a limited liability partnership each time a partner dies or the entity dissolves; this may result in the LLP being more expensive than an LLC, inasmuch as filing fees in most states are per partner, not per entity.

(3) An LLC can elect to be taxed as a corporation, S Corporation, or sole proprietorship, but generally an LLC will elect to be taxed as a partnership. One-member LLCs file Schedule C (sole proprietorship) because by definition, one member cannot be a partnership. Two or more members will file Form 1065 (Partnership Information Return).

(4) An LLC is a legal entity separate from its members—it owns its own assets and is liable for its debts. The personal assets of LLC members generally are beyond the reach of LLC creditors or those of the members.

(5) LLCs also have flexible ownership (some states require two members, others require only one) and capital structure, as well as centralized management.

(6) Disadvantages include no free transferability of ownership interests, poor tax treatment of fringe benefits, and limited flexibility in selecting a tax year. Some states may not recognize one-person LLCs or permit certain lines of business to use the LLC structure.

3. Corporations

  A. S Corporations

    (1) An S Corporation is treated as a pass-through entity under federal income tax laws. This means that S Corporation shareholders can receive business profits as dividends.

    (2) An S Corporation has several general characteristics:

      (a) Limited owner liability

      (b) Free transferability of ownership interests (as long as there are no more than 75 owners)

      (c) Centralized management and continuity of life through stock ownership

    (3) Disadvantages include poor tax treatment of fringe benefits, limited flexibility in selecting a tax year, and no ability to retain income at lower current tax cost.

    (4) S Corporations are subject to strict eligibility requirements; an S Corporation must:

      (a) Be a domestic corporation

      (b) Have no more than 75 shareholders

      (c) Have no shareholders other than individuals who are U.S. citizens or resident aliens, estates, or certain types of trusts

      (d) Have only one class of stock

    (5) If requirements are not met, resulting profits are subject to double taxation.

  B. C Corporations

    (1) A C Corporation is an artificial entity that comes into existence upon the proper filing of articles of incorporation and issuance by the state of a certificate of incorporation.

    (2) A number of different parties are involved with the corporation.

      (a) Shareholders are the owners of the corporation; shareholders elect directors to oversee the corporation.

      (b) Directors are elected by shareholders to direct the main course of the corporation.

(c) Officers are chosen by the directors to run the day-to-day business of the corporation as agents for the corporation.

(3) A C Corporation has several general characteristics:

(a) It is a separate legal entity; the corporation is a separate person. It is separate from the persons who formed the corporation or who currently own it.

(b) The owners have limited liability. The shareholders can lose only what they invest in the corporation (what they pay or promise to pay for the stock of the corporation).

(c) The corporation is taxed separately from its owners because the corporation is a new, separate entity in the eyes of the taxing authorities.

(d) Corporate tax rates are generally lower than individual rates for high-income individuals.

(e) It offers better tax treatment for owner fringe benefits, the ability to select a tax year, and the ability to take loans from qualified retirement plans.

(f) When a business intends to retain all its earnings for an indefinite period in order to finance its growth, differences in tax rates make corporations a better choice than dividend pass-through structures.

(g) It is able to have continuous life. The corporation continues in existence even after a shareholder dies. This is true even if there is only one shareholder.

(h) It allows its owners to transfer ownership. Stock, unless restricted at issuance, is freely transferable.

(4) C Corporation income is subject to double taxation.

(a) A dollar is earned by the corporation, which pays a tax on it at the corporate rate.

(b) What is left of the dollar is paid as a dividend to the shareholders, each of whom pays a tax on it at his or her individual rate.

(c) *The solution*: Keep the dollar in the corporation, avoiding taxation at the individual level, or pay the dollar to the individual as a salary, avoiding taxation at the corporate level.

(5) The tax advantage of corporate tax rates on earnings accumulated by the corporation is limited somewhat by the accumulated-earnings tax.

(a) The accumulated earnings tax is a penalty tax designed to prevent tax avoidance through the accumulation of earnings within the corporation beyond expected needs of the business.

(b) The corporation can accumulate up to a minimum credit of $250,000 of earnings and profits without encountering any problem with the accumulated earnings tax—beyond this amount, it must demonstrate to the IRS that the accumulation is for reasonable needs of the business.

(c) If the corporation cannot demonstrate this need, the IRS imposes the accumulated earnings tax at a rate of 38.6 percent (in 2002) on all accumulated taxable income.

(6) A C Corporation is created by following the process of incorporation.

(7) To raise capital, a C Corporation is allowed to issue stock. A company will always have at least one class of stock but can also have a second class.

(8) Extraordinary transactions such as merger, consolidation, or sale of all assets must have special approval.

(9) A dissolution will terminate the corporation's existence. It is not complete until the winding up of affairs and distribution of assets have occurred.

C. Professional corporation (PC)

    (1) The formalities associated with the operation of a professional corporation (PC) are similar to those of any other commercial corporation.

    (2) Virtually all professional corporation statutes limit the ownership of a professional corporation to licensed members of the profession.

    (3) The professional corporation is formed as a separate legal entity under state law and provides for a continuity of life beyond that of its shareholders.

        (a) At the death, disability, or termination of employment of a professional, the stock held by the professional can be (1) transferred to another licensed professional or (2) redeemed by the corporation.

        (b) A problem can arise if no buyer can be found or if the corporation has inadequate surplus for the redemption. To some extent, this may limit the continuity of life of the professional corporation.

    (4) The limited-liability shelter of the corporate form of ownership offers a distinct advantage over the operation of the business in an unincorporated form—includes protection from contractual obligations of the corporation and generally from the actions of other shareholders and employees.

    (5) Individual shareholders-professionals remain liable for their own negligent actions—a professional acting as an employee of the professional corporation retains unlimited liability for professional malpractice—and for actions of corporate employees directly under supervision.

    (6) There is benefit from the corporate tax structure.

4. Association

    A. An association is a group of persons banded together for a specifically defined purpose.

    B. Some associations operate under tax-exempt status.

    C. To be considered for tax-exempt status under Section 501(a), an association must have a written document, such as "Articles of Association," showing its creation, which must be signed by at least two persons and must be dated.

    D. The definition of an association can vary under state law.

5. Business trust

    A. A trustee takes legal title to the business assets and manages the business for the owners, and the beneficiaries are shareholders.

    B. Business trusts are taxed according to the economic reality of the business.

        (1) If the trust is a sham or façade with no economic reality, it will be ignored and the tax liability will be placed directly on the individual who formed the trust—this includes estate taxes.

        (2) If the trust has only one individual who funded it and operates it, it will generally be treated as a sole proprietorship.

        (3) If it has two or more individuals who control it (i.e., if it resembles a partnership), it will generally be treated as a partnership.

        (4) If the trust is registered as a corporation under state or federal statutes, it will be treated as a corporation.

    C. Federal income tax reporting requirements for business trusts

        (1) If the trust actually operates as a sole proprietorship, the income and expenses should be reported on Schedule C of the Form 1040 of the individual who actually owns and operates it.

      (2) If the trust actually operates as a partnership, the income and expenses should be reported on a Form 1065, U.S. Partnership Income Tax Return, and passed through to the partners on a Schedule K-1.

      (3) If the trust has been granted a corporate charter under any state or federal law, then it should report its income and expenses on a Form 1120, U.S. Corporation Income Tax Return, or a Form 1120S, U.S. Small Business Corporation Income Tax Return.

6. Selection of business form

  A. Sole proprietorship

    (1) When to use:

      (a) When there is only a single owner and single member, or LLCs are not permitted by state law

      (b) When adequate liability insurance is available at an acceptable cost

      (c) When the business is in its infancy

      (d) When the owner is not concerned with transferring future interests of the business

    (2) When not to use:

      (a) When the business begins generating significant income and wealth for the owner—probably best to establish a limited-liability entity

      (b) When concerned about having all personal assets at risk, through unlimited liability

      (c) When the business will involve the delivery of financial services with the inherent risk of errors and omission claims

      (d) When there is more than one employee—this raises the possibility of increased theft, unauthorized borrowing and spending.

  B. General partnership

    (1) When to use:

      (a) When the business begins operations and generates significant start-up losses that can be passed through to the partners without being affected by the various restrictions of S Corporations. Because partnerships are non–tax-paying entities, items of income, gain, deduction, loss, and credit are passed through to the partners, who then take those items into account in their own tax returns.

      (b) When the business is a professional practice in which pass-through taxation can be combined with specially tailored ownership interests that reflect each member's contributions to the practice

      (c) When there are cash distributions received that can reduce the partner's basis in his or her interest. Only distributions in excess of cost basis trigger taxable gain to the partner.

    (2) When not to use:

      (a) When there are partners who do not want to be responsible for the activities of other partners

      (b) When there is a concern about having all personal assets at risk through unlimited liability

      (c) When the business will involve the delivery of financial services with the inherent risk of errors and omission claims

C. Limited partnership

(1) When to use:

    (a) When members want pass-through taxation with no active management

    (b) When there is a concern about having all personal assets at risk through unlimited liability

    (c) When members do not want to be subject to the double taxation of C Corporations

    (d) When members do not want to be subject to the strict S Corporation qualification rules

    (e) When members want tax-free distributions of appreciated property and create different types of partnership interests with varying rights to cash flow, liquidation proceeds, and tax allocations, which S Corporations cannot do

(2) When not to use:

    (a) When partners have active participation in management

    (b) When qualifying as an LLP or LLC is allowed

    (c) When qualifying as an S Corporation is more convenient and partners want the transferability of ownership through stock

D. Limited liability partnership (LLP)

(1) When to use:

    (a) When the members want pass-through taxation and cannot operate as a limited partnership because of the active management of all the firm's partners

    (b) When state law prohibits the use of an LLC—an LLP can be used instead.

    (c) When it is easier to convert an existing general partnership into an LLP rather than an LLC

    (d) When members do not want to be subject to the double taxation of C Corporations

    (e) When members do not want to be subject to the strict S Corporation qualification rules

    (f) When LLCs are subject to certain types of state taxation, such as in Texas, which taxes LLCs on an entity level that does not exist for LLPs

    (g) When members want tax-free distributions of appreciated property and create different types of partnership interests with varying rights to cash flow, liquidation proceeds, and tax allocations, which S Corporations cannot do

(2) When not to use:

    (a) When state law does not offer LLC-like liability protection to LLP partners

    (b) If state law does not permit it

    (c) When qualifying as an S Corporation is more convenient and partners want the transferability of ownership through stock

    (d) If the partner can "zero out" the double taxation of C Corporations with deductible payments to or for the benefit of the owners

E. Limited liability company (LLC)

(1) When to use:

    (a) For professional practices where state law permits its use

    (b) As estate planning vehicles whereby older generations can gift LLC ownership interests to younger family members, yet retaining control while functioning as managers

(c) For corporate joint ventures in which the corporate co-owners desire both pass-through taxation and limited liability

(d) For business start-up companies that expect to have losses in the initial years that are passed through to investors

(e) For real estate investment development activities, because the partnership taxation rules allow the investors to obtain basis from entity-level debt and because special tax allocations can be made to benefit investors

(f) For venture capital investments in which the partnership rules allow pass-through taxation

  (2) When not to use:

(a) When state law does not permit its use in general or in lines of banking or insurance

(b) When shares of stock will continuously be issued to represent ownership interests

(c) If unsure of an income tax outcome, inasmuch as LLC laws are new

F. S Corporation

  (1) When to use:

(a) When limiting owner liability is a key issue

(b) When the eligibility rules can be met

(c) When there will be only one owner, and one-person LLCs are not available. S Corporations are strongly preferred over sole proprietorships.

  (2) When not to use:

If one-person LLCs are available. They hold significant tax advantages over S Corporations.

G. C Corporation

  (1) When to use:

(a) When limiting owner liability is a critical concern

(b) When there will be only one owner, and single-member LLCs are not permitted by state law

(c) When the benefits of pass-through taxation are not required

(d) When owners want the ability to borrow against their qualified retirement plan accounts

(e) When an owner wants to retain all earnings to finance capital expenditures and expansions—lower taxes at corporate level

  (2) When not to use:

(a) When owners do not want to be hit with double taxation. Double taxation can appear in dividend distributions, on the sale of stock, on liquidation, or from appreciating assets, such as real estate. If real estate assets can be owned by a pass-through entity, which, in turn, is owned by the C Corporation shareholders, the real estate can then be leased back to the C Corporation. With this arrangement, the C Corporation can reduce its taxable income by making deductible rental payments that benefit its shareholders. Any gains on the eventual sale of the appreciated assets owned by the pass-through entity will not be subject to double taxation.

(b) When the business distributes most of its income to the owners. Such a business should operate as one of the pass-through entities.

7. Acquisition and disposition

   A. Types

      (1) Liquidation of business—Corporation's properties are distributed to shareholders and the corporate stock is cancelled.

         (a) Liquidations are often an inappropriate way to sell a business, because the tax treatment is unfavorable

         (b) The corporation pays tax on its capital gain when it sells assets or distributes assets to shareholders.

         (c) Shareholders are taxed on the gain equal to the difference between the fair market value of what they receive from the corporation and their basis in their stock.

         (d) S Corporations avoid double taxation on liquidations because of the pass-through of corporate income to shareholders and the basis rule.

      (2) Taxable sale of business

         (a) The vast majority of business sales are taxable.

         (b) Stock sale results in a taxable gain to the business's selling shareholders that is equal to the difference between the selling price and their basis. Sale of stock does not affect the cost basis of assets.

         (c) Asset sale results in a taxable gain to the corporation if the selling price exceeds the corporation's basis, and the shareholders are also taxed on the capital gain when the proceeds from the sale are distributed to them in liquidation. Asset sale may result in a new cost basis for assets.

      (3) Tax-free dispositions of business

         (a) Stock sale will qualify if at least 80 percent of the voting power and at least 80 percent of the other stock in the seller are transferred to the acquiring organization in exchange for only voting stock in the buyer.

         (b) Asset sale will qualify if substantially all of the seller's net assets are transferred to the acquiring organization in exchange for only voting stock in the buyer.

         (c) Tax consequences of a tax-free sale are as follows:

            i. There is no tax to the seller or to the selling corporation at the time of the transaction.

            ii. The seller receives stock in the acquiring corporation at a basis equal to the seller's basis in the property sold—that is, a carryover basis.

            iii. The exchange is tax free, but the seller will be taxed when he or she sells the stock. The gain on the sale can be avoided if the stock is held until death.

   B. Planning the taxable sale

      (1) Installment sales

         (a) A seller's gain can be spread ratably over the period during which installment payments are made.

         (b) A buyer's interest payments are deductible (within limits) when made, and taxable to the seller when received.

         (c) Imputed interest rules apply—interest on an installment note that is regulated by a minimum rate of interest defined in the Internal Revenue Code. Imputed interest is imposed for tax purposes if an installment sale does not provide for an adequate rate of interest, and it is taxed over the installment period by a complex set of rules—in sum, the sale cannot be planned to avoid the tax on interest to the seller by understating the interest at artificially low rates.

(2) Private annuity

   (a) Payments are made for the rest of seller's life—based on actuarial factors.

   (b) Part of each annuity payment is a tax-free return of basis, part is capital gain, and part is interest—similar to an installment sale—but only until the seller reaches life expectancy, and the annuity factor makes the calculations somewhat different and the amount of income tax payable may be significantly different from that in an installment sale.

TOPIC 16: CHARACTERISTICS AND CONSEQUENCES OF PROPERTY TITLING

1. Common law versus community property

   A. Common law is a body of law that is based on custom and general principles and is embodied in case law. It is applied to situations not covered by statute. A husband and wife have equal ownership in all property under common law.

   B. Community property is all property that has been acquired by the efforts of either spouse during their marriage while living in a community property state. It does not include property acquired by only one of the spouses by gift, devise, bequest, or inheritance, or acquired by either spouse prior to their marriage—both spouses own community property equally.

   C. Classifying income in community property states

      (1) *California rule*. Income from community property is community property, as well as anything bought with that income. Income from separate property is separate property, as well as anything bought with that income.

      (2) *Texas rule (Texas, Idaho, and Louisiana)*. Income earned from separate property during the marriage is community property, but the gain on separate property when sold is separate property.

      (3) *Example*: Steve and Liz live in California, a community property state. Steve owned a convertible Corvette before their marriage, which Liz now uses. Last year Liz's father gave her 1,000 shares of XYZ stock, which pays a quarterly dividend. Liz used the last dividend check to buy a mountain bike. Steve bought a kayak from money saved from his July paycheck. The stock and bike are Liz's separate property. The Corvette is Steve's separate property. All the other assets, including both salaries and the kayak, are community property.

2. Sole ownership

   Complete ownership with all rights

3. Joint tenancy with right of survivorship (JTWROS)

   A. On the death of one co-owner, the decedent's interest automatically passes to the surviving owner(s).

   B. The automatic right of survivorship inherent in joint tenancy prevails over other means of transfers at death, including a will and a trust instrument.

   C. In most states, one cotenant can unilaterally *sever* the joint tenancy without the knowledge or consent of the other tenant(s).

   D. Joint tenancies are commonly created among family members.

4. Tenancy by the entireties

   A. *Tenancy by the entirety* is like a joint tenancy in that it carries the right of survivorship, but it can be created only between husband and wife.

  B. It is unlike joint tenancy, in that neither spouse may transfer the property without the consent of the other.

  C. Where such a title is recognized, since it is available only to married couples, a divorce will cause a tenant by the entirety title to automatically convert into a tenant in common form of title.

5. Tenancy in common

  A. Like joint tenancy, *tenants in common* interests are held by two or more persons, each having an undivided right to possess property.

  B. Unlike joint tenancy, *tenants in common* interests may be owned in unequal percentages, and when one owner dies, the remaining owners do not automatically succeed in ownership.

  C. The decedent's interest passes through his or her estate, by will or by the laws of intestate succession. The interest can also be transferred to the trustee of a trust and passed according to the provisions of the trust.

  D. Tenancy in common is a preferred titling for nonrelatives.

6. Trust ownership

  A. A trust is a fiduciary relationship in which one person (the *trustee*) is holder of the title to property (the *trust estate* or *trust corpus*), subject to an equitable obligation to keep or use the property for the benefit of another (the *beneficiary*).

  B. The trust instrument is a written agreement between the *settlor* (the person creating and funding the trust) and the *trustee* that sets forth for whose benefit the trust is created, how the trust estate is to be managed, the duration of the trust, and the distribution of the corpus when the trust terminates.

  C. A trust passes property outside of probate.

7. Uniform Transfer to Minors Act (UTMA) and Uniform Gifts to Minors Act (UGMA)

  A. UGMA allows a simple method of making gifts to minors—no court supervision is required. UGMA allows transfer of securities, cash, life insurance, and annuities, but does not allow real property to be held in custodial form.

  B. UTMA was designed to replace UGMA. UTMA allows any property interest to be transferred, including real property.

  C. There are characteristics shared by UGMA and UTMA that are different from those of trusts.

   (1) A custodial gift may be created for only one person. In contrast, a trust can provide for multiple beneficiaries.

   (2) UGMA/UTMA is not a separate taxpayer—all income is taxable to the minor. In contrast, an irrevocable trust is a separate taxpayer offering preferential tax treatment.

   (3) Under UGMA/UTMA, donees usually receive the custodial property outright by age 21, but distributions from trusts may be delayed for a later age.

TOPIC 17: FINANCIAL SERVICES INDUSTRY REGULATION REQUIREMENTS

1. Registration and licensing

  A. National Association of Security Dealers, Inc. (NASD)

   (1) Anyone who sells stocks, bonds, tax-sheltered investments, options, mutual funds, or other securities must register with the NASD in addition to the SEC.

(2) The NASD is an independent group overseen by the SEC and is a self-governing organization that polices its own members.

(3) Registration with the NASD is accomplished by completing a Uniform Application for Securities Industry Registration, a Form U-4, and receiving a passing grade on one or more exams, depending on the products the adviser wishes to sell. Passing the exam(s) and being given the right to sell makes the individual a registered representative (Registered Representative).

(4) Qualification and registration requirements for security licenses:

   (a) *Series 3—Futures and Commodities*. For individuals who wish to sell commodities or futures contracts

   (b) *Series 4—Registered Options Principal*. For managers supervising options sales personnel or supervising compliance

   (c) *Series 6—Investment Companies*. For individuals who wish to sell only mutual funds and variable annuities

   (d) *Series 7—General Securities Representative*. For individuals who wish to trade securities

   (e) *Series 9 and 10 (also known as Series 8)—General Sales Supervisor*. For New York Stock Exchange (NYSE) managers to supervise branch activities

   (f) *Series 11—Assistant Representative*. For sales assistants who wish to accept unsolicited customer orders

   (g) *Series 24—General Securities Principal*. For licensing NYSE managers to supervise branch activities

   (h) *Series 27—General Financial/Operations Principal*. Required for the chief financial officer of NASD member firms

   (i) *Series 55—Registered Equity Trader*. Required for persons participating in equity trading

   (j) *Series 63—Uniform State Law*. Required for most individuals who solicit orders for any type of security in a particular state

   (k) *Series 65—Registered Investment Adviser*. Required by many states for individuals who act as investment advisers

   (l) *Series 66—Combined Registered Investment Adviser/Uniform State Law*. Combines the Series 65 and Series 63 licenses

B. The insurance buyer makes contact with the insurer in any of three ways and must be registered as such.

   (1) *Agent*. Representative of the insurance company (also called *principal*). An agent has authority to act on behalf of the principal in business transactions and has the power to bind a company to a risk by acceptance.

   (2) *Broker*. A marketing intermediary between the insurer and the policy owner, who represents the policy owner instead of the insurer. This generally permits sales representatives to sell products from a number of companies, primarily as the representative of the insurance buyer. In regard to insurance consultants and financial planners, many states require anyone who presents him- or herself as providing advice regarding insurance, including financial planners, to have a license.

   (3) *Service representatives*. These are salaried individuals hired by insurers to assist agents in selling and servicing insurance. A license is usually not required by the state to act as a service representative.

C. SEC Release No. IA-770

    (1) The SEC has taken the position that the Investment Advisors Act of 1940 is the statutory body of law that should control the area of regulation of financial planners.

    (2) SEC Release No. IA-770 sets forth three separate tests for determining whether a financial planner's activities fall under the Investment Advisors Act of 1940. All three tests must be answered in the affirmative for the Investment Advisors Act of 1940 to apply to the financial planner.

        (a) Investment advice is clearly a part of the person's primary business.

        (b) The advice is specific and action oriented.

        (c) The adviser receives compensation for the advice.

    (3) If a financial adviser passes all of these tests, the SEC assumes that he or she is in the business of investment advice and requires that person to register unless otherwise exempted.

D. The Investment Advisors Act of 1940 specifies six areas set forth in Section 202(a)(11) that eliminate the need for financial service professionals to be subject to the mandates of the statute. The Investment Advisors Act of 1940 does not apply to any of their activities if they fall within the following categories:

    (1) Any bank or holding company that is not an investment company

    (2) Any lawyer, accountant, engineer, or teacher, when the advisory services are "solely incidental" to the practice of his or her profession

    (3) Any broker, dealer, or registered representative whose performance of advisory services is solely incidental to his or her performance as a broker or dealer and who receives no specific compensation for these services

    (4) The publishers of newspapers, newsmagazines, or business or financial publications of general or regular circulation

    (5) Any person whose advice, analysis, or reports relate only to securities that are direct obligations of or publications guaranteed as to principal or interest by the United States of America

    (6) Any other persons not within the intent of law as specified by the SEC

E. There are five other groups of individuals who fall within the definition of investment adviser but are exempt from registration with the Securities and Exchange Commission under Section 203(b) of the Investment Advisors Act of 1940:

    (1) Any investment adviser whose clients are all residents of the state in which the adviser maintains his or her principal office and place of business and who does not provide advice or analysis in regard to listed securities or on any securities admitted to unlisted trading privileges on any national securities exchange

    (2) Any investment adviser whose primary clients are insurance companies

    (3) Any investment adviser who has fewer than 15 clients in a year and does not present him- or herself as an investment adviser to the public

    (4) Any investment adviser that is a charitable organization or employed by a charitable organization and provides advice and analysis only to charitable organizations

    (5) Any investment adviser who provides investment advice exclusively to church employee pension plans

F. Investment Advisors Supervision Coordination Act of 1996—Enacted in 1997, the Investment Advisors Supervision Coordination Act of 1996 changed the landscape in regard to the Investment Advisors Act of 1940. The primary outcome is that financial planners need to be registered with the SEC or state authorities, but not both.

(1) Any adviser with $30 million or more of assets under control will still have to register with the SEC, but will be exempt from state registration.

(2) Those with less than $30 million in managed assets will have to register with the state. Any adviser with between $25 million and $30 million of managed assets can register with either the state or the SEC.

(3) All other areas of the Investment Advisors Act of 1940, with the exclusion of registration, will still apply to Registered Investment Advisers (RIAs).

(4) States retain jurisdiction in regard to fraud and illegal activity as it applies to Registered Investment Advisers.

(5) A *national* de minimis *standard* rule was introduced, stating that investment advisers may not be required to register in a state unless the adviser has a place of business in that state or, during the preceding 12 months, has had more than five clients who are residents of the state.

(6) Record keeping rules put forth that no state may require more stringent requirements than the resident state of the adviser.

(7) The Act allows the denial of registration to felons if within 10 years of the conviction

(8) The Act mandated a new consumer information hotline allowing for inquiry regarding disciplinary actions and proceedings against any RIA or associates

G. Regulation of the insurance industry

(1) *Legislative action.* The legislative branch of the government of each of the 50 states enacts laws that govern the insurance industry.

(2) *Judicial action.* The role of the courts in regulating insurance is to interpret the meaning of policy terms, rule on the constitutionality of state insurance laws, and adjudicate disputes between insurers and policyholders when other available avenues of dispute resolution fail.

(3) *Administrative action.* The Commissioner of Insurance in each state is charged with the administration of the state's insurance laws. The Commissioner makes rulings that have the binding force of law and may exercise judicial power in interpreting and enforcing the insurance code.

2. Reporting

A. Form ADV

(1) When an investment adviser is required to register with the SEC, he or she must also file SEC Form ADV and pay the required filing fees. Form ADV contains two sections:

(a) Part I contains general and background information regarding the applicant and questions regarding the applicant's expected clients.

(b) Part II is more detailed, requiring information about the adviser's fee structure, specific types of services offered, and the method of business operation, as well as questions in regard to the direct involvement of the adviser in securities transactions for his or her clients.

(2) Once registration is complete, the investment adviser may use the official title of Registered Investment Adviser, but not the initials "RIA," which may suggest that an exam or class work was completed and a professional designation obtained.

(3) Form ADV generally restricts advisers from "performance-based" fees in regard to the performance of assets under management; however, there is not any restriction placed

on the adviser in basing fees as a percentage of the total assets under management with a client. Rule 205-3 says performance-based fees are permitted when the (1) client is a registered investment company, (2) the adviser manages more than $750,000 of the client's assets, or (3) the adviser believes that the client's net worth exceeds $1.5 million.

  B. Brochure rule

    (1) Since January 1979, Registered Investment Advisers are required to deliver a written disclosure, a requirement commonly called the "brochure rule." The disclosure is to be delivered to the client within 48 hours of entering into an investment advisory agreement or when the contract is signed if the client has the right to terminate the contract within five days of signing.

    (2) Form ADV, Part II, can be used to meet the requirement of the brochure rule.

3. Compliance

  A. The SEC requires a detailed file of record keeping.

  B. Section 206 of the Investment Advisors Act of 1940 has also come to be known as the "antifraud provision," making any illegal actions by the adviser equivalent to fraud. The Act puts the adviser in a fiduciary position.

  C. Should an adviser fail to meet any of the requirements of the Investment Advisors Act of 1940, the registration process, or the continued registration requirements, the SEC may investigate and confiscate all books and records as well as levy fines for noncompliance.

  D. The Insider Trading and Securities Fraud Enforcement Act of 1988 mandates that investment advisers maintain a clearly written set of rules and policies in order to prevent the likelihood of insider trading on nonpublic information.

4. State securities and insurance laws

  A. State securities

    (1) Advisers should be knowledgeable of the " blue sky laws" mandated by states requiring the registration of advisers.

    (2) Currently, 49 states require the registration of investment advisors.

    (3) Many states require a minimum capitalization amount as a prerequisite for granting investment adviser registration.

  B. Insurance laws

    (1) In contrast to securities, the insurance industry is regulated at the state level. Advisers wishing to sell insurance products must be licensed for all products they wish to sell within the state in which they work. This means that advisers wishing to sell all types of insurance must pass exams for each type as specified by each state.

    (2) Keep in mind that variable life and variable annuities contain investments and, therefore, require the adviser to also have a Series 6 securities license.

TOPIC 18: BUSINESS LAW

The "Contracts," "Agency," and "Negotiable instruments" sections were taken from *CPA Fast Track Examination Review*, 2nd ed. (Joe Ben Hoyle, New York: John Wiley & Sons, Inc., 2001).

1. Contracts

  A. Definitions that are important to contract law

    (1) *Offeree.* Person to whom an offer is made

    (2) *Offeror.* Person who makes an offer

B. Legal requirements for contracts—For a valid contract to exist, five elements must exist: offer and acceptance, genuine assent, adequate consideration, capacity, and legality.

(1) *Offer and acceptance.* One party must make a definite, unqualified offer, and the other party must accept this offer in total. Three conditions must exist for there to be a valid offer: intent, communication, and definiteness. Three conditions must exist for there to be a valid acceptance: bilateral contract or a unilateral contract, content, and communication.

(2) *Genuineness of assent.* It is important that both parties are bound by their promises. There are certain conditions that would cause a lack of assent so that no valid contract exists:

   (a) Misrepresentation

   (b) Duress, indicating a condition of coercion

   (c) Undue influence, indicating a lack of assent by the offeree

   (d) A unilateral mistake, whereby one party knows or should realize that the other party is relying on a mistaken belief or incorrect information

   (e) A mutual mistake, indicating a contract that contains latent ambiguities and can be avoided by either the offeror or the offeree

   (f) A lack of mutuality exists in a situation in which a statement has been made that sounds like a promise but does not, in reality, bind the person making the statement to do anything.

(3) *Adequate consideration.* Consideration is something that is bargained for and exchanged in a contract.

(4) *Legal capacity.* The parties to an enforceable contract must be capable of entering into the contract in the eyes of the law. There are certain parties who lack legal capacity.

   (a) A minor lacks legal capacity.

   (b) An insane person lacks legal capacity.

   (c) An intoxicated person may lack legal capacity.

(5) *Legality.* The terms of a contract cannot require any laws to be broken.

C. Types of contracts

(1) Nature of the promise

   (a) *Bilateral contract.* The promise of one party is exchanged for the promise of the other party. Both parties make promises that are legally enforceable.

   (b) *Unilateral contract.* The promise of one party is exchanged for the other party's performing some act or refraining from some act. Only one party can be forced to comply with the contract. For example, insurance contracts are unilateral. Only the insurer is legally bound to do something. The insured makes no promise to do anything. Of course, if the insured does not pay the renewal premium, the policy is canceled.

(2) Legal validity and enforceability

   (a) *Enforceable contract.* All conditions and elements are present and clear.

   (b) *Void contract.* A void contract has no legal standing because it lacks one or more of the requirements specified by law for a valid contract.

   (c) *Voidable contract.* A voidable contract is a legally enforceable contract, but one from which at least one of the parties can escape liability because of lack of capacity, lack of mutuality, duress, misrepresentation, undue influence, or mistake.

      (d) *Quasi-contract.* Not actually a contract, but can act like one. It serves as a remedy where someone has unjustly received a benefit but where there was no contract.

      (e) *Unenforceable contract.* A contract can exist because it has all of the elements of a valid contract. However, at least one of the parties may have a defense that can be used to render it unenforceable, such as the Statute of Frauds or a material breach of contract.

D. Two topics in contract law, which are unrelated to each other, concern written agreements.

    (1) The *Statute of Frauds* states in general that a contract does not have to be in writing in order to be enforceable. However, there are exceptions to this general rule. The following contracts must be in writing to be enforceable:

      (a) A promise to answer for debts of another. For example, one person promises to pay a debt and another person guarantees that promise. The guarantee must be in writing to be enforceable.

      (b) A contract to transfer an interest in real estate must be in writing.

      (c) A contract that cannot, by its terms, be performed within one year from the date of agreement must be in writing.

      (d) The Uniform Commercial Code (UCC) on the sale of goods of $500 or more must be in writing.

    (2) The *parol evidence rule* also impacts written contracts. When a contract is in writing, this rule limits the evidence that can be introduced at trial to prove what the terms of the contract are. The contract as written will be binding on both parties.

E. Any nonperformance of a contract is a breach of the contract. However, there are times when nonperformance of the terms of a contract is excused.

    (1) If one party has committed a material breach, the other party is excused from performance.

    (2) Death excuses a party from the duty to perform services, but not from the contractual duty to deliver goods or convey real estate.

    (3) If a breach of contract has occurred, there are various remedies available to the nonbreaching party. The nonbreaching party can be awarded monetary damages.

      (a) The general measure of monetary damages is the amount of money that will put the nonbreaching party in the position that he or she would have occupied had there been no breach. Such damages are known as *compensatory damages*.

      (b) *Punitive damages* are damages aimed at punishing the breaching party rather than merely compensating the nonbreaching party. Punitive damages are not usually allowed in breach-of-contract cases.

      (c) *Liquidated damages* are damages for breach of contract where the monetary amount was agreed to at the time the contract was made. Courts allow such damages only if the amount is reasonable.

      (d) Under certain circumstances, the nonbreaching party can be awarded equity.

2. Torts

A. A person can commit two classes of wrongs: public and private.

    (1) A public wrong is a violation of one of the laws that govern the relationships of the individual with the rest of society. It is called a *crime* and is subject to criminal law.

    (2) A private wrong is an infringement of the rights of another individual. A private wrong is called a *tort*, and the person who commits such a wrong is called a *tortfeasor*. A tort

may give the person whose rights were violated a right of action for damages against the tortfeasor. This action is called a civil action.

B. Torts are divided into two types: intentional and unintentional.

   (1) *Intentional torts* include infringements on the rights of others such as assault and battery, libel, slander, false arrest or imprisonment, trespass, and invasion of privacy. Individuals who suffer injury as a result of these intentional torts have the right to sue for damages.

   (2) *Unintentional torts* are those that result from negligence or carelessness, and in these cases, the injured party may also be entitled to damages in a civil action even though the tortfeasor had no malicious intent as in an intentional tort.

C. An individual's exposure to financial loss associated with liability may arise from three sources: (1) criminal acts, (2) torts, and (3) legal liability arising out of breach of contract.

D. Liability insurance is rarely concerned with the legal penalties resulting from criminal behavior or intentional torts. In liability insurance, we are concerned primarily with unintentional torts or losses arising from negligence.

3. Agency

   A. The term *agency* refers to a two-party relationship in which one party (an agent) is authorized to act on behalf of the other (a principal).

   B. Certain general characteristics are found in this type of relationship:

   (1) In acting for a principal, the agent has a fiduciary duty to act for the benefit of the principal and not in the agent's own self-interest.

   (2) The agent may be subject to the control of the principal.

      (a) If the agent is an independent contractor, the principal has no control.

      (b) If the agent is an employee of the principal, the agent is subject to the control of the principal.

   C. The principal will be bound by an agent's contracts made with third parties as long as the agent has one of the following kinds of authority:

   (1) *Express authority.* Authority specifically granted by a principal to an agent by means of an agency agreement

   (2) *Implied authority.* The authority that an agent has as necessary to carry out acts needed to exercise his or her express authority

   (3) *Apparent authority.* Authority that, in the absence of contrary action by the principal, appears to a reasonable person to be possessed by the principal's agent

   D. A principal is liable for all torts committed by its agents in the scope of employment.

   E. An agent will have liability to a third party for the agent's own torts and contracts.

   (1) An agent is liable along with the principal for the agent's own torts.

   (2) For contracts, the general rule is that the principal is liable and the agent is not, as long as the agent acted within the scope of the agent's authority and the identity of the principal was fully disclosed. This rule holds regardless of how authority arose.

   F. The relationship between a principal and an agent can be terminated. The relationship can be terminated by operation of law. The following automatically terminate an agency:

   (1) Death of either the principal or the agent

   (2) Insanity of either the principal or the agent

   (3) Bankruptcy of the principal

   (4) Illegality of agency purpose

4. Negotiable instruments

   A. A negotiable instrument is a written contract that can be used as a substitute for money. In general, there are two types of negotiable instruments:

      (1) A promissory note is a written promise to make payment.
      (2) A draft is a written order to make payment, but three parties are involved. Even if a single party occupies two of these positions, it is still a three-party instrument.

   B. A *holder in due course* of a negotiable instrument is entitled to payment despite most defenses that the maker or drawer may have. There are several exceptions to the rule that a holder in due course takes the negotiable instrument free of personal defenses:

      (1) Infancy is a defense against a holder in due course. Thus, a minor who signs a promissory note cannot be held liable.
      (2) An exception arises if the instrument was created under extreme duress.
      (3) An exception arises in case of bankruptcy of the party designated to make payment.
      (4) An exception arises if a fraud occurred that the signer of the instrument had no opportunity to detect.

   C. Several steps are necessary for a party to become a holder in due course of a negotiable instrument.

      (1) A document is considered a negotiable instrument only if it has a particular form.

         (a) It must be in writing and signed by the maker or drawer.
         (b) It must contain an unconditional promise or order to pay.
         (c) It must be for a sum certain in money.
         (d) It must be payable at a definite time or on demand.
         (e) It must be payable to order of a party or payable to the bearer of the instrument (except for checks).
         (f) It must contain no other obligation, promise, or requirements.

      (2) The person trying to assert status as a holder in due course of the instrument must be a holder. The person is a holder if the instrument was properly negotiated to him or her.

   D. The relationship that exists between a bank and its customers is also important. The bank (the drawee on a check) has an obligation to a customer (the drawer of a check). A bank must also follow a customer's order not to pay.

      (1) An oral stop order is valid for 14 days.
      (2) A written stop order is valid for six months.

   E. A person who presents an instrument for payment and a person who transfers an instrument to another party make, by operation of law, certain warranties regarding the instrument. The warranties in these two cases differ slightly, but, in general, they are as follows:

      (1) The person has good title to the instrument that is being presented or transferred.
      (2) All signatures are genuine or authorized.
      (3) There are no known defenses to the instrument.

5. Professional liability

   A. Because of the nature of a practitioner-client relationship, services and recommendations provided by financial planning practitioners carry a certain level of liability exposure; it is inherent to the profession. The Practice Standards, however, should assist the practitioner in managing that risk.

   B. The potential of common law liability to clients includes liability based on (1) breach of contract, (2) tort or negligence, and (3) fraud.

C. According to federal securities laws, the financial planner can also have liability under the Securities Act of 1933, Securities Exchange Act of 1934, Investment Advisors Act of 1940, Investment Advisors Supervision Coordination Act of 1996, and National Association of Security Dealers.

D. There are two forms of insurance used to protect professionals from financial loss as a result of being sued for professional lapses. First, malpractice insurance is used by those who can cause physical harm to others (such as physicians, dentists, and surgeons). Second, errors and omissions insurance protects those (attorneys, accountants, architects, real estate agents, and insurance agents) where risk involves property damage (includes intangible property).

6. Fiduciary liability—A fiduciary is similar to a trustee in that the fiduciary must act for the benefit of the beneficiary of the fiduciary relationship. There is no need for a trust to exist as there is for trustees. Fiduciaries are held to a very high standard of responsibility.

7. Arbitration and mediation are alternatives to litigation. In arbitration, a disinterested third party hears both sides and makes a binding determination as to the resolution of a dispute. In mediation, a disinterested third party helps the two sides come to an agreement. The mediator makes no judgment.

TOPIC 19: QUANTITATIVE ANALYSIS

1. *Probability analysis* is used to determine the likelihood that a certain event will or will not happen. It is used in evaluating insurance risk and the development of insurance rates. When used with investments, it helps determine the likelihood that a certain return will be earned and may be used to evaluate the likelihood that the economy will be reacting in a specific way at a particular time in the future.

2. *Modeling* and *simulation* are tools that permit evaluation of various decisions under differing environmental circumstances before committing money to a specific investment or project. When probability theory is combined with the various models and/or simulations, the probability of each scenario can be evaluated and decisions made that will provide the best result, using the most likely scenario and/or the least damaging result under the least favorable scenario.

3. *Sensitivity analysis* involves the degree of change in results that arises from small changes in inputs. The independent variable (input) is changed to see how sensitive the dependent variable is to the input. This can be used to evaluate the volatility of various investment alternatives. For example, you can see how sensitive a stock's price is by changes in sales.

TOPIC 20: MONETARY SETTLEMENT PLANNING

1. A *structured settlement* is designed to spread out the payments to the recipient. The primary reason for a structured product is that it simplifies the need for managing money and reduces the problem of running out of funds before death.

2. When money comes from a legal action, it is paid as a *legal settlement*. Legal settlements can be paid as lump sums or as structured settlements.

3. Lottery winnings and monetary windfalls

A. The biggest problem facing those who come into a lot of money is the number of people who want part of it. The vast majority of lottery winners have little to show after five years.

B. Purchasing a new house and car, taking several vacations, and gifting to friends and family result in an erosion of the uniform estate and gift tax credit and may well result in transfer taxes being owed.

C. Lottery winnings, gambling winnings, and the like are subject to income taxes.

4. Lump sum retirement distributions

   A. This is a distribution from a qualified plan that represents the participant's entire account balance. To be qualified as a lump sum distribution, the distribution must meet certain conditions.

      (1) The client must have been a plan participant for at least five years.
      (2) The funds must be distributed to the client within one taxable year.
      (3) The distribution must represent the entire account balance or benefit.
      (4) The amount distributed must be payable only upon death, attainment of age 59½, separation of service, or disability.

   B. A decision must be made as to whether to pay the tax on the lump sum right away or to postpone the tax by rolling over the money into an IRA. If the latter decision is made, the money must be rolled over to an IRA within 60 days or directly transferred.

5. Insurance proceeds

   A. Alternatives to receiving insurance proceeds

      (1) *As a lump sum payment.* All proceeds are received in one lump sum payment.
      (2) *As an annuity payment.* Life insurance allows for the distribution of a sum of money on an actuarial basis for fixed intervals.

   B. Tax consequences

      (1) A lump sum payment is income tax free. This is the most popular choice of life insurance settlement. A cash settlement allows the beneficiary to retire outstanding debt, pay funeral costs, provide for an emergency fund, and allow for investing in the market.
      (2) An annuity payment is partially taxable. Each annuity payment represents a combination of the return of principal and interest and dividends on the principal. The principal portion has already been taxed and will not be taxed again when the payments are received. The interest and dividends are generally taxed as income.

   C. Fixed annuity versus variable annuity

      (1) A fixed annuity guarantees a stated return during the life of the contract.
      (2) Variable annuity payments are made to a variety of investment opportunities—stocks, bonds, and managed accounts—that fluctuate on the basis of investment results. Investors can switch their funds from one investment option to another without having to pay taxes. The risk of return transfers from the insurance company to the policyholder. Variable annuities serve as a hedge against inflation, whereas fixed annuities do not.

6. Systematic withdrawal plans

   A. Transferring or rolling over a lump sum amount from a qualified retirement account into an IRA account
   B. Systematic distribution from an IRA account, generally on a monthly basis to supplement income
   C. The goal is to invest in securities—stocks, bonds, and cash—that provide inflation-adjusted income with a return on principal.
   D. The client and adviser would need to determine the after-tax income.

Chapter 2

INSURANCE PLANNING AND RISK MANAGEMENT

TOPIC 21: PRINCIPLES OF INSURANCE

1. Definition and application

A. *Risk* is defined as the *possibility of loss*. The definition of risk refers to the possibility, not the probability, of loss. It does not suggest an element of measurability. There are different classifications of risk:

(1) *Financial and nonfinancial risk.* Risk may involve financial loss in some cases; in other cases, there is no financial loss. Insurance is concerned with those risks that involve a financial loss.

(2) *Static and dynamic risk.* Dynamic risks are those resulting from changes in the economy. Changes in price level, consumer tastes, income and output, and technology may cause financial loss to members of the economy. Static risks involve those losses that would occur even if there were no changes in the economy, such as the perils of nature and the dishonesty of other individuals. Static risks are more suited to treatment of insurance than are dynamic risks.

(3) *Fundamental and particular risks.* Fundamental risks involve group risks, caused by conditions more or less beyond the control of the individuals who suffer the losses. These risks are the responsibility of society rather than the individual, such as unemployment and occupational disability. Particular risks involve losses that arise out of individual events and are felt by individuals rather than by an entire group. Particular risks are more appropriate for insurance than fundamental risks.

(4) *Pure and speculative risks.* Pure risk is used to designate those situations that involve only the chance of loss or no loss. Speculative risk describes situations in which there is a possibility of loss, but also a possibility of gain. Gambling is an example of a speculative risk. Only pure risks are generally insurable.

B. There are different elements for determining an insurable risk:

(1) The risk of loss must be definable and measurable.
(2) There must be a large enough number of similar exposure units to make potential losses somewhat predictable.
(3) A potential loss must be fortuitous or accidental.
(4) The loss must not be catastrophic.

C. *Peril* is a cause of a loss. Examples of perils are fire, windstorm, hail, and theft. Each of these is a cause of a loss that occurs.

D. *Hazard* is a condition that may create or increase the chance of a loss arising from a given peril. It is possible for something to be both a peril and a hazard. Hazards are normally classified in three categories:

(1) *Physical hazards* consist of those physical properties that increase the chance of loss from the various perils. Examples of physical hazards that increase the possibility of loss from a peril of fire are the type of construction and the location of a property.

(2) *Moral hazard* refers to the increase in the probability of loss that results from the dishonest tendencies of an insured in an attempt to defraud an insurance company.

(3) *Morale hazard* results from the careless attitude of an insured person toward the occurrence of losses. The purchase of insurance may create a morale hazard, inasmuch as the realization that the insurance company will bear a loss may lead the insured to exercise less care than if forced to bear the loss alone.

E. Law of large numbers

    (1) As the number of independent trials is increased, the actual results will come ever closer to the results that would be expected to occur based on the underlying probability.

    (2) For example, the law of large numbers can be explained by flipping a penny; half the time it will come up heads, and half the time it will come up tails.

    (3) If there are enough observations of an event, its outcome can be predicted with some accuracy. Insurance companies do such predicting. Based on years of historical information, insurance companies can predict, with reasonable accuracy, how many claims will be made and the amount of the claims for an entire group. They cannot predict the claims for an individual.

F. Adverse selection—It is the tendency for those who know that they are highly vulnerable to specific pure risks to be most likely to acquire and to retain insurance to cover that loss.

2. Response to risk

A. *Risk retention* is perhaps the most common method of handling risk. The retention may be voluntary or involuntary. As a general rule, risks that should be retained are those that lead to relatively small certain losses. Risk retention is characterized by low frequency and low severity.

B. *Risk transfer* is the transfer of risk from one individual to another who is more willing to bear the risk. Insurance is the most widely used means for reducing risk by transfer. Risk transfer is characterized by low frequency and high severity.

C. *Risk control*—ways to minimize losses—includes risk avoidance and risk reduction. In contrast, *risk financing*—ways to pay for those losses that happen—includes risk transfer and risk retention.

D. *Risk reduction* is achieved through loss prevention and control. Safety programs and means of loss prevention include medical care, fire departments, night security guards, sprinkler systems, and burglar alarms. Risk reduction is characterized by high frequency and low severity.

E. *Risk avoidance* occurs when an individual refuses to accept a risk even for an instant. This is accomplished by merely not engaging in the action that gives rise to risk. The avoidance of risk is one method of dealing with risk, but it is a negative rather than a positive technique. Personal advancement of the individual and progress in the economy both require risk taking. If avoidance were utilized extensively, both the individual and society would suffer. Risk avoidance is characterized by high frequency and high severity.

3. Mortality versus morbidity

A. Mortality is the rate at which a population dies.

B. Morbidity deals with the likelihood of disability.

C. Mortality and morbidity rates are applicable to a group, but only marginally useful when applied to individuals.

D. When insurance companies gather enough information about a certain population, such as nonsmoking females age 37, they can develop premium rates that reflect the expected death or disability rate for the group. Companies tend to skew this rate toward the healthier group, lowering the premiums. This is often done for competitive reasons.

E. To avoid adverse selection, the companies evaluate applicants for insurance.

TOPIC 22: ANALYSIS AND EVALUATION OF RISK EXPOSURES

1. Personal

   A. *Death*. The primary purpose of life insurance is to permit a person's dependents to live in a similar manner that was enjoyed before the person's death. Two approaches evaluate the risk of premature death:

      (1) *Human life value*. This is the present value of that portion of estimated future earnings that is necessary to support dependents. For example, assume future income is estimated at $90,000 per year, but the economic value to dependents is only $65,000. The life value at age 35 is measured by an amount, invested at a reasonable rate, yielding an income of $65,000 per year for 30 years (up until retirement age of 65). If the discount rate used is 6 percent, the present value is $894,714. The present value of an individual reduces over time until finally disappearing at retirement age.

      (2) *Needs analysis*. Needs analysis requires determining needs that arise or continue to exist after a person's death and comparing them to sources that already exist, such as employer-provided life insurance and retirement accounts. For example, there may be a need to provide a source of funds to support the living expenses of the family or to pay for the college education of children.

   B. *Disability*. This is the inability to work because of sickness or accident, resulting in loss of income to the individual or family. There is a tendency by individuals to underestimate the frequency and severity of long-term disability.

   C. *Poor health*. Individuals often find themselves in need of protection against financial consequences of poor health.

   D. *Unemployment*. In a volatile economy, unemployment is always a possibility. Unemployment can be a significant cash drain to a family. Emergency funds should be well funded in order to deal with temporary lapses in income.

   E. *Outliving one's capital*. The risk of living too long is called *superannuation*. The risk is caused by individuals not saving enough by the time retirement arrives, and the assets that have been accumulated do not last for the rest of the individual's life. One product offered by insurance companies to protect against retirement risk is a life-income annuity.

2. Property

   A. *Real*. Land and anything attached and affixed to it, and all rights inherent in ownership. Real property is subject to loss from many different perils, and insurance policies provide protection.

   B. *Personal*. Tangible (other than real estate) and intangible assets that are subject to ownership. These include such things as clothes, furniture, china, artwork, vehicles, patents, and copyrights. Personal property coverage is also categorized under named perils or open perils.

   C. *Auto*. Auto insurance is considered a necessity for individuals who drive. There are severe financial consequences that arise from auto accidents on a daily basis.

3. Liability

   A. *Torts* are divided into two types: intentional or unintentional. *Intentional torts* include such infringements on the rights of others as assault and battery, libel, slander, false arrest or imprisonment, trespass, and invasion of privacy. *Unintentional torts* are those that result from *negligence* or carelessness.

(1) *Negligence* is conduct that is below the standard of care established by law for the protection of others against unreasonable risk of harm within the scope of reasonable expectation.

(2) Those things that must be proven to establish tort liability for negligence are as follows:

    (a) A duty owed by the wrongdoer to the plaintiff

    (b) The wrongdoer failed to conduct him- or herself in accordance with the duty owed (breach of duty).

    (c) Measurable damage to property or injury to the plaintiff has occurred.

    (d) The breach of the duty is the proximate cause of the damage or injury.

(3) For obvious reasons, mentally incompetent persons are generally exempted from the definition of behaving as a reasonable and prudent individual. In addition, infants cannot be held negligent if they have not reached the *age of reason*. The age of reason varies among states.

(4) Normally, the burden of proof for negligence lies with the injured party. However, there are also three doctrines that impose liability by statute or shift the burden of proof from the injured party to the defendant.

    (a) *Negligence per se*, or negligence "as a matter of law," may exist when a person violates a statute. Consider, for example, the speed limits established by law around schools, put in place to protect children. These speed limits amount to the establishment of rules that no reasonable person should violate. If the rules are violated, the injured party is relieved of the obligation of proving that the speed was unreasonable.

    (b) *Absolute liability (strict liability)* arises when a person who commits certain types of torts will be liable for any injury inflicted on another, regardless of willful wrongdoing or negligence on his or her part. This is sometimes referred to as "liability without fault." Workers' compensation laws impose absolute liability on employers for injuries to employees.

    (c) *Res ipsa loquitur* is translated as "the thing speaks for itself." Under this uncommon provision in the law, a defendant is presumed guilty unless he or she can prove innocence. In the eyes of the law, the fact that the accident occurred is evidence that the defendant was negligent. For example, if a man walks down the street and a safe being lowered by a rope falls on him, he is not required to prove that the person lowering the safe failed to exercise due care.

(5) When someone is accused of negligence, there are four defenses available that may reduce or eliminate the liability.

    (a) *Assumption of the risk* occurs when the injured party reasonably should have recognized and understood the danger involved in an activity and voluntarily chose to pursue the activity anyway. For example, a plaintiff who took boxing lessons would have learned about all of the dangers of boxing.

    (b) *Contributory negligence* is the lack of ordinary care on the part of an injured person, which combined with the defendant's negligence and contributed to the injury as a proximate cause. Contributory negligence on the part of an injured party will defeat his or her claim, no matter how slight the negligence.

    (c) *Comparative negligence* means that damages will be diminished in proportion to the amount of negligence attributable to the person injured or to the owner or person in control of the damaged property.

(d) *Last clear chance* means that the contributory negligence of an injured party will not bar his or her recovery if the defendant immediately prior to the accident had a "last clear chance" to prevent the accident but did not act on that opportunity.

(6) The *collateral source rule* is further protection against a negligent act.

(a) Under the *collateral source rule*, an injured person may receive the full compensation awarded by the court in a negligence suit and still obtain the benefits of any personal insurance available to him or her.

(b) The collateral source rule prevents the defendant from escaping the penalty merely because the injured party provided his or her own insurance coverage.

(7) *Vicarious liability* can result from negligence.

(a) This type of liability is ascribed to one person or entity because of the acts of another. It is based on the common law principle of *repondeat superior*, "Let the master answer."

(b) A principal has vicarious liability because of the tortuous conduct or negligence of his or her agent. Parents are generally liable for the acts of their children.

(8) *Survival of tort actions* extends beyond the death of the plaintiff and defendant. The estate or heirs have a right to sue for loss.

B. *Libel* is an intentional tort. Libel is writing untrue information about someone that defames him or her.

C. *Slander* is also an intentional tort. Slander is verbal or spoken information about someone that defames him or her.

D. *Malpractice* is alleged professional misconduct or lack of ordinary skills in the performance of a professional act. A practitioner is liable for damages or injuries caused by malpractice.

4. Business-related risk

A. Workers' compensation laws impose absolute liability on employers for injuries to employees.

B. Death or disability of a partner or proprietor may cause serious problems for the existence of a business.

5. Calculation of benefits

A. Property and casualty insurance calculation

(1) The coverage on the dwelling and other structures under homeowners forms is on a *replacement cost basis*. If the amount of insurance covering the building is at least 80 percent, the loss will be paid on a replacement basis (without deduction for depreciation) rather than on an *actual cash basis* (replacement cost less depreciation).

(2) If the amount of insurance is less than 80 percent replacement cost, the company will pay the larger of the following two amounts:

(a) The actual cash value (ACV)

(b) The proportion of the replacement cost of the loss that the amount of insurance bears to 80 percent of the replacement cost value of the building

(3) *Example*: John's house would cost $150,000 to rebuild; 80 percent of that amount is $120,000. John has only $100,000 of coverage. If he has a kitchen fire that does $30,000 worth of damage, how much will the insurance company pay?

(4) *Solution*: Because the house is 30 years old, depreciation on the damaged part of the house is 50 percent. So the ACV coverage would be $15,000. Alternatively, John has

$100,000 of the required $120,000 of coverage. That is 83 percent of the required amount. Take 83.33 percent of the $30,000 loss, which is $25,000. If John has a $500 deductible, the insurance company will pay $24,500.

B. Health insurance calculation

(1) The *deductible* is the retained risk. When covered expenses are incurred, the first part of the expenses is applied to the deductible, which is paid by the insured.

(2) After the deductible is paid, the next provision is *coinsurance*. Coinsurance, also known as co-payment, is a split between the insured and the insurance company. The most common is 80/20. If an insured has a $1,500 medical bill, a $300 deductible, and 80/20 coinsurance, the insured pays the first S300 and 20 percent of the next $1,200. The insurance company pays 80 percent of that $1,200.

(3) Next is the *stop-loss limit*, sometimes called the maximum out-of-pocket expense. Its use becomes vital in cases of catastrophic medical expenses where the coinsurance provision may result in an individual's paying a large sum of cash. For example, a plan may have a $200 deductible and an 80 percent coinsurance provision that applies to the next $5,000. In this case, the most the individual pays out of pocket is $1,200 (S200 + $1,000).

C. Life insurance calculation

(1) There are three primary factors used to calculate the premiums of a life insurance policy.

(a) *Mortality*. The probability of dying or living at a certain age. An actuary determines the rate of death at each age and lists an arbitrary number of lives at each age.

(b) *Interest*. Insurance companies do not need to collect the full amount of future losses from the members of the group, because they earn interest on the funds that are collected. The allowance for interest is made by discounting the future claims to obtain their present value.

(c) *Loading*. The portion of the premium that is designed to cover the expenses, profit, and margin for contingencies

(2) Mortality and interest are used to calculate the *net premium* of insurance, excluding operating expenses. The *gross premium* adds net premium and operating expenses and is the amount that the insured pays for the policy.

(3) Under level premium plans, the insured pays more than the cost of protection in the early years of the policy. The difference between what the insured pays and the cost of protection is the policy *reserves*. The reserves represent the cash value of the policy. Reserves equal present value of future benefits minus present value of future premiums.

TOPIC 23: LEGAL ASPECTS OF INSURANCE

1. Indemnity

A. Insurance contracts are *contracts of indemnity*. This means that the insurer promises to reimburse the insured up to the extent of the insured's covered financial loss, or the amount of coverage, whichever is less.

B. There are three principles that support insurance as a contract of indemnity:

(1) *Doctrine of insurable interest* (discussed later)

(2) *Actual cash value.* This arrangement ensures enforcement of the principle of indemnity because the insured is generally not reimbursed by being provided with new property as a replacement for old property.

(3) *Subrogation.* The common law doctrine of subrogation gives the insurer whatever rights the insured possessed against the responsible third parties. This means that if you are injured by someone else and your health insurance pays the bills, your insurer has the right to sue the person who injured you to be paid back before you can collect anything from that party.

2. Insurable interest—Insurance is issued only if the applicant has an insurable interest in the subject matter being insured. For example, a homeowner has an insurable interest in his or her home because he or she would suffer a financial loss if the home were damaged or destroyed.

3. Contract requirements—For a valid contract to exist, five elements must exist: offer and acceptance, genuine assent, adequate consideration, capacity, and legality. (See Topic 18 for a complete discussion on contracts.)

4. Contract characteristics

   A. Characteristics of insurance contracts

      (1) *An insurance contract is a personal contract.* This means that the policy is personal to the insured. With the exception of life insurance, it may not be assigned to anyone else without the approval of the insurer.

      (2) *Insurance contracts are unilateral.* Under the terms of a unilateral contract, only one party can be forced to comply with the contract. Under the terms of a bilateral contract, both parties make promises that are legally enforceable. Insurance contracts are unilateral.

      (3) *An insurance contract is a contract of adhesion.* The insured can accept or reject the contract only as written. Thus, the policy is not drawn up through negotiations.

      (4) *Insurance contracts are aleatory contracts.* An aleatory contract is one in which one party may receive benefits greatly in excess of the benefits to be received by the other party. An insurance contract is aleatory because the insured may receive benefits far in excess of the premium paid.

      (5) *Insurance contracts are also contracts of utmost good faith.* If the information provided by the applicant is false or incomplete, the insurer may be able to void the contract on grounds of breach of warranty, misrepresentation, or concealment.

   B. Other characteristics within the legal framework of insurance contracts

      (1) *Misrepresentation* is a false statement. If a misrepresentation is *intentional* and *material*, it is usually basis for voiding the contract. For life insurance policies, the misrepresentation must be discovered within the one- or two-year contestable period.

      (2) *Warranty* is a statement made by one party to a contract, which, if untrue, renders the policy voidable by the other party. *Representation* is information given that is true to the best of the individual's knowledge. Courts generally hold that insurance contracts may not be voided because of a breach of warranty or misrepresentation unless the violation was material and/or increased the risk that contributed to the loss. Such decisions are obviously more favorable for the insured.

      (3) *Concealment* is the failure to disclose known material information. Information is material if it would have led the insurer to make a different underwriting decision had the withheld information been known. Intentional concealment (intent to defraud the insurer) is grounds for voiding the contract.

(4) *Estoppel* prevents one from denying a fact if the fact was admitted to be true by previous actions. If one party to a contract waives its right to enforce a part of the contract, and the other party relies on that waiver, the first party is prevented (estopped) from enforcing it later.

(5) *Rescission*. An insurance policy may be rescinded if one party can prove that the other party misrepresented material information in the preparation or negotiation of the insurance contract.

(6) *Reformation* is the changing of an existing contract, not the creation of a new one. It is done when both parties agree to change the new contract from what was originally intended.

(7) *Conditional*. The insurance company is obligated to pay a claim on the condition that a covered loss is sustained.

C. Categories for analyzing insurance contracts

(1) *Declarations* are factual statements identifying the specific person, property, or activity being insured and the parties to the insurance transaction.

(2) The *definitions* section of the policy is an explanation of the key policy terms.

(3) The *insuring agreement* is the heart of the insurance policy. This agreement(s) spells out the basic premise of the insurance company. An example is an agreement to pay the face amount of the policy in the event of the insured's death.

(4) *Exclusions* are items that the insurer does not intend to cover. A practical result of exclusions is to hold down the premium cost of coverage for policy owners.

(5) *Conditions*. The insuring agreement is a qualified promise that is enforceable only if the policy owner fulfills the conditions that are spelled out in the policy. An example of these conditions is timely payment of premiums.

(6) *Policy continuation*. One of the most important miscellaneous provisions of a policy relates to the right of the owner to continue coverage. These policy renewal provisions fall into five categories:

   (a) *Noncancelable*. This gives the policy owner the right to renew the coverage at each policy anniversary date, and future rates in the coverage are guaranteed in the contract itself.

   (b) *Guaranteed renewable*. Like a noncancelable policy, a guaranteed renewable policy gives the policy owner the right to renew the coverage at each policy anniversary date, but the insurer does not guarantee future rates for the coverage.

   (c) *Nonrenewable for stated reasons only*. These policies often qualify as guaranteed renewable, but allow the insurer to refuse to renew the policy for conditions specifically listed in the policy.

   (d) *Optional renewable*. This gives the insurer the unilateral right to refuse to renew a policy at the end of any period for which premiums have been paid.

   (e) *Cancelable*. A few property and liability policies are cancelable during the period for which premiums have been paid.

(7) *Valuation of losses*. Another type of miscellaneous provision concerns a required sharing in the amount of the loss by the insured. For example, deductibles are common in homeowners insurance, auto insurance, and medical expense insurance.

(8) *Endorsements and riders*. An endorsement—or, in life insurance, a rider—is a provision added to the policy, generally for an extra premium charge. As a general legal principle, whenever the wording in an endorsement or rider conflicts with the terms of the policy to which it is attached, the endorsement or rider takes precedence.

TOPIC 24: PROPERTY AND CASUALTY INSURANCE

1. Real and personal property

   A. Land and anything attached and affixed to it, and all the rights inherent in ownership. It includes such things as mineral rights, air rights, dwellings, and those things permanently attached to buildings. Real property is subject to loss from many different perils. Insurance policies help provide protection for some of these perils.

      (1) *Named perils.* The named-perils policy contains a list of covered perils. If the peril is not listed, then any loss associated with that peril will not be covered.

      (2) *All-risk (open perils).* This policy covers all losses to property unless peril is specifically excluded from coverage.

   B. There are eight standard homeowners forms.

      (1) *HO-1—Basic Form.* Designed for owner-occupants of one- to four-family dwelling units. Provides named perils coverage for 12 perils, insuring the dwelling, other structures, and personal property.

Homeowners Forms

Coverage	Form HO-2	Form HO-3	Form HO-4	Form HO-6	Form HO-8
A: Dwelling	Amount based on replacement cost, $15,000 minimum	Amount based on replacement cost, $20,000 minimum	Not covered	$1,000 on owner's additions and alterations to the unit	Amount based on actual cash value of the home, $15,000 minimum
B: Other Structures	10% of Part A	10% of Part A	Not covered	Included in Part A coverage	10% of Part A
C: Personal Property	50% of Part A	50% of Part A	$6,000 minimum	$6,000 minimum	50% of Part A
D: Loss of Use	30% of Part A	30% of Part A	30% of Part C	40% of Part C	10% of Part A
Perils covered	Perils 1–18	All perils except those specifically excluded from building; perils 1–18 on personal property	Perils 1–18	Perils 1–18	Perils 1–12

Perils 1–12 are fire, lightning, windstorm, hail, riot or civil commotion, aircraft, vehicles, smoke, vandalism or malicious mischief, explosion, theft, and volcanic eruption.

Perils 1–18 are Perils 1–12 plus (13) falling objects, (14) weight of ice, snow, or sleet, (15) accidental discharge or overflow of water or steam, (16) sudden and accidental tearing apart, cracking, burning, or bulging, (17) freezing of plumbing, heating, air-conditioning system, or appliances, and (18) damage from artificially generated electricity.

(2) *HO-2—Broad Form.* Designed for owner-occupants of one- to four-family dwelling units. Provides named perils coverage for 18 perils (broad form), insuring the dwelling, other structures, and personal property.

(3) *HO-3—Special Form.* Designed for owner-occupants of one- to four-family dwelling units. Provides open perils coverage for insuring the dwelling and other structures. Personal property is subject to the named perils covered in HO-2.

(4) *HO-4—Contents Broad Form.* HO-4 is designed for renters. It has no dwelling coverage. Provides named perils coverage (18 perils—broad form) for personal property.

(5) *HO-5—Comprehensive Form.* Designed for owner-occupants of one- to four-family dwelling units. Provides open perils coverage for dwelling, other structures, and personal property.

(6) *HO-6—Unit-Owners Form.* HO-6 is designed for the owners of condominiums. Provides named perils coverage (18 perils—broad form) for personal property.

(7) *HO-8—Modified Coverage Form.* Designed for owner-occupants of one- to four-family dwelling units. Provides protection for dwellings that have a fair market value (FMV) less than the replacement value of the dwelling. Reduced named perils coverage for 12 perils, insuring dwelling, other structures, and personal property. The HO-8 policy was created to provide coverage where housing prices are so low that the cost to rebuild a structure exceeds the cost of the identical house next door and the land it is on.

(8) *HO-15—Homeowners Special Personal Property Coverage Form.* Provides open perils coverage of personal property and is used in combination with an HO-3 policy.

C. Each homeowner form has two major sections.

   (1) Section I provides property coverage, which contains five categories of property coverage.

       (a) Coverage A for the dwelling
       (b) Coverage B for the other structures
       (c) Coverage C for personal property
       (d) Coverage D for loss of use
       (e) Additional coverage that provides protection for assorted situations

   (2) Section II provides liability and medical payment coverage.

   (3) The coverage under Section II is identical for all forms, and it is only in respect to Section I that the forms differ.

D. Coverage A—Dwelling

   (1) This is the part of the policy that insures the house and anything attached to it.

   (2) Land is specifically excluded.

   (3) It is important to remember that the insurance coverage is based on the cost to rebuild or repair, not the market value of a house. House prices are affected more by market conditions than construction costs.

E. Coverage B—Other Structures

   (1) This insures other structures such as a shed, detached garage, or fence.

   (2) Three exclusions under Coverage B:

       (a) Structures used for a business are not covered.
       (b) Structures that are rented to nonresidents of the house are not covered unless it is the garage that is rented, which may be rented to anyone if used exclusively for garage purposes.
       (c) Coverage does not extend to land.

F. Coverage C—Personal Property

    (1) This insures the personal property of the homeowner at its actual cash value.

    (2) It is broad form unless open perils coverage is added.

    (3) This coverage applies to personal property owned or used by any insured while anywhere in the world. The coverage is provided on both owned and borrowed property. For example, if the insured or a family member borrows property from a friend, and the property is damaged as a result of a peril, the homeowners policy will cover the property as if it had been owned by the insured.

    (4) Some personal property is excluded under contents.

        (a) Articles that are separately described and specifically insured under the homeowners policy or any other insurance policy—those covered under floaters or inland marine coverage

        (b) Animals, birds, and fish

        (c) Motorized land vehicles

        (d) Aircraft and their parts

        (e) Property contained in an apartment regularly rented or held for rental to others by the insured

        (f) Property of roomers, boarders, and other tenants not related to the insured

        (g) Property rented or held for rental to others away from the premises

        (h) Business property

        (i) Credit cards or fund transfer cards

    (5) Personal property coverage contains limits in the blanket policy.

        (a) $200 limits include cash.

        (b) $250 limit includes property away from the building used for business purposes.

        (c) $1,000 limit includes personal records, collectibles, electronic equipment, and securities.

        (d) $2,000 limit includes firearms.

        (e) $2,500 limit includes property at the dwelling used for business and the theft of silver- and gold-ware.

        (f) If these items are insured for a larger amount, they must be scheduled.

G. Coverage D—Loss of Use. Pays for time in a hotel when the owner must stay away from the house while it is being repaired

H. Additional coverage

    (1) This covers such things as debris removal; reasonable repair; damage to trees, plants, and shrubs; fire department service charge; damage to property removed; and losses from credit cards.

    (2) $500 per tree; $500 limit for credit cards

I. Coverage E—Personal Liability

    (1) This coverage provides insurance in case someone is injured on the property or through the negligence of the owner, and that injured person sues.

    (2) The minimum amount of coverage is $100,000 per occurrence.

J. Coverage F—Medical Payments to Others

    (1) The insurer agrees to pay all reasonable medical expenses (defined to include funeral expenses) incurred by persons who are injured while on the insured premises with the permission of any insured, or who are injured away from the premises if the injury

results from an activity of the insured or a member of the insured's family, even if insured is not liable.

(2) The coverage does not apply to the insured and members of the insured's household.

(3) Medical payment coverage is not liability coverage and is not based on fault. If the insured was liable, Coverage E is used.

(4) Coverage will generally be up to $1,000 for medical payments to others.

K. Conditions under Section I

(1) The insured has specific duties following a loss.

(a) Give notice to the company.
(b) Protect the property from further damage.
(c) Prepare an inventory of the damages, indicating items and amount of loss.
(d) Submit a signed statement within 60 days of the loss.
(e) If theft occurs, the insured is also required to notify the police and/or credit card company.

(2) The loss settlement provision states that losses to personal property or other structures will be on an actual cash value basis not to exceed the cost of repairing or replacing the property. For the building, the conditions apply the replacement cost provision and limitations of replacement cost. In effect, the dwelling must be insured up to 80 percent of its replacement value for the insurer to pay the face amount of the claim, less the deductible.

(3) A *pair and sets clause* prevents the insured from collecting for a total loss when part of a pair is lost.

(4) An *appraisal provision* is used when the insured and insurer cannot agree on the amount of loss. In effect, each party selects an appraiser and the appraisers then select an umpire. This does not dispute whether a loss is actually covered or not. Such disputes are settled in courts.

(5) The *loss payment clause* requires the insurance company to pay for the loss within 30 days after an agreement has been reached as to the amount of loss.

L. General conditions applicable to Sections I and II

(1) The policy will be void if the insured willfully misrepresented or concealed any material fact concerning the insurance.

(2) The *liberalization clause* allows for any new form or endorsement made by the insurer during the term of the policy to broaden the policy without additional premium.

(3) No waiver is valid unless in writing.

(4) The insured can cancel the policy immediately, and the insurer can cancel only under certain conditions and must give the insured advanced written notice.

(5) If the insurance company decides not to renew, then 30 days' written notice is required prior to expiration.

(6) Assignment of a policy is not valid unless the insurance company gives written consent.

(7) There is a subrogation clause in the policy.

M. Perils covered under Section I

(1) Section I—general exclusions: ordinance or law, earth movement, flood and/or water, power failure, neglect, intentional losses, nuclear waste, accident, war

(2) There are 12 basic named perils covered under an HO-1 (no longer commonly sold) and HO-8 policy: fire, lightning, windstorm, hail, riot or civil commotion, aircraft, vehicles, smoke, vandalism or malicious mischief, explosion, theft, and volcanic eruption.

(3) There are 18 total perils covered under broad named perils—the 12 basic named perils plus the following 6 perils:

    (a) Falling objects

    (b) Weight of ice, snow, and sleet

    (c) Accidental discharge or overflow of water or steam

    (d) Sudden and accidental tearing apart, cracking, burning, or bulging of a steam, hot water, air-conditioning, or automatic fire protective sprinkler system, or from within a household appliance

    (e) Freezing of a plumbing, heating, air-conditioning, or automatic fire sprinkler system, or of a household appliance

    (f) Sudden and accidental damage from artificially generated electrical currents

N. The majority of perils are self-explanatory, but further explanation of some perils is necessary for a full understanding of the coverage permitted for that peril.

(1) Not all fires are covered under the fire peril. A friendly fire is one that burns within the confines in which it was intended. A hostile fire is one that has escaped its intended confines. Only hostile fires are covered under the fire peril.

(2) Windstorm and hail peril excludes any damage to the interior of a building unless the roof or exterior walls are first damaged by the wind or hail. For example, if damage is caused to the walls and carpet because the insured left the window open, there is no coverage. In contrast, if the wind broke the window, there would be coverage.

(3) Explosions are covered, regardless of whether they are internal or external.

(4) Damages to the interior of a building caused by falling objects, such as a tree, are covered to the extent that the loss due to the falling object first damages the exterior of the building.

(5) If snow melts and leaks into a residence, causing damage, it is not covered. It is only the damage caused by the weight of snow, ice, or sleet that is covered.

(6) Sudden and accidental damage from artificially generated electrical currents excludes damage to tubes, transistors, and electronic components (television sets and stereos are not covered).

(7) The policy requires the insured to give immediate notice to the police if an article is stolen. There are three general exclusions for theft:

    (a) Theft committed by any insured

Covered Perils in HO Policies

	Form HO-2	Form HO-3	Form HO-4	Form HO-6	Form HO-8
A: Dwelling	Broad	Open peril	N/A	Broad	Basic
B: Other Structures	Broad	Open peril	N/A	N/A	Basic
C: Personal Property	Broad	Broad	Broad	Broad	Basic
D: Loss of Use	Broad	Open peril/broad	Broad	Broad	Basic

    (b) Theft in or from a dwelling under construction or of materials or supplies for use in the construction until the dwelling is completed and occupied

    (c) Theft from any part of a residence rented by an insured to anyone except another insured

  (8) In addition to the three general exclusions for theft, there are three more exclusions for off-premises theft.

    (a) Property at any other residence owned, rented to, or occupied by any insured is not covered for loss by theft except while the insured is residing at the location. For example, theft coverage does not apply at an individual's summer cottage unless the individual is actually residing at the cottage. This also applies to students, unless the student has been at the residence anytime during 45 days immediately preceding the loss.

    (b) Theft from watercrafts or their furnishings, equipment, and outboard motors

    (c) Campers and trailers stolen while away from the premises

O. Inland marine coverage

  (1) Inland marine coverage is insurance on specific items of personal property either as an endorsement to the homeowners (HO) policy (scheduled floater) or as a separate policy, because coverage may be limited or excluded under the general HO policy.

  (2) This coverage is sometimes called *scheduled personal property endorsement* or *personal articles floater.*

P. Comprehensive personal liability coverage for the individual

  (1) Purchasing liability insurance

    (a) It may be purchased as a separate comprehensive personal liability policy, generally referred to as a CPL.

    (b) It is included as Section II of the homeowners policy, which provides essentially the same coverage as the separate CPL.

    (c) It is included in other contracts. For example, an individual's automobile policy provides the coverage.

  (2) Comprehensive personal liability coverage

    (a) Liability insurance is comprehensive because it is designed to protect against all types of hazards.

    (b) The insured under the liability coverage of CPL:

      i. The named insured and the individual's spouse if a resident of the same household

      ii. Relatives of either spouse who are residents of the household and anyone else under age 21 in the care of any of the foregoing (i.e., children and other minors living with the insured)

      iii. A child while away at college

      iv. Anyone legally responsible for animals or watercraft to which the insurance applies. (This provides coverage for individuals to whom the insured may have loaned such animals or watercraft, or who have custody for other reasons.)

      v. Any vehicle to which the policy applies for anyone while working for the insured or any person named previously; also any other individuals using the insured vehicle with the insured's consent

(c) Section II general *exclusions* for liability and medical payments: the CPL policy does not apply to auto/boat/plane, intentional damage, business pursuits, uninsured locations, war/nuclear waste, criminal activities, or damages covered by workers' compensation.

(3) Optional personal injury liability endorsements expand homeowners liability protection for tort action, such as libel, slander, defamation of character, false arrest, or invasion of right of privacy.

2. Automobile and recreational vehicle

A. Personal Auto Policy (PAP) is a package policy, similar to a homeowners policy, that provides both property and liability insurance for family members. PAP provides four types of insurance:

(1) *Part A*. Liability coverage

(2) *Part B*. Medical payments coverage

(3) *Part C*. Uninsured motorists coverage

(4) *Part D*. Coverage for damage to the policyholder's auto

(5) The policy also contains two sections—Part E and Part F—that explain the duties of the insured following an incident or loss, and includes other policy provisions.

B. *Part A*—Liability coverage

(1) The PAP defines an insured as

(a) The insured or any family member for the ownership, maintenance, or use of *any* auto or trailer

(b) Any person using the insured's covered auto with permission

(2) PAP defines the covered auto as

(a) Any vehicle shown in the declarations

(b) Any newly acquired auto—always covered automatically for 14 days

(c) Any trailer the insured owns, or any auto or trailer the insured does not own while used as a temporary substitute for any other vehicle

(3) Coverage

(a) For the named insured and family members, coverage applies to any auto, including borrowed or rented autos.

(b) Persons other than the named insured and family members are covered while using the auto if there is a reasonable belief that the person has the right to do so.

(c) The coverage is not extended to automobiles used in any business or occupation.

(4) There may be situations in which two policies will apply to the same loss.

(a) *Example*: If Steve borrows Megan's car, Megan's policy will provide coverage for both Steve and Megan in the event of a loss. Megan is covered as the named insured, and Steve is covered as a permissive user. Steve also has coverage under his own policy as the named insured while using a borrowed auto with permission.

(b) When two policies apply to the same loss, the policy of the auto being driven is primary and the policy of the permissive user is excess.

(5) PAP is written with split limits, such as $25,000/$50,000/$10,000. These limits apply to each accident.

(a) The first limit is the maximum amount that will be paid to any one person for bodily injury claims.

(b) The second limit represents the aggregate that will be paid for all bodily injury claims.

(c) The third limit applies to aggregate property damage claims.

(d) *Example*: Harry's PAP provides for $250,000/$500,000/$50,000. Harry gets into an auto accident and injures two people in the other car. The courts award one of the injured people damages of $300,000, and the other is awarded damages of $200,000. Their car was totally demolished and cost $65,000.

(e) *Solution*: The insurer will pay only $250,000 of the $300,000 award because the per person policy limit is $250,000. The policy will pay the full $200,000 to the other individual. The policy will pay only $50,000 for the damage to the car because the property damage limit is $50,000.

C. *Part B—Medical coverage*

(1) Medical payments in the auto policy cover the cost of medical services for the insured, relatives, and anyone else in the insured's car. Coverage is provided to the named insured while occupying an owned or nonowned automobile. Coverage also applies to the named insured and family members if, while any of them is a pedestrian, he or she is struck by any motor vehicle designated for use of public roads. Payment is made under the *pedestrian provision*.

(2) This coverage does not apply to pedestrians or to occupants of the other vehicle. In contrast, we learned that homeowners insurance provides coverage for medical payments to others.

(3) The advantage of medical payment coverage in addition to liability insurance is that the payment is prompt because there is no time wasted in determining liability.

D. *Part C—Uninsured motorists*

(1) This part of the PAP protects the driver against those who have no coverage or are underinsured. It also covers hit-and-run situations.

(2) It is necessary to show that the other driver was at fault in order to collect on a claim.

(3) This type of policy applies only to bodily injury.

E. *Part D—Coverage for damage to insured's auto*

(1) Comprehensive physical damage

(a) Comprehensive insurance protects the car against breakage of glass, theft, vandalism, falling objects, fire, hail, water, flood, riot, earthquake, and contact with a bird or animal.

(b) This coverage does not apply to cars damaged in a collision with another car or object, or to normal wear and tear on a car.

(c) The extent and deductible of the coverage varies from policy to policy.

(2) Collision

(a) *Collision* is defined as the upset of a covered auto or its impact with another vehicle or object.

(b) Collision coverage applies to the covered auto regardless of fault.

(c) Collision insurance includes a deductible amount.

F. *Part E—Duties after accident or loss*

In the case of a claim, the policyholder must do the following:

(1) Send the insurance company accident-related paperwork.

(2) Authorize the insurance company to obtain medical and other pertinent records.

   (3) Submit proof of loss.
   (4) Cooperate with the insurance company in every way.

G. *Part F*—General provisions

   The key provisions are

   (1) The term of the policy may be changed or waived only by an endorsement signed by the company.
   (2) The policy provides that the insurer will not provide coverage for any insured that has made fraudulent statements with any accident or loss.
   (3) The policyholder may cancel the policy by notifying the company in writing.
   (4) There is a subrogation clause that applies to all coverage.

H. Many companies give discounts for at least some of the following: higher deductibles; elimination of collision coverage for older cars; no accident for some period of time, generally three years; smoking avoidance; students with good grades; driver's education course for young drivers; a defensive driving course; airbags and automatic seat belts in vehicle; other policies with the same company; travel short distances to work; individuals over age 25; women (versus men); and married people (versus single).

I. There are three primary areas in auto insurance that may not be covered.

   (1) When someone is living in the same house as the owner but is not listed on the insurance policy. It is vital to include all appropriate family members on the insurance policy. It is generally recommended to insure children under the owner's policy, even if the children are away at school.
   (2) When the accident occurs during business use
   (3) When travelers reject insurance coverage through a rental company; their insurance policy may not fully cover rental cars, especially if accidents happen outside of the United States

3. Business and business activity

   A. *Commercial property insurance.* Protecting real and personal property used in business. The coverage applies to losses from most perils other than those that relate to crime, transportation, and boiler explosion.
   B. *Business income insurance.* Protects against loss of income after the occurrence of direct physical damage to business property
   C. *Boiler and machinery insurance.* Covers a wide range of damage to personal and real property and can be written to provide business income and extra expense coverage. Generally used to cover items not covered by commercial property and business income insurance.
   D. *Inland marine insurance.* Specialized transportation insurance characterized by coverage of specific goods in transit
   E. *Crime insurance.* Protects the business against losses that arise from illegal activities such as burglary, robbery, extortion, forgery, employee dishonesty, and theft
   F. *Commercial general liability (CGL) insurance.* Protects business owner against claims by members of the public who are injured or suffer a loss in, or as a result of, the business. The policy provides little or no coverage for (a) liability to employees, (b) liability arising from rendering or failure to render professional services, and (c) liability arising from automobile, aircraft, or watercraft. A client who suffers a financial loss because a financial planner implemented an incorrect investment transaction is not covered by CGL insurance.

G. *Commercial auto insurance.* When an auto is not eligible for PAP, it is generally provided similar coverage under a commercial auto policy.

H. *Workers' compensation and employers' liability (WC&EL) insurance.* If an employee is hurt on the job, even because of his or her own negligence, the injury is covered.

4. Umbrella policy

A. An umbrella liability policy provides liability coverage in excess of the limits or exposures in basic liability policies. Coverage is typically $1 million or more.

B. The two functions of the umbrella policy are

(1) To provide increased coverage when the limits of the basic coverage are inadequate to cover future judgments

(2) To provide broader coverage than that provided by the basic policy or policies (the homeowners and auto policies would both be basic policies)

C. The umbrella insurer requires the insured to have adequate underlying basic liability policies before an umbrella liability policy will be issued. For example, a typical insurer may insist that the insured have auto liability limits of $100,000/$300,000/$50,000 and minimum CPL coverage of $300,000.

D. If the policy owner fails to maintain adequate underlying coverage, the insurer will pay only the amount it would be required to pay had the underlying policy been in force. For example, assume a $1 million umbrella policy with the required underlying limit of $250,000 per person under an auto liability policy, but the insured's liability limits are only $50,000. If an injured party obtains a legal judgment of $750,000 against the insured, the underlying auto policy will pay $50,000 and the umbrella policy will pay $500,000. The insured would have an uninsured loss of $200,000.

E. Exclusions to umbrella liability insurance include

(1) Owned or leased aircraft and watercraft

(2) Business pursuits (unless these exposures are covered by a basic policy or policies)

(3) Rendering or failure to render professional services

(4) Claims normally covered by workers' compensation

(5) Intentional injury

(6) Damage to property owned by the insured, or damage to nonowned property in the insured's care, custody, and control

TOPIC 25: GENERAL BUSINESS LIABILITY

1. *Professional liability insurance* provides coverage for legal liability arising from the failure of a person to use the care and the degree of skill expected of a practitioner in his or her profession. The liability coverage available to professionals is two forms:

A. *Errors and omissions insurance* covers exposures to financial and property damage liability (including intangible property). This coverage is designed primarily for insurance agents, lawyers, accountants, architects, and real estate agents. This is the form used by financial planners.

B. *Malpractice insurance* is used to cover exposures to bodily injury liability. This coverage is designed for doctors, dentists, and hospitals.

2. *Directors and officers (D&O) liability insurance*

A. A corporation purchases this insurance, and the corporation is the policyholder but not the insured. The officers and directors are the insureds.

B. It protects officers and directors against lawsuits brought by stockholders, creditors, competitors, and governments.

C. Exclusions include bodily injury and damage to tangible property, fraudulent acts, violations of securities laws, and acts that result in personal gain to which the director or officer is not entitled.

3. *Product liability insurance* protects against claims resulting from a product that is produced or manufactured by a business.

TOPIC 26: HEALTH INSURANCE (INDIVIDUAL)

1. Hospital-surgical

   A. These plans provide benefits only for individuals who are hospitalized or need surgery. There are no benefits for visits to the physician's office.

   B. The policy is inadequate for prolonged sickness and serious accidents, as well as medical expenses outside the hospital setting.

   C. Hospital coverage is provided for a limited number of days, and surgical coverage is paid on a fee-schedule basis. A fee-schedule basis repays the patient an amount stated in the contract for each day of hospitalization and for listed surgical procedures, regardless of the actual cost.

   D. These plans tend to have the lowest premiums because they pay the least benefits.

2. Major medical

   A. These plans usually provide $1 million or more in coverage and cover almost everything related to illness or injury. They typically have a deductible, coinsurance, and a stop-loss that apply to a wide range of covered expenses.

   B. Major medical plans share several characteristics:

      (1) In most cases, the insured has complete freedom to choose any medical provider without reduced benefits. In some cases, the insured receives reduced benefits if a medical provider is chosen outside the network.

      (2) These plans do not make use of a gatekeeper (i.e., primary care physician).

      (3) Major medical plans do not provide benefits for preventative care.

      (4) Major medical plans differ in their coverage of prescription drugs. Some plans require a policy rider for drug coverage, and others carry limitations, such as a maximum benefit.

3. Traditional indemnity

   A. Indemnity plans—comprehensive medical expense plan

      (1) Coverage includes diagnostic, medical, hospital, and surgical services.

      (2) Reimbursement amounts are capped; the plan pays up to policy or lifetime limit.

      (3) Patients are allowed to visit any doctor for any number of visits.

      (4) Escalating costs have resulted in managed care plans: *preferred provider organizations* (PPO), *health maintenance organizations* (HMO), and *point-of-service* (POS) *plans*.

   B. Managed care plans share the following characteristics:

      (1) *Controlled access to providers.* Managed care programs control costs by limiting which physicians or hospitals can be used. They also use primary care physicians to determine the necessity of specialized care in order to control costs.

      (2) *Comprehensive case management.* This includes treatment, ongoing care, and reviews.

(3) *Preventative care.* To keep costs down, managed care plans encourage a healthy lifestyle to prevent illness in later years.

(4) *Risk sharing.* If physicians share in the financial consequences of their decisions, managed care programs can possibly eliminate unnecessary tests and expenses.

(5) *High-quality care.* The quality of care must be high to encourage individuals to participate.

4. Preferred provider organization (PPO)

A. Benefit plans that contract with preferred providers to offer medical services to plan participants at a reduced rate

B. There are several characteristics of a PPO:

(1) Medical providers are paid on a fee-for-service basis.

(2) The insured has the choice to use network or out-of-network providers. There are incentives to use network providers, including such benefits as lower deductibles and co-payments and broader type of covered care.

(3) Most PPOs do not use a primary care physician as a gatekeeper. Therefore, participants do not need referrals to see specialists.

(4) PPOs are slightly more costly than HMOs.

5. Health maintenance organization (HMO)

A. An organized system of health care that provides a broad range of medical services on a prepaid basis to subscribers within a particular geographic region

B. There are several characteristics of an HMO:

(1) Highest degree of review, including financial incentives and disincentives for providers

(2) Offers a comprehensive package of health care with an emphasis on preventative care

(3) Subscribers pay an annual premium to receive medical services. They generally pay no deductible or co-payment, except in some cases where there may be a small co-payment for certain services.

(4) Subscribers are required to see providers who are affiliated with the HMO. Out-of-area or out-of-network coverage is possible, but only in the case of medical emergencies.

(5) Emphasizes treatment by primary care physicians; therefore, access to specialists is controlled.

6. Medicare supplement insurance

A. Provides benefits for specific expenses not covered by Medicare. These include

(1) Deductibles, coinsurance, or co-payments

(2) Expenses that are excluded from coverage, such as prescription drugs and treatment outside the United States

B. Medigap insurance is Medicare supplement insurance in the individual marketplace. The objective is to fill in the gaps when Medicare is exhausted.

C. The National Association of Insurance Commissioners designed 10 standard plans for the federal government. The 10 plans are identified by the letters A–J. Insurance companies cannot provide benefits that differ from these available options, with two exceptions:

(1) Companies can offer high-deductible Medigap standard policies when used with medical savings accounts. These are identical to plans A–J except in the amount of the deductible.

(2) The Medicare SELECT program can limit or exclude benefits for medical services if a nonnetwork provider is used. A Medicare SELECT policy is identical to plans A–J except in the treatment of benefits when using nonnetwork providers.

D. There are three basic benefits that are included in plans A–J:

    (1) Hospitalization

    (2) Medical expenses

    (3) Blood

E. The difference between the Medigap plans is their treatment of the following benefits: skilled nursing facility, Part A deductible, Part B deductible, Part B excess charges, foreign travel emergency, at-home recovery, preventive medical care, and prescription drugs.

F. For prescription drugs, Medigap plans H, I, and J pay 50 percent of outpatient drug charges after a $250 deductible, with either a $1,250 (plans H and I) or a $3,000 (plan J) calendar year limit.

7. Point-of-service (POS) plans

A. Hybrid of HMOs and PPOs. These are similar to HMOs for network services and like PPOs for nonnetwork services.

B. Two basic types of POS plans:

    (1) Open-ended HMO provides traditional HMO coverage with the flexibility to visit a nonnetwork provider.

    (2) Gatekeeper PPO requires the participant to elect a primary care physician. This controls the participant in seeing a network specialist. However, the participant can always elect to go outside the network at a higher cost and less coverage.

Medicare Supplement (Medigap) Insurance

Benefits	A	B	C	D	E	F	G	H	I	J
Basic	X	X	X	X	X	X	X	X	X	X
Skilled-nursing facility			X	X	X	X	X	X	X	X
Part A deductible		X	X	X	X	X	X	X	X	X
Part B deductible			X			X				X
Part B excess charges						100%	80%		100%	100%
Foreign travel emergency			X	X	X	X	X	X	X	X
At-home recovery				X			X		X	X
Preventive medical care					X					X
Prescription drugs								$1,250	$1,250	$3,000

Chart taken from Burton Beam, David Bickelhaupt, Robert Crowe, and Barbara Poole, *Fundamentals of Insurance for Financial Planning*, 3rd ed., Bryn Mawr, Pennsylvania: The American College, Huebner School Series, 2002.

8. Blue Cross and Blue Shield are organizations formed for the purpose of prepaying subscribers for medical care expenses.

   A. Blue Cross plans provide coverage primarily for hospital expenses.
   B. Blue Shield plans provide coverage primarily for physicians' services. Physician expense insurance covers nonsurgical physicians' fees, whereas surgical expense insurance covers surgeons' fees.

TOPIC 27: DISABILITY INCOME INSURANCE (INDIVIDUAL)

1. Occupational definitions and application

   A. No benefit is payable if the injury or illness is not disabling. There are four basic types of definitions of total disability found in current policies.

      (1) *Own occupation.* This is the inability to engage in one's own occupation.
      (2) *Modified any occupation.* This is the inability to engage in an occupation for which fitted by education, training, or experience.
      (3) *Any occupation.* This is the inability to engage in any occupation. It is the most restrictive and is used by only a few companies.
      (4) *Loss of income.* This provision pays when the insured has a reduction of income due to an illness or injury that is at least at a specified level. It measures only income.

   B. A number of companies use a so-called *split definition* of disability. A split definition is *own occupation* for some period of time, such as two years, then a modified *own occupation* definition. This is found in group policies more often than individual policies.

   C. Many short-term disability income policies do not provide disability income benefits for illnesses or accidents resulting from occupational exposures. In most cases, occupational disabilities are covered by workers' compensation laws mandating coverage. Policies excluding occupational disabilities are known as *nonoccupational* policies. Long-term policies often provide benefits for both occupational and nonoccupational disabilities.

   D. Beyond the basic definition, many policies provide different benefit levels for disabilities that are total, partial, and/or residual disabilities.

      (1) *Total disability* benefits provide for the full policy benefit.
      (2) *Partial benefits* promise to pay a reduced benefit if the insured can perform some but not all of the important daily duties of his or her occupation. The partial disability benefit is usually 50 percent of the total disability benefit. The benefit is usually paid for only a short time. Six months is the most common benefit period.
      (3) *Residual benefits* are usually paid after a total disability and are designed to allow the insured to return to work without losing all benefits. Benefits are usually paid based on the percentage of lost income. These are better than partial disability benefits in that there is typically no limit for the length of time that reduced benefits are available.

2. Benefit period

   A. Short-term disability provides benefits for a limited period of time, usually up to six months, subject to a one- to seven-day waiting period for sickness and no waiting period for accidents. Some plans have the same waiting period for sickness and accidents, and other plans have no waiting period. Benefits rarely exceed beyond one year.
   B. Long-term disability provides extended benefits—up to two years or life—subject to a three-month or six-month waiting period. Six-month waiting periods are the most common. The waiting periods for sickness and accident are the same.

3. Elimination period (waiting period) is the deductible for a disability income insurance policy. The purpose of the waiting period is to eliminate coverage for short-term disabilities and to help control the moral hazard. By denying replacement of income for a period, the insurer can deter the insured from faking a disability to enjoy a paid vacation. The longer the elimination period, the lower the premium.

4. Benefit amount

   A. Disability income plans are designed to provide a benefit level that replaces a percentage of regular earnings (excluding bonuses and overtime).

      (1) Short-term disability plans range from 50 to 100 percent, but 70 percent is usually the upper limit. Some short-term plans use different percentages—for example, paying 100 percent of earnings for four weeks and then 70 percent of earnings for the rest of the time.

      (2) Long-term disability plans typically provide benefits in the range of 50 to 70 percent of an employee's gross income; 60 and 66⅔ are the most common percentages.

   B. These plans often place a maximum dollar amount on the benefit that is provided.

5. Riders

   A. *Cost-of-living allowance (COLA) riders* provide for periodic increases in the disability income benefit after the insured becomes disabled.

   B. The *presumptive disability* provision states that the loss of the use of two bodily members or the loss of sight or hearing will be presumed to be total disability, whether or not the insured is able to do any work for compensation.

   C. The *guaranteed insurability* provision permits the insured to purchase additional amounts of coverage if his or her income has increased.

   D. The *automatic benefit increase* provision increases the benefit each month to reflect the increased cost.

   E. A *waiver of premium* provision exists if the insured becomes totally disabled and the disability lasts for a period of time.

   F. The *Social Security substitute rider* permits the coordination of disability insurance with the Social Security insurance program.

   G. The *probation period* is the period of time after issuance of a policy in which specified illnesses or injuries will be excluded from coverage.

   H. The *preexisting conditions clause* covers a physical condition that the insured had before the disability income policy was issued. Preexisting conditions are typically excluded from coverage under individual disability income policies.

   I. The *change of occupation* provision allows the insurer to reduce the benefit payable if the insured changes to a more hazardous occupation.

   J. The *relation of earnings to insurance clause* (also called *average earnings clause*) states that if the total disability income provided by all policies exceeds the insured's earned income, or average earned income for the preceding two years (whichever is greater), the income benefits under the policy will be reduced proportionately. The clause is designed to protect the insurer from the moral hazard associated with a situation in which the disability benefits payable may exceed the normal income of the insured.

   K. Policy continuation provisions

      (1) *Noncancelable policy.* The insurer may not cancel or increase premiums.

      (2) *Guaranteed renewable policy.* The insurer may not cancel, but may increase premiums for an entire class of policy owners.

(3) *Conditionally renewable policy.* The insurer has the right to terminate the contract by not renewing it.

(4) *Policy renewable at the company's option (optionally renewable).* Usually tied to association-type plans. The insurance company has the right to cancel the insured's policy at the end of the policy year.

(5) *Policy with no provision.* The insurer has complete flexibility to renew or refuse to renew the policy. The insured must apply for new coverage rather than a renewal.

(6) *Cancelable policy.* This is an even more common clause used in association with group plans. The insurer can terminate this policy anytime during its term.

6. Taxation of benefits

A. If disability benefits are received from an employer-provided disability policy, such benefits are totally included in taxable income.

B. If disability benefits are received from an employee-paid disability policy, such benefits are excluded from taxable income.

C. If disability benefits are received from a policy paid by both an employer and an employee, then benefits are included in income to the extent of the employer pro rata share of premiums. *Example:* Steve is covered under a long-term disability income insurance plan of his employer. Steve pays 75 percent of the premium cost, and the employer pays 25 percent of the premium cost. The income tax treatment is as follows:

(1) The employer's contributions are deductible and are not taxable as income to Steve.

(2) Steve's contributions are not tax deductible.

(3) 25 percent of any disability income payments are tax free to Steve, and 75 percent are taxable as income.

TOPIC 28: LONG-TERM CARE INSURANCE (INDIVIDUAL AND JOINT)

1. Basic provisions

A. The National Association of Insurance Commissioners (NAIC) model legislation emphasizes two areas, policy provisions and marketing provisions.

B. Policy provisions

(1) Certain terms can be used in the policy only if defined. These include *adult day care, skilled-nursing care,* and the like.

(2) The renewal provisions are only guaranteed renewable and noncancelable.

    (a) *Guaranteed renewable.* Premiums can be adjusted.

    (b) *Noncancelable.* Premiums cannot be changed.

(3) Exclusions are prohibited except for some conditions.

    (a) A maximum look-back period of six months relating to preexisting conditions

    (b) Mental and nervous disorder (but not including Alzheimer's disease)

    (c) Alcoholism and drug addiction

    (d) Suicide and war

    (e) Services available under Medicare and other social insurance programs

(4) A policy must offer the ability to purchase more coverage.

(5) It must offer the right to purchase a nonforfeiture option.

(6) An inflation protection benefit must be offered.

(7) The policy must have a provision that waives premiums if the insured has been receiving benefits for a specified period of time, such as 60 or 90 days.

(8) After two years, the policy must be incontestable based on misrepresentation. It can still be contested if the applicant intentionally misrepresented facts pertaining to his or her health.

(9) There is a prohibition of a prior hospitalization requirement in order to qualify for nursing home care, and a prohibition on requiring prior nursing home care in order to qualify for home health care benefits.

(10) Group coverage must provide for continuation or conversion.

C. Marketing provisions

(1) The prospective applicant must receive an outline of coverage, a shopper's guide, and a free 30-day look at the policy. Therefore, a full refund of premiums must be paid up to 30 days after the policy is purchased if the applicant chooses not to keep the contract.

(2) The insurer must ensure fair and accurate comparisons with other competitors.

(3) The insurer must provide unambiguous and clear wording in the application to ascertain the applicant's health.

(4) The policy cannot be issued until the applicant is given the option to identify a third party to be notified of any pending lapses because of failure to pay premiums.

(5) If a policy replaces another policy, the new policy must waive any time period pertaining to preexisting conditions and probationary periods for comparable benefits.

(6) Insurers must report lapse rates, replacement sales, and denied claims each year.

(7) Advertising materials used by insurance companies must be filed with the state regulatory authority.

(8) The contracts must have a defined incontestability period and require that conditions be defined for rescission of the policy by the insurance company.

2. Eligibility

A. The Health Insurance Portability and Accountability Act (HIPAA) created a definition for qualified long-term care (LTC) plans. HIPAA provides favorable tax treatment only for *qualified long-term care insurance contracts*.

(1) Only qualified long-term care insurance can be provided.

(2) The policy cannot pay for expenses reimbursed under Medicare.

(3) The policy cannot have a cash surrender value or loan provision.

(4) Refunds of premiums and policy dividends must be used to reduce future premiums or increase future benefits.

(5) The policy must comply with consumer protection provisions, such as those adopted in the NAIC model Act.

B. HIPAA defines *qualified long-term care services* as necessary diagnostic, preventive, therapeutic, curing, treating, and rehabilitative services and maintenance or personal care services that are required by a *chronically ill* person and are provided by a plan of care prescribed by a licensed health care practitioner.

C. A chronically ill person is one who meets the following requirements:

(1) The inability to perform at least two *activities of daily living* (ADLs) for a period of at least 90 days. The Act identifies ADLs as eating, bathing, dressing, transferring from bed to chair, using the toilet, and maintaining continence. A qualified long-term care policy must contain at least five of the six.

(2) Substantial services are required to protect the individual from threats of health and safety due to cognitive impairment.

3. Benefit amount and period

   A. Amount

      (1) Benefits are primarily a specified amount per day. They are sold in increments of $10 per day up to $500 per day.

      (2) Benefits can be provided on an indemnity basis that covers 80 to 100 percent of charges up to a maximum amount.

   B. Period

      (1) The duration of an LTC policy benefit is impacted by the elimination period and a maximum benefit period.

      (2) The longer the elimination period, the lower the premium. In contrast, the longer the maximum benefit period, the higher the premium.

4. Elimination protection—Benefits do not begin until a specified period of time passes after the individual starts receiving LTC. This period can be as short as 0 days and as long as 365 days.

5. Inflation protection—The cost is built into the initial premium. Therefore, premiums do not increase at the time of the annual increase.

6. Nursing home and in-home care

   A. *Skilled-nursing care.* This requires a registered nurse who is under a licensed physician's supervision. The nurse is available 24 hours a day.

   B. *Intermediate care.* This care requires fewer nurses per 100 persons for whom nursing care is being provided and must be based on doctor's orders.

   C. *Custodial care.* This is care for which medical services are not needed. Custodial care requires a low nurse-to-patient ratio. The main services and functions provided are food preparation, food service, bathing, and moving patient from bed to chair and subsequently from chair to bed.

   D. *Home health care.* Allowed when a person is capable of providing limited service for him- or herself. Daily or weekly nurse visits are common.

   E. *Assisted-living care.* This is provided by facilities that care for the elderly who do not need the same level of care as provided in nursing homes.

   F. *Respite care.* This is occasional full-time care at home for a person receiving home health care. It gives family members a break from providing care.

7. Comparing and selecting policies

   A. The policy should be guaranteed renewable for life.

   B. A three-month waiting period generally offers the best value for the premium dollars paid.

   C. The policy should provide coverage for skilled and intermediate care, as well as for custodial care, which does not require the engagement of licensed medical professionals.

   D. Long-term care at home can be more attractive than care in a residential or nursing facility.

   E. Select a policy that does not require the insured to be hospitalized before entering a nursing home for care.

   F. Select a policy that provides long-term care coverage for patients with Alzheimer's disease.

   G. Choose a policy that provides for the anticipated rise in the cost of long-term care.

   H. Select a policy that provides for a waiver of premiums in the event of disability and provides level premiums for life.

   I. Select a policy that provides a favorable benefit period.

8. Tax implications and qualifications—Qualified long-term care contracts have favorable tax benefits:

A. Individuals can deduct premiums paid for LTC in excess of 7.5 percent of adjusted gross income. There are limits to the maximum amount that can be deducted, subject to the covered individual's age.

B. Employer contributions are deductible to the employer and result in no taxable income to the employee.

C. Benefits are received tax free with one exception. For contracts written on a per diem basis, proceeds are excludible from income up to $210 per day (2002, indexed annually).

9. Appropriateness of coverage

The elderly are not the only ones in need of long-term care. Younger people who are unable to care for themselves as a result of accident, sickness, or disabilities may also be in need of long-term care.

TOPIC 29: LIFE INSURANCE

1. Fundamentals

A. Certain basic characteristics are common among all life insurance policies.

(1) It is not the possibility of death that is insured, but rather an untimely death.

(2) Life insurance is not a contract of indemnity. It does not attempt to put the individual in the same financial position as before the loss.

(3) An insurable interest must exist at the onset of the contract.

B. Life insurance is divided into two types:

(1) Term insurance

(a) Term insurance is sometimes called pure insurance. It pays a death benefit if a person dies during a specified time period.

(b) There is no cash value or loan element.

(c) There are increasing premiums in later years when the policy is renewed.

(d) Key points common with term policies are *renewability* and *convertibility*.

i. *Renewability.* The right to renew the contract *without* a medical examination or other evidence of insurability

ii. *Convertibility.* Allows the policyholder to exchange the term policy for a permanent policy *without* evidence of insurability

(2) Permanent insurance

(a) The protection afforded by permanent insurance never expires, and the policy never has to be renewed or converted.

(b) The protection is guaranteed as long as policyholders continue to pay premiums or pay up their policies, regardless of health.

(c) Permanent policies have a cash value and a loan element.

(d) There is an advantage of tax-deferred investment income with the cash value.

(e) Permanent insurance includes whole life insurance, endowment insurance, universal life insurance, adjustable life insurance, and variable life insurance.

C. The cash value of a permanent insurance policy acts as a savings fund for the policyholder.

(1) The *level premium concept* helps explain how a cash value reserve accumulates over time for the insured. This means that the insurance company will receive the same premium amount regardless of the age of the insured. In the early years of the policy,

the insured pays more than the cost of pure life insurance protection. In later years, the insured is actually paying less than the cost of pure life insurance.

(2) The policy can be viewed as having two parts: the portion of the cash value and the pure insurance. The effective amount of insurance is the difference between the face amount and the reserve. This amount is called the *net amount at risk*. Life insurance is seen as a decreasing term (net amount of risk) and an increasing amount of investment (the growing reserve). These two elements always equal the face amount of the policy.

(3) The cash value reserve is not solely the property of the insured. It is the insured's only if and when the policy is surrendered. There are three distinct advantages in the use of a cash reserve:

    (a) By paying an amount in excess of the cost of pure insurance during the early years of the contract, the insured avoids a rising premium in the later years.

    (b) If the insured survives, he or she has accumulated a savings fund that can be used for income in old age.

    (c) Cash value policies permit borrowing on the policy up to a specified percentage of cash value, usually at a guaranteed interest rate.

2. Types

  A. Term insurance

    (1) A *yearly renewable term* (YRT) policy is a one-year term contract renewable for successive periods of one year each. It is a policy that typically has a low first-year premium that increases every year while the face amount is fixed.

    (2) *Level-term insurance* guarantees level premiums and face value for up to 10 years, and there are some policies that project level premiums for 20 years or more.

    (3) *Decreasing term insurance* provides systematic decreases in the amount of benefit from year to year. Decreasing term insurance is often used to provide funds for paying off a mortgage. Such policies typically have a level premium.

  B. Whole life insurance

    (1) Whole life insurance was devised as an alternative to the increasing premium payment associated with term insurance. The level premium is the result of spreading out the increasing annual insurance costs over the life of the insured (see Topic 29, Section 1.C.)

    (2) Whole life policies involve the fixed payment of premiums over a very long period of time. Premiums must be paid when due or when the policy lapses.

    (3) These policies provide a guaranteed but fixed death benefit.

    (4) Whole life policies offer a balance between protection and cash accumulation.

    (5) The insured does not control the investment vehicle in a whole life policy. Instead, the insurance company invests the premiums in investment-grade bonds and high-quality mortgages. The result is a modest return on invested funds. Thus, whole life policies do not provide a hedge against inflation. The cash values lose purchasing power during inflationary periods.

    (6) The policyholder can discontinue making premium payments and choose among the different nonforfeiture options.

    (7) There are four primary types of whole life insurance:

      (a) *Ordinary whole life* assumes that the premium rate will be payable throughout the insured's life. It has the lowest premium rate for any whole life policy and a lower cash value than other whole life policies.

    (b) *Limited-pay whole life* is for someone who wants protection for life without paying premiums in retirement. This type of whole life policy differs from a traditional whole life policy in three ways: (1) Premium payments do not continue for life even though it provides lifetime protection, (2) the premium rate is higher than that of whole life because the period of time is limited, and (3) the policy builds up cash value faster than whole life.

    (c) *Single-premium whole life (SPWL)* is a whole life policy in which a single premium is paid up front as a lump sum for life protection. The compelling reason for buying an SPWL is to use a life insurance policy as a tax-deferred investment.

    (d) *Graded premium whole life* has a relatively low initial premium that increases each year for five to seven years. When it levels out, it is usually higher than the whole life premium that would have been charged at the beginning of the policy's life, but lower than if the policy were taken out at the end of the increasing premium period. It is designed to allow individuals who want income to catch up with permanent insurance premiums.

C. Universal life insurance

    (1) Universal life (UL) permits a policyholder to increase or decrease the death benefit coverage with satisfactory evidence of insurability.

    (2) It provides extreme flexibility by allowing the policyholder to increase or decrease the amount and frequency of premium payments as long as the cash value is sufficient to cover the cost of continuing the policy.

    (3) Interest credited to the policy's cash value is geared to current interest rates, but is subject to a minimum amount, such as 4 percent. This provides a hedge against inflation.

    (4) As interest rates increase, the policy's cash value increases more than that of whole life, and this results in more tax-deferred investment income.

    (5) Changes in interest rate can also be viewed as a disadvantage inasmuch as future yield potential may be uncertain.

    (6) Universal life is often called *unbundled* insurance—it is possible to see the entire operation (operating expenses, mortality charges, and cash value buildup) of the policy in the annual statement.

    (7) A UL policy differs from a whole life policy in specific ways:

        (a) The premium payment is flexible.

        (b) The death benefit is adjustable.

        (c) The investment and mortality risks are shifted from the insurance company to the policyholder.

    (8) There are two choices of death benefit designs:

        (a) Universal life, Option A (or 1)—level death benefit

            i. The death benefit is the face amount of the policy. Hence, the death benefit includes the cash accumulation fund.

            ii. The mortality charges are based on the net amount at risk or protection element, the face amount of the policy minus the accumulation fund.

            iii. *One exception*: If the cash value gets high enough and represents a large proportion of the death benefit, the policy will increase the death benefit even though it is called a level death benefit contract. This is a rare occurrence, and tax law defines the specified proportion of the death benefit derived from the net amount at risk.

     (b) Universal life, Option B (or 2)

        i. This form of universal life pays the state face amount plus its cash value at the insured's death.

        ii. There is always a constant net amount at risk over the policy's cash value.

        iii. The death benefit increases when the cash value increases, whereas a reduction in cash value will reduce the death benefit.

        iv. The monthly mortality charges are based on the face amount of the policy every year.

        v. This option is more expensive than Option A (or 1).

D. Variable life insurance

  (1) The policy owner selects the investments to which the savings element will be directed.

  (2) There is no guaranteed cash value or crediting rate.

  (3) Investments are in separate accounts that look much like mutual funds, but technically are different. Policies generally have between 5 and 15 separate accounts from which to choose, one of which is always a conservative interest-bearing account.

  (4) In a down market, a policyholder runs the risk of being surprised with a premium notice that a substantial payment must be made just to keep the policy in force.

  (5) A variable life insurance policy shifts the investment risk to the insured and lets the insured direct some or all of the policy's cash value into the securities market. This permits the insured to participate in the returns of the equity market.

  (6) Must be sold with a prospectus and can be sold only by licensed insurance and securities agents

  (7) Guaranteed minimum death benefit only equal to the initial face amount of the policy

  (8) Above the minimum, the death benefit depends on the performance of the policyowner's selected investments.

  (9) Allows policy loans, but at a smaller percentage than traditional whole and universal life insurance

  (10) Contains the usual range of nonforfeiture options

E. Variable whole life insurance

  (1) Fixed premiums of whole life

  (2) Guaranteed death benefit of whole life

  (3) Investment flexibility of variable life

  (4) The big difference from other types of whole life insurance is that it has no guaranteed cash values.

F. Variable universal life insurance

  (1) Premium flexibility of universal life

  (2) Death benefit design flexibility of universal life

  (3) Investment flexibility of variable life

  (4) The big difference from ordinary universal life insurance is that it has no guaranteed cash values.

G. Endowment policies

  (1) Death benefit equals cash value at maturity.

  (2) Purchaser can specify the policy's maturity date (10-, 15-, 20-, 25-, 30-year endowments, and longer).

  (3) Whole life insurance is identical in design to an endowment at age 100, when cash value equals the death benefit.

(4) The 1984 change in the federal income tax law eliminated the tax-advantaged buildup of an endowment's cash value. The current sale of endowment contracts is very limited in the United States.

H. Joint-life insurance

(1) A *first-to-die policy* is specifically for business continuation agreements. All of the owners are insured under the same policy. When the first owner dies, the insurance company makes a payment that is used to buy the deceased owner's share of the business.

(2) A *second-to-die policy* is popular for estate tax payment.

(a) It is usually purchased as a policy on the lives of both spouses. Upon the death of a married person, the entire estate passes to the surviving spouse free of federal estate taxes. However, upon the death of the second spouse, estates of more than $1 million (in 2003) are taxable. The taxes can be paid with the proceeds from a second-to-die policy.

(b) This policy eliminates any liquidity problems.

(c) If the deceased owned the policy, it is included in the estate of the deceased, even if the deceased is not the beneficiary.

(3) A *family income policy* is a combination of decreasing term insurance and some form of whole life insurance. The whole life insurance pays a lump sum, and the term rider provides income designed to end at a specified date in the future.

(4) A *family life insurance policy* has a base policy on one adult in the household. This is typically whole life. The policy also covers other members of the family. The policies are usually sold in "units." A typical unit may be $25,000 on the primary insured, $15,000 on the spouse, and $5,000 on each child.

3. Contractual provisions

A. *Participating versus nonparticipating policies*

(1) Nonparticipating policies do not pay any policy owner dividends. In contrast, participating policies charge a small extra margin in the premium with intent to return a part of the premium in the form of dividends.

(2) Participating policies have the ability to respond to changes in the economy. When interest rates soared in the late 1970s and early 1980s, it was participating policies that kept up with the changes and did not lock policy owners into very low interest earnings in their policies.

B. *Entire contract.* The policy, including the attached application, is the whole contract. There are no other documents that control it.

C. *Ownership.* Life insurance is owned by someone with an insurable interest in the insured. The contract can be transferred in whole or in part by the owner, but the transfer is effective only if the insurance company is notified in writing.

D. *Beneficiary.* The beneficiary or beneficiaries are named in the application. The owner may change the beneficiary unless that designation has been made irrevocable. Any change must be in writing to the insurance company to be effective.

(1) *Primary beneficiary.* The individual first designated to receive the proceeds of an insurance policy

(2) *Contingent beneficiary.* A beneficiary who is entitled to receive proceeds if the primary beneficiary has died

E. *Collateral assignment.* Allows the owner to use the policy as collateral. This is often done in a business setting.

F. *Incontestable clause.* This clause gives the insurance company two years during the life of the insured to discover any information about the insured that would have affected issuance of the policy. If material adverse information is found, the company has the right to void the contract. If the information is found after the two years, the policy stays in force (fraud is an exception).

G. *Misstatement of age.* If, at death, the death certificate shows the insured was older or younger than stated in the application, the death benefit will be adjusted to what the premium would have purchased.

H. *Grace period.* This is the automatic extension for premium payment, usually to 31 days after due date. Without this provision, if a premium is received after the due date, the policy lapses.

I. *Reinstatement.* If the premium arrives after the grace period, the policy lapses. The reinstatement provision permits the owner, if insurable interest still exists and if the insured is still insurable, to reinstate a policy that has lapsed for nonpayment of premium. If a policy was surrendered for its cash value, it may not be reinstated. Generally, reinstatement is automatic if requested within 30 days of the end of the grace period.

J. *Automatic premium loan.* If the premium has not been paid at the end of the grace period, the company will automatically lend the owner the premium, using the cash value of the policy as collateral. This prevents the policy from lapsing. It is used only in cash value policies.

K. *Suicide clause.* Adverse selection would occur if insurance companies had to honor death claims for suicides that occurred shortly after a life insurance policy is taken out. In most states, if the insured commits suicide within the first two years after the policy was issued, the insurance company will pay only the cumulative premiums plus interest.

L. *Aviation and war clauses.* These eliminate coverage for any death that is aviation related or due to war. Few if any policies currently have these provisions.

M. *Policy loans.* Permanent policies permit owners to borrow from the insurance company at a specified interest rate, using the policy as collateral. The policy loan clause describes that right and contains specific provisions.

N. *Simultaneous death clause.* If the insured and the beneficiary die simultaneously, it will be presumed that the beneficiary died first. The proceeds will be distributed as if the insured survived the beneficiary and will be paid to the secondary beneficiary or to the insured's estate.

O. *Common disaster clause.* Settlement of the policy proceeds is withheld for a designated number of days after the death of the insured (usually 30), and any beneficiary surviving the insured but dying within the specified period is considered to have predeceased the insured. Therefore, the proceeds are distributed as if the insured survived the beneficiary.

P. *Guaranteed purchase option.* This option protects the policy owner against the chance of becoming uninsurable by allowing the insured to purchase additional amounts of insurance at specified times or ages without showing evidence of insurability.

Q. *Waiver of premium.* If the insured becomes disabled, the insurance company will waive premiums on the life insurance policy during the continuance of the insured's disability.

R. *Accelerated benefits provision (accelerated death benefit).* This allows a terminally ill insured to withdraw a portion of the policy's death benefit before death. The amount received is income tax free.

S. *Prohibited provisions found in life insurance.* (1) Nonpayment of a loan is not a cause for forfeiture, and (2) an insurance company cannot promise something in the declarations and take it away in the fine print.

4. Dividend options—Participating life insurance policies offer several dividend options:

    A. *Cash.* Dividend is paid to the owner in cash. Such payments are considered a return of premium and are income tax free.

    B. *Reduction of premiums.* The dividend is used to reduce the current premium.

    C. *Accumulation at interest.* The insurance company holds on to the funds and pays interest on the accumulated funds. The interest is taxed as ordinary income. This is similar to a savings account.

    D. *Purchase of paid-up additions.* The annual dividend is used to purchase small amounts of paid-up permanent insurance (no future premiums due).

    E. *Purchase of term insurance.* Used in combination with one of the other options. Part of the dividend is used to purchase one-year term insurance in the amount of the guaranteed cash value of the policy.

    F. Many companies also permit the owner to apply the dividend to any interest or principal of a policy loan.

5. Nonforfeiture option—A number of choices are available regarding how a life insurance policy owner can use the policy's cash value:

    A. *Surrender for cash.* The policy owner can withdraw the cash value (called cash surrender value) of the policy. All surrenders must be made in cash.

    B. *Purchase an annuity.* The policy owner can purchase an annuity to provide income for life or a specified time period.

    C. *Buy a reduced amount of paid-up permanent insurance.* This option permits the owner to have a zero premium policy of a reduced amount.

    D. *Buy the same amount of extended term insurance.* The amount of the term insurance is the same as the face amount of the original policy, but the period of coverage will be only for the time frame identified in the policy.

6. Settlement options

    A. An *interest-only option* can be used to "buy time" before a final settlement is chosen. When interest only is chosen, the insurance company typically sends a quarterly check representing interest earned during the quarter.

    B. A *lump sum payment* is income tax free. This is the most popular choice of life insurance settlement. A cash settlement allows the beneficiary to retire outstanding debt, pay funeral costs, provide for an emergency fund, and allow for investing in the market.

    C. There are several *fixed annuity options* that provide partial taxability:

        (1) *Fixed income option.* The recipient tells the insurance company how much income is needed each month. The insurance company tells the recipient how long the payments will continue.

        (2) *Fixed period option.* The recipient tells the insurance company how long the money must last. The company then calculates the amount of each payment.

        (3) There are four *life income options.*

            (a) *Straight life income.* The beneficiary receives a specified amount for as long as he or she lives, but nothing is paid after his or her death. This option provides the largest monthly benefit per $1,000 of proceeds.

(b) *Life income with period certain.* The beneficiary is paid a life income for as long as he or she lives, with a guaranteed minimum number of payments to be made, regardless of how long he or she lives.

(c) *Life income with refund.* The beneficiary is paid a life income for as long as he or she lives, and if the amount of the original lump sum has not been paid out by the time the beneficiary dies, the remainder of the proceeds will be paid to the secondary beneficiary in a lump sum or continued installments.

(d) *Joint-and-survivor income.* After the death of one payee, the benefit payments continue until the death of the second payee. The monthly income is reduced when benefits are payable based on two lives.

D. A *variable annuity option* can also be chosen as a settlement choice. The limitation of the fixed annuity option is that it is, in effect, a savings account that earns a fixed rate of interest. As such, it does not serve as a hedge against inflation. In contrast, a variable annuity offers a return that is consistent with the market by investing the proceeds in a family of mutual funds. The risk of return transfers from the insurance company to the policyholder.

7. Policy replacement

A. Sometimes an agent or planner will suggest that an existing life insurance policy be allowed to lapse and that a new and improved policy be purchased to replace the old one.

B. These are some reasons that may justify replacement of a policy:

(1) The insurance company that issued the policy is in financial trouble, and the policy is performing very poorly.

(2) The policy was issued as a "smoker's" policy, the insured quit smoking three years ago, and the insurance company will not consider changing it to a "nonsmoker's" policy.

(3) It is a relatively small term insurance policy, and by replacing it with a very large policy, the cost per thousand of insurance will drop substantially.

(4) All needed life insurance is being purchased by an irrevocable life insurance trust.

(5) Certain provisions and/or riders available with the replacement policy may not be available with the original policy.

C. There are some reasons that replacement may not be appropriate for a client:

(1) The client will have to pay policy acquisition costs again. New underwriting and commission costs must be covered, and any dividends and cash values on the new policy will be small or nonexistent for several years.

(2) The new policy will have a new contestable period and a new suicide clause.

(3) Some provisions and/or riders in the new policy may be less favorable to the client than those in the old policy.

(4) The new premium will be based on the insured's attained age at the time of the replacement.

(5) Although most policies have a policy fee, the savings by eliminating the fee from an old policy generally do not offset the financial losses associated with replacement.

8. Tax issues and strategies

A. Income taxation of death proceeds

(1) The Internal Revenue Code (IRC), under Section 101(a), defines life insurance. If a policy does not qualify under the law as life insurance, the earnings each year (above the premiums paid) are considered ordinary income for tax purposes. If it does qualify as life insurance, all earnings are tax deferred and the death benefit is income tax free.

(2) There are two tests the IRS uses to determine whether a policy meets the definition of life insurance.

(a) The first is called the *cash value accumulation test*. The most that can be paid into a policy is an amount that would be the "net single premium" to pay up the policy. This rule applies to traditional life insurance policies.

(b) The second test is the *guideline premium and corridor test*. This test first defines the maximum premium that can go into the policy at any given point in time. It then compares the cash value with the death benefit. There are limits as to what percentage of the death benefit the cash value can be. As this test is generally applied to universal life–type policies, the death benefit of the policies generally increases automatically if the cash value vastly increases, so the policy will continue to qualify as life insurance.

(3) The *transfer for value* rule states that when a life insurance policy is transferred from one owner to another for "valuable consideration," then a transfer for value has occurred and the income tax exclusion is lost. Only the amount paid for the policy and any subsequent premiums are recovered income tax free by the transferee-owner. There are exceptions to this exception. A transfer for value does not cause this loss of tax-free benefit if it can be categorized as one of the following transfers:

(a) A transfer to the insured

(b) A transfer to a partner of the insured or a partnership in which the insured is a partner

(c) A transfer to a corporation in which the insured is a shareholder or officer

(d) A transfer in which the basis for the new owner is the same as the basis of the original owner. (This is typically a gift of a policy from an insured to his or her spouse or children.)

(4) Death proceeds distributed from a series of payments have a return of principal portion that is not taxable and an interest earned element that is taxable.

B. Income taxation of living proceeds

(1) *Inside cash buildup*. A cash buildup in a life insurance policy is not subject to taxation as long as it stays in the policy. If cash is taken out or loaned, it is not taxable unless the life insurance policy is a *modified endowment contract* (MEC). An MEC is a policy that failed the seven-pay test.

(a) The policy is an MEC if the total premium actually paid into the policy at any time during the seven-year testing period is more than the sum of the net level premiums that would be needed to result in a paid-up policy after seven years.

(b) If this happens, the death benefit remains income tax free, but there are other changes affecting the loan value.

(1) If the policy cash value exceeds the premiums paid and the policy owner borrows against the policy, then the amount of the loan that is part of the gain in the policy is taxed as ordinary income.

(2) If the owner is under age 59½, there is a 10 percent penalty tax for taking out the loan.

(3) If the loan is repaid, it is considered an addition to the basis in the policy.

(c) An MEC is subject to a *last-in first-out* (LIFO) tax treatment with respect to loans and distributions from the policy. In contrast, if the policy qualifies as life insurance and is not an MEC, it is taxed as *first-in first-out* (FIFO).

(2) *Taxation of dividends.* The IRS has taken the position that dividends paid on life insurance policies are a return of excess premium. When a policy owner receives dividends from a life insurance company, those dividends are income tax free. If the cumulative dividends paid exceed the cumulative premiums paid for the policy, the excess dividends are reportable as ordinary income for tax purposes.

(3) *Taxation of cash surrender.* The taxable amount is the total surrendered value minus the policy owner's current basis in the policy.

    (a) Surrender value = policy loan + net cash value.

    (b) Tax basis = premiums paid − dividends.

    (c) Taxable gain = surrender value − tax basis.

(4) *IRC Section 1035 Exchange.* Under IRC Section 1035, a life insurance policy or an annuity may be exchanged for a similar contract with no adverse income tax consequences.

    (a) The funds must be transferred company to company, not through the hands of the policy owner.

    (b) The basis in the original policy becomes the basis in the new policy.

    (c) The new policy cannot have a later maturity date than the original policy. This means that an endowment at age 65 may not be exchanged for a whole life policy that endows at age 100.

    (d) A life insurance policy may be exchanged for an annuity, but an annuity may not be exchanged for a life insurance policy.

    (e) The new policy must cover the same insured(s) or annuitant(s).

C. Gift taxation of life insurance

    (1) If a life insurance policy is transferred from one individual to another, or to a trust, there is a potential gift tax. The value of the policy is the *interpolated terminal reserve.* For the most part, this is close to the cash value of the policy.

    (2) Gift tax can apply if a policy owned by one individual on another's life matures by reason of the insured's death and a person other than the policy owner is named beneficiary. For example, if a wife owns a policy on her husband's life and the children are beneficiaries, the proceeds are payable to the children instead of to her. In this case, the policy owner (wife) has made a gift to the beneficiaries (children).

D. Estate taxation of life insurance is influenced by ownership.

    (1) If an insured owns a policy on his or her life, then at death the death benefit will be included in his or her estate in determining whether any estate taxes are due.

    (2) If the insured had an incident of ownership within three years of death, the proceeds of the policy will be included in his or her estate.

9. Policy ownership issues and strategies, including split-dollar

A. The following are the three popular ownership choices available to purchasers in order to avoid having the proceeds included in the estate of the deceased:

    (1) If an irrevocable trust is the owner of the policy, the insured makes payments to the trust to cover the premiums on the life insurance policy. The trust is the beneficiary and designates how the benefits are to be distributed. However, the proceeds are added back into the estate if death occurs within three years after the transfer of the insurance policy to the trust.

    (2) A charity chosen by the client can be the owner and beneficiary of an insurance policy. A yearly tax-deductible gift to the charity pays the policy's premium.

(3) The insured can make children the beneficiaries and owners of a policy. Parents can pay premiums without paying gift taxes, if under limits. The child receives the face amount free from federal income and estate tax when the parent dies.

B. Split-dollar life insurance: The owner can be either the insured's employer or the insured.

(1) *Endorsement method*. The employer owns the policy and has the primary responsibility for paying premiums.

(2) *Collateral assignment method*. The insured employee owns the policy and has primary responsibility for paying premiums.

TOPIC 30: VIATICAL AGREEMENTS

1. Legal principles

A. In a viatical agreement, a policy owner (the *viator*) who is terminally ill or chronically ill sells a life insurance policy to a third party (the *viatical settlement provider*) in return for a lump sum cash settlement.

B. The lump sum is a percentage of the death benefit (generally 40 to 80 percent).

2. Requirements

A. The insured must be terminally ill—expected to live less than two years—or chronically ill—permanently and severely disabled or unable to perform at least two activities of daily living for at least 90 days.

B. The viatical settlement provider generally must be licensed with the state. If the state does not require this, then the provider must meet the requirements of the NAIC Model Act.

3. Tax implications

A. Viatical agreements are income tax free if the requirements are met. If transferred for value, capital gains may result on the difference between the settlement received and the total premium paid.

B. If the insured lives beyond 24 months, the insured does not have to pay tax.

4. Planning

A. Alternatives to consider before using a viatical agreement include an accelerated death benefit provision, accessing cash value in the form of a loan, and using cash value as collateral for a loan from a bank or family member.

B. The proceeds may make the viator ineligible for assistance that he or she would otherwise receive, such as Medicaid and Supplemental Security Income.

C. The proceeds may be subject to creditor's claims.

D. When choosing a viatical settlement provider, financial planners should help clients to consider the provider's reputation, financial strength, privacy provision, state licenses, and overall return.

5. Ethical concepts and planning

A. A contractual agreement regarding privacy should be considered to ensure that the viator's personal information (i.e., life expectancy) is not shared with outside sources.

B. The viator may not receive an adequate payment, and investing in such a contract may be difficult for some investors. The earlier an insured dies, the larger the return provided to the investor.

C. The new policy owner has no insurable interest in the life of the insured, which can provide an incentive for foul play.

TOPIC 31: INSURANCE NEEDS ANALYSIS AND RATIONALE

1. Life insurance amount required

   A. Liquidity and survivor income needs

      (1) A *financial needs analysis* approach is used to determine how much life insurance a family needs if the principal sum is to be liquidated in the process of meeting the client's financial objectives for his or her survivors.

      (2) The risk associated with the *liquidation approach*—use of investment earnings and capital—is running out of funds while the beneficiary still needs them. The *nonliquidation approach*—use of investment earnings only—provides a smaller monthly income for the beneficiary, but the income will continue indefinitely because the principal is not used.

      (3) Life insurance should fund the unfunded portions of lump sum and ongoing income needs.

         (a) Determine the financial objectives after death.

         (b) Determine the extent to which these objectives are satisfied by current cash, investments, and insurance.

         (c) Determine the amount of life insurance necessary to meet the gap between current sources of funds and needs.

      (4) Find the present value of future additional income needs—usually broken into component segments—in which the total income need is the sum of the present values of each of the separate, individually calculated segments.

   B. Capital needs analysis (capital retention)

      (1) Does not liquidate the lump sum principal received after death, and uses a high capitalization rate to provide income benefits from the investment income only

      (2) Additional capital needs used to meet the desired objective are calculated by dividing the amount of additional income need by the after-tax interest rate anticipated on the capital sum. For example, if $75,000 per year of additional income is needed, the capital sum generating this income payment (assume a 5 percent after-tax return) is $1,500,000 ($75,000 ÷ .05).

   C. Human life value

      (1) This concept is credited to Solomon Huebner. It is not possible to place a value on a human life. It is only possible to place a relative value on a human life. It must be related to what will be lost if a person dies.

      (2) This is the present value of that portion of a person's estimated future earnings that will be used to support dependents.

      (3) For example, assume an individual takes home $50,000 per year, and $10,000 of that can be directly attributed to his or her expenses. As a result, the family loses $40,000 if that person dies. Assuming the individual is 40 years old today, and normal retirement for Social Security is age 67 for that person, the dependents will lose the present value of $40,000 per year, adjusted for expected increases over 27 years. The present value of an annuity due for 27 years, using a $40,000 shortfall as the payment and a conservative discount rate of 5 percent, is $585,721. This may seem like a lot, but calculate how much this individual would be earning 27 years from now by inflating $40,000 at 5 percent (annual salary increase) for 27 years. The result is an annual income of approximately $149,000.

(4) If an individual has no dependents, this approach to determining his or her value would result in a value of zero.

2. Disability insurance

A. The difference between income needs (i.e., expenses) and income sources is the financial risk in the event of an illness or accident that results in disability.

B. Having no dependents may eliminate the need for life insurance, but an individual with no dependents still has a need for disability insurance.

C. Disability payments generally do not go on for life and commonly end at age 65. As such, protection should be provided for the worst possible outcome—disability for life. It is important that the disability protection program help the individual save for retirement just as it would if he or she were without disability.

3. Long-term care insurance

A. The United Seniors Health Council (a nonprofit organization) recommends that individuals buying LTC insurance meet a minimum threshold before purchasing it in order to afford premiums to continue coverage: $75,000 in assets in addition to a home, plus a yearly income of $25,000 for singles and $35,000 for couples.

B. It is generally advisable to purchase LTC insurance when an individual is around age 60. At an earlier age, it is difficult to determine how much coverage an individual needs and what facilities are needed.

C. The amount of coverage is determined in a similar way to life insurance: Take the present value of the estimated future expense that is necessary to support an LTC facility.

4. Health insurance

A. The primary consideration for health insurance is protection against catastrophic loss.

B. There is generally a five-step process for determining the ideal health plan.

(1) Select the plan that best meets the family's needs.

(2) Analyze the coverage of the plan in regard to the medical needs of the family.

(3) Choose a reasonably priced plan offering the most desirable services.

(4) Check the quality of care—this information can be obtained from the National Committee for Quality Assurance (a nonprofit organization).

(5) Check the location and accessibility of the medical facility.

5. Property insurance

A. Insure against significant risk, and bear the small risks that can be financially covered.

B. Reduce risk through preventative measures (such as antitheft devices for homes and cars).

6. Liability insurance

A. It is imperative that the liability limits of the homeowners and auto policies are coordinated with the deductible under an umbrella policy. For example, assume an insured has a $100,000 limit under the homeowners and auto policies but has a $300,000 deductible under an umbrella policy. If a claim is $500,000, the first $100,000 is covered under either the homeowners or auto policy, and the amount of $300,000 is covered by the umbrella policy, but the gap of $200,000 is not covered.

B. It is often recommended that the homeowners, auto, and umbrella policies be purchased from the same insurance company to avoid any gaps in coverage.

C. The amount of liability insurance should be based on the risk exposure of the individual—this is commonly based on the risk of a profession and the amount of personal assets and income that is exposed to claims and lawsuits.

TOPIC 32: TAXATION OF DISABILITY, LONG-TERM CARE, AND LIFE INSURANCE

This topic is covered under various other topics, as follows:

Disability Income Insurance   Topic 27, Section 6, Taxation of benefits
Long-Term Care Insurance   Topic 28, Section 8, Tax implications and qualifications
Life Insurance   Topic 29, Section 8, Tax issues and strategies, and Section 9, Policy ownership issues and strategies

TOPIC 33: INSURANCE POLICY SELECTION

1. Purpose of coverage

   A. *Protecting existing assets.* It is vital to have the right proportion of homeowners insurance to replacement value of a house. An adequate level of auto insurance is necessary to protect against major property loss through an accident or theft.

   B. *Protecting income.* Life insurance will allow for an uninterrupted replacement of income caused by death. Disability insurance will provide income when the ability to earn income is not possible because of an accident or illness.

   C. *Protecting both income and assets.* An adequate level of liability insurance and health insurance prevents a deterioration of existing assets and the potential use of income for unexpected lawsuits and emergencies.

2. Length of time required—Life insurance

   (1) Term insurance is used for short-term needs.

      (a) Term insurance can be used to hedge a mortgage or loan. An entrepreneur can use term insurance to protect his or her family from any speculative business dealings.

      (b) A parent with young children is likely to need more insurance while the children are dependent than when they are self-sufficient.

   (2) Permanent insurance is used for long-term needs.

      (a) Is used to augment or maximize retirement income many years later. A client has safety of principal and death protection, while benefiting from a cash value savings.

      (b) The most appealing factor of permanent life insurance as an investment is its role in simultaneously meeting the opposing risks of premature death and outliving savings.

   (3) Life insurance is not a pure savings vehicle. An individual who has no need for death protection but purchases life insurance as an investment incurs costs for death benefits and commissions that are avoided with other investments.

3. Risk tolerance

   A. *Investment choice.* A variable form of insurance introduces a certain degree of risk. Generally, anyone who is risk averse is better off with a traditional form of insurance than with a variable form.

   B. *Emphasis on protection only.* Term insurance should be considered for the client.

   C. *Flexibility with premium payments.* If premium payment flexibility is important to a client, universal life and variable universal life are appropriate.

   D. *Survivors' needs.* If the principal need for funds is at the death of the main income earner, a single-owner policy is appropriate. If the need for funds is to provide estate liquidity when the surviving spouse dies, consider a joint or survivorship life (second-to-die) policy.

E. *Inflation protection.* Variable life, universal life, or variable universal life insurance can provide protection against inflation.

F. *Length of time planned for paying premiums.* The periodic payment is higher if the period is shorter. Limited-pay whole life should be considered if the client wants to confine premium payments to working years only. Moreover, ordinary whole life can be considered if dividends or a nonforfeiture option is available to avoid lifelong premium payments.

4. Cash flow constraints

A. Families should buy adequate disability and health insurance even if it means a sacrifice in the amount of life insurance coverage.

B. A higher deductible will lower the premium of an insurance policy.

C. Risk reduction can reduce the cost of insurance policies; risk retention will eliminate the cost of insurance.

TOPIC 34: INSURANCE COMPANY SELECTION AND DUE DILIGENCE

1. Financials

A. The primary measure used in evaluating an insurance company is its financial strength. The selection of an insurance company by consumers generally involves six factors:

(1) Financial strength
(2) Willingness and ability to pay claims
(3) Lines of coverage offered
(4) Service before and after a claim
(5) Cost of the coverage
(6) Age of the company

B. Only after adequately identifying sound companies should a planner compare products.

C. A company's primary line of business and policy size provide important information. The following are generalities to consider:

(1) Companies selling only life insurance, with a substantial portion of permanent insurance, will have better financial stability than those companies dabbling in many product lines.

(2) Companies dealing mostly with term insurance are less stable because the price of term insurance is so competitive, and poor underwriting can create substantial financial stress.

2. Ratios

A. Another reference for insurance company analysis is the NAIC Watch-list. This Insurance Regulatory Information System (IRIS) is a series of 12 financial ratios designed to measure the financial strength of insurers. A company that has a number of bad ratios can be put on the NAIC Watch-list. The insurance commissioners then tend to keep a close eye on the company to see how it is doing relative to improving those ratios.

B. *Risk-based capital* (RBC) *ratio* is a method developed by the NAIC to measure the minimum amount of capital that an insurance company needs to maintain to support its overall operations. The RBC ratio is used as a warning sign for insurance commissioners to keep track of companies having financial problems. Currently there are four major categories of risk that must be measured to arrive at an overall risk-based capital amount: asset risk, credit risk, underwriting risk, and off-balance-sheet risk.

C. The *lapse ratio* is based on the percentage of policies that are canceled. A high lapse ratio can make profitability difficult.

D. *Policy persistency* is a measure of longevity of policies. The most profitable policies are those that remain in force for a long time.

3. Ratings

   A. Ratings of financial strength are best obtained from the five primary established rating organizations: (1) A. M. Best, (2) Fitch (formed by merger of Duff & Phelps and Fitch IBCA), (3) Moody's, (4) Standard & Poor's, and (5) Weiss.

   B. Ratings are generally based on the analysis of five factors:

      (1) Underwriting results
      (2) Economy of management
      (3) Adequacy of reserves for undischarged liabilities
      (4) Adequacy of policyholders' surplus to absorb shocks
      (5) Soundness of investments

   C. The following list identifies the lowest rating system used by each rating agency in identifying a good insurance company—a higher rating indicates a stronger company, and a lower rating indicates a weaker company.

A. M. Best	FPR 5 Good
Fitch	BBB- Good
Moody's	Baa3 Adequate
Standard & Poor's	BBB- Adequate
Weiss	B- Good

   D. It is often suggested that before any insurance company is recommended, it should have one of the top three ratings from at least three of the previously listed organizations.

4. Mutual versus stock

   A. Stock insurance companies

      (1) Capital stock insurance companies are profit-making ventures in which stockholders assume the risk from individual insureds.
      (2) Stockholders own the company and elect a board of directors.
      (3) The premium charged by the company is final.
      (4) Earnings are distributed to shareholders in the form of dividends.
      (5) Capital invested by stockholders provides a surplus to protect against adverse contingencies.

   B. Mutual insurance companies

      (1) Policyholders own the company. Ownership is acquired when they purchase a policy from the mutual insurer. There is no vested right of ownership except in the case of liquidation.
      (2) The premium charged by the company is not fixed.
      (3) There is a lack of capital stock and distribution of earnings.
      (4) The company must accumulate a surplus to protect against adverse contingencies.

5. Reinsurance

   A. Reinsurance is insurance for insurers.
   B. The purpose is the diversification of losses when catastrophic events occur. In this way, it enhances the financial strength of the insurance company.
   C. Reinsurance also enhances the growth of small companies by having a reinsurer take over part of the requirement for maintaining adequate reserve.
   D. The policyowner looks to the primary insurer for paying a claim. The primary insurer is then reimbursed by the reinsurer.

6. Investments

   A. Premiums received are invested by insurers as a way of lowering the cost of insurance and as a source of profit.

   B. The way insurers can invest funds is highly regulated by state laws—the strictest regulation applies to life insurers.

   C. Life insurers invest most funds in long-term securities. Liquidity of investments is not a major consideration in investing funds. In 2000, the general makeup for life insurance companies was 11 percent invested in government bonds, 40 percent in corporate bonds, and 30 percent in stocks. The remaining amount was in the form of cash equivalents, real estate mortgage loans, policy loans, and other investments.

   D. Non-life insurers invest a larger holding in government bonds than life insurers because property and liability contracts are of a short duration and have no savings element. In 2000, the general invested makeup was 36 percent government bonds, 21 percent corporate bonds, and 21 percent stocks.

7. Underwriting

   A. Underwriting is the selection and classification of insurance applications. The selection process involves accepting some applicants while rejecting other applicants.

   B. The primary purpose of underwriting is to identify adverse selection, inasmuch as it can be disastrous to an insurer.

   C. The agent and the home office conduct underwriting at the time of original application and at each renewal. The home office serves as the primary underwriter of an insurance contract.

   D. Underwriting information is obtained from the applicant, the agent, the claims department, insurer bureaus and associations, and outside agencies.

8. Federal and state law

   A. There are three methods available to the government for providing insurance regulation: legislative action, administrative action, and judicial action.

   B. The National Association of Insurance Commissioners (NAIC) drafted a law that became known as the McCarran-Ferguson Act, which became law on March 9, 1945. The law explicitly grants the states the power to regulate the insurance business.

   C. The NAIC has a broad range of regulation, but no legal power over insurance regulation.

      (1) The NAIC recommends legislation, but each state may accept or reject its recommendations.

      (2) There are several areas regulated by the NAIC.

         (a) *Solvency regulation.* Licensing of companies, reporting and financial analysis, risk-based capital (RBC), examination of companies, regulation of reserves, investments, dealing with insolvencies, state insolvency funds, and the NAIC state accreditation program

         (b) *Marketing regulation.* Unfair practices, policy forms, competence of agents, consumer complaints and assistance, and regulation of rates

   D. The NAIC's role is to enforce the laws in a state to discourage twisting and rebating.

      (1) *Twisting* is the persuading of an insurance policyowner to replace an existing policy with a policy issued by another company, to the detriment of the insured.

      (2) *Rebating* is the illegal return of part of the premium paid to the policyowner as a price-cutting sales inducement.

Chapter 3

EMPLOYEE BENEFITS PLANNING

TOPIC 35: EMPLOYEE BENEFIT PLANS

1. Group life insurance

    A. Types and basic provisions

        (1) Group term insurance

            (a) *Must* satisfy four requirements:

                i. Plan must provide a general death benefit, which is excludible from income.

                ii. Plan must be provided to a group of employees as compensation for personal services as employees.

                iii. Insurance must be provided under a policy carried directly or indirectly by the employer.

                iv. Amount of insurance provided to each employee must be computed by a formula that precludes individual selection; the formula can be based on age, years of service, compensation, or position.

            (b) Most inexpensive form of group insurance

            (c) Easiest and least expensive to administer

            (d) Master contract between employer and insurance company; individual employees receive a certificate as evidence of coverage.

            (e) Evidence of insurability is *not* required = guaranteed issue; coverage is between $5,000 and $100,000.

            (f) Premium waiver

            (g) Payout is usually a lump sum distribution to the beneficiary (spouse and/or children of the insured), although an installation method may be permitted in the master contract.

            (h) A terminated employee may convert the group term policy to an individual cash value policy without evidence of insurability; the premium would be based on the age of the participant on the conversion date. Cost can be prohibitive at older ages.

            (i) For retired participants, the employer may set up a "retired lives reserve."

        (2) Group permanent

            (a) The employee receives a permanent benefit because the policy provides an "economic value" that extends over more than one year.

            (b) Evidence of insurability is *not* required = guaranteed issue.

            (c) There are generally three different types of group insurance: *group paid up, group ordinary, and group universal life (UL)*

        (3) Dependent coverage—supplemental coverage

            (a) Dependents' group life

                i. Group life coverage for an employee's spouse and unmarried children (age 14 days to age 19, age 24 if full-time student)

                ii. Limit for children of employee is $500 for age 14 days to 6 months, thereafter $1,000 to 2,000. Limit for spouse is usually $5,000 to $10,000.

                iii. May be convertible to individual policies

            (b) Supplemental group term

                i. Additional group term coverage for specific class of employees, but not for individuals

                ii. Must be provided on a nondiscriminatory basis

iii. Evidence of insurability required because there is potential for adverse selection

(c) Group carve-out

   i. Individual, discriminatory benefits provided to selective employees (i.e., executives)

   ii. Cost of the coverage must be included in the executive's gross income and is deductible to the employer.

   iii. Sometimes referred to as a *premium bonus plan*

   iv. May be used to bring group term coverage into compliance

   v. Policy owned by the employee—fully portable when employee leaves employer

B. Income tax implications

(1) Plans can be established as

(a) *Contributory plan.* Employee pays some of the cost (i.e., premium).

   i. Employee contributions are usually made with after-tax dollars.

   ii. Employee can use pretax dollars for contributions if plan is part of a cafeteria plan (IRC Section 125).

(b) *Noncontributory plan.* Employer pays the *entire* cost.

(2) Nondiscrimination rules: Any plan that qualifies as group term insurance (under IRC Section 79) *must* satisfy one of the following four conditions:

(a) It must benefit at least 70 percent of the employees.

(b) No more than 15 percent of the participants can be "key employees."

(c) Benefits are either a flat amount or a uniform percentage of salary.

(d) Plan is part of a cafeteria plan (IRC Section 125) and is covered under IRC Section 125 nondiscrimination provisions.

(3) Income tax considerations

(a) Group term insurance less than $50,000 coverage

   i. Premiums are deductible by the employer.

   ii. Premiums are not taxable to the employee.

   iii. Key employee in a discriminatory plan—premiums are taxable based on a rate schedule, referred to as Table 1, provided by IRS regulations.

(b) Group term insurance greater than $50,000 coverage

   i. Premiums are deductible by the employer.

   ii. Premiums are taxable to the employee—based on Table 1 costs less employee contributions.

   iii. Key employee in a discriminatory plan—premiums are taxable based on a rate schedule, referred to as Table 1, provided by IRS regulations.

(c) Group term or permanent life in a qualified plan—any face amount of coverage

   i. Premiums are deductible by the employer.

   ii. Premiums are taxable to the employee.

     • Permanent equals lesser of one-year term rate of P.S. 58 (provided by the federal government to measure the taxable economic benefit received by employees from the pure insurance protection provided by split-dollar plans and qualified retirement plans).

- Term equals lesser of premium of P.S. 58.

    iii. Key employee in a discriminatory plan—premiums are taxable and handled in same way as for employee.

  (d) Group permanent life insurance—any face amount of coverage

    i. Premiums are deductible by the employer, only if the employee has vested rights to the insurance.

    ii. Premiums are taxable to the employee.

- Permanent equals premium costs.
- Permanent and term equals allocation formula less employee contributions.

    iii. Key employee in a discriminatory plan—premiums are taxable.

  (e) Employee contributions toward coverage are subtracted from the cost of employer-provided coverage greater than $50,000. *Exceptions*: Cost of excess coverage is not taxed to the employee if

    i. The beneficiary is a charity.

    ii. The employee is disabled.

    iii. The employee is one of certain retirees (i.e., retired before 1984, or age 55 before 1984).

  (f) The cost of employer-provided insurance coverage up to $2,000 on dependents is excludible from income as a *de minimis* fringe benefit. Cost of coverage over $2,000 is fully taxable to the employee.

  (g) Dividends from permanent insurance may be taxable to the employee. Amount taxable to the employee for dividends received (either actually or constructively) is offset by employee contributions.

  (4) Death benefit is income tax free.

2. Group disability insurance—basic provisions and limitations

  (1) Definition of disability (See Topic 27)

  (2) Own occupation limits (See Topic 27)

  (3) Integrated with Social Security, workers' compensation, or other income. There is a reduction of disability benefits payable under a disability contract to the extent that other benefits are available.

  (4) Income tax implications (See Topic 27)

    (a) Employer-paid premiums are deductible to the employer (if benefits are paid to employee).

    (b) Benefits attributable to employer-paid premiums are taxable to the employee.

    (c) Premiums paid by employer are nontaxable to the employee.

3. Group medical insurance

  A. Types and basic provisions

    (1) Indemnity: comprehensive medical expense plan (See Topic 26)

    (2) Preferred provider organization (PPO) (See Topic 26)

    (3) Health maintenance organization (HMO) (See Topic 26)

    (4) Dental and vision plans

      (a) Dental exclusions

        i. Cosmetic services (Orthodontics are usually covered.)

        ii. Replacement of dentures

        iii. Services that have no professional endorsement

        iv. Occupational injuries that are covered under workers' compensation laws

   (b) Dental limitations

        i. Limit benefits to the least expensive type of accepted dental treatment for a given condition.

        ii. Usually have overall benefit limits

        iii. Limit frequency with which benefits are paid (e.g., allowing only two cleanings per year)

   (c) Vision plans do not pay for necessary eye surgery or treatment of eye disease because such services are covered under medical health insurance. Benefits are available to improve vision, such as LASIK surgery.

B. Employee benefit analysis and application—nondiscrimination rules

   (1) Insured group health plans (i.e., HMO, PPO) are not required to meet discriminatory tests.

   (2) Self-funded plans are required to meet at least one of the following:

      (a) Benefits at least 70 percent of all employees

      (b) Benefits at least 80 percent of eligible employees if 70 percent or more of all employees are eligible

      (c) Benefits a class of employees that is considered nondiscriminatory

   (3) Nondiscrimination requirements for benefits—The same type and amount of benefit is available to all employees regardless of compensation level; that is, benefits available to a highly compensated employee (HCE) must be equally available to other participants.

C. Income tax implications

   (1) *Employer pays premium.* Deductible to the employer and not taxable to the employee

   (2) *Employee receives benefit.* Reimbursement for medical expenses are not taxable to the employee.

D. COBRA (Consolidated Omnibus Budget Reconciliation Act of 1985)

   (1) COBRA requires some employers to offer the right to continued health coverage to employees and their families who have had a *qualifying event.*

   (2) Continuation coverage requirements

      (a) *Employees.* Qualifying events include voluntary or involuntary termination (for reasons other than gross misconduct) and change from full-time to part-time status.

      (b) *Spouses and other dependents of covered employee.* Qualifying events include employee's death, divorce, legal separation, and eligibility for Medicare.

      (c) *Children of covered employee.* Qualifying events include loss of dependent status due to plan age limitations or marriage.

   (3) Qualified beneficiary has 60-day window after the qualifying event to elect to continue coverage and 45 days to pay the premium for the period prior to the election.

   (4) Continuation coverage for the qualified beneficiary continues until the earliest of:

      (a) 18 months

      (b) 29 months if beneficiary is totally disabled (Social Security definition) during the first 60 days of COBRA coverage

    (c) 36 months if a second qualifying event (death or divorce of terminated employee) occurs during continuing coverage period

    (d) The date the plan terminates for all employees

    (e) The date the premium for coverage is not paid on time

    (f) The qualified beneficiary becomes covered under another employer-sponsored health plan.

    (g) The qualified beneficiary becomes eligible for Medicare.

    (h) The widowed or divorced spouse remarries and becomes covered under the new spouse's employer-sponsored health plan.

(5) Coverage must be identical to coverage provided to employees.

(6) Coverage cannot be conditioned on evidence of insurability.

(7) At the end of continuation coverage, a qualified beneficiary must be offered the right to convert to an individual plan.

(8) Long-term care is not subject to COBRA rules.

(9) COBRA charges may not exceed 102 percent of the cost of the plan.

(10) Notification of the right to COBRA coverage

    (a) Must be made at two distinct times.

        i. When the plan becomes subject to COBRA rules or employee becomes covered under a plan subject to COBRA

        ii. When a qualifying event occurs

    (b) Penalty of $100/day/qualified beneficiary for failure to notify; may not apply to minor or good-faith violations.

(11) Exemptions from COBRA rules

    (a) Employers who have fewer than 20 employees for at least half of the prior year (i.e., applies to ≥ 20 employees)

    (b) Government and church employers

(12) Full coverage of preexisting conditions

4. Cafeteria plans and flexible spending accounts

  A. Basic provisions and eligible benefits

    (1) Cafeteria plan (IRC Section 125)

      (a) Written plan under which employees may choose between two or more benefits consisting of two mandatory components:

        i. Cash—taxable to the employee as compensation

        ii. One or more *qualified benefits*

          • Medical expense benefit via individual or group—nontaxable

          • Cost of group term insurance in excess of $50,000—taxable

      (b) Core benefits include life insurance, health insurance, and disability insurance.

      (c) Credits for selection of additional benefits:

        i. Credits may be allocated according to age, salary, and service.

        ii. Credits may purchase enhanced core benefits or additional benefits: flexible spending account, dental insurance, dependent child care, additional vacation days (cannot carry over), and 401(k) plans (salary reduction) or 401(m) plans (after-tax contributions) with or without employer matching.

        iii. May not select

- Retirement plan or deferred compensation
- Scholarships and fellowships
- Transportation/commuter benefits
- Educational assistance
- Employee discounts
- Noncash (*de minimis*) fringe benefits
- Long-term care insurance (added by the Health Insurance Portability and Accountability Act [HIPAA])

    (d) Plan may offer a choice of prepackaged benefit plan combinations.

    (e) If a plan is discriminatory in favor of the HCE, the HCE will be taxed on employer contributions to the plan to the extent of the cost of all taxable benefits that are available to the HCE.

  (2) Flexible spending account (FSA)

    (a) A type of cafeteria plan funded through salary reductions, stand-alone plan, or included as part of an IRC Section 125 plan

    (b) Allows an employee to fund certain benefits with pretax dollars

    (c) Employee commits a specific salary reduction dollar amount for the coming year for benefits.

    (d) Key phrase: *Use it or lose it!* Employer gets the forfeiture.

    (e) Benefits provided include medical and dental expenses not otherwise covered, such as vision; dependent care expenses for children or parents; health insurance premiums; disability insurance premiums; extra vacation; and contributions to 401(k) plan.

B. Income tax implications

  (1) Cafeteria plans that comply with Section 125 (i.e., do not discriminate) are not subject to the doctrine of *constructive receipt* and generate no taxable income to the extent an employee chooses the types of benefits that are normally nontaxable.

    (a) The choice of cash is a taxable benefit.

    (b) Life insurance in excess of $50,000 is taxable.

  (2) FSAs allow for the funding of benefits with pretax dollars.

5. Other employee benefits

A. Fringe benefits

  (1) Employees are taxed on the fair market value of certain noncash fringe benefits provided by the employer because these benefits are treated as compensation and will be included in gross income.

    (a) Personal use of company car, airplane, or lodging

    (b) No-additional-cost services and qualified employee discounts to HCE if not available to rank-and-file employees

    (c) Country club dues paid on behalf of an employee

    (d) Season tickets to theatrical or sporting events furnished by the employer

    (e) Employer-sponsored van pools

  (2) There are some fringe benefits that are not taxable:

      (a) No-additional-cost services normally provided to the public, such as hotel rooms or airline, bus, or cruise seats, which would remain unused if employee did not use them

      (b) Qualified employee discounts on goods and services offered for sale to the customers, not to exceed employer's gross profit percentage or for services, cannot exceed 20 percent.

      (c) Working condition fringe benefits such as property or services that the employee could deduct as business expenses if not employer provided

      (d) *De minimis* fringe benefits so small as to make accounting impractical or unreasonable

      (e) Use of employer-operated or on-premises athletic facilities

      (f) Meals furnished to the employee for the employer's convenience and on the employer's premises, and lodging furnished for the employer's convenience and the employee is required to accept as a condition of employment

      (g) Dependent care assistance program benefits

      (h) Business use of employer-provided automobile

      (i) Transportation benefits, such as free parking, at the employer's place of business

      (j) Moving expense reimbursement

   (3) If the benefit is not considered to be exempt as a qualified noncash fringe benefit, then it will be included in Federal Insurance Contributions Act (FICA) and Federal Unemployment Tax Act (FUTA) taxes.

B. Voluntary employee beneficiary association (VEBA)

   (1) A type of multiple-employer trust that can be used to prefund employee benefits

   (2) Employer receives tax-favored treatment—employer deposits into the trust are immediately tax deductible.

      (a) Must have at least 10 participating employers, generally members of a professional organization

      (b) The plan is structured to be a welfare benefit plan that cannot be considered a deferred compensation plan.

   (3) VEBAs that comply with IRC Section 501(c)(9) (nondiscrimination) and Section 505 (maximum $200,000 limit on compensation for benefit formulas) are *exempt* from income tax on earnings. *Note*: Earnings in a *welfare benefit trust*, another type of multiple-employer trust, are fully taxable to the employer.

   (4) Expensive to set up and administer, and the IRS has more specific rules regarding VEBAs.

   (5) Purpose of a VEBA as stated in Section 501(c)(9)

      (a) To provide "life, sick, accident, and other" benefits designed to "safeguard or improve the health of member . . . against a contingency that . . . impairs a member's earning power."

      (b) Other benefits include vacation, child care, legal services, severance pay, education and job training benefits, supplemental unemployment benefits, and preretirement death benefits.

      (c) Prohibited benefits

         i. Retirement benefits

         ii. Commuting benefits

   (6) Benefit payments

(a) Dollar value of benefit provided and employer's contribution to the VEBA are not included in the employee's gross income.

(b) Only plan benefits may be paid from the VEBA; trust earnings cannot be paid directly to any individual.

(c) Benefits paid to employees are subject to the same tax treatment as benefits paid through similar individual plans; employee is *not* taxed on the contributions to the VEBA.

(7) Membership in VEBA

(a) Voluntary for the employee

(b) The employee's designated beneficiaries may also join.

(c) Noncurrent employees may become members, but the number of such "nonemployees" cannot be greater than 10 percent of the total membership.

C. Salary continuation plans

(1) Employer can supplement current salary of an employee/executive with a salary continuation agreement to take place at death or retirement of the selected executive.

(2) Employer can negotiate with executive to defer some of his or her current salary and provide additional compensation at death to a beneficiary or at the retirement of the executive.

D. Prepaid legal services

(1) The purpose is for an employer to provide an employee with legal services, such as in a divorce, drafting a will or trust, home purchase closings, and others.

(2) Tax implications should be carefully considered.

E. Group long-term care insurance

(1) Group programs generally provide benefits for three to five years.

(2) Individually owned long-term care (LTC) insurance is more flexible with waiting periods, benefit payment periods, types of facilities, and premium waiver.

TOPIC 36: EMPLOYEE STOCK OPTIONS

1. Basic provisions

A. Company restrictions—Insiders are subject to insider trading rules that limit the sale of stocks by the employee to within six months of the time he or she has been issued the option.

B. Transferability

(1) *Incentive stock option (ISO)*. Only the employee may exercise the option during his or her lifetime. The employee can transfer only upon death.

(2) *Nonqualified stock option (NSO)*. Option is transferable to family members.

C. Retirement

(1) Systematic repositioning of the portfolio is a consideration if the stock represents a large percentage of the employee's holdings.

(2) A method must be devised to raise cash for exercising the options if the employee wants potential future appreciation.

D. Vesting schedule

(1) *Straight vesting*. Same percentage of options becomes exercisable each year (e.g., 500 options each year).

    (2) *Cliff vesting*. All options become exercisable at one time.

    (3) *Step vesting*. The percentage of exercisable options varies year to year.

    (4) *Performance vesting*. Options become vested in the year the company achieves a particular goal (e.g., revenue or price/share goal).

    (5) *Early vesting* (*accelerated exercise*). In this type of arrangement, employees are allowed to immediately exercise options when they are granted. For each option exercise, they receive a share of "restricted" stock, which is subject to a holding period that is based on the stock option plan's original vesting schedule.

E. Expiration

    (1) Generally, employees have 10 years (or less) to exercise the option.

    (2) Terminated employees may have 30 to 90 days after termination to exercise vested options; the period may extend to six months to one year in the event of death or disability.

F. Availability to nonemployees (directors, board members, etc.)—An individual must be an employee to benefit from an ISO.

G. Cashless exercise/same day sale—No money is exchanged. A broker lends money to the employee to purchase shares and then sells them immediately for a fee.

H. Potential problems include expiration of the option, termination from employment, and overallocation.

2. Incentive stock options (ISO)

A. Income tax implications (regular, AMT, basis)

    (1) *Upon grant*. Income *not* reported; *no* income tax due

    (2) *Upon exercise*. *No* income for calculating regular tax. Difference between the fair market value (FMV) at exercise and exercise price (the bargain element or "spread") is an adjustment item for calculating the alternative minimum tax (AMT).

    (3) *Upon (qualifying) sale*. For AMT, long-term capital gain is difference between FMV at time of sale and FMV at time of exercise. For regular tax, long-term capital gain is difference between FMV at time of sale and exercise price.

    (4) Employer receives *no tax deduction*, unless holding requirement is *not* satisfied.

B. Holding period requirements for a *qualifying sale*—Shares must be held for at least one year after the option is exercised and for at least two years after the option is granted.

    (1) If the holding period requirement is not met, a disqualifying disposition occurs and the appreciation on the sale (untaxed bargain element plus other appreciation) will be taxed as *ordinary income.*

    (2) An employee receiving the ISO is required to continue as an employee from the time of the grant of the options until at least three months before the exercise. If not, options are converted to NSOs.

C. Disqualifying dispositions—If the holding requirements are not satisfied, then a portion of the employee's profit is taxed as compensation and the employer is allowed a deduction for that compensation. The other portion is taxed to the optionee as a short-term capital gain.

D. Employee benefit analysis and application—Options may be granted to executives, key employees, or other groups of employees on a *discriminatory basis*.

3. Nonqualified stock options (NSO)

A. Income tax implications (regular, AMT, basis)

    (1) *Upon grant*. *No* income tax is due.

   (2) *Upon exercise.* The employee realizes income equal to the difference between grant (exercise) price and FMV at time of exercise. This difference is called the *bargain element.* The FMV at time of exercise becomes the new cost basis. The company must withhold federal and state taxes (using the supplemental wage tax—27 percent federal rate until it drops in 2004)—as well as Social Security taxes. Depending on the individual's tax situation, too much or too little tax may have been withheld.

   (3) *Upon sale.* If the employee holds the stock and sells later, the employee recognizes capital gain or loss; may be short or long term, depending on whether it is held for more than one year. The sale will not trigger additional tax unless the selling price exceeds the share basis.

B. Gifting opportunities—may gift to family members, family trusts, charities

   (1) IRS safe harbor allows the gifting of vested options where valuation is based only on Black-Scholes valuation model.

   (2) Gift tax valuation—Options must be valued for gift tax purposes at the time of the gift. If the employer uses *straight vesting* (e.g., 20 percent yearly for five years), the employee can make a completed gift of the vested portions at an earlier date when the options have a low value.

C. Employee benefit analysis and application—Option may be granted to an employee, a member of the board, an independent contractor, a family member, or any other beneficiary of the employee on a *discriminatory basis.*

4. Planning strategies for employees with both incentive stock options and nonqualified stock options

  A. There should be consideration given to exercising options and selling stock over a period of time to take advantage of price averages and risk reduction.

  B. Individuals in high tax brackets should consider early exercise for appreciating stocks to benefit from lower taxes, because the bargaining element is taxed as income for NSOs and possible AMT consequences for ISOs.

  C. It makes sense to hold on to the stock for more than one year after exercise to change tax treatment to long-term capital gain.

  D. Diversification and meeting financial goals may be good reasons for selling options sooner than the end of the exercise period.

5. Election to include in gross income in the year of transfer (Section 83(b) election)

  A. Employee makes an election to include in income the FMV of the stock, less any amount paid for the stock, at the time the stock is issued.

  B. The election can be made only if the stock is subject to *substantial risk of forfeiture* and is not transferable.

  C. After the forfeiture restrictions have lapsed, any subsequent appreciation or depreciation *after* the election date is taxed as capital gain or loss when the employee sells the stock.

TOPIC 37: STOCK PLANS

1. *Employee stock purchase plans (ESPPs).* A form of stock option plan under IRC Section 423; allows a company to sell stock to employees at a discount from the market price

  A. Basic provisions

   (1) The option must be offered to employees on a nondiscriminatory basis.

   (2) *Transferability.* Only the employee may purchase the shares during his or her lifetime.

(3) Purchase price of the stock can be as low as 85 percent of FMV on the offer/grant date or sale date, whichever is less. The offer typically permits employees to purchase stock every six months via payroll withholding.

(4) Maximum FMV of the stock that an employee may accrue the right to purchase in any calendar year cannot exceed $25,000.

B. Income tax implications

(1) *Upon grant*. Income is not recognized = *no* income tax.

(2) *Upon purchase*. Income is not recognized.

(3) *Upon sale*. Whether treated as compensation income or long-term capital gain depends on whether the holding period requirements (as for ISOs) are met and whether the stock is sold for more or less than the purchase price.

C. Qualifying sale (disposition)

(1) Amount of ordinary income recognized equals the lesser of (1) the actual gain (amount by which the sale price exceeds the actual purchase price) or (2) the purchase price discount (when the purchase price is based on the lower of the value of the stock on the first or last day of the offering period, even if it is the higher price). All additional gain on the sale of stock is treated and taxed as long-term capital gain.

(2) *Example*: Assume company uses a 15 percent discount on the lower of the value of the stock on the first or last day of the offering period and that the stock price is $10 per share on the first day of the offering period (which is the purchase date) and $30 when sold. When the stock is sold after satisfying the holding period requirements, recognize ordinary income of $1.50 per share (15 percent of $10) and long-term capital gain of $20 per share ($30 minus ordinary income of $1.50, minus the purchase price of $8.50). The $1.50 will be reported on a W-2.

D. Disqualifying sale (disposition)

(1) Amount of ordinary income is equal to the difference between the FMV of stock at date of purchase and purchase price. Ordinary income is measured as the "spread" on the purchase date, regardless of whether the purchase price is calculated on the first day of the offering period. In addition, any difference between the sale price and the basis will be a capital gain or loss, which will be long-term if the stock has been held for more than one year.

(2) *Example*: Assume a sale is one year after grant but less than two years from purchase. Further assume that the company uses a 15 percent discount and that the stock price is $10 per share on the first day of the offering period, $15 on the last day of the offering period, and $20 when the stock is sold. The individual will recognize ordinary income of $6.50 per share ($15 minus purchase price of $8.50) and long-term capital gain of $5.00 per share ($20 minus $15 basis, which is the sum of the purchase price and the amount of ordinary income recognized) when the stock is sold.

E. Employee benefit analysis and application—ESPP must be offered to all employees who qualify on a nondiscriminatory basis; ISO and NSO may discriminate.

2. Phantom stock and other employee stock plans

A. Phantom stock

(1) Basic provisions

(a) Employee is awarded units analogous to shares using a formula (e.g., based on compensation).

(b) After a time specified in the plan, the employee is entitled to receive deferred compensation in cash and/or stock.

(c) Phantom stock is not real stock but a method of *tracking* the performance of the employer's stock. There is *no* dilution of company stock.

(d) The plan is an unfunded and unsecured promise of the employer to pay cash, stock, or other property. There is no recognized income by the employee.

(e) The employee cannot specify the date on which to exercise the stock.

(2) Income tax implications

(a) No income is recognized on the date the phantom stock is awarded.

(b) Upon exercise, the company generally pays in cash the difference between the current stock value and the value of the phantom stock units. The entire amount received is subject to ordinary income tax rates and the usual withholding tax rules.

B. Stock appreciation right (SAR)—The right of an employee to receive cash and/or stock equal to the increase in the value of the company's stock after the date the SAR is granted. The employee receives payment for the appreciation in stock price *without* exercising the options.

(1) *Basic provisions*. Similar to a phantom stock plan, *except*:

(a) The SAR is generally offered together with a stock option.

(b) It gives the employee the right to appreciation in the stock after the grant date.

(c) The employee has the right to decide when to exercise the SAR.

(2) *Income tax implications*. The amount is taxed as ordinary income in the year of exercise—similar to phantom stock.

C. Restricted stock—Shares of stock are granted to the employee at no cost or at a bargain price *with restrictions*: stock cannot be sold or disposed of before a specified period of time, and employee cannot work for a competitor and /or must stay with the employer for a specified time period and meet performance criteria.

(1) Basic provisions

(a) May be issued to employees on a discriminatory basis

(b) Used as a form of incentive compensation to key employees

(2) Income tax implications

(a) Stocks are subject to risk of substantial forfeiture so income (value of the shares) is not recognized.

(b) When no longer subject to forfeiture (i.e., stock is substantially vested), the value of the stock is recognized as ordinary income to the employee, *and* the employer can take a deduction.

(c) If the employee is confident that the restricted stock will not be forfeited, within 30 days of the date of the grant, the employee can pay income tax and file an 83(b) election on the value of the shares as of the grant date. When the restrictions lapse and the employee sells the stock, the appreciation is taxed as capital gain.

(d) Any appreciation or depreciation *after* the stock is vested is capital gain or loss when the employee sells the stock.

(e) Dividends that are paid on unvested shares are treated as income to the employee and deductible compensation for the employer.

D. Junior stock—Restricted stock that can be converted into common stock of the company but only if performance goals are reached. Its voting, liquidation, and dividend rights are subordinate (i.e., junior) to the regular class of common stock.

    (1) Basic provisions

        (a) Convertible to common stock upon certain events, such as attainment of performance goals

        (b) Conversion at option of employee or may be automatic

        (c) Similar to NSO

    (2) Income tax implications

        (a) When purchased at FMV, there is *no* tax to employee when the junior stock is issued.

        (b) There is no tax when the junior stock is converted to common stock.

        (c) Employee recognizes gain on the date he or she sells the common stock that was exchanged for junior stock. Basis is the amount paid for the junior stock.

E. Performance share/unit plans

    (1) Basic provisions

        (a) Awards are "granted" at the start of a specific time period (usually measured in years, e.g., three to five years) and earned through attaining performance goals.

        (b) Value of shares/units determined by performance results for each performance cycle

        (c) Payments made in cash and/or stock

    (2) Income tax implications—taxed as ordinary income on the date payments are made

TOPIC 38: NONQUALIFIED DEFERRED COMPENSATION

1. Basic provisions and differences from qualified plans

  A. Nonqualified plans are different from qualified plans in the following ways:

    (1) Tax deferred for employees unless considered funded. Tax is always deferred for employees with qualified plans.

    (2) Tax deduction deferred for employers until the benefit has been paid (unless considered funded). Qualified plans always provide immediate deduction for employers.

    (3) Earnings do not accumulate tax free (unless tax shelter is used). Earnings always accumulate tax free for qualified plans.

    (4) No special tax treatment at retirement for employees. Qualified plans offer special tax treatment for rollovers and forward averaging.

    (5) Minimal and inexpensive legal and administrative requirements. Qualified plans are burdensome and expensive.

    (6) Minimal and inexpensive reporting and disclosure requirements. Qualified plans are burdensome and expensive.

    (7) More effective ability to attract, retain, and motivate employees

    (8) Provide retirement benefits in excess of qualified plan limits

  B. Nonqualified plans circumvent qualified plan nondiscrimination rules.

2. Types of plans and applications

Note: Must have a signed *written agreement* for deferring compensation prior to any services being performed (i.e., prior to earning it) to avoid adverse tax consequences. Plans may discriminate. No ERISA requirements need to be satisfied.

A. Pure deferred compensation (i.e., a salary reduction plan)

(1) Employee agrees to give up a specified portion of compensation (e.g., salary, raise, bonus, commissions).

(2) Employer promises to pay a benefit sometime in the future, equal to the amount deferred plus a predetermined rate of interest.

(3) Often referred to as an *in lieu of* plan; employee is accepting a promise in lieu of current income.

(4) A rabbi trust is commonly used to fund this type of plan.

(5) Main consideration for the executive should be the strength of the company making the promise.

B. Supplemental executive retirement plans (SERPs)

(1) Employee does not give up current compensation for the benefit.

(2) Employer makes a commitment to provide the benefit.

(3) Can also be designed to provide additional retirement plan benefits above a company's qualified retirement plan calculations, thus providing an incentive for hiring mid-career executives

(4) Generally available only to executives and selected top management

C. Rabbi trusts

(1) A rabbi trust is an irrevocable trust set up by the employer for a nonqualified deferred compensation (NQDC) plan.

(2) Funds are set aside prior to retirement and secured against unwillingness to pay.

(3) Funds contributed into the trust:

(a) The funds must be available to pay benefits to the employees, and assets cannot revert back to the employer even with a hostile takeover.

(b) The funds are subject to the claims of all general creditors of the company in the event of a bankruptcy.

(c) Notice must be given to the trustee by the firm immediately if the firm becomes bankrupt or insolvent.

(4) The trust cannot contain *insolvency triggers* that hasten payments to executives when the employer's net worth falls below a certain point.

(5) Used as a method to "fund" unfunded deferred compensation plans

(a) Gives the employee the security of a funded plan (except in a bankruptcy)

(b) Tax-deferred benefits of an unfunded plan—*not* taxable to employee (i.e., income deferred) or deductible by employer

(6) Executives can take a hardship withdrawal without triggering constructive receipt.

(7) Such a fund can be useful for an executive in the event of a hostile takeover or merger, but provides no benefit if a firm goes bankrupt.

D. Secular trusts

(1) A secular trust is an irrevocable trust set up to provide nonqualified benefits to an employee.

(2) Funds are set aside prior to retirement and secured against unwillingness to pay.

(3) Employer contributions into the trust are *not* subject to claims of general creditors.

(4) Deferred compensation plans funded by a secular trust result in the employee's being in *constructive receipt* of the contribution. Contributions are taxable to the employee at the later of the date that contributions are made or the date when benefits become

nonforfeitable. The employer gets an immediate deduction for the contribution into the trust.

(5) Provides protection for the employee in the event of the employer's bankruptcy, insolvency, merger, takeover, or outright refusal to pay. The price of this protection is immediate taxation on the contribution.

(6) Potential for double taxation, once at the trust level and again when actually paid out to the employee. Because of tax consequences, secular trusts are not common.

3. Tax implications

   A. Constructive receipt

     (1) An employee is taxed on compensation he or she has a right to receive on demand without any risk of forfeiture. In a NQDC plan, if the employee had a choice to receive the compensation but declined for whatever reason, the IRS will treat the compensation as taxable income to the recipient.

     (2) The tax issue is whether or not a taxpayer can control the timing of the actual receipt of the income.

     (3) Treasury Revenue Ruling 60-31: An employee is *not taxed* on compensation if all three of the following are satisfied:

       (a) The election to defer compensation is made under a written agreement before services are rendered.

       (b) The agreement represents an *unsecured promise to pay*.

       (c) The plan is unfunded, or if funded, there is a substantial risk of forfeiture.

   B. Substantial risk of forfeiture

     (1) Exists if the participant's right to the compensation is conditioned on the future performance of substantial services. The risk of forfeiture must be real and substantial.

     (2) Examples that indicate a substantial risk of forfeiture include:

       (a) Continued employment for a specified time period (e.g., until retirement) or else employee losses benefit

       (b) A noncompete clause after employee leaves employer for a specified time period or in a certain geographic area

       (c) Availability of the employee for consulting services after retirement

     (3) *Note*: Death and disability are *not* considered reasons for substantial risk of forfeiture.

4. Funding methods

   A. Unfunded versus informally funded

     (1) Unfunded: There is only the employer's *promise to pay* an amount sometime in the future.

     (2) Informally funded

       (a) Assets are set aside in a general reserve fund to meet the benefit obligations of the plan.

         i. Employee has no rights or security interest in the assets or fund.

         ii. Funds are always subject to the claims of the company's creditors.

         iii. Funds may be invested in life insurance, mutual funds, or other securities.

         iv. *Promise to pay* is the employee's only security for future benefits.

       (b) There is no taxation to the employee as long as funds are subject to the company's creditors, inasmuch as there is no constructive receipt.

       (c) If the employee has vested benefits, there is no constructive receipt, because the funds are not secured.

   B. Funded

      (1) The deferred compensation is *secured* by property in which the employee has a beneficial interest and is beyond the reach of creditors.

      (2) To avoid taxation, constructive receipt must be avoided.

      (3) Most plans are designed to be unfunded for ERISA and tax purposes.

5. Strategies—The strategies are apparent in the use of different nonqualified plans.

TOPIC 39: EMPLOYER/EMPLOYEE INSURANCE ARRANGEMENTS

1. Business continuation (buy-sell) plans

   A. Buy-sell agreements make sure an estate can sell a business interest for a reasonable price. The contract contains wording that binds the owner of a business to sell his or her share of the business at a specified price to a designated buyer, usually partners in the business.

   B. There are numerous benefits for constructing a buy-sell agreement.

      (1) Guarantees a market for a closely held business

      (2) Provides a source of liquidity for estate taxes owed

      (3) Allows for the continuation of the business with the other owners

      (4) Improved credit risk

   C. Types

      (1) Cross-purchase agreement

         (a) Each owner purchases an insurance policy on other owners.

           i. Policy owner is also the beneficiary.

           ii. Upon the death of an owner, the owner's estate will sell and the other owners will buy the business interest of the deceased.

           iii. Insurance proceeds are used to fund the agreement.

         (b) For example, assume three equal partners and one of them dies. The two surviving partners will each purchase one-half interest of the deceased partner.

         (c) Advantages/disadvantages

           i. The surviving stockholders pay for the stock with after-tax dollars.

           ii. Premiums are paid with money that might have been taxed both to the corporation and to stockholders.

           iii. It is easy to form when there are a small number of stockholders.

           iv. The obligation to purchase the shares falls on younger shareholders who are often not in a position to buy the shares.

           v. This agreement results in fewer legal problems and tax consequences.

      (2) Entity agreement (also called stock-redemption agreement)

         (a) The business buys the insurance on the owners.

           i. The firm is the beneficiary and carries life insurance on each partner.

           ii. Upon the death of an owner, the business will buy the business interest from the deceased owner's estate.

         (b) Advantages/disadvantages

      i. The corporation, not the stockholders, pays the life insurance premiums under the agreement—premiums are paid with money that has been taxed only once to the corporation.

      ii. It is easy to form when there are a large number of stockholders.

      iii. It results in no dividend treatment.

      iv. The corporation may not have enough cash to redeem shares if life insurance is not used.

      v. The corporation can use installment payments of the purchase price to redeem shares.

2. Business overhead disability plan

    A. Proceeds are used to cover ongoing operating costs of a business while the business owner is disabled, such as paying rent, salaries, taxes, and utilities.

    B. The elimination period is short; generally provides a benefit for up to two years.

    C. The purpose of the insurance is to continue to keep staff and premises available until business can resume when the owner returns.

    D. Premiums are deductible and benefits are taxable.

3. Executive/owner benefits (Section 162)—executive-bonus life insurance

    A. This allows an employer to provide life insurance protection for a selected employee on a tax-deductible basis.

    B. Upon the death of the employee, the insurance company pays the death benefit directly to the beneficiary; proceeds are income tax free.

4. Split-dollar

    A. This allows an employer to provide life insurance protection for a selected employee.

    B. The death benefit is split as follows:

      (1) The corporation receives a return of its contributions, which is the cash surrender value.

      (2) The beneficiary receives the *net amount at risk*.

    C. Employer and employee split (share) the premium:

      (1) Employee pays the portion of premium that is attributed to the "economic benefit" (= lesser of P.S. 58 cost or "standard risk," one-year individual term rates) of the insurance protection in that year.

      (2) Employer pays the remaining portion of the premium attributed to the cost of insurance (the amount equal to the annual increase in the cash surrender value).

5. Key employee insurance

    A. Insurance on a key employee and owned by the business who is also the beneficiary

    B. Premiums are *not* deductible to the business.

    C. Death benefits are tax free.

    D. The purpose of key employee insurance is to (1) protect the business against loss of business income and (2) provide funds for locating and training a replacement.

Chapter 4

INVESTMENT PLANNING

TOPIC 40: TYPES AND USE OF INVESTMENT VEHICLES

1. Certificates of deposit and cash equivalents

    A. Certificates of deposit

    (1) A certificate of deposit, or CD, is a time deposit with a specified maturity.

    (2) It is nonnegotiable or negotiable.

        (a) A nonnegotiable CD is one in which the initial depositor must wait until maturity to receive the funds. If funds are withdrawn prior to the maturity date, there is an early withdrawal penalty.

        (b) A negotiable CD allows the depositor to sell the CD in the open market anytime before maturity.

    (3) Depository institutions can sell negotiable CDs or jumbo CDs if an investor has $100,000 or more to invest. Maturities tend to be up to one year. CDs of less than $100,000 are generally nonnegotiable.

    B. Money market mutual funds

    (1) Money market mutual funds specialize in short-term securities. This is an alternative to other money market instruments.

    (2) They are made up of many short-term instruments available in the open market (Treasury bills, commercial paper, banker's acceptances, certificates of deposit, repurchase agreements, etc.).

    C. U.S. Treasury bills

    (1) U.S. Treasury bills are issued by the federal government.

    (2) These securities are in denominations of $1,000 to $100,000 and mature in 3 to 12 months.

    (3) They are sold at a discount.

    (4) Interest is subject to federal income tax but exempt from state and local tax.

    D. Commercial paper

    (1) Commercial paper is unsecured short-term promissory notes issued by corporations.

    (2) Only firms with excellent credit ratings are able to sell commercial paper, so the risk of default is small.

    (3) The maturity of commercial paper is usually less than 270 days.

    (4) Commercial paper is sold at a discount.

    E. Banker's acceptances

    (1) Banker's acceptances are short-term promissory notes guaranteed by a bank. The bank takes ultimate responsibility for repaying these loans to the holder.

    (2) These acceptances are sold on a discounted basis and are common with international trade.

    F. Repurchase agreements

    (1) A repurchase agreement, or "repo," is the sale of a short-term security with the commitment by the seller to buy back the security at a specified price and date.

    (2) The repurchase price is higher than the initial sale price.

    (3) If the term of the loan is one day, it is called an *overnight repo*; if the term is more than one day, it is called a *term repo*.

2. U.S. government and agency securities

    A. Treasury notes and bonds

(1) Treasury notes have maturities in 2 to 10 years in denominations of $1,000 to more than $100,000.

(2) Treasury bonds are the government's long-term debt and have maturities greater than 10 years.

(3) Notes and bonds are issued as coupon securities.

(4) Treasury notes and bonds are the safest intermediate- and long-term investments available for purchase because they are backed by the government. This increased safety results in yields that are lower than those of high-quality corporate debt.

(5) Interest is subject to federal income tax but exempt from state and local tax.

B. U.S. government savings bonds

(1) The Series E bond was designed to encourage more people to save money. It was sold in denominations of $25, $100, $500, and up to $10,000. Series E bonds were sold at a discount and paid no interest, similar to zero coupon bonds.

(2) Treasury issued the new Series EE bond to replace the Series E bond. The rate of interest is a variable rate that allows investors to benefit from increasing interest rates.

(3) Interest earned for both E and EE bonds is not taxable until the bonds are redeemed or reach maturity. However, they do permit recognition of the income in earlier years with a valid election. Recognizing the income from E and EE bonds may be a tax planning strategy for young children who have no other taxable income and will thereby create basis in the bonds.

(4) Interest deferred on Series EE bonds can be further deferred by exchanging the EE bonds for HH bonds. The deferral continues until HH bonds are sold or mature.

(5) Interest from Series EE U.S. government savings bonds may be completely excluded from gross income if the bond proceeds are used to pay qualified higher education expenses.

(6) H and HH bonds are sold at par in larger denominations (minimum of $500). The bonds have a maturity of 20 years, and interest is paid and is fully taxable in the year of payment. There is not an option to accumulate the interest or defer the taxes. Series HH bonds are a new issue that is designed to replace the older series H bonds.

(7) It should be noted that the interest earned form E, EE, H, and HH bonds is U.S. government interest and is not taxable by municipalities.

C. Federal agency debt

(1) Bonds issued by federal agencies are not debt of the federal government. Therefore, their yields are higher than those yields available on U.S. Treasury debt. However, they are extremely safe because they have the backing of the federal government.

(a) This backing in most cases is only moral backing, which, in the case of default, the federal government is not obligated to support the debt.

(b) Other agency debt has a legal backing. In this case, the Treasury is legally bound to assume any obligation contained in the debt's indenture.

(2) Federally related institutions include the Government National Mortgage Association (Ginnie Mae) that is backed by the full faith and credit of the U.S. government. These bonds have no credit risk because there is no chance of default.

(3) The other type of agency debt, government-sponsored entities, includes the Federal National Mortgage Association (Fannie Mae), the Federal Home Loan Bank Corporation (Freddie Mac), and the Student Loan Marketing Association (Sallie Mae). These are privately owned, publicly chartered institutions that were created by the U.S.

government to support a specific need. Investors are exposed to credit risk, but the risk is very unlikely because the government provides a moral backing.

D. Treasury inflation protected securities (TIPS)

    (1) TIPS are securities issued by the federal government that have coupon payments that periodically adjust to changes in the inflation rate.

    (2) Changes in inflation are represented in the principal and not the coupon.

    (3) The *inflation-adjusted principal* is multiplied by the real rate to get the appropriate coupon payment. The real rate represents the fixed coupon rate net of inflation. For example, suppose a par value of $10,000 and a coupon rate of 4 percent. Annualized inflation for the next six months is 5 percent. The coupon payment is calculated as follows:

        (a) First, compute the *inflation-adjusted principal*. If the annual inflation rate is 5 percent, then the semiannual rate is 2.5 percent ($5\% \times \frac{1}{2}$). Apply this to the principal of $10,000 to get an inflation-adjusted principal of $10,250 ($10,000 × 1.025).

        (b) Next, compute the *semiannual coupon payment*. This is found by multiplying the inflation-adjusted principal amount with the semiannual real rate. The semiannual coupon rate equals $205 ($10,250 × 2%).

E. Treasury STRIPS

    (1) In 1985, the Treasury introduced zero coupon bonds called STRIPS, standing for separate trading of registered interest and principal securities.

    (2) STRIPS are direct obligations of the federal government.

    (3) STRIPS do not pay a coupon, but interest is taxed as it accrues. Therefore, it is appealing to purchase STRIPS in retirement accounts because tax in retirement accounts is deferred until funds are withdrawn.

    (4) STRIPS are more volatile than other government bonds during periods of changing interest rates.

    (5) To take advantage of the greater price volatility found in STRIPS, it is better to buy them when interest rates are expected to fall.

3. Municipal bonds—general obligation bonds and revenue bonds

    (1) *General obligation* bonds are backed by the full faith and credit of the taxing power of the issuing government.

    (2) *Revenue bonds* are supported by the revenue of a project.

    (3) General obligation bonds have less risk than revenue bonds because they are supported by taxes, whereas revenue bonds are supported only by the funds generated by a project.

    (4) Municipal bonds tend to lack marketability and liquidity. These issues are traded over the counter and the market is thin, causing a large spread between bid and ask. They trade in denominations of $5,000 face value.

    (5) Most debt issued by state and local governments is a long-term serial issue. Serial bonds offer the benefit to the buyer of knowing when the bonds are going to mature. The bonds are purchased based on the investor's time horizon.

    (6) The federal government does not tax interest earned from municipal bonds. Municipal bond interest may also be tax exempt for various states. For example, Colorado does not tax Colorado municipal bond interest, but taxes municipal interest from other states.

4. Corporate bonds

A. Investment grade

(1) *Investment grade bond* does not indicate a particular type of bond; the term refers to any debt of high quality—rated triple B or higher.

(2) There are several types of corporate bonds that can be investment grade (but these can also be high-yield grade, discussed under Topic 40, Section 4.B.)

(a) Secured versus unsecured bonds

i. *Secured* bonds have a claim to assets of a corporation in the event of default, insolvency, or liquidation. For example, a mortgage bond is secured by real property or buildings.

ii. *Unsecured* bonds are not backed by collateral.

(b) Debentures

i. *Debentures* are promissory notes that are not backed by collateral (they are unsecured), but are supported by the creditworthiness of a firm or government agency.

ii. During bankruptcy, debentures are redeemed only after all secured debt has been paid off. Therefore, debentures pay a higher yield than secured debt because of the added risk.

iii. Some debentures are *subordinated*, and these are even more risky than other debt. Subordinated debentures are paid off after all other unsecured debt is paid off during bankruptcy. Investors are often attracted to subordinated debt because of higher yields and other embedded options, such as convertible provisions.

(c) Zero coupon bonds

i. Bonds sold with no coupon at a discount and redeemed for face value at maturity. Interest is accrued over the life of the bond.

ii. There is no tax avoidance in buying zero coupon bonds.

iii. The tax disadvantage of accrued interest can be circumvented in retirement accounts because tax is deferred until funds are withdrawn.

iv. Zero coupon bonds are extremely volatile in periods of changing interest rates.

v. Zero coupon bonds should be bought when interest rates are expected to fall, to take advantage of the increased bond price.

B. High yield

(1) High-yield securities are often referred to as "junk" bonds. These are bonds that are low quality, speculative grade, usually rated below triple B. The features are the same as investment grade debt. However, the poor quality means they offer higher yields than investment grade debt. Triple B or better is generally considered investment grade.

(2) High-yield securities often have a call feature and sinking fund. They are usually debentures and may be subordinated to a firm's other debt. However, some high-yield securities have collateral (i.e., mortgage bonds).

(3) These bonds are often issued to finance a takeover and merger or to help a start-up firm raise capital.

C. Convertible

(1) Conversion rights allow a bondholder to convert the bond into shares of common stock. The conversion feature acts as a benefit to induce investors to buy the bonds. It allows a

corporation to have a debt instrument in its capital structure, although the conversion feature usually comes at a cost.

- (a) These bonds tend to trade at a lower coupon rate than is available with other bonds.
- (b) They are subordinate to other debt issued by the corporation.

(2) They often have a sinking fund provision and are often called by corporations to force bondholders to convert to common stock.

(3) The true benefit to holding these bonds is the safety of debt with the potential for capital gains. Convertible bonds will increase (decrease) in value as the underlying stock increases (decreases).

(4) Both the underlying stock and interest rates cause variations in the price of convertibles. Convertibles are in double jeopardy during periods of high interest rates and low stock prices.

(5) *Conversion ratio.* The number of shares into which a bond is converted is found by taking the face value of the bond and dividing it by the conversion price. *Example*: If a bond is priced at $1,000 and the conversion price is $25, the conversion ratio equals 40 shares ($1,000/$25).

(6) *Conversion value.* The number of shares into which a bond is converted times the market price of the stock gives the value of the bond in terms of stock. *Example*: If a bond is convertible into 40 shares and the market price of the stock is $23, then the bond's value is worth $920 relative to stock ($23 × $40).

(7) The market price of a convertible bond cannot be less than the conversion value, or an opportunity for arbitrage would exist.

D. Callable

(1) A call provision allows a firm to buy back bonds at a specified price before maturity.

(2) It is often used after a period of high interest rates. If bonds were issued during a period of high interest rates, it may make sense for a firm to refinance new debt at a lower interest rate.

(3) The call price is usually less than the market price. If the call price is higher than the market price, it is not beneficial for the issuer to call the bonds.

(4) There is risk to purchasing a callable bond:

- (a) Increased *interest rate risk*
- (b) Increased *reinvestment risk*
- (c) Reduced potential for capital appreciation

(5) The call price acts like a ceiling in periods of falling interest rates. The price of a bond without a call provision will continue to rise as interest rates fall. There is an advantage to callable bonds when interest rates rise; the price of a callable bond does not fall as much as the price of a straight bond because of the call provision.

E. Ways to retire debt

(1) *Bullet maturity.* Bullet maturity means paying off the entire principal in one payment at the maturity date. These are nonamortizing securities.

(2) *Serial bonds.* A bond issue in which specified bonds mature each year. Interest is paid off at different intervals. Serial bonds are common with state and local governments to finance capital improvements, but are not common with corporations. These are nonamortizing securities.

(3) *Amortizing securities.* Amortizing securities make both interest and principal payments. For example, mortgage-backed and asset-backed securities pay both interest and principal payments each month until maturity, when the entire principal is paid up.

(4) *Sinking funds.* Sinking funds are a series of periodic payments to retire a portion of the bond issue prior to maturity either by using a random selection process (lottery) or through the open market.

(5) *Call provision* (explained under Topic 40, Section 4.D.)

(6) *Refundable versus nonrefundable bonds.* The act of issuing new debt and using the proceeds to retire old debt is called *refunding.* This practice is common with bonds having high coupon rates during a time of low interest rates. Nonrefundable bonds contain restrictions that prevent them from using proceeds from new debt to retire old debt. A bond can be callable but nonrefundable.

F. Different types of embedded options: An embedded option is a right of an issuer or bondholder as indicated in the bond indenture. Embedded options play an important role in the valuation of bonds. They affect the timing and magnitude of cash flows. They also affect the rate of performance for a bond over time. There are several embedded options that are granted to issuers and borrowers.

(1) *Call provision* (discussed under Topic 40, Section 4.D.)

(2) *Prepayment provision.* Prepayment provisions are common with amortizing securities. Such a provision allows the borrower to prepay the loan balances before maturity. It is commonly used with home mortgages and car loans.

(3) *Accelerated sinking fund provision.* The accelerated sinking fund option allows the issuer to retire more bonds than required under a sinking fund.

(4) *Put provision.* The bondholder has an option to sell the bonds back to the issuer for a specified price. This is common when bonds are trading below par because of high interest rates. If an investor anticipates rising interest rates, or wants to hedge against rates increasing, a put option may be an attractive investment.

(5) *Conversion rights* (discussed under Topic 40, Section 4.C.)

5. Promissory notes

   A. These are documents signed by a borrower promising to repay a loan under stated terms.
   B. They are unsecured notes that can be of short- or long-term duration.

6. Insurance-based investments

   A. Guaranteed investment contracts (GICs), now called stable value funds, are securities sold by insurance companies primarily to pension plans. They are called guaranteed investment contracts because the rate of return is guaranteed for a fixed period of time (such as five years). Returns for GICs are generally low because little risk is involved.
   B. Annuities are contracts issued by insurance companies that make regular periodic payments. Annuities may begin now or may be deferred, beginning at some point in the future. There are two general types of annuities: (1) fixed annuities and (2) variable annuities (see Topic 29, (6) Settlement options).

7. Stocks

   A. Common

      (1) Investors often try to match their financial objectives with the particular characteristics of stocks.
      (2) There are six categories of common stock.

(a) *Blue chip stocks*. Highly regarded investment quality companies. They are well established and older and have the ability to pay dividends in both good and bad years.

(b) *Income stocks*. Pay regular and steady dividends and provide consistent current income for investors. These stocks should also appreciate enough to keep up with inflation.

(c) *Growth stocks*. Sales, earnings, and market share grow at rates that are higher than those of an average company or the general economy. Blue chip stocks can also be classified as growth stocks. Little to no dividends are paid.

(d) *Cyclical stocks*. Cyclical stocks tend to prosper in growing and expanding economies and tend to do poorly during down business cycles. Examples include autos, paper, and airlines.

(e) *Interest-sensitive stocks*. The performance of some companies is largely affected by changes in interest rates. For example, the housing industry has more demand when interest rates are low because it is cheaper for consumers to purchase homes. Examples include insurance companies, telephones, utilities, and banks.

(f) *Defensive stocks*. Stocks that are relatively unaffected by general fluctuations in the economy are considered to be defensive stocks. Examples are soft drinks, groceries, alcohol, and tobacco.

(3) Control or voting rights

(a) *Noncumulative*. One share of common stock permits one vote for each member of the board of directors. This noncumulative voting would allow a shareholder of 100 shares of common stock to cast 100 votes for each of the director's positions.

(b) *Cumulative*. Permits a shareholder to cast votes equal to the number of positions on the board of directors times the number of shares owned, allocated in any way the shareholder wishes. *Example*: Three positions on the board of directors would allow a shareholder with 100 shares to cast 300 votes for one position, 150 votes for two positions, 100 votes for three positions, or any combination that does not exceed the 300 allotted votes. Cumulative voting helps to protect minority shareholders' right to management.

(4) Cash dividends are payments to the owners of a corporation.

(a) Stock price adjustment—The price of the stock declines by the amount of the dividend per share on the ex-dividend date. For example, assume a $100-priced stock that pays a $1 dividend. On the ex-date, the stock's price will drop to $99, but the stockholder will receive $1 in dividends, so there is no change in overall value to the stockholder. A firm's balance sheet will adjust too—both cash and retained earnings decline by the amount of dividends paid.

(b) Dividend process

i. *Declaration date*. The declaration date is the date when the board of directors passes a resolution to pay a dividend.

ii. *Ex-dividend date*. In return, brokerage firms and stock exchanges establish the ex-dividend date to make sure the right people get the dividend. The ex-dividend date is two business days before the date of record. If you buy the stock before the ex-dividend date, you are entitled to receive the dividend. If you buy the stock after this date, you will not receive the dividend. Before the date, the stock trades "*cum* dividend."

      iii. Date of record. The corporation prepares a list of all individuals believed to be stockholders. The date of record is then the date on which holders of record are designated to receive the dividend.

      iv. Date of payment. The date of payment is when dividends are mailed to stockholders.

(5) A stock split is an increase in a firm's number of shares outstanding and is expressed as a ratio. For example, a two-for-one stock split means that a stockholder who owns 100 shares will now own 200 shares. A three-for-two stock split means that 100 shares increase to 150 shares ($3 \div 2 \times 100$).

(6) A stock dividend is a payment made by the firm in the form of additional shares instead of cash and is expressed as a percentage. For example, a 20 percent stock dividend means that shareholders receive one new share for every five shares owned. An investor who owns 100 shares will now have 120 shares. The result is a 20 percent increase in the total number of outstanding shares.

(7) Shareholders do not gain value after a stock dividend or split, because the price of the stock declines by the same percentage as the stock dividend or split.

(8) Effect of noncash dividends on the balance sheet

    (a) Cash and stock dividends produce different results on the balance sheet, and stock splits have no effect on the capital structure of a firm.

    (b) Cash dividends result in a reduction in cash and a corresponding reduction in retained earnings.

    (c) Stock dividends increase the total number of outstanding shares, thus increasing the total value of common stock par and paid-in-capital surplus, but there is a reduction in retained earnings to offset. The net effect is no change in total stockholders' equity.

    (d) Stock splits reduce par value but do not change the common equity part of the balance sheet. The shares are increased, but there is a counterbalancing decline in par value. The net effect is no change in total stockholders' equity.

B. Preferred stock

(1) Preferred stock usually pays a fixed dividend that is not guaranteed. It is expressed as a percentage to par or dollar amount. For example, a $5 preferred represents a $5 annual dividend per share. The dividends are paid from earnings and given preference over common stock dividends.

(2) *Cumulative* preferred is preferred stock in which dividends are not paid but accumulate. The dividends are said to be in arrearage. This means they have not been paid but will be at some time in the future before dividends are paid to holders of common stock.

(3) *Noncumulative* preferred is preferred stock in which dividends do not accumulate. In this case, any missed dividend payments are not paid in the future.

(4) Preferred stock is usually purchased by investors seeking a fixed stream of income, as are bonds.

(5) There are some significant differences between preferred stock and bonds.

    (a) Preferred stock is *perpetual*. This means that a firm does not have to generate sufficient money to retire it.

    (b) Preferred stock is less risky than common stock but is more risky than debt. A firm has a legal obligation to make interest payments to bondholders, but does not have to make dividend payments to preferred stockholders.

(c) Preferred stock has greater market fluctuation than bonds. This can be explained by the longer term (perpetual) and uncertainty (risk) associated with dividend payments.

C. Warrants

(1) Warrants are equity call options directly issued by a corporation to buy the underlying stock at a specified price over a specified time period.

(2) The distinguishing difference of a warrant from an ordinary call option is that, if exercised, the company issues more common stock shares to give to the holder of the warrant. Therefore, when warrants are exercised, the total number of outstanding shares increases. The increase in shares is dilutive to the firm's earnings.

(3) Warrants usually give the right to buy one common share. However, they are not limited to this. Some warrants give the option to buy more or less than one share. Sometimes this conversion term is the result of mergers or stock splits.

(4) The theoretical price of a warrant does not necessarily equal the market price. The price of a warrant is usually higher than the theoretical price because investors put a premium on warrants in anticipation that the underlying stock price will rise above the exercise price.

(5) Warrants exhibit more percentage change in price relative to the underlying stock. This is because of the leverage effect.

D. Rights

(1) *Preemptive rights* are the rights of current stockholders to maintain their proportionate ownership in the firm.

(2) Firms that have given preemptive rights present a *rights offering* when they issue new stock. This offering allows existing shareholders to purchase new shares before they are offered to the general public. This right prevents dilution of an investor's ownership percentage when new shares are issued.

(3) The *right* is defined as an option given to stockholders to buy additional shares at a specified price during a specified time period.

8. Derivatives—securities with a value that is tied to the value of underlying securities

A. Options

(1) An option is a contract that gives the owner the right (but not a legal obligation) to trade an underlying asset at a predetermined future date and price. The value of an option depends on the value of an underlying asset. The price paid for the option contract is called the premium.

(2) Options are classified as calls and puts.

(a) A call gives the holder the right to buy an asset at a predetermined price.
(b) A put gives the holder the right to sell the asset at a predetermined price.

(3) The seller of an option contract is called an option writer.

(a) The writer of a call must deliver the asset at a predetermined price.
(b) The writer of a put must purchase the asset at a predetermined price.

(4) Strike price and expiration date

(a) The strike price is the predetermined price for an option. If a call is exercised, the holder buys the asset at the strike price. If a put is exercised, the holder sells the asset at the strike price. If a call writer is assigned, the writer must deliver the asset at the strike price. If a put writer is assigned, the writer must purchase the asset at the strike price.

(b) The predetermined time when the option contract expires is called the expiration date.

(c) For example, one stock option contract generally represents 100 shares of the underlying stock. An XYZ Dec 75 call priced at $2.50 represents an actual cost of $250 dollars (100 shares times $2.50 per share). The contract will expire in December and the stock price is $75.

(5) Definition of in-the-money, out-of-the-money, and at-the-money

(a) *In-the-money.* The option has value.

    i. Call option: if the underlying stock price is greater than the strike price

    ii. Put option: if the underlying stock price is less than the strike price

(b) *Out-of-the-money.* The option has little to no value.

    i. Call option: if the underlying stock price is less than the strike price

    ii. Put option: if the underlying stock price is greater than the strike price

(c) *At-the-money.* The option has minimal value.

    i. Call option: if the underlying stock price is equal to the strike price

    ii. Put option: if the underlying stock price is equal to the strike price

(6) Option expiration—Listed stock options expire on the Saturday following the third Friday of the expiration month. The only exceptions are when legal holidays fall on this Friday or Saturday.

(7) Difference between American and European options

(a) American options allow the holder the right to exercise the option contract at some predetermined price anytime before or at expiration.

(b) European options allow the holder to exercise the option only at expiration.

(c) The majority of options that are traded are American options. It is important to understand that the name of the option has nothing to do with the geography.

(d) American options have more theoretical value than European options because of the early exercise privilege.

(8) Intrinsic value and time value

(a) The intrinsic value is the minimum price an option can command. For call options, it is the stock price minus the strike price for an in-the-money option. Conversely, for put options, it is the strike price minus the stock price for an in-the-money put.

(b) The time value is the premium minus the intrinsic value. For example, a $50 XYZ call is priced at $5. The underlying stock is trading at $53. The intrinsic value is $3 and the time value is $2. An out-of-the-money option consists entirely of time value because there is no intrinsic value.

B. Futures

(1) A futures contract is a formal agreement between a buyer and seller and a commodity exchange.

(2) When purchasing a contract (long position), the buyer agrees to accept a specific commodity at a specified date. When selling a contract (short position), the seller agrees to deliver the specific commodity at a specified date. The long position increases in value if the underlying commodity increases in value; the short position increases in value if the underlying commodity decreases in value.

(3) *Future price*. The price in a contract for the future delivery of a commodity

(4) *Spot price*. The current price of a commodity

(5) Purchasing futures contracts requires a margin account with an initial deposit and a required minimum balance. Futures contracts are settled daily (called marking-to-market). Traders are required to realize losses in cash on a daily basis. If the futures contract increases, the investor is permitted to withdraw the increase in the margin account. If the contract decreases in value below the maintenance margin, the investor must deposit cash or securities to restore the initial margin level.

(6) As the delivery date gets closer, the future price will converge with the spot price for that commodity.

(7) *Daily limit*. The maximum daily change permitted in a commodity future's price.

9. Exchange traded funds (ETFs)

   A. Characteristics of ETFs

   (1) Exchange traded funds offer purchasers the ability to invest in a basket of stocks that closely mirror an underlying benchmark index. They trade daily on exchanges and are priced continuously by the marketplace throughout the day.

   (2) Can be sold short and bought on margin—anything you might do with a stock, you can do with an ETF.

   (3) Most charge lower annual expenses than index mutual funds, but you must pay a commission to buy and sell ETF shares.

   (4) The funds rely on an arbitrage mechanism to keep the prices at which they trade roughly in line with the net asset values of their underlying portfolios.

   (5) Forces of supply and demand determine the market price of an ETF.

   B. ETFs are different from traditional mutual funds in three ways:

   (1) *Trading flexibility*. ETFs trade throughout the day, which allows an investor to buy and sell them at any time.

   (2) *Cost*. In terms of the annual expenses charged to investors, ETFs are considerably less expensive than the vast majority of mutual funds, but this does not include the commissions charged for trading these funds.

   (3) *Taxes*. Most trading in ETFs takes place between shareholders, shielding the fund from any need to sell stocks to meet redemptions. However, ETFs do make capital gains distributions, as they buy and sell stocks to adjust for changes to their underlying benchmark.

10. Index securities

    A. Index securities are a portfolio of underlying equities or bonds seeking to mirror the performance of a like type index.

    B. Advantages include

    (1) *Low costs*. Index fund costs may be 0.15 to 0.25 percent per year, as compared with the internal cost of 0.75 to 1.25 of actively managed funds.

    (2) *Lower taxes*. Managers do not actively buy and sell stocks. Actively managed funds may result in massive capital gain distributions even while losing money, but index funds rarely experience this problem.

    (3) *Keeping pace with the index*. This is a great benefit, inasmuch as the majority of actively managed stock funds underperform the Standard & Poor's (S&P) 500 index.

C. Disadvantages include

    (1) *Downside risk.* Index funds cannot hold cash, which often cushions the fall in a declining market.

    (2) *Tax ramification in a down market.* When nervous investors start to redeem shares, index funds are compelled to sell shares because there is no cash position to act as a buffer. This may hurt after-tax returns.

    (3) *Value added by money managers.* There are some active money managers who have established long-term track records that outperformed the market.

11. Investment companies

A. Unit investment trusts

    (1) Unit investment trusts represent a fixed portfolio of assets and are sold to investors in units of $1,000.

    (2) The assets of a unit investment trust are frozen. That means no new securities are purchased. In addition, the securities already purchased are seldom sold.

    (3) The trust is self-liquidating. After a period of time, the portfolio is sold and the funds are distributed to the stockholders. When funds are received, they are not reinvested in the trust.

    (4) Unit investment trusts are designed to meet specific objectives, such as interest income. Expenses are lower than closed-end and open-end funds because of a fixed portfolio. This generally means that there is no management fee.

B. Open-end mutual funds

    (1) Open-end investment companies are also called mutual funds and do not trade on the secondary markets. These shares are purchased directly from the fund at the net asset value (NAV) plus any applicable sales charge.

        (a) A no-load fund charges no sales fee when an investor is buying and selling shares.

        (b) A load fund charges a sales fee to the investor. The investor pays the offering price. It is determined as

            i. Offering price $= \dfrac{\text{NAV}}{(1 - \text{load})}$

            ii. Assume an investor is looking to purchase an open-end fund with a load of 5.5 percent and net asset value of $10. The offer price is

$$\frac{\$10}{(1 - 0.055)} = \$10.58 \text{ per share.}$$

    (2) When the mutual fund receives money from an investor, it issues new shares and purchases additional assets. If an investor sells the shares, they are redeemed and the fund pays the investor from its cash holdings. In some instances, a fund may have to sell shares within the fund to pay the investor.

    (3) The possibility of buying an open-end fund at a discount and selling it at a premium does not exist.

C. Closed-end investment companies

(1) Closed-end investment companies issue a specified number of shares composed of stock or a combination of stock and debt. The shares cannot be redeemed and new shares are not issued after the initial offering. These shares trade on the open market.

(2) A closed-end investment company can trade at a price that is greater or less than NAV. If it is less than NAV, it is selling at a discount. If it is greater than NAV, it is selling at a premium. The reason for the market price to be different from the NAV is supply and demand.

(3) The NAV is the asset value of all shares owned by the investment company. It is total assets (stock, bonds, cash) *minus* total liabilities (accrued fees) *divided* by the number of shares outstanding.

12. Real estate investment trust (REIT)

A. An REIT is a publicly traded closed-end investment company that invests in a managed, diversified portfolio of real estate or real estate mortgages and construction loans—think of it as a real estate mutual fund.

B. REITs are traded on exchanges and can sell for premiums or discounts to the NAV.

C. Investors must pay the tax on an REIT's earnings as they are distributed. Distributed income is taxed as ordinary income. Capital gains and losses from the sale of assets in the REIT portfolio retain their character and are taxed as gains and losses when distributed.

D. Three types of REITs

(1) *Equity REITs.* Acquire ownership interests in commercial, industrial, and residential properties. Income is primarily received from the rental of these properties.

(2) *Mortgage REITs.* Lending funds for construction loans, mortgages; these types of REITs can invest in mortgage-backed securities.

(3) *Hybrid REITs.* Combinations of equity and mortgage REITs

E. Advantages of REITs include (1) limited liability, (2) no corporate-level tax; REIT shareholders avoid double taxation, (3) ability to leverage, (4) usable as collateral, (5) liquidity, (6) diversification in real estate portfolio, and (7) inflation hedge.

F. Disadvantages of REITs include (1) loss of control, (2) lower potential returns, (3) management fees and administrative charges, and (4) no flow-through of tax benefits—losses cannot be passed through.

13. Real estate (investor managed)

A. Real estate properties are classified as:

(1) Income properties—residential and commercial properties

(2) Speculative properties—raw land and investment properties

B. Framework for determining value in real estate investment analysis:

(1) *Investor objectives* include investment characteristics and constraints and goals.

(2) *Analysis of important features* includes physical property, property rights, time horizon, and geographic area.

(3) *Data collection and determinants of value* include demand, supply, benefits of property, and property transfer process.

(4) *Valuation of property* includes estimating market value and the investment analysis.

C. Estimating market value

(1) *Cost approach.* Evaluates property based on the current cost to rebuild it. It works best for newer properties.

(2) *Comparative sales approach*. Evaluates property relative to comparable properties that have recently sold in the same area.

(3) *Income approach*. Evaluates a property at the present value of all future cash flows. The *capitalization approach* treats net operating income as if it were a perpetuity.

    (a) Market value (V) = annual net operating income (NOI) ÷ market capitalization rate (R).

    (b) Where NOI is gross potential income *less* vacancy and collection losses, and *less* operating expenses including insurance and property taxes. R is the required rate of return for investors.

    (c) *Example*: A building would earn $250,000 if fully occupied. The building has a 5 percent vacancy rate and operating expenses of $50,000. An investor wants a 12 percent return on this investment. The market value is

        Step 1. NOI = $250,000 − (0.05)($250,000) − $50,000 = $187,500.
        Step 2. V = $187,500 ÷ 0.12 = $1,562,500.

D. Investment analysis

    (1) Net present value analysis using after-tax cash flows
    (2) Internal rate of return analysis

14. Private placement

A. Private placements sell securities directly to sophisticated or accredited investors. They do not require a Securities and Exchange (SEC) registration filing and are established for a predetermined amount of time.

B. Rule 504 of Regulation D exempts issuance of securities of up to $1 million in a 12-month period to an unlimited number and type of investors.

C. Rule 505 of Regulation D exempts issuance of up to $5 million in a 12-month period. Sales can be made to no more than 35 nonaccredited investors and to an unlimited number of accredited investors. Accredited investors include banks, savings and loan associations, insurance companies, individuals having a net worth of at least $1 million or annual income of $200,000, and so forth.

D. Rule 506 of Regulation D exempts the issuance of an unlimited amount of securities in a private placement. Requirements are similar to those established under Rule 505. However, any nonaccredited investors must be sophisticated investors or represented by a sophisticated investor. A sophisticated investor is one with knowledge and experience in financial matters.

E. Sales under Rule 505 or 506 of Regulation D are restricted as to resale. These securities (as well as securities sold by a controlling person) may not be resold unless either registered with the SEC (unless exempted by securities laws) or sold per the safe harbor provisions of Rule 144.

15. Limited partnerships

A. Limited partnerships are businesses owned by general and limited partners.

    (1) General partners manage the business. As a result, they can be held accountable and liable for all the actions of the business.

    (2) Limited partners are investors and are liable only up to the amount of their investments. Limited partners who take an active management role in the business can lose their limited liability protection and then be considered general partners.

16. Asset-backed securities

   A. An asset-backed security represents a pool of asset-linked debts.

   B. Investors receive payments on a monthly basis, consisting of scheduled principal and interest, and any unscheduled payments consisting of prepayments.

   C. Unlike prepayments for mortgage-backed securities, prepayments for asset-backed securities are almost unaffected by changes in market interest rates, resulting in relatively predictable cash flows.

   D. All asset-backed securities have one or more credit enhancements that result in a higher credit rating. They offer investors higher yield than corporate bonds of similar quality and maturity.

   E. The market for asset-backed securities is very liquid.

17. Mortgage pass-through securities

   A. A mortgage pass-through security represents a self-amortizing pool of mortgages.

   B. Payments are made on a monthly basis and consist of scheduled principal and interest, as well as any unscheduled payments consisting of prepayments and defaults. The timing and amount of cash flows are largely dependent on prepayments. Payments vary from month to month, and the amount received by the investor also varies each month.

   C. If no prepayments are made, the monthly cash flows will remain constant. It is only the composition of the cash flows between interest, principal, and servicing fees that changes when a loan amortizes.

   D. Mortgage pass-through securities should be evaluated by fixed-income investors because they provide many benefits.

      (1) Their yields can be as much as 200 basis points higher than comparable government and corporate fixed-income debt.

      (2) They are considered to be of higher credit quality than AAA corporate bonds, because mortgage pass-through securities are issued by federal agencies.

      (3) These securities prove to be very liquid in the marketplace. They are more liquid than corporate bonds and as liquid as Treasuries.

      (4) They are a very good source for an investor interested in receiving a monthly income.

   E. Mortgage pass-through securities also carry a degree of risk.

      (1) Interest rate risk

      (2) Reinvestment rate risk

   F. The uncertainty in the monthly payments affects the valuation of a mortgage pass-through security. If mortgages are paid off sooner than expected, the realized return will be higher than the expected return. The opposite is also true: If mortgages are paid off later than expected, the realized return will be smaller than the expected return.

18. Collateralized mortgage obligations (CMOs)

   A. A collateralized mortgage obligation is a derivative of a pass-through security held by a trust in which prepayment and reinvestment risk is reduced.

   B. The CMO is subdivided into different classes (called *tranches*), which receive different cash flow payments. The principal repayment is directed to the first tranche until it is retired and then paid to the next tranche. Principal repayments are not made to the next tranche until the prior tranche is retired. Interest is paid off annually on the amount of the loan in each tranche.

    C. By accepting a later repayment of principal, investors in the longer tranches accept a higher interest rate than investors in the early tranches.

    D. With a mortgage pass-through security, prepayments are spread over the entire life of the security. In the case of a CMO, prepayments are spread over each tranche. The timing of principal repayment becomes slightly more known than that of a mortgage pass-through security. For example, an investor in need of cash is better served by purchasing the first tranche, whereas an investor in little need of cash is better off acquiring a later tranche.

19. Natural resources—investments in timber, oil, and the like. They have an elastic demand, which means they are price sensitive to demand. Increases in demand cause their value to rise, and vice versa.

20. Tangible assets—Tangible assets include collectibles, such as Beanie Babies, baseball cards, coins, stamps, and the like. A strong secondary marketplace and government regulation do not exist for these assets. Liquidity risk and fraud can run high.

21. American depository receipts (ADRs)

    A. Foreign firms can have their shares traded on U.S. exchanges.

        (1) One way is to have their shares directly available for trading by listing them on exchanges. These shares are traded exactly like those of a U.S. company.

        (2) The other way is by issuing American depository receipts (ADRs).

    B. ADRs represent indirect ownership in shares of a foreign company. ADRs are tradable receipts issued by U.S. banks that have possession of physical shares held on deposit by correspondent banks in the home country of the company whose shares are issued. The correspondent bank holding the shares receives the dividends and converts them into U.S. dollars after paying all foreign withholding taxes.

    C. ADRs are an effective means of investing in foreign companies without having to worry about currency risk.

22. Security risk diagram

    A. Risk (and return potential) increases from bottom to top.

    B. Risk (and return potential) increases from left to right.

    C. FDIC-insured CDs are less risky.

    D. Futures and commodities are most risky.

Futures and Commodities				
Speculative Common Stocks and Bonds			Gold, Silver, and Collectibles	
Limited Partnerships		Real Estate	Options	
High-Grade Common Stock			Growth Mutual Funds	
Balanced Mutual Funds		High-Grade Preferred Stock	High-Grade Convertible Securities	
High-Grade Municipal Bonds		Money Market Accounts	High-Grade Corporate Bonds	
FDIC-Insured CDs	U.S. Series EE and HH Bonds	Insurance-Based Investments	Treasure Bills, Notes, and Bonds	FDIC-Insured Checking and Savings Accounts

↑ More risk and return potential →

TOPIC 41: TYPES OF INVESTMENT RISK

1. Inflation risk

    A. Inflation risk, or purchasing power risk, arises from variations in cash flows from a security because of inflation, which reduces the purchasing power of money.

    B. *Example:* If the purchaser buys a bond paying a coupon rate of 5 percent, but inflation later increases to 5.5 percent, then the purchasing power of the cash flow (i.e., money) has declined.

2. Interest rate risk

    A. The prices of bonds and stocks are inversely related to interest rates. When market interest rates increase, the prices of bonds and stocks go down. When market interest rates drop, the prices go up.

    B. The inverse relationship between market yields and bond prices is extended to a bond's coupon. If market yields fall below a bond's coupon, the price of the bond will always exceed its par value. The bond is said to trade at a *premium*. In contrast, when market yield rises above coupons, the price of a bond is always less than its par value. It is said to be trading at a *discount*.

        Premium bond   Coupon rate > market yield → bond price > par value
        Discount bond   Coupon rate < market yield → bond price < par value
        Par bond   Coupon rate = market yield → bond price = par value

    C. If investors anticipate that interest rates will rise, then they are predicting that bond prices will fall. If they predict that interest rates will drop, they are anticipating that bond prices will rise.

    D. The *magnitude* of change in a bond's price is subject to the bond's maturity and coupon. Bonds with *longer maturities* and *lower coupons* are subject to *more price volatility* than bonds with shorter maturities and higher coupons.

    E. There is a deeper relationship between price and yield for bonds.

        (1) As the yield increases, the price curve gets flatter → changes in yields have a smaller effect on the bond's price when yields increase.

        (2) As yields drop, the price curve gets steeper → changes in yields have a large impact on the bond's price.

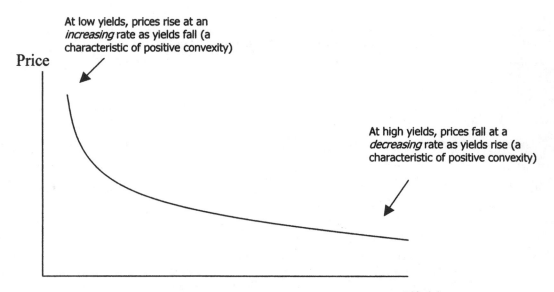

(3) This relationship shows that yields affect price volatility. When yields are high → bond price volatility is low (flatter price curve). When yields are low → bond price volatility is high (steeper price curve).

3. *Systematic risk* includes risks that affect the entire *market* (e.g., market risk, interest rate risk, purchasing power risk, foreign currency risk, and reinvestment risk). Systematic risk cannot be eliminated through diversification because it affects the entire market. Beta is a measure by which systematic risk is determined. Beta is an accurate measure of systematic risk only when calculated for a diversified portfolio.

4. Business risk

   A. *Unsystematic risk.* Risks that are unique to a single business or industry, such as operations and methods of financing. These risks include business risk and financial risk. Unlike systematic risk, unsystematic risk can be eliminated through diversification. Several studies have found that unsystematic risk has been significantly reduced with portfolios of 10 to 15 stocks.

   B. Investment risk equals total risk equals standard deviation equals systematic risk (nondiversifiable risk) plus unsystematic risk (diversifiable risk).

5. Liquidity risk

   A. Marketability risk implies the ease with which a security can be bought or sold. Liquidity risk represents the ease with which the security can be sold at a fair price without risk of loss. Securities can be marketable but not necessarily liquid.

   B. The primary measure of liquidity is the size of the spread between the bid and ask. A larger spread signals an illiquid market. Investors want liquid markets so as to sell their securities quickly at a fair price. In general, liquidity improves when more participants are engaged in trading the security.

6. Reinvestment risk—This risk occurs when amortizing securities repay principal and expose investors to the risk of investing these funds at a lower interest rate.

7. Political risk—Also called regulatory or country risk, political consists of changes in government, restrictions imposed on foreign exchange flows, and environmental and other regulations that impose compliance costs on the firm.

8. Exchange risk

   A. Exchange rate risk, or currency risk, occurs when interest and dividend payments are denominated in a foreign currency and the value of the currency fluctuates relative to the value of the home currency.

   B. If the foreign currency increases against the home currency, each unit (i.e., dollar) will be worth more; if a foreign currency decreases against the home currency, each unit will be worth less.

TOPIC 42: MEASURES OF INVESTMENT RISK

1. Coefficient of determination (R^2)

   A. The coefficient of determination is often referred to as R^2. It gives the variation in one variable explained by another and is an important statistic in investments.

   B. R^2 is systematic risk; $1 - R^2$ is unsystematic risk.

   C. R^2 is calculated by squaring the correlation coefficient (r).

   D. The beta coefficient reports the volatility of some return relative to the market. The strength of the relationship is indicated by R^2. If R^2 equals 0.15, an investor can assume that beta has little meaning because the variation in the return is caused by something other than the movement in the market (unsystematic risk). If R^2 equals 0.95, the variation in the market explains 95 percent of the variation in the return (systematic risk—where beta is a good measure of risk).

2. Covariance

   A. Covariance is a measure of the degree to which two variables move together over time. A positive covariance indicates that variables move in the same direction, and a negative covariance indicates that they move in opposite directions. Larger numbers indicate a stronger relationship, and smaller numbers indicate a weaker relationship.
   B. Covariance is an absolute number and can be difficult to interpret. It is often converted into the correlation coefficient, which is easier than covariance to interpret.
   C. The covariance between securities 1 and 2 is

   $$\text{cov}_{1,2} = (r_{1,2})(\sigma_1)(\sigma_2)$$

3. Correlation coefficient (r)

   A. It is a measure of the relationship of returns between two stocks.

      (1) A correlation coefficient of +1 means that returns always move together in the same direction. They are *perfectly positively correlated.*
      (2) A correlation coefficient of −1 means that returns always move in exactly the opposite directions. They are *perfectly negatively correlated.*
      (3) A correlation coefficient of zero means that there is no relationship between two stocks' returns. They are *uncorrelated.*

   B. There is an inverse relationship between correlation and diversification. The lower the correlation, the greater the diversification. Risk is erased when returns are perfectly negatively correlated.
   C. If the correlation coefficient between securities is less than 1, then the risk of a portfolio will always be less than the simple weighted average of the individual risks of the stocks in the portfolio.
   D. The correlation coefficient between securities 1 and 2 is

   $$r_{1,2} = (\text{cov}_{1,2})/\sigma_1\sigma_2$$

4. Variance

   A. Variance is the standard measure of total risk.
   B. It measures the dispersion of returns around the expected return. The larger the dispersion, the more risk involved with an individual security.
   C. Variance is an absolute number and can be difficult to interpret. It is often converted into standard deviation, which is easier than variance to interpret. The square root of variance is standard deviation.

5. Semivariance measures downside risk, which is the dispersion of returns occurring below a specified target return such as zero or the T-bill rate.

6. Standard deviation (σ)

   A. Standard deviation is a measure of variability of returns of an asset as compared with its mean or expected value. It measures total risk.
   B. There is a direct relationship between standard deviation (σ, sigma) and risk. The larger the dispersion around a mean value, the greater the risk and the larger the standard deviation for a security.

C. Observations will tend to cluster around the expected mean, and the bell-shaped curve is often used to represent the dispersion. The standard deviation is a measure of this dispersion or variability.

    (1) Approximately 68 percent of outcomes fall within ± 1 σ of the mean.
    (2) Approximately 95 percent of outcomes fall within ± 2 σ of the mean.
    (3) Approximately 99 percent of outcomes fall within ± 3 σ of the mean.

D. *Example*: Assume the standard deviation for stock A is 1.03. If stock A has an average return of 15 percent, then 68 percent of all returns fall within 13.97 and 16.03 percent.

E. Standard deviation is an absolute measure of dispersion. That is, it can be influenced by the magnitude of the original numbers. If stock A and stock B had different returns, a comparison of standard deviations may not indicate that B is more diverse. Other measures of risk are useful complements to standard deviation.

F. Steps to calculating *historical* standard deviation

    (1) For each observation, take the difference between the individual observation and the average return.
    (2) Square the difference.
    (3) Sum the squared differences.
    (4) For sample σ, divide this sum by one less than the number of observations. For population σ, divide this sum by the total number of observations (for the CFP® Examination, assume sample unless stated differently).
    (5) Take the square root.

G. *Calculation example*: Great Properties, Inc., has an average return of 12 percent and the following individual returns for the corresponding time periods listed in the following table. What is the standard deviation for Great Properties, Inc.?

Year	Actual Return	Average Return	Difference	Difference Squared
1	12%	6.8%	5.2	27.04
2	10	6.8	3.2	10.24
3	−5	6.8	−11.8	139.24
4	7	6.8	0.2	0.04
5	10	6.8	3.2	10.24
Sum of squared differences =				186.80
The standard deviation is $[186.80 \div (5-1)]^{1/2} = 6.83\%$				

H. The expected rate of return (ER) for a single stock or portfolio of stocks is calculated as follows:

ER stock $= \Sigma(R)(\text{probability})$

ER portfolio $= \Sigma(\text{ER stock})(W\% \text{ of funds invested in each stock})$

ER for a two-stock portfolio $= W_1 ER_2 + W_2 ER_2$

I. The standard deviation of returns for an individual investment is calculated as

σ asset $= [\Sigma(R \text{ actual} - ER)^2(\text{probability})]^{1/2}$

J. *Calculation example:*

Step 1: Expected Return		
Probability	**Return (R)**	**Expected Return**
0.25	5%	1.25%
0.35	15%	5.25%
0.40	25%	10.00%
Sum of expected returns =		16.25%

Step 2: Standard Deviation of Return (standard deviation is square root of variance)				
Probability	**Return (R)**	**ER**	$(R - ER)^2$	$[(R - ER)^2]$ (probability)
0.25	5%	16.25%	0.0127	0.0032
0.35	15%	16.25%	0.0002	0.0001
0.40	25%	16.25%	0.0077	0.0031
Variance =				0.0064
Standard deviation =				0.08

K. The standard deviation of a portfolio is not the average of the standard deviations of the individual stocks. It is *not* a linear combination of the standard deviations of the individual assets. The standard deviation of a portfolio is usually less than the average standard deviation of the stocks in the portfolio.

7. Coefficient of variation

   A. Where standard deviation is a measure of absolute dispersions, the coefficient of variation is a measure of relative dispersions.
   B. It is calculated as follows: Standard deviation ÷ mean.
   C. The larger value indicates greater dispersion relative to the arithmetic mean of the return. *Example*: Assume stock A has a standard deviation of 7.5 and an average rate of return of 4 percent. Stock B has a standard deviation of 9.5 and an average rate of return of 10 percent. The standard deviation indicates that stock B has greater risk than stock A because of a higher standard deviation. However, the relative dispersion is less for stock B than for A. Investment A has a 1.87 (7.5 ÷ 4) coefficient of variation, whereas investment B has only a 0.95 (9.5 ÷ 10) coefficient of variation. Considering the relative dispersion, investors seeking less risk would consider purchasing stock B instead of stock A.

8. Beta

   A. The beta coefficient is a measure of systematic risk and should be used for a diversified portfolio. In the construction of a well-diversified portfolio, all unsystematic risk is removed. A diversified portfolio is a portfolio of systematic risk, and the beta coefficient is a measure of volatility for a diversified portfolio.
   B. If the stock has a beta of 1.0, the implication is that the stock moves exactly with the market. A beta of 1.2 is 20 percent riskier than the market, and 0.8 is 20 percent less risky than the market.

C. Understand that the beta coefficient for an *individual security* may be unstable over time. It is not an accurate predictor of future movements in stock prices. The beta coefficient for a *portfolio of securities* is fairly stable over time. For a portfolio of securities, as one stock's beta increases, another tends to decrease, thus averaging each other out over time.

TOPIC 43: MEASURES OF INVESTMENT RETURNS

1. Annualized return
   A. The annual rate of return is used for comparison purposes among companies. It is referred to as the APR, or annual percentage rate. The annualized return is calculated by multiplying a given rate by the number of compounding periods that annualizes it. For example, if the quarterly rate of return is 4 percent for an investment, the annual rate of return is 16 percent.
   B. Time value of analysis tells us that a 4 percent quarterly return is actually more than a 16 percent annual return. It is actually 16.99 percent [$(1.04)^4$].

2. Real (inflation-adjusted) return
   A. The real return is the earnings from an investment that are above inflation. The real return is determined by the following formula:

   (1) $$\frac{1 + \text{nominal rate}}{1 + \text{inflation rate}} - 1 \times 100$$

   (2) Where the nominal rate is the absolute return, and the inflation rate is the rate of inflation for the period.

   B. *Example*: Assume an individual invests $1,000 at the beginning of the year and earns 10 percent. The inflation over the period is 3 percent. The real return equals

   $$\frac{1.10}{1.03} - 1 \times 100 = 6.79\%$$

3. Risk-adjusted return
   A. In determining the various returns earned by a portfolio, a higher return by itself is not necessarily indicative of superior performance. Alternately, a lower return is not indicative of inferior performance.
   B. There are three major composite equity portfolio measures that combine risk and return to give quantifiable risk-adjusted numbers. These composite performance measures are the Treynor index, the Sharpe index, and the Jensen index (see Topic 46). Investors can use these measures together to determine whether a portfolio or fund manager actually beat the market.
   C. In the simplest way, the risk-adjusted return is calculated by taking the rate of return of a stock or portfolio and dividing it by some risk measure, such as standard deviation or beta.

4. Required rate of return
   The capital asset pricing model (CAPM) determines the required rate of return for any risky asset. It specifies that the return on an investment (r) depends on the return the individual earns on a risk-free asset and a risk premium. The return of a U.S. Treasury bill is used as the risk-free asset. The risk-adjusted return is expressed as

   $r = r_f + (r_m - r_f)$ beta

   where r_f is the risk-free asset and r_m is the return of the market. The risk premium, which is the additional return of the market over the risk-free rate of return ($r_m - r_f$) is adjusted by the systematic risk associated with that asset, the beta coefficient.

5. Expected rate of return

   A. The expected return is the anticipated growth from an investment. It is the return that is expected to occur for the amount of risk undertaken. The expected return is calculated as

   $$E(r) = \frac{E(D)}{P} + E(g)$$

   where $E(r)$ is the expected return (as a percentage); $E(D)$ is the expected dividend [current dividend $\times$ (1 + expected growth rate)]; P is the price of the asset; and $E(g)$ is the expected growth.

   B. *Example*: If the stock is selling at $50 and is expected to pay a $3 dividend, which is expected to grow 5 percent per year, then the expected return is

   $$\frac{\$3}{\$50} + 0.05 = 11\%$$

6. The after-tax return (see Topic 43, Section 12: After-tax yield) is calculated by multiplying the pretax rate by the quantity one minus the marginal tax bracket of the investor. For example, if an asset has a taxable return of 15 percent and the investor is in a 36 percent tax bracket, the after-tax return is $15(1 - 0.36) = 9.6$ percent.

7. Holding period return

   A. The holding period return (HPR) is the total return and is determined by taking the total return divided by the initial cost of the investment:

   $$HPR = \frac{P_1 - P_0 + D}{P_0}$$

   Where, P_1 is the sale price, P_0 is the purchase price, and D is the dividend paid.

   For example, if an individual buys a stock for $10 and collects a $1 dividend and later sells it for $15, the holding period is

   $$HPR = \frac{\$15 - \$10 + \$1}{\$10} = 60\%$$

   B. There is a major weakness in using the holding period. It does not consider how long it took to earn the return. This problem is evident if the stock paid annual dividends of $0.25, and the stock was sold at the end of the fourth year for $15. The return of 60 percent is higher than the true return.

8. Internal rate of return

   A. The internal rate of return is the discounted rate that makes the present value of the cash outflows equal to initial cash inflows such that the net present value is equal to zero.

   B. *Example*: Assume an investor bought a stock for $50 and sold the stock two years later at $65. The internal rate of return can be found using a calculator:

   $$PV = -\$50, FV = \$65, PMT = 0, N = 2 \rightarrow \text{solve for } I = 14.02\%$$

9. Yield to maturity

   A. The yield to maturity is the internal rate of return of a bond if held to maturity. It considers the current interest return and all price appreciation or depreciation. It is also a measure of risk and is the discount rate that equals the present value of all cash flows.

   B. From a firm perspective, it is the cost of borrowing by issuing new bonds. From an investor perspective, it is the internal rate of return that is received if the bond is held to maturity.

C. The yield to maturity can easily be solved using a financial calculator, in the same way as finding the internal rate of return. For example, assume a $1,000 par bond is priced at $950 with a 10 percent semiannual coupon payment. The bond matures in three years. The yield to maturity is found as follows:

$$N = 6; PV = -\$950; FV = \$1,000; PMT = \$50 \rightarrow \text{solve for } I = 6.01 \times 2 = 12.03\%$$

D. Yield to maturity (and internal rate of return) has a shortcoming: It assumes all cash flows are discounted at the same rate and are reinvested at the yield to maturity rate (IRR). If cash flows are not reinvested at the IRR, the realized return does not equal the IRR. This is defined as reinvestment risk.

10. Yield to call

A. The yield to call is used to determine the internal rate of return earned by the bond until it is called or retired by the firm. The yield to call is calculated in a similar way as is the yield to maturity, except

   (1) The expected call date is used in place of the known maturity date.
   (2) The principal plus call penalty is used in place of principal only.

B. Suppose a bond matures after 10 years and pays a 10 percent semiannual coupon rate and is selling for $925. The yield to maturity is 11.26 percent. An investor believes the bond will be called in five years at a penalty of $75 per $1,000 bond. The yield to call is calculated, using a financial calculator, as

$$N = 10, PV = -\$925, FV = \$1,075, PMT = \$50 \rightarrow \text{CPT YTC} = 6.60 \times 2 = 13.2\%$$

where N is the five-year call period multiplied by 2 (semiannual payments).

The yield to call is 13.2 percent, which is greater than the yield to maturity (11.26 percent) because the bond is selling at a discount, and it takes a greater return to erase the discount sooner; if the bond is selling at a premium, the yield to call is less than the yield to maturity because the premium is spread out over a smaller time horizon.

11. Current yield

A. The current yield considers only the coupon component of bonds. It does not include any reinvestment income or price appreciation or depreciation. The current yield is

$$\frac{\text{Annual coupon payment}}{\text{Price of bond}}$$

B. For example, assume a $1,000 par value bond priced at $950 with a 10 percent semiannual coupon rate. The current yield is

$$\frac{\$100}{\$950} = 10.5\%$$

C. The current yield is important to investors interested in income. Those investors who want high yearly income want bonds with a high current yield.

12. After-tax yield

A. The *after-tax yield* on a bond issue after paying taxes is computed as pretax yield on an equivalent but fully taxable bond $\times$ (1 − marginal tax rate).

B. The *taxable equivalent yield* (TEY) is calculated to determine the yield that must be earned on a taxable bond to equal the same yield for a tax-exempt municipal bond. It is calculated as

$$\text{Taxable equivalent yield} = \frac{\text{Tax-exempt yield}}{1 - \text{marginal tax rate}}$$

C. *Example*: Assume a municipal bond yields 4.3 percent. Assume a Treasury security is yielding 6.7 percent. The investor is in the 37 percent tax bracket. Which investment should be purchased?

   (1) The tax equivalent yield is

       (a) $4.3 \div (1 - 0.37) = 6.82\%$

       (b) Because 6.82 percent is greater than 6.7 percent, the investor should choose purchasing the municipal bond because it earns a higher taxable equivalent yield.

   (2) The after-tax yield is

       (a) $6.7\% \times (1 - 0.37) = 4.22\%$

       (b) 4.22 percent is less than 4.3 percent, so the choice again is to purchase the municipal bond. The two equations yield the same result.

13. Realized compound rate

   A. The realized compound rate on an asset is the actual return based on the present value of future cash flows. The realized compound rate is commonly known as the time value of money. The equation is

   $$P_0(1 + r)^n = P_n$$

   where P_0 is the purchase price of the security, r is the rate of return for the period, n is the number of periods, and P_n is the price at which the security is sold.

   B. To find the rate of return, assume a stock was purchased at $50 and later sold at the end of the fifth year at $90. The rate of return is easily solved using a calculator:

   $$PV = -\$50, FV = \$90, N = 5 \rightarrow \text{solve for } I = 12.47\%$$

14. Geometric return

   A. Another way to determine the rate of return over a period of years is to use the geometric average. The standard formula for the geometric average is

   $$G = [(1 + x_1)(1 + x_2) \ldots (1 + X_\infty)]^{1/x} - 1$$

   B. Calculate the geometric average using the annual rate of returns:

Year	Return
1	15%
2	20%
3	−10%
4	−5%
5	15%

   In this example, the returns are redefined to make them positive. This is done by adding 1.0 to the returns. The term $(1 + R_t)$ represents the year ending value relative to the initial investment at the beginning of the year. The calculation is

   $$[(1.15)(1.20)(0.90)(0.95)(1.15)]^{1/5} - 1 = 6.29\%$$

TOPIC 44: TIME-INFLUENCED SECURITY VALUATION CONCEPTS

Note: For present value, future value, and internal rate of return (IRR), see Topic 14.

1. Bond duration

   A. Duration is the average time it takes to capture interest and principal repayments. It seeks to compare bonds with different coupons and maturities by determining how sensitive the price of each bond is to interest rate changes.
   B. Bonds exhibit more price volatility the longer the term to maturity. If two bonds have the same coupon, the bond with the greater maturity will have the longer duration. Low coupon bonds are generally more volatile than high coupon bonds. If two bonds have the same maturity, the bond with the lower coupon will have the longer duration.
   C. The process gets a little more complex for a bond with a shorter (longer) maturity and smaller (larger) coupon. For bonds with different maturities and coupon rates, using duration is an excellent technique for determining which bond is more volatile to changes in interest rates.
   D. The bond with the longer duration will decline more in price with an increase in interest rates; the bond with the longer duration will increase more in price with a decrease in interest rates.
   E. To illustrate how duration is determined, consider a 10 percent semiannual three-year bond. The current interest rate on similar bonds is 12 percent. The bond is currently selling for $950.82. The cash flows are as follows:

Year	Payment
0.5	$50
1.0	$50
1.5	$50
2.0	$50
2.5	$50
3.0	$1,050

   F. The duration of a bond is the sum of the present value of cash flows weighted by a time period (t) in which the payment is received. All individual present values are summed and then divided by the current price of the bond. The following demonstrates this relationship:

Period (t)	Interest	Cash Flow	Solve Present Value (PV)	PV $\times t$
1	6%	$50	$47.17	$47.17
2	6%	$50	$44.50	$90.00
3	6%	$50	$41.98	$125.94
4	6%	$50	$39.60	$158.40
5	6%	$50	$37.36	$186.81
6	6%	$1,050	$740.21	$4,441.25
Sum =				$5,048.57

$$\text{Duration} = \frac{\$5,048.57}{\$950.82} = 5.30 \div 2 = 2.65 \text{ years}$$

G. Because of semiannual compounding: Annual payment and interest rate are divided by 2, the number of payments is multiplied by 2, and duration of 5.30 is divided by 2.

H. The duration of 2.65 years means that the investor collects on average all interest and principal repayment within 2.65 years. Keep in mind that not all payments are received at 2.65 years. Duration represents the weighted average of all payments. Therefore, duration is not the sum of all present values (which is the price of the bond). The longer the term to maturity, the more weight put on the calculation.

I. Duration can be precisely defined as the approximate percentage change in the price of a bond to a small change in interest rates. More specifically, duration is the approximate percentage change in price with a 100 basis point change in interest rates. Therefore, duration of 2.65 means that the price of a bond will change approximately 2.65 percent with a 100 basis point change in interest rates.

J. For large changes in yield (50 or more basis points), duration tends to *underestimate the increase in price* that occurs with a decrease in yield, and *overestimate the decrease in price* that comes with an increase in yield.

2. Bond convexity

A. The price-yield relationship can be represented by a tangent line. The tangent line shows the rate of change in price to changes in yield. The slope of the tangent line is one basis point. The tangent line is strongly related to duration. In fact, duration is used interchangeably with a tangent line because both estimate the rate of change in price. There is more duration the steeper the tangent line and less duration the flatter the tangent line.

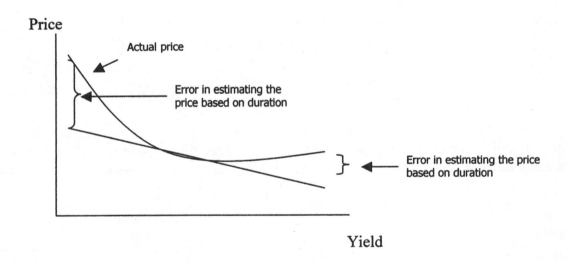

B. There is an interesting relationship between duration (tangent line) and the approximate change in price. The actual price change is greater than the estimated price change when yields decrease; the actual price change is less than the estimated price change when yields increase.

C. Duration becomes less exact with greater changes in yields because the price-yield relationship is not linear, but curved. How curved the path actually is depends on the degree of convexity. The distance between the tangent line (estimated price) and the curvature of the actual path (actual price) is the error in estimating price based on duration. If the degree of convexity is measured, the price of a bond can be estimated with more accuracy.

D. Duration is used to approximate the first percentage change in price. Convexity is used to approximate the second and is added to duration.

TOPIC 45: BOND AND STOCK VALUATION METHODS

1. Capitalized earnings

   A. *Capitalization* treats earnings and dividends as a perpetuity. Preferred stock is a perpetual debt instrument. Its dividends continue indefinitely because there is no maturity on preferred stock. The value of preferred stock is the present value of its dividends discounted at the appropriate interest rate over an infinite period of time. The value of a preferred stock is

   (1) $V_p = \dfrac{D}{k}$

   (2) *Example*: Assume a preferred stock pays an annual dividend of $2 per share. The discount rate for comparable preferred stock is 8 percent. The present value of a share is

       (a) $V_p = \dfrac{\$2}{0.08} = \$25$

       (b) An investor is paying too much if the preferred stock is purchased for more than $25 per share; the stock is relatively cheap if it is trading under $25 per share.

   B. The value of a bond is also found through capitalization. The price of a bond is the present value of future cash flows discounted at the appropriate interest rate.

   (1) The price of a bond is found with a calculator. *Example*: Firm A has issued a five-year bond with a 10 percent coupon and a face value of $1,000. The interest rate for competitive bonds with a similar length of time to maturity and credit risk is 7 percent. Interest is paid annually. The value of the bonds is determined by

       (a) FV = $1,000, PMT = $100, $N = 5$, I = 7 → solve for PV

       (b) The present value of the bond is $1,123, so it is selling at a premium (higher price than the face value) because the bond is paying a 10 percent interest rate, whereas the current market interest rate is only 7 percent.

   (2) If other competitive bonds are paying a current interest rate of 12 percent, the 10 percent coupon is less attractive to bondholders. They are not willing to pay $1,000 for a bond paying a 10 percent interest rate when they can pay the same price for other competitive bonds yielding 12 percent. The price of the bond must drop to yield 12 percent. The calculation is

       (a) FV = $1,000, PMT = $100, $N = 5$, I = 12 → solve for PV

       (b) The price of the bond is $927.90. The bond is said to be selling at a discount (lower price than face value). In this situation, an investor will be competitive with similar bonds and yield 12 percent on the investment.

   (3) Bonds generally pay interest twice a year (semiannually) instead of once a year. The equation previously presented is modified slightly by adjusting the total number of periods and the amount of each payment. The total number of periods becomes 10 (2 × 5 years), the amount of payment is $50 ($100 coupon ÷ 2), and the yield becomes 6 percent (12% ÷ 2). The calculation is as follows: FV = $1,000, PMT = $50, $N = 10$, I = 6 → solve for PV = − $926.39.

2. Dividend growth models

   A. Valuing stock with no dividend growth

   (1) This model uses the same equation as that used to value a preferred stock. The only difference is the required rate of return on the common stock, which tends to account for more risk than that of a preferred stock.

(2) $V = \dfrac{D_0}{k}$

B. Stock value, assuming a one-year holding period

  (1) The value of a stock is the present value of any dividend received during the year, plus the present value of the price of stock at the end of the year. The valuation equation is

$$V = \frac{\text{Dividend to be received}}{(1 + k_e)^1} + \frac{\text{Year-end sale price}}{(1 + k_e)^1}$$

  (2) *Example*: What is the value of a stock that last year paid a $1 dividend that is expected to grow 10 percent next year? The stock will be selling at $25 at year end. The risk-free rate of interest is 4 percent, the market return is 10 percent, and the stock's beta is 1.2.

    (a) *Step 1*. Solve for the discount rate. $K_{\text{stock}} = 4\% + (10\% - 4\%)1.1 = 10.6\%$.

    (b) *Step 2*. Add the future dividend to future stock price. $D_1 = \$1(1.1) = \$1.10$, so add future value of stock and dividend to get $26.10 ($1.10 + $25).

    (c) *Step 3*. Find the present value. $\dfrac{\$26.10}{(1 + 0.106)^1} = \$23.59$.

C. Valuing stock with constant dividend growth

  (1) The constant growth dividend discount model assumes that dividends may increase at a fixed rate on an annual basis in the future. *Example*: If the latest dividend is $1 and dividends grow at an annual rate of 5 percent, the dividend next year is

    (a) $\$1(1 + 0.05)^1 = \$1.05$

    (b) The dividend in the second year is $\$1(1 + 0.05)^2 = \$1.10$.

    (c) The pattern of 5 percent growth is expected to continue into the future.

  (2) The value of a common stock with a constant rate of growth can be determined by

$$V = \frac{D_0(1 + g)}{k - g} \text{ or } \frac{D_1}{k - g}$$

where D_0 is the latest dividend paid per share, D_1 is the expected dividend per share for year 1, k is the required rate of return on the stock, and g is the expected growth rate of dividends.

  (3) *Example*: What is the value of a stock that paid a $2 dividend last year, which is expected to grow annually at 5 percent? The risk-free rate is 4 percent and the expected return on the market is 10 percent. The stock's beta is 1.7.

    (a) *Step 1*. Determine k by using CAPM.

$$k_{\text{stock}} = R_{\text{risk free}} + \text{beta}_{\text{stock}} (R_{\text{market}} - R_{\text{risk free}})$$
$$k_{\text{stock}} = 4\% + 1.7(10\% - 4\%) = 14.2\%$$

    (b) *Step 2*. Use the constant dividend discount model.

$$V_0 = \frac{\$2(1 + 0.05)}{0.142 - 0.05} = \$22.82$$

    (c) If the stock is bought at a lower price than $22.82, its expected return will exceed 14.2 percent. If the stock is bought at a higher price than $22.82, its expected return will not exceed 14.2 percent. For example, if the stock price is currently $25, the

expected return is $(E(r)) = \dfrac{\$2}{\$25} + 0.05 = 13\%$.

(4) The constant growth dividend discount model (DDM) has the following assumptions:

    (a) The stock pays dividends, and they grow constantly forever.

    (b) The constant growth rate continues for an infinite period.

    (c) k must be greater than g.

D. Temporary supernormal growth

    (1) Some companies have supergrowth in the early years that levels out in later years. For these companies, k is less than g. Therefore, the constant growth DDM does not work.

$$\text{Value}_{\text{supernormal growth}} = \frac{D_1}{(1+k)} + \frac{D_2}{(1+k)^2} - \cdots + \frac{\dfrac{D(n+1)}{(k-g)}}{(1+ke)^n}$$

    (2) *Example*: For years 1 through 4, $g = 25$ percent; for years 5 on, $g = 5$ percent; $D_1 = \$1$, and $k = 10$ percent. Solve for the stock's value.

    (a) *Step 1*. Project dividends into the future:

        $D_1 = \$1$, $D_2 = \$1.25$, $D_3 = 1.56$, $D_4 = 1.95$, $D_5 = \$2.04$

    (b) *Step 2*. Find the value of the stock at the end of year 4, using D_5:

        $V_4 = D_5/(k-g) = \$2.04/(0.10 - 0.05) = \$40.80$

    (c) Find the present value using the supernormal growth model:

$$\frac{1.00}{(1+0.10)} + \frac{1.25}{(1+0.10)^2} + \frac{1.56}{(1+0.10)^3} + \frac{1.95}{(1+0.10)^4} + \frac{40.80}{(1+0.10)^4} = \$32.31$$

    Note: The present value of $40.80 is found by discounting four periods, not five periods, because the stock price was found at the end of year 4.

3. Ratio analysis

  A. Price/earnings

    (1) The price/earnings (P/E) ratio (earnings multiplier) is used to determine the value of a stock. The earnings multiplier tells an investor the price being paid for each \$1 of earnings. For example, a stock earning \$5 per share with a 15 P/E means an investor is willing to pay \$75 a share for the stock.

    (2) The expected earnings multiplier is used to value a stock by estimating earnings for the next 12 months. The equation becomes:

    P_0 = Current market price $= \dfrac{E_1 \times P_0}{E_1}$

    (3) The P/E ratio is really just a reinstatement of the dividend discount model. The firm's dividend is related to earnings and the proportion distributed. In dividing both sides of the formula by expected earnings for the next 12 months, E_1, the result is

    (a) $\dfrac{P_0}{E_1} = \dfrac{\dfrac{D_1}{E_1}}{k-g}$

    (b) The previous formula shows that a P/E ratio depends on the same factors to value a stock as those achieved through the use of the dividend discount model. The factors include (1) the dividend payout ratio (dividend divided by earnings, D/E), (2) the required rate of return (k), and (3) the expected growth rate of dividends (g).

(4) *Advantage*: P/E ratio can be applied to stocks that are not paying cash dividends. The dividend discount model assumes the firm is paying or is going to pay a cash dividend.

(5) *Disadvantage*: P/E ratio does not tell whether a stock is overvalued or undervalued to its market price. Investors are required to draw inferences to historical P/E ratios in determining if the P/E ratio is high or low. The dividend discount model allows for comparison to determine whether a stock is overvalued or undervalued to its actual price.

(6) The estimated value of a stock can be determined by using the P/E ratio and applying it to estimated earnings for the next year (E_1).

(7) *Example*: A firm has an expected payout ratio of 50 percent, a required rate of return of 11 percent, and an expected dividend growth rate of 6 percent. Earnings for the current year (E_0) are $2.00. The *future earnings multiplier* is computed as

(a) $P/E_{future\ ratio} = \dfrac{0.50}{0.11 - 0.06} = 10\times$

(b) Current earnings are $2.00 and g is 6 percent, so earnings per share$_{estimate}$ = 2.00(1.06) = $2.12.

(c) The future value of the stock is estimated as $V_1 = (EPS_{estimate}) \times (P/E_{future}) = \$2.12 \times 10 = \$21.20$.

(8) Compare this estimated value (end of year 1) of the stock to its market price to determine whether the stock should be bought or sold—the price and ending dividend must be discounted by the required rate of return of 11 percent. If the present value of the future stock price and dividend payment are greater than the current market price, the stock is undervalued and should be bought. If the present value of the future stock value and dividend payments are less than the current market price, the stock is overpriced and should be avoided.

(9) There is a relationship between the P/E ratio and all components of the dividend discount model. First, the higher the payout ratio, the higher the P/E. Second, the higher the expected growth rate, g, the higher the P/E. Finally, the higher the required rate of return, k, the lower the P/E. The spread between k and g is the main determinant of the P/E ratio, but the dividend payout ratio does have an impact. The expected (P_0/E_1) earnings multiplier is what should be used when valuing stocks, not the historical (P_0/E_0) ratio.

B. Price/free cash flows

(1) The price to cash flow ratio is defined as the market value divided by per-share cash flow.

(2) This ratio is often used in conjunction with the P/E ratio, because emphasis is placed on growth in cash flows versus earnings; earnings are often subject to accounting manipulation, whereas cash flows are often more stable. Cash flows are often used to predict financial strength and potential problems.

C. Price/sales

(1) This ratio is defined as the firm's stock price divided by its per-share sales.

(2) *Advantages*: The ratio is meaningful for distressed firms; sales figures are not as easily manipulated as earnings; less volatile than P/E multiples. *Disadvantage*: It can distort valuation when earnings drop.

(3) A low P/S ratio indicates low valuation, whereas a high P/S ratio indicates high valuation.

D. Price/earnings/growth (PEG)

(1) PEG is calculated by dividing the P/E ratio by the estimated earnings growth rate. If dividends are significant, add the dividend yield to the growth rate when calculating the PEG ratio.

(2) It indicates the price the market placed on earning expectations.

4. Intrinsic value

A. Intrinsic value is the underlying value that a careful evaluation would produce.

B. An efficient market would always price stocks at their intrinsic value; an inefficient market would not necessarily do so.

C. Under the dividend discount model, the intrinsic value of stock is the present value of the stock's expected future dividends, discounted at the stock's required rate of return.

D. If a stock trades above its intrinsic value, the stock should be sold. If a stock trades below its intrinsic value, the stock should be bought.

5. Book value

A. Book value is stockholder's equity divided by outstanding shares. Stockholder's equity includes the sum of stock, additional paid-in capital, and retained earnings on a firm's balance sheet.

B. Value investors pick stocks that trade below book value.

C. The price/book value is defined as the firm's stock price divided by its per-share book value.

(1) A low ratio suggests that a stock is undervalued; a high ratio suggests that it is overvalued.

(2) What is considered high or low is up to the discretion of the analyst, but should be used in comparison with other stocks. It has become an important measure of relative value among stocks.

TOPIC 46: PORTFOLIO MANAGEMENT AND MEASUREMENT CONCEPTS

1. Portfolio theory

A. Understanding the relationship between portfolio risk and correlation is the key to modern portfolio theory.

B. Markowitz portfolio theory is based on several important assumptions. Under these assumptions, a portfolio is considered to be efficient if no other portfolio offers a higher expected return with the same (or lower) risk or if no other portfolio offers lower risk with the same (or higher) return.

(1) Investors view investment alternatives as being represented by a probability distribution of expected returns over the same holding period.

(2) Investors maximize their one-period expected utility.

(3) Investors estimate risk of a portfolio on the basis of variability of expected returns.

(4) Investors base all decisions on expected return and risk.

(5) For a given level of risk, investors prefer higher returns to lower returns, or for a given return level, investors prefer less risk to more risk.

C. The standard deviation of a portfolio is less than the weighted average standard deviation of the individual stocks in the portfolio. An exception exists if the correlation coefficient of the stocks in the portfolio is +1; then the standard deviation of the portfolio is equal to the simple weighted standard deviations of the individual stocks in the portfolio.

D. The covariance of returns between stocks must be found in order to determine the standard deviation of a portfolio. Recall that the covariance of two stocks is $(\text{cov}_{1,2}) = (r_{1,2})(\sigma_1)(\sigma_2)$. This can be rearranged to find the correlation coefficient, which is $r_{1,2} = (\text{cov}_{1,2})/\sigma_1\sigma_2$.

E. The standard deviation of a two-stock portfolio is

$$\sigma \text{ portfolio} = (W_1^2\sigma_1^2 + W_2^2\sigma_2^2 + 2W_1W_2\sigma_1\sigma_2 r_{1,2})^{1/2}$$

F. Note that the correlation impacts only the risk of a portfolio. The equation for expected return for a two-stock portfolio is unchanged. $W_1ER_2 + W_2ER_2$.

G. When you combine stocks of equal returns and equal risk, but change the correlation coefficient to less than +1, the return is constant but the risk is less. Portfolio risk declines when the $r_{1,2}$ goes from +1 to −1. In fact, at −1 there would be no risk. As correlation decreases, diversification increases.

H. What we learn from modern portfolio theory is that the correlation coefficient is the engine that drives the whole theory of portfolio diversification. The lower the correlation coefficient, the greater the diversification.

I. Markowitz (father of the Portfolio Theory) constructed the *efficient frontier*. The efficient frontier represents a set of portfolios that will give an investor the highest return at each level of risk (or the lowest risk for each level of return).

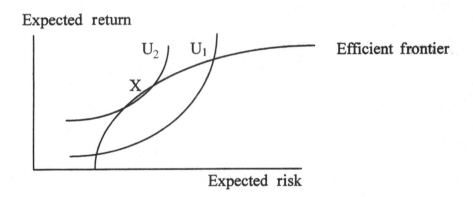

J. Combining the efficient frontier and an investor's indifference curve (U_2, U_1) map indicates which efficient portfolio satisfies the investor's risk/return trade-off. The *optimal portfolio* (point X) for an investor is the highest indifference curve that is tangent to the efficient frontier. The optimal portfolio gives the investor the greatest possible utility. Steep indifference curves represent a conservative investor, and flat indifference curves indicate a less risk-averse investor.

2. Capital market theory

   A. Capital market theory starts where Markowitz left off.
   B. Assumptions to capital market theory

      (1) All investors are Markowitz efficient investors who want to target points on the efficient frontier.
      (2) Investors can borrow and lend any amount of money at the risk-free rate of return.
      (3) All investors have the same homogeneous expectations—they see the same risk/return distribution and cannot buy below the capital market line.
      (4) All investors have the same one-period time horizon.

(5) All investments are infinitely divisible—meaning that it is possible to buy and sell fractional shares of any asset or portfolio.

(6) There are no taxes or transaction costs.

(7) There is no inflation and no interest rates changes.

(8) Capital markets are in equilibrium.

C. The combination of a risk-free asset and a risky asset produces a *linear* risk/return line.

D. The linear (straight) efficient frontier line is called the capital market line (CML). Any two assets falling on this line will be perfectly positively correlated with each other.

E. You can get better portfolios by moving up the efficient frontier until you reach point *M*, which is the best combination (see following graph). Investors hold the risk-free asset and portfolio *M* between R_f and *M*. This means that investors are lending some of their funds at the risk-free rate (buying the risk-free asset). To the right of *M*, investors hold more than 100 percent of portfolio *M*. This means that they are borrowing funds to buy more assets (buying on margin).

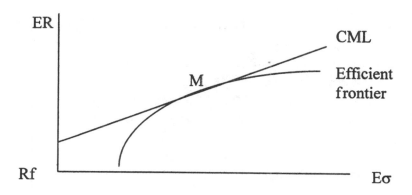

F. The CML tells us that all investors will hold some combination of the risk-free asset and portfolio *M*. Portfolio *M*, called the *market portfolio*, is held by all investors and contains all stocks, bonds, and risky assets in existence. The market portfolio represents the ultimate or completely diversified portfolio.

G. All securities below the CML are inefficient, and according to capital market theory, no one will buy them (all investors have homogeneous expectations), but casual observation tells us that someone will own a security below the CML. The problem is that we have not correctly specified our measure of risk by using standard deviation (unsystematic risk is not rewarded).

H. The proper risk/return relationship is not total risk and return but, rather, systematic risk and return. To quantify the risk/return relationship, we must measure systematic risk. Beta then becomes the measure of risk because it measures only systematic risk.

I. The security market line (SML) uses beta to plot risk. It is a linear line that replaces the CML. The equation of the SML is CAPM.

3. Performance measures

A. Sharpe ratio

(1) Relative measure of the risk-adjusted performance of a portfolio based on *total risk* (= systematic + nonsystematic risk)

(2) Standard deviation (σ) is used as the measure for total risk.

(3) Because Sharpe uses standard deviation, it implies that the portfolio is *not* widely diversified. It is appropriate in working with a smaller portfolio.

(4) Because this is a relative measure, the Sharpe index must be used to compare alternative investments. *Note*: In comparing, *bigger is better*.

(5) If the portfolio is fully diversified (all nonsystematic risk has been eliminated), then the Sharpe index should yield similar results for a comparison of several investments as the Treynor index.

(6) The Sharpe ratio is calculated as

$$S_i = \frac{r_p - r_f}{\sigma}$$

where r_p is the portfolio rate of return, r_f is the risk-free rate of return, and σ is the standard deviation of the portfolio.

B. Treynor ratio

(1) Relative measure of the risk-adjusted performance of a portfolio based on the market risk (i.e., the systematic risk); therefore, use with diversified portfolios.

(2) Risk is measured by the beta coefficient (β).

(3) If the portfolio is fully diversified (all nonsystematic risk has been eliminated), then both indices (Sharpe and Treynor) should yield the same results, because diversification will eliminate all unsystematic risk from the portfolio.

(4) Because this is a relative measure, the Treynor index must be used to compare alternative investments. In comparing, if the $T_i \geq 0$, that is *good*; if < 0, that is *no good*.

(5) The Treynor index should be computed for the market to determine whether a particular portfolio has outperformed the market. The results do not indicate by how much each portfolio outperformed the market.

(6) The Treynor ratio is calculated as

$$T_i = \frac{r_p - r_f}{\text{beta}}$$

where r_p is the realized return of the portfolio and r_f is the risk-free rate of return.

C. Jensen ratio

(1) Alpha, α, is an absolute measure of performance and measures how well a managed portfolio performed relative to an unmanaged portfolio of equal risk.

(2) It determines how much the realized return differs from the required return. The following formula is used to find alpha:

$$\alpha = r_p - [r_f + (r_m - r_f) \text{ beta}]$$

(3) In the equation, the α (referred to as alpha) value indicates whether a portfolio manager is superior or inferior in market timing and stock selection. A positive alpha indicates a superior manager, and a negative alpha indicates an inferior manager.

(4) *Example*: Assume a return of 15 percent with a beta of 1.2 for manager X when the market return is 14.3 percent and the risk-free rate is 7 percent. The alpha is expressed as

(a) $\alpha = 0.15 - [0.07 + (0.143 - 0.07)1.2] = -0.0076$

(b) This indicates inferior performance because it is negative. If portfolio manager Y earns a return of 12.5 percent with a beta of 0.7, then the alpha is expressed as
$\alpha = 0.125 - [0.07 + (0.143 - 0.07)0.7] = 0.0039$

(c) This indicates superior performance because it is positive. The absolute return for manager X is higher, but the risk-adjusted return for manager Y is greater, denoting superior performance. Manager Y not only outperformed manager X but also outperformed the market return on a risk-adjusted basis. In the example, portfolio X performed 0.76 percent less than the market, whereas portfolio Y performed 0.39 percent better than the market.

4. Investment policy statement

  A. An investment policy statement (IPS) creates a structure for making investment decisions and managing the investor's portfolio.

   (1) Establishes risk and return objectives
   (2) Determines constraints—time horizon, tax consequences, liquidity needs, regulations, and unique client needs
   (3) Establishes a standard of agreed-upon goals and other criteria against which investment performance can be measured
   (4) Reduces professional liability exposure by documenting that prudent procedures were followed in making investment decisions

  B. An IPS should be created for each individual client.

5. Appropriate benchmarks—Performance measurements of a portfolio are from the perspective of the entire portfolio's composition or from security classes and segments of the portfolio. It is appropriate to compare a large cap growth fund against the Standard & Poor's (S&P) 500 Index. It would *not* be appropriate to compare a small cap fund against the S&P 500 Index. Planners should make a careful analysis to determine the appropriate benchmark(s) when tracking the return for a portfolio.

6. Dollar- versus time-weighted rate of return

  A. *Dollar-weighted rate of return.* It applies the concept of internal rate of return (IRR) to investment portfolios. The dollar-weighted rate of return is defined as the internal rate of return of a portfolio, taking into account all cash inflows and outflows.

   (1) *Example*: Assume an investor buys one share of stock for $50 at the beginning of the first year, and buys another share for $55 at the end of the first year. The investor earns $1 in dividends in the first year and $2 in the second year. What is the dollar-weighted rate of return if the shares are sold at the end of the second year for $65 each?
   (2) *Step 1.* There are two cash outflows: $50 at time period $t = 0$ and $55 at time period $t = 1$. There are also two cash inflows: $1 at time period $t = 1$ and $132 ($2 dividends plus $130 proceeds) at time period $t = 2$.
   (3) *Step 2.* Group net cash flow by time. The $t = 0$ net cash flow is -50, the $t = 1$ net cash flow is -54 ($-\$55 + 1$), and the $t = 2$ net cash flow is $132 ($130 + $2). The net cash flows can be entered on the calculator to solve the IRR.
   (4) $-50[CF_0]$; $-54[CF_j]$; $132 [CF_j] \rightarrow [IRR] = 17.21\%$

  B. *Time-weighted rate of return.* This method does not weigh the amount of all dollar flows during each time period. It computes the return for each period and takes the average of the results. It finds the holding period for each period and averages them. If the investment is for more than one year, take the geometric mean of the annual returns to find the time-weighted rate of return for the measurement period. Looking back at the previous example:

Holding period 1	($55 − $50 + $1) ÷ $50 = 12%
Holding period 2	($130 − $110 + $2) ÷ $110 = 20%
The geometric return	$[(1.12)(1.20)]^{1/2} - 1 = 15.9\%$

C. In the investment management industry, the time-weighted return is the preferred method of performance measurement because it is not affected by the timing of cash flows. If a client adds funds to an investment portfolio at an unfavorable time, the dollar-weighted return will tend to be depressed. If funds are added at a favorable time, the dollar-weighted return will tend to be elevated.

D. As indicated in the previous example, the time-weighted rate of return is less than the dollar-weighted rate of return because the stock performed better in the second year when the investor owned more shares. If the stock performed better in the first year rather than the second year when the investor had fewer shares, the time-weighted return would have been more than the dollar-weighted return.

7. Probability analysis, including Monte Carlo

A. Monte Carlo simulation is a mathematical technique for numerically solving differential equations. The technique tends to be computer intensive.

B. To understand how the process works, consider an example of how a complex option might be priced. Suppose the option's value is dependent on two underliers, a stock index and an exchange rate. Monte Carlo simulation might be used to price such an option as follows:

(1) Randomly generate 10,000 scenarios for the value, on the option's expiration date, of the two underliers. Do so in a manner that is consistent with an assumed (risk neutral) joint probability distribution of the two variables.

(2) Determine what the option's expiration value would be in each of the 10,000 scenarios.

(3) Form a histogram of those results. This represents a discrete approximation for the probability distribution of the option's expiration value. The discounted mean of the histogram is the estimated option price.

C. Note that this solution yields only an approximate price. By using more scenarios—say 20,000 instead of 10,000—the precision of the result can be improved.

D. A probability distribution is a mathematical function that describes the probabilities of possible events in a sample space. The sum probability of all the possible events in the sample space must equal 1.

TOPIC 47: FORMULA INVESTING

1. Dollar cost averaging

A. Dollar cost averaging is the process of purchasing securities over a period of time by periodically investing a predetermined amount at regular intervals.

B. The goal of dollar cost averaging is to reduce the effects of price fluctuations. When the market is rising, additional shares will benefit from the price increases. When the market is declining, the additional shares purchased will be purchased at lower prices and will yield more shares per dollar invested.

2. Dividend reinvestment plans (DRIP)

A. Shareholders have cash dividends automatically reinvested in additional shares of the firm's common stock. The cost of doing this is low or none.

B. Dividends that are reinvested are treated the same for tax purposes as a dividend received in the form of cash. These dividends, like other dividends, will be reported to the IRS on Form 1099-DIV.

3. Bond ladders

A. A bond ladder is the purchase of bonds with maturities distributed over a period of time. It is created to reduce interest rate risk. *Example*: A $100,000 bond portfolio would require $10,000 worth of bonds that mature each year for 10 years. If interest rates change, the price of bonds with shorter maturities (maturities of 1 to 5 years) will fluctuate less than the price of bonds with greater maturities (maturities of 6 to 10 years).

B. Bond ladders provide three primary benefits:

(1) Interest rate risk is less than that of a portfolio of longer-term maturities.

(2) Interest earned on the portfolio is greater than that of a portfolio of shorter-term maturities.

(3) Cash is available each year when a short-term bond matures.

C. Bond ladders also have a disadvantage: If an investor anticipates a change in interest rates and wants to alter the portfolio, then virtually all the bonds have to be sold.

4. Bond barbells

A. Barbells constitute a strategy of acquiring a portfolio of very long term maturities and very short term maturities. For example, a $100,000 bond portfolio would require $50,000 in bonds that have short-term maturities (6 months to 1 year) and $50,000 in bonds with long-term maturities (20 to 30 years). In this way, an investor needs to sell only half a portfolio in order to adjust to any anticipation of interest rate moves.

B. A barbell strategy will reduce the impact of fluctuating interest rates if an investor correctly anticipates the rate change. It will magnify the impact if the investor is incorrect.

TOPIC 48: INVESTMENT STRATEGIES

1. Market timing (active investing)

A. Market timing is the active management of a portfolio. An investor anticipates the direction of economic conditions and stock prices and adjusts his or her portfolio to these changes.

B. Market timing is in direct conflict with the efficient market hypothesis.

C. The more an investor believes that markets are inefficient, the greater the argument for a market timing strategy.

2. Passive investing

A. Investors are typically not attempting to outperform the market. Rather, investors are looking to immunize their portfolios in an effort to lock in specified rates of return (or terminal values) they deem acceptable, given the risks involved. These strategies do not generate significant transaction costs.

B. A passive asset allocation begins by setting specific percentages for each asset class. These percentages for a passive strategy should be maintained over time; the portfolio will require rebalancing every six months or so.

3. Fundamental analysis

A. Fundamental analysis is the evaluation of a firm and its investment attractiveness based on the firm's financial strength, competitiveness, earnings outlook, managerial strength, and sensitivity to the macroeconomy and industry effects.

B. A top-down approach is used in fundamental analysis. It involves picking the best stocks within the most promising industries in the individual's economic forecast for inclusion in the portfolio. Steps include (1) determining general economic influences, (2) determining industry influences, and (3) company analysis.

4. Buy and hold

   A. Investors hold on to their securities to minimize transaction costs because they do not believe that active management adds any additional returns to their portfolios. For bond investing, investors look for vehicles whose maturities (or duration) approximate their stipulated investment horizon in order to reduce price and reinvestment risk.

   B. A buy-and-hold strategy should not be confused with a passive strategy. With a passive strategy, the asset allocation percentages are maintained over time by rebalancing the portfolio. A buy-and-hold strategy does not rebalance a portfolio.

   C. The purchase of index funds is an example of a buy-and-hold strategy. These funds attempt to match the makeup of an index, such as the S&P 500.

5. Portfolio immunization

   A. Immunization allows an investor to earn a specified rate of return on a bond portfolio regardless of the direction of interest rates. The investor becomes immunized to changes in interest rates over a time horizon.

   B. Active rebalancing of bonds ensures that the duration of a portfolio always equals the investor's time horizon.

   C. Two methods for immunizing a portfolio:

      (1) Purchasing a series of zero-coupon bonds whose maturities correspond with the planning horizon

      (2) Assembling and managing a bond portfolio whose duration is kept equal to the planning horizon. The portfolio of bonds must be rebalanced whenever interest rates change.

   D. Duration declines more slowly than the term to maturity; if interest rates do not change, a bond portfolio may still need to be rebalanced to correspond to the investor's time horizon. Only zero coupon bonds have a duration that decreases at the same rate as their term to maturity.

6. Swaps

   A. A swap is a technique for managing a bond portfolio by selling some bonds and buying others with the proceeds, in order to achieve benefits in the form of tax treatment, yields, maturity structure, or trading profits.

   B. There are several types of swaps.

      (1) *Substitution swap.* The swapping of bonds with virtually identical characteristics (i.e., same maturity, coupon, credit rating, and call and sinking funds) selling at different yields. The price difference is viewed as an arbitrage opportunity.

      (2) *Intermarket spread (sector) swap.* This is a variation of a substitution swap. It is used when the difference in yield between two markets is excessive. An investor may swap a government bond for a triple-A–rated corporate bond if the yield is more favorable.

      (3) *Pure-yield pickup swap.* The sale of a low-yield bond and purchase of a high-yield bond. The swap is usually for a bond with a longer maturity or lower quality in order to benefit from a higher yield.

      (4) *Rate anticipation swap.* Seeks to take advantage or avoid the impact of an expected change in interest rates. If higher interest rates are anticipated, an investor will swap longer-term maturities for shorter-term maturities; if lower rates are anticipated, short-term maturities are swapped for long-term maturities.

      (5) *Tax swap.* An investor attempts to take advantage of locking into a loss by selling a bond and buying a similar bond.

7. Technical analysis

  A. Underlying assumptions of technical analysis

    (1) Prices are determined by supply and demand.
    (2) Supply and demand are driven by rational and irrational behavior.
    (3) Security prices move in trends that persist for long periods of time.
    (4) The actual shift in supply and demand can be observed in market price behavior.

  B. The major challenge of technical analysis is the efficient frontier hypothesis. Efficient markets assume that new information will cause instantaneous price adjustments, past technical relationships cannot be repeated, technical analysis requires too much subjective interpretation, and decision variables change over time.

  C. Technicians believe that the speed with which new information is impounded into prices is slow, whereas fundamentalists believe that prices adjust quickly, and efficient market hypothesis analysts believe it happens almost instantaneously.

  D. There are two types of views.

    (1) *Contrarians* follow the rule of doing the opposite to what the general investor does. Therefore, contrarians believe the majority of traders, investors, and institutional advisers are wrong most of the time.
    (2) *Smart money traders* follow a different logic from contrary opinion technicians. They follow the money movement of what they consider to be sophisticated traders.

  E. Contrarians use the following tools:

    (1) Mutual fund cash positions
    (2) Investor credit balances in brokerage accounts
    (3) Investment advisory opinion
    (4) Over the counter (OTC) versus New York Stock Exchange (NYSE) volume
    (5) Chicago Board Options Exchange (CBOE) put/call ratio

  F. Smart money traders use the following tools:

    (1) The Confidence Index
    (2) T-bill yields and Eurodollar rates
    (3) Short sales by specialists
    (4) Margin debit balances in brokerage accounts

  G. The *Confidence Index* (CI) is found in *Barron's* and is the ratio of Barron's average yield on 10 top-grade corporate bonds to the yield on the Dow-Jones average of 40 bonds. This is given by

    (1) $$CI = \frac{\text{Barron's average yield on 10 top-grade corporate bonds}}{\text{Dow-Jones average of 40 bonds}}$$

    (2) The Confidence Index measures the difference between high-quality bonds and a large cross section of bonds. It is also stated as

    $$CI = \frac{\text{Quality bond yield}}{\text{Average bond yield}}$$

    (3) The Confidence Index rises during periods of confidence as the yield spread narrows and drops during periods of pessimism as the yield spread widens. Therefore, the Confidence Index moves in the opposite direction of yield spreads.

  H. Market indicators used in technical analysis

    (1) *Dow Theory*

(a) Recognizes three movements in security markets: major trends, intermediate trends, and short-term trends. Major trends are broad market movements lasting several years. Intermediate trends, occurring within a major trend, are influenced through current events and resemble waves lasting for several weeks or months. Short-term trends are daily ripples that have no significance.

(b) It is up to the technician to properly calculate the direction of a major trend. The term *bull market* is used for an upward major trend, and the term *bear market* is used for a downward major trend. Bull markets exist when upward rallies pass prior highs and declines stay above previous lows.

(2) *Importance of volume.* Price movement alone does not tell how widespread the excess demand or supply is for a security. This is where volume comes into play. Low volume tells us nothing about market movement. High volume tells the extent of interest in and demand for a stock. A price increase on high volume is a very bullish indicator, whereas a price decrease on strong volume is a very bearish indicator.

(3) *Breadth of the market.* This measures the number of advancing stocks in relation to the number of decreasing stocks.

(4) *Short interest ratio.* This measures the cumulative number of shares sold short by investors divided by the daily volume of trading on an exchange.

(5) *Support and resistance levels.* Stocks generally trade in ranges. The lower limit is a stock's support level, and the higher limit is its resistance level. The support level is the level at which technicians believe a stock should be purchased, whereas the resistance level is the level at which a stock should be sold. Technicians state that if a stock were to break its support level, rapid decline would occur before another support level would be defined. If a stock were to penetrate its resistance level, it would quickly move to the upside before reaching a new resistance level.

(6) *Relative strength ratio.* Once a trend begins, it must continue until an event occurs to stop it. The relative strength indicator tells whether the trend is stock specific or caused by market movements. If the ratio increases over time, technicians would expect superior performance to continue. The ratio works in declining markets too. If the price of the stock does not decline as much as the rest of the market, the stock's relative strength ratio will increase. Technicians believe that if the ratio remains stable or rises in down markets, then the stock should do very well in rising markets.

(7) *Moving average lines.* Moving averages allow technicians to find trends in stock prices. Stocks will trade above their moving average if the trend is up and will trade below the moving average if the trend is down. The most commonly used moving average line is a stock's 200-day moving average.

TOPIC 49: ASSET ALLOCATION AND PORTFOLIO DIVERSIFICATION

1. Strategic asset allocation

   A. This is based on an investment policy that determines a suitable mix of assets for a client's portfolio.

   B. Application of client life cycle analysis

      (1) A client's risk tolerance can be deduced from an analysis of his or her life cycle. As discussed in Topic 10, there are four life cycle phases: accumulation phase, consolidation phase, spending phase, and gifting phase.

      (2) In the accumulation phase, individuals are accepting of *high-risk investments for above-average returns*. In the consolidation phase, individuals are accepting of

moderate-risk investments. In the spending phase, individuals are accepting of *low-risk investments.* In this phase, the overall portfolio is less risky than during the consolidation years, but individuals still need to have some risky growth investments, such as common stock, for inflation protection. The gifting phase risk level is comparable to the spending phase.

C. Client risk tolerance measurement and application

(1) It is vital to find a portfolio that matches the investor's risk tolerance level while helping the investor achieve his or her return objectives.

(2) In certain cases, measuring risk tolerance can be objective, but it is generally a subjective measure of the emotional and financial ability of an investor to withstand financial loss. A careful analysis of the client's risk tolerance should precede any discussion of return objectives.

(3) Asset allocation portfolios are generally marketed as follows:

(a) Aggressive growth
(b) Growth
(c) Growth and income
(d) Balanced
(e) Fixed income

(4) Both the return and risk level decrease as we move from aggressive growth to growth, growth to growth and income, and so on.

D. Asset class definition and correlation

(1) Investments are distributed among three broad asset classes.

(a) Stocks
(b) Bonds
(c) Cash and money market instruments

(2) The correlation coefficient is the driving force of asset allocation. As mentioned earlier, as the correlation coefficient decreases from +1, there is an increase in diversification. Diversification can increase the return of a portfolio while decreasing the risk.

(3) Keep in mind that the standard deviation of a portfolio is less than the weighted standard deviation of the individual stocks in the portfolio.

2. Tactical asset allocation uses *security selection* as its main approach to building a portfolio, whereas asset allocation uses an *investment policy* that determines a suitable mix of assets for a client's portfolio.

3. Passive versus active portfolio management (see Topic 48)

A. A *passive strategy* begins by setting specific percentages for each asset class. The portfolio will be rebalanced occasionally to maintain these percentages. A passive strategy should not be confused with a buy-and-hold strategy.

B. An *active strategy* is often referred to as *market timing*, whereas tactical asset allocation is driven by *security selection* as the reason for rebalancing.

4. Strategies for dealing with concentrated positions

A. Rebalancing a portfolio to maintain asset allocation percentages is most appropriate for a tax-deferred retirement account, because gains on the sale of securities are not taxed. It is also appropriate for a regular account, but frequent rebalancing may cause complicated tax reporting headaches.

B. The basic rule of rebalancing is that it should be used at regular intervals, say every quarter or every six months.

TOPIC 50: EFFICIENT MARKET THEORY (EMH)

1. Introduction—The EMH does not state that an individual cannot outperform the market. It states that an individual cannot outperform the market on a risk-adjusted basis over an extended period of time, because security prices fully reflect all available information and are consistent with the risk involved.

2. Strong form

   A. The strong-form EMH states that stock prices fully reflect all public and private information. The strong form includes all types of information: *market, nonmarket public,* and *private information*. Not even access to inside information can produce superior returns. It assumes that inside information cannot be kept inside.

   B. This does not assume an investor cannot be expected to achieve success, only that success should not be expected.

   C. An investor who accepts both the semistrong-form and strong-form EMH will generally avoid all active managers inasmuch as superior returns cannot be expected.

3. Semistrong form

   A. The semistrong-form EMH states that stock prices fully reflect all public information. Security prices include *market* and *nonmarket public* information. This includes a company's past history and information learned from studying financial statements, the industry, and the economic environment.

   B. An investor cannot expect to achieve superior returns using fundamental analysis. This does not assume that an individual cannot achieve superior returns, just that superior returns should not be expected.

4. Weak form

   A. The weak form assumes that stock prices fully reflect all available market information. The weak-form EMH believes that security returns are independent of each other and that correlation between stock prices over time is virtually nothing.

   B. The weak form can be explained by the *random walk theory*. Historical, price behavior, and technical indicators cannot produce superior returns. Information utilized by technical analysis has no predictive value.

   C. The weak-form EMH does state that using good research may produce superior returns; fundamental analysis may have value.

5. Anomalies

   A. Tests of the EMH

      (1) Testing the weak-form EMH

         (a) *Statistical tests* of the independence of security returns
         (b) *Trading rule tests* to examine whether mechanical trading rules can generate excess returns

      (2) Testing the semistrong-form EMH

         (a) *Time-series tests* and *cross-sectional tests* to predict future rates of return based on public information

      (b) Event studies that examine the stock price reaction to significant economic events such as stock splits, initial public offerings, exchange listings, and announcements of dividend and accounting changes

    (3) Testing the strong-form EMH—*Academic tests* are used to look at the legal use of private information and exclude illegal insider trading.

B. Anomalies from time-series tests

    (1) Studies show that *dividend yield, default spread,* and *term structure spread* can be used to determine the returns on stocks and bonds.

    (2) *Quarterly earnings reports* show that the market may not have adjusted stock prices as quickly as expected to reflect earning surprises.

    (3) The *January effect* shows that stocks tend to perform well in January. To take advantage of the January effect, investors would buy securities in December and sell in January. There is also a *day of the week effect* (or *weekend effect*). Research has suggested that the weekend generates a lower return. This implies that investors anticipating the purchase of a stock should not purchase the stock on Friday, but wait until Monday.

C. Anomalies from cross-sectional tests

    (1) The *P/E effect* shows that low P/E stocks produce superior returns relative to the market, and high P/E stocks produce inferior returns.

    (2) The *small-firm effect* (or *small cap*) indicates that small firms consistently produce superior returns relative to larger firms. The return of a firm diminishes as its market capitalization gets bigger.

    (3) The *neglected firm effect* states that a firm that has a small number of analysts following it tends to produce higher returns than those firms covered by many analysts.

    (4) Stocks with high *book-to-price ratios* have a higher risk-adjusted return, representing evidence against the EMH.

D. Anomalies from strong-form academic tests

    (1) Stock exchange specialists have monopolistic access to information and derive above-average returns from the information.

    (2) Corporate insiders also have monopolistic access to information, which produces excess returns.

E. Conclusions of the three forms of market efficiency

    (1) Results support the weak-form EMH.

    (2) Results are mixed for the semistrong form of the EMH. Event studies support the semistrong-form EMH, but time-series and cross-sectional tests give evidence that markets are not always semistrong-form efficient.

    (3) Results support the strong-form EMH except for corporate insiders and specialists.

TOPIC 51: ASSET PRICING MODELS

1. Capital asset pricing model (CAPM)

    A. The CAPM determines the required rate of return for any risky asset. The required return is comprised of the risk-free rate an investor can earn by investing in a riskless security such as a U.S. Treasury bill and the risk premium. According to the CAPM, the risk premium is both the additional return an investor earns above the risk-free rate and the volatility of a particular security to that of the market. Therefore, the required rate (k) of return is

$$k_{stock} = R_{risk\ free} + (R_{market} - R_{risk\ free})\ beta_{stock}$$

B. If the difference between the market rate and the risk-free rate widens, a stock's risk premium will grow. This is an important concept in stock valuation. The larger risk premium causes the stock's intrinsic value to decrease unless the stock can grow faster to keep up with the added risk. If growth cannot keep up with the high-risk premium, the stock's current value may come crashing down.

C. The CAPM can be used to identify undervalued and overvalued assets.

    (1) Compare expected return to the required return (k)

        (a) If the expected return is greater than the required return, the asset is undervalued.
        (b) If the expected return is lower than the required return, the asset is overvalued.
        (c) If the expected return equals the required return, the asset is properly valued.

    (2) Any stock not plotting on the security market line (SML) is mispriced.

        (a) If a stock's expected return falls below the SML, the stock is overpriced → the expected return is too low.
        (b) If a stock's expected return rises above the SML, the stock is undervalued → it is offering a return that is greater than its systematic risk.

2. Multifactor asset pricing model (APM)

  A. Also called the arbitrage pricing theory (APT)
  B. The CAPM is a one-factor model that considers only market risk. Because there are many factors that drive stock return, a multifactored model was developed.
  C. The APT relies on few assumptions:

    (1) Capital markets are competitive.
    (2) Investors prefer more wealth to less wealth.
    (3) The process generating asset returns is represented by the K-factor model.

  D. The APT does not rely on the following CAPM assumptions:

    (1) Investors have quadratic utility functions.
    (2) Security returns are normally distributed.
    (3) The market portfolio contains all securities and is mean variance efficient.

  E. The model assumes K unspecified factors. For example, let F_i represent the risk premium for the ith risk factor and B_i represents the responsiveness of the asset's returns to that risk factor.

$$ER = R_f + B_iF_i + B_2F_2 + B_3F_3 + .\ .\ . + B_nF_n$$

  F. The major drawback of the APT is that it does not specify the risk factors.
  G. If the APT had only one risk factor, that being market risk, it would equal the CAPM.

3. Option pricing model (Black-Scholes)

  A. Determines the value of a call option
  B. The model assumes that the call option is European (exercisable only on expiration date) and not American (exercisable at any time) style.
  C. There are five variables in Black-Scholes model.

    (1) Call values *increase* with an increase in four variables.

      (a) Time to maturity

      (b) Interest rates

      (c) Price of the underlying stock

      (d) Volatility

    (2) Call values *decrease* with an increase in one variable, the strike price.

4. Put-call parity

   A. This determines the value of a put option.

   B. Put-call parity means that there is a relationship between the prices of puts and calls and the underlying stock. It keeps the prices in check so that an opportunity for arbitrage does not happen. Arbitrage is the opportunity to make money without making an investment.

   C. Put-call parity makes certain that the prices of a call and put change with each other and the underlying stock. The put and call can be considered too expensive or cheap, but one cannot be more expensive or cheaper than the other.

TOPIC 52: LEVERAGE OF INVESTMENT ASSETS

1. Margin requirements

   A. When an investor purchases stock on margin, he or she makes an initial payment similar to a down payment on a house and borrows the remaining funds necessary to make the purchase. The investor is buying securities with borrowed money.

   B. The Federal Reserve sets the *initial* margin requirement, which is currently 50 percent. For example, if the initial margin requirement is 50 percent on a $20,000 transaction, the investor must deposit $10,000.

   C. The stock exchanges and brokerage houses set the *maintenance* margin requirement. The maintenance margin is the *minimum equity* an investor must have for a margin position. The maintenance margin protects the brokerage firm from being exposed to too much risk. For example, if the maintenance margin requirement is 35 percent, this means that the borrower must provide 35 percent of the funds and the brokerage firm lends the remaining 65 percent. The investor pays interest on the borrowed funds.

   D. Margin provides significant leverage to an investor. If the price of a stock goes up, the customer's profits accumulate much faster. The same can be said in regard to the downside. If the price of a stock drops, the percentage loss is greater. The leverage factor can be calculated as (1 ÷ margin %). *Example*: At a 35 percent margin requirement, the leverage rate is 2.85 (1 ÷ 0.35). If the rate of return on the stock is 10 percent, the rate of return using a 2.85 leverage rate is 28.5 percent, or 185 percent more.

2. Margin calls

   A. If a stock or portfolio declines sufficiently in price, a margin call will result. A margin call happens when the equity in the account has dropped below the margin requirement. The investor must increase his or her equity by depositing cash or securities or by selling assets.

   B. The following formulas are used to indicate what stock price will trigger a margin call.

    (1) $\text{Long} = \dfrac{[\text{original price } (1 - \text{initial margin \%})]}{1 - \text{maintenance margin \%}}$

    (2) $\text{Short} = \dfrac{[\text{original price } (1 + \text{initial margin \%})]}{1 + \text{maintenance margin \%}}$

C. For example, an investor buys stock at $50. The initial margin requirement is 50 percent and the maintenance margin requirement is 35 percent. If the stock drops to $38½ the investor will get a margin call. The calculation is

$$\text{Long} = \frac{\$50(1 - 0.50)}{1 - 0.35} = \$38.50$$

D. Consider a different way this problem can be posed. If stock drops to $40/share, how much cash will you be required to put up, assuming you bought 100 shares of XYZ stock for $60 per share with an initial margin of 50 percent and a 30 percent maintenance margin?

   (1) Solve current equity → $4,000 (stock value) *less* $3,000 (loan amount) → $1,000 equity.
   (2) Find required equity → $4,000 × 30% → $1,200.
   (3) Subtract (1) from (2) → $1,000 *less* $1,200 → $200.

3. Calculating the rate of return on a margin transaction

   A. The rate of return is calculated by solving the net profit and total investment in a transaction.

      Net profit ÷ investment = % gain or loss

   B. For example, assume Sarah short sells 100 shares of XYZ at $57 with a 50 percent initial margin. XYZ pays a dividend of $2 per share after she sells the stock. She then buys back the stock for $54. The rate of return is

      (1) Investment is $100 × $57 × 0.5 = $2,850.
      (2) Net profit is $5,700 (proceeds) less $5,400 (cost) less $200 (dividend payments) (short the position). The result is $100.
      (3) $100 divided by $2,850 = 3.5%

TOPIC 53: HEDGING AND OPTION STRATEGIES

(See Topic 40 for introduction to options.)

1. Strategy of buying calls

   A. A call is an option to buy a specified amount of shares (usually 100) at a specified price (strike price) within a specified time period (expiration date).
   B. Investors should buy calls when they expect the underlying stock or index to rise.
   C. A long call position can be used in a speculative way through leverage, or conservatively as an insurance policy. The percentage increase in a call often exceeds that of the stock in a rising market. When the price of the underlying stock decreases, the percentage loss in the call is often greater than the stock. This is the effect of leverage. The *absolute gain* or *loss* on the call is less than it is when the stock is owned, because options are less expensive.
   D. The maximum gain is unlimited. The maximum loss is the premium paid for the options. The breakeven equals the strike price plus the premium.
   E. Time decay accelerates as the option approaches expiration.

2. Strategy of buying puts

   A. A put is an option to sell a specified number of shares (usually 100) at a specified price (strike price) within a specified time period.
   B. The objective in buying puts is for a trader to profit from or protect against a price decline in the underlying stock. Put buying is a speculative strategy using leverage or a conservative strategy of insurance.

    C. The maximum gain increases as the stock price decreases and is only limited by the stock going to $0. The maximum loss is the premium paid for the options. The breakeven equals the strike price minus the premium.

    D. Time decay accelerates as the option approaches expiration.

    E. For an investor wanting to protect against downside loss without selling his or her stock position, puts are insurance against falling stock prices. These are known as *protective puts*.

    F. Puts can be used as an alternative to short selling.

    G. An interesting point to note is that purchasing puts against a long position is the same as buying calls outright. Both strategies have limited loss (the premium paid) with unlimited gain. Therefore, if puts are bought as insurance on a stock, it turns the position into a call option for the life of the option.

3. Strategy of selling naked calls

    A. The act of selling an option is known as *writing*. This strategy is also known as *naked call writing*.

    B. Selling naked calls exposes an investor to considerable risk. If the call is exercised because the price of the stock rises, the option writer is obligated to buy the stock back and deliver it to the buyer. The price of the stock can be significantly higher than when the call was originally sold. It is important to understand that the strategy for naked call writing does not involve ownership of the underlying stock (a strategy known as *covered call writing*).

    C. The maximum gain with this strategy is the premium received. The maximum loss is unlimited. The breakeven is the strike price plus the premium.

    D. The motivation for selling calls is to take advantage of volatility and time decay.

        (1) If expected volatility is high, the premium for the call is larger, resulting in more money coming in for the seller.

        (2) An investor can take advantage of time decay by selling an option in the final weeks before expiration. This is when time decay accelerates.

4. Strategy for selling naked puts

    A. The act of selling an option is known as *writing*. Therefore, investors may *write naked puts*.

    B. Naked put selling is a strategy in which the option trader assumes the risk of the underlying security in exchange for the premium. The writer puts an emphasis on the underlying stock's price not declining.

    C. The maximum gain is the premium received. The maximum loss is the cost of buying the stock at the strike price. The loss continues to grow as the underlying stock declines below the strike price. The breakeven is the strike price minus the premium.

    D. The motivation for selling puts is to take advantage of volatility and time decay.

5. Strategy of covered call writing

    A. Covered call selling (or *writing*) is taking a short call with a long stock position in the underlying stock. If the option is exercised, the seller supplies the stock at the strike price.

    B. The call seller limits the gain on the stock by the premium received plus the strike price minus the price paid for the underlying stock. For example, assume a seller receives $5 for selling a 50 XYZ call and pays $52 for 100 shares of XYZ stock. The maximum gain is $3.

    C. The maximum gain is made when the stock trades above the strike price at expiration. The maximum loss is the price paid for the security minus the premium received from selling the call. That means that by selling calls to receive a premium, an investor partially hedges against his or her stock position. The breakeven is also the price paid for the underlying security minus the premium received.

    D. This strategy is used if an investor expects a stable stock price.

6. Strategy of covered put writing

   A. The investor sells the stock short and sells the put in order to construct the covered put. If the put is exercised, the investor buys the shares and uses this to cover the short position. This is the opposite to covered calls in which the investor sells existing shares if the call is exercised.

   B. This strategy is used if an investor expects a stable stock price. The investor is neutral to slightly bearish. For example, assume a stock trades at $53 and the strike price of a put is $55 with a premium of $5. An investor short sells the stock and sells the put. If the stock stays below $58, the investor makes a profit. The maximum profit is $3 (the time premium). The maximum loss is unlimited if the stock price rises.

7. Short sales

   A. A short sell is the sale of borrowed securities in anticipation of a price drop. The short seller profits by selling the securities first with the intention of purchasing them back at a lower price. *Example*: An investor sells 100 shares of XYZ stock short at $100 and later buys those shares back at $70, resulting in a $3,000 profit.

   B. Short selling occurs when an investor believes a stock is overpriced and expects the price to drop. The maximum loss can be unlimited if the price continues to rise.

   C. The investor does not own the securities that are being sold short. These securities are sold short with a contract for future delivery. In effect, the broker borrows shares held in a margin account and lends them to the short seller (shares held in a cash account cannot be lent to a short seller). The proceeds are not delivered to the seller but are held by the broker. These proceeds are used at a later date to buy back the shares (covering the short).

   D. Three technical points affect short sales.

   (1) Investors can short sell only when the last trade for a stock is an uptick or zero uptick. If the price of a stock moves up from the previous trade, that is an uptick. If the price of a stock declines from the previous trade, that is a downtick. If the price of a stock does not change from a previous uptick, that is a zero uptick. The reason for this rule is to prevent traders from manipulating the market.

   (2) Short sellers must pay all dividends that are owed to the lender of the security.

   (3) The short seller must deposit margin money to guarantee the repurchase of the security. For example, assume the margin requirement is 50 percent. If an investor short sells 100 shares of XYZ stock at $70, the initial deposit must be $7,000 × 50 percent, or $3,500. This money is returned to the short seller with any gain or loss when the short position is covered.

TOPIC 54: TAX-EFFICIENT INVESTING

1. Mutual funds

   A. Turnover

   (1) Funds with a greater portfolio turnover ratio generate more tax consequences for their investors.

   (2) The mutual fund turnover ratio identifies the amount of buying and selling happening in a specified mutual fund. *Example*: A turnover ratio of 50 percent means that a fund is expected to replace 50 percent of its investments over a year.

   B. Short-term/long-term/unrealized capital gains

   (1) The return of a mutual fund is stated before tax, but an investor gets to keep only the after-tax return. *Tax efficiency* is defined as the ability to generate returns without generating large amounts of tax obligations.

(2) There is no tax obligation if a fund does not receive income or realize capital gains (i.e., unrealized capital gains). If a fund sells securities within its portfolio, each sale results in a taxable event. If these are short-term sales, then tax is paid at the stockholder's marginal federal income tax rate. If a fund rarely sells it investments, then the likelihood of long-term gains is greater.

(3) Many funds indicate a date when capital gains and income are distributed to shareholders. Investors should be alert to this date. The majority of funds make two distributions.

    (a) Mid-year distribution; consists of income

    (b) Year-end distribution; consists of income and capital gains

(4) *Example*: Assume an investor purchases shares just prior to the distribution date. The investor is the holder of record and responsible for paying any tax of income and capital gains even though the rise in price occurred much earlier. It makes sense to delay the purchase and buy shares when the fund goes ex-dividend.

(5) Hidden capital gains result in unexpected taxes, but hidden capital losses offer tax-free gains. *Example*: If the fund per share price drops from $10 to $5, it has an unrealized loss of $5. Assume an investor purchases the shares at the net asset value of $5. If the shares rise to $10 and are redeemed by the fund, the investor does not incur any capital gains tax as long as the shares continue to be held. However, unrealized losses are not always an opportunity if the price decline is a result of poor management.

2. Stocks

A. Tax management states that the returns of a portfolio must ultimately be measured by the after-tax return.

B. Wash sale rule

(1) Selling shares at a loss and then buying them back within 30 days negates the ability to deduct such losses on your tax return. The disallowed loss amount can be added to the cost basis of the additional shares that were purchased. When these additional shares are sold, any taxable gain or loss includes the loss incurred on the original shares.

(2) The wash sale rule applies not only to stocks but also mutual funds and bonds.

3. Bonds

A. Taxable equivalent yield (see Topic 43)

TEY = Tax-exempt municipal yield divided by (1 − marginal tax rate)

B. Premium/discount considerations

(1) If a bond was purchased at a premium, an investor may elect to amortize a part of the premium each year and reduce his or her basis by the amount deductible, which reduces current income from the bond. The taxpayer can also elect not to amortize the premium, and potentially take a capital loss deduction when the bonds are sold, called, or mature.

(2) When an investor sells a market discount bond, his or her gain is generally treated as interest income (ordinary income) to the extent of market discount accrued up to the date of disposition. Only gain in excess of the amount of accrued market discount may be treated as capital gain. However, if the investor elected to include market discount in income annually as it accrued, and to increase his or her basis, the gain would not include previously included market discount.

C. SEC yield

    (1) A standard yield calculation developed by the Securities and Exchange Commission (SEC) that allows for fairer comparisons among bond funds. It is based on the most recent 30-day period covered by the fund's filings with the SEC. The yield figure reflects the dividends and interest earned during the period after deduction of the fund's expenses for the period.

    (2) It captures the effective rate of interest that an investor can receive in the future.

TOPIC 55: INVESTMENT STRATEGIES IN TAX-ADVANTAGED ACCOUNTS

1. Capital gain versus ordinary income

    A. Every gain or loss is characterized as either ordinary or capital.

    B. Capital gain or loss results from the sale of a capital asset, such as stocks and bonds. Any gain or loss that does not meet this definition is ordinary in nature, such as dividends and interest payments.

2. Tax advantages—Individuals pay no taxes on capital gains and income in tax-deferred accounts if the proceeds and payments are left in the account.

3. Net unrealized appreciation (NUA) is nontaxable. If a distribution is made from a tax-advantaged account, some or all of the distribution would be taxed as ordinary income and not capital gains.

4. Appropriate assets for tax-advantaged versus taxable accounts

    A. Tax-advantaged accounts

        (1) High-income–producing assets

        (2) Stocks held for short-term appreciation

        (3) Zero coupon bonds

        (4) Treasury inflation protected securities (TIPS)

    B. Taxable accounts

        (1) Municipal bonds

        (2) Treasury bills, notes, and bonds

        (3) Growth stocks with long-term appreciation

TOPIC 56: TAXATION OF INVESTMENT VEHICLES

1. Mutual funds

    A. Basis determination

        (1) The basis is the cash investments plus reinvested dividends and capital gains minus returns of capital received.

        (2) Front-end and other sales charges adjust the share purchase price. This tends to increase the basis.

        (3) Back-end loads and redemption charges reduce the proceeds received from the sale of the securities.

        (4) Undistributed capital gains occur when the mutual fund retains the gain from a sale of securities. Taxpayers report their share of income but are allowed a credit for taxes paid by the mutual fund company. The taxpayer has an increase in basis of the difference between the total gain and the tax paid by the mutual fund company.

B. Taxation

    (1) There are two methods for computing the basis of mutual funds.

        (a) *Cost basis.* Actual cost of the mutual funds

            i. Specific identification (ID). To adequately identify shares, the taxpayer must

- Specify the specific shares that are sold
- Receive written confirmation of the identification and sale from the broker

            ii. First-in first-out (FIFO). The oldest shares are sold first.

        (b) *Average basis.* Total cost of shares owned divided by the total number of shares owned

            i. Single-category method. Average share is computed using all shares regardless of whether they are held short or long term.

            ii. Double-category method. The average basis per share is computed in two categories, short and long term.

    (2) Specific ID and FIFO cannot be used if the average basis method is used for sale of any shares in the same mutual fund.

    (3) Year-end distributions include any income paid during the year plus any distributions declared by December 31 and paid by January 31 of the following year.

2. Stocks

  A. Dividends

    (1) Dividends are reported on an annual Form 1099-DIV, and interest is reported on Form 1099-INT. The IRS receives copies of these forms and makes sure that they match the income reported by the investor on Schedule B, Form 1040.

    (2) Dividend reinvestments are considered constructive receipt and taxed as ordinary income.

  B. Basis determination

    (1) Capital gains and losses are recognized on the trade date, not the settlement date. Securities acquired by purchase have a cost basis that includes the security price *plus* any commission charges. Selling expenses are netted against the gross sales price in the computation of the amount realized on sale.

    (2) Realized capital gain from the sale of a security is the amount realized over the cost basis in the security. Realized capital loss is the excess of basis over the amount realized.

    (3) If an investor elects to have dividends reinvested in corporate stock or mutual funds to buy additional shares, the reinvested dividends become the cost basis of new shares.

  C. Capital gains and losses (see Topic 66) are reported on Form 1099-B; an individual investor fills out Schedule D, Form 1040.

  D. Liquidations—Taxes are due in the year a sale has occurred in a taxable account. For a tax-deferred account, taxes do not occur until the liquidation of the account and are subject only to ordinary income.

  E. Stock splits/dividends/rights

    (1) The receipt of a stock split, stock dividend, and right is a nontaxable event, because it is simply dividing an existing investment into more parts.

    (2) *Exceptions*: Distributions of stock are considered taxable events if

        (a) The shareholder chooses to receive additional shares in lieu of cash.

      (b) The distribution affects the shareholder's proportionate interest in the corporation.

      (c) There are distributions of certain preferred stock.

    (3) *Taxable distributions.* They are reported as income. The taxable dividend equals the FMV of the stock on the date of distribution. The holding period begins on the date of the stock dividend distribution.

    (4) *Nontaxable distributions.* Affect the basis in the old shares. The cost basis of the old stock is divided by the total number of shares held after the distribution. The holding period of new shares starts on the same date as the holding period of the old shares.

  F. Warrants

    (1) The exercise of a warrant is not a taxable event.

    (2) The cost basis of the common stock is the purchase price of the warrant plus the cost to exercise.

    (3) The holding period of the stock begins at the time of exercise.

3. Bonds

  A. U.S. government

    (1) Interest on U.S. government debt instruments is subject to federal income tax but totally exempt from state and local taxes.

    (2) *Treasury bills.* The difference between the purchase price and the amount paid at maturity (or when sold) is the interest earned.

    (3) *Treasury notes and bonds.* Interest is paid semiannually and reported in the year it is earned.

  B. Agency

    (1) Agency issues are taxed at both federal and state/local levels.

    (2) Interest is taxed as ordinary income. Capital gain and loss treatment is applicable if bonds have appreciated or depreciated in value.

  C. Municipal

    (1) Interest income earned on state and local government debt instruments is excluded from federal taxes. State and local bond interest *may* be taxed by the state or locality in which the investor resides.

    (2) Capital gains or loss treatment applies when the bonds are sold.

    (3) Interest on tax-exempt private activity bonds issued by any state or local government after August 7, 1986, is a preference item for alternative minimum tax (AMT) purposes. As a result, individuals in high tax brackets cannot assume that they will benefit from tax-exempt status.

    (4) Ordinary dividend distributions that constitute interest income from a mutual fund invested in state and local municipal bonds are tax exempt.

    (5) No deduction is allowed for interest expense paid or accrued on a loan to buy or carry tax-exempt obligations.

  D. Zero coupon

    (1) The accrued interest is taxed as if it were received.

    (2) *Original issue discount (OID).* When a long-term debt instrument is issued at a price lower than its par value, the difference is called OID. Investors cannot defer recognition of the interest income represented by the original issue discount. OID rules do not apply to short-term debt obligation (maturity dates of one year or less).

    (3) Interest is reported on Form OID. The amount of interest shown is generally accurate for only the original bondholder, because the company that issued the bond does not track its activity in the secondary market.

    (4) For bonds purchased on the secondary market, the amount of interest will have to be adjusted if a bond was purchased at a price that was different from the stated issue price plus accrued interest.

E. Treasury inflation protected securities (TIPS)

    (1) The principal is adjusted up or down for inflation or deflation in addition to having a fixed interest rate.

    (2) The interest is paid semiannually. Inflation-adjusted principal is not paid until the bond matures.

    (3) Investors pay federal income taxes on the increasing principal amount as well as coupon interest. The entire gain is taxed as ordinary income, not just the coupon interest.

F. Convertible bonds

    (1) The conversion to common stock is not a taxable event.

    (2) The cost basis for the common stock is the original cost of the convertible bond.

    (3) The holding period for the shares is from the time the convertible was originally purchased.

G. Accrued interest

    (1) *Seller.* Reports the accrued interest in gross income. For example, a bond costing $10,000 is sold for $10,500. The sale price includes $400 of interest accrued. The seller reports interest income of $400 and capital gain income of $100.

    (2) *Purchaser.* Deducts the accrued interest from the next interest payment as a return of capital. For example, if the purchaser of the $10,500 bond in the previous example receives total interest of $600 for the year, $200 is taxable interest income ($600 total − $400 accrued interest). The bond basis is $10,100 ($10,500 purchase price reduced by $400 accrued interest).

4. U.S. savings bonds—Interest is subject to federal taxation but exempt from state and local taxes. The taxpayer can report interest annually or upon redemption.

5. Annuities

A. The investor is not taxed on the yearly buildup in the value of the investment. Tax is deferred, but the gain in an annuity will eventually be taxed as ordinary income when distributed.

B. The portion representing a return of basis is not taxed; the portion representing a distribution of accumulated earnings is taxed as ordinary income.

C. Interest earnings are always assumed to be withdrawn first and then principal, unless an annuity option is selected, and then only a portion of each annuity payment is taxable as ordinary income. *Exception:* Annuity contracts executed before August 13, 1982, retain the right to receive tax-free early withdrawals of investment in contract first (FIFO method).

D. Annuities are fully taxable if

    (1) The taxpayer did not contribute to the cost.

    (2) The taxpayer's entire cost has been recovered.

E. Partially taxable distributions

   (1) *Three-year rule*. Repealed for annuities starting after July 1, 1986. This allows the taxpayer to recover the tax-free basis in the first three years of receiving distributions.

   (2) *General rule*. The percentage of each annuity payment excluded from gross income is total after-tax contribution of employee divided by annual payment times life expectancy.

   (3) *Simplified method*. The nontaxable portion of each annuity payment received is

      (a) Total after-tax contribution of employee divided by number of expected payments

      (b) The number of expected payments is set forth in a government table and is based on the annuity start date and age of the participant at annuity start date.

   (4) *Note*: The general rule must be used unless the distribution qualifies for treatment under the simplified method. The simplified rule cannot be used for any of the following:

      (a) Nonqualified plans

      (b) Qualified plan if annuitant is age 75 or older and the annuity payments are guaranteed for at least five years

      (c) Individual retirement accounts (IRAs)

   (5) *Annuities starting after December 31, 1997*. If the annuity is payable to a primary annuitant and to more than one survivor annuitant, the combined age is the age of the primary annuitant plus the youngest survivor annuitant. If the annuity is payable to more than one survivor annuitant and there is no primary annuitant, the combined age is the age of the oldest survivor annuitant plus the youngest survivor annuitant.

F. A 10 percent excise tax applies for withdrawals taken before the applicant turns age 59½. The penalty tax applies only to the portion that is subject to income tax. The penalty does not apply if the contract holder becomes disabled or if the distribution is over the life of an annuitant.

G. If the annuitant dies before recovering his or her investment, the unrecovered portion is allowed as an itemized deduction on his or her final Form 1040.

6. General and limited partnerships (see Topic 61)

7. Unit investment trusts (UITs) are not actively managed, and securities are not purchased and sold during their life. UITs are subject to federal and state taxation, with capital gains treatment the norm upon liquidation or sale.

Chapter 5

INCOME TAX PLANNING

TOPIC 57: INCOME TAX LAW FUNDAMENTALS

1. Sources of authority

   A. Primary

      (1) Statutory laws

         (a) *Internal Revenue Code of 1986.* The primary source of tax law
         (b) *Taxpayer Relief Act of 1997.* Included more than 300 new provisions and 800 changes to the Internal Revenue Code of 1986
         (c) Tax legislative process begins with the House Ways and Means Committee and later goes to the House of Representatives. If the House approves the bill, it is submitted to the Senate Finance Committee and then to the entire Senate. If approved with no changes, it goes to the president for approval or veto. If there are changes, the Joint Conference Committee will address them and submit the bill back to the House and Senate.

      (2) Administrative pronouncements

         (a) *Treasury regulations.* The official interpretation of a statutory tax rule written and published by the U.S. Treasury; the highest source of authority next to the Internal Revenue Code. Treasury regulations have the full force and effect of the law.
         (b) *Revenue rulings.* Represent the official position of the Internal Revenue Service (IRS), but carry less authority than the Code and regulations. They provide interpretations of the tax law and give guidance to taxpayers.
         (c) *Revenue procedures.* These also represent the official position of the IRS. They are generally related to compliance matters such as tax tables, inflation-indexed amounts, asset class lives, and so forth.
         (d) *Letter rulings.* More specific interpretations by the national office of the IRS related to the tax consequences of a contemplated transaction at the request of the taxpayer. A letter ruling is applicable only to the taxpayer who requested it and cannot be used by another taxpayer in a dispute.

      (3) Judicial decision

         (a) Taxpayers can escalate any tax dispute to a regional appeals office of the IRS.
         (b) If a case is unresolved, the taxpayer can take it to federal court for judicial review, consisting of three *trial courts.*

            i. *U.S. Tax Court.* Refuse to pay deficiency. No jury trial.
            ii. *U.S. District Court.* Pay the deficiency and sue for a refund. Provides a jury trial.
            iii. *U.S. Court of Federal Claims.* Pay the deficiency and sue for a refund. No jury trial.

         (c) If the case is still unresolved, the taxpayer can appeal to the U.S. Circuit Court of Appeals (appellate court); 13 courts, based on jurisdiction.
         (d) The final appeal is to the U.S. Supreme Court, which may agree to hear the case or refuse to hear it. Any ruling is equivalent to law.

   B. Secondary sources of tax information consist mainly of books, periodicals, articles, newsletters, and editorial judgments in tax services.

2. Research sources—Research of a tax question involves the following steps:

   A. Gather all the facts.
   B. Diagnose the problem.

C. Locate the authority.
D. Evaluate the authority.
E. Derive the solution.
F. Communicate the answer.

TOPIC 58: TAX COMPLIANCE

1. Filing requirements

   A. Every individual U.S. citizen and resident alien must file an income tax return when gross income exceeds the standard deduction amount *plus* the applicable personal exemption for the individual's filing status. *Example*: A married couple filing jointly for 2002 with $6,000 personal exemption must file a tax return if their income exceeded $13,850 ($7,850 standard deduction + $6,000 personal exemption). The return must be filed whether or not any tax is due.

   B. The previous rules do not apply to an individual who is claimed as a dependent by another. The dependent must file a return if

      (1) His or her unearned income is more than $750 (for 2003) plus any additional standard deduction claimed because of age or blindness

      (2) His or her total gross income is more than the standard deduction.

   C. No return is necessary for a child if the parents elect to include the child's income in the parents' return under the "kiddie tax" rules (see Topic 59, Section 12.).

   D. The following individuals have to file a tax return even if their gross income is below the required amount:

      (1) An individual who has $400 or more net earnings from self-employment

      (2) Individuals who have received tips from which Social Security tax was not withheld

      (3) Individuals owing alternative minimum tax

      (4) Employees of certain religious and other church-controlled organizations

      (5) Nonresident alien individuals

      (6) Individuals who have changed their country of residence or citizenship during the year

      (7) Individuals who must pay tax from an IRA or qualified retirement plan

      (8) Individuals who must pay tax from recapture of investment credit, low-income housing credit, or federal mortgage subsidy

   E. Most individuals are required to file Form 1040 by April 15 of the following year. Individuals who have adopted a fiscal year must file by the 15th day of the fourth month following the close of the taxable year. Corporations must file a tax return before the 15th day of the third month after the end of their tax year.

   F. The law permits individuals to file an *automatic* four-month extension (three-month extension for partnerships, trusts, and estates and six-month extension for corporations). The extension is only for filing the return, not for paying tax. From the government's perspective, taxpayers who are late in paying taxes are receiving a loan from the government. The IRS bills these taxpayers for interest owed from the required payment date to the date the delinquent tax is actually paid.

   G. Corporations may deduct the interest paid on a tax deficiency as a business expense. For individual filers, the interest paid is nondeductible personal interest.

2. Authority to represent the clients before the IRS (Circular 230)—Certified public accountants (CPAs), attorneys, and enrolled agents have authority to represent a client before the IRS. Enrolled agents receive certification to practice before the IRS by passing a tax exam written and administered by the IRS.

3. Audits

   A. There are several ways in which the IRS chooses tax returns for audit.

      (1) *Discriminate Functions System (DIF) Score.* Method of screening all returns based on a precomputed set of weighted norms used in selecting returns to audit. Based on the weighted score, the program ranks the returns from most auditworthy to least auditworthy. The higher the score, the greater the chance of audit. The DIF selection process is a closely guarded secret of the IRS. The following are 10 items that practitioners consider topics of audit:

         (a) 1040 business returns with total gross receipts (TGR) of $100,000 or more, or with substantial business losses
         (b) 1040 nonbusiness returns with total positive income (TPI) of $50,000 or more
         (c) Returns with tax shelter activity
         (d) Returns prepared by an individual or firm on the Problem Preparer's List of the IRS
         (e) Travel and entertainment expenses
         (f) Business automobile expenses
         (g) Casualty losses
         (h) Barter income
         (i) Deduction for office-in-the-home expenses
         (j) "Hobby" losses

      (2) *Taxpayer Compliance Measurement Program (TCMP).* Designed to compute the norms used by DIF, thereby determining where taxpayers are most likely to fail in complying with the law (55,000 returns every two years)

      (3) *Targeted programs.* Target professions with income derived from tips and the like, or specific situations

      (4) *Document matching programs.* Match specific documents such as W-2s, 1099s, and so forth, to determine discrepancies

      (5) *Random sample*

   B. *Correspondence examinations.* The most common and simplest form of audit is usually conducted by telephone or mail.

   C. *Office examination* takes place at the IRS district office; *field examination* takes place at the taxpayer's business. Field audits are broader in scope than office examinations.

4. Penalties

   A. Late-filing and late-payment penalty—A combined penalty that equals 5 percent of the *balance of tax due* for each month that the return is late, up to 5 months (until penalty equals 25 percent of balance due). After 5 months, the penalty is 0.5 percent for each month late, for an additional 45 months.

   B. Statute of limitations

      (1) The government's cashing a taxpayer's check or mailing a refund does *not* mean that the IRS has accepted the accuracy of the return as filed.

      (2) The statute of limitations gives the IRS three years from the *later* of the statutory due date (usually April 15) or the date on which the return was actually filed to examine a return for mistakes.

      (3) The statute of limitations is extended for six years if the taxpayer omits an amount of gross income exceeding 25 percent of the gross income reported.

   C. Negligence

(1) The penalty equals 20 percent of any underpayment of tax attributable to the taxpayer's failure to make a reasonable attempt to comply with the law or intentional disregard of the law.

(2) The IRS has the *burden of production* to show that the taxpayer was negligent rather than he or she made an honest mistake. This means the IRS must show a *preponderance of evidence* that negligence occurred.

D. Civil fraud

(1) The penalty is 15 percent for each month a return is late, up to a maximum of 75 percent. Fraud is defined as an intentional act of trying to cheat the government.

(2) The burden of proof for establishing fraud falls on the IRS. The IRS must show *clear and convincing evidence* that fraud actually occurred.

E. Criminal fraud

(1) Also known as *tax evasion*, this it is a felony offense, punishable by severe monetary fines (up to $100,000 for an individual and $500,000 for a corporation) and by imprisonment in a federal jail.

(2) There must be guilt *beyond a reasonable doubt* for a person to be convicted.

F. Tax return preparer penalties

(1) An income tax preparer is any person who prepares tax returns (or employs other people to prepare returns) for compensation.

(2) If the preparer understates the amount of tax, and he or she knows (or should know) that the position has no merit, the IRS can impose a $250 penalty. If there is a willful attempt to understate taxes, the fine increases to $1,000.

TOPIC 59: INCOME TAX FUNDAMENTALS AND CALCULATIONS

1. Filing status

A. Single—A taxpayer is single if, on December 31, he or she is unmarried or legally separated.

B. Married filing jointly (MFJ)

(1) Taxpayers may file jointly if, on December 31, they are:

(a) Married and living together

(b) Married and living apart, but not legally separated or divorced

(c) Living in common law marriage, if recognized in the state where they reside

(2) If a spouse dies, the survivor can file jointly if one of the preceding tests were met during the year, assuming the survivor did not remarry.

C. Married filing separately (MFS)

(1) Taxpayers who are married at the end of the year can elect to file separately.

(2) Reasons to file separately:

(a) No joint liability

(b) Lower taxes for some couples. The tax brackets for MFS are exactly half those for MFJ. Spouses generally pay the same amount of tax under MFS as they would under MFJ unless one spouse has medical expenses, casualty losses, or employee business expenses subject to the percentage limitation based on adjusted gross income (AGI).

(3) Potential disadvantages:

      (a) If separate returns are filed and itemized deductions are elected by one spouse, the other spouse must also itemize deductions.

      (b) Increase in taxable Social Security benefits

      (c) Credit losses

      (d) Loss of the special $25,000 allowance for rental real estate

D. Head of household (HOH)

  (1) The taxpayer must meet *all* of the following tests to file as head of household:

    (a) The taxpayer is not married at end of year.

    (b) The taxpayer pays more than half the cost of the home.

    (c) The home was the main home for more than half the year for:

      i. The taxpayer's child, stepchild, adopted child, or grandchild

- An unmarried child does not need to be a dependent.
- A married child generally must be a dependent.

      ii. Foster child who is a dependent

      iii. Another relative who is the taxpayer's dependent:

- Parent or grandparent
- Sibling, stepsibling, or halfsibling
- Mother-, father-, daughter-, son-, brother-, or sister-in-law
- Uncle, aunt, nephew, or niece

      iv. Relatives not listed and unrelated persons may be the taxpayer's dependents if they lived in the taxpayer's household for *one full* year.

    (d) The taxpayer was a U.S. citizen or resident during the full year.

  (2) Parents do *not* have to live with the taxpayer half of the year for the taxpayer to qualify as HOH. The taxpayer qualifies by paying more than half the cost of a parent's home. The home must be the main home of the parent for the entire year. The parent must be a dependent of the taxpayer. Paying half of a nursing home qualifies. The taxpayer must still meet tests (1) (a), the taxpayer is not married at end of year, and (1) (d), the taxpayer was a U.S. citizen or resident during the full year.

  (3) A married taxpayer can file as HOH if *all* of the following are met:

    (a) The taxpayer files a separate tax return.

    (b) The taxpayer pays more than half the cost of the home.

    (c) The spouse did not live in the home during the last six months of the tax year.

    (d) The home was the main home for more than half the year for the taxpayer's child, stepchild, or adopted or foster child.

    (e) The taxpayer was a U.S. citizen or resident during the full year.

E. Qualifying widow(er)

  (1) If the taxpayer's spouse died within two years preceding the year for which the taxpayer's return is being filed, the surviving spouse can qualify to use the married filing jointly tax rate and standard deductions.

  (2) The surviving spouse must meet *all* of the following:

    (a) The taxpayer was entitled to file a joint return with decedent in year of death.

    (b) The taxpayer did not remarry before the end of the current year.

    (c) The taxpayer paid more than half the cost of the home.

    (d) The home was the main home, for the entire year, of the taxpayer's child, stepchild, or adopted or foster child.

2. Gross income

    A. Included income

        (1) Wages, salaries, commissions, and fees
        (2) Taxable noncash fringe benefits
        (3) Allocated and unreported tips
        (4) Gains from real estate, securities, and other property
        (5) Rents
        (6) Interest from bank accounts, CDs, securities, loans, etc.
        (7) Accrued interest form zero coupon bonds
        (8) Dividends
        (9) Royalties
        (10) Alimony and separate maintenance payments
        (11) Annuities, pensions, IRA distributions
        (12) Income from an estate or trust, but not a gift or bequest
        (13) Prizes and awards
        (14) For some taxpayers, up to 85 percent of their Social Security benefits
        (15) All cash and property received, unless it is specifically excluded by federal tax laws

    B. Income excluded from tax

        (1) Gifts and inheritances
        (2) Interest on certain municipal bonds and interest from mutual funds that hold such bonds
        (3) Returns of capital (e.g., loan principal repayments)
        (4) Reimbursements for business expenses
        (5) Exclusions of up to $250,000 ($500,000 for married filing jointly) in gain from the sale of a home
        (6) Some or all of Social Security benefits
        (7) Compensation for injury or sickness, including workers' compensation and certain disability payments
        (8) Employer-paid health coverage
        (9) Employer-provided education assistance up to $5,250
        (10) Qualified foster care payments
        (11) Proceeds of life insurance paid because of death or chronic illness
        (12) Payments received under accident, health, and long-term care insurance policies
        (13) Amounts contributed to a Medical Savings Account (MSA)
        (14) Employer-provided child or dependent care services
        (15) Scholarships and fellowships
        (16) Employer-paid group life insurance up to $50,000

3. Adjusted gross income (AGI)—The following *deductions* are subtracted from gross income to arrive at AGI:

    A. Trade or business expense
    B. Self-employed medical insurance premiums up to a limit
    C. Moving expenses for work
    D. Fifty percent of self-employment tax
    E. Amounts forfeited to a bank or savings institution for premature withdrawal of funds from a deposit account
    F. Alimony and separate maintenance payments
    G. Employee expenses that are reimbursed by the employer

H. Contributions to tax-favored retirement plans for self-employed
I. Contributions to individual retirement accounts (IRAs)
J. The total taxable amount of a lump sum distribution from a retirement plan to participants who reached age 50 before 1986
K. Deductions in connection with property held for the production of rents or royalties
L. Deduction for interest on qualified education loans
M. Payments made in tax years beginning after 2001 for deductible higher education expenses
N. Contributions to Medical Savings Account
O. Losses from the sale or exchange of property

4. Standard deduction (2003)

A. Married, filing jointly; and surviving spouse = $7,950
B. Married, filing separately = $3,975
C. Additional amount(s) for preceding two statuses if:

   (1) 65 or older = $950
   (2) Blind = $950

D. Single = $4,750
E. Head of household = $7,000
F. Additional amount(s) for preceding two statuses if:

   (1) 65 or older = $1,150
   (2) Blind = $1,150

G. Standard deduction for dependents

   (1) A dependent is an individual for whom another taxpayer claims a dependency exemption.
   (2) Dependents are not eligible to claim the regular standard deduction amounts on their own tax returns.
   (3) The special standard deduction allowable on a dependent's tax return is the *greater* of:

       (a) A sum equal to the amount of the dependent's earned income for the year plus $250, but not more than the regular standard deduction amount
       (b) $750 (for 2003)
       (c) *Example*: If a dependent has earned income of $1,000, he or she is entitled to a standard deduction of $1,250 ($1,000 + $250). If the dependent's earned income was $450, he or she is entitled to a standard deduction of $750.

5. Itemized deductions

A. These deductions are claimed on Schedule A. They are deductions taken from AGI in determining taxable income and are called "below-the-line" deductions. Deductions taken from gross income in determining AGI are called "above-the-line" deductions.
B. Types

   (1) Medical expense

       (a) Medical expenses are those paid for the taxpayer, his or her dependents, and anyone who would have been a dependent except for the income test.
       (b) The actual deduction is the cost in excess of 7.5 percent of AGI.
       (c) Medical expense deductions are allowed for

           i. All expenses made to maintain or improve health
           ii. Central air-conditioning when a family member suffers from respiratory ailments

      iii. New siding when the homeowner is allergic to old siding

      iv. Swimming pool for therapeutic purposes

(d) Unreimbursed expenses and insurance premiums paid for long-term care are deductible as medical expenses.

(e) Nondeductible medical expenses include

      i. Baby-sitting and child care

      ii. Costs covered by insurance

      iii. Cosmetic surgery

      iv. Funeral expenses

      v. Health club dues

      vi. Nonprescription drugs and medicines

      vii. Nutritional supplements

      viii. Weight loss program *unless* doctor recommends

(2) State and local income tax

  (a) State and local income taxes are deductible, but not the amount paid for federal income taxes.

  (b) If a deduction is taken in the year of payment but a refund is later received, the refund is taxable income in later years.

(3) Real estate and personal property tax

  (a) Real estate taxes are deductible even if paid to a foreign country.

  (b) Real estate taxes are deductible for *all* property owned by the taxpayer; mortgage interest deduction is limited to two homes.

  (c) If property is owned for just part of the year, only that portion is included.

  (d) Personal property taxes are deductible if based on the value of the property.

(4) Mortgage interest on primary and one secondary home—combined total of the debt

  (a) *Acquisition debt.* Deduction is limited to the interest on the first $1,000,000 of qualified debt.

  (b) *Home equity debt.* Deduction is limited to the *lesser* of the interest on:

      i. The fair market value (FMV) of the home minus the total acquisition indebtedness

      ii. $100,000 for the main and second homes combined

  (c) *Example*: The FMV of a home is $100,000 and the current balance on the original mortgage (home acquisition cost) is $90,000. The bank offers a home equity loan of 125 percent of the FMV of the home less any outstanding mortgages or other liens. To consolidate some other debts, the homeowner takes out the full $35,000 home equity loan [(125% × 100,000) − 90,000] with the bank. The home equity debt deduction is limited to $10,000, which is the smaller of:

      i. $100,000 maximum limit

      ii. The amount that the FMV of $100,000 exceeds the home acquisition debt of $90,000

  (d) Rules regarding a second home

      i. If a second home is rented, the taxpayer must use it more than 14 days or 10 percent of the number of days the home is rented at FMV, whichever is longer.

   ii. More than one second home

- Can treat only one as a qualified second home for the year
- Can choose a different one each year if neither of the second homes is rented out

(e) If a home is used for business and personal use, only the portion used for residential living counts as a qualified residence.

(f) IRS says that a taxpayer cannot deduct interest paid on behalf of another person; however, tax law has allowed deductions where the taxpayer is an "equitable owner" of the personal residence.

(g) Loan origination fees, maximum loan charge, loan discount, and discount points are tax deductible in the year paid if secured by the principal residence.

(h) If a seller pays points, they are deductible by the buyer in the year paid, but the buyer must reduce the basis in the home by the amount paid by the seller.

(5) Charitable contributions (see Topic 71)

(a) Must be made to a qualified charitable organization. Payment must be made, not just pledged. Credit card payments are deductible.

(b) Services provided to a charity are not deductible, but out-of-pocket costs incurred for those services are deductible.

(6) Casualty and theft losses

(a) Include damage, destruction, or loss of property resulting from an identifiable event that is *sudden, unexpected,* or *unusual.* The amount of casualty loss is the difference between the *lesser* of

   i. FMV before event less the FMV after event (if stolen, the FMV after event is 0)
   ii. The adjusted basis

(b) Losses are reduced by any insurance recovery.

(c) Reduction for $100 and 10 percent AGI floors. A $100 floor applies to each incident, but a 10 percent AGI floor is applied to the aggregate casualty loss amount for the year.

(d) *Example*: Steve had his Babe Ruth autographed ball stolen. It was valued at $15,000, with a basis of $10,000. Steve's salary for the year was $40,000. The itemized deduction is calculated as $10,000 (lesser of basis or reduction in FMV) minus $4,000 (10 percent AGI) minus $100 floor. The itemized deduction for casualty loss equals $5,900.

(7) Employee business expenses

(a) This section is not applicable if *all* of the following are true:

   i. The employee fully accounted all work-related expenses to his or her employer.
   ii. The employee received full reimbursement for expenses.
   iii. The employer required the employee to return any excess reimbursement.
   iv. Box 12 of the employee's W-2 shows no amount.

(b) Employees can deduct unreimbursed business-related expenses for (1) travel, (2) entertainment, (3) gifts, and (4) transportation.

(c) Travel versus transportation expenses: Transportation expenses do *not* include expenses incurred while traveling away from home overnight. Those expenses are travel expenses.

(8) Investment interest

    (a) Investment interest costs are limited to the amount of investment income.

    (b) Capital gains may be included in investment income at the election of the taxpayer. The trade-off is that any capital gain included in investment income is not eligible for preferential long-term capital gain rates.

(9) Miscellaneous itemized deductions

    (a) Deductions subject to a 2 percent limit

        i. Unreimbursed employee expenses
        ii. Tax preparation fees
        iii. Other expenses

    (b) Deductions not subject to the 2 percent limit

        i. Amortizable premium on taxable bonds
        ii. Federal estate tax on income in respect to decedent
        iii. Gambling losses up to the extent of gambling winnings
        iv. Unrecovered investment in an annuity
        v. Expenses of officials paid on a fee basis
        vi. Repayments of more than \$3,000 under claim or right
        vii. Impairment-related work expenses of persons with disabilities

    (c) Nondeductible expenses

        i. Broker's commissions paid in connection with property or account
        ii. Burial or funeral expenses
        iii. Capital expenses
        iv. Fees and licenses, such as car license, marriage license, or dog tags
        v. Hobby losses
        vi. Home repairs, insurance, and rents
        vii. Losses from the sale of a home
        viii. Personal disability insurance premiums
        ix. Lobbying expenses

C. Limitations—itemized deduction phaseout (3 percent/80 percent rule)

    (1) A taxpayer's allowable deductions are reduced by the *lesser* of (a) 3 percent of the excess of AGI over a specified amount or (b) 80 percent of the allowable itemized deductions for the year, but not including deductions for medical expenses, investment interest, nonbusiness casualty and theft losses, and gambling losses. The specified amount for 2003 is \$139,500 (\$69,750 if married filing separately).

    (2) *Example*: A husband and wife have AGI of \$175,000 in 2003. Their itemized deductions total \$30,000, including \$3,500 in investment interest, but no medical or casualty losses. The amount by which their AGI exceeds \$139,500 is \$35,500. This amount is multiplied by 3 percent to get \$1,065. Next, take 80 percent of the allowable itemized deductions, which is (30,000 − 3,500) × 80% = \$21,200. The lesser of the two calculations is \$1,065. The total amount of itemized deductions that can be used to reduce taxable income is \$30,000 − \$1,065 = \$28,935.

6. Personal and dependency exemptions

    A. Deduction for personal exemption

    (1) Each taxpayer is allowed a personal exemption for him- or herself and spouse, and may qualify for additional exemptions for each dependent.
    (2) In 2003, the amount is $3,050 for each exemption claimed.
    (3) An individual who is claimed as a dependent by another cannot claim a personal exemption for him- or herself.
    (4) A child cannot claim a personal exemption even if the parent does not take the dependency exemption.

    B. Exemption for dependents—An individual qualifies as a dependent of the taxpayer if *all* of the following conditions are met:

    (1) The person is related to the taxpayer or is a member of the taxpayer's household for the entire year. Certain relatives (child, grandchild, brother, sister, parent, etc.) do not have to live with the taxpayer to qualify.
    (2) The person's gross income does not equal or exceed the exemption amount. This test does not apply to certain children:

        (a) A child under age 19 at the end of the year
        (b) A student under age 24 at the end of the year

    (3) The taxpayer generally provides more than half the support to the person.
    (4) The person does not file a joint return under certain conditions. Suppose, for example, you supported your daughter for the entire year while her husband was overseas on military duty. The couple files a joint return. You cannot take an exemption for your daughter.
    (5) The person meets tests concerning citizenship or is a resident of the United States, Canada, or Mexico.

    C. Phaseout of personal exemption

    (1) The exemption amount will be reduced by 2 percent for each $2,500 ($1,250 for MFS), or fraction of that amount, by which the AGI of a taxpayer exceeds (2003):

        (a) $209,250 MFJ
        (b) $104,625 MFS
        (c) $139,500 Single
        (d) $174,400 HOH
        (e) $209,250 Surviving Spouse

    (2) *Example*: Taxpayers (MFJ) have an AGI of $255,000. The taxpayers have five personal and dependency exemptions. Calculate their actual personal and dependency exemption:

        Step 1 Exemption amount = 5 × $3,050 = $15,250
        Step 2 Difference = $255,000 (AGI) − $209,250 (threshold) = $47,750
        Step 3 Divide by $2,500 = 18.3
        Step 4 Round up to 19
        Step 5 Multiply by 2% = 38%
        Step 6 Loss due to threshold → 38% × $15,250 = $5,795
        Step 7 Personal and dependency exemption after phaseout = $15,250 − $5,795 = $9,455

7. Taxable income is AGI reduced by the greater of allowable itemized deductions or the standard deduction and personal exemptions.

8. Tax liability

   A. Determine tax by using either *tax tables* if taxable income is under $100,000 or *tax rate schedules* if taxable income is $100,000 or more.

   B. Tax credits such as child care, foreign tax credit, and credit for elderly must be taken into consideration in calculating total tax due. Moreover, other taxes such as self-employment tax and AMT may result in increasing total tax due.

   C. Steps for calculating tax liability:

Step 1	Determine total gross income.
Step 2	Subtract deductions from gross income to find AGI.
Step 3	Determine itemized deductions to find out whether they exceed the standard deduction amount. Deduct the greater of total itemized deductions or the standard deduction.
Step 4	Subtract the total itemized deductions or the standard deduction amount.
Step 5	Determine how many personal exemptions can be claimed.
Step 6	To determine taxable income, subtract the personal exemptions from the total found in Step 4.
Step 7	Find the tax amount from either the tax tables or the tax schedules.
Step 8	Subtract tax credits, if any, from taxes determined in Step 7.

   D. Under current law (2003), the tax rates will be gradually reduced until the year 2006, as follows (the lowest marginal rates—10 and 15 percent—will remain unchanged):

Tax Years	Third Marginal Rate	Fourth Marginal Rate	Fifth Marginal Rate	Highest Marginal Rate
2003	27%	30%	35%	38.6%
2004–2005	26%	29%	34%	37.6%
2006 and later	25%	28%	33%	35%

9. Tax credits (See Topic 11 for Hope Credit and Lifetime Learning Credit)

   A. Tax credits are dollar-for-dollar reductions in the actual tax paid; deductions limit only the amount of income subject to tax.

   B. Child tax credit

   (1) The amount of the child tax credit increases as follows:

Tax Year	Amount of Credit
2003–2004	$600
2005–2008	$700
2009	$800
After 2009	$1,000

   (2) The credit amount applies per qualifying child. A qualifying child is one who can be claimed for a dependency exemption.

   (3) The credit is phased out by $50 for each $1,000, or fraction thereof, by which modified AGI exceeds the threshold amount. The phaseout begins at the following levels: MFJ = $110,000; MFS = $55,000; Single = $75,000. *Example*: MFJ taxpayers would have no child credit if their modified AGI exceeds $121,000.

    (4) In 2003 through 2004, the credit is refundable (i.e., payable even if you have no tax liability) to the extent of 10 percent of earned income in excess of $10,000. Beginning in 2005, the 10 percent figure is increased to 15 percent.

C. Child and dependent care credit

    (1) The credit is 35 percent (2003) of expenses incurred by a taxpayer with AGI of $15,000 or less. The percentage decreases by 1 percent for each $2,000 (or fraction of that amount) of AGI over $15,000, but not below 20 percent. For taxpayers with AGI of more than $43,000, the applicable percentage is 20 percent.

    (2) The maximum amount of related expenses that can be used to compute the credit is $3,000 for one qualifying child or $6,000 for two or more qualifying individuals.

    (3) To qualify for the credit, the taxpayer must furnish more than half the cost of maintaining the home and pay child and dependent care expenses in order to work or look for work.

    (4) A qualifying child is someone under age 13 for whom the taxpayer is entitled a dependency deduction, or a dependent who is physically or mentally incapable of caring for him- or herself regardless of age.

D. Credit for elderly and disabled persons

    (1) The credit is available to any individual who:

        (a) Reaches 65 before the end of the tax year

        (b) Is under 65 at the end of the tax year, but is retired with a permanent and total disability and receives disability income

    (2) The credit is eliminated for joint filers with AGI of at least $25,000 (if both are over 65) or $20,000 (if one is over 65), and for a single person with AGI of $17,500 or more.

E. Earned income credit

    (1) The credit is based on the percentage of earned income and is phased out if earned income exceeds a certain dollar amount.

    (2) The percentage depends on whether the taxpayer has no children, one child, or more than one child.

    (3) This credit is different from other credits in that it is *refundable* (other refundable credits are listed under "Other credits").

F. Adoption credit

    (1) There is a tax credit of up to $10,000 for qualifying expenses paid to adopt an eligible child, which is indexed for inflation after 2002.

    (2) An eligible child is either under the age of 18 or is physically or mentally incapable of self-care.

    (3) Any credit for adoption expenses disallowed can be carried forward to the next five years and used on a first-in first-out (FIFO) basis.

G. Foreign tax credit

    (1) U.S. citizens are subject to tax on their worldwide income. To avoid double taxation, a foreign credit is allowed when income is subject to both foreign and U.S. tax.

    (2) Computing the credit

        (a) The credit is generally the lesser of:

            i. The amount of foreign tax paid

            ii. The amount of U.S. tax that would be due on the foreign income

(b) To the extent that the credit is disallowed in the current year, it may be carried back two years and forward five years.

(c) The foreign tax credit is allowed against both regular tax and AMT, but must be recomputed for AMT purposes.

(3) Taxpayers are allowed to treat the amount of foreign taxes paid either as a deduction from income or as a refundable tax credit. The credit will generally be preferable, as it provides dollar-for-dollar tax savings.

H. Retirement savings contributions credit

(1) For tax years 2002 through 2006, the 2001 Economic Growth and Tax Relief Reconciliation Act (EGTRRA) added a nonrefundable personal credit based on an eligible individual's qualified retirement savings contributions.

(2) An eligible individual is a taxpayer who meets *all* of the following:

(a) Must be at least 18 years old

(b) Must not be eligible to be claimed as a dependent by another

(c) Must not be a full-time student during five or more months of the calendar year

(d) Must have adjusted gross income below certain thresholds

(3) Qualified retirement savings contributions include those to:

(a) Section 401(k) and Section 457 plans

(b) Traditional or Roth IRA accounts

(c) Simplified employee pensions (SEPs)

(d) Simple IRA accounts

(e) Tax-exempt or public school annuities

(f) In the case of voluntary after-tax contributions, qualified retirement plans

(4) The maximum credit is $1,000.

I. Other credits

(1) Other nonrefundable credits (credits reduce tax to zero, but excess is not refunded): mortgage interest credit, credit for prior year minimum tax, and credit for electric vehicles

(2) Other refundable credits (any excess is refunded to taxpayer): credit for excess Social Security tax withheld, credit for tax on undistributed capital gain, and health insurance credit

10. Payment of tax

A. Most individuals are required to file Form 1040 by April 15 of the following year. Individuals who have adopted a fiscal year must file by the 15th day of the fourth month following the close of the taxable year.

B. The law permits individuals to file an *automatic* four-month extension, but the individual will pay the IRS interest for the delinquent payment.

11. Estimated payment and withholding requirements

A. Estimated payments are amounts paid throughout the year by self-employed taxpayers or those taxpayers owing taxes in the prior years. Tax law does not permit a taxpayer to wait until the date for filing returns to pay all taxes.

B. Withholding requirements are amounts withheld from employer paychecks throughout the year.

C. Employers must withhold income tax from wages paid to employees but not from amounts paid to independent contractors. Employees are entitled to additional withholding exemptions or allowances.

D. Estimated tax is due the middle of April, June, September, and January.

12. Kiddie tax

A. Kiddie tax rules were established to prevent the abuse of transferring income-earning property from high income tax brackets to low income tax brackets.

B. Kiddie tax rules apply to children if (in 2003)

(1) Unearned income (investment income) is above $1,500.
(2) Child is under age 14.
(3) Either parent was alive during the year.

C. For a child under age 14 by the close of the tax year, the first $750 of unearned income is not taxed, the next $750 of unearned income is taxed at the child's tax rate, and the excess of the child's unearned income is taxed at the parent's marginal rate.

D. For a child at or above age 14 by the close of the tax year, the first $750 of unearned income is not taxed, and any additional unearned income is taxed only at the child's rate. None will be taxed at the parent's rate.

E. Parents of children who are subject to the kiddie tax rule may elect to report the child's income on their own tax return (versus the child's filing a separate return). To make the election, the income must consist solely of dividends, interest, or capital gain distributions that amount to no more than $7,500.

F. Advantages of reporting the child's income on the parent's tax return:

(1) There is no need to file a separate return for the child.
(2) Parent's investment income is increased, which may allow for a greater investment interest deduction.
(3) The ceiling for charitable contributions is increased.

G. Disadvantages of reporting the child's income on the parent's tax return:

(1) Higher aggregate gross income

(a) Can accelerate phaseout of itemized deductions
(b) May reduce $25,000 rental loss allowance for active participants
(c) Deduction for IRA contributions may be phased out.
(d) May reduce or phase out several tax credits

(2) Lost deductions

(a) A child's itemized deductions are not allowed on a parent's return.
(b) The combined exemption for AMT may be reduced.

H. If the child is under 14, the kiddie tax can be avoided by transferring or investing in assets that appreciate and do not generate any taxable income until they are sold.

13. Imputed interest

A. Imputed interest rules were established to prevent individuals from shifting income from high tax brackets to low tax brackets and from shifting interest income to capital gain income by raising the purchase price and charging less interest.

B. If the interest rate is below the applicable federal rates (AFR), the seller may be required to add imputed interest to income.

C. If the AFR is above the interest rate charged at time of transfer, the seller reports the additional interest income, and the buyer is allowed an additional interest deduction.

D. Exceptions

    (1) Loans up to $10,000 to purchase non–income-producing property

    (2) Loans up to $100,000 if the borrower's net investment income is under $1,000

    (3) Compensation-related loans up to $10,000 between an employer and employee or independent contractor

    (4) Loans up to $10,000 between a corporation and a shareholder of a corporation

E. The AFR is set monthly by the federal government according to type and term of loan.

TOPIC 60: TAX ACCOUNTING METHODS

1. Cash method

    A. Recognize income when received; recognize expenses when paid.

    B. Include all items of income constructively received; deduct all bills paid.

    C. Expenses paid in advance are deducted when they apply.

    D. Use with service-oriented businesses and businesses with little or no inventory.

2. Accrual method

    A. Recognize income when earned; recognize expenses when incurred.

    B. Match income and expenses in the correct year.

    C. Items of income are included when they are earned, even though payment may be received in another tax year.

    D. All events that fix the individual's right to receive the income must have happened, and the individual must be able to figure the amount with reasonable accuracy.

    E. Only the accrual method may be used for purchase and sales of inventory.

3. Hybrid method

    A. Any combination of the cash method and the accrual method may be used if the combination clearly shows income.

    B. Applies to businesses with both service and inventory

4. Long-term contracts—building, installation, construction, or manufacturing contracts that are not completed in the tax year in which they are entered into (i.e., manufacturing contract, machinery contract)

5. Installment sale

    A. Installment sale treatment occurs when payments are received in a year other than the year of sale.

    B. Each payment usually consists of three parts: (1) interest, (2) gain on sale, and (3) recovery of basis.

    C. Interest must be charged at a rate at least equal to the IRS minimum. The amount of interest is subtracted from the total of payments made, and the remainder is split between gain on sale and recovery of basis.

    D. The following sales are not reported under the installment method:

        (1) Sale resulting in loss

        (2) Sale of inventory in the ordinary course of a trade or business

        (3) Sale by a dealer of personal or real property, except for certain farm or time-share dispositions

        (4) Publicly traded stocks or bonds

        (5) Sale of a personal residence when the gain has been excluded under $250,000/$500,000 limits

        (6) Portion of a sale resulting in ordinary income due to depreciation recapture

(7) Sale of depreciable property to a related person

(8) Sale when the gain has been deferred under the like-kind exchange rules

(9) Sale in which the taxpayer has elected not to use the installment method

E. A taxpayer would want to elect out of installment treatment for the following reasons:

(1) Taxpayer has a net operating loss (NOL) carryforward.

(2) Taxpayer has a long-term capital loss carryforward.

(3) Taxpayer has a large amount of suspended investment interest expense and can make an election to have the capital gain on the installment sale treated as investment income.

(4) Taxpayer has tax credits available.

F. Reasons for doing an installment sale:

(1) It defers tax.

    (a) Higher principal earns more interest.

    (b) Client may be in a lower tax bracket in the future.

(2) The note should carry higher interest rates than a bank.

(3) It makes the property easier to sell.

(4) Seller is willing to bear the risk of repossession in order to earn a higher profit.

(5) Reselling the note gives the seller greater liquidity.

(6) It may be the only way to sell closely held stock.

(7) It may prevent Social Security benefits from becoming taxable.

G. Get a large down payment to minimize potential foreclosure when selling on the installment basis.

H. A taxpayer may elect to report the entire gain in the year of sale even though the payments will be made in installments.

I. The seller must recognize a portion of the profit each year.

(1) The gross profit percentage is determined in the year the installment sale is made to determine how much of each payment is profit.

Gross profit percentage = Gross profit ÷ Contract price

(2) The contract price includes the total of all principal payments to be made by the buyer over the term of the installment sale.

J. Ordinary income recapture

(1) If property is subject to depreciation recapture, recaptured income must be fully reported by taxpayer in year of disposition as ordinary income.

(2) Recaptured income must be added back to adjusted basis before calculating gross profit percentage.

K. *Exception*: Related party rule: If sale occurs to family member who in turn sells the purchased property within two years, the original seller must recognize all gain deferred by installment sale.

6. Accounting periods

A. The annual time period over which a taxpayer calculates tax liability

B. Taxpayers file on a calendar-year basis.

C. The tax year can be changed only with permission of the IRS.

7. Method changes

A. Once a business entity or individual has adopted an accounting method or accounting period, a change in the method or period requires permission of the IRS even if the original method was incorrect. Such corrections cannot be made by filing an amended tax return.

B. Changes in method include going from cash basis to accrual basis or from one inventory valuation method to another (i.e., FIFO, LIFO [last-in first-out]).

TOPIC 61: TAX CHARACTERISTICS OF ENTITIES

1. Taxation at entity level

    A. Only corporations pay income tax at the entity level.

    (1) Corporations report taxable income on Form 1120.
    (2) Corporations are not subject to the passive activity loss rules.
    (3) Taxable income paid and net income reported on financial statements are usually not the same.
    (4) Corporations generally have tax rates that are more favorable than individual rates.

    B. Dividends received deduction: If a corporation receives dividends from another corporation, it is entitled to a deduction.

    (1) If recipient corporation owns less than 20 percent of the stock of the paying corporation, the deduction is 70 percent of dividends received.
    (2) If recipient corporation owns 20 percent but less than 80 percent of the stock of the paying corporation, the deduction is 80 percent of dividends received.
    (3) If recipient corporation owns 80 percent or more of the stock of the paying corporation, the deduction is 100 percent of dividends received.

    C. Net operating losses can be carried back only 2 years or forward 20 years to offset other corporate income. They are not passed through to shareholders.

    D. Capital gains and losses recognized by corporations are taxed at the same rate as ordinary income and are not subject to the reduced capital gains rate. Deductions for capital losses can offset capital gains only, and no amount can be used to offset ordinary income. Net capital losses can be carried back three years and forward five years to offset capital gains.

    E. Tax-advantaged employee benefits for corporations

    (1) Nontaxable to employee and immediately deductible by corporation

        (a) Premium for group term insurance less than $50,000
        (b) Travel and entertainment
        (c) Health and accident insurance
        (d) Meals and lodging for convenience of employee

    (2) Tax-deferred to employee and immediately deductible by corporation: qualified pension and profit sharing plans

    (3) Immediately taxable to employee and immediately deductible by corporation

        (a) Group term insurance greater than $50,000
        (b) Additional cash salary
        (c) Group legal services

2. Flow through of income and losses to corporations

    A. Getting cash out of the corporation

    (1) Shareholders serve as corporate executives, therefore, receiving salary that is taxed only once at the individual level, while providing a tax deduction for the corporation.
    (2) Shareholders serve as creditors.

        (a) By lending money to a corporation; the interest paid to the shareholder becomes a deductible expense for the corporation.

(b) By leasing property to the corporation, the shareholders receive rent payments that are deductible expenses for the corporation.

(3) Dividends are paid with after-tax dollars (double taxation), but salaries, interest, and rent are paid with before-tax dollars.

B. Constructive dividend: a distribution by a corporation to a shareholder that the corporation classifies as salary, interest, rent, or some other type of payment but that the IRS classifies as a dividend

C. Using closely held corporations as a tax shelter

(1) Corporations generally offer lower tax rates than the high individual tax rates.

(2) Corporations avoid double taxation by accumulating earnings, thus increasing the value of the stock. The unrealized appreciation of stock is not taxable.

(3) When the stock is sold or liquidated at some future time, corporations recognize a taxable gain while indirectly paying a second tax on the accumulated earnings. This strategy reduces the present value of the second tax.

(4) Three factors create tax savings:

(a) Spread between the corporate and individual tax rates
(b) Deferral of tax payments
(c) Conversion of ordinary income (dividend payments) to capital gain income

3. Flow through of income and losses to partnerships and S Corporations

A. Tax basis

(1) A partner's initial basis equals initial investment of cash or property *plus* the share of partnership debt for which the partner may ultimately be held responsible. Suppose, for example, three individuals each deposit $10,000 into a partnership in which they are equal general partners. The partnership borrows $15,000 from a bank to buy supplies and equipment. Each partner's basis is $15,000: the initial cash contributions plus a proportionate share of the partnership debt.

(2) A shareholder's initial basis in stock of an S Corporation equals the cash plus the adjusted basis of any property transferred in exchange for the stock. No debt is included in the shareholder's stock basis because there is no personal liability in S Corporations. However, a shareholder can have a *separate* basis in a debt obligation.

B. Reporting requirements—Partnerships and S Corporations are not taxable entities. Taxable income is measured and characterized at the entity level and taxed directly to the partners or shareholders.

C. Tax consequences to partners

(1) Each partner receives a Schedule K-1 that details information about the partner's *distributive share* of the partnership's income or loss from business items and separately stated items, such as dividend income, capital gains, and charitable donations.

(2) The cash flow from the business is irrelevant to the computation of the partner's tax liability. Thus, the partner is taxed on his or her distributive share of the partnership income whether or not the amount is actually distributed.

(3) General partners are required to pay self-employment (SE) tax on their distributive share of ordinary business income. Limited partners are not considered self-employed and are not required to pay SE tax on their distributive share of ordinary income.

D. Tax consequences to shareholders of an S Corporation

      (1) Shareholders receive a Schedule K-1 (same as partnerships) to incorporate into their individual tax returns.

      (2) The cash flow from the S Corporation is irrelevant to the computation of the shareholder's tax liability.

      (3) Shareholders can also be employees of the corporation. The employee and corporation pay Federal Insurance Contributions Act (FICA) payroll taxes, and the corporation withholds federal income tax. The corporation issues a W-2 form to any shareholder/employee along with a K-1. Shareholders are *not* subject to SE tax.

  E. Adjusting the basis in a partnership

      (1) The basis in a partnership *increases* by ordinary business income, capital gains, and dividend income and *decreases* from ordinary business loss, capital loss, and cash distributions.

      (2) If a partner is allocated income (taxable) but receives no cash distribution from that income, the partner is making an additional investment in the partnership. The cash distribution in future years is considered a nontaxable return on investment. Thus, cash distributions are generally nontaxable for pass-through entities.

      (3) Partners may deduct their distributive share of partnership losses for the year. However, this results in a reduction of their cost basis in the partnership interest.

      (4) The basis cannot be reduced below zero. If a partner's share of loss exceeds the basis, the excess cannot be deducted in the current year. It can be carried forward to future years, but the basis must be restored in order to deduct the carryforward.

  F. Adjusting the basis of S Corporation stock

      (1) Shareholders *increase* the basis of stock by their share of the corporation's income and gain; they decrease the basis of stock by their share of the corporation's losses.

      (2) The cash distribution is considered a nontaxable return of investment that reduces their stock basis. Thus, cash distributions are generally nontaxable for pass-through entities.

      (3) Losses are deductible to the extent of the owner's equity investment and debt obligation.

      (4) In both cases, the basis cannot be reduced below zero. For example, Steve has a basis in stock of $90,000 and a basis in debt of $30,000. Therefore, Steve has an equity investment and an investment as a corporate creditor. If the corporation passes through a loss of $150,000 to Steve (reflected on his K-1), the most that can be deducted is $120,000 on his Form 1040. The $30,000 nondeductible loss is carried forward.

  G. Maximizing tax benefits of start-up firms: Losses immediately pass through to partners or shareholders. For a C Corporation, losses may be trapped at the entity level as loss carryforwards.

  H. Partnerships offer the ability to shift income to family members.

      (1) By dividing income among a number of family members, the total tax burden may shrink to the extent that the division causes income to be taxed at a lower tax bracket.

      (2) Family partnerships are common for shifting income, but the IRS closely restricts their use as income-shifting devices.

4. Special taxes at entity level for flow-through entities

  A. Built-in gains tax

      (1) When one corporation is acquired by another, there are limits in the extent to which the built-in gains of one corporation (gain corporation) can be used to offset the preacquisition losses of the other corporation. If either corporation is a gain

corporation, then any income attributable to built-in gains within five years of the acquisition date cannot be offset by the preacquisition loss of another corporation.

   (2) This rule does not apply if there was a control relationship within a five-year period from the acquisition date.

B. LIFO recapture

   (1) The LIFO recapture amount is excess FIFO inventory over that of LIFO. A C Corporation must include the LIFO recapture amount in its income when it converts to an S Corporation.

   (2) The tax calculated on the LIFO recapture is paid in four equal installments over four tax years.

C. Excess net passive income tax

   (1) An S Corporation that was originally a C Corporation will owe excess net passive income tax if passive income is greater than 25 percent of all gross income. The tax is imposed at 35 percent of the excess net passive income.

   (2) The tax makes an S Corporation with undistributed C Corporation earnings undesirable for holding rental properties or other income-generating assets.

D. Personal holding company

   (1) This is a corporation in which 50 percent of more of the value of the outstanding stock is owned by five or fewer individuals and which creates most of its income from investment or passive activities, such as dividends, interest, rents, and royalties.

   (2) The tax equals 38.6 percent (in 2003) of *undistributed* corporate earnings.

E. Personal service corporation

   (1) Corporations performing services in the fields of health, law, engineering, architecture, accounting, actuarial science, the performing arts, or consulting

   (2) Subject to a flat tax rate of 35 percent and passive loss limitations

F. Accumulated earnings tax

   (1) The tax advantage of corporate tax rates on earnings accumulated by the corporation is limited somewhat by the accumulated earnings tax.

   (2) The accumulated earnings tax is a penalty tax designed to prevent tax avoidance through the accumulation of earnings within the corporation beyond expected needs of the business.

   (3) A corporation can accumulate up to a minimum credit of $250,000 of earnings and profits without encountering any problem with the accumulated earnings tax; beyond this amount, it must demonstrate to the IRS that the accumulation is for reasonable needs of the business.

   (4) If the corporation cannot demonstrate this need, the IRS imposes the accumulated earnings tax at a rate of 38.6 percent (in 2003) on all accumulated taxable income.

5. Use of losses

A. As mentioned earlier, a partner and a shareholder are allowed to deduct losses that are passed through against income from other sources.

B. The basis cannot be reduced below zero. If a partner's or shareholder's share of loss exceeds the basis, the excess cannot be deducted in the current year. It can be carried forward to future years, but the basis must be restored in order to deduct the carryforward.

TOPIC 62: INCOME TAXATION OF TRUSTS AND ESTATES

1. General issues

   A. Filing requirements

      (1) A trustee must file Form 1041 if the trust is not tax-exempt and if

         (a) The trust has any taxable income for the year,

         (b) The trust has gross income of $600 or more, or

         (c) Any beneficiary is a nonresident alien

      (2) The executor or administrator must file Form 1041 for a domestic estate that has

         (a) Gross income of $600 or more, or

         (b) Any beneficiary who is a nonresident alien

      (3) Trusts and estates are required to file a tax return in each calendar year that it has taxable income. Trusts and estates use Form 1041 to report income and distributions. Taxable income distributed to beneficiaries is passed through on a Schedule K-1. The trust pays tax on undistributed income.

   B. Deadlines—For calendar-year estates and trusts, file Form 1041 and Schedule K-1 on or before April 15. For fiscal-year estates and trusts, file by the 15th day of the fourth month following the close of the tax year. An automatic extension of three months is available.

   C. Choice of taxable year

      (1) Trusts must use a calendar year unless they are tax-exempt, charitable, or grantor trusts. Estates can use either a calendar or fiscal year.

      (2) The time allowed for selection of a calendar year for an estate cannot extend beyond 12 months after the decedent's death.

   D. Tax treatment of distributions to beneficiaries

      (1) The beneficiary, not the trust or decedent's estate, pays income tax on his or her distributive share of income. Schedule K-1 (Form 1041) is used to notify beneficiaries of amounts to be included on their income tax returns. The distributed income maintains the same form it had in the trust or estate. Income is taxed to the trust or estate if it is retained.

      (2) The composition of distributable net income (DNI) (discussed later) determines the type of income distributed and taxed to beneficiaries. If 75 percent of DNI is taxable income and 25 percent is tax-exempt interest, then 75 percent of DNI allocated to beneficiaries is taxable income and 25 percent is tax-exempt.

      (3) Schedule K-1 reports the amounts taxable to beneficiaries.

   E. Rate structure—Trusts and estates compute their tax under a separate, unfavorable tax rate schedule that has five brackets and quickly reaches the top marginal rate.

2. Grantor trusts—A trust grantor or another person with significant control over a trust and its property may be taxed on its income as the owner of the trust. A grantor trust is not treated as a separate trust for tax purposes, and income from the trust is taxed to the grantor.

3. Simple trusts

   A. These trusts are required to distribute *all* of their *trust accounting income* to beneficiaries. They have a standard deduction of zero and are allowed deductions similar to those of individuals, except that the personal exemption amount is only $300.

   B. No distributions are allowed for charitable purposes.

4. Complex trusts—A trust that does not meet the definition of a simple trust is a complex trust. Such trusts can accumulate income, make charitable contributions, and distribute principal to

beneficiaries. They have a standard deduction of zero and are allowed the same deductions as simple trusts, except that the personal exemption amount is only $100.

5. Trust income

A. Trust accounting income—This income includes interest, dividends, rents, royalties, and other items. Capital gains may also be included in the income of the trust if allowed by state law. Accounting income does not include DNI.

B. Trust taxable income

(1) The taxable income of a trust is calculated in the same manner as that of an individual unless indicated otherwise. A trust's taxable income equals accounting income less any deduction, which is limited to DNI.

(2) Interest that is tax-exempt to an individual is also tax-exempt to a trust. Capital gain and capital loss rules that apply to individuals also apply to estates and trusts. The rules that apply to reporting ordinary gains and losses for an individual also apply to trusts and estates.

(3) Trusts and estates are subject to the passive activity loss rules and the at-risk rules. If an owner of rental property actively participates in the management of the rental property, he or she can offset against other income up to $25,000 of net losses. The offset is phased out when modified AGI exceeds $100,000 and eliminated at $150,000. A trust is *not* allowed to use the offset. An estate is allowed to use the offset for taxable years ending within two years of the decedent's death.

(4) The rules for individual taxpayers claiming a deduction generally carry over to estates and trusts.

C. Distributable net income (DNI)

(1) The trust or estate receives a deduction based on the taxable income distributed to the beneficiaries during the year. The deductible amount is computed on Schedule B, Form 1041. The income distribution deduction allowed by estates and trusts for funds distributed to beneficiaries is limited to DNI.

(2) Any type of income that includes DNI determines the taxability of the distribution, not the type of property received as distribution.

(3) Any amount distributed that is greater than the DNI is considered undistributed net income (UNI) or corpus. This excess amount receives no current deduction. If distributions are less than DNI, only the amount distributed can be deducted.

6. Estate income tax

A. Estate income tax is calculated as follows:

Step 1	Determine adjusted total income.
Step 2	Determine DNI.
Step 3	Subtract DNI from adjusted total income.
Step 4	The amount remaining is subject to tax at the estate or trust level.

B. In calculating taxable income, an estate may use a personal exemption of $600. If a trust (simple) must distribute all of its trust accounting income immediately, it is allowed a $300 exemption. All other trusts (complex) are allowed a $100 exemption.

TOPIC 63: BASIS

1. Original basis

A. The calculation of any assets depends on how the asset was acquired by the owner. Original basis can be summarized as follows:

(1) *Gifts*. FMV for losses or the donor's basis for gains (double basis rule)

(2) *Inherited assets*. Fair market value on date of death

(3) *Assumption of debt*. Buyer includes any debt assumed in the purchase price in his original basis.

B. Adjusted basis—The property's original basis adjusted to the date of disposition equals cost plus capital additions minus capital recoveries.

C. Original issue discount (OID)

(1) When a long-term debt instrument is issued at a price lower than its par value, the difference is called OID. Investors cannot defer recognition of the interest income represented by the original issue discount. OID rules do not apply to short-term debt obligations (maturity dates of one year or less).

(2) Interest is reported on Form OID. The amount of interest shown is generally accurate for only the original bondholder, because the company that issued the bond does not track its activity in the secondary market.

D. Carryover basis

(1) Adjusted basis of purchased property

(a) Purchase price plus acquisition costs (if any) plus improvements

(b) Factors that would reduce adjusted basis include depreciation (cost recovery deduction), Section 179 expense deduction, and return of capital.

(c) Acquisition cost includes freight, setup and installation, legal and professional fees associated with the purchase, settlement and recording fees, closing costs, and commissions.

(2) Adjusted basis if property acquired through an inheritance: Basis equals FMV on date of death or alternative valuation date (six months from date of death), if elected. Also referred to as "stepped-up basis."

(3) Adjusted basis of gifting—Basis cannot be determined until sale occurs.

(a) Sales price *exceeds* both donor's cost and FMV on date of gift: basis equals donor's cost.

(b) Sales price is *less* than both donor's cost and FMV on date of gift; basis equals the item that would result in smallest loss.

(c) Sales price is *between* donor's cost and FMV on date of gift; basis equals sales price (no gain or loss).

(4) Adjusting basis if gift taxes are paid—This applies only if the FMV of the property at the date of disposition exceeds the donor's adjusted basis. This allows the donee to calculate a new gain basis using:

$$\text{Donor's adjusted basis} + \frac{\text{Unrealized appreciation}}{\text{FMV}} \times \text{Gift tax paid}$$

Example: Mike gave Martha stock with an FMV of $50,000 and paid gift tax of $11,000. Mike originally acquired the stock for $15,000. What is Martha's basis in the stock?

Answer: $15,000 + \dfrac{\$35,000}{\$50,000} \times \$11,000 = \$22,700$ basis

(5) Holding period for gifts

(a) *For gain basis*. The holding period starts on the date the donor acquired the property.

(b) *For loss basis*. The holding period starts on the date of the gift.

E. Stepped-up basis

(1) Assets included in a taxable estate of a decedent receive a stepped-up basis. The receivers of the bequests receive a basis in those assets equal to the fair market value at date of the decedent's death or, alternately, six months after the death. The step-up in basis is available only for those assets in the taxable estate. If assets are kept out of the estate, such as gifts, they will not enjoy the step-up in basis.

(2) *Common law* states have a step-up basis for half of the assets; a step-up in basis for the decedent's share of ownership but not for the survivor's share.

(3) *Community property* states have a full step-up in basis. For tax purposes at death, the new cost basis is the fair market value (FMV) at the date of death for both halves of the community property, even though only one-half is included in the decedent spouse's estate.

(4) Property owned solely by a decedent generally receives a full step-up basis for the person who acquires it.

   Example: Bart owned stock in XYZ, which he purchased for $1,000 in 1935, until his death in 2003, when it passed on to his son John. At Bart's death, the stock was worth $250,000. John kept the stock for six months and sold it for $270,000. John has a realized long-term capital gain of $20,000 between the sale price and the date-of-death value (because it was acquired from the decedent, the holding period for the property is automatically considered long term).

(5) For *joint tenancy with right of survivorship*, two rules are followed in deciding what is included in a decedent's estate and the surviving owner's new basis.

   (a) *Husband and wife rule*. Where the only joint tenants are husband and wife, half of the FMV at the date of death is included in the decedent's estate and the surviving spouse's new basis will equal half the total predeath basis and half the FMV at the date of death.

   (b) *Consideration furnished rule*. Where joint tenants include nonspouses, the decedent's gross estate includes that proportion of the property as the decedent's share of the consideration bears to the total consideration. The new basis for each surviving co-owner's interest is his or her old basis plus an increase by the amount included in the decedent's estate split equally among the surviving joint tenants.

(6) For *tenancy in common*, the surviving spouse's cost basis at death is the amount included in the deceased spouse's estate. If left to a co-owner, the new basis is his or her old basis plus an increase by the amount included in the decedent's estate.

   Example: Lyle, Joel, and Dan purchased property as tenants in common. Of the $100,000 purchase price, Lyle paid $50,000 and took a 50 percent interest, Joel paid $30,000 and took a 30 percent interest, and Dan paid $20,000 and took a 20 percent interest. Years later when Joel died, the property was worth $250,000 and his estate included $75,000 because he owned a 30 percent interest. If Joel left his interest to his widow, Betty, her basis would be $75,000. If he instead left his interest to co-owner Dan, Dan's total basis in the 50 percent interest he would then own would be $95,000 ($75,000 plus his $20,000 contribution).

F. Impact of community property and common law on basis

(1) Community property states provide a decided advantage over common law states in regard to basis adjustments at death.

(2) Couples residing in community property states should hold appreciated property as community property. On the other hand, if property has decreased in value, community property will receive a full step-down in basis at the first death and some other form of title may be preferred.

TOPIC 64: COST RECOVERY CONCEPTS

1. Definition of depreciable property

  A. Property used in a trade or business or held to produce income
  B. Property must lose its value over time.
  C. Property must have a determinable life of greater than one year.

2. What cannot be depreciated

  A. Property placed in service and disposed of in the same year
  B. Land
  C. Inventory
  D. Equipment used to build capital improvements

3. Modified accelerated cost recovery system (MACRS)

  A. Depreciation rules that apply to assets placed in service between 1981 and 1986 are often referred to as the "accelerated cost recovery system" (ACRS). Assets that are placed in service after 1986 fall under a modified cost recovery system, which is called the "modified accelerated cost recovery system" (MACRS).
  B. ACRS generally provided faster recovery than MACRS, but only certain property placed in service under ACRS is still in service for tax purposes.
  C. The term *accelerated* means any cost recovery method that provides a higher deduction in the earlier years of the asset's recovery period than would have been provided in a straight-line recovery method.
  D. The estimated useful life of an asset is irrelevant in the computation of tax depreciation with MACRS. This often results in different numbers relative to what a firm reports as taxable income and what it reports as tax expense on its financial statements.
  E. MACRS is used for most tangible assets in a business or in the production of income after 1986. Eight cost recovery periods are used for property: 3, 5, 7, 10, 15, 20, 27½, and 39 years. The most important recovery periods to know are those for computer software, at 3 years; cars and computer hardware, at 5 years; office furniture and fixtures, at 7 years; residential real estate, at 27½ years; and nonresidential rental property, at 39 years.
  F. Assets with a 3-, 5-, 7-, or 10-year recovery period are depreciated using a 200 percent declining-balance method. Assets with a 15-year or 20-year recovery period are depreciated using a 150 percent declining-balance method. The depreciation method switches to straight-line when a straight-line computation over the remaining recovery period results in a greater reduction. There is no salvage value below 200 percent and 150 percent declining-balance. For property with a life of 27½ or 39 years, straight-line depreciation must be used. MACRS is an accelerated cost recovery system in name only for these assets.
  G. Cost basis

    (1) Depreciation allows for the recovery of the cost of assets purchased for use in a trade or business.

      (a) Reduces the cost basis of an asset, thus increasing future gains
      (b) Reduces current income by providing a deduction in calculating net income for a business

(2) *Example*: Rental property cost $50,000, sold for $90,000, and had $15,000 in depreciation. The amount of gain is

> *Step 1*   Adjusted basis = Basis ($50,000) − Depreciation ($15,000)
> *Step 2*   Gain = Proceeds ($90,000) − Adjusted basis ($35,000) = $55,000

(3) *Allowed or allowable rule*. Even if depreciation was *not* deducted on the taxpayer's return, the basis must be reduced by the depreciation that was allowable for that year.

H. Half-year convention

(1) The half-year convention means that in the first year of the recovery period, six months of depreciation is allowed regardless of when the asset was purchased. The firm later claims six months of depreciation in the year in which the asset is disposed of.

(2) This applies to all assets with a recovery period of 3 to 20 years.

(3) *Exception*: If more than 40 percent of the depreciable assets acquired during a taxable year are placed in service during the last three months of the year, the firm must use the midquarter convention.

I. Midquarter convention

(1) If the midquarter convention is used, then it must be used for all assets (recovery period of 3 to 20 years) placed in service during the year.

(2) Assets placed in service or disposed of in any quarter are assumed to be placed in service, or disposed of, at the midpoint of the quarter.

4. Repairs

A. When a cost incurred in regard to an asset will lengthen its useful life or increase its market value, the cost is considered a betterment and must be added to the cost of the asset and depreciated over the life of the associated asset.

B. If the cost is incurred only to bring the asset back to its normal use, then it will be considered a *repair* and can be expensed to reduce current income.

5. Special elections (Section 179 deduction)

A. A special election is an election to deduct all or part of the cost of certain qualifying property in the year it is placed in service, instead of taking depreciation deductions over a specified recovery period.

B. Taking the deduction on Form 4562 makes the election. Election can be revoked only with IRS consent.

C. Limitations

(1) The aggregate cost that may be taken into account for any taxable year cannot exceed the following applicable amount: $25,000 (2003 or later).

(2) The applicable maximum deduction for any year is reduced (but not below zero) by the amount of qualifying property placed in service during the tax year that exceeds $200,000.

(3) The total cost that can be deducted is limited to taxable income from the active conduct of any trade or business during the tax year. No loss can be created or increased by Section 179. The limit applies at both the business entity level and the individual level.

(4) If a deduction is fully used for the year, amounts above the limit can be considered for depreciation.

D. Property that qualifies

(1) Certain tangible property (except most buildings and their structural components), including "luxury" autos having a gross weight of more than 6,000 pounds

(2) Leased property usually does not qualify, with exceptions for

(a) Property manufactured or produced by the lessor

(b) Certain property that is subject to a short-term lease

E. Section 179 is not permitted if business use is 50 percent or less.

F. Section 179 recapture is required if business use drops to 50 percent or less.

G. For partnerships and S Corporations, the Section 179 deduction passes through to the owners but is limited by the Section 179 dollar limitation regardless of how many businesses the individual owns.

6. Amortization

A. Amortization is used for intangible assets that have a definite life—for example, a patent or copyright.

B. There is a 15-year amortization for intangibles beginning in the month of acquisition.

C. Certain intangibles are specifically excluded:

(1) Interests in corporations, partnerships, trusts, and estates

(2) Interests in land

(3) Computer software not acquired in connection with the purchase of a business or which is readily available to the general public

(4) Sports franchises

(5) Professional fees and transportation costs incurred in a corporate organization or reorganization

TOPIC 65: TAX CONSEQUENCES OF LIKE-KIND EXCHANGES

1. Reporting requirements

A. Form 8824 is used for like-kind exchanges. It must be filed in the current year of exchange and for two years following the year of a related party exchange.

B. Property received must be *identified* within 45 days after the date on which the property is transferred, and *received* within 180 days after the date on which the old property is transferred, but not later than the due date of the tax return (including extensions) for the year that the old property is transferred.

2. Qualifying transaction

A. Only the disposition and receipt of qualifying property can result in a nontaxable exchange.

B. No gain or loss is recognized on the exchange of property

(1) Used in a trade or business

(2) Held for investment

(3) The following guidelines are also considered when (1) and (2) apply:

(a) Such property must be exchanged solely for property used in a trade or business or held for investment.

(b) The taxpayer's intent is important in determining if property is held for investment or trade or business.

(c) The length of time the new property is used for investment or trade or business is important.

(d) *Example*: Steve exchanges his apartment building in Denver for a condo in Vail that he rents out. Five months after the exchange, he moves into the condo with the intention to live there for two years. At that time, he plans to sell the condo for a nontaxable gain under tax laws for a residence ($250,000/$500,000 limitations). The IRS would argue that he never intended to use the condo as rental property.

C. Gain may be recognized when cash or unlike property is received in addition to like-kind property. The gain is the lesser of

  (1) FMV of boot (nonqualifying property or cash) received
  (2) The gain realized

D. Treatment of losses

  (1) *No loss is recognized* when a taxpayer

      (a) Receives unlike property in the exchange of property
      (b) Receives cash in the exchange

  (2) If the taxpayer conveys unlike property in an exchange transaction, *loss is recognized* to the extent that the adjusted basis of unlike property (other than cash) exceeds fair market value.

  (3) Always increases cost basis for realized but not unrecognized losses.

E. The sale of property for cash followed by the purchase of another property does not qualify as a like-kind exchange. For example, if clients sell their property, put the money in a separate bank account, and later use it for a deposit on a new property, the transaction is not a like-kind exchange.

F. Like-kind exchanges are determined separately for buyer and seller. It is possible for only one of them to treat the property as a like-kind exchange.

G. If a property is used for both business and personal use, then an allocation of respective values must be made.

H. Property excluded from the definition of like-kind exchanges (if any of this property is received, it is treated as boot):

  (1) Stocks, bonds, and notes
  (2) Inventory property used for business
  (3) Partnership interests (a limited partnership interest can be exchanged for a general partnership in the same partnership)
  (4) Certificates of trust of beneficial interests
  (5) Foreign real estate
  (6) Contractual rights
  (7) Livestock of different sexes (swap a bull for a breeding heifer)

I. Real estate treatment in like-kind exchanges

  (1) *Like-kind* refers to the character of property, not to its quality. The following are considered like-kind exchanges:

      (a) City real estate for a ranch or farm
      (b) Improved real estate for unimproved real estate
      (c) Office building for a hotel or for developed or underdeveloped land

  (2) Intangible property qualifies for Section 1031 treatment if sold for like-kind property. If the nature of the rights are the same as the character of the underlying property, it is like-kind.

      (a) A like-kind transaction is an exchange of a copyright on a book for a copyright on another book. It is *not* the exchange of a copyright on a book for copyright on a song.
      (b) Goodwill does not qualify for a like-kind exchange.

(3) Depreciable tangible personal property must be in the same asset or product class. For example, the exchange does not qualify for Section 1031 if a half-ton truck is traded for a two-ton truck.

3. Multiple properties

A. The exchange is considered one of multiple properties if the transferred properties are separable into more than one *exchange group*. An exchange group consists of all properties transferred and received within an exchange that are of the same asset class or product class.

B. *Example*: An exchange of a boat for a boat and trailer creates two exchange groups. Each exchange group must transfer and receive at least one property.

C. Typical three-cornered exchange involves three parties and qualifies for Section 1031 treatment:

(1) *Buyer*. Wants to purchase property

(2) *Trader*. Wants to sell property, but only for other like-kind property, to avoid taxes

(3) *Seller*. Wants to sell property, but owns no new property

(4) Buyer wants Trader's property, and Trader wants Seller's property. Seller wants to sell.

(a) The property given up is not converted into cash.

(b) Intent of trade is established—wording must be included in the escrow instructions for Section 1031 exchange.

D. The purchase, sale, and exchange are usually simultaneous, but this is not required. When property is sold at different times, the exchange period begins on the date of the first exchange. In a delayed exchange, the replacement property must be designated within 45 days of closing escrow on the relinquished property and close within 180 days.

E. Exchange of one business for another generally does not qualify for Section 1031 treatment, because the assets of one business cannot be grouped together and treated as one asset.

4. Liabilities—When a taxpayer gives up property that is subject to a liability, and the transferee assumes the liability, then the taxpayer is treated as having received cash in the transaction equal to the amount of the liability being transferred. If the taxpayer has liability that is assumed, and in turn assumes a liability on the replacement property, the liabilities are netted together to calculate the cash received or paid.

5. Boot

A. Characteristics

(1) All property other than like-kind (nonqualifying property)

(2) Cash

B. Exchange of mortgage properties

(1) Relief of debt is boot received whether loan or mortgage (treated as cash received).

(2) Assumption of debt is boot given (treated as cash paid).

Example: ABC and XYZ exchange property A and property B as follows:

Property A—XYZ   FMV = $670,000, debt = $175,000, basis = $200,000
Property B—ABC   FMV = $495,000, debt = $0, basis = $415,000)

Tax Consequences of Exchange		
	ABC	**XYZ**
Amount realized:		
Value of realty acquired	$495,000	$670,000
Boot received (debt relief)	175,000	0
	$670,000	$670,000
Basis of property surrendered:		
Realty	($200,000)	(415,000)
Boot paid (debt assumed)	0	(175,000)
Gain realized	$470,000	$80,000
Gain recognized*	$175,000	$0
Gain deferred	295,000	80,000
	$470,000	$80,000

*Lesser of FMV of boot received or gain realized

C. Basis of assets received

    (1) Reduced by

        (a) Cash (boot) received
        (b) Loss recognized
        (c) Liabilities conveyed

    (2) Increased by

        (a) Cash (boot) paid
        (b) Gain recognized
        (c) Liabilities assumed

Basis Computation		
	ABC	**XYZ**
Basis of realty surrendered	$200,000	$415,000
Boot paid	0	175,000
Gain recognized	175,000	0
Boot received	(175,000)	0
Basis of realty acquired	$200,000	$590,000

D. If both parties are subject to a mortgage, only the *net* amount of debt is considered boot given and boot received.

    Example: ABC and XYZ enter into a like-kind exchange. The property surrendered by ABC is subject to a $125,000 mortgage; property surrendered by XYZ is subject to a $100,000 mortgage. ABC has boot of $25,000 from the exchange (debt relief). XYZ paid $25,000 of boot in the exchange (debt assumption). ABC must recognize $25,000 of realized gains, whereas XYZ has a tax-free exchange.

E. There is net cash boot when cash is both given and received.

F. An offset is allowed where a taxpayer is relieved of debt (boot received) and pays cash or other boot. For example, ABC transfers property subject to a $50,000 debt and $30,000 of cash in exchange for property with no debt. The *net* boot received is $20,000 [$50,000 debt relief/boot received minus $30,000 cash paid (boot given)].

G. No offset is allowed where a taxpayer assumes debt (boot given) and receives cash or other boot. For example, ABC transfers property with no debt for property subject to a $50,000 mortgage (debt assumption) and $35,000 of cash. ABC has $35,000 in boot because netting is not allowed, even though ABC gave $50,000 in boot and received only $35,000 in cash.

If this happens, the other party should take the $35,000 of cash and pay down the $50,000 of debt. As a result, the boot would be reduced by $35,000.

6. Related party transactions

A. A transaction between parties who share a common economic interest or objective and who may not be dealing at arm's length

B. A like-kind exchange of property between related parties qualifies for nonrecognition treatment.

C. If the property transferred is disposed of within two years after the date of transfer, the original property will not qualify for nonrecognition treatment. The gain or loss that was not recognized must now be recognized on the date of disposition.

D. The following dispositions will not invalidate the nonrecognition treatment of the original exchange:

(1) Dispositions or exchanges for which the avoidance of income tax was not the primary reason

(2) Dispositions due to death

(3) Dispositions due to the involuntary conversion of property

(4) Dispositions of property in nonrecognition transactions

(5) Transactions that do not involve shifting of basis

7. Involuntary conversion—Section 1033 (added by author—not part of CFP Board's 101 Topics, but can be tested on)

A. An involuntary conversion is caused by the theft, destruction, seizure, sale or exchange under threat, or condemnation of taxpayer's property.

B. It is an exception to the two-year holding period under like-kind exchanges.

C. It allows a taxpayer who realizes a gain on the involuntary conversion of property to elect to defer the gain if two conditions are met.

(1) The taxpayer must reinvest the amount realized in property similar or related in service or use.

(2) Replacement of involuntarily converted property must occur within two taxable years following the year in which the conversion took place.

D. Rules for nonrecognition

(1) If the cost of qualifying replacement property equals or exceeds the amount realized on an involuntary conversion, none of the realized gain is recognized.

(2) If the amount reinvested in qualifying replacement property is less than the amount realized, realized gain is recognized to the amount that is deficient.

(3) The amount not reinvested is treated as boot and must be recognized as gain.

(4) Unrecognized gain is deferred until a later time in the future when the property is disposed of.

E. The basis of the replacement property is its cost less unrecognized gain.

F. Section 1033 applies only to gains, not to losses.

TOPIC 66: TAX CONSEQUENCES OF GAIN OR LOSS ON SALE OF ASSETS

1. Holding period

   A. Capital gains and losses are based on three holding periods.

      (1) *Short-term capital gains or losses* result from the sale of securities owned for one year or less. These are taxed as ordinary income.

      (2) *Long-term capital gains or losses* result from the sale of securities owned for more than one year. These receive a preferential tax rate.

      (3) *Qualified five-year gain property for sales after December 31, 2000, and held for more than five years*. These receive a preferential tax rate of 18 percent.

   B. The holding period generally starts the day after acquisition and runs through the date of disposition. If the asset is acquired through an exchange, and the basis in the acquired property is determined by the asset given up, then the holding period of the asset received includes the holding period of the property given up.

   C. If the property is received by gift and later sold at a gain, then the donee's holding period includes the time the donor held the property. If the property is sold at a loss, then the donee's holding period does not include the time held by the donor.

   D. Property acquired through a bequest is always considered to be held by the recipient for more than one year unless purchased by the estate for distribution to the recipient.

2. Sale of residence

   A. $500,000 in gain for joint filers ($250,000 for single individuals)

   B. Taxpayer must live at primary residence two out of last five years before sale.

   C. The exclusion is to be used only every two years.

   D. Changes in employment, health problems, or unforeseen circumstances before reaching two-year exclusion requirement

      (1) The numerator of the ratio is the shorter of

         (a) The aggregate time period of ownership/use of the residence

         (b) The time period between the earlier sale of a residence for which gain was excluded and the current sale

      (2) The denominator is equal to two years.

      (3) *Example*: A single taxpayer has lived in her first house for 18 months. She is forced to sell the house because of a new job accepted in a different state. The amount of gain excluded cannot exceed $187,500 ($250,000 × (18 ÷ 24)). If she realizes a gain of $75,000, the entire amount is excludible.

3. Capital assets (Section 1221)

   A. The IRC defines capital assets by exception. Every asset is a capital asset unless it falls in one of eight categories:

      (1) Business inventories

      (2) Business accounts or notes receivable

      (3) Business supplies

      (4) Real or depreciable business property and intangible business assets subject to amortization

      (5) Creative assets (copyright, composition, or artwork if held by the creator)

      (6) U.S. government publications

    (7) Commodities derivatives

    (8) Hedging transaction properties

B. Capital assets for businesses are any assets held for long-term investment rather than active business use. Equity and creditor interests in other firms are capital in nature. Self-created patents are capital assets. Goodwill is a capital asset.

C. Capital losses can be deducted only to the extent of capital gains.

D. Capital loss carrybacks and carryforwards vary among individuals and businesses.

    (1) Individuals can carry capital losses forward indefinitely.

    (2) Businesses can carry capital losses back three years and forward five years. Capital losses are used as a deduction only against capital gains recognized during the eight-year period.

E. Rules for netting capital gains and losses

    (1) Short-term losses are used to offset short-term gains, and long-term losses are used to offset long-term gains.

    (2) If there is a net short-term loss, it is used to offset long-term gains. If net short-term losses are less than long-term gains, the resulting amount is taxed as long-term capital gain.

    (3) If there is a net long-term loss, it is used to offset short-term gains. If net long-term losses are less than short-term gains, the resulting amount is taxed as short-term capital gain.

    (4) If there is a net short-term or long-term capital loss after deducting long-term and short-term capital gains, the capital loss is used to offset against other income, such as dividends and interest. Only $3,000 of the net capital loss can be allowed as a deduction against AGI. The nondeductible amount of the loss is carried forward indefinitely against future capital gains and losses. The long-term capital loss carryforward is netted against 28 percent rate gain before other long-term gain.

F. Preferential rates exist for individuals.

    (1) The 28 percent tax rate is a *maximum* rate of 28 percent. This category recognizes realized gains and losses from the sale of collectibles such as works of art, antiques, gems, stamps, and coins.

    (2) Other long-term gain is taxed at a 20 percent rate. Any portion of such gain that would be taxed at 15 percent under the ordinary rate structure is taxed at only 10 percent.

    (3) For the sale of securities held for more than five years, the capital gain rate is decreased from 10 percent to 8 percent. The rate is also decreased from 20 percent to 18 percent, with one restriction. The holding period for property must begin after 2000. The 18 percent rate cannot apply until 2006.

G. In general, taxpayers prefer capital gains to ordinary gains; they prefer ordinary losses to capital losses.

4. Depreciation recapture

A. Personal or real property used in trade or business (Section 1231)

    (1) Section 1231 assets are certain assets used in trade or business that are held for more than one year. These assets include depreciable tangible and intangible personal property, as well as real property that is depreciable or not. Section 1231 assets do not include inventory.

(2) If a taxpayer has a Section 1231 net gain in the current year but had a Section 1231 net loss in any of the five previous years, the taxpayer must recapture the previous year's loss by treating an equivalent amount of current year gain as ordinary income.

(3) Section 1231 netting procedure

Step 1	Net all Section 1231 gains and losses.
Step 2	If combined result is a net loss, the loss is treated as ordinary; if the result is a gain, the gain is treated as a capital gain.
Exception	If a net gain applies to the current year but the taxpayer had Section 1231 net losses in any of the five previous years, the previous year's losses must be recaptured—an equivalent amount of current year gain is treated as ordinary income.

(4) The depreciation recapture rule requires that gains attributable to previous year depreciation or amortization deductions be characterized as ordinary income (Section 1245 or 1250), rather than Section 1231 gain.

   (a) *Full recapture rule*. The amount of gain equal to accumulated depreciation or amortization through date of sale is recharacterized as ordinary income.

   Example: ABC purchased an asset for $100,000. The asset has accumulated $60,000 MACRS depreciation over the last three years. This results in an adjusted cost basis of $40,000. If the asset is sold for $100,000, ABC recognizes a $60,000 gain. The entire gain is attributable to depreciation of the asset and, as such, is characterized as ordinary income. If the recapture requirement did not exist, the entire gain would be a Section 1231 capital gain.

   (b) *Partial recapture rule for realty*. Applies to buildings, improvements, and other permanent attachments. Only accelerated depreciation in excess of straight-line depreciation is recaptured.

(5) Capital gains are always classified as Section 1231 and never as Section 1245 or 1250, whereas ordinary income is never Section 1231 but either Section 1245 or 1250.

(6) If the sales price is less than the adjusted basis, the loss will be classified as a Section 1231 loss.

B. Rules for personal property (Section 1245)

(1) Section 1245 applies to personal property.

(2) A gain on the distribution of Section 1245 property is treated as ordinary income to the extent of depreciation or amortization allowed. Any remaining gain is usually treated as Section 1231 gain.

(3) This section does not apply to losses—Section 1231 rules are used.

(4) A Section 179 expense election is treated as a depreciation deduction for Section 1245 recapture purposes.

C. Rules for real property (Section 1250)

(1) Section 1250 applies to real property (typically buildings and structural components).

(2) Where property was held more than one year, there is no depreciation recapture if it was depreciated straight-line.

(3) This section does not apply to losses—Section 1231 rules are used.

D. Exceptions—recapture under Sections 1245 and 1250 do not apply to:

(1) *Gifts*. Recapture potential carries over to the donee.

(2) *Death*. There is no recapture.

(3) *Charitable transfers*. Recapture potential reduces the amount of charitable contribution deductions.

(4) *Certain nontaxable transactions*. Recapture potential carries over to the transferee.

(5) *Like-kind exchanges*. Any remaining recapture potential carries over to the property received.

(6) *Involuntary conversions*. Any remaining recapture potential carries over to the property received.

5. Related parties

   A. A gain on the sale of assets to a related party is treated the same as any other gain.
   B. If a loss is realized on a sale to a related party, however, it is not recognized for tax purposes until the related party sells the asset to an unrelated third party.
   C. Related parties include the immediate family members, closely held corporations (who owns more than 50 percent), sister corporations, and the like.

6. Wash sales

   A. Selling shares at a loss and then buying them back within 30 days negates the ability to deduct such losses on a tax return. The disallowed loss amount can be added to the cost basis of the additional shares that were purchased. When these additional shares are sold, any taxable gain or loss includes the loss incurred on the original shares.
   B. The wash sale rule applies not only to stocks but also mutual funds and bonds.

7. Bargain sales—When an asset is sold for an amount below fair market value, the difference is a bargain element.

   A. *Individual*. The difference between the sale price and the FMV is treated as a gift.
   B. *Employee*. The difference is taxed as ordinary income.
   C. *Shareholder*. The difference is a constructive dividend and taxable as ordinary income.
   D. *Charitable organization*. The difference is treated as part sale and part contribution.

8. Section 1244 stock (small business stock election)

   A. Security losses generally are capital in nature. However, Section 1244 allows for ordinary losses if the loss is sustained by an individual who acquires the securities directly from the corporation.
   B. Section 1244 losses are limited to $50,000 annually ($100,000 for joint filers).
   C. The corporation must receive less than $1,000,000 in capital stock at time of issue in order to qualify for Section 1244 treatment.
   D. Section 1244 applies to losses only on the investment and *not* on the income.
   E. Section 1244 must be elected in initial incorporation.

TOPIC 67: ALTERNATIVE MINIMUM TAX (AMT)

1. Individual and corporate AMT

   A. Mechanics

      (1) A parallel system of income taxation. It applies when the calculation of AMT results in a higher tax liability than the calculation of regular income taxation.
      (2) The purpose is to ensure that an individual does not lower his or her tax liability below a reasonable level by using certain tax benefits targeted by AMT. Certain tax benefits available under regular income taxation are not available under AMT.
      (3) It is mandatory tax paid only if it exceeds the regular tax liability. It is not an "alternative" or optional tax.

(4) A base exemption amount that is determined by the filing status for regular tax purposes is permitted to reduce the alternative minimum taxable income (AMTI). The base exemption deduction permitted to a taxpayer is diminished under the phaseout rules by 25 percent of AMTI that exceeds certain levels. AMTI amount resulting in no exemption (in 2002) is $346,000 for married filing jointly and $255,500 for single. In 2002, the base exemption is

Married filing jointly and surviving spouse	$49,000
Unmarried taxpayer	$35,750
Married filing separately	$24,500

(5) There are two tier levels relating to AMT:

  (a) Tier 1 is a flat 26 percent rate that is applied to the first $175,000 of alternative minimum taxable income (AMTI).

  (b) Tier 2 is a flat 28 percent rate that is applied to all of the AMTI in excess of $175,000.

(6) Capital gains distributions or reported long-term capital gains on Form 1040 are subject to tax at a maximum rate of 20 percent for both regular and AMT purposes.

(7) The following is an outline of how AMT for individuals is calculated:

Alternative Minimum Tax Structure

Regular taxable income before deduction for personal exemption

Plus	Regular tax net operating loss (NOL)
Minus	Itemized deduction limitations
Plus	Positive and negative adjustments
Plus	Tax preferences
Minus	AMT NOL
Equals	Alternative minimum taxable income (AMTI)
Minus	Exemption allowed
Equals	AMTI
Times	AMT rate: 26 percent on first $175,000 and 28 percent on excess over $175,000
Equals	Tentative alternative minimum tax (TMT) before credits
Minus	AMT foreign tax credits
Equals	TMT after credits
Minus	Regular tax liability
Equals	Alternative minimum tax (AMT)

B. Preferences and adjustments

  (1) Preferences are tax benefits that are restricted under the AMT system. Preferences are always positive. Adjustments can be either positive or negative amounts.

  (2) A child under age 14 has substantial adjustments or preferences subject to the AMT rules; the child may be subject to AMT.

  (3) There are several common adjustments and preferences.

    (a) *Standard and itemized deductions.* No standard deduction is allowed. Itemized deductions are not allowed for taxes, certain interest, and most miscellaneous expenses. Medical expense deduction is allowed but subject to a 10 percent floor. The overall limitation on itemized deductions does not apply in calculating AMTI.

(b) *Passive activities.* AMT passive rules are similar to regular rules, except that income and deductions are calculated using the AMT system rather than regular tax rules.

(c) *Post-1998 depreciation.* For property placed in service after 1998:

Section 1250 property	No adjustment
Other tangible property in which the straight-line (SL) method was used	SL method using the same recovery period and convention used for regular tax
All other tangible property	150 percent declining balance, switching to straight-line depreciation for the first tax year in which using straight-line method yields a higher allowance, using the same recovery period and convention used for regular tax

(d) *Post-1986 and pre-1999 depreciation.* For property placed in service after 1986 and before 1999:

Section 1250 property	SL method over 40 years using the same midmonth convention used for regular tax purposes
Other tangible property in which the SL method was used	SL method using the same recovery period and convention used for regular tax
All other tangible property	150 percent declining balance, switching to straight-line depreciation for the first tax year in which using straight-line method yields a higher allowance, using the same recovery period and convention used for regular tax

(e) *Adjusted gain or loss.* Gain or loss from the sale or exchange of property must be recomputed with regard to AMT adjustments.

(f) *Loss limitations.* Gains and losses from conduit activities for which the taxpayer has basis or at-risk limitations must be recomputed under AMT.

(g) *Certain tax-exempt interest income.* Interest on certain private activity bonds issued after August 7, 1986, is included in the AMT tax base. These bonds are issued by state and local governments to finance activities that are not associated with the issuing government.

(h) *Incentive stock options.* Excess of fair market value over option price at the earlier of the date the option rights become transferable or are no longer subject to a substantial risk of forfeiture must be included in the AMT tax base.

(i) *Qualified small business stock.* One-half of the gain is excluded from regular taxable income, but 42 percent of this gain must be included in AMT.

(j) *Stock gain exclusion.* Income from the sale or exchange of qualified small business stock must be included in the AMT tax base.

C. Exclusion items versus deferral items

(1) Certain itemized deductions are deductible *in full* under AMT. Allowable itemized deductions include

(a) Casualty losses

(b) Miscellaneous itemized deductions *not* subject to the 2 percent AGI requirement

(c) Returns of amounts included in income (claim right)

(d) Estate tax paid on income with respect to a decedent

(e) Charitable contributions

(f) Interest on indebtedness used to acquire or improve a qualified residence of the taxpayer

(g) Investment interest not in excess of qualified net investing income

(h) Medical expenses in which the floor is 10 percent

(2) Certain itemized deductions are completely *disallowed* under AMT.

(a) State and local taxes (This disallowance is the most common reason that AMT is applied.)

(b) Miscellaneous itemized deductions subject to the 2 percent AGI floor

(c) Home mortgage interest that was not used to buy, build, or substantially improve a primary residence or secondary home

(3) Recovery of a tax that is included in gross income for regular income tax is not included in AMT. For example, state income tax refunds are required to be included under gross income but not AMT.

(4) Net operating loss (NOL). If a taxpayer had an NOL from business activity, the NOL may be used to eliminate up to 90 percent of the taxpayer's AMTI. NOL can be different from that used for regular income tax because it is adjusted for any preference items.

D. Credit (creation, usage, and limitations)

(1) Any AMT paid in a given year because of the deferral (not the elimination) of deductions can be used to offset regular tax in future years when the deductions are used to reduce AMT below the regular tax.

(2) The minimum tax credit (MTC) can be used only against the regular tax liability. It cannot reduce the regular tax liability below the AMT liability for the year.

(3) The MTC is used only after all other nonrefundable credits have been utilized and there remains a regular tax liability in excess of the AMT.

(4) The MTC can be carried forward indefinitely; it cannot be carried back.

2. Small business exemption

A. AMT does not apply to S Corporations and partnerships.

B. C Corporations are generally subject to the AMT, but are exempt if they fit the definition of a "small corporation."

C. Corporations must meet an average annual gross receipt test to be excluded from AMT.

(1) For new corporations, average annual gross receipts must not exceed $5 million for the corporation's first three taxable years. After the initial test is passed, corporations cannot have three-year annual gross receipts in excess of $7.5 million.

(2) For corporations in existence before 1997, a $5 million average annual gross receipts test is applied to the three taxable years, beginning with the first taxable year ending after December 31, 1993. After the initial test is passed, corporations cannot have three-year annual gross receipts in excess of $7.5 million.

D. Corporations subject to AMT

(1) "Adjusted current earnings," or ACE adjustment, applies to corporations, not individuals, in calculating AMT. This adjustment includes items that are not treated as taxable income for regular tax purposes but are treated as "book" income for accounting purposes.

(2) An ACE adjustment item is book income attributable to life insurance owned by a corporation. Death benefits and increases in cash value raise the adjustment; premiums paid on a life insurance contract reduce the adjustment.

TOPIC 68: TAX MANAGEMENT TECHNIQUES

1. Tax credits (see Topic 59 for more details on tax credits)

   A. Deduction or exclusion versus tax credit

      (1) Which is better? The answer depends on the tax bracket. A deduction or exclusion reduces the amount of taxable income that falls within a person's tax bracket. A credit reduces, dollar for dollar, the amount of tax computed on taxable income.

      (2) *Example*: Suppose you are in the 27 percent tax bracket. The choice is between claiming a $1,000 deduction or a $250 credit. The deduction should be claimed because it saves you $270 ($1,000 × 27%) in taxes. The credit saves only $250 in taxes. On the other hand, if you were in the 15 percent tax bracket, the credit should be claimed.

   B. Child and dependent care credit

      (1) Any employer-provided dependent care assistance reduces the maximum amount on a dollar-for-dollar basis.

      (2) If there is a choice between claiming the child and dependent care credit or participating in a dependent care flexible spending account (FSA), an individual will save more taxes by paying child care expenses with FSA money.

      (3) If someone is hired to care for your children and provide the care in your home, the IRS generally considers you an employer. If you pay the worker more than $1,300 per year, you are liable for the employer's share of FICA tax.

   C. Education tax credits

      (1) Tuition paid in December 2002 for a course that begins in January 2003 is counted toward the 2002 credit, not the 2003 credit.

      (2) A taxpayer may be able to reduce the amount of federal income tax withholding based on the estimated tax benefits of education credits and deductions.

2. Alternative minimum tax (AMT planning)

   A. Incentive stock options

      (1) Although no taxable income is recognized when an option is granted or exercised, the difference between the fair market value and the exercise price is an item of AMT tax preference and can trigger a significant AMT liability in the year of exercise if a large amount of appreciated stock is involved.

      (2) When the stock is sold, most of the AMT liability will be recovered as an AMT credit against regular tax if the value of the stock has not decreased after the exercise of the option.

      (3) The AMT gain is the difference between the fair market value of the stock at the time of the sale and the fair market value of the stock at the time of exercise.

      (4) Regular tax gain is the difference between the fair market value at the time of the sale and the exercise price.

      (5) Because regular tax liability will generally exceed the AMT tentative minimum, most or all of the credit for the previously paid AMT is typically claimed against regular tax in the year of sale.

(6) *Example*: In 1998, an employee receives 10,000 shares of employer stock at $10 a share. There are no tax consequences in 1998. In 1999, the employee exercises the option. The fair market value at exercise is $50. The exercise results in no regular income tax in 1999. For AMT purposes, there is a tax preference of $400,000 (($50 − $10) × 10,000). For simplicity, assume the employee pays AMT liability of $112,000 on the $400,000 preference ($400,000 × 28%). In 2000 and 2001, the tentative minimum tax and the regular tax are exactly equal, so none of the credit is used against regular income.

If the employee sells all shares in 2002 at $60 a share, he will recognize a long-term capital gain of $500,000 (($60 FMV − $10 cost) × 10,000 shares). This results in a tax liability of $100,000 ($500,000 × 20% long-term capital gain rate). However, the long-term AMT capital gain is only $100,000 (($60 FMV − $50 AMT basis) × 10,000) and the tentative minimum tax on the gain is only $20,000 ($100,000 × 20%). *Note*: The 20 percent long-term capital gain rate applied is the same for regular tax and AMT. The AMT basis of each share of stock is increased from $10 to $50 by the $40 gain previously recognized in 1999 for AMT. Assume that the tentative minimum tax is exactly the same as the regular tax liability without regard to the regular tax long-term capital gain. If we consider the long-term capital gain, tentative minimum tax is $80,000 less than regular tax liability. Therefore, an $80,000 AMT tax credit against regular tax liability can be claimed. The remaining $32,000 ($112,000 − $80,000) unused AMT credit is carried forward to future years.

(7) If the stock price drops significantly after exercise, it may be difficult to recover the AMT credit.

(8) An AMT tax preference is not created at exercise if the employee cannot sell the stock right away or it is subject to a substantial risk of forfeiture. With this type of stock, a "Section 83(b)" election can be taken to avoid AMT liability.

(9) No AMT adjustment is required if the incentive stock option (ISO) is exercised and sold in the same tax year.

B. Charitable gifts—Gifts of appreciated property (such as stock) have a significant tax advantage by giving a charitable contribution deduction for the full appreciated value of the property, for both regular and AMT purposes (in addition to the avoidance of the capital gain tax).

C. Stock redemption agreements

(1) The IRS defines a redemption of stock as an acquisition by a corporation of its own stock from a shareholder in exchange for property, whether or not stock so acquired is canceled, retired, or held as Treasury stock.

(2) For tax planning purposes, the primary objective in arranging a stock redemption is to achieve capital gain treatment as opposed to dividend treatment on the exchange of stock for money or other property.

(3) The redemption proceeds will be taxable as ordinary income if the transaction is treated as a dividend distribution.

(4) A three-part tax treatment applies to a corporate distribution to a shareholder. The rules apply regardless of whether the distribution to the shareholder is made pursuant to a redemption of stock or paid with respect to the shareholder's ownership in stock (as shown in the following example).

(a) The portion of the distribution not in excess of the corporation's current and accumulated earnings and profits is treated as a dividend and taxed as ordinary income.

(b) The portion of the distribution in excess of the corporation's current and accumulated earnings and profits is then treated as a nontaxable return of capital to the extent of the shareholder's basis in his or her stock.

(c) The portion of the distribution not treated as a dividend that exceeds the shareholder's basis in his or her stock is taxed as capital gain.

(d) *Example*: Steve is sole shareholder of a corporation that has $50,000 in current accumulated earnings and profits. His basis in the stock is $5,000. The corporation distributes $70,000, which is not compensation; $50,000 is treated as dividends and taxed as ordinary income, $5,000 is treated as a return of capital investment (basis is reduced to zero), and $15,000 is treated as capital gain.

(5) *Constructive dividends* are not intended by the corporation to be treated as dividends for tax purposes; however, if the economic effect of such a transaction is the same as that of a dividend distribution, the IRS may recharacterize the transaction as a taxable dividend. Dividends can be in the form of property other than money. The taxation is measured by the fair market value of the property distributed.

(6) *Section 302* allows for capital gain treatment of four types of redemptions, in which the redemptions materially affect a shareholder's percentage of ownership.

(a) A redemption that is not essentially equivalent to a dividend

(b) A substantially disproportionate redemption

(c) A complete redemption

(d) A distribution to a noncorporate shareholder in a partial liquidation of the distributing corporation

(7) *Section 303 redemptions* apply to estates in which stock of a closely held corporation constitutes a substantial portion of total assets. For Section 303 redemptions, the beneficiary or estate receives a stepped-up basis in a decedent's assets that is generally equal to the value of the assets at the date of death of the decedent. If the stock increased in value from time of redemption and decedent's death, any amount in excess of the adjusted basis will be taxed as long-term gain.

3. Accelerated deductions

A. The acceleration of deductions (and deferral of income) reduces taxes in the current year. It is an effective strategy if the marginal tax rate for the client in future years will be the same or less. If the rate jumps up, then it makes little sense to defer income or accelerate deductions.

B. There are several strategies for accelerating deductions.

(1) *Early payment of state income or property taxes.* These are generally due on the 15th of the month after the tax year. If payments are made prior to the end of the tax year, a greater deduction can be taken.

(2) *Early payment of mortgage and qualified education loan interest.* The first mortgage payment in the next year can be paid in the current year to accelerate the mortgage interest deduction. The same is used for qualified education loan interest if the deductible limits have not been reached in the current year.

(3) *Year-end charitable contributions.* Make contributions before year end.

(4) *Year-end expenses.* Make repairs and perform maintenance of rental property before year end.

(5) *Year-end purchase of assets.* Take full use of a Section 179 depreciation for assets used in trade or business.

(6) *Review of asset acquisitions.* Ensure that assets are classified under the shortest period for depreciation.

(7) *Year-end purchases.* Tangible assets can depreciate a half-year if purchased in the last month of the year. This election is not possible if more than 40 percent of total tangible personal property is placed in service during the last 3 months of the year (the midquarter convention is used).

(8) *Education payments.* Next year's payments that qualify for credits should be paid in the current year, such as the Hope Credit or Lifetime Learning Credit.

(9) *Purchase of supplies.* Inventory and supplies can be expensed for businesses.

4. Deferral of income—There are several strategies for deferring income.

   A. *Tax-advantaged retirement savings.* Qualified retirement plans defer taxes on earnings and generally use pretax income for contributions.

   B. *Deferred sales.* Tax savings can be significant if sales of investments are deferred until death. The cost basis becomes the fair market value of such assets at death. Hedging strategies can be used to postpone the recognition of capital gains for stocks.

   C. *Deferred collections.* For a self-employed individual using the cash method, delay year-end billings until late enough in the year that payments will not be received before the end of the year.

   D. *Delayed bonus payment.* Employee year-end bonuses may be paid in the next year. The employer generally does not lose its deduction for the current year, as long as its obligation to pay the employee is fixed before the end of the tax year and paid within 2½ months of the close of its tax year.

   E. *Stock options.* In order to obtain favorable long-term capital gain treatment, stock acquired under an ISO may not be sold before the *later* of two years from the date of the grant of the option or one year from the date of exercise of the option.

   F. *Deferred compensation.* Nonqualified deferred compensation plans can defer receipt of income to selected employees for several years.

   G. *Installment sales.* The use of an installment sale does not affect the tax treatment of a gain as capital gain or ordinary income, but does affect its timing. Installment sales may allow an individual to reduce total tax on the sale by preventing taxable gain from pushing him or her into a higher tax bracket in the year of sale.

   H. *Exchange of like-kind assets.* A carefully structured and implemented exchange can defer tax liability.

   I. *Annuities.* Earnings on contributions accrue tax-deferred.

5. Estimated taxes and withholdings

   A. The required annual payment for most taxpayers is the *lower* of 90 percent of the tax shown on the current year's return or 100 percent of the tax shown on the prior year's return.

   B. To avoid an underpayment penalty, an individual must pay 25 percent of a "required annual payment" by April 15, June 15, September 15, and January 15.

   C. There is no underpayment penalty if the tax shown on the return is less than $1,000.

   D. Corporations have estimated payments of 100 percent of the past year's tax or 100 percent of the current year's tax. If taxable income is above $1 million, the corporation cannot use last year's tax.

   E. Estimated payments are made on a payment voucher Form 1040-ES or by phone using a credit card and calling 1-800-2PAY-TAX or 1-800-ALL-TAXX.

6. Net operating losses (NOL)

A. An NOL is the excess of business deductions over gross income in a particular tax year. An NOL deduction is allowed as a carryback or carryover to other tax years where gross income exceeded business deductions.

B. NOL deduction is allowed for individuals, corporations, estates, and trusts; NOL deduction is not allowed for partnerships and S Corporations.

C. NOL can be carried back two years and forward 20 years. A decedent's NOL can be carried back, but not forward. Farming losses can be carried back five years.

D. *Note*: Do not confuse NOL with NCL (net capital losses), which a corporation can carry back three years and carry forward five years to offset capital gains. An individual can carry forward NCL indefinitely (see Topic 66 for more details).

TOPIC 69: PASSIVE ACTIVITY AND AT-RISK RULES

1. Definitions

A. *At-risk rules* limit a taxpayer's deductible loss to the amount that the taxpayer actually has at risk of loss.

B. At-risk rules apply to the following:

   (1) Individuals
   (2) Estates and trusts
   (3) Partners
   (4) Shareholders in S Corporations
   (5) Most C Corporations

C. The amount at risk is equal to the *sum* of:

   (1) The amount of cash and adjusted basis of other property contributed to the activity by the taxpayer
   (2) Amounts borrowed for use in the activity for which the taxpayer is personally liable
   (3) Amounts borrowed for use in the activity that are secured by property of the taxpayer that is not used in the activity (to the extent of FMV of the property)
   (4) A taxpayer's share of *qualified nonrecourse financing* that is secured by the real property used in the activity. Nonrecourse financing generally means loans from banks, savings and loans, credit unions, and so on. Nonrecourse financing does not include borrowing from any person who has an interest in the activity other than a creditor, or from a related person.

D. Interplay of the amount at risk and the computation of the partner's outside basis (tax basis in his or her interest in the partnership):

   (1) The partner's basis is increased by qualified nonrecourse debt.
   (2) The deductible loss from the activity is limited to the amount at risk.

E. *Passive activity rules*. If a loss qualifies for recognition under at-risk rules, it may also be subject to passive activity rules. Passive activity losses may be used only to offset passive activity income (this does not include portfolio income). A passive activity loss for the year is the amount by which the aggregate losses from *all* passive activities exceed the aggregate income from *all* passive activities for that year. Passive activities are those activities that involve the conduct of a trade or business in which the taxpayer does not materially participate. Rental activities are always passive.

F. Taxpayers subject to passive activity rules:

   (1) Individuals
   (2) Estates

(3) Trusts

(4) Personal service corporations

(5) Closely held C Corporations (Five or fewer individuals own more than 50 percent of the stock.)

(6) Publicly traded partnerships (PTP)—partnership interests that are traded on an established securities market

(a) Net passive income from a PTP cannot be offset by losses from other passive activities.

(b) A net passive loss from a PTP cannot offset income from other passive activities.

(7) Owners of pass-through entity interests on their distributive shares of income or loss from those interests

G. Taxpayers not subject to passive activity rules:

(1) Corporations (other than those listed earlier)

(2) Partnerships (other than those listed earlier)

(3) S Corporations

H. Keep in mind that although partnerships and S Corporations are not subject to passive activity rules, the individual who receives the pass-through items is subject to such rules.

I. There are two kinds of passive activity losses:

(1) Rentals

(2) Businesses in which the taxpayer does not materially participate on a regular, continuous, and substantial basis

J. Income and losses from the following activities are generally *passive*:

(1) Equipment leasing

(2) Rental real estate

(3) Sole proprietorship in which the taxpayer does not materially participate

(4) Limited partnerships, with some exceptions

(5) Partnerships, S Corporations, and limited liability companies in which the taxpayer does not materially participate

(6) PTPs that are not treated as corporations

K. Income and losses from the following activities are generally *nonpassive*:

(1) Salaries, wages, and 1099 commission income

(2) Guaranteed payments

(3) Interest and dividends

(4) Stocks and bonds

(5) Sale of undeveloped land or other investment property

(6) Royalties from ordinary course of business

(7) Businesses in which the taxpayer materially participates

(8) Partnerships, S Corporations, and limited liability companies in which the taxpayer materially participates

(9) Trusts in which the fiduciary materially participates

L. Material participation rules are applied to any trade or business activity. If material participation rules are met, the income or loss from that activity is treated as nonpassive. There are six different ways for an individual to meet this requirement:

(1) Participates more than 500 hours per year in day-to-day operations

(2) Participation essentially constitutes all significant participation in the work involved in the activity.

(3) Participates more than 100 hours, but not more than 500 hours, but more than anyone else

(4) Material participation in an activity for any 5 of the past 10 years

(5) Material participation in a personal service activity for any three prior years

(6) There are relevant facts and circumstances showing the taxpayer was a material participant.

2. Computations—There are five steps for determining deductibility of losses on Form K-1:

A. Determine whether the partner has sufficient basis.

B. Determine whether the partner has sufficient amount at risk.

C. Determine whether the passive activity rules apply.

D. If the partner passes all of the preceding tests, the loss still may not be deductible because of other limitations:

(1) Net operating loss limitation

(2) Capital loss limitation

E. If the deductibility of the partner's losses is limited because of insufficient basis or inadequate amount at risk, the suspended losses may be absorbed in subsequent years, depending on the amount of income in those years.

3. Treatment of disallowed losses

A. Net passive activity losses are suspended and carried forward to offset future passive activity income.

B. At-risk rules are applied before the passive loss rules. If a loss is not allowed because of the at-risk limitation, it is not a suspended loss under the passive loss rules. It is a suspended loss under the at-risk rules.

4. Disposition of passive activities

If the entire interest in a passive activity is disposed of, the suspended losses are fully deductible against other income.

5. Real estate exceptions

A. Rental real estate losses up to $25,000 may be deducted *in full* by anyone whose modified adjusted gross income is less than $100,000 (ignoring passive losses). The taxpayer must *actively participate* to qualify for the $25,000 offset. The $25,000 deduction is phased out at a rate of 50 cents for every dollar the modified adjusted gross income is over $100,000. It is completely phased out when modified adjusted gross income exceeds $150,000.

B. Active participation is participation by a natural person who

(1) Has at least a 10 percent interest in any rental real estate activity

(2) Participates in management decisions in a bona fide sense

C. Many vacation rentals have low periods of customer use. As a result, the activity falls outside the definition of a rental and the $25,000 offset does not apply. An activity is not rental under any of the following six conditions:

(1) Average customer use is seven days or less.

(2) Average customer use is 30 days or less, and the owner provides significant personal service.

(3) The owner provides extraordinary services.

(4) The rental activity is incidental to a nonrental activity of the taxpayer.

(5) The property is customarily made available during business hours for nonexclusive use by customers (golf courses).

(6) The property is used in a partnership, S Corporation, or joint venture in which the owner has an interest, and activity is not a rental activity.

TOPIC 70: TAX IMPLICATIONS OF CHANGING CIRCUMSTANCES

1. Marriage

   A. Filing status

      (1) If married on the last day of the year, taxpayers may choose to file either jointly or separately. In general, filing jointly is more beneficial to a couple.

      (2) In some instances, spouses who file jointly pay more taxes than they would if they were able to file as two single taxpayers. This is often called the "marriage penalty."

         (a) In 2003, the standard deduction is $7,950 for married filing jointly, and $9,500 for two single taxpayers.

         (b) In 2003, the 27 percent tax bracket begins at $47,450 for married filing jointly, and $56,800 for two single taxpayers. Penalties exist at each successive tax bracket.

         (c) Social Security benefits are taxable for a married couple when AGI plus half their benefits reaches $32,000 and as high as $25,000 for single taxpayers.

   B. Children

      (1) Tax treatment of dependent child's income

         (a) Earned income only: Income up to the standard deduction is *not* taxable, regardless of age.

         (b) Unearned income only

            i. For a child under age 14 by the close of the tax year (kiddie tax applies), the first $750 of unearned income is not taxed, the next $750 of unearned income is taxed at the child's tax rate, and the excess of the child's unearned income is taxed at the parent's marginal rate.

            ii. For a child at or above age 14 by the close of the tax year, the first $750 of unearned income is not taxed, and any additional unearned income is taxed only at the child's rate. No unearned income will be taxed at the parent's rate.

         (c) Earned and unearned income

            i. For child under age 14

               • *Unearned.* The first $750 of unearned income is not taxed, the next $750 of unearned income is taxed at the child's tax rate, and the excess of the child's unearned income is taxed at the parent's marginal rate.

               • *Earned.* Earned income minus the remaining amount of the standard deduction is taxed at the child's rate.

            ii. For a child age 14 and over

               Earned and unearned income. Income up to the standard deduction is not taxable; income over the standard deduction is at the child's tax rate.

      (2) A child with income who qualified as a dependent on the parent's tax return cannot claim a personal exemption on his or her own tax return. Exemption can be claimed only by the parents, even if they choose not to claim the exemption.

   C. Common law and community property

      (1) Common law

         (a) Common law is a body of law that is based on custom and general principles and is embodied in case law. It serves as precedent or is applied to situations not covered by statute. A husband and wife have equal ownership in all property under common law.

   (b) Common law states have a stepped-up basis for half of the assets: a step -up in basis for the decedent's share of ownership, but not the survivor's share.

(2) Community property—recognized in nine states

   (a) Community property is all property that has been acquired by the efforts of either spouse during their marriage while living in a community property state, except property acquired by only one of the spouses by gift, devise, bequest, or inheritance or acquired by either spouse prior to their marriage. The two spouses own community property equally.

   (b) Community property states have a full step-up in basis. For tax purposes at death, the new cost basis is the fair market value (FMV) at the date of death for both halves of the community property even though only one-half is included in the decedent spouse's estate.

   (c) Couples residing in community property states should hold appreciated property as community property. On the other hand, if property has decreased in value, community property will receive a full step-down in basis at the first death, and some other form of title may be preferred.

2. Divorce

   A. Alimony

      (1) A series of payments from one spouse to another or to a third party on behalf of the receiving spouse

      (2) Taxable income to the recipient and tax deductible expense to the payor

      (3) Payments are alimony only if all of the following conditions are met:

         (a) Payments must be made in cash.
         (b) Payments must end at death of payee.
         (c) Payor and payee cannot live together.
         (d) Agreement or decree does not specify that the payments are not alimony.
         (e) Front loading is avoided.

      (4) Front loading

         (a) A measure to discourage property settlements as alimony
         (b) There may be alimony recapture if there is more than a $15,000 decrease in alimony payments between any of the first three years.
         (c) Another rule applies to the extent that the payments in the second year exceed the payments in the third year by more than $15,000.
         (d) Alimony recapture affects the third year of alimony payments only. Recapture in the third year is claimed as income by the original payor and claimed as a deduction from income by the payee.

   B. Child support

      (1) Established by the courts and based on the ratio of each parent's income, the percentage of time the child spends with each parent, and the amount of alimony payments made to the custodial parent

      (2) Is not deductible by the payor and not included in the income of the recipient

      (3) The child can be counted as an exemption by only one parent, but the exemption can be traded back and forth each year.

      (4) Only the custodial parent is entitled to claim both the child and the dependent care credit.

C. Qualified Domestic Relations Order (QDRO)

   (1) A QDRO is an order from the court that tells a trustee or administrator of a qualified retirement plan how much to pay out to the nonowner spouse pursuant to a divorce.

   (2) A QDRO ensures that property from a qualified retirement plan can be divided up without negative tax consequences.

   (3) Benefits begin when the participant reaches "earliest retirement age," defined as the earlier of

      (a) The earliest date benefits are payable to the participant under the plan

      (b) The later of the date when participant reaches age 50 or the date on which the participant could start benefits if separated from service

3. Death (final income tax return)

   A. An income tax return must be filed for a decedent for the year of death.

   B. The decedent has a short tax year that ends at the date of death; however, deductions, exemptions, and credits can be taken in full.

   C. *Income in respect of decedent* is income that comes after death and will become part of the decedent's estate.

   D. The surviving spouse can file jointly in the year of death. If the surviving spouse has a minor child, he or she can file as surviving spouse for two additional years following death.

   E. Medical expenses paid during the year following death may be filed either on the decedent's final return or estate tax return.

   F. Any charitable contributions that cannot be used on the final return because of AGI limitations are lost.

TOPIC 71: CHARITABLE CONTRIBUTIONS AND DEDUCTIONS

1. Qualified entities

   A. Public charities

      (1) Churches

      (2) Educational organizations

      (3) Hospitals and medical research organizations

      (4) Government entities

      (5) Publicly supported organizations that receive a substantial amount of support from the general public or governmental units

         (a) Red Cross and Salvation Army

         (b) Boys & Girls Clubs of America

   B. Private charities

      (1) Veterans organizations

      (2) Fraternal orders

      (3) Certain private nonoperating foundations

2. Deduction limitations

   A. Public versus private charities

      (1) Contributions to public charities cannot exceed 50 percent of the taxpayer's AGI. A 30 percent ceiling generally applies to long-term capital gain (LTCG) property. *Exception*: The 30 percent limit does not apply if election is made to reduce the FMV of the property by the amount of the long-term capital gain if the property had been sold.

(2) Contributions to private charities cannot exceed 30 percent of the taxpayer's AGI. A 20 percent ceiling applies to *all* LTCG property.

B. Capital gain property, for purposes of charitable contributions, is property that has been held for more than 12 months. There are two types of capital gain property:

   (1) Real and intangible personal property

      (a) A gift of stock is considered intangible personal property, and appreciated land is an example of real property.

      (b) For contributions made to public charities, the deduction cannot exceed 30 percent of AGI if the full market value of the gift is deducted. The 30 percent limit can be increased to 50 percent of AGI for public charities if the donor is willing to decrease the value of the gifts by 100 percent of the potential gain. This means reducing the fair market value to the property's cost basis.

      (c) *Example*:

         i. Mark donates stock worth $45,000 to the Red Cross (public charity). The stock cost $25,000 when it was purchased five years ago. Mark has AGI of $50,000. Therefore, his maximum deduction for the year is $15,000 ($50,000 × 30%). The remaining $30,000 ($45,000 FMV − $15,000 current deduction) can be carried forward for five years and applied against future income.

         ii. *Exception*: If Mark excludes 100 percent of the potential gain, the deductible value is decreased to $25,000 (cost basis). Mark could deduct the entire $25,000, because 50 percent of his AGI is $25,000. The current year deduction is increased with this election.

      (d) For contributions to private charities, the deduction cannot exceed 20 percent of AGI. There is a full deduction for fair market value only.

   (2) Tangible personal property

      (a) A car or jewelry is tangible personal property.

      (b) A distinction is made between gifts that are used by the charity and gifts that are not used.

         i. *Use related*. Such property would include a painting given to a museum that is shown in public galleries.

            • For contributions to public charities, the deduction cannot exceed 30 percent of AGI if the full market value of the gift is deducted. The 30 percent limit can be increased to 50 percent of AGI if the donor is willing to reduce the value of the gift by 100 percent of the potential gain.

            • For contributions to private charities, the deduction is 20 percent of the donor's cost basis.

         ii. *Use unrelated*. The painting mentioned earlier would be use unrelated if it was sold by the museum or if it was given to the Boy Scouts.

            • For contributions made to public and private charities, the fair market value of the gift must be reduced by 100 percent of the potential gain. This means that the amount of deduction is the donor's cost basis.

            • For contributions to public charities, the deduction cannot exceed 50 percent of AGI. For donations to private charities, the deduction cannot exceed 20 percent of AGI.

C. Ordinary income property

    (1) Ordinary income property is an asset that would have resulted in ordinary income (rather than capital gains) on the date of contribution if it were sold.

    (2) Ordinary income property includes

        (a) Capital assets held 12 months or less at time of contribution

        (b) Art, books, and jewelry, but only if given by the person who created them

        (c) Businessperson's stock in trade and inventory

    (3) The deduction is limited to the donor's cost basis.

D. The following table summarizes charitable contribution deduction limitations.

Charitable Contribution Deduction Limitation			
Type of Property	**Donee**	**Limitations of AGI**	**Amount Deductible**
(A) Cash	Public	50%	Full deduction
	Private	30%	Full deduction
(B) Capital gain property:			
(1) Real and intangible personal property	Public	30%, or 50% on election	Full deduction for FMV Donor's cost basis
	Private	20%	Full deduction for FMV
(2) Tangible personal property:			
Use related	Public	30%, or 50% on election	Full deduction for FMV Donor's cost basis
	Private	20%	Donor's cost basis
Use unrelated	Public	50%	Donor's cost basis
	Private	20%	Donor's cost basis
(C) Ordinary income property	Public	50%	Donor's cost basis
	Private	30%	Donor's cost basis

Chart revised from James Ivers III, *Fundamentals of Income Taxation*, 3rd ed., Huebner School Series (Bryn Mawr, PA: The American College, 2002).

3. Carryover periods

  A. Contributions that exceed the AGI limit for the current tax year can be carried over to each of the next five years.

  B. Carryover contributions are subject to the original percentage limits in the carryover years and are deducted after deducting allowable contributions for the current year.

  C. Use the earlier year carryover if there are carryovers from two or more years.

4. Partial interest gifts to charity

Contributions that are less than the entire interest in a property are generally not deductible. *Exceptions*:

  A. A gift of a partial interest in property if that is the donor's entire interest

  B. Property held in a charitable lead trust or a charitable remained trust

5. Nondeductible contributions

   A. *Note*: Gifts to some organizations may not be deductible as charitable contributions, but may be deductible as ordinary and necessary business expenses.

   B. There are certain nondeductible contributions.

      (1) Money or property given to

          (a) Civic leagues, social and sports clubs, labor unions, and chambers of commerce
          (b) Foreign organizations
          (c) Groups that are run for personal profit
          (d) Groups whose purpose is to lobby for law changes
          (e) Homeowners associations
          (f) Individuals
          (g) Political groups or candidates for public office

      (2) Cost of lotto and bingo tickets
      (3) Dues and fees to country clubs
      (4) Tuition
      (5) Value of blood given to a blood bank
      (6) Contributions consisting of the *right to use* property (such as a rent-free lease to the Boy Scouts)

   C. Payments made to a college or university in exchange for the right to buy tickets to a sporting event qualify for a charitable deduction of 80 percent of the amount paid. Any amount actually paid for tickets is not deductible.

      Example: Steve graduated from ABC University and donated $3,000 to the athletic department to guarantee priority to purchase two premium season tickets to home football games. Steve then purchased two season tickets at a regular price of $200 each. The charitable contribution for the current year is $2,400 (80 percent of $3,000). The $400 expenditure for the tickets cannot be claimed.

6. Appraisals

   A. Appraisals are generally required if a contribution is more than $5,000. Fees paid for the appraisal are not deductible as contributions. They can be claimed as a miscellaneous itemized deduction on Schedule A, subject to the 2 percent of AGI limit.

   B. A qualified appraisal is not required for publicly traded securities if quotations are published on a daily basis or readily available, even if the amount exceeds $5,000.

7. Substantiation requirements

   A. Donations of less than $250

      (1) Cash donations need receipts or other reliable written records with date, amount, and name of organization.
      (2) Noncash donations do not require receipts where it is impractical to get them.

   B. Donations of $250 or more

      (1) Cash donations of $250 or more in any one day to any one organization must have written substantiation from the organization.
      (2) Noncash donations require a written acknowledgement from the charitable organization. For contributions if more than $500, the taxpayer must show the means of acquisition of the property, the date acquired, and the adjusted basis. Most contributions of more than $5,000 require a written appraisal. Form 8283 must be filed for noncash contributions over $500.

    C. Do not combine separate contributions. For example, donations of $25 each week to a church are considered separate payments that should not be combined.

8. Charitable contributions by business entities

    A. Corporations can deduct up to 10 percent of taxable income after adding back any deduction for NOL or capital loss carrybacks or carryforwards and dividends received.

    B. Excess contributions are carried forward five years.

    C. Contributions from pass-through entities are reflected on the returns of the owners.

Chapter 6

RETIREMENT PLANNING

TOPIC 72: RETIREMENT NEEDS ANALYSIS

1. Assumptions for Retirement Planning

    A. *Inflation.* The costs of goods and services that retirees use most often increase faster than the general rate of inflation measured by the Consumer Price Index (CPI).

    B. *Retirement period and life expectancy.* Retirement period is contingent on various factors: years until retirement, years in retirement, and family history/longevity.

    C. *Lifestyle.* Before retiring, have your clients attempt to live on 80 percent of their current income. You can offer to invest the remainder. Most clients need more than 100 percent to maintain their current standard of living.

    D. *Total return.* Project investment return and project the tax rate.

2. Financial needs

    A. Living costs

    B. Charitable and beneficiary gifting objectives: To stretch your client's retirement income, you may want to explore charitable estate planning strategies and reduce your client's current, ongoing contributions to charity.

    C. Medical costs, including long-term care needs analysis

    D. Other (trust and foundation funding, education funding, etc.): current residence, food costs, car loans, auto insurance costs, clothing cost, health insurance premiums, recreation costs, future savings, and income taxes

3. Income sources

    A. Total return assumptions

        (1) Return assumptions include all sources of future income, such as qualified retirement plans, tax-deferred plans, and Social Security.

        (2) Retirement income-need analysis calculation—comprehensive example:

PV	Present value
I	Interest rate
N	Number of periods
FV	Future value
PMT	Payment

Jim Parker is currently age 37 and Sarah Parker is age 34. The Parkers would like to retire when Jim is age 65 (preretirement period of 28 years). The retirement income need is $70,000 in today's dollars. They will need to provide for retirement income until Sarah has reached age 95 (postretirement period of 33 years). They expect to earn an after-tax return of 8 percent, and inflation of 3 percent. The planner anticipates Social Security income to be $15,000 at retirement.

Step 1. Adjust income deficit for inflation over preretirement period. Solve future value of income deficit in first year of retirement. Subtract Social Security income to arrive at a net amount of $55,000.

PV = $55,000, I = 3%, N = 28, solve FV → $125,836

Determine retirement fund needed to meet income deficit. Solve lump sum needed at beginning of retirement (present value annuity due) to fund annual income deficit that increases annually with inflation (i.e., a growing annuity).

Find inflation-adjusted rate of return

$[(1.08/1.03) - 1] \times 100 = 4.85\%$

The inflation-adjusted rate of return is a serial payment. It increases each year by the assumed inflation rate.

Calculator should be set to "begin" mode, because payments are expected at the beginning of each year.

PMT = \$125,836; I = 4.85; N = 33; FV = 0; solve PV → \$2,150,395

Change calculator back to "end" mode.

Step 2. Analyze current assets and project growth from now to retirement. This amount is compared with the need projected in Step 1.

The Parkers have \$150,000 in assets targeted for retirement purposes. Find the future value of these assets at retirement.

PV = \$150,000; I = 8; N = 28; solve FV → \$1,294,065

Shortfall is \$2,150,395 − \$1,294,065 = \$856,329

Step 3. Determine additional savings needs by solving for yearly payments. Use level payment or serial payment.

Level payment accounts for inflation. Remember that an 8 percent after-tax return is the nominal rate. In basic terms, the nominal return = real rate + inflation rate. Solve for payment.

FV = \$856,329; N = 28; I = 8%, PV = 0; solve PMT → \$8,982

The Parkers will need to save \$8,982 each year during the accumulation phase to reach the shortfall of \$856,329 in assets.

Serial payments provide an inflation adjustment during the accumulation years because the payments increase each year by the inflation rate (this was automatically done during the level payment calculation). In order to calculate the first year serial payment, inflation must be removed from the future value of current assets because it will be accounted for in the serial payments and cannot be counted twice.

The shortfall value of \$856,329 is deflated for inflation.

FV = \$856,329; N = 28; I = 3%, PMT = 0; solve PV → \$374,281

The inflation-adjusted interest rate is used for serial payments. It was earlier calculated as [(1.08/1.03) − 1] × 100 = 4.85%. Calculate first year serial payments.

FV = \$374,281; N = 28; I = 4.85; PV = 0; solve PMT → \$6,562

This amount is increased by the inflation rate to provide the first year serial payments.

\$6,562 × 1.03 = \$6,759

If this amount is increased for inflation each year, the total future value at retirement will equal \$856,329. Therefore, either using the level payment method or the serial payment method will yield the same result at retirement.

B. Probabilistic analysis assumptions

    (1) The Monte Carlo system uses baseline information, such as age and the current value and composition of investments, along with certain assumptions about the unknown future, such as changing inflation rates, life expectancy and investment returns. Then

the program runs through hundreds or thousands of random combinations to determine how much a client can safely spend at retirement.

(2) Monte Carlo can be misleading if a planner uses the wrong assumptions.

4. Alternatives to compensate for projected cash-flow shortfalls

   A. Consider making the maximum contribution to qualified retirement plans.
   B. Decrease current and future expenditures.
   C. Participate in more aggressive investments.
   D. Advance the retirement age or lower the desired amount of income.
   E. Accept more risk by increasing the expected rate of return in forecasts.
   F. Consider serial (increasing) annual payments versus level annual payments.

TOPIC 73: SOCIAL SECURITY

1. Eligibility and benefit

   A. Terminology

      (1) Fully insured = 40 quarters of coverage (total of 10 years in covered work).
      (2) Currently insured = 6 quarters of coverage during the full 13-quarter period ending with the calendar quarter in which the person died, became entitled to disability benefits, or became entitled to retirement benefits.
      (3) In 2002, workers receive one quarter of coverage for each $870 of earnings up to a maximum of four quarters.

   B. Retirement

      (1) Entitled to retirement benefits if

         (a) Fully insured
         (b) At least age 62

      (2) The retirement benefit at normal retirement age (age 65, but gradually increasing to age 67 for those born after 1960) equals the worker's primary insurance amount (PIA).
      (3) If benefits are received prior to normal retirement age, an individual will receive a monthly benefit equal to only a percentage of PIA. For a retired worker, PIA is reduced by ⅚ of 1 percent for each of the first 36 months the worker is under normal retirement age when payments commence and by ⁵⁄₁₂ of 1 percent for each such month in excess of 36.
      (4) *Here is the important point*: There are advantages and disadvantages to taking the benefit before full retirement age. The advantage is that the individual collects benefits for a longer period of time. The disadvantage is that the benefit is permanently reduced.
      (5) An individual can obtain a higher retirement benefit by working past normal retirement age up to age 70.

   C. Disability

      (1) A person is entitled to disability benefits if he or she meets *all* of the following requirements.

         (a) Is insured for disability benefits
         (b) Is under the age of 65
         (c) Has been disabled for 12 months, or is expected to be disabled for 12 months
         (d) Has filed application for disability benefits
         (e) Has completed a five-month waiting period or is exempted from this period.

(2) A person must be so severely impaired, physically or mentally, that he or she cannot perform any other gainful work. The impairment must last 12 months or more. The determination is based on medical evidence.

(3) To qualify for disability, an individual must be fully insured and have at least 20 quarters of coverage during a 40-quarter period ending with the quarter in which the person is disabled. The quarterly period requirement is met if a person worked 5 years of the last 10 years before disability.

(4) Special insured status is required to qualify for disability benefits if an individual is disabled before age 31. Special insured status is established if a person:

    (a) Is disabled before the quarter in which age 31 is attained, and

    (b) Has credits in one-half of the quarters during the period beginning with the quarter after the quarter in which the person attained age 21 and ending with the quarter in which the person became disabled. If disabled before age 24, the person must have six quarters of coverage in the 12-quarter period.

D. Survivor—The following benefits are payable to the survivors of a deceased insured worker:

(1) *Mother's and father's benefit.* Monthly benefit for widow(er), regardless of age if caring for at least one child, under 16 or disabled before age 22, of a deceased worker

(2) *Child's benefit.* Monthly benefit for each child who is

    (a) Under age 18

    (b) Over age 18 and disabled before age 22

    (c) Under age 19 and a full-time student

(3) *Widow(er)'s benefit.* Monthly benefit for widow(er), or surviving divorced widow(er), age 60 or older

(4) *Disabled widow(er)'s benefit.* Monthly benefit for a disabled widow(er), age 50 to 60

(5) *Parent's benefit.* Monthly benefit for parent age 62 or older who was dependent on deceased worker for support

(6) Lump sum death payment of $255 (in 2002)

E. Family limitations

(1) A spouse is entitled to up to 50 percent of employee's full retirement benefit. The spouses' benefit ends when certain events happen:

    (a) The spouse dies.

    (b) The worker dies (in which case the spouse is entitled to widow(er)'s, mother's, or father's benefits).

    (c) The worker's entitlement to disability benefits ends and he or she is not entitled to retirement benefits.

    (d) The spouse is under age 62 and there is no longer a child of the worker under 16 or disabled who is entitled to child's benefits

    (e) The spouse becomes entitled to retirement or disability benefits and his or her PIA is equal to or larger than one-half of the worker's PIA.

    (f) The spouse and worker are divorced before the spouse reaches age 62 and before the spouse and worker had been married for 10 years.

    (g) The divorced spouse marries someone other than the worker.

(2) Each qualified child may receive a monthly payment up to 50 percent of the employee's full retirement benefit amount, but there is a limit to the amount that can be paid to the family as a whole. This total depends on the amount of the employee's benefit and the

number of family members who also qualify on the employee's record. The total varies, but it is generally equal to about 150 to 188 percent of PIA for retirement and survivors. The child's benefit ends when certain events happen:

(a) The child dies.

(b) The child marries (but not if the child is a disabled child over age 18 and the child marries another Social Security beneficiary).

(c) The child's parent is no longer entitled to disability benefits, unless entitlement ended because the insured parent became entitled to retirement benefits or died.

(d) The child reaches age 18 and is neither under disability or a full-time student.

(3) A grandchild is considered the child of the worker if

(a) The grandchild's natural parents are deceased or disabled at the time the worker becomes entitled to retirement or disability benefits or dies.

(b) The grandchild was legally adopted by the worker's surviving spouse.

(c) The grandchild is dependent on the insured.

(4) The spouse can lose benefits if he or she is under normal retirement age and earnings exceed $11,520 (in 2003). A child can lose benefits if he or she works and earns more than $11,520 in 2003.

(5) A widow or widower may receive employee's full benefit (100 percent PIA) at 65 or older, or reduced benefit as early as age 60 (or age 50 to 59 and disabled). Children under age 18 also receive 75 percent of the deceased employee's benefit.

Benefit Table										
Benefits for workers and their families					Benefits for survivors of deceased workers				Maximum family benefit for retirement and survivor	Maximum family benefit for disability
FRA retirement benefit or disability benefit	Age 62 retirement benefit	Benefits for family members			Spouse not caring for child		One child	Spouse and one child; or two children		
		Spouse not caring for child		Child or spouse caring for child		Age 60 or age 50–59 and disabled				
		FRA	Age 62		Age 65					
100% of PIA	77½% of PIA	50% of PIA	36¼% of PIA	50% of PIA	100% of PIA	71½% of PIA	75% of PIA	150% of PIA	150–188% of PIA	100–150% of PIA

Adapted from Mercer, *2003 Guide to Social Security and Medicare,* 31st ed., Louisville, KY: Mercer Human Resources Consulting, Inc., 2002.

2. How benefits are calculated

A. The primary insurance amount (PIA) is the basic unit used to determine the amount of each monthly benefit. A disabled or retired worker receives the full PIA if benefits start at normal retirement age.

B. It is necessary to know the average indexed monthly Earnings (AIME) to calculate PIA. AIME is based on an individual's lifetime earnings history.

C. Social Security benefits depend on an average of 35 years of worker's best earnings (after indexing) to figure AIME. If there are fewer than 35 years of earnings, zero is used for each remaining year. The index factors given for each year make past earnings comparable to the level of earnings today.

D. AIME is computed by dividing the total earnings (sum of the highest 35 years of indexed earnings) by 420 (35 years × 12 months). This number is then used to find PIA.

E. The PIA formula for persons attaining age 62 in 2002, or becoming disabled or dying before age 62 in 2002, is

(1) 90 percent of the first $592 of AIME, *plus*

(2) 32 percent of the next $2,975 of AIME, *plus*

(3) 15 percent of AIME in excess of $3,567

(4) The dollar amount in the PIA formula after 2002 is adjusted annually by changes in the national indexing average wage. The PIA resulting from the formula is increased annually to reflect changes in the cost of living.

F. The PIA formula for persons who attained age 62 before 2002 (born before 1940) uses a different index factor multiplier and PIA benefit formula, but the steps are similar for those attaining age 62 in 2002.

3. Working after retirement

A. No benefits are lost for those older than normal retirement age.

B. If a person is under the normal retirement age, the following apply:

(1) If no more than $30,000 is earned in 2002 by a worker who reaches normal retirement age in 2002, no benefits are lost for that year.

(2) If more than $30,000 is earned in 2002 before the month the beneficiary reaches normal retirement age, $1 of benefits is lost for each $3 of earnings over $30,000.

(3) If no more than $11,520 is earned in 2003 by a worker under normal retirement age for the entire year, no benefits are lost for that year.

(4) If more than $11,520 is earned in 2003 by a worker under the normal retirement age for the entire year, $1 of benefits is lost for each $2 of earnings over $11,520.

4. Taxation of Social Security

A. FICA (Social Security and Medicare) tax

(1) 7.65 percent FICA tax for employers and employees

(2) For 2003, the 6.20 percent Social Security tax is computed on the first $87,000 of the employee's wages. The 1.45 percent Medicare tax is computed on the employee's total wages.

B. Self-employment tax is imposed on self-employed people at a rate of 15.3 percent. This is a combination of 12.40 percent Social Security tax and 2.9 percent Medicare tax (no ceiling).

C. Income taxes on benefits (in 2003)

(1) *Benefits 50 percent taxable.* Fifty percent of benefits are included in gross income if a person's income plus half of his or her Social Security benefits is more than the following base amounts for that person's filing status.

(a) $32,000 for married couples filing jointly

(b) $0 for married couples filing separately, and the person lived with the spouse at any time during the year

(c) $25,000 for all other taxpayers

(2) *Benefits 85 percent taxable.* Eighty-five percent of benefits are included in gross income if a person's income plus half of his or her Social Security benefits is more than the following base amounts for that person's filing status.

(a) $44,000 for married couples filing jointly

(b) $0 for married couples filing separately, and the person lived with the spouse at any time during the year

(c) $34,000 for all other taxpayers

(3) If a person is married filing separately and lived with the spouse at any time during the year, up to 85 percent of benefits are included in gross income.

TOPIC 74: MEDICARE

1. Eligibility

   A. Medicare Part A

      (1) Anyone over 65 who is eligible for retirement benefits is eligible for Medicare Part A.
      (2) Disabled persons are covered after two years of disability benefits.
      (3) Others include persons requiring kidney transplants.
      (4) Many people under the original Medicare plan have a Medigap policy to pay for costs that the original plan does not cover (see Topic 26).

   B. Medicare Part B

      (1) Anyone eligible for Part A is automatically eligible for Part B.
      (2) Voluntary enrollment—a person can opt out of Part B.
      (3) A monthly premium payment is required.

   C. Medicare + Choice (Part C). A person must have both Medicare Parts A and B to join a Medicare + Choice plan, which provides managed care under contract to Medicare.

2. Coverage provided by Parts A and B

   A. Benefits covered by Medicare Part A

      (1) Hospital coverage

         (a) Hospital expenses are paid in full for 60 days during the benefit period. This is followed by 30 additional days with co-payment and a 60-day lifetime reserve.
         (b) A benefit period begins when a Medicare recipient is hospitalized and ends only when the recipient has been out of the hospital or skilled-nursing facility for 60 consecutive days.
         (c) There is no limit on the amount of benefit periods a person can have in a lifetime.
         (d) The 60-day lifetime reserve may be used if the 90-day period has been exhausted.

      (2) Skilled nursing facility

         (a) Benefits in a skilled-nursing facility are provided only if a physician certifies that skilled-nursing care or rehabilitative services are needed for a condition that was treated in the hospital resulting in a stay of at least 3 days within the last 30 days.
         (b) Benefits are paid in full for 20 days, and an additional 80 days are covered with a co-payment. After 100 days of coverage, the patient must pay the full cost of skilled-nursing facility care.
         (c) Every patient must be under the supervision of a full-time nurse and a physician, and the physician must be available at all time for emergencies.
         (d) It is important to note that sole custodial care is *not* provided under any part of Medicare. However, there is a degree of custodial care provided when skilled-nursing or rehabilitative services are needed and covered under the plan.

      (3) Home health care

         (a) Medicare pays home health care benefits in full.
         (b) To receive these benefits, a person must be confined to his or her home and be treated under a home health plan established by a physician.

      (4) Hospice

(a) Hospice benefits are available under Medicare for individuals who are certified as being terminally ill with a life expectancy of less than six months.

(b) Benefits are provided primarily in the patient's home by a Medicare-approved hospice.

B. Benefits covered by Medicare Part B: Physicians' and surgeons' fees, diagnostic tests, physical therapy, drugs that cannot be self-administered, medical supplies such as splints and casts, rental of medical equipment such as wheelchairs, mammograms and Pap smears, prosthetic devices, ambulance services, diabetes glucose monitoring, colorectal and prostrate cancer screening, and bone mass measurements

C. Benefits *not* covered under Medicare: The original Medicare plan does not cover health care for a person traveling outside the United States (there are exceptions for emergencies in Mexico and Canada); it does not cover custodial care, dental work, cosmetic surgery (except after an accident), routine foot care, eye and hearing exams, prescription glasses and hearing aids, most prescription drugs, private room in hospital or nursing home, services covered under workers' compensation, most chiropractic care, acupuncture, or most immunizations.

D. Benefits covered by Medicare + Choice (Part C): Covers *all* the services covered under Part A and Part B and additional services such as prescription drugs

3. Cost of coverage

A. Medicare Part B costs are $54 per month (in 2002).

B. Medicare + Choice Plans *and* Medigap premiums vary among companies.

TOPIC 75: TYPES OF RETIREMENT PLANS

1. Characteristics

A. Qualified retirement plans (QRP)

(1) The retirement plan is afforded special tax treatment for meeting a multitude of requirements of the Internal Revenue Code (IRC). Obvious *tax advantages* for a QRP include

(a) Employer (E/ER) is allowed an *immediate* tax deduction for amount contributed to the plan for a particular year.

(b) Employee/participant (E/EE) pays *no current* income tax on the amounts contributed by the E/ER on his or her behalf.

(c) Earnings are tax-exempt, allowing for tax-free accumulation of income and gains on investments.

(d) Reduced income tax *may* apply to lump sum distributions to certain participants.

(e) Income taxes on certain types of distributions may be deferred by rolling over (R/O) the distribution to an individual retirement account (IRA) or another (qualified or nonqualified) retirement plan.

(f) Incomes taxes on certain types of distributions to a deceased participant's spouse may be deferred by R/O distribution to an IRA.

(g) Installment or annuity payments are taxed only when they are received.

(2) Two major types of qualified plan categories

(a) Defined benefit plan (DBP)

  i. The maximum allowable benefit payable from the plan is the lesser of 100 percent of salary or $160,000 per year (in 2003).

  ii. The maximum compensation base that can be used is $200,000 (in 2003).

      iii. Generally subject to Pension Benefit Guaranty Coporation (PBGC) insurance

      iv. Must satisfy minimum participation rule of Code Section 401(a)(26)

      v. Retirement benefit is *certain.*

      vi. Each DBP is subject to the minimum funding standard.

      vii. Deductible contribution is based on actuarial calculations and can vary from year to year.

(b) Defined contribution plan (DCP)

      i. The maximum allowable annual contribution is the lesser of 100 percent of salary or $40,000 (in 2003).

      ii. The maximum compensation base that can be used is $200,000 (in 2003). Note that $40,000 is only 20 percent of $200,000.

      iii. Not subject to PBGC insurance

      iv. Not subject to minimum participation rule

      v. Deductible contribution limited to 25 percent of aggregate compensation

      vi. Retirement benefit is *uncertain.*

B. Nonqualified plans

  (1) Characteristics and objectives

    (a) Alternative to qualified plans for executives

    (b) Few design restrictions regarding benefit structure, vesting requirements, or coverage

    (c) Designed to defer the payment of income taxes by employees until benefits are paid out

    (d) Employer deduction is deferred to the time of payout; deduction is matched to employee income.

    (e) Assets must be available to pay claims of creditors in order to avoid current taxation.

    (f) Limited benefit security for participants

  (2) Nonqualified deferred compensation plan designs

    (a) *Salary reduction plan.* Gives participants the option to *defer* regular compensation, bonuses, or commissions

    (b) *Supplemental executive retirement plan (SERP).* Additional employer-provided benefits

C. Government plans (Section 457 plans)

  (1) Section 457 of the Internal Revenue Code gives rules for governing nonqualified plans of government entities and nonprofit organizations.

  (2) Characteristics

    (a) Election to defer compensation must be made before the compensation is earned.

    (b) The employer may discriminately choose any employee for coverage.

    (c) Such plans are similar to a 401(k) plan, in which the maximum deferral limit that applies is $12,000 for 2003.

2. Types of qualified plans

A. Money purchase

  (1) Employer is required to make contributions based on contribution formula—contributions are allocated as a percentage of compensation regardless of age (unlike target benefit plan).

(2) The plan is subject to minimum funding standard, whether or not the company made a profit.

(3) Forfeitures may be reallocated to remaining participants' accounts *or* applied to reduce employer contributions.

(4) Investment in sponsoring company's stock is limited to 10 percent.

(5) The plan can be integrated with Social Security.

(6) *Younger employees* accumulate more than they would with a DBP

(7) The plan generally does not produce as large a contribution and deduction for *older employees* as DBP.

(8) No guarantee of future benefits; the investment risk rests on the employee.

B. Profit sharing

(1) Employer contributions must be "substantial and recurring."

(2) Profits are not required in order to make contributions.

(3) Forfeitures may be reallocated among the remaining participants.

(4) Nondiscriminatory allocation of contributions

(5) No limit on how much can be invested in the sponsoring company's stock

(6) Can be integrated with Social Security

(7) Benefits the younger employee more than the older employee (owner). Younger employees accumulate more than they would with a DBP over time because of earnings, forfeitures, compounding effect, tax-deferred accumulation

(8) Profit sharing plans are usually recommended for upstart companies because:

    (a) Profits may be nonexistent in the beginning years.

    (b) Contributions are flexible.

    (c) Earnings fluctuate from year to year.

(9) Do not provide as large a contribution deduction as a DBP

(10) No guarantee of future benefits; the investment risk rests on the employee.

C. Age-weighted

(1) An age-weighted profit sharing plan uses age and compensation to allocate contributions to participants. In this way, its concept is similar to that of a target benefit plan. The plan, therefore, benefits older employees because they have fewer years to retirement.

(2) To satisfy nondiscrimination requirements, this plan is tested under cross-testing rules.

D. New comparability plan

(1) A new comparability plan is a profit sharing plan or money purchase pension plan in which the contribution percentage formula for one group of participants is greater than for another group of participants.

(2) To satisfy nondiscrimination requirements, this plan is tested under cross-testing rules.

E. Tandem plan

(1) Employer adopts a money-purchase plan and a profit sharing plan.

(2) Employer gains flexibility in plan.

    (a) Profit sharing contributions are not required annually.

    (b) Money-purchase contributions are still required annually.

(3) Oriented toward younger, higher-paid employees

F. Section 401(k) plan (also called cash or deferred arrangement or CODA)

    (1) A Section 401(k) plan *cannot* exist on its own—it is *not* a stand-alone plan.

        (a) *Must* be combined with a qualified retirement plan

            i. Profit sharing plan

            ii. Stock bonus (employee stock ownership plan, ESOP)

            iii. Pre-ERISA (Employment Retirement Income Security Act) money-purchase plan

        (b) May be combined with a salary reduction simplified employee pension (SARSEP) if established before January 1, 1997

        (c) May be combined with a Savings Incentive Match Plan for Employees (SIMPLE)

    (2) Types of 401(k) plans

        (a) Traditional Section 401(k) is much like a profit sharing plan.

            i. Can be funded entirely from employee salary reduction

            ii. Nondiscrimination testing, such as actual deferral percentage (ADP) and top-heavy rules apply.

        (b) SIMPLE 401(k) plans and safe harbor 401(k) plans

            i. Exempt from nondiscrimination testing (ADP/ACP) actual contribution percentage

            ii. Funding requirements for employer

    (3) *Traditional and safe harbor 401(k) plans*. Employee elective deferral amount is $12,000 in 2003. Catch-up contributions by employees age 50 or older is $2,000 in 2003.

    (4) *SIMPLE 401(k) plans*. Lower annual elective deferral limits of $8,000 in 2003; catch-up amount is $1,000 in 2003.

    (5) Two types of contributions

        (a) *Cash or deferred arrangement (CODA)*. Employee has the option of receiving an employer contribution (e.g., annual bonus)

            i. In *cash* and having it taxed currently, or

            ii. *Deferring* the cash by making it a tax-deferred retirement plan contribution (i.e., 401(k) plan)

        (b) *Salary reduction*. Employee defers the receipt and taxation. The reduction amount is deducted from the paycheck and contributed to a retirement fund and accumulates tax-deferred.

    (6) In-service withdrawals by employees for certain "hardships" are permitted; these are not available in qualified pension plans.

    (7) May not provide adequate retirement savings for employees who enter the plan at later ages

    (8) All elective deferrals from all employer plans that cover the employee must be aggregated; deferrals are characterized as employer contributions to ensure that the sum of employee and employer tax-favored contributions do not exceed the 25 percent payroll limit and the limit on annual additions.

    (9) Employees bear investment risk under the plan.

    (10) Meets the employer's requirement of *substantial and recurring* contributions in profit sharing plans

    (11) No integration with Social Security for just 401(k) plan

G. Employee stock ownership plan (ESOP)

  (1) An ESOP must invest primarily in employer stock.

  (2) Portfolio is 100 percent company stock; there are special diversification requirements for participants over age 55 with 10 years of service.

  (3) May borrow to buy company stock: *leverage* ESOP (LESOP)

  (4) ESOP can be integrated with Social Security; a LESOP cannot be integrated with Social Security.

  (5) An ESOP plan (and stock bonus plan) makes sense for a corporation by

    (a) Providing a market for the owner's closely held stock

    (b) Giving tax deductions while having no effect on cash flows

    (c) Protecting company stock from hostile takeovers

H. Stock bonus plan

  (1) Benefit payments are usually made in shares of company stock. The participant can receive cash in lieu of stock.

  (2) Diversified portfolio

  (3) May *not* borrow to buy company stock

  (4) Can integrate with Social Security

I. Thrift or savings plan

  (1) Contributions are *after-tax* dollars; earnings are tax-deferred.

  (2) Employees are required to contribute (up to 6 percent) in order to be eligible to receive the employer's matching contribution.

  (3) Hardship withdrawals are more liberal than with 401(k) plans.

  (4) In a rollover: after-tax money to participant and earnings to IRA

J. Target benefit

  (1) Forfeitures may be reallocated to remaining participants' accounts *or* applied to reduce employer contributions.

  (2) Allocation of employer contributions is based on age-weighted formula—favors older employee.

  (3) Investment in sponsoring company's stock is limited to 10 percent.

  (4) Can be integrated with Social Security

  (5) Provisions shared with defined contribution plan

    (a) Employee assumes investment risk—no guarantee of future benefits.

    (b) *No* ongoing actuarial determinations

    (c) Forfeitures may be reallocated *or* used to reduce employer contribution.

  (6) Provisions shared with defined benefit plan

    (a) Plan benefits *older* employees (older employees may not receive a benefit as great as with a DBP).

    (b) Actuarial determination for initial contribution level and formula for allocation contributions

    (c) Subject to minimum funding standard: *mandatory* annual employer contributions

K. Defined benefit plan

  (1) Retirement benefits are definitely determinable—the benefit is defined by the formula in the plan.

  (2) When the interest rate earned on plan assets is higher or lower than the actuarial assumptions, the employer increases or decreases its future contributions to the plan as needed to match the promised benefit (unlike target benefit plan).

(3) Plan formulas are geared to retirement benefits and not contributions (unlike cash balance plans).

(4) Actuary determines required contribution each year—*minimum funding standard.*

(5) Forfeitures *must* be used to reduce the employer's contribution.

(6) Employees accrue retirement benefits when eligible to participate, but are not vested until a minimum period of time is worked.

(7) Benefits *must* be paid to plan participants even if the plan is terminated.

(8) The plan can be integrated with Social Security.

(9) Greater tax-deductible contributions than through DCP.

(10) Rewards long-term employees with a substantial benefit even if close to normal retirement age

(11) Larger contribution to older employee—more beneficial to participants closer to retirement

(12) Investment risk rests on employer.

(13) Higher administration costs

(14) Plan benefits are *not* portable.

(15) Retirement benefits/distributions are *not* adjusted for cost of living (i.e., inflation).

L. Cash balance plan

(1) A cash balance plan is a defined benefit plan with features similar to those of a defined contribution plan.

(2) The distinguishing feature of a cash balance plan is that a separate account is established for each participant, using a hypothetical account balance. These hypothetical allocations and earnings are designed to imitate the actual contributions and earnings that would occur to an employees account under a defined contribution plan.

(3) Employee balances grow based on hypothetical earnings (i.e., interest credits). The interest rate varies from year to year and is communicated to the employee at the start of each year. The rate is not tied to actual performance of investments and is determined independently; the minimum rate cannot be more than the lowest standard interest rate, and the maximum rate cannot be less than the highest standard interest rate.

(4) Actuary determines required contribution each year—*minimum funding standard.*

(5) Plan can be integrated with Social Security.

(6) Greater tax-deductible contributions than through DCP

(7) Forfeitures *must* be used to reduce employer's contribution.

(8) More beneficial to younger participants

(9) Employer *must* pay benefits in accordance with plan provisions even in low- or no-profit years.

(10) Investment risk rests on employer.

(11) Higher administration costs

(12) Benefits *must* be paid to plan participants even if the plan is terminated.

(13) Plan benefits are *not* portable.

(14) Retirement benefits/distributions are *not* adjusted for cost of living (i.e., inflation).

Comparison of Defined Contribution Plans			
	Profit Sharing Plan	**Stock Bonus or ESOP Plan**	**Money Purchase Plan**	**Target Benefit Plan**
Employer Contribution (maximum deduction)	25% of covered payroll[1]			
Mandatory Employer Contribution	No, but "substantial and recurring"		Yes, as percentage of compensation or flat sum	Yes, as stated in plan formula
Employee Contribution	401(k) provisions, if permitted		401(k) provisions are not permitted, but after-tax contributions are permitted	
Forfeitures	Reallocated or used to reduce employer contribution[2]			
Maximum "Annual Additions"[3] to Participant's Account	100% of compensation or $40,000 whichever is less			
Discriminatory Plan Test	Coverage tests, ADP/ACP test, and top heavy test			
Social Security Integration	Yes[4], except LESOP only			

[1]LESOP only equals 25 percent deduction limit for principal payments and unlimited interest deduction.

[2]Forfeitures are generally reallocated for discretionary contribution plans.

[3]"Annual additions" are employer contributions (including 401(k) elective deferrals), forfeiture allocations, and employee nondeductible contributions.

[4]No integration with Social Security for only 401(k) provision.

TOPIC 76: QUALIFIED PLAN RULES AND OPTIONS

1. Feasibility of installation of a qualified plan

   A. Client objectives

      (1) *Personal objectives.* Maximize personal tax benefits; maximize personal retirement benefits; achieve retirement income goal; provide estate protection.

      (2) *Business objectives.* Reduce corporate income tax; reward valued employees; motivate employees; reduce employee turnover; increase employee job satisfaction.

      (3) *Altruistic objectives.* Provide employees with retirement income; promote employee savings; provide flexible compensation; share profits; share ownership.

   B. Constraints (to provide a plan that will meet the needs of the client.)

      (1) Personnel characteristics, profile (age, service, compensation, etc.)

      (2) Profits and cash flows (variable, stable, etc.)

      (3) Profile of employees (long-term, part-time, etc.)

      (4) Profile of the business owner (age, financial situation, etc.)

(5) Client sophistication and commitment (fiduciary responsibility, contributing for employees, administrative costs, etc.)

(6) Types of retirement plans available for specific forms of businesses

Eligible Business Entities for Each Retirement Plan								
Business Form	**Target Benefit**	**Defined Benefit**	**Money Purchase**	**Profit Sharing**	**Stock Bonus and ESOP**	**Section 401(k)**	**SIMPLE & SEP**	**457 Plan**
Sole Proprietor	Y	Y	Y	Y	NO	Y	Y	NO
General Partnership	Y	Y	Y	Y	NO	Y	Y	NO
C Corp	Y	Y	Y	Y	Y	Y	Y	Y
S Corp	Y	Y	Y	Y	Y	Y	Y	NO
Tax-Exempt 501(c)(3)	Y	Y	Y	Y	NO	Y	Y	Y
Public School	Y	Y	Y	Y	NO	NO	Y	Y
State/Local Government	Y	Y	Y	Y	NO	NO	Y	Y

2. Qualified plan coverage and eligibility requirements

   A. Age and service requirements—Employees must be eligible to participate in a qualified retirement plan within *six months* after the later of:

      (1) *21 and 1 (vesting schedule)*. Employee has reached age 21 *and* has met one-year service requirement: The employee is included in the plans vesting schedule.

      (2) *21 and 2 (100 percent vesting)*. Employee has reached age 21, *and* if the service requirement exceeds one year but does *not* exceed two years of service, the plan must provide full and immediate vesting of benefits.

      (3) *Important*. For 401(k) plans the maximum is one year.

      (4) An employer can exclude employees who are

         (a) Covered by a collective bargaining agreement
         (b) Nonresident aliens
         (c) Part-time employees who have worked less than 1,000 hours per year
         (d) Employees who have worked less than one year
         (e) Employees under age 21

   B. Coverage requirements

      (1) These requirements ensure that the "highly compensated employee" (HCE) is not getting more benefits at the expense of the "non-highly-compensated employee" (NHCE).

      (2) One of two coverage tests must be satisfied for a plan to receive favorable tax treatment:

(a) *The ratio percentage test.* The percentage of NHCEs who benefit under the retirement plan must equal at least 70 percent of the percentage of HCEs who benefit under the plan.

    Example: The Wise Corporation's defined benefit plan covers 70 percent of its NHCEs and 85 percent of its HCEs in the plan year. Does the company's plan meet the ratio percentage test? Yes, the plan does meet the ratio percentage test because the ratio percentage for the year is 82.3 percent (0.70 ÷ 0.85).

(b) *The average benefits test.* This is a two-prong test, and both conditions must be satisfied.

    i. The plan must benefit a class of employees that qualifies under the classification set up by the employer and found by the IRS not to be discriminatory in favor of HCEs.

    ii. The average benefit percentage for the eligible NHCEs must be 70 percent of the average benefit percentage for the eligible HCEs.

C. Minimum participation

(1) Occasionally referred to as the 50/40 test. For years after 1996, it applies to defined benefit plans only. For defined benefit plans, minimum participation must benefit the *lesser* of:

(a) 50 employees, or

(b) 40 percent of all employees

(2) *Example*: A law office has 125 employees. All employees are covered by the firm's defined benefit plan except for 70 associate attorneys and paralegals. The minimum participation requirement is satisfied because the plan covers at least the lesser of (1) 50 employees (125 − 70 = 55) or (2) 40 percent of all employees (150 × 40% = 60). *Note*: The plan is also required to meet the minimum coverage requirement.

(3) Combining different plans of the same employer does not satisfy the requirement.

D. Actual deferral percentage test/actual contribution percentage test

(1) These are specific nondiscrimination tests for plans allowing salary deferrals and matching contributions (i.e., 401(k) plans).

(2) Actual deferral percentage test (ADP)

(a) This test compares the deferral rates of NHCEs relative to their compensation with the deferral rates of HCEs.

(b) The ADP of HCEs is limited by the ADP of NHCEs. If the ADP of HCEs is greater than the limit, HCEs must decrease their deferrals.

(c) The ADP of HCEs must not exceed the greater of:

    i. The ADP of all other employees times 125 percent, or

    ii. The lesser of

       • The ADP of all other employees plus 2 percent, or

       • The ADP of all other employees times 2

(d) Consider the following chart and illustration:

If the NHCEs defer (on average)						
0.75%	2%	4%	6%	8%	10%	12%
Then the HCEs defer (on average)						
1.5%	4%	6%	8%	10%	12.5%	15%

If the ADP of NHCEs is less than 2 percent, HCEs may defer up to two times. If the ADP of NHCEs is 2 percent to 8 percent, HCEs may defer an additional 2 percent.

If the ADP of NHCEs is more than 8 percent, HCEs may defer up to 125 percent.

(3) Actual contribution percentage (ACP) test

    (a) Applies to employer *matching* contributions and after-tax employee contributions under all qualified DCP and employee contributions under a DBP, to the extent they are allocated to a separate account for each individual participant

    (b) The ACP test is similar to the ADP test.

E. Highly compensated—To determine whether an employee is a highly compensated active employee for the determination year, two calculations are required: (1) look-back year and (2) determination year.

(1) In the *look-back* year:

    (a) The employee owns 5 percent of the employer, *or*

    (b) Received compensation from the employer greater than $90,000 (as indexed in 2003); and, if the employer elects, is among the top-paid group of employees (top-paid 20 percent of employees ranked by compensation)

    (c) If the employer elects to use membership in the top-paid group, then the employer can choose to include fewer employees in the HCE group, even if those employees make more than $90,000. For example, if 35 percent of the employees earn more than $90,000 (as adjusted), including 5 percent owners, the top-paid group election will limit the selection of HCE group to 20 percent of employees.

(2) In the *determination* year:

    (1) The employee owns 5 percent of the employer *only*.

(3) *Important*: The employee is an HCE if he or she meets *either* the look-back year or determination year conditions.

(4) *Example*: Assume an employer elects to use membership in the top-paid group. Jim, who started employment in 2001, has earned the following salaries each year:

Year	Compensation	Status
2001	$100,000	Excluded
2002	$105,000	Excluded
2003	$110,000	Excluded

Jim has earned more than $90,000 each year, but has been excluded from the HCE group because he is not a 5 percent owner or a member of the top-paid group. Now assume the employer does not elect to use membership in the top-paid group for 2002. For 2003, Jim is an HCE because for the look-back years he earned more than $90,000.

F. Controlled group—IRS rules prevent employers from setting up multiple businesses whereby one business entity provides retirement plan benefits to key employees and another business entity that employs common-law workers provides zero benefits. When a control group relationship exists, all employees of the group are considered employees of a single employer for the purpose of satisfying rules that govern QRP. A control group exists when there are:

(1) *Parent-subsidiary relationships*. There is ≥ 80 percent common ownership by one or more companies in the group and the parent owns 80 percent of at least one company. Consider the following example:

Example: Corporation A owns 80 percent of Corporations B and C, and Corporations B and C each own 40 percent of Corporation D. Therefore, Corporation D is part of the parent-subsidiary controlled group because it is 80 percent owned by firms within the group.

(2) *Brother-sister relationships*. (1) Five or fewer people own 80 percent or more of the stock value *and* (2) the same five or fewer people own more than 50 percent of the stock or voting power of *each corporation*, taking into account the ownership of each person only to the extent that such ownership is identical with respect to each business (i.e., identical ownership test).

Example: ABC Corporation and XYZ Corporation are owned by four unrelated shareholders.

	Percentage of Ownership	
Shareholder	ABC Corporation	XYZ Corporation
Chris	80%	20%
Mark	10	50
Emma	5	15
Stan	5	15
TOTAL	100%	100%

The four shareholders together own more than 80 percent or more of the stock of each corporation, but they do not own more than 50 percent of the stock of each corporation, taking into account only the identical ownership as demonstrated:

Shareholder	Identical Ownership Percentage
Chris	20%
Mark	10
Emma	5
Stan	5
TOTAL	40%

ABC Corporation and XYZ Corporation do not constitute a controlled group of corporations.

(3) *Affiliated service groups*. Consist of a *first service organization* (FSO) and one or more "A" or "B" organizations. These groups were used to circumvent the controlled group rules originally set forth in ERISA.

An FSO must be a *professional service organization* whose principal business is the performance of professional services of one or more of the following: CPA, actuary, architect, attorney, doctor, and engineer.

(a) "A" organization

    i. Is an owner (a shareholder or partner) of an FSO and

    ii. Regularly performs services for the FSO

(b) "B" organization

    i. A significant portion of "B" organization's business is the performance of services for the FSO, or "A" organization.

    ii. At least 10 percent owned by officers, HCEs, or owners of the FSO, or "A" Organization

3. Qualified plan vesting schedule

  A. Types

    (1) Employee contributions are 100 percent vested immediately.

    (2) Employer matching contributions (i.e., contributions made by an employer on account of an employee contribution or elective deferral, or forfeiture allocated on the basis of employee contributions, matching contributions, or elective deferrals) made after 2001 must vest under a faster vesting schedule than in earlier years.

      (a) *Three-year vesting (also called Cliff vesting)*. 100 percent after three years

      (b) *Two- to six-year vesting*. Graded vesting that must be at least as fast as the following schedule:

Years of Service	Vested Percentage
2	20
3	40
4	60
5	80
6	100

    (3) This faster vesting schedule is also applicable to top-heavy plans, both before 2002 and after 2001.

    (4) The portion of the benefit or account attributable to employer contributions *other than matching contributions* in years after 2001 remain subject to the five-year and three- to seven-year vesting standard.

    (5) SIMPLE and SEP provide *immediate* 100 percent vesting.

  B. Top-heavy plans—Accelerated vesting schedule is either a three-year Cliff or a two- to six-year graded vesting.

4. Integration with Social Security/disparity limits

  A. Social Security provides greater benefit coverage for workers making less than the taxable wage base (TWB) and provides no additional coverage to those workers making more than the TWB. In other words, higher-income workers receive less retirement benefit than lower-income workers (i.e., less than the TWB) with respect to the Social Security retirement benefit.

  B. The *disparity* in retirement benefit for the higher-income versus the lower-income workers can be "corrected" by integrating the Social Security benefit with the qualified retirement plan benefit. The disparity is allowed by the IRC as long as it is *not* considered discriminatory and regulatory limits are observed.

  C. Defined benefit plan

    (1) *Excess method* of integration with Social Security. The plan defines a compensation level called the *integration level*. The plan then provides a higher rate of benefits for compensation above the integration level.

      Example: A plan has an annual benefit that is 30 percent of final average annual compensation plus 25 percent of compensation above the integration level. Steve retires with a final average compensation of $40,000. The integration level is $37,000. His annual retirement benefit is

      (a) 30 percent of final average compensation of $40,000, plus

      (b) 25 percent of $3,000 ($40,000 − $37,000)

      (c) The total benefit equals $12,750 ($12,000 + $750).

(2) The percentage spread between the benefit as a percentage of compensation above and below the integration level is restricted.

    (a) *Base benefit percentage*. The percentage of compensation provided for compensation below the integration level

    (b) *Excess benefit percentage*. The percentage of compensation above the integration level

    (c) The excess benefit percentage cannot exceed the base percentage by more than ¾ of one percentage point for any year of service, or participant's years of service up to 35.

    (d) *Example*: If a plan provides a benefit of 30 percent of final average compensation below the integration level, it cannot provide more than 56.25 percent of compensation above the integration level (the spread of 26.25 percent equals ¾ percent multiplied by 35 years).

    (e) The maximum excess allowance—the spread between the base and excess benefit percentage—cannot be greater than the base benefit percentage. If a plan provides 10 percent of final average compensation below the integration level, then the excess benefit *cannot* exceed 20 percent. (A spread of 26.25 percent calculated from 35 years of service exceeds the maximum excess allowance.)

(2) *Offset method* of integration with Social Security. There is no integration level. The plan formula is reduced by a fixed amount or some formula amount designed to represent the existence of Social Security.

    (a) No more than half of the benefit provided under the formula without the offset may be taken away by an offset.

    (b) *Example*: If a plan provides for 50 percent of final average compensation with an offset, the lowest-paid employee must receive at least 25 percent of final average compensation.

D. Defined contribution plan

    (1) Excess method only

    (2) If the integration level equals the Social Security taxable wage base in effect ($87,000 in 2003), the spread in the allocation percentages above and below the integration level can be no more than the lesser of

        (a) The percentage contribution below the integration level, or

        (b) The greater of

            i. 5.7 percent

            ii. The old age portion of the Social Security tax rate

    (3) *Example*: If a plan allocates a matching contribution plus forfeitures at the rate of 15.7 percent of compensation above the integration level, then it must allocate at least 10 percent of compensation below the level (making the difference 5.7 percent).

E. Plans with no Social Security integration: (1) LESOP, (2) SARSEP, (3) Employer-matching 401(k) elective contributions.

5. Factors affecting qualified plan contributions or benefits

A. Tax consideration

    (1) Deductible expense to the employer in the year of contribution

    (2) Excluded from employer and employee current income

    (3) Contribution is made from *pre-tax* dollars.

    (4) Earnings are tax-deferred until distribution at retirement.

B. Nature of defined benefit—The highest annual benefit payable under the plan must not exceed the *lesser* of

    (1) 100 percent of the participant's compensation averaged over the three years of highest compensation, or

    (2) $160,000 (in 2003, and adjusted in $5,000 increments under a cost-of-living indexing formula). This limit is adjusted actuarially for retirement ages before age 62 and later than age 65.

C. Nature of defined contribution

    (1) The "annual additions" payable under the plan must not exceed the *lesser* of:

        (a) 100 percent of the participant's annual compensation, or

        (b) $40,000 (in 2003, and subject to increments of $1,000)

    (2) *Annual additions* include employer contributions, employee salary reductions, employee contributions, and plan forfeitures reallocated from other accounts.

D. Comparison of defined contribution and defined benefit

    (1) Only the first $200,000 of each employee's annual compensation (in 2003) can be taken into account in the plan's benefit or contribution formula.

    (2) The $200,000 compensation limit is scheduled to be indexed for inflation in increments of $5,000.

    (3) *Example*: If an employee has a 10 percent money-purchase plan and earned $300,000 in 2003, the maximum contribution for that employee is $20,000 (10 percent of $200,000).

E. Definition of compensation

    (1) Wages, salaries, fees for professional services, and other amounts received (without regard to whether an amount is paid in cash) for personal services rendered in the course of employment to the extent that the amounts are includible in income, whether earned from sources inside or outside the United States.

    (2) Elective or salary reduction contributions to a 401(k), or to 403(b) or SIMPLE plans or a similar arrangement

    (3) SEP contributions

    (4) Amounts contributed or deferred under a 457 plan

    (5) Elective or salary reduction contributions to a cafeteria plan (Section 125)

F. Multiple plans

    (1) Multiple plans will still be aggregated in applying the maximum contribution/benefit.

    (2) The administrative cost of multiple plans is higher than that of single plans.

G. Special rules for self-employed

    (1) A Keogh plan is a qualified retirement plan that covers one or more self-employed individuals of an unincorporated business.

    (2) A Keogh plan covers self-employed individuals who are not technically considered employees.

    (3) Any qualified retirement plan can be designed to cover self-employed individuals. It is usually designed as a profit-sharing plan or money-purchase plan.

    (4) The maximum contribution under a defined contribution Keogh plan is $40,000 in 2003.

    (5) "Earned income" takes the place of "compensation" for the self-employed in applying qualified plan rules.

(a) Earned income is defined as the self-employed individual's net income from the business after all deductions, including the deduction for Keogh plan contributions.

(b) A deduction for one-half of self-employment tax must be taken before determining the Keogh deduction.

(6) Adjusted percentage formula = plan contribution percentage (1 + plan contribution percentage).

(a) Maximum money-purchase plan contribution percentage = 100 percent/(1 + 100 percent) = 50 percent.

(b) Maximum profit-sharing plan contribution percentage = 25 percent/(1 + 25 percent) = 20 percent.

6. Top-heavy plans

A. Definitions

(1) *Defined benefit plan.* Top-heavy when more than 60 percent of the present value of the accrued benefits is allotted for key employees

(2) *Defined contribution plan.* Top-heavy when more than 60 percent of the total amount in the accounts of all employees is allotted to key employees

(3) SIMPLE 401(k) and safe harbor 401(k) plans are exempt from top-heavy requirements.

(4) A key employee (KE) is (in 2003)

(a) A more than 5 percent owner

(b) An officer with compensation in excess of $130,000

(c) A more than 1 percent owner with compensation in excess of $150,000

B. Vesting—If a plan is top-heavy, it must provide 100 percent vesting after three years of service or six-year graded vesting.

C. Effects on contributions or benefits

(1) If a plan is top-heavy, it must also provide minimum benefits or contributions for non-key employees.

(a) For defined benefit plans, the benefit for each non-key employee during a top-heavy year must be at least 2 percent of compensation multiplied by the employee's years of service, up to 20 percent. The average compensation used for this formula is based on the highest five years of compensation.

(b) For defined contribution plans, employer contributions during a top-heavy year must be at least 3 percent of compensation.

(2) Super-top-heavy plan, if more than 90 percent of the total plan benefits are in favor of the key employees

(a) For DCP, contributions must be increased from 3 percent to 4 percent.

(b) For DBP, multiple is increased from 2 percent to 3 percent.

7. Loans from qualified plans

A. Allowed for *all qualified plans* if incorporated in the plan documents

B. For a loan not to be considered a "prohibited transaction," certain rules must be followed:

(1) Loans must be available to all participants and beneficiaries.

(2) Loans cannot be available to HCEs in greater proportions than to NHCEs.

(3) The loan must be made in accordance with plan documents.

(4) The loan must be made at a reasonable interest rate.

(5) The loan must be adequately secured (i.e., collateralized).

C. To avoid the loan's being characterized as a distribution

(1) The term of the loan must *not* exceed five years, unless used to acquire a principal residence.

(2) The loan amount must be the *lesser* of

(a) $50,000, or

(b) 50 percent of the present value of the employee's vested account balance (or accrued benefit, in the case of a defined benefit plan)

(3) The plan document may allow a $10,000 minimum loan, even if this amount is greater than half of the present value. For example, an individual with an account balance of $17,000 could borrow up to $10,000.

D. Loans to self-employed persons (Keogh plans) are allowed as long as loans are available to all employees [Economic Growth and Tax Relief Reconciliation Act (EGTRRA) 2001].

TOPIC 77: OTHER TAX-ADVANTAGED RETIREMENT PLANS

1. Traditional IRA

A. Characteristics

(1) Eligible individuals can contribute up to the maximum contribution amount and possibly deduct this amount from current taxable income.

(2) Investment earnings are tax-deferred.

(3) Premature withdrawals are subject to a 10 percent penalty.

(4) Withdrawals are not eligible for the special averaging tax computation that applies to certain lump sum distributions from qualified plans.

(5) An IRA cannot be established at age 70½, and withdrawals are required by April 1 of the year after the year in which the individual reaches age 70½.

(6) Loans are not available.

B. Prohibited investments include collectibles: artworks, rugs, antiques, metals, gems, stamps, coins, and other tangible property. An exception exists for U.S. gold coins, silver coins, and platinum coins.

C. Contribution rules

(1) Deduction limits

(a) Maximum annual deductible IRA contribution is the *lesser* of

i. Maximum annual contribution amount, or

ii. 100 percent of the individual's earned income, less contributions to a Roth IRA

(b) The maximum annual contribution amount is $3,000 in 2003 and 2004.

(c) For individuals who have attained age 50 before the close of the tax year, an additional "catch-up" is allowed, $500 in 2003 through 2004.

(2) Active participant restrictions

(a) An "active participant" is defined as an individual who actively participates in a qualified retirement plan, SEP, SIMPLE plan, TSA, or government plan.

(b) An individual is not an active participant in a defined contribution plan if only earnings are allocated to the individual's account. However, the individual is an active participant if contributions and forfeitures are made to his or her defined contribution plan.

(c) An individual is an active participant in a *defined benefit plan* if he or she is eligible but declines to participate.

(d) Individuals who are not active participants can deduct contributions to an IRA regardless of what they earn.

(e) For an active participant, fully deductible contributions are allowed only if the taxpayer has AGI below specified limits. The deduction begins to decrease (phase out) when income rises above a certain amount and is eliminated altogether when it reaches a higher amount. These amounts vary, depending on filing status.

IRA Active Participant AGI Phaseout Ranges			
Year	**Single**	**Married Filing Jointly**	**Married Filing Separately**
2003	$40,000 to $50,000	$60,000 to $70,000	$0 to $10,000

(f) For taxpayers whose AGI falls between the phaseout levels, the following calculation can be performed to determine the deduction amount:

Deductible amount = maximum contribution
− [maximum contribution × (AGI − filing status floor)/phaseout range)]

(g) *Example*: Steve and Julie are married filing jointly. They are both active participants and have combined adjusted gross income of $65,000 for 2003. They can each make a full contribution of $3,000 ($6,000 total) to their IRA account, but only a portion is deductible. Because the AGI is $5,000 more than the lower-level limit, they will each lose half of the deductible contribution. To calculate:

$3,000 − [$3,000 × ($65,000 − $60,000)/$10,000] = $1,500.

So each can deduct $1,500 ($3,000 total) for the tax year.

(h) For married taxpayers, the rules are different when only one spouse is an active participant. In this case, a $3,000 *deductible* IRA contribution is available for the nonactive participant spouse as long as the couple's AGI does not exceed $150,000. The deduction is phased out from $150,000 to $160,000, and is gone completely if the AGI is $160,000 or more. A deductible contribution is not available for the nonactive spouse if the couple file separate tax returns.

(i) *Example*: Assume that Rita is an active participant in a qualified retirement plan and her husband, Steve, is not. The combined AGI of Rita and Steve for the year is $200,000. Neither Rita nor Steve is entitled to a deductible contribution to an IRA in 2003.

(3) Time limits

(a) An IRA can be established any time prior to the due date of an individual's tax return, without extensions (even if given). The cutoff date is April 15 for most taxpayers.

(b) Because earnings are tax deferred, it is recommended to make contributions as early as possible to benefit from compounding.

(4) Nonrefundable credit—A limited nonrefundable tax credit is available for low-income taxpayers who make contributions to an traditional IRA.

D. Distributions taken before 59½

   (1) Nondeductible contributions are withdrawn tax free on a pro rata basis. Deductible contributions and earnings are treated as ordinary income and are subject to federal income tax.

   (2) The formula for determining the nontaxable portion of an IRA distribution is

   (Total nondeductible contributions/aggregate
   IRA year-end account balances plus amount of IRA distribution) × IRA distribution

   (3) *Example*: Assume that Margaret has made a deductible IRA contribution of $1,800 and a nondeductible contribution of $2,200 over the last two years. Margaret takes $1,000 out of her IRA on January 1. At the end of the year, her account balance is $4,500. Of the $1,000 withdrawn, $415 is treated as a partial return of nondeductible contributions. It is calculated as follows:

   $$\frac{\$2,200}{\$4,500 + \$1,000} \times \$1,000 = \$400$$

   Thus, $600 ($1,000 – $400) is included in Margaret's tax return.

   (4) A 10 percent penalty tax is imposed unless an exception applies. The 10 percent penalty tax is imposed on the recipient of the distribution and applies only to the portion of the distribution included in gross income. The portion that represents the cost recovery (i.e., nondeductible contributions) is not subject to the 10 percent penalty.

   (5) *Example*: Jim receives a $40,000 distribution from his IRA, of which $25,000 represents his nondeductible contributions. Because no exception applies, a 10 percent penalty of $1,500 [($40,000 – $25,000) × 10%] is imposed on Jim.

E. Excess contribution penalty

   (1) If an individual contributes more to an IRA account than is allowed, the excess contribution is subject to a 6 percent excise tax. The penalty will be charged each year the excess contribution remains in the account. The individual can avoid paying the tax by withdrawing the excess contribution and any earnings before the due date of the federal income tax return.

   (2) The earnings on the excess contributions are treated as gross income for the taxable year.

2. Roth IRA, including conversion analysis

   A. Characteristics

      (1) The contribution amount is limited each year, and is eliminated beyond a certain AGI level.

      (2) Qualified withdrawals are entirely tax-free (this includes investment income, capital gains, and other gains).

      (3) Premature withdrawals in excess of contributions are taxed in full and are subject to a 10 percent penalty.

      (4) Contribution eligibility is not restricted by active participation.

      (5) Contributions can be made after age 70½.

      (6) A Roth IRA is not subject to minimum distribution rules until the death of the owner.

      (7) Loans are not available.

   B. Contribution rules

      (1) Contribution limit

(a) The maximum annual deductible IRA contribution is the *lesser* of

    i. Maximum annual contribution amount, or

    ii. 100 percent of the individual's earned income, less contributions to traditional IRAs

(b) Nondeductible contribution = after-tax contribution.

(c) The maximum annual contribution amount is $3,000 in 2003 and 2004.

(d) For individuals who have attained age 50 before the close of the tax year, an additional "catch-up" is allowed, $500 in 2003 and 2004.

(2) Contribution AGI phaseout limits

(a) AGI used for these limits is "modified" AGI, which excludes taxable income from a conversion of a traditional IRA to a Roth IRA.

(b) The phaseout limits are as follows:

Unmarried individuals	$95,000 to $110,000
Married joint return filers	$150,000 to $160,000
Married separate filers	$0 to $10,000

Example: Helen is a single taxpayer and has an AGI of $105,000 for 2003. Helen may make a contribution of up to $1,000 to the Roth IRA, computed as follows:

AGI	$105,000
Less: Applicable dollar amount	$95,000
Difference	$10,000
Reduction to $3,000 (in 2003) limitation ($3,000 × $10,000 /$15,000)	$2,000
Maximum Roth IRA contribution ($3,000 − $2,000)	$1,000

(3) *Time limits.* Same as for traditional IRA

(4) *Nonrefundable credit.* Same as for traditional IRA

(5) *Employer-sponsored Roth IRAs.* Employers can sponsor a Roth IRA for an employee as a limited alternative to qualified plans.

(6) *Qualified Roth contribution programs.* After 2005, employers can amend their Section 401(k) and Section 403(b) plans to provide that a participant's elective deferrals go into a qualified Roth contribution program. This would be a separate account under a 401(k) or 403(b).

C. Rollovers (Roth conversions)

(1) An individual may make a qualified rollover contribution to a Roth IRA from a traditional IRA unless

(a) The individual's modified AGI exceeds $100,000, or

(b) The individual is married and files a separate return (There is one *exception*: See the following Section (4))

(2) The $100,000 AGI limit applies to both single individuals and married individuals filing joint returns.

(3) *Example*: Bart and Jill are married and file separate returns. Their combined AGI is $105,000. Neither Bart nor Jill can make a rollover from an IRA to a Roth IRA, because a married individual filing a separate return is ineligible to make this rollover. Therefore, this would also be true if their combined AGI were less than $100,000.

(4) *Exception*: The only exception to this joint filing requirement is for an individual who has lived apart from the spouse for the entire taxable year. In this case, the individual can be treated as not married and can file a separate tax return.

(5) The disadvantage of conversion of a traditional IRA to a Roth IRA is that the amount is fully taxable to the owner's ordinary income. The conversion amount is not included in AGI in determining whether the $100,000 limit has been reached. Thus, conversion accelerates all taxes on a traditional IRA that would otherwise be deferred.

(6) Qualified retirement plans must first be rolled over to a traditional IRA and then converted to a Roth IRA.

D. Conversion analysis (is it advisable to convert a traditional IRA to a Roth IRA?)

(1) For the same investment rates and tax rates, studies show that the Roth IRA always produces more money at retirement. If taxpayers invest the full contribution limit, the full amount is at work in a Roth and only the net investment is at work in a traditional IRA (because taxes will eventually be owed).

(2) *Example*: A taxpayer in the 28 percent marginal tax bracket when making a $3,000 (in 2003) contribution to a traditional IRA is really making only a net investment of $2,160; however, the taxpayer is investing the full $3,000 in the Roth IRA, not $2,160. It is highly likely that the taxpayer will find the $3,000 after-tax dollars to take full advantage of the ROTH IRA maximum contribution amount.

(3) Studies further show that a Roth IRA *conversion* produces better results than would be produced if the assets were left in a traditional IRA. This advantage is more pronounced if taxes are not paid out of the amount converted.

(4) The longer assets remain in a Roth IRA before withdrawal, the greater the advantage from the conversion.

(5) *Exception*: Because all income taxes are paid up front in the year of conversion, if future income tax rates are *drastically* reduced, the benefit of conversion diminishes.

E. Distribution rules

(1) A distribution from a Roth IRA is not includible in the owner's gross income if it is a "qualified distribution."

    (a) Distributions of earnings are tax-free if the participant is at least age 59½ *and* the Roth IRA has been established for five or more years.

    (b) Contributions are made with after-tax dollars and are never taxed.

    (c) A five-year clock starts with the initial contribution to a Roth IRA.

(2) Withdrawals from a Roth are deemed to occur in a specific order.

    (a) *From excess contributions*. Amounts that exceed the annual contribution limits. These generally are free from federal income tax except for gains (which may be subject to a 10 percent penalty if the individual is less than 59½ years old).

    (b) *From annual Roth IRA contributions*. Sum of the aggregate annual contributions, for which no deduction was allowed (referred to as the contribution-first recovery rule). These are always recovered without federal income tax liability or penalty.

    (c) *From the taxed income component resulting from the first conversion contribution*. These distributions are previously taxed amounts (basis) and are not subject to federal income tax. They may be subject to a 10 percent penalty.

    (d) *From conversion contributions made in later taxable years*. Conversion contributions are considered on a first-in, first-out basis, and for this purpose all conversions that occur within a single taxable year are aggregated. These distributions are not subject to federal income tax. They may be subject to a 10 percent penalty.

    Note: These first four categories are returned income tax-free.

(e) *From earnings (gain) on all contributions.* Earnings on contributions are subject to federal income tax unless they are received in a qualified distribution. Taxable earnings are also subject to a 10 percent penalty if the individual is less than 59½ years old or an exception does not apply.

(3) Special rule for a conversion contribution distributed when a taxpayer is less than 59½ years old and before the end of the five-year period starting with the year in which the conversion was made: The distribution is subject to the 10 percent premature distribution penalty, unless an exception under Section 72(t) applies. (*Note*: The special rule closes the loophole for the converted amount to be withdrawn immediately without penalty.)

(4) *Example*: Betty, age 29, converted and established a Roth IRA. She made an annual contribution of $100 in 2003. In the same year, she also converted a traditional deductible IRA worth $10,000 to a Roth IRA, which is credited with a $50 gain. In 2004, Betty removes $10,150 from her Roth IRAs. The following is a summary of taxable events:

   (a) With respect to the 2003 conversion, Betty will have to include $10,000 (the taxable amount) on her federal income tax return for the year 2003.

   (b) The $100 is treated as distributable first, but is not a qualified distribution. Nonetheless, the $100 amount is not taxable because of the ordering rules and is not subject to penalty.

   (c) The $10,000 is treated as distributed next. This amount is not taxable for the same reason, but is subject to the 10 percent penalty tax unless a Section 72(t) exception applies. Under the special rule, the 5-year period started in 2002, the year in which the conversion amount being withdrawn was contributed.

   (d) The $50 gain is treated as distributed last. The $50 is not a qualified distribution because Betty is less than 59½ years old. It is subject to federal income tax and 10 percent penalty tax, unless 72(t) applies.

3. Simplified employee pension (SEPs)

   A. Characteristics common to defined contribution plans

      (1) Annual employer tax-deductible contributions limited to 25 percent of compensation for common-law employees; for owner/employee the limit is 20 percent of net earnings.

      (2) Subject to funding by the employer only

      (3) Section 415(c), annual additions are limited to the *lesser* of 100 percent compensation or $40,000—this is the maximum amount that can be allocated to each participant. The same applies to other defined contribution type plans.

      (4) The $200,000 (in 2003) compensation cap that applies to qualified plans also applies to SEPs.

      (5) Nondiscrimination rules and top-heavy rules apply.

      (6) Controlled group/affiliated services group rules apply.

      (7) Participation in a SEP satisfies "active participant status" for determining deductible IRA contribution.

      (8) The plan may integrate with Social Security.

      (9) Direct employer contributions are not subject to Social Security (FICA) or federal unemployment (FUTU) taxes. Salary reductions are subject to FICA and FUTA.

      (10) Plans established prior to January 1, 1997 may allow 401(k) provisions; that is, SARSEPs are "grandfathered" but *no new* such plans after January 1, 1997.

B. Characteristics UNIQUE to SEP

    (1) Special coverage requirements:

        (a) Covers all employees who are at least age 21, and

        (b) Worked during three of the past five years, including contribution year (part-time employment counts in determining years of service), and

        (c) Received compensation of more than $450 (in 2003)

    (2) May exclude employee as "eligible" if he or she is

        (a) A member of a collective bargaining unit

        (b) A nonresident alien

    (3) Contributions are *fully discretionary*, which gives employer full control and maximum flexibility; substantial and recurring contributions are *not* required.

    (4) Deadline for contributions to a SEP is April 15, *including* extensions.

    (5) Administration costs are very low; there are no annual filing requirements.

    (6) The plan is totally portable because employees are always 100 percent vested.

    (7) Distributions are not eligible for special averaging.

    (8) Loans are *not* permitted.

C. Appropriate plan usage

    (1) A SEP is a good choice for a small employer because

        (a) Coverage rules are easier to work with than those of qualified plans.

        (b) Shorter-term employees can be eliminated from the plan (less than three years).

        (c) There are lower costs and administrative expenses.

    (2) A SEP is a poor choice if an employer has many long-term part-time employees, because they will have to be covered by the plan.

    (3) A profit-sharing plan should be chosen if an employer wants a more aggressive age-weighted or cross-tested allocation formula that benefits older, more highly compensated employees.

D. Distributions—same as traditional IRA

E. Salary reduction SEPs (SARSEPs)

    (1) Plan must have been in place before January 1, 1997. Ongoing contributions and new participants may be added to "grandfathered" plans.

    (2) Employer must have ≤ 25 eligible employees in the preceding years.

    (3) At least 50 percent of the eligible employees *must* participate.

    (4) The employee must add together, each year, all elective deferrals to (1) salary reduction SEPs, (2) Section 401(k) plans, (3) SIMPLE IRAs, and (4) Section 403(b) plans. Elective deferrals are limited to $12,000 in 2003. The total must not exceed $14,000 in 2003. Employees who have reached age 50 have a catch-up provision of $2,000 in 2003.

    (5) Special ADP test applies: Deferral percentage of *each* HCE must not exceed the ADP of all eligible NHCEs multiplied by 125 percent.

4. SIMPLE IRAs

A. Characteristics

    (1) Plan is easy to administer.

    (2) Benefits of a SIMPLE IRA are totally portable because employees are always 100 percent vested.

(3) Individuals can benefit from a broad range of investments.

(4) Plan can be funded in part from salary reductions by employees.

(5) Annual contributions are restricted to lesser amounts than provided by a qualified plan.

(6) Distributions are not eligible for 10-year averaging.

(7) If an employer adopts a SIMPLE IRA plan, it cannot maintain a qualified plan, SEP, 403(a) annuity, 403(b) plan, or 457 plan.

(8) Employee elective deferrals are excludable for income, employer contributions are deductible, earnings are tax-deferred.

(9) Direct employer contributions are not subject to FICA and FUTA taxes. Employee salary reduction contributions are subject to FICA and FUTA.

(10) There are no nondiscrimination testing and top-heavy rules.

(11) Two conditions *must* be met in order to be eligible to *establish* plan:

    (a) Employer has no more than 100 employees (counting only those employees earning at least $5,000 in compensation). If the employer grows beyond the 100-employee limit, the law does allow the employer to sponsor the plan for an additional two-year grace period.

    (b) Employer cannot maintain any other qualified plan, 403(b), 403(a) annuity, 457 plan, or SEP at the same time it has a SIMPLE.

B. Contributions

(1) Employees who earned at least $5,000 from the employer in any two preceding years, and are expected to earn $5,000 in the current year, can contribute $8,000 in 2003. Catch-up is $1,000 in 2003.

(2) Participants must be age 21 or older with one year of service (1,000 hours).

(3) The employer is required to make a contribution equal to either

    (a) A dollar-for-dollar contribution up to a limit of 3 percent of the employee's compensation. This is permitted to be reduced at the option of the employer if

        i. The limit is not reduced below 1 percent.

        ii. The limit is not reduced for more than two years of a five-year period that ends (and includes) the year for which the election is effective.

        iii. Employees are notified of the reduced limit within a reasonable period of time.

Important: For the 3 percent match, the annual compensation limit does not apply.

Example: Baby Corporation sets-up a SIMPLE IRA plan in 2002. The president, Jim, earns compensation of $220,000. If Jim elects to defer $7,000, Baby Corporation must match an additional $6,600 (220,000 × 3%). Therefore, a total of $13,600 will be contributed to Jim's SIMPLE IRA.

    (b) A 2 percent nonelective contribution for the matching contribution, but only if

        i. Eligible employees are notified that a 2 percent nonelective contribution will be made instead of a matching contribution, and

        ii. This notice is provided within a reasonable period of time.

Important: For purposes of the 2 percent nonelective contribution, the annual compensation limitation ($200,000 in 2003) does apply.

Example: Assume the same facts as in the earlier example, except that Baby Corporation has elected to make a nonelective contribution of 2 percent of compensation. Therefore, the total contribution made to Jim's SIMPLE IRA will equal $11,000 [$7,000 + $4,000 (2% × 200,000)].

C. Distributions

    (1) Rollovers permitted:

        (a) SIMPLE plan to SIMPLE plan

        (b) SIMPLE plan to IRA or SEP if in SIMPLE plan for two years

    (2) Discontinuing participation after two years, a SIMPLE is treated as a traditional IRA.

    (3) Early withdrawals:

        (a) 25 percent penalty if withdrawal is during first two years of participation

        (b) 10 percent penalty after two years of participation

    (4) Loans are *not* permitted.

    (5) There is *no* protection under anticreditor provisions.

5. Section 403(b) plans (also called tax-deferred annuity plans or tax-sheltered annuity plans)

  A. Eligibility

    (1) If offered, such a plan must be offered to all employees regardless of age, service, or union affiliation.

    (2) An organization must be one of the following to adopt a Section 403(b) plan:

        (a) A tax-exempt employer described in Section 501(c)(3) of the Code

        (b) An educational organization (most public schools and colleges)

    (3) A self-employed duly ordained or licensed minister of a church who works for an employer that is not a qualified tax-exempt organization is treated as working for such an organization for the purposes of participating in a tax-sheltered annuity (TSA) plan.

  B. Plan characteristics

    (1) Funded by employee contributions

    (2) Permitted rollovers:

        (a) TSA to TSA, 401(k), or 457 plan maintained by a state/local government

        (b) TSA to traditional IRA

    (3) Not considered a qualified plan, although subject to similar restrictions

    (4) A TSA is subject to ERISA if an employer contributes.

        (a) Subject to ERISA's minimum vesting schedules, but seldom used—usually 100 percent vested

        (b) Must comply with nondiscrimination tests

    (5) A TSA is not subject to ERISA if the following conditions are met:

        (a) Employee participation is voluntary.

        (b) All rights under the annuity contract or the custodial account are controlled by the participant, participant's beneficiary, or his or her designee.

        (c) The employer's involvement is primarily limited to activities such as collecting salary reductions for deposit into TSA accounts or providing information of the TSA vendors to the participants.

  C. Plan investments limited to

    (1) Annuity contracts

    (2) Mutual fund shares

    (3) Life insurance, with some restrictions

    (4) Retirement income accounts (DCP) maintained by churches or certain church-related organizations

D. Contribution Limits

    (1) Employee salary reductions are subject to an annual limit—$12,000 in 2003.

    (2) The limit of salary deferrals applies in the aggregate of all elective deferrals under 403(b), 401(k), SARSEP, and SIMPLE plans. Section 457(b) plans have separate limits that are *not* reduced by contributions to either a 401(k) or 403(b) plan.

    (3) Salary reduction catch-up

        (a) If an employee has completed 15 years of service for the employer, and the employer is (1) an educational organization, (2) a hospital, (3) a home health care agency, or (4) a church, synagogue or related organization, the elective deferral limit is increased by an additional sum equal to the lesser of

            i. $3,000,

            ii. $15,000, reduced by any amounts excluded from gross income for prior taxable years by reason of the catch-up provision, or

            iii. $5,000 times the employee's years of service with the employer, less all prior salary reductions with the employer

        (b) Participants who are age 50 and over are eligible for additional elective deferrals—$2,000 in 2003.

    (4) Total amount of tax-deferred employer and employee contributions to the employee's account is subject to the annual Section 415 limitation of the lesser of

        (a) 100 percent of compensation, or

        (b) $40,000

    (5) For all employers, only the first $200,000 (in 2003) of each participant's compensation can be taken into account in any plan contribution formula.

E. Distributions

    (1) Distributions are subject to the qualified plan distribution rules.

    (2) In-service distribution

        (a) Hardship withdrawals allowed

        (b) Loans—subject to plan document

6. Section 457 plans

A. Eligibility—can be offered to all employees, or any group of employees, or even a single employee

    (1) Employee of state and local governments, their agencies

    (2) Employee of tax-exempt organization—Section 501(c)(3) organization, *excluding* church, synagogue, or any organization controlled by a church or synagogue

B. Funding the plan

    (1) Governmental plans *must* be funded per the Small Business Job Protection Act (SBJPA) 1996 [Section 457(g)]. The governmental 457 plan holds all plan assets and income in trust, or in custodial accounts or annuity contracts, for the exclusive benefit of the participants and beneficiaries.

    (2) A funded 457 plan for a *nongovernmental* tax-exempt organization is subject to ERISA. Such organizations can avoid ERISA requirements if they are designed to take advantage of ERISA exemptions—for example, "unfunded plans" for highly compensated members only (i.e., top hat plans).

      (a) *Unfunded* means that the 457 assets remain the property of the employer and subject to the claims of the employer's creditors. The employee does not have any rights or security interest in the assets.

      (b) If the assets are subject to the claims of the company's general creditors, there is *no constructive receipt* by the participant, and therefore there is *no* receipt of income and taxes are deferred.

  (3) Unfunded assets may be set aside in a reserve fund by the employer to provide the deferred compensation.

C. Contributions

  (1) The amount deferred annually by an employee cannot exceed the lesser of 100 percent of compensation or applicable dollar limit—$12,000 in 2003.

  (2) Participants in a 457 plan of a *government employer* who are age 50 and older are eligible for additional salary reduction contributions—$2,000 in 2003.

  (3) Three-year catch-up provision—intended to provide an employee who did not make maximum annual deferrals in prior years to make higher contributions in anticipation of retirement

      (a) Applied during the last three years prior to plan's retirement, the limit of deferral is increased to the lesser of

        i. Twice the amount of the regularly applicable dollar limit, or

        ii. The sum of

          • The otherwise applicable limit for the year, plus

          • The amount by which the applicable limit in preceding years exceeded the participant's actual deferral for those years

      (b) The "final three-year" provisions cannot be used if the new "aged 50+ catch-up" provision is being used.

      (c) Applies to all eligible 457 plans (not just eligible 457 governmental plans)

D. Distributions

  (1) Plan distributions cannot be made before

      (a) The calendar year in which the participant attains age 70½

      (b) Severance from employment

      (c) An unforeseeable emergency as defined in the regulations

  (2) In-service distributions

      (a) A one-time distribution by participant is allowed under the following conditions:

        i. Total amount payable may not exceed $5,000.

        ii. No deferred compensation has been made for at least two years.

        iii. Participant has not used this option previously.

      (b) Mandatory cashout by the 457 plan—used to close small, inactive accounts in order to reduce administrative costs; allowed under following conditions:

        i. The accounts do not exceed $5,000.

        ii. No deferred compensation has been made for at least two years.

        iii. There has been no previous use of the cashout provision.

  (3) Because this is *not* a QRP, there is no forward averaging option.

  (4) Loans are permitted if allowed in the plan document.

  (5) Participant may delay distribution one time if elected prior to start of distribution.

TOPIC 78: REGULATORY CONSIDERATIONS

1. Employee Retirement Income Security Act (ERISA)

   A. Fiduciary is any person (e.g., trustee, plan administrator, employer—officer and director—plan sponsor, or investment adviser) who

      (1) Exercises any discretionary authority or control over plan management
      (2) Exercises any authority or control over management or disposition of plan assets
      (3) Renders investment advice for a fee or other compensation
      (4) Has discretionary authority or responsibility over plan administration

   B. IRS involvement

      (1) All new plans must be submitted to the IRS for approval
      (2) Monitors operation of existing plans
      (3) Interprets existing law and issue regulations to be applied to all plans
      (4) Rules on matters of employer deductibility of plan contributions

   C. Department of Labor (DOL) involvement

      (1) Monitors investment of plan assets and the actions of those in charge of administering plans
      (2) Shares with the IRS oversight of prohibited transactions

   D. Created the Pension Benefit Guarantee Corporation (PBGC)

      (1) Mandatory insurance for *defined benefit plans*; annual premium $19/year/participant
      (2) Plan termination insurance under PBGC

         (a) Guaranteed (basic) benefits—nonforfeitable

            i. Retirement benefits
            ii. Death benefits in pay status
            iii. Survivor benefits in pay status
            iv. Disability benefits owed or in pay status

         (b) Benefit must be a "pension benefit."
         (c) Participant must be eligible for benefit at time of plan termination.
         (d) Nonguaranteed benefits

            i. Retirement benefits in excess of PBGC limit
            ii. Medical insurance premiums/benefit

         (e) Limitations

            i. Monthly payments only—*no lump sum*
            ii. Guaranteed monthly benefit cannot be greater than employee's gross monthly income during the five consecutive years of highest earnings.
            iii. Maximum age 65 monthly benefit adjusted annually along with the Social Security wage base (SSWB) changes ($3,579 in 2002)

   E. Qualified plan terminations

      (1) General information

         (a) QRP are established for the benefit of the participant and his or her beneficiaries.
         (b) The plan must be permanent.

      (2) Termination of plan

         (a) Termination cannot be implemented arbitrarily.
         (b) Termination must be because of business necessity.

(c) Termination must follow specific rules governing allocation of plan assets.

(3) Voluntary termination

(a) *Standard termination*. A single employer may terminate under this type of termination if the plan has sufficient assets for benefit liabilities. Plan assets must be distributed according to ERISA.

(b) *Distress termination*. A single employer may terminate under distress termination if the plan *does not* have sufficient assets to pay vested benefits (where employer is in bankruptcy (BK) proceedings or will be able to continue in business only if relieved of outstanding pension liabilities). Employer must provide to PBGC actuarial certification of asset values and benefit liabilities.

(4) Involuntary termination. The PBGC may terminate an underfunded plan for one or more of the following reasons:

(a) Plan does not comply with minimum funding standard.

(b) Plan cannot pay benefits when due.

(c) Plan has unfunded liabilities following a distribution of more than $10,000 to an owner.

(d) If plan is not terminated, loss to the PBGC is expected to be unacceptably high.

(5) Switching from DBP to DCP

(a) Requires the DBP to be terminated

(b) Creation of a new DCP

(c) Voluntary standard termination

(d) 100 percent vesting of affected participants

(e) Distribution of plan assets in accordance with ERISA

(6) Switching from a DBP to a cash balance plan

(a) Requires only amending the DBP

(b) *Avoids* vesting, distribution, and plan termination

(7) Priority for allocating plan assets (must precede asset reversion)

(a) Employee voluntary contributions

(b) Employee mandatory contributions

(c) Certain annuity payments in pay status

(d) Other guaranteed (insured) benefits

(e) Other vested benefits that are not guaranteed

(f) All other plan-provided benefits

(8) Reversion of residual assets to employee

(a) 50 percent penalty on assets reversions

(b) Penalty reduced to 20 percent if employer (1) transfers 25 percent of potential reversion amount to a replacement plan, or (2) increases the participants' accrued benefits by at least 20 percent.

2. Department of Labor (DOL) regulations—ERISA of 1974

A. Established guidelines for qualified and nonqualified employee benefit plans involving retirement income

B. Established nondiscriminatory rules for favored employee groups: highly compensated employees and key employees

C. Established vesting schedules for employees

D. Requires adequate funding of pension plans

3. Fiduciary obligations: ERISA requires that a fiduciary act "solely in the interest of the participants and their beneficiaries." A fiduciary must

   A. Act for the exclusive purpose of providing benefits to participants and their beneficiaries and defraying reasonable expenses of administrating the plan

   B. Act "with the care, skill, prudence, and diligence under the circumstances then prevailing that a prudent man acting in a like capacity and familiar with such matters would use in the conduct of an enterprise of a like character and with like aims." This is the Prudent Man Rule.

   C. Diversify investments of the plan "in order to minimize the risk of large losses, unless under the circumstances it is clearly prudent not to do so"

   D. Act "in accordance with the plan document and instruments governing the plan inasmuch as these documents and instruments are consistent with ERISA provisions." This rule requires the fiduciary to strictly follow the terms of the plan document when making decisions.

4. Prohibited transactions (between a retirement plan and a disqualified person/party)

   A. There are six prohibited transactions:

      (1) Sale, exchange, or lease of property
      (2) Lending money or extending credit
      (3) Furnishing goods, services, or facilities
      (4) Transfer to or use of plan assets by a disqualified person
      (5) If a fiduciary, dealing with plan income or assets in own account
      (6) If a fiduciary, receiving consideration for own account from a party involved in the plan transaction (cannot receive outside pay)

   B. *Disqualified persons/party* for the purposes of Prohibited Transactions Rules

      (1) A fiduciary
      (2) Any person providing services to the plan
      (3) An employer or employee organization, any of whose members are covered by the plan
      (4) A 50 percent owner of (3)
      (5) A member of the family of (1), (2), (3), or (4)
      (6) A corporation, partnership, trust, or estate that is 50 percent or more owned by (1), (2), (3), or (4)
      (7) An officer, director, 10 percent or more shareholder, highly compensated employee (earning at least 10 percent of the employer's total payroll), or a 10 percent or more partner or joint venture of person in (3), (4), or (5)

   C. Tax consequences imposed on a plan committing prohibited transaction(s)—this is a two-tier penalty:

      (1) A penalty tax equal to 15 percent of the amount involved in the prohibited transaction is imposed on all disqualified persons involved (individually and together) for *each year or part thereof* that the transaction remains uncorrected. The 15 percent penalty carries over from year to year, and a new 15 percent penalty is assessed each year. Because it is *both* a continuing transaction and a new transaction each year, this penalty tax pyramids.

      (2) An additional penalty tax equal to 100 percent of the amount involved is imposed if the prohibited transaction is not timely corrected.

D. Exemptions from Prohibited Transactions Rules

    (1) Receipt of benefits under terms of the plan

    (2) Distribution of plan assets according to allocation provisions

    (3) Loans available to plan participants and beneficiaries (see Topic 76)

    (4) Loans made to an ESOP

    (5) Purchase or sale of qualifying employer securities by an individual account, profit sharing, stock bonus, thrift or savings plan, or ESOP, for adequate consideration and without commission

    (6) Providing office space/services for the plan for "reasonable" compensation

5. Reporting requirements

    A. Advance Determination Letter for new plans (i.e., not prototypes)

    B. Prototype/model plans—IRS preapproved plans

    C. Summary plan descriptions (SPD)—for communicating plan benefits to the participants and their beneficiaries

TOPIC 79: PLAN SELECTION FOR BUSINESSES

Key factors affecting selection

1. Owner's personal objectives

    A. *Tax considerations*. Maximize personal tax benefits.

    B. *Capital needs at retirement*. Maximize personal retirement benefits and achieve retirement income goals/objectives.

    C. *Capital needs at death*. Provide estate protection.

2. Business's objectives

    A. *Tax considerations*. Reduce corporate income tax.

    B. *Cash flow situation and outlook*. Variable, stable, or increasing cashflow; projected cash flow in the future

    C. *Employee demographics*. Reward valued employees, motivate employees, reduce turnover, increase employee satisfaction.

    D. Comparison of defined contribution and defined benefit plan alternatives

        (1) Maximize the proportion of plan costs that benefit highly compensated employees.

            (a) *Defined benefit plans*. These provide the maximum benefit for key employees when key employees are generally older than rank-and-file employees; they include service-based contributions or benefit formulas that are in favor of key employees.

            (b) *Age-weighting*. Age-weighted plans constitute an allocation method to increase the contributions to a QRP for the benefit of the older HCEs by weighting for age and compensation. This is not discriminatory as long as the allocation method is applied uniformly to all participants.

            (c) *Cross-testing*. With this method, nondiscrimination in a defined contribution plan is determined by looking at projected benefits under the plan at each employee's retirement age, rather than looking at the amounts contributed by the employer each year. New comparability plans are tested under cross-testing rules to satisfy nondiscrimination requirements.

                i. A new comparability plan is one in which the compensation percentage formula for one category (rather than strictly age) of participants is greater than the formula for other participants.

      ii. The plan must contain a definite predetermined formula for allocating contributions made to the plan participants.

      iii. Typically, substantial contributions are made for the favored and older employees, and much lower contributions for other employees.

  (d) *Section 401(k) plans.* Traditional plans allow a higher rate of contribution to HCEs under the ADP test, as long as there is maximum participation by NHCEs. Safe harbor plans and SIMPLE 401(k) plans allow employers to avoid ADP/ACP testing.

  (e) *Social Security integration.* Recall that Social Security favors the lower-income employees, that is, below the SSWB. It is, by design, discriminatory *against* the business owner and the more highly compensated employee.

(2) Provide a savings medium that employees perceive as valuable.

  (a) *Defined contribution plans.* Every defined contribution plan has individual accounts, so each employee knows how much his or her personal benefit is worth.

  (b) *Cash balance plans.* These plans tend to provide greater benefits to younger employees with shorter service, as compared with other defined benefit plans.

  (c) *Plans with employee participation.* Section 401(k) plans allow an employee to make before-tax salary reductions.

(3) Provide adequate replacement income for each employee's retirement. A defined benefit plan is the best vehicle if adequate replacement income is an employer's objective. The following is a list of reasons:

  (a) Defined benefit plans provide benefit based on final compensation, not necessarily years of service. Defined contribution plans provide benefits directly related to years of service, because newer employees cannot accumulate substantial savings.

  (b) The employer guarantees the benefit. There is no investment risk for employees in a defined benefit plan.

  (c) Employer funding is mandatory.

  (d) The plan can provide maximum life insurance.

(4) Create an incentive for employees to maximize performance.

  (a) Profit-sharing plans

  (b) ESOP/stock bonus plans

  (c) Any other defined contribution plan or cash balance plan

(5) Minimize turnover.

  (a) Defined benefit plan versus defined contribution plan. Both plans reward employees who stay until retirement. Defined benefit plans provide benefits that are generally based on years of service; defined contribution plans have benefits that continue to grow with each year of service. However, defined contribution plans are generally portable, allowing employees to move between jobs.

  (b) Graduated vesting—minimizes the cost of covering short-service employees.

(6) Encourage retirement. Defined benefit plan works best to encourage retirement because:

  (a) No further benefits can be earned upon reaching designated retirement age in the plan.

  (b) It designs a subsidized early retirement incentive.

(7) Maximize employer contribution flexibility. Profit sharing plans and SEPs offer the most flexibility. Other types of plans have less flexibility in one way or another.

TOPIC 80: INVESTMENT CONSIDERATIONS FOR RETIREMENT PLANS

(Fiduciary considerations and prohibited transactions are part of Topic 80, but are covered under Topic 78.)

1. Suitability

   A. Time horizon: the time in which a specific financial goal is expected to be reached
   B. Liquidity and marketability: *Liquidity* is the ability to readily convert an investment into cash *without* loss of principal; *marketability* is the degree to which there is an active market in which the investment can be traded
   C. Tax considerations

      (1) General concerns with respect to retirement plans

         (a) When selecting asset classes and investment vehicles, compare the expected return on different investments on a *before-tax basis*.
         (b) Prior to distribution, retirement plan assets are exempt from income taxes.
         (c) Investment strategies must be appropriate for tax-exempt growth (consider the use of annuities in an IRA).

      (2) Unrelated business taxable income (UBTI)

         (a) UBTI is gross income (in excess of $1,000) that is generated by a qualified retirement plan trust that is directly carrying on a trade or business not substantially related to the purpose of the trust.
         (b) IRS has ruled that a qualified retirement plan that invests funds into a common trust fund has UBTI from the trust fund to the same extent as it would have had it made the same investment directly.
         (c) If a common trust fund operated an active business, or an IRA purchased a limited partnership interest, income from that business or partnership would be UBTI when passed through to the qualified retirement plan or IRA.
         (d) Passive income is *not* considered UBTI—dividends, interests, annuities, royalties, rents from real property, rents from debt-financed real property, and gains from the sale or exchange of capital assets.
         (e) Nonpassive income considered UBTI

            i. Income from oil and gas drilling or other *non-real-estate partnership interest*. A QRP that invests in a publicly traded *limited partnership* (LP) is considered to be working in the partnership's business as if it were a general partner. Income (minus expenses) received by the QRP from this publicly traded LP is considered UBTI.
            ii. Dividends from stock purchased on margin, that is, *debt-financed dividends*

   D. Risk tolerance considerations

      (1) The risk tolerance level of the small business owner is an important determinant as to what asset classes and investment vehicles are selected, and the expected return for the QRP portfolio.
      (2) The risk tolerance level assumed by the plan is based on the client's emotional temperament and attitudes.
      (3) The required liquidity and marketability will impact the risk assumed in the portfolio.
      (4) Recall the relationship between risk and return. The QRP portfolio should be structured to *maximize* the return for given level of risk, or in other words, *minimize* the risk for a given rate of return.
      (5) Investment strategy will differ between DBP and DCP.

    (a) Defined benefit plan

        i. Participant's benefits are fixed.

        ii. Employer contributions vary.

        iii. Employer assumes the investment risk.

        iv. Prefers a conservative investment strategy to avoid wide swings in employer contributions, that is, actuarial determination for contributions to the plan are relatively consistent year to year.

    (b) Defined contribution plan

        i. Participant's benefits are variable.

        ii. Employer contributions are fixed.

        iii. Employee assumes the investment risk.

        iv. Investments may be more aggressive.

E. Diversification and regulatory concerns

    (1) Construct a diversified portfolio with investments that are *not* subject to the same investment risk. ERISA's fiduciary standards require portfolio diversification.

    (2) Diversification will depend on fiduciary standards and the business owners' risk tolerance.

    (3) An exception to diversification can occur when the investments can be prudently invested without diversifying.

    (4) The plan's fiduciary must meet ERISA's definition and standards.

    (5) The plan's trustee prepares a statement of investment policy and objectives.

    (6) Asset classes and investments are monitored periodically.

2. Life insurance—allowed in QRP if the benefits are "incidental" to the overall plan

  A. Defined contribution plan—cost of insurance (i.e., cost of current protection)

    (1) For an ordinary policy (whole life), the premiums paid by the plan cannot exceed 50 percent of the contributions made to the plan on the participant's behalf.

    (2) For a nonordinary policy [term, Universal Life (UL)], the premium cannot exceed 25 percent of the contribution made to the plan on the participant's behalf.

    (3) The contract must be distributed to the participant or converted to a payout option of the start of benefits upon retirement.

  B. Defined benefit plan—For an ordinary or nonordinary policy, the plan benefit (i.e., the insurance benefit) is limited to not greater than 100 times the expected monthly retirement income benefit. For example, if the potential pension benefit is $1,500/month, then the plan trustee could apply for $150,000 of insurance on the participant's life. The participant would be taxed (ordinary rates) on the term cost of insurance.

TOPIC 81: DISTRIBUTION RULES, ALTERNATIVES, AND TAXATION

1. Premature distributions

  A. Penalties

    (1) Distribution prior to age 59½

    (2) Subject to 10 percent nondeductible penalty *and* taxed as ordinary income

    (3) *Exception*: Distribution or payment from a SIMPLE IRA within two years of the opening of the SIMPLE IRA is subject to a 25 percent penalty tax.

    (4) The participant always has 60 days to undo the distribution.

B. Hardship withdrawal

   (1) For qualified plans and 403(b) only: The participant must have a triggering event to qualify for a hardship withdrawal. A triggering event has occurred when the participant has demonstrated to the plan administrator an "immediate and heavy financial need."

   (2) The IRS has issued safe harbor guidelines that define what constitutes an "immediate and heavy financial need" in order to give the employer guidance. The following is a list of safe harbor triggering events:

      (a) Medical care for the participant, spouse, or any dependents of the participant

      (b) Purchase of principal residence—applies only to the purchase, not mortgage payments

      (c) Tuition and related education fees—must be for postsecondary education of participant, spouse, or children

      (d) Prevention of eviction or foreclosure

   (3) The client should understand that (1) he or she must still pay the 10 percent penalty, (2) the full distribution will be taxed as ordinary income, and (3) a six-month blackout exists on elective deferrals after a hardship withdrawal.

   (4) The participant must exhaust all other options before taking out a hardship withdrawal.

C. IRC Section 72(t) for qualified plans. The following is a list of allowable distributions that will exclude an individual from paying the 10 percent penalty tax under IRC Section 72(t) for qualified plans only:

   (1) Distributions made on or after the date on which the participant attains age 59½

   (2) Distributions made to a beneficiary on or after the death of the participant

   (3) Distributions attributable to the participant's becoming disabled

   (4) Distributions that are part of a series of substantially equal periodic payments (not less frequently than annually) made for life (or life expectancy) of the participant or the joint lives of the participant and his or her designated beneficiary. Distributions under this exception generally cannot be modified for five years unless another exception applied to the distribution when it initially commenced.

   (5) Distributions made to an employee after separation from service after attainment of age 55

   (6) A payment to an alternate payee pursuant to a qualified domestic relations order (QDRO)

   (7) Distributions used to pay qualified higher education expenses (including graduate education expenses) for the individual, the individual's spouse, or any child or grandchild of either

   (8) Distributions made on account of an IRS levy

   (9) A dividend paid with respect to certain stock held by an ESOP

   (10) Amounts transferred to an IRA of a spouse or former spouse under a divorce or separation instrument

   (11) Corrective distributions

D. IRC Section 72(t) for tax-advantaged retirement plans. Tax-advantaged plans (IRA, Roth IRA, SEP, and SIMPLE) do not need a triggering event for the owner to remove funds. The owner can remove funds at anytime but is subject to a 10 percent penalty tax, in addition to the balance being taxed as ordinary income. The following is a list of allowable distributions that will exclude an individual from paying the 10 percent penalty tax under IRC Section 72(t) for tax-advantaged retirement plans only:

   (1) Distributions made on or after the date on which the participant attains age 59½

   (2) Distributions made to a beneficiary on or after the death of the participant

   (3) Distributions attributable to the participant's becoming disabled

   (4) Distributions that are part of a series of substantially equal periodic payments (not less frequently than annually) made for life (or life expectancy) of the participant or the joint lives of the participant and his or her designated beneficiary. Distributions under this exception generally cannot be modified for five years unless another exception applied to the distribution when it initially commenced.

   (5) Distributions for medical expenses in excess of 7½ percent of adjusted gross income.

   (6) Distributions for health insurance premiums made to an unemployed individual after separation from employment if the individual has received unemployment compensation for 12 consecutive weeks under any federal or state unemployment compensation law

   (7) Distributions used to pay qualified higher education expenses (including graduate education expenses) for the individual, the individual's spouse, or any child or grandchild of either

   (8) Distributions made for a first-time home buyer's expenses. There is a lifetime maximum of $10,000. The distribution must be used within 120 days to buy, build, or rebuild the principal residence of the individual, his or her spouse, or any child, grandchild, or ancestor of either. A person qualifies as a first-time home buyer if he or she had no present ownership interest in a principal residence during the preceding two years.

   (9) Distributions made on account of an IRS levy

  (10) Amounts transferred to an IRA of a spouse or former spouse under a divorce or separation instrument

  (11) Corrective distributions

E. Substantially equal periodic payments (Section 72(t))

   (1) There is no minimum age requirement.

   (2) IRS does not require reason for taking withdrawals.

   (3) Payments must be made at least annually.

   (4) Three methods to calculate:

     (a) Life-expectancy method [e.g., required minimum distribution (RMD)]

       i. Results in the exact annual payment required

       ii. Results in the smallest payment

     (b) Amortization method: The account balance is amortized over the participant's life expectancy (or joint life expectancy) using a reasonable interest rate (i.e., expected investment return).

     (c) Annuitization method

       i. Divide the account balance by an annuity factor that is based on a reasonable interest rate (e.g., 8 percent) and mortality factors (UP-84 Mortality Table).

       ii. Results in the largest payment

   (5) Payments *must* continue for five years or until participant is age 59½ whichever is *longer*. If payment is changed (increased *or* decreased) prior to satisfying either condition, the 10 percent penalty is assessed back to *dollar one* plus interest.

   (6) Accounts need not be aggregated to begin Section 72(t) distribution.

F. The EGTRRA 2001 changed the operative phrase "separation from service" to "severance from employment." This allows distributions from plans that terminate after a merger or spin-off because the participant has severed his or her relationship with the original employer. This repeals the "same desk rule."

G. Differences in comparing qualified plans to IRAs under IRC Section 72(t). The following exceptions apply to IRAs, but not to qualified plans under IRC Section 72(t):

    (1) IRAs allow distributions for health insurance premiums made to an unemployed individual after separation from employment if the individual has received unemployment compensation for 12 consecutive weeks under any federal or state unemployment compensation law.

    (2) IRAs allow distributions made for a first-time home buyer. There is a lifetime maximum of $10,000.

    (3) IRAs allow distributions used to pay qualified higher education expenses (including graduate education expenses) for the individual, the individual's spouse, or any child or grandchild of either.

H. The following exceptions apply to qualified plans, but not to IRAs under IRC Section 72(t):

    (1) Distributions made to an employee after severance from service after attainment of age 55

    (2) A payment to an alternate payee pursuant to a QDRO

    (3) A dividend paid with respect to certain stock held by an ESOP

2. Election of distribution options

A. Lump sum distributions

    (1) *Must* satisfy four conditions:

        (a) Must be distributed in one taxable year

        (b) Must represent the full account balance to the participant's credit from all qualified plans of a single type

        (c) Lump sum payable

            i. For common-law employees, (i.e., rank and file)

                • Attainment of age 59½

                • Death (available to designated beneficiary)

                • Separation from service ("severance from employment")

            ii. For the self-employed owner

                • Attainment of age 59½

                • Death (available to designated beneficiary)

                • Disability

        (d) Must be made *from*

            i. Qualified pension plan (money purchase plan, target benefit, DBP)

            ii. Profit sharing plan

            iii. Stock bonus plan

    (2) Taxation of a lump sum distribution

        (a) Taxed as ordinary income

        (b) Taxed-deferred if distribution is rolled over

            i. QRP to another QRP

            ii. QRP to tradition IRA or conduit IRA

(c) May qualify for *10-year forward-averaging tax treatment* if the participant was born before January 1, 1936 (i.e., age 50 by January 1, 1986) if four conditions met:

    i. Participant must be at least age 59½.

    ii. Forward averaging must be applied to all lump sum distributions received during the year.

    iii. Employee must have been a plan participant for at least five years (waiver if distribution is due to death).

    iv. Only one forward-averaging election is allowed in a lifetime.

B. Annuity options

  (1) All qualified pension plans must provide two forms of survivorship benefits for spouses:

    (a) Automatic lifetime survivor benefit in the form of a *qualified joint and survivor annuity* (QJSA).

      i. Must provide annuity for life of the participant with a survivor annuity for the life of the participant's spouse.

      ii. Must provide survivor annuity that is not less than 50 percent nor greater than 100 percent of the annuity payable during the joint lives of the participant and spouse. For example, if $1,000 per month is payable during the joint lives, the annuity to the surviving spouse can be any specified amount from $500 per month to $1,000 per month.

      iii. The spouse's annuity must continue even if the spouse remarries.

    (b) Automatic lifetime survivor benefit in the form of a *qualified preretirement survivor annuity* (QPSA)

      i. Provides survivor benefit if participant dies before retirement

      ii. The survivor annuity payable is the amount that would have been paid under a QJSA.

  (2) Consent of nonparticipant spouse to waiver (or electing out) of QPSA and QJSA in favor of an optional benefit form selected by the participant must

    (a) Be in writing,

    (b) Acknowledge the effect of the waiver, and

    (c) Be witnessed, either by a plan representative or a notary public

  (3) Stock bonus, profit sharing, and ESOPs generally are exempt from the QJSA and QPSA requirements if two conditions are satisfied:

    (a) There are no annuity options.

    (b) The plan participant's account balance is payable to the participant's spouse in the event of the participant's death.

  (4) *Life annuity* is an automatic form of benefit for an unmarried participant—provides monthly payments for life.

  (5) *Period certain annuity* is another form, as an option to joint or single life annuity—period certain provides payments for a specified period of time.

  (6) Other annuity benefit options

    (a) A wide range of options increases the administrative costs of a qualified plan.

    (b) The IRA makes it difficult to withdraw benefit options once they are established.

  (7) Taxation of annuity payments

(a) *Noncontributory basis (no cost basis)*. Full amount of benefit payment is includible in the participant's gross income and taxed as ordinary income.

(b) *Contributory basis (taxable and nontaxable amount)*. The benefit payment consists of a taxable (includible) and a nontaxable (excludible) portion in gross income.

(c) The participant's cost basis includes:

   i. Total after-tax contributions made by the employee

   ii. Total cost of life insurance protection reported as taxable income by the participant, if plan distribution is received under the same contract that provides the life insurance protection

   iii. Any employer contributions that were previously taxed to employee (nonqualified plan later becomes qualified)

   iv. Amount of any plan loans included in income as a taxable distribution

(d) *In-service (partial) distribution*. Partial distribution taken out before termination of employment

   i. Nontaxable and taxable amounts

   ii. Nontaxable amount equals

$$\text{Distribution} \times \frac{\text{Employee's cost basis}}{\text{Total account balance}}$$

   iii. Pre-1987 "grandfathered" rule—after-tax money can be withdrawn first (FIFO).

   iv. Taxable in-service distribution may be subject to early distribution penalty, and a mandatory withholding at 20 percent, unless transferred to an eligible retirement plan as a direct rollover.

(e) *Total distribution*. If an employee has a cost basis, one of two tables is used to determine the excludable portion of each monthly payment.

   i. For a single-life annuity, based on the age of the annuitant

Age of Participant	Number of Monthly Payments
55 and under	360
56–60	310
61–65	260
66–70	210
70 and over	160

   ii. For a joint and survivor annuity, based on the ages of both annuitants

Combined Ages of Both Participants	Number of Monthly Payments
Not more than 110	410
111–120	360
121–130	310
131–140	260
More than 140	210

(f) Once the cost basis is fully recovered, payments received subsequently are fully taxable. If the participant dies before the cost basis is fully recovered, an income tax deduction for the unrecovered basis is allowed on the participant's final income tax return.

C. Rollover

   (1) Participant has constructive receipt of the money.

   (2) Beginning in 2002, amounts in Section 401(a) plans, Section 403(b) arrangements, or Section 457(b) plans maintained by a state or local government generally can be rolled over to another Section 401(a) plan, Section 403 (b) arrangement, Section 457 (b) plan maintained by state or local government, or IRA.

   (3) Beginning in 2002, after-tax employee contributions can be rolled over to other plans and IRAs.

   (4) Beginning in 2002, contributory IRA amounts can be rolled over to a Section 401(a) plan, Section 403(b) arrangement, Section 457(b) plan maintained by a state or local government, or another IRA.

   (5) Surviving spouses can roll over distributions into their own 401(k), 403(b), IRA, or governmental 457.

   (6) After two years in a SIMPLE plan, it may be rolled over to a traditional IRA or SEP plan without penalty. A SIMPLE to SIMPLE rollover is permitted at any time.

   (7) A rollover must be completed within a 60-day period, unless waived by the IRS if it deems the account owner has undergone a personal or natural disaster beyond his or her control.

   (8) Only one rollover per account per one year period is permitted.

   (9) A rollover will be subject to 20 percent withholding if money is from QRP to participant.

   (10) Distributions *not* eligible for rollover:

      (a) Amounts distributed to satisfy RMD

      (b) Amounts that are part of a series of equal periodic payments

      (c) Hardship withdrawals

      (d) Nontaxable portion of a distribution

      (e) Elective contributions that are returned as a result of Section 415 limitations

      (f) Corrective distributions of excess contributions and excess deferrals

      (g) Loans in default that are deemed distributions

      (h) Dividends on employer securities in an ESOP

      (i) Cost of life insurance coverage

D. Direct transfer

   (1) Transfer of QRP or IRA assets *directly* from custodian/trustee-to-custodian/trustee

   (2) Participant *does not* have constructive receipt of the funds.

   (3) Avoids the 20 percent mandatory withholding

   (4) Multiple transfers are permitted via this method.

3. Required minimum distribution (RMD)

A. Rules

   (1) RMD applies to qualified plans, IRAs, SEPs, SIMPLE IRAs, and Section 457 government deferred compensation plans.

   (2) Minimum distributions must begin no later than April 1 of the calendar year following the *later* of

      (a) The calendar year in which the employee attains age 70½

      (b) The employee retires (not available for 5 percent owners of business or for an IRA owner)

   (3) Use the balance as of December 31 of the year prior to the distributions year as the RMD calculation base.

(4) RMD is calculated separately for each IRA, but distributions can be taken from any account to satisfy the minimum.

B. Calculations

    (1) Life expectancy method

        (a) The required minimum is determined by dividing the owner's account balance by the appropriate life expectancy.

        (b) To satisfy RMD rules, the entire interest must be distributed by the required beginning date, or the interest must be distributed over one of the following periods:

            i. Over the lifetime of the participant

            ii. Over the joint and survivor lives of the participant and a designated beneficiary

            iii. Over a period that does not extend beyond the life expectancy of the participant

            iv. Over a period that does not extend beyond the joint and survivor life expectancy of the participant and a designated beneficiary

    (2) Three life expectancy tables

        (a) Uniform Lifetime Table

            i. Table for determining minimum required distributions during the lifetime of the participant when the retirement benefit is in the form of an account balance

            ii. Used in situations in which the employee's spouse is either

                • Not the sole designated beneficiary

                • Is the sole designated beneficiary but is not more than 10 years younger than the employee

Uniform Lifetime Table (2002 final regulations)			
Age of Employee	**Distribution Period**	**Age of Employee**	**Distribution Period**
70	27.4	86	14.1
71	26.5	87	13.4
72	25.6	88	12.7
73	24.7	89	12.0
74	23.8	90	11.4
75	22.9	91	10.8
76	22.0	92	10.2
77	21.2	93	9.6
78	20.3	94	9.1
79	19.5	95	8.6
80	18.7	96	8.1
81	17.9	97	7.6
82	17.1	98	7.1
83	16.3	99	6.7
84	15.5	100	6.3
85	14.8	101	5.9

      iii. Example: Mike reaches age 72 in 2003. His account balance in an IRA was $500,000 as of the end of 2002. His required distribution for 2002 is $19,532 ($500,000 ÷ 25.6).

  (b) Joint and Last Survivor Table

      i. The joint life expectancy of the participant and the spouse is used in situations in which the employee's spouse is either

- Sole designated beneficiary, or
- More than 10 years younger than the participant

      ii. If the designated beneficiary is changed to anyone other than the spouse, this table cannot be used.

  (c) Single Life Table

      i. Used by designated beneficiaries, including spouse

- Spouse can recalculate each year.
- Nonspouse beneficiaries do not recalculate, but determine life expectancy for first year of distributions and subtract one year for each subsequent year.

      ii. Also applies to Roth IRA nonspouse beneficiaries

      iii. Example: Steve Brown dies in 2002 at age 61. He owns a Roth IRA worth $35,000. His son, Bill, inherits the Roth IRA at age 25. Bill must begin taking minimum distributions (tax-free) by December 2003, using the Single Life Table. The initial life expectancy of 58.2 years to given in the table.

Single Life Table (2002 final regulations)			
Age	**Life Expectancy**	**Age**	**Life Expectancy**
0	82.4	60	25.2
5	77.7	65	21.0
10	72.8	70	17.0
15	67.9	75	13.4
20	63.0	80	10.2
25	58.2	85	7.6
30	53.3	90	5.5
35	48.5	95	4.1
40	43.6	100	2.9
45	38.8	105	1.9
50	34.2	110	1.1
55	29.6	111	1.0

C. Penalties

  (1) There is a 50 percent penalty on the amount not distributed that should be distributed.

  (2) If the account value has decreased below the calculated minimum based on the December 31 balance, the account can be depleted with no 50 percent penalty for not taking the full amount required.

(3) A 50 percent penalty for shortfalls in RMD applies to traditional IRAs and may pertain to Roth IRAs. Roth IRAs are not subject to minimum required distributions during the lifetime of the participant. Therefore, there is no required beginning date during the lifetime of the participant. However, Roth IRAs are subject to minimum required distributions after the death of the participant.

4. Beneficiary considerations

   A. Designated beneficiary

      (1) Must be determined by September 30 of year following year of death
      (2) Must be beneficiary as of the date of death

         (a) Beneficiaries can be eliminated by a disclaimer, but not replaced or added after owner's death.
         (b) To make a qualified disclaimer, the beneficiary must meet all of the following requirements:

            i. The disclaimer must be in writing.
            ii. The disclaimer must be received by the transferor of the asset no later than nine months after the date of death.
            iii. The person making the disclaimer cannot have accepted any of the assets prior to execution of the qualified disclaimer.
            iv. The person making the disclaimer cannot direct the assets being disclaimed.

         (c) Disclaimers can stretch IRAs—for example, the primary beneficiary may disclaim and allow the IRA to pass to a much younger contingent beneficiary.

      (3) Executors or trustees do not have the ability to choose a beneficiary after date of death.
      (4) The first required distribution must be withdrawn by December 31 of the year following the year of death.
      (5) If a beneficiary dies during the period between owner's death and the designation date of beneficiaries, the required distributions are calculated using the life expectancy of the beneficiary (as if designated).

         Example: A father dies in 2002 and names his daughter as beneficiary. The daughter dies later in 2002, prior to being named as designated beneficiary (September 30 of 2003). The grandchild inherits the retirement plan and must use the daughter's life expectancy in the new tables.

      (6) Beneficiaries must be named under the plan documentation. If a beneficiary is named by the estate or will, he or she cannot be a designated beneficiary and cannot use the Single Life Expectancy table for calculating distributions.

   B. Death of owner prior to *required beginning date* (RBD)

      (1) The entire benefit must be distributed within five years of the death of the participant. This rule has been dubbed the "five-year rule." An exception to the five-year rule exists. The life expectancy rule applies in all cases in which a deceased owner has a designated beneficiary. This means that distributions are made over the life expectancy of the designated beneficiary.
      (2) Designated beneficiary is not the surviving spouse of the participant:

         (a) To satisfy the life expectancy rule, the entire interest of the participant must be distributed over the life expectancy of the designated beneficiary.
         (b) Minimum required distributions must begin by December 31 of the year following the year when the participant died.

(c) The applicable distribution period is determined by using the life expectancy table. For each subsequent distribution calendar year, the previous year's life expectancy is reduced by 1.

(3) Designated beneficiary is the surviving spouse of the participant:

(a) To satisfy the life expectancy rule, the entire interest of the participant must be distributed over the life expectancy of the spouse.

(b) Minimum required distributions must begin by December 31 of the later of:

   i. The year following the year in which the participant died, or

   ii. The year in which the participant would have attained age 70½ had the participant survived.

(c) If the surviving spouse dies before benefits must begin under the life expectancy rule, the surviving spouse will be treated as if he or she were the participant. This means that the next beneficiary is the designated beneficiary of the now-deceased surviving spouse. This successor beneficiary is subject to the life expectancy rule or the five-year rule.

(4) If no designated beneficiary is named by the participant, the five-year rule applies.

(5) Roth IRAs

(a) All Roth IRA owners die before their required beginning dates.

(b) Distributions must be made in accordance with the five-year rule or the life expectancy rule.

(6) Switch available for beneficiaries:

(a) If owner died before RBD prior to 2002, designated beneficiaries subject to the five-year rule can switch to the life expectancy rule by December 31, 2003.

(b) If the life expectancy method was chosen for an inherited IRA, a switch to the new tables could be done in 2002. This is required in 2003.

C. Death of owner *after RBD*

(1) The entire balance must be distributed "at least as rapidly" as was the case before the participant died. The *at least as rapidly* rule is satisfied by using the longer of (using the Single Life Table):

(a) The life expectancy of the designated beneficiary determined as of the year following the year when the participant died, or

(b) The remaining life expectancy of the participant, using the participant's birthday during the year of death, reduced by 1

(2) Sole designated beneficiary is the surviving spouse of the participant:

(a) Take distributions over his or her life expectancy by December 31 of the year following the owner's death.

(b) Recalculate for each subsequent year using the Single Life Table.

(3) Designated beneficiary is not solely the surviving spouse of the participant:

(a) The *at least as rapidly rule* is satisfied by using the larger of the two numbers.

(b) For each subsequent distribution calendar year, further reduce the number by 1.

(4) If no designated beneficiary is named, the distribution period is the deceased owner's life expectancy calculated in the year of death and reduced by 1 for each subsequent year.

(5) In the year of death, the heirs must take the decedent's required distribution based on the method under which the decedent had been taking distributions. In later years, the required distributions depend on who is the chosen beneficiary.

(6) If the designated beneficiary is older than the owner, the designated beneficiary can use the owner's remaining life expectancy. For example, if a daughter dies after RBD and her father is beneficiary, the father can use the daughter's life expectancy for calculating RMD.

D. Election by surviving spouse to treat IRA of Rollover to IRA as owned by spouse

(1) If the surviving spouse makes a spousal rollover to an IRA, minimum distributions for the surviving spouse's life expectancy do not have to begin until April 1 of the year following the year the *surviving spouse* attains age 70½.

(2) The minimum distribution is based on the Uniform Lifetime Table in regard to the surviving spouse. The surviving spouse can name a new beneficiary, such as a child.

(3) *Example*: Steve dies at age 82 having named his spouse, Sarah, age 75, as the beneficiary of his IRA. Sarah names their child, Bart, as the sole beneficiary. Sarah uses the uniform lifetime table to calculate the minimum distribution. In the year following Steve's death, Sarah is age 76 and her distribution period is 22. When Sarah dies, minimum distributions to Bart are determined based on his single life expectancy.

E. Designated beneficiary must be recalculated in accordance with the new provisions for IRA owner who died prior to January 1, 2003.

(1) Look at the year following the year of owner's death and determine designated beneficiary as of September 30 of that year.

2) Reconstruct the proper distribution period beginning on or after January 1, 2003.

F. Multiple beneficiaries and separate accounts

(1) If more than one beneficiary is designated, required distributions are based on the age of the oldest beneficiary.

(2) Separate accounts can be established for each beneficiary at any time.

(a) But for each beneficiary to use his or her own life expectancy to calculate distributions, the separate accounts must be established by December 31 of the year following the year of the owner's death.

(b) Post-death investment gains and losses are allocated to the separate accounts on a pro rata basis.

(3) The separate accounts must be established by the designation date of September 30 to avoid the possibility of calculating a first-year distribution based on the life expectancy of the oldest designated beneficiary.

(4) If separate accounts are not created and beneficiaries that cannot be designated exist (charity), the account will be subject to the five-year rule. Consider paying off the charity's portion in full and then set up separate accounts for designated beneficiaries.

G. Trust as beneficiary

(1) There is a provision allowing an underlying beneficiary of a trust to be an owner's designated beneficiary for determining RMD when the trust is beneficiary

(2) Beneficiary documentation certifying designated beneficiaries on September 30 must be provided to the plan administrator by October 31 of the year following the year of the employee's death.

(3) If a trust is named beneficiary and a spouse is the sole beneficiary of the trust, the spouse cannot roll over the account into his or her own IRA account.

(4) Individual trusts cannot split into separate accounts, but if the IRA is payable to multiple trusts, then the rules for separate accounts can be used if divided prior to December 31.

(5) A beneficiary can be disregarded in determining the oldest beneficiary if the individual is a successor to the interest of another beneficiary.

(6) Clients should review documents to ensure designated beneficiaries are correct, especially if multiple IRAs exist or multiple beneficiaries have been designated.

5. Qualified domestic relations order (QDRO)

A. A domestic relations order is a judgment, decree, or order (including the approval of a property settlement) that is made pursuant to state domestic relations law (community property law) and that relates to the provision of child support, alimony payments, or marital property rights for the benefit of the spouse, former spouse, child, or other dependent of a participant.

B. A QDRO is a domestic relations order that creates or recognizes the existence of an alternate payee's right to, or assigns to an alternate payee the right to, receive all or a portion of the benefits payable with respect to the participant under a qualified retirement plan and that complies with certain special requirements:

(1) Name and address of participant and alternate payee covered by the order,

(2) Amount or percentage of the participant's benefit to be paid by the QRP to each alternate payee or the manner in which such amount or percentage is to be determined,

(3) Number of payments or period to which the order applies, and

(4) The QRP to which the order applies

C. A state authority, usually a court or state agency or instrumentality, *must issue* the judgment, order, or decree or approve the property settlement before it can be a domestic relations order under ERISA.

D. Applies to all qualified retirement plans, 403(b) plans, and 457 plans

E. QDRO rules *do not* apply to IRAs, but the transfer of an individual's interest in an IRA to his or her spouse or former spouse under a divorce or separation agreement is *not* considered a taxable transfer made by the individual; and thereafter the IRA is treated as maintained for the benefit of the spouse or former spouse.

F. IRAs can be used to implement a QDRO if a direct transfer of the participant's interest in a retirement plan to the spouse is otherwise prohibited.

G. QDRO rules *do not* apply to nonqualified plans. However, there have been rulings that life insurance benefits under an employer-sponsored nonqualified plan, "are"subject to QDRO rules if a divorce decree specifies how the life insurance benefits must be distributed.

6. Taxation of distributions

A. Waiver (discussed earlier in regard to this topic but worth considering again)

Consent of nonparticipant spouse to waiver (or electing out) of QPSA and QJSA in favor of an optional benefit form selected by the participant must

(1) Be in writing,

(2) Acknowledge the effect of the waiver, and

(3) Be witnessed, either by a plan representative or by a notary public

B. Cost basis recovery (see also, taxation of annuity basis in Topic 81)

(1) No tax is paid on contributions until a distribution is made. Tax is paid on net distribution, where the cost basis is recovered tax-free.

(2) Cost basis consists of the following:

(a) All employee contributions that have not been treated as deductions for federal income tax purposes

(b) Any loans that were included in the employee's income

(c) Any employee contributions that were included in the employee's income

(d) Any life insurance (PS-58) costs that were included in the employee's income
   Note: Self-employed cannot include insurance cost in cost basis.

(3) Capital gains treatment. Lump sum distributions may be eligible for capital gains treatment.

(a) Only pre-1974 employer contributions are eligible.

(b) Only participants in a QRP who have attained age 50 by January 1, 1986 are eligible.

(c) Long-term capital gains tax rate is 20 percent.

(4) Net unrealized appreciation (NUA)

(a) If a lump sum distribution includes employer securities, the NUA in the value of the securities will not be taxed to the employee at the time of distribution.

(b) The amount of appreciation will be taxed when the employee sells the securities at long-term capital gains tax rates.

(c) Employee may elect to pay the tax on the amount of appreciation at the time the securities are distributed by including the amount in income.

Chapter 7

ESTATE PLANNING

TOPIC 82: METHODS OF PROPERTY TRANSFER AT DEATH

1. The probate process: Probate is the process by which a court validates the will of a deceased individual. Probate also involves all other matters in regard to the settlement of estates of deceased persons.

   A. Testate succession

      (1) When a person dies leaving a will

      (2) This obligates the *executor* named in the will (after probate) to dispose of the decedent's property.

   B. Intestate succession

      (1) When a person dies without leaving a will

      (2) An *administrator* is appointed by the court to dispose of the decedent's property.

      (3) The state determines how the assets will be conveyed.

      (4) Intestate succession laws

         (a) Per stirpes *distribution*. Gives larger distributions to descendents of a closer degree of consanguinity (blood relationship) to the decedent

         (b) Per capita *distribution*. Requires that all eligible descendents receive an equal share of the property

   C. Advantages and disadvantages of probate

      (1) Advantages

         (a) Protects creditors

         (b) Provides clean title to heirs or legatees

         (c) Provides for the orderly administration of property

         (d) Establishes title to property where there may be some question as to ownership

      (2) Disadvantages

         (a) Excessive cost

         (b) Excessive delays

         (c) Open to public scrutiny

   D. Assets subject to probate

      (1) Assets in which the decedent has sole title

      (2) Assets held by tenancy in common

      (3) Assets held as community property

      (4) Assets disposed of by will

      (5) Contract proceeds that are payable to the estate

   E. Techniques of avoiding probate

      (1) Creating joint tenancy with right of survivorship

      (2) Creating a tenancy by its entirety

      (3) Using trusts

      (4) Establishing a funded revocable living trust

      (5) Establishing a beneficiary (other than the estate) to transfer by contract, such as life insurance contracts and retirement plans

   F. Ancillary probate

      (1) This occurs when a person domiciled in one state dies and owns property in another state (usually real estate).

      (2) It creates a special probate proceeding in the state in which the property is held.

      (3) The will should contain a provision that appoints an ancillary executor for disposing the property.

2. Operation of law (title)

  A. *Operation of law* refers to the passing of rights to a property from one person to another by the application of the established laws. This action uses laws specific to the situation and is done without any effort by the persons involved.

  B. Examples of operation of law as it relates to property interests

    (1) Joint tenancy with right of survivorship (JTWROS)

      (a) Equal ownership and automatic survivorship
      (b) Involves an undivided right to possess the property
      (c) Not subject to probate

    (2) Interests by the entirety

      (a) This is like joint tenancy, but can be created only between a husband and wife.
      (b) It is unlike joint tenancy, in that neither spouse can transfer property without the consent of the other spouse.
      (c) Not subject to probate

    (3) Tenancy in common (TC)

      (a) Can be unequal ownership and includes no automatic survivorship
      (b) Involves an undivided right to possess the property
      (c) Subject to probate

    (4) Community property (CP)

      (a) Exists only between spouses
      (b) CP is created immediately on acquisition of the property.
      (c) No automatic survivorship—Decedent's share can be transferred to someone other than spouse, with the use of a will.
      (d) Decedent's share is subject to probate.

    (5) The extent of ownership interest in property

      (a) *Fee simple.* Complete ownership with all rights (sell, gift, transfer, etc.). Property will pass through probate.
      (b) *Life estate.* Ownership interest ceases at death. For example, Steve assigns his interest in a house to Sarah, his close friend, for her use to enjoy until her death. Sarah has received a life estate in the house.

3. Transfers through trusts

  A. A trust is created to hold, manage, and distribute assets to the beneficiaries as indicated by the grantor of the trust. Property held in a trust is called the *principal* (also called the *corpus* or *trust estate*). Almost any form of property or asset can be included in a trust.

  B. There are three major parties to a trust:

    (1) *Trustor (also called grantor, settlor, or creator).* The person who creates the trust and whose property is used to fund the trust
    (2) *Trustee.* The person or entity that takes legal title and manages the trust assets
    (3) *Beneficiary.* The person who enjoys the beneficial interest in the trust

  C. There are two principal forms of trusts:

    (1) Inter vivos *or living trust.* Activated immediately upon its creation. It is generally funded during the life of the trustor.

   (2) *Testamentary trust.* Written into the will and implemented upon death. The funding mechanism is the probate process.

D. Transfers through trusts occur for five primary reasons:

   (1) To provide for multiple beneficiaries
   (2) To manage property in the event of incapacitation
   (3) To protect beneficiaries from themselves and others
   (4) To avoid probate
   (5) To reduce transfer taxes

4. Transfers by contract

A. *Transfer by contract* refers to the passing of assets through

   (1) Life insurance contracts
   (2) Annuities
   (3) Qualified retirement plans
   (4) Buy-sell agreements
   (5) Prenuptial agreements

B. Transfer by contract avoids probate if the beneficiary is someone other than the estate.

TOPIC 83: ESTATE PLANNING DOCUMENTS

1. Wills

A. Legal requirements

   (1) A will provides the *testator* with an opportunity to control the passing of his or her property and thus avoid intestacy.
   (2) Requirements for making a will

      (a) Generally any person 18 or older of sound mind
      (b) Less mental capacity is required by law to make a will than to make a contract. The testator must know the nature and extent of the property and the natural objects of his or her bounty.
      (c) Typically must be in writing, signed by the testator, and witnessed by at least two persons

   (3) A will is revocable—revised or amended by codicils. Codicils are supplements to wills, executed under the same rules as wills.

B. Types of wills

   (1) *Holographic will.* One written entirely by the testator, which is valid in some states without the formality of witnesses
   (2) *Nuncupative will.* An oral will spoken by the testator during the last illness in the presence of the required number of witnesses
   (3) *Living will.* A legal document executed by the testator declaring what medical treatment and procedures, such as life support, may or may not be used in the event that he or she becomes unconscious or incompetent
   (4) *Joint wills (also called mutual or reciprocal wills).* Two separate wills that share reciprocal provisions for the disposition of property in the event of death by one of the parties
   (5) *Pour-over will.* A will that distributes, at the testator's death, probate assets to a trust previously created

C. Avoiding will contests—An *in terrorem* clause provides that if a beneficiary unsuccessfully contests the validity of a will, the beneficiary bequest is void.

2. Powers of attorney

   A. Defined

      (1) A power of attorney is created by an individual, giving authority to another entity to act on the behalf of the individual. The power of attorney is usually witnessed and accredited.

      (2) The person executing the power is called the principal, and the person appointed by the power is the attorney-in-fact.

   B. Durable feature

      (1) A *durable power of attorney* is not terminated by subsequent disability or incapacity of the principal. It is designed to cover the situation in which the principal becomes incompetent. A power of attorney that is not a durable power of attorney terminates upon disability or incompetence.

      (2) A *springing power of attorney* does not become effective until the occurrence of a specified event.

   C. For health care

      (1) Applies to all situations in which the principal is unable to give "informed consent" with respect to a particular medical decision. It often gives the power to use or not to use artificial life-support systems.

      (2) It always springs on incapacity.

      (3) Such powers are recognized in almost all states, but state law varies in terms of the scope of authority of the attorney-in-fact.

      (4) A major drawback is that this power is so *powerful*: It can place reluctant family members in the position of having to make a decision that is regretted later in life.

   D. For property

      (1) Durable power of attorney for property appoints a person to make decisions in regard to the principal's assets.

      (2) It is generally effective upon execution (no springing) and continues until death of the principal.

      (3) It is often used in place of a trust for smaller estates.

      (4) It is often used for purposes of gift giving by the attorney-in-fact when the principal is elderly, and/or seriously ill, and not legally competent.

   E. Special or limited powers

      (1) A limited power is a special power.

      (2) The extent of the power is limited only by the desires of the principal.

   F. General powers

      (1) An unlimited power is a general power.

      (2) Broad general powers are intended to give the attorney-in-fact the right to act to the same extent the principal could have acted if available.

3. Advance medical directives (e.g., living wills)

   A. An advance medical directive establishes a medical situation in which the testator no longer wants life-sustaining treatment (i.e., life-support systems to prolong life). A living will is a medical life-support directive.

   B. It does not designate an agent to make medical decisions.

C. There are several drawbacks to living wills. They are generally very brief and vague, covering only a narrow range of outcomes, which are mostly in the area of life-sustaining treatment. No living will, no matter how detailed, can cover all possible medical outcomes. Most living wills apply only to terminal patients.

D. In some states, it may be appropriate to execute both a living will and durable power of attorney for health care to cover all areas.

4. Trusts

A. Clients may create trusts to manage their property if they become incapacitated or upon death.

B. Where the disabled (or decedent) settlor was serving as trustee at the time of the disability or death, most state laws allow a *successor* trustee to immediately take over the administration of the estate.

C. A living trust can be used for managing the disposition of property upon disability or death.

   (1) Similarities of a living trust and a will

      (a) Both serve as a guide for the disposition of property.
      (b) Both have a fiduciary who is responsible for managing property.
      (c) Both instruments are revocable and amendable, at least up until death of the person creating the instrument (a living trust generally becomes irrevocable at death of the grantor).

   (2) Differences between a living trust and a will

      (a) Dispose of different types of property. A living trust disposes of property owned by the trustee in trust for the trustor (decedent). A will disposes of probate property owned by the decedent at death.
      (b) A living trust *appoints* a trustee, whereas a will *nominates* an executor.
      (c) Formal execution requirements are stricter for a will. Witnesses are not required when signing the trust documents. However, the mental capacity necessary is at a higher standard for a trust.

D. Testamentary trusts are also a principal document of property disposition.

   (1) This trust takes effect after death at the end of the probate process.
   (2) It contains all provisions commonly found in a will and includes unique cases that relate to the trust documents.
   (3) A testamentary trust must appoint a trustee and nominate an executor.

5. Marital agreements

There are some issues that may have to be addressed in planning a marriage. Premarital agreements are among the most widely used vehicles for marriage planning.

6. Business agreements (see Topic 39)

Buy-sell agreements make sure an estate can sell a business interest for a reasonable price. The contract contains wording that binds the owner of a business to sell his or her share of a business at a specified price to a designated buyer, usually a partner(s) in the business.

TOPIC 84: GIFTING STRATEGIES

1. Suitability of gifting as a planning strategy

The following are the requirements for a transfer to be viewed as a valid gift:

A. The donor must be capable of transferring property.

B. The donee must be capable of receiving and possessing the property.

C. There must be delivery to, and some form of acceptance by, the donee or the donee's agent.

D. The donor must not maintain any interest in the property.

2. Techniques for gift-giving

When designing a gifting program, a planner should consider:

A. Giving assets with high rates of return, as opposed to assets with lower rates. This strategy can help avoid a buildup of revenue in the estate that would be taxed at the donor's tax rate.

B. Giving income-producing property to eliminate the income tax payable by the donor on the property. For example, if the donor is in the highest tax bracket and the donee is in a low tax bracket, substantial tax savings within a family unit can result if the income-producing property is given to the donee.

C. Giving growth assets rather than stagnant assets. This plan will prevent the post-gift appreciation from being taxed in the donor's gross estate.

D. Giving assets with a high basis rather than a low basis. If an asset with a low basis is held until death, the receiver of the asset is subject to a step-up in basis equal to the fair market value at the time of death. If the asset is gifted, the basis remains the same for the donor and the donee.

E. Selling assets whose value is less than their basis. Selling these assets results in a loss to the owner, which may possibly be deducted from the donor's income taxes.

F. Avoid gifting installment obligations. The donor will have to recognize the entire untaxed proceeds at the time of transfer.

G. Before gifting stock in an S Corporation to a trust, make sure the gift will not cause the loss of S Corporation status.

3. Appropriate gift property

A. Income-producing property, such as rental property

B. Property that is likely to grow substantially in value, such as life insurance, common stock, antiques and art, or real estate

C. Property owned by the donor in a state other than his or her own state of residence. Such a gift will avoid ancillary probate at the time of the donor's death.

D. Property, which has already appreciated, if the donor is contemplating selling it and the donee is in a lower tax bracket than the donor

E. It is generally *not* a good idea to give away property that would result in a loss if sold, inasmuch as the donee cannot use the donor's loss. The appropriate strategy would be for the donor to sell the property, take the loss, and give away the cash proceeds.

4. Strategies for closely held business owners—Stock in a closely held corporation can often be an ideal asset for gift purposes, but care must be taken so that not too much stock is given away. If an estate retains too little closely held stock, it may fail the percentage tests that qualify it for privileged treatment. A minimum of 35 percent of the value of the adjusted gross estate (AGE) must consist of closely held stock to qualify for the Section 303 redemption or for the Section 6166 installment payment of estate taxes.

5. Gifts of present and future interest

A. The gift tax exclusion is available only for gifts of present interest; the exclusion does not apply to gifts of future interest.

B. For a gift to be considered a gift of present interest, the donee must have the immediate right to use, possess, or enjoy the property. A gift will be considered one of future interest if the right to use, possess, or enjoy the property is delayed.

C. In making a gift to a trust, the gift will be considered to be of present interest only if the beneficiary has the right to demand immediate custody of the property transferred.

D. The most common types of future interests

(1) *Reversion*. A future interest in property that is retained by the transferor after he or she transfers interest in property

   Example: Steve transfers property in trust to Sarah for her life. The document does not explain what will happen to the property after Sarah's death. Steve has retained a reversionary interest. The trust property will belong to Steve when Sarah dies. If Steve dies before Sarah, the property will belong to his estate.

(2) *Remainders*. The right to use, possess, and enjoy property after all prior owners' interests end

   Example: A businessperson gives money to a trust, which states that the income is to be paid currently to his or her child and upon termination of the trust the principal is to be transferred to his or her grandchildren. The value of the remainder interest to the grandchildren would not be eligible for the annual gift tax exclusion.

(3) The *income beneficiaries* receive a life estate or estate for years in the trust income (present value interest); *remaindermen* (beneficiary of trust corpus at termination of all other interests) receive the remainder at termination of the income interests (future value interest).

E. Statutory exceptions to present interest requirement

(1) Minor's trust or Section 2503(c) trust

   (a) Considered a present interest gift and thus will qualify for the annual exclusion

   (b) The property passes to the minor on attaining the age of 21 years. In the event of the minor's death before attaining age 21, it will be payable to the estate of the minor or as he or she may appoint under a general power of appointment.

(2) Uniform Gift to Minors Act (UGMA) or Uniform Transfer to Minors Act (UTMA)

   (a) Considered a present interest gift and thus will qualify for the annual exclusion

   (b) Each state has one or the other, UTMA being the more modern version of UGMA. These are statutory creations, requiring a custodial institution (usually a bank, securities institution, etc.) to hold the funds for the minor and a custodian to be the person responsible for the account.

   (c) The funds stay under the domain of the custodian until the beneficiary is 21 (by statute in almost all states, although at least one state allows an 18-year-old to take control of his or her account). At age 21, the beneficiary has full rights and control over the balance of the funds.

   (d) If the donor dies while being the custodian, the value is brought back into the donor's estate.

   (e) Established for education purposes

(3) Section 529 plans

   (a) The donor can donate this year's and the next four years' annual exclusion at one time and still qualify for annual exclusion.

   (b) If the donor dies before the completion of the years for which the gift was made, the portion of the original transfer attributable to years in which the donor did not survive will be included in the donor's taxable estate.

   (c) The donor may remain in control without inclusion in estate. The donor may change beneficiaries within a range of related parties if the original beneficiary does not need the money for college.

F. Common law exemption—Crummey power

    (1) For use in a trust that does not satisfy the requirements of Section 2503(c)

    (2) Gifts placed in an irrevocable trust are a gift of a future interest, but by placing a lapsing power (Crummey power) to withdraw, a future interest is converted to a present interest. A Crummey power makes a transfer to a trust a gift of a present interest.

6. Tax implications

A. Income

    (1) The main reason for making a gift of income-producing property is to eliminate the income tax payable by the donor on the property. For example, the tax savings are obvious when the donor is in a high income tax bracket and the donee is in a low income tax bracket.

    (2) The age of the receiver matters. If the donee happens to be a child under the age of 14, the "kiddie tax" will be imposed on the net unearned income of the child.

B. Gift

    (1) A planned gift program can minimize a donor's overall estate, minimize gift taxes, and maximize the overall after-tax income available to a family unit during the donor's lifetime.

    (2) Valuation of gift

        (a) The value of a gift is its fair market value on the date of the gift.

        (b) Any consideration received by the donor reduces the value of the gift.

    (3) Transfers made within three years

        (a) Any gift tax paid on gifts within three years of death must be added to the gross estate. This is called the "gross-up" approach, which prevents the amount of the gift tax from escaping the estate tax.

        (b) Gifts made within three years of death are not included in the gross estate of the donor. They are treated in the same way as any other post-1976 taxable gift (i.e., added to taxable estate). Exceptions to this general rule include property under Section 2036, transfers with life estate; Section 2037, transfers taking effect at death; Section 2038, revocable transfers; and Section 2042, proceeds of life insurance.

    (4) Creation of joint ownership (see Topic 87)

        (a) When property is purchased with the funds of one person and titled jointly, a completed gift is made.

        (b) The most notable exceptions to this are titling of property jointly between husband and wife and titling of joint bank accounts and United States Savings Bonds.

        (c) In the case of a joint bank account or United States Savings Bond, a completed gift is not made until the noncontributing joint owner draws upon the bank account or surrenders part of the bond for cash.

    (5) Exercise of a general power of appointment (see also, Topic 89)

        (a) A general power of appointment is subject to gift tax (versus a limited or special power of appointment).

        (b) A general power of appointment is the power of the holder to appoint to the holder, the holder's estate, the holder's creditors, or the creditors of the holder's estate.

        (c) This section must be kept in mind when creating trusts with *Crummey* powers, as *Crummey* powers are general powers of appointment.

(d) Events that trigger gift tax to holder of power of appointment

    i. Section 2514. Provides that the exercise or release of a general power of appointment shall be deemed a transfer of property by the individual possessing such power.

    ii. Section 2514(e). Treats the lapse of a power as a release only to the extent that the property, which could have been appointed by exercise of such lapsed power, exceeds in value the greater of $5,000 or 5 percent of assets.

(6) Transfer of property cost basis

(a) *Basic rule*: Recipient (aka donee or transferee) takes donor's basis.

    i. Exception 1: When the transferred property is included in the donor's taxable estate at death, by being subject to Section 2036, 2037, or 2038, the inclusion gives the recipient a date-of-death fair market value as the basis.

    ii. Exception 2: When property is gifted that has a fair market value less than the donor's adjusted cost basis, the recipient's basis for future loss is the fair market value as of the date of the transfer and the recipient's basis for gain is the donor's original adjusted cost basis.

(b) *Example*: Bob has 100 shares of flyinghigh.com for which he paid $100 each. Today they are worth $5 each. Bob gives the shares to his daughter Samantha. Samantha now has two bases, one for future loss and one for future gain. Should she sell the stock for $4 each, she will have a loss (for purposes of offsetting other capital gains) of $1 per share. The possible tax benefit from the loss from $100 to $5 is forever gone. However, should the stock go up to $50, Samantha's basis is $100 (Bob's original adjusted basis), and thus there would be no loss or gain on the sale. Note that had Bob sold the stock for $50, he would have been able to claim a $50 per share loss to offset other gains. Samantha cannot take advantage of this loss. If the stock goes up to $150, Samantha's gain will be $50, the same as Bob would have had.

C. Estate

(1) The unified credit is a dollar-for-dollar reduction of any gift or estate tax due. Estate and gift taxes will no longer be "unified," in that the exclusion amounts for each will be different beginning in 2004. The gift tax unified credit is $345,800 in 2002 to 2009, which is equivalent to an exemption of $1 million.

(2) *Example*: Ben and his wife, Martha, make a $1 million present interest gift in 2003 to their only son. The computation for each spouse is as follows:

Gift (split)	$500,000
Annual exclusion	$10,000
Net gift	$490,000
Tax on net gift	$152,400
Unified credit	$345,800
Net tax due	$0

To the extent that the credit is used during lifetime, it will have the effect of reducing the credit available against the estate tax. For estate tax purposes, there will be only a $193,400 credit left for each spouse (in 2003). Additional credits will be available as the unified credit increases in subsequent years.

(3) Gift tax rates are cumulative. As a donor makes gifts that are subject to gift tax over the years, the previous years' gifts are added together with gifts made in the current year in order to determine the gift tax bracket for current gifts.

TOPIC 85: GIFT TAXATION AND COMPLIANCE

1. Filing requirements

   A. After giving a gift, the donor is required to complete a U.S. gift tax return, Form 709. The tax return must be filed before April 15 following the year of the gift.
   B. A gift tax return must be filed by the donor in any calendar year that he or she gives:

   (1) More than the annual exclusion to the donee
   (2) A gift of a future interest, regardless of how small it is
   (3) Total gifts exceeding $100,000 (indexed) to a noncitizen spouse
   (4) A gift for which spouses elect gift splitting, even if the amount is less than the annual exclusion for each after the split

2. Calculation

   A. Annual exclusion and applicable credit

   (1) In 2003, the first $11,000 of gifts of a present interest made by a donor to each donee in each calendar year is excluded from the amount of the donor's taxable gifts.
   (2) The first $110,000 by a donor to a spouse who is not a U.S. citizen is excluded.
   (3) The annual exclusion is doubled to $22,000 (in 2003) by gift splitting with a spouse. Each spouse is deemed to have given half the gift, even though one spouse in actuality made the entire gift.
   (4) Rules regarding annual gift tax exclusion

      (a) A gift in trust is treated as a gift to a trust's beneficiary in determining how many annual exclusions are allowed.
      (b) The amount of income interest in a trust qualifies for the annual exclusion if the trustee is required to distribute the income annually.
      (c) The gift that is contingent upon survivorship is a gift of a future interest.
      (d) A gift is a future interest if the donor's enjoyment depends on the exercise of a trustee's discretion.
      (e) A gift must have an ascertainable value to qualify for the exclusion.

   (5) The gift tax unified credit is $345,800 in 2002 to 2009, which is equivalent to an exemption of $1 million.

   B. Split gifts

   (1) Available only to married couples who file a joint return
   (2) Must be selected on a Form 709. It is filed by one taxpayer, and the other signs a consent for the gift splitting.
   (3) Gifts of community property do not require gift splitting because each spouse is considered to own one-half of the community property.
   (4) For any one year in which gift splitting is selected, all gifts made by either spouse (whether taxable or not) are considered to be split.
   (5) Each gift that is split is considered to have been made one-half by each spouse, totally without regard to the source of the funds or assets actually transferred.
   (6) *Example*: Myron and Myrna made the following gifts in 2002: Myron gave their daughter, Mona, 1,000 shares of ABC stock, which was trading at $22.50 per share. Myrna gave her mother's wedding ring to her daughter by her first marriage, Midge.

The ring was worth about $15,000. They write a $30,000 check to their son, Michael, to help him with a down payment on a house. At the end of the year, Myrna gives Michael $5,000 cash to help him with personal expenses.

(7) *Solution*: Gift tax reporting is on Form 709, due on or before April 15, 2003, in either Myron's or Myrna's name and Social Security number, with the other signing as consenting. The gifts are listed in the following table:

Gift	FMV (Fair Market Value)	Annual Exclusion in 2003		Taxable Gift	
		Myron	**Myrna**	**Myron**	**Myrna**
ABC stock to Mona	$22,500	$11,000	$11,000	$250	$250
Ring to Midge	$15,000	$7,500	$7,500	0	0
Check to Michael	$30,000	$11,000	$11,000	$4,000	$4,000
Cash to Michael	$5,000	0	0	$2,500	$2,500
Total				$6,750	$6,750

C. Prior taxable gifts

(1) No prior taxable gifts: If this is the case, the tax rates from the unified federal estate and gift tax rate schedule are applied to the current year taxable gifts. Gift tax computation:

Total current year's gross gifts (fair market value)

Less:	One-half of value of gifts split with spouse
	Annual exclusions
	Marital deduction
	Charitable deduction
Equals:	Total taxable gifts
Calculate:	Tentative tax on total taxable gifts
Less:	Unified credit (not to exceed tentative tax)
Equals:	Current gift tax

Example: In 2003, Mary made a gift of XYZ stock worth $730,000 to her brother, Ralph. This is the first taxable gift ever made by Mary. The tentative tax on a $719,000 estate ($11,000 annual exclusion) is $236,830. When $236,830 of Mary's unified credit ($345,800 in 2003) is applied, no gift tax is due.

Note: Total gifts cannot include political contributions, direct payments for medical and hospital expenses, or direct payments of tuition.

(2) With prior taxable gift: Tax on gifts is cumulative. Previous taxable gifts "gross-up" present taxable gifts for tax computation purposes. That is, once you have used the lower tax rates, future taxable gifts will be at the progressively higher rates in the Code—that is, you can use each lower bracket only once; any subsequent taxable transfer must be taxed at the higher rates.

(3) The method to determine the effective tax on all subsequent taxable transfers is as follows:

Total current year's gross gifts (fair market value)

Less:	Annual exclusion(s) and deductions
Equals:	Current taxable gift
Plus:	Total prior taxable gift
Equals:	Total (current and prior) taxable gifts
Calculate:	Tentative tax on total taxable gifts
Less:	Tentative tax on total prior taxable gifts
Equals:	Tentative tax of current taxable gifts
Less:	Unused unified credit (not to exceed tentative tax)
Equals:	Current gift tax

Example: In 2003, Mary (see earlier example) gave an additional $511,000 of XYZ stock to her friend, Betty. The gift tax is as follows:

Total current year's gross gifts		$511,000
Less:	Annual exclusion(s) and deductions	($11,000)
Equals:	Current taxable gift	$500,000
Plus:	Total prior taxable gift	$719,000
Equals:	Total (current and prior) taxable gifts	$1,219,000
Tentative tax on total taxable gifts		$435,590
Less:	Tentative tax on total prior taxable gifts	($236,830)
Equals:	Tentative tax of current taxable gift	$198,760
Less:	Unused unified credit ($345,800 − $236,830)	($108,970)
Equals:	Current gift tax	$89,790

D. Education and medical exclusions

(1) Qualified payments made directly to an educational institution for tuition are fully excluded from being taxable gifts.

(2) Qualified payments made directly to a provider of medical care are fully excluded from being taxable gifts.

(3) Gifts to political organizations are excluded from being taxable gifts.

E. Marital and charitable deductions

(1) Gifts to a U.S. citizen spouse are fully deductible, provided that they are not terminable interests.

(2) Charitable gifts are fully deductible.

F. Tax liability

(1) Taxable gifts

(a) Gifts made during life, which are either in excess of a donor's annual exemption or are not a present interest

(b) To the extent that tax is due, the taxpayer *must* utilize available unified credit.

(c) To the extent that unified credit is not available, the taxpayer must pay the tax by April 15 of the year following the year of the gift, to avoid penalties and interest.

(d) Any gift tax actually paid (no unified credit used) within three years of death will be included in the decedent's taxable estate. This equalizes the difference between "tax inclusive" and "tax exclusive" transfers.

(2) Net gifts occur when the donee agrees to pay any gift tax due. In this way, the gross amount of a gift is reduced by the amount of gift tax the donee pays. Rules for net gifts:

(a) The actual gift tax liability is lowered because the gift taxes paid reduce the value of the taxable gift.

(b) The donor's unified credit must be used to compute the donee's gift tax liability.

(c) For estate tax purposes, only the net amount of the gift is considered in the estate tax computation as an adjusted taxable gift.

(d) For income tax purposes, a net gift is treated as part sale and part gift to the extent that the gift tax paid by the donee exceeds the donor's basis in the property.

TOPIC 86: INCAPACITY PLANNING

1. Disability or incapacity can be defined as the inability to act on one's own behalf.
2. Care of client's dependents—guardianships (also called conservatorships)

   A. A guardianship is a state-imposed arrangement that results from an action brought by an interested party; it requires a finding such as "mental illness," "incompetence," or the like.

   B. The parties involved in a guardianship are

   (1) The ward or protected person
   (2) The guardian or conservator
   (3) The state

   C. Voluntary guardianship allows the ward to choose the guardian. It provides the protection of the court and state law, but it is relatively simple to dissolve and thus is often useful only as an interim arrangement in times of crisis or pending completion of other arrangements.

3. Care of person and property (see also, Topic 83)

   A. Planning scenarios

   (1) Provisions for managing the financial affairs of clients in the event they are unable to do so themselves (durable power of attorney, revocable living trust, and nominations of persons to serve as guardian or conservator)
   (2) Providing support for clients who are no longer self-supporting and have not accumulated enough assets to maintain their cost of living
   (3) Planning for long-term health care
   (4) Protecting property from claims of the state or other government
   (5) Planning for changing taxes

   B. Comparison of management techniques

   (1) *Durable power of attorney versus conservatorship.* The advantages of using the former for managing an incompetent person's property are as follows:

   (a) It avoids both public proceedings and the need to determine the status of the principal.
   (b) Various legal expenses and delays are avoided inasmuch as court appointment of a fiduciary is unnecessary.
   (c) It is relatively uncomplicated and inexpensive to create and is easy for the principal and agent to understand.
   (d) Title to the assets remains with the principal.

   (2) *Living trust versus conservatorship.* The advantages of using the former for managing an incompetent person's property are as follows:

   (a) The greater flexibility of a trust
   (b) The determination by the grantor of what provisions will be included in the trust document, such as who will be the fiduciary (trustee), what the standard for incompetency will be, what the trustee's powers will be, and so forth

     (c) Smaller administration costs, because a conservatorship requires frequent court approval of transactions

     (d) Wider management authority, allowing the trustee to conduct more kinds of transactions with the grantor's property than would be possible under a guardianship or conservatorship

     (e) *Exception*: With less court supervision, overreaching and abuse of power are more likely.

   (3) *Living trust versus durable power of attorney.* The advantages of using the former for managing an incompetent person's property are as follows:

     (a) Assurance that the transactions will be accomplished. Although some third parties may not recognize the authority of an agent under a durable power of attorney, the trustee's power to act according to the trust agreement must be honored (although most states will not compel a third party to follow the directions of an attorney-in-fact, states generally will compel others to recognize a trustee's authority over trust property).

     (b) The management and distribution terms are usually more detailed in a trust.

     (c) *Exception*: A trust is more costly to create and maintain.

4. Disability insurance—features of a good disability policy (see also, Topic 27)

  A. Select a policy that covers partial disability, not total disability.

  B. Select a policy that uses "your occupation" definition, not "any job" definition.

  C. Select a policy that is guaranteed renewable and noncancelable.

  D. Choose a policy that covers disability resulting from both accident and illness.

  E. Choose a policy that pays at least through age 65.

  F. Select a policy that pays at least 60 percent of take-home pay.

  G. A three-month waiting period generally offers the best value for the premium dollars paid.

  H. Cost-of-living adjustments should be included in the policy.

  I. Standard-of-living adjustments should be included in the policy so that the insured can increase the benefit amount without a medical exam.

5. Long-term care insurance—features of a good long-term care policy (see also, Topic 28)

  A. The policy should be guaranteed renewable for life.

  B. A three-month waiting period generally offers the best value for the premium dollars paid.

  C. The policy should provide coverage for skilled and intermediate care, as well as for custodial care, which does not require the engagement of licensed medical professionals.

  D. Long-term care at home can be more attractive than a residential or nursing facility.

  E. Select a policy that does not require the insured to be hospitalized before entering a nursing home for care.

  F. Select a policy that provides long-term care coverage for Alzheimer's disease.

  G. Choose a policy that provides for the anticipated rise in the cost of long-term care.

  H. Select a policy that provides for a waiver of premiums in the event of disability and provides level premiums for life.

  I. Select a policy that provides a favorable benefit period.

6. Medicaid planning

  A. Medicaid is a joint federal and state program that provides assistance for health care to certain aged, disabled, or blind individuals. The intent is to provide help to needy individuals. This can be integrated with the requirements for Supplemental Security Income (SSI).

B. If a client's assets exceed a certain dollar value, the individual will be ineligible to receive Medicaid benefits. The income of the individual and spouse is also considered.

C. Distributions from an annuity do count for purposes of the income test, but do not count under the assets test.

D. The individual's personal residence is generally not included as an asset for purposes of Medicaid eligibility, but this really depends on the state law.

E. There are strict limits on transfers of assets to achieve Medicaid eligibility. For example, the value of any transfer of assets within 36 months before the individual makes an application for Medicaid will be considered an available resource. There are some exceptions, including transfers to children who are caretakers for their parents.

F. In general, for assets transferred to trusts, the look-back period is 60 months from the date the individual makes a Medicaid application or the date an individual enters a nursing home.

G. Assets in a revocable trust are considered to be available resources, regardless of when the trust was created. A 60-month look-back period applies to transfers between trusts.

H. Irrevocable special needs trust

    (1) This is a bypass trust, which is not included in the gross estate of the beneficiary, and its assets are not counted for purposes of eligibility under Medicaid.

    (2) The settlor retains the following powers:

        (a) While competent, the power to act as trustee

        (b) While not competent, the right to invade principal on the basis of health, education, maintenance, and support

        (c) The power to appoint an unlimited amount of trust property to family members other than the trustor

        (d) The power to change beneficiaries in order to reallocate the estate amount among the children

7. Viatical settlements (see Topic 30)

8. Business disability coverage (see also, Topic 39)

A. The disability of business owners or key employees poses a serious risk to a business's financial health. The problem is especially evident in small businesses in which the workforce may not be large enough to have a backup for critical tasks. Even if the primary business is halted because of the disability of the owner or a key person, certain aspects of the business must continue (e.g., accounts payable and receivable).

B. Disability insurance can be written to cover business overhead, key person disability, salary continuation for owners or key persons, or a disability buy-sell agreement.

    (1) Business overhead policies cover many of the ongoing operation costs of a business while the owner is totally disabled.

    (2) Key person insurance allows a business to find a temporary replacement for a key person who has become disabled, replace lost revenue, fund the search for a replacement, and fund costs of training when a new person is found.

    (3) Salary continuation is simply a plan to continue the salary of the disabled person.

    (4) A buy-sell plan shifts the ownership of the company to one or more individuals. The cost of the buy-sell can be paid in a lump sum or in installments.

9. Social Security disability benefits (see Topic 73)

TOPIC 87: ESTATE TAX CALCULATION AND COMPLIANCE

1. The gross estate

    A. Inclusions

        (1) Section 2033 includes in the gross estate the value of "all property to the extent of the (decedent's) interest therein."

            (a) Generally includes property or interests considered "owned" by decedent
            (b) Generally includes contingent interest
            (c) Income in Respect of a Decedent

                i. Rights to unpaid income possessed by decedent
                ii. Subject to income tax and estate tax
                iii. Income tax deduction for estate tax attributable to included value of the income right [Section 691(c)]
                iv. Retirement plans and annuities are major sources of Income in Respect of a Decedent (IRD).

        (2) Section 2034 includes in the gross estate dower and curtesy interest (fully deductible under the marital deduction).
        (3) Section 2035 includes in the gross estate any gift tax paid on gifts within three years of death.
        (4) Sections 2036, 2037, and 2038 cover transfers with retained interest (Section 2036), reversionary interest (Section 2037), or power to amend, alter, or revoke (Section 2038).

            (a) Purpose of Sections 2036, 2037, and 2038

                i. Premised on the notion that the decedent has made a gift of property, but has retained a certain degree of control and enjoyment over the property, so the property is included in the gross estate
                ii. All require that the decedent has made a transfer of property for less than full consideration in money or money's worth.

            (b) Section 2036 covers transfers with retained interest.

                i. Section 2036(a)(1) includes in the gross estate the value of any property in which the decedent has retained a life estate. The Code does not use the words *life estate,* but instead refers to the "the possession or enjoyment of, or the right to the income from, the property."

                    • *Example*: A person transfers to his son real estate as a gift, reserving a life estate.
                    • *Example*: A person transfers to his daughter a residence as a gift. The transferor continues to live in the residence rent free until death.

                ii. Section 2036(a)(2) includes property for which the decedent reserved the right either alone or in conjunction with any person to designate the persons who shall possess or enjoy the property or the income therefrom.

                    • *Example*: A decedent created a trust and was one of three trustees of the trust. The trust provided that the trustees, in their sole discretion, could pay trust income to the beneficiary or accumulate the income.
                    • A power limited by an ascertainable standard (support, health, education, or maintenance) is not within Section 2036(a)(2).

                iii. Section 2036(b) states that the retention of right to vote shares of stock of a controlled corporation is considered a retention.

   (c) Section 2037 covers transfers taking effect at death.

     i. Two conditions must exist:

- Possession or enjoyment of the property can, through ownership of such interest, be obtained only by surviving the decedent.
- The decedent has retained a reversionary interest in the property, and the value of such reversionary interest immediately before the death of the decedent exceeds 5 percent of the value of such property.

     ii. The statute says the term *reversionary interest* includes a possibility that property transferred by the decedent may return to the decedent or his or her estate or may be subject to a power of disposition by him or her.

     iii. The 5 percent test is only a test. If the 5 percent requirement is met, then the entire value of the interest subject to the reversion is included in the decedent's gross estate.

   (d) Section 2038 includes transfers involving the power to alter, amend, revoke, or terminate.

     i. Generally synonymous with the power to designate the persons who shall possess or enjoy the property or the income therefrom

     ii. Under Section 2038, the property must be subject to the power at the time of the decedent's death.

  (5) Section 2039 requires inclusion in the gross estate the value of any annuity or other payment received by the beneficiary. If an annuity pays a survivorship benefit to a named beneficiary, the present value of the future payments to the beneficiary is included in the decedent's gross estate. This applies to pension and retirement plans that provide for a survivorship benefit.

  (6) Section 2041 includes in the gross estate any property subject to a general power of appointment at the time of the decedent's death.

  (7) Estate taxation of life insurance (see Topic 93)

 B. Exclusions

  (1) Interests arising at death are not included (e.g., a wrongful death action).

  (2) Frequently, creating an irrevocable life insurance trust or having other family members own the policy is done in an effort to keep the proceeds of the policy out of the estate.

  (3) A power of appointment that is limited by an ascertainable standard relating to health, education, support, or maintenance is not a general power of appointment.

2. Deductions

 A. Funeral expenses

 B. Administrative expenses, including commissions, fees, court costs, and selling expenses for asset dispositions

 C. Debt and mortgages

 D. Certain taxes payable at death

 E. Losses from administering the estate (such as casualty losses)

3. Adjusted gross estate (AGE) is defined in Section 6166 as gross estate less expenses, debts, and losses.

4. Deductions from the adjusted gross estate

 A. Charitable contributions (see Topic 92)

 B. Transfers to surviving spouse (see Topic 95)

5. Taxable estate is found by subtracting charitable deduction and marital deduction from the AGE.
6. Adjusted taxable gifts rule
    A. Adjusted taxable gifts are defined as the taxable portion of all post-1976 gifts. A gift is taxable to the extent it exceeds any allowable (1) annual gift tax exclusion, (2) gift tax marital deduction (similar to the estate tax marital deduction, but for lifetime gifts to a spouse), or (3) gift tax charitable deduction.
    B. The sole purpose of the adjusted taxable gifts coming into the estate tax equation is to move the decedent's taxable estate up into the appropriate marginal rates.
    C. Gross estate versus taxable estate
        (1) If a gift is added to the gross estate, the value of the gift is the fair market value of the property as of the date of death (or alternative valuation date, if elected). Gifts that for any reason have been includable in a decedent's gross estate are not considered adjusted taxable gifts.
        (2) If the taxable gift is added to the taxable estate, the value at the date of the gift applies.
7. Add the adjusted taxable gifts to the taxable estate to arrive at the *tentative tax base.*
8. Tentative tax calculation—The tentative estate tax is determined by applying the unified transfer tax rate from Section 2001(c) to the tentative tax base.
9. Credits
    A. Gift tax payable
        (1) The tentative tax is reduced by the gift tax paid or payable on gifts included in the tax base.
        (2) Gift tax paid is a reduction of estate tax and *not* a credit.
        (3) It is the dollar amount after application of the unified credit.
    B. Unified credit
        (1) The credit must be used the first time a gift tax or an estate tax is required to be paid. A taxpayer does not have the right to pay tax in lieu of using the unified credit.
        (2) The total tax on the net gift or estate is calculated, then some or all of the credit as may be necessary is applied against total tax due and owing on a dollar-for-dollar basis. The balance, if any, is the net tax due.
        (3) If the credit is not fully utilized in one transaction, the balance will carry over to another, later transaction. If credit remains after calculating any tax due at death, that credit vanishes and no one gets the benefit of it.
        (4) The amounts of unified credit, and their applicable exclusion amounts, are as follows:

Year	Unified Credit	Exclusion Amount
2003	345,800	1,000,000
2004	555,800	1,500,000
2005	555,800	1,500,000
2006	780,800	2,000,000
2007	780,800	2,000,000
2008	780,800	2,000,000
2009	1,455,800	3,500,000

After 2009, estate tax is repealed.

C. Prior transfer credit

(1) The *credit for taxes on prior transfers* is available where the same property has been taxed in the estate of a person who died within 10 years before or 2 years after the decedent's death.

(2) The credit for tax on prior transfers is limited to the smaller of

(a) The amount of the federal estate tax attributable to the transferred property in the transferor's estate

(b) The amount of federal estate tax attributable to the transferred property in the decedent's estate

(3) If the transferor died within two years before or two years after the present decedent's death, the credit is the smaller of the two limitations. If the transferor died more than 2 years before the decedent, the credit is reduced by 20 percent for each 2 years by which the death of the transferor preceded the decedent's death, up to 10 years.

D. State death tax

It does not reduce the total estate tax. It merely divides the total death taxes between the federal and state governments.

E. Federal estate taxes

(1) No prior gifts:

Gross Estate

Less:	Total deductions
Equals:	Taxable estate
Calculate:	Tentative estate tax
Less:	Unified credit
Equals:	Total death taxes
Less:	State death tax credit
Less:	Other credits
Equals:	Federal estate tax

(2) With prior gifts:

Gross Estate

Less:	Total deductions
Equals:	Taxable estate
Plus:	*Adjusted taxable gifts (post-1976)*
Equals:	*Estate tax base*
Calculate:	Tentative estate tax
Less:	*Gift taxes payable on post-1976 taxable gifts*
Less:	Unified credit
Equals:	Total death taxes
Less:	State death tax credit
Less:	Other credits
Equals:	Federal estate tax

TOPIC 88: SATISFYING LIQUIDITY NEEDS

1. Sale of assets during lifetime

   A. Assets that have a built-in loss are generally the *best* to sell. Death eliminates this potential tax benefit by stepping down the basis to date-of-death value.
   B. High-basis assets are also good to sell because there is little or no taxable gain.
   C. Low-basis assets are the least attractive to sell. Tax on these assets is eliminated if held until death, and the beneficiary receives a new basis at fair market value.

2. Life insurance (see Topic 93)

TOPIC 89: POWERS OF APPOINTMENT

1. Use and purpose

   A. A power of appointment is a power to name someone to receive a beneficial interest in property. The grantor of the power is called the *donor*. The person receiving the power is called the *holder* or *donee*. The parties to whom the holder gives property by exercising the power are called the *appointees*. The persons who receive the property if the holder permits the power to lapse are called the *takers in default*.
   B. A power of appointment is "general" if there are no restrictions on the donee's choice of appointees. If there are restrictions, then the power is termed a "limited" or "special" power.
   C. A power of appointment is used

      (1) When the estate owner wants someone else to make decisions concerning his or her property
      (2) When the estate owner does not know the future needs of his or her beneficiaries or how many beneficiaries there will be
      (3) When the assets would be subject to the generation-skipping transfer tax (GSTT) upon a taxable termination of the trust. The inclusion of assets in the estate of the holder results in a lower tax than GSTT because of a graduated rate schedule rather than a flat tax rate at the highest estate tax rate.
      (4) When the estate owner desires to qualify assets for the marital deduction but would like to have a right to designate who will receive the property

2. General and special (limited) powers

   A. 5 + 5 power

      (1) The "5 or 5" power is useful for avoiding estate taxes as well as gift taxes. The right of invasion must be made noncumulative.
      (2) Property subject to a general power will be included in the estate of the holder only to the extent that the property that could have been appointed by the exercise of the power, but has lapsed, *exceeds* the greater of:

         (a) $5,000
         (b) 5 percent of the total value of the funds subject to the power as valued at the time of the lapse

      (3) Estate tax consequences

         (a) *Example*: Mark was the income beneficiary of a trust with assets of $200,000. Assume the value of the trust does not change. Mark was given a noncumulative power to withdraw $10,000 per year. He did not exercise the power, which resulted in a lapse each year. When Mark dies, only $10,000 is included in his gross estate.

The lapse in prior years is ignored because the amount does not exceed the greater of $5,000 or 5 percent of the corpus of $200,000.

    (b) *Example*: Marge was income beneficiary of a trust with assets of $70,000. Marge was also given a noncumulative power to withdraw $10,000 per year (which she did not exercise). At the expiration of each year, Marge has released a general power to the extent of $5,000 (i.e., a $10,000 lapse *minus* the greater of $5,000 or 5 percent of $70,000 [$3,500]).

    (c) If Marge dies in the sixth year of the trust's existence and assets remain constant, Marge's gross estate would include $35,000 on account of this trust. The $35,000 consists of $10,000 on account of the power held by the decedent at the time of death and $25,000 on account of the lapse of the power in each of the prior five years.

  (4) Gift tax consequences: Failure to exercise results in gifts to the remaindermen of the trust, with a reduction each year by the amount of the holder's (Marge) life estate in the lapsed amounts.

  (5) Income tax consequences: If the beneficiary has a 5 or 5 power and fails to exercise the power in a given year, the beneficiary becomes the grantor of that portion of the trust over which the power has lapsed.

B. Crummey provisions

  (1) Gifts placed in an irrevocable trust are gifts of a future interest, but by placing a lapsing power (Crummey power) to withdraw, a future interest is converted to a present interest. A Crummey power makes a transfer to a trust a gift of a present interest.

  (2) The beneficiary has a noncumulative right to withdraw a specified amount of property transferred to a trust within a specified period.

  (3) If the right is not exercised, the annual transfer for the year remains in the trust for management by the trustee. If the right is exercised, the trustee must deliver the fund to the beneficiary.

  (4) The lapse of the withdrawal power to the extent it exceeded the *greater* of $5,000 or 5 percent of trust corpus causes a taxable gift by the power holder to the remaindermen of the trust. Because the remaindermen (possibly unknown) do not have the power to withdraw the gift from the trust, the beneficiary made a future interest gift, which does not qualify for the annual exclusion.

  (5) Two negative tax consequences of this taxable gift by the Crummey trust beneficiary:

    (a) The beneficiary made a transfer subject to gift tax, which would use up some of his or her unified credit.

    (b) The property subject to the lapsed power would be included in the beneficiary's estate for estate tax purposes as a transfer in which the interest has been retained, because the beneficiary usually has some continuing right to the trust (i.e., a life estate) property.

  (6) The gift tax problem created by the lapse of a general power to trust property in excess of $5,000 or 5 percent of the trust corpus is resolved by the following:

    (a) No gift tax is due by reserving in the beneficiary a power that keeps the lapse from being a completed gift. This is the power to direct where the trust property will go upon lapse of the withdrawal power.

    (b) The estate tax problem is not avoided, but most Crummey trusts are intended to be paid out during the beneficiary's lifetime, so this should not be a problem.

C. Distribution for health, education, maintenance, and support

A power that is limited by an ascertainable standard relating to health, education, maintenance, or support (HEMS) is not a general power of appointment.

3. Tax implications

A. General power implications

(1) Section 2514 provides that the exercise or release of a general power of appointment shall be deemed a transfer of property by the individual possessing such power.

(2) Section 2514(e) treats the lapse of a power as a release only to the extent that the property, which could have been appointed by exercises of such lapsed power, exceeds in value the greater of $5,000 or 5 percent.

(3) Section 2041 includes, in the donee's gross estate, property subject to a general power of appointment at the time of the decedent's death.

B. Special or limited power implications

(1) The existence of a special power of appointment or the exercise, release, or lapse of such a right will not cause inclusion in the power holder's gross estate.

(2) No gift tax is imposed by the exercise, release, or lapse of a special power of appointment.

TOPIC 90: TYPES, FEATURES, AND TAXATION OF TRUSTS

1. Classification

A. Simple and complex

(1) A simple trust is considered merely a conduit for forwarding income to the beneficiaries, but no principal is distributed. The trust passes its income through to the beneficiaries, who then report the income with the same character that it had for the trust and who pay taxes on it according to their own marginal tax brackets.

(2) A complex trust is an irrevocable trust that can either accumulate some fiduciary accounting income (FAI) (i.e., does not pay out all of the FAI for the year) or distribute principal.

B. Revocable and irrevocable

(1) Revocable living trust

(a) Subject to the right of rescind and amend
(b) Becomes irrevocable at the grantor's death
(c) Includable in estate
(d) No gift tax at time of creation

(2) Irrevocable living trust

(a) Cannot be revoked by the grantor after its creation except upon the consent of all the beneficiaries
(b) Gift tax may apply at time of transfer.
(c) Has income and estate tax benefits

2. Rule against perpetuities

A. The rule against perpetuities is a law that requires a time period for a trust to terminate and distribute its property to a person.

B. To satisfy the requirements of the rule, an interest must vest within 21 years after the death of someone at the moment of the transferor into an irrevocable trust. The interest must vest or fail to vest no later than 21 years after *some life in being* at the creation of the interest.

C. A violation of the rule will cause the particular interest to be void and revert to the transferor or the transferor's successors.

D. The rule does not take a wait-and-see approach; it does not allow us to wait and see whether any grandchildren are born after the grantor's death.

E. It typically enables the transferor to control the disposition of property for his or her life, for the lives of the children, and for the grandchildren's lives, but no longer. A great-grandchild's interest will typically (but not always) vest after the 21-year period and thus will fail.

3. Selected provisions

A. Spendthrift clause

(1) A spendthrift provision (or spendthrift trust) is designed to protect trust assets from the "spendthrift" propensities of a trust's beneficiaries. A trust provision may prohibit a trust beneficiary from assigning his or her interest in the trust corpus. Such a provision will prevent creditors from reaching the trust assets by any legal or equitable process.

(2) Once trust income is paid to the beneficiary, the funds lose their trust character and may be attacked by creditors.

B. Perpetuity clause

(1) A clause in a will or trust that prevents interests from being ruled invalid under the rule against perpetuities

(2) Identifies the lives of all people in a trust that can be calculated

C. Other

(1) A sprinkling provision gives the trustee authority to allocate income and corpus among the trust beneficiaries in accordance with their needs. Thus, the trustee of a sprinkle trust has considerable flexibility to use discretion in providing for the unique needs of beneficiaries.

(2) A support provision limits the trustee's right of distribution to only as much of the trust's assets (income or principal) as the trustee deems necessary to discharge the grantor's obligation of support to one or more specified beneficiaries.

4. Taxation of trusts and estates

A. Trust income and federal estate income tax (see Topic 62)

B. Federal gift tax implications

(1) *Revocable trust.* The transfer of property to a revocable trust does not result in a taxable gift because there has not been a completed gift.

(2) *Irrevocable trust.* The transfer of property to an irrevocable trust usually results in a taxable gift.

(a) The grantor is subject to gift tax liability on the actuarial value of both the income stream and the remainder interest transferred to the trust beneficiaries.

(b) The actuarial value of the gift may be reduced by the gift tax annual exclusion if a beneficiary has a "present interest," which can be created by giving a trust beneficiary an unrestricted right to the immediate use, possession, or enjoyment of property or income.

C. Federal estate tax implications

    (1) *Revocable trust.* Assets are included in the deceased grantor's gross estate.

    (2) *Irrevocable trust.* Assets transferred to an irrevocable trust will avoid both probate and inclusion in the deceased grantor's gross estate, if the grantor does not retain prohibited rights:

        (a) A life income interest or right to use or enjoy trust property

        (b) A right to change the beneficiary designation

        (c) A right to change the trustee (unless the grantor's power is limited to parties not related or subordinate to the grantor)

        (d) A right to determine the beneficial enjoyment of trust assets

        (e) A reversionary interest of more than 5 percent

TOPIC 91: QUALIFIED INTEREST TRUSTS

1. Grantor retained income trusts (GRITs)

    A. The acronym GRIT is used to refer to all grantor retained income trusts, including common law GRITs, GRATs, and GRUTs (see following sections (2) and (3)). Property is transferred into an irrevocable trust, where the grantor retains the right to income for a period of years, after which the trust ends and the property is transferred to the remaindermen. If the transferor survives the income period, all beneficial interest in the trust ceases, and the asset is out of the transferor's estate. However, the taxable gift value is included in the estate tax base as an adjusted taxable gift. If the transferor does not survive the income term, Section 2036(a) applies and the assets are included in the grantor's estate.

    B. The primary purpose of a GRIT is to leverage the applicable exclusion amount (AEA) to avoid estate tax, not gift tax. The value of the gift made is calculated by taking the FMV of the property and reducing it by the retained interest. This equals the remainder interest that is considered a gift. This remainder interest is a future interest and is discounted. Therefore, the longer the term of the trust and the higher the Section 7520 rate, the smaller the gift value. The result is to freeze the value in the grantor's interest and transfer growth in value to the children, escaping larger gift and estate tax.

    C. There is no reason to create a GRIT of any kind with a term that goes beyond 2009, because the estate tax is repealed at that time. In the post-EGTRRA (Economic Growth and Tax Relief Reconciliation Act) era, a GRIT is beneficial only if the term ends before the settlor dies and the settlor dies before 2010. If a settlor dies after 2009, assuming the estate tax remains repealed, the now distributed GRIT turns out to be a waste of time. The remaindermen receive the trust assets with a carryover basis. If the settlor had simply held on to the assets, the increase in basis would have been allocated to them.

2. Grantor retained annuity trusts (GRATs)—make fixed payments to grantor at least annually

3. Grantor retained unitrust (GRUTs)—The required payment is determined each year as a percentage of the fair market value of the trust property. The value of the assets are recalculated each year.

4. Qualified personal residence trusts (QPRTs, or House-GRITs)

    A. QPRTs can hold an interest in only one residence.

    B. The grantor who survives the term of a QPRT does not have to vacate the residence, because he or she can rent it as a remainderman. The transaction must be at arm's length and at fair rental value.

    C. The residence cannot be purchased from the trustee by the settlor, the settlor's spouse, or an entity controlled by them.

5. Tangible personal property trusts

   A. The problem with setting up these trusts is that it is difficult to value a term interest for tangible personal property.

   B. The zero valuation rule of Section 2702 does not apply to tangible property where:

      (1) The failure of the interest holder to exercise rights would not have a substantial impact on the remainder interest.

      (2) No depreciation deduction is allowed.

6. Limitations on the valuation of remainder interests of qualified interest trusts

   A. Section 2702 limits the advantage of a grantor retained trust by valuing the income interest at zero when the transfer is made to a family member. This means that the entire value of the transferred property is subject to immediate gift tax (i.e., it is not discounted by the term). For gift tax purposes, the *nonqualified* retained interests are treated as if they were not retained.

   B. To be *qualified*, a retained income interest must be paid annually and there must be a precise way of calculating the amount. There are four types of Section 2702 GRITs that avoid the zero valuation rule for the retained interest.

      (1) GRATs
      (2) GRUTs
      (3) QPRTs
      (4) Tangible personal property trusts

   C. If the retained interest is a qualifying one, the zero valuation rule is avoided. If Section 2702 applies and the retained interest is not a qualified one, the interest is given a zero value.

   D. *Example*: Jerry transfers $1 million into a trust, retaining the right to all income for 15 years. His two children are the remaindermen. The income interest is valued at zero because it is neither a GRAT nor a GRUT. The result is that the entire $1 million value is a taxable gift.

TOPIC 92: CHARITABLE GIVING

1. Considerations for contributions and transfers

   A. An unlimited amount of property can be transferred to qualified charities without incurring federal gift taxes. As with the marital deduction, there is no limit to the size of the gift tax charitable deduction.

   B. The charitable organization incurs no income tax liability as a result of the gift and is not subject to income tax on the income derived from the property transferred.

   C. A transfer made during an individual's life will not only provide an income tax deduction but will also remove property from the taxpayer's estate. In contrast, a testamentary bequest to a qualified organization will only remove property from the taxpayer's estate.

   D. Reasons for making a lifetime gift to a charity (rather than to a noncharitable beneficiary) : To use the unlimited charitable deduction to either reduce or avoid gift tax liability while removing the value of the asset (including any appreciation) from the donor's potential gross estate

2. To qualify for a charitable income tax deduction

   A. Public charities are the charitable, educational, scientific, religious, medical, and related nonprofit organizations that are publicly supported. Examples include Red Cross, United Way, universities, hospitals, churches, synagogues, and the like. Groups that aid or prevent cruelty to children or animals and governmental units that use donations solely for public purposes are included in this category.

B. Contributions qualifying as charitable deductions for income tax purposes must meet the following requirements:

    (1) They must be made to qualifying organizations.

    (2) They must be gifts of property and not the value of time or services provided.

    (3) They must be made before the close of the year in which the deduction is to be claimed.

    (4) They must have a value greater than any benefit received from the qualifying organization. (Only the value in excess of the benefit received is deductible.)

    (5) They must be gifts of the donor's entire interest in the property, unless made in accordance with special rules.

    (6) They must be claimed by the taxpayer as itemized deductions. (No charitable deduction has been allowed to nonitemizers since 1986.)

3. Charitable remainder trusts (CRTs)

A. Characteristics

    (1) The donor retains a limited right to enjoy the property while receiving an income tax deduction and reducing federal estate tax.

    (2) The CRT must have at least one noncharitable income beneficiary.

    (3) The CRT must have an irrevocable remainder interest to be held for or paid to a charity.

    (4) The grantor has the right to change the charitable remaindermen without causing inclusion in the grantor's estate.

    (5) The funding date is critical for determining whether a trust qualifies as a CRT. If the trust is not funded, an income tax charitable deduction cannot be claimed and the assets are included in the estate.

    (6) The beneficiary may receive the income for a period not exceeding 20 years or for life, and the remainder goes to the charity.

B. Charitable remainder unitrusts (CRUTs)

    (1) The income tax deduction *equals* the total value of property *minus* present value of retained interest income.

    (2) The income recipient is a noncharitable beneficiary, which is usually the donor.

    (3) *A fixed percentage of the net fair market value* of the principal, revalued annually, must be payable to the noncharitable beneficiary.

    (4) The percentage payable to the noncharitable beneficiary must be not less than 5 percent or more than 50 percent of the *annual value*.

    (5) The remainder interest at inception must be greater than or equal to 10 percent of the original value of the property transferred to the trust.

    (6) The remainderman is the charity.

    (7) Additional contributions are permitted.

    (8) May have sprinkling provision

    (9) When income is insufficient for payout, the trustee can pay up to income and make up the deficiency in subsequent years.

    (10) Can hold tax-exempt securities

C. Charitable remainder annuity trusts (CRATs)

    (1) The income tax deduction *equals* the total value of property *minus* present value of retained interest income.

    (2) The income recipient is a noncharitable beneficiary, which is usually the donor.

     (3) *A fixed amount or fixed percentage of the initial value* of the trust must be payable to the noncharitable beneficiary.

     (4) The annuity percentage must be not less than 5 percent or more than 50 percent of the *initial fair market value* of all the property transferred in trust.

     (5) The remainder interest at inception must be ≥ 10 percent of the original value of the property transferred to the trust.

     (6) The remainderman is the charity.

     (7) Additional contributions are *not* allowed.

     (8) May have sprinkling provision

     (9) Must invade corpus when income is insufficient for payout

   (10) Can hold tax-exempt securities

4. Charitable lead trusts

  A. Characteristics

     (1) A charitable lead trust differs radically from the charitable remainder trusts in that the donor in the charitable lead trust gives away an income stream and receives a remainder interest.

     (2) The donor places income-producing property in a reversionary trust and directs that the trust income be transferred to a designated charity for a period of time not to exceed 20 years. At the end of this "lead" time, the property reverts to the donor or to some other noncharitable beneficiary.

     (3) The benefit the donor receives is a very large income tax deduction in the year that the trust is funded, the value of the deduction being the present value of the total anticipated income during the lead period when the charity receives the income. If done right, the value of the remainder interest can equal zero, resulting in a full deduction of the current value of property transferred to the trust.

     (4) The trust must be set up as a grantor trust, making the annual income taxable to the donor (but can purchase tax-exempt securities to lower tax liability of the donor), unless it is established at the grantor's death. As such, these trusts are generally established at the transferor's death.

  B. Charitable lead unitrusts (CLUTs)

     (1) *A fixed percentage of the net fair market value* of the principal, revalued annually, must be payable to the charitable beneficiary.

     (2) The percentage payable to the charitable beneficiary must be not less than 5 percent or more than 50 percent of the *annual value*.

     (3) Additional contributions are permitted.

     (4) Can pay up to income and make up deficiency in subsequent years

  C. Charitable lead annuity trusts (CLATs)

     (1) *A fixed amount or fixed percentage of the initial value* of the trust must be payable to the charitable beneficiary.

     (2) The annuity percentage must be not less than 5 percent or more than 50 percent of the *initial fair market value* of all the property transferred in trust.

     (3) Additional contributions are *not* allowed.

     (4) Must invade corpus when income is insufficient for payout

5. Pooled income funds

  A. Created and maintained by a public charity instead of a private donor

  B. The donor must contribute an irrevocable, vested remainder interest to the charity.

    C. The property is commingled with property transferred by other donors.

    D. The funds cannot invest in tax-exempt securities.

    E. No donor or income beneficiary can be a trustee.

    F. The donor must retain for him- or herself (or one or more named income beneficiaries) a life income interest.

    G. Each income beneficiary must receive a pro rata share of income, annually, based on the rate of return earned by the fund.

    H. Sprinkling is *not* allowed.

    I. Additional contributions are allowed.

6. Private foundations

    A. A private foundation can be set up by either a corporation or a trust and is generally organized by a family to accomplish charitable goals. The foundation allows the family and other interested parties to make contributions, gifts, and bequests, which the foundation will then distribute to public charities.

    B. Many family foundations are created to perpetuate the family name in a charitable setting while simultaneously acting as a conduit for charitable distributions to be made.

    C. Private foundations differ from public ones in that instead of merely collecting and distributing for charitable activities, they conduct charitable activities of their own.

    D. Properly organized and operated, a foundation is exempt from federal income tax, and gifts and bequests made to it are deductible.

7. Other types of charitable gifts

    A. Net income with makeup CRUT (NIMCRUT)

        (1) Payments to the beneficiary are limited to the lower of

            (a) The set percentage

            (b) The actual income of the trust

        (2) Allows for a provision to "make up" when income is less than the set percentage.

        (3) Used as an alternative to pension plans by investing in low-income–producing assets in early years (when donor's income is high) and high-income–producing assets in later years (when donor's income is low).

    B. Wealth replacement trust: irrevocable life insurance trust used in conjunction with a charitable remainder trust to replace the asset the heirs of the donor would be losing

8. Income tax charitable deduction limitations

    A. Tax and non-tax characteristics of specific forms of charitable transfers including alternative minimum tax considerations

        (1) A charitable contribution to a qualified charity reduces current income taxes (assuming the donor itemizes deductions). Because the top marginal income tax bracket is currently 38.6 percent (in 2003), the income tax savings to an individual making a gift to charity will generally be greater than previously when the top marginal rate was lower.

        (2) No federal gift tax is payable on a gift to a qualified charity regardless of the size of the gift.

        (3) Gifts to qualified charities can reduce the federal estate tax, with the amount of the deduction limited only by the value of the gift (i.e., the donor's entire estate can be left to charity, and a deduction will be allowed for the entire gift).

        (4) The charity itself will pay no tax upon the receipt of either a lifetime gift or a bequest.

(5) Generally, no income tax will be payable by a qualified charity on income earned by donated property.

(6) If an otherwise deductible charitable contribution to a college or university entitles the donor to purchase tickets for athletic events, 80 percent of the contribution will be deductible.

B. For federal income tax purposes, there are percentage limitations on the amount that can be claimed as a charitable contribution deduction; these depend on the types of property transferred (see Topic 71).

TOPIC 93: USE OF LIFE INSURANCE IN ESTATE PLANNING

1. Advantages and disadvantage

    A. Advantages

    (1) To provide an income to the decedent's family

    (2) To provide cash for payment of the decedent's debts, estate expenses, and taxes—at a "discount," and if arranged properly, with no associated probate costs or death taxes

    (3) To fund business continuation agreements

    B. Disadvantage: If set up improperly, death proceeds may be included in the gross estate.

2. Ownership and beneficiary designation

    A. Selecting owner and beneficiary when the estate is less than the applicable exclusion amount (AEA)

    (1) No transfer taxes are expected, so there are no tax consequences.

    (2) The selection is easy and flexible.

    B. Spouse as owner and beneficiary when estate is likely to exceed AEA

    (1) Naming either spouse as owner or beneficiary of a policy on the life of a spouse will subject the proceeds to transfer taxation at least at the second death. To minimize taxes, neither spouse should be designated owner or beneficiary of an insurance policy on the life of the other.

    (2) A taxable gift occurs when the noninsured spouse is named owner and someone else is beneficiary. To minimize taxes, name whichever spouse is selected as both the owner and beneficiary to avoid gift tax consequences.

    C. Child as owner and beneficiary

    (1) If a child is named owner and beneficiary, he or she can turnover the proceeds to provide liquidity to the estate. However, any transfer of funds to the estate is treated as a gift unless the child is the sole beneficiary of the estate.

    (2) To avoid making a gift, the child could purchase estate assets or lend money to the estate.

3. Life insurance trusts

    Irrevocable trust as owner and beneficiary

    A. Irrevocable life insurance trust (ILIT) is best choice.

    (1) The trust must be irrevocable or IRC Section 2038 will draw the insurance proceeds into the trustor's estate.

    (2) The trustor cannot be named as beneficiary because of Section 2036(a). The trustee is both the owner and beneficiary (usually the uninsured spouse).

(3) A second-to-die policy should be considered if the sole purpose is to pay estate taxes at the death of the second spouse. A term policy should be considered if the couple are younger and have less wealth and the purpose is to replace the financial contribution of the deceased spouse.

B. Impressive outcomes of an ILIT

(1) Excludes the insurance proceeds from income taxation and estate taxation for both spouses

(2) Excludes the insurance proceeds from the probate estates of both spouses

(3) The annual exclusion can be used for gifts to the trust to pay premiums

(4) Ensures that the responsible party will have the needed liquidity after death

(5) Makes proceeds available to the surviving spouse for health, education, maintenance, and support

4. Gift and estate taxation

A. Estate taxation

(1) The decedent's adjusted taxable gift includes the date-of-gift value less the annual exclusion for any life insurance policy the decedent transferred after 1976 and more than three years before death (Section 2001).

(2) If the decedent owned a life insurance policy on the life of another person, the replacement cost of the policy is included in the decedent's gross estate (Section 2033). The three-year rule does not apply to a policy on another's life.

(3) Life insurance proceeds on the life of the decedent are included in the gross estate if the decedent made a transfer of any incidents of ownership in the policy within three years of death [Section 2035(a)].

(4) Life insurance proceeds receivable by a personal representative or receivable by other beneficiaries are included in the gross estate if the decedent possessed any of the incidents of ownership at death (Section 2042).

(5) The transfer must be complete and irrevocable. The donor must give up all incidents of ownership.

(a) The insured must survive three years after the transfer of ownership in order for the insurance to be effectively moved from the estate [Section 2035(a)].

(b) The proceeds of a policy may be included in a decedent's estate even though he or she possessed incidence of ownership in only a fiduciary capacity—for example, as trustee.

(c) Paying premiums is not an incident of ownership.

B. Gift taxation

(1) Transfers of life insurance

(a) Transfers of ownership during life will trigger a gift in the approximate amount of the cash value of the policy.

(b) Gift tax can arise at the death of the insured if the owner and beneficiary are different. For example, assume a wife buys a policy on her husband and names her daughter beneficiary. When the husband dies, she has made a gift to her daughter for the amount of the proceeds.

(c) If a donor makes a gift of a life insurance policy and then dies within three years of making the gift, the value of the proceeds will be brought back into the donor's estate.

        (d) Premiums paid within three years by the insured on a policy the insured does not own will not be pulled back into the estate under Section 2035. These premiums may constitute a taxable gift if they exceed the annual exclusion.

        (e) A transfer by gift of a policy of insurance is subject to gift tax, based on the valuation of the policy at the time of the gift, not on the value of the proceeds at the time of death.

    (2) Gifts of life insurance are valued under different rules:

        (a) If the gift is a paid-up life insurance policy, its value is the replacement cost for a comparable contract with the same company.

        (b) If the gift is a new policy purchased for another person or is transferred immediately after purchase, the value of the gift is the gross premium paid by the donor.

        (c) If the gift is an existing policy for which future premiums are payable, its value is the policy's "interpolated terminal reserve" plus the unearned portion of the paid premium. (This means that the value of the policy's reserve at the date of gift plus the amount of the gross premium paid, which is not yet earned by the insurer, would be the value of the policy.) Note that the portion of the premium the insurer has not earned yet by providing insurance coverage is really owed to the premium payer, who has already paid for the protection not yet received.

        (d) *Note*: If a life insurance policy is transferred to an irrevocable trust, the transfer is a gift of a future interest to the beneficiary of the trust. The value of the gift will be determined by whichever of the previous three rules would be applicable. The donor-grantor cannot use the $11,000 (in 2003) annual exclusion, because a gift in trust is a gift of a future interest, not a present interest.

5. Income taxation

    A. The general rule is that the proceeds of a life insurance policy paid by reason of death are not includible in the deceased's or the beneficiary's gross income for federal income tax purposes.

    B. There is an exception to this general rule, the *transfer for value rule*. If the life insurance policy is acquired by another for a valuable consideration, the difference between the policy's death proceeds and the purchaser's cost basis is includible in the beneficiary's gross income.

    C. The transfer for value rule does not apply to gifts of policies. In addition, the rule does not apply to the following purchasers:

       (1) The insured (or the insured's grantor trust)

       (2) The insured's partner or a partnership in which the insured is a partner

       (3) A corporation in which the insured is a shareholder or officer

       (4) The insured's spouse or incidental to a divorce

       (5) A purchaser whose adjusted basis is determined by reference to the transferor's adjusted basis

    D. The IRS has issued regulations allowing chronically ill and terminally ill insureds to receive "living" or accelerated benefits from their insurance policies, and beneficiaries can avoid income tax on the death benefit.

TOPIC 94: VALUATION ISSUES

1. Estate freezes

   A. Definition of estate freezes

      (1) The primary goal is a reduction in estate taxes by fixing the value of estate assets at current levels. The owner accomplishes the freeze by transferring the appreciation rights to another individual during the owner's lifetime.

      (2) It often is a transaction involving a corporation or partnership, in which the owner of the business transfers interests in property (i.e., common stock) with anticipated future appreciation to a younger family member, while retaining rights in income and principal in the property (i.e., preferred stock).

   B. Corporate and partnership recapitalizations (Section 2701)

      (1) Section 2701 is known as the special gift tax valuation rule, which addresses estate freezes. The gift tax value of a transfer is determined by using Section 2701 special valuation rules to value the interests in the property retained by the transferor.

      (2) Code Section 2701 values certain retained interest at zero, resulting in a higher value of the transferred interest, unless an exception exists.

      (3) The special valuation rules of Section 2701 apply if the following occur:

          (a) A transfer of an interest in a corporation or partnership to a family member of the transferor is made.

          (b) Immediately after the transfer, the transferor or family member holds a retained interest.

      (4) The following types of transfers are excluded from coverage under Code Section 2701:

          (a) Transfers for which market quotations on an established securities market are readily available on the date of transfer for either the interest transferred or for the interest retained by the transferor

          (b) Transfers in which the retained interest is of the same class or proportionately the same class as the transferred interest

          (c) Transfers that proportionately reduce each class of interest held by the transferor and applicable family members immediately before transfer

   C. Transfers in trust

      (1) In determining the value of a transfer of an interest in trust for the benefit of a family member, the value of the retained interest is zero unless the retained interest is a qualified interest. The rule does not apply to incomplete gifts or a transfer of an interest in a personal residence that is inhabited by the holder of a term of interest.

      (2) A qualified interest is as follows:

          (a) Any interest that consists of a right to receive fixed payments at least annually

          (b) Any interest that consists of a right to receive amounts that are payable at least annually and are a fixed percentage of the fair market value of the property in trust

          (c) Any noncontingent remainder interest if all other interests in the trust consist of interests described in the items listed previously

2. Valuation issues with family partnerships and limited liability companies (LLCs)

   A. Purpose and requirements

      (1) Advantages

(a) Gifts of family limited partnership interests are advantageous, because discounts for lack of marketability and minority interests are available to reduce the gift tax value of limited partnership interests. These discounts mean substantial reduction from the value of the underlying business assets, thereby saving transfer costs.

(b) Limited partnership interests can provide some protection against creditors.

(c) The family partnership is more likely to stay intact when there are failed marriages among the owner's children, because the business assets themselves are not under the control of the children.

(2) A family partnership must meet the following three requirements:

(a) Capital invested in the business must be a material income-producing factor. A personal service partnership is not a good candidate for a family partnership.

(b) The donor of the partnership interests must be paid reasonable compensation for services to the partnership.

(c) The share of partnership income attributed to a donee's interest cannot be proportionately greater than the income interest attributed to the donor's interest. Nevertheless, if the donor's interest is a 10 percent general partnership interest and the donees receive 90 percent limited partnership interests, the donees are entitled to 90 percent of the partnership net income.

(3) Family limited partnerships are generally not recommended unless the owners have a net worth of approximately $3 million. Setting up a family limited partnership requires attorney's fees and appraisal fees for the limited partnership interests. Appraisal fees are also required at the time gifts are made of limited partnership interests. Preparation of partnership returns and K-1s will also require some accounting fees.

B. Minority discounts

(1) A minority discount is a valuation discount allowed for an interest in a business because the interest is not a controlling interest.

(2) In most situations, more than 50 percent of the voting shares constitutes a controlling interest, and less than 50 percent is a minority interest.

(3) A minority interest discount is based on a number of factors, including the inability of a minority owner to realize his or her pro rata share of the entity's net assets by liquidating his or her interests in the entity and his or her lack of control over corporate policy.

(4) For transfer tax valuation, minority discounts between 15 and 50 percent are obtainable.

(5) Factors influencing the size of the discount include the overall quality of management, composition of other share holdings, size of the business, history of profitability, existence of business opportunities not currently being exploited, and degree of the company's financial leverage.

C. Marketability discounts

(1) Because of the lack of an established market (i.e., restricted stock, stock in a closely held business, and partnership interest), certain stocks are invariably more difficult to sell than business stock that is publicly traded.

(2) For transfer tax valuation, marketability discounts between 15 and 50 percent are obtainable.

(3) These discounts apply to both minority and majority interests.

(4) Factors influencing the size of the discount include the extent of the resale restrictions, Securities and Exchange Commission (SEC) restraints on marketability, the dollar

value of the stock, the firm's growth expectations, and the size of the company's total assets and equity.

D. Blockage discounts

(1) Large quantities of a stock listed on an exchange can receive a blockage discount if selling them at one time could have a depressing effect on the market price.

(2) If the block represents a controlling interest in the corporation, possibly even triggering a higher price, a premium may be attached to its value.

(3) Blockage discounts may be available for other property, such as a large number of paintings left in the estate of a prominent artist.

E. Key person discounts

(1) A discount may be allowed for a business that lost a key person (i.e., the decedent) who was responsible for its goodwill.

(2) In practice, the IRS will require an executor to show that the loss could not have been avoided by such actions as the purchase of key person life insurance or by other means.

3. Valuation techniques and the federal gross estate tax

A. Selecting valuation date for estate accounts

(1) Date of death
(2) Alternative valuation date

B. Fair market value: For federal transfer taxes, the fundamental principle of valuation is that tax is generally imposed on the fair market value of the property as of the date of the transfer. Fair market value is defined as the price that a willing buyer would pay a willing seller where both had reasonable knowledge of the relevant facts of the transaction and neither was under any compulsion to buy or to sell.

C. The principle of fair market value applies to a wide variety of properties and situations, but there are important exceptions.

(1) Valuing real estate

(a) The value of real property depends on the location, size, shape, condition, defects, physical quality, zoning laws, and any other factors unique to the land.

(b) A *co-ownership discount* is available where one of the co-owners refuses to sell his or her interest either to the estate or to a third party and refuses to buy the interest held by the estate. This lack of cooperation impairs the marketability, and thus the value, of the real property, so a discount is allowed.

(2) Valuing insurance policies

(a) When the donor (owner) of a life insurance policy is not the insured, the value of the gift is the replacement cost of the policy.

(b) Replacement cost is determined in different ways for different policies.

  i. On a paid-up or a single-premium policy, the value is the replacement cost, which is the single premium the insurer would charge for a comparable contract of equal face value on the life of a person who was the insured's age (i.e., at the time of death).

  ii. On an established whole life policy, the value is found by adding any unearned portion of the last premium to the interpolated terminal reserve. The interpolated terminal reserve is the value of the reserve held by the insurer for a policy and calculated as of a given date.

iii. For a term policy, the value of the policy is the unused premium. The same rules apply to valuing a life insurance policy when the deceased owned the policy but was not the insured.

(3) Valuing annuities

   (a) Commercial annuities are annuity contracts issued by companies regularly engaged in sales of annuities, and they are valued at the price at which the company issues comparable contracts.

   (b) For a private annuity contract, the value is determined by the present value of the future payments required under the contract.

(4) Valuing bonds

   (a) The fair market value of publicly traded bonds is the mean between the highest and lowest quoted selling price on the date of death (or alternate valuation date).

   (b) If there was no trading in the bond on the valuation date, the mean prices on the closest trading dates are weighted inversely by the number of days from the valuation date.

   (c) Series EE bonds are valued at their redemption price (market value) as of the date of death. These bonds are neither negotiable nor transferable, and the only definitely ascertainable value is the amount at which the Treasury will redeem them.

   (d) Certain U.S. Treasury bonds, called "flower bonds," may be redeemed at par value if they were owned by the decedent at date of death and are used to pay federal estate taxes. These bonds are valued at the higher of market price or par value.

(5) Valuing stock

   (a) The fair market value of publicly traded stock is the mean between the highest and lowest quoted selling prices on the applicable valuation date.

   (b) If there was no trading of the stock on the valuation date, IRS regulations require use of the mean of the high and low prices on the nearest trading dates before and after the valuation date and then weighting these mean prices. The mean price calculated for a trading date two days from the valuation date will be weighted twice as much as a mean price for a trading date four days from the valuation date.

   (c) *Example*: If the mean price was $10 two days after (or before) the valuation date and was $11 four days before (or after) the date, the valuation date price will be $10.33.

   (d) *Solution*: ($10 × 4 + $11 × 2) / 6 = $10.33

(6) Valuing closely held stock—Valuing the stock of a closely held corporation is difficult because of the lack of an organized market. As with real estate, there are many factors to consider in valuing closely held stock. Among of the factors to consider are the following:

   (a) Nature of the business and history of the enterprise

   (b) Outlook for the economy and for the specific industry in which the company operates

   (c) Book value of the stock

   (d) Earning capacity of the company

   (e) The company's dividend paying capacity

   (f) Goodwill

   (g) Any recent sales of the stock and the size of the block of stock being valued

(h) Fair market value of the stock of comparable companies in the same or similar business and whose stock is publicly traded

(7) Valuing life estates, remainders, and reversions

(a) The fair market value of life estates, remainders, and reversions is their present value.

(b) The calculation of present value is done by consulting the appropriate IRS tables for the present worth of an annuity, of an income interest, and of a remainder interest. The tables show the factors for these three present worth calculations at various interest rates (or discount rates).

(c) There is a separate table showing the factors to use when the annuity or income interest is for a term certain (fixed number of years) and when the annuity or income interest is payable for the life of a designated person. Another table provides the factors to use when an annuity or income interest is payable for the joint lives of "A" and "B"; that is, the income is paid to "A" and "B" and then to the survivor for life.

TOPIC 95: MARITAL DEDUCTION

Note: The estate tax will probably be eliminated for estates of decedents who die after 2009. As such, most estate planning will focus on postponing taxes, with the hope that at least one spouse lives to 2010 or beyond.

1. Characteristics

   A. There is currently no limitation on the amount of property that may qualify for the marital deduction.

   B. The deduction does not apply to a terminable interest.

   C. Advantages of the 100 percent marital deduction

      (1) Simple and inexpensive

      (2) Surviving spouse gets complete control over the assets.

   D. Disadvantages of the 100 percent marital deduction

      (1) Decedent's unified credit is unused.

      (2) The estate tax between the two spouses may be higher for the reason stated in the preceding item (1), assuming the second death occurs before 2010. Both estates are taxed as one estate at the death of the surviving spouse, so the larger the estate, the higher the rate of tax on the top dollar.

2. Terminal interest rule and exceptions

   A. A terminable interest is defined as an interest that ends upon an event or contingency. For example, a spouse initially gets an interest in the property, but this interest terminates upon some event (usually death) and the interest then passes to someone else.

   B. A terminal interest is defined as a property interest with three characteristics:

      (1) It is subject to some future absolute or contingent termination of the surviving spouse's interest.

      (2) The possibility of termination is created by the decedent, and there will be a shift in the interest.

      (3) Some other person or entity (other than the surviving spouse and his or her estate) will possess or own the property.

   C. Exceptions to terminable interest

(1) Under Section 2056(b)(3), if the only condition whereby the surviving spouse's interest may terminate is death in a common disaster or within six months of the decedent's death and such death does not occur

(2) Under Section 2056(b)(5), if the surviving spouse is entitled to all the income for life and the surviving spouse has a general power of appointment

(3) Under Section 2056(b)(7), if the personal representative elects to deduct the value of qualified terminable interest property (QTIP)

(4) Under Section 2056(b)(8), if property is transferred to a qualified charitable remainder trust, where the surviving spouse is the only noncharitable beneficiary

3. QTIP planning and the prior transfer credit

A. The first spouse to die has power of the ultimate disposition of property.

B. For a property transfer to receive QTIP treatment, the following two conditions apply:

(1) An irrevocable election must be made by the donor spouse or by the executor for QTIP, and

(2) The surviving spouse must receive a qualified income interest for life. Income from the trust must be paid at least annually to the surviving spouse.

C. A "qualified income interest" is defined as follows:

(1) The surviving spouse must be entitled to receive all income from the property; in other words:

(a) Some form of distribution of income is mandatory.

(b) Accumulation is not permitted.

(c) Only a spouse can receive the income; no other beneficiaries are permitted.

(2) Income must be paid at least annually.

(3) No person may assign any part of the property to any person other than the surviving spouse.

(4) For federal estate tax purposes, the value of the property is taxable in the surviving spouse's gross estate.

D. Property treated as QTIP and that qualifies for the marital deduction in the owner's estate tax return must be included in the surviving spouse's gross estate. When such QTIP property is later dispersed from the surviving spouse's estate, the executor of the estate is entitled to seek repayment from the recipients for estate taxes paid on the surviving spouse's estate. If reimbursement is not sought, the beneficiaries of the estate may be deemed to have made a gift to the persons from whom reimbursement could have been obtained.

E. Sometimes called a "C" trust or a "Q" trust

4. Special planning for noncitizen spouses

A. IRC Section 2056(d) disallows the marital deduction if the surviving spouse is not a U.S. citizen.

B. If the spouse becomes a citizen before the federal estate tax return is filed (within nine months), IRC Section 2056(d) does not apply. However, the spouse must have been a U.S. resident at the time of the decedent's death.

C. The marital deduction is allowed for property placed in a qualified domestic trust (QDOT) that passes to a non-U.S. surviving spouse.

(1) The executor makes an irrevocable election.

(2) Requires at least one trustee to be a U.S. citizen or U.S. corporation

(3) The trustee has the right to withhold estate tax on distribution.

(4) U.S. laws preside over the qualified domestic trust (QDOT), so whenever a trustee distributes any principal from the trust, estate taxes must be paid to the U.S. Treasury.

(5) U.S. Treasury is given the right to collect taxes at the second death, no matter where the spouse is domiciled. This rule prevents a surviving spouse from taking a marital deduction in the United States and then exiting the country to avoid estate taxes.

(6) To qualify for the marital deduction, the property passing to the QDOT for the noncitizen spouse must also meet all rules pertaining to the marital deduction.

5. Marital deduction and bypass planning

A. A bypass trust (also known as a nonmarital trust or a "B" trust) is generally used to take advantage of the unified credit. Planners sometimes use a method in which a testator's assets are placed in A, B, and Q trusts.

B. A bypass trust is funded with assets equal to the exemption equivalent, and the remaining property is divided in any desired proportion between an A and a QTIP trust.

C. The assets transferred to the bypass trust are taxed at the first spouse's death even though the use of the unified credit results in no tax being due. It bypasses the surviving spouse's estate (or some other income beneficiary's estate) for tax purposes.

D. The bypass trust gives the spouse a right to income, as well as access to principal for purposes of health, education, support, or maintenance, without the property being included in his or her estate at death.

E. Highly appreciated assets are often placed in a bypass trust to freeze the value for estate tax purposes at the death of the first spouse.

F. Upon the death of the first spouse, trusts B and C are funded and become irrevocable. The surviving spouse can control the distribution of assets only according to the terms of those trusts. (He or she may or may not be given a limited power to appoint corpus or to withdraw limited to an ascertainable standard—health, education, maintenance, and support.

G. Trust A can be amended or revoked by the surviving spouse.

TOPIC 96: DEFERRAL AND MINIMIZATION OF ESTATE TAXES

1. Deductions and credits—There are many ways to obtain deductions from and credits for estate taxes:

A. *Interspousal gifting.* Can create significant estate tax savings. By making gifts from a "wealthier" spouse to a "poorer" spouse, large amounts of property can be removed from an estate.

B. *Charitable deductions.* Outright transfers to qualified charities are 100 percent deductible for both estate and gift tax purposes.

C. *Funeral, debts, losses.* Cost of the funeral, debts of the decedent, losses incurred during estate administration, and debts of the estate are all deductible from estate taxes.

D. *Credit for pre-1977 gifts.* The amount of this credit is limited to the lesser of the gift tax or the estate tax on property that is included in the estate.

E. *Prior transfer credit.* A tax credit is allowed where property is included in the transferor's taxable estate and the transferee dies within 10 years of the transferor. The inherited property does not have to be found in the transferee's estate.

F. *Foreign death taxes.* A credit is allowed for most, but not all, foreign death taxes paid on property that is included in the U.S. gross estate and situated in a foreign country.

2. Lifetime planning techniques—Developing an estate plan should result in a set of recommendations that allow for the best use, conservation, and transfer of the client's wealth. In 1996, the Certified Financial Planner Board of Standards, Inc., identified the following steps in the financial planning process:

   A. The planner must take the lead in explaining to the client the estate planning process. Planners must make their role clear and should set forth their responsibilities in an engagement letter, spelling out the services to be preformed. Planners must also make the client aware of his or her own tasks, including gathering data, working with the planner to implement the plan, and informing the planner of any changes that may affect the original plan.

   B. A planner must obtain sufficient information about the client and the client's family in order to make recommendations that are worthwhile. Estate planning opportunities exist for wealthy married couples seeking to transfer an estate to the next generation, single wealthy parents, young couples with minor children, couples whose children are grown, or any other of a myriad of family statuses. The planner may want to consider family members for positions such as executor, guardian, and trustee. The planner must be sensitive to special concerns (e.g., health needs, children with drug addictions). In these situations, consider trust planning that provides for long-term asset management.

   C. After gathering the essential information, the planner reviews the facts and prepares preliminary recommendations; the planner should be prepared to offer alternatives as well. The most common recommendations fall into two areas: planning for property transfers and planning for the client's incapacity and/or death.

   D. The key purpose of the plan is to efficiently distribute the client's wealth to the appropriate persons, in the appropriate amounts, and at the appropriate time. To do this, the planner must keep in mind the following considerations that relate to more specific estate planning goals:

      (1) Deciding whether to use a trust or some other means to avoid probate

      (2) Examining alternatives to reduce and possibly eliminate transfer taxes at the death of the client and the client's spouse

      (3) Considering lifetime transfers, partly to reduce transfer costs and partly to shift taxable income to a person in a lower tax bracket

      (4) Arranging to provide the needed liquidity at the client's death or disability

      (5) Devising a strategy to unwind the client's business affairs in a manner that maintains the greatest income and value for the survivors

   E. After the planner and the client iron out the specifics of the plan, together they should start the process of implementing the plan. Contact an attorney to draft transfer documents that will be executed by the client. Use an insurance agent to prepare the appropriate insurance contracts. If necessary, contact the bank that houses the trust department the client wishes to use as a trustee. The client should feel comfortable with the bank's trust department personnel, including their investment philosophy and how they relate to trust beneficiaries.

   F. Laws change, and the client's personal situation and objectives may change. The planner should, from time to time, meet with the client and monitor the plan's progress. By keeping current, the planner can periodically suggest appropriate revisions to the plan. Events that are likely to require plan revision include marriage, divorce, birth of a child, new legislation, and new court decisions.

3. Postmortem planning techniques

   A. Defined—There are almost always many decisions to make after a death occurs. Postmortem estate planning primarily entails:

(1) Filing the appropriate tax returns
(2) Making the proper elections
(3) Planning estate distributions
(4) Determining whether any disclaimers can and should be made
(5) Selecting the appropriate valuation date for assets

B. Qualified disclaimers

(1) A disclaimer is one means of changing the original estate plan. A disclaimer is simply a formal refusal of an inheritance of property from a decedent. Such a refusal is still a taxable gift unless one satisfies the IRC requirements for a "qualified disclaimer." Under the qualified disclaimer rules, an estate beneficiary may avoid receipt of the property bequeathed by the deceased, thereby avoiding any gift tax.

(2) A qualified disclaimer must meet the following requirements:

   (a) The disclaimer must be irrevocable and unqualified.
   (b) The disclaimer must be in writing.
   (c) The disclaimer must be delivered to the grantor or grantor's legal representative within nine months of the date of transfer or within nine months after a minor turns 21 years of age.
   (d) The disclaiming person must not receive any benefit from the property disclaimed and must not have any control over the disposition of the property after disclaiming.

(3) A qualified disclaimer is also used to reduce estate taxes.

(4) *Example*: The Beaver disclaims a bequest from his father. The property may then pass to June, his mother, under the residuary clause of his father's (Ward) will. This transfer will be eligible for the marital deduction, and no estate tax will be due on the transferred property. On the other hand, June may elect to disclaim a bequest from Ward to reduce the amount of property qualifying for the marital deduction and to take advantage of the unified credit (i.e., using a bypass trust). This disclaimer will reduce the estate tax when June dies, thus reducing overall estate taxes on both estates.

(5) Some estate planners use a disclaimer trust. A disclaimer trust is created under the terms set forth in the will of a decedent. A disclaimer trust has the following attributes:

   (a) It is irrevocable.
   (b) Any property the surviving spouse disclaims will be transferred to the trust.
   (c) Earnings from the trust will be paid to the spouse at specified intervals.
   (d) The surviving spouse cannot retain any rights to invade the principal.
   (e) If the surviving spouse remarries, at his or her death the trust assets will pass to a beneficiary other than the surviving spouse.
   (f) The surviving spouse has only a life interest, so the assets will not be included in the gross estate of the surviving spouse.
   (g) The trust assets will not qualify for the marital deduction, so the decedent's estate will make greater use of the unified estate tax credit.

C. Alternative valuation date

(1) An executor can make election to value an estate six months after the date of death, only if it reduces the value of the estate for tax purposes.

(2) The alternate valuation date is used when property within an estate declines in value after the decedent's death. Likely candidates for this valuation method are securities or stock in a closely held business, which can decline during the period of estate settlement.

(3) All assets disposed of between the date of death and the alternative valuation date are valued on the date of disposition.

(4) All wasting assets are valued as of the date of death, regardless of selecting the alternative valuation date.

    (a) Annuities

    (b) Leases

    (c) Patents

    (d) Installment sales

D. Relief provisions for business owners' and farmers'/ranchers' estates

  (1) Deferral of estate taxes (Section 6166)

    (a) Allows estate tax for a closely held business to be paid over 14 years

      i. The first four payments are interest-only payments starting on the one-year anniversary of the original due date.

      ii. Starting in the fifth year, the estate pays the estate tax in 10 installments.

    (b) The interest paid on the deferred tax is at a lower rate than the regular rate for underpaid tax payments.

    (c) Three conditions must be satisfied.

      i. The value of the decedent's interest in the business must be at least 35 percent of the value of the adjusted gross estate.

      ii. Must be an interest in a closely held business

        • Sole proprietorship

        • Partnership in which at least 20 percent of the capital interest is included in the decedent's gross estate or that has 15 or fewer partners

        • A corporation in which at least 20 percent of the voting stock is included in the decedent's gross estate or that has 15 or fewer shareholders

      iii. The business must have been carrying on trade at the time of the decedent's death.

  (2) Corporate stock redemptions (Section 303)

    (a) In general, when closely held corporations buy back stock from its shareholders, the proceeds must be treated as dividend income unless it falls under Section 303.

    (b) If an estate qualifies for Section 303, the proceeds received from the redemption are classified as capital gain, usually long-term; if an estate does not qualify for Section 303, the proceeds are treated as ordinary income.

    (c) Under this rule, stock may be redeemed from an estate equal to the total amount of all estate taxes, inheritances taxes, estate administration costs, and funeral expenses.

    (d) The owner's death steps up the adjusted basis in the stock, so there is little to no gain reported.

    (e) Certain requirements must be met to qualify for this tax treatment:

      i. The stock to be redeemed must be included in the decedent's gross estate.

      ii. The value of the stock included in the gross estate must exceed 35 percent of the decedent's AGE.

        • Stock in two or more corporations may be combined for this percentage requirement if 20 percent or more of the outstanding stock of each corporation is included in the decedent's gross estate.

- This percentage test must be met both before and after adding to the gross estate the property transferred within three years of death.

    iii. One cannot redeem more than the total of federal and state death taxes, GSTT, administration and funeral expenses. The executor cannot use the Section 303 redemption to pay debts of the estate.

    iv. Only those beneficiaries responsible for paying estate taxes can employ the Section 303 redemption. If stock is left to one heir and the taxes are payable out of the residuary estate passing to a different heir, the Section 303 redemption is not available.

(3) Special use valuation [Section 2032(a)]

    (a) Under Section 2032(a) of the Internal Revenue Code, an executor may elect special use valuation for real estate used in a closely held business or for farming.

    (b) The reduced valuation is made on the basis of the current actual use rather than its highest and best use.

    (c) *Example*: Assume a farm was originally located outside a city, but urban growth has approached the farm. The FMV of the farm is significantly higher than the value of its actual use. If taxes were levied on its FMV, the heirs would probably have to sell the farm. However, valuation at its actual use enables the heirs to continue to carry on with business.

    (d) The maximum reduction allowed by special use valuation is $820,000 in 2002. The maximum reduction of $820,000 will be indexed for inflation.

    (e) There are five requirements under Section 2032(a).

        i. The property must be held for "qualified use" and actively managed by the decedent and the decedent's family for five out of eight years prior to the decedent's death.

        ii. The value of the real *and* personal property ("qualified property") portion must equal at least 50 percent of the gross estate after deduction of secured debt and mortgages.

        iii. The real property portion must be at least 25 percent of the gross estate after deduction of secured debt and mortgages.

        iv. The qualifying property must pass to qualifying heirs. The heirs sign a recapture agreement stating that the taxes saved will be recaptured by the government if the heirs do not continue the qualified use for at least 10 years after the decedent's death.

        v. On the date of the decedent's death, the real estate must be used as a farm or in a closely held business.

(4) Qualified family-owned business exclusion (Section 2057)

    (a) The family-owned business deduction is coordinated with the unified credit, so the unified credit increases as the deduction decreases.

    (b) The family-owned business deduction is an exclusion equal to the difference between $1,300,000 and the AEA for the year the business owner died.

    (c) That is, an estate of a person dying in 2003 can claim a deduction of $300,000 and have an AEA of $1,000,000 (i.e., a unified credit of $345,800) or some other in-between combination, as long as the total does not exceed $1,300,000.

    (d) This deduction is eliminated for estates of decedents dying after 2003.

    (e) To claim this deduction, the following requirements must be met:

      i. The decedent must have been a citizen or resident of the United States at the time of death.

     ii. The decedent must have materially participated in the business for five of the eight years preceding the decedent's death.

    iii. The interest must be a "qualified" family-owned business.

    iv. The net value of the business interest that passes to "qualified heirs" must equal at least 50 percent of the decedent's AGE. In contrast to the requirements in Section 2032(a), unsecured debts (claims against the estate) as well as mortgages and liens are deducted to arrive at AGE.

     v. The executor must make the election on the estate tax return and file a tax recapture agreement signed by all qualified heirs.

4. Optimal QTIP planning

  A. The QTIP election is yet another postmortem planning technique that can reduce federal estate taxes. The QTIP election allows an executor to qualify property for the marital deduction that under normal circumstances would not have met the requirements.

  B. As stated earlier, to qualify property for the estate tax marital deduction, property left to the spouse cannot be terminable. The QTIP allows for an exception to this rule. If the executor chooses QTIP treatment, the property will provide a life income for the surviving spouse, but *must* be included in his or her gross estate.

  C. The QTIP is not always desirable. If the surviving spouse already has a large estate, adding more property to it will result in increased estate taxes at his or her death.

TOPIC 97: INTRAFAMILY AND OTHER BUSINESS TRANSFER TECHNIQUES

1. Characteristics

  A. Family partnership

    (1) A single or multiple type of partnership interest owned solely and exclusively by a member of a family

    (2) Partnership interests are often gifted from an older family member to a younger one.

  B. Stock recapitalization or partnership capital freeze

    (1) Involves restructuring of an entity's capital structure through the creation of at least two capital classes (corporate shares or partnership interests), and then the exchange of one capital class for another

    (2) With a recapitalization, a senior family member usually exchanges common shares that bear all future appreciation for preferred voting shares that have a fixed (par) value. The common shares are then gifted to a junior family member.

    (3) With a partnership capital freeze, a senior family member usually exchanges a regular partnership interest for a fixed partnership interest that has a preferred right to income distribution. Through gifts, junior family members usually receive regular partnership interests that have sole rights to any partnership appreciation.

  C. Personal holding company

    (1) A C Corporation formed for the purpose of transferring appreciated property in other companies to the new holding company in exchange for its stock

    (2) The corporation is taxed as a personal holding company if it meets two concurrent tests: (1) Five or fewer shareholders must own more than one-half of outstanding stock, and (2) at least 60 percent of the company's adjusted ordinary gross income must be

"personal holding company income" such as dividends, interest, rents, or amounts received in return for personal services.

(3) It is usually capitalized with a large amount of nonvoting common stock and a small amount of voting common stock. The owner maintains control through the voting stock while systematically gifting the nonvoting common stock to other family members to limit the future appreciation includable in his or her own estate to that on the smaller number of voting shares.

2. Techniques

A. Buy-sell agreements

(1) A buy-sell agreement is a contract binding the owner of a business interest to sell the business interest for a specified or determinable price at his or her death or disability and a designated purchaser to buy at that time.

(2) If a fixed price is used in the buy-sell agreement, the IRS will take a long look at it. Planners should suggest the client use a formula that allows for the business value to increase or decrease as time passes. If a formula is not appealing, then an appraisal of the business at the time of the decedent's death will help avoid the IRS's scrutinizing the value of the agreement.

B. Installment notes

(1) Installment sales provide for payment of the purchase price over a period of years. Such sales allow the estate to recognize the capital gains as payments are received, rather than all at once.

(2) This technique can also be beneficial to the buyer, inasmuch as the buyer is not required to complete the buy-sell agreement with one lump sum. Sometimes an installment sale is part of a family transaction.

C. Self-canceling installment notes (SCIN)

(1) A self-canceling note in usually triggered by the death of the person holding the note. The note may be canceled before full payment is received.

(2) The initial value of an SCIN is less than an installment note, so the buyer has to give additional consideration in the form of a higher principal amount or higher interest rate.

(3) In determining the higher principal payments, the IRS tables can be used to determine the likelihood of the note holder's death. The older the individual, the greater the consideration.

(4) Planners may recommend an SCIN when estate tax rates exceed marginal income tax rates.

D. Private annuities

(1) A private annuity is an exchange of an asset for an unsecured promise by the buyer to pay an annuity for the life of the transferor.

(2) A private annuity commonly provides life payments to the annuitant. Taking the payments in this way allows the annuitant to spread the capital gains from the sale, rather than accepting them in one lump sum.

(3) The private annuity contract must be unsecured, so the annuitant-to-be should make sure the entity making the annuity payments is sound financially.

(4) A private annuity allows a person with a large estate to remove possible future appreciation from the estate and spread out capital gains, both actions reducing current income tax.

E. Transfer in trust

    (1) If a grantor seeks to freeze estate values, a transfer in trust will often fill the need.

    (2) Transfers in trust work by splitting property into two parts: remainder interest and income interest.

3. Federal income, gift, and estate implications

    A. Buy-sell agreements

        (1) Gift taxation: Generally, there is no gift taxation unless the buyout agreement gives the purchaser an unqualified present purchase right at a contract price below fair market value.

        (2) Income taxation

            (a) The selling owner, usually the estate of the deceased, sells a capital asset subject to capital gain treatment. However, there is usually no capital gain treatment because the buyer receives a stepped-up basis at fair market value.

            (b) The selling party is taxed on the proceeds of the business as dividends, to the extent of the corporation's earnings, unless the corporation qualifies for IRC Sections 302 and 303.

        (3) Estate taxation

            (a) To set the estate tax value of a business equal to its buyout agreement price, agreements must meet Section 2703(b) requirements:

                i. The agreement must be a bona fide arrangement.

                ii. The agreement must not be a device to transfer the property to members of the decedent's family for less than full and adequate consideration.

                iii. The terms of the agreement must be comparable to similar arrangements entered into by persons in an arm's-length transaction.

            (b) The requirements ensure a value reasonably close to the value of the business interest at time of transfer.

            (c) *Example*: If a surviving owner, a son, is allowed to buy the decedent parent's $1 million business interest at $250,000, this would be in violation of the first two requirements.

    B. Installment notes

        (1) Gift taxation: No gift tax consequences if it is a bona fide sale for full and adequate consideration

        (2) Income taxation

            (a) Can defer capital gains over several years

            (b) Interest paid to seller is treated as ordinary income (tax-deductible for buyer if qualified); principal is return of capital and capital gain.

            (c) Losses are never reported.

            (d) Two events trigger immediate recognition of remaining gain to the seller:

                i. The seller sells the installment note.

                ii. The seller cancels the installment note.

            (e) Consequences of (1) and (2): The seller has received taxable income. The income is equal to the difference between the cost basis and the value of the payments forgiven.

        (3) Estate taxation

(a) Keeps postsale appreciation out of the seller's gross estate

(b) When the holder of an installment note dies, only the present value of the installment note is included in his or her gross estate.

(c) If the transfer was a partial gift (less than full and adequate consideration paid), the date-of-death value of the property sold less actual consideration paid is included in the estate.

C. Self-canceling installment notes

(1) Gift taxation—To avoid gift taxes, the buyer will have to make additional principal payments or pay higher interest rates. In determining the higher principal payments, the IRS tables can be used to determine the likelihood of the note holder's death.

(2) Income taxation

(a) The decedent note holder must report the difference between the fair market value and the basis on the estate's income tax return upon cancellation. The gain is income in respect of decedent.

(b) No income tax deduction is allowed, inasmuch as the note is not in the gross estate.

(3) Estate taxation: The value of the SCIN at the note holder's death will not have to be included in the holder's gross estate.

D. Private annuities

(1) Gift taxation

(a) No taxable gift

(b) Value of property transferred equals present value of annuity.

(2) Income taxation

(a) Each payment is split into three parts:

    i. *Investment in the contract.* Tax free

    ii. *Gain in asset.* Taxed as capital gain

    iii. *Balance after investment in the contract and the gain in asset are removed.* Taxed as ordinary income

(b) Once the annuitant reaches original life expectancy, all investments in contract and gains have been paid, and future payments are solely ordinary income.

(c) The unrecovered basis is deductible as a loss if the annuitant does not reach life expectancy.

(d) The person or entity making the annuity payments cannot deduct any portion of the payments.

(3) Estate taxation

(a) No estate tax

(b) Lifetime annuity terminates at the death of the annuitant.

(c) If the annuity is worth less than the property transferred, then the original transaction is ruled a gift and the gross estate includes the entire date-of-death value of the property, reduced by payments already received. This is deemed a Section 2036(a) transfer with a retained interest.

E. Transfers in trust (general tax objectives)

(1) Gift taxation

(a) Keeps retained interest value at zero

(b) No gift tax for transfers to qualified charities

(2) Income taxation

(a) Grantor pays trust income.

(b) Grantor has income tax deduction for charitable trusts.

(3) Estate taxation—removes assets and/or postappreciation from the estate

TOPIC 98: DISPOSITION OF ESTATE

1. Tax and nontax consequences of various estate plans (outright distributions, transfers in trust, etc.)

   A. Tax implications

      (1) *Income tax.* Income (dividends, etc.) generated by the property will be taxed to the donee after the transfer. The donee's basis is the lesser of

         (a) The fair market value (FMV)

         (b) The donor's basis, with an adjustment for the gift tax paid

      (2) *Gift tax.* Complete versus incomplete gifts. If a donor can unilaterally retrieve the gifted property, there has not been a completed transfer. Therefore, the gift tax is not triggered (contrast the tax implications of this with a completed gift with a retained interest). However, if the transfer is a completed gift, the donor will have a gift tax liability to the extent that the FMV of the gift on the date of the transfer is greater than the available annual exclusion and/or any permissible charitable or marital deductions.

      (3) *"Tax exclusive" nature of gifts.* A donor will not pay gift tax on the funds that are used to pay the gift tax. In contrast, the estate tax is "tax inclusive," meaning that the estate will pay taxes on the funds that will be used to pay the estate taxes. Consequently, if all other factors are equal, from a transfer tax perspective, it is less expensive to transfer assets during lifetime than at death.

      (4) *Impact of gifting on the estate tax.* A completed gift that does not involve a retained interest will usually affect a decedent's potential estate tax calculation by

         (a) Decreasing the value of the gross estate

         (b) Increasing the value of the adjusted taxable gift

         (c) Decreasing the tax base

   B. Custodial gifts (UGMA and UTMA)

      (1) Income from custodial property is taxed to the minor (at a rate based on the kiddie tax) whether distributed or not, except to the extent that it is used to discharge a parental obligation of support (in the latter situation, it is taxed to the parent).

      (2) Gift tax liability is triggered by the irrevocable transfer. Because the child is legal title holder, the gift is one of a present interest, qualifying each dollar of gifted custodial property for a dollar of annual exclusion (up to the applicable maximum annual limit).

   C. Section 2503(b) mandatory income trust

      (1) Income tax: Unlike a custodial account, the trust is a taxable entity separate from the beneficiaries. However, because income must be distributed to the income beneficiaries, it is taxable to them at the appropriate tax rate.

      (2) Gift tax liability is triggered by the irrevocable transfer. The mandatory distribution of income creates a present interest qualifying for an annual exclusion. However, because the gift to the trust is split between the income (present interest) and remainder (future interest) beneficiaries, only part of each dollar of gift property (the portion going to the income beneficiary) will qualify for the annual exclusion.

D. Section 2503(c) minor's trust

(1) The trust is a separate taxable entity. Any income distributed to the minor is taxable to the minor in the year received. Income that is accumulated is taxed to the trust. Distribution at the termination of the trust is made tax free to the minor; the throwback rule does not apply to minors.

(2) Because the federal tax code mandates present interest treatment of gifts to a Section 2503(c) trust, the gift tax results are the same as for custodial accounts.

E. Crummey trust

(1) Income tax: Because the transfer is irrevocable, there are no income tax implications to the grantor unless rights prohibited under the grantor trust rules have been retained.

(2) An irrevocable transfer creates a completed gift that can be offset by the annual exclusions, limited by the aggregate amount that the holders of the Crummey right are entitled to withdraw, because it is the withdrawal right that creates a present interest.

2. Estate planning for nontraditional relationships

A. Children of another relationship: Techniques to avoid disinheritance are placing property in joint tenancy with right of survivorship (WROS), establishing trusts, and lifetime gifting.

B. Cohabitation

(1) Not eligible to take advantage of the marital deduction. This means that estate taxes cannot be deferred.

(2) Liquidity is a primary consideration.

(3) Wills containing specific bequests are very important.

C. Adoptions

For probate, an adopted child is able to inherit from the adopted parent but not from the natural parent who gave up the child.

D. Same-sex relationships

(1) Not eligible to take advantage of the marital deduction. This means that estate taxes cannot be deferred.

(2) Liquidity is a primary consideration.

(3) Wills containing specific bequests are very important.

E. Communal relationships

(1) Not eligible to take advantage of the marital deduction. This means that estate taxes cannot be deferred.

(2) Liquidity is a primary consideration.

(3) Wills containing specific bequests are very important.

TOPIC 99: GENERATION-SKIPPING TRANSFER TAX (GSTT)

1. Transfers subject to the GSTT

A. If at an individual's death property is passed to someone two generations younger than the owner, a generation-skipping transfer tax will be imposed. The tax deters grandparents from passing assets to their grandchildren and thus denying the government of tax dollars for another generation. The IRS wants property in an estate to be taxed in each generation. This tax is imposed at the highest federal estate and gift tax rate (49 percent in 2003). The amount of gift tax depends on whether the transfer involves a direct skip, a taxable distribution, or a taxable termination.

B. Direct skip

   (1) A transfer subject to an estate or gift tax, made to a skip person

   (2) *Example*: A gift from a grandparent to his or her grandchild, or a transfer to a trust in which all the beneficiaries are skip persons

   (3) The transferor pays the GST tax in a direct skip at the time of transfer.

   (4) The tax in a direct skip is *tax exclusive*. The taxable amount does not include the amount of generation-skipping tax.

   (5) *Example*: A grandfather makes a lifetime gift to his granddaughter, Martha, in 2003. Assume no exemptions are available. The grandfather pays a generation-skipping tax of $490,000. However, the tax is paid out of additional assets of the grandparent, and not out of the gift. The full $1,120,000 is passed to the grandchild.

C. Taxable distributions

   (1) Any distribution of income or corpus from a trust to a skip person that is not otherwise subject to estate or gift tax

   (2) *Example*: A distribution from a trust to a grandson of the grantor is considered a skip-person distribution.

   (3) The transferee pays the GST tax in a taxable distribution. If the trust pays the tax for the transferee, the payment is treated as an additional taxable distribution.

   (4) The tax payable upon a taxable distribution is *tax inclusive*. This means the amount subject to tax includes

      (a) The property
      (b) GST tax itself

   (5) *Example*: If a trustee makes a taxable distribution of $9,000 of trust income to a grandchild in 2003, the tax is 49 percent of $9,000, or $4,410. It must be paid out of the property passing to the grandchild. Therefore, the grandchild nets only $5,590.

D. Taxable terminations

   (1) Termination by death, lapse of time, release of power, or otherwise, of an interest in property held in trust results in the skip person's holding all the interests in the trust.

   (2) *Example*: Ben leaves his life income to his son, Bart, and the remainder goes to his granddaughter, Melanie. The son's death terminates his life interest and it passes to Melanie, a skip person.

   (3) A taxable termination cannot occur as long as one nonskip person has a present interest in the property.

   (4) There is no taxable termination if an estate or gift tax is imposed on the nonskip person at termination.

   (5) The trustee pays the GST tax in a taxable termination.

   (6) The tax payable upon a taxable termination is *tax inclusive* because the property subject to the transfer includes the generation-skipping tax.

2. Impact of the GSTT on lifetime transfers

A. Outright transfer of cash or property

   (1) A generation-skipping transfer (GST) is any transfer of property by gift or at death, to any person who, under federal tax law, is assigned to a generation that is two or more generations below that of the transferor.

   (2) *Two or more generations* refers to grandchildren and great nieces and nephews and any generations beyond. People belonging to these generations are referred to as *skip persons*.

(3) GSTT is a separate tax from the unified gift and estate tax and is in addition to these taxes. It is possible that the total cost of making a property transfer can exceed the value of the gift.

(4) A flat tax equal to the highest gift and estate tax rate is imposed on every generation-skipping transfer.

(5) There is a special rule called the *predeceased ancestor exception*. This rule will "move up" lower generations if the parent in the line of descent dies before the transfer. The predeceased ancestor exception applies only if the parent was deceased at the time of transfer.

(6) The GSTT applies to

    (a) Property placed in trust
    (b) Transfers involving the creation of life estates
    (c) Remainders
    (d) Insurance and annuity contracts

(7) Generation assignment

    (a) Related persons are assigned to the ancestral chain relating back to the grandparents of the transferor, except that the spouse of the transferor is always assigned to the same generation as the transferor or descendant.

    (b) Unrelated persons are assigned to the transferor's generation if they are not more than 12½ years younger than the transferor; otherwise, unrelated persons are assigned to succeeding generations on the basis of 25 years for each generation (i.e., first younger generation—12½ to 37½ years younger than transferor).

B. Transfer in trust

(1) A gift in trust that qualifies for the gift tax annual exclusion may still be subject to the GSTT. The gift in trust will qualify for the GSTT annual exclusion only if the trust meets the following two requirements:

    (a) The trust must state that it will make no distribution to any person other than the beneficiary during his or her lifetime.

    (b) At the beneficiary's death, the trust assets must be includable in the beneficiary's gross estate for federal estate tax purposes.

(2) To fulfill these requirements, grandparents often set up a separate trust for each grandchild. Crummey trusts or Section 2503(c) trusts can generally be designed to take advantage of the GSTT annual exclusion.

3. Exemptions and exclusions for the GSTT

A. Outright lifetime gifts that qualify for the gift tax annual exclusion are excluded from GST tax.

B. The GSTT exemption

(1) For a married couple, each spouse has a GSTT exemption. Therefore, each spouse can use some or all of his or her GSTT exemption to avoid GST tax. In this way, the exemption can be doubled.

(2) A flat tax equal to the gift and estate tax at the highest rate is imposed on every generation-skipping transfer.

Year	Exemption	GSTT Rate
2003	$1,060,000*	49%
2004	$1.5 million	48%
2005	$1.5 million	47%
2006	$2 million	46%
2007	$2 million	45%
2008	$2 million	45%
2009	$3.5 million	45%
2010	Tax repealed	Tax repealed

*Plus increases for indexing for inflation

C. Qualified transfer payments (educational and medical): Payments of educational or medical expenses are excluded from GST tax.

TOPIC 100: FIDUCIARY RESPONSIBILITIES

1. Duties of fiduciary

   A. "Fiduciary" is simply a generic title given to individuals and organizations that have been given the power to manage assets owned by another. Persons considered fiduciaries include an executor, administrator, personal representative, and custodian.

   B. The following duties generally apply to fiduciaries:

   (1) *Exercise loyalty in making decisions concerning the estate.* As a fiduciary, one is expected to act for the benefit of the estate's beneficiaries. Confidentiality is implied in this duty.

   (2) *Exercise care, diligence, and prudence in handling the estate's property.* This duty requires the fiduciary to act "with the skill and care that a prudent man or woman would exercise in administering his or her own affairs."

   (3) *Preserve and protect estate assets.* Preservation can include providing adequate security for coin, stamp, art, and other types of collections. It also includes a duty to protect capital and to make investment assets productive. In dealing with investments, it is the fiduciary's conduct, rather than investment results, that is reviewed.

2. Selection of fiduciary

   A. Look for the following qualities when selecting a fiduciary:

   (1) Likelihood of the person chosen to outlive the testator
   (2) Skill in managing legal and financial affairs
   (3) Familiarity with the testator's estate and the testator's wishes
   (4) Strong integrity coupled with loyalty to the testator
   (5) Impartiality and absence of conflicts of interest

   B. The following are three of the most often used fiduciaries:

   (1) Family member or friend

   (a) Choosing a family member or a friend will often help with administration costs, and such persons normally possess a strong degree of loyalty.
   (b) Weakness: Knowledge of legal and financial issues is usually limited. Longevity may also be an issue.

   (2) Corporate executor

       (a) Banks usually do an adequate job in managing estate assets. They have experience in handling legal and financial affairs, their longevity is strong, and they can be impartial when dealing with conflicts.

       (b) Weakness: Banks are usually unfamiliar with the decedent's family and may have trouble deciding who gets minor personal effects for which the decedent did not give guidance. Many banks also require the estate to be of a certain size before agreeing to be executor.

   (3) Attorney

       (a) Probate attorneys usually do a good job in managing assets during the probate period, because they possess substantial knowledge in this area. Depending on the attorney, financial dealings may or may not be a strong point.

       (b) Weakness: Administration costs will usually be high, because an attorney executor may hire another attorney to represent the estate. There may be conflicts of interest; an attorney who anticipates becoming a fiduciary may insert an exculpation clause in the will, which would shelter the attorney from simple negligence acts.

TOPIC 101: INCOME IN RESPECT OF A DECEDENT (IRD)

1. IRD assets

   A. From Treasury Regulation Section 1.691 (a)-1(b):

> In general, the term "income in respect of a decedent" refers to those amounts to which a decedent was entitled as gross income but which were not properly includible in computing his [or her] taxable income for the taxable year ending with the date of his [or her] death or for a previous taxable year under the method of accounting employed by the decedent.

   B. IRD is income that the decedent earned but, because of his or her death, was not constructively received and is not includable in his or her taxable income. An example is salary earned but not paid. Because the taxpayer was not paid until after his or her death, it could not be included on his or her final income tax return.

   C. Examples of IRD

     (1) If the decedent completed all events sufficient to close a sale, but did not collect the proceeds before death, the amount collected after death will be IRD.

     (2) If the decedent had a contingent claim to sales proceeds, the completion of the agreement after death will result in IRD.

     (3) Dividends on stocks paid after the stockholder's death

     (4) The forgiveness of debt on an installment note

     (5) Distributions made after death from a qualified plan or IRA

2. IRD income tax deduction

   A. IRD is subject to both the estate tax and income tax. Some of this double taxation can be offset:

     (1) The recipient of the IRD is entitled to an income tax deduction for that portion of the estate taxes attributed to including IRD in the gross estate.

     (2) An income tax deduction is allowed for generation-skipping transfer taxes ascribed to IRD items included in a taxable termination, or direct skips caused by the transferor's death.

   B. A deduction is allowed each year the IRD is included in income. To compute the deduction, all items treated as IRD in the gross estate are aggregated. The total is reduced by all DRD (deductions in respect of a decedent) to arrive at net value. The value of the IRD is the lesser of the amount included in the gross estate or the amount included in income. Once the net value is determined, estate taxes are recomputed by excluding the net value from the gross estate. The difference between the original estate tax and the recomputed estate tax is the IRD deduction.

BIBLIOGRAPHY

Beam, B. T., D. L. Bickelhaupt, and R. M. Crowe. *Fundamentals of Insurance For Financial Planning*. Bryn Mawr, PA: The American College, 2000.

Bost, J. B. *Estate Planning and Taxation*. 2001-2002 ed. Dubuque, IO: Kendall/Hunt Publishing Company, 2001.

CCH. *CCH Financial and Estate Planning Guide*. 13th ed. Chicago: CCH Incorporated, 2001.

CCH. *CCH Guide to Tax Planning for Individuals and Small Businesses*. 2nd ed. Chicago: CCH Incorporated, 2002.

CCH. *CCH Tax Planning Strategies*. 2002–2003 ed. Chicago: CCH Incorporated, 2002.

Cordell, D. M. *Fundamentals of Financial Planning*. 4th ed. Bryn Mawr, PA: The American College, 1999.

Gear Up, Inc. *1040 Individual Income Tax (2002)*. Portland, OR: Gear Up, Inc., 2002.

Graber, R. S. and W. J. Woerheide. *Fundamentals of Investments For Financial Planning*. 2nd ed. Bryn Mawr, PA: The American College, 2002.

Hearth, D. and J. K. Zaima. *Contemporary Investments: Security and Portfolio Analysis*. 3rd ed. Fort Worth, TX: Harcourt, Inc., 2001.

Hoyle, B. J. *Wiley CPA Examination Review Fast Track Study Guide*. 2nd ed. New York: John Wiley & Sons, Inc., 2001.

Jones, C. P. *Investments: Analysis and Management*. 7th ed. New York: John Wiley & Sons, Inc., 2000.

Jones, M. J. *The Pension Answer Book*. Special Supplement—Final Regulations Governing Minimum Required Distributions. New York: Panel Publishers, 2002.

Jones, S. M. *Principles of Taxation for Business and Investment Planning*. 2002 ed. New York: McGraw-Hill Irwin, 2002.

Krass, S. J. *The Pension Answer Book*. 2002 ed. New York: Panel Publishers, 2002.

Kurlowicz, T., J. F. Ivers, and J. J. McFadden. *Planning for Business Owners and Professionals*. 8th ed. Bryn Mawr, PA: The American College, 2002.

Leimberg, S. R., J. A. Kasner, S. N. Kandell, R. G. Miller, M. S. Rosenbloom, H. L. Levy, and T. C. Polacek. *The Tools & Techniques of Estate Planning*. 12th ed. Cincinnati, OH: The National Underwriter Company, 2001.

Leimberg, S. R., M. J. Satinsky, R. T. LeClair, and R. J. Doyle. *The Tools & Techniques of Financial Planning*. 6th ed. Cincinnati, OH: The National Underwriter Company, 2002.

Leimberg, S. R. and J. J. McFadden. *The Tools & Techniques of Employee Benefit and Retirement Planning*. 7th ed. Cincinnati, OH: The National Underwriter Company, 2001.

Lesser, G. S., S. D. Diehl, and G. Kolojeski. *Roth IRA Answer Book*. 2nd ed. New York: Panel Publishers, 2000.

Littell, D. A. and K. B. Tacchino. *Planning for Retirement Needs*. 5th ed. Bryn Mawr, PA: The American College, 2001.

Lockwood, S. G., D. R. Levy, and M. Fleisher. *Individual Retirement Account Answer Book*. 8th ed. New York: Panel Publishers, 2002.

Martin, A. R. *Limited Liability Company & Partnership Answer Book*. 2nd ed. New York: Panel Publishers, 2001.

Mayo, H. B. *Investments: An Introduction.* 6th ed. Mason, OH: South-Western College Publishing, 2002.

Mercer. *2003 Guide to Social Security and Medicare.* 31st ed. Louisville, KY: Mercer Human Resource Consulting, Inc., 2002.

Mitchell, W. D. *Estate and Retirement Planning Answer Book.* 3rd ed. New York: Panel Publishers, 2001.

Mittra, Sid. *Practicing Financial Planning for Professionals.* 7th ed. Rochester Hills, MI: RH Publishing, 2002.

The National Underwriter Company. *Social Security Manual (2002).* Cincinnati, OH: The National Underwriter Company, 2002.

Reilly, F. K. and E. A. Norton. *Investments.* 5th ed. New York: Harcourt, Inc., 1999.

RIA. *RIA Federal Tax Handbook.* 2002 ed. New York: Research Institute of America, 2001.

TMI Tax Services. *Form 1040 Quickfinder—2001 Tax Year.* 2002 ed. Minnetonka, MN: TMI Tax Services, Inc., 2001.

Shilling, D. *Financial Planning for The Older Client.* 5th ed. Cincinnati, OH: The National Underwriter Company, 2001.

Vaughan, E. J. and T. Vaughan. *Fundamentals of Risk and Insurance.* 9th ed. Hoboken, NJ: John Wiley & Sons, Inc., 2003.

INDEX

SCHAUM'S OUTLINE OF

THEORY AND PROBLEMS

OF

FINANCIAL MANAGEMENT
Second Edition

WITHDRAWN

•

JAE K. SHIM, Ph.D.
Professor of Business Administration
California State University at Long Beach

JOEL G. SIEGEL, Ph.D., CPA
Professor of Finance and Accounting
Queens College
City University of New York

•

SCHAUM'S OUTLINE SERIES
McGRAW-HILL

New York   San Francisco   Washington, D.C.   Auckland   Bogotá   Caracas   Lisbon
London   Madrid   Mexico City   Milan   Montreal   New Dehli
San Juan   Singapore   Sydney   Tokyo   Toronto

JAE K. SHIM is currently Professor of Business Administration at California State University at Long Beach. He received his M.B.A. and Ph.D. from the University of California at Berkeley. Professor Shim has published numerous articles in such journals as *Financial Management*, *Decision Sciences*, *Econometrica*, *Journal of Urban Economics*, *Long Range Planning*, and *Business Economics.* He is a coauthor of Schaum's Outlines of *Financial Accounting*, *Personal Finance*, and *Managerial Accounting.* Dr. Shim has over forty-five books to his credit and is a recipient of the 1982 Credit Research Foundation Award for his article on financial management.

JOEL G. SIEGEL is Professor of Finance and Accounting at Queens College of the City University of New York. He received his Ph.D. in accounting from Bernard M. Baruch College and is a certified public accountant. In 1972, Dr. Siegel received the Outstanding Educator of America Award. He has written on numerous finance topics in professional journals, including *The Financial Executive* and *The Financial Analyst Journal.* Dr. Siegel is the author of *How to Analyze Businesses, Financial Statements and Quality of Earnings* and is a coauthor of Schaum's Outlines of *Financial Accounting*, *Personal Finance*, and *Managerial Accounting.*

Material from the *CFA Examinations,* Copyright © 1983, 1982, 1981, 1980, 1979, 1978, 1977, 1976, 1975, and 1974 by the Chartered Financial Analysis, is reprinted (or adapted) with permission.

Material from the *Certificate in Management Accounting Examinations*, Copyright © 1983, 1982, 1981, 1980, 1979, 1978, 1977, 1976, 1975, 1974, 1973 and 1972 by the National Association of Accountants, is reprinted (or adapted) with permission.

Schaum's Outline of Theory and Problems of
FINANCIAL MANAGEMENT

4 5 6 7 8 9 10 11 12 13 14 15 16 17 18 19 20 PRS PRS 9 0 2 1 0

ISBN 0-07-057922-9

Sponsoring Editor: Barbara Gilson
Editing Supervisor: Maureen B. Walker
Production Supervisor: Sherri Souffrance

Library of Congress Cataloging-in-Publication Data

Shim, Jae K.
    Schaum's outline of financial management / Jae K. Shim, Joel G.
Siegel. -- 2nd ed.
        p. cm. -- (Schaum's outline series)
    Enl. ed. of: Schaum's outline of theory and problems of managerial
finance. c1986.
    Includes index.
    ISBN 0-07-057922-9 (paper)
    1. Business enterprises- -Finance. 2. Corporations--Finance.
3. Managerial accounting.   I. Siegel, Joel G.   II. Shim, Jae K.
Schaum's outline of theory and problems of managerial finance.
III. Title.
HG4026.S455 1998
658. 15--dc21   97-53255
                                                                CIP

McGraw-Hill

A Division of The McGraw·Hill Companies

Preface

Financial Management, designed for finance and business students, presents the theory and application of corporate finance. As in the preceding volumes in the Schaum's Outline Series in Accounting, Business, and Economics, the solved-problems approach is used, with emphasis on the practical application of principles, concepts, and tools of financial management. Although an elementary knowledge of accounting, economics, and statistics is helpful, it is not required for using this book since the student is provided with the following:

1. Definitions and explanations that are clear and concise.
2. Examples that illustrate the concepts and techniques discussed in each chapter.
3. Review questions and answers.
4. Detailed solutions to representative problems covering the subject matter.
5. Comprehensive examinations, with solutions, to test the student's knowledge of each chapter; the exams are representative of those used by 2- and 4-year colleges and M.B.A. programs.

In line with the development of the subject, two professional designations are noted. One is the Certificate in Management Accounting (CMA), which is a recognized certificate for both management accountants and financial managers. The other is the Chartered Financial Analyst (CFA), established by the Institute of Chartered Financial Analysts. Students who hope to be certified by either of these organizations may find this outline particularly useful.

This book was written with the following objectives in mind:

1. To supplement formal training in financial management courses at the undergraduate and graduate levels. It therefore serves as an excellent study guide.
2. To enable students to prepare for the business finance portion of such professional examinations as the CMA and CFA examinations. Hence it is a valuable reference source for review and self-testing.

This edition expands in scope to cover new developments in finance such as agency problems, the Aribitrage Pricing Model (APM), financial derivatives such as options, the Black-Scholes Option Pricing Model. It updates tax changes such as Modified Accelerated Cost Recovery System (MACRS). A new chapter, Multinational Finance, is added.

Financial Management was written to cover the common denominator of managerial finance topics after a thorough review was made of the numerous managerial finance, financial management, corporate finance, and business finance texts currently available. It is, therefore, comprehensive in coverage and presentation. In an effort to give readers a feel for the types of questions asked on the CMA and CFA examinations, problems from those exams have been incorporated within this book.

Our appreciation is extended to the National Association of Accountants and the Institute of Chartered Financial Analysts for their permission to incorporate their examination questions in this book. Selected materials from the CMA examinations, copyrighted by the National Association of Accountants, bear the notation (CMA, adapted). Problems from the CFA examinations bear the notation (CFA, adapted).

Finally, we would like to thank our assistants, Su-chin Tsai and Jackie Steinke, for their assistance and our wives, Chung and Roberta, who helped with the typing.

JAE K. SHIM
JOEL G. SIEGEL

Contents

Chapter 1

Introduction

1.1 THE GOALS OF MANAGERIAL FINANCE

Typical goals of the firm include (1) stockholder wealth maximization; (2) profit maximization; (3) managerial reward maximization; (4) behavioral goals; and (5) social responsibility. Modern managerial finance theory operates on the assumption that the primary goal of the firm is to *maximize the wealth of its stockholders*, which translates into *maximizing the price of the firm's common stock*. The other goals mentioned above also influence a firm's policy but are less important than stock price maximization. Note that the traditional goal frequently stressed by economists—*profit maximization*—is not sufficient for most firms today.

Profit Maximization versus Stockholder Wealth Maximization

Profit maximization is basically a single-period or, at the most, a short-term goal. It is usually interpreted to mean the maximization of profits within a given period of time. A firm may maximize its short-term profits at the expense of its long-term profitability and still realize this goal. In contrast, stockholder wealth maximization is a long-term goal, since stockholders are interested in future as well as present profits. Wealth maximization is generally preferred because it considers (1) wealth for the long term; (2) risk or uncertainty; (3) the timing of returns; and (4) the stockholders' return. Table 1-1 provides a summary of the advantages and disadvantages of these two often conflicting goals.

Table 1-1.   Profit Maximization versus Stockholder Wealth Maximization

Goal	Objective	Advantages	Disadvantages
Profit maximization	Large amount of profits	1. Easy to calculate profits 2. Easy to determine the link between financial decisions and profits	1. Emphasizes the short term 2. Ignores risk or uncertainty 3. Ignores the timing of returns 4. Requires immediate resources
Stockholder wealth maximization	Highest market value of common stock	1. Emphasizes the long term 2. Recognizes risk or uncertainty 3. Recognizes the timing of returns 4. Considers stockholders' return	1. Offers no clear relationship between financial decisions and stock price 2. Can lead to management anxiety and frustration

1

EXAMPLE 1.1 Profit maximization can be achieved in the short term at the expense of the long-term goal, that is, wealth maximization. For example, a costly investment may experience losses in the short term but yield substantial profits in the long term. Also, a firm that wants to show a short-term profit may, for example, postpone major repairs or replacement, although such postponement is likely to hurt its long-term profitability.

EXAMPLE 1.2 Profit maximization does not consider risk or uncertainty, whereas wealth maximization does. Consider two products, A and B, and their projected earnings over the next 5 years, as shown below.

Year	Product A	Product B
1	$10,000	$11,000
2	10,000	11,000
3	10,000	11,000
4	10,000	11,000
5	10,000	11,000
	$50,000	$55,000

A profit maximization approach would favor product B over product A. However, if product B is more risky than product A, then the decision is not as straightforward as the figures seem to indicate. It is important to realize that a trade-off exists between risk and return. Stockholders expect greater returns from investments of higher risk and vice versa. To choose product B, stockholders would demand a sufficiently large return to compensate for the comparatively greater level of risk.

1.2 THE ROLE OF FINANCIAL MANAGERS

The financial manager of a firm plays an important role in the company's goals, policies, and financial success. The financial manager's responsibilities include:

1. *Financial analysis and planning:* Determining the proper amount of funds to employ in the firm, i.e., designating the size of the firm and its rate of growth

2. *Investment decisions:* The efficient allocation of funds to specific assets

3. *Financing and capital structure decisions:* Raising funds on as favorable terms as possible, i.e., determining the composition of liabilities

4. *Management of financial resources* (such as working capital)

5. *Risk management:* protecting assets

In a large firm, these financial responsibilities are carried out by the treasurer, controller, and financial vice president (chief financial officer). The treasurer is responsible for managing corporate assets and liabilities, planning the finances, budgeting capital, financing the business, formulating credit policy, and managing the investment portfolio. He or she basically handles *external* financing matters. The controller is basically concerned with *internal* matters, namely, financial and cost accounting, taxes, budgeting, and control functions. The chief financial officer (CFO) supervises all phases of financial activity and serves as the financial adviser to the board of directors.

The Financial Executives Institute, an association of corporate treasurers and controllers, distinguishes their functions as shown in Table 1-2. (For a typical organization chart highlighting the structure of financial activity within a firm, see Problem 1.4.)

The financial manager can affect stockholder wealth maximization by influencing

1. Present and future earnings per share (EPS)

2. The timing, duration, and risk of these earnings

3. Dividend policy

4. The manner of financing the firm

Table 1-2. Functions of Controller and Treasurer

Controller	Treasurer
Planning for control	Provision of capital
Reporting and interpreting	Investor relations
Evaluating and consulting	Short-term financing
Tax administration	Banking and custody
Government reporting	Credits and collections
Protection of assets	Investments
Economic appraisal	Insurance

1.3 AGENCY PROBLEMS

An agency relationship exists when one or more persons (called principals) employ one or more other persons (called agents) to perform some tasks. Primary agency relationships exist (1) between shareholders and managers and (2) between creditors and shareholders. They are the major source of agency problems.

Shareholders versus Managers

The *agency problem* arises when a manager owns less than 100 percent of the company's ownership. As a result of the separation between the managers and owners, managers may make decisions that are not in line with the goal of maximizing stockholder wealth. For example, they may work less eagerly and benefit themselves in terms of salary and perks. The costs associated with the agency problem, such as a reduced stock price and various "perks," is called *agency costs*. Several mechanisms are used to ensure that managers act in the best interests of the shareholders: (1) golden parachutes or severance contracts; (2) performance-based stock option plans; and (3) the threat of takeover.

Creditors versus Shareholders

Conflicts develop if (1) managers, acting in the interest of shareholders, take on projects with greater risk than creditors anticipated and (2) raise the debt level higher than was expected. These actions tend to reduce the value of the debt outstanding.

1.4 FINANCIAL DECISIONS AND RISK-RETURN TRADE-OFF

Integral to the theory of finance is the concept of a risk-return trade-off. All financial decisions involve some sort of risk-return trade-off. The greater the risk associated with any financial decision, the greater the return expected from it. Proper assessment and balance of the various risk-return trade-offs available is part of creating a sound stockholder wealth maximization plan.

EXAMPLE 1.3 In the case of investment in stock, the investor would demand higher return from a speculative stock to compensate for the higher level of risk.

In the case of working capital management, the less inventory a firm keeps, the higher the expected return (since less of the firm's current assets is tied up), but also the greater the risk of running out of stock and thus losing potential revenue.

A financial manager's role is delineated in part by the financial environment in which he or she operates. Three major aspects of this environment are (1) the organization form of the business; (2) the financial institutions and markets; and (3) the tax structure. In this book, we limit the discussion of tax structure to that of the corporation.

1.5 BASIC FORMS OF BUSINESS ORGANIZATION

Finance is applicable both to all economic entities such as business firms and nonprofit organizations such as schools, governments, hospitals, churches, and so on. However, this book will focus on finance for business firms organized as three basic forms of business organizations. These forms are (1) the sole proprietorship; (2) the partnership; and (3) the corporation.

Sole Proprietorship

This is a business owned by one individual. Of the three forms of business organizations, sole proprietorships are the greatest in number. The advantages of this form are:

1. No formal charter required
2. Less regulation and red tape
3. Significant tax savings
4. Minimal organizational costs
5. Profits and control not shared with others

The disadvantages are :

1. Limited ability to raise large sums of money
2. Unlimited liability for the owner
3. Limited to the life of the owner
4. No tax deductions for personal and employees' health, life, or disability insurance

Partnership

This is similar to the sole proprietorship except that the business has more than one owner. Its advantages are:

1. Minimal organizational effort and costs
2. Less governmental regulations

Its disadvantages are:

1. Unlimited liability for the individual partners
2. Limited ability to raise large sums of money
3. Dissolved upon the death or withdrawal of any of the partners

There is a special form of partnership, called a *limited partnership*, where one or more partners, but not all, have limited liability up to their investment in the event of business failure.

1. The general partner manages the business
2. Limited partners are not involved in daily activities. The return to limited partners is in the form of income and capital gains
3. Often, tax benefits are involved

Examples of limited partnerships are in real estate and oil and gas exploration.

Corporation

This is a legal entity that exists apart from its owners, better known as stockholders. Ownership is evidenced by possession of shares of stock. In terms of types of businesses, the corporate form is not the greatest in number, but the most important in terms of total sales, assets, profits, and contribution to national income. Corporations are governed by a distinct set of state or federal laws and come in two forms: a state *C Corporation* or *federal Subchapter S*.

The advantages of a C corporation are:

1.   Unlimited life
2.   Limited liability for its owners, as long as no personal guarantee on a business-related obligation such as a bank loan or lease
3.   Ease of transfer of ownership through transfer of stock
4.   Ability to raise large sums of capital

Its disadvantages are:

1.   Difficult and costly to establish, as a formal charter is required
2.   Subject to double taxation on its earnings and dividends paid to stockholders
3.   Bankruptcy, even at the corporate level, does not discharge tax obligations

Subchapter S Corporation

This is a form of corporation whose stockholders are taxed as partners. To qualify as an S corporation, the following is necessary:

1.   A corporation cannot have more than 35 shareholders
2.   It cannot have any nonresident foreigners as shareholders
3.   It cannot have more than one class of stock
4.   It must properly elect Subchapter S status

The S corporation can distribute its income directly to shareholders and avoid the corporate income tax while enjoying the other advantages of the corporate form. *Note:* not all states recognize Subchapter S corporations.

1.6   THE FINANCIAL INSTITUTIONS AND MARKETS

A healthy economy depends heavily on efficient transfer of funds from savers to individuals, businesses, and governments who need capital. Most transfers occur through specialized *financial institutions* (see Fig. 1-1) which serve as *intermediaries* between suppliers and users of funds.

It is in the *financial markets* that entities demanding funds are brought together with those having surplus funds. Financial markets provide a mechanism through which the financial manager may obtain funds from a wide range of sources, including financial institutions. The financial markets are composed of money markets and capital markets. Figure 1-1 depicts the general flow of funds among financial institutions and markets.

Money markets are the markets for short-term (less than 1 year) debt securities. Examples of money market securities include U.S. Treasury bills, federal agency securities, bankers' acceptances, commercial paper, and negotiable certificates of deposit issued by government, business, and financial institutions.

Capital markets are the markets for long-term debt and corporate stocks. The New York Stock Exchange, which handles the stocks of many of the larger corporations, is a prime example of a capital market. The American Stock Exchange and the regional stock exchanges are still another example. In addition, securities are traded through the thousands of brokers and dealers on the *over-the-counter market*, a term used to denote all buying and selling activities in securities that do not take place on an organized stock exchange.

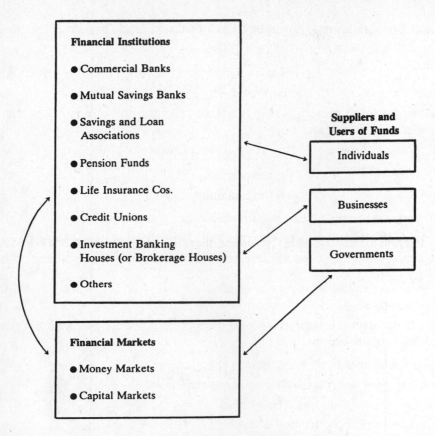

Fig. 1-1   General flow of funds among financial institutions and financial markets

1.7   CORPORATE TAX STRUCTURE*

In order to make sound financial and investment decisions, a corporation's financial manager must have a general understanding of the corporate tax structure, which includes the following:

1. Corporate tax rate schedule
2. Interest and dividend income
3. Interest and dividends paid by a corporation
4. Operating loss carryback and carryforward
5. Capital gains and losses
6. Alternative "pass-through" entities

Corporate Tax Rate Schedule

Corporations pay federal income tax on their taxable income, which is the corporation's gross income reduced by the deductions permitted under the Internal Revenue Code of 1986. Federal income

---

*Section 1.7 (Corporate Tax Structure) was contributed by Professor Michael Constas, Department of Accountancy, College of Business Administration, California State University, Long Beach.

taxes are imposed at the following tax rates:

> 15% on the first $50,000
>
> 25% on the next $25,000
>
> 34% on the next $25,000
>
> 39% on the next $235,000
>
> 34% on the next $9,665,000
>
> 35% on the next $5,000,000
>
> 38% on the next $3,333,333
>
> 35% on the remaining income

EXAMPLE 1.4   If a firm has $20,000 in taxable income, the tax liability is $3,000 ($20,000 × 15%).

EXAMPLE 1.5   If a firm has $20,000,000 in taxable income, the tax is calculated as follows:

Income ($)	× Marginal Tax Rate (%)	= Taxes ($)
50,000	15	7,500
25,000	25	6,250
25,000	34	8,500
235,000	39	91,650
9,665,000	34	3,286,100
5,000,000	35	1,750,000
3,333,333	38	1,266,667
1,666,667	35	583,333
20,000,000		7,000,000

Financial managers often refer to the federal tax rate imposed on the next dollar of income as the "marginal tax rate" of the taxpayer. Because of the fluctuations in the corporate tax rates, financial managers also talk in terms of the "average tax rate" of a corporation. Average tax rates are computed as follows:

$$\text{Average Tax Rate} = \text{Tax Due/Taxable Income}$$

EXAMPLE 1.6   The average tax rate for the corporation in Example 1.5 is 35% (7,000,000/20,000,000). The marginal tax rate for the corporation in Example 1.5 is 35%.

As suggested in Example 1.6, at taxable incomes beyond $18,333,333, corporations pay a tax of 35% on all of their taxable income. This fact demonstrates the reasoning behind the patch-quilt of corporate tax rates. The 15%–25%–34% tax brackets demonstrate the intent that there should be a graduated tax rate for small corporate taxpayers. The effect of the 39% tax bracket is to wipe out the early low tax brackets. At $335,000 of corporate income, the cumulative income tax is $113,900, which results in an average tax rate of 34% ($113,900/$335,000). The income tax rate increases to 35% at taxable incomes of $10,000,000. The purpose of the 38% tax bracket is to wipe out the effect of the 34% tax bracket and to raise the average tax rate to 35%. This is accomplished at taxable income of $18,333,333. The income tax on $18,333,333 of taxable income is $6,416,667, which results in an average tax rate of 35% ($6,416,667/$18,333,333). Thereafter, the tax rate is reduced back to 35%.

Interest and Dividend Income

Interest income is taxed as ordinary income at the regular corporate tax rate.

Corporate income is subject to "double taxation." A corporation pays income tax on its taxable income, and when the corporation pays dividends to its individual shareholders, the dividends are subject to a second tax.

If a corporation owns stock in another corporation, then the income of the "subsidiary" corporation could be subject to triple taxation (income tax paid by the "subsidiary," "parent" and the individual shareholder). To avoid this result, corporate shareholders are entitled to reduce their income by a portion of the dividends received in a given year. Generally, the amount of the reduction depends upon the percentage of the stock of the "subsidiary" corporation owned by the "parent" corporation as shown below:

Percentage of Ownership by Corporate Shareholder	Deduction Percentage
Less than 20%	70%
20% or more, but less than 80%	80%
80% or more	100%

EXAMPLE 1.7   ABC Corporation owns 2% of the outstanding stock of XYZ Corporation, and ABC Corporation receives dividends of $10,000 in a given year from XYZ Corporation. As a result of these dividends, ABC Corporation will have ordinary income of $10,000 and an offsetting dividends received deduction of $7,000 (70% × $10,000), which results in a net $3,000 being subject to federal income tax. If ABC Corporation is in the 35% marginal tax bracket, its tax liability on the dividends is $1,050 (35% × $3,000). As a result of the dividends received deduction, these dividends are taxed at an effective federal tax rate of 10.5%.

Interest and Dividends Paid

Interest paid is a tax-deductible business expense. Thus, interest is paid with *before-tax* dollars. Dividends on stock (common and preferred), however, are not deductible and are therefore paid with *after-tax* dollars. This means that our tax system favors debt financing over equity financing.

EXAMPLE 1.8   Yukon Corporation has an operating income of $200,000, pays interest charges of $50,000, and pays dividends of $40,000. The company's taxable income is:

$$\begin{array}{ll} \$200,000 & \text{(operating income)} \\ \underline{-50,000} & \text{(interest charge, which is tax-deductible)} \\ \$150,000 & \text{(taxable income)} \end{array}$$

The tax liability, as calculated in Example 1.5, is $48,750. Note that dividends are paid with after-tax dollars.

Operating Loss Carryback and Carryforward

If a company has an operating loss, the loss may be applied against income in other years. The loss can be carried back 3 years and then forward for 15 years. The corporate taxpayer may elect to first apply the loss against the taxable income in the 3 prior years. If the loss is not completely absorbed by the profits in these 3 years, it may be carried forward to each of the 15 following years. At that time, any loss remaining may no longer be used as a tax deduction. To illustrate, a 1997 operating loss may be used to recover, in whole or in part, the taxes paid during 1994, 1995, and 1996. If any part of the loss remains, this amount may be used to reduce taxable income, if any, during the 15-year period of 1998 through 2012. The corporation may choose to forgo the loss carryback, and to instead carry the net operating loss to future years only.

EXAMPLE 1.9   The Loyla Company's taxable income and associated tax payments for the years 1994 through 2001 are presented below:

Year	Taxable Income ($)	Tax Payments ($)
1994	100,000	22,250
1995	100,000	22,250
1996	100,000	22,250
1997	(700,000)	0
1998	100,000	22,250
1999	100,000	22,250
2000	100,000	22,250
2001	100,000	22,250

In 1997, Loyla Company had an operating loss of $700,000. By carrying the loss back 3 years and then forward, the firm was able to "zero-out" its before-tax income as follows:

Year	Income Reduction ($)	Remaining 1997 Net Operating Loss ($)	Tax Savings ($)
1994	100,000	600,000	22,250
1995	100,000	500,000	22,250
1996	100,000	400,000	22,250
1997	0	400,000	0
1998	100,000	300,000	22,250
1999	100,000	200,000	22,250
2000	100,000	100,000	22,250
2001	100,000	0	22,250
Total	700,000		155,750

As soon as the company recognized the loss of $700,000 in 1997, it was able to file for a tax refund of $66,750 ($22,250 + $22,250 + $22,500) for the years 1994 through 1996. It then carried forward the portion of the loss not used to offset past income and applied it against income for the next four years, 1998 through 2001.

Capital Gains and Losses

Capital gains and losses are a major form of corporate income and loss (see also Chapter 8). They may result when a corporation sells investments and/or business property (not inventory). If depreciation has been taken on the asset sold, then part or all of the gain from the sale may be taxed as ordinary income.

Like all taxpayers, corporations net any capital gains and capital losses that they have. Corporations include any net capital gains as part of their taxable income. Individuls pay tax on their capital gains at reduced rates. Unlike individuals, corporations pay tax on their capital gains at the same rate as any other income. If an individual has a net capital loss, the individual may deduct up to $3,000 of that loss in the year incurred. The remaining capital loss is carried forward to future years indefinitely. Unlike individuals, corporations may not deduct any net capital losses. Instead, corporations may carry back the net capital loss to the 3 previous years and/or carry forward the net capital to the next 5 years. These capital loss carrybacks and carryforwards may be used to offset net capital gains in the past and/or future years.

Modified Accelerated Cost Recovery System (MACRS)

For all assets acquired after 1986, depreciation for tax purposes ("cost recovery") is calculated using the Modified Accelerated Cost Recovery System ("MACRS"). MACRS is discussed in depth in Chapter 8.

Alternative "Pass-Through" Tax Entities

As noted above, a disadvantage of corporations, compared to other forms of doing business (e.g., general partnerships), is double taxation. The net income of a corporation is taxed to the corporation. Later, should the corporation distribute that income to its shareholders, the distribution is taxed a second time to the recipient shareholders. Despite this disadvantage, corporations are popular because they have many advantages, including the fact that the liability of their shareholders, who are active in their business, for corporate debts is generally limited to the shareholders' investment in the corporation.

Two entities have developed (S Corporations and Limited Liability Companies), which allow investors limited liability and yet avoid double taxation. With these entities, owners of the entities are taxed on their share of the entities' income. Later, when that income is distributed to the owners, the distribution can be tax-free.

The importance of avoiding double taxation can be seen in the following example. Assume that a business has $100,000 of net income, and it has one shareholder, who is in the 28% marginal tax bracket. Assume that the business is either a corporation or a pass-through entity:

	Corporation	Pass-Through Entity
Entity's Taxable Income:	$100,000	$100,000
Tax on Entity Level:	(22,250)	(0)
Distribution to Owner:	$ 77,750	$100,000
Tax on Owner:	(21,770)	(28,000)
After-tax Distribution:	$ 55,980	$ 72,000

Double taxation costs the investor $16,020 or approximately 16% in the above example. This percentage increases as the corporation's marginal tax rate increases.

Generally, the pass-through entity merely files an informational tax return with the Internal Revenue Service, and informs its owners of their share of the entity's taxable income or loss. The owners will be taxed on their share of the corporation's income. Afterwards, the distribution of any accrued income to the owners generally is tax-free.

S Corporations

Corporations, if they meet certain requirements, may elect to be taxed as S Corporations. This is merely a tax classification, and corporations who make this election are still treated as general corporations for other legal purposes. In order to qualify for this treatment, the corporation must make a timely election with the Internal Revenue Service. In addition, the corporation must meet other requirements, which include:

- The corporation is a domestic (not foreign) corporation

- The corporation has no more than 35 shareholders

- The corporation does not have any shareholders who are nonresident aliens, corporations or certain trusts

- The corporation has only one class of stock

If an S Corporation fails to meet any of the specified requirements, or if it voluntarily chooses to do so, its S Corporation status will terminate. Upon termination, the corporation will be taxed as a general corporation. Generally, after such a termination, the corporation must wait 5 years before it may elect S Corporation tax treatment again.

Limited Liability Companies

Limited Liability Companies ("LLC"s) are a relatively recent development. Most states permit the establishment of LLCs. LLCs are typically not permitted to carry on certain service businesses (e.g., law, medicine, and accounting). According to recent IRS regulations, an LLC may elect whether it wishes to be taxed as a corporation or as a pass-through entity (a partnership). Provided that the appropriate election is made, then the LLC will enjoy pass-through status.

Review Questions

1. Modern financial theory assumes that the primary goal of the firm is the maximization of stockholder _____ , which translates into maximizing the _____ of the firm's common stock.

2. _____ is a short-term goal. It can be achieved at the expense of the firm and its stockholders.

3. A firm's stock price depends on such factors as present and future earnings per share, the timing, duration, and _____ of these earnings, and _____ .

4. A major disadvantage of the corporation is the _____ on its earnings and the _____ paid to its owners (stockholders).

5. A _____ is the largest form of business organization with respect to the number of such businesses in existence. However, the corporate form is the most important with respect to the total amount of _____ , assets, _____ , and contribution to _____ .

6. A corporation is a(n) _____ that exists separately from its owners, better known as _____ .

7. A partnership is dissolved upon the _____ or _____ of any one of the _____ .

8. The sole proprietorship is easily established with no _____ and does not have to share _____ or _____ with others.

9. Corporate financial functions are carried out by the _____ , _____ , and _____ .

10. The financial markets are composed of money markets and _____ .

11. Money markets are the markets for short-term (less than 1 year) _____ .

12. The _____ is the term used for all trading activities in securities that do not take place on an organized stock exchange.

13. Commercial banks and credit unions are two examples of _____ .

14. _____ represent the distribution of earnings to the stockholders of a corporation.

15. _____ are the rates applicable for the next dollar of taxable income.

16. In order to avoid triple taxation, corporations may be entitled to deduct a portion of the _____ that they receive.

17. If a corporation has a net operating loss, the loss may be _____ and then _____ .

18. Unlike individuals, corporations are taxed on their capital gains at the same _____ as other income.

19. A corporation is entitled to carryback any net capital loss _____ years and/or carryforward that loss _____ years.

20. Two entities that offer active investors limited liability and avoid double taxation are _____ and _____ .

Answers: (1) wealth, market price; (2) Profit maximization; (3) risk, dividend policy; (4) double taxation, dividends; (5) sole proprietorship, sales, profits, national income; (6) legal entity, stockholders; (7) withdrawal, death, partners; (8) formal charter, profits, control; (9) treasurer, controller, financial vice-president; (10) capital markets; (11) debt securities; (12) over-the-counter market; (13) financial institutions (or intermediaries); (14) Dividends; (15) Marginal tax rates; (16) dividends; (17) carried back, carried forward; (18) income tax rates; (19) 3 years, 5 years; (20) S Corporations, Limited Liability Companies.

Solved Problems

1.1 **Profit Maximization versus Stockholder Wealth Maximization.** What are the disadvantages of profit maximization and stockholder wealth maximization as the goals of the firm?

SOLUTION

The disadvantages are

Profit Maximization	**Stockholder Wealth Maximization**
Emphasizes the short run	Offers no clear link between financial decisions and stock price
Ignores risk	
Ignores the timing of returns	Can lead to management anxiety and frustration
Ignores the stockholders' return	

1.2 **The Role of Financial Managers.** What are the major functions of the financial manager?

SOLUTION

The financial manager performs the following functions:

1. Financial analysis, forecasting, and planning
   (*a*) Monitors the firm's financial position
   (*b*) Determines the proper amount of funds to employ in the firm
2. Investment decisions
   (*a*) Makes efficient allocations of funds to specific assets
   (*b*) Makes long-term capital budget and expenditure decisions

3. Financing and capital structure decisions
   (a) Determines both the mix of short-term and long-term financing and equity/debt financing
   (b) Raises funds on the most favorable terms possible
4. Management of financial resources
   (a) Manages working capital
   (b) Maintains optimal level of investments in each of the current assets

1.3 Stock Price Maximization. What are the factors that affect the market value of a firm's common stock?

SOLUTION

The factors that influence a firm's stock price are:
1. Present and future earnings
2. The timing and risk of earnings
3. The stability and risk of earnings
4. The manner in which the firm is financed
5. Dividend policy

1.4 Organizational Chart of the Finance Function. Depict a typical organizational chart highlighting the finance function of the firm.

SOLUTION

See Fig. 1-2.

1.5 Tax Liability and Average Tax Rate. A corporation has a taxable income of $15,000. What is its tax liability and average tax rate?

SOLUTION

The company's tax liability is $2,250 ($15,000 × 15%). The company's average tax rate is 15 percent.

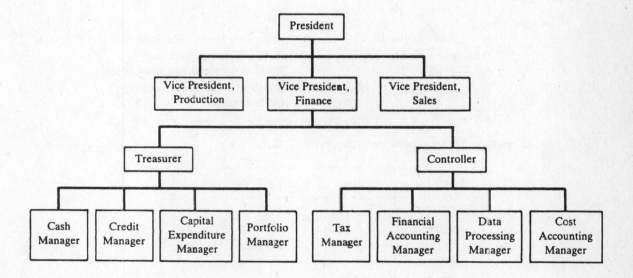

Fig. 1-2

1.6   Tax Liability. A corporation has $120,000 in taxable income. What is its tax liability?

SOLUTION

Income ($)	× Marginal Tax Rate (%)	= Taxes ($)
50,000	15	7,500
25,000	25	6,250
25,000	34	8,500
20,000	39	7,800
120,000		30,050

The company's total tax liability is $30,050.

1.7   Average Tax Rate. In Problem 1.6, what is the average tax rate of the corporation?

SOLUTION

Average tax rate = total tax liability ÷ taxable income = $30,050/$120,000 = 25.04%.

1.8   Dividends Received Deduction. Rha Company owns 30% of the stock in Aju Corporation and receives dividends of $20,000 in a given year. Assume that Rha Company is in the 35% tax bracket. What is the company's tax liability?

SOLUTION

Rha Company will include the $20,000 in its income, but generally, will receive an offsetting deduction equal to 80% of the dividends received (80% × $20,000 = $16,000). As a result of this deduction, Rha Company will be taxed on a net amount of $4,000.

1.9   Dividends Received Deduction. Yousef Industries had operating income of $200,000 in 1997. In addition, it received $12,500 in interest income from investment and another $10,000 in dividends from a wholly owned subsidiary. What is the company's total tax liability for the year?

SOLUTION

Taxable income:

$200,000	(operating income)
12,500	(interest income)
10,000	(dividend income)
(10,000)	(100% dividend received deduction for 100% subsidiary)
$212,500	(taxable income)

The company's total tax liability is computed as follows:

Income ($)	× Marginal Tax Rate (%)	= Taxes ($)
50,000	15	7,500
25,000	25	6,250
25,000	34	8,500
112,500	39	43,875
212,500		66,125

1.10   **Interest and Dividends Paid.** Johnson Corporation has operating income of $120,000, pays interest charges of $60,000, and pays dividends of $20,000. What is the company's tax liability?

SOLUTION

The company's taxable income is:

$120,000   (operating income)
−60,000   (interest charge)
$ 60,000   (taxable income)

The tax liability is then calculated as follows:

Income ($)	×	Marginal Tax Rate (%)	=	Taxes ($)
50,000		15		7,500
10,000		25		2,500
60,000				10,000

Note that since dividends of $20,000 are paid out of after-tax income, the dividend amount is not included in the computation.

1.11   **Net Operating Loss Carryback and Carryforward.** The Kenneth Parks Company's taxable income and tax payments/liability for the years 1994 through 2000 are given below.

Year	Taxable Income ($)	Tax Payments ($)
1994	50,000	7,500
1995	100,000	22,250
1996	50,000	7,500
1997	(200,000)	0
1998	100,000	22,250
1999	50,000	7,500
2000	50,000	7,500

Compute the Company's tax refund in 1997.

SOLUTION

Year	Income Reduction ($)	Remaining 1997 Net Operating Loss ($)	Tax Savings ($)
1994	50,000	150,000	7,500
1995	100,000	50,000	22,250
1996	50,000	0	7,500
Total	200,000		37,250

As soon as the corporation recognizes the $200,000 loss in 1997, it may file for a tax refund of $37,250 ($7,500 + $22,250 + $7,500) for the years 1994 through 1996.

1.12   **Net Operating Loss Carryback and Carryforward.** Assume that the Kenneth Parks Company anticipates that corporate tax rates will decline in future years, and, therefore, elects to forgo the carryback and to instead carry the net operating loss forward. Calculate the company's tax benefit in the future years assuming no change in tax rates.

SOLUTION

Year	Income Reduction ($)	Remaining 1997 Net Operating Loss ($)	Tax Savings ($)
1998	100,000	100,000	22,250
1999	50,000	50,000	7,500
2000	50,000	0	7,500
Total	200,000		37,250

1.13   **Capital Gain–Maximum Tax Rate.** The Theisman Company and its sole shareholder John Theisman each have a net capital gain of $100,000. John Theisman is in the maximum individual capital gain tax bracket (28%) and the Theisman Company is in the maximum corporate tax bracket (35%). What is the tax liability resulting from the capital gain?

SOLUTION

The Theisman Company: $35\% \times \$100,000 = \$35,000$
John Theisman: $28\% \times \$100,000 = \$28,000$

1.14   **Capital Loss–Tax Benefit.** The taxpayers in Problem 1.11 have a net capital loss of $100,000 in the following year. What is the tax benefit liability resulting from the capital loss?

SOLUTION

The Theisman Company: May carryback the $100,000 net capital loss to the previous year, and offset the capital gain described in Problem 1.11. The Theisman Company will receive a refund of the $35,000 paid in the previous year on the capital gain.

John Theisman: Will deduct $3,000 of the net capital loss against its operating income. This should save David $1,188 in taxes in the current year. The remaining net capital loss will be carried forward to future years indefinitely.

1.15   **Alternative "Pass-Through" Tax Entities.** Davidson Company is a limited liability company. It earned $100,000 in its first year of operation. It may elect to be taxed as a corporation or as a pass-through entity. Davidson Company intends to distribute all of its earnings to its sole shareholder David Davidson, who is in the 39.6% tax bracket. Should it elect to be taxed as a corporation or as a pass through entity in its first year?

SOLUTION

	Corporation	Pass-Through Entity
Entity's Taxable Income:	$100,000	$100,000
Tax on Entity Level:	(22,250)	(0)
Distribution to Owner:	$77,750	$100,000
Tax on Owner:	(30,789)	(39,600)
After-tax Distribution:	$ 46,961	$ 60,400

Focussing only on the first year, the sole shareholder will receive a larger after-tax distribution if it elects to be taxed as a pass-through entity.

1.16   Alternative "Pass-Through" Tax Entities. Assume that in Problem 1.15, the Davidson Company intends to use its earnings in the business and will not distribute any earnings to its shareholder. Under these circumstances, should it elect to be taxed as a corporation or as a pass-through entity in its first year?

SOLUTION

	Corporation	Pass-Through Entity
Entity's Taxable Income:	$100,000	$100,000
Tax on Entity Level:	(22,250)	(0)
Distribution to Owner:	$ 0	$ 39,600
Tax on Owner:		(39,600)
Total Retained by Entity:	$ 77,750	$ 61,400

Focussing only on the first year, if no distributions are anticipated, the entity can retain more of its earnings if it elects to be taxed as a corporation.

Chapter 2

Financial Analysis

2.1 THE SCOPE AND PURPOSE OF FINANCIAL ANALYSIS

Financial analysis is an evaluation of both a firm's past financial performance and its prospects for the future. Typically, it involves an analysis of the firm's financial statements and its flow of funds. *Financial statement analysis* involves the calculation of various ratios. It is used by such interested parties as creditors, investors, and managers to determine the firm's financial position relative to that of others. The way in which an entity's financial position and operating results are viewed by investors and creditors will have an impact on the firm's reputation, price/earnings ratio, and effective interest rate.

Funds flow analysis is an evaluation of the firm's statement of cash flows in order to determine the impact that its sources and uses of funds have on the firm's operations and financial condition. It is used in decisions that involve corporate investments, operations, and financing.

2.2 FINANCIAL STATEMENT ANALYSIS

The financial statements of an enterprise present the summarized data of its assets, liabilities, and equities in the balance sheet and its revenue and expenses in the income statement. If not analyzed, such data may lead one to draw erroneous conclusions about the firm's financial condition. Various measuring instruments may be used to evaluate the financial health of a business, including *horizontal*, *vertical*, and *ratio analyses*. A financial analyst uses the ratios to make two types of comparisons:

1. *Industry comparison*. The ratios of a firm are compared with those of similar firms or with industry averages or norms to determine how the company is faring relative to its competitors. Industry average ratios are available from a number of sources, including:

    (a) *Dun & Bradstreet*. Dun & Bradstreet computes 14 ratios for each of 125 lines of business. They are published annually in *Dun's Review* and *Key Business Ratios*.

    (b) *Robert Morris Associates*. This association of bank loan officers publishes *Annual Statement Studies*. Sixteen ratios are computed for more than 300 lines of business, as well as a percentage distribution of items on the balance sheet and income statement (common size financial statements).

2. *Trend analysis*. A firm's present ratio is compared with its past and expected future ratios to determine whether the company's financial condition is improving or deteriorating over time.

After completing the financial statement analysis, the firm's financial analyst will consult with management to discuss their plans and prospects, any problem areas identified in the analysis, and possible solutions.

2.3 HORIZONTAL ANALYSIS

Horizontal analysis is used to evaluate the trend in the accounts over the years. A $3 million profit year looks very good following a $1 million profit year, but not after a $4 million profit year. Horizontal analysis is usually shown in comparative financial statements (see Examples 2.1 and 2.2). Companies often show comparative financial data for 5 years in annual reports.

18

EXAMPLE 2.1

The Ratio Company
Comparative Balance Sheet
(In Thousands of Dollars)
December 31, 19X3, 19X2, and 19X1

	19X3	19X2	19X1	Increase or (Decrease) 19X3–19X2	Increase or (Decrease) 19X2–19X1	Percentage of Increase or (Decrease) 19X3–19X2	Percentage of Increase or (Decrease) 19X2–19X1
ASSETS							
Current assets							
Cash	$ 30.0	$ 35	$ 35	$ (5.0)	—	(14.3)	—
Accounts receivable	20.0	15	10	5.0	$ 5	33.3	50.0
Marketable securities	20.0	15	5	5.0	10	33.3	200.0
Inventory	50.0	45	50	5.0	(5)	11.1	(10.0)
Total current assets	$120.0	$110	$100	$10.0	$10	9.1	10.0
Plant assets	100.0	90	85	10.0	5	11.1	5.9
Total assets	$220.0	$200	$185	$20.0	$15	10.0	8.1
LIABILITIES							
Current liabilities	$ 55.4	$ 50	$ 52	$ 5.4	$ (2)	10.8	(3.8)
Long-term liabilities	80.0	75	70	5.0	5	6.7	7.1
Total liabilities	$135.4	$125	$122	$10.4	$ 3	8.3	2.5
STOCKHOLDERS' EQUITY							
Common stock, $10 par value, 4,500 shares	$ 45.0	$ 45	$ 45	—	—	—	—
Retained earnings	39.6	30	18	$ 9.6	$12	32.0	66.7
Total stockholders' equity	$ 84.6	$ 75	$ 63	$ 9.6	$12	12.8	19.0
Total liabilities and stockholders' equity	$220.0	$200	$185	$20.0	$15	10.0	8.1

EXAMPLE 2.2

The Ratio Company
Comparative Income Statement
(In Thousands of Dollars)
For the Years Ended December 31, 19X3, 19X2, and 19X1

	19X3	19X2	19X1	Increase or (Decrease) 19X3–19X2	Increase or (Decrease) 19X2–19X1	Percentage of Increase or (Decrease) 19X3–19X2	Percentage of Increase or (Decrease) 19X2–19X1
Sales	$100.0	$110	$50	$(10.0)	$60	(9.1)	120.0
Sales returns and allowances	20.0	8	3	12.0	5	150.0	166.7
Net sales	$ 80.0	$102	$47	$(22.0)	$55	(21.6)	117.0
Cost of goods sold	50.0	60	25	(10.0)	35	(16.7)	140.0
Gross profit	$30.0	$ 42	$22	$(12.0)	$20	(28.6)	90.9
Operating expenses							
Selling expenses	$ 11.0	$ 13	$ 8	$ (2.0)	$ 5	(15.4)	62.5
General expenses	4.0	7	4	(3.0)	3	(42.9)	75.0
Total operating expenses	$ 15.0	$ 20	$12	$ (5.0)	$ 8	(25.0)	66.7
Income from operations	15.0	$ 22	$10	$ (7.0)	$12	(31.8)	120.0
Nonoperating income	3.0	0	1	3.0	(1)	—	(100.0)
Income before interest expense and taxes	$ 18.0	$ 22	$11	$ (4.0)	$11	(18.2)	100.0
Interest expense	2.0	2	1	—	1	—	100.0
Income before taxes	$ 16.0	$ 20	$10	$ (4.0)	$10	(20.0)	100.0
Income taxes (40% rate)	6.4	8	4	(1.6)	4	(20.0)	100.0
Net income	9.6	12	6	(2.4)	6	(20.0)	100.0

Because horizontal analysis stresses the trends of the various accounts, it is relatively easy to identify areas of wide divergence that require further attention. In the income statement shown in Example 2.2, the large increase in sales returns and allowances coupled with the decrease in sales for the period 19X2 to 19X3 should cause concern. One might compare these results with those of competitors to determine whether the problem is industrywide or just within the company.

Note that it is important to show both the dollar amount of change and the percentage of change, because either one alone might be misleading. For example, although the interest expense from 19X1 to 19X2 increased 100 percent (Example 2.2), it probably does not require further investigation since the dollar amount of increase is only $1,000. Similarly, a large change in dollar amount might result in only a small percentage change and therefore not be a cause for concern.

When an analysis covers a span of many years comparative financial statements may become cumbersome. To avoid this, the results of horizontal analysis may be presented by showing trends relative to a base year. In this method, a year representative of the firm's activity is chosen as the base. Each account of the base year is assigned an index of 100. The index for each respective account in succeeding years is found by dividing the account's amount by the base year amount and multiplying by 100. For example, if we let 19X1 be the base year in the balance sheet of Example 2.1, Accounts Receivable would be given an index of 100. In 19X2, the index would be 150 [(15/10) × 100], and in 19X3 it would be 200 [(20/10) × 100]. A condensed form of the balance sheet using *trend analysis* is shown in Example 2.3.

EXAMPLE 2.3

The Ratio Company
Trend Analysis of the Balance Sheet
(Expressed as Percent)
Dec. 31, 19X3, 19X2, and 19X1

	19X3	19X2	19X1
ASSETS			
Current assets	120	110	100
Plant assets	117.6	105.9	100
Total assets	118.9	108.1	100
LIABILITIES AND			
STOCKHOLDERS' EQUITY			
Liabilities			
Current liabilities	106.5	96.2	100
Long-term liabilities	114.3	107.1	100
Total liabilities	111.0	102.5	100
Stockholders' equity			
Common stock	100	100	100
Retained earnings	220	166.7	100
Total stockholders' equity	134.3	119	100
Total liabilities and stockholders' equity	118.9	108.1	100

2.4 VERTICAL ANALYSIS

In *vertical analysis*, a significant item on a financial statement is used as a base value, and all other items on the financial statement are compared to it. In performing vertical analysis for the balance sheet, total assets is assigned 100 percent. Each asset account is expressed as a percentage of total assets. Total liabilities and stockholders' equity is also assigned 100 percent. Each liability and equity account is then expressed as a percentage of total liabilities and stockholders' equity. In the income statement, net sales is given the value of 100 percent and all other accounts are evaluated in comparison to net sales. The resulting figures are then given in a *common size statement*. The common size analysis of Ratio Company's income statement is shown in Example 2.4.

EXAMPLE 2.4

The Ratio Company
Income Statement and
Common Size Analysis
(In Thousands of Dollars)
For the Years Ended Dec. 31, 19X3 and 19X2

	19X3		19X2	
	Amount	%	Amount	%
Sales	$100.0	125.0%	$110	107.8%
Sales returns and allowances	20.0	25.0	8	7.8
Net sales	$ 80.0	100.0	$102	100.0
Cost of goods sold	50.0	62.5	60	58.8
Gross profit	$ 30.0	37.5	$ 42	41.2
Operating expenses				
Selling expenses	$ 11.0	13.8	$ 13	12.7
General expenses	4.0	5.0	7	6.9
Total operating expenses	$ 15.0	18.3	$ 20	19.6
Income from operations	$ 15.0	18.7	$ 22	21.6
Nonoperating income	3.0	3.8		
Income before interest				
expense and taxes	S 18.0	22.5	$ 22	21.6
Interest expense	2.0	2.5	2	2.0
Income before taxes	S 16.0	20.0	$ 20	19.6
Income taxes	6.4	8.0	8	7.8
Net income	$ 9.6	12.0%	$ 12	11.8%

Vertical analysis is used to disclose the internal structure of an enterprise. It indicates the existing relationship between each income statement account and revenue. It shows the mix of assets that produces the income and the mix of the sources of capital, whether by current or long-term liabilities or by equity funding. In addition to making such internal evaluation possible, the results of vertical analysis are also used to further assess the firm's relative position in the industry.

As with horizontal analysis, vertical analysis is not the end of the process. The financial analyst must be prepared to probe deeper into those areas that either horizontal or vertical analysis, or both, indicate to be possible problem areas.

2.5   RATIO ANALYSIS

Horizontal and vertical analyses compare one figure to another within the same category. It is also essential to compare figures from different categories. This is accomplished through *ratio analysis*. There are many ratios that an analyst can use, depending upon what he or she considers to be important relationships.

Financial ratios can be classified into five groups:

1. Liquidity ratios
2. Activity ratios

3. Leverage ratios
4. Profitability ratios
5. Market value ratios

Some of the most useful ones in each category are discussed next.

Liquidity Ratios

Liquidity is a company's ability to meet its maturing short-term obligations. Liquidity is essential to conducting business activity, particularly in times of adversity, such as when a business is shut down by a strike or when operating losses ensue due to an economic recession or a steep rise in the price of a raw material or part. If liquidity is insufficient to cushion such losses, serious financial difficulty may result. Poor liquidity is analogous to a person having a fever—it is a symptom of a fundamental problem.

Analyzing corporate liquidity is especially important to creditors. If a company has a poor liquidity position, it may be a poor credit risk, perhaps unable to make timely interest and principal payments.

Liquidity ratios are static in nature as of year-end. Therefore, it is also important for management to look at expected *future* cash flows. If future cash outflows are expected to be high relative to inflows, the liquidity position of the company will deteriorate.

A description of various liquidity measures follows.

Net Working Capital.   Net working capital[1] is equal to current assets less current liabilities. *Current assets* are those assets that are expected to be converted into cash or used up within 1 year. *Current liabilities* are those liabilities that must be paid within 1 year; they are paid out of current assets. Net working capital is a safety cushion to creditors. A large balance is required when the entity has difficulty borrowing on short notice.

$$\text{Net working capital} = \text{current assets} - \text{current liabilities}$$

The net working capital for the Ratio Company for 19X3 is:

$$\$120,000 - \$55,400 = \$64,600$$

In 19X2, net working capital was $60,000. The increase in net working capital is a favorable sign.

Current Ratio.   The current ratio is equal to current assets divided by current liabilities. This ratio, which is subject to seasonal fluctuations, is used to measure the ability of an enterprise to meet its current liabilities out of current assets. A high ratio is needed when the firm has difficulty borrowing on short notice. A limitation of this ratio is that it may rise just prior to financial distress because of a company's desire to improve its cash position by, for example, selling fixed assets. Such dispositions have a detrimental effect upon productive capacity. Another limitation of the current ratio is that it will be excessively high when inventory is carried on the last-in, first-out (LIFO) basis.

$$\text{Current ratio} = \frac{\text{current assets}}{\text{current liabilities}}$$

The Ratio Company's current ratio for 19X3 is:

$$\frac{\$120,000}{\$55,400} = 2.17$$

In 19X2, the current ratio was 2.2. The ratio showed a slight decline over the year.

---

[1]Some textbooks define *working capital* as current assets less current liabilities. Therefore, the terms *net working capital* and *working capital* are often used interchangeably throughout those books.

Quick (Acid-Test) Ratio.   The quick ratio, also known as the acid-test ratio, is a stringent test of liquidity. It is found by dividing the most liquid current assets (cash, marketable securities, and accounts receivable) by current liabilities. Inventory is not included because of the length of time needed to convert inventory into cash. Prepaid expenses are also not included because they are not convertible into cash and so are not capable of covering current liabilities.

$$\text{Quick ratio} = \frac{\text{cash} + \text{marketable securities} + \text{accounts receivable}}{\text{current liabilities}}$$

The quick ratio for the Ratio Company in 19X3 is:

$$\frac{\$30,000 + \$20,000 + \$20,000}{\$55,400} = 1.26$$

The ratio was 1.3 in 19X3. The ratio went down slightly over the year.

Activity (Asset Utilization) Ratios

Activity ratios are used to determine how quickly various accounts are converted into sales or cash. Overall liquidity ratios generally do not give an adequate picture of a company's *real* liquidity, due to differences in the kinds of current assets and liabilities the company holds. Thus, it is necessary to evaluate the activity or liquidity of specific current accounts. Various ratios exist to measure the activity of receivables, inventory, and total assets.

Accounts Receivable Ratios.   Accounts receivable ratios consist of the accounts receivable turnover ratio and the average collection period. The *accounts receivable turnover ratio* gives the number of times accounts receivable is collected during the year. It is found by dividing net credit sales (if not available, then total sales) by the average accounts receivable. *Average accounts receivable* is typically found by adding the beginning and ending accounts receivable and dividing by 2. Although average accounts receivable may be computed annually, quarterly, or monthly, the ratio is most accurate when the shortest period available is used. In general, the higher the accounts receivable turnover, the better since the company is collecting quickly from customers and these funds can then be invested. However, an excessivly high ratio may indicate that the company's credit policy is too stringent, with the company not tapping the potential for profit through sales to customers in higher risk classes. Note that here, too, before changing its credit policy, a company has to weigh the profit potential against the risk inherent in selling to more marginal customers.

$$\text{Accounts receivable turnover} = \frac{\text{net credit sales}}{\text{average accounts receivable}}$$

Ratio Company's average accounts receivable for 19X3 is:

$$\frac{\$15,000 + \$20,000}{2} = \$17,500$$

The accounts receivable turnover ratio for 19X3 is:

$$\frac{\$80,000}{\$17,500} = 4.57 \text{ times}$$

In 19X2, the accounts receivable turnover ratio was 8.16. The drop in this ratio in 19X3 is significant and indicates a serious problem in collecting from customers. The company needs to reevaluate its credit policy, which may be too lax, or its billing and collection practices, or both.

The *collection period* (days sales in receivables) is the number of days it takes to collect on receivables.

$$\text{Average collection period} = \frac{365}{\text{accounts receivable turnover}}$$

The Ratio Company's average collection period for 19X3 is:

$$\frac{365}{4.57} = 79.9 \text{ days}$$

This means that it takes almost 80 days for a sale to be converted into cash. In 19X2, the average collection period was 44.7 days. With the substantial increase in collection days in 19X3, there exists a danger that customer balances may become uncollectible. One possible cause for the increase may be that the company is now selling to highly marginal customers. The analyst should compare the company's credit terms with the extent to which customer balances are delinquent. An *aging schedule*, which list the accounts receivable according to the length of time they are outstanding, would be helpful for this comparison.

Inventory Ratios.   If a company is holding excess inventory, it means that funds which could be invested elsewhere are being tied up in inventory. In addition, there will be high carrying cost for storing the goods, as well as the risk of obsolescence. On the other hand, if inventory is too low, the company may lose customers because it has run out of merchandise. Two major ratios for evaluating inventory are inventory turnover and average age of inventory.

Inventory turnover is computed as:

$$\text{Inventory turnover} = \frac{\text{cost of goods sold}}{\text{average inventory}}$$

Average inventory is determined by adding the beginning and ending inventories and dividing by 2.
    For the Ratio Company, the inventory turnover in 19X3 is:

$$\frac{\$50,000}{\$47,500} = 1.05 \text{ times}$$

In 19X2, the inventory turnover was 1.26 times.
    The decline in the inventory turnover indicates the stocking of goods. An attempt should be made to determine whether specific inventory categories are not selling well and if this is so, the reasons therefore. Perhaps there are obsolete goods on hand not actually worth their stated value. However, a decline in the turnover rate would not cause concern if it were primarily due to the introduction of a new product line for which the advertising effects have not been felt yet.

Average age of inventory is computed as follows:

$$\text{Average age of inventory} = \frac{365}{\text{inventory turnover}}$$

The average age of inventory in 19X3 is:

$$\frac{365}{1.05} = 347.6 \text{ days}$$

In 19X2, the average age was 289.7 days. The lengthening of the holding period shows a potentially greater risk of obsolescence.

Operating Cycle

The *operating cycle* of a business is the number of days it takes to convert inventory and receivables to cash. Hence, a short operating cycle is desirable.

Operating cycle = average collection period + average age of inventory

The operating cycle for the Ratio Company in 19X3 is:

79.9 days + 347.6 days = 427.5 days

In 19X2, the operating cycle was 334.4 days. This is an unfavorable trend since an increased amount of money is being tied up in noncash assets.

Total Asset Turnover. The total asset turnover ratio is helpful in evaluating a company's ability to use its asset base efficiently to generate revenue. A low ratio may be due to many factors, and it is important to identify the underlying reasons. For example, is investment in assets excessive when compared to the value of the output being produced? If so, the company might want to consolidate its present operation, perhaps by selling some of its assets and investing the proceeds for a higher return or using them to expand into a more profitable area.

$$\text{Total asset turnover} = \frac{\text{net sales}}{\text{average total assets}}$$

In 19X3 the total asset turnover ratio for the Ratio Company is:

$$\frac{\$80,000}{\$210,000} = 0.381$$

In 19X2, the ratio was 0.530 ($102,000/$192,500). The company's use of assets declined significantly, and the reasons need to be pinpointed. For example, are adequate repairs being made? Or are the assets getting old and do they need replacing?

Interrelationship of Liquidity and Activity to Earnings. A trade-off exists between liquidity risk and return. *Liquidity risk* is minimized by holding greater current assets than noncurrent assets. However, the rate of return will decline because the return on current assets (i.e., marketable securities) is typically less than the rate earned on productive fixed assets. Also, excessively high liquidity may mean that management has not aggressively searched for desirable capital investment opportunities. Maintaining a proper balance between liquidity and return is important to the overall financial health of a business.

It must be pointed out that high profitability does not necessarily infer a strong cash flow position. Income may be high but cash problems may exist because of maturing debt and the need to replace assets, among other reasons. For example, it is possible that a growth company may experience a decline in liquidity since the net working capital needed to support the expanding sales is tied up in assets that cannot be realized in time to meet the current obligations. The impact of earning activities on liquidity is highlighted by comparing *cash flow from operations* to net income.

If accounts receivable and inventory turn over quickly, the cash flow received from customers can be invested for a return, thus increasing net income.

Leverage (Solvency, Long-Term Debt) Ratios

Solvency is a company's ability to meet its long-term obligations as they become due. An analysis of solvency concentrates on the long-term financial and operating structure of the business. The degree of long-term debt in the capital structure is also considered. Further, solvency is dependent upon profitability since in the long run a firm will not be able to meet its debts unless it is profitable.

When debt is excessive, additional financing should be obtained primarily from equity sources. Management might also consider lengthening the maturity of the debt and staggering the debt repayment dates.

Some leverage ratios follow.

Debt Ratio. The debt ratio compares total liabilities (total debt) to total assets. It shows the percentage of total funds obtained from creditors. Creditors would rather see a low debt ratio because there is a greater cushion for creditor losses if the firm goes bankrupt.

$$\text{Debt ratio} = \frac{\text{total liabilities}}{\text{total assets}}$$

For the Ratio Company, in 19X3 the debt ratio is:

$$\frac{\$135,400}{\$220,000} = 0.62$$

In 19X2, the ratio was 0.63. There was a slight improvement in the ratio over the year as indicated by the lower degree of debt to total assets.

Debt/Equity Ratio.   The *debt/equity ratio* is a significant measure of solvency since a high degree of debt in the capital structure may make it difficult for the company to meet interest charges and principal payments at maturity. Further, with a high debt position comes the risk of running out of cash under conditions of adversity. Also, excessive debt will result in less financial flexibility since the company will have greater difficulty obtaining funds during a tight money market. The debt/equity ratio is computed as:

$$\text{Debt/equity ratio} = \frac{\text{total liabilities}}{\text{stockholders' equity}}$$

For Ratio Company, the debt/equity ratio was 1.60 in 19X3 ($135,400/$84,600) and 1.67 in 19X2. The ratio remained fairly constant. A desirable debt/equity ratio depends on many variables, including the rates of other companies in the industry, the access for further debt financing, and the stability of earnings.

Times Interest Earned (Interest Coverage) Ratio.   The times interest earned ratio reflects the number of times before-tax earnings cover interest expense.[2] It is a safety margin indicator in the sense that it shows how much of a decline in earnings a company can absorb. The ratio is computed as follows:

$$\text{Times interest earned ratio} = \frac{\text{earnings before interest and taxes (EBIT)}}{\text{interest expense}}$$

In 19X3, interest of Ratio Company was covered 9 times ($18,000/$2,000), while in 19X2 it was covered 11 times. The decline in the coverage is a negative indicator since less earnings are available to meet interest charges.

Profitability Ratios

An indication of good financial health and how effectively the firm is being managed is the company's ability to earn a satisfactory profit and return on investment. Investors will be reluctant to associate themselves with an entity that has poor earning potential since the market price of stock and dividend potential will be adversely affected. Creditors will shy away from companies with deficient profitability since the amounts owed to them may not be paid. Absolute dollar profit by itself has little significance unless it is related to its source.

Some major ratios that measure operating results are summarized below.

Gross Profit Margin.   The gross profit margin reveals the percentage of each dollar left over after the business has paid for its goods. The higher the gross profit earned, the better. Gross profit equals net sales less cost of goods sold.

$$\text{Gross profit margin} = \frac{\text{gross profit}}{\text{net sales}}$$

The gross profit margin for the Ratio Company in 19X3 is:

$$\frac{\$30,000}{\$80,000} = 0.38$$

---

[2] Note that some textbooks use *after*-tax earnings to calculate this ratio.

In 19X2 the gross profit margin was 0.41. The decline in this ratio indicates the business is earning less gross profit on each sales dollar. The reasons for the decline may be many, including a higher relative production cost of merchandise sold.

Profit Margin.   The ratio of net income to net sales is called the profit margin. It indicates the profitability generated from revenue and hence is an important measure of operating performance. It also provides clues to a company's pricing, cost structure, and production efficiency.

$$\text{Profit margin} = \frac{\text{net income}}{\text{net sales}}$$

In 19X3, the Ratio Company's profit margin is:

$$\frac{\$9,600}{\$80,000} = 0.120$$

In 19X2, the ratio was also 0.120. The constant profit margin indicates that the earning power of the business remained static.

Return on Investment.   Return on investment (ROI) is a key, but rough, measure of performance. Although ROI shows the extent to which earnings are achieved on the investment made in the business, the actual value is generally somewhat distorted.

There are basically two ratios that evaluate the return on investment. One is the return on total assets, and the other is the return on owners' equity.

The *return on total assets* (ROA) indicates the efficiency with which management has used its available resources to generate income.

$$\text{Return on total assets} = \frac{\text{net income}}{\text{average total assets}}$$

For the Ratio Company in 19X3, the return on total assets is:

$$\frac{\$9,600}{(\$220,000 + \$200,000)/2} = 0.0457$$

In 19X2, the return was 0.0623. The productivity of assets in deriving income deteriorated in 19X3.

The Du Pont formula shows an important tie-in between the profit margin and the return on total assets. The relationship is:

$$\text{Return on total assets} = \text{profit margin} \times \text{total asset turnover}$$

Therefore,

$$\frac{\text{Net income}}{\text{Average total assets}} = \frac{\text{net income}}{\text{net sales}} \times \frac{\text{net sales}}{\text{average total assets}}$$

As can be seen from this formula, the ROA can be raised by increasing either the profit margin or the asset turnover. The latter is to some extent industry dependent, with retailers and the like having a greater potential for raising the asset turnover ratio than do service and utility companies. However, the profit margin may vary greatly within an industry since it is subject to sales, cost controls, and pricing. The interrelationship shown in the Du Pont formula can therefore be useful to a company trying to raise its ROA since the area most sensitive to change can be targeted.

For 19X3, the figures for the Ratio Company are:

$$\text{Return on total assets} = \text{profit margin} \times \text{total asset turnover}$$
$$0.0457 = 0.120 \times 0.381$$

We know from our previous analysis that the profit margin has remained stable while asset turnover has deteriorated, bringing down the ROI. Since asset turnover can be considerably higher, Ratio Company might first focus on improving this ratio while at the same time reevaluating its pricing policy, cost controls, and sales practices.

The *return on common equity* (ROE) measures the rate of return earned on the common stockholders' investment.

$$\text{Return on common equity} = \frac{\text{earnings available to common stockholders}}{\text{average stockholders' equity}}$$

In 19X3, Ratio Company's return on equity is:

$$\frac{\$9,600}{(\$84,600 + \$75,000)/2} = 0.1203$$

In 19X2, the ROE was 0.17. There has been a significant drop in the return earned by the owners of the business.

ROE and ROA are closely related through what is known as the *equity multiplier* (leverage, or debt ratio) as follows:

$$\text{ROE} = \text{ROA} \times \text{equity multiplier}$$

$$= \text{ROA} \times \frac{\text{total assets}}{\text{common equity}}$$

or

$$= \frac{\text{ROA}}{1 - \text{debt ratio}}$$

In 19X3, the Ratio Company's debt ratio was 0.62. Thus,

$$\text{ROE} = \frac{0.0457}{1 - 0.62} = 0.1203$$

Note that ROA = 0.0457 and ROE = 0.1203. This means that through the favorable use of leverage (debt), the Ratio Company was able to increase the stockholders' return *significantly*.

Market Value Ratios

A final group of ratios relates the firm's stock price to its earnings (or book value) per share. It also includes dividend-related ratios.

Earnings per Share. Earnings per share indicates the amount of earnings for each common share held. When preferred stock is included in the capital structure, net income must be reduced by the preferred dividends to determine the amount applicable to common stock. When preferred stock does not exist, as is the case with the Ratio Company, earnings per share is equal to net income divided by common shares outstanding. Earnings per share is a useful indicator of the operating performance of the company as well as of the dividends that may be expected.

$$\text{Earnings per share} = \frac{\text{net income} - \text{preferred dividends}}{\text{common stock outstanding}}$$

In 19X3, earnings per share is:

$$\frac{\$9,600}{4,500 \text{ shares}} = \$2.13$$

In 19X2, earnings per share was $2.67. The decline in earnings per share should be of concern to investors.

Almost all of the Ratio Company's profitability ratios have declined in 19X3 relative to 19X2. This is a very negative sign.

Price/Earnings Ratio (Multiple). Some ratios evaluate the enterprise's relationship with its stockholders. The often quoted price/earnings (P/E) ratio is equal to the market price per share of stock divided by the earnings per share. A high P/E multiple is good because it indicates that the investing public considers the company in a favorable light.

$$\text{P/E ratio} = \frac{\text{market price per share}}{\text{earnings per share}}$$

Let us assume that the market price per share of Ratio Company stock was $20 on December 31, 19X3, and $22 on December 31, 19X2. Therefore, the P/E ratio in 19X3 is:

$$\frac{\$20}{\$2.13} = 9.39$$

The ratio in 19X2 was 8.24 ($22/$2.67). The rise in the P/E multiple indicates that the stock market has a favorable opinion of the company.

Book Value per Share. Book value per share is net assets available to common stockholders divided by shares outstanding, where net assets is stockholders' equity minus preferred stock. Comparing book value per share with market price per share gives another indication of how investors regard the firm.

The Ratio Company book value per share in 19X3 equals:

$$\text{Book value per share} = \frac{\text{total stockholders' equity} - \text{preferred stock}}{\text{shares outstanding}}$$

$$= \frac{\$34,600 - 0}{4,500} = \$18.80$$

The book value per share in 19X2 was $16.67.

If we assume the stock market has a market price of $20 per share, then Ratio Company's stock is favorably regarded by investors since its market price exceeds book value.

Dividend Ratios. Many stockholders are primarily interested in receiving dividends. The two pertinent ratios are *dividend yield* and *dividend payout.*

$$\text{Dividend yield} = \frac{\text{dividends per share}}{\text{market price per share}}$$

$$\text{Dividend payout} = \frac{\text{dividends per share}}{\text{earnings per share}}$$

Obviously, a decline in these ratios signals a decline in the value of dividends and would cause concern on the part of stockholders. (See Problem 2.12 for a computation of the dividend ratios.)

EXAMPLE 2.5

Summary of Financial Ratios

Ratio	Formula	19X2	19X3	Evaluation of Trend
Liquidity Net working capital	Current assets − current liabilities	$60,000	$64,600	Improved
Current ratio	$\dfrac{\text{Current assets}}{\text{Current liabilities}}$	2.2	2.17	Deteriorated
Quick ratio	$\dfrac{\text{Cash + marketable securities + receivables}}{\text{Current liabilities}}$	1.3	1.26	Deteriorated

(*continued*)

Summary of Financial Ratios (*cont.*)

Ratio	Formula	19X2	19X3	Evaluation of Trend
Activity				
Accounts receivable turnover	$\dfrac{\text{Net credit sales}}{\text{Average accounts receivable}}$	8.16	4.57	Deteriorated
Average collection period	$\dfrac{365}{\text{Accounts receivable turnover}}$	44.7 days	79.9 days	Deteriorated
Inventory turnover	$\dfrac{\text{Cost of goods sold}}{\text{Average inventory}}$	1.26	1.05	Deteriorated
Average age of inventory	$\dfrac{365}{\text{Inventory turnover}}$	289.7 days	347.6 days	Deteriorated
Operating cycle	Average collection period + average age of inventory	334.4 days	427.5 days	Deteriorated
Total asset turnover	$\dfrac{\text{Net sales}}{\text{Average total assets}}$	0.530	0.381	Deteriorated
Leverage				
Debt ratio	$\dfrac{\text{Total debt}}{\text{Total assets}}$	0.63	0.62	Improved
Debt/equity ratio	$\dfrac{\text{Total liabilities}}{\text{Stockholders' equity}}$	1.67	1.60	Improved
Times interest earned	$\dfrac{\text{Earnings before interest \& taxes}}{\text{Interest expense}}$	11 times	9 times	Deteriorated
Profitability				
Gross profit margin	$\dfrac{\text{Gross profit}}{\text{Net sales}}$	0.41	0.38	Deteriorated
Profit margin	$\dfrac{\text{Net income}}{\text{Net sales}}$	0.12	0.12	Constant
Return on total assets	$\dfrac{\text{Net income}}{\text{Average total assets}}$	0.0623	0.0457	Deteriorated
Return on common	$\dfrac{\text{Net income}}{\text{Common equity}}$	0.17	0.1203	Deteriorated
Market value				
Earnings per share	$\dfrac{\text{Net income} - \text{preferred dividends}}{\text{Common stock outstanding}}$	$2.67	$2.13	Deteriorated
Price/earnings ratio	$\dfrac{\text{Market price per share}}{\text{Earnings per share}}$	8.24	9.39	Improved
Book value per share	$\dfrac{\text{Stockholders' equity} - \text{preferred stock}}{\text{Common stock outstanding}}$	$16.67	$18.80	Improved
Dividend yield	$\dfrac{\text{Dividends per share}}{\text{Market price per share}}$			
Dividend payout	$\dfrac{\text{Dividends per share}}{\text{Earnings per share}}$			

Collective Inference of All the Ratios

By examining the trend in the company's ratios from 19X2 to 19X3, shown in Example 2.5, we find from the decline in the current and quick ratios that there has been a slight deterioration in liquidity. However, net working capital has improved. A significant deterioration in the activity ratios has taken place, indicating that better credit and inventory policies are needed. Ratio Company should improve its collection efforts. The increased age in inventory may point to obsolescence problems. On a positive note, the company's leverage has improved, so it is generally better able to meet long-term debt. However, less earnings are available to meet interest charges. Ratio Company's profitability has worsened over the year. As a result, the return on the owner's investment and the return on assets have gone down. Part of the reason for the earnings decrease may be the company's higher cost of short-term financing. The higher costs may have come about because of the problems with receivables and inventory that forced a decline in the liquidity and activity ratios. Also, as receivables and inventory turn over fewer times per year, earnings will drop from a lack of sales and the costs associated with holding higher current asset balances.

2.6 SUMMARY AND LIMITATIONS OF RATIO ANALYSIS

Financial statement analysis is an attempt to work with the reported financial figures in order to assess the entity's financial strengths and weaknesses.

Most analysts tend to favor certain ratios. They may leave out some of those mentioned in this chapter and include some not mentioned. Although other ratios may be of interest, depending on one's perspective (i.e., manager, stockholder, investor, creditor), there is no use in computing ratios of unrelated items such as sales returns to income taxes.

A banker, for example, is concerned with the firm's liquidity position in deciding whether to extend a short-term loan. On the other hand, a long-term creditor has more interest in the entity's earning power and operating efficiency as a basis to pay off the debt at maturity. Stockholders are interested in the long-run profitability of the firm since that will be the basis for dividends and appreciation in the market price of stock. Management, naturally, is interested in all aspects of financial analysis since they are concerned with how the firm looks to both the investment and credit communities.

Once a ratio is computed, it is compared with related ratios of the company, the same ratios from previous years, and the ratios of competitors. The comparisons show trends over a period of time and hence the ability of an enterprise to compete with others in the industry. Ratio comparisons do not mark the end of the analysis of the company, but rather indicate areas needing further attention.

Although ratio analysis is useful, it does have its limitations, some of which are listed below.

1. Many large firms are engaged in multiple lines of business, so that it is difficult to identify the industry group to which the firm belongs. Comparing their ratios with those of other corporations may be meaningless.

2. Operating and accounting practices differ from firm to firm, which can distort the ratios and make comparisons meaningless. For example, the use of different inventory valuation methods (LIFO versus FIFO) and different depreciation methods would affect inventory and asset turnover ratios.

3. Published industry average ratios are only approximations. Therefore, the company may have to look at the ratios of its major competitors, if such ratios are available.

4. Financial statements are based on historical costs and do not take inflation into account.

5. Management may hedge or exaggerate their financial figures; thus, certain ratios will not be accurate indicators.

6. A ratio does not describe the quality of its components. For example, the current ratio may be high but inventory may consist of obsolete goods.

7. Ratios are static and do not consider future trends.

2.7 CASH BASIS OF PREPARING THE STATEMENT OF CHANGES IN FINANCIAL POSITION

The statement of changes in financial position prepared on the *cash basis* typically provides more information for financial analysis. Its preparation is shown in the following example.

EXAMPLE 2.6   In addition to the information presented in the following balance sheet for the beginning and end of 19X1, Long Beach Corporation had a net income after taxes of $182 million and paid out $40 million in cash dividends.

Long Beach Corporation
Balance Sheet
(In Millions of Dollars)

	Jan. 1, 19X1	Dec. 31, 19X1	Source	Use
ASSETS				
Cash	$ 51	$ 27	$ 24	
Marketable securities	30	2	28	
Receivables	62	97		$ 35
Inventories	125	211		86
Total current assets	$268	$337		
Gross fixed assets	$225	$450		225
Less: Accumulated depreciation	(62)	(85)	23	
Net fixed assets	$163	$365		
Total assets	$431	$702		
LIABILITIES AND EQUITY				
Accounts payable	$ 65	$ 74	9	
Notes payable	45	9		36
Other current liabilities	21	45	24	
Long-term debt	24	78	54	
Common stock	114	192	78	
Retained earnings	162	304	142	
Total liabilities and equity	$431	$702	$382	$382

Note the purchase of fixed assets in the amount of $225 million and depreciation expense of $23 million. Prepare the statement of changes in financial position.

Long Beach Corporation
Statement of Changes in Financial Position
(In Millions of Dollars)

	Amount	% of Total
SOURCES		
From operations		
Net income	$182	45.73%
Depreciation	23	5.78
Sale of marketable securities	28	7.04
Increase in accounts payable	9	2.26
Increase in other liabilities	24	6.03
Issuance of long-term debt	54	13.57
Sale of common stock	78	19.60
Total sources	$398	100.00%
USES		
Payment of dividends	$ 40	9.48%
Increase in receivables	35	8.29
Increase in inventories	86	20.38
Decrease in notes payable	36	8.53
Purchase of fixed assets	225	53.32
Total uses	$422	100.00%
Decrease in cash	$ 24	

An analysis of the statement of changes in financial position shows the following information. Large investments were made in fixed assets and inventories (53.32 percent and 20.38 percent, respectively). Funds were also used to reduce outstanding notes payable and to increase accounts receivable. The uses of funds were met from internal sources, which provided 51.51 percent of the funds used (45.73 percent from retained earnings and 5.78 percent from depreciation), while another 33.17 percent of the total funds were raised through new issues of long-term debt and common stock (33.17% = 13.57% + 19.60%).

2.8   THE STATEMENT OF CASH FLOWS

The statement of cash flows shows the sources and uses of cash, which is a basis for cash flow analysis for financial managers. The statement aids him/her in answering vital questions like "where was money obtained?" and "where was money put and for what purpose?" The following provides a list of more specific questions that can be answered by the statement of cash flows and cash flow analysis:

1. Is the company growing or just maintaining its competitive position?
2. Will the company be able to meet its financial obligations?
3. Where did the company obtain funds?
4. What use was made of net income?
5. How much of the required capital has been generated internally?
6. How was the expansion in plant and equipment financed?
7. Is the business expanding faster than it can generate funds?
8. Is the company's dividend policy in balance with its operating policy?
9. Is the company's cash position sound and what effect will it have on the market price of stock?

Cash is vital to the operation of every business. How management utilizes the flow of cash can determine a firm's success or failure. Financial managers must control their company's cash flow so that bills can be paid on time and extra dollars can be put into the purchase of inventory and new equipment or invested to generate additional earnings.

FASB Requirements

Management and external interested parties have always recognized the need for a cash flow statement. Therefore, in recognition of the fact that cash flow information is an integral part of both investment and credit decisions, the Financial Accounting Standards Board (FASB) has issued Statement No. 95, "Statement of Cash Flows." This pronouncement requires that enterprises include a statement of cash flows as part of the financial statements. A statement of cash flows reports the cash receipts, payments, and net change in cash on hand resulting from the *operating*, *investing* and *financing* activities of an enterprise during a given period. The presentation reconciles beginning and ending cash balances.

Accrual Basis of Accounting

Under Generally Accepted Accounting Principles (GAAP), most companies use the accrual basis of accounting. This method requires that revenue be recorded when earned and that expenses be recorded when incurred. Revenue may include credit sales that have not yet been collected in cash and expenses incurred that may not have been paid in cash. Thus, under the accrual basis of accounting, net income will generally not indicate the net cash flow from operating activities. To arrive at net cash flow from operating activities, it is necessary to report revenues and expenses on a cash basis. This is accomplished by eliminating those transactions that did not result in a corresponding increase or decrease in cash on hand.

EXAMPLE 2.7   During 19X1, the Eastern Electric Supply Corporation earned $2,100,000 in credit sales, of which $100,000 remained uncollected as of the end of the calendar year. Cash that was actually collected by the corporation in 19X1 can be calculated as follows:

Credit sales	$2,100,000
Less: Credit sales uncollected	
at year end	100,000
Actual cash collected	$2,000,000

A statement of cash flows focuses only on transactions involving the cash receipts and disbursements of a company.

As previously stated, the statement of cash flows classifies cash receipts and cash payments into operating, investing, and financing activities.

Operating Activities

Operating activities include all transactions that are not investing or financing activities. They only relate to income statement items. Thus cash received from the sale of goods or services, including the collection or sale of trade accounts and notes receivable from customers, interest received on loans, and dividend income are to be treated as cash from operating activities. Cash paid to acquire materials for the manufacture of goods for resale, rental payments to landlords, payments to employees as compensation, and interest paid to creditors are classified as cash outflows for operating activities.

Investing Activities

Investing activities include cash inflows from the sale of property, plant, and equipment used in the production of goods and services, debt instruments or equity of other entities, and the collection of principal on loans made to other enterprises. Cash outflows under this category may result from the purchase of plant and equipment and other productive assets, debt instruments or equity of other entities, and the making of loans to other enterprises.

Financing Activities

The financing activities of an enterprise involve the sale of a company's own preferred and common stock, bonds, mortgages, notes, and other short- or long-term borrowings. Cash outflows classified as financing activities include the repayment of short- and long-term debt, the reacquisition of treasury stock, and the payment of cash dividends.

EXAMPLE 2.8   The basic form of the statement of cash flows for Long Beach Corporation in Example 2.6 is illustrated below.

Long Beach Corporation
Statement of Cash Flows
For the Year Ended December 31, 19X1
(In Millions of Dollars)

Cash flows from operating activities:		
Net income	182	
Add (deduct) to reconcile net income to net cash flow		
Depreciation	23	
Increase in accounts payable	9	
Increase in other liabilities	24	
Increase in accounts receivable	(35)	
Increase in inventory	(86)	
Net cash provided by operating activities		117
Cash flows from investing activities:		
Cash paid to purchase fixed assets	(225)	
Sale of marketable securities	28	(197)
Net cash provided by investing activities		
Cash flows from financing activities:		
Decrease in notes payable	(36)	
Issuance of long-term debt	54	
Sale of common stock	78	
Cash paid for dividends	(40)	
Net cash used in financing activities		56
Net decrease in cash and cash equivalents		(24)
Cash and cash equivalents at the beginning of the year		51
Cash and cash equivalents at the end of the year		27

Review Questions

1. Comparing an account to the same account in a prior year is known as _____ .

2. In a common size income statement, _____ is given the value of 100 percent.

3. _____ is the ability of a company to meet its current liabilities out of current assets.

4. The current ratio is equal to _____ divided by _____ .

5. _____ is included in computing the current ratio but not the quick ratio.

6. Accounts receivable turnover is equal to _____ divided by _____ .

7. The number of days for converting inventory sold on credit into cash is found by adding the _____ to the _____ .

8. The ratio of total liabilities to _____ is used to determine the degree of debt in the capital structure.

9. The number of times interest is earned is equal to _____ divided by _____ .

10. Return on owners' equity is found by dividing _____ by _____ .

11. The price/earnings ratio is equal to the _____ per share divided by the _____ per share.

12. Two measures that are of interest to stockholders in evaluating the dividend policy of a firm are the dividend _____ and the dividend _____ ratios.

13. When the comparison of ratios indicates a significant change in a company's financial position, the analyst should investigate further: (*a*) true; (*b*) false.

14. The Statement of Cash Flows seeks to explain the changes in _____ and _____ rather than ambiguous terms such as _____ .

15. The _____ is the breakdown of the return on total assets into the profit margin and _____ .

16. Depreciation expense is one of the items that must be _____ to net income to determine the cash flows from _____ .

17. The three major categories of the Statement of Cash Flows are cash flows associated with _____ activities, investing activities, and _____ activities.

18. The return on equity is the return on total assets multiplied by _____ .

19. A stock dividend (is/is not) shown in the Statement of Cash Flows.

20. Financial statement analysis should combine _____ and industry comparisons.

Answers: (1) horizontal analysis; (2) net sales; (3) Liquidity; (4) current assets, current liabilities; (5) Inventory; (6) net credit sales, average accounts receivable; (7) collection period, average age of inventory; (8) stockholders' equity; (9) income before interest and taxes, interest expense; (10) net income, average stockholders' equity; (11) market price, earnings; (12) yield, payout; (13) (*a*); (14) cash, cash equivalents, funds; (15) Du Pont formula, total asset turnover; (16) added back, operating activities; (17) operating, financing; (18) equity multiplier; (19) is not; (20) trend analysis.

Solved Problems

2.1   Horizontal Analysis. Smith Corporation provides the following comparative income statement:

Smith Corporation
Comparative Income Statement
For the Years Ended Dec. 31, 19X3 and 19X2

	19X3	19X2
Sales	$570,000	$680,000
Cost of goods sold	200,000	170,000
Gross profit	$370,000	$510,000
Operating expenses	100,000	210,000
EBIT	$270,000	$300,000

(*a*) Calculate the percentage change using horizontal analysis and (*b*) evaluate the results.

SOLUTION

(*a*)   *Smith Corporation*
Comparative Income Statement
For the Years Ended Dec. 31, 19X3 and 19X2

	19X3	19X2	% Increase or (Decrease)
Sales	$570,000	$680,000	(16.2)
Cost of goods sold	200,000	170,000	17.6
Gross profit	$370,000	$510,000	(27.5)
Operating expenses	100,000	210,000	(52.4)
EBIT	$270,000	$300,000	(10.0)

(*b*)   Gross profit declined 27.5 percent due to the combined effects of lower sales and higher cost of sales. However, operating expenses were sharply cut. This kept the decline in net income to only 10 percent.

2.2   Index Numbers. Jones Corporation reports the following for the period 19X1 to 19X3:

	19X3	19X2	19X1
Current liabilities	$34,000	$25,000	$20,000
Long-term liabilities	$60,000	$45,000	$50,000

The base year is 19X1. Using trend analysis, determine the appropriate index numbers.

SOLUTION

	19X3	19X2	19X1
Current liabilities	170	125	100
Long-term liabilities	120	90	100

2.3   Vertical Analysis. The Lyons Corporation reported the following income statement data:

	19X2	19X1
Net sales	$400,000	$250,000
Cost of goods sold	$280,000	$160,000
Operating expenses	$75,000	$56,000

(*a*) Prepare a comparative income statement for 19X2 and 19X1 using vertical analysis, and (*b*) evaluate the results.

SOLUTION

(*a*)

The Lyons Corporation
Income Statement and
Common Size Analysis
For the Years Ended Dec. 31, 19X2 and 19X1

	19X2		19X1	
	Amount	%	Amount	%
Net sales	$400,000	100	$250,000	100
Cost of goods sold	280,000	70	160,000	64
Gross profit	$120,000	30	$ 90,000	36
Operating expenses	75,000	18.8	56,000	22.4
EBIT	$ 45,000	11.2%	$ 34,000	13.6%

(*b*)   Cost of goods sold may have increased because of higher costs in buying merchandise. Expenses may have dropped due to better cost control. However, the drop in expenses has not offset the rise in the cost of goods sold and so the company's profits have declined from 19X1 to 19X2.

2.4   Net Working Capital, Current Ratio, and Quick Ratio. Charles Corporation's balance sheet at December 31, 19X7, shows the following:

Current assets	
Cash	$ 4,000
Marketable securities	8,000
Accounts receivable	100,000
Inventories	120,000
Prepaid expenses	1,000
Total current assets	$233,000
Current liabilities	
Notes payable	$ 5,000
Accounts payable	150,000
Accrued expenses	20,000
Income taxes payable	1,000
Total current liabilities	$176,000
Long-term liabilities	$340,000

Determine the following: (*a*) net working capital; (*b*) current ratio; and (*c*) quick ratio.

SOLUTION

(*a*)
$$\text{Net working capital} = \text{current assets} - \text{current liabilities}$$
$$= \$223,000 - \$176,000 = \$57,000$$

(*b*)
$$\text{Current ratio} = \frac{\text{current assets}}{\text{current liabilities}} = \frac{\$233,000}{\$176,000} = 1.32$$

(*c*)
$$\text{Quick ratio} = \frac{\text{cash} + \text{marketable securities} + \text{accounts receivable}}{\text{current liabilities}}$$

$$\frac{\$4,000 + \$8,000 + \$100,000}{\$176,000} = \frac{\$112,000}{\$176,000} = .64$$

2.5   Liquidity Position. Based upon the answer to Problem 2.4, does Charles Corporation have good or poor liquidity if industry average for current ratio is 1.29 and quick ratio is 1.07?

SOLUTION

While the company's current ratio is slightly better than the industry norm, its quick ratio is significantly below the norm. Charles Corporation has more current liabilities than highly liquid assets and so has a poor liquidity position.

2.6   Accounts Receivable. The Rivers Company reports the following data relative to accounts receivable:

	19X2	19X1
Average accounts receivable	$ 400,000	$ 416,000
Net credit sales	$2,600,000	$3,100,000

The terms of sale are net 30 days. (*a*) Compute the accounts receivable turnover and the collection period, and (*b*) evaluate the results.

SOLUTION

(*a*)
$$\text{Accounts receivable turnover} = \frac{\text{net credit sales}}{\text{average accounts receivable}}$$

For 19X2:
$$\frac{\$2,600,000}{\$400,000} = 6.5 \text{ times}$$

For 19X1:
$$\frac{\$3,100,000}{\$416,000} = 7.45 \text{ times}$$

$$\text{Collection period} = \frac{365}{\text{accounts receivable turnover}}$$

For 19X2:
$$\frac{365}{6.5} = 56.2 \text{ days}$$

For 19X1:
$$\frac{365}{7.45} = 49 \text{ days}$$

(*b*) The company's management of accounts receivable is poor. In both years, the collection period exceeded the terms of net 30 days. The situation is getting worse, as is indicated by the significant increase in the collection period in 19X2 relative to 19X1. The company has significant funds tied up in accounts receivable that otherwise could be invested for a return. A careful evaluation of the credit policy is needed; perhaps too many sales are being made to marginal customers.

2.7 **Net Sales.** Utica Company's net accounts receivable were $250,000 as of December 31, 19X8, and $300,000 as of December 31, 19X9. Net cash sales for 19X9 were $100,000. The accounts receivable turnover for 19X9 was 5.0. What were Utica's total net sales for 19X9?

SOLUTION

$$\text{Average accounts receivable} = \frac{\text{beginning accounts receivable} + \text{ending accounts receivable}}{2}$$

$$\frac{\$250,000 + \$300,000}{2} = \$275,000$$

$$\text{Accounts receivable turnover} = \frac{\text{net credit sales}}{\text{average accounts receivable}}$$

$$5 = \frac{\text{net credit sales}}{\$275,000}$$

$$\text{Net credit sales} = 5 \times \$275,000 = \$1,375,000$$

Since the cash sales were $100,000, the total net sales must be $1,475,000.

2.8 **Inventory.** On January 1, 19X6, the River Company's beginning inventory was $400,000. During 19X6, River purchased $1,900,000 of additional inventory. On December 31, 19X6, River's ending inventory was $500,000. (*a*) What is the inventory turnover and the age of inventory for 19X6? (*b*) If the inventory turnover in 19X5 was 3.3 and the average age of the inventory was 100.6 days, evaluate the results for 19X6.

SOLUTION

(*a*)   First determine the cost of goods sold:

Beginning inventory	$ 400,000
Purchases	1,900,000
Cost of goods available	$2,300,000
Ending inventory	500,000
Cost of goods sold	$1,800,000

$$\text{Average inventory} = \frac{\text{beginning inventory} + \text{ending inventory}}{2} = \frac{\$400,000 + \$500,000}{2} = \$450,000$$

$$\text{Inventory turnover} = \frac{\text{cost of goods sold}}{\text{average inventory}} = \frac{\$1,800,000}{\$450,000} = 4$$

$$\text{Average age of inventory} = \frac{365}{\text{inventory turnover}} = \frac{365}{4} = 91.3 \text{ days}$$

(*b*)   River Company's inventory management improved in 19X6, as evidenced by the higher turnover rate and the decrease in the number of days that inventory was held. As a result, there is less liquidity risk and the company's profitability will benefit from the increased turnover of merchandise. Note that this is only a conjecture, based on an evaluation of two ratios in isolation; keep in mind that if the rapid turnover was accomplished by offering excessive discounts, for example, profitability ratios may not show an improvement.

2.9 **Operating Cycle.** Based on your answer to Problem 2.8, what is the River Company's operating cycle in 19X6 if it is assumed that the average collection period is 42 days?

SOLUTION

Average age of inventory	91.3
Average collection period	42.0
Operating cycle	133.3 days

2.10 Financial Ratios. A condensed balance sheet and other financial data for the Alpha Company appear below.

Alpha Company
Balance Sheet
Dec. 31, 19X1

ASSETS

Current assets	$100,000
Plant assets	150,000
Total assets	$250,000

LIABILITIES AND
**   STOCKHOLDERS' EQUITY**

Current liabilities	$100,000
Long-term liabilities	75,000
Total liabilities	$175,000
Stockholders' equity	75,000
Total liabilities and stockholders' equity	$250,000

Income statement data appear below.

Net sales	$375,000
Interest expense	4,000
Net income	22,500

The following account balances existed at December 31, 19X0:

Total assets	$200,000
Stockholders' equity	$65,000

The tax rate is 35 percent. Industry norms as of December 31, 19X1, are:

Debt/equity ratio	1.75
Profit margin	0.12
Return on total assets	0.15
Return on stockholders' equity	0.30
Total asset turnover	1.71

Calculate and evaluate the following ratios for Alpha Company as of December 31, 19X1: (a) debt/equity ratio; (b) profit margin; (c) return on total assets; (d) return on stockholders' equity; and (e) total asset turnover.

SOLUTION

(a)
$$\text{Debt/equity ratio} = \frac{\text{total liabilities}}{\text{stockholders' equity}} = \frac{\$175,000}{\$75,000} = 2.33$$

Alpha's debt/equity ratio is considerably above the industry norm, indicating a solvency problem. Excessive debt may make it difficult for the firm to meet its obligations during a downturn in business. A high debt position will also make it difficult for Alpha Company to obtain financing during a period of tight money supply.

(b)
$$\text{Profit margin} = \frac{\text{net income}}{\text{net sales}} = \frac{\$22,500}{\$375,000} = 0.06$$

Alpha's profit margin is far below the industry norm. This indicates that the operating performance of the company is poor because the profitability generated from revenue sources is low.

(c)
$$\text{Return on total assets} = \frac{\text{net income}}{\text{average total assets}} = \frac{\$22,500}{(\$200,000 + \$250,000)/2} = \frac{\$22,500}{\$225,000} = 0.10$$

Alpha's return on total assets is below the industry norm; therefore, the company's efficiency in generating profit from assets is low. Profit generation is, of course, different from revenue (sales) generation because for the former, corporate expenses are deducted from sales.

(d)
$$\text{Return on stockholders' equity} = \frac{\text{net income}}{\text{average stockholders' equity}}$$

$$= \frac{\$22,500}{(\$65,000 + \$75,000)/2} = \frac{\$22,500}{\$70,000} = 0.32$$

Since the return earned by Alpha's stockholders is slightly more than the industry norm, investment in the firm relative to competition was advantageous to existing stockholders. This may be due to a currently low stockholders' equity investment in the firm. Note also that although stockholders earned a good return, some ratios show that their investment is riskier than most. Whether the return is good enough to warrant the risk of continued investment in Alpha is a decision each stockholder must make individually.

(e)
$$\text{Total asset turnover} = \frac{\text{net sales}}{\text{average total assets}} = \frac{\$375,000}{\$225,000} = 1.67$$

Alpha's ratio is about the same as the industry norm. Therefore, the company's ability to utilize its assets in obtaining revenue is similar to that of competition. The utilization of assets has a bearing upon the ultimate profitability to stockholders.

2.11   Financial Ratios. The Format Company reports the following balance sheet data:

Current liabilities	$280,000
Bonds payable, 16%	$120,000
Preferred stock, 14%, $100 par value	$200,000
Common stock, $25 par value, 16,800 shares	$420,000
Paid-in capital on common stock	$240,000
Retained earnings	$180,000

Income before taxes is $160,000. The tax rate is 40 percent. Common stockholders' equity in the previous year was $800,000. The market price per share of common stock is $35. Calculate (a) net income; (b) preferred dividends; (c) return on common stock; (d) times interest earned; (e) earnings per share; (f) price/earnings ratio; and (g) book value per share.

SOLUTION

(a)
Income before taxes	$160,000
Taxes (40% rate)	64,000
Net income	$ 96,000

(b)   Preferred dividends = 14% × $200,000 = $28,000

(c)   Common stockholders' equity is computed as follows:

Common stock	$420,000
Paid-in capital on common stock	240,000
Retained earnings	180,000
Common stockholders' equity	$840,000

$$\text{Return on common stock} = \frac{\text{net income} - \text{preferred dividends}}{\text{average common stockholders' equity}}$$

$$= \frac{\$96,000 - \$28,000}{(\$800,000 + \$840,000)/2} = \frac{\$68,000}{\$820,000} = 0.08$$

(d)   Income before interest and taxes equals:

Income before taxes	$160,000
Interest expense (16% × $120,000)	19,200
Income before interest and taxes	$179,200

$$\text{Times interest earned} = \frac{\text{income before interest and taxes}}{\text{interest expense}}$$

$$= \frac{\$179,200}{\$19,200} = 9.33 \text{ times}$$

(e) $$\text{Earnings per share} = \frac{\text{net income} - \text{preferred dividends}}{\text{common stock outstanding}} = \frac{\$96,000 - \$28,000}{16,800 \text{ shares}} = \$4.05$$

(f) $$\text{Price/earnings ratio} = \frac{\text{market price per share}}{\text{earnings per share}} = \frac{\$35.00}{\$4.05} = 8.64 \text{ times}$$

(g) $$\text{Book value per share} = \frac{\text{stockholders' equity} - \text{preferred stock}}{\text{common stock outstanding}}$$

$$= \frac{\$840,000}{16,800 \text{ shares}} = \$50 \text{ per share}$$

2.12   Dividends. Wilder Corporation's common stock account for 19X3 and 19X2 showed:

Common stock, $10 par value $45,000

The following data are provided relative to 19X3 and 19X2:

	19X3	19X2
Dividends	$2,250	$3,600
Market price per share	$20	$22
Earnings per share	$2.13	$2.67

(a) Calculate the dividends per share, dividend yield, and dividend payout, and (b) evaluate the results.

SOLUTION

(a)

$$\text{Dividends per share} = \frac{\text{dividends}}{\text{outstanding shares}}$$

For 19X3: $\dfrac{\$2,250}{4,500 \text{ shares}} = \$0.50$

For 19X2: $\dfrac{\$3,600}{4,500 \text{ shares}} = \$0.80$

$$\text{Dividend yield} = \frac{\text{dividends per share}}{\text{market price per share}}$$

For 19X3: $\dfrac{\$0.50}{\$20.00} = 0.025$

For 19X2: $\dfrac{\$0.80}{\$22.00} = 0.036$

$$\text{Dividend payout} = \frac{\text{dividends per share}}{\text{earnings per share}}$$

For 19X3: $\dfrac{\$0.50}{\$2.13} = 0.23$

For 19X2: $\dfrac{\$0.80}{\$2.67} = 0.30$

(b)   The decline in dividends per share, dividend yield, and dividend payout from 19X2 to 19X3 will cause concern to both stockholders and management.

Stockholders will want to determine the reason for the decline. For example, do they know that the company is investing heavily to reposition itself for greater competitiveness in the future? Has the entire industry suffered a decline or only Wilder? Is the company on solid financial footing or is it borderline? What is the company's—and the industry's—potential for the future?

Management will want to deal with similar questions and find solutions to other problems, such as how to manage their finances so as not to lose investors in the short term while ensuring financial health in the long term. Whatever the reasons for the decline in the ratios, this is a situation where management cannot safely ignore the short term and may therefore choose to sacrifice some long-term goals in order to turn the ratios around. The extent to which a company may choose to do this depends on many factors, including its relative financial health, its reputation in the financial world, how much risk managers are willing (or able) to take, what the actual problems are, and what options are available as solutions.

2.13   Financial Ratios. Jones Corporation's financial statements appear below.

Jones Corporation
Balance Sheet
Dec. 31, 19X1

ASSETS

Current assets		
Cash	$100,000	
Marketable securities	200,000	
Inventory	300,000	
Total current assets		$ 600,000
Plant assets		500,000
Total assets		$1,100,000

LIABILITIES AND STOCKHOLDERS' EQUITY

Liabilities		
Current liabilities	$200,000	
Long-term liabilities	100,000	
Total liabilities		$ 300,000
Stockholders' equity		
Common stock, $1 par value,		
100,000 shares	$100,000	
Premium on common stock	500,000	
Retained earnings	200,000	
Total stockholders' equity		800,000
Total liabilities and stockholders' equity		$1,100,000

Jones Corporation
Income Statement
For the Year Ended Dec. 31, 19X1

Net sales	$10,000,000
Cost of goods sold	6,000,000
Gross profit	$ 4,000,000
Operating expenses	1,000,000
Income before taxes	$ 3,000,000
Income taxes (50% rate)	1,500,000
Net income	$ 1,500,000

Additional information includes a market price of $150 per share of stock, total dividends of $600,000 for 19X1, and $250,000 of inventory as of December 31, 19X0.

Compute the following ratios: (*a*) current ratio; (*b*) quick ratio; (*c*) inventory turnover; (*d*) average age of inventory; (*e*) debt/equity ratio; (*f*) book value per share; (*g*) earnings per share; (*h*) price/earnings ratio; (*i*) dividends per share; and (*j*) dividend payout.

SOLUTION

(*a*) $$\text{Current ratio} = \frac{\text{current assets}}{\text{current liabilities}} = \frac{\$600,000}{\$200,000} = 3.0$$

(*b*) $$\text{Quick ratio} = \frac{\text{cash} + \text{marketable securities}}{\text{current liabilities}} = \frac{\$300,000}{\$200,000} = 1.5$$

(*c*) $$\text{Inventory turnover} = \frac{\text{cost of goods sold}}{\text{average inventory}} = \frac{\$6,000,000}{(\$250,000 + \$300,000)/2} = 21.82$$

(*d*) $$\text{Average age of inventory} = \frac{365}{\text{inventory turnover}} = \frac{365}{21.82} = 16.7 \text{ days}$$

(*e*) $$\text{Debt/equity ratio} = \frac{\text{total liabilities}}{\text{stockholders' equity}} = \frac{\$300,000}{\$800,000} = 0.375$$

(*f*) $$\text{Book value per share} = \frac{\text{stockholders' equity} - \text{preferred stock}}{\text{common shares outstanding}} = \frac{\$800,000}{100,000 \text{ shares}} = \$8$$

(g) $$\text{Earnings per share} = \frac{\text{net income}}{\text{outstanding common shares}} = \frac{\$1,500,000}{100,000 \text{ shares}} = \$15$$

(h) $$\text{Price/earnings ratio} = \frac{\text{market price per share}}{\text{earnings per share}} = \frac{\$150}{\$15} = 10$$

(i) $$\text{Dividends per share} = \frac{\text{dividends}}{\text{outstanding shares}} = \frac{\$600,000}{100,000 \text{ shares}} = \$6$$

(j) $$\text{Dividend payout} = \frac{\text{dividends per share}}{\text{earnings per share}} = \frac{\$6}{\$15} = 0.4$$

2.14 **Financial Ratios.** The 19X9 financial statements for Johanson Co. are reproduced below.

Johanson Co.
Statement of Financial Position
(In Thousands of Dollars)
Dec. 31, 19X8 and 19X9

	19X8	19X9
ASSETS		
Current assets		
Cash and temporary investments	$ 380	$ 400
Accounts receivable (net)	1,500	1,700
Inventories	2,120	2,200
Total current assets	$4,000	$4,300
Long-term assets		
Land	$ 500	$ 500
Building and equipment (net)	4,000	4,700
Total long-term assets	$4,500	$5,200
Total assets	$8,500	$9,500
LIABILITIES AND STOCKHOLDERS' EQUITY		
Liabilities		
Current liabilities		
Accounts payable	$ 700	$1,400
Current portion of long-term debt	500	1,000
Total current liabilities	$1,200	$2,400
Long-term debt	4,000	3,000
Total liabilities	$5,200	$5,400
Stockholders' equity		
Common stock	$3,000	$3,000
Retained earnings	300	1,100
Total stockholders' equity	$3,300	$4,100
Total liabilities and stockholders' equity	$8,500	$9,500

Johanson Company
Statement of Income and Retained Earnings
(In Thousands of Dollars)
For the Year Ended Dec. 31, 19X9

Net sales		$28,800
Less: Cost of goods sold	$15,120	
Selling expenses	7,180	
Administrative expenses	4,100	
Interest	400	
Income taxes	800	27,600
Net income		$ 1,200
Retained earnings January 1		300
Subtotal		$ 1,500
Cash dividends declared and paid		400
Retained earnings December 31		$ 1,100

For 19X9, find (a) the acid-test ratio; (b) the average number of days sales were outstanding; (c) the times interest earned ratio; (d) the asset turnover; (e) the inventory turnover; (f) the operating income margin; and (g) the dividend payout ratio. (CMA, adapted.)

SOLUTION

(a) $$\text{Acid-test ratio} = \frac{\text{cash} + \text{net receivables} + \text{marketable securities}}{\text{current liabilities}} = \frac{\$400 + \$1,700}{\$2,400} = 0.875 \cong 0.9$$

(b) $$\text{Accounts receivable turnover ratio} = \frac{\text{net credit sales}}{\text{average accounts receivable}} = \frac{\$28,000}{(\$1,500 + \$1,700)/2} = 18$$

$$\text{Number of days sales outstanding} = \frac{365}{\text{accounts receivable turnover ratio}} = \frac{365}{18} = 20.3$$

(c) $$\text{Times interest earned ratio} = \frac{\text{net income} + \text{taxes} + \text{interest expense}}{\text{interest expense}}$$

$$= \frac{\$1,200 + \$800 + \$400}{\$400} = 6.0$$

(d) $$\text{Asset turnover ratio} = \frac{\text{sales}}{\text{average assets during year}}$$

$$= \frac{\$28,800}{(\$8,500 + \$9,500)/2} = 3.2$$

(e) $$\text{Inventory turnover ratio} = \frac{\text{cost of sales}}{\text{average inventory}} = \frac{\$15,120}{(\$2,120 + \$2,200)/2} = 7.0$$

(f) $$\text{Operating income margin} = \frac{\text{net income from operations before taxes}}{\text{net sales}}$$

$$= \frac{\$1,200 + \$800 + \$400}{\$28,800} = 8.3\%$$

(g) $$\text{Dividend payout ratio} = \frac{\text{dividends}}{\text{net income}} = \frac{\$400}{\$1,200} = 33.3\%$$

2.15   Financial Ratios. Warford Corporation was formed 5 years ago through a public subscription of common stock. Lucinda Street, who owns 15 percent of the common stock, was one of the organizers of Warford and is its current president. The company has been successful, but it is currently experiencing a shortage of funds. On June 10, Street approached the Bell National Bank, asking for a 24-month extension on two $30,000 notes, which are due on June 30, 19X2 and September 30, 19X2. Another note of $7,000 is due on December 31, 19X2, but Street expects to have no difficulty in paying this note on its due date. Street explained that Warford's cash flow problems are primarily due to the company's desire to finance a $300,000 plant expansion over the next 2 fiscal years through internally generated funds.

The commercial loan officer of Bell National Bank requested financial reports for the last 2 fiscal years. These reports are reproduced below.

Warford Corporation
Income Statement
For the Fiscal Years Ended Mar. 31, 19X1 and 19X2

	19X1	19X2
Sales	$2,700,000	$3,000,000
Cost of goods sold[a]	1,720,000	1,902,500
Gross margin	$ 980,000	$1,097,500
Operating expenses	780,000	845,000
Net income before taxes	$ 200,000	$ 252,500
Income taxes (40%)	80,000	101,000
Income after taxes	$ 120,000	$ 151,500

[a] Depreciation charges of $100,000 on the plant and equipment and $102,500 for fiscal years ended March 31, 19X1 and 19X2, respectively, are included in cost of goods sold.

Warford Corporation
Statement of Financial Position
Mar. 31, 19X1 and 19X2

	19X1	19X2
ASSETS		
Cash	$ 12,500	$ 16,400
Notes receivable	104,000	112,000
Accounts receivable (net)	68,500	81,600
Inventories (at cost)	50,000	80,000
Plant and equipment (net of depreciation)	646,000	680,000
Total assets	$881,000	$970,000
LIABILITIES AND OWNERS' EQUITY		
Accounts payable	$ 72,000	$ 69,000
Notes payable	54,500	67,000
Accrued liabilities	6,000	9,000
Common stock (60,000 shares, $10 par)	600,000	600,000
Retained earnings[a]	148,500	225,000
Total liabilities and owners' equity	$881,000	$970,000

[a] Cash dividends were paid at the rate of $1 per share in fiscal year 19X1 and $1.25 per share in fiscal year 19X2.

Calculate the following items for Warford Corporation: (a) current ratio for fiscal years 19X1 and 19X2; (b) quick (acid-test) ratio for fiscal years 19X1 and 19X2; (c) inventory turnover for fiscal year 19x2; (d) return on assets for fiscal years 19X1 and 19X2; and (e) percentage change in sales, cost of goods sold, gross margin, and net income after taxes from fiscal year 19X1 to 19X2. (CMA, adapted.)

SOLUTION

(a)
$$\text{Current ratio} = \frac{\text{current assets}}{\text{current liabilities}}$$

For 19X1:
$$\frac{\$235,000}{\$132,500} = 1.77$$

For 19X2:
$$\frac{\$290,000}{\$145,000} = 2.00$$

(b)
$$\text{Quick ratio} = \frac{\text{current assets} - \text{inventories}}{\text{current liabilities}}$$

For 19X1:
$$\frac{\$185,000}{\$132,500} = 1.40$$

For 19X2:
$$\frac{\$210,000}{\$145,000} = 1.45$$

(c)
$$\text{Inventory turnover} = \frac{\text{cost of goods sold}}{\text{average inventory}}$$

For 19X2:
$$\frac{\$1,902,500}{(\$50,000 + \$30,000)/2} = 29 \text{ times}$$

(d)
$$\text{Return on assets} = \frac{\text{net income}}{\text{total assets}}$$

For 19X1:
$$\frac{\$120,000}{\$881,000} = 13.6\%$$

For 19X2:
$$\frac{\$151,500}{\$970,000} = 15.6\%$$

(e)   Percent changes are as follows (in thousands of dollars):

	Amounts		% increase
	19X2	19X1	
Sales	$3,000.0	$2,700.0	$\frac{\$300.0}{\$2,700.0} = 11.11\%$
Cost of goods sold	$1,902.5	$1,720.0	$\frac{\$182.5}{\$1,720.0} = 10.61\%$
Gross margin	$1,097.5	$ 980.0	$\frac{\$117.5}{\$980.0} = 11.99\%$
Net income after taxes	$ 151.5	$ 120.0	$\frac{\$31.5}{\$120.0} = 26.25\%$

2.16   Financial Ratios. Ratio analysis is employed to gain insight into the financial character of a firm. The calculation of ratios can often lead to a better understanding of a firm's financial position and performance. A specific ratio or a number of selected ratios can be calculated and used to measure or evaluate a specific financial or operating characteristic of a firm. (*a*) Identify and explain what financial characteristic of a firm would be measured by an analysis in which the following four ratios were calculated: (1) current ratio; (2) acid-test ratio; (3) accounts receivable turnover ratio; and (4) inventory turnover ratio. (*b*) Do the ratios in part (*a*) provide adequate information to measure this characteristic or are additional data needed? If so, provide two examples of other data that would be required. (*c*) Identify and explain what specific characteristic regarding a firm's operations would be measured by an analysis in which the following three ratios were calculated: (1) gross profit margin; (2) operating income margin; and (3) net income to sales (profit margin). (*d*) Do these ratios provide adequate information to measure this characteristic or are additional data needed? If so, provide two examples of other data that would be required.

SOLUTION

(*a*) These four ratios are used to measure short-term liquidity and to evaluate the management of net working capital of a firm, i.e., the ability to meet financial obligations in the near future.

(*b*) For a thorough analysis of the firm's ability to meet its financial obligations in the near future, we would also need to know the normal and/or industry standards for these ratios in order to have a basis of comparison. In addition, we would need to know if any current assets are pledged or restricted for any reason, if open lines of credit are available to the firm, the firm's credit rating, and any capital investment plans that might require an inordinate amount of cash.

(*c*) These three ratios are used to measure the profitability of a firm; respectively, each ratio relates sales revenue with (1) the cost of goods or services sold; (2) the costs of operating the business, which would include the cost of goods sold, the marketing expenses, the administrative expenses, and other general operating expenses; and (3) the final net result of all the corporate financial activity for the accounting period.

(*d*) These ratios do provide an indication of the firm's profitability. However, to complete a thorough analysis, it would be necessary to determine the return on investment, earnings per share, inventory valuation methods, depreciation methods, and any nonrecurring items included in the statement. In addition, data about the cost/volume/profit relationships would be useful. All this information should be evaluated while considering industry averages, results of prior periods, and future projections.

2.17 **The Du Pont Formula and Return on Total Assets.** Industry A has three companies whose income statements and balance sheets are summarized below.

	Company X	Company Y	Company Z
Sales	$500,000	(*d*)	(*g*)
Net income	$25,000	$30,000	(*h*)
Total assets	$100,000	(*e*)	$250,000
Total asset turnover	(*a*)	(*f*)	0.4
Profit margin	(*b*)	0.4%	5%
Return on total assets (ROA)	(*c*)	2%	(*i*)

First supply the missing data in the table above. Then comment on the relative performance of each company.

SOLUTION

(*a*)
$$\text{Total asset turnover} = \frac{\text{sales}}{\text{average total assets}} = \frac{\$500,000}{\$100,000} = 5 \text{ times}$$

(*b*)
$$\text{Profit margin} = \frac{\text{net income}}{\text{sales}} = \frac{\$25,000}{\$500,000} = 5\%$$

(c)
$$\text{ROA} = \frac{\text{net income}}{\text{average total assets}}$$

If we multiply both the numerator and denominator by sales, we get

$$\text{ROA} = \frac{\text{net income}}{\text{sales}} \times \frac{\text{sales}}{\text{average total assets}}$$
$$= \text{profit margin} \times \text{total asset turnover}$$
$$= 5\% \ [\text{from } (b)] \times 5 \ [\text{from } (a)] = 25\%$$

(d)
$$\text{Profit margin} = \frac{\text{net income}}{\text{sales}}$$

$$\text{Sales} = \frac{\text{net income}}{\text{profit margin}} = \frac{\$30,000}{0.004} = \$7,500,000$$

(e)
$$\text{ROA} = \frac{\text{net income}}{\text{average total assets}}$$

$$\text{Average total assets} = \frac{\text{net income}}{\text{ROA}} = \frac{\$30,000}{0.02} = \$1,500,000$$

(f)
$$\text{Total asset turnover} = \frac{\text{sales}}{\text{average total assets}}$$

$$= \frac{\$7,500,000 \ [\text{from } (d)]}{\$1,500,000 \ [\text{from } (e)]} = 5 \text{ times}$$

(g)
$$\text{Total asset turnover} = \frac{\text{sales}}{\text{average total assets}}$$

$$\text{Sales} = \text{total asset turnover} \times \text{average total assets}$$
$$= 0.4 \times \$250,000 = \$100,000$$

(h)
$$\text{Profit margin} = \frac{\text{net income}}{\text{sales}}$$

$$\text{Net income} = \text{profit margin} \times \text{sales}$$
$$= 5\% \times \$100,000 \ [\text{from } (g)] = \$5,000$$

(i)
$$\text{ROA} = \text{total asset turnover} \times \text{profit margin}$$
$$= 0.4 \times 5\% = 2\%$$

or

$$\text{ROA} = \frac{\text{net income}}{\text{average total assets}}$$

$$= \frac{\$5,000 \ [\text{from } (h)]}{\$250,000} = 2\%$$

Summarizing the results of (a) through (i) gives:

	Company X	Company Y	Company Z
Total asset turnover	5 times	5 times	0.4 times
Profit margin	5%	0.4%	5%
ROA	25%	2%	2%

Company X performed best. It appears that companies Y and Z are in trouble. Company Y turns over its assets as often as company X, but Y's margin on sales is much lower. Thus, company Y must work on improving its margin. The following questions may be raised about company Y: Is the low margin due to inefficiency? Is it due to excessive material, labor, or overhead, or all three?

Company Z, on the other hand, does just as well as company X in terms of profit margin but has a much lower turnover of capital than X. Therefore, company Z should take a close look at its investments. Is there too much tied up in inventories and receivables? Are there unused fixed assets? Is there idle cash sitting around?

2.18   **ROA and ROE.** The following ratios have been computed for Los Alamitos Company and are compared with the industry averages:

	Los Alamitos	Industry
Return on total assets (ROA)	6.2%	6.0%
Return on common equity (ROE)	16.5%	8.5%

Comment on the comparison of the company to the industry.

SOLUTION

Los Alamitos Company shows a satisfactory return on total investment (6.20 percent versus 6 percent for the industry). The company's 16.5 percent return on common stockholders' investment compares very favorably with that of the industry (16.5 percent versus 8.5 percent). This higher-than-average return reflects the firm's above-average use of financial leverage. Through the favorable use of debt, the firm was able to increase significantly the return earned on the stockholders' investment which would favorably affect its stock price.

2.19   **Financial Statement Analysis and Loan Decision.** The Konrath Company, a wholesaler in the midwest, is considering extending credit to the Hawk Company, a retail chain operation that has a number of stores in the midwest. The Konrath Company has had a gross margin of approximately 60 percent in recent years and expects to have a similar gross margin on the Hawk Company order, which is estimated at $2 million per year. The Hawk Company's order is approximately 15 percent of the Konrath Company's present sales. Recent statements of the Hawk Company are given below.

Hawk Company
Balance Sheet
(In Millions of Dollars)
As of Dec. 31, 19X1, 19X2, and 19X3

	19X1	19X2	19X3
ASSETS			
Current assets			
Cash	$ 2.6	$ 1.8	$ 1.6
Government securities (cost)	0.4	0.2	
Accounts and notes receivable (net)	8.0	8.5	8.5
Inventories	2.8	3.2	2.8
Prepaid assets	0.7	0.6	0.6
Total current assets	$14.5	$14.3	$13.5
Property, plant, and equipment (net)	4.3	5.4	5.9
Total assets	$18.8	$19.7	$19.4

LIABILITIES AND STOCKHOLDERS' EQUITY

Liabilities

Current liabilities

Notes payable	$ 3.2	$ 3.7	$ 4.2
Accounts payable	2.8	3.7	4.1
Accrued expenses and taxes	0.9	1.1	1.0
Total current liabilities	$ 6.9	$ 8.5	$ 9.3
Long-term debt, 6%	3.0	2.0	1.0
Total liabilities	$ 9.9	$10.5	$10.3
Stockholders' equity	8.9	9.2	9.1
Total liabilities and stockholders' equity	$18.8	$19.7	$19.4

Hawk Company
Income Statement
(In Millions of Dollars)
For the Years Ended Dec. 31, 19X1, 19X2, and 19X3

	19X1	19X2	19X3
Net sales	$24.2	$24.5	$24.9
Cost of goods sold	16.9	17.2	18.0
Gross margin	$ 7.3	$ 7.3	$ 6.9
Selling expenses	$ 4.3	$ 4.4	$ 4.6
Administrative expenses	2.3	2.4	2.7
Total expenses	$ 6.6	$ 6.8	$ 7.3
Earnings (loss) before taxes	$ 0.7	$ 0.5	$(0.4)
Income taxes	0.3	0.2	(0.2)
Net income	$ 0.4	$ 0.3	$(0.2)

Hawk Company
Statement of Changes in Financial Position
(In Millions of Dollars)
For the Years Ended Dec. 31, 19X1, 19X2, and 19X3

	19X1	19X2	19X3
Sources of funds			
Net income (loss)	$ 0.4	$ 0.3	$(0.2)
Depreciation	0.4	0.5	0.5
Funds from operations	$ 0.8	$ 0.8	$ 0.3
Sale of building	0.2		
Sale of treasury stock		0.1	0.1
Total sources	$ 1.0	$ 0.9	$ 0.4
Uses of funds			
Purchase of property, plant, and equipment	$ 1.2	$ 1.6	$ 1.0
Dividends	0.1	0.1	
Retirement of long-term debt		1.0	1.0
Total uses	$ 1.3	$ 2.7	$ 2.0
Net increase (decrease) in net working capital	$(0.3)	$(1.8)	$(1.6)

(a) Calculate for the year 19X3 the following ratios: (1) return on total assets; (2) acid-test ratio; (3) profit margin; (4) current ratio; and (5) inventory turnover.

(b) As part of the analysis to determine whether or not Konrath should extend credit to Hawk, assume the ratios below were calculated from Hawk Co. statements. For each ratio indicate whether it is a favorable, unfavorable, or neutral statistic in the decision to grant Hawk credit. Briefly explain your choice in each case.

	19X1	19X2	19X3
(1) Return on total assets	1.96%	1.12%	(0.87)%
(2) Profit margin	1.69%	0.99%	(0.69)%
(3) Acid-test ratio	1.73	1.36	1.19
(4) Current ratio	2.39	1.92	1.67
(5) Inventory turnover (times)	4.41	4.32	4.52
Equity relationships			
Current liabilities	36.0%	43.0%	48.0%
Long-term liabilities	16.0	10.5	5.0
Shareholders' equity	48.0	46.5	47.0
	100.0%	100.0%	100.0%
Asset relationships			
Current assets	77.0%	72.5%	69.5%
Property, plant, and equipment	23.0	27.5	30.5
	100.0%	100.0%	100.0%

(c) Would you grant credit to Hawk Co.? Support your answer with facts given in the problem.

(d) What additional information, if any, would you want before making a final decision? (CMA, adapted.)

SOLUTION

(a) (1) $$\text{Return on total assets} = \frac{\text{net income} + \text{interest expense}}{\text{average assets}} = \frac{-0.2 + 0.45^a}{(19.7 + 19.4)/2} = 0.01$$

$^a \dfrac{(2.0 + 1.0)0.06}{2} = \$0.09$ interest; 0.45 net of taxes.

(2) $$\text{Acid-test ratio} = \frac{\text{cash} + \text{accounts and notes receivable (net)}}{\text{current liabilities}} = \frac{1.6 + 8.5}{9.3} = 1.086$$

(3) $$\text{Profit margin} = \frac{\text{net income}}{\text{sales}} = \frac{-0.2}{24.9} = -0.8\%$$

(4) $$\text{Current ratio} = \frac{\text{current assets}}{\text{current liabilities}} = \frac{13.5}{9.3} = 1.45$$

(5) $$\text{Inventory turnover} = \frac{\text{cost of goods sold}}{\text{average inventory}} = \frac{18.0}{(3.2 + 2.8)/2} = 6$$

(b) (1)   The return on total assets is unfavorable. The rate is low and has been declining.

(2)   The profit margin is unfavorable. The rate is low and has been declining.

(3)   The acid-test ratio is favorable. The direction of change is unfavorable, but ratio itself is probably more than adequate.

(4) The current ratio is unfavorable. The decline has been sharp and the ratio is probably too low.

(5) The inventory turnover is neutral. Inventory turnover has been fairly constant, and we don't know enough about the business to determine if the turnover is adequate.

(*c*) The facts available from the problem are inadequate to make a final judgment; additional information would be necessary. However, the facts given do not present a good overall picture of Hawk. The company doesn't appear to be in serious trouble at the moment, but most of the trends reflected in the ratios are unfavorable. The company appears to be developing liquidity problems: cash and securities are declining; inventories and plant and equipment are an increasing portion of the assets; and current liabilities are an increasing portion of capital.

The operations of the company also show unfavorable trends: cost of goods sold is increasing as a percent of sales; administrative expenses are increasing as a percent of sales; and if we recognize that prices have risen, it appears that physical volume at Hawk might have actually decreased.

On the basis of these observations and the fact that Hawk would be a very large customer (thus a potentially large loss if the accounts became uncollectible), credit should be extended to Hawk only under carefully controlled and monitored conditions.

(*d*) For a final decision on whether to grant credit to Hawk, the additional information needed is: quality of management of the Hawk Company, locations of the Hawk stores, current activities of Hawk that have increased plant and equipment but not inventories, industry position of the Hawk Company, credit rating of the Hawk Company, current economic conditions, capacity of the Konrath Company to handle such a large single account, and normal ratios for the industry.

2.20 **Corporate and Economic Factors.** What factors (*a*) within the company and (*b*) within the economy have affected and are likely to affect the degree of variability in the (1) earnings per share; (2) dividends per share; and (3) market price per share of common stock? (CFA, adapted.)

SOLUTION

(*a*) Within the company
   (1) Earnings
       a. accounting policies
       b. sales volume
       c. new product introduction
   (2) Dividends
       a. capital expenditure
       b. stability of earnings
       c. replacement of fixed assets
   (3) Market price
       a. management quality
       b. growth in earnings
       c. financial leverage

(*b*) Economy
   (1) Earnings
       a. trend in economy
       b. governmental regulation
       c. labor relations
   (2) Dividends
       a. tax law
       b. recessionary conditions
   (3) Market price
       a. investor confidence
       b. cyclical changes

2.21 Transactions and the Statement of Cash Flows. Classify each transaction in the first three columns by its correct cash flow activity.

		Type of activity		
		Operating	Investing	Financing
(a)	Issued common stock for cash			
(b)	Purchased treasury stock			
(c)	Paid an account payable			
(d)	Declared a cash dividend			
(e)	Issued a bond payable			
(f)	Purchased land			
(g)	Sold a machine at book value			

SOLUTION

		Operating	Investing	Financing
(a)	Issued common stock for cash			X
(b)	Purchased treasury stock		X	
(c)	Paid an account payable	X		
(d)	Declared a cash dividend			X
(e)	Issued a bond payable			X
(f)	Purchased land		X	
(g)	Sold a machine at book value		X	

2.22 Activity Classification. Classify each of the following transactions as an operating activity, an investing activity, or a financing activity. Also indicate whether the activity is a source of cash or a use of cash.

1. A plant was sold for $550,000.
2. A profit of $75,000 was reported.
3. Long-term bonds were retired.
4. Cash dividends of $420,000 were paid.
5. Four hundred thousand shares of preferred stock were sold.
6. A new high-tech robotics was purchased.
7. A long-term note payable was issued.
8. A 50 percent interest in a company was purchased.
9. A loss for the year was reported.
10. Additional common stock was sold.

SOLUTION

1. Investing—source of cash
2. Operating—source of cash

3. Financing—use of cash

4. Financing—use of cash

5. Financing—source of cash

6. Investing—use of cash

7. Financing—source of cash

8. Investing—use of cash

9. Operating—use of cash

10. Financing—source of cash

2.23 Statement Analysis of Financial Position. The financial statements for XYZ Company for the years 19X1 and 19X2 are given below.

XYZ Company
Balance Sheet
Dec. 31, 19X1 and 19X2

	19X2	19X1
ASSETS		
Current assets		
Cash	$ 200	$ 150
Accounts receivable	600	300
Inventory	600	700
Total current assets	$1,400	$1,150
Fixed assets		
Plant and equipment	$ 900	$ 700
Less: Accumulated depreciation	(200)	(150)
Net fixed assets	$ 700	$ 550
Long-term investments	$ 300	$ 400
Total assets	$2,400	$2,100
LIABILITIES AND STOCKHOLDERS' EQUITY		
Current liabilities		
Accounts payable	$ 800	$ 400
Taxes payable	50	100
Total current liabilities	$ 850	$ 500
Bonds payable	$ 150	$ 500
Stockholders' equity		
Capital stock	$ 800	$ 700
Retained earnings	600	400
Total stockholders' equity	$1,400	$1,100
Total liabilities and stockholders' equity	$2,400	$2,100

XYZ Company
Income Statement
For the Year Ended Dec. 31, 19X2

Sales		$900
Cost of goods sold		200
Gross margin		$700
Operating expenses		
Selling expense	$100	
Administrative expense	150	
Depreciation expense	50	
Total expenses		300
Net income		$400

XYZ Company
Statement of Retained Earnings
For the Year Ended Dec. 31, 19X2

Retained earnings, Dec. 31, 19X1	$400
Add: Net income	400
	$800
Deduct: Dividends paid	200
Retained earnings, Dec. 31, 19X2	$600

Prepare (*a*) the statement of changes in financial position on a net working capital basis, and (*b*) the statement of changes in financial position on a cash basis with percentages. (*c*) Briefly summarize your findings.

SOLUTION

(*a*)   **XYZ Company**
Statement of Changes in Financial Position
For the Year Ended Dec. 31, 19X2

Sources of net working capital		
From operations		
Net income	$ 400	
Add: Depreciation	50	
Total funds from operations	$ 450	
From sale of long-term investments	100	
From sale of capital stock	100	
Total sources	$ 650	
Uses of net working capital		
To pay dividends	$ 200	
To purchase plant and equipment	200	
To retire bonds payable	350	
Total uses	$ 750	
Decrease in net working capital	$(100)	

XYZ Company
Statement of Changes in Financial Position (Cash Basis)
For the Year Ended Dec. 31, 19X2

	Dollars	%
Sources		
From operations		
Net income	$ 400	34.78%
Depreciation	50	4.35
Decrease in inventory	100	8.7
Increase in accounts payable	400	34.78
From sale of long-term investments	100	8.7
From sale of capital stock	100	8.7
Total sources	$1,150	100.00%
Uses		
Increase in accounts receivable	$ 300	27.27%
Decrease in taxes payable	50	4.55
Payment of dividends	200	18.18
Purchase plant and equipment	200	18.18
Retire bonds payable	350	31.82
Total uses	$1,100	100.00%
Increase in cash	$ 50	

(*c*) Major sources for the XYZ Company during 19X2 were internal (39.13 percent) and an increase in accounts payable (34.78 percent). External sources accounted for 17.4 percent of XYZ's funds through the sale of long-term investments and capital stock. The largest uses of funds were for the retirement of long-term bonds (31.82 percent) and an increase in accounts receivable (27.27 percent). There were also additions to plant and equipment (18.18 percent).

2.24 **Statement of Changes in Financial Position.** The consolidated balance sheets for CSULB Seasonal Products, Inc., at the beginning and end of 19X1 are presented below (in millions of dollars).

	Jan. 1, 19X1	Dec. 31, 19X1
ASSETS		
Cash	$ 12	$ 9
Accounts receivable	14	24
Inventories	4	12
Total current assets	$ 30	$ 45
Gross fixed assets	$120	$145
Less: Accumulated depreciation	45	55
Net fixed assets	$ 75	$ 90
Total assets	$105	$135

LIABILITIES AND EQUITY

Accounts payable	$ 14	$ 11
Notes payable	10	10
Long-term debt	10	25
Common stock	30	30
Retained earnings	41	59
Total liabilities and equity	$105	$135

CSULB earned $20 million after taxes during the year and paid cash dividends of $2 million. The annual depreciation expense during 19X1 was $10 million. The company purchased $25 million of fixed assets.

(*a*) Add a source and use column to the balance sheet; (*b*) prepare a statement of changes in financial position on the cash basis, and include percentage computations; and (*c*) summarize your findings.

SOLUTION

(*a*)

CSULB Seasonal Products
Balance Sheet
(In Millions of Dollars)

	Jan. 1, 19X1	Dec. 31, 19X1	Source	Use
ASSETS				
Cash	$ 12	$ 9	$ 3	
Accounts receivable	14	24		$10
Inventories	4	12		8
Total current assets	$ 30	$ 45		
Gross fixed assets	$120	$145		25
Less: Accumulated depreciation	45	55	10	
Net fixed assets	$ 75	$ 90		
Total assets	$105	$135		
LIABILITIES AND EQUITY				
Accounts payable	$ 14	$ 11		3
Notes payable	10	10		
Long-term debt	10	25	15	
Common stock	30	30		
Retained earnings	41	59	18	
Total liabilities and equity	$105	$135	$46	$46

(b)

CSULB Seasonal Products
Statement of Changes in Financial Position

	Millions of Dollars	% of Total
Sources		
From operations		
Net income	$20	44.44%
Depreciation	10	22.22
Issuance of long-term debt	15	33.33
Total sources	$45	100.00%
Uses		
Pay cash dividends	$ 2	4.17%
Increase in accounts receivable	10	20.83
Increase in inventories	8	16.67
Decrease in accounts payable	3	6.25
Purchase of fixed assets	25	52.08
Total uses	$48	100.00%
Decrease in cash	$ 3	

(c) Most of CSULB's funds were obtained from operations (over 66 percent) along with a relatively large amount of long-term debt (about 33 percent). CSULB allocated these funds primarily to the purchase of fixed assets (52.08 percent), accounts receivable (20.83 percent), and inventories (16.67 percent). It is important to realize that the company does not have an optimal mix of financing since a relatively large portion of long-term debt went toward the purchase of short-term assets, namely accounts receivable and inventories. Furthermore, since the company's sales are seasonal, it could end up with rather costly excess cash on hand if the additional investment in inventories and accounts receivable is not needed.

2.25 Adjustments to Net Income. Indicate whether each of the events described below will be added to or deducted from net income in order to compute cash flow from operations.

1. Gain on sale of an asset
2. Increase in accounts receivable
3. Decrease in prepaid insurance
4. Depreciation expense
5. Increase in accounts payable
6. Uncollectible accounts expense
7. Decrease in wages payable
8. Increase in inventory
9. Amortization of a patent

SOLUTION

1. Deducted from
2. Deducted from
3. Added to
4. Added to
5. Added to
6. Added to

7. Deducted from

8. Deducted from

9. Added to

2.26 Statement of Cash Flows. Acme Manufacturing has provided the following financial statements:

Acme Manufacturing
Comparative Balance Sheets
For the Years Ended December 31, 19X4 and 19X5

	19X4	19X5
ASSETS		
Cash	$ 112,500	$ 350,000
Accounts receivable	350,000	281,250
Inventories	125,000	150,000
Plant and equipment	1,000,000	1,025,000*
Accumulated depreciation	(500,000)	(525,000)
Land	500,000	718,750
Total assets	$1,587,500	$2,000,000
LIABILITIES AND EQUITY		
Accounts payable	$ 300,000	$ 237,500
Mortgage payable	—	250,000
Common stock	75,000	75,000
Contributed capital in excess of par	300,000	300,000
Retained earnings	912,500	1,137,500
Total liabilities and equity	$1,587,500	$2,000,000

Income Statement
For the Year Ended December 31, 19X5

Revenues	$1,200,000
Gain on sale of equipment	50,000
Less: Cost of goods sold	(640,000)
Less: Depreciation expense	(125,000)
Less: Interest expense	(35,000)
Net income	$ 450,000

Other information:

(a) Equipment with a book value of $125,000 was sold for $175,000 (original cost was $225,000).

(b) Dividends of $225,000 were declared and paid.

Prepare a statement of cash flows.

SOLUTION

Acme Manufacturing
Statement of Cash Flows
For the Year Ended December 31, 19X5

CASH FLOWS FROM
OPERATING ACTIVITIES:

Net income	$450,000	
Add (deduct) adjusting items:		
Gain on sale of equipment	(50,000)	
Decrease in accounts receivable	68,750	
Increase in inventory	(25,000)	
Depreciation expense	125,000	
Decrease in accounts payable	(62,500)	
Net Operating Cash		$506,250

CASH FLOWS FROM
INVESTING ACTIVITIES:

Sale of equipment	$175,000	
Purchase of equipment	(250,000)	
Purchase of land	(218,750)	
Net cash from investing activities		(293,750)

CASH FLOWS FROM
FINANCING ACTIVITIES:

Mortgage received	$250,000	
Dividends	(225,000)	
Net cash from financing activities		25,000
Net increase in cash		$237,500

_____

*Beginning equipment	$1,000,000	
Purchases	250,000	
Less sales	(225,000)	
Ending equipment	$1,025,000	

2.27 Financial Analysis. Motel Enterprises operates and owns many motels throughout the United States. The company has expanded rapidly over the past few years, and company officers are concerned that they may have overexpanded.

The following financial statements and other financial data have been supplied by the controller of Motel Enterprises.

Motel Enterprises
Income Statement
(*In Thousands of Dollars*)
For Years Ending Oct. 31, 19X1 and 19X2
(*Unaudited*)

	19X1	19X2
Revenue	$1,920	$2,230
Cost and expenses		
Direct room and related services	$ 350	$ 400
Direct food and beverage	640	740
General and administrative	250	302
Advertising	44	57
Repairs and maintenance	82	106
Interest expense	220	280
Depreciation	95	120
Lease payment	73	100
Total costs and expenses	$1,754	$2,105
Income before taxes	$ 166	$ 125
Provision for income tax	42	25
Net income	$ 124	$ 100

Motel Enterprises
Statement of Financial Position
(*For Thousands of Dollars*)
As of Oct. 31, 19X1 and 19X2
(*Unaudited*)

	19X1	19X2
ASSETS		
Current assets		
Cash	$ 125	$ 100
Accounts receivable (net)	200	250
Inventory	50	60
Other	5	5
Total current assets	$ 380	$ 415
Long-term investments	$ 710	$ 605
Property and equipment		
Buildings and equipment (net)	$2,540	$3,350
Land	410	370
Construction in progress	450	150
Total property and equipment	$3,400	$3,870
Other assets	$ 110	$ 110
Total assets	$4,600	$5,000

LIABILITIES AND
STOCKHOLDERS' EQUITY

Liabilities

  Current liabilities

Accounts payable	$ 30	$ 40
Accrued liabilities	190	190
Notes payable to bank	10	30
Current portion of long-term notes	50	80
Total current liabilities	$ 280	$ 340

Long-term debt

Long-term notes	$2,325	$2,785
Subordinated debentures (due May 1989)	800	800
Total long-derm debt	$3,125	$3,585
Total liabilities	$3,405	$3,925

Stockholders' equity

Common stock ($1 par)	$ 300	$ 300
Paid-in capital in excess of par	730	730
Net unrealized loss on long-term investments		(105)
Retained earnings	165	150
Total stockholders' equity	$1,195	$1,075
Total liabilities and stockholders' equity	$4,600	$5,000

(a) Prepare the statement of changes in financial position (net working capital basis) for Motel Enterprises.

(b) Compute the following ratios for 19X1 and 19X2: (1) debt/equity ratio; (2) times interest earned; (3) return on total assets; (4) current ratio; (5) return on common stock equity; and (6) accounts receivable turnover.

(c) Evaluate the financial condition based on the trend analysis and the statement of changes in financial position. (CMA, adapted.)

SOLUTION

(a)

Motel Enterprises
Statement of Changes in Financial Position
(In Thousands of Dollars)
For the Year Ending Oct. 31, 19X2

Sources of funds		
Net income	$100	
Noncash items		
Gain on land sale	(20)	
Depreciation	120	
Total funds from operations		$200
Sale of land		100
Increases in long-term debt		460
Total resources provided		$760
Applications of funds		
Purchase of building and land	$620	
Construction-in-progress, building	50	
Dividends	115	
Total funds applied		$785
Decrease in net working capital		$(25)

(b) 1.

$$\text{Debt/equity ratio} = \frac{\text{total liabilities}}{\text{stockholders' equity}}$$

For 19X1: $\dfrac{\$3{,}405}{\$4{,}600} = 74.0\%$

For 19X2: $\dfrac{\$3{,}925}{\$5{,}000} = 78.5\%$

2.

$$\text{Times interest earned} = \frac{\text{EBIT}}{\text{interest expense}}$$

For 19X1: $\dfrac{\$386}{\$220} = 1.75$

For 19X2: $\dfrac{\$405}{\$280} = 1.45$

3.

$$\text{Return on total assets} = \frac{\text{net income}}{\text{average total assets}}$$

For 19X1: $\dfrac{\$124}{\$4{,}600} = 2.7\%$

For 19X2: $\dfrac{\$100}{(\$4{,}600 + \$5{,}000)/2} = 2.1\%$

4.

$$\text{Current ratio} = \frac{\text{current assets}}{\text{current liabilities}}$$

For 19X1: $\dfrac{\$380}{\$280} = 1.36$

For 19X2: $\dfrac{\$415}{\$340} = 1.22$

5. $\qquad$ Return on common stock equity $= \dfrac{\text{earnings available to common stockholders}}{\text{average stockholders' equity}}$

For 19X1 estimated: $\dfrac{\$124}{\$1,195} = 10.4\%$

For 19X2: $\dfrac{\$100}{(\$1,195 + \$1,075)/2} = 8.8\%$

6. $\qquad$ Accounts receivable turnover $= \dfrac{\text{net credit sales}}{\text{average accounts receivable}}$

For 19X1 estimated: $\dfrac{\$1,920}{\$200} = 9.6$ (every 38 days)

For 19X2: $\dfrac{\$2,230}{(\$200 + \$250)/2} = 9.91$ (every 37 days)

(c) Based on the trend analysis for 19X1 and 19X2, the company's financial condition has deteriorated to some degree in this period, and there is going to be a serious liquidity problem as is evidenced by the decline in the current ratio and the decline of net working capital.

In addition, the company's interest coverage has declined and large amounts of debt are coming due in the near future. The statement of changes in financial position shows that a large portion of capital expenditures were financed through long-term debt.

Chapter 3

Financial Forecasting, Planning, and Budgeting

3.1 FINANCIAL FORECASTING

Financial forecasting, an essential element of planning, is the basis for budgeting activities and estimating future financing needs. Financial forecasts begin with forecasting sales and their related expenses. The basic steps involved in projecting financing needs are:

1. Project the firm's sales. Most other forecasts (budgets) follow the sales forecast. The statistical methods of forecasting sales include:

   (*a*) Time-series analysis
   (*b*) Exponential smoothing
   (*c*) Regression analysis
   (*d*) Box-Jenkins method

   (These methods are discussed in other disciplines such as managerial economics and statistics and are not covered here.)

2. Project variables such as expenses.

3. Estimate the level of investment in current and fixed assets that is required to support the projected sales.

4. Calculate the firm's financing needs.

3.2 PERCENT-OF-SALES METHOD OF FINANCIAL FORECASTING

When constructing a financial forecast, the sales forecast is used traditionally to estimate various expenses, assets, and liabilities. The most widely used method for making these projections is the *percent-of-sales method*, in which the various expenses, assets, and liabilities for a future period are estimated as a percentage of sales. These percentages, together with the projected sales, are then used to construct pro forma (planned or projected) balance sheets.

The calculations for a pro forma balance sheet are as follows:

1. Express balance sheet items that *vary directly with sales* as a percentage of sales. Any item that does not vary directly with sales (such as long-term debt) is designated *not applicable* (n.a.).

2. Multiply the percentages determined in step 1 by the sales projected to obtain the amounts for the future period.

3. Where no percentage applies (such as for long-term debt, common stock, and capital surplus), simply insert the figures from the present balance sheet in the column for the future period.

4. Compute the projected retained earnings as follows:

   > Projected retained earnings = present retained earnings
   >
   > + projected net income − cash dividends paid

   (You'll need to know the percentage of sales that constitutes net income and the dividend payout ratio.)

5. Sum the asset accounts to obtain a total projected assets figure. Then add the projected liabilities and equity accounts to determine the total financing provided. Since liability plus equity must balance the assets when totaled, any difference is a *shortfall*, which is the amount of external financing needed.

EXAMPLE 3.1   For the following pro forma balance sheet, net income is assumed to be 5 percent of sales and the dividend payout ratio is 4 percent.

Pro Forma Balance Sheet
(In Millions of Dollars)

	Present (19X1)	% of Sales (19X1 Sales = $20)	Projected (19X2 Sales = $24)	
ASSETS				
Current assets	$2.0	10%	$24 × 10% = $2.4	
Fixed assets	4.0	20%	4.8	
Total assets	$6.0		$7.2	
LIABILITIES AND STOCKHOLDERS' EQUITY				
Current liabilities	$2.0	10%	$2.4	
Long-term debt	2.5	n.a.[a]	2.5	
Total liabilities	$4.5		$4.9	
Common stock	$0.1	n.a.[a]	$0.1	
Capital surplus	0.2	n.a.[a]	0.2	
Retained earnings	1.2		1.92[b]	
Total equity	$1.5		$2.22	
Total liabilities and stockholders' equity	$6.0		$7.12	Total financing provided
			$0.08[c]	External financing needed
			$7.2	Total

[a] Not applicable (n.a.). These figures are assumed not to vary with sales.
[b]   19X2 Retained earnings = 19X1 retained earnings + projected net income − cash idividends paid
$$= \$1.2 + 5\%(\$24) - 40\%[5\%(\$24)]$$
$$= \$1.2 + \$1.2 - \$0.48 = \$2.4 - \$0.48 = \$1.92$$
[c]   External financing needed = projected total assets − (projected total liabilities + projected equity)
$$= \$7.2 - (\$4.9 + \$2.22) = \$7.2 - \$7.12 = \$0.08$$

Although the forecast of additional funds required can be made by setting up pro forma balance sheets as described in Example 3.1, it is often easier to use the following simple formula:

$$\begin{bmatrix} \text{external} \\ \text{funds} \\ \text{needed} \end{bmatrix} = \begin{bmatrix} \text{required} \\ \text{increase} \\ \text{in assets} \end{bmatrix} - \begin{bmatrix} \text{spontaneous} \\ \text{increase in} \\ \text{liabilities} \end{bmatrix} - \begin{bmatrix} \text{increase in} \\ \text{retained} \\ \text{earnings} \end{bmatrix}$$

$$\text{EFN} = \left(\frac{A}{S}\right)\Delta S - \left(\frac{L}{S}\right)\Delta S - (PM)(PS)(1 - d)$$

where EFN = external funds needed
     A/S = assets that increase spontaneously with sales as a percentage of sales
     L/S = liabilities that increase spontaneously with sales as a percentage of sales
     ΔS = change in sales
     PM = profit margin on sales
     PS = projected sales
      d = dividend payout ratio

EXAMPLE 3.2   From Example 3.1:

$$\frac{A}{S} = \frac{\$6}{\$20} = 30\%$$

$$\frac{L}{S} = \frac{\$2}{\$20} = 10\%$$

$$\Delta S = \$24 - \$20 = \$4$$

$$PM = 5\% \text{ on sales}$$

$$PS = \$24$$

$$d = 40\%$$

Inserting these figures into the formula, we get

$$EFN = \left(\frac{A}{S}\right)\Delta S - \left(\frac{L}{S}\right)\Delta S - (PM)(PS)(1 - d)$$
$$= 0.3(\$4) - 0.1(\$4) - (0.05)(\$24)(1 - 0.4)$$
$$= \$1.2 - \$0.4 - \$0.72 = \$0.08$$

The $80,000 in external financing can be raised by issuing notes payable, bonds, or stocks, singly or in combination.

One important limitation of the percent-of-sales method is that the firm is assumed to be operating at full capacity. On the basis of this assumption, the firm does not have sufficient productive capacity to absorb projected increases in sales and thus requires an additional investment in assets.

The major advantage of the percent-of-sales method of financial forecasting is that it is simple and inexpensive to use. To obtain a more precise projection of the firm's future financing needs, however, the preparation of a cash budget is required (see the following sections).

3.3   THE BUDGET, OR FINANCIAL PLAN

A company's annual financial plan is called a *budget*. The budget is a set of formal (written) statements of management's expectations regarding sales, expenses, production volume, and various financial transactions of the firm for the coming period. Simply put, a budget is a set of pro forma statements about the company's finances and operations. A budget is a tool for both planning and control. At the beginning of the period, the budget is a plan or standard; at the end of the period, it serves as a control device to help management measure the firm's performance against the plan so that future performance may be improved.

3.4   THE STRUCTURE OF THE BUDGET

The budget is classified broadly into two categories: the *operational budget*, which reflects the results of operating decisions; and the *financial budget*, which reflects the financial decisions of the firm. The operating budget consists of:

1. Sales budget, including a computation of expected cash receipts
2. Production budget
3. Ending inventory budget
4. Direct materials budget, including a computation of expected cash disbursements for materials
5. Direct labor budget
6. Factory overhead budget
7. Selling and administrative expense budget
8. Pro forma income statement

The financial budget consists of:

1. Cash budget
2. Pro forma balance sheet

The major steps in preparing the budget are:

1. Prepare a sales forecast
2. Determine production volume
3. Estimate manufacturing costs and operating expenses
4. Determine cash flow and other financial effects
5. Formulate projected financial statements.

Follow the illustration of the Johnson Company (Examples 3.3 to 3.12), a manufacturer of a single product, as its annual budget is created for the year 19X2. The company develops its budget on a quarterly basis. The example will highlight the variable cost–fixed cost breakdown throughout.

The Sales Budget

The sales budget is the starting point in preparing the operating budget, since estimated sales volume influences almost all other items appearing throughout the annual budget. The sales budget gives the quantity of each product expected to be sold. (For the Johnson Company, there is only one product.) Basically, there are three ways of making estimates for the sales budget:

1. Make a statistical forecast (using any one or a combination of the methods mentioned in Section 3.1) on the basis of an analysis of general business conditions, market conditions, product growth curves, etc.
2. Make an internal estimate by collecting the opinions of executives and sales staff.
3. Analyze the various factors that affect sales revenue and then predict the future behavior of each of those factors.

After sales volume has been estimated, the sales budget is constructed by multiplying the estimated number of units by the expected unit price. Generally, the sales budget includes a computation of cash collections anticipated from credit sales, which will be used later for cash budgeting. See Example 3.3.

EXAMPLE 3.3 Assume that of each quarter's sales, 70 percent is collected in the first quarter of the sale; 28 percent is collected in the following quarter; and 2 percent is uncollectible.

The Johnson Company
Sales Budget
For the Year Ended Dec. 31, 19X2

| | Quarter | | | | |
	1	2	3	4	Total
Expected sales in units	800	700	900	800	3,200
Unit sales price ($)	×80	×80	×80	×80	×80
Total sales	$64,000	$56,000	$72,000	$64,000	$256,000

Schedule of Expected Cash Collections

| | Quarter | | | | |
	1	2	3	4	Total
Accounts receivable, Dec. 31, 19X1	$ 9,500				$ 9,500
1st-qtr. sales ($64,000)	44,800[a]	$17,920[b]			62,720
2d-qtr. sales ($56,000)		39,200	$15,680		54,880
3d-qtr. sales ($72,000)			50,400	$20,160	70,560
4th-qtr. sales ($64,000)				44,800	44,800
Total cash collections	$54,300	$57,120	$66,080	$64,960	$242,460

[a] $64,000 × 0.70 = $44,800
[b] $64,000 × 0.28 = $17,920

The Production Budget

After sales are budgeted, the production budget can be determined. The number of units expected to be manufactured to meet budgeted sales and inventory is set forth. The expected volume of production is determined by subtracting the estimated inventory at the beginning of the period from the sum of units to be sold plus desired ending inventory. See Example 3.4.

EXAMPLE 3.4 Assume that ending inventory is 10 percent of the next quarter's sales and that the ending inventory for the fourth quarter is 100 units.

The Johnson Company
Production Budget
For the Year Ended Dec. 31, 19X2

| | Quarter | | | | |
	1	2	3	4	Total
Planned sales (Example 3.3)	800	700	900	800	3,200
Desired ending inventory	70	90	80	100	100
Total needs	870	790	980	900	3,300
Less beginning inventory[a]	80	70	90	80	80
Units to be produced	790	720	890	820	3,220

[a] The same amount as the previous quarter's ending inventory.

The Direct Materials Budget

When the level of production has been computed, a direct materials budget is constructed to show how much material will be required and how much of it must be purchased to meet production requirements. The purchase will depend on both expected usage of materials and inventory levels. The formula for computing the purchase is

$$
\begin{bmatrix} \text{amount of materials} \\ \text{to be purchased} \\ \text{in units} \end{bmatrix} = \begin{bmatrix} \text{materials needed} \\ \text{for production} \\ \text{in units} \end{bmatrix} + \begin{bmatrix} \text{desired ending} \\ \text{material inventory} \\ \text{in units} \end{bmatrix} - \begin{bmatrix} \text{beginning} \\ \text{material inventory} \\ \text{in units} \end{bmatrix}
$$

The direct materials budget is usually accompanied by a computation of expected cash payments for the purchased materials.

EXAMPLE 3.5   Assume that ending inventory is 10 percent of the next quarter's production needs; the ending materials inventory for the fourth quarter is 250 units; and 50 percent of each quarter's purchases are paid in that quarter, with the remainder being paid in the following quarter. Also, 3 pounds of materials are needed per unit of product at a cost of $2 per pound.

The Johnson Company
Direct Materials Budget
For the Year Ended Dec. 31, 19X2

	Quarter				
	1	**2**	**3**	**4**	**Total**
Units to be produced (Example 3.4)	790	720	890	820	3,220
Material needs per unit (pounds)	×3	×3	×3	×3	×3
Material needs for production	2,370	2,160	2,670	2,460	9,660
Desired ending inventory of materials	216	267	246	250	250
Total needs	2,586	2,427	2,916	2,710	9,910
Less: Beginning inventory of materials[a]	237	216	267	246	237
Materials to be purchased	2,349	2,211	2,649	2,464	9,673
Unit price ($)	×2	×2	×2	×2	×2
Purchase cost	$4,698	$4,422	$5,298	$4,928	$19,346

Schedule of Expected Cash Disbursements

Accounts payable, Dec. 31, 19X1	$2,200				$ 2,200
1st-qtr. purchases ($4,698)	2,349	$2,349			4,698
2d-qtr. purchases ($4,422)		2,211	$2,211		4,422
3d-qtr. purchases ($5,298)			2,469	$2,649	5,298
4th-qtr. purchases ($4,928)				2,464	2,464
Total disbursements	$4,549	$4,560	$4,860	$5,113	$19,082

[a] The same amount as the prior quarter's ending inventory.

The Direct Labor Budget

The production budget also provides the starting point for the preparation of the direct labor cost budget. The direct labor hours necessary to meet production requirements multiplied by the estimated hourly rate yields the total direct labor cost.

EXAMPLE 3.6   Assume that 5 hours of labor are required per unit of product and that the hourly rate is $5.

The Johnson Company
Direct Labor Budget
For the Year Ended Dec. 31, 19X2

	Quarter				
	1	**2**	**3**	**4**	**Total**
Units to be produced (Example 3.4)	790	720	890	820	3,220
Direct labor hours per unit	×5	×5	×5	×5	×5
Total hours	3,950	3,600	4,450	4,100	16,100
Direct labor cost per hour ($)	×5	×5	×5	×5	×5
Total direct labor cost	$19,750	$18,000	$22,250	$20,500	$80,500

The Factory Overhead Budget

The factory overhead budget is a schedule of all manufacturing costs other than direct materials and direct labor. Using the contribution approach to budgeting requires the development of a pre-determined overhead rate for the variable portion of the factory overhead. In developing the cash budget, remember that depreciation does not entail a cash outlay and therefore must be deducted from the total factory overhead in computing cash disbursements for factory overhead.

EXAMPLE 3.7   For the following factory overhead budget, assume that:

1. Total factory overhead is budgeted at $6,000 per quarter plus $2 per hour of direct labor.
2. Depreciation expenses are $3,250 per quarter.
3. All overhead costs involving cash outlays are paid in the quarter in which they are incurred.

The Johnson Company
Factory Overhead Budget
For the Year Ended Dec. 31, 19X2

	Quarter				
	1	**2**	**3**	**4**	**Total**
Budgeted direct labor hours (Example 3.6)	3,950	3,600	4,450	4,100	16,100
Variable overhead rate ($)	×2	×2	×2	×2	×2
Variable overhead budgeted	$ 7,900	$ 7,200	$ 8,900	$ 8,200	$32,000
Fixed overhead budgeted	6,000	6,000	6,000	6,000	24,000
Total budgeted overhead	$13,900	$13,200	$14,900	$14,200	$56,200
Less: Depreciation	3,250	3,250	3,250	3,250	13,000
Cash disbursements for overhead	$10,650	$ 9,950	$11,650	$10,950	$43,200

The Ending Inventory Budget

The ending inventory budget provides the information required for constructing budgeted financial statements. First, it is useful for computing the cost of goods sold on the budgeted income statement. Second, it gives the dollar value of the ending *materials* and *finished goods inventory* that will appear on the budgeted balance sheet.

EXAMPLE 3.8 For the ending inventory budget, we first need to compute the unit variable cost for finished goods, as follows:

	Unit Cost	Units	Total
Direct materials	$2	3 pounds	$ 6
Direct labor	$5	5 hours	25
Variable overhead	$2	5 hours	10
Total variable manufacturing cost			$41

The Johnson Company
Ending Inventory Budget
For the Year Ended Dec. 31, 19X2

Ending Inventory

	Units	Unit Costs	Total
Direct materials	250 pounds	$2	$500
Finished goods	100 units	$41	$4,100

The Selling and Administrative Expense Budget

The selling and administrative expense budget lists the operating expenses involved in selling the products and in managing the business.

EXAMPLE 3.9 The variable selling and administrative expenses amount of $4 per unit of sale, including commissions, shipping, and supplies; expenses are paid in the same quarter in which they are incurred, with the exception of $1,200 in income tax, which is paid in the third quarter.

The Johnson Company
Selling and Administrative Expense Budget
For the Year Ended Dec. 31, 19X2

	Quarter 1	2	3	4	Total
Expected sales in units	800	700	900	800	3,200
Variable selling and administrative expense per unit ($)	×4	×4	×4	×4	×4
Budgeted variable expense	$ 3,200	$ 2,800	$ 3,600	$ 3,200	$12,800
Fixed selling and administrative expenses					
Advertising	1,100	1,100	1,100	1,100	4,400
Insurance	2,800				2,800
Office salaries	8,500	8,500	8,500	8,500	34,000
Rent	350	350	350	350	1,400
Taxes			1,200		1,200
Total budgeted selling and administrative expenses	$15,950	$12,750	$14,750	$13,150	$56,600

The Cash Budget

The cash budget is prepared in order to forecast the firm's future financial needs. It is also a tool for cash planning and control. Because the cash budget details the expected cash receipts and disbursements for a designated time period, it helps avoid the problem of either having idle cash on hand or suffering a cash shortage. However, if a cash shortage is experienced, the cash budget indicates whether the shortage is temporary or permanent, i.e., whether short-term or long-term borrowing is needed.

The cash budget typically consists of four major sections:

1. The receipts section, which gives the beginning cash balance, cash collections from customers, and other receipts

2. The disbursements section, which shows all cash payments made, listed by purpose

3. The cash surplus or deficit section, which simply shows the difference between the cash receipts section and the cash disbursements section

4. The financing section, which provides a detailed account of the borrowings and repayments expected during the budget period

EXAMPLE 3.10   For this example, assume the following:

1. The company desires to maintain a $5,000 minimum cash balance at the end of each quarter.

2. All borrowing and repayment must be in multiples of $500 at an interest rate of 10 percent per annum. Interest is computed and paid as the principal is repaid. Borrowing takes place at the beginning and repayments at the end of each quarter.

3. The cash balance at the beginning of the first quarter is $10,000.

4. A sumn of $24,300 is to be paid in the second quarter for machinery purchases.

5. Income tax of $4,000 is paid in the first quarter.

The Johnson Company
Cash Budget
For the Year Ended Dec. 31, 19X2

	From Example	Quarter 1	Quarter 2	Quarter 3	Quarter 4	Total
Cash balance, beginning	Given	$10,000	$ 9,401	$ 5,461	$ 9,106	$ 10,000
Add receipts						
Collection from customers	3.3	54,300	57,120	66,080	64,960	242,460
Total cash available		$64,300	$66,521	$71,541	$74,066	$252,460
Less disbursements						
Direct materials	3.5	$ 4,549	$ 4,560	$ 4,860	$ 5,113	$ 19,082
Direct labor	3.6	19,750	18,000	22,250	20,500	80,500
Factory overhead	3.7	10,650	9,950	11,650	10,950	43,200
Selling and administrative	3.9	15,950	12,750	14,750	13,150	56,600
Machinery purchase	Given		24,300			24,300
Income tax	Given	4,000				4,000
Total disbursements		$54,899	$69,560	$53,510	$49,713	$227,682
Cash surplus (deficit)		$ 9,401	$(3,039)	$18,031	$24,353	$ 24,778
Financing						
Borrowing			$ 8,500			$ 8,500
Repayment				(8,500)		(8,500)
Interest				(425)		(425)
Total financing			$ 8,500	$(8,925)		$ (425)
Cash balance, ending		$ 9,401	$ 5,461	$ 9,106	$24,353	$ 24,353

The Budgeted Income Statement

The budgeted income statement summarizes the various component projections of revenue and expenses for the budgeting period. For control purposes, the budget can be divided into quarters, for example, depending on the need.

EXAMPLE 3.11

The Johnson Company
Budgeted Income Statement
For the Year Ended Dec. 31, 19X2

	From Example		
Sales (3,200 units @ $80)	3.3		$256,000
Less: Variable expenses			
Variable cost of goods sold (3,200 units @ $41)	3.8	$131,200	
Variable selling and administrative	3.9	12,800	144,000
Contribution margin			$112,000
Less: Fixed expenses			
Factory overhead	3.7	$ 24,000	
Selling and administrative	3.9	43,800	67,800
Net operating income			$ 44,200
Less: Interest expense	3.10		425
Net income before taxes			$ 43,775
Less: Income taxes (20%)			8,755
Net income			$ 35,020

The Budgeted Balance Sheet

The budgeted balance sheet is developed by beginning with the balance sheet for the year just ended and adjusting it, using all the activities that are expected to take place during the budget period. Some of the reasons why the budgeted balance sheet must be prepared are:

1. To disclose any potentially unfavorable financial conditions
2. To serve as a final check on the mathematical accuracy of all the other budgets
3. To help management perform a variety of ratio calculations
4. To highlight future resources and obligations

EXAMPLE 3.12

The Johnson Company
Balance Sheet
For the Year Ended Dec. 31, 19X1

ASSETS		LIABILITIES AND STOCKHOLDERS' EQUITY	
Current assets		Current liabilities	
Cash	$ 10,000	Accounts payable	$ 2,200
Accounts receivable	9,500	Income tax payable	4,000
Materials inventory	474	Stockholders' equity	
Finished goods inventory	3,280	Common stock, no par	70,000
	$ 23,254	Retained earnings	37,054
Fixed assets			
Land	$ 50,000		
Building and equipment	100,000		
Accumulated depreciation	(60,000)		
	$ 90,000	Total liabilities and	
Total assets	$113,254	stockholders' equity	$113,254

The Johnson Company
Budgeted Balance Sheet
For the Year Ended Dec. 31, 19X2

ASSETS		LIABILITIES AND STOCKHOLDERS' EQUITY	
Current assets		Current liabilities	
Cash	$ 24,353[a]	Accounts payable	$ 2,464[g]
Accounts receivable	23,040[b]	Income tax payable	8,755[h]
Materials inventory	500[c]		
Finished goods inventory	4,100[c]	Stockholders' equity	
	$ 51,993	Common stock, no par	70,000[i]
		Retained earnings	72,074[j]
Fixed assets			
Land	$ 50,000[d]		
Buildings and equipment	124,300[e]		
Accumulated depreciation	(73,000)[f]		
	$101,300		
		Total liabilities and	
Total assets	$153,293	stockholders' equity	$153,293

[a] From Example 3.10 (each budget).
[b] From Example 3.3 (sales budget).
$$\text{Accounts receivable} = \text{Beginning balance} + \text{sales} - \text{receipts}$$
$$= \$9,500 + \$256,000 - 242,460 = \$23,040$$
[c] From Example 3.8 (ending inventory budget).
[d] Unchanged from 19X1 balance sheet.
[e] $100,000 (from 19X1 balance sheet) + $24,300 (from Example 3.10) = $124,300
[f] $60,000 (from 19X1 balance sheet) + $13,000 (from Example 3.7) = $73,000
[g] Accounts payable = beginning balance + purchase cost − disbursements for materials
$$= \$2,200 + \$19,346 \text{ (Example 3.5)} - \$19,082 \text{ (Example 3.5)} = \$2,464$$
or 50% of 4th-quarter purchase = 50% ($4,928) = $2,464.
[h] From Example 3.11 (budgeted income statement).
[i] Unchanged from 19X1 balance sheet.
[j] $37,054 (from 19X1 balance sheet) + $35,020 (from net income, Example 3.11) = $72,074

3.5   A SHORTCUT APPROACH TO FORMULATING THE BUDGET

Example 3.3 to 3.12 show a detailed procedure for formulating a budget. However, in practice a shortcut approach to budgeting is quite common and may be summarized as follows:

1. A pro forma income statement is developed using past percentage relationships between relevant expense and cost items and the firm's sales. These percentages are then applied to the firm's forecasted sales. This is a version of the percent-of-sales method discussed in Section 3.2.

2. A pro forma balance sheet is estimated by determining the desired level of certain balance sheet items, then making additional financing conform to those desired figures. The remaining items, thus, are estimated to make the balance sheet balance.

There are two basic assumptions underlying this approach:

1. The firm's past financial condition is an accurate predictor of its future condition.
2. The value of certain variables such as cash, inventory, and accounts receivable can be forced to take on specified *desired* values.

3.6   COMPUTER-BASED MODELS FOR FINANCIAL PLANNING AND BUDGETING

More and more companies are developing computer-based quantitative models for constructing a profit planning budget. The models help managerial decision makers answer a variety of *what-if* questions. The resultant calculations provide a basis for choice among alternatives under conditions of uncertainty. There are primarily two approaches to modeling the corporate budgeting process: *simulation* and *optimization*.

Review Questions

1. _____ , an essential element of planning, is the basis for budgeting activities.

2. The most widely used method for forecasting future financing needs is _____ .

3. In a forecast of additional funds, external funds needed equal required increase in assets minus the sum of _____ plus _____ .

4. Budgeting is a tool for _____ and _____ .

5. The cash budget contains four major sections. They are the _____ section, _____ section, _____ section, and the financing section.

6. How much to produce is contingent upon expected sales in units and the _____ and _____ inventories of finished goods.

7. Production budget is prepared after the _____ budget is completed. It is prepared in _____ .

8. Cash budgets should include noncash charges such as depreciation: (*a*) true; (*b*) false.

9. Cash budgets are prepared on a short-term basis such as on a monthly, quarterly, or even weekly basis: (*a*) true; (*b*) false.

10. Operating budgets would include cash budgets: (*a*) true; (*b*) false.

11. The pro forma _____ shows the expected operating results for the budgeting year, while the pro forma _____ shows the expected financial condition at the end of budgeting period.

12. Desired ending inventory figures appear on both budgeted _____ and _____ .

13. The idea behind preparing cash budgets is to avoid unnecessary cash _____ and _____ .

14. _____ are often used to develop budgets in order to evaluate alternative courses of action.

15. A shortcut approach to formulating a budget uses a version of the _____ .

Answers: (1) Financial forecasting; (2) the percent-of-sales method; (3) spontaneous increase in liabilities, increase in retained earnings; (4) planning, control; (5) cash receipt, cash disbursement, cash surplus (or deficit); (6) beginning, ending; (7) sales, physical units; (8) (*b*); (9) (*a*); (10) (*b*); (11) income statement, balance sheet; (12) income statement (or cost of goods sold), balance sheet; (13) surplus, deficit; (14) Computer-based financial planning models; (15) percent-of-sales method.

Solved Problems

3.1   Behavior of Balance Sheet Items. Which of the following balance sheet items generally vary directly with sales?

(*a*)	Common stock	(*f*)	Marketable securities
(*b*)	Accounts payable	(*g*)	Debentures
(*c*)	Retained earnings	(*h*)	Accrued wages
(*d*)	Inventory	(*i*)	Preferred stock
(*e*)	Taxes payable	(*j*)	Mortgage bonds

SOLUTION

(*b*), (*d*), (*e*), (*f*), (*h*)

3.2   Financial Forecasting and External Funds Needed. The following financial data pertain to Barret Company:

Income Statement
(In Millions of Dollars)

Sales	$16.0
Cost of goods sold	13.0
Gross profit	$ 3.0
Operating expenses	1.0
Net profit before taxes	$ 2.0
Tax	1.0
Profit after taxes	$ 1.0
Dividends	0.7
Retentions	$ 0.3

Balance Sheet
(In Millions of Dollars)

ASSETS

Current assets	
Cash	$ 2.0
Receivables	2.0
Inventories	4.0
Total current assets	$ 8.0
Fixed assets	8.0
Total assets	$16.0

LIABILITIES AND NET WORTH

Current liabilities	$ 5.0
Long-term debt	2.0
Total debt	$ 7.0
Common stock	7.0
Retained earnings	$ 2.0
Total liabilities and net worth	$16.0

Barret expects its sales to increase by $2,000,000 next year. In this problem, all the asset accounts (including fixed assets) and current liabilities vary with sales. Barret is operating at full capacity. (*a*) Forecast Barret's need for external funds by (1) constructing a pro forma balance sheet and (2) using the simple formula. (*b*) Discuss the limitation of the percent-of-sales method.

SOLUTION

(*a*) (1)

Pro Forma Balance Sheet
(*In Millions of Dollars*)

	Present	% of Sales (Sales = $16.0)	Next Year (Projected Sales = $18.0)	
ASSETS				
Current assets	$ 8.0	50	$ 9.0000	
Fixed assets	8.0	50	9.0000	
Total assets	$16.0		$18.0000	
LIABILITIES AND NET WORTH				
Current liabilities	$ 5.0	31.25	$ 5.6250	
Long-term debt	2.0	n.a.	2.0000	
Total liabilities	$ 7.0		$ 7.6250	
Common stock	$ 7.0	n.a.	$ 7.0000	
Retained earnings	2.0		2.3375[a]	
Total net worth	$ 9.0		$ 9.3375	
Total liabilities and net worth	$16.0		$16.9625	Total financing provided
			$ 1.0375[b]	External financing needed
			$18.0000	Total

---

[a] Next year's retained earnings = present year's retained earnings + projected net income (after taxes) − cash dividends paid. Note that after-tax net income = $1.0/$16.0 = 6.25% and dividend payout ratio = 0.7/1.0 = 7%. Therefore.

Next year's retained earnings = $2.0 + 6.25%($18.0) − 0.7[5.25%($18)] = $2.0 + $1.125 − $0.7875 = $2.3375.

[b] External funds needed = projected total assets − (projected total liabilities + projected equity) = $18.0 − $16.9625 = $1.0375

(2)

$$EFN = \left(\frac{A}{S}\right)\Delta S - \left(\frac{L}{S}\right)\Delta S - (PM)(PS)(1 - d)$$

where $\dfrac{A}{S} = \dfrac{\$16.0}{\$16.0} = 100\%$

$\dfrac{L}{S} = \dfrac{\$5.0}{\$16.0} = 31.25\%$

$\Delta S = \$18.0 - \$16.0 = \$2.0$

$PM = \$1.0/\$16.0 = 6.25\%$

$PS = \$18.0$

$d = \$0.7/\$1.0 = 70\%,\ or\ 1 - d = 30\%$

Thus,

$$EFN = 100\%(\$2) - 31.25\%(\$2) - (6.25\%)(\$18)(1 - 0.7)$$
$$= \$2 - \$0.625 - \$0.3375 = \$1.0375$$

(b)   The calculations for both the pro forma balance sheet and the simple formula are based on percentage of sales. The limitations of the percent-of-sales method are (1) the relationship between sales and the expense item, asset, or liability being projected is assumed to be pure, i.e., free of any other influences; and (2) the method does not provide accurate forecasts when a firm has extra capacity to absorb all or a portion of the projected increase in sales and the related investment in assets.

3.3   Determination of External Funds Needed. Ina Corporation is thinking of purchasing a new machine. With this new machine, the company expects sales to increase from \$8,000,000 to \$10,000,000.

The company knows that its assets, accounts payable, and accrued expenses vary directly with sales. The company's profit margin on sales is 8 percent, and the company plans to pay 40 percent of its after-tax earnings in dividends. The company's current balance sheet is given below.

Balance Sheet

Current assets	$ 3,000,000
Fixed assets	12,000,000
Total assets	$15,000,000
Accounts payable	$ 4,000,000
Accrued expenses	1,000,000
Long-term debt	3,000,000
Common stock	2,000,000
Retained earnings	5,000,000
Total liabilities and net worth	$15,000,000

(a)   Prepare a pro forma balance sheet.

(b)   Use the simple formula to determine the external funds needed by the company based on the answer in part (a).

(c)   Determine, using the simple formula, the external funds needed under each of the following conditions:

(1)   The profit margin rises from 8 percent to 10 percent.

(2)   The profit margin is 8 percent, but the dividend payout ratio is reduced from 40 percent to 20 percent.

(d)   Comment on the results from part (c).

SOLUTION

(a)

Pro Forma Balance Sheet
(In Millions of Dollars)

	Present Level	% of Sales	Projected (Based on Sales of $10)
Current assets	$ 3	37.5	$ 3.75
Fixed assets	12	150.0	15.00
Total assets	$15		$18.75
Accounts payable	$ 4	50.0	$ 5.00
Accrued expenses	1	12.5	1.25
Long-term debt	3	n.a.	3.00
Common stock	2	n.a.	2.00
Retained earnings	5	n.a.	5.48[a]
Total liabilities and net worth	$15		$16.73 Total funds provided
			$ 2.02 Additional funds needed

[a] Retained earnings = $5 + 8\%($10) - (0.4)[8\%($10)]$
$= \$5 + \$0.8 - \$0.32 = 5.48$

(b)
$$\text{EFN} = \left(\frac{A}{S}\right)\Delta S - \left(\frac{L}{S}\right)\Delta S - (PM)(PS)(1-d)$$

where $\dfrac{A}{S} = \dfrac{\$15}{\$8} = 187.5\%$

$\dfrac{L}{S} = \dfrac{\$5}{\$8} = 62.5\%$

$\Delta S = \$10 - \$8 = \$2$

$PM = 8\%$

$PS = \$10$

$d = 40\%$

$\text{EFN} = 187.5\%(\$2) - 62.5\%(\$2) - 8\%(\$10)(1-0.4)$
$= \$3.75 - \$1.25 - \$0.48 = \$2.02$

(c) (1)
$PM = 10\%$
$\text{EFN} = 187.5\%(\$2) - 62.5\%(\$2) - 10\%(\$10)(1-0.4)$
$= \$3.75 - \$1.25 - \$0.6 = \$1.9$

(2)
$d = 20\%$
$\text{EFN} = 187.5\%(\$2) - 62.5\%(\$2) - 8\%(\$10)(1-0.2)$
$= \$3.75 - \$1.25 - \$0.64 = \$1.86$

(d)   As is evident from part (c), an improved profit margin [(c)(1)] or a lower dividend payout ratio [(d)(2)] will decrease the amount of external funds needed.

3.4   Filling in Blanks and Financial Forecasting. The following data pertain to ABC Company:

Balance Sheet Items
On Dec. 31, 19X1
(In Thousands of Dollars)

	19X1	% of Sales (19X1 Sales = $400)	Pro Forma Balance Sheet on Dec. 31, 19X2 (Projected Sales = $600)
Cash	$ 10	2.5	$ 15
Receivables	90	22.5	135
Inventories	200	50.0	300
Total current assets	$300	75.0	$450
Net fixed assets	300	75.0	450
Total assets	$600	150.0	$900
Accounts payable	$ 40	10.0	$ 60
Notes payable	20	n.a.	(c)
Accrued wages and taxes	40	10.0	60
Total current liabilities	$100		(b)
Mortgage bonds	$140	n.a.	(d)
Common stock	60	n.a.	(f)
Retained earnings	300	n.a.	324
Total	$600		(e) Funds provided
			(a) Additional funds needed

In addition, ABC Company must maintain a total debt/total assets ratio at or below 40 percent and a current ratio at or above 2.5. Within these constraints, ABC would prefer to finance using short-term rather than long-term debt or long-term debt rather than equity.

Fill in the missing terms on the December 31, 19X2, pro forma balance sheet.

SOLUTION

(a)

$$\begin{bmatrix} \text{external} \\ \text{funds} \\ \text{needed} \end{bmatrix} = \begin{bmatrix} \text{required} \\ \text{increase} \\ \text{in assets} \end{bmatrix} - \begin{bmatrix} \text{spontaneous} \\ \text{increase in} \\ \text{liabilities} \end{bmatrix} - \begin{bmatrix} \text{increase in} \\ \text{retained} \\ \text{earnings} \end{bmatrix}$$

$$= (\$900 - \$600) - \begin{bmatrix} \text{increase in} \\ \text{accounts} \\ \text{payable} \\ \text{accrued wages} \\ \text{and taxes} \end{bmatrix} - (\$324 - \$300)$$

$$= \$300 - [(\$60 - \$40) + (\$60 - \$40)] - \$24$$
$$= \$300 - \$40 - \$24 = \$236$$

(b)

$$\text{Current ratio} = \frac{\text{current assets}}{\text{current liabilities}}$$

$$2.5 \text{ (minimum)} = \frac{\$450}{\text{current liabilities}}$$

Current liabilities = $180, which is the maximum allowed.

(c)   Notes payable = current liabilities − (accounts payable + accrued wages and taxes)

$$= \$180 - (\$60 + \$60) = \$180 - \$120 = \$60$$

(d)

$$\frac{\text{Total debt}}{\text{Total assets}} = 40\% \text{ (maximum)}$$

$$\frac{\text{Current liabilities + mortgage bonds}}{\text{Total assets}} = \frac{\$180 + \text{mortgage bonds}}{\$900}$$

$$\text{Mortgage bonds} = 40\% (\$900) - \$180 = \$180$$

(e)   Total funds provided = total assets − additional funds needed

$$= \$900 - \$236 \text{ [from } (a)] = \$664$$

(f)   Common stock = total funds provided − (mortgage bonds + retained earnings)

$$= \$664^a - (\$180^b + \$324) = \$664 - \$504 = \$160$$

_____

[a] From (e).
[b] From (d).

3.5   Credit Sales and Cash Collections. The following sales budget is given for Van Dyke Sales Co. for the second quarter of 19X1:

	April	May	June	Total
Sales budget	$45,000	$50,000	$60,000	$155,000

Credit sales are collected as follows: 70 percent in month of sale, 20 percent in month following sale, 8 percent in second month following sale, and 2 percent uncollectible. The accounts receivable balance at the beginning of the second quarter is $18,000, of which $3,600 represents uncollected February sales, and $14,400 represents uncollected March sales.

Compute (a) the total sales for February and March, and (b) the budgeted cash collections from sales for each month February through June. Without prejudice to answer (a), assume February sales equal $40,000 and March sales equal $50,000.

SOLUTION

(a)   February sales $(1 - 0.7 - 0.2) = \$3,600$

$$\text{February sales} = \frac{\$3,600}{1 - 0.9} = \$36,000$$

March sales $(1 - 0.7) = \$14,400$

$$\text{March sales} = \frac{\$14,400}{0.3} = \$48,000$$

(b)

	April	May	June
Cash collections			
February			
40,000 (8%)	$ 3,200		
March			
50,000 (20%)	10,000		
50,000 (8%)		$ 4,000	
April			
45,000 (70%)	31,500		
45,000 (20%)		9,000	
45,000 (8%)			$ 3,600
May			
50,000 (70%)		35,000	
50,000 (20%)			10,000
June			
60,000 (70%)			42,000
Total cash collections	$44,700	$48,000	$55,600

3.6 **Cash Collections.** The following data are given for Erich From Stores:

	September, Actual	October, Actual	November, Estimated	December, Estimated
Cash sales	$7,000	$6,000	$8,000	$6,000
Credit sales	$50,000	$48,000	$62,000	$80,000
Total sales	$57,000	$54,000	$70,000	$86,000

Past experience indicates net collections normally occur in the following pattern: No collections are made in the month of sale, 80 percent of the sales of any month are collected in the following month, 19 percent of sales are collected in the second following month, and 1 percent of sales are uncollectible.

Compute (a) total cash receipts for November and December, and (b) accounts receivable balance at November 30 if the October 31 balance is $50,000.

SOLUTION

(a)

	November	December
Cash receipts		
Cash sales	$ 8,000	$ 6,000
Cash collections		
September sales		
50,000 (19%)	9,500	
October sales		
48,000 (80%)	38,400	
48,000 (19%)		9,120
November sales		
62,000 (80%)		49,600
Total cash receipts	$55,900	$64,720

(b)   Accounts receivable (Nov. 30) = $50,000 + $62,000 − $9,500 − $38,400 = $64,100

3.7 **Cash Collections and Discount Policy.** The treasurer of John Loyde Co. plans for the company to have a cash balance of $91,000 on March 1. Sales during March are estimated at $900,000. February sales amounted to $600,000, and January sales amounted to $500,000. Cash payments for March have been budgeted at $580,000. Cash collections have been estimated as follows: 60 percent of the sales for the month to be collected during the month, 30 percent of the sales for the preceding month to be collected during the month, and 8 percent of the sales for the second preceding month to be collected during the month.

The treasurer plans to accelerate collections by allowing a 2 percent discount for prompt payment. With the discount policy, she expects to collect 70 percent of the current sales and will permit the discount reduction on these collections. Sales of the preceding month will be collected to the extent of 15 percent with no discount allowed, and 10 percent of the sales of the second preceding month will be collected with no discount allowed. This pattern of collection can be expected in subsequent months. During the transitional month of March, collections may run somewhat higher. However, the treasurer prefers to estimate collections on the basis of the new pattern so that the estimates will be somewhat conservative.

Estimate (a) cash collections for March and the cash balance at March 31 under the present policy, and (b) cash collections for March and the cash balance at March 31 according to the new policy of allowing discounts. (c) Is the discount policy desirable?

SOLUTION

(*a*) and (*b*)

	(*a*) Cash Collection under the Present Policy:	(*b*) Cash Collection under the Discount Policy:
Balance, March 1	$ 91,000	$ 91,000
Collections		
From March sales	540,000 ($900,000 × 60%)	617,400[a]
From February sales	180,000 ($600,000 × 30%)	90,000 ($600,000 × 15%)
From January sales	40,000 ($500,000 × 8%)	50,000 ($500,000 × 10%)
Total cash available	$851,000	$848,400
Less: Disbursements	580,000	580,000
Balance, March 31	$271,000	$268,400

[a]$900,000 × 70% × 98% = $617,400

(*c*) No, the discount policy is not, since, under the discount policy, the March 31 cash balance will be smaller.

3.8 Cash Disbursements. Eastmark Stores wants to estimate cash disbursements for cash budgeting purposes for the first 3 months of 19X2 from the data given below.

1. Cost of merchandise sold, estimated:

19X1: December	$225,000
19X2: January	$250,000
February	$280,000
March	$210,000

The cost of merchandise is to be paid for as follows: 35 percent in the month of sale and 65 percent in the following month.

2. Wages for each month are estimated as follows:

19X1: December	$23,000
19X2: January	$26,000
February	$31,000
March	$25,000

All are paid as incurred.

3. Utilities are to be paid every other month at the amount of $320 per month. The first payment is to be made in February.

4. Six months' rent and insurance amounting to a total of $9,700 is to be paid in January.

5. An income tax of $12,500 is to be paid in March.

6. Depreciation on office equipment has been estimated at $7,500 for the year.

7. New equipment costing $50,000 is to be acquired in February, with a down payment of $4,000 required at date of purchase.

8. Other operating expenses have been estimated at $2,250 per month, which are to be paid each month.

Prepare a cash disbursement budget for each of the first 3 months of 19X2.

SOLUTION

Cash Disbursements Budget
For 3 Months, 19X2

	January	February	March	Total
Cost of merchandise sold				
35% current	$ 87,500	$ 98,000	$ 73,500	$259,000
65% preceding month	146,250	162,500	182,000	490,750
Total	$233,750	$260,500	$255,500	$749,750
Wages	26,000	31,000	25,000	82,000
Utilities		320		320
Rent and insurance	9,700			9,700
Income tax			12,500	12,500
Equipment, down payment		4,000		4,000
Other operation expenses	2,250	2,250	2,250	6,750
Total disbursements	$271,700	$298,070	$295,250	$865,020

3.9 Cash Budget. Some key figures from the budget of Moore Company for the first quarter of operations for 19X2 are shown below.

	January	February	March
Credit sales	$80,000	$70,000	$86,000
Credit purchases	34,000	32,000	40,000
Cash disbursements			
Wages and salaries	4,000	3,500	4,200
Rent	1,500	1,500	1,500
Equipment purchases	25,000		2,000

The company estimates that 10 percent of its credit sales will never be collected. Of those that will be collected, 50 percent will be collected in the month of sale and the remainder will be collected in the following month. Purchases on account will all be paid for in the month following purchase. 19X2 December sales were $90,000.

Using the preceding information, complete the following cash budget.

	January	February	March
Beginning cash balance	$100,000	_____	_____
Cash receipts			
Cash collections from credit sales	_____	_____	_____
Total cash available	_____	_____	_____
Cash disbursements			
Purchases	_____	_____	_____
Wages and salaries	_____	_____	_____
Rent	_____	_____	_____
Equipment purchases	_____	_____	_____
Total disbursements	_____	_____	_____
Ending cash balance	_____	_____	_____

SOLUTION

	January	February	March
Beginning cash balance	$100,000	$146,000	$174,500
Cash receipts			
Cash collections from credit sales	76,500[a]	67,500[b]	70,200[c]
Total cash available	$176,500	$213,500	$244,700
Cash disbursements			
Purchases		$ 34,000	$ 32,000
Salaries	$ 4,000	3,500	4,200
Rent	1,500	1,500	1,500
Fixed assets	25,000		2,000
Total disbursements	$ 30,500	$ 39,000	$ 39,700
Ending cash balance	$146,000	$174,500	$205,000

---

[a] From December sales: $\dfrac{\$90,000 - (\$90,000 \times 0.1)}{2} = \$40,500$

January sales: $\dfrac{\$80,000 - (\$80,000 \times 0.1)}{2} = \dfrac{36,000}{\$76,500}$

[b] From January sales: $36,000$

February sales: $\dfrac{\$70,000 - (\$70,000 \times 0.1)}{2} = \dfrac{31,500}{\$67,500}$

[c] From February sales: $\$31,500$

March sales: $\dfrac{\$86,000 - (\$86,000 \times 0.1)}{2} = \dfrac{38,700}{\$70,200}$

3.10 Incomplete Data on Sales. The following information pertains to merchandise purchased by Westwood Plumbing Co. for July, August, September, and October. During any month, 60 percent of the merchandise to be sold in the following month is purchased. The balance of the merchandise is purchased during the month of sale. Gross margin averages 20 percent of sales.

	Purchases	
	For the Following Month	For the Current Month
July	$87,000	$92,000
August	$96,000	$100,000
September	$120,000	$89,000
October	$110,000	$92,000

Estimate the sales revenue for August, September, and October.

SOLUTION

Cost of sales:

August:	$87,000 ÷ 0.6 = $145,000
September:	$96,000 ÷ 0.6 = $160,000
October:	$120,000 ÷ 0.6 = $200,000

Since gross margin averages 20 percent of sales, cost of goods sold is equal to 80 percent of sales. Thus, sales:

August: $145,000 ÷ 0.8 = $181,250
September: $160,000 ÷ 0.8 = $200,000
October: $200,000 ÷ 0.8 = $250,000

3.11 **Selling and Administrative Expense Budget.** Foster Company has gathered the following information for the month of July, 19X1:

Sales: $200,000
Sales commissions: 10% of sales
Advertising expenses: $5,000 + 2% of sales
Miscellaneous selling expense: $1,000 + 1% of sales
Office salaries: $7,000
Office supplies: 0.5% of sales
Travel and entertainment: $4,000
Miscellaneous administrative expense: $1,750

Prepare a selling and administrative budget.

SOLUTION

Foster Company
Selling and Administrative Expense Budget
For the Month of July, 19X1

Selling expenses	
Sales staff commissions	$20,000
Advertising expense	9,000
Miscellaneous selling expense	3,000
Total	$32,000
Administrative expenses	
Office salaries	$ 7,000
Office supplies	1,000
Miscellaneous expense	1,750
Travel and entertainment	4,000
Total	$13,750
Total selling and administrative expenses	$45,750

3.12 **Budgeted Income Statement.** In the fiscal quarter ended December 31, 19X1, Eric Wills Lumber Company plans to sell 52,000 board feet lumber at a price of $125 per board foot. There are to be 5,500 board feet on hand October 1, with a cost of $65 per board foot. The company plans to manufacture 53,000 board feet of lumber during the quarter, with the following manufacturing costs:

Direct materials: $971,500
Direct labor: $2,000,000
Factory overhead: (25% of direct labor costs)

The company uses the last-in, first-out (LIFO) method of inventory costing. Selling expenses are estimated at 25 percent of sales, and administrative expenses are expected to be 10 percent more than the previous quarter's $950,000.
Prepare a budgeted income statement.

SOLUTION

Eric Wills Lumber Co.
Budgeted Income Statement
For the Quarter Ended Dec. 31, 19X1

Sales (52,000 @ $125)		$6,500,000
Less: Cost of goods sold		
Beginning inventory		
(5,500 @ $65)	$ 357,500	
Direct materials	971,500	
Direct labor	2,000,000	
Factory overhead		
(25% of $2,000,000)	500,000	
Cost of goods available for sale	$3,829,000	
Less: Ending inventory		
(6,500 units)[a]	423,000[b]	3,406,000
Gross profit		$3,094,000
Less operating expenses		
Selling expenses		
(25% of $6,500,000)	$1,625,000	
Administrative expenses		
(110% of $950,000)	1,045,000	2,670,000
Net income		$ 424,000

[a]
$$5{,}500 \text{ units} + 53{,}000 \text{ units} - x = 52{,}000 \text{ units}$$
$$x = 6{,}500 \text{ units}$$

[b] The unit cost for the last quarter of 19X1 is calculated as follows:

Unit cost = cost of goods manufactured/number of units
$$= (\$971{,}500 + \$2{,}000{,}000 + \$500{,}000)/53{,}000 \text{ board feet} = \$65.50$$

Then,

5,500 units @ $65.00	$357,500
1,000 units @ $65.50	65,500
6,500 units	$423,000

3.13   Budgeted Income Statement. The Moore Distributor, Inc., has just received a franchise to distribute dishwashers. The company started business on January 1, 19X1, with the following assets:

Cash	$45,000
Inventory	$94,000
Warehouse, office, and delivery facilities and equipment	$800,000

All facilities and equipment have a useful life of 20 years and no residual value. First-quarter sales are expected to be $360,000 and should be doubled in the second quarter. Third-quarter sales are expected to be $1,080,000. One percent of sales are considered to be uncollectible. The gross profit margin should be 30 percent. Variable selling expenses (except uncollectible accounts) are budgeted at 12 percent of sales and fixed selling expenses at $48,000 per quarter, exclusive of depreciation. Variable administrative expenses are expected to be 3 percent of sales, and fixed administrative expenses should total $34,200 per quarter, exclusive of depreciation.

Prepare a budgeted income statement for the second quarter, 19X1.

SOLUTION

The Moore Distributor, Inc.
Budgeted Income Statement
For the Second Quarter, 19X1

Sales		$720,000
Cost of goods sold (70%)		504,000
Gross profit (30%)		$216,000
Operating expenses		
Uncollectible accounts (1%)	$ 7,200	
Depreciation^a	10,000	
Selling		
Variable (12%)	86,400	
Fixed	48,000	
Administrative		
Variable (3%)	21,600	
Fixed	34,200	207,400
Income before income tax		$ 8,600

^{a} $\frac{1}{4}$($800,000 \div 20$ years) = $10,000

3.14   Pro Forma Balance Sheet. Given the following data on the Dunes Corporation, project its balance sheet for the coming year:

> Present sales: $500,000
> Next year's sales: $800,000
> After-tax profits: 5% of sales
> Dividend payout ratio: 40%
> Present retained earnings: $200,000
> Cash as a percent of sales: 4%
> Accounts receivable as a percent of sales: 10%
> Inventory as a percent of sales: 30%
> Net fixed assets as a percent of sales: 35%
> Accounts payable as a percent of sales: 7%
> Accruals as a percent of sales: 15%
> Next year's common stock: $200,000

Dunes Corporation
Balance Sheet
Dec. 31, 19X1

ASSETS		LIABILITIES AND EQUITIES	
Cash	(a)	Accounts payable	(f)
Accounts receivable	(b)	Notes payable	(g)
Inventory	(c)	Accruals	(h)
Net fixed assets	(d)	Common stock	(i)
		Retained earnings	(j)
Total	(e)	Total	(k)

SOLUTION

The completed balance sheet is as follows:

Dunes Corporation
Balance Sheet
Dec. 31, 19X1

ASSETS		LIABILITIES AND EQUITIES	
Cash	$ 32,000	Accounts payable	$ 56,000
Accounts receivable	80,000	Notes payable	32,000
Inventory	240,000	Accruals	120,000
Net fixed assets	280,000	Common stock	200,000
		Retained earnings	224,000
Total	$632,000	Total	$632,000

The calculations are outlined below.

(a)   Cash = 4% of sales = 0.04($800,000) = $32,000

(b)   AR = 10% of sales = 0.1($800,000) = $80,000

(c)   Inventory = 30% of sales = 0.3($800,000) = $240,000

(d)   Net fixed assets = 35% of sales = 0.35($800,000) = $280,000

(e) $632,000

(f)   AP = 7% of sales = 0.07($800,000) = $56,000

(g)   Notes payable = total assets $- \left(\begin{array}{l} \text{accounts} \\ \text{payable} \end{array} + \text{accruals} + \begin{array}{l} \text{common} \\ \text{stock} \end{array} + \begin{array}{l} \text{retained} \\ \text{earnings} \end{array} \right)$

$\qquad$ = $632,000 − ($56,000 + $120,000 + $200,000 + $224,000)
$\qquad$ = $632,000 − $600,000 = $32,000

(h)   Accruals = 15% of sales = 0.15($800,000) = $120,000

(i)   Given, $200,000

(j)   Retained earnings next year = retained earnings of the present year + after-tax profits − dividends
$\qquad$ = $200,000 + 5% ($800,000) − 0.4[5% ($800,000)] = $224,000

(k) $632,000

3.15   The Tony DeBenedictis Company's 19X2 sales is expected to be $12 million. The following financial statement items vary directly with sales by the percentages given.

Cash:	4%
Accounts receivable:	15%
Inventories:	20%
Net fixed assets:	35%
Accounts payable:	18%
Accruals:	15%
Profit margin on sales:	6%

The dividend payout ratio is 40 percent; the 19X1 retained earnings was $4 million; and notes payable, common stock, and retained earnings are equal to the amounts shown on the balance sheet below:

Complete the following pro forma balance sheet:

Pro Forma Balance Sheet
(In Thousands of Dollars)

Cash	$ (a)	Accounts payable	$ (h)
Accounts receivable	(b)	Notes payable	1,200
Inventories	(c)	Accruals	(i)
Total current assets	$ (d)	Total current liabilities	$ (j)
Net fixed assets	(e)	Debentures	(k)
		Common stock	1,000
		Retained earnings	1,680
Total assets	$ (f)	Total liabilities and equity	$ (g)

SOLUTION

The completed balance sheet is as follows:

Pro Forma Balance Sheet
(In Thousands of Dollars)

Cash	$ 480	Accounts payable	$2,160
Accounts receivable	1,800	Notes payable	1,200
Inventories	2,400	Accruals	1,800
Total current assets	$4,680	Total current liabilities	$5,160
Net fixed assets	4,200	Debentures	1,040
		Common stock	1,000
		Retained earnings	1,680
Total assets	$8,880	Total liabilities and equity	$8,880

The calculations are outlined below.

(a)   Cash = 4% of sales = 0.04($12,000) = $480
(b)   Accounts receivable = 0.15($12,000) = $1,800
(c)   Inventories = 0.20($12,000) = $2,400
(d)   Total current assets = $480 + $1,800 + $2,400 = $4,680
(e)   Net fixed assets = 0.35($12,000) = $4,200
(f)   Total assets = $4,200 + $4,680 = $8,880
(g)   Therefore, total liabilities and equity is also $8,880
(h)   Accounts payable = 0.18($12,000) = $2,160
(i)   Accruals = 0.15($12,000) = $1,800
(j)   Total current liabilities = $2,160 + $1,200 + $1,800 = $5,160
(k)   Therefore, debentures = $8,880 − $5,160 − $1,000 − $1,680 = $1,040

3.16   **Budgeted Income Statement and Balance Sheet.** A budget is being prepared for the first and second quarters of 19X2 for Aggarwal Retail Stores, Inc. The balance sheet as of December 31, 19X1, is given below

Aggarwal Retail Stores, Inc.
Balance Sheet
Dec. 31, 19X1

ASSETS		LIABILITIES AND EQUITIES	
Cash	$ 65,000	Accounts payable	$ 83,000
Accounts receivable	52,000	Income tax payable	20,000
Merchandise inventory	75,000	Capital stock	70,000
		Retained earnings	19,000
Total assets	$192,000	Total liabilities and equities	$192,000

Actual and projected sales are:

19X1, 3d quarter (actual):	$250,000
19X1, 4th quarter (actual):	$300,000
19X2, 1st quarter (estimated):	$200,000
19X2, 2d quarter (estimated):	$230,000
19X2, 3d quarter (estimated):	$220,000

Experience has shown that 60 percent of sales will be collected during the first quarter of sales and 35 percent of sales will be collected in the following quarter. Gross profit averages 30 percent of sales. There is a basic inventory of $20,000. The policy is to purchase in each quarter the additional inventory needed for the following quarter's sales; payments are made in the quarter following the quarter of purchase. Selling and administrative expenses for each quarter are estimated at 4 percent of sales plus $15,000 and are paid as incurred. Income tax is equal to 40 percent of taxable income. The income tax liability as of December 31, 19X1, is to be paid during the first quarter of 19X2.

Prepare (a) a budgeted income statement for the first and second quarter of 19X2 and (b) a budgeted balance sheet as of June 30, 19X2.

SOLUTION

(a)

Aggarwal Retail Stores, Inc.
Budgeted Income Statement
For the 6 Months Ended June 30, 19X2

	Quarter		
	1	**2**	**Total**
Sales	$200,000	$230,000	$430,000
Less: Cost of goods sold (70%)	140,000	161,000	301,000
Gross margin	$ 60,000	$ 69,000	$129,000
Less: Selling and administrative expenses ($15,000 + 4% of sales)	23,000	24,200	47,200
Net income before tax	$ 37,000	$ 44,800	$ 81,800
Income tax (40%)	14,800	17,920	32,720
Net income	$ 22,200	$ 26,880	$ 49,080

(b)

Aggarwal Retail Stores, Inc.
Budgeted Balance Sheet as of June 30, 19X2

ASSETS		LIABILITIES AND EQUITIES	
Cash	$ 89,800[a]	Accounts payable	$ 97,000[d]
Accounts receivable	49,000[b]	Income tax payable	32,720[e]
Merchandise inventory	129,000[c]	Capital stock	70,000
		Retained earnings	68,080[f]
Total assets	$267,800	Total liabilities and equity	$267,800

The supporting calculations for the balance sheet are as follows:

| | Quarter | | |
	1	2	Total
CASH RECEIPTS			
60% of current sales	$120,000	$138,000	$258,000
35% of prior quarter's sales	105,000	70,000	175,000
Total receipts	$225,000	$208,000	$433,000
CASH DISBURSEMENTS			
Merchandise purchases[g]	$160,000	$181,000	$341,000
Selling and administrative expenses ($15,000 + 4% of sales per month)	23,000	24,200	47,200
Income tax (for previous quarter)	20,000		20,000
Total disbursements	$203,000	$205,200	$408,200

[a] Cash = beginning balance + cash receipts − disbursements
= $65,000 + $433,000 − $408,200 = $89,800

[b] Accounts receivable = beginning balance + sales − cash receipts
= $52,000 + ($200,000 + $230,000) − $433,000 = $49,000

[c] Merchandise inventory = beginning balance + purchases − cost of goods sold
= $75,000 + ($181,000 + $174,000) − 70%($430,000) = $129,000

[d] Accounts payable = Beginning balance + purchases + selling and administrative expenses
− disbursements (for purchases and selling and administrative expenses)
= $83,000 + $355,000 + $47,200 − ($341,000 + $47,200) = $97,000

[e] Income tax payable = beginning balance + net income after tax − income tax payment
= $20,000 + $32,720 − $20,000 = $32,720

[f] Retained earnings = beginning balance + net income = $19,000 + $49,080 = $68,080

[g] **MERCHANDISE**

| Purchases | Quarter | | | |
	4	1	2	Total
($20,000 basic + 70% of the quarter's sales)	$160,000	$181,000	$174,000	$515,000
Cash disbursements for merchandise purchases		$160,000	$181,000	$341,000

Chapter 4

The Management of Working Capital

4.1 MANAGING NET WORKING CAPITAL

Working capital is equal to current assets. *Net* working capital is equal to current assets less current liabilities.

EXAMPLE 4.1   Ace Company has the following selected assets and liabilities:

Cash:	$10,000
Accounts receivable:	$30,000
Inventory:	$42,000
Machinery:	$90,000
Long-term investments:	$36,000
Patent:	$4,000
Accounts payable:	$12,000
Taxes payable:	$3,000
Accrued expenses payable:	$5,000
Bonds payable:	$50,000
Common stock:	$70,000

The net working capital is:

CURRENT ASSETS		
Cash	$10,000	
Accounts receivable	30,000	
Inventory	42,000	$82,000
CURRENT LIABILITIES		
Accounts payable	$12,000	
Taxes payable	3,000	
Accrued expenses payable	5,000	20,000
Net working capital		$62,000

Management of net working capital involves regulating the various types of current assets and current liabilities. Management of net working capital also requires decisions about how current assets should be financed, for example, through short-term debt, long-term debt, or equity. Net working capital is increased when current assets are financed through noncurrent sources.

The liquidity of current assets will affect the terms and availability of short-term credit. The greater the liquidity, the easier it becomes, generally, to obtain a short-term loan at favorable terms. Short-term credit, in turn, affects the amount of cash balance held by a firm.

Working Capital Management and Risk-Return Trade-Off

The management of net working capital requires consideration for the trade-off between return and risk. Holding more current than fixed assets means a reduced liquidity risk. It also means greater flexibility, since current assets may be modified easily as sales volume changes. However, the rate of return will be less with current assets than with fixed assets. Fixed assets typically earn a greater return than current assets. Long-term financing has less liquidity risk associated with it than short-term debt, but it also carries a higher cost.

For example, when a company needs funds to purchase seasonal or cyclical inventory, it uses short-term, not long-term financing. The short-term debt gives the firm flexibility to meet its seasonal needs within its ability to repay the loan. On the other hand, the company's permanent assets should be financed with long-term debt. Because the assets last longer, the financing can be spread over a longer time. Financing assets with liabilities of similar maturity is called *hedging*.

4.2   CURRENT ASSETS

By optimally managing cash, receivables, and inventory, a company can maximize its rate of return and minimize its liquidity and business risk. The financial manager should determine the amount to be invested in a given current asset. The amount invested may vary from day to day and require close evaluation of the account balances. Current assets are improperly managed if funds tied up in an asset could be used more productively elsewhere. Financing such assets with debt incurs unnecessary interest expense. Also, large account balances indicate risk since, for example, inventory may not be saleable and/or accounts receivable may not be collectible. On the other hand, inadequate current asset levels may be costly as, for example, when business is lost because lack of inventory does not permit the timely fulfillment of customer orders.

4.3   CASH MANAGEMENT

Cash refers to currency and demand deposits. *Cash management* involves having the optimum, neither excessive nor deficient, amount of cash on hand at the right time. Proper cash management requires that the company know how much cash it needs, as well as how much it has and where that cash is at all times. This is especially essential in an inflationary environment.

The objective of cash management is to invest excess cash for a return while retaining sufficient liquidity to satisfy future needs. The financial manager must plan when to have excess funds available for investment and when money needs to be borrowed.

The amount of cash to be held depends upon the following factors:

1.   Cash management policies
2.   Current liquidity position
3.   Management's liquidity risk preferences
4.   Schedule of debt maturity
5.   The firm's ability to borrow
6.   Forecasted short- and long-term cash flow
7.   The probabilities of different cash flows under varying circumstances

The company should not have an excessive cash balance since no return is being earned upon it. The least amount of cash a firm should hold is the greater of (1) compensating balances (a deposit held by a bank to compensate it for providing services) or (2) precautionary balances (money held for emergency purposes) plus transaction balances (money needed to cover checks outstanding).

Cash management also requires knowing the amount of funds available for investment and the length of time for which they can be invested. A firm may invest its funds in the following:

1.   Time deposits, including savings accounts earning daily interest, long-term savings accounts, and certificates of deposit
2.   Money market funds, which are managed portfolios of short-term, high-grade debt instruments such as Treasury bills and commercial paper
3.   Demand deposits that pay interest
4.   U.S. Treasury securities

When cash receipts and disbursements are highly synchronized and predictable, a firm may keep a small cash balance. The financial manager must accurately forecast the amount of cash needed, its source, and its destination. These data are needed on both a short- and a long-term basis. Forecasting assists the manager in properly timing financing, debt repayment, and the amount to be transferred between accounts.

In deciding whether to adopt a cash management system, the financial manager should consider its associated costs versus the return earned from implementation of the system. Costs related to cash management systems include bank charges, financial manager's time, and office employee salaries. Some cash management systems use the firm's computer to make transactions with the computers of banks and money market funds. Computer systems are also useful for purchasing and selling securities in the money market.

Companies with many bank accounts should guard against accumulating excessive balances. Less cash needs to be kept on hand when a company can borrow quickly from a bank, such as under a *line of credit agreement*, which permits a firm to borrow instantly up to a specified maximum amount. A company may also find some cash unnecessarily tied up in other accounts, such as advances to employees. Excess cash should be invested in marketable securities for a return. Note however that cash in some bank accounts may not be available for investment. For instance, when a bank lends money to a company, the bank often requires the company to keep funds on hand as collateral. This deposit is called a compensating balance, which in effect represents *restricted* cash for the company.

Holding marketable securities serves as protection against cash shortages. Companies with seasonal operations may buy marketable securities when they have excess funds and then sell the securities when cash deficits occur. A firm may also invest in marketable securities when funds are being held temporarily in anticipation of short-term capital expansion. In selecting an investment portfolio, consideration should be given to return, default risk, marketability, and maturity date.

The thrust of cash management is to accelerate cash receipts and delay cash payments. Each bank account should be analyzed as to its type, balance, and cost so that corporate return is maximized.

Acceleration of Cash Inflow

To accelerate cash inflow, the financial manager must (1) know the bank's policy regarding fund availability; (2) know the source and location of company receipts; and (3) devise procedures for quick deposit of checks received and quick transfer of receipts in outlying accounts into the main corporate account.

The various types of check processing delays that must be analyzed are: (1) mail float—the time required for a check to move from a debtor to a creditor; (2) processing float—the time it takes for a creditor to deposit the check after receipt; and (3) deposit collection float—the time required for a check to clear.

Mail float can be minimized by having the collection center located near the customer. Local banks should be selected to speed the receipt of funds for subsequent transfer to the central corporate account. As an alternative, strategic post office lockboxes may be used for customer remissions. The local bank collects from these boxes periodically during the day and deposits the funds in the corporate account. The bank also furnishes the company with a computer listing of payments received by account and a daily total. Because the lockbox system has a significant per-item cost, it is most cost-effective with low-volume, high-dollar remissions. However, the system is becoming increasingly more available to companies with high-volume, low-dollar deposits as technological advances (such as machine-readable documents) lower the per-item cost of lockboxes.

Before a lockbox system is implemented, the company should make a cost–benefit analysis that considers the average dollar amount of checks received, the costs saved by having lockboxes, the reduction in mailing time per check, and the processing cost.

EXAMPLE 4.2   Chaset Corporation obtains average cash receipts of $200,000 per day. It usually takes 5 days from the time a check is mailed to its availability for use. The amount tied up by the delay is:

$$5 \text{ days} \times \$200,000 = \$1,000,000$$

EXAMPLE 4.3 It takes Travis Corporation about 7 days to receive and deposit payments from customers. Therefore, a lockbox system is being considered. It is expected that the system will reduce the float time to 5 days. Average daily collections are $500,000. The rate of return is 12 percent.

The reduction in outstanding cash balances arising from implementing the lockbox system is:

$$\text{2 days} \times \$500,000 = \$1,000,000$$

The return that could be earned on these funds is:

$$\$1,000,000 \times 0.12 = \$120,000$$

The maximum monthly charge the company should pay for this lockbox arrangement is therefore:

$$\frac{\$120,000}{12} = \$10,000$$

EXAMPLE 4.4 Charles Corporation is exploring the use of a lockbox system that will cost $100,000 per year. Daily collections average $350,000. The lockbox arrangement will reduce the float period by 2 days. The firm's rate of return is 15 percent.

The cost–benefit analysis is shown below.

Return on early collection of cash	
$0.15 \times 2 \times \$350,000$	$105,000
Cost	100,000
Advantage of lockbox	$ 5,000

A corporate financial manager should determine whether it would be financially advantageous to split a geographic collection region into a number of parts.

EXAMPLE 4.5 Travis Company has an agreement with Charter Bank in which the bank handles $3 million in collections a day and requires a $700,000 compensating balance. Travis is thinking of canceling the agreement and dividing its western region so that two other banks will handle its business instead. Bank A will handle $1 million a day of collections, requiring a compensating balance of $300,000, and bank B will handle the other $2 million a day, asking for a compensating balance of $500,000. Travis's financial manager anticipates that collections will be accelerated by $\frac{1}{4}$ day if the western region is divided. The company's rate of return is 14 percent.

The financial manager decided that the new arrangement should be implemented, based on the following analysis:

Acceleration in cash receipts	
$3 million per day $\times \frac{1}{4}$ day	$750,000
Additional compensating balance	
required	100,000
Increased cash flow	$650,000
Rate of return	$\times$ 0.14
Net annual savings	$ 91,000

Concentration banking should also be considered for use. With this method funds are collected by several local banks and transferred to a main *concentration* account in another bank. The transfer of funds between banks should be accomplished through the use of depository transfer checks (DTCs) or wire transfers. In the DTC arrangement, there exists a resolution statement with the bank in which signatureless checks are allowed to be deposited. As the initial banks collect the funds, information is immediately transferred to the concentration bank, which then issues a DTC to collect the outlying funds. The funds may be available the same day.

Once remissions have been accelerated, freed cash should be used for investment in marketable securities or to pay off short-term debt. Thus, the freed cash will generate interest revenue to the business. The revenue derived can be determined for a given month by multiplying the monthly average accounts receivable balance times the associated monthly interest rate (i.e., the interest rate on marketable securities or the interest rate applicable to short-term debt).

EXAMPLE 4.6   A firm's weekly average cash balances are as follows:

Week	Average Cash Balance
1	$12,000
2	17,000
3	10,000
4	15,000
Total	$54,000

The monthly average cash balance is:

$$\frac{\$54,000}{4} = \$13,500$$

If the annual interest rate is approximated at 12 percent, the monthly return earned on the average cash balance is:

$$\$13,500 \times 0.1 = \$135$$

For a cash acceleration system to be feasible, the return earned on the freed cash must exceed the cost of the system.

Delay of Cash Outflow

There are various ways to delay cash disbursements, including:

1. Using drafts to pay bills since drafts are not due on demand. When a bank receives a draft it must return the draft to the issuer for acceptance prior to payment. When the company accepts the draft, it then deposits the required funds with the bank; hence, a smaller average checking balance is maintained.

2. Mailing checks from post offices having limited service or from locations where the mail must go through several handling points, lengthening the payment period.

3. Drawing checks on remote banks or establishing cash disbursement centers in remote locations so that the payment period is lengthened. For example, someone in New York can be paid with a check drawn on a California bank.

4. Using credit cards and charge accounts in order to lengthen the time between the acquisition of goods and the date of payment for those goods.

The cash disbursements of a firm may be controlled by centralizing its payable operation so that it satisfies its obligations at optimum times. Centralization will also facilitate the prediction of the disbursement float.

Payments to vendors should be delayed to the maximum as long as there is no associated finance charge or impairment of the company's credit rating. Of course, bills should not be paid prior to their due dates because of the time value of money.

A company can minimize its cash balances by using probabilities related to the expected time that checks will clear. Deposits, for example, may be made to a payroll checking account based on the expected time needed for the checks to clear.

Although not a delay of cash outflow, a company may reduce its cash outflow by the early repayment of a loan, thus avoiding some payment of interest. The company should consider the wire transfer of funds if a quick payment method is called for, especially if the payment is to be made to a distant location.

EXAMPLE 4.7   Every 2 weeks, company X disburses checks that average $500,000 and take 3 days to clear. How much money can the company save annually if it delays transfer of funds from an interest-bearing account that pays 0.0384 percent per day (annual rate of 14 percent) for those 3 days?

The interest for 3 days is:

$$\$500,000 \times (0.000384 \times 3) = \$576$$

The number of 2-week periods in a year is:

$$\frac{52 \text{ weeks}}{2 \text{ weeks}} = 26$$

The savings per year is:

$$\$576 \times 26 = \$14,976$$

Opportunity Cost of Forgoing a Cash Discount

An *opportunity cost* is the net revenue lost by rejecting an alternative action. A firm should typically take advantage of a discount offered by a creditor because of the associated high opportunity cost. For example, if the terms of sale are 2/10, net/30, the customer has 30 days to pay the bill but will get a 2 percent discount if he or she pays in 10 days. Some companies use seasonal datings such as 2/10, net/30, July 1 dating. Here, with an invoice dated July 1, the discount can be taken until July 10.

The following formula may be used to compute the opportunity cost in percentage, on an annual basis, of not taking a discount:

$$\text{Opportunity cost} = \frac{\text{discount percent}}{100 - \text{discount percent}} \times \frac{360}{N}$$

where N = the number of days payment can be delayed by forgoing the cash discount
            = days credit is outstanding − discount period

The numerator of the first term (discount percent) is the cost per dollar of credit, whereas the denominator (100 − discount percent) represents the money made available by forgoing the cash discount. The second term represents the number of times this cost is incurred in a year.

EXAMPLE 4.8   The opportunity cost of not taking a discount when the terms are 3/15, net/60 is computed as follows:

$$\text{Opportunity cost} = \frac{3}{100 - 3} \times \frac{360}{60 - 15} = \frac{3}{97} \times \frac{360}{45} = 24.7\%$$

Determination of the Optimal Cash Balance

There are two techniques for deciding how much cash to maintain at any given point, considering that both holding cash and investing it have both advantages and disadvantages. The purpose of cash models is to satisfy cash requirements at the least cost.

Baumol's Model

It attempts to determine the optimum amount of transaction cash under conditions of certainty. The objective is to minimize the sum of the fixed costs of transactions and the opportunity cost of holding cash balances. These costs are expressed as:

$$b \times \frac{\text{(T)}}{\text{C}} + \frac{i(\text{C})}{2}$$

where b = the fixed cost of a transaction, T = the total cash needed for the time period involved, i = the interest rate on marketable securities, and C = cash balance.

The optimal level of cash is determined using the following formula:

$$C^* = \sqrt{\frac{2bT}{i}}$$

EXAMPLE 4.9   You estimate a cash need for $4,000,000 over a 1-month period where the cash account is expected to be disbursed at a constant rate. The opportunity interest rate is 6% per annum, or 0.5 percent for a 1-month period. The transaction cost each time you borrow or withdraw is $100.

The optimal transaction size (the optimal borrowing or withdrawal lot size) and the number of transactions you should make during the month follow:

$$C^* = \sqrt{\frac{2bT}{i}} = \sqrt{\frac{2(100)(4,000,000)}{0.005}} = \$400,000$$

The optimal transaction size is $400,000. The average cash balance is:

$$\frac{C^*}{2} = \frac{\$400,000}{2} = \$200,000$$

The number of transactions required are:

$$\frac{\$4,000,000}{\$400,000} = 10 \text{ transactions during the month.}$$

The Miller–Orr Model

The Miller–Orr model is a stochastic model for cash management where *uncertainty* exists for cash payments. In other words, there is irregularity of cash payments. The Miller–Orr model places an upper and lower limit for cash balances. When the upper limit is reached a transfer of cash to marketable securities or other suitable investments is made. When the lower limit is reached a transfer from securities to cash occurs. A transaction will not occur as long as the cash balance falls within the limits.

The Miller–Orr model takes into account the fixed costs of a securities transaction (b), assumed to be the same for buying as well as selling, the daily interest rate on marketable securities (i), and the variance of daily net cash flows (s^2). A major assumption is the randomness of cash flows. The two control limits in the Miller–Orr model may be specified as "h" dollars as an upper limit and zero dollars at the lower limit. When the cash balance reaches the upper level, h less z dollars of securities are bought and the new balance equals zero, z dollars of securities are sold and the new balance again reaches z.

The optimal cash balance z is computed as follows:

$$z = \sqrt[3]{\frac{3bs^2}{4i}}$$

The optimal value for h is computed as $3z$. The average cash balance will approximate $(z + h)/3$.

EXAMPLE 4.10   Delta Inc. has experienced a stochastic demand for its product, which results in fluctuating cash balances randomly. The following information is supplied:

Fixed cost of a securities transaction	$10
Variance of daily net cash flows	$50
Daily interest rate on securities (10%/360)	0.0003

The optimal cash balance, the upper limit of cash needed, and the average cash balance follow:

$$z = \sqrt[3]{\frac{3(10)(50)}{4(0.0003)}} = \sqrt[3]{\frac{3(10)(50)}{0.0012}} = \sqrt[3]{\frac{1.500}{0.0012}}$$

$$= 3\sqrt{1,250,000} = \$102$$

The optimal cash balance is \$102. The upper limit is \$306(3 × \$102). The average cash balance is

$$\frac{(\$102 + \$306)}{3} = \$136$$

When the upper limit of \$306 is reached, \$204 of securities (\$306 − \$102) will be purchased to bring you to the optimal cash balance of \$102. When the lower limit of zero dollars is reached, \$102 of securities will be sold to again bring you to the optimal cash balance of \$102.

4.4 MANAGEMENT OF ACCOUNTS RECEIVABLE

Consideration should be given to the company's investment in accounts receivable since there is an opportunity cost associated with holding receivable balances. The major decision regarding accounts receivable is the determination of the amount and terms of credit to extend to customers. The credit terms offered have a direct bearing on the associated costs and revenue to be generated from receivables. For example, if credit terms are tight, there will be less of an investment in accounts receivable and less bad debt losses, but there will also be lower sales and reduced profits.

In evaluating a potential customer's ability to pay, consideration should be given to the firm's integrity, financial soundness, collateral to be pledged, and current economic conditions. A customer's credit soundness may be evaluated through quantitative techniques such as regression analysis. Such techniques are most useful when a large number of small customers are involved. Bad debt losses can be estimated reliably when a company sells to many customers and when its credit policies have not changed for a long period of time.

The collection period for accounts receivable partly depends on the firm's credit policy and economic conditions, such as a recessionary environment, a period of limited or tight credit, or both.

In managing accounts receivable, the following procedures are recommended. First, establish a *credit policy*:

1. A detailed review of a potential customer's soundness should be made prior to extending credit. Procedures such as a careful review of the customer's financial statements and credit rating, as well as a review of financial service reports (e.g., Dun & Bradstreet), are common.

2. As customer financial health changes, credit limits should be revised.

3. Marketing factors must be noted since an excessively restricted credit policy will lead to lost sales.

4. If seasonal datings are used, the firm may offer more liberal payments than usual during slow periods in order to stimulate business by selling to customers who are unable to pay until later in the season. This policy is financially appropriate when the return on the additional sales plus the lowering in inventory costs is greater than the incremental cost associated with the additional investment in accounts receivable.

Second, establish policy concerning *billing*:

1. Customer statements should be sent within 1 day subsequent to the close of the period.

2. Large sales should be billed immediately.

3. Customers should be invoiced for goods when the order is processed rather than when it is shipped.

4. Billing for services should be done on an interim basis or immediately prior to the actual services. The billing process will be more uniform if cycle billing is employed.

5. The use of seasonal datings should be considered. (See item 4, concerning credit policy.)

Finally, establish policy concerning *collection*:

---

[1] Aging is simply determining the length of time an account is past due.

1. Accounts receivable should be aged[1] in order to identify delinquent and high-risk customers. The aging should be compared to industry norms.

2. Collection efforts should be undertaken at the very first sign of customer financial unsoundness.

EXAMPLE 4.11 Jones Corporation sells on terms of net/60. Its accounts are on the average 30 days past due. Annual credit sales are $500,000. The investment in accounts receivable is:

$$\frac{90}{360} \times \$500,000 = \$125,000$$

EXAMPLE 4.12 The cost of a given product is 40 percent of selling price, and carrying cost is 12 percent of selling price. On average, accounts are paid 90 days subsequent to the sale date. Sales average $40,000 per month. The investment in accounts receivable from this product is:

Accounts receivable:	
3 months × $40,000 sales =	$120,000
Investment in accounts receivable:	
$120,000 × (0.40 + 0.12) =	$ 62,400

EXAMPLE 4.13 A company has accounts receivable of $700,000. The average manufacturing cost is 40 percent of the sales price. The before-tax profit margin is 10 percent. The carrying cost of inventory is 3 percent of selling price. The sales commission is 8 percent of sales. The investment in accounts receivable is:

$$\$700,000(0.40 + 0.03 + 0.08) = \$700,000(0.51) = \$357,000$$

EXAMPLE 4.14 If a company's credit sales are $120,000, the collection period is 60 days, and the cost is 80 percent of sales price, what is (*a*) the average accounts receivable balance and (*b*) the average investment in accounts receivable?

(*a*)   Accounts receivable turnover: $\dfrac{360}{60} = 6$

$$\text{Average accounts receivable} = \frac{\text{credit sales}}{\text{turnover}} = \frac{\$120,000}{6} = \$20,000$$

(*b*)   Average investment in accounts receivable = $20,000 × 0.80 = $16,000

It pays for a firm to give a discount for early payment by customers when the return on the funds received early is greater than the cost of the discount.

EXAMPLE 4.15 Lakeside Corporation provides the following data:

Current annual credit sales	$12,000,000
Collection period	2 months
Terms	net/30
Rate of return	15%

Lakeside proposes to offer a 3/10, net/30 discount. The corporation anticipates 25 percent of its customers will take advantage of the discount. As a result of the discount policy, the collection period will be reduced to $1\frac{1}{2}$ months. Should Lakeside offer the new terms?

The discount policy is disadvantageous, as indicated below.

Current average accounts receivable balance ($12,000,000/6)	$2,000,000
Average accounts receivable balance—after policy change ($12,000,000/8)	1,500,000
Reduction in average accounts receivable	$ 500,000
Rate of return	×0.15
Dollar return earned	$ 75,000
Cost of discount (0.25 × $12,000,000 × 0.03)	$ 90,000
Disadvantage of discount policy ($90,000 − $75,000)	$ 15,000

A firm may consider offering credit to customers with a higher-than-normal risk rating. Here, the profitability on additional sales generated must be compared with the amount of additional bad debts expected, higher investing and collection costs, and the opportunity cost of tying up funds in receivables for a longer period of time. When idle capacity exists, the additional profitability represents the incremental contribution margin (sales less variable costs) since fixed costs remain the same. The incremental investment in receivables represents the average accounts receivable multiplied by the ratio of per-unit cost to selling price.

EXAMPLE 4.16 Joseph Corporation, which has idle capacity, provides the following data:

Selling price per unit	$80
Variable cost per unit	$50
Fixed cost per unit	$10
Annual credit sales	300,000 units
Collection period	2 months
Rate of return	16%

The corporation is considering a change in policy that will relax its credit standards. The following information applies to the proposal:

1. Sales will increase by 20 percent.
2. Collection period will go to 3 months.
3. Bad debt losses are expected to be 3 percent of the increased sales.
4. Collection costs are expected to increase by $20,000.

The analysis of its proposed credit policy change follows:

Concerning incremental profitability:

Increased unit sales (300,000 × 0.20)	60,000
Per-unit contribution margin ($80 − $50)	× $30
Incremental profit	$1,800,000

Concerning additional bad debts:

Incremental dollar sales (60,000 × $80)	$4,800,000
Bad debt percentage	× 0.03
Additional bad debts	$ 144,000

New average unit cost is:

	Units	Unit Cost	Total Cost
Current	300,000	$60	$18,000,000
Increment	60,000	$50[a]	3,000,000
Total	360,000		$21,000,000

$$\text{New average unit cost} = \frac{\$21,000,000}{360,000} = \$58.33$$

---

[a] Since idle capacity exists, the per-unit cost on the incremental sales is solely the variable cost of $50.

Additional cost of higher investment in average accounts receivable is:

Investment in average accounts receivable after the change in policy	$5,249,700[a]
Current investment in average accounts receivable	3,000,000[b]
Incremental investment in average accounts receivable	$2,249,700
Rate of return	× 0.16
Additional cost	$ 359,952

$$^a \frac{\text{Credit sales}}{\text{turnover}} \times \frac{\text{unit cost}}{\text{selling price}} = \frac{\$28,800,000}{4} \times \frac{\$58.33}{\$80.00} = \$5,249,700$$

$$^b \quad \frac{\$24,000,000}{6} \times \frac{\$60}{\$80} = \$3,000,000$$

The net advantage/disadvantage is:

Incremental profitability		$1,800,000
Less: Additional bad debts	$144,000	
Additional collection costs	20,000	
Opportunity cost	359,952	523,952
Net advantage/disadvantage		$1,276,048

Since the net advantage is considerable, Joseph Corporation should relax its credit policy.

EXAMPLE 4.17 Wise Corporation is considering liberalizing its credit policy to encourage more customers to purchase on credit. Currently, 80 percent of sales are on credit and there is a gross margin of 30 percent. Other relevant data are:

	Currently	Proposal
Sales	$300,000	$450,000
Credit sales	$240,000	$360,000
Collection expenses	4% of credit sales	5% of credit sales
Accounts receivable turnover	4.5	3

An analysis of the proposal yields the following results:

Average accounts receivable balance (credit sales/accounts receivable turnover)	
Expected average accounts receivable ($360,000/3)	$120,000
Current average accounts receivable ($240,000/4.5)	53,333
Increase	$ 66,667
Gross profit	
Expected increase in credit sales ($360,000 − $240,000)	$120,000
Gross profit rate	0.30
Increase	$ 36,000
Collection expenses	
Expected collection expenses (0.05 × $360,000)	$ 18,000
Current collection expenses (0.04 × $240,000)	9,600
Increase	$ 8,400

Wise Corporation would benefit from a more liberal credit policy.

When a company is considering initiating a sales campaign in order to improve income, incremental profitability is compared to the cost of the discount and the opportunity cost associated with the higher investment in accounts receivable.

EXAMPLE 4.18 Drake Company is planning a sales campaign, during which Drake will offer credit terms of 4/20, net/60. Drake anticipates its collection period will rise from 70 days to 90 days. Data for the contemplated campaign are:

	% of Sales Prior to Campaign	% of Sales During Campaign
Cash sales	30	20
Payment from		
1–20	50	45
21–100	20	35

The proposed sales strategy will likely increase sales from $6 million to $7 million. The gross profit rate is 20 percent, and the rate of return is 12 percent. Sales discounts are given on cash sales.

An analysis of the proposed sales campaign is as follows:

Sales Campaign

	Without Campaign		**With Campaign**	
Gross profit		$1,200,000		$1,400,000
Sales subject to discount				
0.8 × $6,000,000	$4,800,000			
0.65 × $7,000,000			$4,550,000	
Sales discount	× 0.4	−192,000	× 0.04	−182,000
Investment in average accounts receivable				
70/360 × $6,000,000 × 0.8	$ 933,333			
90/360 × $7,000,000 × 0.8			$1,400,000	
Rate of return	× 0.12	−112,000	× 0.12	−168,000
Net profit		$ 896,000		$1,050,000

Drake should initiate the sales program since it will generate an additional profit of $154,000.

A business may wish to evaluate a credit policy that would extend credit to currently limited-credit or no-credit customers. Full credit should only be given to a customer category if net earnings ensue.

EXAMPLE 4.19 TGD Corporation has three credit categories (X, Y, Z) and is considering changing its credit policy for categories Y and Z. The pertinent data are:

Category	Bad Debt (%)	Collection Period (Days)	Credit Terms	Additional Annual Sales if Credit Restrictions Are Eased
X	2	30	Full	$100,000
Y	5	50	Restricted	$400,000
Z	13	80	No credit	$900,000

Gross profit approximates 15 percent of sales. The rate of return is 16 percent.

Analysis of the data yields the following results:

	Category Y	**Category Z**
Gross profit		
$400,000 × 0.15	$60,000	
$900,000 × 0.15		$135,000
Increment in bad debts		
$400,000 × 0.05	−20,000	
$900,000 × 0.13		−117,000
Incremental average in accounts receivable		
50/360 × 0.85 × $400,000	$47,222	
80/360 × 0.85 × $900,000		$170,000
Rate of return	× 0.16	× 0.16
Additional cost	−7,556	−27,200
Net profitability	$32,444	$ −9,200

Credit should be eased only for category Y. Extending credit to category Z is likely to incur a loss for the company.

4.5 INVENTORY MANAGEMENT

The three types of inventory are: (1) raw materials, which are materials acquired from a supplier that will be used in the manufacture of goods; (2) work-in-process, which is partially completed goods at the end of the accounting period; and (3) finished goods, which are completed goods awaiting sale.

In managing inventory, the financial manager should:

1. Appraise the adequacy of the raw materials level, which depends on expected production, condition of equipment, and any seasonal considerations of business.

2. Forecast future movements in raw materials prices, so that if prices are expected to increase, additional material is purchased at the lower price.

3. Discard slow-moving products to reduce inventory carrying costs and improve cash flow.

4. Guard against inventory buildup, since it is associated with substantial carrying and opportunity costs.

5. Minimize inventory levels when liquidity and/or inventory financing problems exist.

6. Plan for a stock inventory balance that will guard against and cushion the possible loss of business from a material shortage.

7. Examine the quality of merchandise received. In this connection, the ratio of purchase returns to purchases should be examined. A sharp increase in the ratio indicates that a new supplier may be needed.

8. Keep a careful record of back orders. A high back order level indicates that less inventory balances are required. This is because back orders may be used as indicators of the production required, resulting in improved production planning and procurement. The trend in the ratio of the dollar amount of back orders to the average per-day sales will prove useful.

9. Appraise the acquisition and inventory control functions. Any problems must be identified and rectified. In areas where control is weak, inventory balances should be restricted.

10. Closely supervise warehouse and materials handling staff to guard against theft loss and to maximize efficiency.

11. Minimize the lead time in the acquisition, manufacturing, and distribution functions. The lead time in receiving goods is determined by dividing the value of outstanding orders by the average daily purchases. This ratio may indicate whether an increase in inventory stocking is required or whether the purchasing pattern should be altered.

12. Examine the time between raw materials input and the completion of production to see if production and engineering techniques can be implemented to hasten the production operation.

13. Examine the degree of spoilage.

14. Maintain proper inventory control, such as through the application of computer techniques and operations research.

The financial manager must also consider the risk associated with inventory. For example, technological, perishable, fashionable, flammable, and specialized goods usually have a high realization risk. The nature of the risk associated with the particular inventory item should be taken into account in computing the desired inventory level.

Inventory management involves a trade-off between the costs associated with keeping inventory versus the benefits of holding inventory. Higher inventory levels result in increased costs from storage, insurance, spoilage, and interest on borrowed funds needed to finance inventory acquisition. However, an increase in inventory lowers the possibility of lost sales from stockouts and the incidence of production slowdowns from inadequate inventory. Further, large volume purchases will result in greater purchase discounts. Inventory levels are also influenced by short-term interest rates. For example, as short-term interest rates increase, the optimum level of holding inventory will be reduced.

Inventory should be counted at regular, cyclic intervals because this provides the ability to check inventory on an ongoing basis as well as to reconcile the book and physical amounts. Cyclic counting has the following advantages:

1. It allows for an efficient use of a few full-time experienced counters throughout the year.

2. It enables the timely detection and correction of the causes of inventory error.

3. It does not require a plant shutdown, as does a year-end count.

4. It facilitates the modification of computer inventory programs if needed.

A quantity discount may be received when purchasing large orders. The discount serves as a reduction of the acquisition cost of materials.

EXAMPLE 4.20   A company purchases 1,000 units of an item having a list price of $10 each. The quantity discount is 5 percent. The net cost of the item is:

Acquisition cost (1,000 × $10)	$10,000
Less: Discount (0.05 × $10,000)	500
Net cost	$ 9,500

The average investment in inventory should be considered.

EXAMPLE 4.21   Savon Corporation places an order for 5,000 units at the beginning of the year. Each unit costs $10. The average investment is:

Average inventory[a]	2,500 units
Unit cost, $	× $10
Average investment	$25,000

[a]
$$\frac{\text{Quantity } (Q)}{2} = \frac{5,000}{2}$$

The more frequently a company places an order, the lower will be the average investment.

Carrying and Ordering Costs

Inventory carrying costs include those for warehousing, handling, insurance, and property taxes. A provisional cost for spoilage and obsolescence should also be included in an analysis of inventory. In addition, the opportunity cost of holding inventory balances must be considered. Assuming that the carrying cost per unit is constant, then

$$\text{Carrying cost} = \frac{Q}{2} \times C$$

where $Q/2$ represents average quantity and C is the carrying cost per unit.

Inventory order costs are the costs of placing an order and receiving the merchandise. They include freight charges and the clerical costs to place an order. In the case of produced items, they also include the scheduling cost. The ordering cost per unit is assumed to be constant.

$$\text{Ordering cost} = \frac{S}{Q} \times P$$

where S = total usage
   Q = quantity per order
   P = cost of placing an order
The total inventory cost is therefore:

$$\frac{QC}{2} + \frac{SP}{C}$$

A trade-off exists between ordering and carrying costs. A greater order quantity will increase carrying costs but lower ordering costs.

Economic Order Quantity (EOQ)

The economic order quantity (EOQ) is the optimum amount of goods to order each time an order is placed so that total inventory costs are minimized.

$$\text{EOQ} = \sqrt{\frac{2SP}{C}}$$

The number of orders to be made for a period is the usage (S) divided by the EOQ.

EXAMPLE 4.22   Winston Corporation needs to know how frequently to place their orders. They provide the following information:

$$S = 500 \text{ units per month}$$
$$P = \$40 \text{ per order}$$
$$C = \$4 \text{ per unit}$$

$$\text{EOQ} = \sqrt{\frac{2SP}{C}} = \sqrt{\frac{2(500)(40)}{4}} = \sqrt{10,000} = 100 \text{ units}$$

The number of orders required each month is:

$$\frac{S}{\text{EOQ}} = \frac{500}{100} = 5$$

Therefore, an order should be placed about every 6 days (31/5).

EXAMPLE 4.23   Apex Appliance Store is determining its frequency of orders for toasters. Each toaster costs $15. The annual carrying costs are approximated at $200. The ordering cost is $10. Apex expects to sell 50 toasters each month. Its desired average inventory level is 40.

$$S = 50 \times 12 = 600$$
$$P = \$10$$

$$C = \frac{\text{purchase price} \times \text{carrying cost}}{\text{average investment}} = \frac{\$15 \times \$200}{40 \times \$15} = \$5$$

$$\text{EOQ} = \sqrt{\frac{2SP}{C}} = \sqrt{\frac{2(600)(10)}{5}} = \sqrt{\frac{12,000}{5}} = \sqrt{2,400} = 49 \text{ (rounded)}$$

The number of orders per year is:

$$\frac{S}{\text{EOQ}} = \frac{600}{49} = 12 \text{ orders (rounded)}$$

Apex Appliance should place an order about every 30 days (365/12).

During periods of inflation and tight credit, a company should be flexible in its inventory management policies. For example, its EOQ model will have to be modified to reflect rising costs.

Stockouts

Stockout of raw materials or work-in-process can result in a shutdown or slowdown in the production process. In order to avoid a stockout situation, a safety stock level should be maintained. Safety stock is the minimum inventory amount needed for an item, based on anticipated usage and the expected delivery time of materials. This cushion guards against unusual product demand or unexpected delivery problems.

EXAMPLE 4.24 Winston Corporation places an order when its inventory level reaches 210 rather than 180 units. Its safety stock is 30 units. In other words, the company expects to be stocked with 30 units when the new order is received.

The optimum safety stock level is the point where the increased carrying cost equals the opportunity cost associated with a potential stockout. The increased carrying cost is equal to the carrying cost per unit multiplied by the safety stock.

$$\text{Stockout cost} = \text{number of orders} \left(\frac{\text{usage}}{\text{order quantity}} \right) \times \text{stockout units}$$
$$\times \text{ unit stockout cost} \times \text{probability of a stockout}$$

EXAMPLE 4.25 Tristar Corporation uses 100,000 units annually. Each order placed is for 10,000 units. Stockout is 1,000 units; this amount is the difference between the maximum daily usage during the lead time less the reorder point, ignoring a safety stock factor. The stockout probability management wishes to take is 30 percent. The per-unit stockout cost is $2.30. The carrying cost per unit is $5. The inventory manager must determine (*a*) the stockout cost and (*b*) the amount of safety stock to keep on hand.

(a) $\text{Stockout cost} = \dfrac{\text{usage}}{\text{order quantity}} \times \text{stockout units} \times \text{unit stockout cost} \times \text{probability of a stockout}$

$$= \frac{100,000}{10,000} \times 1,000 \times \$2.30 \times 0.3 = \$6,900$$

(*b*)   Let X = safety stock

$$\text{Stockout cost} = \text{carrying cost of safety stock}$$
$$\$6,900 = \$5X$$
$$1,380 \text{ units} = X$$

Economic Order Point (EOP)

The economic order point is the inventory level that signals the time to reorder merchandise at the EOQ amount. Safety stock is provided for in the computation.

$$\text{EOP} = SL + z\sqrt{S(\text{EOQ})(L)}$$

where L = the lead time
z = the stockout acceptance factor

EXAMPLE 4.26 Blake Corporation provides the following data:

S = 2,000 units per month
EOQ = 75 units
$L = \frac{1}{4}$ of a month
z = 1.29, which represents the acceptable stockout level of 10 percent
(from normal probability distribution table—Appendix E)

$$EOP = SL + z\sqrt{S(EOQ)(L)} = (2{,}000)(\tfrac{1}{4}) + 1.29\sqrt{2{,}000(75)(\tfrac{1}{4})}$$
$$= 500 + 1.29\sqrt{37{,}500} = 500 + 1.29(193.6) = 750 \text{ (rounded)}$$

The financial manager should attempt to determine the inventory level that results in the greatest savings.

EXAMPLE 4.27 Frost Corporation is thinking of revising its inventory policy. The current inventory turnover is 16 times. Variable costs are 70 percent of sales. If inventory levels are increased, Frost anticipates additional sales generated and less of an incidence of inventory stockouts. The rate of return is 17 percent.

Actual and estimated sales and inventory turnover are as follows:

Sales	Turnover
$700,000	16
$780,000	14
$850,000	11
$940,000	7

Frost's financial manager can now compute the inventory level that will result in the highest net savings.

A	B	C	D	E	F
		Average Inventory	Opportunity Cost Associated with Additional	Additional	Net Savings
Sales	Turnover	(A ÷ B)	Inventory[a]	Profitability[b]	(E − D)
$700,000	16	$ 43,750			
$780,000	14	$ 55,714	$2,034	$24,000	$21,966
$850,000	11	$ 77,273	$3,665	$21,000	$17,335
$940,000	7	$134,286	$9,692	$27,000	$17,308

[a] Incremental average inventory balance × 0.17 (the rate of return).
[b] Incremental sales × 0.30 (contribution margin).

The best inventory level is 55,714 units, since the greatest savings result at this point.

ABC Inventory Control Method

The ABC method of inventory control requires the classification of inventory into one of three groups, A, B, or C. Group A items are most expensive, group B less expensive, and group C the least expensive. The higher the value of the inventory items, the more control should be exercised over them.

Inventory should be analyzed frequently when using the ABC method. The procedure for constructing an ABC analysis follows:

1. Separate each type of inventory, such as finished goods, work-in-process, and raw materials.
2. Calculate the annual dollar usage for each type of inventory by multiplying the unit cost times the expected future annual usage.
3. Rank each inventory type from high to low, based on annual dollar usage.
4. Classify the inventory as A, B, or C, based on the top 20 percent, the next 30 percent, and the last 50 percent valuation, respectively.
5. Tag the inventory with ABC classifications and record those classifications in the item inventory master records.

Figure 4-1 illustrates the ABC distribution.

Inventory Classification	Population (%)	$ Usage (%)
A	20	80
B	30	15
C	50	5

Fig. 4-1   ABC inventory distribution

The ABC analysis become a tool with which the materials manager checks the accuracy of his or her records. More time is spent checking A category items than B and C items. The financial manager should establish an audit program for those records and items that have the greatest impact on profitability based on the ABC analysis.

Review Questions

1. _____ equals current assets less current liabilities.

2. In managing working capital, one should consider the trade-off between _____ and _____.

3. The financing of long-term assets with long-term debt is referred to as _____.

4. Cash consists of _____ and _____.

5. Cash held for emergency purposes is referred to as a(n) _____ balance.

6. Excess cash that will be needed in the near future should be temporarily invested in _____ securities.

7. The term _____ refers to funds retained by the bank on a loan made to the company.

8. The time required for a check to go from the maker to the payee is referred to as _____.

9. The time needed for a check to clear is referred to as _____.

10. A(n) _____ system is one in which a local bank picks up customer remissions from a post office box.

11. _____ is a system of collection in which a local bank receives funds and transfers them to a main concentration bank account.

12. One way to defer a cash payment is by the use of a(n) _____, because the bank must first secure approval from the company before the instrument is paid.

13. The terms of a $1,000 sale are 3/20, net/40. If collection is received in 14 days, the amount received is $_____.

14. Partially completed merchandise at year-end is referred to as _____ inventory.

15. Inventory consisting of fashionable merchandise has high _____ risk.

16. _____ refers to the cost of holding inventory.

17. As the order size increases, carrying cost _____ and ordering cost _____.

18. The optimum amount to order each time is referred to as the _____.

19. The optimum inventory level requiring a reorder of goods is referred to as the _____.

20. The _____ method requires that greater control be exercised over higher-valued merchandise.

Answers: (1) Net working capital; (2) risk, return; (3) hedging; (4) currency, demand deposits; (5) precautionary; (6) marketable; (7) compensating balance; (8) mail float; (9) deposit collection float; (10) lockbox; (11) Concentration banking; (12) draft; (13) 970; (14) work-in-process; (15) realization; (16) Carrying cost; (17) increases, decreases; (18) economic order quantity (EOQ); (19) economic order point (EOP); (20) ABC.

Solved Problems

4.1   Net Working Capital. Winston Corporation has the following selected assets and liabilities:

Cash	$15,000
Accounts receivable	$20,000
Inventory	$37,000
Land	$70,000
Building	$190,000
Goodwill	$26,000
Accounts payable	$13,000
Salaries payable	$7,000
Taxes payable	$19,000
Mortgage payable	$80,000
Common stock	$100,000
Retained earnings	$82,000

Determine the company's net working capital.

SOLUTION

CURRENT ASSETS

Cash	$15,000	
Accounts receivable	20,000	
Inventory	37,000	$72,000

CURRENT LIABILITIES

Accounts payable	$13,000	
Salaries payable	7,000	
Taxes payable	19,000	39,000
Net working capital		$33,000

4.2 **Delay in Cash Receipt.** Blake Corporation receives average daily cash receipts of $140,000. The finance manager has determined that the time period between the mailing of a check and its actual availability for corporate use is 4 days. What is the amount of cash being tied up because of the delay?

SOLUTION

$$4 \text{ days} \times \$140,000 = \$560,000$$

4.3 **Lockbox.** It typically takes Lawrence Corporation 8 days to receive and deposit customer remissions. Lawrence is considering a lockbox system and anticipates that the system will reduce the float time to 5 days. Average daily cash receipts are $220,000. The rate of return is 10 percent.

(*a*) What is the reduction in cash balances associated with implementing the system? (*b*) What is the rate of return associated with the earlier receipt of the funds? (*c*) What should be the maximum monthly charge associated with the lockbox proposal?

SOLUTION

(*a*) $$\$220,000 \times 3 \text{ days} = \$660,000$$

(*b*) $$0.10 \times \$660,000 = \$66,000$$

(*c*) $$\frac{\$66,000}{12} = \$5,500$$

4.4 **Lockbox.** Doral Corporation is considering a lockbox arrangement that will cost $216,000 per year. Average daily collections are $450,000. As a result of the system, the float time will be reduced by 3 days. The rate of return is 14 percent. Should the lockbox arrangement be instituted?

SOLUTION

Cost	$216,000
Return on freed cash (0.14 × 3 × $450,000)	189,000
Disadvantage of lockbox	$ 27,000

The lockbox should not be used.

4.5 **Dividing of Region.** Boston Corporation has an arrangement with XYZ Bank in which the bank handles $5 million a day in collections but requires a $420,000 compensating balance. The company is considering withdrawing from the arrangement and dividing its southern region so that two other banks will handle the business instead. Bank S will handle $3 million a day of collections and require a $450,000 compensating balance, and bank T will handle the other $2 million a day and require a compensating balance of $350,000. By dividing the southern region, collections will be accelerated by $\frac{1}{2}$ day. The rate of return is 17 percent. Should the southern region be divided?

SOLUTION

Accelerated cash inflow	
$5 million per day $\times \frac{1}{2}$ day	$2,500,000
Incremental compensating balance	
required	380,000
Increased cash flow	$2,120,000
Rate of return	$\times 0.17$
Net annual savings	$ 360,400

Yes, the southern region should be divided, as doing so will save the company $360,400 per year.

4.6 **Average Cash Balance.** Dane Company's weekly average cash balances are:

Week	Average Cash Balance
1	$15,000
2	19,000
3	12,000
4	17,000
Total	$63,000

(*a*) What is the monthly average cash balance? (*b*) Assuming an annual interest rate of 15 percent, what is the monthly rate of return earned on the average cash balance?

SOLUTION

(*a*)
$$\frac{\$63,000}{4} = \$15,750$$

(*b*)
$$\$15,750 \times (0.15 \div 12) = \$196.88$$

4.7 **Book Balance versus Bank Balance.** Company P writes checks averaging $30,000 per day that require 4 days to clear. By what amount will its book balance be less than its bank balance?

SOLUTION

$$\$30,000 \times 4 \text{ days} = \$120,000$$

4.8 **Opportunity Cost of Not Taking Discount.** What is the opportunity cost of not taking a discount when the terms are 2/20, net/45?

SOLUTION

$$\text{Opportunity cost} = \frac{\text{discount percent}}{100 - \text{discount percent}} \times \frac{360}{N} = \frac{2}{98} \times \frac{360}{25} = 29.4\%$$

4.9   Optimal Cash Transaction Size. Green Corporation anticipates a cash requirement of $1,000 over a 1-month period. It is expected that cash will be paid uniformly. The annual interest rate is 24 percent. The transaction cost of each borrowing or withdrawal is $30. (*a*) What is the optimal transaction size? (*b*) What is the average cash balance?

SOLUTION

(*a*)   The optimum transaction size is:

$$C = \sqrt{\frac{2bT}{i}} = \sqrt{\frac{2(30)(1,000)}{0.24 \div 12^a}} = \sqrt{\frac{60,000}{0.02}} = \$1,732.05$$

(*b*)   The average cash balance is:

$$\frac{C}{2} = \frac{\$1,732.05}{2} = \$866.03$$

----

^{a} Monthly interest rate $= \dfrac{0.24 \text{ annual interest rate}}{12 \text{ months}} = 0.02$

4.10   The Miller–Orr Model. Heavenly Company has experienced a stochastic demand for its product, which results in fluctuating cash balances randomly. The following information is supplied:

Fixed cost of a securities transaction	$100
Variance of daily net cash flows	$1,000
Daily interest rate on securities (6%/360)	0.000167

Determine the optimal cash balance, upper and lower limit of cash needed, and average cash balance.

SOLUTION

The optimal cash balance, the upper limit of cash needed, and the average cash balance follow:

$$z = \sqrt[3]{\frac{3(100)(1000)}{4(0.000167)}}$$
$$= 3\sqrt{449,910,000,000} = \$7,663$$

The optimal cash balance is $7,663. The upper limit is $22,989 (3 × $7,663). The lower limit is zero. The average cash balance is

$$\frac{(\$7,663 + \$22,989)}{3} = \$10,217.33$$

When the upper limit of $22,989 is reached, $15,326 of securities ($22,989 − $7,663) will be purchased to bring you to the optimal cash balance of $7,663. When the lower limit of zero dollars is reached, $7,663 of securities will be sold to again bring you to the optimal cash balance of $7,663.

4.11   Date of Cash Receipt. The terms of sale are 3/20, net/45, May 1 dating. What is the last date the customer may pay in order to receive the discount?

SOLUTION

May 20.

4.12   Average Investment in Accounts Receivable. Milch Corporation sells on terms of net/90. Their accounts receivable are on average 20 days past due. If annual credit sales are $800,000, what is the company's average investment in accounts receivable?

SOLUTION

$$\frac{90 + 20}{360} \times \$800,000 = \$244,444$$

4.13   Average Investment in Accounts Receivable. The cost of product X is 30 percent of its selling price, and the carrying cost is 8 percent of selling price. Accounts are paid on average 60 days after sale. Sales per month average $25,000. What is the investment in accounts receivable?

SOLUTION

Accounts receivable = 2 months × $25,000 sales = $50,000

Investment in accounts receivable = $50,000 × 0.38 = $19,000

4.14   Average Investment in Accounts Receivable. Levine Corporation has accounts receivable of $400,000. Its manufacturing cost approximates 35 percent of selling price. The before-tax profit margin is 16 percent, and the inventory carrying cost is 4 percent of the selling price. Sales commissions are 7 percent of sales. What is Levine's average investment in accounts receivable?

SOLUTION

Average   investment   in   accounts   receivable = $400,000(0.35 + 0.04 + 0.07) = $400,000(0.46)
= $184,000

4.15   Average Investment in Accounts Receivable. Ajax Company's credit sales are $300,000, and the collection period is 90 days. Cost is 70 percent of selling price. Determine Ajax's average investment in accounts receivable.

SOLUTION

$$\text{Accounts receivable turnover} = \frac{360}{90} = 4$$

$$\text{Average accounts receivable} = \frac{\$300,000}{4} = \$75,000$$

$$\text{Average investment in accounts receivable} = \$75,000 \times 0.70 = \$52,500$$

4.16   Discount Policy. Stevens Company presents the following information:

Current annual credit sales:	$24,000,000
Collection period:	3 months
Terms:	net/30
Rate of return:	18%

The company is considering offering a 4/10, net/30 discount. It anticipates that 30 percent of its customers will take advantage of the discount. The collection period is expected to decrease to 2 months. Should the discount policy be implemented?

SOLUTION

Current average accounts receivable balance ($24,000,000/4)	$6,000,000
Average accounts receivable balance—after change in policy ($24,000,000/6)	4,000,000
Reduction in average accounts receivable	$2,000,000
Interest rate	× 0.18
Rate of return	$ 360,000
Cost of discount (0.30 × $24,000,000 × 0.04)	$ 288,000
Advantage of discount policy ($360,000 − $288,000)	$ 72,000

Yes, Stevens Company should implement the discount policy.

4.17   Credit Policy. Nelson Corporation reports the following information:

Selling price per unit	$70
Variable cost per unit	$45
Fixed cost per unit	$15
Annual credit sales	400,000 units
Collection period	3 months
Rate of return	19%

The company is considering easing its credit standards. If it does, the following is expected to result: Sales will increase by 25 percent; collection period will increase to 4 months; bad debt losses are anticipated to be 4 percent on the incremental sales; and collection costs will increase by $34,000.

Should the proposed relaxation in credit standards be implemented?

SOLUTION

Incremental profitability:

Increased unit sales (400,000 × 0.25)	100,000
Contribution margin per unit ($70 − $45)	× $25
Incremental profit	$2,500,000

Increased bad debts:

Incremental dollar sales (100,000 × $70)	$7,000,000
Uncollectibility percentage	× 0.04
Additional bad debts	$ 280,000

To determine the opportunity cost of the increased investment in accounts receivable, we first need to calculate the new average unit cost, as follows:

	Units	Unit Cost	Total Cost
Present	400,000	$60	$24,000,000
Increment	100,000	$45	4,500,000
Total	500,000		$28,500,000

$$\text{New average unit cost} = \frac{\$28,500,000}{500,000} = \$57$$

Additional cost:

Investment in average accounts receivable [(credit sales/turnover) × (unit cost/selling price)]	
After change in policy [($35,000,000/3) × ($57/$70)]	$9,500,000
Current [($28,000,000/4) × ($60/$70)]	6,000,000
Incremental	$3,500,000
Rate of return	× 0.19
Opportunity cost	$ 665,000

Net advantage/disadvantage of proposal:

Additional profitability		$2,500,000
Less: Increased bad debts	$280,000	
Increased collection costs	34,000	
Opportunity cost	665,000	979,000
Net advantage		$1,521,000

Thus, the Nelson Corporation would benefit from relaxing its credit policy as proposed.

4.18 **Credit Policy.** Simon Corporation is evaluating a relaxation of its credit policy. At present, 70 percent of sales are on credit and there is a gross margin of 20 percent. Additional data are:

	Current	Anticipated
Sales	$500,000	$640,000
Credit sales	$410,000	$520,000
Collection expenses	3% of credit sales	4% of credit sales
Collection period	72 days	90 days

Using 360 days in a year, answer the following questions: (a) What is the change in gross profit associated with the proposal? (b) What is the incremental change in collection expenses? (c) What is the change in average accounts receivable?

SOLUTION

(a)

Incremental credit sales	$110,000
Gross profit rate	× 0.20
Increase in gross profit	$ 22,000

(b)

Collection expenses with proposal (0.04 × $520,000)	$ 20,800
Collection expenses currently (0.03 × $410,000)	12,300
Increase in collection expenses	$ 8,500

(c) Average accounts receivable after change in policy are:

Credit sales/accounts receivable turnover ($520,000/4)	$130,000
Current average accounts receivable ($410,000/5)	82,000
Increase in average accounts receivable	$ 48,000

4.19 Sales Campaign. Jones Corporation is considering a sales campaign in which it will offer credit terms of 3/15, net/80. The finance manager expects that the collection period will increase from 90 days to 110 days. Information before and during the proposed campaign follows:

	% of Sales before Campaign	% of Sales during Campaign
Cash sales	20	10
Payment from		
1–15	35	25
16–120	45	65

The sales campaign is expected to raise sales from $5 million to $6 million. The gross profit rate is 30 percent and the rate of return is 16 percent. Sales discounts are given on cash sales. Should the sales campaign be initiated?

SOLUTION

	Without Sales Campaign		With Sales Campaign	
Gross profit		$1,500,000		$1,800,000
Sales subject to discount				
0.55 × $5,000,000	$2,750,000			
0.35 × $6,000,000			$2,100,000	
Sales discount	× 0.03	−82,500	× 0.03	−63,000
Investment in average accounts receivable				
(90/360) × $5,000,000 × 0.7	$ 875,000			
(110/360) × $6,000,000 × 0.7			$1,283,333	
Rate of return	× 0.16	−140,000	× 0.16	−205,333
Net profit		$1,277,500		$1,531,667

The sales campaign should be implemented because it results in an incremental profit of $254,167.

4.20 Credit Policy. Wilder Corporation is considering granting credit to currently limited customers or no-credit customers. The following information is given:

Category	Bad Debt Percentage	Collection Period	Credit Terms	Incremental Annual Sales Accompanying Relaxation in Credit Standards
A	3%	20 days	Full	$250,000
B	6%	45 days	Restricted	$540,000
C	10%	90 days	No credit	$800,000

Gross profit approximates 12 percent of sales. The rate of return is 18 percent. Should credit be extended to categories B and C?

SOLUTION

	Category B	Category C
Gross profit		
$540,000 × 0.12		
$800,000 × 0.12	$64,800	$96,000
Less: Increased bad debts		
$540,000 × 0.06	−32,400	
$800,000 × 0.10		−80,000
Incremental investment in average accounts receivable		
(45/360) × 0.88 × $540,000	$59,400	
(90/360) × 0.88 × $800,000		$176,000
Rate of return	× 0.18	× 0.18
Opportunity cost	−10,692	−31,680
Net profit	$21,708	−$15,680

Credit should be extended only to category B.

4.21 Materials Cost. Grason Corporation purchases 3,000 units of a raw material at a list price of $5 each. The supplier offers a quantity discount of 4 percent. What is the material cost of the item?

SOLUTION

Acquisition cost (3,000 × $5)	$15,000
Less: Discount (0.04 × $15,000)	600
Net cost	$14,400

4.22 Average Investment in Inventory. West Corporation orders 4,000 units of a product at the beginning of the period for $7 each. What is West Corporation's average investment in inventory?

SOLUTION

Average inventory ($Q/2 = 4,000/2$)	2,000 units
Unit cost ($)	$\times 7$
Average investment	$14,000

4.23 Ordering Cost. Charles Corporation uses 8,500 units per year. Each order is for 200 units. The cost per order is $13. What is the total ordering cost for the year?

SOLUTION

$$\frac{8,500}{200} \times \$13 = \$552.50$$

4.24 Economic Order Quantity. Luster Corporation presents the following data: Usage is 400 units per month, cost per order is $20, and carrying cost per unit is $6.

Given these data, answer the following questions: (*a*) What is the economic order quantity? (*b*) How many orders are required each month? (*c*) How often should each order be placed?

SOLUTION

(*a*)
$$EOQ = \sqrt{\frac{2SP}{C}} = \sqrt{\frac{2(400)(20)}{6}} = \sqrt{\frac{16,000}{6}} = 52 \text{ (rounded)}$$

(*b*)
$$\frac{S}{EOQ} = \frac{400}{52} = 8 \text{ (rounded)}$$

(*c*)
$$\frac{31}{8} = \text{every 4 days}$$

4.25 Stockout Cost. Boston Corporation uses 30,000 units. Each order placed is for 1,500 units. The stockout units is 300. Management is willing to accept a stockout probability of 40 percent. The stockout cost per unit is $3.20. What is the total stockout cost?

SOLUTION

$$\text{Stockout cost} = \frac{\text{usage}}{\text{order quantity}} \times \text{stockout units} \times \text{unit stockout cost} \times \text{probability of stockout}$$

$$= \frac{30,000}{1,500} \times 300 \times \$3.20 \times 0.4 = \$7,680$$

4.26 Economic Order Point. Met Corporation reports the following data regarding one of its inventory items: Usage is 5,000 units per month, EOQ is units, and lead time is $\frac{1}{2}$ month. The stockout acceptance factor is 1.29, which represents an acceptable stockout percentage of 10 percent.

Determine the economic order point.

SOLUTION

$$EOP = SL + z\sqrt{S(EOQ)(L)}$$
$$= (5,000)(\tfrac{1}{2}) + 1.29\sqrt{5,000(100)(\tfrac{1}{2})}$$
$$= 2,500 + 1.29\sqrt{250,000} = 2,500 + 1.29(500) = 3,145$$

4.27 **Inventory Management.** XYZ Appliance Store sells an average of 160 units per month. Each order the store places is for 300 units. The cost per unit is $5. The cost per order is $12. Carrying cost is $0.15 per dollar invested per year. The rate of return is 18 percent. The tax rate is 46 percent.

(a) What is the investment in average inventory? (b) What is the annual ordering cost? (c) What is the annual holding cost? (d) What is the opportunity cost of holding inventory? (e) What is the total cost of the inventory excluding the purchase price?

SOLUTION

(a)
$$\text{Average inventory} = \frac{Q}{2} = \frac{300}{2} = 150$$

$$\text{Investment in average inventory} = 150 \times \$5 = \$750$$

(b)
$$\text{Ordering cost} = \frac{S}{Q} \times P = \frac{160 \times 12}{300} \times \$12 = \$76.80$$

(c)
$$\text{Holding cost} = \text{carrying cost} \times \text{investment in average inventory}$$
$$= 0.15 \times \$750 = \$112.50$$

(d)
$$\text{Opportunity cost} = \text{rate of return} \times \text{investment in average inventory}$$
$$= 0.18 \times \$750 = \$135$$

(e)
$$\text{Inventory cost (excluding purchase price)}$$
$$= (100 - \text{tax rate}) \times (\text{ordering cost} + \text{holding cost}) + \text{opportunity cost}$$
$$= 0.54(\$76.80 + \$112.50) + \$135 = \$237.22$$

4.28 **Optimum Inventory Level.** Saft Corporation is considering changing its inventory policy. At present, the inventory turns over 12 times per year. Variable costs are 60 percent of sales. The rate of return is 21 percent. Sales and inventory turnover data follow:

Sales	Turnover
$800,000	12
$870,000	10
$950,000	7
$1,200,000	5

Determine the inventory level that results in the greatest net savings.

A	B	C	D	E	F
		Average Inventory	**Opportunity Cost Associated with Additional**	**Additional**	**Net Savings**
Sales	**Turnover**	**(A ÷ B)**	**Inventory**[a]	**Profitability**[b]	**(E − D)**
$800,000	12	$66,666			
$870,000	10	$87,000	$4,270	$28,000	$23,730
$950,000	7	$135,714	$10,230	$32,000	$21,770
$1,200,000	5	$240,000	$21,900	$100,000	$78,100

[a] Incremental average inventory balance × 0.21.
[b] Incremental sales × 0.40.

The inventory level that results in the greatest net savings is 240,000 units.

4.29 Lockbox System. Tunequip, Inc., is a wholesale distributor of specialized audio equipment, tapes, and records. Annual sales are projected at $27 million for the 19X1 fiscal year, and the average accounts receivable balance is estimated at $2.5 million. The average invoice size is $1,000. Customers pay their accounts by check, which are mailed to corporate headquarters in Florida.

The finance manager of Tunequip is examining the firm's cash-handling techniques to find ways to reduce borrowing requirements and financing costs. One alternative under consideration is the establishment of a lockbox system to handle collections from customers in the western United States. Those customers are expected to account for $10.8 million of Tunequip's total projected sales in 19X1. Tunequip could acquire the use of the funds a day earlier if the western customers mailed their checks to a post office box in Utah. The Utah National Bank would process the payments mailed to the post office box; they would deposit the checks in Tunequip's account in Utah National, wire transfer the money to the Florida National Bank (Tunequip's primary bank), and send the payment information by mail. Utah National Bank's charge for operating the lockbox system would be a flat fee of $80 per month plus $0.10 for each paid invoice handled; in addition the Utah bank would require Tunequip to maintain a $5,000 minimum cash balance with the bank.

There would be no change in Tunequip's relationship with Florida National Bank. The finance manager estimates that Tunequip would be able to borrow funds from Florida National Bank during 19X1 at an interest rate of 9 percent.

(*a*) If Tunequip, Inc., established the lockbox system for its western customers, calculate (1) the annual cost of operating the lockbox system, and (2) the dollar amount of the change in the level of accounts receivable and the reduction in borrowing which will result from this system.

(*b*) What factors other than those referred to in (*a*) should Tunequip consider in its evaluation of the lockbox system?

(*c*) Do your calculations support the establishment of a lockbox system for Tunequip's western customers? Explain your answer. (CMA, adapted.)

SOLUTION

(*a*) (1) The annual cost of operating the lockbox system is:

$$\text{Estimated number of invoices} = \frac{\text{western sales}}{\text{average invoice size}}$$

$$= \frac{\$10,800,000}{\$1,000/\text{invoice}} = 10,800 \text{ invoices}$$

Estimated handling fee (10,800 × $0.10)	$1,080
Fixed fee (12 months × $80)	960
Cost of compensating balance ($5,000 × 0.09)	450
Estimated annual operating cost	$2,490

(2) The use of the lockbox will permit Tunequip to acquire the use of the funds 1 day earlier. This will have the effect of reducing the average accounts receivable by 1 day's sales and reduce the need for borrowing by the same amount. This amounts to $30,000 as is shown below.

$$\text{Reduction in average accounts receivable} = \frac{\text{western sales}}{\text{days in year}} = \frac{\$10,800,000}{360} = \$30,000$$

(*b*) Other factors to be considered when changing to the lockbox system include the following: What is the cost of the wire transfers? Will there be a delay in recording receivables thus affecting customer attitudes? Will customers be upset because their lockbox checks will be cashed earlier? What is the impact of changes on costs in the main office? What other alternatives, such as tightening credit terms and slowing payments, of cash management can be used to reduce borrowing needs?

(c)   The financial manager makes the following recommendation:

Reduction in borrowing	$30,000
Interest rate	0.09
Annual savings	$ 2,700
Estimated annual operating cost	2,490
Estimated savings	$ 210

These projections give marginal support for the establishment of a lockbox because annual savings exceed costs by $210. However, the other items outlined in (b) should be considered in arriving at a final decision.

4.30   Credit Policy. The Heap Corporation finds itself with excess manufacturing capacity. The company has lost a portion of its share of the market over the past several years. This, in part, may be due to Heap having a more conservative credit policy than is common in the industry.

	Heap Corporation	**Industry**
Terms	2/10, net/30	2/10, net/60
Credit granted as percent of applicants by credit class		
A	100%	100%
B	100%	100%
C	25%	70%
D	11%	40%
E	2%	20%
F	0%	5%
Average collection period	30 days	60 days

The vice-president for finance recommends that Heap Corporation relax its credit standards, with the expectation that sales and profitability will increase. Staff studies show that credit sales can be expected to increase to $92 million, bad debt losses will be approximately $2.4 million, inventory will need to be increased by $5.67 million, and average collection of accounts receivable will be 60 days. The 19X2 Heap income statement is given below.

Heap Corporation
Income Statement
(In Thousands of Dollars)
For Year Ended December 31, 19X2

Revenue		
Credit sales	$72	
Cash sales	8	$80
Costs and other charges		
Manufacturing expenses[a]	$57.4	
Administrative expenses[b]	3.0	
Selling expenses[c]	9.6	70
Net income before taxes		$10
Federal income tax		5
Net income		$ 5

[a] Materials and supplies	$10.0
Labor	40.0
Fixed overhead	7.4
	$57.4
[b] All fixed	$ 3.0
[c] Selling expenses	
Variable expense	$ 8.0
Bad debt loss estimate	1.6
	$ 9.6

(a) Estimate the accounts receivable balance at December 31, 19X2. (b) Assuming total assets at December 31, 19X2 equal 40 million dollars: (1) What is Heap Corporation's return on corporate assets? (2) What is the asset turnover? (c) What profit margin will Heap Corporation earn if the predictions are correct? (d) What return should be expected on corporate assets if the policy is adopted and the predictions are correct? (e) Will the company be better off financially if the proposed change in credit policy is made? Explain your answer. (CMA, adapted.)

SOLUTION

(a)

Credit sales	$72,000,000
Allowance for bad debts	$ 1,600,000
Net credit sales	$70,400,000
Average collection period	30 days
Accounts receivable turnover	12 times

$$\text{Net receivables balance, Dec. 31, 19X2} = \frac{\$70,400,000}{12} = \$5,866,667$$

(b) (1) $$\text{Return on corporate assets} = \frac{\text{net income}}{\text{total assets}} = \frac{5,000,000}{40,000,000} = 12.5\%$$

(2) $$\text{Asset turnover} = \frac{\text{sales}}{\text{assets}} = \frac{80,000,000}{40,000,000} = 2$$

(c)

Heap Corporation
Pro Forma Income Statement
(In Millions of Dollars)
For Year Ended Dec. 31, 19X3

Credit sales		$92.00	
Cash sales		8.00	$100.00
Manufacturing expense			
Materials and supplies	$12.50		
Labor	50.00		
Fixed overhead	7.40	$69.90	
Administrative expense		3.00	
Selling expense			
Variable	$10.00		
Bad debt loss estimate	2.40	12.40	85.30
Net income before taxes			$ 14.70
Federal income tax			7.35
Net income			$ 7.35

(d)

Total assets	
Prior assets	$40,000,000
Increase in receivables[a]	9,066,666
Increase in inventory	5,670,000
	$54,736,666

---

[a]

$92,000,000 (credit sales)

  2,400,000 (bad debt)

$89,600,000 (net credit sales)

$$\frac{360}{60} = 6 \quad \text{(receivables turnover)}$$

$$\frac{\$89,600,000}{6} = \$14,933,333$$

Change in receivables = $14,933,333 − $5,866,667 = $9,066,666

$$\text{Return on assets} = \frac{\$7,350,000}{\$54,736,666} = 13.4\%$$

(e) Since the overall return on assets has increased after the credit policy change, the company may be considered to be in better financial condition. However, it should be noted that the nature and cost of financing the current asset expansion have not been considered. If the incremental financing is available only at a comparatively high cost, the change in credit policy may not be desirable.

Chapter 5

Short-term Financing

5.1 INTRODUCTION

This chapter discusses the advantages and disadvantages of the various short-term financing sources. "Short term" refers to financing that will be repaid in 1 year or less. Short-term financing may be used to meet seasonal and temporary fluctuations in a company's funds position as well as to meet permanent needs of the business. For example, short-term financing may be used to provide extra net working capital, finance current assets, or provide interim financing for a long-term project.

When compared to long-term financing, short-term financing has several advantages; for example, it is easier to arrange, it is less expensive, and it affords the borrower more flexibility. The drawbacks of short-term financing are that interest rates fluctuate more often, refinancing is frequently needed, and delinquent repayment may be detrimental to the credit rating of a borrower who is experiencing a liquidity problem.

The sources of short-term financing are trade credit, bank loans, bankers' acceptances, finance company loans, commercial paper, receivable financing, and inventory financing.

The merits of the different alternative sources of short-term financing are usually considered carefully before a firm borrows money. The factors bearing upon the selection of the source of short-term financing include:

1. Cost.
2. Effect on credit rating. Some sources of short-term financing may negatively affect the firm's credit rating.
3. Risk. The firm must consider the reliability of the source of funds for future borrowing.
4. Restrictions. Certain lenders may impose restrictions, such as requiring a minimum level of net working capital.
5. Flexibility. Certain lenders are more willing than others to work with the borrower, for example, to periodically adjust the amount of funds needed.
6. Expected money market conditions.
7. The inflation rate.
8. Corporate profitability and liquidity positions.
9. The stability of the firm's operations.

5.2 TRADE CREDIT

Trade credit (accounts payable) refers to balances owed to suppliers. It is a spontaneous financing source since it comes from normal business operations. Trade credit is the least expensive form of financing inventory. The benefits of trade credit are: It is readily available, since suppliers want business; collateral is not required; interest is typically not demanded or, if so, the amount is minimal; it is convenient; and trade creditors are frequently lenient in the event of corporate financial problems. A company having liquidity problems may stretch its accounts payable; however, among the disadvantages of doing so are the giving up of any cash discount offered and the probability of lowering the firm's credit rating.

EXAMPLE 5.1 Tristar Corporation purchases $475 worth of merchandise per day from suppliers. The terms of purchase are net/45, and the company pays on time. How much is Tristar's accounts payable balance?

$$\$475 \text{ per day} \times 45 \text{ days} = \$21,375$$

5.3 BANK LOANS

To be eligible for a bank loan, a company must have sufficient equity and good liquidity. When a short-term bank loan is taken, the debtor usually signs a note, which is a written statement that the borrower agrees to repay the loan at the due date. A note payable may be paid at maturity or in installments.

Bank loans are not spontaneous financing as is trade credit. Borrowers must apply for loans, and lenders must grant them. Without additional funds, a firm may have to restrict its plans; therefore, as a company's need for funds changes, it alters its borrowings from banks. One example is a self-liquidating (seasonal) loan which is used to pay for a temporary increase in accounts receivable or inventory. As soon as the assets realize cash, the loan is repaid.

Loans, of course, earn interest, and the prime interest rate is the lowest interest rate applied to short-term loans from a bank. Banks charge only their most creditworthy clients the prime rate; other borrowers are charged higher interest rates.

Bank financing may take any of the following forms:

1. Unsecured loans
2. Secured loans
3. Lines of credit
4. Installment loans

Unsecured Loans

Most short-term unsecured loans are self-liquidating. This kind of loan is recommended for use by companies with excellent credit ratings for financing projects that have quick cash flows. They are appropriate when the firm must have immediate cash and can either repay the loan in the near future or quickly obtain longer-term financing. The disadvantages of this kind of loan are that, because it is made for the short term, it carries a higher interest rate than a secured loan and payment in a lump sum is required.

Secured Loans

If a borrower's credit rating is deficient, the bank may lend money only on a secured basis, that is, with some form of collateral behind the loan. Collateral may take many forms including inventory, marketable securities, or fixed assets. In some cases, even though the company is able to obtain an unsecured loan, it may still give collateral in exchange for a lower interest rate.

Lines of Credit

Under a line of credit, the bank agrees to lend money to the borrower on a recurring basis up to a specified amount. Credit lines are typically established for a 1-year period and may be renewed annually. Construction companies often use such an arrangement because they usually receive only minimal payments from their clients during construction, being compensated primarily at the end of a job.

The advantages of a line of credit for a company are the easy and immediate access to funds during tight money market conditions and the ability to borrow only as much as needed and repay immediately when cash is available. The disadvantages relate to the collateral requirements and the additional financial information that must be presented to the bank. Also, the bank may place restrictions upon the company, such as a ceiling on capital expenditures or the maintenance of a minimum level of working capital. Further, the bank will charge a commitment fee on the amount of the unused credit line.

When a company borrows under a line of credit, it may be required to maintain a deposit with the bank that does not earn interest. This deposit is referred to as a compensating balance and is stated as a percentage of the loan. The compensating balance effectively increases the cost of the loan. A compensating balance may also be placed on the unused portion of a line of credit, in which case the interest rate would be reduced.

EXAMPLE 5.2　A company borrows $200,000 and is required to keep a 12 percent compensating balance. It also has an unused line of credit in the amount of $100,000, for which a 10 percent compensating balance is required. What amount is the minimum balance that the business must maintain?

$$(\$200,000 \times 0.12) + (\$100,0000 \times 0.10) = \$24,000 + \$10,000 = \$34,000$$

The bank may test a borrower's financial capability by requiring the borrower to "clean up," that is, repay the loan for a brief time during the year (e.g., for 1 month). A company that is unable to repay a short-term loan should probably finance with long-term funds. The payment shows the bank that the loan is actually seasonal rather than permanent financing.

Installment Loans

An installment loan requires monthly payments. When the principal on the loan decreases sufficiently, refinancing can take place at lower interest rates. The advantage of this kind of loan is that it may be tailored to satisfy a company's seasonal financing needs.

Computation of Interest

Interest on a loan may be paid either at maturity (ordinary interest) or in advance (discounting the loan). When interest is paid in advance, the proceeds from the loan are reduced and the effective (true) interest cost is increased.

EXAMPLE 5.3　Acme Company borrows $30,000 at 16 percent interest per annum and repays the loan 1 year hence. The interest paid is $30,000 × 0.16 = $4,800. The effective interest rate is 16 percent.

EXAMPLE 5.4　Assume the same facts as in Example 5.3, except the note is discounted. The proceeds of this loan are smaller than in the previous example.

$$\text{Proceeds} = \text{principal} - \text{interest} = \$30,000 - \$4,800 = \$25,200$$

The true interest rate for this discounted loan is:

$$\text{Effective interest rate} = \frac{\text{interest}}{\text{proceeds}} = \frac{\$4,800}{\$25,000} = 19\%$$

EXAMPLE 5.5　Prestige Bank will give a company a 1-year loan at an interest rate of 20 percent payable at maturity, while Heritage Bank will lend on a discount basis at a 19 percent interest rate. Which bank charges the lowest effective rate?

$$\begin{array}{ll} \text{Prestige Bank} & 20\% \\ \text{Heritage Bank} & \dfrac{19\%}{81\%} = 23.5\% \end{array}$$

The loan from Prestige Bank has the better interest rate.

When a loan has a compensating balance requirement associated with it, the proceeds received by the borrower are decreased by the amount of the balance. The compensating balance will increase the effective interest rate.

EXAMPLE 5.6　The effective interest rate associated with a 1-year, $600,000 loan that has a nominal interest rate of 19 percent, with interest due at maturity and requiring a 15 percent compensating balance is computed as follows:

$$\text{Effective interest rate (with compensating balance)} = \frac{\text{interest rate} \times \text{principal}}{\text{proceeds, } \% \times \text{principal}}$$

$$= \frac{0.19 \times \$600,000}{(1.00 - 0.15) \times \$600,000} = \frac{\$114,000}{\$510,000} = 22.4\%$$

EXAMPLE 5.7 Assume the same facts as in Example 5.6, except that the loan is discounted. The effective interest rate is:

$$\text{Effective interest rate (with discount)} = \frac{\text{interest rate} \times \text{principal}}{(\text{proceeds, } \% \times \text{principal}) - \text{interest}}$$

$$= \frac{0.19 \times \$600,000}{(0.85 \times \$600,000) - \$114,000} = \frac{\$114,000}{\$396,000} = 28.8\%$$

EXAMPLE 5.8 Jones Company has a line of credit in the amount of $400,000 from its bank, but it must maintain a compensating balance of 13 percent on outstanding loans and a compensating balance of 10 percent on the unused credit. The interest rate on the loan is 18 percent. The company borrows $275,000. What is the effective interest rate on the loan?

The required compensating balance is:

$0.13 \times \$275,000$	$35,750
$0.10 \times 125,000$	12,500
	$48,250

$$\text{Effective interest rate (with line of credit)} = \frac{\text{interest rate (on loan)} \times \text{principal}}{\text{principal} - \text{compensating balance}}$$

$$= \frac{0.18 \times \$275,000}{\$275,000 - \$48,250} = \frac{\$49,500}{\$226,750} = 21.8\%$$

On an installment loan, the effective interest rate computation is more involved. Assuming a 1-year loan is to be paid in equal monthly installments, the effective rate must be based on the average amount outstanding for the year. The interest to be paid is computed on the face amount of the loan.

EXAMPLE 5.9 A company borrows $40,000 at an interest rate of 10 percent to be paid in 12 monthly installments. The average loan balance is $40,000/2 = $20,000. The effective interest rate is $4,000/$20,000 = 20%.

EXAMPLE 5.10 Assume the same facts as in Example 5.9, except that the loan is discounted. The interest of $4,000 is deducted in advance so the proceeds received are $40,000 − $4,000 = $36,000. The average loan balance is $36,000/2 = $18,000. The effective interest rate is $4,000/$18,000 = 22.2%.

5.4 BANKERS' ACCEPTANCES

A banker's acceptance is a draft, drawn by an individual and accepted by a bank, that orders payment to a third party at a later date. The creditworthiness of the draft is of good quality because it has the backing of the bank, not the drawer. It is, in essence, a debt instrument created by the creditor out of a self-liquidating business transaction. Bankers' acceptances are often used to finance the shipment and handling of both domestic and foreign merchandise. Acceptances are classed as short-term financing because they typically have maturities of less than 180 days.

EXAMPLE 5.11 A United States oil refiner arranges with its United State commercial bank for a letter of credit to a Saudi Arabian exporter with whom the United States refiner has undertaken a transaction. The letter of credit provides the information regarding the shipment and states that the exporter can draw a time draft for a given amount on the United States bank. Because of the letter of credit, the exporter draws a draft on the bank and negotiates it with a local Saudi Arabian bank, receiving immediate payment. The Saudi Arabian bank sends the draft to the United States bank and when the latter accepts the draft, there is an acceptance to meet the obligation on the maturity date.

5.5   COMMERCIAL FINANCE COMPANY LOANS

When credit is unavailable from a bank, a company may have to go to a commercial finance company (e.g., CIT Financial). The finance company loan has a higher interest rate than a bank, and generally is secured. Typically, the amount of collateral placed will be greater than the balance of the loan. Collateral includes accounts receivable, inventories, and fixed assets. Commercial finance companies also finance the installment purchases of industrial equipment by firms. A portion of their financing is sometimes obtained through commercial bank borrowing at wholesale rates.

5.6   COMMERCIAL PAPER

Commercial paper can be issued only by companies possessing the highest credit ratings. Therefore, the interest rate is less than that of a bank loan, usually $\frac{1}{2}$ percent below prime. Commercial paper is unsecured and sold at a discount in the form of short-term promissory notes. The maturity date is usually less than 270 days, otherwise Securities and Exchange Commission (SEC) registration is needed. When a note is sold at a discount, it means that interest is immediately deducted from the face of the note by the creditor, but the debtor will pay the full face value. Commercial paper may be issued through a dealer or directly placed to an institutional investor.

The benefits of commercial paper are that no security is required, the interest rate is typically less than through bank or finance company borrowing, and the commercial paper dealer often offers financial advice. The drawbacks are that commercial paper can be issued only by large, financially sound companies, and commercial paper dealings relative to bank dealings are impersonal.

EXAMPLE 5.12   Travis Corporation's balance sheet appears below.

ASSETS		LIABILITIES AND STOCKHOLDERS' EQUITY	
Current assets	$ 540,000	Current liabilities	
Fixed assets	800,000	Notes payable to banks	$ 100,000
		Commercial paper	650,000
		Total current liabilities	$ 750,000
		Long-term liabilities	260,000
		Total liabilities	$1,010,000
		Stockholders' equity	330,000
		Total liabilities and	
Total assets	$1,340,000	stockholders' equity	$1,340,000

The amount of commercial paper issued by Travis is a high percentage of both its current liabilities, 86.7 percent ($650,000/$750,000), and its total liabilities, 64.4 percent ($650,000/$1,010,000). Probably Travis should do more bank borrowing because in the event of a money market squeeze, the company would find it advantageous to have a working relationship with a bank.

EXAMPLE 5.13   Able Company sells $500,000 of commercial paper every 2 months at a 13 percent rate. There is a $1,000 placement cost each time. The percentage cost of the commercial paper is:

Interest ($500,000 × 0.13)	$65,000
Placement cost ($1,000 × 6)	6,000
Cost	$71,000

$$\text{Percentage cost of commercial paper} = \frac{\$71,000}{\$500,000} = 14.2\%$$

EXAMPLE 5.14 Ajax Corporation issues $300,000 worth of 18 percent, 90-day commercial paper. However, the funds are needed for only 70 days. The excess funds can be invested in securities earning 17 percent. The brokerage fee associated with the marketable security transaction is 1.5 percent. The dollar cost to the company in issuing the commercial paper is:

Interest expense	
[0.18 × $300,000 × (90/360)]	$13,500
Brokerage fee (0.015 × $300,000)	4,500
Total cost	$18,000
Less: Return on marketable securities	
[0.17 × $300,000 × (20/360)]	2,833
Net cost	$15,167

EXAMPLE 5.15 Charles Corporation anticipates it will need $500,000 cash for February 19X2 in order to purchase inventory. There are three ways to finance this purchase, as follows:

(a) Set up a 1-year credit line for $500,000. The bank requires a 1 percent commitment fee. The interest rate is 18 percent on borrowed funds. Funds are needed for 30 days.

(b) Do not take advantage of a 1/10, net /40 discount on a $500,000 credit purchase.

(c) Issue $500,000 of commercial paper for 30 days at 17 percent.

Which is the least expensive method of financing?

(a) Set up a credit line:

Commitment fee	
[0.01 × $500,000 × (11/12)]	$ 4,583
Interest [0.18 × $500,000 × (1/12)]	7,500
	$12,083

(b) Do not take advantage of discount:

$$0.01 \times \$500,000 = \$5,000$$

(c) Issue commercial paper:

$$0.17 \times \$500,000 \times (1/12) = \$7,083$$

The financing with the least dollar cost is to not take the discount, as specified in (b).

5.7 RECEIVABLE FINANCING

The financing of accounts receivable can generally take place if:

1. Receivables are at a minimum of $25,000

2. Sales are at a minimum of $250,000

3. Individual receivables are at a minimum of $100

4. Receivables apply to selling merchandise rather than rendering services

5. Customers are financially strong

6. Sales returns are not great

7. Title to the goods is received by the buyer at shipment

Receivable financing has several advantages, including avoiding the need for long-term financing and obtaining a recurring cash flow base. Accounts receivable financing has the drawback of high administrative costs when there are many small accounts. However, with the use of computers these costs can be curtailed.

Accounts receivable may be financed under either a factoring or assignment arrangement. *Factoring* refers to the outright sale of accounts receivable to a bank or finance company *without recourse*. The purchaser takes all credit and collection risks. The proceeds received by the selling company are equal to the face value of the receivables less the commission charge, which is typically 2 to 4 percent higher than the prime interest rate. The cost of the factoring arrangement is the factor's commission for credit investigation, interest on the unpaid balance of advanced funds, and a discount from the face value of the receivables where high credit risks exist. Remissions by customers are made directly to the factor.

The advantages of factoring include:

1. Immediate availability of cash
2. Reduction in overhead since the credit examination function is no longer required
3. Utilization of financial advice
4. Receipt of advances as needed on a seasonal basis
5. Strengthening of the balance sheet position

The drawbacks to factoring include both the high cost and the poor impression left with customers because of the change in ownership of the receivables. Also, factors may antagonize customers by their demanding methods of collecting delinquent accounts.

In an *assignment*, there is no transfer of the ownership of the accounts receivable. Receivables are given to a finance company *with recourse*. The finance company typically advances between 50 and 85 percent of the face value of the receivables in cash. The borrower is responsible for a service charge, interest on the advance, and any resulting bad debt losses. Customer remissions continue to be made directly to the company.

The assignment of accounts receivable has a number of advantages, including the immediate availability of cash, cash advances available on a seasonal basis, and avoidance of negative customer feelings. The disadvantages include the high cost, the continuance of the clerical function associated with accounts receivable, and the bearing of all credit risks.

The financial manager should be aware of the impact of a change in accounts receivable policy on the cost of financing receivables.

EXAMPLE 5.16 When accounts receivable are financed, the cost of financing may rise or fall under different conditions. For instance: (1) when credit standards are relaxed, costs increase; (2) when recourse for defaults is given to the finance company, costs decrease; and (3) when the minimum invoice amount of a credit sale is increased, costs decrease.

The finance manager should compute the costs of accounts receivable financing and select the least expensive alternative.

EXAMPLE 5.17 A factor will purchase Ryan Corporation's $120,000 per month accounts receivable. The factor will advance up to 80 percent of the receivables for an annual charge of 14 percent, and a 1.5 percent fee on receivables purchased. The cost of this factoring arrangement is:

Factor fee [0.015 × ($120,000 × 12)]	$21,600
Cost of borrowing [0.14 × ($120,000 × 0.8)]	13,440
Total cost	$35,040

EXAMPLE 5.18 Tristar Corporation needs $250,000 and is weighing the alternatives of arranging a bank loan or going to a factor. The bank loan terms are 18 per cent interest, discounted, with a compensating balance of 20 percent required. The factor will charge a 4 percent commission on invoices purchased monthly, and the interest rate on the purchased invoices is 12 percent, deducted in advance. By using a factor, Tristar will save $1,000 monthly credit department costs, and uncollectible accounts estimated at 3 percent of the factored accounts receivable will not occur. Which is the better alternative for Tristar?

The bank loan which will net the company its desired $250,000 in proceeds is:

$$\frac{\text{Proceeds}}{100\% - (\text{percent deducted})} = \frac{\$250,000}{100\% - (18\% + 20\%)} = \frac{\$250,000}{1.0 - 0.38} = \frac{\$250,000}{0.62} = \$403,226$$

The effective interest rate associated with the bank loan is:

$$\text{Effective interest rate} = \frac{\text{interest rate}}{\text{proceeds, \%}} = \frac{0.18}{0.62} = 29.0\%$$

The amount of accounts receivable that should be factored to net the firm $250,000 is:

$$\frac{\$250,000}{1.0 - 0.16} = \frac{\$250,000}{0.84} = \$297,619$$

The total annual cost of the bank arrangement is:

Interest ($250,000 × 0.29)	$72,500
Additional cost of not using a factor:	
Credit costs ($1,000 × 12)	12,000
Uncollectible accounts ($297,619 × 0.03)	8,929
Total cost	$93,429

The effective interest rate associated with factoring accounts receivable is:

$$\text{Effective interest rate} = \frac{\text{interest rate}}{\text{proceeds, \%}} = \frac{12\%}{100\% - (12\% + 4\%)} = \frac{0.12}{0.84} = 14.3\%$$

The total annual cost of the factoring alternative is:

Interest ($250,000 × 0.143)	$35,750
Factoring ($297,619 × 0.04)	11,905
Total cost	$47,655

Factoring should be used since it will cost almost half as much as the bank loan.

EXAMPLE 5.19 System Corporation's factor charges a 3 percent fee per month. The factor lends the firm up to 75 percent of receivables purchased for an additional 1 percent per month. The company's credit sales are $400,000 per month. As a result of the factoring arrangement, the company saves $6,500 per month in credit costs and a bad debt expense of 2 percent of credit sales.

XYZ Bank has offered an arrangement where it will lend the firm up to 75 percent of the receivables. The bank will charge 2 percent per month interest plus a 4 percent processing charge on receivable lending.

The collection period is 30 days. If System Corporation borrows the maximum allowed per month, should the firm stay with the factor or switch to XYZ Bank?

Cost of factor:

Purchased receivables (0.03 × $400,000)	$12,000
Lending fee (0.01 × $300,000)	3,000
Total cost	$15,000

Cost of bank financing:

Interest (0.20 × $300,000)	$ 6,000
Processing charge (0.04 × $300,000)	12,000
Additional cost of not using the factor:	
Credit costs	6,500
Bad debts (0.02 × $400,000)	8,000
Total cost	$32,500

System Corporation should stay with the factor.

EXAMPLE 5.20 Davis Company is considering a factoring arrangement. The company's sales are $2,700,000, accounts receivable turnover is 9 times, and a 17 percent reserve on accounts receivable is required by the factor. The factor's commission charge on average accounts receivable payable at the point of receivable purchase is 2.0 percent. The factor's interest charge is 16 percent on receivables after subtracting the commission charge and reserve. The interest charge reduces the advance. What is the annual effective cost under the factoring arrangement?

$$\text{Average accounts receivable} = \frac{\text{credit sales}}{\text{turnover}} = \frac{\$2,700,000}{9} = \$300,000$$

Davis will receive the following amount by factoring its accounts receivable:

Average accounts receivable	$300,000
Less: Reserve ($300,000 × 0.17)	−51,000
Commission ($300,000 × 0.02)	−6,000
Net prior to interest	$243,000
Less: Interest [$243,000 × (16%/9)]	4,320
Proceeds received	$238,680

The annual cost of the factoring arrangement is:

Commission ($300,000 × 0.02)	$ 6,000
Interest [$243,000 × (16%/9)]	4,320
Cost each 40 days (360/9)	$10,320
Turnover	×9
Total annual cost	$92,880

The annual effective cost under the factoring arrangement based on the amount received is:

$$\frac{\text{Annual cost}}{\text{Average amount received}} = \frac{\$92,880}{\$238,680} = 38.9\%$$

5.8 INVENTORY FINANCING

Financing inventory typically occurs when a company has fully used its borrowing capacity on receivables. Inventory financing requires the existence of marketable, nonperishable, and standardized goods that have quick turnover. The merchandise should not be subject to rapid obsolescence. Good collateral inventory is that which can be marketed apart from the borrower's marketing organization. Inventory financing should take into account the price stability of the inventory and the expenses associated with selling it.

In the case of marketable inventory, the advance is high. In general, the financing of raw materials and finished goods is about 75 percent of their value. The interest rate approximates 3 to 5 points (i.e., 3 to 5 percent) over prime.

The disadvantages of inventory financing include the high interest rate and the restrictions on some of the company's inventory.

The vehicles of inventory financing include a floating (blanket) lien, warehouse receipt, and trust receipt. In the case of a *floating lien*, the creditor's security lies in the aggregate inventory rather than in its components. Even though the borrower sells and restocks, the lender's security interest continues. With a *warehouse receipt*, the lender receives an interest in the borrower's inventory stored at a public warehouse; however, the fixed costs of this arrangement are quite high. There may be a field warehouse arrangement where the warehouser sets up a secured area directly at the debtor's location. The debtor has access to the goods but must continually account for them. With a *trust receipt* loan, the creditor has title to given goods but releases them to the borrower to sell on the creditor's behalf. As goods are sold, the borrower remits the funds to the lender. A good example of trust receipt use is in automobile dealer financing. The drawback of the trust receipt arrangement is that a trust receipt must be given for specific items.

A collateral certificate may be issued by a third party to the lender guaranteeing the existence of pledged inventory. The advantage of a collateral certificate is flexibility since merchandise does not have to be segregated or possessed by the lender.

EXAMPLE 5.21 Jackson COrporation wishes to finance its $500,000 inventory. Funds are needed for 3 months. A warehouse receipt loan may be taken at 16 percent with a 90 percent advance against the inventory's value. The warehousing cost is $4,000 for the 3-month period. The cost of financing the inventory is:

Interest [$0.16 \times 0.90 \times \$500,000 \times (3/12)$]	$18,000
Warehousing cost	4,000
Total cost	$22,000

EXAMPLE 5.22 Hardy Corporation has been showing growth in its operations but is currently experiencing liquidity problems. Six large financially sound companies are Hardy customers, being responsible for 75 percent of Hardy's sales. On the basis of the following information for 19X1, would Hardy Corporation be able to borrow on receivables or inventory?

Balance sheet data are as follows:

ASSETS

Current assets		
Cash	$ 27,000	
Receivables	380,000	
Inventory (consisting of 55% of work-in-process)	320,000	
Total current assets		$727,000
Fixed assets		250,000
Total assets		$977,000

LIABILITIES AND STOCKHOLDERS' EQUITY

Current liabilities		
Accounts payable	$260,000	
Loans payable	200,000	
Accrued expenses	35,000	
Total current liabilities		$495,000
Bonds payable		110,000
Total liabilities		$605,000
Stockholders' equity		
Common stock	$250,000	
Retained earnings	122,000	
Total stockholders' equity		372,000
Total liabilities and stockholders' equity		$977,000

Selected income statement data are as follows:

Sales	$1,800,000
Net income	$130,000

Receivable financing can be expected since a high percentage of sales are made to only six large financially healthy firms. Receivables will therefore show good collectibility. It is also easier to control a few large customer accounts.

Inventory financing is not likely, due to the high percentage of partially completed items. Lenders are reluctant to finance inventory when a large work-in-process balance exists since the goods will be difficult to further process and sell by lenders.

5.9 OTHER ASSETS

Assets other than inventory and receivables may be used as security for short-term bank loans such as real estate, plant and equipment, cash surrender value of life insurance policies, and securities. Also, lenders are usually willing to advance a high percentage of the market value of bonds. The owner's personal assets may be pledged when the company's financial position is very weak. In addition, loans may be made based on a guaranty of a third party.

Review Questions

1. Short-term financing refers to the issuance of debt having a maturity of less than _____ .

2. Short-term financing makes the borrower more susceptible to _____ fluctuations.

3. The least expensive source of short-term financing is _____ .

4. Accounts payable is a(n) _____ financing source.

5. Accounts payable should not be stretched too far because of a possible reduction in the firm's _____ .

6. A note payable may be payable at _____ or in _____ .

7. _____ loans are those in which the loan is paid as soon as the financed assets realize cash.

8. The rate charged by banks to their best clients is called the _____ interest rate.

9. _____ loans require no collateral.

10. When a(n) _____ is given, the bank agrees to lend the borrower money on a continual basis up to a given amount.

11. A(n) _____ refers to the deposit, which does not earn interest, that a company must maintain at the bank as collateral for a loan.

12. In a(n) _____ loan, monthly payments are required.

13. Interest on a loan may be paid at _____ or _____ .

14. When a loan is discounted, the _____ interest rate will be higher.

15. A(n) _____ is a draft drawn by an individual and accepted by the bank requiring future payment to a third party.

16. The interest rate on _____ is less than the interest rate on a bank loan.

17. The outright sale of accounts receivable to a third party is called _____ .

18. In a(n) _____ , accounts receivable are transferred to a third party with recourse.

19. In the case of inventory financing, a(n) _____ lien applies to the aggregate inventory rather than the components.

20. In a(n) _____ loan, the creditor has title to goods but releases them to the borrower to sell on the creditor's behalf.

Answers: (1) 1 year; (2) interest rate; (3) trade credit; (4) spontaneous; (5) credit rating; (6) maturity, installments; (7) Self-liquidating; (8) prime; (9) Unsecured; (10) line of credit; (11) compensating balance; (12) installment; (13) maturity, in advance; (14) effective; (15) bankers' acceptance; (16) commercial paper; (17) factoring; (18) assignment; (19) floating (blanket); (20) trust receipt.

Solved Problems

5.1 Accounts Payable. James Corporation purchases $750 per day from suppliers on terms of net/30. Determine the accounts payable balance.

SOLUTION

$$\$750 \text{ per day} \times 30 \text{ days} = \$22,500$$

5.2 Compensating Balance. Carl Corporation borrows $150,000 from a bank. A 10 percent compensating balance is required. What is the amount of the compensating balance?

SOLUTION

$$\$150,000 \times 0.10 = \$15,000$$

5.3 Compensating Balance. Wilson Company borrows $500,000 from the bank and is required to maintain a 15 percent compensating balance. Further, Wilson has an unused line of credit of $200,000, with a required 11 percent compensating balance. What is the total required compensating balance the firm must maintain?

SOLUTION

$$(\$500,000 \times 0.15) + (\$200,000 \times 0.11) = \$97,000$$

5.4 Effective Interest Rate. Charles Corporation borrows $70,000 at 19 percent annual interest. Principal and interest is due in 1 year. What is the effective interest rate?

SOLUTION

The effective interest rate is 19 percent.

5.5   **Proceeds of Loan.** Assume the same information as in Problem 5.4, except that interest is deducted in advance. (*a*) What is the amount of proceeds the company will receive at the time of the loan? (*b*) What is the effective interest rate?

SOLUTION

(*a*)
$$\text{Interest} = \$70,000 \times 0.19 = \$13,300$$
$$\text{Proceeds} = \text{principal} - \text{interest} = \$70,000 - \$13,300 = \$56,700$$

(*b*)
$$\text{Effective interest rate} = \frac{\text{interest}}{\text{proceeds}} = \frac{\$13,300}{\$56,700} = 23.5\%$$

5.6   **Interest Cost.** Ajax Corporation is deciding which of two banks to borrow from on a 1-year basis. Bank A charges an 18 percent interest rate payable at maturity. Bank B charges a 17 percent interest rate on a discount basis. Which loan is cheaper?

SOLUTION

$$\text{Bank A} \qquad\qquad 18\%$$
$$\text{Bank B} \qquad \frac{17\%}{83\%} = 20.5\%$$

Ajax should borrow from bank A since the effective interest rate is lower.

5.7   **Effective Interest Rate.** Tech Corporation takes out a $70,000 loan having a nominal interest rate of 22 percent payable at maturity. The required compensating balance is 12 percent. What is the effective interest rate?

SOLUTION

$$\text{Effective interest rate} = \frac{\text{interest rate}}{\text{proceeds, \%}} = \frac{0.22}{1.00 - 0.12} = \frac{0.22}{0.88} = 25\%$$

5.8   **Effective Interest Rate.** Assume the same information as in Problem 5.7 except that interest is payable in advance. What is the effective interest rate?

SOLUTION

$$\text{Effective rate} = \frac{\text{interest rate}}{\text{proceeds, \%}} = \frac{0.22}{0.88 - 0.22} = \frac{0.22}{0.66} = 33.3\%$$

5.9   **Effective Interest Rate and Compensating Balance.** Wilson Corporation has a credit line of $800,000. The compensating balance requirement on outstanding loans is 14 percent, and 8 percent on the unused credit line. The company borrows $500,000 at a 20 percent interest rate. (*a*) What is the required compensating balance? (*b*) What is the effective interest rate?

SOLUTION

(*a*)   The required compensating balance is:

Loan 0.14 × $500,000	$70,000
Unused credit 0.08 × $300,000	24,000
	$94,000

(*b*) $$\text{Effective interest rate} = \frac{\text{interest}}{\text{proceeds}} = \frac{0.20 \times \$500,000}{\$500,000 - \$94,000} = \frac{\$100,000}{\$406,000} = 24.6\%$$

5.10   Average Loan Balance. Wise Corporation borrows $70,000 payable in 12 monthly installments. The interest rate is 15 percent. (*a*) What is the average loan balance? (*b*) What is the effective interest rate?

SOLUTION

(*a*) $$\text{Average loan balance} = \frac{\$70,000}{2} = \$35,000$$

(*b*) $$\text{Effective interest rate} = \frac{0.15 \times \$70,000}{\$35,000} = \frac{\$10,500}{\$35,000} = 30\%$$

5.11   Average Loan Balance. Assume the same information as in Problem 5.10, except that the loan is on a discount basis. (*a*) What is the average loan balance? (*b*) What is the effective interest rate?

SOLUTION

(*a*) $$\text{Proceeds} = \$70,000 - \$10,500 = \$59,500$$
$$\text{Average loan balance} = \frac{\$59,500}{2} = \$29,750$$

(*b*) $$\text{Effective interest rate} = \frac{\$10,500}{\$29,750} = 35.3\%$$

5.12   Commercial Paper. Boston Corporation's balance sheet follows:

ASSETS	
Current assets	$ 700,000
Fixed assets	1,600,000
Total assets	$2,300,000

LIABILITIES AND STOCKHOLDERS' EQUITY	
Current liabilities	
Bank loans payable	$ 500,000
Commercial paper	100,000
Total current liabilities	$ 600,000
Long-term liabilities	300,000
Total liabilities	$ 900,000
Stockholders' equity	1,400,000
Total liabilities and stockholders' equity	$2,300,000

The company has an excellent credit rating and can issue additional commercial paper if it wishes. Should Boston Corporation issue additional commercial paper?

SOLUTION

Yes. Commercial paper is a low percentage of current liabilities, 16.7 percent ($100,000/$600,000), and of total liabilities, 11.1 percent ($100,000/$900,000). Since the cost of commercial paper is less than a bank loan and since the percentage of commercial paper to total debt financing is low, additional commercial paper should be issued.

5.13   Cost of Commercial Paper. Nelson Corporation issues $800,000 of commercial paper every 3 months at a 16 percent rate. Each issuance involves a placement cost of $2,000. What is the annual percentage cost of the commercial paper?

SOLUTION

Interest ($800,000 × 0.16)	$128,000
Placement cost ($2,000 × 4)	8,000
Total cost	$136,000

$$\text{Cost of commercial paper} = \frac{\$136,000}{\$800,000} = 17.0\%$$

5.14   Cost of Commercial Paper. Cho Corporation issues $500,000, 20 percent, 120-day commercial paper. However, the funds are needed for only 90 days. The excess funds can be invested in securities earning 19 percent. The brokerage fee for the marketable security transaction is 1.0 percent. What is the net cost to the company for issuing the commercial paper?

SOLUTION

Interest [0.20 × $500,000 × (120/360)]	$33,333
Brokerage fee (0.01 × $500,000)	5,000
Total cost	$38,333
Less: Return on marketable securities	
[0.19 × $500,000 × (30/360)]	7,917
Net cost	$30,416

5.15   Financing Strategy. Johnson Company expects that it will need $600,000 cash for March 19X2. Possible means of financing are: (*a*) Establish a 1-year credit line for $600,000. The bank requires a 2 percent commitment fee. The interest rate is 21 percent. Funds are needed for 30 days. (*b*) Fail to take a 2/10, net/40 discount on a $600,000 credit purchase. (*c*) Issue $600,000, 20 percent commercial paper for 30 days. Which financing strategy should be selected?

SOLUTION

(*a*)   The credit line cost is:

Commitment fee [0.02 × $600,000 × (11/12)]	$11,000
Interest [0.21 × $600,000 × (1/12)]	10,500
Total cost	$21,500

(*b*)   The cost of not taking discount is:

$$0.02 \times \$600,000 = \$12,000$$

(c)   The cost of commercial paper is:

$$0.20 \times \$600,000 \times \tfrac{1}{12} = \$10,000$$

Strategy (c) is best since issuance of commercial paper involves the least cost.

5.16   Cost of Accounts Receivable Financing. What is the effect of each of the following situations on the cost of accounts receivable financing? (a) A more thorough credit check is undertaken. (b) Receivables are sold without recourse. (c) The minimum invoice amount for a credit sale is decreased. (d) Credit standards are tightened.

SOLUTION

(a)   Decrease   (c)   Increase
(b)   Increase   (d)   Decrease

5.17   Cost of Factoring. Drake Company is contemplating factoring its accounts receivable. The factor will acquire $250,000 of the company's accounts receivable every 2 months. An advance of 75 percent is given by the factor on receivables at an annual charge of 18 percent. There is a 2 percent factor fee associated with receivables purchased. What is the cost of the factoring arrangement?

SOLUTION

Factor fee $(0.02 \times \$250,000 \times 6)$	$30,000
Cost of advance $(0.18 \times \$250,000 \times 0.75)$	33,750
Total cost	$63,750

5.18   Bank versus Factor. Forest Corporation needs $400,000 additional financing. The company is considering the choice of financing with a bank or a factor. The bank loan carries a 20 percent interest rate on a discount basis with a required compensating balance of 16 percent. The factor charges a 3 percent commission on invoices purchased monthly. The interest rate associated with these invoices is 11 percent with interest deductible in advance. If a factor is used, there will be a monthly savings of $1,500 per month in credit department costs. Further, an uncollectible accounts expense of 2 percent on the factored receivables will not exist.

(a) What amount of principal must the company borrow from the bank to receive $400,000 in proceeds? (b) What amount of accounts receivable must be factored to net the firm $400,000? (c) What is the effective interest rate on the bank loan? (d) What is the total annual cost of the bank arrangement? (e) What is the effective interest rate associated with the factoring arrangement? (f) What is the total annual cost of factoring?

SOLUTION

(a)
$$\frac{\text{Principal}}{\text{Proceeds}} = \frac{1.00}{1.00 - (0.20 + 0.16)}$$

$$\frac{\text{Principal}}{\$400,000} = \frac{1}{1 - 0.36} = \frac{\$400,000}{1.0 - 0.36} = \frac{\$400,000}{0.64} = \$625,000$$

(b)
$$\text{Accounts receivables to factor} = \frac{\$400,000}{1.0 - 0.14} = \frac{\$400,000}{0.86} = \$465,116$$

(c)
$$\text{Effective interest rate of bank loan} = \frac{\text{interest rate}}{\text{proceeds, \%}} = \frac{0.20}{0.64} = 31.3\%$$

(*d*) The cost of the bank loan is:

Interest ($400,000 × 0.313)	$125,200
Credit costs ($1,500 × 12)	18,000
Uncollectible accounts ($465,116 × 0.02)	9,302
Total annual cost	$152,502

(*e*) The effective interest rate of factoring is:

$$\frac{0.11}{0.86} = 12.8\%$$

(*f*) The cost of factoring is:

Interest ($400,000 × 0.128)	$51,200
Factoring ($465,116 × 0.03)	13,953
Total annual cost	$65,153

5.19 **Bank versus Factor.** Wayne Corporation's factor charges a 4 percent monthly fee. The factor lends Wayne up to 85 percent of receivables purchased for an additional $1\frac{1}{2}$ percent per month. The monthly credit sales are $350,000. With the factoring arrangement, there is a savings in corporate credit checking costs of $4,200 per month and in bad debts of 3 percent on credit sales.

Trust Bank has offered to lend Wayne up to 85 percent of the receivables, at an interest charge of 2.5 percent per month plus a 5 percent processing charge on receivable lending.

The collection period is 30 days, and Wayne borrows the maximum amount permitted each month. Should Wayne Corporation accept the bank's offer?

SOLUTION

Cost of factor:

Purchased receivables (0.04 × $350,000)	$14,000
Lending fee (0.015 × $350,000 × 0.85)	4,463
Total cost	$18,463

Cost of bank financing:

Interest (0.025 × $350,000 × 0.85)	$ 7,438
Processing charge (0.05 × $350,000 × 0.85)	14,875
Additional cost of not using factor	
Credit costs	4,200
Bad debts (0.03 × $350,000)	10,500
Total cost	$37,013

Wayne Corporation should stay with the factor, since the cost of the bank's offer is more than twice the cost of factoring.

5.20 **Factoring Accounts Receivable.** Grafton Corporation is considering factoring its accounts receivable. Its sales are $3,600,000, and accounts receivable turnover is two times. The factor requires: (1) an 18 percent reserve on accounts receivable; (2) a commission charge of 2.5 percent on average accounts receivable, payable when receivables are purchased; and (3) an interest charge of 19 percent on receivables after deducting the commission charge and reserve. The interest charge reduces the advance.

Given the facts, answer the following questions: (*a*) What is the average accounts receivable? (*b*) How much will Grafton receive by factoring its accounts receivable? (*c*) What is the annual cost of the factoring arrangement? (*d*) What is the effective annual cost of factoring?

SOLUTION

(*a*)
$$\text{Average accounts receivable} = \frac{\text{credit sales}}{\text{turnover}} = \frac{\$3,600,000}{2} = \$1,800,000$$

(*b*) The proceeds from factoring are:

Average accounts receivable	$1,800,000
Less: Reserve ($1,800,000 × 0.18)	−324,000
Commission ($1,800,000 × 0.025)	−45,000
Net prior to interest	$1,431,000
Less: Interest [$1,431,000 × (19%/2)]	135,945
Proceeds received	$1,295,055

(*c*) The cost of factoring is:

Commission ($1,800,000 × 0.025)	$ 45,000
Interest [$1,431,000 × (19%/2)]	135,945
Cost each 180 days (360/2)	$180,945
Turnover	×2
Total annual cost	$361,890

(*d*)
$$\text{Effective annual cost of factoring} = \frac{\text{annual cost}}{\text{average amount received}} = \frac{\$361,890}{\$1,295,055} = 27.9\%$$

5.21 Financing Cost of Inventory. Blake Company desires to finance its $300,000 inventory. Funds are required for 4 months. Under consideration is a warehouse receipt loan at an annual interest rate of 17 percent, with an 85 percent advance against the inventory's value. The warehousing cost is $5,000 for the 4-month period. Determine the financing cost.

SOLUTION

Interest [0.17 × 0.85 × $300,000 × (4/12)]	$14,450
Warehousing cost	5,000
Total cost	$19,450

5.22 Receivable Financing or Inventory Financing. Large Corporation has liquidity problems. Most of its sales are made to small customer accounts. Relevant balance sheet data for 19X1 are:

ASSETS		
Current assets		
Cash	$ 35,000	
Receivables	410,000	
Inventory (primarily consisting of finished goods and raw materials)	360,000	
Total current assets		$ 805,000
Fixed assets		600,000
Total assets		$1,405,000

LIABILITIES AND STOCKHOLDERS' EQUITY

Current liabilities		
Accounts payable	$350,000	
Loans payable	320,000	
Accrued expenses	56,000	
Total current liabilities		$ 726,000
Bonds payable		225,000
Total liabilities		$ 951,000
Stockholders' equity		
Common stock	$300,000	
Retained earnings		
Total stockholders' equity	154,000	454,000
Total liabilities and stockholders' equity		$1,405,000

Relevant income statement data are:

Sales	$2,400,000
Net income	$480,000

Given the balance sheet and income statement data: (*a*) Is receivable financing likely? (*b*) Is inventory financing likely?

SOLUTION

(*a*) No, receivable financing is not likely since receivables are made to many small customer accounts. Control over receivables will therefore be a problem. (*b*) Yes, inventory financing is likely since inventory consists of a large proportion of finished goods and raw materials which are readily salable.

5.23   **Cost of Issuing the Commercial Paper.** Cartele, Inc., will need $4 million over the next year to finance its short-term requirements. The company is considering financing alternatives—bank financing and the sale of commercial paper.

Addison Union Bank is willing to loan Cartele the necessary funds providing the company maintains a 20 percent compensating balance. The effective cost of the bank loan, considering the compensating balance requirement, is 10.4 percent on a pretax basis.

Under the other alternative Cartele would sell $4 million of 90-day maturity commercial paper every 3 months. The commercial paper will carry a rate of $7\frac{3}{4}$ percent; the interest rate is expected to remain at this level throughout the year. The commercial paper dealer's fee to place the issue would be a one-time charge of $\frac{1}{8}$ percent. The commercial paper dealer will require Cartele to establish a $400,000 compensating balance.

Management prefers the flexibility of bank financing. However, if the cost of bank financing should exceed the cost of the commercial paper by more than 1 percent, Cartele plans to issue the commercial paper.

(*a*) Calculate the effective cost on a pretax basis of issuing the commercial paper and, based solely upon your cost calculations, recommend the method of financing Cartele, Inc., should select. (*b*) Identify the characteristics Cartele should possess in order to deal regularly in the commercial paper market. (CMA, adapted.)

SOLUTION

(*a*)
$$\text{Cost of commercial paper} = \frac{\text{costs incurred by using commercial paper}}{\text{net funds available from commercial paper}}$$

The cost of commercial paper in the first quarter is:

Cost of issuing commercial paper

Interest ($4,000,000 \times 0.0775 \times \frac{1}{4}$)		$ 77,500
Placement fee ($4,000,000 \times 0.00125$)		5,000
1st-quarter cost		$ 82,500

Funds available for use

Funds raised		$4,000,000
Less: Compensating balance	$400,000	
Interest and placement	82,500	482,500
Net funds available in the 1st quarter		$3,517,500

$$\text{Cost of commercial paper in the 1st quarter} = \frac{\$82,500}{\$3,517,500} = 2.345\%$$

Cost of issuing commercial paper per quarter

Interest ($4,000,000 \times 0.0775 \times \frac{1}{4}$)		$ 77,500

Funds available for use

Funds raised		$4,000,000
Less: Compensating balance	$400,000	
Interest	77,500	477,500
Net funds available per quarter		$3,522,500

$$\text{Cost of commercial paper per quarter} = \frac{\$77,500}{\$3,522,500} = 2.20\%$$

The total annual effective cost of commercial paper is:

Effective cost = 1st-qtr. cost + 3(cost per quarter − for 2d, 3d, 4th qtrs.)
= 0.02345 + 3(0.02200) = 0.02345 + 0.06600 = 0.089545 = 8.95%

Cartele, Inc., should choose commercial paper because the cost of bank financing (10.4 percent) exceeds the cost of commercial paper (8.95 percent) by greater than 1 percent.

(b) The characteristics Cartele, Inc., should possess in order to deal regularly in the commercial paper market include the following:

1. Have a prestigious reputation, be financially strong, and have a high credit rating.
2. Have flexibility to arrange for large amounts of funds through regular banking channels.
3. Have large and frequently recurring short-term or seasonal needs for funds.
4. Have the ability to deal in large denominations of funds for periods of 1 to 9 months and be willing to accept the fact that commercial paper cannot be paid prior to maturity.

5.24 Establishing a Line of Credit. Luther Company produces and sells a complete line of infant and toddler toys. Its sales, characteristic of the entire toy industry, are very seasonal. The company offers favorable credit to those customers who will place their Christmas orders early and who will accept a shipment schedule arranged to fit the production schedules of Luther. The customer must place orders by May 15 and be willing to accept shipments beginning August 15; Luther guarantees shipment no later than October 15. Customers willing to accept these conditions are not required to pay for their Christmas purchases until January 30.

The suppliers of the raw materials used by Luther in the manufacture of toys offer more normal credit terms. The usual terms for the raw materials are 2/10, net/30. Luther Company makes payment within the 10-day discount period during the first 6 months of the year; however, in the summer and fall, it does not even meet the 30-day terms. The company regularly pays invoices for raw materials 80 to 90 days after the invoice date during this latter period. Suppliers have come to accept this pattern because it has existed for many years. In addition, this payment pattern has not affected Luther's credit rating or ability to acquire the necessary raw materials.

Luther recently hired a new financial vice-president. He feels quite uncomfortable with the unusually large accounts receivable and payable balances in the fall and winter and with the poor payment practice of Luther. He would like to consider alternatives to the present method of financing the accounts receivable.

One proposal being considered is to establish a line of credit at a local bank. The company could then draw against this line of credit in order to pay the invoices within the 10-day discount period and pay off the debt in February when the accounts receivable are collected. The effective interest rate for this arrangement would be 12 percent.

(a) Would establishing a line of credit reduce Luther's cost of doing business? Support your answer with appropriate calculations. (b) Would long-term financing (debt and common stock) be a sound alternative means of financing Luther's generous accounts receivable terms? (CMA, adapted.)

SOLUTION

(a) No, the line of credit alternative would not reduce Luther Company's cost of doing business. The cost of not taking the cash discount is calculated as follows:

$$\text{Cost} = \frac{\text{discount percent}}{(1.00 - \text{discount percent})} \times \frac{360}{\text{payment date} - \text{discount period}}$$

If Luther pays its invoices within 80 days, the cost of the cash discount forgone is 10.5 percent as shown below.

$$\text{Cost} = \frac{0.02}{(1.00 - 0.02)} \times \frac{360}{(80 - 10)} = \frac{0.02}{0.98} \times \frac{360}{70} = 10.5\%$$

Therefore, given the assumptions that Luther Company's credit rating or supply sources would not suffer due to late payment, the cost of the trade credit and forgoing the cash discount is lower than the 12 percent effective cost of the line of credit arrangement that would be used to take advantage of the 2 percent cash discounts.

(b) No, long-term financing is not an appropriate financing alternative to either the present method or the proposed line of credit for Luther Company.

Luther's financing need is primarily short term and seasonal. If long-term financing is employed, Luther would probably have excess funds for 6 months of each year. The use of long-term financing to meet seasonal needs usually is impractical and can affect the company's profits and financing flexibility adversely. Generally, the matching of asset lives and liability maturity provides less risk because the return on and proceeds from the sale of the assets provide the funds necessary to pay off the debt when due. For example, noncurrent assets should be financed with long-term debt rather than short-term obligations.

5.25   Costs of Alternative Sources of Short-term Financing. On March 1, 19X1, National Corporation purchased $100,000 worth of inventory on credit with terms of 1/20, net/60. In the past, National has always followed the policy of making payment 1 month (30 days) after the goods are purchased.

A new member of National's staff has indicated that the company she had previously worked for never passed up its cash discounts, and she wonders if that is not a sound policy. She has also pointed out to National that if it does not take advantage of the cash discount, it should wait the entire 60-day period to pay the full bill rather than paying within 30 days.

If National were to take advantage of the discount and pay the bill on March 20 rather than on March 30, the firm would have to borrow the necessary funds for the 10 extra days. National's borrowing terms with a local bank are estimated to be at $8\frac{1}{2}$ percent (annual rate), with a 15 percent compensating balance for the term of the loan. Most members of National's staff feel that it makes little sense to take out an $8\frac{1}{2}$ percent loan with a compensating balance of 15 percent in order to save 1 percent on its $100,000 by paying the account 10 days earlier than it had planned.

(a) Just in terms of true interest cost, would it be to National's advantage to take the 1 percent discount by paying the bill 10 days earlier than usual if to do this it borrowed the necessary amount on the above-mentioned terms? (b) If National ordinarily paid 60 days after purchase (instead of 30 days); would the company benefit by taking the discount if it had to borrow the money on the above-mentioned terms? (c) Compare your answers to (a) and (b) and explain what makes the discount more (less) desirable under the conditions stated in (b) than in (a). (CMA, adapted.)

SOLUTION

(a)   The cost of not paying by the twentieth day is $1,000. The company pays on the thirtieth day; thus, it is paying $1,000 to borrow $99,000 for 10 days. The annual interest cost is:

$$\frac{\$1,000}{\$99,000} \times \frac{360}{10} = 36.36\%$$

It would be necessary to borrow $116,471 from the bank to satisfy the 15 percent compensating balance and pay $99,000 to the suppliers ($99,000 ÷ 0.85). The interest charges for the 10-day period would be $116,471 × 0.085 × 10/360 = $275.00. The interest rate on the $99,000 would be:

$$\frac{\$275}{\$99,000} \times \frac{360}{10} = 10.00\%$$

It is to National's advantage to borrow from the bank in order to earn the discount.

(b)   Waiting 40 days past the discount date to pay the bill changes the annual interest cost of the discount to 9.09 percent.

$$\frac{\$1,000}{\$99,000} \times \frac{360}{40} = 9.09\%$$

The interest charges at the bank would be $116,471 × 0.085 × 40/360 = $1,100.
    The interest rate on the $99,000 would be:

$$\frac{\$1,100}{\$99,000} \times \frac{360}{40} = 10.00\%$$

It is not in National's best interest to borrow from the bank in this case.

(c)   The reason the borrowing alternative is no longer desirable in (b) is the change in the number of days that the borrowing covers. The $1,000 discount is a fixed charge for the 40-day period; it is unchanged by the number of days that lapse between the twentieth day and the day of payment. However, the interest charges vary with the number of days. Changing the borrowing period from 10 to 40 days increases the interest charges from $275 to $1,100.

5.26   Factoring. The Jackson Company has been negotiating with the Wright Bank with the hope of finding a cheaper source of funds than their current factoring arrangements. Forecasts indicate that, on average, they will need to borrow $180,000 per month this year—which is approximately 30 percent more than they have been borrowing on their receivables during the past year. Sales are expected to average $900,000 per month, of which 70 percent are on credit.

As an alternative to the present arrangements, Wright Bank has offered to lend the company up to 75 percent of the face value of the receivables shown on the schedule of accounts. The bank would charge 15 percent per annum interest plus a 2 percent processing charge per dollar of receivables assigned to support the loans. Jackson Company extends terms of net 30 days, and all customers who pay their bills do so by the 30th of the month.

The company's present factoring arrangement costs them a $2\frac{1}{2}$ percent factor fee plus an additional $1\frac{1}{2}$ percent per month on advances up to 90 percent of the volume of credit sales. Jackson Company saves $2,500 per month that would be required to support a credit department and a $1\frac{3}{4}$ percent bad debt expense on credit sales.

(a) Calculate the expected monthly cost of the bank financing proposal. (b) Calculate the expected monthly cost of factoring. (c) Discuss three advantages of factoring. (d) Discuss three disadvantages of factoring. (e) Would you recommend that the firm discontinue or reduce its factoring arrangement in favor of Wright Bank's financing plan? Explain your answer. (CMA, adapted.)

SOLUTION

(a) The expected monthly cost of bank financing is the sum of the interest cost, processing cost, bad debt expense, and credit department cost. The calculations are as follows:

Interest [(0.15/12) × $180,000]	$ 2,250
Processing [0.02 × ($180,000/0.75)]	4,800
Additional cost of not using factor:	
credit department	2,500
Bad debt expense	
(0.0175 × 0.7 × $900,000)	11,025
Expected monthly cost of bank financing	$20,575

(b) The expected monthly cost of factoring is the sum of the interest cost and the factor cost. The calculations are as follows:

Interest (0.015 × $180,000)	$ 2,700
Factor (0.025 × 0.7 × $900,000)	15,750
Expected monthly cost of factoring	$18,450

(c) The following are possible advantages of factoring: (1) Using a factor eliminates the need to carry a credit department. (2) Factoring is a flexible source of financing because as sales increase, the amount of readily available financing increases. (3) Factors specialize in evaluating and diversifying credit risks.

(d) The following are possible disadvantages of factoring: (1) The administrative costs may be excessive when invoices are numerous and relatively small in dollar amount. (2) Factoring removes one of the most liquid of the firm's assets and weakens the position of creditors. It may mar the firm's credit rating and increase the cost of other borrowing arrangements. (3) Customers could react unfavorably to a firm's factoring their accounts receivable.

(e) Based upon the calculations in parts (a) and (b), the factoring arrangement should be continued. The disadvantages of factoring are relatively unimportant in this case, especially since Jackson Company has been using the factor in the past. Before arriving at a final decision, the other services offered by the factor and bank would have to be evaluated, as well as the margin of error inherent in the estimation of the source data used in the calculations for parts (a) and (b). The additional borrowing capacity needed by Jackson Company is irrelevant because the firm needs only $180,000, the bank will loan $472,500 ($900,000 × 0.70 × 0.75), and the factor will lend $567,000 ($900,000 × 0.70 × 0.90).

Examination I

Chapters 1–5

1. What are the principal functions of the financial manager?

2. Charles Corporation reports the following for 19X1:

Accounts receivable—Jan. 1	$100,000
Accounts receivable—Dec. 31	$150,000
Inventory—Jan. 1	$40,000
Inventory—Dec. 31	$55,000
Net credit sales	$800,000
Cost of goods sold	$450,000

Compute: (*a*) accounts receivable turnover; (*b*) collection period; (*c*) inventory turnover; (*d*) age of inventory; and (*e*) operating cycle.

3. Column A lists the name of a ratio and column B indicates how the ratio is computed. For each ratio name given in column A identify the ratio computation from column B.

Column A		**Column B**
(1) Profit margin	(*a*)	$\dfrac{\text{Net income} - \text{preferred dividends}}{\text{common stock outstanding}}$
(2) Dividend payout	(*b*)	$\dfrac{\text{Market price per share}}{\text{Earnings per share}}$
(3) Earnings per share	(*c*)	$\dfrac{\text{Net income}}{\text{Sales}}$
(4) Dividend yield	(*d*)	$\dfrac{\text{Dividends per share}}{\text{Earnings per share}}$
(5) Quick ratio	(*e*)	$\dfrac{\text{Current assets}}{\text{Current liabilities}}$
(6) Interest coverage	(*f*)	$\dfrac{\text{Cash} + \text{marketable securities} + \text{accounts receivable}}{\text{Current liabilities}}$
(7) Current ratio	(*g*)	$\dfrac{\text{Dividends per share}}{\text{Market price per share}}$
(8) Price/earnings ratio	(*h*)	$\dfrac{\text{Income before interest and taxes}}{\text{Interest expense}}$

154

4. Classify each transaction in the first three columns by its correct cash flow activity.

Type of Activity

		Operating	Investing	Financing	Not applicable
(a)	Purchased land				
(b)	Sold corporate plant				
(c)	Declared a stock dividend				
(d)	Appropriated retained earnings				
(e)	Issued common stock				
(f)	Payments for material purchase				

5. Sale terms call for a 2 percent discount if paid within the first 10 days of the month after sale. Based on prior experience, 70 percent of the sales are collected within the discount period, 20 percent are collected by the end of the month after sale, 8 percent are collected in the following month, and 2 percent are uncollectible. Actual sales for October and November are $10,000 and $20,000, respectively. Compute the cash collections forecast for December.

6. Wise Corporation is considering entering into a lockbox arrangement which will have a yearly cost of $115,000. Average daily collections are $380,000. The lockbox system will reduce float time by 2 days. The rate of return is 16 percent. Should the lockbox system be implemented?

7. Geller Corporation provides the following data:

Current annual credit sales $30,000,000
Collection period 2 months
Terms net/30
Rate of return 15%

The business is considering offering a 3/10, net/30 discount. It is expected that 25 percent of the customers will take advantage of the discount. The collection period is anticipated to decrease to 1 month. Is it financially feasible to implement the discount policy?

8. William Company provides the following information: Usage is 300 units per month, cost per order is $15, and carrying cost per unit is $8.
Determine: (a) economic order quantity; (b) the number of orders required each month; and (c) the number of days that should elapse between orders.

9. What is the opportunity cost of not taking a discount when the terms are 4/10, net/60?

10. Scott Corporation makes an $80,000 loan having a nominal interest rate of 18 percent. Interest is payable in advance and there is a required compensating balance of 10 percent. What is the effective interest rate of the loan?

11. Remsen Corporation's factor charges a 5 percent monthly fee. It lends Remsen up to 90 percent of receivables purchased for an additional 2 percent per month. Monthly credit sales are $400,000. With the factoring arrangement, there is a savings in corporate credit checking costs of $3,600 per month and in bad debts of 3.5 percent on credit sales.

Service Bank offers to lend the company up to 90 percent of the receivables. The bank's interest charge will be 2.5 percent per month plus a 4 percent processing charge on receivable lending. The collection period is 30 days, the company borrows the maximum allowed each month.

Is it less expensive to finance with the factor or bank?

Answers to Examination I

1. The prime functions of the financial manager are: (*a*) obtaining financing; (*b*) investing funds; (*c*) managing assets; (*d*) paying out the appropriate amount of dividends; and (*e*) financial forecasting.

2. (*a*) $\text{Accounts receivable turnover} = \dfrac{\text{net credit sales}}{\text{average accounts receivable}} = \dfrac{\$800,000}{\$125,000} = 6.4 \text{ times}$

(*b*) $\text{Collection period} = \dfrac{365}{\text{accounts receivable turnover}} = \dfrac{365}{6.4} = 57 \text{ days}$

(*c*) $\text{Inventory turnover} = \dfrac{\text{cost of goods sold}}{\text{average inventory}} = \dfrac{\$450,000}{\$47,500} = 9.47 \text{ times}$

(*d*) $\text{Age of inventory} = \dfrac{365}{\text{inventory turnover}} = \dfrac{365}{9.47} = 38.5 \text{ days}$

(*e*)   The operating cycle is:

Collection period	57.0 days
Age of inventory	38.5 days
Operating cycle	95.5 days

3. (1) (*c*); (2) (*d*); (3) (*a*); (4) (*g*); (5) (*f*); (6) (*h*); (7) (*e*); (8) (*b*).

4.

		Operating	Investing	Financing	Not applicable
(*a*)	Purchased land		×		
(*b*)	Sold corporate plant		×		
(*c*)	Declared a stock dividend				×
(*d*)	Appropriated retained earnings				×
(*e*)	Issued common stock			×	
(*f*)	Payment for material purchase	×			

5. The cash collections forecast for December is:

October sales ($10,000 × 0.08)		$ 800
November sales		
Discount ($20,000 × 0.70 × 0.98)	$13,720	
No discount ($20,000 × 0.20)	4,000	17,720
Total cash collections		$18,520

6. The proposed lockbox arrangement for Wise Corporation is:

Cost	$115,000
Return on freed cash ($0.16 \times 2 \times \$380,000$)	121,600
	$ 6,600

The lockbox system would save the company $6,000 and should be implemented.

7.

Current average accounts receivable balance ($30,000,000/6$)	$5,000,000
Average accounts receivable balance—after change in policy ($30,000,000/12$)	2,500,000
Reduction in average accounts receivable	$2,500,000
Rate of return	$\times 0.15$
Dollar return	$ 375,000
Cost of discount ($0.25 \times \$30,000,000 \times 0.03$)	$ 225,000
Advantage to discount policy ($\$375,000 - \$225,000$)	$ 150,000

The discount policy is financially feasible.

8. (a)
$$\text{EOQ} = \sqrt{\frac{2SP}{C}} = \sqrt{\frac{2(300)(15)}{8}} = \sqrt{\frac{9,000}{8}} = 34 \text{ (rounded)}$$

(b)
$$\frac{S}{\text{EOQ}} = \frac{300}{34} = 9 \text{ (rounded)}$$

(c)
$$\frac{31}{9} = \text{every 3 days (rounded)}$$

9.
$$\text{Opportunity cost of not taking discount} = \frac{\text{discount percent}}{100 - \text{discount percent}} \times \frac{360}{N} = \frac{4}{96} \times \frac{360}{50} = 30.0\%$$

10.
$$\text{Effective interest rate} = \frac{\text{interest rate} \times \text{principal}}{(\text{proceeds, \%} \times \text{principal}) - \text{interest}}$$
$$= \frac{18\% \times \$80,000}{(90\% \times \$80,000) - \$14,400} = \frac{\$14,400}{\$57,600} = 25\%$$

11. The cost of financing with a factor is:

Purchased receivable ($0.05 \times \$400,000$)	$20,000
Lending fee ($0.02 \times \$400,000 \times 0.90$)	7,200
Total cost	$27,200

The cost of financing with a bank is:

Interest ($0.025 \times \$400,000 \times 0.90$)	$ 9,000
Processing charge ($0.04 \times \$400,000 \times 0.90$)	14,400
Additional cost of not using factor	
Credit costs	3,600
Bad debts ($0.035 \times \$400,000$)	14,000
Total cost	$41,000

It is less expensive to use the factor.

Chapter 6

Time Value of Money

6.1 INTRODUCTION

Time value of money is a critical consideration in financial and investment decisions. For example, *compound interest* calculations are needed to determine future sums of money resulting from an investment. Discounting, or the calculation of *present value*, which is inversely related to compounding, is used to evaluate future cash flow associated with capital budgeting projects. There are plenty of applications of time value of money in finance. The chapter discusses the concepts, calculations, and applications of future values and present values.

6.2 FUTURE VALUES—COMPOUNDING

A dollar in hand today is worth more than a dollar to be received tomorrow because of the interest it could earn from putting it in a savings account or placing it in an investment account. Compounding interest means that interest earns interest. For the discussion of the concepts of compounding and time value, let us define:

F_n = future value = the amount of money at the end of year n
P = principal
i = annual interest rate
n = number of years

Then,

F_1 = the amount of money at the end of year 1
   = principal and interest = $P + iP = P(1 + i)$
F_2 = the amount of money at the end of year 2
   = $F_1(1 + i) = P(1 + i)(1 + i) = P(1 + i)^2$

The future value of an investment compounded annually at rate i for n years is

$$F_n = P(1 + i)^n = P \cdot \text{FVIF}_{i,n}$$

where $\text{FVIF}_{i,n}$ is the future value interest factor for \$1 and can be found in Appendix A.

EXAMPLE 6.1 George Jackson placed \$1,000 in a savings account earning 8 percent interest compounded annually. How much money will he have in the account at the end of 4 years?

$$F_n = P(1 + i)^n$$
$$F_4 = \$1,000(1 + 0.08)^4 = \$1,000 \cdot \text{FVIF}_{8,4}$$

From Appendix A, the FVIF for 4 years at 8 percent is 1.3605. Therefore,

$$F_4 = \$1,000(1.3605) = \$1,360.50$$

EXAMPLE 6.2 Rachael Kahn invested a large sum of money in the stock of TLC Corporation. The company paid a \$3 dividend per share. The dividend is expected to increase by 20 percent per year for the next 3 years. She wishes to project the dividends for years 1 through 3.

$$F_n = P(1 + i)^n$$
$$F_1 = \$3(1 + 0.2)^1 = \$3(1.2000) = \$3.60$$
$$F_2 = \$3(1 + 0.2)^2 = \$3(1.4400) = \$4.32$$
$$F_3 = \$3(1 + 0.2)^3 = \$3(1.7280) = \$5.18$$

Intrayear Compounding

Interest is often compounded more frequently than once a year. Banks, for example, compound interest quarterly, daily, and even continuously. If interest is compounded m times a year, then the general formula for solving for the future value becomes

$$F_n = P\left(1 + \frac{i}{m}\right)^{n \cdot m} = P \cdot \text{FVIF}_{i/m, n \cdot m}$$

The formula reflects more frequent compounding $(n \cdot m)$ at a smaller interest rate per period (i/m). For example, in the case of semiannual compounding $(m = 2)$, the above formula becomes

$$F_n = P\left(1 + \frac{i}{2}\right)^{n \cdot 2} = P \cdot \text{FVIF}_{i/2, n \cdot 2}$$

As m approaches infinity, the term $(1 + i/m)^{n \cdot m}$ approaches $e^{i \cdot n}$, where e is approximately 2.71828, and F_n becomes

$$F_n = P \cdot e^{i \cdot n}$$

The future value increases as m increases. Thus, continuous compounding results in the maximum possible future value at the end of n periods for a given rate of interest.

EXAMPLE 6.3   Assume that $P = \$100$, $i = 12\%$ and $n = 3$ years. Then for

Annual compounding $(m = 1)$: $F_3 = \$100(1 + 0.12)^3 = \$100(1.404)^3 = \$140.49$

Semiannual compounding $(m = 2)$: $F_3 = \$100\left(1 + \dfrac{0.12}{2}\right)^{3 \cdot 2}$

$\qquad\qquad\qquad\qquad\qquad = \$100(1 + 0.06)^6 = \$100(1.4185) = \$141.85$

Quarterly compounding $(m = 4)$: $F_3 = \$100\left(1 + \dfrac{0.12}{4}\right)^{3 \cdot 4} = \$100(1 + 0.03)^{12}$

$\qquad\qquad\qquad\qquad\qquad = \$100(1.4257) = \$142.57$

Monthly compounding $(m = 12)$: $F_3 = \$100\left(1 + \dfrac{0.12}{12}\right)^{3 \cdot 12}$

$\qquad\qquad\qquad\qquad\qquad = \$100(1 + 0.01)^{36} = \$100(1.4307) = \$143.07$

Continuous compounding $(e^{i \cdot n})$: $F_3 = \$100 \cdot e^{(0.12 \cdot 3)} = \$100(2.71828)^{0.36}$

$\qquad\qquad\qquad\qquad\qquad = \$100(1.4333) = \$143.33$

Future Value of an Annuity

An *annuity* is defined as a series of payments (or receipts) of a fixed amount for a specified number of periods. Each payment is assumed to occur at the *end* of the period. The future value of an annuity is a compound annuity which involves depositing or investing an equal sum of money at the end of each year for a certain number of years and allowing it to grow.

Let S_n = the future value of an n-year annuity

$\qquad A$ = the amount of an annuity

Then we can write

$$S_n = A(1 + i)^{n-1} + A(1 + i)^{n-2} + \cdots + A(1 + i)^0$$
$$= A[(i + I)^{n-1} + (1 + i)^{n-2} + \cdots + (1 + i)^0]$$
$$= A \cdot \sum_{t=0}^{n-1} (1 + i)^t = A \cdot \text{FVIFA}_{i,n}$$

where $\text{FVIFA}_{i,n}$ represents the future value interest factor for an n-year annuity compounded at i percent and can be found in Appendix B.

EXAMPLE 6.4   Jane Oak wishes to determine the sum of money she will have in her savings account at the end of 6 years by depositing $1,000 at the end of each year for the next 6 years. The annual interest rate is 8 percent. The FVIFA$_{8\%,6\text{years}}$ is given in Appendix B as 7.336. Therefore,

$$S_6 = \$1,000(\text{FVIFA}_{8,6}) = \$1,000(7.336) = \$7,336$$

6.3   PRESENT VALUE—DISCOUNTING

Present value is the present worth of future sums of money. The process of calculating present values, or *discounting*, is actually the opposite of finding the compounded future value. In connection with present value calculations, the interest rate i is called the *discount rate*.

Recall that

$$F_n = P(1 + i)^n$$

Therefore,

$$P = \frac{F_n}{(1 + i)^n} = F_n \left[\frac{1}{(1 + i)^n} \right] = F_n \cdot \text{PVIF}_{i,n}$$

Where PVIF$_{i,n}$ represents the present value interest factor for $1 and is given in Appendix C.

EXAMPLE 6.5   Ron Jaffe has been given an opportunity to receive $20,000 6 years from now. If he can earn 10 percent on his investments, what is the most he should pay for this opportunity? To answer this question, one must compute the present value of $20,000 to be received 6 years from now at a 10 percent rate of discount. F_6 is $20,000, i is 10 percent, which equals 0.1, and n is 6 years. PVIF$_{10,6}$ from Appendix C is 0.5645.

$$P = \$20,000 \left[\frac{1}{(1 + 0.1)^6} \right] = \$20,000(\text{PVIF}_{10,6}) = \$20,000(0.5645) = \$11,290$$

This means that Ron Jaffe, who can earn 10 percent on his investment, could be indifferent to the choice between receiving $11,290 now or $20,000 6 years from now since the amounts are time equivalent. In other words, he could invest $11,290 today at 10 percent and have $20,000 in 6 years.

Present Value of Mixed Streams of Cash Flows

The present value of a series of mixed payments (or receipts) is the sum of the present value of each individual payment. We know that the present value of each individual payment is the payment times the appropriate PVIF.

EXAMPLE 6.6   Candy Parker has been offered an opportunity to receive the following mixed stream of revenue over the next 3 years:

Year	Revenue
1	$1,000
2	$2,000
3	$500

If she must earn a minimum of 6 percent on her investment, what is the most she should pay today? The present value of this series of mixed streams of revenue is as follows:

Year	Revenue ($)	× PVIF	= Present Value
1	1,000	0.943	$ 943
2	2,000	0.890	1,780
3	500	0.840	420
			$3,143

Present Value of an Annuity

Interest received from bonds, pension funds, and insurance obligations all involve annuities. To compare these financial instruments, we need to know the present value of each. The present value of an annuity (P_n) can be found by using the following equation:

$$P_n = A \cdot \frac{1}{(1+i)^1} + A \cdot \frac{1}{(1+i)^2} + \cdots + A \cdot \frac{1}{(1+i)^n}$$

$$= A \left[\frac{1}{(1+i)^1} + \frac{1}{(1+i)^2} + \cdots + \frac{1}{(1+i)^n} \right]$$

$$= A \cdot \sum_{t=1}^{n} \frac{1}{(1+i)^t} = A \cdot \text{PVIFA}_{i,n}$$

where $\text{PVIFA}_{i,n}$ represents the appropriate value for the present value interest factor for a $1 annuity discounted at i percent for n years and is found in Appendix D.

EXAMPLE 6.7   Assume that the revenues in Example 6.6 form an annuity of $1,000 for 3 years. Then the present value is

$$P_n = A \cdot \text{PVIFA}_{i,n}$$
$$P_3 = \$1,000(\text{PVIFA}_{6,3}) = \$1,000(2.6730) = \$2,673$$

Perpetuities

Some annuities go on forever. Such annuities are called *perpetuities*. An example of a perpetuity is preferred stock which yields a constant dollar dividend indefinitely. The present value of a perpetuity is found as follows:

$$\text{Present value of a perpetuity} = \frac{\text{receipt}}{\text{discount rate}} = \frac{A}{i}$$

EXAMPLE 6.8   Assume that a perpetual bond has an $80-per-year interest payment and that the discount rate is 10 percent. The present value of this perpetuity is:

$$P = \frac{A}{i} = \frac{\$80}{0.10} = \$800$$

6.4   APPLICATIONS OF FUTURE VALUES AND PRESENT VALUES

Future and present values have numerous applications in financial and investment decisions, which will be discussed throughout the book. Five of these applications are presented below.

Deposits to Accumulate a Future Sum (or Sinking Fund)

An individual might wish to find the annual deposit (or payment) that is necessary to accumulate a future sum. To find this future amount (or sinking fund) we can use the formula for finding the future value of an annuity.

$$S_n = A \cdot \text{FVIFA}_{i,n}$$

Solving for A, we obtain:

$$\text{Sinking fund amount} = A = \frac{S_n}{\text{FVIFA}_{i,n}}$$

EXAMPLE 6.9   Mary Czech wishes to determine the equal annual end-of-year deposits required to accumulate $5,000 at the end of 5 years when her son enters college. The interest rate is 10 percent. The annual deposit is:

$$S_5 = \$5,000$$
$$\text{FVIFA}_{10,5} = 6.1051 \quad \text{(from Appendix B)}$$
$$A = \frac{\$5,000}{6.1051} = \$818.99 \cong \$819$$

In other words, if she deposits $819 at the end of each year for 5 years at 10 percent interest, she will have accumulated $5,000 at the end of the fifth year.

Amortized Loans

If a loan is to be repaid in equal periodic amounts, it is said to be an *amortized loan*. Examples include auto loans, mortgage loans, and most commercial loans. The periodic payment can easily be computed as follows:

$$P_n = A \cdot \text{PVIFA}_{i,n}$$

Solving for A, we obtain: Amount of loan $= A = \dfrac{P_n}{\text{PVIFA}_{i,n}}$

EXAMPLE 6.10 Jeff Balthness has a 40-month auto loan of $5,000 at a 12 percent annual interest rate. He wants to find out the monthly loan payment amount.

$$i = 12\% \div 12 \text{ months} = 1\%$$
$$P_{40} = \$5,000$$
$$\text{PVIFA}_{1,40} = 32.8347 \quad \text{(from Appendix D)}$$

Therefore, $A = \dfrac{\$5,000}{32.8347} = \$152.28$

So, to repay the principal and interest on a $5,000, 12 percent, 40-month loan, Jeff Balthness has to pay $152.28 a month for the next 40 months.

EXAMPLE 6.11 Assume that a firm borrows $2,000 to be repaid in three equal installments at the end of each of the next 3 years. The bank wants 12 percent interest. Compute the amount of each payment.

$$P_3 = \$2,000$$
$$\text{PVIFA}_{12,3} = 2.4018$$

Therefore, $A = \dfrac{\$2,000}{2,4018} = \$832.71$

Each loan payment consists partly of interest and partly of principal. The breakdown is often displayed in a *loan amortization schedule*. The interest component is largest in the first period and subsequently declines, whereas the principal portion is smallest in the first period and increases thereafter, as shown in the following example.

EXAMPLE 6.12 Using the same data as in Example 6.11, we set up the following amortization schedule:

Year	Payment	Interest	Repayment of Principal	Remaining Balance
1	$832.71	$240,00[a]	$592.71	$1,407.29
2	$832.71	$168.88	$663.83	$ 743.46
3	$832.68[b]	$ 89.22	$743.46[c]	

[a] Interest is computed by multiplying the loan balance at the beginning of the year by the interest rate. Therefore, interest in year 1 is $2,000(0.12) = $240; in year 2 interest is $1,407.29(0.12) = $168.88; and in year 3 interest is $743.46(0.12) = $89.22. All figures are rounded.

[b] Last payment is adjusted downward.

[c] Not exact because of accumulated rounding errors.

Annual Percentage Rate (APR)

Different types of investments use different compounding periods. For example, most bonds pay interest semiannually; banks generally pay interest quarterly. If an investor wishes to compare investments with different compounding periods, he or she needs to put them on a common basis. The *annual percentage rate* (APR), or effective annual rate, is used for this purpose and is computed as follows:

$$APR = \left(1 + \frac{r}{m}\right)^m - 1.0$$

where r = the stated, nominal or quoted rate and m = the number of compounding periods per year.

EXAMPLE 6.13   If the nominal rate is 6 percent, compounded *quarterly*, the APR is

$$APR = \left(1 + \frac{r}{m}\right)^m - 1.0 = \left(1 + \frac{0.06}{4}\right)^4 - 1.0 = (1.015)^4 - 1.0 = 1.0614 - 1.0 = 0.0614 = 6.14\%$$

This means that if one bank offered 6 percent with quarterly compounding, while another offered 6.14 percent with annual compounding, they would both be paying the same effective rate of interest.

Rates of Growth

In finance, it is necessary to calculate the *compound annual interest rate*, or rate of growth, associated with a stream of earnings.

EXAMPLE 6.14   Assume that the Geico Company has earnings per share of $2.50 in 19X1, and 10 years later the earnings per share has increased to $3.70. The compound annual rate of growth of the earnings per share can be computed as follows:

$$F_n = P \cdot FVIF_{i,n}$$

Solving this for FVIF, we obtain:

$$FVIF_{i,n} = \frac{F_n}{P}$$

$$FVIF_{i,10} = \frac{\$3.70}{\$2.50} = 1.48$$

From Appendix A an FVIF of 1.48 at 10 years is at $i = 4\%$. The compound annual rate of growth is therefore 4 percent.

Bond Values

Bonds call for the payment of a specific amount of interest for a stated number of years *and* the repayment of the face value at the bond's maturity. Thus, a bond represents an annuity plus a lump sum. Its value is found as the present value of this payment stream. The interest is usually paid semiannually.

$$V = \sum_{t=1}^{n} \frac{I}{(1+r)^t} + \frac{M}{(1+r)^n}$$
$$= I(PVIFA_{r,n}) + M(PVIF_{r,n})$$

where I = interest payment per period
   M = par value, or maturity value, usually $1,000
   r = investor's required rate of return
   n = number of periods

This topic is covered in more detail in Chapter 7, "Risk, Return, and Valuation."

EXAMPLE 6.15 Assume there is a 10-year bond with a 10 percent coupon, paying interest semiannually and having a face value of $1,000. Since interest is paid semiannually, the number of periods involved is 20 and the semiannual cash inflow is $100/2 = $50.

Assume that investors have a required rate of return of 12 percent for this type of bond. Then, the present value (V) of this bond is:

$$V = \$50(\text{PVIFA}_{6,20}) + \$1,000(\text{PVIF}_{6,20})$$
$$= \$50(11.4699) + \$1,000(0.3118) = \$573.50 + \$311.80 = \$885.30$$

Note that the required rate of return (12 percent) is higher than the coupon rate of interest (10 percent), and so the bond value (or the price investors are willing to pay for this particular bond) is less than its $1,000 face value.

Review Questions

1. _____ is a critical consideration in many financial and investment decisions.

2. The process of determining present value is often called _____ and is the reverse of the _____ process.

3. $F_n = P(1 + i/m)^{n \cdot m}$ is a general formula used for _____ .

4. _____ results in the maximum possible future value at the end of n periods for a given rate of interest.

5. A(n) _____ is a series of payments (or receipts) of a fixed amount for a specified number of periods.

6. The _____ , or effective annual rate, is used to compare investments with different _____ on a common basis.

7. The present value of a mixed stream of payments (or receipts) is the _____ of present values of _____ .

8. A(n) _____ is an annuity in which payments go on forever.

9. The _____ is the annual deposit (or payment) of an amount that is necessary to accumulate a specified future sum.

10. If a loan is to be repaid in equal periodic amounts, it is said to be a(n) _____ .

Answers: (1) Time value of money; (2) discounting, compounding; (3) intrayear compounding; (4) Continuous compounding; (5) annuity; (6) annual percentage rate (APR), compounding periods; (7) sum, the individual payments; (8) perpetuity; (9) sinking fund; (10) amortized loan.

Solved Problems

6.1 **Future Value.** Compute the future values of (*a*) an initial $2,000 compounded annually for 10 years at 8 percent; (*b*) an initial $2,000 compounded annually for 10 years at 10 percent; (*c*) an annuity of $2,000 for 10 years at 8 percent; and (*d*) an annuity of $2,000 for 10 years at 10 percent.

SOLUTION

(*a*) To find the future value of an investment compounded annually, use:

$$F_n = P(1 + i)^n = P \cdot \text{FVIF}_{i,n}$$

In this case, $P = \$2,000$, $i = 8\%$, $n = 10$, and $\text{FVIF}_{8\%,10\text{yr}} = 2.1589$. Therefore,

$$F_{10} = \$2,000(1 + 0.08)^{10} = \$2,000(2.1589) = \$4,317.80$$

(*b*) $$F_n = P(1 + i)^n = P \cdot \text{FVIF}_{i,n}$$

Here $P = \$2,000$, $i = 10\%$, $n = 10$, and $\text{FVIF}_{10,10} = 2.5937$. Therefore,

$$F_{10} = \$2,000(1 + 0.10)^{10} = \$2,000(2.5937) = \$5,187.40$$

(*c*) For the future value of an annuity, use:

$$S_n = A \cdot \text{FVIFA}_{i,n}$$

In this case $A = \$2,000$, $i = 8\%$, $n = 10$, and $\text{FVIFA}_{8\%,10\text{yr}} = 14.486$. Therefore,

$$S_{10} = \$2,000(14.486) = \$28,972$$

(*d*) $$S_n = A \cdot \text{FVIFA}_{i,n}$$

Here, $A = \$2,000$, $i = 10\%$, and $\text{FVIFA}_{10,10} = 15.937$. Therefore,

$$S_{10} = \$2,000(15.937) = \$31,874$$

6.2 **Intrayear Compounding.** Calculate how much you would have in a savings account 5 years from now if you invest $1,000 today, given that the interest paid is 8 percent compounded: (*a*) annually; (*b*) semiannually; (*c*) quarterly; and (*d*) continuously.

SOLUTION

A general formula for intrayear compounding is:

$$F_n = P(1 + i/m)^{n \cdot m} = P \cdot \text{FVIF}_{i/m, n \cdot m}$$

For this problem $P = \$1,000$ and $n = 5$ years.

(*a*) When $m = 1$, $i = 8\%$, and $\text{FVIF}_{(8\%/1),5 \cdot 1} = 1.4693$,

$$F_5 = \$1,000\left(1 + \frac{0.08}{1}\right)^{5 \cdot 1} = \$1,000(1.4693) = \$1,469.30$$

(*b*) When $m = 2$ and $\text{FVIF}_{(8\%/2),5 \cdot 2} = \text{FVIF}_{4,10} = 1.4802$,

$$F_5 = \$1,000(1.4802) = \$1,480.20$$

(*c*) $m = 4$ and $\text{FVIF}_{(8\%/4),5 \cdot 4} = \text{FVIF}_{2,20} = 1.4859$,

$$F_5 = \$1,000(1.4859) = \$1,485.90$$

(*d*) For continuous compounding, use:

$$F_n = P \cdot e^{i \cdot n}$$

$$F_5 = \$1,000(2.71828)^{0.08 \cdot 5} = \$1,000(2.71828)^{0.4}$$

$$= \$1,000(1.4918) = \$1,491.80$$

6.3 **Present Value.** Calculate the present value, discounted at 10 percent, of receiving: (*a*) $800 at the end of year 4; (*b*) $200 at the end of year 3 and $300 at the end of year 5, (*c*) $500 at the end of year 4 and $300 at the end of year 6, and (*d*) $500 a year for the next 10 years.

SOLUTION

(*a*)

$$P = F_n \left[\frac{1}{(1+i)^n} \right] = F_n \cdot \text{PVIF}_{i,n}$$

Here $n = 4$, $F_4 = \$800$, and $i = 10\%$.

$$\text{PVIF}_{10,4} = 0.6830$$
$$P = \$800(0.6830) = \$546.40$$

(*b*)
$$P = \$200(\text{PVIF}_{10,3}) + \$300(\text{PVIF}_{10,5})$$
$$= \$200(0.7513) + \$300(0.6209) = \$150.26 + \$186.27 = \$336.53$$

(*c*)
$$P = \$500(\text{PVIF}_{10,4}) + \$300(\text{PVIF}_{10,6}) = \$500(0.6830) + \$300(0.5645)$$
$$= \$341.50 + \$169.35 = \$510.85$$

(*d*)   For the present value of an annuity, use:

$$P_n = A \cdot \text{PVIFA}_{i,n}$$

Here $A = \$500$, $n = 10$, and $i = 10\%$. Therefore,

$$P_{10} = \$500(\text{PVIFA}_{10,10}) = \$500(6.1446) = \$3,072.30$$

6.4 **Present Value.** Calculate the present value of the following future cash inflows discounted at 10 percent: (*a*) $1,000 a year for years 1 through 10; (*b*) $1,000 a year for years 5 through 10; and (*c*) $1,000 a year for years 1 through 3, nothing in years 4 through 5, then $2,000 a year for years 6 through 10.

SOLUTION

(*a*)
$$P_n = A \cdot \text{PVIFA}_{i,n}$$

Here $A = \$1,000$, $i = 10\%$, and $n = 10$ years. Therefore,

$$P_{10} = \$1,000(\text{PVIFA}_{10,10}) = \$1,000(6.1446) = \$6,144.60$$

(*b*)
$$P = \$1,000(\text{PVIFA}_{10,10}) - \$1,000(\text{PVIFA}_{10,4})$$
$$= \$1,000(6.1446) - \$1,000(3.1699) = \$6,144.60 - \$3,169.90 = \$2,974.70$$

This type of annuity is called a *deferred annuity*.

(*c*)
$$P = \$1,000(\text{PVIFA}_{10,3}) + [\$2,000(\text{PVIFA}_{10,10}) - \$2,000(\text{PVIFA}_{10,5})]$$
$$= \$1,000(2.4869) + [\$2,000(6.1446) - \$2,000(3.7908)]$$
$$= \$2,486.90 + [\$12,289.2 - \$7,581.60] = \$2,466.90 + \$4,707.60 = \$7,194.5$$

6.5 **Present Value.** Your favorite uncle has offered you the choice of the following options. He will give you either $2,000 1 year from now or $3,000 4 years from now. Which would you choose if the discount rate is (*a*) 10 percent? (*b*) 20 percent?

SOLUTION

$$P = F_n \cdot \text{PVIF}_{i,n}$$

(*a*)   Option 1: $2,000 one year from now. In this case $i = 10\%$, $n = 1$, $F_1 = \$2,000$, and $\text{PVIF}_{10,1} = 0.9091$. Therefore,

$$P = \$2,000(0.9091) = \$1,818.20$$

Option 2: $3,000 four years from now. In this case $i = 10\%$, $n = 4$, $F_4 = \$3,000$, and $\text{PVIF}_{10,4} = 0.6830$. Therefore,

$$P = \$3,000(0.6830) = \$2,049$$

At 10 percent, the best choice is $3,000 four years from now.

(b)   Option 1: $2,000 one year from now. In this case $i = 20\%$, $n = 1$, $F_1 = \$2,000$, and $\text{PVIF}_{20,1} = 0.8333$. Therefore,

$$P = \$2,000(0.8333) = \$1,666.60$$

Option 2: $3,000 four years from now. In this case $i = 20\%$, $n = 4$, $F_4 = \$3,000$, and $\text{PVIF}_{20,4} = 0.4823$. Therefore,

$$P = \$3,000(0.4823) = \$1,446.9$$

At 20 percent, the best choice is $2,000 one year from now.

6.6   **Present value.** A 55-year-old executive will retire at age 65 and expects to live to age 75. Assuming a 10 percent rate of return, calculate the amount he must have available at age 65 in order to receive $10,000 annually from retirement until death. (CFA, adapted.)

SOLUTION

This problem involves finding the present value of an annuity. The executive must have $61,446 available at age 65, calculated as follows:

$$P_n = A \cdot \text{PVIFA}_{i,n}$$

Here $A = \$10,000$, $n = 10$, $i = 10\%$, and $\text{PVIFA}_{10,10} = 6.1446$. Therefore,

$$P_{10} = \$10,000(6.1446) = \$61,446$$

6.7   **Present Value.** Your father is about to retire. His firm has given him the option of retiring with a lump sum of $20,000 or an annuity of $2,500 for 10 years. Which is worth more now, if an interest rate of 6 percent is used for the annuity?

SOLUTION

$$P_n = A \cdot \text{PVIF}_{i,n}$$

Here $A = \$2,500$, $i = 6\%$, $n = 10$, and $\text{PVIFA}_{6,10} = 7.3601$. Therefore,

$$P_{10} = \$2,500(\text{PVIFA}_{6,10}) = \$2,500(7.3601) = \$18,400.25$$

The lump sum of $20,000 is worth more now.

6.8   **Perpetuities.** What is the present value of a perpetuity of $80 per year if the discount rate is 11 percent.

SOLUTION

$$\text{The present value of a perpetuity} = \frac{A}{i} = \frac{\$80}{11\%} = \$727.27$$

6.9   **Deposits Required.** If you need $6,000 5 years from now, how much of a deposit must you make in your savings account each year, assuming an 8 percent annual interest rate?

SOLUTION

Solving $S_n = A \cdot \text{FVIFA}_{i,n}$ for A yields:

$$A = \frac{S_n}{\text{FVIFA}_{i,n}}$$

In this problem $S_5 = \$6,000$, $i = 8\%$, $n = 5$, and $\text{FVIFA}_{8,5} = 5.8666$. Therefore,

$$A = \frac{\$6,000}{5.8666} = \$1,022.74$$

6.10   Sinking Fund. A $1 million bond issue is outstanding. Assume deposits earn 8 percent per annum. Calculate the amount to be deposited to a sinking fund each year in order to accumulate enough money to retire the entire $1 million issue at the end of 20 years. (CFA, adapted.)

SOLUTION

$$A = \frac{S_n}{\text{FVIFA}_{i,n}}$$

In this problem, $S_{20} = \$1,000,000$ and $\text{FVIFA}_{8,20} = 45.762$. Therefore,

$$A = \frac{\$1,000,000}{45.762} = \$21,852.19$$

6.11   Loan Amortization. You have applied for a home mortgage of $75,000 to finance the purchase of a new home for 30 years. The bank requires a 14 percent interest rate. What will be the annual payment?

SOLUTION

Solving $P_n = A \cdot \text{PVIFA}_{i,n}$ for A yields:

$$A = \frac{P_n}{\text{PVIFA}_{i,n}}$$

Here $P_{30} = \$75,000$ and $\text{PVIFA}_{14,30} = 7.0027$. Therefore,

$$A = \frac{\$75,000}{7.0027} = \$10,710.16$$

6.12   Loan Amortization. A commercial bank is willing to make you a loan of $10,000. The bank wants a 12 percent interest rate and requires five equal annual payments to repay both interest and principal. What will be the dollar amount of the annual payment?

SOLUTION

$$A = \frac{P_n}{\text{PVIFA}_{i,n}}$$

Here $P_5 = \$10,000$ and $\text{PVIFA}_{12,5} = 3.6048$. Therefore,

$$A = \frac{\$10,000}{3.6048} = \$2,774.08$$

6.13   Loan Amortization Schedule. Set up an amortization schedule for a $5,000 loan to be repaid in equal installments at the end of each of the next 3 years. The interest rate is 15 percent.

SOLUTION

First, find the amount of equal installment by using the following formula:

$$A = \frac{P_n}{PVIFA_{i,n}}$$

In this problem $P_3 = \$5,000$ and $PVIFA_{15,3} = 2.2832$. Therefore,

$$A = \frac{\$5,000}{2.2832} = \$2,189.91$$

The amortization schedule is as follows:

Year	Payment	Interest[a]	Repayment of Principal	Remaining Balance
1	$2,189.91	$750	$1,439.91	$3,560.09
2	$2,189.91	$534.01	$1,655.90	$1,904.19
3	$2,189.82[b]	$285.63	$1,904.19[c]	

[a] Interest is computed by multiplying the loan balance at the beginning of the year by the interest rate. Therefore, interest in year 1 is $5,000(0.15) = \$750$; in year 2 interest is $3,560.09(0.15) = \$534.01$; etc.

[b] Last payment is adjusted downward.

[c] Not exact because of accumulated rounding errors.

6.14 **Annual Percentage Rate (APR).** Suppose that a company borrows $20,000 for 1 year at a stated rate of interest of 9 percent. What is the annual percentage rate (APR) if interest is paid to the lender (*a*) annually? (*b*) semiannually? (*c*) quarterly?

SOLUTION

$$APR = \left(1 + \frac{r}{m}\right)^m - 1.0$$

In this problem $r = 9\% = 0.09$.

(*a*) If interest is paid at the end of the year, $m = 1$ and

$$APR = \left(1 + \frac{0.09}{1}\right)^1 - 1.0 = 1.09 - 1.0 = 0.09 = 9.0\%$$

(*b*) If the interest is paid at the end of each 6-month period, $m = 2$ and

$$APR = \left(1 + \frac{0.09}{2}\right)^2 - 1.0 = (1.045)^2 - 1.0$$

$$= 1.092 - 1.0 = 0.092 = 9.2\%$$

(*c*) If interest is paid at the end of each quarter, $m = 4$ and

$$APR = \left(1 + \frac{0.09}{4}\right)^4 - 1.0 = (1.0225)^4 - 1.0$$

$$= 1.093 - 1.0 = 0.093 = 9.3\%$$

More frequent payment of interest increases the effective annual cost paid by the company.

6.15 **Rate of Growth.** If a firm's earnings increase from $3.00 per share to $4.02 over a 6-year period, what is the rate of growth?

SOLUTION

Solving $F_n = P \cdot \text{FVIF}_{i,n}$ for FVIF yields:

$$\text{FVIF}_{i,n} = \frac{F_n}{P}$$

Here, $P = \$3.00$ and $F_6 = \$4.02$. Therefore,

$$\text{FVIF}_{i,6} = \frac{\$4.02}{\$3.00} = 1.340$$

From Appendix A, an FVIF of 1.340 at 6 years is at $i = 5\%$. The rate of growth of earnings is therefore 5 percent.

6.16 **Annual Rate of Interest.** You borrowed \$20,000, to be repaid in 12 monthly installments of \$1,891.20. What is the annual interest rate?

SOLUTION

Solving $P_n = A \cdot \text{PVIFA}_{i,n}$ for PVIFA yields:

$$\text{PVIFA}_{i,n} = \frac{P_n}{A}$$

In this problem $P_{12} = \$20,000$ and $A = \$1,891.20$. Therefore,

$$\text{PVIFA}_{i,12} = \frac{\$20,000}{\$1,891.20} = 10.5753$$

From Appendix D, a PVIFA of 10.5753 for 12 periods is at $i = 2\%$. The annual interest rate is therefore $2\% \times 12 = 24\%$.

6.17 **Bond Value.** What amount should an investor be willing to pay for a \$1,000, 5-year United States government bond which pays \$50 interest semiannually and is sold to yield 8 percent?

SOLUTION

The semiannual interest is 4 percent. The value of the bond is:

$$\begin{aligned}
V &= I(\text{PVIFA}_{r,n}) + M(\text{PVIF}_{r,n}) \\
&= \$50(\text{PVIFA}_{4,10}) + \$1,000(\text{PVIF}_{4,10}) \\
&= \$50(8.1109) + \$1,000(0.6756) = \$405.55 + \$675.60 = \$1,081.15
\end{aligned}$$

6.18 **Bond Values.** Calculate the value of a bond with a face value of \$1,000, a coupon interest rate of 8 percent paid semiannually, and a maturity of 10 years. Assume the following discount rates: (a) 6 percent; (b) 8 percent; and (c) 10 percent.

SOLUTION

$$\text{Semiannual interest} = \frac{8\%(\$1,000)}{2} = \$40$$

$$\text{Number of periods} = 10 \times 2 = 20 \text{ periods}$$

(a)
$$\begin{aligned}
V &= I(\text{PVIA}_{r,n}) + M(\text{PVIF}_{r,n}) \\
&= \$40(\text{PVIFA}_{3,20}) + \$1,000(\text{PVIF}_{3,20}) \\
&= \$40(14.8775) + \$1,000(0.5537) = \$595.10 + \$553.7 = \$1,148.80
\end{aligned}$$

(b)
$$\begin{aligned}
V &= \$40(\text{PVIFA}_{4,20}) + \$1,000(\text{PVIF}_{4,20}) \\
&= \$40(13.5903) + \$1,000(0.4564) = \$543.61 + \$456.40 = \$1,000 \text{ (rounded)}
\end{aligned}$$

(c)
$$\begin{aligned}
V &= \$40(\text{PVIFA}_{5,20}) + \$1,000(\text{PVIF}_{5,20}) \\
&= \$40(12.4622) + \$1,000(0.3769) = \$498.49 + \$376.90 = \$875.37
\end{aligned}$$

Chapter 7

Risk, Return, and Valuation

7.1 RISK DEFINED

Risk (or uncertainty) refers to the variability of expected returns associated with a given investment. Risk, along with the concept of return, is a key consideration in investment and financial decisions. This chapter will discuss procedures for measuring risk and investigate the relationship between risk, returns, and security valuation.

Probability Distributions

Probabilities are used to evaluate the risk involved in a security. The *probability* of an event taking place is defined as the chance that the event will occur. It may be thought of as the percentage chance of a given outcome.

EXAMPLE 7.1   A weather forecaster may state, "There is a 30 percent chance of rain tomorrow and a 70 percent chance of no rain." Then we could set up the following probability distribution:

Outcome	Probability
Rain	30% = 0.3
No rain	70% = 0.7
	100% = 1.00

Expected Rate of Return

Expected rate of return ($\bar{r}$) is the weighted average of possible returns from a given investment, weights being probabilities. Mathematically,

$$\bar{r} = \sum_{i=1}^{n} r_i p_i$$

where r_i = ith possible return
  p_i = probability of the ith return
  n = number of possible returns

EXAMPLE 7.2   Consider the possible rates of return that you might earn next year on a $50,000 investment in stock A or on a $50,000 investment in stock B, depending upon the states of the economy: recession, normal, and prosperity.
For stock A:

State of Economy	Return (r_i)	Probability (p_i)
Recession	−5%	0.2
Normal	20%	0.6
Prosperity	40%	0.2

For stock B:

State of Economy	Return (r_i)	Probability (p_i)
Recession	10%	0.2
Normal	15%	0.6
Prosperity	20%	0.2

171

Then the expected rate of return ($\bar{r}$) for stock A is computed as follows:

$$\bar{r} = \sum_{i=1}^{n} r_i p_i = (-5\%)(0.2) + (20\%)(0.6) + (40\%)(0.2) = 19\%$$

Stock B's expected rate of return is:

$$\bar{r} = (10\%)(0.2) + (15\%)(0.6) + 20\%(0.2) = 15\%$$

Measuring Risk: The Standard Deviation

The standard deviation (σ), which is a measure of dispersion of the probability distribution, is commonly used to measure risk. The smaller the standard deviation, the tighter the probability distribution and, thus, the lower the risk of the investment.

Mathematically,

$$\sigma = \sqrt{\sum_{i=1}^{n} (r_i - \bar{r})^2 p_i}$$

To calculate σ, take the following steps:

Step 1.   Compute the expected rate of return ($\bar{r}$).

Step 2.   Subtract each possible return from $\bar{r}$ to obtain a set of deviations ($r_i - \bar{r}$).

Step 3.   Square each deviation, multiply the squared deviation by the probability of occurrence for its respective return, and sum these products to obtain the *variance* (σ^2):

$$\sigma^2 = \sum_{i=1}^{n} (r_i - \bar{r})^2 p_i$$

Step 4.   Finally, take the square root of the variance to obtain the standard deviation (σ).

To follow this step-by-step approach, it is convenient to set up a table.

EXAMPLE 7.3   Using the data given in Example 7.2, compute the standard deviation for each stock and set up the tables as follows for stock A:

Return (r_i) (%)	Probability (p_i)	Step 1 $r_i p$ (%)	Step 2 ($r_i - \bar{r}$)(%)	($r_i - \bar{r}$)^2	Step 3 ($r_i - \bar{r}$)$^2 p_i$(%)
−5	0.2	−1	−24	576	115.2
20	0.6	12	1	1	0.6
40	0.2	8	21	441	88.2
		$\bar{r} = $ 19			$\sigma^2 = 204$

Knowing $\sigma^2 = 204$, we proceed with Step 4 and

$$\sigma = \sqrt{204} = 14.28\%$$

For stock B:

Return (r_i) (%)	Probability (p_i)	Step 1 $r_i p_i$ (%)	Step 2 ($r_i - \bar{r}$)(%)	($r_i - \bar{r}$)^2	Step 3 ($r_i - \bar{r}$)$^2 p_i$(%)
10	0.2	2	−5	25	5
15	0.6	9	0	0	0
20	0.2	4	5	25	5
		$\bar{r} = $ 15			$\sigma^2 = 10$

Knowing $\sigma^2 = 10$, we take Step 4 and

$$\sigma = \sqrt{10} = 3.16\%$$

Statistically, if the probability distribution is *normal*, 68 percent of the returns will lie in ± 1 standard deviation, 95 percent of all observations will lie between ± 2 standard deviations, and 99 percent of all observations will lie between ± 3 standard deviations of the expected value.

EXAMPLE 7.4   Using the results from Example 7.3,

	Stock A	Stock B
Expected return ($\bar{r}$)	19%	15%
Standard deviation (σ)	14.28%	3.16%

For stock A, there is a 68 percent probability that the actual return will be in the range of 19 percent plus or minus 14.28 percent or from 4.72 percent to 33.28 percent. Since the range is so great, stock A is risky; it is likely to either fall far below its expected rate of return or far exceed the expected return. For stock B, the 68 percent range is 15 percent plus or minus 3.16 percent or from 11.84 percent to 18.16 percent. With such a small σ, there is only a small probability that stock B's return will be far less or greater than expected; hence, stock B is not very risky.

Measure of Relative Risk: Coefficient of Variation

One must be careful when using the standard deviation to compare risk since it is only an absolute measure of dispersion (risk) and does not consider the dispersion of outcomes in relationship to an expected value (return). Therefore, when comparing securities that have different expected returns, use the coefficient of variation. The coefficient of variation is computed simply by dividing the standard deviation for a security by expected value: $\sigma / \bar{r}$. The higher the coefficient, the more risky the security.

EXAMPLE 7.5   Again, using the results from Example 7.3:

	Stock A	Stock B
$\bar{r}$	19%	15%
σ	14.28%	3.16%
$\sigma / \bar{r}$	0.75%	0.21%

Although stock A is expected to produce a considerably higher return than stock B, stock A is overall more risky than stock B, based on the computed coefficient variation.

Types of Risk

The various risks that must be considered when making financial and investment decisions are as follows:

1. *Business risk* is caused by fluctuations of earnings before interest and taxes (operating income). Business risk depends on variability in demand, sales price, input prices, and amount of operating leverage.

2. *Liquidity risk* represents the possibility that an asset may not be sold on short notice for its market value. If an asset must be sold at a high discount, then it is said to have a substantial amount of liquidity risk.

3. *Default risk* is the risk that a borrower will be unable to make interest payments or principal repayments on debt. For example, there is a great amount of default risk inherent in the bonds of a company experiencing financial difficulty.

4. *Market risk* is the risk that a stock's price will change due to changes in the stock market atmosphere as a whole since prices of all stocks are correlated to some degree with broad swings in the stock market.

5. *Interest rate risk* is the risk resulting from fluctuations in the value of an asset as interest rates change. For example, if interest rates rise (fall), bond prices fall (rise).

6. *Purchasing power risk* is the risk that a rise in price will reduce the quantity of goods that can be purchased with a fixed sum of money.

7.2   PORTFOLIO RISK AND CAPITAL ASSET PRICING MODEL (CAPM)

Most financial assets are not held in isolation; rather, they are held as parts of portfolios. Therefore, risk-return analysis (discussed in Section 7.1) should not be confined to single assets only. It is important to look at portfolios and the gains from diversification. What is important is the return on the portfolio, not just the return on one asset, and the portfolio's risk.

Portfolio Return

The expected return on a portfolio (r_p) is simply the weighted average return of the individual assets in the portfolio, the weights being the fraction of the total funds invested in each asset:

$$r_p = w_1 r_1 + w_2 r_2 + \cdots + w_n r_n = \sum_{j=1}^{n} w_j r_j$$

where r_j = expected return on each individual asset
           w_j = fraction for each respective asset investment
           n = number of assets in the portfolio

$$\sum_{j=1}^{n} w_j = 1.0$$

EXAMPLE 7.6   A portfolio consists of assets A and B. Asset A makes up one-third of the portfolio and has an expected return of 18 percent. Asset B makes up the other two-thirds of the portfolio and is expected to earn 9 percent. What is the expected return on the portfolio?

Asset	Return (r_j)	Fraction (w_j)	$w_j r_j$
A	18%	$\frac{1}{3}$	$\frac{1}{3} \times 18\% = $ 6%
B	9%	$\frac{2}{3}$	$\frac{2}{3} \times 9\% = $ 6%
			$r_p = $ 12%

Portfolio Risk

Unlike returns, the risk of a portfolio (σ_p) is not simply the weighted average of the standard deviations of the individual assets in the contribution, for a portfolio's risk is also dependent on the correlation coefficients of its assets. The correlation coefficient (ρ) is a measure of the degree to which two variables "move" together. It has a numerical value that ranges from -1.0 to 1.0. In a two-asset (A and B) portfolio, the portfolio risk is defined as:

$$\sigma_p = \sqrt{w_A^2 \sigma_A^2 + w_B^2 \sigma_B^2 + 2 w_A w_B \cdot \rho_{AB} \sigma_A \sigma_B}$$

where σ_A and σ_B = standard deviations of assets A and B, respectively

w_A and w_B = weights, or fractions, of total funds invested in assets A and B

ρ_{AB} = the correlation coefficient between assets A and B

Portfolio risk can be minimized by *diversification*, or by combining assets in an appropriate manner. The degree to which risk is minimized depends on the correlation between the assets being combined. For example, by combining two *perfectly negative* correlated assets ($\rho = -1$), the overall portfolio risk can be completely eliminated. Combining two *perfectly positive* correlated assets ($\rho = +1$) does nothing to help reduce risk. (See Example 7.7.) An example of the latter might be ownership of two automobile stocks or two housing stocks.

EXAMPLE 7.7 Assume the following:

Asset	σ	w
A	20%	$\frac{1}{3}$
B	10%	$\frac{2}{3}$

The portfolio risk then is:

$$\sigma_p = \sqrt{w_A^2 \sigma_A^2 + w_B^2 \sigma_B^2 + 2 w_A w_B \cdot \rho_{AB} \sigma_A \sigma_B}$$
$$= \sqrt{(\tfrac{1}{3})^2 (0.2)^2 + (\tfrac{2}{3})^2 (0.1)^2 + 2\rho_{AB}(\tfrac{1}{3})(\tfrac{2}{3})(0.2)(0.1)}$$
$$= \sqrt{0.0089 + 0.0089\rho_{AB}}$$

(a) Now assume that the correlation coefficient between A and B is +1 (a perfectly positive correlation). This means that when the value of asset A increases in response to market conditions, so does the value of asset B, and it does so at exactly same rate as A. The portfolio risk when $\rho = +1$ then becomes:

$$\sigma_p = \sqrt{0.0089 + 0.0089\rho_{AB}} = \sqrt{0.0089 + 0.0089(1)} = \sqrt{0.0178} = 0.1334 = 13.34\%$$

(b) If $\rho = 0$, the assets lack correlation and the portfolio risk is simply the risk of the expected returns on the assets, i.e., the weighted average of the standard deviations of the individual assets in the portfolio. Therefore, when $\rho_{AB} = 0$, the portfolio risk for this example is:

$$\sigma_p = \sqrt{0.0089 + 0.089\rho_{AB}} = \sqrt{0.0089 + 0.0089(0)} = \sqrt{0.0089} = 0.0943 = 9.43\%$$

(c) If $\rho = -1$ (a perfectly negative correlation coefficient), then as the price of A rises, the price of B declines at the very same rate. In such a case, risk would be completely eliminated. Therefore, when $\rho_{AB} = -1$, the portfolio risk is

$$\sigma_p = \sqrt{0.0089 + 0.0089\rho_{AB}} = \sqrt{0.0089 + 0.0089(-1)} = \sqrt{0.0089 - 0.0089} = \sqrt{0} = 0$$

When we compare the results of (a); (b); and (c), we see that a positive correlation between assets increases a portfolio's risk above the level found at zero correlation, while a perfectly negative correlation eliminates that risk.

EXAMPLE 7.8 To illustrate the point of diversification, assume the data on the following three securities are as follows:

Year	Security X (%)	Security Y (%)	Security Z (%)
19X1	10	50	10
19X2	20	40	20
19X3	30	30	30
19X4	40	20	40
19X5	50	10	50
r_j	30	30	30
σ_j	14.14	14.14	14.14

Note here that securities X and Y have a perfectly negative correlation, and securities X and Z have a perfectly positive correlation. Notice what happens to the portfolio risk when X and Y, and X and Z are combined. Assume that funds are split equally between the two securities in each portfolio.

Year	Portfolio XY (50%–50%)	Portfolio XZ (50%–50%)
19X1	30	10
19X2	30	20
19X3	30	30
19X4	30	40
19X5	30	50
r_p	30	30
σ_p	0	14.14

Again, see that the two perfectly negative correlated securities (XY) result in a zero overall risk.

Capital Asset Pricing Model (CAPM)

A security risk consists of two components—diversifiable risk and nondiversifiable risk. *Diversifiable risk*, sometimes called *controllable risk* or *unsystematic risk*, represents the portion of a security's risk that can be controlled through diversification. This type of risk is unique to a given security. Business, liquidity, and default risks fall into this category. *Nondiversifiable risk*, sometimes referred to as *noncontrollable risk* or *systematic risk*, results from forces outside of the firm's control and is therefore not unique to the given security. Purchasing power, interest rate, and market risks fall into this category. Nondiversifiable risk is assessed relative to the risk of a diversified portfolio of securities, or the *market portfolio*. This type of risk is measured by the *beta* coefficient.

The capital asset pricing model (CAPM) relates the risk measured by beta to the level of expected or required rate of return on a security. The model, also called the security market line (SML), is given as follows:

$$r_j = r_f + b(r_m - r_f)$$

where r_j = the expected (or required) return on security j
r_f = the risk-free security (such as a T-bill)
r_m = the expected return on the market portfolio (such as Standard & Poor's 500 Stock Composite Index or Dow Jones 30 Industrials)
b = beta, an index of nondiversifiable (noncontrollable, systematic) risk

The key component in the CAPM, beta (b), is a measure of the security's volatility relative to that of an average security. For example: b = 0.5 means the security is only half as volatile, or risky, as the average security; b = 1.0 means the security is of average risk; and b = 2.0 means the security is twice as risky as the average risk.

The whole term $b(r_m - r_f)$ represents the risk premium, the additional return required to compensate investors for assuming a given level of risk.

Thus, in words, the CAPM (or SML) equation shows that the required (expected) rate of return on a given security (r_j) is equal to the return required for securities that have no risk (r_f) plus a risk premium required by investors for assuming a given level of risk. The higher the degree of systematic risk (b), the higher the return on a given security demanded by investors. Figure 7.1 graphically illustrates the CAPM as the *security market line*.

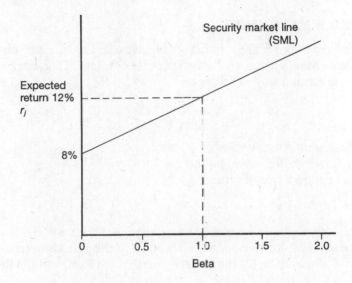

Fig. 7-1 CAPM as security market line

EXAMPLE 7.9 Assuming that the risk-free rate (r_f) is 8 percent, and the expected return for the market (r_m) is 12 percent, then if

$b = 0$ (risk-free security)	$r_j = 8\% + 0(12\% - 8\%) = 8\%$
$b = 0.5$	$r_j = 8\% - 0.5(12\% - 8\%) = 10\%$
$b = 1.0$ (market portfolio)	$r_j = 8\% + 1.0(12\% - 8\%) = 12\%$
$b = 2.0$	$r_j = 8\% + 2.0(12\% - 8\%) = 16\%$

The Arbitrage Pricing Model (APM)

The CAPM assumes that required rates of return depend only on one risk factor, the stock's *beta*. The Arbitrage Pricing Model (APM) disputes this and includes any number of risk factors:

$$r = r_f + b_1 RP_1 + b_2 RP_2 + \cdots + b_n RP_n$$

where r = the expected return for a given stock or portfolio
   r_f = the risk-free rate
   b_i = the sensitivity (or reaction) of the returns of the stock to unexpected changes in economic forces i ($i = 1, \ldots, n$)
   RP_i = the market risk premium associated with an unexpected change in the ith economic force
   n = the number of relevant economic forces

Roll and Ross suggest the following five economic forces:

1. Changes in expected inflation

2. Unanticipated changes in inflation

3. Unanticipated changes in industrial production

4. Unanticipated changes in the yield differential between low- and high-grade bonds (the default-risk premium)

5. Unanticipated changes in the yield differential between long-term and short-term bonds (the term structure of interest rates)

7.3 BOND AND STOCK VALUATION

The process of determining security valuation involves finding the present value of an asset's expected future cash flows using the investor's required rate of return. Thus, the basic security valuation model can be defined mathematically as follows:

$$V = \sum_{t=1}^{n} \frac{C_t}{(1+r)^t}$$

where V = intrinsic value or present value of an asset
C_i = expected future cash flows in period $t = 1, \ldots, n$
r = investor's required rate of return

Bond Valuation

The valuation process for a bond requires a knowledge of three basic elements: (1) the amount of the cash flows to be received by the investor, which is equal to the periodic interests to be received and the par value to be paid at maturity; (2) the maturity date of the loan; and (3) the investor's required rate of return.

Incidentally, the periodic interest can be received annually or semiannually. The value of a bond is simply the present value of these cash flows. Two versions of the bond valuation model are presented below:

If the interest payments are made annually, then

$$V = \sum_{t=1}^{n} \frac{I}{(1+r)^t} + \frac{M}{(1+r)^n} = I(\text{PVIFA}_{r,n}) + M(\text{PVIF}_{r,n})$$

where I = interest payment each year = coupon interest rate × par value
M = par value, or maturity value, typically \$1,000
r = investor's required rate of return
n = number of years to maturity
PVIFA = present value interest factor of an annuity of \$1 (which can be found in Appendix D)
PVIF = present value interest factor of \$1 (which can be found in Appendix C)

EXAMPLE 7.11   Consider a bond, maturing in 10 years and having a coupon rate of 8 percent. The par value is \$1,000. Investors consider 10 percent to be an appropriate required rate of return in view of the risk level associated with this bond. The annual interest payment is \$80(8% × \$1,000). The present value of this bond is:

$$V = \sum_{t=1}^{n} \frac{I}{(1+r)^t} + \frac{M}{(1+r)^n} = I(\text{PVIFA}_{r,n}) + M(\text{PVIF}_{r,n})$$

$$= \sum_{t=1}^{10} \frac{\$80}{(1+0.1)^t} + \frac{\$1,000}{(1+0.1)^{10}} = \$80(\text{PVIFA}_{10\%,10}) + \$1,000(\text{PVIF}_{10\%,10})$$

$$= \$80(6.1446) + \$1,000(0.3855) = \$491.57 + \$385.50 = \$877.07$$

If the interest is paid *semiannually*, then

$$V = \sum_{t=1}^{2n} \frac{I/2}{(1+r/2)^t} + \frac{M}{(1+r/2)^{2n}} = \frac{I}{2}(\text{PVIFA}_{r/2,2n}) + M(\text{PVIF}_{r/2,2n})$$

EXAMPLE 7.12   Assume the same data as in Example 7.11, except the interest is paid semiannually.

$$V = \sum_{t=1}^{2n} \frac{I/2}{(1+r/2)^t} + \frac{M}{(1+r/2)^{2n}} = \frac{I}{2}(\text{PVIFA}_{r/2,2n}) + M(\text{PVIF}_{r/2,2n})$$

$$= \sum_{t=1}^{20} \frac{\$40}{(1+0.05)^t} + \frac{\$1,000}{(1+0.05)^{20}}$$

$$= \$40(\text{PVIFA}_{5\%,20}) + \$1,000(\text{PVIF}_{5\%,20}) = \$40(12.4622) + \$1,000(0.3769) = \$498.49 + \$376.90 = \$875.39$$

Common Stock Valuation

Like bonds, the value of a common stock is the present value of all future cash inflows expected to be received by the investor. The cash inflows expected to be received are dividends and the future price at the time of the sale of the stock. For an investor holding a common stock for only 1 year, the value of the stock would be the present value of both the expected cash dividend to be received in 1 year (D_1) and the expected market price per share of the stock at year-end (P_1). If r represents an investor's required rate of return, the value of common stock (P_0) would be:

$$P_0 = \frac{D_1}{(1+r)^1} + \frac{P_1}{(1+r)^1}$$

EXAMPLE 7.13 Assume an investor is considering the purchase of stock A at the beginning of the year. The dividend at year-end is expected to be $1.50, and the market price by the end of the year is expected to be $40. If the investor's required rate of return is 15 percent, the value of the stock would be:

$$P_0 = \frac{D_1}{(1+r)^1} + \frac{P_1}{(1+r)^1} = \frac{\$1.50}{(1+0.15)} + \frac{\$40}{(1+0.15)} = \$1.50(0.870) + \$40(0.870) = \$1.31 + \$34.80 = \$36.11$$

Since common stock has no maturity date and is held for many years, a more general, multiperiod model is needed. The general common stock valuation model is defined as follows:

$$P_0 = \sum_{t=1}^{\infty} \frac{D_t}{(1+r)^t}$$

There are three cases of growth in dividends. They are (1) zero growth; (2) constant growth; and (3) nonconstant, or supernormal, growth.

In the case of zero growth, if

$$D_0 = D_1 = \cdots = D_\infty$$

then the valuation model

$$P_0 = \sum_{t=1}^{\infty} \frac{D_t}{(1+r)^t}$$

reduces to the formula:

$$P_0 = \frac{D_1}{r}$$

EXAMPLE 7.14 Assuming D equals $2.50 and r equals 10 percent, then the value of the stock is:

$$P_0 = \frac{\$2.50}{0.1} = \$25$$

In the case of constant growth, if we assume that dividends grow at a constant rate of g every year [i.e., $D_t = D_0(1+g)^t$], then the above model is simplified to:

$$P_0 = \frac{D_1}{r-g}$$

This formula is known as the *Gordon growth model*.

EXAMPLE 7.15 Consider a common stock that paid a $3 dividend per share at the end of the last year and is expected to pay a cash dividend every year at a growth rate of 10 percent. Assume the investor's required rate of return is 12 percent. The value of the stock would be:

$$D_1 = D_0(1 + g) = \$3(1 + 0.10) = \$3.30$$

$$P_0 = \frac{D_1}{r - g} = \frac{\$3.30}{0.12 - 0.10} = \$165$$

Finally, consider the case of nonconstant, or supernormal, growth. Firms typically go through life cycles, during part of which their growth is faster than that of the economy and then falls sharply. The value of stock during such supernormal growth can be found by taking the following steps: (1) Compute the dividends during the period of supernormal growth and find their present value; (2) find the price of the stock at the end of the supernormal growth period and compute its present value; and (3) add these two PV figures to find the value (P_0) of the common stock.

EXAMPLE 7.16   Consider a common stock whose dividends are expected to grow at a 25 percent rate for 2 years, after which the growth rate is expected to fall to 5 percent. The dividend paid last period was $2. The investor desires a 12 percent return. To find the value of this stock, take the following steps:

1.   Compute the dividends during the supernormal growth period and find their present value. Assuming D_0 is $2, g is 15 percent, and r is 12 percent:

$$D_1 = D_0(1 + g) = \$2(1 + 0.25) = \$2.50$$
$$D_2 = D_0(1 + g)^2 = \$2(1.563) = \$3.125$$
or
$$D_2 = D_1(1 + g) = \$2.50(1.25) = \$3.125$$

$$\text{PV of dividends} = \frac{D_1}{(1 + r)^1} + \frac{D^2}{(1 + r)^2} = \frac{\$2.50}{(1 + 0.12)} + \frac{\$3.125}{(1 + 0.12)^2}$$
$$= \$2.50(\text{PVIF}_{12\%,1}) + \$3.125(\text{PVIF}_{12\%,2})$$
$$= \$2.50(0.8929) + \$3.125(0.7972) = \$2.23 + \$2.49 = \$4.72$$

2.   Find the price of the stock at the end of the supernormal growth period. The dividend for the third year is:

$$D_3 = D_2(1 + g'), \text{ where } g' = 5\%$$
$$= \$3.125(1 + 0.05) = \$3.28$$

The price of the stock is therefore:

$$P_2 = \frac{D_3}{r - g'} = \frac{\$3.28}{0.12 - 0.05} = \$46.86$$
$$\text{PV of stock price} = \$46.86(\text{PVIF}_{12\%,2}) = \$46.86(0.7972) = \$37.36$$

3.   Add the two PV figures obtained in steps 1 and 2 to find the value of the stock.

$$P_0 = \$4.72 + \$37.36 = \$42.08$$

Expected Rate of Return on a Bond: Yield to Maturity

The expected rate of return on a bond, better known as the bond's *yield to maturity*, is computed by solving the following equation (the bond valuation model) for r:

$$V = \sum_{t=1}^{n} \frac{I}{(1 + r)^t} + \frac{M}{(1 + r)^n} = I(\text{PVIFA}_{r,n}) + M(\text{PVIF}_{r,n})$$

where V is the market price of the bond.

Finding the bond's yield, r, involves trial and error. It is best explained by example.

EXAMPLE 7.17   Suppose you were offered a 10-year, 8 percent coupon, $1,000 par value bond at a price of $877.07. What rate of return could you earn if you bought the bond and held it to maturity? Recall that in Example 7.11 the value of the bond, $877.07, was obtained using the required rate of return of 10 percent. Compute this bond's yield to see if it is 10 percent.

First, set up the bond valuation model:

$$V = \$877.07 = \sum_{t=1}^{10} \frac{\$80}{(1+r)^t} + \frac{\$1,000}{(1+r)^{10}}$$

$$= \$80(\text{PVIFA}_{r,10}) + \$1,000(\text{PVIF}_{r,10})$$

Since the bond is selling at a discount under the par value ($877.07 versus $1,000), the bond's yield is above the going coupon rate of 8 percent. Therefore, try a rate of 9 percent. Substituting factors for 9 percent in the equation, we obtain:

$$V = \$80(6.4177) + \$1,000(0.4224) = \$513.42 + \$422.4 = \$935.82$$

The calculated bond value, $935.82, is *above* the actual market price of $877.07, so the yield is *not* 9 percent. To lower the calculated value, the rate must be *raised*. Trying 10 percent, we obtain:

$$V = \$80(6.1446) + \$1,000(0.3855) = \$491.57 + \$385.50 = \$877.07$$

This calculated value is exactly equal to the market price of the bond; thus, *10 percent* is the bond's yield to maturity.

The formula that can be used to find the *approximate* yield to maturity on a bond is:

$$\text{Yield} = \frac{I + (M - V)/n}{(M + V)/2}$$

where I = dollars of interest paid per year
        M = the par value, typically $1,000 per share
        V = a bond's value
        n = number of years to maturity

This formula can also be used to obtain a starting point for the trial-and-error method discussed in Example 7.17.

EXAMPLE 7.18   Using the same data as in Example 7.17 and the shortcut method, the rate of return on the bond is:

$$\text{Yield} = \frac{I + (M - V)/n}{(M + V)/2} = \frac{\$80 + (\$1,000 - \$877.60)/10}{(\$1,000 + \$877.60)/2} = \frac{\$80 + \$12.24}{\$938.80} = \frac{\$92.24}{\$938.80} = 9.8\%$$

which is very close to the exact rate of 10 percent.

Expected Rate of Return on Common Stock

The formula for computing the expected rate of return on common stock can be derived easily from the valuation models.

The single-period return formula is derived from:

$$P_0 = \frac{D_1}{(1+r)} + \frac{P_1}{(1-r)}$$

Solving for r gives:

$$r = \frac{D_1 + (P_1 - P_0)}{P_0}$$

In words,

$$\text{Rate of return} = \frac{\text{dividends} + \text{capital gain}}{\text{beginning price}}$$

$$= \text{dividend yield} + \text{capital gain yield}$$

EXAMPLE 7.19   Consider a stock that sells for $50. The company is expected to pay a $3 cash dividend at the end of the year, and the stock's market price at the end of the year is expected to be $55 a share. Thus, the expected return would be:

$$r = \frac{D_1 + (P_1 - P_0)}{P_0} = \frac{\$3.00 + (\$55 - \$50)}{\$50} = \frac{\$3.00 + \$5.00}{\$50} = 16\%$$

or:

$$\text{Dividend yield} = \frac{\$3.00}{\$50} = 6\%$$

$$\text{Capital gain yield} = \frac{\$5.00}{\$50} = 10\%$$

$$r = \text{dividend yield} + \text{capital gain yield}$$

$$= 6\% + 10\% = 16\%$$

Assuming a constant growth in dividend, the formula for the expected rate of return on an investment in stock can be derived as follows:

$$P_0 = \frac{D_1}{r - g}$$

$$r = \frac{D_1}{P_0} + g$$

EXAMPLE 7.20   Suppose that ABC Company's dividend per share was $4.50, expected to grow at a constant rate of 6 percent. The current market price of the stock is $30. Then the expected rate of return is:

$$r = \frac{D_1}{P_0} + g = \frac{\$4.50}{\$30} + 6\% = 15\% + 6\% = 21\%$$

7.4   DETERMINING INTEREST-RATE RISK

Interest-rate risk of a debt instrument such as a bond can be determined in two ways. One way is to look at the term structure of a debt security by measuring its average term to maturity – a *duration*. The other way is to measure the sensitivity of changes in a debt security's price associated with changes in its yield to maturity. We will discuss two measurement approaches: Macaulay's duration coefficient and the interest elasticity.

Duration

Duration (D), more exactly known as *Macaulay's Duration Coefficient*, is an attempt to measure risk in a bond by considering the maturity and the time pattern of cash inflows (i.e., interest payments and principal). It is defined as the number of years until a bond pays back its principal.

EXAMPLE 7.21   A bond pays a 7 percent coupon rate annually on its $1,000 face value if it has 3 years until its maturity and has a YTM of 6 percent. The computation of duration involves the following three steps:

Step 1   Calculate the present value of the bond for each year.

Step 2   Express present values as proportions of the price of the bond.

Step 3   Multiply proportions by years' digits to obtain the weighted average time.

	(1)	(2)	(3)	(Step 1) (4)	(Step 2) (5)	(Step 3) (6)
Year	Cash flow		PV factor @ 6%	PV of Cashflow	PV as proportion of price of bond	(6) = (1) × (5) Column (5)
1	$70		0.9434	$66.04	0.0643	0.0643
2	70		0.8900	62.30	0.0607	0.1214
3	1,070		0.8396	898.39	0.8750	2.6250
				$1,026.73	1.0000	2.8107

This 3-year bond's duration is a little over 2.8 years. Although duration is expressed in years, think of it as a percentage change. Thus, 2.8 years means this particular bond will gain (lose) 2.8 percent of its value for each 1 percentage drop (rise) in interest rates. Note, however, that duration will not tell you anything about the credit quality or yield of your bonds.

Interest Rate Elasticity

A bond's interest rate elasticity (E) is defined as

$$E = \frac{\text{Percentage change in bond price}}{\text{Percentage change in YTM}}$$

Since bond prices and YTMs always move inversely, the elasticity will always be a negative number. Any bond's elasticity can be determined directly with the above formula. Knowing the duration coefficient (D), we can calculate the E using the following simple formula:

$$(-1)E = D\frac{\text{YTM}}{(1+\text{YTM})}$$

EXAMPLE 7.22   Using the same date in Example 7.21, the elasticity is calculated as follows:
   $(-1) E = 2.8107 [0.06/(1.06)] = 0.1591$, which means that the bond will lose or gain 15.91% of principal value for each 1 percentage point move in interest rates.

Review Questions

1. _____ refers to the variability of _____ associated with a given investment.

2. Expected rate of return is the _____ of possible returns from a given investment, with the weights being _____ .

3. The smaller the standard deviation, the "tighter" the _____ and, thus, the lower the _____ of the investment.

4. The higher the coefficient of _____ , the greater the risk of the security.

5. _____ depends on _____ in demand, sales price, input prices, and so on.

6. _____ refers to the change in a stock's price that results from changes in the stock market as a whole.

7. Total risk is the sum of _____ and _____ .

8. Portfolio risk can be reduced by _____ .

9. $\rho_{AB} = -1.0$ means that assets A and B have a(n) _____ .

10. The _____ , or _____ , equation shows that the required rate of return on a security is equal to the risk-free rate plus _____ .

11. The valuation process involves finding the _____ of an asset's expected future cash flows using the investor's required rate of return.

12. The expected rate of return on a stock is the sum of _____ yield and _____ yield.

13. The _____ computes the value of a common stock when dividends are expected to grow at a constant rate.

14. The three cases of dividend growth are: _____ , _____ , and _____ .

15. The one-period return on stock investment is dividends plus _____ , divided by the beginning price.

16. _____ is an index of systematic risk.

17. Unlike the Capital Asset Pricing Model (CAPM), the _____ includes any number of risk factors.

18. There are two ways to measure interest rate risk of a bond: one is _____ and the other is the interest rate elasticity.

Answers: (1) Risk, expected return (or earnings); (2) weighted average, probabilities; (3) probability distribution, risk; (4) variation; (5) Business risk, variability; (6) Market risk; (7) unsystematic risk, systematic risk; (8) diversification; (9) perfectly negative correlation; (10) capital asset pricing model (CAPM), security market line (SML), a risk premium; (11) present value; (12) dividend, capital gain; (13) Gordon growth model; (14) zero growth, constant growth, supernormal growth; (15) capital gain; (16) Beta; (17) Arbitrage Pricing Model (APM); duration or Macaulay's duration coefficient.

Solved Problems

7.1   **Expected Return and Standard Deviation.** Assuming the following probability distribution of the possible returns, calculate the expected return ($\bar{r}$) and the standard deviation (σ) of the returns.

Probability (p_i)	Return (r_i)
0.1	−20%
0.2	5%
0.3	10%
0.4	25%

SOLUTION

$$r = \sum r_i p_i$$

$$\sigma = \sqrt{\sum (r_i - \bar{r})^2 p_i}$$

It is convenient to set up the following table:

$r_i(\%)$	p_i	$r_i p_i(\%)$	$(r_i - \bar{r})(\%)$	$(r_i - \bar{r})^2$	$(r_i - \bar{r})^2 p_i(\%)$
−20	0.1	−2	−32	1,024	102.4
5	0.2	1	−7	49	9.8
10	0.3	3	−2	4	1.2
25	0.4	10	13	169	67.6
		$\bar{r} = 12$			$\sigma^2 = 181$

Since $\sigma^2 = 181$, $\sigma = \sqrt{181} = 13.45\%$.

7.2 **Return and Measures of Risk.** Stocks A and B have the following probability distributions of possible future returns:

Probability (p_i)	A (%)	B (%)
0.1	−15	−20
0.2	0	10
0.4	5	20
0.2	10	30
0.1	25	50

(a) Calculate the expected rate of return for each stock and the standard deviation of returns for each stock. (b) Calculate the coefficient of variation. (c) Which stock is less risky? Explain.

SOLUTION

(a) For stock A:

$r_i(\%)$	p_i	$r_i p_i(\%)$	$(r_i - \bar{r})(\%)$	$(r_i - \bar{r})^2$	$(r_i - \bar{r})^2 p_i(\%)$
−15	0.1	−1.5	−20	400	40
0	0.2	0	−5	25	5
5	0.4	2	0	0	0
10	0.2	2	5	25	5
25	0.1	2.5	20	400	40
		$\bar{r} = 5.0$			$\sigma^2 = 90$

Since $\sigma^2 = 90$, $\sigma = \sqrt{90} = 9.5\%$.
   For stock B:

$r_i(\%)$	p_i	$r_i p_i(\%)$	$(r_i - \bar{r})(\%)$	$(r_i - \bar{r})^2$	$(r_i - \bar{r})^2 p_i(\%)$
−20	0.1	−2	−39	1,521	152.1
10	0.2	2	−9	81	16.2
20	0.4	8	1	1	0.4
30	0.2	6	11	121	24.2
50	0.1	5	31	961	96.1
		$\bar{r} = 19$			$\sigma^2 = 289$

Since $\sigma^2 = 289$, $\sigma = \sqrt{289} = 17\%$.

(b)   The coefficient of variation is $\sigma/\bar{r}$. Thus, for stock A:

$$\frac{9.5\%}{5\%} = 1.9$$

For stock B:

$$\frac{17.0\%}{19\%} = 0.89$$

(c)   Stock B is less risky than stock A since the coefficient of variation (a measure of relative risk) is smaller for stock B.

7.3   Absolute and Relative Risk. Ken Parker must decide which of two securities is best for him. By using probability estimates, he computed the following statistics:

Statistic	Security X	Security Y
Expected return ($\bar{r}$)	12%	8%
Standard deviation (σ)	20%	10%

(a) Compute the coefficient of variation for each security, and (b) explain why the standard deviation and coefficient of variation give different rankings of risk. Which method is superior and why?

SOLUTION

(a)   For the X coefficient of variation ($\sigma/\bar{r}$) is 20/12 = 1.67. For Y it is 10/8 = 1.25.

(b)   Unlike the standard deviation, the coefficient of variation considers the standard deviation of securities relative to their average return. The coefficient of variation is therefore the more useful measure of relative risk. The lower the coefficient of variation, the less risky the security relative to the expected return. Thus, in this problem, security Y is relatively less risky than security X.

7.4   Diversification Effects. The securities of firms A and B have the expected return and standard deviations given below; the expected correlation between the two stocks (ρ_{AB}) is 0.1.

	$\bar{r}$	σ
A	14%	20%
B	9%	30%

Compute the return and risk for each of the following portfolios: (a) 100 percent A; (b) 100 percent B; (c) 60 percent A–40 percent B; and (d) 50 percent A–50 percent B.

SOLUTION

(a) $\qquad\qquad$ 100 percent A: $\bar{r} = 14\%$; $\sigma = 20\%$; $\sigma/\bar{r} = \dfrac{20}{14} = 1.43$

(b) $\qquad\qquad$ 100 percent B: $\bar{r} = 9\%$; $\sigma = 30\%$; $\sigma/\bar{r} = \dfrac{30}{9} = 3.33$

(c)   60 percent A – 40 percent B:

$$r_p = w_A r_A + w_B r_B = (0.6)(14\%) + (0.4)(9\%) = 12\%$$

$$\sigma_p = \sqrt{w_A^2 \sigma_B^2 + w_B^2 \sigma_B^2 + 2 w_A w_B \rho_{AB} \sigma_A \sigma_B}$$

$$= \sqrt{(0.6)^2(0.2)^2 + (0.4)^2(0.3)^2 + 2(0.6)(0.4)\rho_{AB}(0.2)(0.3)}$$

$$= \sqrt{0.0144 + 0.0144 + 0.0288\rho_{AB}} = \sqrt{0.0288 + 0.0288(0.1)} = \sqrt{0.03168} = 0.1780 = 17.8\%$$

(d)   50 percent A–50 percent B:

$$r_p = (0.5)(14\%) + (0.5)(9\%) = 11.5\%$$
$$\sigma_p = \sqrt{(0.5)^2(0.2)^2 + (0.5)^2(0.3)^2 + 2(0.5)(0.5)\rho_{AB}(0.2)(0.3)}$$
$$= \sqrt{0.01 + 0.0225 + 0.03\rho_{AB}} = \sqrt{0.0325 + 0.03\rho_{AB}}$$
$$= \sqrt{0.0325 + 0.03(0.1)} = \sqrt{0.0355} = 0.1884 = 18.84\%$$

7.5   **Diversification Effects.** Use the same facts as for Problem 7.4, except for this problem assume the expected correlation between the two stocks (ρ_{AB}) = −1.0.

SOLUTION

(a) and (b)   The answers are the same as in Problem 7.4.

(c) $r_p = 12\%$
$$\sigma_p = \sqrt{0.0288 + 0.0288(-1.0)} = \sqrt{0} = 0\%$$

(d) $r_p = 11.5\%$
$$\sigma_p = \sqrt{0.0325 + 0.03(-1.0)} = \sqrt{0.0025} = 0.05 = 5\%$$

7.6   **Beta and Expected Return.** Assume that the risk-free rate of return is 8 percent, the required rate of return on the market is 13 percent, and stock X has a beta coefficient of 1.5. (a) What is stock X's required rate of return? (b) What if the beta increases to 2? (c) What if the risk-free rate decreases to 6 percent, assuming the beta is still 1.5?

SOLUTION

$$r = r_f + b(r_m - r_f)$$
(a) $r = 8\% + 1.5(13\% - 8\%) = 8\% + 1.5(5\%) = 15.5\%$
(b) $r = 8\% + 2(13\% - 8\%) = 8\% + 10\% = 18\%$
(c) $r = 6\% + 1.5(13\% - 6\%) = 5\% + 10.5 = 16.5\%$

7.7   **Required Rate of Return and Beta.** Moe Corporation is considering several securities. The rate on Treasury bills is currently 8.25 percent, and the expected return for the market is 11.5 percent. What should be the required rates of return for each security?

Security	Beta
A	1.15
B	0.85
C	1.00
D	1.50

SOLUTION

Security	$r_f(\%)$	+	$b[r_m(\%) - r_f(\%)]$	=	$r(\%)$
A	8.25		$(1.15)(11.5 - 8.25)$		11.9875
B	8.25		$(0.85)(11.5 - 8.25)$		11.0125
C	8.25		$(1.00)(11.5 - 8.25)$		11.5
D	8.25		$(1.50)(11.5 - 8.25)$		13.125

7.8   **CAPM.** If Treasury bills yield 10 percent, and Alpha Company's expected return for next year is 18 percent and its beta is 2, what is the market's expected return for next year? Assume the capital asset pricing model (CAPM) applies and everything is in equilibrium.

SOLUTION

$$r = r_f + b(r_m - r_f)$$
$$18\% = 10\% + 2(r_m - 10\%)$$
$$0.18 = 0.1 + 2r_m - 0.2$$
$$0.28 = 2r_m$$
$$r_m = \frac{0.28}{2} = 0.14 = 14\%$$

7.9   **Beta.** Assuming the CAPM applies, if the market's expected return is 13 percent, the risk-free rate is 8 percent, and stock A's required rate of return is 16 percent, what is the stock's beta coefficient?

SOLUTION

$$r = r_f + b(r_m - r_f)$$
$$16\% = 8\% + b(13\% - 8\%)$$
$$0.16 = 0.08 + b(0.05)$$
$$0.08 = b(0.05)$$
$$b = 1.6$$

7.10   **Security Market Line (SML).** The risk-free rate is 7 percent, and the expected return on the market portfolio is 12 percent. (*a*) What is the equation for the security market line (SML)? (*b*) Graph the SML.

SOLUTION

(*a*)   The SML equation is:

$$r = r_f + b(r_m - r_f) = 7\% + b(12\% - 7\%) = 7\% + b(5\%)$$

(*b*)   See Fig.7-2.

7.11   **CAPM.** Assume the following: the risk-free rate is 8 percent, and the market portfolio expected return is 12 percent.

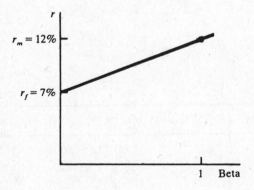

Fig. 7-2

Portfolio	Beta
A	0.6
B	1.0
C	1.4

(*a*) Calculate for each of the three portfolios the expected return consistent with the capital asset pricing model. (*b*) Show graphically the expected portfolio returns in (*a*). (*c*) Indicate what would happen to the capital market line if the expected return on the market portfolio were 10 percent. (CFA, adapted.)

SOLUTION

(*a*)   Portfolio A: $r = 8\% + 0.6(12\% - 8\%) = 10.4\%$

Portfolio B: $r = 8\% + 1.0(12\% - 8\%) = 12.0\%$

Portfolio C: $r = 8\% + 1.4(12\% - 8\%) = 13.6\%$

(*b*)   See Fig. 7-3.

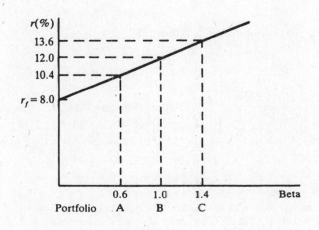

Fig. 7-3

(*c*)   A lower expected return for the market portfolio would change the slope of the market line downward, as is shown in Fig. 7-4.

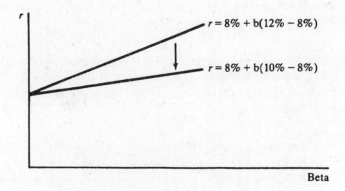

Fig. 7-4

7.12 **CAPM.** During a 5-year period, the relevant results for the aggregate market are that the r_f (risk-free rate) is 8 percent and the r_m (return on market) is 14 percent. For that period, the results of four portfolio managers are as follows:

Portfolio Manager	Average Return (%)	Beta
A	13	0.80
B	14	1.05
C	17	1.25
D	13	0.90

(a) Calculate the expected rate of return for each portfolio manager and compare the actual returns with the expected returns. (b) Based upon your calculations, select the manager with the best performance. (c) What are the critical assumptions in the capital asset pricing model (CAPM)? What are the implications of relaxing these assumptions? (CFA, adapted.)

SOLUTION

(a)   Use the CAPM equation:

$$r_j = r_f + b(r_m - r_f)$$

The expected rates of return are as follows:

Portfolio Manager	Average Return (%)	Expected Return (%)	Actual Return (%)	Difference between Actual and Expected Returns (%)
A	13	$r_A = 8\% + 0.80(14\% - 8\%) = 12.8$	13	+0.2
B	14	$r_B = 8\% + 1.05(14\% - 8\%) = 14.3$	14	−0.3
C	17	$r_C = 8\% + 1.25(14\% - 8\%) = 15.5$	17	+1.5
D	13	$r_D = 8\% + 0.90(14\% - 8\%) = 13.4$	13	−0.4

(b)   Portfolio managers A and C did better than expected, since A exceeded the expected return by 1.56 percent ($0.2\% \div 12.8\%$) and C bettered the expected return by 9.68 percent ($1.5\% \div 15.5\%$). C therefore showed the best performance.

(c)   The critical assumptions in CAPM are perfect capital markets and homogeneous expectations.

Relaxation of the perfect capital markets assumption results in limitations to the effectiveness of predicting and computing expected return on stock. Certain securities may have values and expected returns that are not entirely explained by the security market line. Residual risk may be important, particularly where bankruptcy costs are significant. When expectations of market participants are not homogeneous, each investor has his or her own capital market line. The important thing to stress, however, is that in market equilibrium, there still will exist an implied risk-return trade-off for securities where risk is represented by the undiversifiable risk, as opposed to the total risk of the security.

7.13 **Value of Bond.** Trooper Corporation has a bond issue with a coupon rate of 10 percent per year and 5 years remaining until maturity. The par value of the bond is $1,000. What is the value of the bond when the going rate of interest is (a) 6 percent; (b) 10 percent; and (c) 12 percent? The bond pays interest annually.

SOLUTION

$$\text{Annual interest} = 10\% \times \$1,000 = \$100$$

$$V = \sum_{i=1}^{n} \frac{I}{(1+r)^i} + \frac{M}{(1+r)^n} = \frac{\$100}{(1+r)^1} + \frac{\$100}{(1+r)^2} + \cdots + \frac{\$100}{(1+r)^5} + \frac{\$1,000}{(1+r)^5}$$

$$= \$100(\text{PVIFA}_{r,n}) + \$1,000(\text{PVIF}_{r,n})$$

(a) $\text{Value} = \$100(\text{PVIFA}_{6\%,5}) + \$1,000(\text{PVIF}_{6\%,5})$

$= \$100(4.2124) + \$1,000(0.7473) = \$421.24 + \$747.30 = \$1,168.54$

(b) $\text{Value} = \$100(\text{PVIFA}_{10\%,5}) + \$1,000(\text{PVIF}_{10\%,5})$

$= \$100(3.7908) + \$1,000(0.6209) = \$379.08 + \$620.90 = \$999.98$

(c) $\text{Value} = \$100(\text{PVIFA}_{12\%,5}) + \$1,000(\text{PVIF}_{12\%,5})$

$= \$100(3.6048) + \$1,000(0.5674) = \$360.48 + \$567.40 = \$927.88$

7.14 Value of Bond. Assume the same data and questions as in Problem 7.13, except that in this problem, the bond pays interest semiannually.

SOLUTION

$$\text{Semiannual interest} = \frac{\$100}{2} = \$50$$

$$\text{Number of periods} = 5 \text{ years} \times 2 = 10 \text{ periods}$$

$$V = \sum_{t=1}^{2n} \frac{i/2}{(1 + r/2)^t} + \frac{M}{(1 + r/2)^{2n}}$$

$$= \frac{\$50}{(1 + r/2)} + \frac{\$50}{(1 + r/2)^2} \cdots \frac{\$50}{(1 + r/2)^{10}} + \frac{\$1,000}{(1 + r/2)^{10}}$$

$$= \$50(\text{PVIFA}_{r/2,10}) + \$1,000(\text{PVIF}_{r/2,10})$$

(a) $V = \$50(\text{PVIFA}_{3\%,10}) + \$1,000(\text{PVIF}_{3\%,10})$

$= \$50(8.5302) + \$1,000(0.7441) = \$426.51 + \$744.10 = \$1,170.61$

(b) $V = \$50(\text{PVIFA}_{5\%,10}) + \$1,000(\text{PVIF}_{5\%,10})$

$= \$50(7.7217) + \$1,000(0.6139) = \$386.09 + \$613.90 = \$999.99$

(c) $V = \$50(\text{PVIFA}_{6\%,10}) + \$1,000(\text{PVIF}_{6\%,10})$

$= \$50(7.3601) + \$1,000(0.5584) = \$368.01 + \$558.40 = \$926.41$

7.15 Stock Valuation—Single Period. Mary Czech is considering the purchase of stock X at the beginning of the year. The dividend at year-end is expected to be $3.25, and the market price by the end of the year is expected to be $25. If she requires a rate of return of 12 percent, what is the value of the stock?

SOLUTION

$$P_0 = \frac{D_1}{(1 + r)} + \frac{P_1}{(1 + r)} = \frac{\$3.25}{(1 + 0.12)} + \frac{\$25}{(1 + 0.12)}$$

$$= \$3.25(0.893) + \$25(0.893) = \$2.90 + \$22.33 = \$25.23$$

7.16 Stock Valuation—Finite Periods. The Ohm Company paid a $2.50 dividend per share at the end of the year. The dividend is expected to grow by 10 percent each year for the next 3 years, and the stock's market price per share is expected to be $50 at the end of the third year. Investors require a rate of return of 14 percent. At what price per share should the Ohm stock sell?

SOLUTION

$$P_0 = \sum_{t=1}^{3} \frac{D_t}{(1 - r)^t} + \frac{P_3}{(1 + r)^3}$$

Note that

$$D_0 = \$2.50$$
$$D_1 = \$2.50(1 + 0.10) = \$2.50(1.10) = \$2.75$$
$$D_2 = \$2.50(1 + 0.10)^2 = \$2.50(1.21) = \$3.03$$
$$D_3 = \$2.50(1 + 0.10)^3 = \$2.50(1.331) = \$3.33$$

$$P_0 = \frac{\$2.75}{(1 + 0.14)} + \frac{\$3.03}{(1 + 0.14)^2} + \frac{\$3.33}{(1 + 0.14)^3} + \frac{\$50}{(1 + 0.14)^3}$$
$$= \$2.75(0.877) + \$3.03(0.770) + \$3.33(0.675) + \$50(0.675)$$
$$= \$2.41 + \$2.33 + \$2.25 + \$33.75 = \$40.74$$

The stock should sell for \$40.74 per share.

7.17   Stock Valuation—No Growth in Dividends. Susan O'Reilly invests in a stock of company X which expects no growth in dividends. The company paid a \$2.75 dividend per share. If Susan requires a rate of return of 10 percent, what would be the value of the stock?

SOLUTION

If $D_0 = D_1 = D_2 = \cdots = D_\infty$, then

$$P_0 = \frac{D}{r}$$

Therefore,

$$P_0 = \frac{\$2.75}{0.1} = \$27.50$$

7.18   The Gordon Dividend Growth Model. Develop the Gordon growth model, assuming constant growth of dividends, i.e., $D_t = D_0(1 + g)^t$.

SOLUTION

Since $D_t = D_0(1 + g)^t$

$$P_0 = \frac{D_0(1 + g)}{(1 + r)} + \frac{D_0(1 + g)^2}{(1 + r)^2} + \cdots + \frac{D_0(1 + g)^\infty}{(1 + r)^\infty}$$

If both sides of this expression are multiplied by $(1 + r)/(1 + g)$ and then this is subtracted from the product, the result is:

$$\frac{P_0(1 + r)}{(1 + g)} - P_0 = D_0 - \frac{D_0(1 + g)^\infty}{(1 + r)^\infty}$$

If $r > g$, which should normally be true, the term on the far right-hand side approaches zero. As a result,

$$\frac{P_0(1 + r)}{(1 + g)} - P_0 = D_0$$

$$P_0\left(\frac{1 + r}{1 + g}\right) - P_0\left(\frac{1 + g}{1 + g}\right) = D_0$$

$$P_0\left[\frac{(1 + r) - (1 + g)}{(1 + g)}\right] = D_0$$

$$P_0(r - g) = D_0(1 + g)$$

If we assume dividends grow at a constant rate g, then

$$D_t = D_0(1 + g)^t \qquad \text{and} \qquad t = 1$$

and

$$P_0 = \frac{D_1}{r - g}$$

7.19 **Stock Valuation.** Investors require a rate of return of 12 percent. At what price will the stock sell if the next expected dividend D_1 is S1 per share and investors expect the dividends and earnings to grow (a) at 8 percent; (b) at 10 percent; (c) at 12 percent; and (d) at 14 percent?

SOLUTION

$$P_0 = \frac{D_1}{r-g}$$

(a)
$$P_0 = \frac{\$1}{0.12 - 0.08} = \$25$$

(b)
$$P_0 = \frac{\$1}{0.12 - 0.1} = \$50$$

(c)
$$P_0 = \frac{\$1}{0.12 - 0.12} = \text{undefined}$$

The formula is invalid since a necessary condition is $r > g$.

(d)
$$P_0 = \frac{\$1}{0.12 - 0.14} = \text{undefined}$$

7.20 **Beta and Stock Valuation.** The risk-free rate is 6 percent, the required rate of return on the market is 12 percent, and stock A has a beta coefficient of 1.2. If the dividend expected during the coming year is $2 and the growth rate of dividends and earnings is 7 percent, at what price should stock A sell?

SOLUTION

$$r = r_f + b(r_m - r_f) = 6\% + 1.2(12\% - 6\%) = 6\% + 7.2\% = 13.2\%$$

Therefore,

$$P_0 = \frac{D_1}{r-g} = \frac{\$2}{13.2\% - 7\%} = \frac{\$2}{0.062} = \$32.26$$

7.21 **Stock Valuation.** Investors require a 20 percent per year return on the stock of M Company. Yesterday M Company paid a $2 dividend (dividends are paid annually). The dividend is expected to grow 30 percent per year for the next 2 years and at 8 percent per year thereafter. At what price should the stock sell?

SOLUTION

$$D_0 = \$2$$
$$D_1 = \$2(1 + 0.3) = \$2.60$$
$$D_2 = \$2(1 + 0.3)^2 = \$2(1.69) = \$3.38$$
$$D_3 = \$3.38(1 + 0.08) = \$3.65$$

Present value of dividends for the first 2 years are:

$$\frac{\$2.60}{(1 + 0.2)} + \frac{\$3.38}{(1 + 0.2)^2} = \$2.60(\text{PVIF}_{20\%,1}) + \$3.38(\text{PVIF}_{20\%,2})$$

$$= \$2.60(0.8333) + \$3.38(0.6944) = \$2.17 + \$2.35 = \$4.52$$

Find P_2:

$$P_2 = \frac{D_3}{r-g} = \frac{\$3.65}{0.2 - 0.08} = \$30.42$$

Present value of $30.42 is:

$$\frac{\$30.42}{(1+0.2)^2} = \$30.42(\text{PVIF}_{20\%,2}) = \$30.42(0.6944) = \$21.12$$

Add these two PV figures to obtain P_0:

$$P_0 = \$4.52 + \$21.12 = \$25.64$$

7.22   Stock Valuation. Investors require a 10 percent per year return on the stock of the Take-Two Corporation, which anticipates a nonconstant growth pattern for dividends. The company paid a $2 per share dividend. The dividend is expected to grow by 15 percent per year until the end of year 4 (i.e., for the next 3 years) and 7 percent thereafter.

(a) Project dividends for years 1 through 4. (b) Compute the present value of the dividends in part (a). (c) Project the dividend for the fifth year (D_5). (d) Find the present value of all future dividends beginning with the fifth year's dividend. The present value you find will be at the end of the fourth year. Use the formula $P_4 = D_5/(r-g)$. (e) Discount back the value found in part (d) for 4 years at 10 percent. (f) Determine the value of the stock P_0.

SOLUTION

(a)
$$D_0(\text{given}) = \$2$$
$$D_1 = \$2(1+0.15) = \$2.30$$
$$D_2 = \$2.30(1+0.15) = \$2.65$$
$$D_3 = \$2.65(1+0.15) = \$3.05$$
$$D_4 = \$3.05(1+0.15) = \$3.51$$

(b)   PV of dividends $= \dfrac{\$2.30}{(1+0.1)} + \dfrac{\$2.65}{(1+0.1)^2} + \dfrac{\$3.05}{(1+0.1)^3} + \dfrac{\$3.51}{(1+0.1)^4}$

$\quad = \$2.30(\text{PVIF}_{10\%,1}) + \$2.65(\text{PVIF}_{10\%,2}) + \$3.05(\text{PVIF}_{10\%,3}) + \$3.51(\text{PVIF}_{10\%,4})$

$\quad = \$2.30(0.9091) + \$2.65(0.8264) + \$3.05(0.7513) + \$3.51(0.6830)$

$\quad = \$2.09 + \$2.19 + \$2.29 + \$2.40 = \$8.97$

(c)
$$D_5 = \$3.51(1+0.15) = \$4.04$$

(d)
$$P_4 = \frac{D_5}{r-g} = \frac{\$4.04}{0.1-0.07} = \frac{\$4.04}{0.03} = \$134.67$$

(e)   Therefore, $\dfrac{\$134.67}{(1+0.1)^4} = \$134.67(\text{PVIF}_{10\%,4}) = \$134.67(0.6830) = \$91.98$

(f)   The value of the stock, P_0, is:

$$P_0 = \$8.97 + \$91.98 = \$100.95$$

7.23   Stock Valuation. On December 31, 19X2, the shares of Amacom, Inc., closed at $20. The company subsequently paid a year-end dividend in each of the years 19X3 through 19X7 as follows:

$$19X3:\ \$1.00 \qquad 19X6:\ \$1.25$$
$$19X4:\ \$1.00 \qquad 19X7:\ \$1.25$$
$$19X5:\ \$1.10$$

Suppose you had purchased a share of Amacom stock on December 31, 19X2. Find the price at which you must sell your share at 19X7 year-end in order to realize an annual compounded total rate of return of 10 percent on your initial investment (before commissions and taxes). (CFA, adapted.)

SOLUTION

$$P_0 = \sum_{t=1}^{5} \frac{D_t}{(1+r)^t} + \frac{P_5}{(1+r)^5}$$

Substituting the value given yields:

$$\$20 = \sum_{t=1}^{5} \frac{D_t}{(1+0.1)^t} + \frac{P_5}{(1+0.1)^5}$$

First compute the present value of dividends for the years 19X3 through 19X7.

$$\frac{\$1.00}{(1+0.1)^1} + \frac{\$1.00}{(1+0.1)^2} + \frac{\$1.10}{(1+0.1)^3} + \frac{\$1.25}{(1+0.1)^4} + \frac{\$1.25}{(1+0.1)^5}$$

$$= \$1.00(0.9091) + \$1.00(0.8264) + \$1.10(0.7513) + \$1.25(0.6830) + \$1.25(0.6209)$$

$$= \$0.91 + \$0.83 + \$0.83 + \$0.85 + \$0.78 = \$4.20$$

Therefore,

$$\$20 = \$4.20 + \frac{P_5}{(1+0.1)^5}$$

$$\$20 = \$4.20 + P_5(\text{PVIF}_{10\%,5})$$

$$\$20 = \$4.20 + P_5(0.6209)$$

$$P_5(0.6209) = \$20 - \$4.20$$

$$P_5(0.6209) = \$15.80$$

$$P_5 = \frac{\$15.80}{0.6209} = \$25.45$$

7.24   Yield to Maturity. The Rite Company's bonds have 3 years remaining until maturity. Interest is paid annually, the bonds have a $1,000 par value, and the coupon interest rate is 10 percent. What is the yield to maturity at a current market price of: (*a*) $1,052; (*b*) $1,000; and (*c*) $935?

SOLUTION

$$\text{Annual interest} = \$100 \qquad (10\% \times \$1,000)$$

$$V = \sum_{t=1}^{n} \frac{I}{(1+r)^t} + \frac{M}{(1+r)^n}$$

$$= I(\text{PVIFA}_{r,n}) + M(\text{PVIF}_{r,n})$$

(*a*)

$$\$1,052 = \frac{\$100}{(1+r)^1} + \frac{\$100}{(1+r)^2} + \cdots + \frac{\$100}{(1+r)^3} + \frac{\$1,000}{(1+r)^3}$$

$$\$1,052 = \$100(\text{PVIFA}_{r,3}) + \$1,000(\text{PVIF}_{r,3})$$

Since the bond is selling above par value, the bond's yield is below the coupon rate of 10 percent. At $r = 8\%$:

$$V = \$100(2.5771) + \$1,000(0.7938) = \$257.71 + \$793.80 = \$1,051.51$$

Therefore, the annual yield to maturity of the bond is 8 percent.
Alternatively, the shortcut formula yields:

$$\text{Yield to maturity of a bond} = \frac{I + (M - V)/n}{(M + V)/2}$$

$$= \frac{\$100 + (\$1,000 - \$1,052)/3}{(\$1,000 + \$1,052)/2} = \frac{\$82.67}{\$1,026} = 8.05\%$$

(b)
$$\$1{,}000 = \$100(PVIFA_{r,3}) + \$1{,}000(PVIF_{r,3})$$

Since the bond is selling at par value, the bond's yield should be the same as the coupon rate. At $r = 10\%$:

$$V = \$100(2.4869) + \$1{,}000(0.7513) = \$248.69 + \$751.30 = \$999.99$$

Or, using the shortcut formula:

$$\text{Yield} = \frac{\$100 + (\$1{,}000 - \$1{,}000)/3}{(\$1{,}000 + \$1{,}000)/2} = \frac{\$100}{\$1{,}000} = 10\%$$

(c)
$$\$935 = \$100(PVIFA_{r,3}) + \$1{,}000(PVIFA_{r,3})$$

Since the bond is selling at a discount under the par value, the bond's yield is above the going coupon rate of 10 percent. At $r = 12\%$:

$$V = \$100(2.4018) + \$1{,}000(0.7118) = \$240.18 + \$711.80 = \$951.98$$

At 10 percent, the bond's value is above the actual market value of $935, so we must raise the rate. At $r = 13\%$:

$$V = \$100(2.361) + \$1{,}000(0.693) = \$236.10 + \$693 = \$929.10$$

Since the bond value of $935 falls between 12 percent and 13 percent, find the yield by interpolation, as follows:

	Bond Value	
12%	$951.18	$951.18
True yield	935.00	
13%		929.10
Difference	$ 16.18	$ 22.08

$$\text{Yield} = 12\% + \frac{16.18}{22.08}(1\%) = 12\% + 0.73(1\%) = 12.73\%$$

Alternatively, using the shortcut method:

$$\text{Yield} = \frac{\$100 + (\$1{,}000 - \$935)/3}{(\$1{,}000 + \$935)/2} = \frac{\$121.67}{\$967.5} = 12.58\%$$

7.25   Yield to Maturity. Assume a bond has 4 years remaining until maturity and that it pays interest semiannually (the most recent payment was yesterday). (a) What is the yield to maturity of the bond if its maturity value is $1,000, its coupon yield is 8 percent, and it currently sells for $821? (b) What if it currently sells for $1,070?

SOLUTION

$$V = \sum_{t=1}^{2n} \frac{I/2}{(1 + r/2)^t} + \frac{M}{(1 + r/2)^{2n}}$$
$$= I/2(PVIFA_{r/2,2n}) + M(PVIF_{r/2,2n})$$

(a)
$$\text{Semiannual interest} = \frac{8\%(\$1{,}000)}{2} = \$40$$

$$\$821 = \frac{\$40}{(1 + r/2)^1} + \frac{40}{(1 + r/2)^2} + \cdots + \frac{40}{(1 + r/2)^8} + \frac{\$1{,}000}{(1 + r/2)^8}$$
$$\$821 = \$40(PVIFA_{r/2,8}) + \$1{,}000(PVIF_{r/2,8})$$

By trial and error, we find that when $r/2 = 7\%$:

$$V = \$40(5.9713) + \$1{,}000(0.5820) = \$238.85 + \$582 = \$820.85$$

Therefore, the annual yield is $7\% \times 2 = 14\%$.

Using the shortcut formula:

$$\text{Yield} = \frac{I + (M - V)/n}{(M + V)/2} = \frac{\$80 + (\$1{,}000 - \$821)/4}{(\$1{,}000 + \$821)/2} = \frac{\$124.75}{\$910.5} = 13.7\%$$

(b)
$$\$1{,}070 = \frac{\$40}{(1 + r/2)^1} + \frac{40}{(1 + r/2)^2} + \cdots + \frac{40}{(1 + r/2)^8} + \frac{\$1{,}000}{(1 + r/2)^8}$$

$$\$1{,}070 = \$40(\text{PVIFA}_{r/2,3}) + \$1{,}000(\text{PVIF}_{r/2,8})$$

By trial and error, we get the semiannual interest of 3 percent:

$$V = \$40(7.0197) + \$1{,}000(0.7894) = \$280.79 + \$789.40 = \$1{,}070.19$$

Therefore, the annual yield is $3\% \times 2 = 6\%$.
Alternatively, using the shortcut method:

$$\text{Yield} = \frac{\$80 + (\$1{,}000 - \$1{,}070)/4}{(\$1{,}000 + \$1{,}070)/2} = \frac{\$62.5}{\$1{,}035} = 6\%$$

7.26 Yield of a Note. You can buy a note at a price of \$13,500. If you buy the note, you will receive 10 annual payments of \$2,000, the first payment to be made immediately. What rate of return, or yield, does the note offer?

SOLUTION

$$V = \sum_{t=1}^{n} \frac{C_t}{(1 + r)^t}$$

$$\$13{,}500 = \$2{,}000 + \frac{\$2{,}000}{(1 + r)^1} + \frac{\$2{,}000}{(1 + r)^2} + \cdots + \frac{\$2{,}000}{(1 + r)^9}$$

$$\$13{,}500 = \$2{,}000(1 + \text{PVIFA}_{r,9})$$

$$(1 + \text{PVIFA}_{r,9}) = \frac{\$13{,}500}{\$2{,}000} = 6.75$$

$\text{PVIFA}_{r,9} = 6.75 - 1 = 5.75$, which is very close to 10 percent as found in Appendix D.

7.27 Expected Return on Stock Investment. You are considering the purchase of a share of stock in a firm for \$40. The company is expected to pay a \$2.50 dividend at the end of the year, and its market price after the payment of the dividend is expected to be \$45 a share. What is the expected return on the investment in this stock?

SOLUTION

$$r = \frac{\text{dividends} + (\text{ending price} - \text{beginning price})}{\text{beginning price}} = \frac{D_1 + (P_1 - P_0)}{P_0}$$

$$= \frac{\$2.50 + (\$45 - \$40)}{\$40} = 18.75\%$$

Alternatively, we set the current market price equal to the present value of the dividend, plus the expected market price, as follows:

$$\$40 = \frac{\$2.50}{(1 + r)} + \frac{\$45}{(1 + r)}$$

Solving this equation for r:

$$\$40(1 + r) = \$2.50 + \$45$$

$$1 + r = \frac{\$2.50 + \$45}{\$40}$$

$$r = \frac{\$2.50 + \$45}{\$40} - 1 = \frac{\$47.50}{40} - 1 = 1.1975 - 1 = 18.75\%$$

7.28   **Expected Return on Stock Investment.** Tom Laboratory's common stock is currently selling at $60 per share. The next annual dividend is expected to be $3 per share, and the earnings, dividends, and stock prices are expected to grow at a rate of: (*a*) 0 percent; (*b*) 4 percent; and (*c*) 6 percent. What is the expected total return in each case from the purchase of the common stock?

SOLUTION

$$r = \frac{D_1}{P_0} + g$$

(*a*)

$$r = \frac{\$3}{\$60} + 0 = 5\%$$

(*b*)

$$r = \frac{\$3}{\$60} + 4\% = 5\% + 4\% = 9\%$$

(*c*)

$$r = \frac{\$3}{\$60} + 6\% = 5\% + 6\% = 11\%$$

7.29   **Dividend Yield and Capital Gain Yield.** N Company's last dividend, D_0, was $1. Earnings and dividends are expected to grow at a 5 percent rate. The required rate of return on the stock is 13 percent. The current stock price is $25. What is the expected dividend yield and expected capital gains yield for the coming year?

SOLUTION

$$\text{Dividend yield} = \frac{\$1.00(1 + 0.05)}{\$25} = \frac{\$1.05}{\$25} = 4.2\%$$

$$\text{Capital gain yield} = \text{rate of return} - \text{dividend yield} = 13\% - 4.2\% = 8.8\%$$

7.30   **The Arbitrage Pricing Model (APM).** Suppose a three-factor APM holds and the risk-free rate is 6 percent. You are interested in two particular stocks: A and B. The returns on both stocks are related to factors 1 and 2 as follows:

$$r = 0.06 + b_1(0.09) - b_2(0.03) + b_3(0.04)$$

The sensitivity coefficients for the two stocks are given below.

Stock	b_1	b_2	b_3
A	0.70	0.80	0.20
B	0.50	0.04	1.20

Calculate the expected returns on both stocks. Which stock requires a higher return?

SOLUTION

For stock A: $r = 0.06 + (0.70)(0.09) - (0.80)(0.03) + (0.20)(0.04)$
                              $= 10.70\%$

For stock B: $r = 0.06 + (0.50)(0.09) - (0.04)(0.03) + (1.20)(0.04)$
                              $= 14.10\%$

Stock B requires a higher return, indicating it is the riskier of the two. Part of the reason is that its return is substantially more sensitive to the third economic force than stock A's is.

7.31   Duration. You have a 9 percent bond with 4 years to maturity paid interest annually. Its YTM is 10 percent and its market value is $968.29 per bond. What is the duration of the bond?

SOLUTION

The computation of duration involves the following three steps:

Step 1   Calculate the present value of the bond for each year.

Step 2   Express present values as proportions of the price of the bond.

Step 3   Multiply proportions by years' digits to obtain the weighted average time.

			(Step 1)	(Step 2)	(Step 3)
(1)	(2)	(3)	(4)	(5)	(6)
Year	Cash flow	PV factor @10%	PV of Cashflow	PV as proportion of price of bond	Column (1) × Column (5)
1	$ 90	0.9091	$ 81.82	0.0845	0.0845
2	90	0.8264	74.38	0.0768	0.1536
3	90	0.7513	67.62	0.0698	0.2094
4	1,090	0.6830	744.47	0.7689	3.0756
			$968.29	1.0000	3.5231

The duration of the bond is 3.52 years.

7.32   Interest Rate Sensitivity. What is the interest rate elasticity of the bond in Problem 7.31? What does that mean?

SOLUTION

The formula is:

$$(-1)E = D\frac{YTM}{(1 + YTM)}$$

(-1) $E = 3.5231$ $(0.10/1.10) = 0.3203$, which means that the bond will lose or gain 32.03% of principal value for each 1 percentage point move in interest rates.

Chapter 8

Capital Budgeting
(Including Leasing)

8.1 CAPITAL BUDGETING DECISIONS DEFINED

Capital budgeting is the process of making long-term planning decisions for investments. There are typically two types of investment decisions: (1) selection decisions concerning proposed projects (for example, investments in long-term assets such as property, plant, and equipment, or resource commitments in the form of new product development, market research, re-funding of long-term debt, introduction of a computer, etc.); and (2) replacement decisions (for example, replacement of existing facilities with new facilities).

8.2 MEASURING CASH FLOWS

The *incremental* (or relevant) after-tax cash flows that occur with an investment project are the ones that are measured. In general the cash flows of a project fall into the following three categories: (1) the initial investment; (2) the incremental (relevant) cash inflows over the life of the project; and (3) the terminal cash flow.

Initial Investment

The initial investment (*I*) is the initial cash outlay necessary to purchase the asset and put it in operating order. It is determined as follows:

$$\text{Initial investment} = \frac{\text{cost of asset} + \text{installation cost}}{+ \text{working capital investments}} - \frac{\text{proceeds from}}{\text{sale of old asset}} \pm \frac{\text{taxes on sale}}{\text{of old asset}}$$

The proceeds from the sale of old assets are subject to some type of tax. There are three possibilities:

1. The asset is sold for more than its book value.
2. The asset is sold for its book value.
3. The asset is sold for less than its book value.

Additional working capital (in the form of increased inventory, cash, and receivables) is usually required to support a new investment project. This should be included in the project's initial outlay. At the end of the project's life, it should be recaptured as part of the project's terminal cash flow.

EXAMPLE 8.1 Assume that an asset has a book value of $60,000 and initially cost $100,000. Assume further that the firm's ordinary marginal tax rate is 34 percent. Consider each of the three possible tax situations dealing with the sale of the old asset.

1. The old asset is sold for $80,000. In this case, the total gain is simply recapture of depreciation and taxed at the ordinary rate. Therefore,

$$(\$80,000 - \$60,000)(0.34) = \$6,800$$

2. The old asset is sold for $60,000. In this case, no taxes result since there is neither a gain nor a loss on the sale.

3. The old asset is sold for $50,000. In this case there is a loss, which results in tax savings. The *tax savings* are as follows:

$$(\$60,000 - \$50,000)(0.34) = \$3,400$$

200

Taxes on the gain from the sale of an old asset or the tax savings on a loss must be considered when determining the amount of the initial investment of a new asset.

EXAMPLE 8.2 XYZ Corporation is considering the purchase of a new machine for $250,000, which will be depreciated on a straight-line basis over 5 years with no salvage value. In order to put this machine in operating order, it is necessary to pay installation charges of $50,000. The new machine will replace an existing machine, purchased 3 years ago at a cost of $240,000, that is depreciated on a straight-line basis (with no salvage value) over its 8-year life (i.e., $30,000 per year depreciation). The old machine can be sold for $255,000 to a scrap dealer. The company is in the 34 percent tax bracket. The machine will require an increase in w/p inventory of $5,000.

The key calculation of the initial investment is the taxes on the sale of the old machine. The total gain, which is the difference between the selling price and the book value, is $105,000 ($255,000 − $150,000). The tax on this $105,000 total gain is $35,700 (34% × $105,000). Therefore, the amount of initial investment is:

Purchase price of the machine	$250,000
+ Installation cost	50,000
+ Increased investment in inventory	5,000
− Proceeds from sales of old machine	255,000
+ Taxes on sale of old machine	35,700
Initial investment	$ 85,700

Incremental (Relevant) Cash Inflows

The relevant cash inflows over a project's expected life involve the incremental after-tax cash flows resulting from increased revenues and/or savings in cash operating costs. Cash flows are not the same as accounting income, which is not usually available for paying the firm's bills. The differences between accounting income and cash flows are such noncash charges as depreciation expense and amortization expense.

The computation of relevant or incremental cash inflows after taxes involves the following two steps:

1. Compute the after-tax cash flows of each proposal by adding back any noncash charges, which are deducted as expenses on the firm's income statement, to net profits (earnings) after taxes; that is:

    After-tax cash inflows = net profits (or earnings) after taxes + depreciation

2. Subtract the cash inflows after taxes resulting from use of the old asset from the cash inflows generated by the new asset to obtain the relevant (incremental) cash inflows after taxes.

EXAMPLE 8.3 XYZ Corporation has provided its revenues and cash operating costs (excluding depreciation) for the old and the new machine, as follows:

	Annual		Net Profits before
	Revenue	**Cash Operating Costs**	**Depreciation and Taxes**
Old machine	$150,000	$70,000	$ 80,000
New machine	$180,000	$60,000	$120,000

Recall from Example 8.2 that the annual depreciation of the old machine and the new machine will be $30,000 and $50,000, respectively.

To arrive at net profits after taxes, we first have to deduct depreciation expenses from the net profits before depreciation and taxes, as follows:

	Net Profits after Taxes	Add Depreciation	After-Tax Cash Inflows
Old machine	($80,000 − $30,000)(1 − 0.46) = $27,000	$30,000	$57,000
New machine	($120,000 − $50,000)(1 − 0.46) = $37,800	$50,000	$87,800

Subtracting the after-tax cash inflows of the old machine from the cash inflows of the new machine results in the relevant, or incremental, cash inflows for each year.

Therefore, in this example, the relevant or incremental cash inflows for each year are $87,800 − $57,000 = $30,800.

Alternatively, the incremental cash inflows after taxes can be computed, using the following simple formula:

$$\text{After-tax } \textit{incremental} \text{ cash inflows} = \text{(increase in revenues)}(1 - \text{tax rate})$$
$$-\text{(increase in cash charges)}(1 - \text{tax rate})$$
$$+\text{(increase in depreciation expenses)}(\text{tax rate})$$

EXAMPLE 8.4   Using the data in Example 8.3, after-tax incremental cash inflows for each year are:

Increase in revenue × (1 − tax rate):	
($180,000 − $150,000)(1 − 0.46)	$16,200
−Increase in cash charges × (1 − tax rate):	
($60,000 − $70,000)(1 − 0.46)	−(−5,400)
+Increase in depreciation expense ×	
tax rate: ($50,000 − $30,000)(0.46)	9,200
	$30,800

Terminal Cash Flow

Cash flows associated with a project's termination generally include the disposal value of the project plus or minus any taxable gains or losses associated with its sale. The way in which to compute these gains or losses is very similar to the method for computing the taxes on the sale of an old asset. In most cases, the disposal value at the end of the project's useful life results in a taxable gain since its book value (or undepreciated value) is usually zero. The terminal cash flow must include the recapture of working capital investments required in the initial outlay.

8.3   CAPITAL BUDGETING TECHNIQUES

Several methods of evaluating investment projects are as follows:

1. Payback period
2. Accounting rate of return (ARR)
3. Net present value (NPV)
4. Internal rate of return (IRR)
5. Profitability index (or benefit/cost ratio)

The NPV method and the IRR method are called discounted cash flow (DCF) methods. Each of these methods is discussed below.

Payback Period

The payback period measures the length of time required to recover the amount of initial investment. It is computed by dividing the initial investment by the cash inflows through increased revenues or cost savings.

EXAMPLE 8.5 Assume:

Cost of investment	$18,000
Annual after-tax cash savings	$ 3,000

Then, the payback period is:

$$\text{Payback period} = \frac{\text{initial investment cost}}{\text{increased revenues or lost savings}} = \frac{\$18,000}{\$3,000} = 6 \text{ years}$$

Decision rule: Choose the project with the shorter payback period. The rationale behind this choice is: The shorter the payback period, the less risky the project, and the greater the liquidity.

EXAMPLE 8.6 Consider two projects whose after-tax cash inflows are not even. Assume each project costs $1,000.

	Cash Inflow	
Year	A ($)	B ($)
1	100	500
2	200	400
3	300	300
4	400	100
5	500	
6	600	

When cash inflows are not even, the payback period has to be found by trial and error. The payback period of project A is ($1,000 = $100 + $200 + $300 + $400) 4 years. The payback period of project B is ($1,000 = $500 + $400 + $100):

$$2 \text{ years} + \frac{\$100}{\$300} = 2\frac{1}{3} \text{ years}$$

Project B is the project of choice in this case, since it has the shorter payback period.

The *advantages* of using the payback period method of evaluating an investment project are that (1) it is simple to compute and easy to understand, and (2) it handles investment risk effectively.

The *shortcomings* of this method are that (1) it does not recognize the time value of money, and (2) it ignores the impact of cash inflows received after the payback period; essentially, cash flows after the payback period determine profitability of an investment.

Accounting Rate of Return

Accounting rate of return (ARR) measures profitability from the conventional accounting standpoint by relating the required investment—or sometimes the average investment—to the future annual net income.

Decision rule: Under the ARR method, choose the project with the higher rate of return.

EXAMPLE 8.7 Consider the following investment:

Initial investment	$6,500
Estimated life	20 years
Cash inflows per year	$1,000
Depreciation per year (using straight line)	$325

The accounting rate of return for this project is:

$$\text{ARR} = \frac{\text{net income}}{\text{investment}} = \frac{\$1,000 - \$325}{\$6,500} = 10.4\%$$

If *average* investment (usually assumed to be one-half of the original investment) is used, then:

$$\text{ARR} = \frac{\$1,000 - \$325}{\$3,250} = 20.8\%$$

The *advantages* of this method are that it is easily understandable, simple to compute, and recognizes the profitability factor.

The *shortcomings* of this method are that it fails to recognize the time value of money, and it uses accounting data instead of cash flow data.

Net Present Value

Net present value (NPV) is the excess of the present value (PV) of cash inflows generated by the project over the amount of the initial investment (I):

$$\text{NPV} = \text{PV} - \text{I}$$

The present value of future cash flows is computed using the so-called cost of capital (or minimum required rate of return) as the discount rate. In the case of an annuity, the present value would be

$$\text{PV} = \text{A} \cdot \text{PVIFA}$$

where A is the amount of the annuity. The value of PVIFA is found in Appendix D.

Decision rule: If NPV is positive, accept the project. Otherwise, reject it.

EXAMPLE 8.8 Consider the following investment:

Initial investment	$12,950
Estimated life	10 years
Annual cash inflows	$3,000
Cost of capital (minimum required rate of return)	12%

Present value of the cash inflows is

$$\text{PV} = \text{A} \cdot \text{PVIFA} = \$3,000 \times \text{PVIFA}_{12\%,10}$$

$= \$3,000 (5.6502)$	$16,950.60
Initial investment (I)	12,950.00
Net present value (NPV = PV − I)	$ 4,000.60

Since the NPV of the investment is positive, the investment should be accepted.

The *advantages* of the NPV method are that it obviously recognizes the time value of money and it is easy to compute whether the cash flows form an annuity or vary from period to period.

Internal Rate of Return

Internal rate of return (IRR) is defined as the rate of interest that equates I with the PV of future cash inflows. In other words, at IRR,

$$I = PV$$

or

$$NPV = 0$$

Decision rule: Accept the project if the IRR exceeds the cost of capital. Otherwise, reject it.

EXAMPLE 8.9   Assume the same data given in Example 8.8, and set the following equality (I = PV):

$$\$12,950 = \$3,000 \times PVIFA$$

$$PVIFA = \frac{\$12,950}{\$3,000} = 4.317$$

which stands somewhere between 18 percent and 20 percent in the 10-year line of Appendix D. The interpolation follows:

		PV Factor	
18%		4.494	4.494
IRR		4.317	
20%			4.192
Difference		0.177	0.302

Therefore,

$$IRR = 18\% + \frac{0.177}{0.302}(20\% - 18\%)$$

$$= 18\% + 0.586(2\%) = 18\% + 1.17\% = 19.17\%$$

Since the IRR of the investment is greater than the cost of capital (12 percent), accept the project.

The *advantage* of using the IRR method is that it does consider the time value of money and, therefore, is more exact and realistic than the ARR method.

The *shortcomings* of this method are that (1) it is time-consuming to compute, especially when the cash inflows are not even, although most business calculators have a program to calculate IRR, and (2) it fails to recognize the varying sizes of investment in competing projects and their respective dollar profitabilities.

When cash inflows are not even, IRR is computed by the trial-and-error method, as follows:

1.   Compute NPV at cost of capital, denoted here as r_1.
2.   See if NPV is positive or negative.
3.   If NPV is positive, then pick another rate (r_2) much higher than r_1. If NPV is negative, then pick another rate (r_2) much smaller than r_1. The true IRR, at which NPV = 0, must lie somewhere in between these two rates.
4.   Compute NPV using r_2.
5.   Interpolate to get the exact rate.

EXAMPLE 8.10   Consider the following investment whose cash flows are different from year to year:

Year	After-Tax Cash Inflows ($)
1	1,000
2	2,500
3	1,500

Assume that the amount of initial investment is $3,000 and the cost of capital is 14 percent.

1.   NPV at 14 percent:

Year	Cash Inflow ($)	PV Factor at 14%	Total PV ($ Rounded)
1	1,000	0.8772	877
2	2,500	0.7695	1,924
3	1,500	0.6750	1,013
			3,814

Therefore,

$$NPV = \$3,814 - \$3,000 = \$814$$

2.   We see that NPV = $813 is positive at $r_1 = 14\%$.

3.   Pick, say, 30 percent to play safe as r_2.

4.   Computing NPV at $r_2 = 30\%$:

Year	Cash Inflow ($)	PV Factor at 30%	Total PV ($ Rounded)
1	1,000	0.7694	769
2	2,500	0.5921	1,480
3	1,500	0.4558	684
			2,933

Therefore,

$$NPV = \$2,933 - \$3,000 = -\$67$$

5.   Interpolate:

	NPV	
14%	$814	$814
IRR	0	
30%		$-(-67)$
Difference	$814	$881

Therefore,

$$IRR = 14\% + \frac{\$814}{\$881}(30\% - 14\%)$$

$$= 14\% + 0.924(16\%) = 14\% + 14.78\% = 28.78\%$$

Profitability Index (Benefit/Cost Ratio)

The profitability index is the ratio of the total PV of future cash inflows to the initial investment, that is, PV/I. This index is used as a means of ranking projects in descending order of attractiveness. If the profitability index is greater than 1, then accept the project.

Decision rule: If the profitability index is greater than 1, then accept the project.

EXAMPLE 8.11 Using the data in Example 8.8, the profitability index is

$$\frac{PV}{I} = \frac{\$16,950}{\$12,950} = 1.31$$

Since this project generates $1.31 for each dollar invested (i.e., its profitability index is greater than 1), accept the project.

8.4 MUTUALLY EXCLUSIVE INVESTMENTS

A project is said to be *mutually exclusive* if the acceptance of one project automatically excludes the acceptance of one or more other projects. In the case where one must choose between mutually exclusive investments, the NPV and IRR methods may result in contradictory indications. The conditions under which contradictory rankings can occur are:

1. Projects that have different life expectancies.
2. Projects that have different sizes of investment.
3. Projects whose cash flows differ over time. For example, the cash flows of one project increase over time, while those of another decrease.

The contradictions result from different assumptions with respect to the reinvestment rate on cash flows from the projects.

1. The NPV method discounts all cash flows at the cost of capital, thus implicitly assuming that these cash flows can be reinvested at this rate.
2. The IRR method implies a reinvestment rate at IRR. Thus, the implied reinvestment rate will differ from project to project.

The NPV method generally gives correct ranking, since the cost of capital is a more realistic reinvestment rate.

EXAMPLE 8.12 Assume the following:

	Cash Flows					
	0	1	2	3	4	5
A	(100)	120				
B	(100)					201.14

Computing IRR and NPV at 10 percent gives the following different rankings:

	IRR	NPV at 10%
A	20%	9.01
B	15%	24.90

The NPVs plotted against the appropriate discount rates form a graph called a NPV profile (Fig. 8-1).

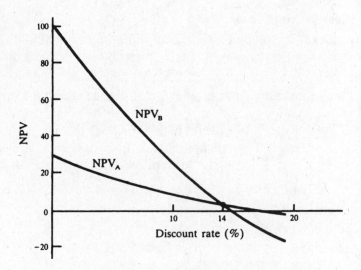

Fig. 8-1 NPV profile

At a discount rate larger than 14 percent, A has a higher NPV than B. Therefore, A should be selected. At a discount rate less than 14 percent, B has the higher NPV than A, and thus should be selected. The correct decision is to select the project with the higher NPV, since the NPV method assumes a more realistic reinvestment rate, that is, the cost of capital.

8.5 THE MODIFIED INTERNAL RATE OF RETURN (MIRR)

When the IRR and NPV methods produce a contradictory ranking for mutual exclusive projects, the modified IRR, or MIRR, overcomes the disadvantage of IRR.

The MIRR is defined as the discount rate which forces

I = PV of terminal (future) value compounded at the cost of capital

The MIRR forces cash flow reinvestment at the cost of capital rather than the project's own IRR, which was the problem with the IRR.

1. MIRR avoids the problem of multiple IRRs.
2. Conflicts can still occur in ranking mutually exclusive projects with differing sizes. NPV should again be used in such a case.

EXAMPLE 8.13 In Example 18.12, Project A's MIRR is:

First, compute the project's terminal value at a 10% cost of capital.

$$120 \text{ FVIF}_{10,4} = 12 \times 1.4641 = 175.69$$

Next, find the IRR by setting:

$$100 = 175.69 \text{ PVIF}_{\text{MIRR,5}}$$

$$\text{PVIF} = 100/175.69 = 0.5692, \text{ which gives MIRR} = \text{about } 12\%$$

Now we see the consistent ranking from both the NPV and MIRR methods.

	MIRR	NPV at 10%
A	12%	$ 9.01
B	15	$24.90

8.6 COMPARING PROJECTS WITH UNEQUAL LIVES

A replacement decision typically involving two mutually exclusive projects. When these two mutually exclusive projects have significantly different lives, an adjustment would be necessary. We discuss two approaches: (1) the replacement chain (common life) approach and (2) the equivalent annual annuity approach.

The Replacement Chain (Common Life) Approach

This procedure extends one, or both, projects until an equal life is achieved. For example, Project A has a 6-year life, while Project B has a 3-year life. Under this approach, the projects would be extended to a common life of 6 years. Project B would have an adjusted NPV equal to the NPV_B plus the NPV_B discounted for 3 years at the project's cost of capital. Then the project with the higher NPV would be chosen.

EXAMPLE 8.14 Sims Industries, Inc. is considering two machines to replace an old machine. Machine A has a life of 10 years, will cost $24,500, and will produce net cash savings of $4,800 per year. Machine B has an expected life of 5 years, will cost $20,000, and will produce net cash savings in operating costs of $6,000 per year. The company's cost of capital is 14 percent. Project A's NPV is

$$NPV_A = PV - I = \$4,800 \ PVIFA_{10,14} - \$24,500$$
$$= \$4,800(5.2161) - \$24,500 = \$25,037.28 - \$24,500$$
$$= \$537.28$$

Project B's extended time line can be set up as follows:

0	1	2	3	4	5	6	7	8	9	10	
−200	60	60	60	60	60	60	60	60	60	60	(in hundredths)
						−200					

$$Adjusted \ NPV_B = PV - I = \$6,000 \ PVIFA_{10,14} - \$20,000 \ PVIF_{5,14} - \$20,000 \ PVIF_{5,14} - \$20,000$$
$$= \$6,000(5.2161) - \$20,000(0.5194) - \$20,000$$
$$= \$31,296.60 - \$10,388.00 - \$20,000$$
$$= \$908.60$$

Or, alternatively,

$$NPV_B = PV - I = \$6,000 \ PVIFA_{5,14} - \$20,000$$
$$= \$6,000(3.4331) - \$20,000$$
$$= \$20,598.60 - \$20,000$$
$$= \$598.60$$

$$Adjusted \ NPV_B = NPV_B + NPV_B \ discounted \ for \ 5 \ years$$
$$= \$598.60 + \$598.60 \ PVIF_{5,14}$$
$$= \$598.60 + \$598.60(0.5194)$$
$$= \$598.60 + \$310.91$$
$$= \$909.51 \ (due \ to \ rounding \ errors)$$

The Equivalent Annual Annuity (EAA) Approach

It is often cumbersome to compare projects with different lives. For example, one project might have a 4-year life versus a 10-year life for the other. This would require a replacement chain analysis over 20 years, the lowest common denominator of the two lives. In such a case, it is often simpler to use an alternative approach, the *equivalent annual annuity method.*

This procedure involves three steps:

1. Determine each project's NPV over its original life.

2. Find the constant annuity cash flow or EAA, using

$$\frac{\text{NPV of each project}}{\text{PVIFA}_{n,i}}$$

3. Assuming infinite replacement, find the infinite horizon (or perpetuity) NPV of each project, using

$$\frac{\text{EAA of each}}{\text{cost of capital}}$$

EXAMPLE 8.15   From Example 8.14, $\text{NPV}_A = \$537.28$ and $\text{NPV}_B = \$598.60$.
To obtain the constant annuity cash flow or EAA, we do the following:

$$\text{EAA}_A = \$537.28/\text{PVIFA}_{10,14} = \$537.28/5.2161 = \$103.00$$
$$\text{EAA}_B = \$598.60/\text{PVIFA}_{5,14} = \$598.60/3.4331 = \$174.36$$

Thus, the infinite horizon NPVs are as follows:

$$\text{Infinite horizon NPV}_A = \$103.00/0.14 = \$735.71$$
$$\text{Infinite horizon NPV}_B = \$174.36/0.14 = \$1,245.43$$

8.7   THE CONCEPT OF ABANDONMENT VALUE

The notion of abandonment value recognizes that abandonment of a project before the end of its physical life can have a significant impact on the project's return and risk. This distinguishes between the project's economic life and physical life. Two types of abandonment can occur:

1. Abandonment of an asset since it is being unprofitable.

2. Sale of the asset to some other party who can extract more value than the original owner.

EXAMPLE 8.16   ABC Company is considering a project with an initial cost of $5,000 and net cash flows of $2,000 for next three years. The expected abandonment cash flows for years 0,1,2, and 3 are $5,000, $3,000, $2,500, and $0. The firm's cost of capital is 10 percent. We will compute NPVs in three cases.

Case 1.   NPV of the project if kept for 3 years

$$\text{NPV} = \text{PV} - \text{I} = \$2,000 \text{ PVIFA}_{10,3} = \$2,000(2.4869) - \$5,000$$
$$= \$26.20$$

Case 2.   NPV of the project if abandoned after Year 1

$$\text{NPV} = \text{PV} - \text{I} = \$2,000 \text{ PVIF}_{10,1} + \$3,500 \text{ PVIF}_{10,2} - \$5,000$$
$$= \$2,000(0.9091) + \$3,000(0.9091) - \$5,000$$
$$= \$1,818.20 + \$2,717.30 - \$5,000 = -\$454.50$$

Case 3. NPV of the project if abandoned after Year 2

$$\text{NPV} = \text{PV} - \text{I} = \$2,000 \text{ PVIF}_{10,1} + \$2,000 \text{ PVIF}_{10,2} + \$1,500 \text{ PVIF}_{10,2} - \$5,000$$
$$= \$2,000(0.9091) + \$2,000(0.8264) + \$2,500(0.8264) - \$5,000$$
$$= \$1,818.20 + \$1,652.80 + \$2,066.00 - \$5,000 = \$537$$

The company should abandon the project after Year 2.

8.8 CAPITAL RATIONING

Many firms specify a limit on the overall budget for capital spending. *Capital rationing* is concerned with the problem of selecting the mix of acceptable projects that provides the *highest overall NPV*. The profitability index is used widely in ranking projects competing for limited funds.

EXAMPLE 8.17 A company with a fixed budget of $250,000 needs to select a mix of acceptable projects from the following:

Projects	I ($)	PV ($)	NPV ($)	Profitability Index	Ranking
A	70,000	112,000	42,000	1.6	1
B	100,000	145,000	45,000	1.45	2
C	110,000	126,500	16,500	1.15	5
D	60,000	79,000	19,000	1.32	3
E	40,000	38,000	−2,000	0.95	6
F	80,000	95,000	15,000	1.19	4

The ranking resulting from the profitability index shows that the company should select projects A, B, and D:

	I	PV
A	$ 70,000	$112,000
B	100,000	145,000
D	60,000	79,000
	$230,000	$336,000

Therefore,

$$\text{NPV} = \$336,000 - \$230,000 = \$106,000$$

Unfortunately, the profitability index method has some limitations. One of the more serious is that it breaks down whenever more than one resource is rationed.

A more general approach to solving capital rationing problems is the use of *mathematical* (or *zero-one*) programming.[1] Here the objective is to select the mix of projects that maximizes the NPV subject to a budget constraint.

EXAMPLE 8.18 Using the data given in Example 8.13 set up the problem as a mathematical programming problem. First label project A as X_1, B as X_2, and so on; the problem can be stated as follows: Maximize

$$\text{NPV} = \$42,000X_1 + \$45,000X_2 + \$16,500X_3 + \$19,000X_4 - \$2,000X_5 + \$15,000X_6$$

---

[1] A comprehensive treatment of the problem appears in H. Martin Weingartner, "Capital Budgeting of Interrelated Projects—Survey and Synthesis," *Management Science*, vol. 12, March 1966, pp. 485–516.

subject to

$$\$70{,}000X_1 + \$100{,}000X_2 + \$110{,}000X_3 + \$60{,}000X_4 + \$40{,}000X_5 + \$80{,}000X_6 \leq \$250{,}000$$
$$X_i = 0, 1_- \ (i = 1, 2, \ldots, 6)$$

Using the mathematical program solution routine, the solution to this problem is:

$$X_1 = 1, \quad X_2 = 1, \quad X_4 = 1$$

and the NPV is $106,000. Thus, projects A, B, and D should be accepted.

8.9   CAPITAL BUDGETING DECISIONS AND THE MODIFIED ACCELERATED COST RECOVERY SYSTEM (MACRS)

Although the traditional depreciation methods still can be used for computing depreciation for book purposes, 1981 saw a new way of computing depreciation deductions for tax purposes. The current rule is called the *Modified Accelerated Cost Recovery System* (MACRS) rule, as enacted by Congress in 1981 and then modified somewhat in 1986 under the Tax Reform Act of 1986. This rule is characterized as follows:

1.   It abandons the concept of useful life and accelerates depreciation deductions by placing all depreciable assets into one of eight age property classes. It calculates deductions, based on an allowable percentage of the asset's original cost (see Tables 8-1 and 8-2).

With a shorter asset tax life than useful life, the company would be able to deduct depreciation more quickly and save more in income taxes in the earlier years, thereby making an investment more attractive. The rationale behind the system is that this way the government encourages the company to invest in facilities and increase its productive capacity and efficiency. (Remember that the higher d, the larger the tax shield (d)(t).)

2.   Since the allowable percentages in Table 8-1 add up to 100%, there is no need to consider the salvage value of an asset in computing depreciation.

3.   The company may elect the straight-line method. The straight-line convention must follow what is called the *half-year convention*. This means that the company can deduct only half of the regular straight-line depreciation amount in the first year. The reason for electing to use the MACRS optional straight-line method is that some firms may prefer to stretch out depreciation deductions using the straight-line method rather than to accelerate them. Those firms are the ones that just start out or have little or no income and wish to show more income on their income statements.

EXAMPLE 8.19   Assume that a machine falls under a 3-year property class and costs $3,000 initially. The straight-line option under MACRS differs from the traditional straight-line method in that under this method the company would deduct only $500 depreciation in the first year and the fourth year ($3,000/3 years = $1,000; $1,000/2 = $500). The table below compares the straight-line with half-year convention with the MACRS.

Year	Straight-line (half-year) Depreciation	Cost		MACRS %	MACRS Deduction
1	$ 500	$3,000	×	33.3	$ 999
2	1,000	3,000	×	44.5	1,335
3	1,000	3,000	×	14.8	444
4	500	3,000	×	7.4	222
	$3,000				$3,000

EXAMPLE 8.20   A machine costs $10,000. Annual cash inflows are expected to be $5,000. The machine will be depreciated using the MACRS rule and will fall under the 3-year property class. The cost of capital after taxes is

Table 8-1. Modified accelerated cost recovery system classification of assets

Year	Property class					
	3-year	5-year	7-year	10-year	15-year	20-year
1	33.3%	20.0%	14.3%	10.0%	5.0%	3.8%
2	44.5	32.0	24.5	18.0	9.5	7.2
3	14.8^a	19.2	17.5	14.4	8.6	6.7
4	7.4	11.5^a	12.5	11.5	7.7	6.2
5		11.5	8.9^a	9.2	6.9	5.7
6		5.8	8.9	7.4	6.2	5.3
7			8.9	6.6^a	5.9^a	4.9
8			4.5	6.6	5.9	4.5^a
9				6.5	5.9	4.5
10				6.5	5.9	4.5
11				3.3	5.9	4.5
12					5.9	4.5
13					5.9	4.5
14					5.9	4.5
15					5.9	4.5
16					3.0	4.4
17						4.4
18						4.4
19						4.4
20						4.4
21						2.2
Total	100%	100%	100%	100%	100%	100%

^{a} Denotes the year of changeover to straight-line depreciation.

10%. The estimated life of the machine is 4 years. The salvage value of the machine at the end of the fourth year is expected to be $1,200. The tax rate is 30%.

The formula for computation of after-tax cash inflows $(S - E)(1 - t) + (d)(t)$ needs to be computed separately. The NPV analysis can be performed as follows:

	Present value factor @ 10%	Present value
Initial investment: $10,000:	1.000	$(10,000.00)
$(S - E)(1 - t)$:		
$5,000 (1 - 0.3) = $3,500 for 4 years	3.170(a)	$ 11,095.00

$(d)(t)$:

Year	Cost		MACRS %	d	(d)(t)		
1	$10,000	×	33.3	$3,330	$ 999	0.909(b)	908.09
2	$10,000	×	44.5	4,450	1,335	0.826(b)	1,102.71
3	$10,000	×	14.8	1,480	444	0.751(b)	333.44
4	$10,000	×	7.4	740	222	0.683(b)	151.63

Table 8.2. MACRS tables by property class

MACRS Property Class & Depreciation Method	Useful Life (ADR Midpoint Life) "a"	Examples of Assets
3-year property 200% declining balance	4 years or less	Most small tools are included; the law specifically excludes autos and light trucks from this property class.
5-year property 200% declining balance	More than 4 years to less than 10 years	Autos and light trucks, computers, typewriters, copiers, duplicating equipment, heavy general-purpose trucks, and research and experimentation equipment are included.
7-year property 200% declining balance	10 years or more to less than 16 years	Office furniture and fixtures and most items of machinery and equipment used in production are included.
10-year property 200% declining balance	16 years or more to less than 20 years	Various machinery and equipment, such as that used in petroleum distilling and refining and in the milling of grain, are included.
15-year property 150% declining balance	20 years or more to less than 25 years	Sewage treatment plants, telephone and electrical distribution facilities, and land improvements are included.
20-year property 150% declining balance	25 years or more	Service stations and other real property with an ADR midpoint life of less than 27.5 years are included.
27.5-year property Straight-line	Not applicable	All residential rental property is included.
31.5-year property Straight-line	Not applicable	All nonresidential real property is included.

"a" The term ADR midpoint life means the "useful life" of an asset in a business sense; the appropriate ADR midpoint lives for assets are designated in the Tax Regulations.

Salvage value:

$1,200 in year 4: $1,200 (1 − 0.3) = 840(c)	0.683(b)	573.72
Net present value (NPV)		$ 4,164.59

(a) PVIFA$_{10\%,4}$ = 3.170 (from Appendix D).

(b) PVIF values obtained from Appendix C.

(c) Any salvage value received under the MACRS rules is a *taxable gain* (the excess of the selling price over book value, $1,200 in this example), since the book value will be zero at the end of the life of the machine.

Since NPV = PV − I = $4,164.59 is positive, the machine should be bought.

8.10 LEASING

Leasing provides an alternative to purchasing an asset in order to acquire its services without directly incurring any fixed debt obligation. There are two basic types of leases available to the business firm:

1. *An operating lease* is basically a short-term lease. It is cancelable at the option of the firm leasing the asset (the lessee). Such leases are commonly used for leasing such items as computer hardware, cash registers, vehicles, and equipment.

2. *A financial (capital) lease* is a longer-term lease than an operating lease. It constitutes a noncancelable contractual commitment on the part of the lessee to make a series of payments to the firm that actually owns the asset (the lessor) for the use of the asset.

Accounting for Leases

Prior to 1977, most financial (capital) leases were not included in the balance sheets of the lessee. Instead, they were reported in the footnotes of the balance sheet. However, in November 1976, the Financial Accounting Standards Board (FASB), which is a part of the American Institute of Certified Public Accountants, issued a statement that requires any lease meeting one or more of the following criteria[2] to be included in the body of the balance sheet of the lessor.

1. The lease transfers ownership of the property to the lessee by the end of the lease term.

2. The lease contains a bargain repurchase option.

3. The lease term is equal to 75 percent or more of the estimated economic life of the leased property.

4. The present value of the minimum lease payments equals or exceeds 90 percent of the excess of the fair value of the property over any related investment tax credit retained by the lessor.

The Lease-Purchase Decision

The lease-purchase decision is a decision that commonly confronts firms considering the acquisition of new assets. It is a hybrid capital budgeting decision which forces a company to compare the leasing and purchasing alternatives. To make an intelligent decision, an *after-tax, cash outflow, present value* comparison is needed. There are special steps to take when making this comparison.

When considering a lease, take the following steps:

1. Find the annual lease payment. Since the annual lease payment is typically made in advance, the formula to be used is:

$$\text{Amount of lease} = A + A(\text{PVIFA}_{i,n-1}) \quad \text{or} \quad A = \frac{\text{amount of lease}}{1 + \text{PVIFA}_{i,n-1}}$$

Notice we use $n - 1$ rather than n.

[2] Financial Accounting Standards Board, *Statement of Accounting Standards No. 13*, "Accounting for Leases," November 1976, Stamford, CN.

2. Find the after-tax cash outflows.

3. Find the present value of the after-tax cash outflows.

When considering a purchase, take the following steps:

1. Find the annual loan amortization by using:

$$A = \frac{\text{amount of loan for the purchase}}{\text{PVIFA}_{i,n}}$$

This step may not be necessary since this amount is usually available.

2. Calculate the interest. The interest is segregated from the principal in each of the annual loan payments because only the interest is tax-deductible.

3. Find the cash outflows by adding interest and depreciation (plus any maintenance costs), and then compute the after-tax outflows.

4. Find the present value of the after-tax cash outflows, using Appendix C.

EXAMPLE 8.12 A firm has decided to acquire an asset costing $100,000 that has an expected life of 5 years, after which the asset is not expected to have any residual value. The asset can be purchased by borrowing or it can be leased. If leasing is used, the lessor requires a 12 percent return. As is customary, lease payments are to be made in advance, that is, at the end of the year prior to each of the 10 years. The tax rate is 50 percent and the firm's cost of capital, or after-tax cost of borrowing, is 8 percent.

First compute the present value of the after-tax cash outflows associated with the leasing alternative.

1. Find the annual lease payment:

$$A = \frac{\text{amount of lease}}{1 + \text{PVIFA}_{i,n-1}}$$

$$= \frac{\$100,000}{1 + \text{PVIFA}_{12\%, 4\text{ years}}} = \frac{\$100,000}{1 + 3.3073} = \frac{\$100,000}{4.3073} = \$23,216 \text{ (rounded)}$$

Steps 2 and 3 can be done in the same schedule, as follows:

Year	(1) Lease Payment ($)	(2) Tax Savings ($)	(3) = (1) − (2) After-Tax Cash Outflow ($)	(4) PV at 8%	(5) = (3) × (4) PV of Cash Outflow ($, Rounded)
0	23,216		23,216	1.000	23,216
1–4	23,216	11,608[a]	11,608	3.3121[b]	38,447
5		11,608	(11,608)	0.6806[c]	(7,900)
					53,763

[a] $23,216 × 50%

[b] From Appendix D.

[c] From Appendix C.

If the asset is purchased, the firm is assumed to finance it entirely with a 10 percent unsecured term loan. Straight-line depreciation is used with no salvage value. Therefore, the annual depreciation is $20,000 ($100,000/5 years). In this alternative, first find the annual loan payment by using:

$$A = \frac{\text{amount of loan}}{\text{PVIFA}_{i,n}}$$

$$= \frac{\$100,000}{\text{PVIFA}_{10\%, 5\text{ years}}} = \frac{\$100,000}{3.7906} = \$26,381 \text{ (rounded)}$$

2. Calculate the interest by setting up a loan amortization schedule.

Year	(1) Loan Payment ($)	(2) Beginning-of-Year Principal ($)	(3) = (2)(10%) Interest ($)	(4) = (1) − (3) Principal ($)	(5) = (2) − (4) End-of-Year Principal ($)
1	26,381	100,000	10,000	16,381	83,619
2	26,381	83,619	8,362	18,019	65,600
3	26,381	65,600	6,560	19,821	45,779
4	26,381	45,779	4,578	21,803	23,976
5	26,381	23,976[a]	2,398	23,983[a]	

[a] Because of rounding errors, there is a slight difference between (2) and (4).

Steps 3 (cash outflows) and 4 (present values of those outflows) can be done as follows:

Year	(1) Loan Payment ($)	(2) Interest ($)	(3) Depreciation ($)	(4) = (2) + (3) Total Deductions ($)	(5) = (4)(50%) Tax Savings ($)	(6) = (1) − (5) Cash Outflow ($)	(7) PV at 8%	(8) = (6) × (7) PV of Cash Outflow ($)
1	26,381	10,000	20,000	30,000	15,000	11,381	0.9259	10,538
2	26,381	8,362	20,000	28,362	14,181	12,200	0.8573	10,459
3	26,381	6,560	20,000	26,560	13,280	13,101	0.7938	10,400
4	26,381	4,578	20,000	24,578	12,289	14,092	0.7350	10,358
5	26,381	2,398	20,000	22,398	11,199	15,182	0.6806	10,333
								52,088

The sum of the present values of the cash outflows for leasing and purchasing by borrowing shows that purchasing is preferable because the PV of borrowing is less than the PV of leasing ($52,088 versus $53,763). The *incremental* savings would be $1,675 ($53,763 − $52,088).

8.11 CAPITAL BUDGETING AND INFLATION

The accuracy of capital budgeting decisions depends on the accuracy of the data regarding cash inflows and outflows. For example, failure to incorporate price-level changes due to inflation in capital budgeting situations can result in errors in the predicting of cash flows and thus in incorrect decisions.

Typically, an analyst has two options dealing with a capital budgeting situation with inflation: Either restate the cash flows in nominal terms and discount them at a nominal cost of capital (minimum required rate of return) or restate both the cash flows and cost of capital in constant terms and discount the constant cash flows at a constant cost of capital. The two methods are basically equivalent.

EXAMPLE 8.22 A company has the following projected cash flows estimated in real terms:

Real Cash Flows (000s)

Period	0	1	2	3
	−100	35	50	30

The nominal cost of capital is 15 percent. Assume that inflation is projected at 10 percent a year. Then the first cash flow for year 1, which is $35,000 in current dollars, will be 35,000 × 1.10 = $38,500 in year 1 dollars. Similarly the cash flow for year 2 will be 50,000 × (1.10)2 = $60,500 in year 2 dollars, and so on. If we discount these nominal cash flows at the 15 percent nominal cost of capital, we have the following net present value (NPV):

Period	Cash Flows	PVIF (Appendix C)	Present Values
0	−100	1.000	−100
1	38.5	0.870	33.50
2	60.5	0.756	45.74
3	39.9	0.658	26.25
		NPV =	5.49 or $5,490

Instead of converting the cash-flow forecasts into nominal terms, we could convert the cost of capital into real terms by using the following formula:

$$\text{Real cost of capital} = \frac{1 + \text{nominal cost of capital}}{1 + \text{inflation rate}} - 1$$

In the example, this gives

$$\text{Real cost of capital} = (1 + 0.15)/(1 + 0.10) - 1$$
$$= 1.15/1.10 - 1$$
$$= 1.045 - 1$$
$$= 0.045 \text{ or } 4.5\%$$

We will obtain the same answer except for rounding errors ($5,490 versus $5,580).

Period	Cash Flows	PVIF = $1/(1 + 0.045)^n$	Present Values
0	−100	1.000	−100
1	35	$1/(1 + 0.045) = 0.957$	33.50
2	50	$1/(1.045)2 = 0.916$	45.80
3	30	$1/(1.045)3 = 0.876$	26.28
		NPV =	5.58 or $5,580

Review Questions

1. The initial investment is _____ plus installation cost minus _____ plus or minus _____ .

2. The total gain is split into _____ and _____ . These breakdowns are subject to _____ tax rates.

3. After-tax cash inflows equal net profits after taxes plus _____ .

4. The NPV method and the IRR method are called _____ methods.

5. _____ is the process of making _____ decisions.

6. _____ is the _____ divided by the cash inflow through increased revenues or cash savings in operating expenses.

7. The shorter the _____, the less risky the project and the greater the _____.

8. Accounting rate of return does not recognize the _____.

9. Internal rate of return is the rate at which _____ equals _____.

10. Accept the investment if its IRR exceeds _____.

11. IRR is difficult to compute when the cash flows are _____.

12. In _____, the NPV and the IRR methods may produce _____.

13. _____ is used widely in ranking the investments competing for limited funds.

14. The _____ method discounts all cash flows at the _____, thus implicitly assuming that these cash flows can be reinvested at this rate.

15. MACRS rules abandon the concept of _____.

16. _____ is taken in the year in which an asset is first placed into service.

17. The straight-line depreciation method with _____ allows the company to deduct only half of the regular straight-line deduction amount in the _____ year.

18. Immediate disposal of an old machine usually results in _____ that is fully deductible from current income for tax purposes.

19. The FASB requires firms to _____ certain financial (capital) leases and to restate their _____.

20. Lease payments represent a desired rate of return to the _____.

21. If two mutually exclusive projects have unequal lives, either of the two methods may be used for the analysis: the _____ and the _____.

22. The _____ overcomes many of the IRR's disadvantages.

Answers: (1) cost (purchase price) of the asset, the proceeds from sale of the old asset, taxes on the sale of old asset; (2) a capital gain, recapture of depreciation, different; (3) depreciation; (4) discounted cash flow (DCF); (5) Capital budgeting, long-term investment; (6) Payback period, initial amount of investment; (7) payback period, liquidity; (8) time value of money; (9) present value of cash inflows, the initial investment; (10) the cost of capital; (11) not even; (12) mutually exclusive investments, conflicting rankings; (13) Profitability index (or benefit/cost ratio); (14) NPV, cost of capital; (15) useful life; (15) Investment tax credit (ITC); (17) the half-year convention, first; (18) a loss; (19) capitalize, balance sheets; (20) lessor; (21) replacement chain (common life) approach, equivalent annual annuity (EAA); (22) modified internal rate of return (MIRR).

Solved Problems

8.1   **Capital Gain (Loss) and Recapture of Depreciation.** For each of the following cases, compute the total taxes resulting from the sale of the asset. Assume a 34 percent ordinary tax rate. The asset was purchased for $75,000 3 years ago and has a book value (undepreciated value) of $40,000. (*a*) The asset is sold for $80,000. (*b*) The asset is sold for $70,000. (*c*) The asset is sold for $40,000. (*d*) The asset is sold for $38,000.

SOLUTION

(*a*)   Total gain = selling price − book value
                                   = $80,000 − $40,000 = $40,000

   Total taxes are: $13,600 (34% × $40,000)

(*b*)   Gain: $70,000 − $40,000 = $30,000

       Tax: $30,000 × 0.34 = $10,200

(*c*)   No tax.

(*d*)   Loss: $38,000 − $40,000 = $2,000

       Tax saving: $2,000 × 0.34 = $680

8.2   **Calculation of Initial Investment.** A firm is considering replacing an old machine with another. The new machine costs $90,000 plus $10,000 to install. For each of the four cases given in Problem 8.1, calculate the initial investment of the replacement.

SOLUTION

	(*a*)	(*b*)	(*c*)	(*d*)
Cost of new machine	$90,000	$90,000	$90,000	$90,000
+ Installation cost	10,000	10,000	10,000	10,000
− Proceeds from sale of old machine	80,000	70,000	40,000	38,000
+ Taxes on sale of old machine	17,500	13,800	0	(920)
Initial investment	$37,500	$43,800	$60,000	$61,080

8.3   **Incremental Cash Inflows.** National Bottles Corporation is contemplating the replacement of one of its bottling machines with a new one that will increase revenue from $25,000 to $31,000 per year and reduce cash operating costs from $12,000 to $10,000 per year. The new machine will cost $48,000 and have an estimated life of 10 years with no salvage value. The firm uses straight-line depreciation and is subject to a 46 percent tax rate. The old machine has been fully depreciated and has no salvage value. What is the incremental (relevant) cash inflows generated by the replacement?

SOLUTION

$$\text{Annual depreciation of the new machine} = \frac{\text{cost}}{\text{expected life}}$$

$$= \frac{\$48,000}{10} = \$4,800 \text{ per year}$$

	Annual		**Net Profits before**
	Revenue	**Cash Operating Costs**	**Depreciation and Taxes**
Old	$25,000	$12,000	$13,000
New	$31,000	$10,000	$21,000

Net profits after taxes and after-tax cash inflows for both machines are computed as follows:

	Net Profits after Taxes	**Add Depreciation**	**After-Tax Cash Inflows**
Old	($13,000 − 0)(1 − 0.46) = $7,020	$ 0	$ 7,020
New	($21,000 − $4,800)(1 − 0.46) = $8,748	$4,800	$13,548

Therefore, the relevant incremental cash inflows for each year are:

$$\$13,548 - \$7,020 = \$6,528$$

Alternatively, use the shortcut formula, as follows:

Increase in revenue $\times$ (1 − tax rate):	
($31,000 − $25,000)(1 − 0.46)	$3,240
− Increase in cash charges $\times$ (1 − tax rate):	
($10,000 − $12,000)(1 − 0.46)	−(−1,080)
+ Increase in depreciation $\times$ tax rate:	
($4,800 − 0)(0.46)	2,208
After-tax cash inflows	$6,528

8.4 **Basic Evaluation Methods.** The following data are given for the Alright Aluminum Company:

Initial cost of proposed equipment	$75,000
Estimated useful life	7 years
Estimated annual savings in cash operating expenses	$18,000
Predicted residual value at the end of the useful life	$3,000
Cost of capital	12%

Compute the: (*a*) payback period; (*b*) present value of estimated annual savings; (*c*) present value of estimated residual value; (*d*) total present value of estimated cash inflows; (*e*) net present value (NPV); and (*f*) internal rate of return (IRR).

SOLUTION

(*a*) $$\text{Payback period} = \frac{\text{initial investment}}{\text{annual savings}} = \frac{\$75,000}{\$18,000} = 4.167 \text{ years}$$

(*b*) $$PV = A \times PVIFA_{12\%, 7\,years} = \$18,000 \times 4.5638 = \$82,148 \text{ (rounded)}$$

(*c*) $$PV = \$3,000 \times PVIF_{12\%, 7\,years} = \$3,000 \times 0.4523 = \$1,357 \text{ (rounded)}$$

(*d*) $$\text{Total PV} = \$82,148 + \$1,357 = \$83,505$$

(*e*) $$NPV = PV - I = \$83,505 - \$75,000 = \$8,505$$

(*f*)   At IRR, I = PV. Thus,

$$\$75,000 = \$18,000 \times PVIFA_{r,7}$$

$$PVIFA_{r,7} = \frac{\$75,000}{\$18,000} = 4.1667$$

which is somewhere between 14 percent and 15 percent in the 7-year line.

Using interpolation,

	PVIFA	
14%	4.2883	4.2883
True rate	4.1667	
15%		4.1604
Difference	0.1216	0.1279

$$\text{IRR} = 14\% + \frac{4.2883 - 4.1667}{4.2883 - 4.1604}(15\% - 14\%)$$

$$= 14\% + \frac{0.1216}{0.1279}(1\%) = 14\% + 0.95\% = 14.95\%$$

8.5 Payback Period and ARR. The John-in-the-Box Store is a fast food restaurant chain. Potential franchisees are given the following revenue and cost information:

Building and equipment	$490,000
Annual revenue	$520,000
Annual cash operating costs	$380,000

The building and equipment have a useful life of 20 years. The straight-line method for depreciation is used. The income tax is 40 percent. Given these facts: (*a*) What is the payback period? (*b*) What is the accounting rate of return?

SOLUTION

$$\text{Net profits before depreciation and taxes} = \$520,000 - \$380,000 = \$140,000$$

$$\text{Annual depreciation} = \frac{\$490,000}{20 \text{ years}} = \$24,500$$

Therefore,

$$\text{Net profit after taxes} = (\$140,000 - \$24,500)(1 - 0.4) = \$69,300$$

$$\text{After-tax cash inflows} = \$69,300 + \$24,500 = \$93,800$$

(*a*) $$\text{Payback period} = \frac{\text{Initial investment}}{\text{annual cash flow}} = \frac{\$490,000}{\$93,800} = 5.22 \text{ years}$$

(*b*) $$\text{Accounting rate of return} = \frac{\text{net income}}{\text{investment}} = \frac{\$69,300}{\$490,000} = 14.14\%$$

or using average investment in the denominator gives:

$$\text{ARR} = \frac{\$69,300}{\$490,000/2} = 28.28\%$$

8.6 Basic Evaluation Methods. The Rango Company is considering a capital investment for which the initial outlay is $20,000. Net annual cash inflows (before taxes) are predicted to be $4,000 for 10 years. Straight-line depreciation is to be used, with an estimated salvage value of zero. Ignore income taxes. Compute the: (*a*) payback period; (*b*) accounting rate of return (ARR); (*c*) net present value (NPV), assuming a cost of capital (before tax) of 12 percent; and (*d*) internal rate of return (IRR).

SOLUTION

(a)
$$\text{Payback period} = \frac{\text{initial investment}}{\text{annual cash flow}} = \frac{\$20,000}{\$4,000/\text{year}} = 5 \text{ years}$$

(b)
$$\text{Accounting rate of return (ARR)} = \frac{\text{net income}}{\text{initial investment}}$$

$$\text{Depreciation} = \frac{\$20,000}{10 \text{ years}} = \$2,000/\text{year}$$

$$\text{Accounting rate of return} = \frac{(\$4,000 - \$2,000)/\text{year}}{\$20,000} = 0.10 = 10\%$$

(c)   Net present value (NPV) = PV of cash inflows [discounted at the cost of capital (12%)]

$$-\text{initial investment}$$

$$\$4,000 \times (\text{PVIFA}_{12\%,10}) - \$20,000 = \$4,000(5.6502) - \$20,000 = \$2,600.80$$

(d) Internal rate of return (IRR) is the rate which equates the amount invested with the present value of cash inflows generated by the project.

$$\$20,000 = \$4,000(\text{PVIFA}_{r,10})$$

$$\text{PVIFA}_{r,10} = \frac{\$20,000}{\$4,000} = 5$$

which is between 15 percent and 16 percent in Appendix D. Using interpolation,

	PVIFA	
15%	5.0188	5.0188
True rate	5.0000	
16%		4.8332
Difference	0.0188	0.1856

$$\text{IRR} = 15\% + \left(\frac{5.0188 - 5.0000}{5.0188 - 4.8332}\right)(16\% - 15\%) = 15\% + \frac{0.0188}{0.1856}(1\%)$$

$$= 15\% + 0.101\% = 15.101\%$$

8.7 **Basic Capital Budgeting Decisions.** Consider an investment which has the following cash flows:

Year	Cash Flow ($)
0	(31,000)
1	10,000
2	20,000
3	10,000
4	10,000
5	5,000

(a) Compute the: (1) payback period; (2) net present value (NPV) at 14 percent cost of capital; and (3) internal rate of return (IRR).

(b) Based on (2) and (3) in part (a), make a decision about the investment. Should it be accepted or not?

SOLUTION

(*a*) (1)   The payback period is computed as follows:

Year	Cash Flow	Recovery of Initial Outlay		Payback Period
		Needed	**Balance**	
1	$10,000	$31,000	$21,000	1.00
2	$20,000	$21,000	$ 1,000	1.00
3	$10,000	$ 1,000		0.10
				2.1^a

^{a} Payback period in years.

(2) NPV is computed as follows:

Year	Cash Flow ($)	PV Factor at 14%	PV ($)
0	(31,000)	1.000	(31,000)
1	10,000	0.8772	8,772
2	20,000	0.7695	15,390
3	10,000	0.6750	6,750
4	10,000	0.5921	5,921
5	5,000	0.5194	2,597
		NPV	8,430

(3)   By definition, IRR is the rate at which PV = I or NPV = 0. From part (2), NPV at 14% = $8,430. Try 30 percent to determine what happens to NPV.

Year	Cash Flow ($)	PV Factor at 30%	PV ($)
0	(31,000)	1.000	(31,000)
1	10,000	0.7694	7,694
2	20,000	0.5921	11,842
3	10,000	0.4558	4,558
4	10,000	0.3509	3,509
5	5,000	0.2702	1,351
			(2,046)

True IRR is somewhere between 14 percent and 30 percent. Use interpolation to determine the amount.

	NPV	
14%	$8,430	$ 8,430
True rate	0	
30%		−(−2,046)
Difference	$8,430	$10,476

Therefore,

$$IRR = 14\% + \frac{\$8,430}{\$8,430 - (-\$2,046)}(30\% - 14\%)$$

$$= 14\% + \frac{\$8,430}{\$10,476}(16\%) = 14\% + 12.875\% = 26.875\%$$

(b) Under the NPV method, accept the project since the NPV is positive ($8,430). Under the IRR method, accept the project since the IRR of 26.875 percent exceeds the cost of capital of 14 percent.

8.8 **Comprehensive Capital Budgeting Decision.** The Chellin Company purchased a special machine 1 year ago at a cost of $12,000. At that time the machine was estimated to have a useful life of 6 years and no salvage value. The annual cash operating cost is approximately $20,000. A new machine has just come on the market which will do the same job but with an annual cash operating cost of only $17,000. This new machine costs $21,000 and has an estimated life of 5 years with zero salvage value. The old machine can be sold for $10,000 to a scrap dealer. Straight-line depreciation is used, and the company's income tax rate is 40 percent.

Assuming a cost of capital of 8 percent after taxes, calculate: (a) the initial investment; (b) the incremental cash inflow after taxes; (c) the NPV of the new investment; and (d) the IRR on the new investment.

SOLUTION

(a) The initial investment is:

Cost of new machine	$21,000
− Proceeds from sale of old machine	10,000
	$11,000

Since the selling price ($10,000) is the same as the book value ($12,000 − $2,000 = $10,000), no taxable gain or loss results.

(b) The incremental cash inflow may be computed by using the shortcut formula:

Annual cash savings	
[$3,000 × (1 − 0.4)]	$1,800
+ Increase in depreciation × tax rate	
[($4,200 − $2,000)(0.4)]	880
After-tax cash inflow	$2,680

(c)
$$NPV = PV - I$$
$$= \$2,680(PVIFA_{8,5}) - \$11,000 = \$2,680(3.9927) - \$11,000$$
$$= \$10,700 - \$11,000 = -\$300 \text{ (rounded)}$$

(d) IRR is the rate at which I = PV. Thus,

$$I = PV$$
$$\$11,000 = \$2,680 \, PVIFA_{r, 5 \text{years}}$$
$$PVIFA_{r,5} = \frac{\$11,000}{\$2,680} = 4.1045$$

which is about 7 percent in the 5-year line of Appendix D.

8.9 **Supplying Missing Data.** Fill in the blanks for each of the following independent cases. Assume in all cases the investment has a useful life of 10 years.

Annual Cash Inflow	Investment	Cost of Capital	IRR	NPV
$100,000	$449,400	14%	(a)	(b)
$70,000	(c)	14%	20%	(d)
(e)	$200,000	(f)	14%	$35,624
(g)	$300,000	12%	(h)	$39,000

SOLUTION

(a)
$$I = PV$$
$$\$449,400 = \$100,000 \text{ PVIFA}_{r,10}$$
$$\text{PVIFA}_{r,10} = \frac{\$449,400}{\$100,000} = 4.494$$

From Appendix D, the present value factor of 4.494 at 10 years gives a rate of 18%.

(b)
$$NPV = PV - I$$
$$= \$100,000 \text{ PVIFA}_{14,10} - \$449,400$$
$$= \$100,000(5.2161) - \$449,400 = \$521,610 - \$449,400 = \$72,210$$

(c)
$$I = PV$$
$$= \$70,000 \text{ PVIFA}_{20,10} = \$70,000(4.1925) = \$293,475$$

(d)
$$NPV = PV - I$$
$$= \$70,000 \text{ PVIFA}_{14,10} - \$293,475$$
$$= \$70,000(5.2161) - \$293,475 = \$365,127 - \$293,475 = \$71,652$$

(e) At IRR 14%, PV = I.
$$\text{Cash inflow} \times \text{PVIFA}_{14,10} = \text{investment}$$
$$\text{Cash inflow} = \frac{\text{investment}}{\text{PVIFA}_{14,10}} = \frac{\$200,000}{5.2161} = \$38,343 \text{ (rounded)}$$

(f)
$$NPV = PV - I$$
$$\$35,624 = PV - \$200,000$$
$$\$35,624 + \$200,000 = PV = \text{cash inflow (PVIFA}_{r,10})$$
$$\$235,624 = \$38,343 \text{ PVIFA}_{r,10}$$
$$\frac{\$235,624}{\$38,343} = \text{PVIFA}_{r,10}$$
$$6.1451 = \text{PVIFA}_{r,10}$$

Since this is the present value factor for 10 percent at 10 years, the cost of capital is 10 percent.

(g)
$$PV = NPV + 1$$
$$\text{Cash inflow (PVIFA}_{12,10}) = NPV + I = \$39,000 + \$300,000 = \$339,000$$
$$\text{Cash inflow} = \frac{\$339,000}{\text{PVIFA}_{12,10}} = \frac{\$339,000}{5.6502} = \$59,998 \text{ (rounded)}$$

(h)
$$I = PV$$
$$\$300,000 = \$59,998 \ \text{PVIFA}_{r,10}$$
$$\text{PVIFA}_{r,10} = \frac{\$300,000}{\$59,998} = 5.0002$$

Since this PVIFA value is about halfway between 15 percent and 16 percent at 10 years, IRR is estimated at about 15.5 percent.

8.10 **NPV Analysis.** Kim Corporation invested in a 4-year project. Kim's cost of capital is 8 percent. Additional information on the project follows:

Year	After-Tax Cash Inflow	Present Value of $1 at 8%
1	$2,000	0.926
2	$2,200	0.857
3	$2,400	0.794
4	$2,600	0.735

Assuming an NPV of $700, what was the initial investment?

SOLUTION

Year	Cash Inflow	PV	Total PV
1	$2,000	0.926	$1,852
2	$2,200	0.857	1,885
3	$2,400	0.794	1,906
4	$2,600	0.735	1,911
			$7,554

$$NPV = PV - I$$
$$I = PV - NPV$$
$$= \$7,554 - \$700 = \$6,854$$

8.11 **IRR.** XYZ, Inc., invested in a machine with a useful life of 6 years and no salvage value. The machine was depreciated using the straight-line method and it was expected to produce annual cash inflow from operations, net of income taxes, of $2,000. The present value of an ordinary annuity of $1 for six periods at 10 percent is 4.3553. The present value of $1 for six periods at 10 percent is 0.5645. Assuming that XYZ used an internal rate of return of 10 percent, what was the amount of the original investment?

SOLUTION

By definition, at IRR, PV = I or NPV = 0.
To obtain the amount of initial investment find the present value of $2,000 a year for 6 periods.

$$PV = \$2,000 \times 4.3553 = \$8,710.60$$

8.12 **Ranking.** Data relating to three investment projects are given below.

	A	B	C
Investment (I)	$30,000	$20,000	$50,000
Useful life	10 years	4 years	20 years
Annual cash savings	$6,207	$7,725	$9,341

Rank the projects according to their attractiveness using the: (a) payback period; (b) IRR; and (c) NPV at 14 percent cost of capital.

SOLUTION

(a)

$$\text{Payback period} = \frac{\text{initial investment}}{\text{increased revenue or savings}}$$

Project	Payback Period	Rank
A	$\dfrac{\$30,000}{\$6,207} = 4.833$ years	2
B	$\dfrac{\$20,000}{\$7,725} = 2.588$ years	1
C	$\dfrac{\$50,000}{\$9,341} = 5.353$ years	3

(b)   The IRR ranking is:

Project	Closed Rate[a]	Rank
A	16%	3
B	20%	1
C	18%	2

[a] $PV = I$

Cash inflow $\times$ PVIFA $= I$

$$PVIFA = \frac{I}{\text{Cash inflow}}$$

For A: $PVIFA_{r,10} = \dfrac{\$30,000}{\$6,207} = 4.8333$

For B: $PVIFA_{r,4} = \dfrac{\$20,000}{\$7,725} = 2.589$

For C: $PVIFA_{r,20} = \dfrac{\$50,000}{\$9,341} = 5.3527$

(c)   NPV at 14 percent is:

Project	Annual Savings	PV Factor	Total PV	I	NPV (PV − I)	Rank
A	$6,207	5.2161	$32,376	$30,000	$ 2,376	3
B	$7,725	2.9137	$22,508	$20,000	$ 2,508	2
C	$9,341	6.6231	$61,866	$50,000	$11,866	1

8.13   Capital Rationing. Rand Corporation is considering five different investment opportunities. The company's cost of capital is 12 percent. Data on these opportunities under consideration are given below.

Project	Investment ($)	PV at 12% ($)	NPV ($)	IRR (%)	Profitability Index (Rounded)
1	35,000	39,325	4,325	16	1.12
2	20,000	22,930	2,930	15	1.15
3	25,000	27,453	2,453	14	1.10
4	10,000	10,854	854	18	1.09
5	9,000	8,749	(251)	11	0.97

Based on these data: (a) rank these five projects in the descending order of preference, according to NPV, IRR, and profitability index (or benefit/cost ratio). (b) Which ranking would you prefer? (c) Based on your answer to part (b), which projects would you select if $55,000 is the limit to be spent?

SOLUTION

(a)

| | Order of Preference | | |
| | | | Profitability |
Project	NPV	IRR	Index
1	1	2	2
2	2	3	1
3	3	4	3
4	4	1	4
5	5	5	5

(b) The profitability index approach is generally considered the most dependable method of ranking projects competing for limited funds. It is an index of relative attractiveness, measured in terms of how much is returned for each dollar invested.

(c) Based on the answer in part (b), choose projects (2) and (1), for which the combined NPV would be $7,255 ($2,930 + $4,325) with the limited budget of $55,000.

8.14 Capital Rationing and Mathematical Programming. Express the capital rationing problem given in Problem 8.13 as a mathematical programming problem.

SOLUTION

Labeling project (1) as X_1, project (2) as X_2, and so on, the problem can be stated as follows: Maximize

$$NPV = \$4,325X_1 + \$2,930X_2 + \$2,453X_3 + \$854X_4 - \$251X_5$$

subject to

$$\$35,000X_1 + \$20,000X_2 + \$25,000X_3 + \$10,000X_4 + \$9,000X_5 \leq \$55,000$$
$$X_i = 0, 1 \ (i = 1, 2, \ldots, 5)$$

8.15 NPV Analysis. In Problem 8.3, should National Bottles Corporation buy the new machine? Base your answer on the NPV method, assuming that the cost of capital is 8 percent after taxes.

SOLUTION

From Problem 8.3,

$$I = \$48,000$$
$$n = 10 \text{ years}$$
$$A = \$6,528/\text{year}$$

Therefore,

$$NPV = PV - I = A \cdot PVIFA - I$$
$$= \$6,528(6.7101) - \$48,000 = \$43,804 - \$48,000 = -\$4,196 \text{ (rounded)}$$

National Bottles Corporation should not purchase the machine, because the NPV is negative.

8.16   Computerized Bookkeeping System and NPV Analysis. Zeta Corporation is contemplating the purchase of a minicomputer in order to reduce the cost of its data-processing operations. Currently, the manual bookkeeping system in use involves the following annual cash expenses:

Salaries	$ 84,000
Payroll taxes and fringe benefits	24,000
Forms and supplies	6,000
	$114,000

The present equipment is fully depreciated and has no salvage value. The cost of the computer, including installation and software, is $100,000. This entire amount is depreciable for income tax purposes on a double declining basis at the rate of 20 percent per annum.

Annual costs of the computerized bookkeeping system are estimated and given below.

Salaries	$40,000
Payroll taxes and fringe benefits	8,000
Forms and supplies	6,000
	$54,000

The computer is expected to be obsolete in 3 years, at which time its salvage value is $10,000.

(*a*) Compute after-tax cash savings. Assume a 40 percent tax rate. (*b*) Decide whether or not to purchase the computer, using the NPV method. Assume a cost of capital of 10 percent after taxes.

SOLUTION

(*a*)

Annual cash expenses of the manual system	$114,000
Annual cash expenses of computerized bookkeeping	54,000
Annual cash savings	$ 60,000

Double-declining-balance method:

Year 1	$20,000	($100,000 × 20%)
Year 2	16,000	($80,000 × 20%)
Year 3	12,800	($64,000 × 20%)
	$48,800	

Therefore, after-tax cash savings are computed as follows:

	Year 1	Year 2	Year 3
Annual cash savings	$60,000	$60,000	$60,000
Depreciation	20,000	16,000	12,800
Net profits before tax	$40,000	$44,000	$47,200
Tax (40%)	16,000	17,600	18,880
Net profits after tax	$24,000	$26,400	$28,320
Depreciation	20,000	16,000	12,800
After-tax cash inflow	$44,000	$42,400	$41,120

(b)

Year	After-Tax Cash Inflow ($)	PV of $1 at 10%	Total PV ($, Rounded)
1	44,000	0.9091	40,000
2	42,400	0.8264	35,039
3	41,120	0.7513	30,893
	10,000[a]	0.7513	7,513
	16,480[b]	0.7513	12,381
			125,826

[a] Salvage.

[b] $16,480 is the tax savings from the loss on the disposal of the computer at the end of year 3, computed as follows:

Salvage value	$ 10,000
Book value ($100,000 − $48,800)	51,200
Loss on disposal	$(41,200)
Tax (40%)	
Tax savings (0.4 × $41,200)	$ 16,480

8.17 Computerized Bookkeeping System and NPV Analysis. Rework Problem 8.16 using the sum-of-years'-digits method of depreciation for the computer.

SOLUTION

(a) The sum-of-years'-digits depreciation is:

Year	Rate	Depreciation	
1	3/6	$ 50,000	($100,000 × 3/6)
2	2/6	33,333	($100,000 × 2/6)
3	1/6	16,667	($100,000 × 1/6)
		$100,000	

Therefore, after-tax cash savings are computed as follows:

	Year 1	Year 2	Year 3
Annual cash savings	$60,000	$60,000	$60,000
Depreciation	50,000	33,333	16,667
Net profits before tax	$10,000	$26,667	$43,333
Tax (40%)	4,000	10,667	17,333
Net profits after tax	$ 6,000	$16,000	$26,000
Depreciation	50,000	33,333	16,667
After-tax cash inflow	$56,000	$49,333	$42,667

(b)

Year	After-Tax Cash Inflow ($)	PV of $1	Total PV ($, Rounded)
1	56,000	0.9091	$50,910
2	49,333	0.8264	40,769
3	42,667	0.7513	32,056
	6,000[a]	0.7513	4,508
			$128,243

[a] The $6,000 cash inflow is computed as follows:

Salvage value	$10,000
Book value	0
Gain	$10,000
Tax (40%)	4,000
After-tax gain	$ 6,000

$$NPV = PV - 1$$
$$= \$128,243 - \$100,000 = \$28,243$$

Since NPV is positive, the company should purchase the computer, replacing the manual bookkeeping system.

8.18   **Replacement Decision.** Wisconsin Products Company manufactures several different products. One of the firm's principal products sells for $20 per unit. The sales manager of Wisconsin Products has stated repeatedly that he could sell more units of this product if they were available. In an attempt to substantiate his claim the sales manager conducted a market research study last year at a cost of $44,000 to determine potential demand for this product. The study indicated that Wisconsin Products could sell 18,000 units of this product annually for the next 5 years.

The equipment currently in use has the capacity to produce 11,000 units annually. The variable production costs are $9 per unit. The equipment has a book value of $60,000 and a remaining useful life of 5 years. The salvage value of the equipment is negligible now and will be zero in 5 years.

A maximum of 20,000 units could be produced annually on new machinery. The new equipment costs $300,000 and has an estimated useful life of 5 years, with no salvage value at the end of 5 years. Wisconsin Products' production manager has estimated that the new equipment, if purchased, would provide increased production efficiencies that would reduce the variable production costs to $7 per unit.

Wisconsin Products Company uses straight-line depreciation on all its equipment for tax purposes. The firm is subject to a 40 percent tax rate, and its after-tax cost of capital is 15 percent.

The sales manager felt so strongly about the need for additional capacity that he attempted to prepare an economic justification for the equipment although this was not one of his responsibilities. His analysis, presented below and on the next page, disappointed him because it did not justify acquisition of the equipment.

He computed the required investment as follows:

Purchase price of new equipment		$300,000
Disposal of existing equipment		
Loss on disposal	$60,000	
Less tax benefit (40%)	24,000	36,000
Cost of market research study		44,000
Total investment		$380,000

He computed the annual returns as follows:

Contribution margin from product	
Using the new equipment	
[18,000 × ($20 − $7)]	$234,000
Using the existing equipment	
[11,000 × ($20 − $9)]	121,000
Increase in contribution margin	$113,000
Less depreciation	60,000
Increase in before-tax income	$ 53,000
Income tax (40%)	21,200
Increase in income	$ 31,800
Less 15% cost of capital on the additional investment required (0.15 × $380,000)	57,000
Net annual return on proposed investment in new equipment	$(25,200)

The controller of Wisconsin Products Company plans to prepare a discounted cash flow analysis for this investment proposal. The controller has asked you to prepare corrected calculations of (a) the required investment in the new equipment and (b) the recurring annual cash flows. Explain why your corrected calculations differ from the original analysis prepared by the sales manager. (c) Calculate the net present value of the proposed investment in the new equipment.

SOLUTION

(a) The initial investment is:

Purchase price of new equipment	$300,000
−Tax savings from loss on disposal[a]	24,000
	$276,000

[a]Tax savings are computed as follows:

Loss = selling price − book value	
= ($0 − $60,000) = $60,000	
Tax rate	0.4
Tax savings	$24,000

(b) Using the shortcut method, the annual cash flows are computed by first determining the increased cash flows resulting from change in contribution margin:

Using new equipment	
[18,000 ($20 − $7)][a]	$234,000
Using existing equipment	
[11,000 ($20 − $9)]	121,000
Increased cash flows	$113,000
Taxes (0.40 × $113,000)	45,200
Increased cash flows after taxes	$ 67,800

Next, compute the increase in depreciation:

Depreciation on new equipment ($300,000 ÷ 5)	$60,000	
Depreciation on existing equipment ($60,000 ÷ 5)	12,000	
Increased depreciation charge	$48,000	
Tax rate	0.4	
		19,200
Recurring annual cash flows		$ 87,000

---

[a] The new equipment is capable of producing 20,000 units, but Wisconsin Products can sell only 18,000 units annually.

The sales manager made several errors in his calculations of required investment and annual cash flows.

Concerning the required investment, the sales manager made two errors: First, the cost of the market research study ($44,000) is a sunk cost because it was incurred last year and will not change regardless of whether the investment is made or not. Second, the loss on the disposal of the existing equipment does not result in an actual cash cost as shown by the sales manager. The loss on disposal results in a reduction of taxes which reduces the cost of the new equipment.

In computing the annual cash flows, the sales manager made three errors: First, he considered only the depreciation on the new equipment rather than just the additional depreciation which would result from the acquisition of the new equipment. Second, he failed to consider that the depreciation is a noncash expenditure which provides a tax shield. Third, the sales manager's use of the discount rate (i.e., cost of capital) was incorrect. The discount rate should be used to reduce the value of future cash flows to their current equivalent at time period zero.

(c) $\text{NPV} = \text{PV} - \text{I} = \text{cash flow } (\text{PVIFA}_{15,5}) - \text{I}$
$= (\$87,000 \times 3.3522) - \$276,000 = \$291,641 - \$276,000 = \$15,641$

8.19 Mutually Exclusive Investments. The Wan-Ki Manufacturing Company must decide between investment projects A and B, which are mutually exclusive. The data on these projects are as follows (in thousands of dollars):

		Cash Flows, per Year			
Project	**0**	**1**	**2**	**3**	**4**
A	(100)	$120.00			
B	(100)				$193.80

(a) For each project, compute the NPV at 12 percent cost of capital, and the IRR. (b) Explain why the rankings conflict. Recommend which project should be chosen.

SOLUTION

(a)   The NPV at 12 percent is:

Project	Cash Inflow	PV at $1[a]	PV	NPV (PV − I)
A	$120.00	0.8929	$107.15	$ 7.15
B	$193.80	0.6355	$123.16	$23.16

---

[a] $\text{PVIF}_{12,1}$ for A and $\text{PVIF}_{12,4}$ for B; both from Appendix C.

The IRR is:

Project	I/Cash Flow	PVIF	IRR
A	$\dfrac{\$100}{\$120.00} = 0.8333$ (at 1 year)		20%
B	$\dfrac{\$100}{\$193.80} = 0.516$ (at 4 years)		13%

(b) The conflicting ranking results from different assumptions regarding the reinvestment rate on the cash inflows released by the project. The NPV method assumes the cost of capital (12 percent in this problem) as the rate for reinvestment, whereas the IRR method assumes the cash inflows are reinvested at their own internal rate of return (20 percent in the case of project A). The use of NPV for ranking mutually exclusive investments is recommended since the cost of capital is a more realistic reinvestment rate. Therefore, project B should be chosen.

8.20 NPV, IRR, and Mutually Exclusive Investments. The Bitter Almond Company was confronted with the two mutually exclusive investment projects, A and B, which have the following after-tax cash flows:

	Cash Flows, per Year ($)				
Project	0	1	2	3	4
A	(12,000)	5,000	5,000	5,000	5,000
B	(12,000)				25,000

Based on these cash flows: (a) Calculate each project's NPV and IRR. (Assume that the firm's cost of capital after taxes is 10 percent.) (b) Which of the two projects would be chosen according to the IRR criterion? (c) How can you explain the differences in rankings given by the NPV and IRR methods in this case?

SOLUTION

(a) The NPV for project A is:

Year	Cash (Outflow) or Inflow	Present Value of $1 at 10%	Net Present Value of Cash Flow
0	$(12,000)	1.000	$(12,000)
1–4	$5,000	3.1699	15,850
			$ 3,850

The NPV for project B is:

Year	Cash (Outflow) or Inflow	Present Value of $1 at 10%	Net Present Value of Cash Flow
0	$(12,000)	1.000	$(12,000)
4	$25,000	0.6830	17,075
			$ 5,075

The IRR for project A is:

$$\$12,000 = \$5,000 \ (\text{PVIFA}_{r,4})$$

$$\text{PVIFA}_{r,4} = \frac{\$12,000}{\$5,000} = 2.4$$

Using interpolation:

	PV	
24%	2.4043	2.4043
True rate	2.4000	
28%		2.2410
Difference	0.0043	0.1633

$$\text{IRR} = 24\% + \frac{0.0043}{0.1633}(4\%) = 24\% + 0.11\% = 24.11\%$$

The IRR for project B is:

Year	Cash (Outflow) Inflow	Present Value of $1 at 20%	Net Present Value of Cash Flow	Present Value of $1 at 22%	Net Present Value of Cash Flow
0	$(12,000)	1.000	$(12,000)	1.000	$(12,000)
4	$25,000	0.4823	12,058	0.4526[a]	11,315
			$ 58		$ (685)

	NPV	
20%	$50	$ 50
True rate	0	
22%		$-(-685)$
Difference	$50	$735

$$\text{IRR} = 20\% + \frac{\$50}{\$735}(2\%) = 20\% + 0.14\% = \$20.14$$

(b) In summary,

Projects	NPV	IRR
A	$3,850	24.11%
B	$5,075	20.14%

Under the NPV method, choose B over A. Under the IRR method, choose A over B.

(c) The decision of which project to choose hinges on assumptions made about reinvestment of cash inflow. Theory suggests resorting to the NPV method because the cost of capital reinvestment assumption implicit in this method is considered to be a more realistic assumption than the IRR, where a reinvestment at the IRR is assumed. Therefore, choose B rather than A, using the NPV ranking.

8.21 **The Modified Internal Rate of Return (MIRR).** Refer to Problem 8.20. Compute MIRRs for projects A and B. Compare the ranking by MIRR with the one by NPV.

SOLUTION

First, compute the terminal value (TV) compounded at the cost of capital 10 percent.

$$\text{A: TV} = 5,000 \ \text{FVIFA}_{10,3} = 5,000 \times 3.3100 = 16,550.00$$

Next, find the IRR by setting:

$$12,000 = 16,390.50 \text{ PVIF}_{MIRR,4}$$

$$\text{PVIF} = 12,000/16,390.50 = 0.7321, \text{ which gives MIRR} = \text{about } 12\%$$

Now we see the consistent ranking from both the NPV and MIRR methods.

	MIRR	NPV at 10%
A	12%	$3,850
B	20.14	5,075

8.22 Replacement Decisions with Unequal Lives. Consider two projects, X and Y:

Project	Cost	Life	Annual after-tax cash inflow
X	$50,000	10 years	$9,000
Y	50,000	15	7,500

The company's cost of capital is 10 percent.

1. Determine the adjusted NPV for each project, using the replacement chain procedure.
2. Determine the equivalent annual annuity for each project.
3. Which project should be taken?

SOLUTION

1. First, determine each project's original NPV as follows:

$$\begin{aligned}
\text{NPV}_X &= \$9,000 \text{ PVIFA}_{10,10} - \$50,000 \\
&= \$9,000(6.1446) - \$50,000 \\
&= \$55,301.40 - \$50,000 \\
&= \$5,301.40 \\
\text{NPV}_Y &= \$7,500 \text{ PVIFA}_{15,10} - \$50,000 \\
&= \$7,500(7.6061) - \$50,000 \\
&= \$57,045.75 - \$50,000 \\
&= \$7,045.75
\end{aligned}$$

Then, compute adjusted NPV for each project at a common life of 30 years:

$$\begin{aligned}
\text{Adjusted NPV}_X &= \$5,301.40 + \$5,301.40 \text{ PVIF}_{10,10} + \$5,301.40 \text{ PVIF}_{20,10} \\
&= \$5,301.40 + \$5,301.40(0.3855) + \$5,301.40(0.1486) \\
&= \$5,301.40 + \$2,043.69 + \$787.79 \\
&= \$8,132.88 \\
\text{Adjusted NPV}_Y &= \$7,045.75 + \$7,045.75 \text{ PVIF}_{15,10} \\
&= \$7,045.75 + \$7,045.75(0.2394) \\
&= \$7,045.75 + \$1,686.75 \\
&= \$8,732.50
\end{aligned}$$

2. Based on the original NPVs, we get:

$$\begin{aligned}
\text{EAA}_X &= \$5,301.40/\text{PVIFA}_{10,10} = \$5,301.40/6.1446 = \$862.77 \\
\text{EAA}_Y &= \$7,045.75/\text{PVIFA}_{15,10} = \$7,045.75/7.6061 = \$926.33
\end{aligned}$$

Thus, the infinite horizon NPVs are as follows:

$$\text{Infinite horizon NPV}_X = \$862.77/0.10 = \$8,627.70$$
$$\text{Infinite horizon NPV}_Y = \$926.33/0.10 = \$9,263.30$$

8.23   **Abandonment.** Henteleff, Inc. is considering a project with the following data:

Year	Initial Investment and Net Cash Flow	Abandonment Value in Year t
0	($8,000)	$8,000
1	4,000	4,500
2	4,000	3,000
3	4,000	0

The firm's cost of capital is 10 percent. What should the company do?

SOLUTION

We will compute NPVs in three cases.

Case 1.   NPV of the project if kept for 3 years

$$\text{NPV} = \text{PV} - \text{I} = \$4,000 \ \text{PVIFA}_{10,3} = \$4,000(2.4869) - \$8,000$$
$$= \$1,947.60$$

Case 2.   NPV of the project if abandoned after Year 1

$$\text{NPV} = \text{PV} - \text{I} = \$4,000 \ \text{PVIF}_{10,1} + \$4,500 \ \text{PVIF}_{10,2} - \$8,000$$
$$= \$4,000(0.9091) + \$4,500(0.9091) - \$8,000$$
$$= \$3,636.40 + \$4,090.95 - \$8,000 = -\$272.65$$

Case 3.   NPV of the project if abandoned after Year 2

$$\text{NPV} = \text{PV} - \text{I} = \$4,000 \ \text{PVIF}_{10,1} + \$4,000 \ \text{PVIF}_{10,2} + \$3,000 \ \text{PVIF}_{10,2} - \$8,000$$
$$= \$4,000(0.9091) + \$4,000(0.8264) + \$3,000(0.8264) - \$8,000$$
$$= \$3,636.40 + \$3,305.60 + \$2,479.20 - \$8,000 = \$1,421.20$$

The company should keep the project for 3 years.

8.24   **NPV Analysis.** Two new machines are being evaluated for possible purchase. Forecasts related to the machines are:

	Machine 1	Machine 2
Purchased price	$50,000	$60,000
Estimated life (straight-line depreciation)	4 years	4 years
Estimated scrap value	None	None
Annual cash benefits before income tax:		
Year 1	$25,000	$45,000
Year 2	25,000	19,000
Year 3	25,000	25,000
Year 4	25,000	25,000
Income tax rate	40%	40%

Compute the net present value of each machine. Assume a cost of capital of 8%.

SOLUTION

After-tax cash benefit:

Cash Benefit Year	(a)	Depreciation	Taxable Income	Income Tax (b)	Net After-Tax Cash Inflow (a)−(b)
			Machine 1		
1	$25,000	$12,500	$12,500	$5,000	$20,000
2	25,000	12,500	12,500	5,000	20,000
3	25,000	12,500	12,500	5,000	20,000
4	25,000	12,500	12,500	5,000	20,000
			Machine 2		
1	$45,000	$15,000	$30,000	$12,000	$33,000
2	19,000	15,000	4,000	1,600	17,400
3	25,000	15,000	10,000	4,000	21,000
4	25,000	15,000	10,000	4,000	21,000

Net present value:

Year	Cash (Outflow) Inflow	Present Value of $1 8 Percent	Net Present Value of Cash Flow
		Machine 1	
0	$(50,000)	1.000	$(50,000)
1–4	20,000	3.312	66,240
		Net present value	$ 16,240
		Machine 2	
0	$(60,000)	1.000	$(60,000)
1	33,000	0.926	30,558
2	17,400	0.857	14,912
3	21,000	0.794	16,674
4	21,000	0.735	15,435
		Net present value	$ 17,579

8.25   Computerized Bookkeeping and NPV Analysis. A medium-sized index manufacturing company is considering the purchase of a small computer in order to reduce the cost of its data-processing operations. At the present time, the manual bookkeeping system in use involves the following direct cash expenses per month:

Salaries	$7,500
Payroll taxes and fringe benefits	1,700
Forms and supplies	600
	$9,800

Existing furniture and equipment are fully depreciated in the accounts and have no salvage value. The cost of the computer, including alterations, installation, and accessory equipment, is $100,000. This entire amount is depreciable for income-tax purposes on a double-declining basis at the rate of 20 percent per annum.

Estimated annual costs of computerized data processing are as follows:

Supervisory salaries	$15,000
Other salaries	24,000
Payroll taxes and fringe benefits	7,400
Forms and supplies	7,200
	$53,600

The computer is expected to be obsolete in 3 years, at which time its salvage value is expected to be $20,000. The company follows the practice of treating salvage as inflow at the time it is likely to be received.

1.   Compute the savings in annual cash expenses after taxes.
2.   Decide whether or not to purchase the computer, using the net present value method. Assume a minimum rate of return of 10 percent after taxes.

SOLUTION

1.

Annual cash expenses of the manual bookkeeping machine system, $9,800 × 12	$117,600
Annual cash expenses of computerized data processing	53,600
Annual cash savings	$ 64,000

	Year 1	Year 2	Year 3
Annual cash savings (a)	$64,000	$64,000	$64,000
Depreciation	20,000	16,000	12,800
Inflow before tax	$44,000	$48,000	$51,000
Income tax (50%) (b)	22,000	24,000	25,600
Cash inflow after tax (a–b)	$42,000	$40,000	$38,400

2.

	After-Tax Cash Inflow		PV Factor	PV
Year 1	$42,000	×	0.909	$ 38,178
Year 2	40,000	×	0.826	33,040
Year 3	38,400	×	0.750	28,800
Year 3 Salvage	20,000	×	0.750	15,000
Year 3 Tax loss	15,600*	×	0.750	11,700
				$126,718
Investment (I)				100,000
Net present value (NPV)				$ 26,718

---

*The $15,600 tax benefit of the loss on the disposal of the computer at the end of year 3 is computed as follows:

Estimated salvage value		$ 20,000
Estimated book value:		
Historical cost	$100,000	
Accumulated depreciation	48,800	51,200
Estimated loss		$(31,200)
Tax rate		50%
Tax effect of estimated loss		$(15,600)

Since the net present value is positive, the computer should be purchased replacing the manual bookkeeping system.

8.26   **IRR.** The Michener Company purchased a special machine 1 year ago at a cost of $12,000. At that time, the machine was estimated to have a useful life of 6 years and no disposal value. The annual cash operating cost is approximately $20,000.

A new machine that has just come on the market will do the same job but with an annual cash operating cost of only $17,000. This new machine costs $15,000 and has an estimated life of 5 years with no disposal value. The old machine could be used as a trade-in at an allowance of $5,000. Straight-line depreciation is used and the company's income tax rate is 40 percent. Compute the internal rate of return on the new investment.

SOLUTION

(1)   The initial outlay:

Outflows:		
Cost of machine		$15,000
Inflows:		
Salvage value – old machine		−5,000
Tax savings from loss on sale of old machine		
($10,000 − $5,000)(0.4)		−2,000
		$ 8,000

(2) Cash savings (annual):

	Book Income	Cash
Difference in cash operating costs:		
Old machine	$20,000	
New machine	17,000	$3,000
	$ 3,000	
Depreciation expense (annual):		
Old machine ($12,000/6 years)	2,000	
New machine ($15,000/5 years)	3,000	
Additional annual depreciation		1,000
Taxable savings		$2,000
Income tax on savings ($2,000 × 0.40)		−800
Annual cash savings after income tax		$2,200

Internal rate of return factor; $8,000/$2,200 = 3.636 years (about 11.5%).

8.27 MACRS and NPV Analysis. A machine costs $1,000 initially. Annual cash inflows are expected to be $300. The machine will be depreciated using the MACRS rule and will fall in the 3-year property class. No salvage value is anticipated. The cost of capital is 16 percent. The estimated life of the machine is 5 years. The tax rate is 40 percent. Make a decision using NPV.

SOLUTION

	Year(s) Having Cash Flows	Amount of Cash Flows	16% PV Factor	PV
Initial investment	Now	$1,000	1.000	$(1,000)
Annual cash inflows:				
$300				
×60%				
$180	1–5	180	3.274	589

Depreciation deductions:

Year	Cost	MACRS %	Depreciation	Tax Shield				
1	$1,000	33.3	333	133.20	1	133.20	0.862	114.82
2	1,000	44.5	445	178.00	2	178.00	0.743	132.25
3	1,000	14.8	148	59.20	3	59.20	0.641	37.95
4	1,000	7.4	74	29.60	4	29.60	0.552	16.34
						Net Present Value		$(109.32)

We should not buy the machine, since the NPV of −$109.32 is negative.

8.28 MACRS and NPV Analysis. A firm is considering the purchase of an automatic machine for $6,200. The machine has an installation cost of $800 and zero salvage value at the end of its expected life of 5 years. Depreciation is by the straight-line method with the *half-year convention*. The machine is considered a 5-year property. Expected cash savings before tax is $1,800 per year over the 5 years. The firm is in the 40 percent tax bracket. The firm has determined the cost of capital (or minimum required rate of return) of 10 percent after taxes. Should the firm purchase the machine? Use the NPV method.

SOLUTION

	Year(s) Having Cash Flows	Amount of Cash Flows	10% PV Factor	PV
Initial investment	Now	$(7,000)	1.000	$(7,000)
Annual cash inflows:				
$1,800				
×60%				
$1,080	1–5	1,080	3.791	4,094

Depreciation deductions:

Year	Depreciation	Tax Shield at 40%				
1	$ 700	$280	1	$280	0.909	$255
2	1,400	560	2	560	0.826	463
3	1,400	560	3	560	0.751	421
4	1,400	560	4	560	0.683	382
5	1,400	560	5	560	0.621	348
6	700	280	6	280	0.564	158
				Net Present Value		$(879)

The firm should not buy the automatic machine since its NPV is negative.

8.29 MACRS and NPV Analysis. The Wessels Corporation is considering installing a new conveyor for materials handling in a warehouse. The conveyor will have an initial cost of $75,000 and an installation cost of $5,000. Expected benefits of the conveyor are: (*a*) Annual labor cost will be reduced by $16,500, and (*b*) breakage and other damages from handling will be reduced by $400 per month. Some of the firm's costs are expected to increase as follows: (*a*) Electricity cost will rise by $100 per month, and (*b*) annual repair and maintenance of the conveyor will amount to $900.

Assume the firm uses the MACRS rules for depreciation in the 5-year property class. No salvage value will be recognized for tax purposes. The conveyor has an expected useful life of 8 years and a projected salvage value of $5,000. The tax rate is 40 percent.

1. Estimate future cash inflows for the proposed project.
2. Determine the projects NPV at 10 percent. Should the firm buy the conveyor?

SOLUTION

1. Annual cash inflow:

$16,500	Reduction in labor cost
4,800	Reduction in breakage
−1,200	Increase in electricity costs
−900	Increase in repair and maintenance cost
$19,200	

2. Initial amount of investment is:

$$\$75,000 + \$5,000 = \$80,000$$

	Year(s) Having Cash Flows	Amount of Cash Flows	10% PV Factor	PV
Initial investment	Now	$(80,000)	1.000	$(80,000)
Annual cash inflows: $19,200				
×60%				
After-tax cash inflow: $11,520	1–8	11,520	5.335	61,459.20

Depreciation deductions:

Year	Cost	MACRS %	Depreciation	Tax Shield		
1	$80,000	20.0	$16,000	$ 6,400	0.909	$ 5,817.60
2	80,000	32.0	25,600	10,240	0.826	8,458.24
3	80,000	19.2	15,360	6,144	0.751	4,614.14
4	80,000	11.5	9,200	3,680	0.683	2,513.44
5	80,000	11.5	9,200	3,680	0.621	2,285.28
6	80,000	5.8	4,640	1,856	0.564	1,046.78
						$24,735.48

Salvage value, fully taxable since book value will be zero:

$5,000				
×60%	8	3,000	0.467	1,401.00
$3,000				
			Net present value	$ 7,595.68

The JKS Corporation should buy and install the conveyor, since it brings a positive NPV.

8.30 **NPV Analysis.** The JS Company is considering buying a machine at a cost of $800,000, which has the following cash flow pattern. No residual value is expected. Depreciation is by straight-line. Assume that the income tax rate is 40%, and the after-tax cost of capital (minimum required rate of return) is 10%. Should the company buy the machine? Use the NPV method.

Year	Cash Inflow, (1)	Cash Outflow, (2)
1	$800,000	$550,000
2	$790,000	$590,000
3	$920,000	$600,000
4	$870,000	$610,000
5	$650,000	$390,000

SOLUTION

Net cash flow after taxes calculation

Year	Cash Inflow, (1)	Cash Outflow, (2)	Net Cash Flow Before Taxes, (3)=(1)-(2)	Depreciation (Noncash Expense) (4)=0.2×, 800,000	Net Income Before Taxes, (5)=(3)-(4)	Income Taxes (6)=0.4×, (5)	Net Income After Taxes, (7)=(5)-(6)	Net Cash Flow After Taxes, (8)=(3)-(6) or (7)+(4)
1	$800,000	$550,000	$250,000	$160,000	$ 90,000	$36,000	$54,000	$214,000
2	$790,000	$590,000	$200,000	$160,000	$ 40,000	$16,000	$24,000	$184,000
3	$920,000	$600,000	$320,000	$160,000	$160,000	$64,000	$96,000	$256,000
4	$870,000	$610,000	$260,000	$160,000	$100,000	$40,000	$60,000	$220,000
5	$650,000	$390,000	$260,000	$160,000	$100,000	$40,000	$60,000	$220,000

The Net Present Value (NPV) is computed as follows:

Year	Net Cash Flow After Taxes,	10% PV Table Value,	Present Value,
0	$(800,000)	1.000	$(800,000)
1	$214,000	0.909	$194,526
2	$184,000	0.826	$151,984
3	$256,000	0.751	$192,256
4	$220,000	0.683	$150,260
5	$220,000	0.621	$136,620
		NPV =	$ 25,646

The company should buy the machine, since NPV is positive ($25,646).

8.31 Payback Period, ARR, and NPV. The Baxter Company manufactures toys and short-lived-fad-type items. The research and development department came up with an item that would make a good promotion gift for office equipment dealers. Aggressive and effective effort by Baxter's sales personnel has resulted in almost firm commitments for this product for the next 3 years. It is expected that the product's value will be exhausted by that time.

In order to produce the quality demanded Baxter will need to buy additional machinery and rent some additional space. It appears that about 25,000 square feet will be needed: 12,500 square feet of presently unused, but leased, space is available now. (Baxter's present lease with 10 years to run costs $3.00 a square foot.) There is another 12,500 square feet adjoining the Baxter facility which Baxter will rent for 3 years at $4.00 per square foot per year if it decides to make this product.

The equipment will be purchased for about $900,000. It will require $30,000 in modifications, $60,000 for installation, and $90,000 for testing: all of these activities will be done by a firm of engineers hired by Baxter. All of the expenditures will be paid for on January 1, 19X1.

The equipment should have a salvage value of about $180,000 at the end of the third year. No additional general overhead costs are expected to be incurred.

The following estimates of revenues and expenses for this product for the 3 years have been developed.

	19X1	19X2	19X3
Sales	$1,000,000	$1,600,000	$800,000
Material, labor, and incurred overhead	$ 400,000	$ 750,000	$350,000
Assigned general overhead	40,000	75,000	35,000
Rent	87,500	87,500	87,500
Depreciation	450,000	300,000	150,000
	$ 977,500	$1,212,500	$622,500
Income before tax	$22,500	$ 387,500	$117,500
Income tax (40%)	9,000	155,000	71,000
	$ 13,500	$ 232,500	$106,500

1. Prepare a schedule which shows the incremental after-tax cash flows for this project.
2. If the company requires a 2-year payback period for its investment, would it undertake this project? Show your supporting calculations clearly.
3. Calculate the after-tax accounting rate of return for the project.
4. A newly hired business-school graduate recommends that the company consider the use of net present value analysis to study this project. If the company sets a required rate of return of 20 percent after taxes, will this project be accepted? Show your supporting calculations clearly. (Assume all operating revenues and expenses occur at the end of the year.)

SOLUTION

1.

Incremental After-Tax Cash Flow (000 omitted)

	19X1	19X2	19X3
Sales	$1,000	$1,600	$800
Material, labor, overhead	$ 400	$ 750	$350
Added rent	50	50	50
Depreciation	450	300	150
Incremental costs	$ 900	$1,100	$550
Incremental income	$ 100	$ 500	$250
Incremental taxes	40	200	100
Incremental income after taxes	$ 60	$ 300	$150
Add back depreciation	450	300	150
Incremental operation cash flow	$ 510	$ 600	$300
Salvage value			180
Net incremental after-tax cash flow	$ 510	$ 600	$480

Initial investment for project:

Purchase price	$ 900
Modification	30
Installation	60
Testing	90
Total	$1,080

2. The project should be undertaken if the criterion is a 2-year payback.

19X1	$ 510,000
19X2	600,000
	$1,110,000

Payback is in 2 years, which is greater than cost of $1,080,000.
   The payback period is:

$$(510/510) + (570/600) = 1.95 \text{ years}$$

3.

19X1 income	$ 13,500
19X2 income	232,500
19X3 income	106,500
	$352,500

Average income: $117,500 ($352,500/3)
Accounting rate of return: $117,500/$1,080,000 = 10.88%

4. The project should be adopted if a 20 percent after-tax rate of return is required.

Present Value of Cash Flows at 20%

19X1	$0.83 \times 510,000 =$	$ 423,300
19X2	$0.69 \times 600,000 =$	414,000
19X3	$0.58 \times 480,000 =$	278,400
	Present Value	$1,115,700

   The present value of $1,115,700 is greater than the initial outlay of $1,080,000; therefore, the project more than satisfies the 20 percent requirement.

8.32 Income Tax Factors. R. Jack and J. Jill have formed a corporation to franchise a quick food system for shopping malls. They have just completed experiments with a prototype machine which will serve as the basis of the operation. Because the system is new and untried, they have decided to conduct a pilot operation in a nearby mall. When it proves successful, they will aggressively market the franchises.

   The income statements below represent Jack and Jill's best estimates of income from the mall operation for the next 4 years. At the end of the 4-year period they intend to sell the operation and concentrate on the sale of and supervision of franchises. Based upon the income stream projected, they believe the operation can be sold for $190,000; the income tax liability from the sale will be $40,000.

1. Calculate the cash flow for the mall operation for the 4-year period beginning January 1, 19X6, ignoring tax implications.
2. Adjust the cash flows for tax consequences as appropriate.

SOLUTION

1.

	19X6	19X7	19X8	19X9
Recurring cash flows:				
Sales	$120,000	$150,000	$200,000	$230,000
Less: Cash expenditures				
Cost of goods sold	$60,000	$ 75,000	$100,000	$110,000
Wages	24,000	30,000	40,000	44,000
Supplies	2,000	2,300	2,400	3,200
Personal property taxes	1,000	1,200	1,600	1,800
Annual rental charges	12,000	12,000	12,000	12,000
Total cash expenditures	$ 99,000	$120,500	$156,000	$171,000
Total recurring cash flows before taxes	$ 21,000	$ 29,500	$ 44,000	$ 59,000
Nonrecurring cash flows:				
Cash flows at inception:				
Rental charges	$ (36,000)			
Purchase of new machine	(130,000)			
Cash flows at conclusion of mall operation:				
Sale of mall operation	0	0	0	$190,000
Total nonrecurring cash flows	$(166,000)	0	0	$190,000
Total cash flows before taxes	$(145,000)	$ 29,500	$ 44,000	$249,000

2.

Calculation of Income Taxes

	19X6	19X7	19X8	19X9
Income from operations:				
Net income (loss) before taxes as stated	$ (10,000)	$(1,500)	$13,000	$ 28,000
Add: Amount for straight-line depreciation	11,000	11,000	11,000	11,000
Deduct: Amount of S-Y-D depreciation*	(20,000)	(18,000)	(16,000)	(14,000)
Taxable income (loss) before carryforward of operating loss	$ (19,000)	$(8,500)	$ 8,000	$ 25,000
Operating loss carryforward	0	0	(8,000)	(19,500)
Taxable income	0	0	0	$ 5,500
Income tax on income from operations (40%)	0	0	0	$2,200
Income tax from sale of mall operation				40,000
Total income taxes				$ 42,200
Total cash flows before taxes (part I)	$(145,000)	$29,500	$44,000	$249,000
Less: Income taxes	0	0	0	42,200
Total cash flows after taxes	$(145,000)	$29,500	$44,000	$206,800

*S-Y-D depreciation calculation:

Purchase price of equipment	$130,000
Salvage value	20,000
Depreciable base	$110,000

Year	Rate	Depreciation
19X6	10/55	$20,000
19X7	9/55	18,000
19X8	8/55	16,000
19X9	7/55	14,000

8.33 Determination of Cash Flows. The Norman Corporation of Cerritos, CA, maker of a famous electronic component, is considering replacing one of its current hand-operated assembly machines with a new fully automated machine. This replacement would mean the elimination of one employee, generating salary and benefit savings.

Keep:
One full-time machine operator – salary and benefits, $25,000 per year
Cost of maintenance – $2000 per year
Cost of defects – $6000
Original depreciable value of old Machine – $50,000
Annual depreciation – $5000 per year
Expected life – 10 years
Age – 5 years old
No expected salvage value in 5 years
Current salvage value – $5000
Tax rate – 34 percent

Replace:
Cost of new machine – $60,000
Installation fee – $3000
Transportation charge – $3000
Cost of maintenance – $3000 per year
Cost of defects – $3000 per year
Expected life – 5 years
Salvage value – $20,000
Depreciation method by straight-line

1. Given the following information, determine the cash flows associated with this replacement.

2. Assume an after-tax cost of capital of 14 percent, compute:

   (a) Payback period

   (b) Internal rate of return

   (c) Net present value

Should the new machine be bought?

SOLUTION

1. (1) The initial outlay:

Outflows:	
Cost of machine	$60,000
Installation fee	3,000
Shipping fee	3,000
Inflows:	
Salvage value – old machine	−5,000
Tax savings on sale of old machine ($25,000–$5,000) (0.34)	−6,800
	$54,200

(2)   The differential cash flows over the project's life.

	Book Income	Cash Flow
Savings: Reduced salary	$25,000	$25,000
Reduced defects	3,000	3,000
Costs: Increased maintenance	(1,000)	(1,000)
Increased depreciation ($13,200–$5000)*	(8,200)	
Net savings before taxes	$18,800	$27,000
Taxes (0.34)	(6,392)	(6,392)
Annual net cash flow after taxes		$20,608

*Annual depreciation on the new machine = ($60,000 + $3,000 + $3,000)/5 = $13,200.

(3)   The terminal cash flow:

Salvage value – new machine	$20,000
Less: Taxes on gain:	6,800
($20,000 – 0) × 0.34	
	$13,200

Thus, the cash flow in the final year will be equal to the annual net cash flow in that year of $20,608 plus the terminal cash flow of $13,200 for a total of $33,808.

2.   (a)   Payback period = $54,200/$20,608 = 2.63 years

(b)   IRR by trial and error = about 30 percent
$54,200 = $20,608 \text{ PVIFA}_{i,5} + $13,200 \text{ PVIF}_{i,5}$

(c)   NPV = $20,608 \text{ PVIFA}_{14\%,5} + $13,200 \text{ PVIF}_{14\%,5} - $54,200$
= $20,608 (3.433) + $13,200 (0.519) - $54,200$
= $70,726 - $6,850 - $54,200 = $23,376$

The machine should be bought since the IRR is greater than 14% and the NPV is positive.

8.34   Annual Lease Payments. Fairchild Leasing Company is setting up a capital lease with Gemi Trucking, Inc. The lease will cover a $36,000 delivery truck. The terms of the lease call for a 12 percent return to the truck lessor. The lease is to run for 5 years.

Based on these data, determine (a) the annual lease payment and (b) the annual lease payment if the lessor desires 10 percent on its lease.

SOLUTION

(a) $\text{Annual lease payment} = A = \dfrac{\text{amount}}{\text{PVIFA}_{12\%,5}} = \dfrac{\$36,000}{3.6048} = \$9,987 \text{ (rounded)}$

(b) $A = \dfrac{\$36,000}{\text{PVIFA}_{10\%,5}} = \dfrac{\$36,000}{3.7908} = \$9,497 \text{ (rounded)}$

8.35   Annual Lease Payments. Star Wars Leasing, Inc., is setting up a financial lease covering a $36,000 truck. The lease arrangement requires beginning-of-year payments and the life of the lease is 5 years. The company wants equal annual lease payments that will allow it to earn 12 percent on its investment.

Based on these data, determine (a) the annual lease payment and (b) the annual lease payment if the desired rate of return is only 10 percent.

SOLUTION

(a) Since the lease payment is made in advance, the straightforward application of the formula (i.e., A = amount/PVIFA) does not work. The equation can be set up as follows:

$$\$36,000 = A + A \cdot PVIFA_{12\%,4}$$
$$\$36,000 = A(1 + PVIFA_{12\%,4})$$

$$A = \frac{\$36,000}{1 + PVIFA_{12\%,4}} = \frac{\$36,000}{1 + 3.0373} = \frac{\$36,000}{4.0373} = \$8,917 \text{ (rounded)}$$

(b)
$$A = \frac{\$36,000}{1 + PVIFA_{10\%,4}} = \frac{\$36,000}{1 + 3.1699} = \frac{\$36,000}{4.1699} = \$8,633 \text{ (rounded)}$$

8.36 Lease versus Purchase Decision. Carter Company wishes to expand its productive capacity. In order to do so it must acquire a new tractor costing \$40,000. The machine can be purchased or leased. The firm is in the 40 percent tax bracket and its after-tax cost of debt is currently 6 percent.

If the firm purchased the machine, the purchase would be totally financed with a 10 percent loan requiring equal annual end-of-year payments over 5 years. The machine would be depreciated straight-line over its 5-year life. A salvage value of zero is anticipated. The life of a lease would be 5 years. The lessor intends to charge equal annual lease payments that will enable it to earn 15 percent on its investment. In doing the following calculations, round your answers to the nearest dollar.

(a) Calculate the annual lease payment required in order to give the lessor its desired return. (b) Calculate the annual loan payment paying 10 percent interest. (c) Determine the after-tax cash outflows associated with each alternative. (d) Find the present value of the after-tax cash outflows using the after-tax cost of debt. (e) Which alternative (i.e., lease or purchase) would you recommend? Why?

SOLUTION

(a)
$$\text{Annual lease payment} = A = \frac{\$40,000}{PVIFA_{15\%,5}} = \frac{\$40,000}{3.3522} = \$11,932$$

(b)
$$\text{Annual loan payment} = A = \frac{\$40,000}{PVIFA_{10\%,5}} = \frac{\$40,000}{3.7908} = \$10,552$$

(c) and (d) Data pertaining to a lease agreement are as follows:

Year	Payment	After-Tax Cost	PV Factor at 6%	PV of Outflow
1–5	\$11,932	\$7,159	4.2124	\$30,157

Data pertaining to a purchase agreement are as follows:

Year	Payment ($)	Interest ($)	Principal ($)	Balance ($)	Depreciation ($)
1	10,552	4,000	6,552	33,448	8,000
2	10,552	3,345	7,207	26,241	8,000
3	10,552	2,624	7,928	18,313	8,000
4	10,552	1,831	8,721	9,592	8,000
5	10,552	959	9,593		8,000

Year	Total ($) (Interest + Dep.)	Tax Savings ($)	After-Tax Cash Outflow ($)	PV Factor at 6%	PV of Outflow
1	12,000	4,800	5,752	0.9434	$ 5,426
2	11,345	4,538	6,014	0.8900	5,352
3	10,624	4,250	6,302	0.8396	5,291
4	9,831	3,932	6,620	0.7921	5,244
5	8,959	3,584	6,968	0.7473	5,207
					$26,520

(e) The purchase alternative is preferable because the PV of the purchase cash outflow is less than the PV of the lease cash outflow.

8.37 Lease versus Purchase Decision. Sanchez Co. is considering a capital lease providing additional warehouse space for its department stores. The price of the facility is $330,000. The leasing arrangement requires beginning-of-year payments which, for tax purposes, cannot be deducted until the end of the year. The life of the lease is 5 years and the facility has zero expected salvage value. The lessor wants a 5 percent return on its lease. Assume that the firm is in the 40 percent tax bracket and its after-tax cost of debt is currently 7 percent. Find the present value of the after-tax cash outflows using the after-tax cost of debt as the discount rate. Round your answer to the nearest dollar.

SOLUTION

$$\text{Annual lease payment (for the beginning-of-year payment situation)} = \frac{\$330,000}{1 + \text{PVIFA}_{15\%,4}}$$

$$= \frac{\$330,000}{1 + 2.8550} = \frac{\$330,000}{3.8550} = \$85,603$$

Year	Payment	Tax Savings	After-Tax Cost	PV at 7%	PV of Cash Outflow
0	$85,603	0	$85,603	0.9346	$ 80,005
1–4	$85,603	$34,241	$51,362	3.3872	173,973
5		$34,241	($34,241)	0.7130	(24,414)
					$229,564

8.38 Lease versus Purchase Decision. The Marijay Co. has selected a machine that will produce substantial cost savings over the next 5 years. The company can acquire the machine by outright purchase for $240,000 or a lease arrangement from the manufacturer.

Marijay could obtain a 5-year loan from a local bank to pay for the outright purchase. The bank would charge interest at an annual rate of 10 percent on the outstanding balance of the loan and require Marijay to maintain a compensating balance equal to 20 percent of the outstanding balance of the loan. The principal would be paid in five equal installments, and each annual payment of principal and interest would be due at the end of each year. In addition to borrowing the amount needed to purchase the machine, Marijay would have to obtain a loan to cover the compensating balance required by the local bank.

A local financier and investor heard of Marijay's need and offered them an unusual proposition. She would advance the company $240,000 to purchase the machine if the company would agree to pay her a lump sum of $545,450 at the end of 5 years.

The capital lease offered by the manufacturer would allow all the tax benefits of ownership to accrue to Marijay. The title to the machine would be transferred to Marijay at the end of the 5 years at no cost. The manufacturer would be responsible for maintenance of the machine and has included $8,000 per year in the lease payment to cover the maintenance cost. Marijay would pay $70,175 to the manufacturer at the beginning of each year for the 5-year period.

(a) Calculate the before-tax interest rate for each of the three alternatives.

(b) Without prejudice to your answer to (a), what arguments would you present to justify a lease financing alternative even if that arrangement turned out to have a higher interest cost than a regular loan?

(c) Compare the relative effect that the three financing alternatives would have on Marijay's current ratio at the end of the first year. (CMA, adapted.)

SOLUTION

(a) The before-tax interest rates of return for each of the three alternatives are shown below.
     For a local financier

$$\text{PVIF}_{r,5} = \frac{\text{principal}}{\text{total payment}} = \frac{\$240,000}{\$545,450} = 0.44$$

The before-tax interest rate is 18 percent, which is determined by finding the rate for a PVIF of 0.44 for year 5 in Appendix C.
     For a lease:

Annual payment for leasing = $70,175 yearly payment − $8,000 maintenance = $62,175

To find the principal, subtract the first annual payment from the price of the machine, since this payment is made at the *beginning* of the year. Therefore,

$$\text{PVIFA}_{r,4} = \frac{\text{principal}}{\text{annual payment}}$$

$$= \frac{\$240,000 - \$62,175}{\$62,175} = 2.8601$$

From Appendix D, the before-tax interest rate is 15 percent for a PVIFA of 2.8601 at 4 years (4 years, not 5, since payments are made at the beginning of each year).
     For a purchase:

Beginning of Year	Principal Borrowed ($)[a]	Compensating Balance (20%) ($)	(1) Principal for Use (80%) ($)	(2) Interest (10%) on Borrowings ($)	(2 ÷ 1) Effective Rate (%)
1	300,000	60,000	240,000	30,000	12½
2	240,000	48,000	192,000	24,000	12½
3	180,000	36,000	144,000	18,000	12½
4	120,000	24,000	96,000	12,000	12½
5	60,000	12,000	48,000	60,000	12½

[a] One-fifth of loan repaid each year at the end of the year.

(b) Arguments justifying leases are as follows: The commitment for maintenance is limited, the cash budgeting impact of maintenance is known, manufacturer may exchange the machine for improved model at reduced rates, and financing alternatives are expanded.

(c) The effect on the current ratio at the end of the first year differs according to the financing alternative. For the financier there is no effect because the entire transaction is recorded as a long-term debt and there is no current asset or current liability until the end of the fourth year. With a loan, the current ratio will be lower than with the financier arrangement because there will be net cash outlays in the first year and a current liability recorded at the end of the first year. If a lease is chosen, the current ratio will be lower than both prior alternatives. There will be a greater net cash outlay in the first year and a larger current liability recorded at the end of the first year.

Chapter 9

Capital Budgeting Under Risk

9.1 INTRODUCTION

Risk analysis is important in making capital investment decisions because of the large amount of capital involved and the long-term nature of the investments being considered. The higher the risk associated with a proposed project, the greater the rate of return that must be earned on the project to compensate for that risk.

9.2 MEASURES OF RISK

Risk, a measure of the dispersion around a probability distribution, is defined as the variability of cash flow around the expected value. Risk can be measured in either *absolute* or *relative* terms. First, the *expected value*, $\bar{A}$, is

$$\bar{A} = \sum_{i=1}^{n} A_i p_i$$

where
A_i = the value of the *i*th possible outcome
p_i = the probability that the *i*th outcome will occur
n = the number of possible outcomes

Then, the absolute risk is measured by the *standard deviation*:

$$\sigma = \sqrt{\sum_{i=1}^{n} (A_i - \bar{A})^2 p_i}$$

The relative risk is measured by the *coefficient of variation*, which is $\sigma/\bar{A}$. (These three statistics were also discussed in Chapter 7.)

EXAMPLE 9.1 The ABC Corporation is considering investment in one of two mutually exclusive projects. Depending on the state of the economy, the projects would provide the following cash inflows in each of the next 5 years:

State	Probability	Proposal A	Proposal B
Recession	0.3	$1,000	$ 500
Normal	0.4	$2,000	$2,000
Boom	0.3	$3,000	$5,000

To compute the expected value ($\bar{A}$), the standard deviation (σ), and the coefficient of variation, it is convenient to set up the following tables:
For proposal A:

A_i ($)	p_i	$A_i p_i$ ($)	$(A_i - \bar{A})$ ($)	$(A_i - \bar{A})^2 p_i$
1,000	0.3	300	−1,000	300,000
2,000	0.4	800	0	0
3,000	0.3	900	1,000	300,000
		$\bar{A} = 2,000$		$\sigma^2 = $ 600,000

Since $\sigma^2 = 600,000$, $\sigma = 775$. Thus

$$\frac{\sigma}{\bar{A}} = \frac{\$775}{\$2,000} = 0.39$$

For proposal B:

A_i ($)	p_i	$A_i p_i$ ($)	$(A_i - \bar{A})$ ($)	$(A_i - \bar{A})^2$ ($)	$(A_i - \bar{A})^2 p_i$
500	0.3	150	−1,950	3,802,500	1,400,750
2,000	0.4	800	−450	202,500	81,000
5,000	0.3	1,500	2,550	6,502,500	2,601,000
		2,450			$\sigma^2 = 3,822,750$

Since $\sigma^2 = 3,822,750$, $\sigma = \$1,955$. Thus

$$\frac{\sigma}{\bar{A}} = \frac{\$1,955}{\$2,450} = 0.80$$

Therefore, proposal A is relatively less risky than proposal B, as indicated by the lower coefficient of variation.

9.3   RISK ANALYSIS IN CAPITAL BUDGETING

Since different investment projects involve different risks, it is important to incorporate risk into the analysis of capital budgeting. There are several methods for incorporating risk, including:

1.   Probability distributions
2.   Risk-adjusted discount rate
3.   Certainty equivalent
4.   Simulation
5.   Sensitivity analysis
6.   Decision trees (or probability trees)

Probability Distributions

Expected values of a probability distribution may be computed. Before any capital budgeting method is applied, compute the expected cash inflows or, in some cases, the expected life of the asset.

EXAMPLE 9.2   A firm is considering a $30,000 investment in equipment that will generate cash savings from operating costs. The following estimates regarding cash savings and useful life, along with their respective probabilities of occurrence, have been made:

Annual Cash Savings		Useful Life	
$ 6,000	0.2	4 years	0.2
$ 8,000	0.5	5 years	0.6
$10,000	0.3	6 years	0.2

Then, the expected annual saving is:

$$\begin{array}{ll} \$6,000(0.2) = & \$1,200 \\ \$8,000(0.5) = & 4,000 \\ \$10,000(0.3) = & \underline{3,000} \\ & \underline{\$8,200} \end{array}$$

The expected useful life is:

$$4(0.2) = 0.8$$
$$5(0.6) = 3.0$$
$$6(0.2) = \underline{1.2}$$
$$\underline{\underline{5 \text{ years}}}$$

The expected NPV is computed as follows (assuming a 10 percent cost of capital):

$$NPV = PV - I = \$8,200(PVIFA_{10\%,5}) - \$30,000$$
$$= \$8,200(3.7908) - \$30,000 = \$31,085 - \$30,000 = \$1,085$$

The expected IRR is computed as follows: By definition, at IRR,

$$I = PV$$
$$\$30,000 = \$8,200(PVIFA_{v,5})$$
$$PVIFA_{v,5} = \frac{\$30,000}{\$8,200} = 3.6585$$

which is about halfway between 10 percent and 12 percent in Appendix D, so that we can estimate the rate to be ~11 percent. Therefore, the equipment should be purchased, since (1) NPV = \$1,085, which is positive, and/or (2) IRR = 11 percent, which is greater than the cost of capital of 10 percent.

Risk-Adjusted Discount Rate

This method of risk analysis adjusts the cost of capital (or discount rate) upward as projects become riskier. Therefore, by increasing the discount rate from 10 percent to 15 percent, the expected cash flow from the investment must be relatively larger or the increased discount rate will generate a negative NPV, and the proposed acquisition/investment would be turned down.

The use of the risk-adjusted discount rate is based on the assumption that investors demand higher returns for riskier projects. The expected cash flows are discounted at the risk-adjusted discount rate and then the usual capital budgeting criteria such as NPV and IRR are applied.

EXAMPLE 9.3 A firm is considering an investment project with an expected life of 3 years. It requires an initial investment of \$35,000. The firm estimates the following data in each of the next 3 years:

After-Tax Cash Inflow	Probability
−\$ 5,000	0.2
\$10,000	0.3
\$30,000	0.3
\$50,000	0.2

Assuming a risk-adjusted required rate of return (after taxes) of 20 percent is appropriate for the investment projects of this level of risk, compute the risk-adjusted NPV.

First,

$$\bar{A} = -\$5,000(0.2) + \$10,000(0.3) + \$30,000(0.3) + \$50,000(0.2) = \$21,000$$

The expected NPV = \$21,000(PVIFA_{20\%,3}) − \$35,000
$$= \$21,000(2.1065) - \$35,000 = \$44,237 - \$35,000 = \$9,237$$

Certainty Equivalent

The certainty equivalent approach to risk analysis is drawn directly from the concept of utility theory. This method forces the decision maker to specify at what point the firm is *indifferent* to the choice between a certain sum of money and the expected value of a risky sum.

Once certainty equivalent coefficients are obtained, they are multiplied by the original cash flow to obtain the equivalent certain cash flow. Then, the accept-or-reject decision is made, using the normal capital budgeting criteria. The risk-free rate of return is used as the discount rate under the NPV method and as the cutoff rate under the IRR method.

EXAMPLE 9.4   XYZ, Inc., with a 14 percent cost of capital after taxes is considering a project with an expected life of 4 years. The project requires an initial certain cash outlay of $50,000. The expected cash inflows and certainty equivalent coefficients are as follows:

Year	After-Tax Cash Flow ($)	Certainty Equivalent Coefficient
1	10,000	0.95
2	15,000	0.80
3	20,000	0.70
4	25,000	0.60

The risk-free rate of return is 5 percent; compute the NPV and IRR.
The equivalent certain cash inflows are obtained as follows:

Year	After-Tax Cash Inflow ($)	Certainty Equivalent Coefficient	Equivalent Certain Cash Inflow ($)	PV at 5%	PV ($)
1	10,000	0.95	9,500	0.9524	9,048
2	15,000	0.80	12,000	0.9070	10,884
3	20,000	0.70	14,000	0.8638	12,093
4	25,000	0.60	15,000	0.8227	12,341
					44,366

$$\text{NPV} = \$44,366 - \$50,000 = -\$5,634$$

By trial and error, we obtain 4 percent as the IRR. Therefore, the project should be rejected, since (1) NPV = −5,634, which is negative and/or (2) IRR = 4 percent is less than the risk-free rate of 5 percent.

Simulation

This risk analysis method is frequently called the Monte Carlo simulation. It requires that a probability distribution be constructed for each of the important variables affecting the project's cash flows. Since a computer is used to generate many results using random numbers, project simulation is expensive.

Sensitivity Analysis

Forecasts of many calculated NPVs under various alternative functions are compared to see how sensitive NPV is to changing conditions. It may be found that a certain variable or group of variables, once their assumptions are changed or relaxed, drastically alters the NPV. This results in a much riskier asset than was originally forecast.

Decision Trees

Some firms use decision trees (probability trees) to evaluate the risk of capital budgeting proposals. A decision tree is a graphical method of showing the sequence of possible outcomes. A capital budgeting tree would show the cash flows and NPV of the project under different possible circumstances. The decision tree method has the following advantages: (1) It visually lays out all the possible outcomes of the proposed project and makes management aware of the adverse possibilities, and (2) the conditional nature of successive years' cash flows can be expressly depicted. The primary disadvantage is that most problems are too complex to permit a year-by-year depiction. For example, for a 3-year project with three possible outcomes following each year, there are 27 paths. For a 10-year project (again with three possible outcomes following each year) there will be about 60,000 paths.

EXAMPLE 9.5   A firm has an opportunity to invest in a machine which will last 2 years, initially cost $125,000, and has the following estimated possible after-tax cash inflow pattern: In year 1, there is a 40 percent chance that the after-tax cash inflow will be $45,000, a 25 percent chance that it will be $65,000, and a 35 percent chance that it will be $90,000. In year 2, the after-tax cash inflow possibilities depend on the cash inflow that occurs in year 1; that is, the year 2 after-tax cash inflows are *conditional probabilities*. Assume that the firm's after-tax cost of capital is 12 percent. The estimated conditional after-tax cash inflows (ATCI) and probabilities are given below.

If $ATCI_1$ = $45,000		If $ATCI_1$ = $65,000		If $ATCI_1$ = $90,000	
$ATCI_2$ ($)	Probability	$ATCI_2$ ($)	Probability	$ATCI_2$ ($)	Probability
30,000	0.3	80,000	0.2	90,000	0.1
60,000	0.4	90,000	0.6	100,000	0.8
90,000	0.3	100,000	0.2	110,000	0.1

Then the decision tree which shows the possible after-tax cash inflow in each year, including the conditional nature of the year 2 cash inflow and its probabilities, can be depicted as follows:

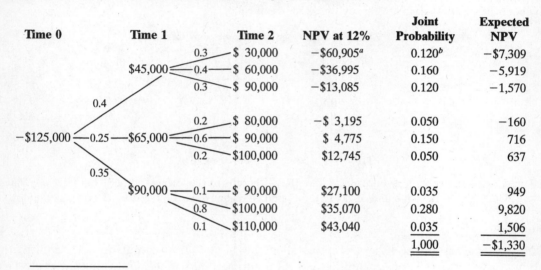

$$^a NPV = PV - I = \frac{\$45,000}{(1 + 0.12)} + \frac{\$30,000}{(1 + 0.12)^2} - \$125,000$$

$$= \$45,000(PVIF_{12\%,1}) + \$30,000(PVIF_{12\%,2}) - \$125,000$$

$$= \$45,000(0.893) + \$30,000(0.797) - \$125,000 = \$40,185 + \$23,910 - \$125,000 = -\$60,905$$

^{b} Joint probability = (0.4)(0.3) = 0.120

The last column shows the calculation of expected NPV, which is the weighted average of the individual path NPVs where the weights are the path probabilities. In this example, the expected NPV of the project is −$1,330, and the project should be rejected.

9.4   CORRELATION OF CASH FLOWS OVER TIME

When cash inflows are independent from period to period, it is fairly easy to measure the overall risk of an investment proposal. In some cases, however, especially with the introduction of a new product, the cash flows experienced in early years affect the size of the cash flows in later years. This is called the *time dependence of cash flows*, and it has the effect of increasing the risk of the project over time.

EXAMPLE 9.6 Janday Corporation's after-tax cash inflows (ATCI) are time-dependent, so that year 1 results (ATCI$_1$) affect the flows in year 2 (ATCI$_2$) as follows:

If ATCI$_1$ is $8,000 with a 40 percent probability, the distribution for ATCI$_2$ is:

0.3	$ 5,000
0.5	$10,000
0.2	$15,000

If ATCI$_1$ is $15,000 with a 50 percent probability, the distribution for ATCI$_2$ is:

0.3	$10,000
0.6	$20,000
0.1	$30,000

If ATCI$_1$ is $20,000 with a 10 percent chance, the distribution for ATCI$_2$ is:

0.1	$15,000
0.8	$40,000
0.1	$50,000

The project requires an initial investment of $20,000, and the risk-free rate of capital is 10 percent.

The company uses the expected NPV from decision tree analysis to determine whether the project should be accepted. The analysis is as follows:

Time 0	Time 1	Time 2	NPV at 10%	Joint Probability	Expected NPV
		0.3 $ 5,000	−$ 8,595[a]	0.12[b]	−$1,031
	$ 8,000	0.5 $10,000	−$ 4,463	0.20	−893
		0.2 $15,000	−$ 331	0.08	−26
	0.4				
		0.3 $10,000	$ 1,901	0.15	285
−$20,000	0.5 $15,000	0.6 $20,000	$10,165	0.30	3,050
		0.1 $30,000	$18,429	0.05	921
	0.1				
	$20,000	0.1 $15,000	$10,576	0.01	106
		0.8 $40,000	$31,238	0.08	2,499
		0.1 $50,000	$39,502	0.01	395
				1.00	$5,306

^{a} NPV = PV − I = $8,000 PVIF$_{10,1}$ + $5,000 PVIF$_{10,2}$ − $20,000

     = $8,000(0.9091) + $5,000(0.8264) − $20,000 = − $8,595

^{b} Joint probability of the first path = (0.4)(0.3) = 0.12

Since the NPV is positive ($5,306), Janday Corporation should accept the project.

9.5 NORMAL DISTRIBUTION AND NPV ANALYSIS: STANDARDIZING THE DISPERSION

With the assumption of *independence* of cash flows over time, the expected NPV would be

$$NPV = PV - I$$

$$= \sum_{t=1}^{n} \frac{\bar{A}_t}{(1 + r)^t} - I$$

The standard deviation of NPVs is

$$\sigma = \sqrt{\sum_{t=1}^{n} \frac{\sigma_t^2}{(1+r)^{2t}}}$$

The expected value ($\bar{A}$) and the standard deviation (σ) give a considerable amount of information by which to assess the risk of an investment project. If the probability distribution is *normal*, some probability statement regarding the project's NPV can be made. For example, the probability of a project's NPV providing an NPV of less or greater than zero can be computed by standardizing the normal variate x as follows:

$$z = \frac{x - \text{NPV}}{\sigma}$$

where x = the outcome to be found
       NPV = the expected NPV
         z = the standardized normal variate whose probability value can be found in Appendix E.

EXAMPLE 9.7   Assume an investment with the following data:

	Period 1	Period 2	Period 3
Expected cash inflow ($\bar{A}$)	$5,000	$4,000	$3,000
Standard deviation (σ)	$1,140	$1,140	$1,140

Assume that the firm's cost of capital is 8 percent and the initial investment is $9,000. Then the expected NPV is:

$$\text{NPV} = \text{PV} - \text{I}$$

$$= \frac{\$5,000}{(1+0.08)} + \frac{\$4,000}{(1+0.08)^2} + \frac{\$3,000}{(1+0.08)^3} - \$9,000$$

$$= \$5,000(\text{PVIF}_{8,1}) + \$4,000(\text{PVIF}_{8,2}) + \$3,000(\text{PVIF}_{8,3}) - \$9,000$$

$$= \$5,000(0.9259) + \$4,000(0.8573) + \$3,000(0.7938) - \$9,000$$

$$= \$4,630 + \$3,429 + \$2,381 - \$9,000 = \$1,440$$

The standard deviation about the expected NPV is

$$\sigma = \sqrt{\sum_{t=1}^{n} \frac{\sigma_t^2}{(1+r)^{2t}}}$$

$$= \sqrt{\frac{\$1,140^2}{(1+0.08)^2} + \frac{\$1,140^2}{(1+0.08)^4} + \frac{\$1,140^2}{(1+0.08)^6}}$$

$$= \sqrt{\$2,888,411} = \$1,670$$

The probability that the NPV is less than zero is then:

$$z = \frac{x - \text{NPV}}{\sigma}$$

$$= \frac{0 - \$1,440}{\$1,670} = -0.862$$

The area of normal distribution that is z standard deviations to the left or right of the mean may be found in Appendix E. A value of z equal to -0.862 falls in the area between 0.1949 and 0.1922 in Appendix E. Therefore, there is approximately a 19 percent chance that the project's NPV will be zero or less. Putting it another way, there is a 19 percent chance that the IRR of the project will be less than the risk-free rate.

9.6   PORTFOLIO RISK AND THE CAPITAL ASSET PRICING MODEL (CAPM)

Portfolio considerations play an important role in the overall capital budgeting process. Through diversification, a firm can stabilize earnings, reduce risk, and thereby increase the market price of the firm's stock.

Beta Coefficient

The capital asset pricing model (CAPM) can be used to determine the appropriate cost of capital. The NPV method uses the cost of capital as the rate to discount future cash flows. The IRR method uses the cost of capital as the cutoff rate. The required rate of return, or cost of capital according to the CAPM, or security market line (SML), is equal to the risk-free rate of return (r_f) plus a risk premium equal to the firm's beta coefficient (b) times the market risk premium $(r_m - r_f)$:

$$r_j = r_f + b(r_m - r_f)$$

EXAMPLE 9.8   A project has the following projected cash flows:

Year 0	Year 1	Year 2	Year 3
$(400)	$300	$200	$100

The estimated beta for the project is 1.5. The market return is 12 percent, and the risk-free rate is 6 percent. Then the firm's cost of capital, or required rate of return, is:

$$r_j = r_f + b(r_m - r_f) = 6\% + 1.5(12\% - 6\%) = 15\%$$

The project's NPV can be computed using 15 percent as the discount rate:

Year	Cash Flow ($)	PV at 15%	PV ($)
0	(400)	1.000	(400)
1	300	0.870	261
2	200	0.756	151
3	100	0.658	66
			78[a]

-----

[a]NPV.

The project should be accepted since its NPV is positive, that is, $78. Also, the project's IRR can be computed by trial and error. It is almost 30 percent, which exceeds the cost of capital of 15 percent. Therefore, by that standard also the project should be accepted.

Calculation of Beta Coefficient

In measuring an asset's systematic risk, beta, an indication is needed of the relationship between the asset's returns and the market returns (such as returns on the Standard & Poor's 500 Stock Composite Index). This relationship can be statistically computed by determining the regression coefficient between asset and market returns. The method is presented below.

$$b = \frac{\text{Cov}(r_j, r_m)}{\sigma_m^2}$$

where $\text{Cov}(r_j, r_m)$ is the covariance of the returns of the assets with the market returns, and σ_m^2 is the variance (standard deviation squared) of the market returns.

An easier way to compute beta is to determine the slope of the least-squares linear regression line

$(r_j - r_f)$, where the excess return of the asset $(r_j - r_f)$ is regressed against the excess return of the market portfolio $(r_m - r_f)$. The formula for b is:

$$b = \frac{\Sigma\, MK - n\bar{M}\bar{K}}{\Sigma\, M^2 - n\bar{M}^2}$$

where $M = (r_m - r_f)$
$\quad K = (r_j - r_f)$
$\quad n$ = number of years
$\quad \bar{M}$ = average of M
$\quad \bar{K}$ = average of K

EXAMPLE 9.9   Compute the beta coefficient, b, using the following data for stock x and the market portfolio:

Historic Rates of Return

Year	r_j (%)	r_m (%)
19X1	−5	10
19X2	4	8
19X3	7	12
19X4	10	20
19X5	12	15

Assume that the risk-free rate is 6 percent. For easy computation, it is convenient to set up the following table:

Year	Stock Return, r_j	Market Return, r_m	Risk-free Rate, r_f	$(r_j - r_f) = K$	$(r_m - r_j) = M$	M^2	MK
19X1	−0.05	0.10	0.06	−0.11	0.04	0.0016	−0.0044
19X2	0.04	0.08	0.06	−0.02	0.02	0.0004	−0.0004
19X3	0.07	0.12	0.06	0.01	0.06	0.0036	0.0006
19X4	0.10	0.20	0.06	0.04	0.14	0.0196	0.0056
19X5	0.12	0.15	0.06	0.06	0.09	0.0081	0.0054
				−0.02	0.35	0.0333	0.0068
				$\bar{K} = -0.004$	$\bar{M} = 0.07$		

Therefore, beta is:

$$b = \frac{\Sigma\, MK - n\bar{M}\bar{K}}{\Sigma\, M^2 - n\bar{M}^2} = \frac{0.0068 - (5)(-0.004)(0.07)}{0.0333 - (5)(0.07)^2} = \frac{0.0082}{0.0088} = 0.93$$

Review Questions

1. _____ is important in the capital budgeting process.

2. Risk can be measured in either _____ or terms _____ .

3. The use of _____ is based on the concept that investors demand _____ for riskier projects.

4. The certainty equivalent approach is directly drawn from the concept of _____ .

5. Under the certainty equivalent approach, _____ is used as the discount rate under the NPV method and as the cutoff rate under the IRR method.

6. Simulation is often called _____ simulation.

7. _____ attempts to determine how sensitive NPV or IRR is to changing conditions.

8. A(n) _____ is a graphical exposition of the _____ of possible outcomes.

9. If the probability distribution is _____ , the expected value and the _____ may be used to compute the probability of a project's providing an NPV of less or greater than zero.

10. The required rate of return on a company's security is equal to the _____ plus a _____ .

11. Riskier projects should be evaluated with a higher discount rate, called a _____ .

12. An easier way to determine beta is to determine the _____ of the least-squares linear regression line, where the _____ of the security is regressed against the _____ of the _____ .

13. Relative risk is measured by the _____ .

14. _____ is an index of _____ risk.

Answers: (1) Risk analysis; (2) absolute, relative; (3) risk-adjusted rates of return, higher returns; (4) utility theory; (5) the risk-free rate; (6) Monte Carlo; (7) Sensitivity analysis; (8) decision tree (or probability tree), sequence; (9) normal, standard deviation; (10) risk-free rate, risk premium; (11) risk-adjusted discount rate; (12) slope, excessive return, excessive return, market portfolio; (13) coefficient of variation; (14) Beta, systematic (noncontrollable, nondiversifiable).

Solved Problems

9.1   **Expected Value and Standard Deviation.** The Lendel Company is considering investment in one of two mutually exclusive projects. They have the following cash inflows for each of the next 3 years:

	Cash Inflows ($)	
Probability	Project A	Project B
0.10	3,000	3,000
0.25	3,500	4,000
0.30	4,000	5,000
0.25	4,500	6,000
0.10	5,000	7,000

Calculate (a) the expected value (expected cash inflow) of each project; (b) the standard deviation of each project; and (c) the coefficient of variation. (d) Which project has the greater degree of risk? Why?

SOLUTION

(a) and (b)
$$\bar{A} = \sum_{i=1}^{n} A_i p_i \qquad \sigma = \sqrt{\sum_{i=1}^{n} (A_i - \bar{A})^2 p_i}$$

For project A:

A_i ($)	p_i	$A_i p_i$ ($)	$A_i - \bar{A}$ ($)	$(A_i - \bar{A})^2$ ($)	$(A_i - \bar{A})^2 p_i$
3,000	0.10	300	−1,000	1,000,000	100,000
3,500	0.25	875	−500	250,000	62,500
4,000	0.30	1,200	0	0	0
4,500	0.25	1,125	500	250,000	62,500
5,000	0.10	500	1,000	1,000,000	100,000
		$\bar{A} = 4,000$			$\sigma^2 = 325,000$

Since $\sigma^2 = 325,000$, $\sigma = \$570.09$.

For project B:

A_i ($)	p_i	$A_i p_i$ ($)	$(A_i - \bar{A})$ ($)	$(A_i - \bar{A})^2$ ($)	$(A_i - \bar{A})^2 p_i$ ($)
3,000	0.10	300	−2,000	4,000,000	400,000
4,000	0.25	1,000	−1,000	1,000,000	250,000
5,000	0.30	1,500	0	0	0
6,000	0.25	1,500	1,000	1,000,000	250,000
7,000	0.10	700	2,000	4,000,000	400,000
		$\bar{A} = 5,000$			$\sigma^2 = 1,300,000$

Since $\sigma^2 = 1,300,000$, $\sigma = \$1,140.18$.

(c) The coefficient of variation is:

	A	**B**
$\dfrac{\sigma}{\bar{A}}$	$\dfrac{\$570.09}{\$4,000} = 0.14$	$\dfrac{\$1,140.18}{\$5,000} = 0.23$

(d) Project B is riskier, since it has the greater coefficient of variation (i.e., 0.23 versus 0.14).

9.2   **Coefficient of Variation.** McEnro wishes to decide between two projects, X and Y. By using probability estimates, he has determined the following statistics:

	Project X	Project Y
Expected NPV	$35,000	$20,000
σ	$22,000	$20,000

(a) Compute the coefficient of variation for each project, and (b) explain why σ and the coefficient of variation give different rankings of risk. Which method is better?

SOLUTION

(a)
$$
\begin{array}{ccc}
 & \textbf{Project X} & \textbf{Project Y} \\
\sigma/\bar{A} & \dfrac{\$22,000}{35,000} = 0.63 & \dfrac{\$20,000}{20,000} = 1.00
\end{array}
$$

(b) The coefficient of variation is a superior measure of risk because it is a relative measure, giving the degree of dispersion relative to the expected value.

9.3 **NPV Analysis Under Risk.** The Connors Company is considering a $60,000 investment in a machine that will reduce operating costs. The following estimates regarding cash savings, along with their probabilities of occurrence, have been made:

Annual Cash Savings		Useful Life	
Event	**Probability**	**Event**	**Probability**
$20,000	0.30	9 years	0.40
$14,000	0.30	8 years	0.40
$12,000	0.40	6 years	0.20

(a) Compute the expected annual cash savings and useful life. Determine whether the machine should be purchased, using the NPV method.

(b) The company wishes to see whether the machine would be a good investment if each of its most pessimistic estimates, but not both at the same time, came true. Determine whether the investment would be desirable if: (1) the useful life is the expected value computed in part (a), and annual cash flows are only $12,000; (2) the annual cash flows are equal to the expected value computed in part (a) and the useful life is only 6 years.

SOLUTION

(a) Determination of expected annual cash savings is:

Event (A_i)	Probabilities (p_i)	Expected Value
$20,000	0.30	$ 6,000
$14,000	0.30	4,200
$12,000	0.40	4,800
	1.00	$15,000

Determination of useful life is:

Event	Probability	Useful Life
9 years	0.40	3.6 years
8 years	0.40	3.2 years
6 years	0.20	1.2 years
	1.00	8.0 years

Expected annual cash savings	$15,000
Present value factor for 8-year annuity at 16%	×4.344
Present value of future flows (PV)	$65,160
Less cost of machine (I)	60,000
Net present value (NPV)	$ 5,160

The purchase of the machine would appear to be wise because of its positive net present value.

(b) (1) The present value of the future cash savings ($52,128) is less than the purchase price ($60,000) and the machine should not be purchased.

Annual cash savings, pessimistic estimate	$12,000
Present value factor, 8-year annuity at 16%	4.344
Present value of future cash flows	$52,128

(2) The present value of the future cash savings ($55,275) is less than the purchase price ($60,000) and the machine should not be purchased.

Annual cash savings, expected value	$15,000
Present value factor, 6-year annuity at 16%	3.685
Present value of future cash flows	$55,275

9.4 **Expected NPV and Risk.** The administrator of ABC Hospital is considering the purchase of new operating room equipment at a cost of $7,500. The surgical staff has furnished the following estimates of useful life and cost savings. Each useful life estimate is independent of each cost savings estimate.

Years of Estimated Useful Life	Probability of Occurrence	Estimated Cost Savings	Probability of Occurrence
4	0.25	$1,900	0.30
5	0.50	$2,000	0.40
6	0.25	$2,100	0.30
	1.00		1.00

Calculate (a) the expected net present value, allowing for risk and uncertainty and using a 10 percent discount rate, and (b) the standard deviation and coefficient of variation for the present value calculations of estimated cost savings before deducting the investment.

SOLUTION

(a)

(1) Estimated Useful Life — Years	(2) Estimated Useful Life — Probability	(3) Estimated Cost Savings — $	(4) Estimated Cost Savings — Probability	(5) Combined Probability (2) × (4)	(6) Present Value Factor 10%	(7) Present Value ($) (Conditional Value) (3) × (6)	(8) Expected Present Value ($) (5) × (7)
	0.25	1,900	0.30	0.075	3.170	6,023	452
4	0.25	2,000	0.40	0.100	3.170	6,340	634
	0.25	2,100	0.30	0.075	3.170	6,657	499
	0.50	1,900	0.30	0.150	3.791	7,203	1,080
5	0.50	2,000	0.40	0.200	3.791	7,582	1,516
	0.50	2,100	0.30	0.150	3.791	7,961	1,194
	0.25	1,900	0.30	0.075	4.355	8,275	621
6	0.25	2,000	0.40	0.100	4.355	8,710	871
	0.25	2,100	0.30	0.075	4.355	9,146	686
				1.000			7,553

Total expected present value	$7,553
Less investment in equipment	7,500
Expected net present value	$ 53

(b)

(1) Present Value ($) (Conditional Value)	(2) Difference from Expected Value ($) ($7,553)	(3) (2) Squared ($)	(4) Probability	(5) (3) × (4) ($)
6,023	−1,530	2,340,900	0.075	175,568
6,340	−1,213	1,471,369	0.100	147,137
6,657	−896	802,816	0.075	60,211
7,203	−350	122,500	0.150	18,375
7,582	29	841	0.200	168
7,961	408	166,464	0.150	24,970
8,275	722	521,284	0.075	39,096
8,710	1,157	1,338,649	0.100	133,865
9,146	1,593	2,537,649	0.075	190,324

$$\sigma^2 = \$789,714$$

$$\sigma = \sqrt{\$789,714} = \$889$$

$$\text{Coefficient of variation} = \frac{\sigma}{\bar{A}} = \frac{\$889}{\$7,553} = 0.12$$

9.5   Risk-Adjusted NPV and Decision. Vilas Corporation is considering two mutually exclusive projects, both of which require an initial investment of $4,500 and an expected life of 10 years. The probability distribution for the cash inflows are as follows (for years 1 through 10):

Project A		Project B	
Cash Inflow	Probability	Cash Inflow	Probability
$ 700	0.10	$ 550	0.2
900	0.80	800	0.3
1,000	0.10	1,000	0.3
		1,400	0.2

The company has decided that the project with higher relative risk should have a required rate of return of 16 percent, whereas the less risky project's required rate of return should be 14 percent.

Compute (a) the coefficient of variation as a measure of relative risk, and (b) the risk-adjusted NPV of each project. Which project should be chosen? (c) What factors other than NPV should be considered when deciding between these two projects?

SOLUTION

(a)   For project A:

$$\bar{A} = \sum_{i=1}^{n} A_i p_i = \$700(0.1) + \$900(0.8) + \$1,000(0.1)$$

$$= \$70 + \$720 + \$100 = \$890$$

$$\sigma = \sqrt{\sum_{i=1}^{n}(A_i - \bar{A})^2 p_i} = \sqrt{(\$700 - \$890)^2(0.1) + (\$900 - \$890)^2(0.8) + (\$1,000 - \$890)^2(0.1)}$$

$$= \sqrt{\$3,610 + \$80 + \$1,210} = \sqrt{\$4,900} = \$70$$

$$\frac{\sigma}{\bar{A}} = \frac{\$70}{\$890} = 0.079$$

For project B:

$$\bar{A} = \$550(0.2) + \$800(0.3) + \$1,000(0.3) + \$1,400(0.2)$$
$$= \$110 + \$240 + \$300 + \$280 = \$930$$

$$\sigma = \sqrt{(\$550 - \$930)^2(0.2) + (\$800 - \$930)^2(0.3) + (\$1,000 - \$930)^2(0.3) + (\$1,400 - \$930)^2(0.2)}$$
$$= \sqrt{\$28,880 + \$5,070 + \$1,470 + \$44,180} = \sqrt{\$79,600} = \$282.13$$

$$\frac{\sigma}{\bar{A}} = \frac{\$282.13}{\$930} = 0.30$$

(b) Project A is relatively less risky than project B. Therefore, project A's expected cash inflow is discounted at 14 percent, while project B's expected cash inflow is discounted at 16 percent.
For project A:

$$\text{Expected NPV} = \text{PV} - \text{I} = \$890(\text{PVIFA}_{14\%,10}) - \$4,500 = \$890(5.216) - \$4,500$$
$$= \$4,642.24 - \$4,500 = \$142.24$$

For project B:

$$\text{Expected NPV} = \$930(\text{PVIFA}_{16\%,10}) - \$4,500 = \$930(4.833) - \$4,500$$
$$= \$4,494.69 - \$4,500 = -\$5.31$$

Because project A has a positive NPV, project A should be chosen.

(c) The company should also consider the potential diversification effect associated with these projects. If the project's cash inflow patterns are negatively correlated with those of the company, the overall risk of the company may be significantly reduced.

9.6   Risk-Adjusted NPV. Kyoto Laboratories, Inc., is contemplating a capital investment project with an expected useful life of 10 years that requires an initial cash outlay of $225,000. The company estimates the following data:

Annual Cash Inflows ($)	Probabilities
0	0.10
50,000	0.20
65,000	0.40
70,000	0.20
90,000	0.10

(a) Assuming a risk-adjusted required rate of return of 25 percent is appropriate for projects of this level of risk, calculate the risk-adjusted NPV of the project. (b) Should the project be accepted?

SOLUTION

(a) $$\bar{A} = \sum_{i=1}^{n} A_i p_i = \$0(0.10) + \$50,000(0.2) + \$65,000(0.4) + \$70,000(0.2) + \$90,000(0.1)$$

$$= \$0 + \$10,000 + \$26,000 + \$14,000 + \$9,000 = \$59,000$$
$$\text{Expected NPV} = \text{PV} - \text{I}$$
$$= \$59,000 \ (\text{PVIFA}_{25\%,10}) - \$225,000 = \$210,689 - \$225,000 = -\$14,311$$

(b) Reject the project, since the expected NPV is negative.

9.7   Certainty Equivalent NPV. Rush Corporation is considering the purchase of a new machine that will last 5 years and require a cash outlay of $300,000. The firm has a 12 percent cost of capital rate and its after-tax risk-free rate is 9 percent. The company has expected cash inflows and certainty equivalents for these cash inflows, as follows:

Year	After-Tax Cash Inflows ($)	Certainty Equivalent
1	100,000	1.00
2	100,000	0.95
3	100,000	0.90
4	100,000	0.80
5	100,000	0.70

Calculate (*a*) the unadjusted NPV, and (*b*) the certainty equivalent NPV. (*c*) Determine if the machine should be purchased.

SOLUTION

(*a*) $NPV = PV - I = \$100,000(PVIFA_{12\%,5}) - \$300,000$

                 $= \$100,000(3.605) - \$300,000 = \$360,500 - \$300,000 = \$60,500$

(*b*)

Year	After-Tax Cash Inflows ($)	Certainty Equivalents	Certain Cash Inflows ($)	PV at 9%	PV ($)
1	100,000	1.00	100,000	0.917	91,700
2	100,000	0.95	95,000	0.842	79,990
3	100,000	0.90	90,000	0.772	69,480
4	100,000	0.80	80,000	0.708	56,640
5	100,000	0.70	70,000	0.650	45,500
					343,310

Certainty equivalent NPV = $343,310 - $300,000 = $43,310

(*c*)   Because of a positive NPV, the machine should be purchased.

9.8   Decision Tree. The Summerall Corporation wishes to introduce one of two products to the market this year. The probabilities and present values of projected cash inflows are given below.

Products	Initial Investment ($)	PV of Cash Inflows ($)	Probabilities
A	225,000		1.00
		450,000	0.4
		200,000	0.5
		−100,000	0.1
B	80,000		1.00
		320,000	0.2
		100,000	0.6
		−150,000	0.2

(*a*) Construct a decision tree to analyze the two products. (*b*) Which product would you introduce? Comment on your decision.

SOLUTION

(*a*)

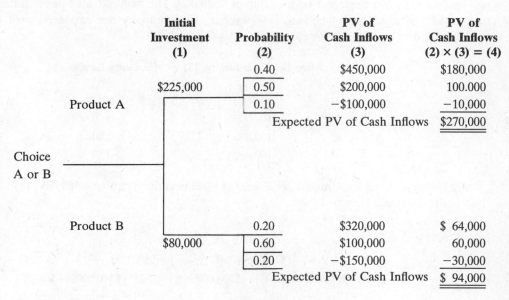

	Initial Investment (1)	Probability (2)	PV of Cash Inflows (3)	PV of Cash Inflows (2) × (3) = (4)
		0.40	$450,000	$180,000
	$225,000	0.50	$200,000	100.000
Product A		0.10	−$100,000	−10,000
			Expected PV of Cash Inflows	$270,000
Product B		0.20	$320,000	$ 64,000
	$80,000	0.60	$100,000	60,000
		0.20	−$150,000	−30,000
			Expected PV of Cash Inflows	$ 94,000

For product A:

$$\text{Expected NPV} = \text{expected PV} - I = \$270,000 - \$225,000 = \$45,000$$

For product B:

$$\text{Expected NPV} = \$94,000 - \$80,000 = \$14,000$$

(*b*) Based on the expected NPV, choose product A over product B; however, this analysis fails to recognize the risk factor in project analysis.

9.9 **Dependent Cash Inflows and Expected NPV.** The Newcome Corporation has determined that its after-tax cash inflow (ATCI) distributions are not independent. Further, the company has estimated that the year 1 results (ATCI$_1$) will affect the year 2 flows (ATCI$_2$) as follows:

If ATCI$_1$ = $40,000 with a 30 percent chance, the distribution for ATCI$_2$ is:

0.2	$20,000
0.6	$50,000
0.2	$80,000

If ATCI$_1$ = $60,000 with a 40 percent chance, the distribution for ATCI$_2$ is:

0.3	$70,000
0.4	$80,000
0.3	$90,000

If ATCI$_1$ = $80,000 with a 30 percent chance, the distribution for ATCI$_2$ is:

0.1	$80,000
0.8	$100,000
0.1	$120,000

Assume that the project's initial investment is $100,000.

(*a*) Set up a decision tree to depict the above cash flow possibilities, and calculate an expected NPV for each 2-year possibility using a risk-free rate of 15 percent. (*b*) Determine if the project should be accepted.

SOLUTION

(*a*)

Time 0	Time 1		Time 2	NPV at 10%	Joint Probability	Expected NPV
		0.2	$ 20,000	−$50,080[a]	0.06[b]	−$ 3,005
	$40,000	0.6	$ 50,000	−$27,400	0.18	−4,912
		0.2	$ 80,000	−$ 4,720	0.06	−283
	0.3					
		0.3	$ 70,000	$ 5,120	0.12	614
−$100,000	0.4—$60,000	0.4	$ 80,000	$12,680	0.16	2,029
		0.3	$ 90,000	$20,240	0.12	2,428
	0.3					
	$80,000	0.1	$ 80,000	$30,080	0.03	902
		0.8	$100,000	$45,200	0.24	10,848
		0.1	$120,000	$60,320	0.03	1,810
					1.00	$10,431

[a] $\text{NPV} = \text{PV} - \text{I} = \dfrac{\$40,000}{(1 + 0.15)} + \dfrac{\$20,000}{(1 + 0.15)^2} - \$100,000$

$= \$40,000(\text{PVIF}_{15\%,1}) + \$20,000(\text{PVIF}_{15\%,2}) - \$100,000$

$= \$40,000(0.87) + \$20,000(0.756) - \$100,000 = \$34,800 + \$15,120 - \$100,000 = -\$50,080$

[b] Joint probability of the first path $= (0.3)(0.2) = 0.06$

The expected NPV is $10,431.

(*b*) Accept the project, since the expected NPV is positive.

9.10 Decision Tree Analysis. The Drysdale Corporation is contemplating the development of a new product. The initial investment required to purchase the necessary equipment is $200,000. There is a 60 percent chance that demand will be high in year 1. If it is high, there is an 80 percent chance that it will continue high indefinitely. If demand is low in year 1, there is a 60 percent chance that it will continue to be low indefinitely. If demand is high, forecasted cash inflow (before taxes) is $90,000 a year; if demand is low, forecasted cash inflow is $30,000 a year.

The corporate income tax rate is 40 percent. The company uses straight-line depreciation and will depreciate the equipment over 10 years with no salvage value.

(*a*) Determine the after-tax cash inflows. (*b*) Set up a decision tree representing all possible outcomes, and compute the expected NPV using a 10 percent risk-free rate of return.

SOLUTION

(*a*) First, compute the annual depreciation.

$$\text{Depreciation} = \text{price/useful life} = \frac{\$200,000}{10 \text{ years}} = \$20,000/\text{year}$$

$$\text{After-tax cash inflow} = \text{after-tax net profits} + \text{depreciation}$$

Therefore, when demand is high:

$$\text{After-tax cash inflow} = (\$90,000 - \$20,000)(1 - 0.4) + \$20,000 = \$62,000$$

When demand is low:

$$\text{After-tax cash inflow} = (\$30,000 - \$20,000)(1 - 0.4) + \$20,000 = \$26,000$$

(b)

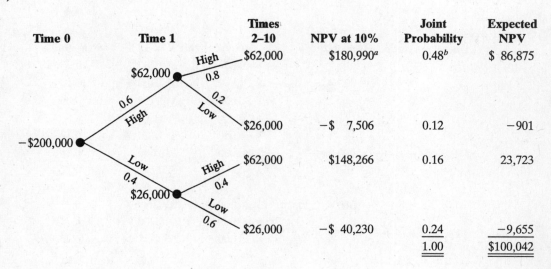

		Times 2–10	NPV at 10%	Joint Probability	Expected NPV

^{a}NPV = PV − I = $\dfrac{\$62,000}{(1+0.1)} + \dfrac{\$62,000}{(1+0.1)^2} + \cdots + \dfrac{\$62,000}{(1+0.1)^{10}} - \$200,000$

$= \$62,000(\text{PVIF}_{10\%,1}) + \$62,000(\text{PVIFA}_{10\%,10} - \text{PVIFA}_{10\%,1}) - \$200,000$

$= \$62,000(0.909) + \$62,000(6.145 - 0.909) - \$200,000$

$= \$56,358 + \$324,632 - \$200,000 = \$180,990$

^{b}Joint probability = (0.6)(0.8) = 0.48

The expected NPV is $100,042.

9.11   Decision Tree Analysis and Expected IRR. The NFL Systems, Inc., is considering the purchase of a minicomputer using the following decision tree:

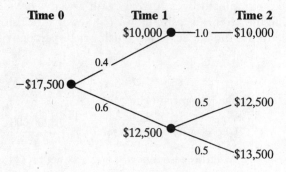

(a) Complete the decision tree by computing IRR, joint probability, and the expected IRR (round to the nearest whole percent of IRR). (b) Should this computer be purchased? (Assume the company's cost of capital is 16 percent.)

SOLUTION

(a)

Time 0	Time 1		Time 2	IRR	Joint Probability	Expected IRR
	$10,000	1.0	$10,000	9%[a]	0.4[b]	3.6
−$17,500						
		0.4				
		0.6	$12,500	25%	0.30	7.5
	$12,500	0.5				
		0.5	$13,500	30%[c]	0.30	9.0
					1.00	20.1%

[a] By definition, at IRR, I = PV.
Thus,

$$\$17,500 = \$10,000(\text{PVIFA}_{r,2})$$

$$\text{PVIFA}_{r,2} = \frac{\$17,500}{\$10,000} = 1.75$$

From Appendix D this value is close to 9 percent.

[b] Joint probability = (0.4)(1.0) = 0.4

[c] I = PV($17,500) = $12,500(\text{PVIF}_{r,1}) + $13,500(\text{PVIF}_{r,2})$
By trial and error, IRR is approximately 30 percent. In other words, at $r = 30$ percent:

I = PV

= $12,500(0.769) + $13,500(0.592) = $9,613 + $7,992 = $17,605

(b) The expected IRR is 20.1 percent, which exceeds the cost of capital of 16 percent. Therefore, the computer should be purchased.

9.12 Normal Distribution and NPV Analysis. The probability distribution of possible NPVs for project A has an expected cash inflow of $30,000 and a standard deviation of $15,000. Assuming a normal distribution, compute the probability that: (a) the NPV will be zero or less; (b) the NPV will be greater than $45,000; and (c) the NPV will be less than $7,500.

SOLUTION

The standardized normal variate is:

$$z = \frac{x - \text{NPV}}{\sigma}$$

(a) For NPV of zero or less:

$$z = \frac{0 - \$30,000}{\$15,000} = -2$$

From Appendix E, $z = \pm 2$ corresponds to a probability of 0.0228 or 2.28 percent.

(b)   For NPV of $45,000 or more:

$$z = \frac{\$45,000 - \$30,000}{\$15,000} = 1.0$$

From Appendix E, the probability for this value of z is 15.77 percent.

(c)   For NPV of $7,500 or less:

$$z = \frac{\$7,500 - \$30,000}{\$15,000} = -1.5$$

From Appendix E, the probability for $z = \pm 1.5$ is 6.68 percent.

9.13   Normal Distribution and NPV Analysis. The Halo Shipping Company is considering an investment in a project that requires an initial investment of $6,000, with a projected after-tax cash inflow generated over the next 3 years as follows:

Period 1		Period 2		Period 3	
Probability	Cash Flow ($)	Probability	Cash Flow ($)	Probability	Cash Flow ($)
0.10	1,000	0.2	1,000	0.3	1,000
0.30	2,000	0.4	2,000	0.4	2,000
0.20	3,000	0.3	3,000	0.1	3,000
0.40	4,000	0.1	4,000	0.2	4,000

Assume that probability distributions are independent and the after-tax risk-free rate of return is 6 percent. Calculate: (a) the expected NPV of the project; (b) the standard deviation of the expected NPV; (c) the probability that the NPV will be zero or less (assume that the probability distribution is normal and continuous); (d) the probability that the NPV will be greater than zero; and (e) the probability that the NPV will be greater than the expected value.

SOLUTION

(a)

Period 1	Period 2	Period 3
$1,000(0.1) = \$ \quad 100$	$1,000(0.2) = \$ \quad 200$	$1,000(0.3) = \$ \quad 300$
$2,000(0.3) = \quad 600$	$2,000(0.4) = \quad 800$	$2,000(0.4) = \quad 800$
$3,000(0.2) = \quad 600$	$3,000(0.3) = \quad 900$	$3,000(0.1) = \quad 300$
$4,000(0.4) = \underline{\quad 1,600}$	$4,000(0.1) = \underline{\quad 400}$	$4,000(0.2) = \underline{\quad 800}$
$\$2,900$	$\$2,300$	$\$2,200$

$$NPV = PV - I$$

$$= \frac{\$2,900}{(1+0.06)} + \frac{\$2,300}{(1+0.06)^2} + \frac{\$2,200}{(1+0.06)^3} - \$6,000$$

$$= \$2,900(PVIF_{6\%,1}) + \$2,300(PVIF_{6\%,2}) + \$2,200(PVIF_{6\%,3}) - \$6,000$$

$$= \$2,900(0.943) + \$2,300(0.89) + \$2,200(0.84) - \$6,000$$

$$= \$2,735 + \$2,047 + \$1,848 - \$6,000 = \$6,630 - \$6,000 \ = \$630$$

(b) Calculations for standard deviation of NPV are as follows:

For period 1:

A	p	$(A - \bar{A})$	$(A - \bar{A})^2$	$(A - \bar{A})^2 p$
$1,000	0.1	$-$1,900	$3,610,000	$ 361,000
$2,000	0.3	$-$ 900	$ 810,000	243,000
$3,000	0.2	$ 100	$ 10,000	2,000
$4,000	0.4	$1,100	$1,210,000	484,000
				$1,090,000[a]
				$ 1,044[b]

[a]$1,090,000 = \sigma^2$
[b]$1,044 = \sigma$

For period 2:

A ($)	p	$(A - \bar{A})$ ($)	$(A - \bar{A})^2$ ($)	$(A - \bar{A})^2 p$ ($)
1,000	0.2	$-1,300$	1,690,000	338,000
2,000	0.4	-300	90,000	36,000
3,000	0.3	700	490,000	147,000
4,000	0.1	1,100	2,890,000	289,000
			$\sigma^2 =$	810,000
			$\sigma = $	800

For period 3:

A ($)	p	$(A - \bar{A})$ ($)	$(A - \bar{A})^2$ ($)	$(A - \bar{A})^2 p$ ($)
1,000	0.3	$-1,200$	1,440,000	432,000
2,000	0.4	-200	40,000	16,000
3,000	0.1	800	640,000	64,000
4,000	0.2	1,800	3,240,000	648,000
			$\sigma^2 =$	1,160,000
			$\sigma = $	1,077

The standard deviation of the expected NPV is:

$$\sigma_{\text{NPV}} = \sqrt{\frac{(\$1,044)^2}{(1 + 0.06)^2} + \frac{(\$900)^2}{(1 + 0.06)^4} + \frac{(\$1,077)^2}{(1 + 0.06)^6}}$$

$$= \sqrt{\$970,039 + \$642,857 + \$727,776} = \sqrt{\$2,340,672} = \$1,530$$

(c)
$$z = \frac{x - \text{NPV}}{\sigma} = \frac{0 - \$630}{\$1,530} = -0.41176$$

From the normal distribution table Appendix E, this value of z gives a probability of 0.3409, or approximately a 34 percent chance that NPV will be zero or less.

(d) The probability of the NPV being greater than zero is the compliment of 34 percent, or 66 percent.

(e)
$$z = \frac{\$630 - \$630}{\$1,530} = 0$$

Reading from Appendix E, at $z = 0$, there is 50 percent probability that the NPV will be greater than the expected value.

9.14   **Portfolio Effects.** The projected cash inflows of three projects—X, Y, and Z—for the period 19X1 to 19X5 are given below.

Year	Project X	Project Y	Project Z
19X1	$2,000	$6,000	$1,000
19X2	$3,000	$4,000	$2,000
19X3	$4,000	$3,000	$3,000
19X4	$5,000	$2,000	$3,000
19X5	$7,000	$1,000	$6,000

	Project X	Project Y	Project Z
$\bar{A}$	$4,200	$3,200	$3,000
σ	$3,847	$3,847	$3,742

(*a*) Calculate the expected cash inflows and standard deviation of cash inflows for project combinations XY and XZ, and (*b*) determine the portfolio effects of the above combinations of projects upon the portfolio risk.

SOLUTION

Since the probabilities associated with the cash inflows are not given (in fact, their cash inflows are equally likely), the formulas for $\bar{A}$ and σ are

$$\bar{A} = \sum A_i/n \quad \text{and} \quad \sigma = \sqrt{\sum_{i=1}^{n} (A_i - \bar{A})^2/n}$$

where n is the number of terms.

(*a*)   For projects XY:

Cash Inflow (A) ($)	$(A - \bar{A})$ ($)	$(A - \bar{A})^2$ ($)
8,000	600	360,000
7,000	−400	160,000
7,000	−400	160,000
7,000	−400	160,000
8,000	600	360,000
37,000		1,200,000

$$\bar{A} = \frac{\$37,000}{5} = \$7,400$$

$$\sigma^2 = \frac{\$1,200,000}{5} = \$240,000$$

Thus

$$\sigma = \$490$$

For projects XZ:

Cash Inflow (A) ($)	$(A - \bar{A})$ ($)	$(A - \bar{A})^2$ ($)
3,000	−4,200	17,640,000
5,000	−2,200	4,840,000
7,000	−200	40,000
8,000	800	640,000
13,000	5,800	33,640,000
36,000		56,800,000

$$\bar{A} = \frac{\$36,000}{5} = \$7,200$$

$$\sigma^2 = \frac{\$56,800,000}{5} = \$11,360,000$$

Thus

$$\sigma = \$3,370$$

(b) The greatest reduction in overall risk occurs when the portfolio combines projects which are negatively correlated such as projects XY (i.e., $\sigma_{XY} = \$490$).

9.15   CAPM and Capital Budgeting Decision. The Taylor Corporation is evaluating some new capital budgeting projects. Their evaluation method involves comparing each project's risk-adjusted return obtained from the capital asset pricing model (CAPM) with the project's average rate of return. The following data are provided:

Projects	Beta
A	−0.5
B	0.8
C	1.2
D	2.0

Possible rates of return and associated probabilities are:

	Rates of return (%)		
	(0.4)	(0.5)	(0.1)
A	4	2	5
B	2	6	12
C	10	15	20
D	−8	25	50

Assume that the risk-free rate of return is 6 percent and the market rate of return is 12 percent. Which projects should be selected?

SOLUTION

Use the CAPM equation to compute:

Projects	$r = r_f + b(r_m - r_f)$
A	$r_A = 6\% + (-0.5)(12\% - 6\%) = 3\%$
B	$r_B = 6\% + (0.8)(12\% - 6\%) = 10.8\%$
C	$r_C = 6\% + (1.2)(12\% - 6\%) = 13.2\%$
D	$r_D = 6\% + (2.0)(12\% - 6\%) = 18\%$

Average rates of return are:

Projects	
A	$4(0.4) + 2(0.5) + 5(0.1) = 3.1\%$
B	$2(0.4) + 6(0.5) + 12(0.1) = 5\%$
C	$10(0.4) + 15(0.5) + 20(0.1) = 13.5\%$
D	$-8(0.4) + 25(0.5) + 50(0.1) = 14.3\%$

Projects A and C should be selected, since their average rates of return exceed the required rates of return provided by the CAPM equation.

9.16 **Beta and NPV Analysis.** The risk-free rate is 5 percent and the expected return on the market portfolio is 13 percent. On the basis of the CAPM, answer the following questions: (*a*) What is the risk premium on the market? (*b*) What is the required rate of return on an investment with a beta equal to 1.2? (*c*) If an investment with a beta of 0.6 offers an expected return of 8.5 percent, does it have a positive NPV? (*d*) If the market expects a return of 12.5 percent from stock A, what is its beta?

SOLUTION

(*a*)
$$\text{Risk premium} = (r_m - r_f) = 13\% - 5\% = 8\%$$

(*b*)
$$rj = r_f + b(r_m - r_f)$$
$$= 5\% + 1.2(13\% - 5\%) = 5\% + 9.6\% = 14.6\%$$

(*c*) The answer is no.

$$r_j = 5\% + 0.6(13\% - 5\%) = 9.8\%$$

Since the required rate of return is 9.8 percent and the expected return from the investment is only 8.5 percent, the project produces a negative NPV.

(*d*)
$$r_j = r_f + b(r_m - r_f)$$
$$12.5\% = 5\% + b(13\% - 5\%)$$
$$b = 0.9375$$

9.17 **Beta and NPV Analysis.** A project has the following forecasted cash flows (in thousands of dollars):

Year 0	Year 1	Year 2	Year 3
($100)	$30	$50	$90

The estimated project beta is 2.0. The market return is 13 percent, and the Treasury bill yield is 6 percent. Compute (*a*) the project's cost of capital and (*b*) the project's NPV.

SOLUTION

(*a*) The project's cost of capital is:

$$r = r_f + b(r_m - r_f)$$
$$= 6\% + 2.0(13\% - 6\%) = 6\% + 14\% = 20\%$$

(*b*) The project's NPV is:

Year	Cash Flow ($)	PV at 20%	PV ($)
0	(100)	1.000	(100)
1	30	0.833	25
2	50	0.694	35
3	90	0.579	52
		NPV =	12

9.18   Calculation of Beta Using Regression Analysis. You are given the following data for stock A and the market portfolio:

Historic Rates of Return

Year	r_j (%)	r_m (%)
19X0	1	-2
19X1	3	7
19X2	14	20
19X3	18	30

Assuming that the risk-free rate is 4 percent, compute (a) the beta coefficient and (b) the required rate of return to be used for capital budgeting decisions in 19X4 when the market rate of return is expected to be 18 percent?

SOLUTION

(a)

Year	Stock Return, r_j	Market Return, r_m	Risk-Free Rate, r_j	Excess Stock Return $(r_j - r_f) = K$	Excess Market Return $(r_f - r_m) = M$	M^2	Cross Product MK
19X0	0.01	-0.02	0.04	-0.03	0.06	0.0036	-0.0018
19X1	0.03	0.07	0.04	-0.01	-0.03	0.0009	0.0003
19X2	0.14	0.2	0.04	0.10	-0.16	0.0256	-0.016
19X3	0.18	0.3	0.04	0.14	-0.26	0.0676	-0.0364
				0.2	-0.39	0.0977	-0.0539

$$\bar{K} = 0.05$$
$$\bar{M} = -0.0975$$

$$b = \frac{\Sigma MK - n\bar{M}\bar{K}}{\Sigma M^2 - n\bar{M}^2} = \frac{-0.0539 - (4)(-0.0975)(0.05)}{0.0977 - (4)(-0.0975)^2} = \frac{-0.0344}{-0.0597} = 0.59$$

(b)
$$r_j = r_f + b(r_m - r_f)$$
$$= 4\% + (0.59)(18\% - 4\%) = 12.26\%$$

Therefore, the 19X4 risk-adjusted rate of return that is required for capital budgeting projects is 16.18 percent.

Chapter 10

Cost of Capital

10.1 COST OF CAPITAL DEFINED

Cost of capital is defined as the rate of return that is necessary to maintain the market value of the firm (or price of the firm's stock). Managers must know the cost of capital, often called the *minimum required rate of return* in: (1) making capital budgeting decisions; (2) helping to establish the optimal capital structure; and (3) making decisions such as leasing, bond refunding, and working capital management. The cost of capital is computed as a weighted average of the various capital components, which are items on the right-hand side of the balance sheet such as debt, preferred stock, common stock, and retained earnings.

10.2 COMPUTING INDIVIDUAL COSTS OF CAPITAL

Each element of capital has a component cost that is identified by the following:

k_i = before-tax cost of debt

$k_d = k_i(1 - t)$ = after-tax cost of debt, where t = tax rate

k_p = cost of preferred stock

k_s = cost of retained earnings (or internal equity)

k_e = cost of external equity, or cost of issuing new common stock

k_o = firm's overall cost of capital, or a weighted average cost of capital

Cost of Debt

The before-tax cost of debt can be found by determining the internal rate of return (or yield to maturity) on the bond cash flows, which was discussed in detail in Chapter 7. However, the following shortcut formula may be used for *approximating* the yield to maturity on a bond:

$$k_i = \frac{I + (M - V)/n}{(M + V)/2}$$

where I = annual interest payments in dollars
   M = par value, usually $1,000 per bond
   V = value or net proceeds from the sale of a bond
   n = term of the bond in years

Since the interest payments are tax-deductible, the cost of debt must be stated on an after-tax basis. The after-tax cost of debt is:

$$k_d = k_i (1 - t)$$

where t is the tax rate.

EXAMPLE 10.1 Assume that the Carter Company issues a $1,000, 8 percent, 20-year bond whose net proceeds are $940. The tax rate is 40 percent. Then, the before-tax cost of debt, k_i, is:

$$k_i = \frac{I + (M - V)/n}{(M + V)/2}$$

$$= \frac{\$80 + (\$1,000 - \$940)/20}{(\$1,000 + \$940)/2} = \frac{\$83}{\$970} = 8.56\%$$

280

Therefore, the after-tax cost of debt is:

$$k_d = k_i(1 - t)$$
$$= 8.56\%(1 - 0.4) = 5.14\%$$

Cost of Preferred Stock

The cost of preferred stock, k_p, is found by dividing the annual preferred stock dividend, d_p, by the net proceeds from the sale of the preferred stock, p, as follows:

$$k_p = \frac{d_p}{p}$$

Since preferred stock dividends are not a tax-deductible expense, these dividends are paid out after taxes. Consequently, no tax adjustment is required.

EXAMPLE 10.2   Suppose that the Carter Company has preferred stock that pays a $13 dividend per share and sells for $100 per share in the market. The flotation (or underwriting) cost is 3 percent, or $3 per share. Then the cost of preferred stock is:

$$k_p = \frac{d_p}{p}$$
$$= \frac{\$13}{\$97} = 13.4\%$$

Cost of Equity Capital

The cost of common stock, k_e, is generally viewed as the rate of return investors require on a firm's common stock. Three techniques for measuring the cost of common stock equity capital are available: (1) the Gordon's growth model; (2) the capital asset pricing model (CAPM) approach; and (3) the bond plus approach.

The Gordon's Growth Model. The Gordon's model was discussed in detail in Chapter 7. The model is:

$$P_0 = \frac{D_1}{r - g}$$

where P_0 = value of common stock
$\quad D_1$ = dividend to be received in 1 year
$\quad\quad r$ = investor's required rate of return
$\quad\quad g$ = rate of growth (assumed to be constant over time)

Solving the model for r results in the formula for the cost of common stock:

$$r = \frac{D_1}{P_0} + g \quad\quad \text{or} \quad\quad k_e = \frac{D_1}{P_0} + g$$

Note that the symbol r is changed to k_e to show that it is used for the computation of cost of capital.

EXAMPLE 10.3   Assume that the market price of the Carter Company's stock is $40. The dividend to be paid at the end of the coming year is $4 per share and is expected to grow at a constant annual rate of 6 percent. Then the cost of this common stock is:

$$k_e = \frac{D_1}{P_0} + g = \frac{\$4}{\$40} + 6\% = 16\%$$

The cost of *new* common stock, or external equity capital, is higher than the cost of existing common stock because of the flotation costs involved in selling the new common stock.

If f is flotation cost in percent, the formula for the cost of new common stock is:

$$k_e = \frac{D_1}{P_0(1-f)} + g$$

EXAMPLE 10.4   Assume the same data as in Example 10.3, except the firm is trying to sell new issues of stock A and its flotation cost is 10 percent. Then:

$$k_e = \frac{D_1}{P_0(1-f)} + g$$

$$= \frac{\$4}{\$40(1-0.1)} + 6\% = \frac{\$4}{\$36} + 6\% = 11.11\% + 6\% = 17.11\%$$

The CAPM Approach. An alternative approach to measuring the cost of common stock is to use the CAPM, which involves the following steps:

1. Estimate the risk-free rate, r_f, generally taken to be the United States Treasury bill rate.
2. Estimate the stock's beta coefficient, b, which is an index of systematic (or nondiversifiable market) risk.
3. Estimate the rate of return on the market portfolio such as the Standard & Poor's 500 Stock Composite Index or Dow Jones 30 Industrials.
4. Estimate the required rate of return on the firm's stock, using the CAPM (or SML) equation:

$$k_e = r_f + b(r_m - r_f)$$

Again, note that the symbol r_j is changed to k_e.

EXAMPLE 10.5   Assuming that r_f is 7 percent, b is 1.5, and r_m is 13 percent, then:
$$k_e = r_f + b(r_m - r_f) = 7\% + 1.5(13\% - 7\%) = 16\%$$

This 16 percent cost of common stock can be viewed as consisting of a 7 percent risk-free rate plus a 9 percent risk premium, which reflects that the firm's stock price is 1.5 times more volatile than the market portfolio to the factors affecting nondiversifiable, or systematic, risk.

The Bond Plus Approach. Still another simple but useful approach to determining the cost of common stock is to add a *risk premium* to the firm's own cost of long-term debt, as follows:

$$k_e = \text{long-term bond rate} + \text{risk premium}$$
$$= k_i(1-t) + \text{risk premium}$$

A risk premium of about 4 percent is commonly used with this approach.

EXAMPLE 10.6   Using the data found in Example 10.1, the cost of common stock using the bond plus approach is:

$$k_e = \text{long-term bond rate} + \text{risk premium}$$
$$= k_i(1-t) + \text{risk premium}$$
$$= 5.14\% + 4\% = 9.14\%$$

Cost of Retained Earnings

The cost of retained earnings, k_s, is closely related to the cost of existing common stock, since the cost of equity obtained by retained earnings is the same as the rate of return investors require on the firm's common stock. Therefore,

$$k_e = k_s$$

10.3   MEASURING THE OVERALL COST OF CAPITAL

The firm's overall cost of capital is the weighted average of the individual capital costs, with the weights being the proportions of each type of capital used. Let k_o be the overall cost of capital.

$$k_o = \sum \left(\begin{array}{ll} \text{\% of total capital} & \text{cost of capital} \\ \text{structure supplied by} \times & \text{for each source} \\ \text{each type of capital} & \text{of capital} \end{array} \right)$$

$$= w_d \cdot k_d + w_p \cdot k_p + w_e \cdot k_e + w_s \cdot k_s$$

where w_d = % of total capital supplied by debt

w_p = % of total capital supplied by preferred stock

w_e = % of total capital supplied by external equity

w_s = % of total capital supplied by retained earnings (or internal equity)

The weights can be historical, target, or marginal.

Historical Weights

Historical weights are based on a firm's existing capital structure. The use of these weights is based on the assumption that the firm's existing capital structure is optimal and therefore should be maintained in the future. Two types of historical weights can be used—book value weights and market value weights.

Book Value Weights. The use of book value weights in calculating the firm's weighted cost of capital assumes that new financings will be raised using the same method the firm used for its present capital structure. The weights are determined by dividing the book value of each capital component by the sum of the book values of all the long-term capital sources. The computation of overall cost of capital is illustrated in the following example.

EXAMPLE 10.7   Assume the following capital structure for the Carter Company:

Mortgage bonds ($1,000 par)	$20,000,000
Preferred stock ($100 par)	5,000,000
Common stock ($40 par)	20,000,000
Retained earnings	5,000,000
Total	$50,000,000

The book value weights and the overall cost of capital are computed as follows:

Source	Book Value	Weights	Cost	Weighted Cost
Debt	$20,000,000	40%	5.14%	2.06%
Preferred stock	5,000,000	10	13.40%	1.34
Common stock	20,000,000	40	17.11%	6.84
Retained earnings	5,000,000	10	16.00%	1.60
Totals	$50,000,000	100%		11.84%

Overall cost of capital = k_o = 11.84%

Market Value Weights. Market value weights are determined by dividing the market value of each source by the sum of the market values of all sources. The use of market value weights for computing a firm's weighted average cost of capital is theoretically more appealing than the use of book value weights because the market values of the securities closely approximate the actual dollars to be received from their sale.

EXAMPLE 10.8 In addition to the data from Example 10.7, assume that the security market prices are as follows:

$$\text{Mortgage bonds} = \$1{,}100 \text{ per bond}$$
$$\text{Preferred stock} = \$90 \text{ per share}$$
$$\text{Common stock} = \$80 \text{ per share}$$

The firm's number of securities in each category is:

$$\text{Mortgage bonds} = \frac{\$20{,}000{,}000}{\$1{,}000} = 20{,}000$$

$$\text{Preferred stock} = \frac{\$5{,}000{,}000}{\$100} = 50{,}000$$

$$\text{Common stock} = \frac{\$20{,}000{,}000}{\$40} = 500{,}000$$

Therefore, the market value weights are:

Source	Number of Securities	Price	Market Value
Debt	20,000	$1,100	$22,000,000
Preferred stock	50,000	$90	4,500,000
Common stock	500,000	$80	40,000,000
			$66,500,000

The $40 million common stock value must be split in the ratio of 4 to 1 (the $20 million common stock versus the $5 million retained earnings in the original capital structure), since the market value of the retained earnings has been impounded into the common stock.

The firm's cost of capital is as follows:

Source	Market Value	Weights	Cost	Weighted Average
Debt	$22,000,000	33.08%	5.14%	1.70%
Preferred stock	4,500,000	6.77	13.40%	0.91
Common stock	32,000,000	48.12	17.11%	8.23
Retained earnings	8,000,000	12.03	16.00%	1.92
	$66,500,000	100.00%		12.76%

$$\text{Overall cost of capital} = k_o = 12.76\%$$

Target Weights

If the firm has determined the capital structure it believes most consistent with its goal, the use of that capital structure and associated weights is appropriate.

Marginal Weights

The use of marginal weights involves weighting the specific costs of various types of financing by the percentage of the total financing expected to be raised using each method. In using target weights, the firm is concerned with what it believes to be the optimal capital structure or target percentage. In using marginal weights, the firm is concerned with the *actual* dollar amounts of each type of financing to be needed for a given investment project.

EXAMPLE 10.9 The Carter Company is considering raising $8 million for plant expansion. Management estimates using the following mix for financing this project:

Debt	$4,000,000	50%
Common stock	2,000,000	25
Retained earnings	2,000,000	25
	$8,000,000	100%

The company's cost of capital is computed as follows:

Source	Marginal Weights	Cost	Weighted Cost
Debt	50%	5.14%	2.57%
Common stock	25	17.11%	4.28
Retained earnings	25	16.00%	4.00
	100%		10.85%

Overall cost of capital $= k_o = 10.85\%$

10.4 LEVEL OF FINANCING AND THE MARGINAL COST OF CAPITAL (MCC)

Because external equity capital has a higher cost than retained earnings due to flotation costs, the weighted cost of capital increases for each dollar of new financing. Therefore, lower-cost capital sources are used first. In fact, the firm's cost of capital is a function of the size of its total investment. A schedule or graph relating the firm's cost of capital to the level of new financing is called the *weighted marginal cost of capital (MCC)*. Such a schedule is used to determine the discount rate to be used in the firm's capital budgeting process. The steps to be followed in calculating the firm's marginal cost of capital are summarized below.

1. Determine the cost and the percentage of financing to be used for each source of capital (debt, preferred stock, common stock equity).

2. Compute the break points on the MCC curve where the weighted cost will increase. The formula for computing the break points is:

$$\text{Break point} = \frac{\text{maximum amount of the lower-cost source of capital}}{\text{percentage financing provided by the source}}$$

3. Calculate the weighted cost of capital over the range of total financing between break points.

4. Construct an MCC schedule or graph that shows the weighted cost of capital for each level of total new financing. This schedule will be used in conjunction with the firm's available investment opportunities schedule (IOS) in order to select the investments. As long as a project's IRR is greater than the marginal cost of new financing, the project should be accepted. Also, the point at which the IRR intersects the MCC gives the optimal capital budget.

Example 10.10 illustrates the procedure for determining a firm's weighted cost of capital for each level of new financing and how a firm's investment opportunity schedule (IOS) is related to its discount rate.

EXAMPLE 10.10 A firm is contemplating three investment projects, A, B, and C, whose initial cash outlays and expected IRR are shown below. IOS for these projects is:

Project	Cash Outlay	IRR
A	$2,000,000	13%
B	$2,000,000	15%
C	$1,000,000	10%

If these projects are accepted, the financing will consist of 50 percent debt and 50 percent common stock. The firm should have $1.8 million in earnings available for reinvestment (internal common). The firm will consider only the effects of increases in the cost of common stock on its marginal cost of capital.

1. The costs of capital for each source of financing have been computed and are given below:

Source	Cost
Debt	5%
Common stock ($1.8 million)	15%
New common stock	19%

If the firm uses only internally generated common stock, the weighted cost of capital is:

$k_o = \Sigma$ percentage of the total capital structure supplied by each source of capital
$\times$ cost of capital for each source

In this case the capital structure is composed of 50 percent debt and 50 percent internally generated common stock. Thus,

$$k_o = (0.5)5\% + (0.5)15\% = 10\%$$

If the firm uses only new common stock, the weighted cost of capital is:

$$k_o = (0.5)5\% + (0.5)19\% = 12\%$$

Range of Total New Financing (In Millions of Dollars)	Type of Capital	Proportion	Cost	Weighted Cost
$0–$3.6	Debt	0.5	5%	2.5%
	Internal common	0.5	15%	7.5
				10.0%
$3.6 and up	Debt	0.5	5%	2.5%
	New common	0.5	19%	9.5
				12.0%

2. Next compute the break point, which is the level of financing at which the weighted cost of capital increases.

$$\text{Break point} = \frac{\text{maximum amount of source of the lower-cost source of capital}}{\text{percentage financing provided by the source}}$$
$$= \frac{\$1,800,000}{0.5} = \$3,600,000$$

3. That is, the firm may be able to finance $3.6 million in new investments with internal common stock and debt without having to change the current mix of 50 percent debt and 50 percent common stock. Therefore, if the total financing is $3.6 million or less, the firm's cost of capital is 10 percent.

4. Construct the MCC schedule on the IOS graph to determine the discount rate to be used in order to decide in which project to invest and to show the firm's optimal capital budget. See Fig. 10-1.

The firm should continue to invest up to the point where the IRR equals the MCC. From the graph in Fig. 10-1, note that the firm should invest in projects B and A, since each IRR exceeds the marginal cost of capital. The firm should reject project C since its cost of capital is greater than the IRR. The optimal capital budget is $4 million, since this is the sum of the cash outlay required for projects A and B.

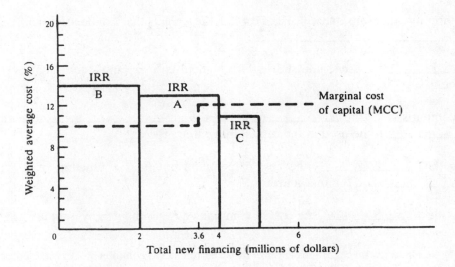

Fig. 10-1 MCC schedule and IOS graph

Review Questions

1. The firm's cost of capital is calculated as a(n) _____ of the costs of the various types of financing.

2. Capital components on the right-hand side of the firm's balance sheet are _____, _____, _____ and _____.

3. There are three techniques for measuring the cost of common stock. They are _____, _____, and _____.

4. The cost of capital, often called the _____, is used in: (1) making _____ decisions; (2) helping to establish the _____; and (3) making such decisions as _____, bond financing, and working capital management.

5. The after-tax cost of debt is k_i times _____.

6. The _____ is found by dividing the annual _____ dividend by the net proceeds from sale.

7. No tax adjustments are necessary for the computation of the costs of _____ and preferred stock.

8. The cost of _____ is higher than the cost of common stock because of _____ involved in its sale.

9. The _____ approach to determining the cost of common stock is to add a _____ to the firm's own cost of long-term debt.

10. Two types of historical weights are used: _____ and _____.

11. In computing the firm's overall cost of capital, the weights that can be used are _____ , _____ , and _____ .

12. The _____ schedule shows the weighted cost of capital for each level of total new financing.

13. The comparison of the _____ and the _____ helps determine the firm's _____ to be used in the capital budgeting process.

14. Using the _____ , the cost of common equity is a function of the risk-free rate, _____ , and the market return.

15. Using the _____ , the cost of common equity is dividend yield plus _____ .

Answers: (1) weighted average; (2) long-term debt, preferred stock, common stock, retained earnings; (3) the Gordon's growth model approach, the CAPM approach, the bond plus approach; (4) required rate of return, capital budgeting, optimal capital structure, leasing; (5) $(1 - \text{tax rate})$; (6) cost of preferred stock, preferred stock; (7) common stock (equity); (8) new common stock, flotation costs; (9) bond plus, risk premium; (10) book value, market value; (11) historical, target, marginal; (12) marginal cost of capital (MCC); (13) MCC, investment opportunity schedule (IOS), optimal capital budget; (14) CAPM, beta; (15) Gordon's growth model, growth rate in earnings and dividends.

Solved Problems

10.1   Cost of Debt. Calculate the after-tax cost of debt under each of the following cases: (*a*) the interest rate is 10 percent, and the tax rate is 40 percent; (*b*) the interest rate is 11 percent, and the tax rate is 50 percent.

SOLUTION

$$k_d = k_i(1 - t)$$

(*a*) $$k_d = 10\% \ (1 - 0.4) = 6\%$$
(*b*) $$k_d = 11\% \ (1 - 0.5) = 5.5\%$$

10.2   Cost of Bonds. XYZ Company has bonds outstanding with 7 years left before maturity. The bonds are currently selling for $800 per $1,000 face value. The interest is paid annually at a rate of 12 percent. The firm's tax rate is 40 percent. Calculate the after-tax cost of debt using (*a*) the regular method, and (*b*) the shortcut method.

SOLUTION

(*a*)   Using the regular method, the yield to maturity is:

$$V = \sum_{t=1}^{n} \frac{I}{(1 + r)^t} + \frac{M}{(1 + r)^n}$$
$$= I(\text{PVIFA}_{r,n}) + M(\text{PVIF}_{r,n})$$
$$\$800 = \$120(\text{PVIFA}_{r,7}) + \$1,000(\text{PVIF}_{r,7})$$

At 17%,

$$V = \$120(3.9215) + \$1,000(0.3338) = \$470.58 + \$333.80 = \$804.38$$

which is close enough to $800; therefore, the yield to maturity or before-tax cost of debt is 17 percent.

The after-tax cost of debt is computed as:

$$k_d = k_i(1 - t)$$
$$= 17\% \, (1 - 0.4) = 10.2\%$$

(b) Using the shortcut method:

$$k_i = \frac{I + [(M - V)/n]}{(M + V)/2} = \frac{\$120 + [(\$1,000 - \$800)/7]}{(\$1,000 + \$800)/2} = \frac{\$120 + \$28.57}{\$900} = 16.51\%$$

Therefore, the after-tax cost of debt is computed as:

$$k_d = 16.51\%(1 - 0.4) = 9.91\%$$

10.3 **Cost of Bonds.** Assume the same data as in Problem 10.2, but now assume the interest is paid semiannually. Calculate the after-tax cost of debt, using (a) the regular method, and (b) the shortcut method.

SOLUTION

(a) Since the interest is paid semiannually, the interest payment is $120 ÷ 2 = $60 and the number of periods is 14. Using the regular method gives:

$$V = I(\text{PVIFA}_{r,n}) + M \, (\text{PVIF}_{r,n})$$
$$\$800 = \$60(\text{PVIFA}_{i,14}) + \$1,000 \, (\text{PVIF}_{i,14})$$

To arrive at a value of $800, first try 8 percent:

$$V = \$60(8.2442) + \$1,000(0.3405) = \$494.65 + \$340.50 = \$835.15$$

Since this is too high, try 9 percent:

$$V = \$60(7.7862) + \$1,000(0.2992) = \$467.17 + \$299.20 = \$766.37$$

Since this value is too low, the cost of debt is somewhere between 8 percent and 9 percent. Using the interpolation:

	8%	9%
PV	$835.15	$835.15
True rate	800.00	
PV		766.37
Difference	$ 35.15	$ 68.78

$$\text{True rate} = 8\% + \frac{\$35.15}{\$68.78}(1\%) = 8\% + 0.51 = 8.51\%$$

$$\text{Annual rate} = 8.51\% \times 2 = 17.02\%$$

Therefore, the after-tax cost of debt is computed as:

$$k_d = k_i(1 - t) = 17.02\%(1 - 0.4) = 10.21\%$$

(b) Using the shortcut method:

$$k_i = \frac{\$60 + [(\$1,000 - \$800)/14]}{(\$1,000 + \$800)/2} = \frac{\$60 + \$14.29}{\$900} = 8.25\%$$

Annual rate $= 8.25\% \times 2 = 16.5\%$

Therefore, the after-tax cost of debt is computed as:

$$k_d = 16.5\%(1 - 0.4) = 9.9\%$$

10.4 **Cost of Preferred Stock.** In its capital structure, ABC Corporation has preferred stock paying a dividend of $5 per share and selling for $23. The company's tax rate is 40 percent. Calculate (a) the before-tax cost of preferred stock, and (b) the after-tax cost of preferred stock.

SOLUTION

(a) The before-tax cost of preferred stock is:

$$k_p = \frac{d_p}{p} = \frac{\$5}{\$23} = 21.7\%$$

(b) The same as the above, since preferred stock dividends are not a tax-deductible expense and are therefore paid out after taxes.

10.5 **Cost of Retained Earnings.** Plato Company's common stock is selling for $50. Last year's dividend was $4.8 per share. Compute the cost of retained earnings (or internal equity) if both earnings and dividends are expected to grow at (a) zero percent and (b) a constant rate of 9 percent.

SOLUTION

(a)

$$D_1 = D_0(1 + g) = \$4.8(1 + 0) = \$4.8$$

$$k_s = \frac{D_1}{P_0} = \frac{\$4.8}{\$50} = 9.6\%$$

(b)

$$D_1 = D_0(1 + g) = \$4.8(1 + 0.09) = \$5.232$$

$$k_s = \frac{D_1}{P_0} + g = \frac{\$5.232}{\$50} + 9\% = 10.5 + 9\% = 19.5\%$$

10.6 **Cost of Retained Earnings (or Internal Equity).** Epsilon Company's last annual dividend was $4 per share, and both earnings and dividends are expected to grow at a constant rate of 8 percent. The stock now sells for $50 per share. The company's beta coefficient is 1.5. The return of a market portfolio is 12 percent, and the risk-free rate is 8 percent. The company's A-rated bonds are yielding 12 percent. Calculate the cost of retained earnings (or internal equity) using: (a) the Gordon's growth model; (b) the bond plus method; and (c) the capital asset pricing model.

SOLUTION

(a) For the Gordon's growth model:

$$D_1 = D_0(1 + g) = \$4.00(1 + 0.08) = \$4.32$$

$$k_s = \frac{D_1}{P_0} + g = \frac{\$4.32}{\$50} + 8\% = 8.64\% + 8\% = 16.64\%$$

(b)

$$k_s = \text{bond yield} + \text{risk premium} = 12\% + {\sim}4\% = 16\%$$

For the bond plus method, a risk premium of about 4 percent is commonly used:

(c)   For the CAPM:

$$k_s = r_f + b(r_m - r_s) = 8\% + 1.5(12\% - 8\%) = 8\% + 6\% = 14\%$$

10.7   Cost of New Common Stock. Assume the data given in Problem 10.5 are for new stock. Compute the cost of new common stock (or external equity). Assume there is a 10 percent flotation cost associated with issuing new common stock.

SOLUTION

(a)

$$D_1 = D_0(1 + g) = \$4.80\,(1 + 0) = \$4.80$$

$$k_e = \frac{D_1}{P_0(1 - f)} + g = \frac{\$4.80}{\$50(1 - 0.1)} + 0 = \frac{\$4.80}{\$45} = 10.67\%$$

(b)

$$D_1 = D_0(1 + g) = \$4.80(1 + 0.09) = \$5.232$$

$$k_e = \frac{D_1}{P_0(1 - f)} = g = \frac{\$5.232}{\$50(1 - 0.1)} + 9\%$$

$$= \frac{\$5.232}{\$45} + 9\% = 11.63\% + 9\% = 20.63\%$$

10.8   Costs of Retained Earnings and New Common Stock. Armon Brothers, Inc., is attempting to evaluate the costs of internal and external common equity. The company's stock is currently selling for $62.50 per share. The company expects to pay $5.42 per share at the end of the year. The dividends for the past 5 years are given below:

Year	Dividend
19X5	$5.17
19X4	$4.92
19X3	$4.68
19X2	$4.46
19X1	$4.25

The company expects to net $57.50 per share on a new share after flotation costs. Calculate: (a) the growth rate of dividends; (b) the flotation cost (in percent); (c) the cost of retained earnings (or internal equity); and (d) the cost of new common stock (or external equity).

SOLUTION

(a)

$$\$5.17 = \$4.25(\text{FVIF}_{i,r\,\text{yrs}})$$

$$\text{FVIF}_{i,4\,\text{yrs}} = \frac{\$5.17}{\$4.25} = 1.216$$

From Appendix A, we obtain 5 percent from the 4-year line.
   Alternatively,

$$\$5.42 = \$4.25(\text{FVIF}_{i,5\,\text{yrs}})$$

$$\text{FVIF}_{i,5\,\text{yrs}} = \frac{\$5.42}{\$4.25} = 1.276$$

From Appendix A, obtain 5 percent in the 5-year line.

(b) The flotation cost percentage is calculated as follows:

$$\frac{\$62.50 - \$57.50}{\$62.50} = \frac{\$5}{\$62.50} = 8\%$$

(c) The cost of retained earnings, k_s, is:

$$k_s = \frac{D_1}{P_0} + g = \frac{\$5.42}{\$62.50} + 5\% = 8.67\% + 5\% = 13.67\%$$

(d) The cost of new common stock, k_e, is:

$$k_e = \frac{D_1}{P_0(1-f)} + g = \frac{\$5.42}{\$62.5(1-0.08)} + 5\% = \frac{\$5.42}{\$57.50} + 5\%$$
$$= 9.43\% + 5\% = 14.43\%$$

10.9 Weighted Average Cost of Capital. The Gamma Products Corporation has the following capital structure, which it considers optimal:

Bonds, 7% (now selling at par)	$ 300,000
Preferred stock, $5.00	240,000
Common stock	360,000
Retained earnings	300,000
	$1,200,000

Dividends on common stock are currently $3 per share and are expected to grow at a constant rate of 6 percent. Market price per share of common stock is $40, and the preferred stock is selling at $50. Flotation cost on new issues of common stock is 10 percent. The interest on bonds is paid annually. The company's tax rate is 40 percent.

Calculate: (a) the cost of bonds; (b) the cost of preferred stock; (c) the cost of retained earnings (or internal equity); (d) the cost of new common stock (or external equity); and (e) the weighted average cost of capital.

SOLUTION

(a) Since the bonds are selling at par, the before-tax cost of bonds (k_i) is the same as the coupon rate, that is, 7 percent. Therefore, the after-tax cost of bonds is

$$k_d = k_i(1-t)$$
$$= 7\%(1-0.4) = 4.20\%$$

(b) The cost of preferred stock is:

$$k_p = \frac{d_p}{p} = \frac{\$5}{\$50} = 10\%$$

(c) The cost of retained earnings is:

$$D_1 = D_0(1+g) = \$3(1+0.06) = \$3.18$$
$$k_s = \frac{D_1}{P_0} + g = \frac{\$3.18}{\$40} + 6\% = 7.95\% + 6\% = 13.95\%$$

(d) The cost of new common stock is:

$$k_e = \frac{D_1}{P_0(1-f)} + g = \frac{\$3.18}{\$40(1-0.1)} + 6\% = 8.83\% + 6\% = 14.83\%$$

(e) The weighted average cost of capital is computed as follows:

Source of Capital	Capital Structure	Percentage	Cost	Weighted Cost
Bonds	$ 300	25%	4.20%	1.05 %
Preferred stock	240	20	10.00%	2.00
Common stock	360	30	13.95%	4.185
Retained earnings	300	25	14.83%	3.708
Totals	$1,200	100%		10.943%

Weighted average cost of capital = 10.943%

10.10 Weighted Average Cost of Capital. Valie Enterprises, Inc., has compiled the following investments:

Type of Capital	Book Value	Market Value	After-Tax Cost
Long-term debt	$3,000,000	$2,800,000	4.8%
Preferred stock	102,000	150,000	9.0%
Common stock	1,108,000	2,500,000	13.0%
	$4,210,000	$5,450,000	

(a) Calculate the weighted average cost of capital, using (1) book value weights and (2) market value weights. (b) Explain the difference in the results obtained in (a).

SOLUTION

(a) (1) Book value weights are computed as follows:

Type of Capital	Book Value	Weight	Cost	Weighted Cost
Long-term debt	$3,000,000	0.713	4.8%	3.422%
Preferred stock	102,000	0.024	9.0%	0.216
Common stock	1,108,000	0.263	13.0%	3.419
	$4,210,000	1.000		7.057%

(2) Market value weights are computed as follows:

Type of Capital	Market Value	Weight	Cost	Weighted Cost
Long-term debt	$2,800,000	0.514	4.8%	2.467%
Preferred stock	150,000	0.028	9.0%	0.252
Common stock	2,500,000	0.458	13.0%	5.954
	$5,450,000	1.000		8.673%

(b) The book value weights give the firm a much greater leverage (or debt position) than the market value weights. The cost of capital based on market value weights is more realistic, since it is based on the prevailing market values. Since common stock usually sells at a higher value than its book value, the cost of capital is higher when using market value weights.

10.11 Cost of Capital. The Conner Company has the following capital structure:

Mortgage bonds, 6%	$ 20,000,000
Common stock (1 million shares)	25,000,000
Retained earnings	55,000,000
	$100,000,000

Mortgage bonds of similar quality could be sold at a net of 95 to yield $6\frac{1}{2}$ percent. Their common stock has been selling for $100 per share. The company has paid 50 percent of earnings in dividends for several years and intends to continue the policy. The current dividend is $4 per share. Earnings are growing at 5 percent per year. If the company sold a new equity issue, it would expect to net $94 per share after all costs. Their marginal tax rate is 50 percent.

Conner wants to determine a cost of capital to use in capital budgeting. Additional projects would be financed to maintain the same relationship between debt and equity. Additional debt would consist of mortgage bonds, and additional equity would consist of retained earnings. (a) Calculate the firm's weighted average cost of capital, and (b) explain why you used the particular weighting system. (CMA, adapted.)

SOLUTION

(a)

	Amount	Proportion	After-Tax Cost	Weighted Average
Bonds	20	20%	3.25%[a]	0.65%
Common stock	25	25	9.0[b]	2.25
Retained earnings	55	55	9.0	4.95
	100	100%		7.85%

[a] 3.25% = 6.5%(1 − 0.5)

[b] The cost of equity capital is:

$$k_e = \frac{D_1}{P_0} + g = \frac{4.00}{100.00} + 0.05 = 9.0\%$$

Market value weighting (in millions) produces the following cost of capital:

Bonds	19	16%	3.25%	0.52%
Common and retained earnings	100	84	9.00%	7.56
	119	100%		8.08%

(b) The weighting to be used should reflect the mix of capital the company intends to use (presumably based upon its understanding of the optimal mix). The problem states that the company intends to maintain the same relationship between debt and equity. If that relationship is defined as the book value relationship, then that should be used to calculate the weighted average cost of capital. If the relationship referred to means the market value weighted average cost of capital, then that relationship should be used.

10.12 Cost of Capital Comparison. The treasurer of a new venture, Start-Up Scientific, Inc., is trying to determine how to raise $6 million of long-term capital. Her investment adviser has devised the alternative capital structures shown below:

Alternative A		Alternative B	
$2,000,000	9% debt	$4,000,000	12% debt
$4,000,000	Equity	$2,000,000	Equity

If alternative A is chosen, the firm would sell 200,000 shares of common stock to net $20 per share. Stockholders would expect an initial dividend of $1 per share and a dividend growth rate of 7 percent.

Under alternative B, the firm would sell 100,000 shares of common stock to net $20 per share. The expected initial dividend would be $0.90 per share, and the anticipated dividend growth rate 12 percent.

Assume that the firm earns a profit under either capital structure and that the effective tax rate is 50 percent. (a) What is the cost of capital to the firm under each of the suggested capital structures? Explain your result. (b) Explain the logic of the anticipated higher interest rate on debt associated with alternative B. (c) Is it logical for shareholders to expect a higher dividend growth rate under alternative B? Explain your answer. (CMA, adapted.)

SOLUTION

(a) The cost of capital for a firm is computed as a weighted average of the component costs of the sources used to raise capital where the weights relate to the percentage of total capital raised. In this case the two components are debt and equity.

$$\text{Cost of debt } (k_d) = (\text{interest rate})(1 - \text{tax rate})$$

$$\text{Cost of equity } (k_e) = \frac{\text{dividend}}{\text{price}} + \text{growth}$$

$$\text{Overall cost of capital } (k_o) = (\text{weight of debt})(k_d) + (\text{weight of equity})(k_e)$$

For alternative A:

$$k_d = 0.09(1 - 0.5) = 4.5\%$$

$$k_e = \frac{\$1}{\$20} + 0.07 = 12\%$$

$$k_o = \tfrac{2}{6} \times 0.045 + \tfrac{4}{6} \times 0.12 = 9.5\%$$

For alternative B:

$$k_d = 0.12(1 - 0.5) = 6\%$$

$$k_e = \frac{\$0.90}{\$20} + 0.12 = 16.5\%$$

$$k_o = \tfrac{4}{6} \times 0.06 + \tfrac{2}{6} \times 0.165 = 9.5\%$$

The weighted average cost of capital is the same for alternatives A and B because the risk = return trade-offs for A and B balance each other.

(b) The interest rate on debt is higher for alternative B because the financial risk is greater due to the increased use of leverage. As a result, the probability of not being able to meet the high fixed payment increases, causing the bond market to have a higher required rate of return to offset this greater risk.

(c) It is logical for shareholders to expect a higher dividend growth rate under alternative B because of the additional financial risk and increased fixed interest requirement. Equity holders will demand a higher return to compensate them for the additional financial risk. Dividends per share should grow at a faster rate than alternative A because earnings per share grow faster due to the greater amount of leverage (smaller base). In addition, assuming a given payout rate, it follows that dividends per share would also grow faster than alternative A.

10.13 Cost of Capital. Timel Company is in the process of determining its capital budget for the coming fiscal year. Timel Company's balance sheet reflects five sources of long-term funds. The current outstanding amounts from these five sources are shown below and represent the company's historical sources of funds fairly accurately.

Source of Funds	$ Amount (in Millions)	%
Mortgage bonds ($1,000 par, $7\frac{1}{2}$%)	135	15.0
Debentures ($1,000 par, 8%, due 19X5)	225	25.0
Preferred stock ($100 par, $7\frac{1}{2}$%)	90	10.0
Common stock ($10 par)	150	16.7
Retained earnings	300	33.3
	900	100.0

Timel will raise the funds necessary to support the selected capital investment projects so as to maintain its historical distribution among the various sources of long-term funds. Thus, 15 percent will be obtained from additional mortgage bonds on new plant, 25 percent from debentures, 10 percent from preferred stock, and 50 percent from some common equity source. Timel's policy is to reinvest the funds derived from each year's earnings in new projects. Timel issues new common stock only after all funds provided from retained earnings have been exhausted.

Management estimates that its net income after taxes for the coming year will be $4.50 per common share. The dividend payout ratio will be 40 percent of earnings to common shareholders ($1.8 per share), the same ratio as the prior 4 years. The preferred stockholders will receive $6.75 million. The earnings retained will be used as needed to support the capital investment program.

The capital budgeting staff, in conjunction with Timel's investment broker, has developed the following data regarding Timel's sources of funds if it were to raise funds in the current market.

Source of Funds	Par Value ($)	Interest or Dividend Rate (%)	Issue Price ($)
Mortgage bonds	1,000	14	1,000.00
Debentures	1,000	$14\frac{1}{2}$	1,000.00
Preferred stock	100	$13\frac{1}{2}$	99.25
Common stock	10		67.50

The estimated interest rates on the debt instruments and the dividend rate on the preferred stock are based upon the rates being experienced in the market by firms which are of the same size and quality as Timel. The investment banker believes that the price of $67.50 for the common stock is justified, since Timel's price/earnings ratio of 15 is consistent with the 10 percent earnings growth rate that the market is capitalizing.

Timel is subject to a 40 percent income tax rate.

Calculate (*a*) the after-tax marginal cost of capital for each of the five sources of capital for Timel Company, and (*b*) Timel Company's after-tax weighted average cost of capital. (*c*) Timel Company follows a practice that 50 percent of any funds raised will be derived from common equity sources. Determine the point of expansion at which Timel's source of common equity funds would switch from retained earnings to new common stock in the coming year. (*d*) If the basic business risks are similar for all firms in the industry in which Timel Company participates, would all firms in the industry have approximately the same weighted average cost of capital? Explain your answer. (CMA, adapted.)

SOLUTION

(a) For a mortgage bond:

$$k_d = \text{current yield } (1 - \text{tax rate}) = 14\%(1 - 0.4) = 8.4\%$$

For a debenture:

$$k_d = \text{current yield } (1 - \text{tax rate}) = 14.5\%(1 - 0.4) = 8.7\%$$

For preferred stock:

$$k_p = \frac{\text{dividend}}{\text{issue price}} = \frac{\$13.5}{\$99.25} = 13.6\%$$

For common stock:

$$k_e = \frac{\text{current dividend}}{\text{current price}} + \text{expected growth rate} = \frac{\$1.80}{\$67.50} + 10\% = 12.67\%$$

For retained earnings:

$$k_s = \text{opportunity rate of return on common stock} = k_e = 12.67\%$$

(b) The weighted average cost of capital is calculated as follows:

Source	Current Component Cost (%)	× Weights	= Weighted Average Cost
Mortgage bond	8.4	0.15	0.0126
Debenture	8.7	0.25	0.0217
Preferred stock	13.6	0.10	0.0136
Common stock	12.67	0.167	0.0212
Retained earnings	12.67	0.333	0.0422
Total			0.1113

The weighted average cost of capital is 11.13 percent.

(c) The maximum expansion from retained earnings before a new common stock is required is calculated as follows (in millions of dollars):

Net income ($4.50/common share × 15 million shares)	$67.5
Less: Dividend payout ($1.80/common share × 15 million shares)	27.0
Preferred stock dividend	6.75
Retained earnings available for expansion	$33.75

If common equity is to be 50 percent of total capital, then the $33.75 million increase in retained earnings would be matched by raising an additional $33.75 million from debt and preferred stock for a total of $67.5 million expansion before common shares would be issued.

(d) The weighted average cost of capital may vary among firms in the industry even if the basic business risk is similar for all firms in the industry. This is true because each firm selects the degree of financial leverage it desires. A firm with a high degree of financial leverage would be assigned a high-risk premium by investors.

10.14 Cost of Capital and Weighting System. Electro Tool Co., a manufacturer of diamond drilling, cutting, and grinding tools, has $1 million of its 8 percent debenture issue maturing on September 1, 19X1. The $1 million that has been accumulated to retire this debt is now going to be used to acquire additional manufacturing machinery. To meet the debt and purchase of machinery, an additional $1 million must be raised. One proposal that has been particularly appealing is the sale and lease-back of the company's general office building. This proposal has a lower interest cost than the financing program proposed by the equipment vendor.

The building would be sold to FHR, Inc., for $1 million and leased back on a 25-year lease. The lease calls for Electro Tool to pay $110,168 annually, which permits FHR, Inc., to recover its investment and earn 10 percent on the investment. Electro Tool will pay for all maintenance costs, property taxes, and insurance during the lease period. At the end of the 25 years Electro Tool will reacquire the building for a very small payment. The sale and lease-back will be treated the same for both financial reporting and income tax purposes.

The current capital structure and cost of the individual components for Electro Tool Co. are shown below.

Capital Component	Amount per Recent Balance Sheet	Before-Tax Component Cost
8% debentures (including the $1,000,000 to be retired)	$ 5,000,000	8%
	1,000,000	9%
9% preferred stock	2,000,000	13%
Common stock	2,000,000	12%
Retained earnings	$10,000,000	

Electro Tool is subject to a 40 percent income tax rate.

(a) Using the data provided, calculate the historical weighted average cost of capital of Electro Tool Co. (1) before the retirement of the debentures and the sale and lease-back action, and (2) after the retirement of the debentures and the sale and lease-back transaction. (b) If the component costs and weightings used to calculate the weighted average cost of capital in (a) (1) are different from those used in (a) (2), explain why. If the amounts used to calculate (a) (1) are the same as those used in (a) (2), explain why. (c) Market values for the capital components were not presented. What arguments are given to support the use of market values in calculating the weighted average cost of capital? (CMA, adapted.)

SOLUTION

(a) (1) The historical weighted average cost of capital before the retirement of the debentures and the sale and lease-back transaction is 8.3 percent, as calculated below.

	(1) Amount per Recent Balance Sheet	(2) % of Total	(3) Before-Tax Cost	(4) After-Tax Cost	(5) Weighted Cost (2) × (4)
8% debentures	$ 5,000,000	50%	0.08	0.048	0.024
9% preferred stock	1,000,000	10	0.09	0.09	0.009
Common stock	2,000,000	20	0.13	0.13	0.026
Retained earnings	2,000,000	20	0.12	0.12	0.024
	$10,000,000	100%			0.083

(2) The historical weighted average cost of capital after the retirement of the debentures and the sale and lease-back transaction is 8.42 percent as calculated below.

	(1) Amount per Recent Balance Sheet	(2) % of Total	(3) Before-Tax Cost	(4) After-Tax Cost	(5) Weighted Cost (2) × (4)
Lease	$ 1,000,000	10%	0.10	0.06	0.006
Debentures	4,000,000	40	0.08	0.048	0.0192
Preferred stock	1,000,000	10	0.09	0.09	0.009
Common stock	2,000,000	20	0.13	0.13	0.026
Retained earnings	2,000,000	20	0.12	0.12	0.024
	$10,000,000	100%			0.0842

(b) The component costs and weightings used to calculate the historical weighted average cost of capital are different in (a) (1) and (a) (2) because lease financing is substituted for a portion of the debentures. Therefore, the debentures now represent only 40 percent of the total capital and the lease 10 percent. The after-tax cost of the lease is $0.10 \times 0.60 = 0.06$, whereas the after-tax cost of the debentures is $0.08 \times 0.60 = 0.048$. The overall cost of capital is increased because a higher cost component replaced a lower cost component.

(c) Market values should be used in calculating the weighted average cost of capital because the cost of capital calculation is used to estimate the current marginal cost of capital for the company. The use of market values: (1) recognizes the current investor attitudes regarding the company's risk position and thus will reflect current rates for capital; (2) recognizes better the capital proportions the company must consider in the capital sources decision; and (3) ignores the influence of past values which are not relevant to future decisions.

10.15 Bond Rating and Cost of Capital. Two bond rating agencies, Moody's and Standard and Poor's, lowered the ratings on Appleton Industries' bonds from triple-A to double-A in response to operating trends revealed by the financial reports of recent years. The change in the ratings is of considerable concern to the Appleton management because the company plans to seek a significant amount of external financing within the next 2 years.

(a) Identify several events or circumstances which could have occurred in the operations of Appleton Industries that might have influenced the factors the bond rating agencies use to evaluate the firm and, as a result, caused the bond rating agencies to lower Appleton's bond rating. (b) If Appleton Industries maintains its present capital structure, what effect will the lower bond ratings have on the company's weighted average cost of capital? Explain your answer. (c) If Appleton Industries' capital structure was at an optimal level before the rating of its bonds was changed, explain what effect the lower bond ratings will have on the company's optimal capital structure. (CMA, adapted.)

SOLUTION

(a) Factors or circumstances which may have caused the rating agencies to lower the bond rating of Appleton Industries include:

1. Lowered long-term solvency reflected by a reduction in the times-interest-earned ratio or a reduction in the fixed-charge-coverage ratio

2. Lowered short-term liquidity reflected by a decrease in the current ratio or quick ratio

3. Lowered profitability reflected by a reduced market share, lower return on sales, or decreased profits

4. An increased risk of financial stability due to major pending litigation which would be damaging to the firm or a large increase in earnings variability

5. A major change in management which is perceived negatively by the financial community

(b) The weighted average cost of capital can be expected to rise. The lower bond rating is usually relied upon as an indication of greater risk being assumed by the bond investors. This change will be noted by the investors of other Appleton securities. Thus the investors in each capital component of Appleton Industries can be expected to require a higher return.

(c) Appleton Industries capital structure will shift toward greater equity with less debt. The fact that the bond rating was lowered would indicate to investors that the risk has increased. To reduce the risk and minimize the increase in the cost of capital, the optimal capital structure will have to shift toward one with an increased percentage of equity.

10.16 **Earnings Multiple and Cost of Capital.** The Jefferson Corporation is contemplating a $50 million expansion project. Over the years, the firm's board of directors has adhered to a policy of rejecting any investment proposal that would jeopardize the market value of the firm's common stock.

A preliminary analysis projected a rate of return on the new project of around 14 percent before taxes. Jefferson has reached tentative agreement with an insurance company to finance the project through a private placement of the $50 million in the form of 10 percent notes.

The firm's common stock has been historically selling at 10 times after-tax earnings. Current earnings per share are $2.70 and the firm faces a 50 percent corporate income tax rate.

Long-term debt (8%)	$ 10,000,000
Common stock ($2 par, 10,000,000 shares outstanding)	20,000,000
Paid-in capital, in excess of par	70,000,000
Retained earnings	100,000,000
Total capitalization	$200,000,000

(a) One of the members of Jefferson Corporation's board of directors argued that the firm should immediately place the notes, since the before-tax marginal cost of capital for the project is only 10 percent (the interest on the notes), and indications are that the project's before-tax rate of return would be greater than 10 percent. Discuss.

(b) Assuming Jefferson's earnings multiple declines to 9, what level of annual earnings must the new project generate in order to meet the director's objective? (CMA, adapted.)

SOLUTION

(a) The board members' conclusion is not valid because the facts seem to indicate the Jefferson Corporation's capitalization is not in equilibrium. The issuance of the notes will move debt from 5 percent of total capitalization (10/200) to 24 percent (60/250). This increases the financial risk that common equity must bear through increased fixed interest payments, and the increased risk can be expected to be manifested by a decline in the earnings multiple. While the marginal cost of capital appears to be 10 percent (the cost of the private placement), the marginal cost of capital is a combination of explicit interest cost on the notes and the additional costs of earnings that must occur to compensate the common stockholders for the decline in the earnings multiple.

Jefferson Corporation should have calculated the weighted average cost of capital according to the following formula:

$$\left(\begin{array}{c} \text{Percent of new funds} \\ \text{raised from debt} \end{array} \right) \times (\text{cost of debt}) + \left(\begin{array}{c} \text{percent of funds} \\ \text{raised from equity} \end{array} \right) \times (\text{additional cost of equity})$$

The 14 percent rate of return on this project should be compared to the firm's average cost of capital. If the project's return is at least as great as the weighted average cost of capital, then the value of the firm's stock will not decrease.

(b) The stock is now selling at 10 times earnings:

$$P_0 = 10(\$2.70) = \$27.00$$

This is the price that must be maintained upon taking on the new project. If the new project causes the P/E ratio to fall to 9 and offers no additional earnings, the price of stock would fall by $2.70 to $24.30.

In order to get the price of stock back up to $27, the earnings provided by the new asset must equal X:

$$\text{(New P/E)(new EPS)} = \$27$$
$$9(\$2.70 + X) = \$27$$
$$\$2.70 + X = \$3$$
$$X = \$0.30$$

This assumes that currently held assets are capable of continuing to provide $2.70 in earnings per share.

The annual earnings the new project must generate to meet Jefferson Corporation's objective are determined as follows:

(1) Required EPS to maintain $27 price with a multiple of 9:

$$\frac{\$27.00}{9} = \$3.00$$

(2) Required earnings after taxes:

$$\$3.00 \times 10,000,000 \text{ shares} = \$30,000,000$$

(3) Required earnings before taxes:

$$\frac{\$30,000,000}{0.5} = \$60,000,000$$

(4) Interest expense:

$$(\$10,000,000)(0.08) + (\$50,000,000)(0.10) = \$800,000 + \$5,000,000 = \$5,800,000$$

(5) Required earnings before interest and taxes:

$$\$60,000,000 + \$5,800,000 = \$65,800,000$$

(6) Old earnings before interest and taxes:

$$\frac{(\$2.70 \times 10,000,000 \text{ shares})}{0.5} + \$800,000 = \$54,800,000$$

(7) Additional before interest and taxes earnings required:

Projected earnings	$65,800,000
Old earnings	54,800,000
	$11,000,000

10.17 The MCC and IOS Schedules. Rhonda Pollak Company is considering three investments whose initial costs and internal rates of return are given below:

Project	Initial Cost ($)	Internal Rate of Return (%)
A	100,000	19
B	125,000	15
C	225,000	12

The company finances all expansion with 40 percent debt and 60 percent equity capital. The after-tax cost is 8 percent for the first $100,000, after which the cost will be 10 percent. Retained earnings in the amount of $150,000 is available, and the common stockholders' required rate of return is 18 percent. If the new stock is issued, the cost will be 22 percent.

Calculate (a) the dollar amounts at which breaks occur, and (b) calculate the weighted cost of capital in each of the intervals between the breaks. (c) Graph the firm's weighted marginal cost of capital (MCC) schedule and investment opportunities schedule (IOS). (d) Decide which projects should be selected and calculate the total amount of the optimal capital budget.

SOLUTION

(a) Breaks (increases) in the weighted marginal cost of capital will occur as follows:
For debt:

$$\frac{\text{Debt}}{\text{Debt/assets}} = \frac{\$100,000}{0.4} = \$250,000$$

For common stock:

$$\frac{\text{Retained earnings}}{\text{Equity/assets}} = \frac{\$150,000}{0.6} = \$250,000$$

The debt break is caused by exhausting the lower cost of debt, while the common stock break is caused by using up retained earnings.

(b) The weighted cost of capital in each of the intervals between the breaks is computed as follows:
With $0–$250,000 total financing:

Source of Capital	Weight	Cost	Weighted Cost
Debt	0.4	8%	3.2%
Common stock	0.6	18%	10.8
			$k_o = 14.0\%$

With over $250,000 total financing:

Source of Capital	Weight	Cost	Weighted Cost
Debt	0.4	10%	4.0%
Common stock	0.6	22%	13.2
			$k = 17.2\%$

(c) See Fig. 10-2.

(d) Accept projects A and B for a total of $225,000, which is the optimal budget.

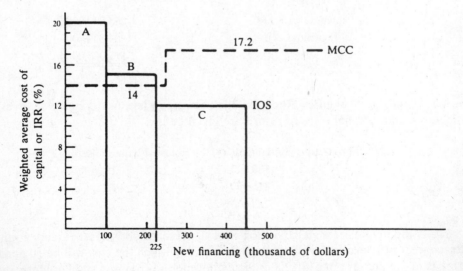

Fig. 10-2

10.18 The MCC and IOS Schedules. John Constas & Company has to decide which of the following four projects should be selected:

Project	Initial Investment ($)	Internal Rate of Return (%)
A	250,000	16
B	300,000	10
C	100,000	12
D	150,000	13

The company has the following capital structure:

Debt (long-term only)	30%
Equity	70%

The company's last earnings per share was $400.

It pays out 50 percent of its earnings as dividends. The company has $210,000 of retained earnings available for investment purposes. The cost of debt (before taxes) is 10 percent for the first $180,000. The cost of any additional debt (before taxes) is 14 percent. The company's tax rate is 40 percent; the current market price of its stock is $43; the flotation cost is 15 percent of the selling price; the expected growth rate in earnings and dividends is 8 percent.

(*a*) How many breaks are there in the MCC schedule, and at what dollar amounts do the breaks occur? (*b*) What is the weighted cost of capital in each of the intervals between the breaks? (*c*) Graph the MCC and IOS schedules. (*d*) Which projects should the company accept and what is the total amount of the optimal capital budget?

SOLUTION

(*a*) There are two breaks in the MCC schedule:

For common stock: $\dfrac{\text{Retained earnings}}{\text{Equity/assets}} = \dfrac{\$210,000}{0.7} = \$300,000$

For debt: $\dfrac{\text{Debt}}{\text{Debt/assets}} = \dfrac{\$180,000}{0.3} = \$600,000$

(*b*) The weighted cost of capital in each of the intervals between the breaks is calculated as follows:
With 0$ − $300,000:

Source of Capital	Weight	After-Tax Cost	Weighted Cost
Debt	0.3	6%[a]	1.8%
Retained earnings	0.7	13%[b]	9.1
			$k_o = \underline{10.9\%}$

[a] $k_d = k_i(1 - t) = 10\%(1 - 0.4) = 6\%$

[b] $k_s = \dfrac{D_1}{P_0} + g = \dfrac{(\$2.00)(1 + 0.08)}{\$43} + 8\% = \dfrac{\$2.16}{\$43} + 8\% = 13.0\%$

With $300,000–$600,000:

Source of Capital	Weight	After-Tax Cost	Weighted Cost
Debt	0.3	6%	1.80%
External equity	0.7	13.9%[a]	9.73
			$k_o = \underline{11.53\%}$

[a] $k_e = \dfrac{D_1}{P_0(1 - f)} + g = \dfrac{(\$2.00)(1 + 0.08)}{\$43(1 - 0.15)} + 8\% = \dfrac{\$2.16}{\$36.55} + 8\% = 13.9\%$

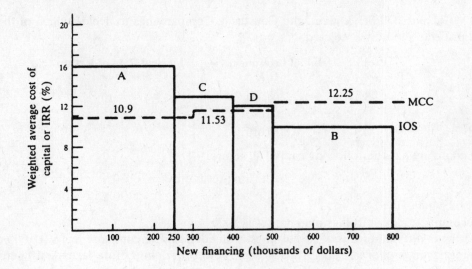

Fig. 10-3

Above $600,000:

Source of Capital	Weight	After-Tax Cost	Weighted Cost
Debt	0.3	8.4%[a]	2.52%
External equity	0.7	13.9%	9.73
			$k_o = $ 12.25%

---

[a] $k_d = k_i(1 - t) = 14\%(1 - 0.4) = 8.4\%$

(c) The MCC and IOS schedules are shown in Fig. 10-3.

(d) The company should select projects A, D, and C for a total optimal capital budget of $500,000.

Chapter 11

Leverage and Capital Structure

11.1 LEVERAGE DEFINED

Leverage is that portion of the fixed costs which represents a risk to the firm. *Operating leverage*, a measure of operating risk, refers to the fixed operating costs found in the firm's income statement. *Financial leverage*, a measure of financial risk, refers to financing a portion of the firm's assets, bearing fixed financing charges in hopes of increasing the return to the common stockholders. The higher the financial leverage, the higher the financial risk, and the higher the cost of capital. Cost of capital rises because it costs more to raise funds for a risky business.

11.2 BREAK-EVEN POINT, OPERATING LEVERAGE, AND FINANCIAL LEVERAGE

A discussion of *break-even analysis*, broadly known as *cost/volume/profit analysis*, is necessary for understanding the nature and importance of operating leverage.

Break-Even Analysis

The *break-even point* is the level of sales at which no profit or loss results. To determine the break-even point, the costs must be divided into (1) *variable costs* which are costs that vary in direct proportion to a change in volume, and (2) *fixed costs*, which are costs that are constant regardless of volume.

The break-even point can be found easily by setting sales just equal to the total of the variable costs plus the fixed costs:

Let   S = Sales ($)
        X = Sales volume in units
        P = Selling price per unit
        V = Unit variable cost
    VC = Variable operating costs
    FC = Fixed operating costs

Then

$$S = VC + FC$$
$$PX = VX + FC$$
$$(P - V)X = FC$$
$$X = \frac{FC}{P - V}$$

or

$$\text{Break-even sales in units} = \frac{\text{fixed operating costs}}{\text{unit selling price} - \text{unit variable cost}}$$

EXAMPLE 11.1 The Wayne Company manufactures and sells doors to home builders. The doors are sold for $25 each. Variable costs are $15 per door, and fixed operating costs total $50,000. The company's break-even point is:

$$X = \frac{FC}{P - V} = \frac{\$50,000}{\$25 - \$15} = 5,000 \text{ doors}$$

Therefore, the company must sell 5,000 doors to break even.

Cash Break-Even Point

If a firm has a minimum of available cash or the opportunity cost of holding excess cash is high, management may want to know the volume of sales that will cover all cash expenses during a period. This is known as the *cash break-even point*.

Not all fixed operating costs involve cash payments. For example, depreciation expenses are noncash charges. To find the cash break-even point, the noncash charges must be subtracted from total fixed operating costs. Therefore, the cash break-even point is lower than the usual break-even point. The formula is:

$$X = \frac{FC - d}{P - V}$$

where d is depreciation expenses.

EXAMPLE 11.2 Assume from Example 11.1 that the total fixed operating costs of $50,000 include depreciation in the amount of $2,000. Then the Wayne Company cash break-even point is:

$$X = \frac{FC - d}{P - V} = \frac{\$50,000 - \$2,000}{\$25 - \$15} = \frac{\$48,000}{\$10} = 4,800 \text{ doors}$$

The company has to sell 4,800 doors to cover only the fixed costs involving cash payments of $48,000 and to break even.

Operating Leverage

Operating leverage is a measure of operating risk and arises from fixed operating costs. A simple indication of operating leverage is the effect that a change in sales has on earnings. The formula is:

$$\text{Operating leverage at a given level of sales } (X) = \frac{\% \text{ change in EBIT}}{\% \text{ change in sales}} = \frac{(P - V)X}{(P - V)X - FC}$$

where

$$\text{EBIT} = \text{earnings before interest and taxes}$$
$$= (P - V)X - FC$$

EXAMPLE 11.3 From Example 11.1, assume that the Wayne Company is currently selling 6,000 doors per year. Its operating leverage is:

$$\frac{(P - V)X}{(P - V)X - FC} = \frac{(\$25 - \$15)(6,000)}{(\$25 - \$15)(6,000) - \$50,000} = \frac{\$60,000}{10,000} = 6$$

which means if sales increase by 10 percent, the company can expect its net income to increase by six times that amount, or 60 percent.

Financial Leverage

Financial leverage is a measure of financial risk and arises from fixed financial costs. One way to measure financial leverage is to determine how earnings per share are affected by a change in EBIT (or operating income).

$$\text{Financial leverage at a given level of sales } (X) = \frac{\% \text{ change in EPS}}{\% \text{ change in EBIT}} = \frac{(P - V)X - FC}{(P - V)X - FC - IC}$$

where EPS is earnings per share, and IC is fixed finance charges, i.e., interest expense or preferred stock dividends. [Preferred stock dividend must be adjusted for taxes i.e., preferred stock dividend/$(1 - t)$.]

EXAMPLE 11.4 Using the data in Example 11.3, the Wayne Company has total financial charges of $2,000, half in interest expense and half in preferred stock dividend. The corporate tax rate is 40 percent. What is their financial leverage? First,

$$IC = \$1,000 + \frac{\$1,000}{(1-0.4)} = \$1,000 + \$1,667 = \$2,667$$

Therefore, Wayne's financial leverage is computed as follows:

$$\frac{(P-V)X - FC}{(P-V)X - FC - IC} = \frac{(\$25 - \$15)(6,000) - \$50,000}{(\$25 - \$15)(6,000) - \$50,000 - \$2,667} = \frac{\$10,000}{\$7,333} = 1.36$$

which means that if EBIT increases by 10 percent, Wayne can expect its EPS to increase by 1.36 times, or by 13.6 percent.

Total Leverage

Total leverage is a measure of total risk. The way to measure total leverage is to determine how EPS is affected by a change in sales.

$$\text{Total leverage at a given level of sales } (X) = \frac{\% \text{ change in EPS}}{\% \text{ change in sales}}$$

$$= \text{operating leverage} \times \text{financial leverage}$$

$$= \frac{(P-V)X}{(P-V)X - FC} \times \frac{(P-V)X - FC}{(P-V)X - FC - IC}$$

$$= \frac{(P-V)X}{(P-V)X - FC - IC}$$

EXAMPLE 11.5 From Examples 11.3 and 11.4, the total leverage for Wayne Company is:

Operating leverage × financial leverage = 6 × 1.36 = 8.16

or

$$\frac{(P-V)X}{(P-V)X - FC - IC} = \frac{(\$25 - \$15)(6,000)}{(\$25 - \$15)(6,000) - \$50,000 - \$2,667}$$

$$= \frac{\$60,000}{\$7,333} = 8.18 \text{ (due to rounding error)}$$

11.3 THE THEORY OF CAPITAL STRUCTURE

The theory of capital structure is closely related to the firm's cost of capital. Capital structure is the mix of the long-term sources of funds used by the firm. The primary objective of capital structure decisions is to maximize the market value of the firm through an appropriate mix of long-term sources of funds. This mix, called the *optimal capital structure*, will minimize the firm's overall cost of capital. However, there are arguments about whether an optimal capital structure actually exists. The arguments center on whether a firm can, in reality, affect its valuation and its cost of capital by varying the mixture of the funds used. There are four different approaches to the theory of capital structure:

1. Net operating income (NOI) approach
2. Net income (NI) approach
3. Traditional approach
4. Modigliani-Miller (MM) approach

All four use the following simplifying assumptions:

1. No income taxes are included; they will be removed later.
2. The company makes a 100 percent dividend payout.
3. No transaction costs are incurred.
4. The company has constant earnings before interest and taxes (EBIT).
5. The company has a constant operating risk.

Given these assumptions, the company is concerned with the following three rates:

1.
$$k_i = \frac{I}{B}$$

where k_i = yield on the firm's debt (assuming a perpetuity)
        I = annual interest charges
        B = market value of debt outstanding

2.
$$k_e = \frac{EAC}{S}$$

where k_e = the firm's required rate of return on equity or cost of common equity
            (assuming no earnings growth and a 100 percent dividend payout ratio)
    EAC = earnings available to common stockholders
        S = market value of stock outstanding

3.
$$k_o = \frac{EBIT}{V}$$

where k_o = the firm's overall cost of capital (or capitalization rate)
   EBIT = earnings before interest and taxes (or operating earnings)
        $V = B + S$ and is the market value of the firm

In each of the four approaches to determining capital structure, the concern is with what happens to k_i, k_e, and k_o when the degree of leverage, as denoted by the debt/equity (B/S) ratio, increases.

The Net Operating Income (NOI) Approach

The net operating income approach suggests that the firm's overall cost of capital, k_o, and the value of the firm's market value of debt and stock outstanding, V, are both independent of the degree to which the company uses leverage. The key assumption with this approach is that k_0 is constant regardless of the degree of leverage.

EXAMPLE 11.6   Assume that a firm has $6,000 in debt at 5 percent interest, that the expected level of EBIT is $2,000, and that the firm's cost of capital, k_o, is constant at 10 percent. The market value (V) of the firm is computed as follows:

$$V = \frac{EBIT}{k_o} = \frac{\$2,000}{0.10} = \$20,000$$

The cost of external equity (k_e) is computed as follows:

$$EAC = EBIT - I = \$2,000 - (\$6,000 \times 5\%)$$
$$= \$2,000 - \$300 = \$1,700$$

$$S = V - B = \$20,000 - \$6,000 = \$14,000$$

$$k_e = \frac{EAC}{S} = \frac{\$1,700}{\$14,000} = 12.14\%$$

The debt/equity ratio is

$$\frac{B}{S} = \frac{\$6,000}{\$14,000} = 42.86\%$$

Assume now that the firm increases its debt from $6,000 to $10,000 and uses the proceeds to retire $10,000 worth of stock and also that the interest rate on debt remains 5 percent.

The value of the firm now is:

$$V = \frac{EBIT}{k_o} = \frac{\$2,000}{0.10} = \$20,000$$

The cost of external equity is

$$EAC = EBIT - I = \$2,000 - (\$10,000 \times 5\%)$$
$$= \$2,000 - \$500 = \$1,500$$

$$S = V - B = \$20,000 - \$10,000 = \$10,000$$

$$k_e = \frac{EAC}{S} = \frac{\$1,500}{\$10,000} = 15\%$$

The debt/equity ratio is now:

$$\frac{B}{S} = \frac{\$10,000}{\$10,000} = 100\%$$

Since the NOI approach assumes that k_o remains constant regardless of changes in leverage, the cost of capital cannot be altered through leverage. Hence this approach suggests that there is no one optimal capital structure, as evidenced in Fig. 11-1.

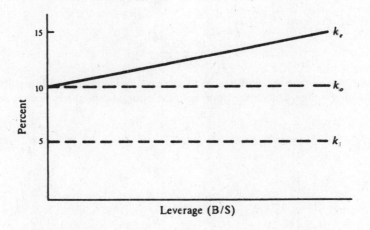

Fig. 11-1   Costs of capital: Net operating income approach

The Net Income (NI) Approach

Unlike the net operating income approach, the net income approach suggests that both the overall cost of capital, k_o and the market value of the firm, V, are affected by the firm's use of leverage. The critical assumption with this approach is that k_i and k_e remain unchanged as the debt/equity ratio increases.

EXAMPLE 11.7   Assume the same data given in Example 11.6 except that k_e equals 10 percent. The value of the firm, V, is computed as follows:

$$EAC = EBIT - I = \$2,000 - (\$6,000 \times 5\%) = \$1,700$$

$$V = S + B = \frac{EAC}{k_e} + B$$

$$= \frac{\$1,700}{0.10} + \$6,000 = \$17,000 + \$6,000 = \$23,000$$

The firm's overall cost of capital is:

$$k_o = \frac{EBIT}{V} = \frac{\$2,000}{\$23,000} = 8.7\%$$

The debt/equity ratio in this case is:

$$\frac{B}{S} = \frac{\$6,000}{\$17,000} = 35.29\%$$

Now assume, as before, that the firm increases its debt from $6,000 to $10,000, uses the proceeds to retire that amount of stock, and that the interest rate on debt remains at 5 percent. Then the value of the firm is:

$$EAC = EBIT - I = \$2,000 - (\$10,000 \times 5\%) = \$1,500$$

$$V = S + B = \frac{EAC}{k_e} + B$$

$$= \frac{\$1,500}{0.10} + \$10,000 = \$15,000 + \$10,000 = \$25,000$$

The overall cost of capital is

$$k_o = \frac{EBIT}{V} = \frac{\$2,000}{\$25,000} = 8\%$$

The debt/equity ratio is now

$$\frac{B}{S} = \frac{\$10,000}{\$15,000} = 66.67\%$$

The NI approach shows that the firm is able to increase its value, V, and lower its cost of capital, k_o, as it increases the degree of leverage. Under this approach, the optimal capital structure is found farthest to the right in Fig. 11-2.

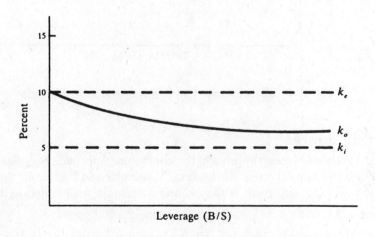

Fig. 11-2   Cost of capital: Net income approach

Traditional Approach

The traditional approach to valuation and leverage assumes that there is an optimal capital structure and that the firm can increase its value through leverage. This is a moderate view of the relationship between leverage and valuation that encompasses all the ground between the NOI approach and the NI approach.

EXAMPLE 11.8   Assume the same data given in Example 11.6. Assume, however, that k_e is 12 percent, rather than the 12.14 percent or 10 percent with the NOI or NI approaches illustrated previously. The value of the firm is:

$$EAC = EBIT - I = \$2,000 - (\$6,000 \times 5\%) = \$1,700$$

$$V = S + B = \frac{EAC}{k_e} + B$$

$$= \frac{\$1,700}{0.12} + \$6,000 = \$14,167 - \$6,000 = \$20,167$$

The overall cost of capital is:

$$k_o = \frac{EBIT}{V} = \frac{\$2,000}{\$20,167} = 9.9\%$$

The debt/equity ratio is:

$$\frac{B}{S} = \frac{\$6,000}{\$14,167} = 42.35\%$$

Assume, as before, that the firm increases its debt from \$6,000 to \$10,000. Assume further that k_i rises to 6 percent and k_e at that degree of leverage is 14 percent. The value of the firm, then, is:

$$EAC = EBIT - I$$
$$= \$2,000 - (\$10,000 \times 6\%) = \$2,000 - \$600 = \$1,400$$

$$V = S + B = \frac{EAC}{k_e} + B$$

$$= \frac{\$1,400}{0.14} + \$10,000 = \$10,000 + \$10,000 = \$20,000$$

The overall cost of capital is:

$$k_o = \frac{EBIT}{V} = \frac{\$2,000}{\$20,000} = 10.0\%$$

The debt/equity ratio is:

$$\frac{B}{S} = \frac{\$10,000}{\$10,000} = 100\%$$

Thus the value of the firm is lower and its cost of capital slightly higher than when the debt is \$6,000. This result is due to the increase in k_e and, to a lesser extent, the increase in k_i. These two observations indicate that the optimal capital structure occurs before the debt/equity ratio equals 100 percent as shown in Fig. 11-3.

Miller-Modigliani (MM) Position

Miller-Modigliani (MM) advocates that the relationship between leverage and valuation is explained by the NOI approach. More specifically, MM's propositions are summarized below.

1. The market value of the firm and its cost of capital are independent of its capital structure.
2. k_e increases so as to exactly offset the use of cheaper debt money.
3. The cutoff rate for capital budgeting decisions is completely independent of the way in which an investment is financed.

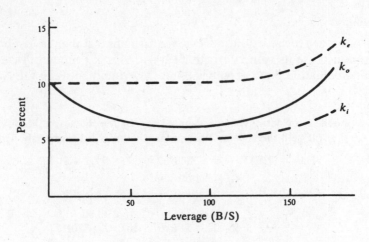

Fig. 11-3

Factors Affecting Capital Structure

Many financial managers believe, in practice, that the following factors influence financial structure:

1. Growth rate of future sales
2. Stability of future sales
3. Competitive structures in the industry
4. Asset makeup of the individual firm
5. Attitude of owners and management toward risk
6. Control position of owners and management
7. Lenders' attitude toward the industry and a particular firm

11.4 EBIT-EPS ANALYSIS

The use of financial leverage has two effects on the earnings that go to the firm's common stockholders: (1) an increased risk in earnings per share (EPS) due to the use of fixed financial obligations, and (2) a change in the level of EPS at a given EBIT associated with a specific capital structure.

The first effect is measured by the degree of financial leverage previously discussed. The second effect is analyzed by means of *EBIT-EPS* analysis. This analysis is a practical tool that enables the financial manager to evaluate alternative financing plans by investigating their effect on EPS over a range of EBIT levels. Its primary objective is to determine the EBIT break-even, or indifference, points among the various alternative financing plans. The indifference points between any two methods of financing can be determined by solving for EBIT in the following equality:

$$\frac{(\text{EBIT} - \text{I})(1 - t) - \text{PD}}{S_1} = \frac{(\text{EBIT} - \text{I})(1 - t) - \text{PD}}{S_2}$$

where
t = tax rate
PD = preferred stock dividends
S_1 and S_2 = number of shares of common stock outstanding after financing for plan 1 and plan 2, respectively.

EXAMPLE 11.9 Assume that ADI Company, with long-term capitalization consisting entirely of $5 million in stock, wants to raise $2 million for the acquisition of special equipment by: (1) selling 40,000 shares of common stock at $50 each; (2) selling bonds, at 10 percent interest; or (3) issuing preferred stock with an 8 percent dividend. The present EBIT is $8 million, the income tax rate is 50 percent, and 100,000 shares of common stock are now outstanding. In order to compute the indifference points, we begin by calculating EPS at a projected level of $1 million.

	All Common	All Debt	All Preferred
EBIT	$1,000,000	$1,000,000	$1,000,000
Interest		200,000	
Earnings before taxes (EBT)	$1,000,000	$ 800,000	$1,000,000
Taxes	500,000	400,000	500,000
Earnings after taxes (EAT)	$ 500,000	$ 400,000	$ 500,000
Preferred stock dividend			160,000
EAC	$ 500,000	$ 400,000	$ 340,000
Number of shares	140,000	100,000	100,000
EPS	$3.57	$4.00	$3.40

Now connect the EPSs at the level of EBIT of $1 million with the EBITs for each financing alternative on the horizontal axis to obtain the EPS-EBIT graphs. We plot the EBIT necessary to cover all fixed financial costs for each financing alternative on the horizontal axis. For the common stock plan, there are no fixed costs, so the intercept on the horizontal axis is zero. For the debt plan, there must be an EBIT of $200,000 to cover interest charges. For the preferred stock plan, there must be an EBIT of $320,000 [$160,000/(1 − 0.5)] to cover $160,000 in preferred stock dividends at a 50 percent income tax rate; so $320,000 becomes the horizontal axis intercept. See Fig. 11-4.

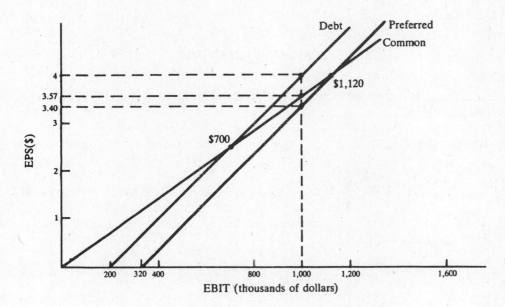

Fig. 11-4

In this example, the indifference point between all common and all debt is:

$$\frac{(\text{EBIT} - \text{I})(1 - t) - \text{PD}}{S_1} = \frac{(\text{EBIT} - \text{I})(1 - t) - \text{PD}}{S_2}$$

$$\frac{(\text{EBIT} - 0)(1 - 0.5) - 0}{140,000} = \frac{(\text{EBIT} - 200,000)(1 - 0.5) - 0}{100,000}$$

Rearranging yields:

$$0.5(\text{EBIT})(100,000) = 0.5(\text{EBIT})(140,000) - 0.5(200,000)(140,000)$$

$$20,000 \text{ EBIT} = 14,000,000,000$$

$$\text{EBIT} = \$700,000$$

Similarly, the indifference point between all common and all preferred would be:

$$\frac{(\text{EBIT} - \text{I})(1 - t) - \text{PD}}{S_1} = \frac{(\text{EBIT} - \text{I})(1 - t) - \text{PD}}{S_2}$$

$$\frac{(\text{EBIT} - 0)(1 - 0.5) - 0}{140,000} = \frac{(\text{EBIT} - 0)(1 - 0.5) - 160,000}{100,000}$$

Rearranging yields:

$$0.5(\text{EBIT})(100,000) = 0.5(\text{EBIT})(140,000) - 160,000(140,000)$$
$$20,000 \text{ EBIT} = 22,400,000,000$$
$$\text{EBIT} = \$1,120,000$$

Based on the above computations, we can draw the following conclusions:

1. At any level of EBIT, debt is better than preferred stock.
2. At a level of EBIT above \$700,000, debt is better than common stock. If EBIT is below \$700,000, the reverse is true.
3. At a level of EBIT above \$1,120,000, preferred stock is better than common. At or below that point, the reverse is true.

Review Questions

1. _____ refers to the incurrence of fixed operating costs in the firm's income statement. It is a measure of _____ .

2. The higher the _____ , the higher the financial risk, and the higher the _____ .

3. The _____ is the level of _____ at which no profit or loss results.

4. To find the _____ , noncash charges such as _____ must be subtracted from total fixed operating costs.

5. A simple indication of _____ is to look at how earnings are affected by a change in sales.

6. Total leverage is a measure of _____ . It measures how _____ is affected by a change in sales.

7. Total leverage is the _____ of _____ and _____ .

8. There are four positions regarding the relationship between valuation and leverage. They are the _____ , the _____ , the _____ , and the _____ .

9. Under the _____ , there is no such thing as optimal capital structure.

10. The key assumption underlying the net income approach is that the cost of _____ and the cost of _____ remain unchanged as the _____ increases.

11. The _____ to valuation and leverage assumes that there is a(n) _____ capital structure and that the firm can increase _____ through _____ .

12. The primary objective of the _____ is to determine the _____ break-even, or _____ , points between the various alternative financing plans.

13. _____ refers to the mix of long-term financing sources used.

14. Debt has a(n) _____ advantage over preferred stock in that _____ is a tax-deductible expense while _____ are not.

15. The theory of capital structure assumes no _____ and no _____ .

Answers: (1) Operating leverage, operating risk; (2) financial leverage, cost of capital; (3) break-even point, sales; (4) cash break-even point, depreciation; (5) operating leverage; (6) total risk, EPS; (7) product, operating leverage, financial leverage; (8) net income (NI) approach, net operating income (NOI) approach, traditional approach, Miller-Modigliani (MM) approach; (9) net operating income (NOI) approach; (10) common equity, debt, debt/equity ratio; (11) traditional approach, optimal, its value, leverage; (12) EBIT-EPS analysis, EBIT, indifference; (13) Capital structure; (14) tax, interest, preferred stock dividends; (15) income taxes, transaction costs.

Solved Problems

11.1 **Break-Even and Cash Break-Even Points.** The following price and cost data are given for firms A, B, and C:

	A	B	C
Selling price per unit	$25	$12	$15
Variable cost per unit	$10	$6	$5
Fixed operating costs	$30,000	$24,000	$100,000

Calculate (*a*) the break-even point for each firm, and (*b*) the cash break-even point for each firm, assuming $5,000 of each firm's fixed costs are depreciation. (*c*) Rank these firms in terms of their risk.

SOLUTION

(*a*)
$$X = \frac{FC}{P - V}$$

Firm A: $\dfrac{\$30,000}{\$15} = 2,000$ units

Firm B: $\dfrac{\$24,000}{\$6} = 4,000$ units

Firm C: $\dfrac{\$100,000}{\$10} = 10,000$ units

(b)
$$X = \frac{FC - d}{P - V}$$

Firm A: $\dfrac{\$30,000 - \$5,000}{\$15} = 1{,}667$ units

Firm B: $\dfrac{\$24,000 - \$5,000}{\$6} = 3{,}167$ units

Firm C: $\dfrac{\$100,000 - \$5,000}{\$10} = 9{,}500$ units

(c) Firm A seems least risky, followed by B and then C, based on increasing break-even points. It is important to recognize, however, that operating leverage is only one measure of risk.

11.2 Operating and Financial Leverages. John Tripper Soft Drinks, Inc., sells 500,000 bottles of soft drinks a year. Each bottle produced has a variable cost of $0.25 and sells for $0.45. Fixed operating costs are $50,000. The company has current interest charges of $6,000 and preferred dividends of $2,400. The corporate tax rate is 40 percent.

(a) Calculate the degree of operating leverage, the degree of financial leverage, and the degree of total leverage. (b) Do part (a) at the 750,000 bottle sales level. (c) What generalizations can you make comparing (a) to (b) after first finding the break-even point?

SOLUTION

(a)
$$\text{Operating leverage} = \frac{(P - V)X}{(P - V)X - FC}$$

$$= \frac{(\$0.45 - \$0.25)(500{,}000)}{(\$0.45 - \$0.25)(500{,}000) - \$50{,}000} = \frac{\$100{,}000}{\$50{,}000} = 2$$

$$\text{Financial leverage} = \frac{(P - V)X - FC}{(P - V)X - FC - IC^a}$$

$$= \frac{(\$0.45 - \$0.25)(500{,}000) - \$50{,}000}{(\$0.45 - \$0.25)(500{,}000) - \$50{,}000 - \$10{,}000} = \frac{\$50{,}000}{\$50{,}000 - \$10{,}000} = 1.25$$

$$^a IC = \$6{,}000 + \frac{\$2{,}400}{1 - 0.4} = \$6{,}000 + \$4{,}000 = \$10{,}000$$

$$\text{Total leverage} = \frac{(P - V)X}{(P - V)X - FC - IC} = \frac{\$100{,}000}{\$40{,}000} = 2.5$$

(b)
$$\text{Operating leverage} = \frac{(0.45 - \$0.25)(750{,}000)}{(\$0.45 - \$0.25)(750{,}000) - \$50{,}000} = \frac{\$150{,}000}{\$100{,}000} = 1.5$$

$$\text{Financial leverage} = \frac{\$100{,}000}{\$100{,}000 - \$10{,}000} = 1.11$$

$$\text{Total leverage} = \frac{\$150{,}000}{\$90{,}000} = 1.667$$

or

$$\text{Total leverage} = 1.5 \times 1.11 = 1.667$$

(c)
$$\text{Break-even point} = \frac{FC}{P - V} = \frac{\$50{,}000}{\$0.45 - \$0.25} = 250{,}000 \text{ units}$$

The degree of operating leverage decreases the further the company moves from break-even operations.

The addition of financial leverage to operating leverage magnifies the effect of a change in sales on earnings per share. With financial leverage the break-even point moves to 300,000 units.

$$\frac{\$50,000 + \$10,000}{\$0.45 - \$0.25} = 300,000 \text{ units}$$

11.3   **Financial Leverage.** Herken Company is a closely held corporation with a capital structure composed entirely of common stock and retained earnings. The stockholders have an agreement with the company that states the company will purchase the stock of a shareholder should a shareholder want to sell his or her holdings in the company. The agreement states that the stock will be purchased at a price equal to the stock's previous year-end book value per share.

Early in October 19X1 Mrs. John Vader, a widow of one of Herken's major stockholders, expressed an interest in selling her stock in accordance with the buy-back pricing arrangement. Mrs. Vader owns 600,000 shares of the 3 million shares of Herken Company common stock.

The board of directors has concluded that the company must replace the capital used to repurchase the shares. The board has assurances that it would be able to finance the acquisition of stock by borrowing the necessary funds on 10-year notes through private placement at an annual interest rate of 10 percent. Thus the company would have capital provided by debt and perhaps be able to take advantage of financial leverage.

The board and Mrs. Vader agreed that the exchange will take place on January 1, 19X2. The book value per share of common stock is projected to be $50 on December 31, 19X1.

The controller of Herken Company had prepared a forecast and pro forma statements for the 19X2 year.

An excerpt of the forecasted earnings statement for the year ended December 31, 19X2, is presented below (in thousands of dollars). Herken used a 40 percent income tax rate in the forecasted statement. The pro forma statements do not reflect the repurchase of Mrs. Vader's shares or the new issue of debt required to pay for the shares.

Income before income taxes	$50,000
Less income taxes (40%)	20,000
Net income	$30,000

(a) Revise the excerpt from Herken Company's forecasted earnings statement for the year ended December 31, 19X2, to reflect the long-term debt financing to be used to purchase Mrs. Vader's common stock. Assume the 40 percent tax rate will still be applicable. (b) Explain the impact the long-term debt financing would have on Herken Company's earnings per share and return on stockholders' equity using the forecasted data for 19X2. (c) Identify and discuss the advantages and disadvantages of financial leverage for a company that has a capital structure similar to that of Herken Company before and after this long-term debt has been added. (CMA, adapted.)

SOLUTION

(a)
Herken Company
Revised Profit Forecast
(In Thousands of Dollars)
For the Year Ended December 31, 19X2

Earnings before interest and taxes	$50,000
Interest—new debt ($30,000 × 10%)	3,000
Earnings before tax	$47,000
Income tax (40%)	18,800
Net income	$28,200

With 2,400 shares outstanding, earnings per share is $11.75 and dividends per share (assuming no change) is $0.

(b)   The effects of the financial leverage is to increase the earnings per share because the reduction in after-tax earnings caused by the after-tax impact of the interest expense is more than offset by the impact of having fewer shares outstanding. Return on equity would also increase because the book value decreases 20 percent while the earnings are only decreasing by 6 percent (from $30,000 to $28,200).

(c)   The basic advantages of financial leverage where the earnings on assets exceed the after-tax cost of the debt are increased earnings per share (EPS) and increased return on equity (ROE). The disadvantages of financial leverage include: (1) the risk that earnings will drop below the cost of debt, which would result in negative financial leverage that would lower both EPS and ROE; (2) increased financial risk to the owners through variability in net income due to the fixed cost associated with debt; and (3) the prospect of increased cost of capital due to creditors' assessment of increased financial risk.

11.4   **The NI Approach.** Equipment Company has earnings before interest and taxes (EBIT) of $10 million. The company currently has outstanding debt of $20 million at a cost of 7 percent. Ignore taxes.

(a) Using the net income (NI) approach and a cost of equity of 12.5 percent; (1) compute the total value of the firm and the firm's overall weighted average cost of capital (k_o), and (2) determine the firm's market debt/equity ratio. (b) Assume that the firm issues an additional $10 million in debt and uses the proceeds to retire stock; the interest rate and the cost of equity remain the same. (1) Compute the new total value of the firm and the firm's overall cost of capital, and (2) determine the firm's market debt/equity ratio.

SOLUTION

(a)
$$\text{EBIT} = \$10,000,000$$
$$I = \$20,000,000 \times 7\% = \$1,400,000$$
$$k_e = 12.5\%$$

(1)   The total value of the firm, V, can be found as follows:

$$\text{EAC} = \text{EBIT} - I = \$10,000,000 - \$1,400,000 = \$8,600,000$$

$$S = \frac{\text{EAC}}{k_e} = \frac{\$8,600,000}{0.125} = \$68,800,000$$

$$V = S + B = \$68,800,000 + \$20,000,000 = \$88,800,000$$

Therefore,

$$k_o = \frac{\text{EBIT}}{V} = \frac{\$10,000,000}{\$88,800,000} = 11.26\%$$

(2) The firm's market debt/equity ratio is:

$$\frac{B}{S} = \frac{\$20,000,000}{\$68,800,000} = 29\%$$

(b)   (1)
$$I = \$30,000,000 \times 7\% = \$2,100,000$$
$$\text{EAC} = \text{EBIT} - I = \$10,000,000 - \$2,100,000 = \$7,900,000$$

$$S = \frac{\text{EAC}}{k_e} = \frac{\$7,900,000}{0.125} = \$63,200,000$$

$$V = S + B = \$63,200,000 + \$30,000,000 = \$93,200,000$$

Therefore,

$$k_o = \frac{EBIT}{V} = \frac{\$10,000,000}{\$93,200,000} = 10.73\%$$

(2)   The debt/equity ratio is:

$$\frac{B}{S} = \frac{\$30,000,000}{\$63,200,000} = 47\%$$

11.5   **The NOI Approach.** Assume the same data as given in Problem 11.4. (*a*) Using the net operating income (NOI) approach and an overall cost of capital of 12 percent; (1) compute the total value, the stock market value of the firm, and the cost of equity; and (2) determine the firm's market debt/equity ratio. (*b*) Determine the answer to (*a*) if the company were to sell the additional $10 million in debt, as in Problem 11.4(*b*).

SOLUTION

(*a*)
$$EBIT = \$10,000,000$$
$$k_o = 12\%$$
$$EAC = \$8,600,000$$

(1)
$$V = \frac{EBIT}{k_o} = \frac{\$10,000,000}{12\%} = \$83,330,000$$

$$S = V - B = \$83,330,000 - \$20,000,000 = \$63,330,000$$

Therefore,

$$k_e = \frac{EAC}{S} = \frac{\$8,600,000}{\$63,330,000} = 13.6\%$$

(2)   The debt/equity ratio is:

$$\frac{B}{S} = \frac{\$20,000,000}{\$63,330,000} = 31.58\%$$

(*b*)   (1)
$$S = V - B = \$83,330,000 - \$30,000,000 = \$53,330,000$$

Therefore,

$$k_e = \frac{EAC}{S} = \frac{\$8,600,000}{\$53,330,000} = 16.1\%$$

(2)   The debt/equity ratio is:

$$\frac{B}{S} = \frac{\$30,000,000}{\$53,330,000} = 56.3\%$$

11.6   **The NI Approach.** Happy-Day Industries, Inc., is financed entirely with 100,000 shares of common stock selling at $50 per share. The firm's EBIT is expected to be $400,000. The firm pays 100 percent of its earnings as dividends. Ignore taxes.

(*a*) Using the NI approach, compute the total value of the firm and the cost of equity. (*b*) The company has decided to retire $1 million of common stock, replacing it with 9 percent long-term debt. Compute the total value of the firm and the overall cost of capital after refinancing.

SOLUTION

(a)   Since there is no debt, B = 0 and I = 0.

$$S = V - B = (100{,}000 \text{ shares} \times \$50) - 0 = \$5{,}000{,}000$$
$$EAC = EBIT - I = \$400{,}000 - 0 = \$400{,}000$$

Therefore,

$$k_e = \frac{EAC}{S} = \frac{\$400{,}000}{\$5{,}000{,}000} = 8\%$$

which is also k_o.

(b)
$$I = \$1{,}000{,}000 \times 9\% = \$90{,}000$$
$$EAC = EBIT - I = \$400{,}000 - \$90{,}000 = \$310{,}000$$

$$S = \frac{EAC}{k_e} = \frac{\$310{,}000}{0.08} = \$3{,}875{,}000$$

$$V = S + B = \$3{,}875{,}000 + \$1{,}000{,}000 = \$4{,}875{,}000$$

Therefore,

$$k_o = \frac{EBIT}{V} = \frac{\$400{,}000}{\$4{,}875{,}000} = 8.2\%$$

11.7   **The NOI Approach.** Assume the same data as given in Problem 11.6. (a) Using the NOI approach and an overall cost of capital of 10 percent, compute the total value, the stock market value of the firm, and the cost of equity. (b) Determine the answers to (a) if the company decided to retire $1 million of common stock, replacing it with 9 percent long-term debt.

SOLUTION

(a)
$$V = \frac{EBIT}{k_o} = \frac{\$400{,}000}{0.10} = \$4{,}000{,}000$$
$$S = V - B = \$4{,}000{,}000 - \$0 = \$4{,}000{,}000$$

Therefore,

$$k_e = \frac{EAC}{S} = \frac{\$400{,}000}{\$4{,}000{,}000} = 10\%$$

(b)
$$S = V - B = \$4{,}000{,}000 - \$1{,}000{,}000 = \$3{,}000{,}000$$

Therefore,

$$k_e = \frac{EAC}{S} = \frac{\$400{,}000}{\$3{,}000{,}000} = 13.3\%$$

11.8   **EPS Calculation.** The balance sheet of the Delta Corporation shows a capital structure as follows:

Current liabilities	$ 0
Bonds (6% interest)	100,000
Common stock	900,000
Total claims	$1,000,000

Its rate of return before interest and taxes on its assets of $1 million is 20 percent. The value of each share (whether market or book value) is $30. The firm is in the 50 percent tax bracket. Calculate its earnings per share.

SOLUTION

EBIT (20% × $1,000,000)	$200,000
Less: Interest (6% × $100,000)	6,000
Earnings before tax (EBIT)	$194,000
Less: Income tax (50%)	97,000
Earnings after tax (EAT)	$ 97,000

Number of common shares outstanding is:

$$\frac{\$900,000}{\$30} = 30,000 \text{ shares}$$

$$EPS = \frac{\$97,000}{30,000 \text{ shares}} = \$3.23$$

11.9   The EBIT-EPS Analysis. DMC Corporation currently has 100,000 shares of common stock outstanding with a market price of $50 per share. It also has $2 million in 7 percent bonds (currently selling at par). The company is considering a $4 million expansion program that it can finance with either (I) all common stock at $50 per share, or (II) all bonds at 9 percent. The company estimates that if the expansion program is undertaken, it can attain, in the near future, $1 million in EBIT.

(a) The company's tax rate is 40 percent. Calculate the EPS for each plan. (b) Draw the EBIT-EPS graph. (c) What is the indifference point between the alternatives? (d) If the expected EBIT for the near future is greater than your answer in (c), what form of financing would you recommend?

SOLUTION

(a)   The EPS is computed as follows:

	(I) All Stock	(II) All Bonds
EBIT	$1,000,000	$1,000,000
Interest	140,000[a]	500,000[b]
EBT	$ 860,000	$ 500,000
Tax (40%)	344,000	200,000
EAT	$ 516,000	$ 300,000
Number of shares	180,000[c]	100,000
EPS	$2.87	$3.00

---

[a] $2,000,000 × 7% = $140,000

[b] $4,000,000 × 9% = $360,000
$360,000 + $140,000 = $500,000

[c] $4,000,000 ÷ $50 per share = 80,000 shares. Therefore,

$$100,000 + 80,000 = 180,000 \text{ shares}$$

(b)   The EBIT-EPS graph is shown in Fig. 11-5.

(c) $$EPS = \frac{(EBIT - I)(1 - t) - PD}{\text{Number of shares outstanding}}$$

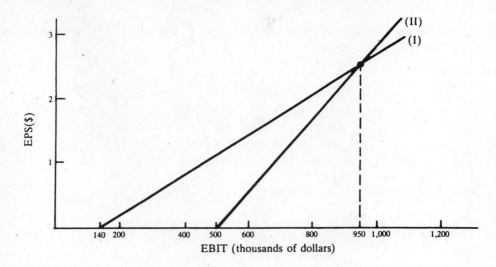

Fig. 11-5

The EBIT-EPS indifference points between plans (I) and (II) are calculated as follows:

EPS under plan (I) = EPS under plan (II)

$$\frac{(\text{EBIT} - 140{,}000)(1 - 0.4) - 0}{180{,}000} = \frac{(\text{EBIT} - 500{,}000)(1 - 0.4) - 0}{100{,}000}$$

$$(0.6\ \text{EBIT} - 84{,}000)(100{,}000) = (0.6\ \text{EBIT} - 300{,}000)(180{,}000)$$

$$48{,}000\ \text{EBIT} = 45{,}600{,}000{,}000$$

$$\text{EBIT} = \$950{,}000$$

(*d*) Plan (II), all bonds, is preferred.

11.10 The EBIT-EPS Analysis. Amsterdam Products, Inc., is evaluating two financing plans. Key data are given below. Assume a 50 percent tax rate and an expected EBIT of $400,000.

	Plan A	Plan B
Bonds	$80,000 at 9%	$150,000 at 10%
Preferred stock	8,000 shares of $3	4,000 shares of $3.50
Common stock	20,000 shares	23,000 shares

Determine (*a*) the EPS for each plan, and (*b*) the financial break-even points for each plan. (*c*) Draw the EBIT-EPS graph. (*d*) At what level of EBIT would the company be indifferent as to which of these two plans is selected?

SOLUTION

(*a*) The earnings per share (EPS) for each plan is given below.

	Plan A	Plan B
EBIT	$400,000	$400,000
Interest	7,200	15,000
EBT	$392,800	$385,000
Tax (0.5)	196,400	192,500
EAT	$196,400	$192,500
Preferred stock dividend	24,000	14,000
EAC	$172,400	$178,500
Number of shares outstanding	20,000 shares	23,000 shares
EPS	$8.62	$7.76

(*b*) In order to draw the EBIT-EPS graph for the two plans, two coordinates are needed and are given by the financial break-even points:

For plan A:

$$\$7,200 + \frac{\$24,000}{0.5} = \$55,200$$

For plan B:

$$\$15,000 + \frac{\$14,000}{0.5} = \$43,000$$

In other words, the company must have $55,200 in EBIT under plan A to cover interest charges and preferred stock dividends. It must have $43,000 in EBIT under plan B to cover its interest charges and preferred stock dividends.

(*c*) The EBIT-EPS chart is shown in Fig. 11- 6.

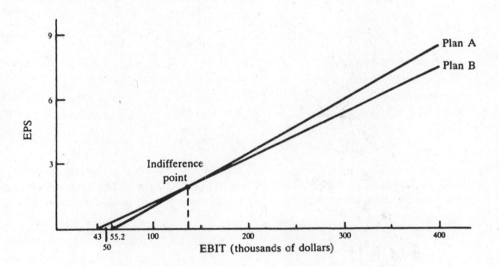

Fig. 11-6

(*d*) The indifference point is calculated as follows:

$$\text{EPS} = \frac{(\text{EBIT} - \text{I})(1 - t) - \text{PD}}{\text{number of shares outstanding}}$$

EPS under plan A = EPS under plan B

$$\frac{(\text{EBIT} - 7,200)(1 - 0.5) - 24,000}{20,000} = \frac{(\text{EBIT} - 15,000)(1 - 0.5) - 14,000}{23,000}$$

$$\frac{0.5\,\text{EBIT} - 3,600 - 24,000}{20,000} = \frac{0.5\,\text{EBIT} - 7,500 - 14,000}{23,000}$$

$$(0.5\,\text{EBIT} - 27,600)(23,000) = (0.5\,\text{EBIT} - 21,500)(20,000)$$

$$1,500\,\text{EBIT} = 204,800,000$$

$$\text{EBIT} = \$136,533$$

Therefore, below the level of $136,533, plan B is preferred; above the level of $136,533, plan A is preferred.

11.11 The EBIT-EPS Analysis. Parker Brothers, Inc., is considering three financing plans. The key information follows. Assume a 50 percent tax rate.

Plan A	Plan B	Plan C
Common stock: $200,000	Bonds at 8%: $100,000	Preferred stock at 8%: $100,000
	Common stock: $100,000	Common stock: $100,000

In each case the common stock will be sold at $20 per share. The expected EBIT is $80,000.

Determine (a) the EPS for each plan, and (b) the financial break-even point for each plan. (c) Draw the EBIT-EPS graph. (d) Indicate over what EBIT range each plan is preferred.

SOLUTION

(a)   The EPS calculation is shown below:

	Plan A	Plan B	Plan C
EBIT	$80,000	$80,000	$80,000
Interest		8,000	
EBT	$80,000	$72,000	$80,000
Tax (50%)	40,000	36,000	40,000
EAT	$40,000	$36,000	$40,000
Preferred stock dividend			8,000
Earnings available to			
common stockholders (EAC)	$40,000	$36,000	$32,000
Number of shares outstanding	10,000	5,000	5,000
EPS	$4.00	$7.20	$6.40

(b)   The financial break-even points are: for plan A, 0; for plan B, $8,000; and for plan C, $8,000 ÷ 0.5 = $16,000. In other words, plan B must have $8,000 in EBIT to cover the interest charge of $8,000; plan C must have $16,000 in EBIT to pay the preferred stock dividend of $8,000.

(c)   See Fig. 11-7.

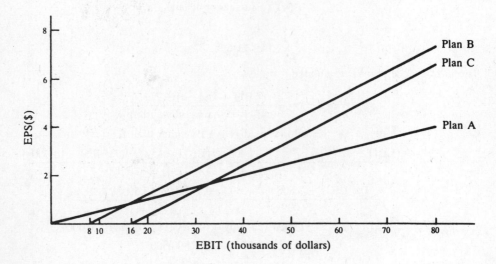

Fig. 11-7

(d)   From Fig. 11-7, the EBIT-EPS graph in (c), we see that plan B will always dominate plan C at any level of EBIT. Thus, only alternatives A versus B and A versus C need be evaluated. The indifference points are computed as follows:

For plan A versus plan B:

$$\frac{(EBIT - 0)(1 - 0.5) - 0}{10,000} = \frac{(EBIT - 8,000)(1 - 0.5) - 0}{5,000}$$

$$0.5\ EBIT(5,000) = (0.5\ EBIT - 4,000)(10,000)$$

$$2,500\ EBIT = 40,000,000$$

$$EBIT = \$16,000$$

For plan A versus plan C:

$$\frac{(EBIT - 0)(1 - 0.5) - 0}{10,000} = \frac{(EBIT - 0)(1 - 0.5) - 8,000}{5,000}$$

$$\frac{0.5\ EBIT}{10,000} = \frac{0.5\ EBIT - 8,000}{5,000}$$

$$0.5\ EBIT(5,000) = (0.5\ EBIT - 8,000)(10,000)$$

$$2,500\ EBIT = 5,000\ EBIT - 80,000,000$$

$$2,500\ EBIT = 80,000,000$$

$$EBIT = \$32,000$$

If EBIT is expected to exceed $16,000, plan B is preferred over plan A. If EBIT is expected to exceed $32,000, plan C is preferred over plan A.

11.12 EBIT-EPS Analysis. The Morton Company is planning to invest $10 million in an expansion program which is expected to increase earnings before interest and taxes by $2.5 million. The company currently is earning $5 per share on 1 million shares of common outstanding. The capital structure prior to the investment is:

Debt	$10,000,000
Equity	30,000,000
	$40,000,000

The expansion can be financed by sale of 200,000 shares at $50 net each, or by issuing long-term debt at a 6 percent interest cost. The firm's recent profit and loss statement was as follows:

Sales	$101,000,000
Variable cost	$ 60,000,000
Fixed cost	30,500,000
	$ 90,500,000
Earnings before interest and taxes	$ 10,500,000
Interest	500,000
Earnings before taxes	$ 10,000,000
Taxes (50%)	5,000,000
Earnings after taxes	$ 5,000,000

(a) Assuming the firm maintains its current earnings and achieves the anticipated earnings from the expansion, what will be the earnings per share (1) if the expansion is financed by debt? (2) if the expansion is financed by equity? (b) At what level of earnings before interest and taxes will the earnings per share under either alternative be the same amount? (c) The choice of financing alternatives influences the earnings per share. The choice might also influence the earnings multiple used by the market. Discuss the factors inherent in the choice between the debt and equity alternatives that might influence the earnings multiple. Be sure to indicate the direction in which these factors might influence the earnings multiple. (CMA, adapted.)

SOLUTION

(a)

	(1) Debt-Financed	(2) Equity-Financed
Earnings before interest and taxes—present	$10,500,000	$10,500,000
Added earnings—expansion	2,500,000	2,500,000
	$13,000,000	$13,000,000
Interest	1,100,000	500,000
	$11,900,000	$12,500,000
Taxes	5,950,000	6,250,000
Net income	$ 5,950,000	$ 6,250,000
Common shares outstanding	1,000,000	1,200,000
Earnings per share	$5.95	$5.21

(b)

$$\text{EPS} = \frac{(\text{EBIT} - I)(1 - t)}{\text{no. of shares}}$$

$$\frac{(\text{EBIT} - 1,100,000)(1 - 0.50)}{1,000,000} = \frac{(\text{EBIT} - 500,000)(1 - 0.50)}{1,200,000}$$

$$\text{EBIT} = \$4,100,000$$

(c) A major factor that is inherent in the choice between debt and equity financing is the change in the risk for the equity holders. If the expansion is financed by debt, the increase in risk appears in two forms. (1) There is increased risk of insolvency because the debt requires regular fixed cash outlay for interest and principal. Equity financing does not incur the legal obligations of the regular cash outlay. (2) The other effect is on the variability of earnings to common stockholders. The fixed charges against income reduces the amount of income available to stockholders. The relative variability of earnings available to common stockholders increases. Both these risks would tend to reduce the earnings multiple. (Note, the market value of a share does not necessarily decrease with the debt expansion.)

11.13 **Rate of Return and Optimal Capital Structure.** Central Furniture Company recently announced plans to expand its production capacity by building and equipping two new factories to operate in parallel with existing production facilities. The expansion will double the assets of the firm. The proposed expansion has received a lot of attention from industry observers due to the cyclical nature of the furniture industry and the size of the project. The new plants will require fewer workers than current plants of similar capacity because the new facilities will be highly automated.

Central Furniture must now decide how the plant expansion will be financed. The project will require $5 million in new funds and the expected return on the new assets is estimated at 12 percent before taxes, the same return that is currently earned on the existing assets. The two alternatives proposed to raise the needed funds are (1) private placement of long-term debt at an interest rate of 10 percent, and (2) issuance of new common stock at $25 per share.

Currently the company is financed equally by debt and equity as follows:

Long-term debt (8%)	$2,500,000
Common stock ($1 par)	$100,000
Paid-in capital on common stock	$400,000
Retained earnings	$2,000,000

Central Furniture's common stock is currently traded on a stock exchange at a market price of $27 per share. Central Furniture is subject to a tax rate of 40 percent. (a) Compute Central Furniture Company's anticipated rate of return on stockholders' equity if the expansion project is financed by (1) private placement of long-term debt, and (2) issuance of common stock. (b) One of the two alternatives—long-term debt or common stock—will move Central Furniture Company to a more optimum capital structure. (1) What criteria are used to judge optimum capital structure? (2) Explain what factors influence the determination of an optimum capital structure. (CMA, adapted.)

SOLUTION

(a) (1)

Earnings before interest and taxes		
($10,000,000 × 0.12)		$1,200,000
Less: Interest expense		
Present debt (0.08 × $2,500,000)	$200,000	
New debt (0.10 × $5,000,000)	500,000	700,000
Earnings before taxes		$ 500,000
Taxes (40%)		200,000
Net income		$ 300,000

$$\text{Return on stockholders' equity} = \frac{\$300,000}{\$2,500,000} = 12\%$$

(2)

Earnings before interest and taxes		
($10,000,000 × 0.12)		$1,200,000
Less: Interest expense		
(0.08 × $2,500,000)		200,000
Earnings before taxes		$1,000,000
Taxes (40%)		400,000
Net income		$ 600,000

$$\text{Return on stockholders' equity} = \frac{\$600,000}{\$7,500,000} = 8\%$$

(b) (1) Optimum capital structure is the lowest weighted average cost of capital that a given firm is able to obtain given its risk constraints. (2) The optimum capital structure for a firm is influenced by the relationship of its return to the risks of earning the return. Specific factors influencing these two items would include:

1. The growth rate of income
2. Cash flow available to service debt
3. The amount of operating risk
4. Lender and investor interpretation of the financial risk of the firm and industry

11.14 Alternative Sources of Financing. The Drew Furniture Company is considering the introduction of a new product line. Plant and inventory expansion equal to 50 percent of present asset levels will be necessary to handle the anticipated volume of the new product line. New capital will have to be obtained to finance the asset expansion. Two proposals have been developed to provide the added capital.

1. Raise the $100,000 by issuing 10-year 12 percent bonds. This will change the capital structure from one with about 20 percent debt to one with almost 50 percent debt. The investment banking house estimates the price/earnings ratio, now 12 to 1, will be reduced to 10 to 1 if this method of financing is chosen.

2. Raise the $100,000 by issuing new common stock. The investment banker believes that the stock can be issued to yield $33⅓. The price/earnings ratio would remain at 12 to 1 if the stock were issued. The present market price is $36.

The company's most recent financial statements are as follows:

Drew Furniture Company
Balance Sheet
As of December 31, 19X1

ASSETS		EQUITIES	
Current	$ 65,000	Debt 5%	$ 40,000
Plant and equipment	135,000	Common stock	100,000
		Retained earnings	60,000
	$200,000		$200,000

Income Statement
For the Year Ended December 31, 19X1

Sales	$600,000
Operating costs	538,000
Operating income	$ 62,000
Interest charges	2,000
Net income before taxes	$ 60,000
Federal income taxes	30,000
Net income	$ 30,000

(a) The vice-president of finance asks you to calculate the earnings per share and the market value of the stock (assuming the price/earnings ratios given are valid estimates) for the two proposals assuming total sales (including the new product line) of: (1) $400,000; (2) $600,000; and (3) $800,000. Costs exclusive of interest and taxes are about 90 percent of sales. (b) Which proposal would you recommend? Your answer should indicate: (1) the criteria used to judge the alternatives; (2) a brief defense of the criteria used; and (3) the proposal chosen in accordance with the criteria. (c) Would your answer change if a sales level of $1,200,000 or more could be achieved? Explain. (d) What reason(s) would the investment broker give to support the estimate of a lower price/earnings ratio if debt is issued? (CMA, adapted.)

SOLUTION

(a) Proposal 1, for 10-year 12 percent bonds:

Drew Furniture Company
Income Statement
For the Year Ended December 31, 19X1

	Estimated Sales Levels		
Sales	$400,000	$600,000	$800,000
Operating costs	360,000	540,000	720,000
Operating income	$ 40,000	$ 60,000	$ 80,000
Interest charges	14,000	14,000	14,000
Net income before taxes	$ 26,000	$ 46,000	$ 66,000
Federal income taxes	13,000	23,000	33,000
Net income	$ 13,000	$ 23,000	$ 33,000

$$\text{Outstanding shares} = \frac{30,000}{3} = 10,000$$

Earnings per share	$1.30	$2.30	$3.30
Price/earnings ratio	10 times	10 times	10 times
Estimated market value	$31	$23	$33

Proposal 2, for common stock issue to yield 33\frac{1}{3}$:

Drew Furniture Company
Income Statement
For the Year Ended December 31, 19X1

	Estimated Sales Levels		
Sales	$400,000	$600,000	$800,000
Operating costs	360,000	540,000	720,000
Operating income	$ 40,000	$ 60,000	$ 80,000
Interest charges	2,000	2,000	2,000
Net income before taxes	$ 38,000	$ 58,000	$ 78,000
Federal income taxes	19,000	29,000	39,000
Net income	$ 19,000	$ 29,000	$ 39,000

$$\text{Outstanding shares} = \frac{100,000}{33\frac{1}{3}} + 10,000 = 13,000 \text{ shares}$$

Earnings per share	$1.46	$2.23	$3.00
Price/earnings ratio	12 times	12 times	12 times
Estimated market value	$17.52	$26.76	$36.00

(b) Within the constraints of this problem, two possible objectives emerge: profit maximization as measured by earnings per share, and wealth maximization as measured by the price of the common stock. If profit maximization is used, the firm should choose to finance the new product by selling bonds, since earnings per share is higher for each of the three levels of sales. On the other hand, wealth maximization would require the sale of new common stock because stock price is higher at each sales level.

Wealth maximization is the preferred criterion for financial decision making. Unlike profit maximization, wealth maximization represents a measure of the total benefits to be enjoyed by the shareholders, adjusted for both the timing of benefits and the risk associated with their receipt. A criterion which ignores these two important determinants of value cannot be expected to provide a proper guide to decision making.

Because wealth maximization is the preferred objective, the sale of common stock is the recommended financing technique.

(c) Proposal 2 would still be the choice because the market value remains above that of proposal 1. The difference is smaller than is shown with the lower sales estimates, which means that proposal 1 would become attractive if sales reached a higher level (approximately $1.6 million).

(d) The investment banker would suggest that the lower price/earnings ratio with debt financing is a reflection of the greater returns demanded by stockholders in compensation for the greater variability in earnings and higher risk of bankruptcy created by the fixed commitment to pay debt interest and principal.

Examination II

I. Put a T (true) or F (false) in the space provided below:

_____ **1.** Finding present values is simply the inverse of compounding.

_____ **2.** A perpetuity is an annuity that continues for 20 years.

_____ **3.** Risk is defined as the variation in returns about a standard deviation.

_____ **4.** Through diversification, an investor can reduce the systematic risk, or beta.

_____ **5.** A proxy for the risk-free rate is the Treasury bills yield.

_____ **6.** The cost of capital is the weighted average of the various capital costs.

_____ **7.** Total leverage is the product of operating leverage and financial leverage.

_____ **8.** The optimal capital structure can be defined as the mix of financing sources that minimize the company's debt cost.

_____ **9.** Projects that are negatively correlated tend to be less risky than those that move together in the same direction.

_____**10.** The NPV method and the IRR approach assume the same rate for reinvestment.

II. Select the best answer:

1. Which of the following takes into account the time value of money?

(*a*) Average rate of return

(*b*) Payback period

(*c*) Internal rate of return

(*d*) None of the above

2. The NPV method and the IRR method may produce conflicting ranking when

(*a*) projects are mutually exclusive

(*b*) projects are independent and not competing for limited funds

(*c*) both of the above

(*d*) none of the above

3. Which of the following is concerned with the relationship between the firm's EBIT and EPS?

(*a*) Beta

(*b*) Operating leverage

(*c*) Sales revenue

(*d*) Financial leverage

4. Through diversification a firm can stabilize its earnings and most effectively reduce its risk when projects are

(*a*) perfectly positively correlated

(*b*) independent of each other

(*c*) perfectly negatively correlated

(*d*) none of the above

5. Under the CAPM, the required rate of return on a security is the sum of a risk premium and

   (a) financial risk
   (b) operating risk
   (c) diversifiable risk
   (d) risk-free rate

6. All the following elements are necessary for the computation of the cost of common stock under the Gordon's growth model, except

   (a) tax rate
   (b) growth rate in dividends or earnings
   (c) market price
   (d) dividend

7. Which one of the following must be adjusted for taxes?

   (a) Cost of retained earnings
   (b) Cost of common stock
   (c) Cost of preferred stock
   (d) Cost of debt

8. Which of the following is not a method for adjusting for risk in capital budgeting?

   (a) Risk-adjusted rate
   (b) Simulation
   (c) Certainty equivalent approach
   (d) Break-even analysis

9. The traditional approach to capital structure implies

   (a) there is a minimum cost of capital that is determined by an optimal capital structure
   (b) there is no such thing as optimal capital structure
   (c) all the above
   (d) none of the above

10. The simple expression for the total value of the firm is

   (a) stocks/bonds
   (b) stocks × bonds
   (c) stocks + bonds
   (d) none of the above

III.

1. If a firm's earnings and dividends grow from $2.15 per share to $4 per share over an 8-year period, what is the rate of growth?

2. How much would you be willing to pay today for an investment that would return $1,250 each year for the next 10 years, assuming a discount rate of 12 percent?

3. The risk-free rate is 5 percent, the market return is 12 percent and the stock's beta coefficient is 1.25. If the dividend expected during the coming year is $3 and grows at an 8 percent rate, at what price should the stock sell?

4. The Sawyer Company has just issued $10 million of $1,000, 8 percent, 10-year bonds. Due to the current market rates the firm had to sell the bonds at a discount of $40 from their face value. (*a*) Calculate the before-tax cost, or yield to maturity, of the bond, using the shortcut formula, and (*b*) calculate the after-tax cost of the bond, assuming the firm's tax rate is 40 percent.

5. The Desert Products Company is considering six investment proposals of similar risk, for which the funds available are limited. The projects are independent and have the following initial investment and present values of cash inflows associated with them:

Project	Initial Cost (I) ($)	PV ($)
A	15,000	21,000
B	8,000	12,000
C	5,000	7,500
D	4,000	6,400
E	2,000	3,500
F	1,000	1,900

(*a*) Compute the profitability index and NPV for each project. (*b*) Under capital rationing, which projects should be selected, assuming a total budget of $25,000? (*c*) Which projects should be selected if the total budget is reduced to $24,000?

6. A firm is considering two alternative plans to finance a proposed $7 million investment. Plan A: Issue debt (9 percent interest rate). Plan B: Issue common stock (at $20 per share, 1 million shares currently outstanding). The company's income tax rate is 40 percent. (*a*) Calculate the indifference level of EBIT, or the break-even point for each plan, and (*b*) plot these two plans on the EBIT-EPS chart.

7. ABC System, Inc., plans to sell new shares of common stock at $35. The flotation cost is 10 percent. What is the cost of external equity? Both earnings and dividends are expected to grow at a constant rate of 6 percent and the annual dividend per share is $2.

8. Alta-Data, Inc., is considering an investment proposal. The company's board of directors indicated that the firm's present 70 percent owners' equity and 30 percent long-term debt structure should be maintained. The company's projected earnings accompanied by periodic common stock sales will permit it to maintain the present 70 percent owners' equity structure of 40 percentage points from retained earnings and 30 percentage points from common stock.

    After consultation with the firm's investment banker, the company has determined that the debt could be sold to yield 9 percent and new common stock could be sold to provide proceeds of $40 per share to the firm. The company is currently paying a dividend of $2 per share, and the dividends are expected to grow at a constant rate of 6 percent. The firm's income tax rate is 40 percent.

    Calculate the after-tax cost of capital that the company can use for its capital budgeting decision.

Answers to Examination II

I. **1.** T; **2.** F; **3.** F; **4.** F; **5.** T; **6.** T; **7.** T; **8.** F; **9.** T; **10.** F

II. **1.** (c); **2.** (a); **3.** (d); **4.** (c); **5.** (d); **6.** (a); **7.** (d); **8.** (d); **9.** (a); **10.** (c)

III.

1.

$$F_n = P \cdot FVIF_{i,n}$$
$$\$4.00 = \$2.15(FVIF_{i,8})$$
$$FVIF_{i,8} = \frac{\$4.00}{\$2.15} = 1.8605$$

From Appendix A, $FVIF_{8\%,8} = 1.8509$. Therefore, the firm's approximate rate of growth is 8 percent.

2.
$$PV = \$1,250(PVIFA_{12\%,10}) = \$1,250(5.6502) = \$7,062.75$$

3.
$$r = r_f + b(r_m - r_f)$$
$$= 5\% + 1.25(12\% - 5\%) = 5\% + 8.75\% = 13.75\%$$
$$P_0 = \frac{D_1}{r-g} = \frac{\$3}{13.75\% - 8\%} = \frac{\$3}{0.0575} = \$52.17$$

4. (a)
$$\text{Yield to maturity} = \frac{I + \frac{(M - V)}{n}}{\frac{(M + V)}{2}} = \frac{\$80 + (\$1,000 - \$960)/10}{(\$1,000 + \$960)/2}$$
$$= \frac{\$80 + \$4}{\$980} = 8.57\%$$

(b) After-tax cost of debt $= 8.57\% (1 - 0.4) = 5.14\%$

5. (a) NPV = PV − I and the profitability index is PV/I.

Project	Initial Cost (I) ($)	NPV ($)	Profitability Index (PI)
A	15,000	6,000	1.40
B	8,000	4,000	1.50
C	5,000	2,500	1.50
D	4,000	2,400	1.60
E	2,000	1,500	1.75
F	1,000	900	1.90

(b)

Project	I	PV	NPV	PI
A	$ 5,100	$21,000	$ 6,000	1.40
C	5,000	7,500	2,500	1.50
D	4,000	6,400	2,400	1.60
F	1,000	1,900	900	1.90
Totals	$25,000	$36,800	$11,800	

No combination within the $25,000 total budget constraint would show as much NPV as the one listed above. Note that project E is not included even though its 1.75 PI is higher than three of the included projects.

(c)

Project	I	PV	NPV	PI
B	$ 8,000	$12,000	$ 4,000	1.50
C	5,000	7,500	2,500	1.50
D	4,000	6,400	2,400	1.60
E	2,000	3,500	1,500	1.75
F	1,000	1,900	900	1.90
Totals	$20,000	$31,300	$11,300	

It is not necessary to use all the available $24,000 budget in order to maximize NPV. For example, two combinations that do use the entire $24,000 but which have lower NPV are shown below.

Project	I	PV	NPV	PI
A	$15,000	$21,000	$ 6,000	1.40
B	8,000	12,000	4,000	1.50
F	1,000	1,900	900	1.90
Totals	$24,000	$34,900	$10,900	

Project	I	PV	NPV	PI
A	$15,000	$21,000	$ 6,000	1.40
C	5,000	7,500	2,500	1.50
D	4,000	6,400	2,400	1.60
Totals	$24,000	$34,900	$10,900	

6. (a)

$$\frac{(\text{EBIT})(1-0.4)}{1,500,000} = \frac{(\text{EBIT} - \$900,000)(1-0.4)}{1,000,000}$$

$$\text{Break-even EBIT} = \$2,700,000$$

(b) See Fig. E-1.

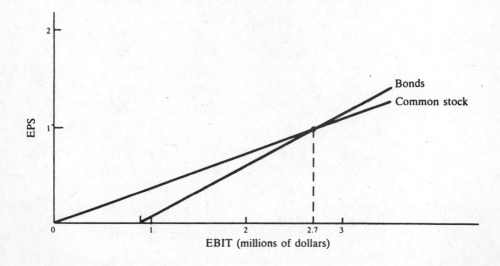

Fig. E-1

7.

$$k_e = \frac{D_1}{P_0(1-f)} + g$$

$$= \frac{\$2.00(1 + 0.06)}{\$35(1 - 0.1)} + 6\% = \frac{\$2.12}{\$31.5} + 6\% = 6.7\% + 6\% = 12.7\%$$

8.

$$\text{After-tax cost of debt} = 9\%(1 - 0.4) = 5.4\%$$

$$\text{Cost of new common stock} = \frac{D_1}{P_0} + g = \frac{\$2.00}{\$40} + 6\% = 11\%$$

$$\text{Cost of retained earnings} = \frac{\$2.00}{\$42} + 6\% = 10.76\%$$

Therefore, the after-tax cost of capital, or weighted average of individual capital component costs, is computed as follows:

	Weights	Weighted Average
Debt, 5.4%	0.3	1.62%
New common stock, 11%	0.4	4.4
Retained earnings, 10.76%	0.3	3.23
After-tax cost of capital		9.25%

Chapter 12

Dividend Policy

12.1 INTRODUCTION

Corporate earnings distributed to stockholders are called dividends. Dividends are paid in either cash or stock and are typically issued quarterly. They may be paid only out of retained earnings and not from invested capital such as capital stock or the excess received over stock par value. In general, the more stable a company's earnings, the more regular its issue of dividends.

A company's dividend policy is important for the following reasons:

1. It bears upon investor attitudes. For example, stockholders look unfavorably upon the corporation when dividends are cut, since they associate the cutback with corporate financial problems. Further, in setting a dividend policy, management must ascertain and fulfill the objectives of its owners. Otherwise, the stockholders may sell their shares, which in turn may bring down the market price of the stock. Stockholder dissatisfaction raises the possibility that control of the company may be seized by an outside group.

2. It impacts the financing program and capital budget of the firm.

3. It affects the firm's cash flow position. A company with a poor liquidity position may be forced to restrict its dividend payments.

4. It lowers stockholders' equity, since dividends are paid from retained earnings, and so results in a higher debt-to-equity ratio.

If a company's cash flows and investment requirements are volatile, the company should not establish a high regular dividend. It would be better to establish a low regular dividend that can be met even in years of poor earnings.

Relevant dates associated with dividends are as follows:

1. *Declaration date.* This is the date on which the board of directors declares the dividend. On this date, the payment of the dividend becomes a legal liability of the firm.

2. *Date of record.* This is the date upon which the stockholder is entitled to receive the dividend.

3. *Ex-dividend date.* The ex-dividend date is the date when the right to the dividend leaves the shares. The right to a dividend stays with the stock until 4 days before the date of record. That is, on the fourth day prior to the record date, the right to the dividend is no longer with the shares, and the seller, not the buyer of that stock, is the one who will receive the dividend. The market price of the stock reflects the fact that it has gone ex-dividend and will decrease by approximately the amount of the dividend.

EXAMPLE 12.1 The date of record for the dividend declared by the Acme Company is October 20. Harris sells Jones her 100 shares of Acme Company on October 18. Harris, not Jones, will receive the dividend on the shares.

4. *Date of payment.* This is the date when the company distributes its dividend checks to its stockholders.

Dividends are usually paid in cash. A cash dividend is typically expressed in dollars and cents per share. However, the dividend on preferred stock is sometimes expressed as a percentage of par value.

EXAMPLE 12.2 On November 15, 19X1, a cash dividend of $1.50 per share was declared on 10,000 shares of $10 par value common stock. The amount of the dividend paid by the company is $15,000 (10,000 × $1.50).

EXAMPLE 12.3 Jones Corporation has 20,000 shares of $10 par value, 12 percent preferred stock outstanding. On October 15, 19X1, a cash dividend was declared to holders of record as of December 15, 19X1. The amount of dividend to be paid by Jones Corporation is equal to:

$$20,000 \text{ shares} \times \$10 \text{ par value} = \$200,000 \times 12\% = \$24,000$$

Some companies allow stockholders to automatically reinvest their dividend in corporate shares instead of receiving cash. The advantage to the stockholder is that he or she avoids the brokerage fees associated with buying new shares. However, there is no tax advantage since the stockholder must still pay ordinary income taxes on the dividend received.

12.2 DIVIDEND POLICY

A finance manager's objective for the company's dividend policy is to maximize owner wealth while providing adequate financing for the company. When a company's earnings increase, management does not automatically raise the dividend. Generally, there is a time lag between increased earnings and the payment of a higher dividend. Only when management is confident that the increased earnings will be sustained will they increase the dividend. Once dividends are increased, they should continue to be paid at the higher rate. The various types of dividend policies are:

1. *Stable dividend-per-share policy.* Many companies use a stable dividend-per-share policy since it is looked upon favorably by investors. Dividend stability implies a low-risk company. Even in a year that the company shows a loss rather than profit the dividend should be maintained to avoid negative connotations to current and prospective investors. By continuing to pay the dividend, the shareholders are more apt to view the loss as temporary. Some stockholders rely on the receipt of stable dividends for income. A stable dividend policy is also necessary for a company to be placed on a list of securities in which financial institutions (pension funds, insurance companies) invest. Being on such a list provides greater marketability for corporate shares.

2. *Constant dividend-payout-ratio (dividend per share/earnings per share) policy.* With this policy a constant percentage of earnings is paid out in dividends. Because net income varies, dividends paid will also vary using this approach. The problem this policy causes is that if a company's earnings drop drastically or there is a loss, the dividends paid will be sharply curtailed or nonexistent. This policy will not maximize market price per share since most stockholders do not want variability in their dividend receipts.

3. *A compromise policy.* A compromise between the policies of a stable dollar amount and a percentage amount of dividends is for a company to pay a low dollar amount per share plus a percentage increment in good years. While this policy affords flexibility, it also creates uncertainty in the minds of investors as to the amount of dividends they are likely to receive. Stockholders generally do not like such uncertainty. However, the policy may be appropriate when earnings vary considerably over the years. The percentage, or extra, portion of the dividend should not be paid regularly; otherwise it becomes meaningless.

4. *Residual-dividend policy.* When a company's investment opportunities are not stable, management may want to consider a fluctuating dividend policy. With this kind of policy the amount of earnings retained depends upon the availability of investment opportunities in a particular year. Dividends paid represent the *residual* amount from earnings after the company's investment needs are fulfilled.

Theoretical Position

Theoretically, a company should retain earnings rather than distribute them when the corporate return exceeds the return investors can obtain on their money elsewhere. Further, if the company obtains a return on its profits that exceeds the cost of capital, the market price of its stock will be maximized.

Capital gains arising from the appreciation of the market price of stock has a tax advantage over dividends. On the other hand, a company should not, theoretically, keep funds for investment if it earns less of a return than what the investors can earn elsewhere. If the owners have better investment opportunities outside the firm, the company should pay a high dividend.

Although theoretical considerations from a financial point of view should be considered when setting dividend policy, the practicality of the situation is that investors expect to be paid dividends. Psychological factors come into play which may adversely affect the market price of the stock of a company that does not pay dividends.

12.3 FACTORS THAT INFLUENCE DIVIDEND POLICY

A firm's dividend policy is a function of many factors, some of which have been described. Other factors that influence dividend policy are as follows:

1. *Company growth rate.* A company that is rapidly growing, even if profitable, may have to restrict its dividend payments in order to keep needed funds within the company for growth opportunities.

2. *Restrictive covenants.* Sometimes there is a restriction in a credit agreement that will limit the amount of cash dividends that may be paid.

3. *Profitability.* Dividend distribution is keyed to the profitability of the company.

4. *Earnings stability.* A company with stable earnings is more likely to distribute a higher percentage of its earnings than one with unstable earnings.

5. *Maintenance of control.* Management that is reluctant to issue additional common stock because it does not wish to dilute its control of the firm will retain a greater percentage of its earnings. Internal financing enables control to be kept within.

6. *Degree of financial leverage.* A company with a high debt-to-equity ratio is more likely to retain earnings so that it will have the needed funds to meet interest payments and debts at maturity.

7. *Ability to finance externally.* A company that is capable of entering the capital markets easily can afford to have a higher dividend payout ratio. When there is a limitation to external sources of funds, more earnings will be retained for planned financial needs.

8. *Uncertainty.* Payment of dividends reduces the chance of uncertainty in stockholders' minds about the company's financial health.

9. *Age and size.* The age and size of the company bear upon its ease of access to capital markets.

10. *Tax penalties.* Possible tax penalties for excess accumulation of retained earnings may result in high dividend payouts.

Stockholder Tax Considerations

The answer to the question of which is preferred by stockholders—income from dividends or from capital gains (sale of stock)—depends on the individual stockholder's tax bracket. Capital gains arising from appreciation in market price is subject to a long-term capital gain deduction. Only 28 percent of the gain on the sale of stock that has been held more than one year is subject to taxation. Of course, a broker's commission will have to be paid on the sale. Dividends are considered ordinary income and are taxed at the full rate (less a $100 dividend exclusion). Taxpayers in low tax brackets or those who rely on a fixed income favor greater dividend distribution. The theoretical dispute regarding dividend policy relates to investor psychology in terms of whether earnings should be taken as capital gains or as dividends.

EXAMPLE 12.4 Ms. Smith is in the 45 percent tax bracket. She sells stock that she has held for more than one year at a gain of $50,000. Her tax computation on the sale follows:

Gain	$50,000
Capital gain deduction	×28%
Tax	$14,000

Controversy

The dividend policy controversy can best be described by presenting the approaches put forth by various authors:

1. Gordon et al. believe that cash flows of a company having a low dividend payout will be capitalized at a higher rate because investors will perceive capital gains resulting from earnings retention to be more risky than dividends.

2. Miller and Modigliani argue that a change in dividends impacts the price of the stock since investors will perceive such a change as being a statement about expected future earnings. They believe that investors are generally indifferent to a choice between dividends or capital gains.

3. Weston and Brigham et al. believe that the best dividend policy varies with the particular characteristics of the firm and its owners, depending on such factors as the tax bracket and income needs of stockholders, and corporate investment opportunities.

12.4 STOCK DIVIDENDS

A stock dividend is the issuance of additional shares of stock to stockholders. A stock dividend may be declared when the cash position of the firm is inadequate and/or when the firm wishes to prompt more trading of its stock by reducing its market price. With a stock dividend, retained earnings decrease but common stock and paid-in capital on common stock increase by the same total amount. A stock dividend, therefore, provides *no change* in stockholders' wealth. Stock dividends increase the shares held, but the proportion of the company each stockholder owns remains the same. In other words, if a stockholder has a 2 percent interest in the company before a stock dividend, he or she will continue to have a 2 percent interest after the stock dividend.

EXAMPLE 12.5 Mr. James owns 200 shares of Newland Corporation. There are 10,000 shares outstanding; therefore, Mr. James holds a 2 percent interest in the company. The company issues a stock dividend of 10 percent. Mr. James will then have 220 shares out of 11,000 shares issued. His proportionate interest remains at 2 percent (220/11,000).

12.5 STOCK SPLIT

A stock split involves issuing a substantial amount of additional shares and reducing the par value of the stock on a proportional basis. A stock split is often prompted by a desire to reduce the market price per share, which will make it easier for small investors to purchase shares.

EXAMPLE 12.6 Smith Corporation has 1,000 shares of $20 par value common stock outstanding. The total par value is $20,000. A 4-for-1 stock split is issued. After the split 4,000 shares at $5 par value will be outstanding. The total par value thus remains at $20,000. Theoretically, the market price per share of the stock should also drop to one-fourth of what it was before the split.

The differences between a stock dividend and a stock split are as follows:

(1) With a stock dividend, retained earnings are reduced and there is a pro rata distribution of shares to stockholders. A stock split increases the shares outstanding but does not lower retained earnings.

(2) The par value of stock remains the same with a stock dividend but is proportionally reduced in a stock split.

The similarities between a stock dividend and a stock split are:

(1) Cash is not paid.

(2) Shares outstanding increase.

(3) Stockholders' equity remains the same.

12.6 STOCK REPURCHASES

Treasury stock is the name given to previously issued stock that has been purchased by the company. Buying treasury stock is an alternative to paying dividends. Since outstanding shares will be fewer after stock has been repurchased, earnings per share will rise (assuming net income is held constant). The increase in earnings per share may result in a higher market price per share.

EXAMPLE 12.7   Travis Company earned $2.5 million in 19X1. Of this amount, it decided that 20 percent would be used to purchase treasury stock. At present there are 400,000 shares outstanding. Market price per share is $18. The company can use $500,000 (20% × $2.5 million) to buy back 25,000 shares through a tender offer of $20 per share.

Current earnings per share is:

$$\text{EPS} = \frac{\text{net income}}{\text{outstanding shares}} = \frac{\$2,500,000}{400,000} = \$6.25$$

The current P/E multiple is:

$$\frac{\text{Market price per share}}{\text{Earnings per share}} = \frac{\$18}{\$6.25} = 2.88 \text{ times}$$

Earnings per share after treasury stock is acquired becomes:

$$\frac{\$2,500,000}{375,000} = \$6.67$$

The expected market price, assuming the P/E ratio remains the same, is:

$$\text{P/E multiple} \times \text{new earnings per share} = \text{expected market price}$$
$$2.88 \times \$6.67 = \$19.21$$

To stockholders, the advantages arising from a stock repurchase include the following: (1) If market price per share goes up as a result of the repurchase, stockholders can take advantage of the capital gain deduction. This assumes the stock is held more than one year and is sold at a gain. (2) Stockholders have the option of selling or not selling the stock, while if a dividend is paid, stockholders must accept it and pay tax.

To the company, the advantages from a stock repurchase include the following:

(1) If there is excess cash flow that is deemed temporary, management may prefer to repurchase stock than to pay a higher dividend that they feel cannot be maintained.

(2) Treasury stock can be used for future acquisitions or used as a basis for stock options.

(3) If management is holding stock, they would favor a stock repurchase rather than a dividend because of the favorable tax treatment.

(4)   Treasury stock can be resold in the market if additional funds are needed.

To stockholders, the disadvantages of treasury stock acquisitions include the following:

(1)   The market price of stock may benefit more from a dividend than a stock repurchase.

(2)   Treasury stock may be bought at an excessively high price to the detriment of the remaining stockholders. A higher price may occur when share activity is limited or when a significant amount of shares are reacquired.

To management, the disadvantages of treasury stock acquisition include the following:

(1)   If investors feel that the company is engaging in a repurchase plan because its management does not have alternative good investment opportunities, a drop in the market price of stock may ensue.

(2)   If the reacquisition of stock makes it appear that the company is manipulating the price of its stock on the market, the company will have problems with the Securities and Exchange Commission (SEC). Further, if the Internal Revenue Service (IRS) concludes that the repurchase is designed to avoid the payment of tax on dividends, tax penalties may be imposed because of the improper accumulation of earnings as specified in the tax code.

Review Questions

1.   The basic types of dividends are _____ and _____ .

2.   Dividends are usually issued _____ .

3.   The date that a dividend becomes a legal liability of the corporation is called the _____ .

4.   The right to a dividend stays with the stock until _____ days before the date of record.

5.   The receipt of dividends is favored by stockholders in _____ tax brackets.

6.   The dividend payout ratio is equal to _____ divided by _____ .

7.   Under a residual-dividend policy, dividends are paid _____ the firm's investment needs have been satisfied.

8.   A stock dividend provides _____ real income for investors.

9.   Mr. X owned 100 shares of $10 par value stock. He then received in exchange 200 shares of $5 par value stock. This is referred to as a(n) _____ .

10.   _____ refers to shares reacquired by the company.

Answers: (1) cash, stock; (2) quarterly; (3) declaration date; (4) 4; (5) lower; (6) dividends per share, earnings per share; (7) after; (8) no; (9) stock split; (10) Treasury stock.

Solved Problems

12.1 **Dividends per Share.** Lakeside Corporation's net income for 19X1 was $300,000. It retained 40 percent. The outstanding shares are 100,000. Determine the dividends per share.

SOLUTION

$$\frac{\text{Dividends}}{\text{Shares}} = \frac{\$300,000 \times 60\%}{100,000 \text{ shares}} = \frac{\$180,000}{100,000} = \$1.80$$

12.2 **Cash Dividend.** The Dover Corporation has 10,000 shares of common stock outstanding. On March 5, the company declared a cash dividend of $5 per share payable to stockholders of record on April 5. What is the amount of the dividend?

SOLUTION

$$10,000 \times \$5 = \$50,000$$

12.3 **Tax.** Ms. Jones is in the 35 percent tax bracket. How much tax will she have to pay in each of the following cases?
(*a*)   Dividend income = $10,000
(*b*)   Long-term capital gain = $10,000

SOLUTION

(*a*) $10,000 − $100 (dividend exclusion) = $9,900 × 35% = $3,465
(*b*) $10,000 × 40% (capital gain rate) = $4,000 taxable × 35% = $1,400

12.4 **Dividend Policy.** Robert Corporation pays out 70 percent of its earnings in the form of dividends.

(*a*) Evaluate this policy assuming most stockholders are senior citizens in low tax brackets.

(*b*) Evaluate this policy assuming most stockholders are in high tax brackets.

SOLUTION

(*a*) A high dividend payout is appropriate in the case of senior citizens since they rely on the fixed income. Because they are in a low tax bracket, capital gains will not help them that much.

(*b*) A low dividend payout is called for with high-tax-bracket stockholders. Dividends serve as ordinary income. Capital gain is most beneficial for them since only 28 percent of the gain is taxable for securities held more than one year.

12.5 **Market Price per Share.** Company A and company B are identical in every respect except for their dividend policies. Company A pays out a constant percentage of its net income (60 percent dividends), while company B pays out a constant dollar dividend. Company B's market price per share is higher than that of company A. The financial manager of company A does not understand why her market price per share is lower even though in some good years company A's dividends exceed those of company B. Explain.

SOLUTION

The reason why company B has a higher market price per share than company A is because the stock market looks favorably upon stable dollar dividends. They reflect less uncertainty about the firm.

12.6   **External Equity to be Issued.** Travis Company's net income for the year was $3 million. It pays out 30 percent of its earnings in dividends. The company will acquire $5 million in new assets of which 35 percent will be financed by debt. What is the amount of external equity that must be issued?

SOLUTION

Net income	$3,000,000
Percent of net income retained	×0.7
Retained earnings	$2,100,000
New assets	$5,000,000
Percent financed by equity	×0.65
Equity financing required	$3,250,000
Retained earnings	2,100,000
External equity to be issued	$1,150,000

12.7   **Dividend Payout.** Most Corporation had a net income of $800,000 in 19X1. Earnings have grown at an 8 percent annual rate. Dividends in 19X1 were $300,000. In 19X2, the net income was $1,100,000. This, of course, was much higher than the typical 8 percent annual growth rate. It is anticipated that earnings will go back to the 8 percent rate in future years. The investment in 19X2 was $700,000.

How much dividend should be paid in 19X2 assuming: (*a*) a stable dividend payout ratio of 25 percent? (*b*) a stable dollar dividend policy is maintained? (*c*) a residual-dividend policy is maintained and 40 percent of the 19X2 investment is financed with debt? (*d*) the investment for 19X2 is to be financed with 80 percent debt and 20 percent retained earnings? Any net income not invested is paid out in dividends.

SOLUTION

(*a*)
$$\$1,100,000 \times 25\% = \$275,000$$

(*b*)   Dividend in 19X2 is:

$$\$300,000 \times 1.08 = \$324,000$$

(*c*)   The equity needed is:

$$\$700,000 \times 60\% = \$420,000$$

Because net income is greater than the equity needed, all the $420,000 of equity investment will be derived from net income.

$$\text{Dividend} = \$1,100,000 - \$420,000 = \$680,000$$

(*d*)
$$\text{Earnings retained} = \$700,000 \times 20\% = \$140,000$$

$$\text{Dividend} = \text{net income} - \text{earnings retained}$$
$$\$960,000 = \$1,100,000 - \$140,000$$

12.8   **Trend in Dividends.** Many corporations attempt to maintain a sustained rather than a fluctuating cash dividend per share payment. The payment is gradually adjusted to changes in earnings over time. As a consequence, corporations apparently establish a target payout ratio range. Explain why corporation managements desire sustained cash dividends per share with an increasing trend and attempt to avoid fluctuating cash dividend payments. (CMA, adapted.)

SOLUTION

Corporations tend to follow a policy of sustained cash dividends per share with an increasing and stable trend over time because they believe that such a dividend policy helps maintain or increase the firm's common stock price over time. Corporations following this policy feel that investors will pay a higher price for the stock of a firm with a stable dividend policy because stability provides investors with a reduced level of uncertainty regarding the cash returns provided by the firm.

Another argument for a stable dividend policy leading to higher stock price is that many investors look at cash dividends as a source of funds for their living expenses. Such investors cannot easily plan their income when dividends are fluctuating. Thus, to assist their planning, investors will pay a premium for stock with stable dividend policies.

12.9   Dividend Payout. The Xylon Company has experienced rapid growth in the past 5 years. In order to finance the growth, the board of directors has followed a policy of controlled borrowing, a low dividend payout ratio, and regular stock dividends.

The percent of debt in the capital structure has remained constant since 19X0. The funds generated from operations have been reinvested in productive assets. Each January, for the past 4 years, Xylon's board of directors has declared and paid a 10 percent dividend. A $0.20 per share cash dividend on the stock outstanding on June 15 has been paid each July for the past 5 years. Management estimates that the earnings for 19X7 will be $250,000. The closing price of Xylon Company's stock at November 30, 19X7 was $25.50 per share.

The board anticipates a challenge to its intention to continue this dividend policy by two stockholders who are survivors of two of the founders. Selected data related to the company's earnings and dividends are presented below:

Year	Earnings ($)	Shares Outstanding as of Dec. 31	Cash Dividends Per Share ($)	Cash Dividends Total Payout ($)	Market Price per Share as of Dec. 31 ($)
19X2	100,000	100,000	0.20	20,000	10.00
19X3	120,000	110,000	0.20	22,000	12.00
19X4	144,000	121,000	0.20	24,200	14.30
19X5	172,800	133,100	0.20	26,620	17.00
19X6	207,360	146,410	0.20	29,282	22.00

Prepare a response from the perspective of Xylon Company's board of directors which (*a*) justifies the low cash dividend payout, and (*b*) rationalizes the use of stock dividends. (CMA, adapted.)

SOLUTION

(*a*)   The low cash dividend payout is required to finance from internal sources investment opportunities which exceed the cost of capital in order to continue the income and market value growth pattern established. Financing growth through retained earnings has been good for the company and the stockholders, as demonstrated by the increased earnings per share, the increased market price per share, and the increase in total cash dividends paid because of the annual stock dividends.

(*b*)   The continued use of stock dividends allows stockholders who need cash to sell a few shares without reducing the original number of shares owned. In addition, those sales can be taxed at the capital gains rate as opposed to ordinary income rates. This may be important to the shareholders of this company because they are wealthy and likely to be in high tax brackets. The use of stock dividends increases the payout in future years even though the dividend rate per share does not increase.

12.10   Stock Dividend. The Benson Corporation has 9,000 shares of common stock having a par value of $120 outstanding. A 10 percent stock dividend is declared. The fair market value of the stock is $124 per share.

(a) By how much will retained earnings be reduced? (b) What is the par value of the common stock to be issued? (c) What is the paid-in capital on common stock?

SOLUTION

(a)   9,000 shares × 10% = 900 shares × $124 = $111,600

(b)   900 shares × $120 = $108,000

(c)   900 shares × $4 = $3,600

12.11 Reformulated Capital Structure. Blake Company's capital structure on December 30, 19X1, was:

Common stock ($1 par, 100,000 shares)	$100,000
Paid-in capital on common stock	20,000
Retained earnings	680,000
Total stockholders' equity	$800,000

The company's net income for 19X1 was $150,000. It paid out 40 percent of earnings in dividends. The stock was selling at $6 per share on December 30.

Assuming the company declared a 5 percent stock dividend on December 31, what is the reformulated capital structure on December 31?

SOLUTION

The stock dividend is 5,000 shares (5% × 100,000 shares). Retained earnings is reduced by the fair market value of the stock dividend of $30,000 ($6 × 5,000 shares), paid-in capital on common stock is increased by $25,000 ($5 × 5,000 shares), and common stock is increased at the par value of the shares issued of $5,000 ($1 × 5,000 shares).

The reformulated capital structure on December 31 is:

Common stock ($100,000 − $5,000)	$105,000
Paid-in capital on common stock ($20,000 + $25,000)	45,000
Retained earnings ($680,000 − $30,000)	650,000
	$800,000

Notice that after the stock dividend, total stockholders' equity remains the same.

12.12 Stock Split. The Simpson Company has 50,000 shares of common stock having a par value of $12 per share. The board of directors decided on a 2-for-1 stock split. The market price of the stock was $20 before the split.

(a) Record the stock split. (b) What will the market price per share be immediately after the split?

SOLUTION

(a) No entry is needed since the company's account balances remain the same. However, there should be a memorandum to the effect that there are now 100,000 shares having a par value of $6 per share.

(b) $10 ($20/2)

12.13 Dividend Last Year. Subsequent to a 3-for-1 stock split, Ace Corporation paid a dividend of $5 per share. This was a 10 percent increase over the prior year's dividend (before the split). Determine the dividend for last year.

SOLUTION

Dividend subsequent to split is: $5 \times 3 = \$15$. Last year's dividend is:

$$\frac{\$15}{1.10} = \$13.64$$

12.14 Earnings per Share. Blake Company's net income for 19X2 was $3 million. Of this amount, 40 percent will be used to purchase treasury stock. Currently, there are 1 million shares outstanding and the market price per share is $9.

(*a*) How many shares can the company buy back through a tender offer of $12 a share? (*b*) What is the current earnings per share? (*c*) What is the current P/E ratio? (*d*) What will earnings per share be after the treasury stock acquisition? (*e*) What is the expected market price per share assuming the present P/E ratio remains the same?

SOLUTION

(*a*)   Funds available for repurchase of stock are computed as follows:

$$\$3 \text{ million} \times 40\% = \$1,200,000$$

Shares to be repurchased are computed as follows:

$$\frac{\$1,200,000}{\$12} = 100,000 \text{ shares}$$

(*b*)
$$\text{EPS} = \frac{\text{net income}}{\text{shares outstanding}} = \frac{\$3,000,000}{1,000,000} = \$3$$

(*c*)
$$\text{P/E ratio} = \frac{\text{market price per share}}{\text{earnings per share}} = \frac{\$9}{\$3} = 3 \text{ times}$$

(*d*)
$$\text{EPS} = \frac{\$3,000,000}{900,000} = \$3.333$$

(*e*)
$$\text{Market price per share} = \text{P/E ratio} \times \text{new EPS}$$
$$3 \times \$3.333 = \$10$$

Chapter 13

Term Loans and Leasing

13.1 INTERMEDIATE-TERM BANK LOANS

Intermediate-term loans are loans with a maturity of more than 1 year. Intermediate-term loans are appropriate when short-term unsecured loans are not, such as when a business is acquired. The interest rate on an intermediate-term loan is generally higher than on a short-term loan because of the longer maturity date. The interest rate may be either fixed or variable (according to, for example, changes in the prime interest rate). The cost of an intermediate-term loan varies with the amount of the loan and the financial strength of the borrower.

Ordinary intermediate-term loans are payable in periodic equal installments except for the last payment, which may be higher (referred to as a balloon payment). The schedule of loan payments should be based on the borrower's cash flow position to satisfy the debt.

The amortization payment in a term loan equals:

$$\text{Amortization payment} = \frac{\text{amount of loan}}{\text{present value factor}}$$

EXAMPLE 13.1 XYZ Company contracts to repay a term loan in five equal year-end installments. The amount of the loan is $150,000 and the interest rate is 10 percent. The amortization payment each year is:

$$\text{Amortization payment} = \frac{\text{amount of loan}}{\text{present value factor}} = \frac{\$150,000}{3.7908^a} = \$39,569.48$$

^{a}Present value of annuity for 5 years at 10 percent.

EXAMPLE 13.2 Charles Company takes out a term loan in 20 year-end annual installments of $2,000 each. The interest rate is 12 percent. The amount of the loan is:

$$\text{Amortization payment} = \frac{\text{amount of loan}}{\text{present value factor}}$$

$$\$2,000 = \frac{\text{amount of loan}}{7.4694^a}$$

$$\text{Amount of loan} = \$2,000 \times 7.4694 = \$14,938.80$$

^{a}Present value of annuity for 20 years at 12 percent.

The amortization schedule for the first 2 years is:

Year	Payment	Interest^a	Principal	Balance
0				$14,938.80
1	$2,000	$1,792.66	S207.34	$14,731.46
2	$2,000	$1,767.78	$232.22	$14,499.24

^{a}12 percent times the balance of the loan at the beginning of the year.

Revolving credit, typically used for seasonal financing, may have a 3-year maturity, but the notes evidencing the revolving credit are short-term, typically 90 days. The advantages of revolving credit are flexibility and readily available credit. Within the time period of the revolving credit agreement, the company may renew a loan or engage in additional financing up to a specified maximum amount.

Compared to a line of credit arrangement, there are generally fewer restrictions on revolving credit but at the cost of a slightly higher interest rate.

Restrictive provisions to protect the lender in an intermediate-term loan agreement may be in the form of:

1. General provisions used in most agreements which vary depending upon the borrower's situation. Examples are working capital and cash dividend requirements.

2. Routine (uniform) provisions that are used universally in most agreements. Examples are the payment of taxes and the maintenance of proper insurance to assure maximum lender protection.

3. Specific provisions that are tailored to a given situation. Examples are the placing of limits on future loans and the carrying of adequate life insurance for executives.

The advantages of intermediate-term loans are:

1. Flexibility in that the terms may be altered as the financing requirements of the company change.

2. Financial information of the company is kept confidential, since no public issuance is involved.

3. The loan may be arranged quickly, compared to a public offering.

4. It avoids the possible nonrenewal of a short-term loan.

5. Public flotation costs are not involved.

The disadvantages of intermediate-term loans are:

1. Collateral and possible restrictive covenants are required, as opposed to none for commercial paper and unsecured short-term bank loans.

2. Budgets and financial statements may have to be submitted periodically to the lender.

3. "Kickers," or "sweeteners," such as stock warrants or a share of the profits are sometimes requested by the bank.

13.2 INSURANCE COMPANY TERM LOANS

Insurance companies and other institutional lenders may extend intermediate-term loans to companies. Insurance companies generally accept loan maturity dates exceeding 10 years, but their rate of interest is often higher than that of bank loans. Insurance companies do not require compensating balances, but usually there is a prepayment penalty involved, which is typically not the case with a bank loan. A company may take out an insurance company loan when it desires a longer maturity range.

13.3 EQUIPMENT FINANCING

Equipment may serve as collateral for a loan. An advance is made against the market value of the equipment. The more marketable the equipment is, the higher the advance will be. Also considered is the cost of selling the equipment. The repayment schedule is designed so that the market value of the equipment at any given time exceeds the unpaid principal balance of the loan.

Equipment financing may be obtained from banks, finance companies, and manufacturers of equipment. Equipment loans may be secured by a chattel mortgage or a conditional sales contract. A chattel mortgage serves as a lien on property except for real estate. In a conditional sales contract, the seller of the equipment keeps title to it until the buyer has satisfied all the agreed terms; otherwise the seller will repossess the equipment. The buyer makes periodic payments to the seller over a specified time period. A conditional sales contract is generally used by small companies with low credit ratings.

13.4 LEASING

The parties involved in a lease are the *lessor*, who legally owns the property, and the *lessee*, who uses it in exchange for making rental payments.

The following types of leases exist:

1. *Operating (service) lease.* This type of lease includes both financing and maintenance services. The lessee leases property that is owned by the lessor. The lessor may be the manufacturer of the asset or it may be a leasing company that buys assets from the manufacturer to lease to others. The lease payments required under the contract are generally not sufficient to recover the full cost of the property. There usually exists a cancelation clause that provides the lessee with the right to cancel the contract and return the property prior to the expiration date of the agreement.

2. *Financial lease.* This type of lease does not typically provide for maintenance services, is noncancelable, and the rental payments equal the full price of the leased property.

3. *Sale and lease-back.* With this lease arrangement, a company sells an asset it owns to another company (usually a financial institution) and then leases it back. This allows the firm to obtain needed cash from the sale and still have the property for its use.

4. *Leveraged lease.* In a leveraged lease, there is a third party who serves as the lender. Here, the lessor borrows money from the lender in order to buy the asset. The property is then leased to the lessee.

Leasing has several advantages, including the following:

1. Immediate cash outlay is not required.

2. Typically, a purchase option exists, permitting the lessee to obtain the property at a bargain price at the expiration of the lease. This provides the lessee with the flexibility to make the purchase decision based on the value of the property at the termination date.

3. The lessor's expert service is made available.

4. There are generally fewer financing restrictions (e.g., limitations on dividends) placed on the lessee by the lessor than are imposed when obtaining a loan to buy the asset.

5. The obligation for future rental payment may not have to be reported on the balance sheet.

6. Leasing allows the lessee, in effect, to depreciate land, which is not allowed if land is purchased.

7. In bankruptcy or reorganization, the maximum claim of lessors against the company is 3 years of lease payments. In the case of debt, creditors have a claim for the total amount of the unpaid financing.

8. The lessee may avoid having the obsolescence risk of the property if the lessor, in determining the lease payments, fails to accurately estimate the obsolescence of the asset.

There are several drawbacks to leasing, including the following:

1. A higher cost in the long run than if the asset is purchased.

2. The interest cost associated with leasing is typically higher than the interest cost on debt.

3. If the property reverts to the lessor at termination of the lease, the lessee must either sign a new lease or buy the property at higher current prices. Also, the salvage value of the property is realized by the lessor.

4. The lessee may have to retain property no longer needed (i.e., obsolete equipment).

5. The lessee cannot make improvements to the leased property without the permission of the lessor.

An operating lease is cancelable by the lessee or lessor. The lessee's accounting entry each year is to debit rental expense and credit cash. In a capital lease, the lessee acquires the property in *substance* but not in legal form. According to the Financial Accounting Standards Board (FASB) Statement No. 13, a capital lease exists when any *one* of the following four criteria are met:

1. The lessee obtains title to the property at the end of the lease.
2. There is a bargain purchase option.
3. The lease term equals 75 percent or more of the life of the property.
4. The present value of future minimum rental payments equals or exceeds 90 percent of the fair market value of the property at the inception of the lease.

With a capital lease, the lessee records the leased asset and related obligation on the books at the present value of the future minimum rental payments. In determining the present value of future rental payments, the discount factor to be used is the lower of the lessor's implicit rate or the lessee's incremental borrowing rate. As each rental payment is made, the liability is debited for the principal amount of the payment and interest expense is charged for the interest portion. Since, in theory, the lessee has acquired the property, he or she will depreciate the asset. The recognition of an asset and long-term liability provides a balance sheet that more appropriately reflects the company's financial position and hence allows for more meaningful ratio analysis.

EXAMPLE 13.3 Smith Corporation leased property under a 6-year lease requiring equal year-end annual payments of $20,000. The lessee's incremental borrowing rate is 12 percent.

At the date of lease, the lessee would report an asset and liability at:

$$\$20,000 \times 4.41114^a = \$82,228$$

> ^{a}PVIFA$_{12,6}$ = present value of
> annuity for 6 years at 12 percent.

An amortization schedule for the first 2 years follows:

Year	Payment	Interest^a	Principal	Balance
0				$82,228
1	$20,000	$9,867	$10,133	$72,095
2	$20,000	$8,651	$11,349	$60,746

> ^{a} 12 percent times present value of the liability at the beginning of
> the year.

The lessee can determine the periodic rental payments to be made under the lease by dividing the value of the leased property by the present value factor associated with the future rental payments.

EXAMPLE 13.4 Wilder Corporation enters into a lease for a $100,000 machine. It is to make 10 equal annual payments at year-end. The interest rate on the lease is 14 percent.

The periodic payment equals:

$$\frac{\$100,000}{5.2161^a} = \$19,171.41$$

> ^{a}The present value of an
> ordinary annuity factor for
> $n = 10$, $i = 14\%$ is 5.2161.

EXAMPLE 13.5 Assume the same facts as in Example 13.5, except that now the annual payments are to be made at the beginning of each year.

The periodic payment equals:

Year	Factor
0	1.0
1–9	4.9464
	5.9464

$$\frac{\$100,000}{5.9464} = \$16,816.90$$

The interest rate associated with a lease agreement can also be computed. Divide the value of the leased property by the annual payment to obtain the factor, which is then used to find the interest rate with the help of an annuity table.

EXAMPLE 13.6 Harris Corporation leased $300,000 of property and is to make equal annual payments at year-end of $40,000 for 11 years. The interest rate associated with the lease agreement is:

$$\frac{\$300,000}{\$40,000} = 7.5$$

Going to the present value of annuity table in Appendix D and looking across 11 years to a factor closest to 7.5, we find 7.4987 at a 7 percent interest rate. Therefore, the interest rate in the lease agreement is 7 percent.

The capitalized value of a lease can be found by dividing the annual lease payment by an appropriate present value of annuity factor.

EXAMPLE 13.7 Property is to be leased for 8 years at an annual rental payment of $140,000 payable at the beginning of each year. The capitalization rate is 12 percent. The capitalized value of the lease is:

$$\frac{\text{Annual lease payment}}{\text{Present value factor}} = \frac{\$140,000}{1 + 4.5638} = \$25,162.66$$

Lease-Purchase Decision

Often a decision must be made as to whether it is better to purchase an asset or lease it. Present value analysis may be used to determine the cheapest alternative. This topic was treated in Chapter 8, "Capital Budgeting Including Leasing."

Review Questions

1. Intermediate-term financing applies to a period greater than _____ .

2. The interest rate on an intermediate-term loan is typically _____ than on a short-term loan.

3. The interest rate may be either _____ or _____ .

4. When the last payment on a loan is higher than the prior periodic installments it is referred to as a(n) _____ payment.

5. In a revolving credit arrangement, the notes evidencing the debt are _____ .

6. Restrictive provisions in a loan agreement that vary, based on the borrower's situation, are referred to as _____ provisions.

7. A restriction in a loan agreement that puts a limitation on the borrower's future loans is referred to as a(n) _____ provision.

8. A chattel mortgage has a lien against property except for _____ .

9. In a(n) _____, the seller of equipment retains title until the purchaser has met the terms of the contract.

10. In a(n) _____ lease, there is a third party who acts as the lender.

11. When a company sells an asset it owns and then leases it back, this is referred to as a(n) _____ arrangement.

12. In an operating lease, the entry each year is to debit _____ and credit _____ .

13. In a(n) _____ lease, the lessee records the leased property on his or her books as an asset at the _____ of future minimum rental payments.

14. One of the criteria for a capital lease is that the lease term equals or exceeds _____ of the life of the property.

15. The lessor can pass the _____ on to the lessee.

Answers: (1) 1 year; (2) higher; (3) fixed, variable; (4) balloon; (5) short-term; (6) general; (7) specific; (8) real estate; (9) conditional sales contract; (10) leveraged; (11) sale and lease-back; (12) rent expense, cash; (13) capital, present value; (14) 75 percent; (15) investment tax credit.

Solved Problems

13.1 Intermediate-Term Loans. What are the advantages and disadvantages to intermediate-term loans?

SOLUTION

The advantages of intermediate-term loans are as follows:

1. Flexibility exists regarding terms, since they may be modified based on the changing financial condition of the entity.
2. No public disclosure of the company's financial data is required.
3. The loan may be obtained quickly relative to a public issuance.

The disadvantages of intermediate-term loans are as follows:

1. The company may have to put up collateral.
2. Budgets and financial statements may have to be periodically submitted to the lender.
3. There is a specified maturity date for repayment.
4. The company may have to give the bank "sweeteners" for the loan, such as a share of its net income.

13.2 Amortization Payment. ABC Company agrees to pay a $50,000 loan in eight equal year-end payments. The interest rate is 12 percent.

(a) What is the annual payment? (b) What is the total interest on the loan?

SOLUTION

(a) $$\text{Amortization payment} = \frac{\text{amount of loan}}{\text{present value factor}} = \frac{\$50,000}{4.9676} = \$10,065.22$$

(b)

Total payments (8 × $10,065.22)	$80,521.76
Principal	50,000.00
Interest	$30,521.76

13.3 Amount of Loan. Bank Corporation takes out a term loan payable in five year-end annual installments of $3,000 each. The interest rate is 10 percent. What is the amount of the loan?

SOLUTION

$$\$3,000 \times 3.7908 = \$11,372.40$$

13.4 Amortization Schedule. Using the data in Problem 13.3: (a) prepare an amortization schedule for the loan repayment; and (b) explain why the interest is declining over the loan period.

SOLUTION

(a)

Year	Payment ($)	Interest ($)	Principal ($)	Balance ($)
0				11,372.40
1	3,000	1,137.24	1,862.76	9,509.64
2	3,000	950.96	2,049.04	7,460.60
3	3,000	746.06	2,253.94	5,206.66
4	3,000	520.67	2,479.33	2,727.33
5	3,000	272.73	2,727.33[a]	

[a] Adjusted for slight rounding difference.

(b) Interest is declining because the balance of the loan decreases over time.

13.5 Leasing. What are the advantages and disadvantages of leasing?

SOLUTION

The advantages of leasing include the following:

1. It is not necessary to pay out cash immediately.
2. The lease contract often provides a bargain purchase option that permits the lessee to buy the property for a nominal sum at the lease termination date.
3. Typically, the service technology of the lessor is made available.

4. There are generally fewer financing restrictions set out by the lessor relative to those imposed under other modes of financing.

5. In an operating lease, the lessee does not have to report a liability on his or her books.

The disadvantages of leasing include the following:

1. In the long run, the cost of leasing is higher than the cost of buying.

2. If the lessor receives the property at the end of the lease, the lessee must either enter into a new lease agreement or purchase the property at high current prices.

3. The lessee may have to keep obsolete property.

13.6   Periodic Payment. Bard Corporation leases a $75,000 machine. It is required to make 15 equal annual payments at year-end. The interest rate on the lease is 16 percent. What is the periodic payment?

SOLUTION

$$\frac{\$75,000}{5.575} = \$13,452.91$$

13.7   Periodic Payment. Assume the same information as in Problem 13.6, except that now the annual payments are to be made at the beginning of the year. What is the periodic payment?

SOLUTION

$$\frac{\$75,000}{1 + 5.468} = \frac{\$75,000}{6.468} = \$11,595.55$$

13.8   Interest Rate. Tint Corporation leased $150,000 of equipment and is to make equal year-end annual payments of $22,000 for 15 years. What is the interest rate on the lease?

SOLUTION

$$\frac{\$150,000}{\$22,000} = 6.818$$

Going to the present value of annuity table in Appendix D and looking across 15 years to a factor closest to 6.818, we find 6.811 at a 12 percent interest rate.

13.9   Capitalized Value of Lease. Property is to be leased for 15 years at an annual rental payment of $40,000 payable at the beginning of each year. The capitalization rate is 10 percent. What is the capitalized value of the lease?

SOLUTION

$$\frac{\text{Annual lease payment}}{\text{Present value factor}} = \frac{\$40,000}{1 + 7.3667} = \$4,780.86$$

Chapter 14

Long-term Debt

14.1 INTRODUCTION

This chapter discusses the characteristics, advantages, and disadvantages of long-term debt financing. In addition to the various types of debt instruments, the circumstances in which a particular form of debt is most appropriate are mentioned. Bond refunding is also highlighted.

In formulating a financing strategy in terms of source and amount, consider the following:

1. The cost and risk associated with alternative financing strategies.
2. The future trend in capital market conditions and how they will affect future fund availability and interest rates.
3. The existing ratio of debt to equity.
4. The maturity dates of present debt instruments.
5. The existing restrictions in loan agreements.
6. The type and amount of collateral required by long-term creditors.
7. The ability to alter financing strategy to adjust to changing economic conditions.
8. The amount, nature, and stability of internally generated funds.
9. The adequacy of present lines of credit for current and future needs.
10. The inflation rate, since with debt the repayment is made in cheaper dollars.
11. The earning power and liquidity position of the firm.
12. The tax rate.

Sources of long-term debt include mortgages and bonds.

14.2 MORTGAGES

Mortgages represent notes payable that have as collateral real assets and require periodic payments. Mortgages can be issued to finance the acquisition of assets, construction of plant, and modernization of facilities. The bank will require that the value of the property exceed the mortgage on that property. Most mortgage loans are for between 70 percent and 90 percent of the value of the collateral. Mortgages may be obtained from a bank, life insurance company, or other financial institution. It is easier to obtain mortgage loans for multiple-use real assets than for single-use real assets.

There are two kinds of mortgages: a *senior* mortgage, which has first claim on assets and earnings, and a *junior* mortgage, which has a subordinate lien.

A mortgage may have a closed-end provision that prevents the firm from issuing additional debt of the same priority against the same property. If the mortgage is open-ended, the company can issue additional first-mortgage bonds against the property.

Mortgages have a number of advantages, including favorable interest rates, less financing restrictions, and extended maturity date for loan repayment.

14.3 BONDS PAYABLE

Long-term debt principally takes the form of bonds payable and loans payable. A bond is a certificate indicating that the company has borrowed a given sum of money that it agrees to repay at a future date. A written agreement, called an *indenture*, describes the features of the particular bond issue. The indenture is a contract between the company, the bondholder, and the trustee. The trustee makes sure that the company is meeting the terms of the bond contract. In many cases, the trustee is the trust department of a commercial bank. Although the trustee is an agent for the bondholder, it is selected by the company prior to the issuance of the bonds. The indenture provides for certain restrictions on the company such as a limitation on dividends and minimum working capital requirements. If a provision of the indenture is violated, the bonds are in default. The indenture may also have a negative pledge clause, which precludes the issuance of new debt that would take priority over existing debt in the event the company is liquidated. The clause can apply to assets currently held as well as to assets that may be purchased in the future.

Interest

Bonds are issued in $1,000 denominations. Many bonds have maturities of 10 to 30 years. The interest payment to the bondholder is called *nominal interest*, which is the interest on the face of the bond. It is equal to the coupon (nominal) interest rate times the face value of the bond. Although the interest rate is stated on an annual basis, interest on a bond is usually paid semiannually. Interest expense is tax-deductible.

EXAMPLE 14.1   A company issues a 20 percent, 20-year bond. The tax rate is 46 percent. The annual after-tax cost of the debt is:

$$20\% \times 54\% = 10.8\%$$

EXAMPLE 14.2   A company issues a $100,000, 12 percent, 10-year bond. The semiannual interest payment is:

$$\$100,000 \times 12\% \times \tfrac{6}{12} = \$6,000$$

Assuming a tax rate of 30 percent, the after-tax semiannual interest dollar amount is:

$$\$6,000 \times 70\% = \$4,200$$

A bond sold at face value is said to be sold at 100. If a bond is sold below its face value, it is being sold at less than 100 and is issued at a discount. If a bond is sold above face value, it is being sold at more than 100, that is, sold at a premium. A bond may be sold at a discount when the interest rate on the bond is below the prevailing market interest rate for that type of security. A bond is sold at a premium when the opposite market conditions exist. The discount or premium is amortized over the life of the bond. The amortized discount is a tax-deductible expense, while the amortized premium is income subject to tax.

Bond issue costs, also a tax-deductible expense, must also be amortized over the life of the bond.

EXAMPLE 14.3   Travis Corporation issues a $100,000, 14 percent, 20-year bond at 94. The maturity value of the bond is $100,000. Annual cash interest payment is:

$$14\% \times \$100,000 = \$14,000$$

The proceeds received for the issuance of the bond is:

$$94\% \times \$100,000 = \$94,000$$

The amount of the discount is:

$$\$100,000 - \$94,000 = \$6,000$$

The annual discount amortization is:

$$\frac{\$6,000}{20} = \$300$$

EXAMPLE 14.4 A bond having a face value of $100,000 with a 25-year life was sold at 102. The tax rate is 40 percent. The bond was sold at a premium since it was issued above face value. The total premium is $2,000 ($100,000 × 0.02). The annual premium amortization is $80 ($2,000/25). The after-tax effect of the premium amortization is $48 ($80 × 60%).

The yield on a bond is the effective interest rate the company is incurring on that bond. The two methods of computing yield are the simple yield and the yield to maturity. These were fully discussed in Chapter 7.

The price of a bond depends on several factors such as its maturity date, interest rate, and collateral.

EXAMPLE 14.5 Harris Corporation's 6 percent income bonds are due in 19X5 and are selling at $855. The company's $5\frac{1}{2}$% first-mortgage bonds are due in 19X0 and are selling at $950. The first-mortgage bonds which have a lower interest rate compared to the income bonds are selling at a higher price because (1) the bonds are closer to maturity, and (2) the bonds are backed by collateral.

Also, interest is not paid on the income bonds unless there are corporate earnings. This makes them unattractive and hence they will be selling at a lower price.

Types of Bonds

The various types of bonds that may be issued are:

1. *Debentures.* Because debentures represent unsecured debt, they can be issued only by large, financially strong companies with excellent credit ratings.

2. *Subordinated debentures.* The claims of the holders of these bonds are subordinated to those of senior creditors. Debt having a prior claim over the subordinated debentures is set forth in the bond indenture. Typically, in the event of liquidation, subordinated debentures come after short-term debt.

3. *Mortgage bonds.* These are bonds secured by real assets.

4. *Collateral trust bonds.* The collateral for these bonds is the issuer's security investments (bonds or stocks), which are given to a trustee for safekeeping.

5. *Convertible bonds.* These may be converted to stock at a later date based on a specified conversion ratio. Convertible bonds are typically issued in the form of subordinated debentures. Convertible bonds are more marketable and are typically issued at a lower interest rate than are regular bonds. Of course, if bonds are converted to stock, debt repayment is not involved. Convertible bonds are discussed in detail in Chapter 16, "Warrants and Convertibles."

6. *Income bonds.* These bonds require the payment of interest only if the issuer has earnings. However, since interest accumulates regardless of earnings, the interest, if bypassed, must be paid in a later year when sufficient earnings exist.

7. *Guaranteed bonds.* These are debt issued by one party with payment guaranteed by another party.

8. *Serial bonds.* A specified portion of these bonds comes due each year. At the time serial bonds are issued, a schedule is given showing the yields, interest rates, and prices applicable with each maturity. The interest rate on the shorter maturities is lower than the interest rate on the longer maturities. Serial bonds are primarily issued by government agencies.

Bond Ratings

Financial advisory services (e.g., Standard and Poor's, and Moody's) rate publicly traded bonds according to risk in terms of the receipt of principal and interest. An inverse relationship exists between the quality of a bond issue and its yield. That is, low-quality bonds will have a higher yield than high-quality bonds. Thus, a risk-return trade-off exists for the bondholder. Bond ratings are important to financial management because they influence marketability and the cost associated with the bond issue.

EXAMPLE 14.6 The following bond ratings are used by Moody's and Standard & Poor's:

Moody's		Standard & Poor's	
Aaa	Prime quality	AAA	Bank investment quality
Aa	High quality	AA	
A	Upper medium grade	A	
Baa	Medium grade	BBB	
Ba	Lower medium grade	BB	Speculative
B	Speculative	B	
Caa, Ca	Very speculative to near or in default	CCC	
C	Lowest grade	CC	
		C	Income bond
		DDD	Bond is in default
		DD	
		D	

14.4 DEBT FINANCING

The advantages of issuing long-term debt include:

1. Interest is tax-deductible, while dividends are not.
2. Bondholders do not participate in superior earnings of the firm.
3. The repayment of debt is in cheaper dollars during inflation.
4. There is no dilution of company control.
5. Financing flexibility can be achieved by including a call provision in the bond indenture. A call provision allows the company to pay the debt before the expiration date of the bond.
6. It may safeguard the company's future financial stability, for example, in times of tight money markets when short-term loans are not available.

The disadvantages of issuing long-term debt include:

1. Interest charges must be met regardless of corporate earnings.
2. Debt must be repaid at maturity.
3. Higher debt infers greater risk in the capital structure, which may increase the cost of capital.
4. Indenture provisions may place stringent restrictions on the company.
5. Overcommitments may arise due to forecasting errors.

To investors, bonds have the following advantages:

1. There is a fixed interest payment each year.
2. Bonds are safer than equity securities.

To investors, bonds have the following disadvantages:

1. They do not participate in incremental profitability.
2. There is no voting right.

The proper mixture of long-term debt to equity in a company depends on the type of organization, credit availability, and after-tax cost of financing. Where a high degree of financial leverage exists, the firm may wish to take steps to minimize other corporate risks.

Debt financing is more appropriate when:

1. Stability in revenue and earnings exists.
2. There is a satisfactory profit margin.
3. There is a good liquidity and cash flow position.
4. The debt/equity ratio is low.
5. Stock prices are currently depressed.
6. Control considerations are a primary factor.
7. Inflation is expected.
8. Bond indenture restrictions are not burdensome.

An entity experiencing financial difficulties may wish to refinance short-term debt on a long-term basis such as by extending the maturity dates of existing loans. This may alleviate current liquidity and cash flow problems.

As the default risk of the firm becomes higher, so the interest rate will become high on the debt to compensate for the greater risk.

EXAMPLE 14.7 Ari Corporation has $10 million of 12 percent mortgage bonds outstanding. The indenture permits additional bonds to be issued provided all the following conditions are satisfied:

1. The pretax times-interest-earned ratio exceeds 5.
2. Book value of the mortgaged assets are at least 1.5 times the amount of debt.
3. The debt/equity ratio is below 0.6.

The following additional information is provided:

1. Income before tax is $9 million.
2. Equity is $30 million.
3. Book value of assets is $34 million.
4. There are no sinking fund payments for the current year. (A sinking fund is money set aside to be used to retire a bond issue.)
5. Half the proceeds of a new issue would be added to the base of mortgaged assets.

Only $7 million more of 12 percent debt can be issued based on the following calculations:

1. The before-tax times-interest-earned ratio is:

$$\frac{\text{Income before tax and interest}}{\text{Interest}} = \frac{\$9,000,000 + \$1,200,000^a}{\$1,200,000 + 0.12X} = 5$$

$$\frac{\$10,200,000}{\$1,200,000 + 0.12X} = 5$$

$$\$10,200,000 = \$6,000,000 + 0.60X$$

$$X = \$7,000,000$$

---

^{a}Interest is:

$$\$10,000,000 \times 0.12 = \$1,200,000$$

2.
$$\frac{\text{Book value of mortgaged assets}}{\text{Debt}} = \frac{\$34,000,000 + 0.5X}{\$10,000,000 + X} = 1.5$$

$$\$34,000,000 + 0.5X = \$15,000,000 + 1.5X$$

$$X = \$19,000,000$$

3.
$$\frac{\text{Debt}}{\text{Equity}} = \frac{\$10,000,000 + X}{\$30,000,000} = 0.6$$

$$\$10,000,000 + X = \$18,000,000$$

$$X = \$8,000,000$$

The first condition is controlling and hence limits the amount of new debt to \$7 million.

14.5 BOND REFUNDING

Bonds may be refunded by the company prior to maturity through either the issuance of a serial bond or exercising a call privilege on a straight bond. The issuance of serial bonds allows the company to refund the debt over the life of the issue. A call feature in a bond enables the issuer to retire it before the expiration date. The call feature is included in many corporate bond issues.

When future interest rates are anticipated to decline, a call provision in the bond issue is recommended. Such a provision enables the firm to buy back the higher-interest bond and issue a lower-interest one. The timing for the refunding depends on expected future interest rates. A call price is usually established in excess of the face value of the bond. The resulting call *premium* equals the difference between the call price and the maturity value. The issuer pays the premium to the bondholder in order to acquire the outstanding bonds before the maturity date. The call premium is generally equal to 1 year's interest if the bond is called in the first year, and it declines at a constant rate each year thereafter. Also involved in selling a new issue are flotation costs. Both the call premium and flotation costs are tax-deductible expenses.

A bond with a call provision typically will be issued at an interest rate higher than one without the call provision. The investor prefers not to have a situation where the company can buy back the bond at its option prior to maturity. This is because the company will tend to buy back high-interest bonds early and issue lower-interest bonds when interest rates decline. The investor would obviously want to hold onto a high-interest bond when prevailing interest rates are low.

EXAMPLE 14.8 A \$100,000, 10 percent, 20-year bond is issued at 95. The call price is 102. Four years after issue the bond is called. The call premium is equal to:

Call price	\$102,000
Face value of bond	100,000
Call premium	\$ 2,000

EXAMPLE 14.9 A \$40,000 callable bond was issued. The call price is 104. The tax rate is 35 percent. The after-tax cost of calling the issue is:

$$\$40,000 \times 0.04 \times 0.65 = \$1,040$$

The desirability of refunding a bond requires present value analysis. The present value technique was discussed in Chapter 8, "Capital Budgeting."

EXAMPLE 14.10 Tracy Corporation has a \$20 million, 10 percent bond issue outstanding that has 10 years to maturity. The call premium is 7 percent of face value. New 10-year bonds in the amount of \$20 million can be issued at an 8 percent interest rate. Flotation costs associated with the new issue are \$600,000.

Refunding of the original bond issue should take place as shown below.

Old interest payments ($20,000,000 × 0.10)	$2,000,000
New interest payments ($20,000,000 × 0.08)	1,600,000
Annual savings	$ 400,000

Call premium ($20,000,000 × 0.07)	$1,400,000
Flotation cost	600,000
Total cost	$2,000,000

Year	Calculation	Present Value
Year 0	−$2,000,000 × 1	−$2,000,000
Years 1–10	$ 400,000 × 6.71[a]	+2,684,000
Net present value		$ 684,000

---

[a] Present value of annuity factor for $i = 8\%$, $n = 10$.

EXAMPLE 14.11 Ace Corporation is considering calling a $10 million, 20-year bond that was issued 5 years ago at a nominal interest rate of 10 percent. The call price on the bonds is 105. The bonds were initially sold at 90. The discount on bonds payable at the time of sale was, therefore, $1 million and the net proceeds received were $9 million. The initial flotation cost was $100,000. The firm is considering issuing $10 million, 8 percent, 15-year bonds and using the net proceeds to retire the old bonds. The new bonds will be issued at face value. The flotation cost for the new issue is $150,000. The company's tax rate is 46 percent. The after-tax cost of new debt ignoring flotation costs, is 4.32 percent ($8\% \times 54\%$). With the flotation cost, the after-tax cost of new debt is estimated at 5 percent. There is an overlap period of 3 months in which interest must be paid on the old and new bonds.

The initial cash outlay is:

Cost to call old bonds ($10,000,000 × 105%)	$10,500,000
Cost to issue new bond	150,000
Interest on old bonds for overlap period ($10,000,000 × 10% × 3/12)	250,000
Initial cash outlay	$10,900,000

The initial cash inflow is:

Proceeds from selling new bond		$10,000,000
Tax-deductible items		
Call premium	$500,000	
Unamortized discount ($1,000,000 × 15/20	750,000	
Overlap in interest ($10,000,000 × 10% × 3/12)	250,000	
Unamortized issue cost of old bond ($100,000 × 15/20)	75,000	
Total tax-deductible items	$1,575,000	
Tax rate	×0.46	
Tax savings		724,500
Initial cash inflow		$10,724,500

The *net* initial cash outlay is therefore:

Initial cash outlay	$10,900,000
Initial cash inflow	10,724,500
Net initial cash outlay	$ 175,500

The annual cash flow for the old bond is:

Interest (10% × $10,000,000)		$1,000,000
Less: Tax-deductible items		
Interest	$1,000,000	
Amortization of discount ($1,000,000/20 years)	50,000	
Amortization of issue cost ($100,000/20 years)	5,000	
Total tax-deductible items	$1,055,000	
Tax rate	×0.46	
Tax savings		485,300
Annual cash outflow with old bond		$ 514,700

The annual cash flow for the new bond is:

Interest		$800,000
Less: Tax-deductible items		
Interest	$800,000	
Amortization of issue cost ($150,000/15 years)	10,000	
Total tax-deductible items	$810,000	
Tax rate	×0.46	
Tax savings		372,600
Annual cash outflow with new bond		$427,400

The net annual cash savings with the new bond compared to the old bond is:

Annual cash outflow with old bond	$514,700
Annual cash outflow with new bond	427,400
Net annual cash savings	$ 87,300

The net present value associated with the refunding is:

	Calculation	Present Value
Year 0	−$175,500 × 1	−$175,500
Years 1–15	$87,300 × 10.38[a]	+906,174
Net present value		$730,674

---

[a] Present value of annuity factor for $i = 5\%$, $n = 15$.

Since a positive net present value exists, the refunding of the old bond should be made.

Sinking fund requirements may exist with regard to a bond issue. With a sinking fund, the company is required to set aside money to purchase and retire a portion of the bond issue each year. Usually, there is a mandatory fixed amount that must be retired, but occasionally the retirement may relate to the company's sales or profit for the current year. If a sinking fund payment is not made, the bond issue may be in default.

In many cases, the company can handle the sinking fund in one of the following two ways:

1. It can call a given percentage of the bonds at a stipulated price each year, for example, 5 percent of the original amount at a price of $1,080.

2. It can buy its own bonds on the open market.

The least expensive alternative should be selected. If interest rates have increased, the price of the bonds will have decreased, and the open market option should be used. If interest rates have decreased, the bond prices will have increased, and so calling the bonds is the preferred choice.

EXAMPLE 14.12　XYZ Company has to reduce bonds payable by $300,000. The call price is 104. The market price of the bonds is 103. The company will elect to buy back the bonds on the open market because it is less expensive, as indicated below.

Call price ($300,000 × 104%)	$312,000
Purchase on open market ($300,000 × 103%)	309,000
Advantage of purchasing bonds on the open market	$ 3,000

Review Questions

1. A(n) _____ mortgage prohibits the company from issuing further debt of the same priority against the property.

2. A(n) _____ is the written agreement specifying the terms of a bond issue.

3. A(n) _____ clause in a bond agreement prevents the issuance of new debt having priority over existing debt.

4. Bonds are stated in $_____ denominations.

5. The interest payment based on the face value of a bond is called _____ interest.

6. As the maturity date of a bond lengthens, the interest rate _____ .

7. When a bond is sold at an amount in excess of its face value, it is sold at a(n) _____ .

8. A(n) _____ is an unsecured bond.

9. A(n) _____ bond pays interest only if the issuer has earnings.

10. Bond issues that mature periodically are called _____ bonds.

11. The issuance of bonds has an advantage in _____ times in that the company will be paying back the debt in _____ dollars.

12. A(n) _____ provision enables the firm to buy back bonds at a date prior to maturity.

13. _____ is tax-deductible, whereas dividends are not.

Answers: (1) closed-end; (2) indenture; (3) negative pledge; (4) 1,000; (5) nominal; (6) increases; (7) premium; (8) debenture; (9) income; (10) serial; (11) inflationary, cheaper; (12) call; (13) Interest.

Solved Problems

14.1 **Interest.** A company issues a $300,000, 10 percent, 20-year bond. The tax rate is 40 percent. What is the after-tax semiannual interest dollar amount?

SOLUTION

$$\$300,000 \times 10\% \times \tfrac{6}{12} = \$15,000 \text{ (before taxes)}$$
$$\$15,000 \times 60\% = \$9,000 \text{ (after taxes)}$$

14.2 **Bond Issuance.** Boxer Corporation issues a $300,000, 16 percent, 10-year bond at 108.

(*a*) What is the maturity value? (*b*) What is the annual cash interest payment? (*c*) What are the proceeds the company receives upon issuance of the bond? (*d*) What is the amount of the premium? (*e*) What is the annual premium amortization?

SOLUTION

(*a*) $300,000

(*b*) $$16\% \times \$300,000 = \$48,000$$

(*c*) $$108\% \times \$300,000 = \$324,000$$

(*d*) $$\$324,000 - \$300,000 = \$24,000$$

(*e*) $$\frac{\$24,000}{10} = \$2,400$$

14.3 **Amortization.** A bond with a face value of $200,000 with a 20-year life was sold at 105. The tax rate is 35 percent. What is the after-tax effect of the premium amortization?

SOLUTION

Total premium is:

$$\$200,000 \times 0.05 = \$10,000$$

Annual premium amortization is:

$$\frac{\$10,000}{20} = \$500$$

After-tax effect of premium amortization is:

$$\$500 \times 0.65 = \$325$$

14.4   Bond Ratings. Match the description in column A with Moody's bond rating in column B.

	Column A		Column B
(a)	Speculative	(1)	C
(b)	Prime quality	(2)	Aaa
(c)	Lowest grade	(3)	Ba
(d)	Lower medium grade	(4)	B
(e)	Near or in default	(5)	Ca

SOLUTION

(a) (4); (b) (2); (c) (1); (d) (3); (e) (5).

14.5   Bond Rating. The two bond rating agencies, Moody's and Standard & Poor's, lowered the ratings on Appleton Industries' bonds from triple-A to double-A in response to operating trends revealed by the financial reports of recent years. The change in the ratings is of considerable concern to the Appleton management because the company plans to seek a significant amount of external financing within the next 2 years.

(a) Identify several events or circumstances which could have occurred in the operations of Appleton Industries which could have influenced the factors the bond rating agencies use to evaluate the firm and, as a result, caused the bond rating agencies to lower Appleton's bond rating. (b) If Appleton Industries maintains its present capital structure, what effect will the lower bond ratings have on the company's weighted average cost of capital? Explain your answer. (c) If Appleton Industries' capital structure was at an optimal level before the rating of its bonds was changed, explain what effect the lower bond ratings will have on the company's optimal capital structure. (CMA, adapted.)

SOLUTION

(a) Factors or circumstances which could have caused the rating agencies to lower the bond rating of Appleton Industries include:

1. Lowered long-term solvency reflected by a reduction in the times-interest-earned ratio or a reduction in the fixed-charge-coverage ratio

2. Lowered short-term liquidity reflected by a decrease in the current or quick ratios

3. Lowered profitability reflected by a reduced market share, lower return on sales, or decreased profits

4. An increased risk of financial stability due to major pending litigation which would be damaging to the firm or a large increase in earnings variability

5. A major change in management which is perceived negatively by the financial community

(b) The weighted average cost of capital can be expected to rise. The lower bond rating is usually relied upon as an indication of greater risk being assumed by the bond investors. This change will be noted by the investors of other Appleton securities. Thus the investors in each capital component of Appleton Industries can be expected to require a higher return.

(c) Appleton Industries' capital structure will shift toward greater equity with less debt. The fact that the bond rating was lowered would indicate to investors that the risk has increased. To reduce the risk and minimize the increase in the cost of capital, the optimal capital structure will have to shift toward one with an increased percentage of equity.

14.6   Amount of Debt. Boston Corporation has $30 million of 10 percent mortgage bonds outstanding. The indenture allows the issuance of additional bonds provided the following conditions are met: (1) The before-tax times-interest-earned ratio exceeds 4; (2) book value of the mortgaged assets is at least two times the amount of debt; and (3) the debt/equity ratio is less than 0.5.

The following additional data are provided: (1) Income before tax is $11 million; (2) equity is $90 million; (3) book value of mortgaged assets is $80 million; and (4) forty percent of the proceeds of a new issue would be added to the base of mortgaged assets.

How much additional debt can be issued?

SOLUTION

The before-tax times-interest-earned ratio is:

$$\frac{\text{Income before tax and interest}}{\text{Interest}} = \frac{\$11,000,000 + \$3,000,000^a}{\$3,000,000 + 0.10X} = 4$$

$$\frac{\$14,000,000}{\$3,000,000 + 0.10X} = 4$$

$$\$14,000,000 = \$12,000,000 + 0.40X$$

$$X = \$5,000,000$$

^{a} Interest $30,000,000 \times 0.10 = \$3,000,000$.

The book value of the mortgaged assets is:

$$\frac{\text{Book value of mortgaged assets}}{\text{Debt}} = \frac{\$80,000,000 + 0.4X}{\$30,000,000 + X} = 2$$

$$\$80,000,000 + 0.4X = \$60,000,000 + 2X$$

$$X = \$12,500,000$$

The debt/equity ratio is:

$$\frac{\text{Debt}}{\text{Equity}} = \frac{\$30,000,000 + X}{\$90,000,000} = 0.5$$

$$\$30,000,000 - X = \$45,000,000$$

$$X = \$15,000,000$$

The first condition is controlling and thus limits the amount of new debt to $5 million.

14.7   Call Premium. Mider Corporation issued a $100,000, 14 percent, 15-year bond at 98. The call price is 104. Seven years after issue the bond is called. What is the call premium?

SOLUTION

Call price	$104,000
Face value of bond	100,000
Call premium	$ 4,000

14.8   After-Tax Cost of Call. A $30,000 callable bond was issued. The call price is 105. The tax rate is 46 percent. What is the after-tax cost of calling the issue?

SOLUTION

$$\$30,000 \times 0.05 \times 0.54 = \$810$$

14.9   Bond Refunding. Smith Corporation has a $40 million, 14 percent bond issue outstanding, with 15 years remaining. The call premium is 8 percent of face value. A new 15-year bond issue for $40 million can be issued at a 10 percent interest rate. Flotation costs applicable to the new issue are $350,000. Should Smith Corporation call the original bond issue?

SOLUTION

Old interest payments ($40,000,000 × 0.14)		$5,600,000
New interest payments ($40,000,000 × 0.10)		4,000,000
Annual savings		$1,600,000
Call premium ($40,000,000 × 0.08)		$3,200,000
Flotation cost		350,000
Total cost		$3,550,000

	Calculations	Present Value
Year 0	−$3,550,000 × 1	−$ 3,550,000
Years 1–15	1,600,000 × 7.6061[a]	+12,169,760
Net present value		$ 8,619,760

---

[a] Present value of annuity factor for $i = 10\%$, $n = 15$.

The company should retire the original bond issue because doing so results in a positive net present value.

14.10 Bond Refunding. Jones Corporation is considering calling a $20 million, 30-year bond that was issued 10 years ago at a face interest rate of 14 percent. The call price on the bonds is 104. The bonds were initially sold at 97. The initial flotation cost was $200,000. The company is considering issuing $20 million, 12 percent, 20-year bonds in order to net proceeds and retire the old bonds. The new bonds will be issued at face value. The flotation costs for the new issue are $225,000. The tax rate is 46 percent. The after-tax cost of new debt ignoring flotation costs is 6.48 percent (12% × 54%). With flotation costs, the after-tax cost of new debt is anticipated to be 7 percent. There is a 2-month overlap in which interest must be paid on the old bonds and new bonds. Should refunding take place?

SOLUTION

The initial cash outlay is:

Cost to call old bonds ($20,000,000 × 104%)	$20,800,000
Cost to issue new bond	225,000
Interest on old bonds for overlap period ($20,000,000 × 14% × 2/12)	466,667
Initial cash outlay	$21,491,667

The initial cash inflow is:

Proceeds from selling new bond		$20,000,000
Tax-deductible items		
Call premium	$ 800,000	
Unamortized discount		
($600,000 × 20/30)	400,000	
Unamortized issue cost of old bond		
($200,000 × 20/30)	133,333	
Overlap in interest		
($20,000,000 × 14% × 2/12)	466,667	
Total tax-deductible items	$1,800,000	
Tax rate	×0.46	
Tax savings		828,000
Initial cash inflow		$20,828,000

The *net* initial cash outlay is therefore:

Initial cash outlay	$21,491,667
Initial cash inflow	20,828,000
Net initial cash outlay	$ 663,667

The annual cash flow for the old bond is:

Interest (14% × $20,000,000)		$2,800,000
Less: Tax-deductible items		
Interest	$2,800,000	
Amortization of discount		
($600,000/30 years)	20,000	
Amortization of issue cost		
($200,000/30 years)	6,667	
Total tax-deductible items	$2,826,667	
Tax rate	×0.46	
Tax savings		1,300,267
Annual cash outflow with old bond		$1,499,733

The annual cash flow for the new bond is:

Interest (12% × $20,000,000)		$2,400,000
Less: Tax-deductible items		
Interest	$2,400,000	
Amortization of issue cost		
($225,000/20 years)	11,250	
Total tax-deductible items	$2,411,250	
Tax rate	×0.46	
Tax savings		1,109,175
Annual cash outflow with new bond		$1,290,825

The net annual cash saving with the new bond compared to the old bond is:

Annual cash outflow with old bond	$1,499,733
Annual cash outflow with new bond	1,290,825
Net annual cash savings	$ 208,908

The net present value associated with the refunding is:

	Calculations	**Present Value**
Year 0	$-\$663,667 \times 1$	$-\$$ 663,667
Years 1–20	$\$208,908 \times 10.59^{a}$	$+2,212,336$
Net present value		$\$1,548,669$

^{a}Present value of annuity factor for $i = 7\%$, $n = 20$.

Since a positive net present value exists, the refunding should take place.

14.11 Purchase of Bonds on the Open Market. Drifter Company has to reduce bonds payable by $500,000. The call price of its bonds is 103. The market price of the bonds is 101. Should the bonds be called or bought back on the open market?

SOLUTION

Call price ($500,000 × 103%)	$515,000
Purchase on open market ($500,000 × 101%)	505,000
Advantage of purchasing bonds on the open market	$ 10,000

The bonds should be bought back.

Chapter 15

Preferred and Common Stock

15.1 INTRODUCTION

This chapter discusses equity financing. The advantages and disadvantages of issuing preferred and common stock are addressed, along with the various circumstances in which either financing source is most suited. Stock rights are also described. Consideration is given to the advantages and disadvantages of public versus private placement, or sale. Also discussed is the role of the investment banker.

15.2 INVESTMENT BANKING

Investment banking involves public flotation, or sale, of a security issue. Investment bankers perform the following functions:

1. *Underwriting.* The investment banker buys a new security issue, pays the issuer, and markets the securities. The underwriter's compensation is the difference between the price at which the securities are sold to the public, and the price paid to the company for the securities.

2. *Distributing.* The investment banker markets the security issue.

3. *Giving advice.* The investment banker provides valuable advice to the company concerning the best way to raise funds. The investment banker is familiar with the various sources of long-term funds, debt and equity markets, and Securities and Exchange Commission (SEC) regulations.

4. *Providing funds.* The investment banker furnishes funds to the issuing company during the distribution period.

When a number of investment bankers get together as a group because a particular issue is large and/or risky, they are referred to as a *syndicate*. A syndicate is a temporary association of investment bankers brought together for the purpose of selling new securities. One investment banker among the group will be selected to manage the syndicate. The investment banker so selected is called the *originating house*, which underwrites the major amount of the issue. One bid price for the issue is made on behalf of the group, but the terms and features of the issue are established by the company.

There are two types of underwriting syndicates, divided and undivided. In a *divided* account, the liability of each member investment banker is limited in terms of participation. Once a member sells the securities assigned, that investment banker has no additional liability regardless of whether the other members are able to sell their portion of the security or not. In an *undivided* account, each member is liable for unsold securities up to the amount of its percentage participation irrespective of the number of securities that investment banker has sold. Most syndicates are based on the undivided account arrangement.

In another approach to investment banking, the investment banker agrees to sell the securities on a best-efforts basis, or as an agent for the company. Here, the investment banker does not serve as underwriter but rather sells the stock and receives a commission on the sale. An investment banker may insist on this type of arrangement when he or she has reservations about the success of the security offering in the market.

Besides investment bankers, there are firms that specialize in more specific financial functions with regard to stock. A *dealer* buys securities and holds them in inventory for later resale, expecting to make a profit on the spread. The *spread* is the price appreciation of the securities. A *broker* receives and forwards purchase orders for securities to the applicable stock exchange or over-the-counter market. The broker is compensated with a commission on each sale.

15.3 PUBLIC VERSUS PRIVATE PLACEMENT OF SECURITIES

Equity and debt securities may be issued either publicly or privately. A consideration in determining whether to issue securities publicly or privately is the type and amount of the needed financing.

In a public issuance, the shares are bought by the general public. In a private placement, the company issues the securities directly to either one or a few large investors. The large investors involved are financial institutions such as insurance companies, pension funds, and commercial banks.

Private placement has the following advantages, when compared to a public issuance:

1. The flotation cost is less. Flotation cost is the expense of registering and selling the stock issue. Examples are brokerage commissions and underwriting fees. The flotation cost for common stock exceeds that for preferred stock. Flotation cost expressed as a percentage of gross proceeds is higher for smaller issues than for larger ones.

2. It avoids SEC filing requirements.

3. It avoids the disclosure of information to the public at large.

4. There is less time involved in obtaining funds.

5. It may not be practical to issue securities in the public market when a company is so small that an investment banker would not find it profitable.

6. The company's credit rating may be low, and as a consequence investors may not be interested in buying securities when the money supply is limited.

Private placement has the following disadvantages, when compared to a public issuance:

1. It is more difficult to obtain significant amounts of money privately compared to publicly.

2. Large investors usually employ stringent credit standards requiring the company to be in a strong financial position.

3. Large institutional investors may watch more closely the company's activities than smaller investors in a public issue.

4. Large institutional investors are more capable of obtaining voting control of the company.

15.4 PREFERRED STOCK

Preferred stock may be issued when the cost of common stock is high. The best time to issue preferred stock is when the company has excessive financial leverage and an issue of common stock might create control problems for the owners. Many utilities offer preferred stock. Preferred stock is a more expensive way to raise capital than a bond issue because the dividend payment is not tax-deductible.

Preferred stock may be cumulative or noncumulative. *Cumulative* preferred stock means that if any previous year's dividend payments have been missed, they must be paid before dividends can be paid to common stockholders. If preferred dividends are in arrears for a long period of time, a company may find it difficult to resume its dividend payments to common stockholders. With *noncumulative* preferred stock, the company need not pay missed preferred dividends. Preferred stock dividends are limited to the rate specified, which is based on the total par value of the outstanding shares.

EXAMPLE 15.1 As of December 31, 19X6, Ace Company has 6,000 shares of $15 par value, 14 percent, cumulative preferred stock outstanding. Dividends have not been paid in 19X4 and 19X5. Assuming the company has been profitable in 19X6, the amount of the dividend to be distributed is:

Par value of stock = 6,000 shares × $15 = $90,000

Dividends in arrears	
($90,000 × 14% × 2 years)	$25,200
Current year dividend ($90,000 × 14%)	12,600
Total dividend	$37,800

Participating preferred stock means that if declared dividends exceed the amount normally given to preferred stockholders and common stockholders, the preferred and common stockholders will participate in the excess dividends. Unless stated otherwise, the distribution of the excess dividends will be based on the relative total par values.

EXAMPLE 15.2   Boston Corporation has the following equity securities outstanding:

Preferred stock, participating—10,000 shares, $10 par value, 12% dividend rate	$100,000
Common stock—4,000 shares, $20 par value	$ 80,000

The dividend rate declared on the common stock is 10 percent. If the dividends declared for the year are $25,000, the amounts assigned to preferred stock and to common stock are:

	Preferred Stock	Common Stock
Regular dividend		
Preferred (12% × $100,000)	$12,000	
Common (10% × $80,000)		$ 8,000
Excess dividend—allocation based on relative par value		
Preferred [($100,000/$180,000) × $5,000]	2,778	
Common [($80,000/$180,000) × $5,000]		2,222
Total dividend	$14,778	$10,222

Preferred stock may be callable, which means that the company can buy it back at a later date at a specified call price. The call provision is advantageous when interest rates decline, since the company has the option of discontinuing payment of dividends at a rate that has become excessive by buying back preferred stock that was issued when bond interest rates were high. Unlike bonds, preferred stock rarely has a maturity date associated with it. However, if preferred stock has a sinking fund associated with it, this, in effect, establishes a maturity date for repayment.

In the event of corporate bankruptcy, preferred stockholders are paid after creditors and before common stockholders. In such a case, preferred stockholders receive the par value of their shares, dividends in arrears, and the current year's dividend. Any asset balance then goes to the common stockholders.

The cost of preferred stock can be determined by dividing the dividend payment by the net proceeds received.

EXAMPLE 15.3   Blick Corporation sells preferred stock amounting to $2 million. The flotation cost is 11 percent of gross proceeds. The dividend rate is 14 percent. The effective cost of the preferred stock is:

$$\frac{\text{Dividend}}{\text{Net proceeds}} = \frac{0.14 \times \$2,000,000}{\$2,000,000 - (0.11 \times \$2,000,000)} = \frac{\$280,000}{\$1,780,000} = 15.7\%$$

The company should estimate the amount it will receive per share and the number of shares it must sell in order to finance the business.

EXAMPLE 15.4   Brady Corporation is considering expanding its operations. It anticipates a need for $5 million to finance the expansion through the issuance of preferred stock. The preferred stock has a par value of $100 and a dividend rate of 10 percent. Similar issues, of preferred stock are currently providing a yield of 12 percent.

For each share, the company will receive:

$$\frac{\text{Dividend}}{\text{Market yield}} = \frac{0.10 \times \$100}{0.12} = \frac{\$10}{0.12} = \$83.33$$

The amount of shares that must be issued is:

$$\frac{\text{Funds required}}{\text{Price per share}} = \frac{\$5,000,000}{\$83.33} = 60,002 \text{ shares (rounded)}$$

To a company, a preferred stock issue has the following advantages:

1. Preferred dividends do not have to be paid, whereas interest on debt must be paid.
2. Preferred stockholders cannot force the company into bankruptcy.
3. Preferred shareholders do not share in unusually high profits of the company.
4. A growth company can generate better earnings for its original owners by issuing preferred stock having a fixed dividend rate than by issuing common stock.
5. Preferred stock issuance does not dilute the ownership interest of common stockholders in terms of earnings participation and voting rights.
6. The company does not have to collateralize its assets as it may have to do if bonds are issued.

To a company, a preferred stock has the following disadvantages:

1. Preferred stock requires a higher yield than bonds.
2. Preferred dividends are not tax-deductible.

To an investor, a preferred stock offers the following advantages:

1. Preferred stock usually provides a constant return in the form of a fixed dividend payment.
2. Preferred stockholders come before common stockholders in the event of corporate bankruptcy.
3. Preferred dividends are subject to an 85 percent dividend exclusion for *corporate* investors. For example, if a company holds preferred stock in another company and receives dividends of $10,000, only 15 percent (or $1,500) is taxable. On the other hand, interest income received on bonds is fully taxable. The *individual* investor does not qualify for the 85 percent dividend exclusion.

To an investor, the disadvantages of a preferred stock are:

1. The return is limited because of the fixed dividend rate.
2. There is greater price fluctuation with preferred stock than with bonds because of the nonexistence of a maturity date.
3. Preferred stockholders cannot require the company to pay dividends if the firm has inadequate earnings.

15.5   COMMON STOCK

The owners of a corporation are called stockholders. They elect the board of directors, who in turn select the officers of the firm. When the election occurs, management sends proxy statements, which ask stockholders to give management the right to vote their stock. Effective control of the corporation can exist with less than 50 percent common stock ownership since many stockholders do not bother to vote. Stockholders have limited liability in that they are not personally liable for the debts of the company.

Authorized shares represent the maximum amount of stock the company can issue according to the corporate charter. *Issued shares* represent the number of authorized shares which have been sold by the firm. *Outstanding shares* are the issued shares actually being held by the investing public. *Treasury stock* is stock that has been reacquired by the firm. It is not retired but, rather, held for possible future resale, a stock option plan, to use in purchasing another company, or to prevent a takeover by an outside group. Outstanding shares are therefore equal to the issued shares less the treasury shares. Dividends are based on the outstanding shares.

The *par value* of a stock is a stated amount of value per share specified in the corporate charter. The firm typically cannot sell stock at a price below par value since stockholders would be liable to creditors for the difference between par value and the amount received.

A closely held corporation is one having only a few stockholders. They keep full control and are not required to publicly disclose financial information about the company. However, a company having 500 or more stockholders must file an annual financial statement with the Securities and Exchange Commission.

A company may issue different classes of common stock. Class A is stock issued to the public and usually has no dividends specified. However, it does have voting rights. Class B stock is usually kept by the company's organizers. Dividends are typically not paid on it until the company has generated sufficient earnings.

Common stockholders enjoy the following rights:

1. The right to receive dividends.

2. The right to receive assets upon the dissolution of the business.

3. The right to vote.

4. The preemptive right to buy new shares of common stock prior to their sale to the general public. In this way, current stockholders can maintain their proportionate percentage ownership in the company.

5. The receipt of a stock certificate which evidences ownership in the firm. The stock certificate may then be sold by the holder to another in the secondary security market.

6. The right to inspect the company's books.

In some states there also exists *cumulative voting*, which allows for multiple votes for a particular director. Cumulative voting is designed to allow a minority group to be able to elect one director.

A number of options exist for equity financing in the case of small businesses, including:

1. Venture capital (investor) groups

2. Issuances directly to institutional investors

3. Issuances to relatives or friends

4. Issuances to major customers and suppliers

A determination of the number of shares that must be issued to raise sufficient funds to meet the capital budget may be required.

EXAMPLE 15.5 Brady Corporation presently has 650,000 shares of common stock outstanding. The capital budget for the upcoming year is $1.8 million.

Assuming new stock may be issued for $16 a share, the number of shares that must be issued to provide the necessary funds to meet the capital budget is:

$$\frac{\text{Funds needed}}{\text{Market price per share}} = \frac{\$1,800,000}{\$16} = 112,500 \text{ shares}$$

The new shareholders will now own 14.8 percent of the total shares outstanding as computed below.

$$\frac{\text{Newly issued shares}}{\text{Total shares}} = \frac{112{,}500}{650{,}000 + 112{,}500} = \frac{112{,}500}{762{,}500} = 14.8\%$$

EXAMPLE 15.6 Smith Corporation wishes to raise $3 million in its first public issue of common stock. After its issuance, the total market value of stock is anticipated to be $7 million. Currently, there are 140,000 outstanding shares that are closely held.

Determine the number of new shares that must be issued to raise the $3 million.

The new shares will have $\frac{3}{7}$ ($3 million/$7 million) of the outstanding shares after the stock issuance. Therefore, current stockholders will be holding $\frac{4}{7}$ of the shares.

$$140{,}000 \text{ shares} = \tfrac{4}{7} \text{ of the total shares}$$
$$\text{Total shares} = 245{,}000$$
$$\text{New shares} = \tfrac{3}{7} \times 245{,}000 = 105{,}000 \text{ shares}$$

Subsequent to the stock issuance, the anticipated price per share is:

$$\text{Price per share} = \frac{\text{market value}}{\text{share outstanding}} = \frac{\$7{,}000{,}000}{245{,}000 \text{ shares}} = \$28.57$$

A company that first issues its common stock publicly is referred to as "going public." The estimated price per share to sell the securities is equal to:

$$\frac{\text{Anticipated market value of the company}}{\text{Total outstanding shares}}$$

For an established company, the market price per share can be computed as follows:

$$\frac{\text{Expected dividend}}{\text{Cost of capital} - \text{growth rate in dividends}}$$

EXAMPLE 15.7 Golden Corporation expects the dividend for the year to be $10 a share. The cost of capital is 13 percent. The growth rate in dividends is expected to be constant at 8 percent. The price per share is:

$$\text{Price per share} = \frac{\text{expected dividend}}{\text{cost of capital} - \text{growth rate in dividends}} = \frac{\$10}{0.13 - 0.08} = \frac{\$10}{0.05} = \$200$$

Another approach to pricing the share of stock for an existing company is through the use of the price/earnings (P/E) ratio, which is equal to:

$$\frac{\text{Market price per share}}{\text{Earnings per share}}$$

EXAMPLE 15.8 Grace Corporation's earnings per share is $7. It is expected that the company's stock should sell at eight times its earnings. The market price per share is therefore

$$\text{P/E} = \frac{\text{market price per share}}{\text{earnings per share}}$$
$$\text{Market price per share} = \text{P/E multiple} \times \text{earnings per share} = 8 \times \$7 = \$56$$

The financial manager may wish to determine the market value of a company's stock. There are a number of different ways to do this.

EXAMPLE 15.9 Assuming an indefinite stream of future dividends of $300,000 and a required rate of return of 14 percent, the market value of the stock equals:

$$\text{Market value} = \frac{\text{expected dividends}}{\text{rate of return}} = \frac{\$300,000}{0.14} = \$2,142,857$$

If there are 200,000 shares, the market price per share is:

$$\frac{\text{Market value}}{\text{Number of shares}} = \frac{\$2,142,857}{200,000} = \$10.71$$

EXAMPLE 15.10 Technical Corporation is considering a public issue of its securities. The average price/earnings multiple in the industry is 15. The company's net income is $400,000. There will be 100,000 shares outstanding subsequent to the issuance of the stock. The expected price per share is:

$$\text{Total market value} = \text{net income} \times \text{price/earnings multiple}$$
$$= \$400,000 \times 15 = \$6,000,000$$
$$\text{Price per share} = \frac{\text{market value}}{\text{number of shares}} = \frac{\$6,000,000}{100,000} = \$60$$

EXAMPLE 15.11 Pinston Corporation issues 400,000 new shares of common stock to present stockholders at a $25 price per share. The price per share prior to the issue is $29. Currently, there are 500,000 outstanding shares. The expected price per share after the new issue is:

Value of outstanding shares (500,000 × $29)	$14,500,000
Value of newly issued shares (400,000 × $25)	10,000,000
Value of entire issue	$24,500,000

$$\text{Value per share} = \frac{\text{value of entire shares}}{\text{total number of shares}} = \frac{\$24,500,000}{900,000} = \$27.22$$

EXAMPLE 15.12 Prider Corporation is considering building a new plant. The firm has typically distributed all its earnings in the form of dividends. Capital expansion has been financed through common stock issuance. In the capital structure, there is no outstanding preferred stock or debt.

The following expectations exist:

Net income	$23,000,000
Shares outstanding	5,000,000
Construction cost of new plant	$16,000,000

Incremental annual earnings expected because of the new plant is $2 million. The rate of return anticipated by stockholders is 12 percent per annum. The total market value of the firm if the plant is financed through the issuance of common stock is:

$$\frac{\text{Total net income}}{\text{Rate of return}} = \frac{\$25,000,000}{0.12} = \$208,330,000$$

The financial manager may wish to compute the company's price/earnings ratio and required rate of return.

EXAMPLE 15.13 Davis Corporation has experienced an 8 percent growth rate in earnings and dividends. Next year, it anticipates earnings per share of $4 and dividends per share of $2.50. The company will be having its first public issue of common stock. The stock will be issued at $50 per share.

The price/earnings ratio is:

$$\frac{\text{Market price per share}}{\text{Earnings per share}} = \frac{\$50}{\$4} = 12.5 \text{ times}$$

The required rate of return on the stock is:

$$\frac{\text{Dividends per share}}{\text{Market price per share}} + \text{growth rate in dividends}$$

$$\frac{\$2.50}{\$50} + 0.08 = 0.13$$

When the degree of financial leverage is excessive, the company would be better off financing with an equity issue.

Financing with common stock has the following advantages:

1. There is no requirement to pay dividends.

2. There is no repayment date.

3. A common stock issue improves the company's credit rating relative to the issuance of debt.

Financing with common stock has the following disadvantages:

1. Dividends are not tax-deductible.

2. Ownership interest is diluted. The additional voting rights could vote to take control away from the current ownership group.

3. Earnings and dividends are spread over more shares outstanding.

4. The flotation costs associated with a common stock issue are higher than with preferred stock and debt financing.

It is always cheaper to finance operations from internally generated funds. Financing out of retained earnings involves no flotation costs.

Stockholders are generally better off when a firm cuts back on its dividends rather than issuing common stock as a source of needed additional funds. First, when earnings are retained rather than new stock issued, the market price per share of existing stock will rise, as indicated by higher earnings per share. Second, if stock is held for more than one year and then sold at a gain, the investor will get a tax advantage with a capital gain deduction. The capital gain is 28 percent, which means that only 28 percent of the gain is taxed. However, cash dividends are fully taxable. Thus, there is a tax benefit to investors, with a reduction in dividends. One caution, however: Lower dividend payments may be viewed negatively in the market and may result in a reduction in the market price of stock due to psychological factors.

15.6 STOCK RIGHTS

Stock rights represent the option to purchase securities at a specified price at a future date. The preemptive right provides that existing stockholders have the first option to buy additional shares in the company. Exercising this right permits them to maintain voting control and protects against dilution in ownership and earnings.

EXAMPLE 15.14 Charles Corporation has 500,000 shares of common stock outstanding and is planning to issue another 100,000 shares through stock rights. Each current stockholder will receive one right per share. Each right enables the stockholder to buy $\frac{1}{5}$ of a share of new common stock (100,000 shares/500,000 shares). Hence, five rights are needed to acquire one share of stock. Hence, a shareholder holding 10,000 shares would be able to purchase 2,000 new shares ($10,000 \times \frac{1}{5}$). By exercising his or her right, the stockholder would now have a total of 12,000 shares, constituting a 2 percent interest (12,000/600,000) in the total shares outstanding. This is the same 2 percent ownership (10,000/500,000) the stockholder held before the rights offering.

In a rights offering, there is a date of record, which states the last day that the receiver of the right must be the legal owner as reflected in the firm's stock ledger. Because of a lag in bookkeeping, stocks are often sold *ex rights* (without rights) 4 business days before the record date. Before this point, the stock is sold *rights on*, which means that purchasers receive the rights.

The recipient of the rights can exercise them, sell them, or let them expire. Since stock rights are transferable, many are traded on the stock exchange and over-the-counter markets. They may be exercised for a given period of time at a *subscription price*, which is set somewhat below the prevailing market price.

After the subscription price has been determined, management must ascertain the number of rights necessary to purchase a share of stock. The total number of shares that must be sold equals:

$$\text{Shares to be sold} = \frac{\text{amount of funds to be obtained}}{\text{subscription price}}$$

The number of rights needed to acquire one share equals:

$$\text{Rights per share} = \frac{\text{total shares outstanding}}{\text{shares to be sold}}$$

EXAMPLE 15.15 Star Corporation wishes to obtain $800,000 by a rights offering. There are currently 100,000 shares outstanding. The subscription price is $40 a share. The shares to be sold equal:

$$\text{Shares to be sold} = \frac{\text{amount of funds to be obtained}}{\text{subscription price}} = \frac{\$800,000}{\$40} = 20,000 \text{ shares}$$

The number of rights needed to acquire one share equals:

$$\text{Rights per share} = \frac{\text{total shares outstanding}}{\text{shares to be sold}} = \frac{100,000}{20,000} = 5$$

Thus, five rights will be required to purchase each new share at $40. Each right enables the holder to buy $\frac{1}{5}$ of a share of stock.

Value of a Right

The value of a right should, theoretically, be the same whether the stock is selling with rights on or with ex rights.

When stock is selling with rights on, the value of a right equals:

$$\text{Value of right} = \frac{\text{market value of stock with rights on} - \text{subscription price}}{\text{number of rights needed to buy one share} + 1}$$

EXAMPLE 15.16 Charles Company's common stock sells for $55 a share with rights on. Each stockholder is given the right to buy one new share at $35 for every four shares held. The value of each right is:

$$\text{Value of right} = \frac{\text{market value with rights on} - \text{subscription price}}{\text{number of rights needed to buy one share} + 1}$$

$$= \frac{\$55 - \$35}{4 + 1} = \frac{\$20}{5} = \$4$$

When stock is traded ex rights, the market price is anticipated to decline by the value of the right. The market value of stock trading ex rights should theoretically equal:

Market value of stock with rights on − value of a right when stock is selling rights on

The value of a right when stock is selling ex rights equals:

$$\text{Value of right} = \frac{\text{market value of stock trading ex rights} - \text{subscription price}}{\text{number of rights needed to buy one new share}}$$

EXAMPLE 15.17 Assuming the same facts as those in Example 15.16, the value of the right of Charles Company stock trading ex rights should equal:

Market value of stock with rights on − value of a right when stock is selling rights on

$$\$55 - \$4 = \$51$$

The value of a right when stock is selling ex rights is therefore:

$$\text{Value of right} = \frac{\text{market value of stock trading ex rights} - \text{subscription price}}{\text{number of rights needed to buy one new share}}$$

$$= \frac{\$51 - \$35}{4} = \frac{\$16}{4} = \$4$$

Notice that the theoretical value of the right is identical when the stock is selling rights on or ex rights.

15.7 STOCKHOLDERS' EQUITY SECTION OF THE BALANCE SHEET

The stockholders' equity section of a company's balance sheet consists of:

1. *Capital stock*, which includes the stock issued by the corporation and stated at par value. The two types of capital stock are preferred and common. Also included in the capital stock section are stock rights.

2. *Paid-in capital*, which represents the excess over par value received by a corporation for the issuance of stock.

3. *Retained earnings*, which refers to the accumulated earnings of the company less any dividends paid out.

The company records the issuance of stock only when it *initially* sells it to the stockholder.

When one stockholder sells his or her shares, the transaction is not entered on the corporation's books. The company need only change the name on its records to that of the new stockholder so that dividends may be properly paid.

Treasury stock is shown in the stockholders' equity section as a deduction when computing total stockholders' equity.

15.8 GOVERNMENTAL REGULATION

When securities are issued publicly, they must conform to federal and state regulations. State rules are referred to as *blue sky laws*. The major federal laws are the Securities Act of 1933 and the Securities Exchange Act of 1934. The 1934 act applies to existing security transactions, while the 1933 act deals with regulation of new security issues. The acts require full disclosure to investors concerning the company's affairs. Prior to the issuance of a new security, the company must prepare a prospectus for investors which contains a condensed version of the registration statement filed with the SEC.

15.9 FINANCING STRATEGY

The corporation financial manager is concerned with selecting the best possible source of financing based on the facts of the situation. This section describes various circumstances in which a particular financing source is most suited.

EXAMPLE 15.18 Tart Corporation is considering issuing either debt or preferred stock to finance the acquisition of a plant costing $1.3 million. The interest rate on the debt is 15 percent. The dividend rate on the preferred stock is 10 percent. The tax rate is 46 percent.

The annual interest payment on the debt is:

$$15\% \times \$1,300,000 = \$195,000$$

The annual dividend on the preferred stock is:

$$10\% \times \$1,300,000 = \$130,000$$

The required earnings before interest and taxes to meet the dividend payment is:

$$\frac{\$130,000}{(1 - 0.46)} = \$240,741$$

If the company anticipates earning $240,741 without difficulty, it should issue the preferred stock.

EXAMPLE 15.19 Charles Corporation has previously used short-term financing. It is now considering refinancing its short-term debt with equity or long-term debt securities. The financial manager decided to list the factors that should be taken into account when selecting an appropriate means of financing. These factors are:

1. The costs of the instruments
2. The company's earnings compared to the cost of debt and preferred stock
3. The recurrence in sales and earnings
4. The degree of financial leverage
5. The maturity and degree of success of the firm
6. The degree of dilution in voting control to be tolerated
7. The firm's solvency status

EXAMPLE 15.20 Pride Corporation has sales of $30 million a year. It needs $6 million in financing for capital expansion. The debt/equity ratio is 68 percent. The company is in a risky industry, and net income is not stable year to year. The common stock is selling at a high P/E ratio relative to the competition. Under consideration is either the issuance of common stock or a convertible bond.

Because the company is in a high-risk industry and has a high debt/equity ratio and fluctuating earnings, the issuance of common stock is preferred.

EXAMPLE 15.21 Wilson Corporation is a mature company in its industry. It has a limited ownership. The company has a fluctuating sales and earnings stream. The firm's debt/equity ratio is 70 percent relative to the industry standard of 55 percent. The after-tax rate of return is 16 percent. Since Wilson's is a seasonal business, there are given times during the year when its liquidity position is deficient. The company is undecided on the best means of financing.

Preferred stock is one possible means of financing. Debt financing is not recommended because of the already high debt/equity ratio, the variability in earnings, and the poor liquidity position. Because of the limited ownership, common stock financing may not be appropriate since this would dilute the ownership.

EXAMPLE 15.22 A new company is established and it plans to raise $15 million in funds. The company anticipates that it will obtain contracts that will provide $1,200,000 a year in before-tax profits. The firm is considering whether to issue bonds only or an equal amount of bonds and preferred stock. The interest rate on AA corporate bonds is 12 percent. The tax rate is 50 percent.

The firm will probably have difficulty issuing $15 million of AA bonds because the interest cost of $1,800,000 (12% × $15,000,000) associated with these bonds is greater than the estimated earnings before interest and taxes. The issuance of debt by a new company is a risky alternative.

Financing with $7.5 million in debt and $7.5 million in preferred stock is also not recommended. While some debt may be issued, it is not feasible to finance the balance with preferred stock. In the event that $7.5 million of

AA bonds were issued at the 12 percent rate, the company would be obligated to pay $900,000 in interest. In this event, a forecasted income statement would look as follows:

Earnings before interest and taxes	$1,200,000
Interest	900,000
Taxable income	$ 300,000
Taxes	150,000
Net income	$ 150,000

The amount available for the payment of preferred dividends is only $150,000. Hence, the maximum rate of return that could be paid on $7.5 million of preferred stock is:

$$\frac{\$150,000}{\$7,500,000} = 0.02$$

Stockholders would not invest in preferred stock that offers only a 2 percent rate of return.
The company should consider financing with common stock.

EXAMPLE 15.23 Boyser Corporation wishes to construct a plant that will take about $1\frac{1}{2}$ years to build. The plant will be used to manufacture a new product line, for which Boyser anticipates a high demand. The new plant will significantly increase the company's size. The following costs are expected to occur:

1. The cost to build the plant, $800,000

2. Funds required for contingencies, $100,000

3. Annual operating costs, $175,000

The asset, debt, and equity positions of the firm are similar to industry standards. The market price of the firm's stock is less than it should be, considering the future earning power of the new product line. What would be an appropriate way to finance the construction?

Because the market price of stock is less than it should be and considering the potential of the product line, convertible bonds and installment bank loans might be appropriate means of financing, since interest expense is tax-deductible. Further, the issuance of convertible bonds might not require repayment, since the bonds are likely to be converted to common stock because of the firm's profitability. Installment bank loans can be gradually paid off as the new product generates cash inflow. Funds required for contingencies can be in the form of open bank lines of credit.

If the market price of the stock was not at a depressed level, financing through equity would be an alternative financing strategy.

EXAMPLE 15.24 Davis Company wishes to acquire Gortman Corporation but has not decided on an optimum means to finance the purchase. The current debt/equity position is within the industry guideline. In previous years, financing has been accomplished through the issuance of short-term debt.

Earnings have shown instability over the years and consequently the market price of the stock has fluctuated. At present, however, the market price of stock is strong.

The company's tax bracket is low.

The acquisition should be financed through the issuance of equity securities for the following reasons:

1. The market price of stock is presently at a high level.

2. The issuance of long-term debt will result in more instability in earnings due to high fixed interest charges. As a result, there will be greater instability in the company's stock price.

3. The issuance of more debt will cause the firm's debt/equity ratio to rise above the industry norm. This will adversely affect the company's cost of capital and availability of financing.

4. Because it will take a long time to derive the funds necessary for the acquisition cost, short-term debt should not be issued. If short-term debt is issued, the debt would have to be met prior to the receipt of the return from the acquired business.

EXAMPLE 15.25 Breakstone Corporation wishes to undertake a capital expansion program and must, therefore, obtain $7 million in financing. The company has a good credit rating. The current market price of its common stock is $60. The interest rate for long-term debt is 18 percent. The dividend rate associated with preferred stock is 16 percent, and Breakstone's tax rate is 46 percent.

Relevant ratios for the industry and the company are:

	Industry	Breakstone
Net income to total assets	13%	22%
Long-term debt to total assets	31%	29%
Total liabilities to total assets	47%	45%
Preferred stock to total assets	3%	0
Current ratio	2.6	3.2
Net income plus interest to interest	8	17

Dividend per share is $8, the dividend growth rate is 7 percent, no sinking fund provisions exist, the trend in earnings shows stability, and the present ownership group wishes to retain control. The cost of common stock is:

$$\frac{\text{Dividends per share}}{\text{Market price per share}} + \text{dividend growth rate}$$

$$\frac{\$8}{\$60} + 0.07 = 20.3\%$$

The after-tax cost of long-term debt is 9.7 percent ($18\% \times 54\%$). The cost of preferred stock is 16 percent. How should Breakstone finance its expansion?

The issuance of long-term debt is more appropriate for the following reasons:

1. Its after-tax cost is the lowest.
2. The company's ratios of long-term debt to total assets and total liabilities to total assets are less than the industry average, pointing to the company's ability to issue additional debt.
3. Corporate liquidity is satisfactory based on the favorable current ratio relative to the industry standard.
4. Fixed interest charges can be met, taking into account the stability in earnings, the earning power of the firm, and the very favorable times-interest-earned ratio. Additional interest charges should be met without difficulty.
5. The firm's credit rating is satisfactory.
6. There are no required sinking fund provisions.
7. The leveraging effect can take place to further improve earnings.

In the case that the firm does not want to finance through further debt, preferred stock would be the next best financing alternative, since its cost is lower than that associated with common stock and no dilution in the ownership interest will take place.

EXAMPLE 15.26 Harris Corporation has experienced growth in revenue and net income but is in a weak liquidity position. The inflation rate is high. At the end of 19X5, the firm needs $600,000 for the following reasons:

New equipment	$175,000
Research and development	95,000
Paying overdue accounts payable	215,000
Paying accrued liabilities	60,000
Desired increase in cash balance	55,000
	$600,000

Presented below are the financial statements for 19X5.

Harris Corporation
Balance Sheet
Dec. 31, 19X5

ASSETS

Current assets

Cash	$ 12,000	
Accounts receivable	140,000	
Notes receivable	25,000	
Inventory	165,000	
Office supplies	20,000	
Total current assets		$362,000
Fixed assets		468,000
Total assets		$830,000

LIABILITIES AND STOCKHOLDERS' EQUITY

Current liabilities

Loans payable	$ 74,000	
Accounts payable	360,000	
Accrued liabilities	55,000	
Total current liabilities		$489,000
Long-term debt		61,000
Total liabilities		$550,000
Stockholders' equity		
Common stock	$200,000	
Retained earnings	80,000	
Total stockholders' equity		280,000
Total liabilities and stockholders' equity		$830,000

Harris Corporation
Income Statement
For the Year Ended Dec. 31, 19X5

Sales	$1,400,000
Cost of sales	750,000
Gross margin	$ 650,000
Operating expenses	480,000
Income before tax	$ 170,000
Tax	68,000
Net income	$ 102,000

It is anticipated that sales will increase on a yearly basis by 22 percent and that net income will increase by 17 percent. What type of financing is best suited for Harris Corporation?

The most suitable source of financing is long-term. A company in a growth stage needs a large investment in equipment, and research and development expenditure. With regard to 19X5, $270,000 of the $600,000 is required for this purpose. A growth company also needs funds to satisfy working capital requirements. Here, 45.8 percent of financing is necessary to pay overdue accounts payable and accrued liabilities. The firm also needs sufficient cash to capitalize on lucrative opportunities. The present cash balance to total assets is at a low 1.4 percent.

Long-term debt financing is recommended for the following reasons:

1. The ratio of long-term debt to stockholders' equity is a low 21.8 percent. The additional issuance of long-term debt will not impair the overall capital structure.

2. The company has been profitable and there is an expectation of future growth in earnings. Internally generated funds should therefore ensue, enabling the payment of fixed interest charges.

3. During inflation, the issuance of long-term debt generates purchasing power gains because the firm will be repaying creditors in cheaper dollars.

4. Interest expense is tax-deductible.

Review Questions

1. The two sources of equity financing are _____ and _____ .

2. A(n) _____ enables the future purchase of stock.

3. A(n) _____ purchases and distributes new securities of a company.

4. When a group of investment bankers handle a large issue, the group is referred to as a(n) _____ .

5. The investment banker who manages the group is called the _____ .

6. The two types of underwriting syndicates are _____ and _____ .

7. A(n) _____ purchases securities and holds them in inventory for later resale.

8. A(n) _____ handles transactions for securities on the stock exchanges.

9. When securities are _____ they are sold to a few institutional investors.

10. The expense related to registering and selling a security is called _____ cost.

11. One advantage of a private placement is that it avoids _____ filing requirements.

12. _____ preferred stock means that if dividends are not paid in a particular year, they must be paid in a later year before any distributions are given to common stockholders.

13. Preferred dividends are based on the total _____ of the outstanding shares.

14. _____ preferred stock means that preferred shareholders will participate with common shareholders in any excess dividends.

15. For corporate investors, dividends received are subject to a(n) _____ dividend exclusion.

16. A(n) _____ statement gives management the right to vote common stockholders' shares.

17. The maximum amount of shares the company can issue as per the corporate charter are the _____ shares.

18. Shares that have been sold to the public are called _____ shares.

19. _____ is stock which has been bought back by the company.

20. _____ equal issued shares less treasury shares.

21. Each stock has a(n) _____ that is specified in the corporate charter.

22. The _____ right allows a stockholder to purchase new shares of stock before they are sold to the general public.

23. The stockholders' equity section of a company's balance sheet consists of the _____ , _____ , and _____ sections.

Answers: (1) common stock, preferred stock; (2) stock right; (3) investment banker; (4) syndicate; (5) originating house; (6) divided, undivided; (7) dealer; (8) broker; (9) privately placed; (10) flotation; (11) SEC; (12) Cumulative; (13) par value; (14) Participating; (15) 85%; (16) proxy; (17) authorized; (18) issued; (19) Treasury stock; (20) Outstanding shares; (21) par value; (22) preemptive; (23) capital stock, paid-in capital, retained earnings.

Solved Problems

15.1   Dividends Payable to Preferred. On December 31, 19X4, Arco Company had 5,000 shares of $10 par value, 15 percent, cumulative preferred stock outstanding. Dividends are in arrears for 3 years. Since 19X4 was a profitable year, the company paid its dividend in full. What is the total dividend payable to preferred stockholders?

SOLUTION

Total par value (5,000 shares × $10)	$50,000
Dividends in arrears ($50,000 × 15% × 3 years)	$22,500
Current year dividend ($50,000 × 15%)	7,500
Total dividend	$30,000

15.2   Dividends. Harris Corporation has the following equity securities outstanding:

Preferred stock, participating, 20,000 shares, $15 par value, 14% dividend rate	$300,000
Common stock, 5,000 shares, $20 par value	$100,000

The dividend rate declared on the common stock is 12 percent, and dividends declared for the year are $60,000. Determine the amount of the dividend to be paid to preferred stockholders and common stockholders.

SOLUTION

	Preferred Stock	Common Stock
Regular preferred dividend (14% × $300,000)	$42,000	
Regular common dividend (12% × $100,000)		$12,000
Excess dividend allocated based on relative par value:		
Preferred $\left(\dfrac{\$300,000}{\$400,000} \times \$6,000\right)$	4,500	
Common $\left(\dfrac{\$100,000}{\$400,000} \times \$6,000\right)$		1,500
Total dividend	$46,500	$13,500

15.3   Effective Cost of Preferred Stock. Star Corporation issued $5 million of preferred stock. The flotation cost was 10 percent of gross proceeds. The dividend rate is 16 percent. What is the effective cost of the preferred stock?

SOLUTION

$$\frac{\text{Dividend}}{\text{Net proceeds}} = \frac{0.16(\$5,000,000)}{\$5,000,000 - 0.10(\$5,000,000)} = \frac{\$800,000}{\$4,500,000} = 17.8\%$$

15.4   Receipt per Share. Appel Corporation is considering expanding. It plans to finance the expansion by issuing $4 million in preferred stock. The preferred stock has a par value of $50 and a dividend rate of 12 percent. Similar issues of preferred stock are presently yielding 14 percent.

(a) How much will the company receive for each share? (b) How many shares must be issued?

SOLUTION

(a) $\dfrac{\text{Dividend}}{\text{Market yield}} = \dfrac{0.12 \times \$50}{0.14} = \dfrac{\$6}{0.14} = \$42.86$

(b) $\dfrac{\text{Funds required}}{\text{Price per share}} = \dfrac{\$4,000,000}{\$42.86} = 93,327 \text{ sharres (rounded)}$

15.5   Shares to Be Sold. Simon Corporation has 800,000 common shares outstanding. The capital budget for the upcoming year is $2 million. New stock may be sold for $20 a share.

(a) What is the number of shares that must be sold to obtain the needed funds? (b) What percent of the total shares outstanding will the new stockholders own?

SOLUTION

(a) $\dfrac{\text{Funds needed}}{\text{Market price per share}} = \dfrac{\$2,000,000}{\$20} = 100,000 \text{ shares}$

(b) $\dfrac{\text{Newly issued shares}}{\text{Total shares}} = \dfrac{100,000}{800,000 + 100,000} = \dfrac{100,000}{900,000} = 11.1\%$

15.6   Expected Price. Saft Corporation wants to obtain $4 million in its first public issue of common stock. After the issuance, the total market value of stock is estimated at $10 million. At present, there are 120,000 closely held shares.

(a) What is the amount of new shares that must be issued to obtain the $4 million? (b) After the stock issuance, what will be the expected price per share?

SOLUTION

(a)   The new shares will be 40 percent ($4 million/$10 million) of the outstanding shares subsequent to the stock issuance. Thus, current stockholders will be holding 60 percent of the shares.

$$120,000 \text{ shares} = 60\% \text{ of the total shares}$$
$$\text{Total shares} = 200,000$$
$$\text{New shares} = 40\% \times 200,000 = 80,000 \text{ shares}$$

(b) $$\text{Price per share} = \frac{\text{market value}}{\text{outstanding shares}} = \frac{\$10,000,000}{200,000} = \$50$$

15.7   Price per Share. Gallagher Corporation anticipates a $6 dividend per share for the year. Its minimum rate of return is 12 percent. The dividend growth rate is 6 percent. What is the price per share?

SOLUTION

$$\frac{\text{Expected dividend}}{\text{Minimum return} - \text{dividend growth rate}} = \frac{\$6}{0.12 - 0.06} = \frac{\$6}{0.06} = \$100$$

15.8   Market Value. A company expects an indefinite stream of future dividends of $200,000 and a required rate of return of 16 percent. There are 100,000 shares.

(a) What is the market value of the stock? (b) What is the market price per share?

SOLUTION

(a) $$\text{Market value} = \frac{\text{expected dividends}}{\text{rate of return}} = \frac{\$200,000}{0.16} = \$1,250,000$$

(b) $$\text{Market price per share} = \frac{\text{market value}}{\text{number of shares}} = \frac{\$1,250,000}{100,000} = \$12.50$$

15.9   Expected Price. Wolinsky Corporation is considering a public issuance of its securities. The average P/E ratio in the industry is 12. The firm's reported earnings are $300,000. After the issuance of the stock, there will be 200,000 shares outstanding. What is the expected price per share?

SOLUTION

$$\text{Total market value} = \text{earnings} \times \text{P/E} = \$300,000 \times 12 = \$3,600,000$$

$$\text{Price per share} = \frac{\text{market value}}{\text{shares outstanding}} = \frac{\$3,600,000}{200,000} = \$18$$

15.10   Expected Price. Nelson Corporation issues 200,000 new shares of common stock to current stockholders at a $15 price per share. The price per share before the issue was $18. At present, there are 300,000 shares outstanding. What is the expected price per share after the new issue?

SOLUTION

Value of outstanding shares	
(300,000 × $18)	$5,400,000
Value of newly issued shares	
(200,000 × $15)	3,000,000
Value of entire issue	$8,400,000

$$\text{Value per share} = \frac{\text{value of entire shares}}{\text{total shares}} = \frac{\$8,400,000}{500,000} = \$16.80$$

15.11 Total Market Value. Stephens Corporation is thinking about constructing a new facility. The company has usually distributed its earnings in the form of dividends. Common stock has typically been issued to finance capital expansion. Preferred stock and debt are not in the capital structure.

The company's expectations follow:

Net income	$18,000,000
Outstanding shares	2,000,000
Construction cost of new facility	$10,000,000

The expected additional earnings due to the new facility is $2 million. The expected stockholder rate of return is 16 percent per annum. What is the total market value of the company, assuming the facility is financed with common stock?

SOLUTION

$$\frac{\text{Total net income}}{\text{Rate of return}} = \frac{\$20,000,000}{0.16} = \$125,000,000$$

15.12 P/E Ratio. Wilson Corporation anticipates a 10 percent growth in net income and dividends. Next year, the company expects earnings per share of $5 and dividends per share of $3. Wilson will be having its first public issuance of common stock. The stock will be issued at $40 per share.

(*a*) What is the P/E ratio? (*b*) What is the required rate of return on the stock?

SOLUTION

(*a*)
$$\frac{\text{Market price per share}}{\text{Earnings per share}} = \frac{\$40}{\$5} = 8 \text{ times}$$

(*b*)
$$\frac{\text{Dividends per share}}{\text{Market price per share}} + \text{dividend growth rate} = \frac{\$3}{\$40} + 0.10 = 17.5\%$$

15.13 Preemptive Right. Barker Company has 400,000 shares of common stock outstanding and is considering issuing another 100,000 shares through stock rights. Each current stockholder will obtain one right per share. Mr. A owns 40,000 shares of common stock.

(*a*) What amount of each new share of common stock can a stockholder acquire by each right? (*b*) How many rights are required to purchase one new share of common stock? (*c*) How many new shares will Mr. A be able to obtain? (*d*) What will Mr. A's percentage interest in the company be after exercising all his rights? (*e*) Did his percentage ownership change after exercising his rights relative to what it was before the rights offering?

SOLUTION

(a)
$$\text{Rights per share} = \frac{\text{shares to be sold}}{\text{shares outstanding}} = \frac{100,000}{400,000} = \frac{1}{4}$$

(b)
$$\text{Rights required for 1 share} = \frac{\text{shares outstanding}}{\text{shares to be sold}} = \frac{400,000}{100,000} = 4$$

(c)   Share available to a stockholder = shares held $\times$ right per share = $\dfrac{40,000 \times 1}{4}$ = 10,000 shares

(d)
$$\% \text{ Ownership} = \frac{\text{shares held} + \text{shares bought on rights}}{\text{total shares outstanding}} = \frac{50,000}{500,000} = 10\%$$

(e)   No. The percentage ownership is the same. Before the rights offering Mr. A also held a 10 percent interest (40,000/400,000).

15.14 Rights per Share. Mason Corporation intends to raise $1.5 million in a rights offering. At present, there are 240,000 shares outstanding. A subscription price of $25 a share is assigned.

(a) How many shares must be sold? (b) How many rights are needed to purchase one share of stock?

SOLUTION

(a)
$$\text{Shares to be sold} = \frac{\text{amount of funds to be obtained}}{\text{subscription price}} = \frac{\$1,500,000}{\$25} = 60,000 \text{ shares}$$

(b)   The number of rights needed to acquire one share equals:
$$\text{Rights per share} = \frac{\text{total shares outstanding}}{\text{shares to be sold}} = \frac{\$40,000}{60,000} = 4$$

15.15 Value per Right. Charles Corporation stock sells at $78 a share with rights on. The subscription price is $60, and five rights are needed to purchase a new share of stock. What is the value of each right?

SOLUTION

$$\text{Value of right} = \frac{\text{market value with rights on} - \text{subscription price}}{\text{number of rights to buy 1 share} + 1} = \frac{\$78 - \$60}{5 + 1} = \frac{\$18}{6} = \$3$$

15.16 Value per Right. Assume the same facts as in Problem 15.15. (a) What will be the market value of the stock trading ex rights? (b) What is the value of a right when the stock is selling ex rights?

SOLUTION

(a)   Value of stock, ex rights = market value of stock with rights on − value of right = $78 − $3 = $75

(b)   Value of right (when stock sells ex rights) = $\dfrac{\text{market value of stock, ex rights} - \text{subscription price}}{\text{number of rights to buy 1 share}}$

$$= \frac{\$75 - \$60}{5} = \frac{\$15}{5} = \$3$$

15.17 Cost of Financing. Mason Corporation is considering the issuance of either debt or preferred stock to finance the purchase of a facility costing $1.5 million. The interest rate on the debt is 16 percent. Preferred stock has a dividend rate of 12 percent. The tax rate is 46 percent.

(*a*) What is the annual interest payment? (*b*) What is the annual dividend payment? (*c*) What is the required income before interest and taxes to satisfy the dividend requirement?

SOLUTION

(*a*) $$\text{Annual interest} = 16\% \times \$1,500,000 = \$240,000$$

(*b*) $$\text{Annual dividend} = 12\% \times \$1,500,000 = \$180,000$$

(*c*) $$\text{Before-tax income required for dividend} = \frac{\text{dividend}}{1-t} = \frac{\$180,000}{(1-0.46)} = \$333,333$$

15.18 Common Stock versus Debt. Blake Corporation has $20 million in sales a year. It requires $3.5 million in financing for capital expansion. The debt/equity ratio is 70 percent. The industry has inherent risk, and earnings show variability. The common stock is selling at a high P/E ratio. The company is considering issuing either common stock or debt. Which type of financing is recommended?

SOLUTION

Since Blake is in a high-risk industry, has a high debt/equity ratio, and shows variability in earnings, issuing more debt would be expensive, restrictive, and potentially dangerous to Blake's future financial health. Common stock should therefore be issued, although this will dilute ownership.

15.19 Type of Financing. Krul Corporation is an established company in its industry. It has a limited ownership. The trend in revenue and earnings has shown variability. The company's debt/equity ratio is considerably higher than the industry norm. The after-tax rate of return is 18 percent. The company's business is seasonal. What method of financing is most suitable?

SOLUTION

Debt financing is inadvisable due to the high debt/equity ratio, the earnings variability, and the seasonal nature of the business. Issuance of common stock is not suggested because of the limited ownership. Preferred stock appears to be the best means of financing.

15.20 Financing Strategy. A new company plans to obtain $18 million in financing. The company expects to obtain a yearly income of $2 million before interest and taxes. The firm is considering issuing bonds or an equal amount of bonds and preferred stock. The interest rate on bonds is 14 percent. The tax rate is 46 percent. What financing strategy would you recommend?

SOLUTION

It would be difficult to issue $18 million in bonds because the interest cost of $2,520,000 ($14\% \times \$18,000,000$) exceeds the anticipated before-tax profit. Also, there is always risk when a new company issues debt.

Financing equally with debt and preferred stock is not advisable. With the issuance of $9 million in debt at 14 percent, the company incurs $1,260,000 in interest charges. The following forecasted income statement applies to this plan:

Income before interest and taxes	$2,000,000
Interest	1,260,000
Taxable income	$ 740,000
Taxes	340,400
Net income	$ 399,600

The amount available to pay preferred dividends is only $399,600. Thus, the maximum return that can be derived on the $9 million of preferred stock is:

$$\frac{\$399,600}{\$9,000,000} = 4.4\%$$

Investors would not be interested in buying preferred stock having a rate of return of only 4.4 percent.

15.21 Means of Financing. Midas Corporation wants to build a new facility that will produce a new product line. The company expects the following costs to arise:

Cost to construct facility	$1,100,000
Funds needed to meet contingencies	$200,000
Annual operating costs	$225,000

The new facility will materially increase the corporate size. The asset and debt ratios of the firm are in conformity with industry norms. Taking into account the future earning potential of the new product line, the company's market price per share is less than what it should be. What is an appropriate means of financing the new facility?

SOLUTION

Since the market price of stock is temporarily depressed and considering the potential success of the product line, convertible bonds appear to be a wise financing strategy. With convertible bonds interest expense is tax-deductible. Also, the issuance of convertible bonds will not mandate repayment because the bonds will probably be converted to common stock as the company becomes more profitable due to the new product line. Another possible financing source is installment bank loans, which may be paid off gradually as cash flow is derived from the new product. Open bank lines of credit may be used to meet possible contingencies.

15.22 Means of Financing. Sunder Corporation wants to acquire another company but is unsure of the best basis to finance the purchase. The company's financial leverage is about the same as the industry average. In prior years, short-term debt has been used for financing. Net income and price per share have shown variability over the years. However, the market price of stock is now strong. The firm is in a low tax bracket.

What means of financing is recommended?

SOLUTION

Equity securities appear to be a good financing source for the following reasons:

1. The price per share is currently high.

2. If long-term debt is issued, there will be higher fixed charges resulting in greater variability in earnings. This in turn will cause instability in the price per share. Also, debt issuance will make the company's degree of financial leverage higher than the industry norm. This may impair the firm's cost of financing and availability of funds.

3. Short-term debt should not be employed, since the debt will have to be met before the receipt of the return from the acquired business.

15.23 Cost of Financing. Morgan Corporation must obtain $8 million in financing for its expansion plans. The firm's credit rating is good. Common stock is now selling at $50 per share. Preferred stock has a dividend rate of 15 percent. Long-term debt has an interest rate of 19 percent. The tax rate is 46 percent.

Applicable ratios for Morgan and the industry are:

	Industry	Morgan
Net income to total assets	15%	24%
Long-term debt to total assets	29%	26%
Total liabilities to total assets	48%	44%
Preferred stock to total assets	4%	0
Current ratio	3.1	3.8
Net income plus interest to interest	9	15

Dividends per share are $6. The growth rate in dividends is 5 percent, there is no sinking fund provision, net income and sales show stability, and the current ownership group wants to maintain its control.

(a) What is the cost of common stock? (b) What is the cost of preferred stock? (c) What is the cost of long-term debt? (d) What source of financing is recommended?

SOLUTION

(a)
$$\frac{\text{Dividends per share}}{\text{Market price per share}} + \text{growth rate in dividends}$$

$$\frac{\$6}{\$50} + 0.05 = 17\%$$

(b)   15%

(c)   19% × 54% = 10.3%

(d)   Long-term debt should be issued for the following reasons:

1. It has the lowest after-tax cost.
2. The firm's debt ratios are below the industry norms, indicating that Morgan can take on additional debt.
3. The company's liquidity is satisfactory, as indicated by the favorable current ratio.
4. Additional interest charges can be satisfied based on the stability in revenue and earnings as well as the favorable interest coverage ratio.
5. The firm has a good credit rating.
6. No sinking fund provisions exist.
7. Assuming the return earned on debt funds exceeds the after-tax interest cost, increased profitability will occur due to the leveraging effect.
8. No dilution in ownership will occur.

15.24 Recommended Financing. Frost Corporation has shown growth in sales and earnings but has a liquidity problem. The rate of inflation is high. At year-end 19X8, the company requires $500,000 for the following reasons:

New machinery	$200,000
Research and development	80,000
Paying overdue obligations	130,000
Paying accrued expenses	25,000
Desired increase in cash balance	65,000
	$500,000

Partial financial statements for 19X8 are shown below.

Frost Corporation
Balance Sheet
Dec. 31, 19X8

ASSETS

Current assets

Cash	$ 10,000	
Other current assets	320,000	
Total current assets		$330,000
Noncurrent assets		570,000
Total assets		$900,000

LIABILITIES AND STOCKHOLDERS' EQUITY

Current liabilities		$500,000
Long-term debt		100,000
Total liabilities		$600,000
Stockholders' equity		
Common stock	$250,000	
Retained earnings	50,000	
Total stockholders' equity		300,000
Total liabilities and stockholders' equity		$900,000

Frost Corporation
Income Statement
For the Year Ended Dec. 31, 19X8

Sales	$1,300,000
Cost of sales	600,000
Gross margin	$ 700,000
Operating expenses	500,000
Income before tax	$ 200,000
Tax	86,000
Net income	$ 114,000

The company expects that sales and earnings will increase by 25 percent and 20 percent, respectively.

What type of financing is recommended?

SOLUTION

The best type of financing is on a long-term basis. A growing company requires a significant investment in machinery and in research and development. In 19X8, 56 percent of the financing is required for this purpose. A growing company also requires financing to meet working capital needs. Here, 31 percent of the financing is required to pay overdue obligations and accrued expenses. Money is also needed to take advantage of favorable business opportunities. At the current time, the ratio of cash to total assets is a low 1.1 percent.

Financing with long-term debt is recommended for the following reasons:

1. The ratio of long-term debt to stockholders' equity is a low 33.3 percent. Further debt issuance will not hurt the overall capital structure.

2. There is growth in revenue and earnings. As a result, internally generated funds will be able to be used to satisfy the fixed interest charges.

3. In inflationary times, the company will be paying back debt in cheaper dollars.

4. Interest is tax-deductible.

15.25 Financing Options. On average over the past 10 years, Tektronix's return on equity has not been sufficient to finance growth of the business, thus an infusion of new capital from outside sources has been required. Most of the additional capital has been in the form of long-term debt, which represented 13 percent of total capital in fiscal 1997 and 21 percent of total capital in fiscal 2001.

With expansion of the business expected to accelerate in the next few years after the current lull, but with return on equity likely to remain somewhat depressed because of competitive factors and costs associated with "preparing for 2000," a need for additional capital is developing. Also, of the $146 million of long-term debt outstanding at the fiscal 2001 year-end, nearly $65 million matures in the fiscal 2002 to fiscal 2004 period. Thus, it is possible that as much as $100 million of capital may have to be raised to meet all requirements.

In anticipation of capital needs, Tektronix in fiscal 2001 borrowed funds in the commercial paper market, and the company intends to replace these commercial paper borrowings at some future time with long-term financing.

Given the foregoing circumstances, and also given that Tektronix common stock currently is quoted on the New York Stock Exchange at 160 percent of book value and that the current interest rate on newly issued triple-A industrial bonds of long maturity is 14 percent, evaluate on an immediate and longer-term basis each of the following options. Include in your answers economic and capital market assumptions. (*a*) Tektronix is selling 2 million shares of common stock at $50 per share; (*b*) Tektronix is selling a $100 million straight debenture issue maturing in 20 years; and (*c*) Tektronix is selling a $100 million bond issue convertible into common stock and maturing in 20 years. (CFA, adapted.)

SOLUTION

(*a*) From the timing viewpoint, selling equity is attractive considering price-to-book rates (160 percent) and comparatively modest dilution (2 million shares represents 11 percent of currently outstanding shares, less impact of after-tax cost of borrowing to be retired). However, price soon could move higher given a better economic environment, earnings recovery, and resultant stronger general stock market. Long-term, selling equity is expensive, as continuing dividend service is with after-tax dollars. Also, immediate return on equity capital will diminish with reduced leverage as debt matures.

(*b*) Increasing debt, net of maturities, to a larger part of total capital is tolerable by most standards. According to the data provided, debt of about $146 million would increase to around $181 million ($146 + $100 − $65), and by 1984 this sum presumably would not represent much more than the current 21 percent subject to earnings retention during the interim. However, this would be an appealing option only if interest rate assumptions indicate other than a rather meaningful decline over the next year or two, and if pro forma interest charge coverage and/or the current lull in the business do not seriously impact the rating and issue price of the bonds. The after-tax cost of debt service will be comparatively low, and so would be the net cost of capital. Another consideration will be sinking fund requirements and call restrictions and price.

(*c*) A convertible bond issue has certain disadvantages but it also has advantages: (1) it can be sold at a lower interest cost than a straight debt; and (2) the potential dilution is less than an issue of common reflecting the premium over the common market.

Examination III

Chapters 12–15

1. Travis Company has 10,000 shares of common stock with a par value of $10 per share. A 4-for-1 stock split is made. The market price of the stock was $16 prior to the split. (*a*) Record the stock split. (*b*) What will the market price per share be immediately subsequent to the stock split?

2. Bravo Corporation's net income for the year was $2.5 million. It pays out 40 percent of its profit in dividends. The company will buy $4 million in new assets, and 55 percent of the assets will be financed by debt. What is the amount of external equity that must be issued?

3. Blake Company had net income of $600,000 in 19X1. Net income has grown at a 5 percent annual rate. Dividends in 19X1 were $200,000. In 19X2, the net income was $700,000. This of course exceeded the 5 percent annual growth rate. It is expected that earnings will return to a 5 percent growth rate in later years.

    What should the dividends paid out in 19X2 be, assuming (*a*) a stable dividend payout ratio of 20 percent, and (*b*) a stable dollar dividend policy is maintained?

4. Whitestone Corporation leases a $60,000 machine. It must make 10 equal year-end annual payments. There is a 14 percent interest rate. What is the annual payment?

5. Mall Corporation leased $120,000 of equipment and is to make year-end annual payments of $19,000 for 16 years. What is the interest rate on the lease?

6. Drake Corporation takes out a term loan payable in 12 year-end annual installments of $5,000 each. The interest rate is 14 percent. (*a*) What is the amount of the loan? (*b*) Prepare an amortization schedule for the loan repayment for the first 2 years.

7. Shillinglaw Corporation has $5 million of 16 percent mortgage bonds outstanding. The indenture permits additional bonds to be issued as long as the following conditions are satisfied: (*a*) The before-tax times-interest-earned ratio is greater than 3. (*b*) Book value of the mortgaged assets are at least four times the amount of debt. (*c*) The debt/equity ratio is less than 0.8.

    The following additional data are given: Income before tax is $12 million, equity is $30 million, book value of mortgaged assets is $60 million, and 20 percent of the proceeds of a new issue would be added to the base of mortgaged assets.

    What amount of additional debt can be issued for each of the conditions (*a*), (*b*), and (*c*)?

8. Blake Company has a $30 million, 12 percent bond issue outstanding with 20 years remaining. The call premium is 7 percent of face value. A new 20-year bond issue for $30 million can be issued at a 10 percent interest rate. Flotation costs related to the new issue are $800,000. Should a refunding of the bond issue take place?

9. Ajax Corporation issued a $400,000, 15 percent, 20-year bond at 96. The call price is 102. Six years after issue the bond is called. What is the call premium?

10. Sharav Corporation has the following equity securities outstanding:

> Preferred stock, participating, 15,000 shares,
> $10 par value, 12% dividend rate $150,000
> Common stock, 10,000 shares, $20 par value $200,000

The dividend rate declared on the common stock is 10 percent, and dividends declared for the year are $50,000.

Determine the amount of the dividend to be paid to preferred stockholders and common stockholders.

11. Smith Corporation issued $6 million of preferred stock. The flotation cost was 15 percent of gross proceeds. The dividend rate is 18 percent. What is the effective cost of the preferred stock?

12. Knab Corporation expects to raise $2 million in a rights offering. Currently, there are 250,000 shares outstanding. A subscription price of $40 a share is assigned. (*a*) How many shares must be sold? (*b*) How many rights are required to purchase one share of stock?

13. Barnum Company stock sells at $70 a share with rights on. The subscription price is $55. Four rights are needed to purchase a new share of stock. What is the value of each right?

14. Assume the same facts as in Problem 13. (*a*) What will be the market value of the stock trading ex rights? (*b*) What is the value of a right when the stock is selling ex rights?

Answers to Examination III

1. (*a*) No entry is required, because the company's account balances remain the same. However, a memorandum is required to the effect that there are now 40,000 shares having a par value of $2.50 per share.

(*b*)
$$\frac{\$16}{4} = \$4$$

2.

Net income	$2,500,000
Percent of net income retained	×0.6
Retained	$1,500,000
New assets	$4,000,000
Percent financed by equity	×0.45
Equity financing required	$1,800,000
Retained earnings	1,500,000
External equity to be issued	$ 300,000

3. (*a*)
$$\$700,000 \times 20\% = \$140,000$$

(*b*)
$$\text{Dividend in 19X1} = \$200,000 \times 1.05 = \$210,000$$

4.
$$\frac{\$60,000}{5.216} = \$11,503.07$$

5.
$$\frac{\$120,000}{\$19,000} = 6.316$$

Looking at the present value of annuity table in Appendix D and going across 16 years to a factor nearest to 6.316 find 6.2651 at a 14 percent interest rate.

6. (a)
$$\$5,000 \times 5.6603 = \$28,301.50$$

(b)

Year	Payment	Interest	Principal	Balance
0				$28,301.50
1	$5,000	$3,962.21	$1,037.79	$27,263.71
2	$5,000	$3,816.92	$1,183.08	$26,080.63

7. (a) The before-tax times-interest-earned ratio is:

$$\frac{\text{Income before tax and interest}}{\text{Interest}} = \frac{\$12,000,000 + \$800,000^a}{\$800,000 + 0.16X} = 3$$

$$\frac{\$12,800,000}{\$800,000 + 0.16X} = 3$$

$$\$12,800,000 = \$2,400,000 + 0.48X$$

$$X = \$21,666,667$$

[a] Interest $5,000,000 × 0.16 = $800,000.

(b)
$$\frac{\text{Book value of mortgaged assets}}{\text{Debt}} = \frac{\$60,000,000 + 0.2X}{\$5,000,000 + X} = 4$$

$$\$60,000,000 + 0.2X = \$20,000,000 + 4X$$

$$X = \$10,526,315$$

(c)
$$\frac{\text{Debt}}{\text{Equity}} = \frac{\$5,000,000 + X}{\$30,000,000} = 0.8$$

$$\$5,000,000 + X = \$24,000,000$$

$$X = \$19,000,000$$

The second condition is controlling and thus restricts the amount of new debt to $10,526,315.

8.

Old interest payments ($30,000,000 × 0.12)		$3,600,000
New interest payments ($30,000,000 × 0.10)		3,000,000
Annual savings		$ 600,000
Call premium ($30,000,000 × 0.07)		$2,100,000
Flotation cost		800,000
Total cost		$2,900,000

	Calculations	Present Value
Year 0	−$2,900,000 × 1	−$2,900,000
Years 1–20	+$600,000 × 8.5136[a]	+5,108,160
Net present value		+$2,208,160

[a] Present value of annuity factor for $i = 10\%$, $n = 20$.

A refunding of the bond issue should occur, since it results in a positive net present value.

9.

Call price	$408,000
Face value of bond	400,000
Call premium	$ 8,000

10.

	Preferred Stock	Common Stock
Regular dividend		
Preferred (12% × $150,000)	$18,000	
Common (10% × $200,000)		$20,000
Excess dividend		
Preferred		
[($150,000/$350,000) × $12,000]	5,143	
Common		
[($200,000/$350,000) × $12,000]		6,857
Total dividend	$23,143	$26,857

11.

$$\frac{\text{Dividend}}{\text{Net proceeds}} = \frac{18\% \times \$6,000,000}{\$6,000,000 - 0.15(\$6,000,000)} = \frac{\$1,080,000}{\$5,100,000} = 21.18\%$$

12. (*a*)

$$\text{Shares to be sold} = \frac{\text{amount of funds to be obtained}}{\text{subscription price}} = \frac{\$2,000,000}{\$40} = 50,000 \text{ shares}$$

(*b*)

$$\text{Rights per share} = \frac{\text{total shares outstanding}}{\text{shares to be sold}} = \frac{250,000}{50,000} = 5$$

13.

$$\frac{\$70 - \$55}{4 + 1} = \frac{\$15}{5} = \$3$$

14. (*a*)

$$\$70 - \$3 = \$67$$

(*b*)

$$\frac{\$67 - \$55}{4} = \frac{\$12}{4} = \$3$$

Chapter 16

Warrants, Convertibles, Options, and Futures

16.1 INTRODUCTION

Warrants and convertibles are unique relative to other types of securities in the sense that they may be converted into common stock at will by the holder. This chapter defines warrants and convertibles, discusses their valuation, presents their advantages and disadvantages, and discusses when their issuance is most appropriate. Options and futures are also introduced as derivative instruments used for hedging and speculating.

16.2 WARRANTS

A *warrant* refers to the option to purchase a given number of shares of stock at a given price. Warrants can be either detachable or nondetachable. A detachable warrant may be sold separately from the bond with which it is associated. Thus, the holder may exercise the warrant but not redeem the bond if he or she wishes. A *nondetachable* warrant is sold with its bond to be exercised by the bond owner simultaneously with the convertible bond.

To obtain common stock the warrant must be given up along with the payment of cash called the *exercise price*. Although warrants typically expire on a given date, some are perpetual, that is, never expire. A holder of a warrant may exercise it by purchasing the stock, sell it on the market to other investors, or continue to hold it. The company cannot force the exercise of a warrant. An investor may wish to hold a warrant rather than exercise or sell it because there exists a possibility of achieving a high rate of return. But there are several drawbacks to warrants, including a high risk of losing money, no voting rights, and no receipt of dividends.

If desired, a company may have the exercise price associated with a warrant vary over time (e.g., increase each year).

If there is a stock split or stock dividend before the warrant is exercised, the option price of the warrant is typically adjusted for it.

Through warrants additional funds are received by the issuer. When a bond is issued with a warrant, the warrant price is typically set between 10 percent and 20 percent above the stock's market price. If the company's stock price goes above the option price, the warrants will, of course, be exercised at the option price. The closer the warrants are to their expiration date, the greater the chance is that they will be exercised.

Valuation of a Warrant

The theoretical value of a warrant may be computed by a formula. The formula value is typically less than the market price of the warrant. This is because the speculative appeal of a warrant permits the investor to obtain a good degree of personal leverage.

Value of a warrant = (market price per share − exercise price)

$\times$ number of shares that may be purchased through exercise of the warrant

EXAMPLE 16.1 A warrant for XYZ stock gives the owner the right to buy one share of common stock at $25 a share. The market price of the common stock is $53. The formula price of the warrant is:

Value of warrant = (market price per share − exercise price)

$\times$ number of shares which may be purchased through exercise

= ($53 − $25) × 1 = $28

If the owner had the right to buy three shares of common stock with one warrant, the theoretical value of the warrant would be

$$(\$53 - \$25) \times 3 = \$84$$

In the event the stock is selling for an amount below the option price, there will be a negative value. Because this is illogical, we use a formula value of zero.

EXAMPLE 16.2   Assume the same facts as in Example 16.1, except that the stock is selling at $21 a share. The formula amount is

$$(\$21 - \$25) \times 1 = -\$4$$

However, zero will be assigned.

Warrants do not have an investment value because there is no interest or dividends paid on them. Hence, the market value of a warrant is solely attributable to its convertibility value into common stock. But the market price of a warrant is typically more than its theoretical value, which is referred to as the *premium* on the warrant. The lowest amount that a warrant will sell for is its theoretical value.

The value of a warrant depends on the remaining life of the option, dividend payments on the common stock, the fluctuation in the price of the common stock, whether the warrant is listed on the exchange, and the opportunity cost of funds for the investor. A high value is associated with a warrant when its life is long, the dividend payment on common stock is small, the stock price is volatile, it is listed on the exchange, and the value of funds to the investor is great (because the warrant requires a lesser investment).

EXAMPLE 16.3   ABC stock currently has a market value of $50. The exercise price of the warrant is also $50. Therefore, the theoretical value of the warrant is $0. However, the warrant will sell at a premium (positive price) as long as there is a possibility that the market price of the common stock will surpass $50 before the expiration date of the warrant. The further into the future the expiration date is, the greater will be the premium, since there is a longer period for possible price appreciation.

Of course, the lower the market price is relative to the exercise price, the less the premium is.

EXAMPLE 16.4   Assume the same facts as in Example 16.3, except that the current market price of the stock is $35. The warrant's premium in this case will be much lower, since it would take a long time for the stock's price to increase above $50 a share. If investors expected that the stock price would not rise above $50 at a later date, the value of the warrant would be $0.

If the market price of ABC stock rises above $50, the market price of the warrant will increase and the premium will decrease. In other words, when the stock price is in excess of the exercise price, the market price of the warrant approximately equals the theoretical value causing the premium to disappear. The reduction in the premium arises because of the lessening of the advantage of owning the warrant compared to exercising it.

Advantages and Disadvantages of Warrants

The advantages of issuing warrants include the following:

1. They allow for balanced financing between debt and equity.
2. They permit the issuance of debt at a low interest rate.
3. They serve as a "sweetener" for an issue of debt or preferred stock.

The disadvantages of issuing warrants include the following:

1. When exercised they will result in a dilution of common stock.
2. They may be exercised at a time when the business has no need for additional capital.

Warrant versus Stock Right

There is a difference between a warrant and a *stock right*. A stock right is given *free* to current stockholders, who may either exercise them by purchasing new shares or sell them in the market. Also, a stock right has a shorter duration than a warrant.

16.3 CONVERTIBLE SECURITIES

A *convertible security* is one that may be exchanged for common stock by the holder according to agreed upon terms. Examples are convertible bonds and convertible preferred stock. A specified number of shares of stock are received by the holder of the convertible security when he or she makes the exchange. This is referred to as the *conversion ratio*, which equals:

$$\text{Conversion ratio} = \frac{\text{par value of convertible security}}{\text{conversion price}}$$

The *conversion price* applies to the effective price the holder pays for the common stock when the conversion is effected. The conversion price and the conversion ratio are set at the time the convertible security is issued. The conversion price should be tied to the growth potential of the company. The greater the potential, the greater the conversion price should be.

A convertible bond is a quasi-equity security because its market value is tied to its value if converted rather than as a bond.

EXAMPLE 16.5 If the conversion price of common stock is $25 per share, a $1,000 convertible bond is convertible into 40 shares ($1,000/$25).

EXAMPLE 16.6 A $1,000 bond is convertible into 30 shares of stock. The conversion price is $33.33 ($1,000/30 shares).

EXAMPLE 16.7 A share of convertible preferred stock with a par value of $50 is convertible into four shares of common stock. The conversion price is $12.50 ($50/4).

EXAMPLE 16.8 A $1,000 convertible bond is issued that entitles the holder to convert the bond into 10 shares of common stock. Hence, the conversion ratio is 10 shares for 1 bond. Since the face value of the bond is $1,000 the holder is tendering this amount upon conversion. The conversion price equals $100 per share ($1,000/10 shares).

EXAMPLE 16.9 An investor holds a $1,000 convertible bond that is convertible into 40 shares of common stock. Assuming the common stock is selling for $35 a share, the bondholder can convert the bond into 40 shares worth $1,400.

EXAMPLE 16.10 Y Company issued a $1,000 convertible bond at par. The conversion price is $40. The conversion ratio is:

$$\text{Conversion ratio} = \frac{\text{par value of convertible security}}{\text{conversion price}} = \frac{\$1,000}{\$40} = 25$$

The conversion value of a security is computed as follows:

$$\text{Conversion value} = \text{common stock price} \times \text{conversion ratio}$$

When a convertible security is issued, it is priced higher than its conversion value. The difference is referred to as the *conversion premium*. The percentage conversion premium is computed in the following manner:

$$\text{Percentage conversion premium} = \frac{\text{market value} - \text{conversion value}}{\text{conversion value}}$$

EXAMPLE 16.11   LA Corporation issued a $1,000 convertible bond at par. The market price of the common stock at the date of issue was $48. The conversion price is $55.

$$\text{Conversion ratio} = \frac{\text{par value of convertible security}}{\text{conversion price}} = \frac{\$1,000}{\$55} = 18.18$$

$$\text{Conversion value of the bond} = \text{common stock price} \times \text{conversion ratio} = \$48 \times 18.18 = \$872$$

The difference between the conversion value of $872 and the issue price of $1,000 represents the conversion premium of $128. The conversion premium may also be expressed as a percentage of the conversion value. The percent in this case is:

$$\text{Percentage conversion premium} = \frac{\text{market value} - \text{conversion value}}{\text{conversion value}} = \frac{\$1,000 - \$872}{\$872} = \frac{\$128}{\$872} = 14.7\%$$

The conversion terms may not be static but may increase in steps over specified time periods. Thus, as time goes on fewer common shares are exchanged for the bond. In some cases, after a specified period of time the conversion option may expire.

Usually the convertible security contains a clause that protects it from dilution caused by stock dividends, stock splits, and stock rights. The clause typically prevents the issuance of common stock at a price lower than the conversion price. Also, the conversion price is reduced by the percentage amount of any stock split or stock dividend. This enables the shareholder of common stock to maintain his or her proportionate interest.

EXAMPLE 16.12   A 3-for-1 stock split takes place, which requires a tripling of the conversion ratio. A 20 percent stock dividend necessitates a 20 percent increase in the conversion ratio.

EXAMPLE 16.13   Assume the same facts as in Example 16.8 coupled with a 4-for-1 split. The conversion ratio now becomes 40, and the conversion price now becomes $25.

The voluntary conversion of a security by the holder depends on the relationship of the interest on the bond compared to the dividend on the stock, the risk preference of the holder (stock has a greater risk than a bond), and the current and expected market price of the stock.

Valuation of Convertibles

In a sense, a convertible security is a hybrid security, since it has attributes that are similar to common stock and bonds. The expectation is that the holder will eventually receive both interest yield and a capital gain. Interest yield relates to the coupon interest relative to the market price of the bond when purchased. The capital gain yield applies to the difference between the conversion price and the stock price at the issuance date and the anticipated growth rate in stock price.

EXAMPLE 16.14   A $10,000, 12 percent, 5-year bond is purchased at 95. The simple interest yield is:

$$\frac{\text{Coupon interest}}{\text{Market price of bond}} = \frac{0.12 \times \$10,000}{\$9,500} = \frac{\$1,200}{\$9,500} = 12.6\%$$

The interest yield of 12.6 percent is above the coupon interest rate of 12 percent because the bond was purchased at a discount of 95 percent from its face value ($9,500). At maturity, the holder will get back the face value of $10,000. By purchasing the bond at a discount, the holder has improved his or her rate of return.

The investment value of a convertible security is the value of the security, assuming it was not convertible but had all other attributes. For a convertible bond, its investment value equals the present value of future interest payments plus the present value of the maturity amount. For preferred stock, the investment value equals the present value of future dividend payments plus the present value of expected selling price.

Conversion value refers to the value of stock received upon converting the bond. As the price of the stock goes up so will its conversion value.

EXAMPLE 16.15 A $1,000 bond is convertible into 18 shares of common stock with a market value of $52 per share. The conversion value of the bond equals:

$$\$52 \times 18 \text{ shares} = \$936$$

EXAMPLE 16.16 At the date a $100,000 convertible bond is issued, the market price of the stock is $18 a share. Each $1,000 bond is convertible into 50 shares of stock. The conversion ratio is thus 50. The number of shares the bond is convertible into is:

$$100 \text{ bonds } (\$100,000/\$1,000) \times 50 \text{ shares} = 5,000 \text{ shares}$$

The conversion value is:

$$\$18 \times 5,000 \text{ shares} = \$90,000$$

If the stock price is expected to grow at 6 percent per year, the conversion value at the end of year 1 is:

Shares	5,000
Stock price ($18 × 1.06)	$ 19.08
Conversion value	$95,400

The conversion value at the end of year 2 is:

Shares	5,000
Stock price ($19.08 × 1.06)	$ 20.22
Conversion value	$101,100

A convertible security will not sell at less than its value as straight debt (nonconvertible security). This is because the conversion privilege has to have some value in terms of its potential convertibility to common stock and in terms of reducing the holder's risk exposure to a declining price in the bond (convertible bonds fall off less in price than straight debt issues). Market value will equal investment value only when the conversion privilege is worthless due to a low market price of the common stock relative to the conversion price.

When convertible bonds are issued, the business expects that the value of common stock will appreciate and that the bonds will eventually be converted. If conversion does take place, the company could then issue another convertible bond. Such a financial policy is referred to as *leapfrog financing*.

Of course, if the market price of common stock declines rather than rises, there will be no conversion of debt into equity. In this case, the convertible security remains as debt and is termed a *hung* convertible.

A convertible security holder may prefer to hold the security rather than convert it even though the conversion value exceeds the price paid for it. First, as the price of the common stock goes up so will the price of the convertible security. Second, the holder receives regular interest payments or preferred dividends. To force conversion, companies issuing convertibles often have a call price. The call price is above the face value of the bond (approximately 10 percent to 20 percent higher). This forces the conversion of stock as long as the price of the stock is greater than the conversion price. Everyone would rather have a higher-value common stock than a lower call price for the bond.

EXAMPLE 16.17 The conversion price on a $1,000 debenture is $40 and the call price is $1,100. In order for the conversion value of the bond to equal the call price, the market price of the stock would have to be $44 ($1,100/25). If the conversion value of the bond is 15 percent higher than the call price, the approximate market price of common stock would be $51 (1.15 × $44). At a $51 price, conversion is virtually guaranteed, since if the investor did not convert he or she would incur a material opportunity loss.

EXAMPLE 16.18   Max Company's convertible bond has a conversion price of $80. The conversion ratio is 10. The market price of the stock is $140. The call price is $1,100. The bondholder would rather convert to common stock with a market value of $1,400 ($140 × 10) than have his or her convertible bond redeemed at $1,100. In this case, the call provision forces the conversion when the bondholder might be tempted to wait longer.

Advantages and Disadvantages of Convertibles

To the company, the advantages of convertible security issuance are:

1. It serves as a "sweetener" in a debt offering by giving the investor an opportunity to take part in the price appreciation of common stock. By selling common stock at a gain if held for more than one year the stockholder will receive a favorable tax treatment in the form of a capital gain deduction. Here, only 28 percent of the gain is subject to tax.

2. The issuance of convertible debt allows for a lower interest rate on the financing relative to issuing straight debt.

3. A convertible security may be issued in a tight money market, when it is difficult for a creditworthy firm to issue a straight bond or preferred stock.

4. There are fewer financing restrictions involved with a convertible security issuance.

5. Convertibles provide a means of issuing equity at prices higher than present market prices.

6. The call provision enables the firm to force conversion whenever the market price of the stock is greater than the conversion price.

7. In the event the company issued straight debt now and common stock later to meet the debt, they would incur flotation costs twice, whereas with convertible debt, flotation costs would occur only once, with the initial issuance of the convertible bonds.

To the holder, the advantages of convertible securities are:

1. They offer the potential of a significant capital gain due to price appreciation of the common stock.

2. They offer the holder protection if corporate performance falls off.

3. The margin requirement associated with buying convertible bonds is lower than that associated with buying common stock. Therefore, more money could be borrowed from the broker to invest in convertibles.

To the company, the disadvantages of convertible security issuance are:

1. If the company's stock price appreciably increases in value, it would have been better off financing through a regular issuance of common stock by waiting to issue it at the higher price instead of allowing conversion at the lower price.

2. The company is obligated to pay the convertible debt if the stock price does not increase.

To the holder, the disadvantages of convertible securities are:

1. The yield on a convertible security is lower than that on a comparable security not having the conversion option.

2. A convertible bond is usually subordinated to other debt obligations. Thus, it typically has a lower bond rating.

Corporate Financing Strategy

When a company's stock price is currently depressed, convertible debt rather than common stock issuance may be called for if the price of stock is expected to rise. Establishing a conversion price above the current market price of stock will involve the issuance of fewer shares when the bonds are converted relative to selling the shares at a current lower price. Also, less share dilution will be involved. Of course, the conversion will take place only if the price of the stock goes above the conversion price. The drawback here, however, is that if the stock price does not rise and conversion does not occur, an additional debt burden is placed upon the firm.

The issuance of convertible debt is recommended when the company wishes to leverage itself in the short run but wishes not to incur interest cost and pay principal on the convertible debt in the long run (due to its conversion).

A convertible issue is often a good financing vehicle for a growth company. The quicker the growth rate, the earlier the conversion. For example, a convertible bond may act as a temporary source of funds in a construction period. It is a relatively inexpensive source for financing growth. A convertible issuance is not recommended for a company with a modest growth rate, since it would take a long time to force conversion. During such a time the company will not be able to easily issue additional financing. A long conversion interval may imply to the investing public that the stock has not done as well as expected. The growth rate of the firm is a prime consideration in determining whether convertibles are the best method of financing.

Financial Statement Analysis

When engaging in financial statement analysis, the creditor should consider a convertible bond having an attractive conversion feature as equity rather than debt since in all probability it will be converted into common stock. The future payment of interest and principal on the debt, then, will not be required.

Convertibles versus Warrants

The differences between convertibles and warrants are as follows:

1. Exercising convertibles does not generally provide additional funds to the firm, while the exercise of warrants does.

2. When conversion takes place the debt ratio is reduced. However, the exercise of warrants adds to the equity position with debt still remaining.

3. Due to the call feature, the company has greater control over the timing of the capital structure with convertibles than with warrants.

16.4   OPTIONS

An option is a contract to give the investor the right – but *not an obligation* – to buy or sell something. It has three main features. It allows you, as an investor, to "lock in":

1. a specified number of shares of stock
2. at a fixed price per share, called strike or exercise price
3. for a limited length of time.

EXAMPLE 16.18   If you have purchased an option on a stock, you have the right to "exercise" the option at any time during the life of the option. This means that, regardless of the current market price of the stock, you have the right to buy or sell a specified number of shares of the stock at the strike price (rather than the current market price).

Calls and puts are types of options. You can buy or sell them in round lots, typically 100 shares.

When you buy a call, you are buying the right to purchase stock at a fixed price. You do this when you anticipate the price of the stock will go up. In buying a call you have the chance to make a significant gain from a small investment if the stock price increases, but you also risk the loss of your entire investment if the stock does not increase in price. Calls are in bearer negotiable form with a life of 1 month to 9 months.

The price per share for 100 shares, which the purchaser may buy at (call), is referred to as the *striking price (exercise price)*. For a put, it is the price at which the stock may be sold. The purchase or sale of the stock is to the writer of the option. The striking price is set for the life of the option on the options exchange. When stock price changes, new exercise prices are introduced for trading purposes reflecting the new value.

The option expires on the last day it can be exercised. Conventional options can expire on any business day while options have a standardized expiration date.

The cost of an option is termed the *premium*. It is the price the purchaser of the call or put has to pay the writer.

Premium for a Call Option

The premium depends on the exchange the option is listed, prevailing interest rates, dividend trend of the related security, trading volume, market price of the stock it applies to, amount of time remaining before the expiration date, variability in price of the related security, and width of the spread in price of the stock relative to the option's exercise price (a wider spread means a higher price).

In-the-Money and Out-of-the-Money

When the market price is greater than the strike price, the call is "in-the-money." When the market price is less than the strike price, the call is "out-of-the-money."

A Call at a $50 Strike Price	
In-the-money	Over $50
At-the-money	$50
Out-of-the-money	Under $50

Call options in-the-money have an intrinsic value equal to the difference between the market price and the strike price.

$$\text{Value of call} = (\text{Market price of stock} - \text{Exercise price of call}) \times 100$$

The market price of stock is at the current date. Of course, the market price will typically change on a stock each day. The exercise (strike) price of the call is fixed for its life. For example, the exercise (strike) price for a 3-month call is the same for the entire period.

EXAMPLE 16.19 The market price per share of a stock is $45, with a strike price of $40. Remember that one call is for 100 shares of stock. The value of the call is

$$\$45 - \$40 = \$5 \times 100 \text{ shares} = \$500$$

Out-of-the-money call options have no intrinsic value.

In effect, the total premium consists of the intrinsic value plus speculative premium (time value) based on factors such as risk, variability, forecasted future prices, expiration date, leverage, and dividend.

$$\text{Total premium} = \text{Intrinsic value} + \text{Speculative premium}$$

The call purchaser takes the risk of losing the entire investment price for the option if a price increase does not take place.

EXAMPLE 16.20 A 2-month call option allows you to buy 500 shares of ABC Company at $20 per share. Within that time period, you exercise the option when the market price is $38. Your gain is $9,000 ($38 − $20 = $18 × 500 shares). If the market price had declined from $20 you would not have exercised the call option, and you would have lost your entire investment.

By purchasing a call you can own common stock for a fraction of the cost of purchasing regular shares. Calls cost significantly less than common stock. Leverage exists because a little change in common stock price can result in a major change in the call option's price. A part of the percentage gain in the price of the call is the speculative premium attributable to the remaining life on the call.

EXAMPLE 16.21   A stock has a current market price of $35. A call can be purchased for $300 allowing the acquisition of 100 shares at $35 each. If the price of the stock increases, the call will also be worth more. Assume that the stock is at $55 at the call's expiration date.

The profit is $20 ($55 − $35) on each of the 100 shares of stock in the call, or a total of $2,000 on an investment of $300. A return of 667 percent ($2,000/$3,000) is earned.

16.5   THE BLACK–SCHOLES OPTION PRICING MODEL (OPM)

The model provides the relationship between call option value and the five factors that determine the premium of an option's market value over its expiration value:

1. Time to maturity. The longer the option period, the greater the value of the option.
2. Stock price volatility. The greater the volatility of the underlying stock's price, the greater its value.
3. Exercise price. The lower the exercise price, the greater the value.
4. Stock price. The higher the price of the underlying stock, the greater the value.
5. Risk-free rate. The higher the risk-free rate, the higher the value.

The formula is:

$$V = P[N(d_1)] - Xe^{-rt}[N(d_2)]$$

where
V = Current value of a call option
P = current price of the underlying stock
$N(d)$ = cumulative normal probability density function = probability that a deviation less than d will occur in a standard normal distribution.
X = exercise or strike price of the option
t = time to exercise date (for example, 3 months means $t = 3/12 = 1/4 = 0.25$)
r = (continuously compounded) risk-free rate of interest
e = 2.71828

$$d_1 = \frac{\ln(P/X) + [r + s^2/2]t}{s\sqrt{t}}$$

$$d_2 = \frac{\ln(P/X) + [r + s^2/2]t}{s\sqrt{t}} \text{ or } = d_1 - s\sqrt{t}$$

s^2 = variance per period of (continuously compounded) rate of return on the stock

The formula, while somewhat imposing, actually requires readily available input data, with the exception of s^2, or volatility. P, X, r, and t are easily obtained.

The implications of the option model are the following:

1. The value of the option increases with the level of stock price relative to the exercise price (P/X), the time to expiration times the interest rate (rt), and the time to expiration times the stock's variability (s^2t).
2. Other properties:
   a. The option price is always less than the stock price.
   b. The optional price never falls below the payoff to immediate exercise ($P - X$ or zero, whichever is larger).
   c. If the stock is worthless, the option is worthless.
   d. As the stock price becomes very large, the option price approaches the stock price less the present value of the exercise price.

EXAMPLE 16.22 You are evaluating a call option which has a $20 exercise price and sells for $1.60. It has 3 months to expiration. The underlying stock price is also $20 and its variance is 0.16. The risk-free rate is 12 percent. The option's value is:

First, calculate d_1 and d_2:

$$d_1 = \frac{\ln(P/X) + [r + s^2/2]t}{s\sqrt{t}}$$

$$= \frac{\ln(\$20/\$20) + [0.12 + (0.16/2)](0.25)}{(0.40)\sqrt{(0.25)}}$$

$$= \frac{0 + 0.05}{0.20} = 0.25$$

$$d_2 = d_1 - s\sqrt{t} = 0.25 - 0.20 = 0.05$$

Next, look up the values for $N(d_1)$ and $N(d_2)$:

$$N(d_1) = N(0.25) = 1 - 0.4013 = 0.5987$$
$$N(d_2) = N(0.05) = 1 - 0.4801 = 0.5199$$

Finally, use those values to find the option's value:

$$V = P[N(d_1)] - Xe^{-rt}[N(d_2)]$$
$$= \$20[0.5987] - \$20e^{(-0.12)(0.25)}[0.5199]$$
$$= \$11.97 - \$19.41(0.5199)$$
$$= \$11.97 - \$10.09 = \$1.88$$

At $1.60, the option is undervalued according to the Black–Scholes model. The rational investor would buy one option and sell 0.5987 shares of stock short.

16.6 FUTURES

A futures is a contract to purchase or sell a given amount of an item for a given price by a certain date (in the future – thus the name "futures market"). The seller of a futures contract agrees to deliver the item to the buyer of the contract, who agrees to purchase the item. The contract specifies the amount, valuation, method, quality, month and means of delivery, and exchange to be traded in. The month of delivery is the expiration date; in other words, the date on which the commodity or financial instrument must be delivered.

Commodity contracts are guarantees by a seller to deliver a commodity (e.g., cocoa or cotton). Financial contracts are a commitment by the seller to deliver a financial instrument (e.g., a Treasury bill) or a specific amount of foreign currency.

Future markets can be used for both hedging and speculating.

EXAMPLE 16.23 Investors use hedging to protect their position in a commodity. For example, a citrus grower (the seller) will hedge to get a higher price for his products while a processor (or buyer) of the item will hedge to obtain a lower price. By hedging an investor minimizes the risk of loss but loses the prospect of sizable profit.

Review Questions

1. The _____ is the cash paid when a warrant is given up to acquire common stock.

2. Dividends are not received on holding _____ .

3. A(n) _____ warrant is sold separately from the bond.

4. The option price must be adjusted for a(n) _____ dividend.

5. Warrants may be issued as _____ for a risky debt or preferred stock issue.

6. If stock has a market price below the option price, the value of the warrant is _____ .

7. The _____ of a warrant relates to its convertibility value into common stock.

8. The longer the remaining life of a warrant, the _____ its value.

9. A(n) _____ dividend payment on common stock means a lower value associated with the warrant.

10. The difference between a warrant and stock right is that the latter is _____ to existing stockholders.

11. The _____ applies to the number of shares received by a holder of a convertible security when he or she makes the exchange.

12. The effective price when a holder pays for common stock to effect conversion is termed the _____ .

13. The market value of a convertible bond relates to its value _____ rather than its bond value.

14. A(n) _____ is a good financing tool for a growth company.

15. Convertible debt involves a(n) _____ interest rate than straight debt.

16. The margin requirement on purchasing convertible bonds is _____ than on purchasing common stock.

17. Interest yield equals _____ divided by the market price of the bond.

18. The investment value of a convertible bond equals the present value of _____ plus the present value of the _____ .

19. _____ is the term used when a new convertible security is issued after an old one has been converted.

20. The term _____ convertible is used when a convertible security continues as debt.

21. For financial statement analysis purposes, a convertible bond with an attractive conversion feature is considered _____ rather than _____ .

22. Options are traded in terms of _____ lots of _____ shares.

23. When the market price is below the strike price, the call is said to be _____ .

24. If you do not exercise a call option, you will lose your _____ .

25. The total premium of an option consists of the intrinsic value plus _____ based on factors such as risk, variability, forecasted future prices, expiration date, leverage, and dividend.

26. The _____ provides the relationship between call option value and the five factors that determine the premium of an option's market value over its expiration value.

27. Future markets can be used for both _____ and _____ .

Answers: (1) exercise price; (2) warrants; (3) detachable; (4) stock; (5) "sweeteners"; (6) zero; (7) market value; (8) higher; (9) high; (10) free; (11) conversion ratio; (12) conversion price; (13) if converted; (14) convertible security; (15) lower; (16) lower; (17) coupon interest; (18) future interest payments, maturity amount; (19) Leapfrog financing; (20) hung; (21) equity, debt; (22) round, 100; (23) out-of-the-money; (24) entire investment; (25) speculative premium (time value); (26) Black–Scholes Option Pricing (OPM); (27) hedging, speculating.

Solved Problems

16.1   **Warrant Value.** A warrant for Ace Corporation stock enables the holder to purchase one share of common stock at $30 a share. The stock has a market price of $47 a share. What is the value of the warrant?

   SOLUTION

   Warrant value = (market price per share − exercise price) × number of shares that may be purchased
   $$= (\$47 - \$30) \times 1 = \$17$$

16.2   **Warrant Value.** Assume the same facts as in Problem 16.1, except that the holder can purchase four shares of common stock for each warrant. What is the value of the warrant?

   SOLUTION

   $$(\$47 - \$30) \times 4 = \$68$$

16.3   **Warrant Value.** Assume the same facts as Problem 16.1, except that the stock has a market price of $28 a share. What is the value of the warrant?

   SOLUTION

   $$(\$28 - \$30) \times 1 = -\$2$$

   Since there can never be a negative value for a warrant, zero is the amount assigned to the warrant.

16.4   **Premium.** The market price of Harris Corporation stock is $45. Its exercise price is similarly $45. Will the stock warrant sell at a premium?

   SOLUTION

   Yes. The warrant will sell at a premium, since there exists the possibility that the market price of the common stock will exceed $45 prior to the expiration date of the warrant.

16.5   **Bond to Common Shares.** The conversion price of common stock is $20 a share. Into how many shares will a $1,000 convertible bond be converted?

SOLUTION

$$\frac{\$1,000}{\$20} = 50 \text{ shares}$$

16.6   Conversion Price. A $1,000 bond is convertible into 60 shares of stock. What is the conversion price?

SOLUTION

$$\frac{\$1,000}{60 \text{ shares}} = \$16.67$$

16.7   Conversion Ratio. A $1,000 convertible bond permits the holder to convert the bond into five shares of common stock. (*a*) What is the conversion ratio? (*b*) What is the conversion price?

SOLUTION

(*a*)   Five shares for each bond

(*b*)

$$\frac{\$1,000}{5 \text{ shares}} = \$200 \text{ per share}$$

16.8   Conversion Ratio. T Corporation issued a $1,000 bond at par. The conversion price is $20. What is the conversion ratio?

SOLUTION

$$\text{Conversion ratio} = \frac{\text{par value of convertible security}}{\text{conversion price}} = \frac{\$1,000}{\$20} = 50$$

16.9   Convertibility. Tristar Corporation issued a $1,000 bond at par. The common stock has a market price of $45. The conversion price is $58. (*a*) Into how many shares can the bond be converted? (*b*) What is the conversion value of the bond? (*c*) What is the conversion premium?

SOLUTION

(*a*)

$$\frac{\$1,000}{\$58} = 17.24 \text{ shares}$$

(*b*)   Conversion value = (common stock price) × (conversion ratio) = $45 × 17.24 = $776

(*c*) $1,000 − $776 = $224

16.10   Percentage Conversion Premium. A $1,000 bond is issued at par. The market price of the common stock at the issue date was $20. The conversion price is $25. (*a*) What is the conversion ratio? (*b*) What is the conversion value? (*c*) What is the percentage conversion premium?

SOLUTION

(*a*)

$$\frac{\$1,000}{\$25} = 40$$

(*b*) $20 × 40 = $800

(*c*) $\text{Percentage conversion premium} = \dfrac{\text{market value} - \text{conversion value}}{\text{conversion value}} = \dfrac{\$1,000 - \$800}{\$800} = \dfrac{\$200}{\$800} = 25\%$

16.11 Conversion Ratio. What effect will a 2-for-1 stock split have on a conversion ratio?

SOLUTION

The conversion ratio will double.

16.12 Conversion Value. A $1,000 bond is convertible into 25 shares of common stock having a market value of $47 per share. What is the conversion value?

SOLUTION

$$\$47 \times 25 \text{ shares} = \$1,175$$

16.13 Conversion Ratio. When a $50,000 convertible bond is issued, the market price of the stock is $25 a share. Each $1,000 bond is convertible into 40 shares of stock. (*a*) What is the conversion ratio? (*b*) What is the conversion value? (*c*) Assuming the stock price is anticipated to grow at 8 percent annually, what is the conversion value at the end of the first year?

SOLUTION

(*a*)
$$\frac{\$50,000}{\$1,000} = 50 \text{ bonds} \times 40 \text{ shares} = 2,000 \text{ shares}$$

(*b*)
$$\$25 \times 2,000 \text{ shares} = \$50,000$$

(*c*)

Shares	2,000
Stock price ($25 × 1.08)	× $27
	$54,000

16.14 Simple Interest Yield. A $30,000, 15 percent, 10-year bond is bought at 102. What is the simple interest yield?

SOLUTION

$$\frac{\text{Coupon interest}}{\text{Market price of bond}} = \frac{0.15 \times \$30,000}{\$30,600} = \frac{\$4,500}{\$30,600} = 14.7\%$$

16.15 Market Price of Stock. For a $1,000 convertible bond, the conversion price is $50. The call price is $1,200. (*a*) If the conversion value of the bond equals the call price, what should the market price of the stock be? (*b*) What is the approximate market price of common stock if the conversion value of the bond is 20 percent higher than the call price?

SOLUTION

(*a*)
$$\frac{\$1,200}{20} = \$60$$

(*b*)
$$\$60 \times 1.20 = \$72$$

16.16 Call Price. Drake Corporation's convertible bond has a conversion price of $90. The conversion ratio is 15. The market price of the stock is $130. The call price is $1,800. Would the bondholder rather convert to common stock or receive the call price?

SOLUTION

Market value of common stock received upon conversion is:

$$\$130 \times 15 = \$1,950$$
$$\text{Call price} = \$1,800$$

The bondholder would rather convert, since he or she receives a benefit of $150.

16.17 Attractiveness of Convertible Debenture. Great Northern Oil Shale Company is a company actively engaged in the oil services industry. The company provides replacement parts for drilling rigs and has just begun to test a device that measures shale oil content in certain rock formations.

The company has an 8 percent convertible subordinated debenture outstanding due in the year 2001. The convertible is callable at 106 and has a conversion price of $50. The common stock is currently paying a dividend of $1.40 on earnings per share of $3. Consensus among analysts is that long-term interest rates will be stable to lower over the next year. The common stock is currently selling for $30 and the convertible bond at 66. Nonconvertible bonds of companies in this industry having similar quality ratings (triple-B) are yielding 14 percent to maturity.

(*a*) Discuss four characteristics of the convertible debenture, and (*b*) explain whether you consider the convertible debenture or the common stock more attractive for purchase. (CFA, adapted.)

SOLUTION

(*a*) Characteristics of this convertible industrial debenture include the following:

(1) The quality of the bond is not high but average for most convertible bonds.

(2) The outlook for interest rates is stable to lower. This is a plus, as bond prices should be stable to rising.

(3) Minimum value as straight debt is around 60, or about 9 percent under current market of 66. This is well within reasonable limits of, say, 15 percent or below.

(4) The current price of the common is 10 percent below the bonds' conversion value. Conversion value is $[(1,000/50) \times \$30]$. This is within reasonable limits of, say, maximum of 20 percent or so.

(5) The current yield on the bond of 12.0 percent seems favorable at more than twice 4.7 percent on the common.

(6) The call risk is remote (call price of 106 versus market price of 66).

(*b*) The convertible looks more attractive because of the modest premiums involved—upside leverage and downside cushion, compared to the common. The convertible also looks more attractive because of the higher income relative to the common, assuming that the common stock price has the potential to rise by a sizable amount from the current price of 33 to the 40-plus level.

16.18 Options. You can buy XZ Company stock at $30 a share, or $3,000 for 100 shares. You can acquire a $33 3-month call for $400. Thus, you could invest $2,600 cash and have the opportunity to buy 100 shares at $33 per share. Assume, however, that you decide to invest your $2,600 in a 3-month CD earning 14 percent interest. The CD will return $91 ($14\% \times \$2,600 \times 3/12$).

(*a*) If the YZ Company stock goes to $16, what is the option worth.

(*b*) If the stock goes to $43, would there be a gain or loss?

SOLUTION

(a) The option will be worthless but the significant loss on the stock of $14 a share did not occur. Instead, the loss is limited to $309 ($400 − $91). However, note that by not buying a stock you may have forgone a dividend.

(b) If the stock went up to $43, the call would be exercised at $33 resulting in a significant gain with little investment.

16.19 The Black–Scholes Option Pricing Model (OPM). Given:

$$\text{Stock price} = \$23$$
$$\text{Exercise price} = \$18$$
$$\text{Risk-free rate} = 0.06$$
$$\text{Time to expire} = 1.0 \ (1 \text{ year})$$
$$\text{Standard deviation of the stock's return} = 0.50 \ (\text{variance is } 0.25)$$

What is the value of this option?

SOLUTION

First, calculate d_1 and d_2:

$$d_1 = \frac{\ln(P/X) + [r + s^2/2]t}{s\sqrt{t}}$$

$$= \frac{\ln(\$23/\$18) + [0.06 + (0.25/2)](1.0)}{(0.50)\sqrt{(1.0)}}$$

$$= 0.86$$

$$d_2 = d_1 - s\sqrt{t} = 0.86 - (0.50)\sqrt{(1.0)} = 0.36$$

Next, look up the values for $N(d_1)$ and $N(d_2)$:

$$N(d_1) = N(0.86) = 1 - 0.195 = 0.805$$
$$N(d_2) = N(0.36) = 1 - 0.3595 = 0.6405$$

Finally, use those values to find the option's value:

$$V = P[N(d_1)] - Xe^{-rt}[N(d_2)]$$
$$= \$23[0.805] - \$18e^{(-0.06)(1.0)}[0.6405]$$
$$= \$7.66$$

Chapter 17

Mergers and Acquisitions

17.1 INTRODUCTION

Internal growth comes about when a company invests in products it has developed, while external growth occurs when a company buys the existing assets of another company through a merger. Financial managers are sometimes required to evaluate the attractiveness of a potential merger as well as participate in merger negotiations. In addition to growth, mergers may allow an organization to diversify.

There are three common ways of joining two or more companies. The following definitions will distinguish the difference between a merger, consolidation, and a holding company:

Merger. A merger is the combination of two or more companies into one, where only the acquiring company retains its identity. Typically, the larger of the two companies is the acquiring company whose identity is maintained.

Consolidation. In a consolidation, two or more companies are combined to form a new company. None of the consolidation firms legally survives. In effect, the consolidating firms are dissolved and a new company is formed.

EXAMPLE 17.1 Companies X and Y give all their assets, liabilities, and stock to the new company, Z, in return for Z's stock, bonds, or cash. The combining of companies X and Y with new company Z emerging is a consolidation.

Holding Company. A holding company holds, or owns, enough shares of common stock to have voting control of one or more other companies. The holding company comprises a group of businesses, each operating as a separate corporate entity. By holding more than 50 percent of the voting rights through common stock, the holding company ensures control of the other companies. In reality, a holding company can have effective control of another company with a smaller percent of ownership, such as 20 percent. The holding company is called the *parent*, and each company controlled is called a *subsidiary*.

Depending on the intent of the combination, there are three common ways businesses get together to gain advantage in their market. The three types of business combinations are:

1. *Vertical.* A vertical merger takes place when a company combines with a customer or supplier. For example, when a furniture manufacturer combines with a chain of furniture stores, the combination is vertical.

2. *Horizontal.* A horizontal combination is when two companies in a similar business combine, for example, when one oil company buys another oil company.

3. *Conglomerate.* A conglomerate is when two companies in unrelated industries combine. For example, when an appliance manufacturer combines with a book publisher, a conglomerate is formed.

17.2 MERGERS

The merger of two companies can be accomplished in one of two ways. The acquiring company can negotiate with management of the other company, which is the preferred approach, or it can make a tender offer directly to the stockholders of the company it wants to take over. A *tender offer* is an offer of cash for shares of stock held by stockholders.

In negotiating with management, often the acquiring company makes a stock offer based on a specified exchange ratio. The merger may take place if the acquired company receives an offer at an acceptable premium over the present market price of its stock. Sometimes to satisfy the management of the acquired business, certain contingent payments, such as stock purchase warrants, are made part of the merger contract. If the negotiations break down, a tender offer may be made directly to the company's stockholders. The tender offer is made at a premium above the market price of the stock and is offered to all stockholders of the company. Tender offers are fully discussed later in this chapter.

There are various financing packages that buyers may use for mergers such as common stock, preferred stock, convertible securities, cash, debt, and warrants. A prime consideration in selecting the final package is its impact on current earnings per share.

When common stock is exchanged, the seller's stock is given in exchange for the buyer's stock. The advantage of a stock trade is that it represents a tax-free exchange. A disadvantage is that issuing the stock increases the buyer's outstanding shares, thus diluting earnings per share. When there is an exchange of cash for common stock, the selling firm's stockholders receive cash for their common stock, resulting in a taxable transaction. Such an exchange may improve earnings per share because the buying company is getting new earnings without increasing outstanding shares.

Reasons for Mergers

There are several reasons why a company would prefer external growth through merger rather than internal growth:

1. The company may want diversification to reduce the risks involved with a seasonal business.

2. A company may expect a synergistic effect by merging with another. Through synergism the results are greater than the sum of the parts. That is, greater earnings may be obtained from the combined company than would be possible from each individual company because of efficiency and cost savings. There is a greater chance of synergistic gains from a horizontal merger, since duplicate facilities may be eliminated.

3. A merger may permit one firm to obtain something it lacks, such as superior management talent or a research capability.

4. A company may improve its ability to raise funds when it combines with another having highly liquid assets and low debt.

5. The net income of the new large company may be capitalized at a low rate, resulting in a high market value for its stock. The stock of a large company is usually more marketable than that of a small one. These attributes may result in a high P/E ratio for the stock.

6. In some cases, it is possible to finance an acquisition when it would not be possible to finance internal expansion. For instance, acquiring another company by exchanging stock may be less costly than constructing a new plant, which requires a substantial cash payment.

7. An acquisition can result in a good return on the investment when the market value of the acquired company is significantly below its replacement cost.

8. By acquiring a company that has been operating at a net loss, the acquiring company may not only get the acquired company at a good price, but will also obtain a tax-loss-carryforward benefit. The acquiring company can use the tax-loss-carryforward benefit to offset its own profitability and thus lower its tax payment. The tax loss may be carried forward for 15 years to reduce the acquiring company's future earnings. In effect, the government is financing part of the acquisition.

EXAMPLE 17.2 Ace Company is considering buying Jones Company. Jones Company has a tax loss of $700,000. Ace expects before-tax profits of $300,000 a year for the next 3 years. The tax rate is 46 percent.

The taxes to be paid for each of the next 3 years after the acquisition follow:

For year 1:

Ace Company's earnings	$300,000
Jones Company's tax loss carryforward	300,000
Taxable income	$ 0
Tax	$ 0

For year 2:

Ace Company's earnings	$300,000
Jones Company's tax loss carryforward	300,000
Taxable income	$ 0
Tax	$ 0

For year 3:

Ace Company's earnings	$300,000
Unused tax loss carryforward ($700,000 − $600,000)	100,000
Taxable income	$200,000
Tax (46% rate)	$ 92,000

Disadvantages of Mergers

The disadvantages that may result from mergers are:

1. A merger may not work out financially because the anticipated benefits (e.g., cost reductions) do not occur.
2. Friction may arise between the management of the two companies.
3. Dissenting minority stockholders may cause problems.
4. Government antitrust action may block or delay the proposed merger.

Evaluating a Potential Merger

In evaluating a possible merger, the financial manager must consider the effect the merger may have on the performance of the company, such as:

1. *Earnings per share.* The merger should improve earnings per share or enhance its stability.
2. *Dividends per share.* The dividends paid prior to the merger should be maintained to stabilize the market price of stock.
3. *Market price per share.* The essential variable to consider is the effect of the merger on the market price of the company's stock.
4. *Risk.* The merger should reduce the business and financial risk of the resulting enterprise.

17.3 ACQUISITION TERMS

When determining the terms of the acquisition, consideration should be given to the following factors:

1. The absolute amount of earnings as well as the earnings growth rate

2. Dividends

3. Market price of the stock

4. Book value per share

5. Net working capital per share

The weight each factor bears on a merger varies, based on the particular circumstances involved.

Earnings.   In ascertaining the value of earnings in a merger, consideration should be given to anticipated future profit and the projected P/E multiple. A company in a rapid growth stage is expected to have a high P/E multiple.

EXAMPLE 17.3   Company S and company T are planning a merger. Company S has the higher P/E ratio. The earnings of company S are expected to show a greater growth rate than that of company T. If the merger occurs, the acquiring company T will be obtaining a company with superior growth potential. Therefore, company T's profitability subsequent to the merger should increase faster than before. The new growth rate will approximate the weighted average growth rates on the individual companies with the weight based on the relative total earnings prior to the merger. The key considerations involved in this analysis are the past and projected growth rates of the business, their size, the P/E multipliers, and the exchange ratio. The combination of these factors influences the EPS of the surviving company.

Dividends.   Dividends impact the acquisition terms, since they constitute income to stockholders. However, the greater a company's growth rate and profitability, the lesser the impact dividends will have on the per share market price of the companies. Conversely, when profits are declining, dividends will have a more significant effect on the market price of the stock.

Market Price of the Stock.   Since the price per share takes into account potential earnings and dividends, current market value must be considered in the merger. The value given to the firm in the acquisition will probably be greater than the current market price per share under the following circumstances:

1. The company is in an industry with financial problems and thus will have a currently depressed market price.

2. The acquired company may have more of a value to the acquirer (e.g., assist in diversification) than to the stock market in general.

3. To encourage stockholders to give up their shares, an amount greater than the current market price may be given.

Book Value per Share.   Generally speaking, book value is not an important ingredient in the merger process because it is based on historical cost rather than current values. But book value may be relevant when it exceeds market price. In such a case, there may be an expectation that the market price of the stock will increase because of new and better management.

Net Working Capital per Share.   Net working capital per share may impact the merger terms due to the liquidity of one of the combining companies. For example, if the acquired company has a very low debt position, the acquiring company may borrow the funds needed for the acquisition by using the acquired company's good liquidity position to meet the loan following the merger. Or the liquid assets of the acquired company can provide needed collateral for the issuance of debt.

17.4 ACQUISITIONS

Acquisition of a Company

The acquisition of a going concern is evaluated through capital budgeting techniques. When a company buys another having a financial structure materially different from its own, the impact of the new capital structure on the company's overall cost of capital must be projected.

EXAMPLE 17.4   Sharav Company is considering purchasing Shillinglaw Corporation for $80,000 in cash. Sharav's current cost of capital is 15 percent. Shillinglaw's estimated overall cost of capital is expected to become 12 percent after the acquisition. The estimated cash inflows from years 1 to 12 are $10,000.

The net present value is:

	Calculations	Present Value
Year 0	−$80,000 × 1	−$80,000
Years 1–12	+$10,000 × 6.194	+61,940[a]
Net present value		−$18,060

---

[a] Using 12 percent as the discount rate.

Since the net present value is negative, the acquisition should not take place.

EXAMPLE 17.5   Boston Corporation is considering acquiring Masters Corporation for $200,000 in cash. Boston's cost of capital is 16 percent primarily due to its high debt position. If the acquisition is made, Boston expects that its overall cost of capital will be 14 percent because Masters Corporation is financed mostly with equity. The acquisition is anticipated to generate yearly cash inflows of $28,000 for the next 10 years.

The net present value is:

	Calculations	Present Value
Year 0	−$200,000 × 1	−$200,000
Years 1–10	+$28,000 × 5.216	+146,048
Net present value		−$ 53,952

Since the net present value is negative, the acquisition should not take place.

Acquisition of Assets for Cash

When one company acquires another for cash, capital budgeting may be used to examine the financial feasibility of the acquisition. To ascertain whether the purchase of assets is financially justifiable, the company must predict the costs and benefits of the assets.

EXAMPLE 17.6   The Davis Company wants to buy certain fixed assets of Boris Company. However, Boris wants to sell out its entire business. The balance sheet for Boris Company follows:

ASSETS

Cash	$ 3,000
Accounts receivable	7,000
Inventories	12,000
Equipment 1	15,000
Equipment 2	25,000
Equipment 3	40,000
Building	100,000
Total assets	$202,000

LIABILITIES AND STOCKHOLDERS' EQUITY

Total liabilities	$ 90,000
Total stockholders' equity	112,000
Total liabilities and stockholders' equity	$202,000

Davis needs only equipment 2 and 3 and the building. The other assets excluding cash can be sold for $30,000. The total cash received is therefore $33,000 ($30,000 + $3,000 initial cash balance). Boris wants $45,000 for the entire business. Davis will thus have to pay a total of $135,000, which is $90,000 in total liabilities and $45,000 for its owners. The actual net cash outlay is therefore $102,000 ($135,000 − $33,000). It is expected that the after-tax cash inflows from the new equipment will be $25,000 per year for the next 6 years. The cost of capital is 10 percent.

The net present value associated with this acquisition follows:

	Calculations	Present Value
Year 0	−$102,000 × 1	−$102,000
Years 1–6	+$25,000 × 4.355	+108,875
Net present value		+$ 6,875

Since the net present value is positive, the acquisition is recommended.

EXAMPLE 17.7   Miles Corporation is thinking of acquiring Piston Corporation for $50,000. Piston has liabilities of $75,000. Piston has equipment that Miles desires. The remaining assets would be sold for $58,000. By acquiring the equipment, Miles will have an increase in cash flow of $17,000 each year for the next 12 years. The cost of capital is 10 percent.

The net cost of the equipment is:

$$\$50,000 + \$75,000 - \$58,000 = \$67,000$$

Miles should make the acquisition since, as indicated below, the net present value is positive.

	Calculations	Present Value
Year 0	−$67,000 × 1	−$ 67,000
Years 1–12	+$17,000 × 6.814	+115,838
Net present value		+$ 48,838

Acquisition by Exchanging Stock

A company is often acquired by exchanging common stock. The exchange will be in accordance with a predetermined ratio. The amount the acquiring firm offers for each share of the acquired business is usually more than the current market price of the traded shares. The *ratio of exchange* is equal to:

$$\frac{\text{Amount paid per share of the acquired company}}{\text{Market price of the acquiring company's shares}}$$

EXAMPLE 17.8   Company A wants to acquire company B. Company A's stock sells for $80 per share. Company B's stock sells for $55 per share. Because of the merger negotiations, company A offers $60 per share. The acquisition is made through an exchange of securities.

$$\text{Ratio of exchange} = \frac{\text{amount paid per share of the acquired company}}{\text{market price of the acquiring company's shares}} = \frac{\$60}{\$80} = 0.75$$

Company A must exchange 0.75 share of its stock for one share of company B's stock.

17.5   THE EFFECT OF A MERGER ON EARNINGS PER SHARE AND MARKET PRICE PER SHARE OF STOCK

When a merger takes place, there may be a favorable or unfavorable effect on net income and market price per share of stock. The effect on earnings per share can easily be seen in Example 17.9.

EXAMPLE 17.9 The following data are presented:

	Company X	Company Y
Net income	$30,000	$54,000
Shares outstanding	4,000	9,000
Earnings per share	$7.50	$6.00
P/E ratio	10	12.5
Market price	$75	$75

Company Y is the acquiring company and will exchange its shares for company X's shares on a one-for-one basis. The exchange ratio is based on the market prices of X and Y. The impact on EPS follows:

	Y Shares Owned after Merger	EPS Prior to Merger	EPS Subsequent to Merger
X stockholders	4,000	$7.50	$6.46[a]
Y stockholders	9,000	$6.00	$6.46[a]
Total	13,000		

---

[a]Total net income is calculated as follows:

4,000 shares × $7.50	$30,000
9,000 shares × $6.00	54,000
New EPS	$84,000

$$\text{EPS} = \frac{\text{total net income}}{\text{total shares}} = \frac{\$84,000}{13,000} = \$6.46$$

EPS decreases by $1.04 for X stockholders but increases by $0.46 for Y stockholders.

The impact on market price is not clear. Assuming the combined company has the same P/E ratio as that of company Y, the market price per share will be $80.75 (12.5 × $6.46). In this example, the stockholders of each firm enjoy a higher market value per share. The increased market value comes about because the net income of the combined company is valued at a 12.5 P/E ratio, the same as company Y, while before the merger, company X had a lower P/E multiple of 10. But if the combined company is valued at company X's multiplier of 10, the market value would be $64.60 (10 × $6.46). In this instance, the stockholders in each firm will have experienced a decline in market value of $10.40 ($75.00 − $64.60).

Since the effect of a merger on market value per share is not clear, EPS is given the prime consideration.

EXAMPLE 17.10 The following data are given:

Case	Market Price per Share of Acquiring Company	Market Price per Share of Acquired Company	Price per Share Offered
1	$60	$20	$25
2	$100	$130	$140

In each of the following cases, the exchange ratio in (1) shares and (2) market price is:

	Exchange Ratio	
Case	Shares	Market Price
1	$25/$60 = 0.42	$25/$20 = 1.25
2	$140/$100 = 1.4	$140/$130 = 1.08

EXAMPLE 17.11 Joy Corporation wishes to acquire Davis Corporation. Data for the companies follow:

	Joy	**Davis**
Net income	$30,000	$14,000
Shares outstanding	22,000	7,000

Joy Corporation issues its shares to make the acquisition. The ratio of exchange is 2.2 to 1. The EPS based on the original shares of each company follows:

$$\text{EPS of the merged entity} = \frac{\text{combined net income}}{\text{total shares}} = \frac{\$30,000 + \$14,000}{22,000 + (7,000 \times 2.2)}$$

$$= \frac{\$44,000}{22,000 + 15,400} = \frac{\$44,000}{37,400 \text{ shares}} = \$1.18$$

EPS of Joy = $1.18

EPS of Davis = $1.18 \times 2.2 = \$2.60$

EXAMPLE 17.12 Andrew Company wants to acquire Stella Company by exchanging 0.6 share of its stock for each share of Stella. Financial data follow:

	Andrew	**Stella**
Net income	$180,000	$36,000
Shares outstanding	60,000	18,000
EPS	$3	$2
Market price	$30	$14
P/E ratio	10	7

Andrew issues its shares to make the acquisition. The shares Andrew has to issue in the acquisition are:

$$18,000 \text{ shares} \times 0.6 = 10,800 \text{ shares}$$

Assuming the earnings of each company remain the same, the EPS after the acquisition is:

$$\frac{\$180,000 + \$36,000}{60,000 + 10,800} = \frac{\$216,000}{70,800 \text{ shares}} = \$3.05$$

The amount earned per share on the original shares of Stella stock is:

$$\$3.05 \times 0.6 = \$1.83$$

The amount earned per share on the original shares of Andrew stock is $3.05.

EXAMPLE 17.13 Arnold Corporation wishes to acquire Jack Corporation by exchanging 1.5 shares of its stock for each share of Jack. Arnold Corporation expects to have the same P/E ratio after the merger as before. The following financial data are presented:

	Arnold	**Jack**
Net income	$400,000	$100,000
Shares	200,000	25,000
Market price per share	$40	$48

The exchange ratio of market price is:

$$\frac{\text{Price per share offered}}{\text{Market price of Jack}} = \frac{\$40 \times 1.5}{\$48} = \frac{\$60}{\$48} = 1.25$$

EPS and P/E multiples for each firm are:

	Arnold	**Jack**
EPS	$400,000/200,000 shares = $2	$100,000/25,000 shares = $4
P/E ratio	$40/$2 = 20 times	$48/$4 = 12 times

The P/E ratio used in obtaining Jack is:

$$1.5 \times \$40 = \$60$$

$$\frac{\$60}{\$4} = 15 \text{ times}$$

The EPS of Arnold after the acquisition is:

$$\frac{\$500,000}{200,000 + (25,000 \times 1.5)} = \frac{\$500,000}{237,500 \text{ shares}} = \$2.11$$

The anticipated market price per share of the merged company is:

$$\$2.11 \times 20 \text{ times} = \$42.20$$

17.6 HOLDING COMPANY

A holding company is one that has the sole purpose of owning the stock of other businesses. A holding company can acquire a small percent of another company (e.g., 10 percent), which may be sufficient to obtain a significant influence over the other, especially when stock ownership is widely disbursed. A holding company that wants to obtain voting control of a business may make a direct market purchase or a tender offer to get the additional shares. What would prompt the officers of a company to turn it into a holding company? A company in a declining industry, for example, may decide to move out of its basic operations by liquidating assets and use the funds obtained to invest in other companies having good growth potential.

Since the operating companies held by the holding company are distinct legal entities, the obligations of any one are isolated from the others. If one of them goes under, there is no claim on the assets of another. However, a loan officer that lends to one company may require a guarantee by the other companies. This will in effect join the assets of the companies. In any case, a major financial setback involving one company is not the responsibility of the others.

The advantages of a holding company arrangement include the following:

1. The ability of the holding company to acquire a large amount of assets with a small investment. In effect, the holding company can control more assets than it could acquire through a merger.

2. There is risk protection because the failure of one of the companies does not cause the failure of the other companies or the holding company. The failure of one invested company would not cost the holding company more than its investment in that firm.

3. It is easy to gain control of another company because all that is involved is buying enough stock in the market place. Unlike a merger in which stockholder or management approval is needed, no approval is needed for a holding company.

The disadvantages of a holding company arrangement are as follows:

1. There is multiple taxation since the income the holding company receives from its subsidiaries is in the form of cash. Before paying dividends, the subsidiary must pay taxes on its earnings. When the earnings are distributed to the holding company as dividends, it must pay tax on the dividends received less the 85 percent dividend exclusion. However, if the holding company

owns 80 percent or more of the subsidiary's stock, there will be a 100 percent dividend exemption. There is no multiple taxation for a subsidiary that is part of a merged company.

EXAMPLE 17.14 A holding company owns 60 percent of another business. Dividends received by the holding company are $15,000. The tax rate is 46 percent. The tax paid on the dividends follows:

Dividend	$15,000
Dividend exclusion (85%)	12,750
Dividend subject to tax	$ 2,250
Tax rate	×46%
Tax	$ 1,035

The effective tax is 6.9% ($1,035/$15,000 or 15% × 46%).

2. A holding company is typically more costly to administer than a single company emanating from a merger. The increased costs arise from not achieving the economies that would normally occur in a merger.

3. The U.S. Department of Justice may consider the holding company a near monopoly and force dissolution of some of the companies by disposal of stock.

4. By acquiring stock ownership in other companies there may occur a financial leverage effect through increased debt which will magnify either earnings or losses. The more the financial leverage involved, the higher the risk of variability in earnings.

A holding company can get a large amount of control for a small investment by obtaining voting control in a company for a minimal amount and then using that firm to gain voting control in another, and so on.

EXAMPLE 17.15 Matz Company holds stock in company X and company Y and has voting control over both. Balance sheet information follows:

Matz Company

Investment		Long-term liabilities	$ 40,000
Company X	$ 30,000	Preferred stock	20,000
Company Y	70,000	Common stock equity	40,000
Total	$100,000	Total	$100,000

Company X

Current assets	$120,000	Current liabilities	$100,000
Noncurrent assets	480,000	Long-term liabilities	350,000
		Common stock equity	150,000
Total	$600,000	Total	$600,000

Company Y

Current assets	$200,000	Current liabilities	$150,000
Noncurrent assets	600,000	Long-term liabilities	400,000
		Common stock equity	250,000
Total	$800,000	Total	$800,000

The percent of total assets controlled by Matz Corporation emanating from its common stock equity is:

$$\frac{\text{Common stock equity of Matz}}{\text{Total assets of company X and company Y}} = \frac{\$40,000}{\$1,400,000} = 2.9\%$$

Assuming another company owns 18 percent of the common stock of Matz and has voting control, the percent of the total assets controlled by the other company's equity is:

$$2.9\% \times 18\% = 0.52\%$$

17.7   TENDER OFFER

The takeover of another company is often accomplished through negotiation. In the event the management of the target company does not want to be merged, the company can be acquired against its will by the buyer making a tender offer. A *tender offer* is made when the buyer goes directly to the stockholders of the target business to *tender* (sell) their shares, typically for cash. The tender in some cases may be shares in the acquiring company rather than cash. If the buyer obtains enough stock, it can gain control of the target company and force the merger. Stockholders are induced to sell when the tender price substantially exceeds the current market price of the target company stock. Typically, there is an expiration date to the tender. Good takeover candidates are cash-rich businesses and those with low debt/equity ratios.

The management of a targeted company can fight the takeover attempt, if it wishes, in the following ways:

1. Furnish publicity against the raider.
2. Purchase treasury stock to make fewer shares available for tendering.
3. Initiate legal action to prevent the takeover, such as by applying antitrust laws.
4. Postpone the tender offer. Many states have laws that can delay the tender offer.
5. Seek out a merger with a different, friendlier, company.
6. Declare an attractive dividend to keep stockholders happy.

With regard to tender offers, the following disclosure requirements exist:

1. The acquiring business must furnish to the management of the potential acquired company and to the SEC, 30 days' notice of its intent to acquire.
2. The name of the group furnishing the money for the acquisition must be disclosed when significant amounts of stock are purchased on the stock exchange. Typically, the acquired stock is in the *street name* of the broker who is acting for the true owner.

Due to the disclosure requirements, competition may arise in the takeover attempt. The competing acquiring companies may increase the acquisition price significantly by bidding higher than the pretakeover market price of stock.

Review Questions

1. A combination of two or more companies into one where only the acquiring company retains its identity is referred to as a(n) _____ .

2. A consolidation is when two or more companies combine to form a(n) _____ company.

3. A(n) _____ company owns common stock of other companies.

4. A(n) _____ business combination is when two companies in a similar business combine.

5. A(n) _____ is when two companies in unrelated industries combine.

6. A good combination may result in a(n) _____ effect.

7. A tax loss may be carried forward _____ years.

8. If a holding company owns 80 percent or more of the subsidiary's stock, there will be a(n) _____ percent dividend exemption.

9. A(n) _____ is made when an acquiring company goes directly to the stockholders of the target business to buy their shares.

Answers: (1) merger; (2) new; (3) holding; (4) horizontal; (5) conglomerate; (6) synergistic; (7) 15; (8) 100; (9) tender offer.

Solved Problems

17.1 Tax-Loss-Carryforward Benefit. In 19X1, Burton Corporation acquires Weiss Corporation, which has a tax-loss-carryforward benefit of $600,000. Burton Corporation has earnings of $500,000 in 19X1 and $800,000 in 19X2. The tax rate is 46 percent. Determine the tax to be paid by Burton in 19X1 and 19X2.

SOLUTION

In 19X1:		
	Burton Corporation earnings	$500,000
	Weiss tax loss carryforward	500,000
	Taxable income	$ 0
	Tax	$ 0

In 19X2:		
	Burton Corporation earnings	$800,000
	Unused Weiss Corporation's tax loss carryforward ($600,000 − $500,000)	100,000
	Taxable income	$700,000
	Tax (46% rate)	$322,000

17.2 Acquisition of a Company. Yohai Corporation is thinking of purchasing Klein Corporation for $70,000 in cash. Yohai's current cost of capital is 16 percent. Klein's estimated overall cost of capital is anticipated to be 14 percent after the acquisition. Forecasted cash inflows from years 1 to 15 are $8,000. Should the acquisition be made?

SOLUTION

	Calculations	Present Value
Year 0	−$70,000 × 1	−$70,000
Years 1–15	+$8,000 × 6.142	+49,136[a]
Net present value		−$20,864

_____

[a]Using 14 percent as the discount rate.

Since the net present value is negative, the acquisition should not be made.

17.3   Acquisition of Assets for Cash. Master Corporation wants to buy certain fixed assets of Smith Corporation. However, Smith Corporation wants to dispose of its entire business. The balance sheet of Smith follows:

ASSETS	
Cash	$ 2,000
Accounts receivable	8,000
Inventories	20,000
Equipment 1	10,000
Equipment 2	20,000
Equipment 3	35,000
Building	90,000
Total assets	$185,000

LIABILITIES AND STOCKHOLDERS' EQUITY	
Total liabilities	$ 80,000
Total stockholders' equity	105,000
Total liabilities and stockholders' equity	$185,000

Master needs only equipment 1 and 2 and the building. The other assets excluding cash can be sold for $35,000. Smith wants $48,000 for the entire business. It is anticipated that the after-tax cash inflows from the new equipment will be $30,000 a year for the next 8 years. The cost of capital is 12 percent.

(a) What is the initial net cash outlay? (b) Should the acquisition be made?

SOLUTION

(a)

Total payment:		
Liabilities	$80,000	
Owners	48,000	$128,000
Cash available ($2,000 + $35,000)		37,000
Initial net cash outlay		$ 91,000

(b)

	Calculations	Present Value
Year 0	−$91,000 × 1	−$ 91,000
Years 1–8	+$30,000 × 4.968	+149,040
Net present value		+$ 58,040

Since the net present value is positive, the acquisition should be made.

17.4   Acquisition of Assets for Cash. Knab Corporation is considering acquiring Deerson Corporation for $40,000. Deerson has liabilities of $62,000. Deerson has machinery that Knab wants, and the remaining assets would be sold for $55,000. The machinery will furnish Knab with an increase in annual cash flow of $7,000 for the next 10 years. The cost of capital is 12 percent.

(a) What is the net cost of the machinery? (b) Should the acquisition be made?

SOLUTION

(a) $40,000 + $62,000 − $55,000 = $47,000$

(b)

	Calculations	Present Value
Year 0	$−\$47,000 \times 1$	$−\$47,000$
Years 1–10	$\$7,000 \times 5.650$	$+39,550$
Net present value		$−\$\ 7,450$

Since the net present value is negative, the acquisition should not be made.

17.5   Acquisition by Exchanging Stock. Company R wishes to acquire company S. Company R's stock sells for $100 per share. Company S's stock sells for $40 a share. Due to merger negotiations, company R offers $50 a share. The acquisition is done through an exchange of securities. What is the ratio of exchange?

SOLUTION

$$\frac{\text{Amount paid per share of the acquired company}}{\text{Market price of the acquiring company's shares}} = \frac{\$50}{\$100} = 0.5$$

17.6   Earnings per Share. The following data concerning companies A and B are presented:

	Company A	Company B
Net income	$35,000	$50,000
Shares outstanding	5,000	10,000
Earnings per share	$7.00	$5.00
P/E ratio	10	14
Market price	$70	$70

Company B is the acquiring company, exchanging its shares on a one-for-one basis for company A's shares. The exchange ratio is based on the market prices of company A and company B stock.

(a) What will earnings per share be subsequent to the merger? (b) What is the change in earnings per share for the stockholders of companies A and B?

SOLUTION

(a)

	B Shares Owned after Merger	EPS before Merger	EPS after Merger
A stockholders	5,000	$7.00	$5.67[a]
B stockholders	10,000	$5.00	$5.67[a]
Total	15,000		

[a]Total net income is calculated as follows:

5,000 shares × $7	$35,000
10,000 shares × $5	50,000
New EPS	$85,000

$$\text{EPS} = \frac{\text{total net income}}{\text{total shares}} = \frac{\$85,000}{15,000} = \$5.67$$

(b)   EPS decreases by $1.33 for company A stockholders but increases by $0.67 for company B stockholders.

17.7   Exchange Ratio. The following information is provided:

Case	Market Price per Share of Acquiring Company	Market Price per Share of Acquired Company	Price per Share Offered
1	$80	$40	$50
2	$120	$160	$130

For each case, determine (*a*) the exchange ratio in shares, and (*b*) the exchange ratio in market price.

SOLUTION

Case	(*a*) Shares	(*b*) Market Price
1	$50/$80 = 0.625	$50/$40 = 1.25
2	$180/$120 = 1.5	$180/$160 = 1.125

17.8   Earnings per Share of Merged Company. Paula Company wants to acquire David Company. Relevant data follow:

	Paula	David
Net income	$40,000	$25,000
Shares outstanding	20,000	5,000

Paula issues its shares to make the acquisition. The ratio of exchange is 2.5. (*a*) What is the earnings per share of the merged company based on the original shares of each company? (*b*) What is the earnings per share of Paula? (*c*) What is the earnings per share of David?

SOLUTION

(*a*)   The merged company's earnings per share is:

$$\frac{\text{Combined net income}}{\text{Total shares}} = \frac{\$65,000}{20,000 + (5,000 \times 2.5)} = \frac{\$65,000}{20,000 + 12,500} = \frac{\$65,000}{32,500 \text{ shares}} = \$2$$

(*b*)   Paula's earnings per share is $2.

(*c*)   David's earnings per share is:

$$\$2 \times 2.5 = \$5$$

17.9   Earnings per Share. Shim Company wishes to acquire Siegel Company by exchanging 0.8 share of its stock for each share of Siegel. Financial data follow:

	Shim	Siegel
Net income	$200,000	$40,000
Shares outstanding	50,000	20,000
Earnings per share	$4	$2
Market price	$40	$16
P/E ratio	10	8

Shim issues its shares to make the acquisition. (*a*) How many shares must Shim issue in the acquisition? (*b*) Assuming the net income of each firm remains the same, what is the earnings per share after the acquisition? (*c*) What is the amount earned per share on the original shares of Siegel stock? (*d*) What is the amount earned per share on the original shares of Shim stock?

SOLUTION

(a)
$$20{,}000 \text{ shares} \times 0.8 = 16{,}000 \text{ shares}$$

(b)
$$\frac{\$200{,}000 + \$40{,}000}{50{,}000 + 16{,}000} = \frac{\$240{,}000}{66{,}000} = \$3.64$$

(c)
$$\$3.64 \times 0.8 = \$2.91$$

(d) $3.64

17.10 EPS, P/E Ratio, and Market Price. Harris Corporation wants to acquire Logo Corporation by exchanging 1.6 shares of its stock for each share of Logo. Harris anticipates having the same P/E ratio subsequent to the merger as prior to it. The following financial data are given:

	Harris	Logo
Net income	$500,000	$150,000
Shares	100,000	25,000
Market price per share	$35	$40

(a) What is the exchange ratio of market prices? (b) What is the EPS and the P/E ratio for each company? (c) What was the P/E ratio used in obtaining Logo? (d) What is the EPS of Harris after the acquisition? (e) What is the expected market price per share of the merged company?

SOLUTION

(a)
$$\frac{\text{Price per share offered}}{\text{Market price of Logo}} = \frac{\$35 \times 1.6}{\$40} = \frac{\$56}{\$40} = 1.4$$

(b)

	Harris	Logo
EPS	$500,000/100,000 shares = $5	$150,000/25,000 shares = $6
P/E ratio	$35/$5 = 7 times	$40/$6 = 6.67 times

(c)
$$1.6 \times \$35 = \$56$$
$$\frac{\$56}{\$6} = 9.33 \text{ times}$$

(d)
$$\frac{\$650{,}000}{\$100{,}000 + (25{,}000 \times 1.6)} = \frac{\$650{,}000}{140{,}000 \text{ shares}} = \$4.64$$

(e)
$$\$4.64 \times 7 \text{ times} = \$32.48$$

17.11 Dividend Exclusion. A holding company owns 40 percent of another business. It received dividends of $20,000. The tax rate is 40 percent. What is the tax to be paid on the dividends?

SOLUTION

Dividend	$20,000
Dividend exclusion (85%)	17,000
Dividend subject to tax	$ 3,000
Tax rate	×40%
Tax	$ 1,200

17.12 Holding Company. Usry Company holds stock in company A and company B and possesses voting control over both. Balance sheet data follow:

Usry Corporation

Investment		Long-term liabilities	$ 30,000
Company A	$ 20,000	Preferred stock	10,000
Company B	80,000	Common stock equity	60,000
Total	$100,000	Total	$100,000

Company A

Current assets	$200,000	Current liabilities	$100,000
Noncurrent assets	300,000	Long-term liabilities	200,000
		Common stock equity	200,000
Total	$500,000	Total	$500,000

Company B

Current assets	$300,000	Current liabilities	$200,000
Noncurrent assets	400,000	Long-term liabilities	350,000
		Common stock equity	150,000
Total	$700,000	Total	$700,000

(a) What is the percent of total assets controlled by Usry Corporation resulting from its common stock equity? (b) Assuming another company owns 25 percent of the common stock of Usry and has voting control, what is the percent of the total assets controlled by the other firm's equity?

SOLUTION

(a)
$$\frac{\text{Common stock equity of Usry}}{\text{Total assets of company A and company B}} = \frac{\$60,000}{\$1,200,000} = 5.0\%$$

(b)
$$5.0\% \times 25\% = 1.25\%$$

Chapter 18

Failure and Reorganization

18.1 INTRODUCTION

When a business fails it can be either reorganized or dissolved depending on the circumstances. A number of ways exist for business failure to occur, including a poor rate of return, technical insolvency, and bankruptcy.

Deficient Rate of Return.   A company may fail if its rate of return is negative or poor. If operating losses exist, the company may not be able to meet its obligations. A negative rate of return will cause a decline in the market price of its stock. When a company does not earn a return greater than its cost of capital, it may fail. If corrective action is not forthcoming, perhaps the firm should liquidate. A poor return, however, does not constitute legal evidence of failure.

Technical Insolvency.   Technical insolvency means that the business cannot satisfy current debt when due even if total assets are greater than total liabilities.

Bankruptcy.   In bankruptcy, liabilities are greater than the fair market value of assets. There exists a negative real net worth.

According to law, failure of a company can be either technical insolvency or bankruptcy. When creditor claims against a business are in question, the law permits creditors recourse against the company.

Some causes of business failure include:

1. Poor management
2. An economic downturn affecting the company and/or industry
3. The end of the life cycle of the firm
4. Overexpansion
5. Catastrophe

18.2 VOLUNTARY SETTLEMENT

A voluntary settlement with creditors permits the company to save many of the costs that would be present in bankruptcy. Such a settlement is done out of court. The voluntary settlement enables the company to either continue or be liquidated and is initiated to enable the debtor firm to recover some of its investment.

A creditor committee may decide to allow the firm to continue to operate if it is expected that the company will recover. Creditors may also continue to do business with the company. In sustaining the firm's existence, there may be:

1. An extension
2. A composition
3. Creditor control
4. Integration of each of the above

Extension

In an *extension*, creditors will receive the balances due but over an extended period of time. Current purchases are made with cash. It is also possible that the creditors may agree not only to lengthen the maturity date for payment but also to subordinate their claims to current debt for suppliers furnishing

432

credit in the extension period. The creditors expect the debtor will be able to work out his or her problems.

The creditor committee may require certain controls, including legal control over the company's assets or common stock, obtaining a security interest in assets, and approval of all cash payments.

If there are creditors dissenting to the extension agreement, they may be paid immediately to prevent them from having the company declared bankrupt.

Composition

In a *composition*, there is a voluntary reduction of the amount the debtor owes the creditor. The creditor obtains from the debtor a stated percent of the obligation in *full* settlement of the debt regardless of how low the percent is. The agreement is designed to allow the debtor to continue to operate. The creditor may try to work with the debtor in handling the firm's financial problems, since a stable customer may ensue. The advantages of a composition are that court costs are eliminated as well as the stigma of a bankrupt company.

If there are dissenting stockholders, they may be paid in full or they may be permitted to recover a higher percentage so that they do not force the business to close.

For an extension or composition to be practical, the following should exist:

1. An ethical debtor who will not use the company's assets for personal use.

2. An expectation that the debtor will recover.

3. Present business conditions must be such as to promote the debtor's recovery.

Creditor Committee Takes Control

A committee of creditors may decide to take control of the business if they are not happy with present management. They will operate the business in order to satisfy their claims. Once paid, the creditors may recommend that new management replace the old before further credit is given. The drawback with such an agreement is the possibility of mismanagement lawsuits brought by stockholders against the creditors.

Integration

The creditors and the company negotiate a plan that involves a combination of extension, composition, and creditor control. For instance, the agreement may allow for a 20 percent cash payment of the balance owed plus five future payments of 12 percent, typically in the form of notes. The total payment is thus 80 percent.

The advantages of negotiated settlements are that:

1. They are less formal than bankruptcy proceedings.

2. They cost less (e.g., they avoid or reduce legal expenses).

3. They are easier to implement than bankruptcy proceedings.

4. They usually provide creditors with the greatest return.

The following disadvantages may arise:

1. If the troubled debtor still has control over its business affairs, there may occur further decline in asset values. Creditor controls can, however, be implemented to provide some degree of protection.

2. Unrealistic small creditors may make the negotiating process a drain by demanding full payment.

18.3   BANKRUPTCY REORGANIZATION

If no voluntary settlement is agreed upon, the company may be put into bankruptcy by its creditors. The bankruptcy proceeding may either reorganize or liquidate the firm.

Bankruptcy takes place when a company cannot pay its bills or when liabilities are greater than the fair market value of the assets. Here, legal bankruptcy may be declared. A company may file for reorganization under which it will formulate a plan for continued life.

Chapter 7 of the Bankruptcy Reform Act of 1978 outlines the procedures to be followed for liquidation. This chapter applies when reorganization is not feasible. Chapter 11 goes into the steps of reorganizing a failed business. If a reorganization is not possible under Chapter 11, the company will be liquidated in accordance with Chapter 7.

The two types of reorganization petitions are:

1. *Voluntary.* The firm petitions for its own reorganization. The company does not have to be insolvent to file for voluntary reorganization.

2. *Involuntary.* Creditors file for an involuntary reorganization of the company. An involuntary petition must establish either that the debtor firm is not meeting its debts when due or that a creditor or another party has taken control over the debtor's assets. In general, most of the creditors or claims must support the petition.

The five steps involved in a reorganization are:

1. A reorganization petition is filed under Chapter 11 in court.
2. A judge approves the petition and either appoints a trustee or lets the creditors elect one to handle the disposition of the assets.
3. The trustee presents a fair plan of reorganization to the court.
4. The plan is given to the creditors and stockholders of the firm for approval.
5. The debtor pays the expenses of the parties rendering services in the reorganization proceedings.

The trustee in a reorganization plan is required to:

1. Value the company
2. Recapitalize the company
3. Exchange outstanding debts for new securities

Valuation

In valuing the firm, the trustee must estimate its liquidation value versus its value as a going concern. Liquidation is called for when the liquidation value exceeds the continuity value. If the firm is more valuable when operating, reorganization is the answer. Future earnings must be predicted when arriving at the value of the reorganized company. The going concern value represents the present value of future earnings.

EXAMPLE 18.1 A petition for reorganization of X Company was filed under Chapter 11. The trustee determined that the company's liquidation value after subtracting expenses was $4.3 million. The trustee estimates that the reorganized business will generate $540,000 in annual earnings. The cost of capital rate is 12 percent. Assuming the earnings would continue indefinitely, the value of X Company as a going concern is:

$$\$540,000 \times \frac{1}{0.12} = \$4,500,000$$

Since the company's value as a going concern ($4.5 million) exceeds the value in liquidation ($4.3 million), reorganization is called for.

Recapitalization

Assuming the trustee recommends reorganization, a plan must be developed to carry it out. The obligations may be extended or equity securities may be issued in substitution of the debt. *Income bonds* may be given for the debentures. With an income bond, interest is paid only when there are earnings. This process of exchanging liabilities for other types of liabilities or equity securities is referred to as *recapitalization*. In recapitalizing the firm, the purpose is to have a mixture of debt and equity that will permit the company to meet its debts and provide reasonable profits for the owners.

EXAMPLE 18.2   The current capital structure of Y Corporation is presented below.

Debentures	$1,500,000
Collateral bonds	3,000,000
Preferred stock	800,000
Common stock	2,500,000
Total	$7,800,000

There exists high financial leverage:

$$\frac{\text{Debt}}{\text{Equity}} = \frac{\$4,500,000}{\$3,300,000} = 1.36$$

Assuming the company is deemed to be worth $5 million as a going concern, the trustee can develop a less leveraged capital structure having a total capital of $5 million as follows:

Debentures	$1,000,000
Collateral bonds	1,000,000
Income bonds	1,500,000
Preferred stock	500,000
Common stock	1,000,000
Total	$5,000,000

The income bond of $1.5 million is similar to equity in appraising financial leverage, since interest is not paid unless there is income. The new debt/equity ratio is safer:

$$\frac{\text{Debt} + \text{collateral bonds}}{\text{Income bonds} + \text{preferred stock} + \text{common stock}} = \frac{\$2,000,000}{\$3,000,000} = 0.67$$

Exchange of Obligations

In exchanging obligations to achieve the best capital structure, priorities must be followed. Senior claims are taken care of before junior claims. Senior debt holders must receive a claim on new capital equal to their prior claims. The last priority goes to common stockholders in receiving new securities. A debt holder usually receives a combination of different securities. Preferred and common stockholders may receive nothing. Usually, however, they retain some small ownership. After the exchange, the debt holders may become the firm's new owners.

EXAMPLE 18.3   A $1 million mortgage bondholder may receive in exchange $500,000 in income bonds, $300,000 in preferred stock, and $200,000 in common stock.

Common stockholders receive nothing in exchange.

18.4   LIQUIDATION DUE TO BANKRUPTCY

When a company becomes bankrupt it may be liquidated under Chapter 7 of the Bankruptcy Reform Act of 1978. The key elements of liquidation are *legal considerations*, *claim priority*, and *dissolution*.

Legal Considerations

When a company is declared bankrupt, creditors must meet between 10 and 30 days subsequent to that declaration. A judge or referee takes charge of the meeting in which the creditors provide their claims. A trustee is appointed by the creditors. The trustee handles the property of the defaulted company, liquidates the business, maintains appropriate records, evaluates the claims of creditors, makes payments, and provides relevant information regarding the liquidation process. Many times three trustees are appointed and/or an advisory committee of at least three creditors is formed.

Claim Priority

Some claims against the company take precedence over others in bankruptcy. The following rank order exists in meeting claims:

1. *Secured claims.* Secured creditors receive the value of the secured assets in support of their claims. If the value of the secured assets is insufficient to satisfy their claims in full, the balance reverts to general creditor status.
2. *Bankruptcy administrative costs.* These costs include any expenses related to handling the bankruptcy such as legal and trustee expenses.
3. *Unsecured salaries and commissions.* These claims are limited to $2,000 per individual and must have been incurred within 90 days of the bankruptcy petition.
4. *Unsecured customer deposit claims.* These claims are limited to $900 each.
5. *Taxes.* Tax claims apply to unpaid taxes due the government.
6. *General creditor claims.* General creditors are those who have loaned money to the company without specific collateral. Included are debentures and accounts payable.
7. *Preferred stockholders.*
8. *Common stockholders.*

In most cases, once creditor obligations have been settled with the remaining assets there is nothing left for stockholders.

Bankruptcy distribution in principle should be based on *absolute priority*, in which creditor claims are satisfied strictly following the priority listing. Junior claims are supposed to be met after senior claims are fully satisfied. However, in practice, courts sometimes use *relative priority* in distributing assets in which junior claims receive a partial distribution even though all senior claims have not been fully met.

Dissolution

After claims have been met in priority order and an accounting made of the proceedings, there may then be instituted an application to *discharge* the bankrupt business. A *discharge* occurs when the court releases the company from legitimate debts in bankruptcy, with the exception of debts that are immune to discharge. As long as a debtor has not been discharged within the prior 6 years and was not bankrupt due to fraud, the debtor may then start a new business.

EXAMPLE 18.4   The balance sheet of Ace Corporation for the year ended December 31, 19X4, follows:

Balance Sheet

Current assets	$400,000	Current liabilities	$475,000
Fixed assets	410,000	Long-term liabilities	250,000
		Common stock	175,000
		Retained earnings	(90,000)
Total assets	$810,000	Total liabilities and stockholders' equity	$810,000

The company's liquidation value is $625,000. Rather than liquidate, there could be a reorganization with an investment of an additional $320,000. The reorganization is expected to generate earnings of $115,000 per year. A multiplier of 7.5 is appropriate. If the $320,000 is obtained, long-term debt holders will receive 40 percent of the common stock in the reorganized business in substitution for their current claims.

If $320,000 of further investment is made, the firm's going-concern value is $862,500 (7.5 × $115,000). The liquidation value is given at $625,000. Since the reorganization value exceeds the liquidation value, reorganization is called for.

EXAMPLE 18.5 Plant and equipment having a book value of $1.5 million was sold for $1.3 million. There are mortgage bonds on the plant and equipment in the amount of $1.8 million. The proceeds from the collateral sale are insufficient to satisfy the secured claim. The unsatisfied portion of $500,000 ($1,800,000 − $1,300,000) of the claim becomes a general creditor claim.

EXAMPLE 18.6 Land having a book value of $1.2 million was sold for $800,000. Mortgage bonds on the land are $600,000. The surplus of $200,000 will be returned to the trustee to pay other creditors.

EXAMPLE 18.7 Charles Corporation is bankrupt. The book and liquidation values follow:

	Book Value	Liquidation Value
Cash	$ 600,000	$ 600,000
Accounts receivable	1,900,000	1,500,000
Inventory	3,700,000	2,100,000
Land	5,000,000	3,200,000
Building	7,800,000	5,300,000
Equipment	6,700,000	2,800,000
Total assets	$25,700,000	$15,500,000

The liabilities and stockholders' equity at the date of liquidation are:

Current liabilities		
Accounts payable	$1,800,000	
Notes payable	900,000	
Accrued taxes	650,000	
Accrued salaries	450,000[a]	
Total current liabilities		$ 3,800,000
Long-term liabilities		
Mortgage on land	$3,200,000	
First mortgage—building	2,800,000	
Second mortgage—building	2,500,000	
Subordinated debentures	4,800,000	
Total long-term liabilities		13,300,000
Total liabilities		$17,100,000
Stockholders' equity		
Preferred stock	$4,700,000	
Common stock	6,800,000	
Retained earnings	(2,900,000)	
Total stockholders' equity		8,600,000
Total liabilities and stockholders' equity		$25,700,000

---

[a] The salary owed to each worker is below $2,000 and was incurred within 90 days of the bankruptcy petition.

Expenses of the liquidation including legal costs were 15 percent of the proceeds. The debentures are subordinated only with regard to the two first-mortgage bonds.

The distribution of the proceeds follows:

Proceeds		$15,500,000
Mortgage on land	$3,200,000	
First mortgage—building	2,800,000	
Second mortgage—building	2,500,000	
Liquidation expenses (15% × $15,500,000)	2,325,000	
Accrued salaries	450,000	
Accrued taxes	650,000	
Total		11,925,000
Balance		$ 3,575,000

The percent to be paid to general creditors is:

$$\frac{\text{Proceeds balance}}{\text{Total owed}} = \frac{\$3,575,000}{\$7,500,000} = 47.66667\%$$

The balance due general creditors follows:

General Creditors	Owed	Paid
Accounts payable	$1,800,000	$ 858,000
Notes payable	900,000	429,000
Subordinated debentures	4,800,000	2,288,000
Total	$7,500,000	$3,575,000

EXAMPLE 18.8 The balance sheet of the Oakhurst Company is presented below.

ASSETS

Current assets		
Cash	$ 9,000	
Marketable securities	6,000	
Receivables	1,100,000	
Inventory	3,000,000	
Prepaid expenses	4,000	
Total current assets		$4,119,000
Noncurrent assets		
Land	$1,800,000	
Fixed assets	2,000,000	
Total noncurrent assets		3,800,000
Total assets		$7,919,000

LIABILITIES AND
STOCKHOLDERS' EQUITY

Current liabilities

Accounts payable	$ 180,000	
Bank loan payable	900,000	
Accrued salaries	300,000[a]	
Employee benefits payable	70,000[b]	
Customer claims—unsecured	80,000[c]	
Taxes payable	350,000	
Total current liabilities		$1,880,000
Noncurrent liabilities		
First mortgage payable	$1,600,000	
Second mortgage payable	1,100,000	
Subordinated debentures	700,000	
Total noncurrent liabilities		3,400,000
Total liabilities		$5,280,000
Stockholders' equity		
Preferred stock (3,500 shares)	$ 350,000	
Common stock (8,000 shares)	480,000	
Paid-in capital	1,600,000	
Retained earnings	209,000	
Total stockholders' equity		2,639,000
Total liabilities and stockholders' equity		$7,919,000

[a]The salary owed to each worker is below $2,000 and was incurred within 90 days of the bankruptcy petition.

[b]Employee benefits payable have the same limitations as unsecured wages and satisfy for eligibility in bankruptcy distribution.

[c]No customer claim is greater than $900.

Additional data are as follows:

1. The mortgages apply to the company's total noncurrent assets.

2. The subordinated debentures are subordinated to the bank loan payable. Therefore, they come after the bank loan payable in liquidation.

3. The trustee has sold the company's current assets for $2.1 million and the noncurrent assets for $1.9 million. Therefore, a total of $4 million was received.

4. The business is bankrupt, since the total liabilities of $5.28 million are greater than the $4 million of the fair value of the assets.

Assume that the administration expense for handling the bankrupt company is $900,000. This liability is not reflected in the above balance sheet.

The allocation of the $4 million to the creditors is shown here.

Proceeds		
Available to secured creditors		$4,000,000
First mortgage—payable from $1,900,000 proceeds of noncurrent assets	$1,600,000	
Second mortgage—payable from balance of proceeds of noncurrent assets	300,000	1,900,000
Balance after secured creditors		$2,100,000
Next priority		
Administrative expenses	$ 900,000	
Accrued salaries	300,000	
Employee benefits payable	70,000	
Customer claims—unsecured	80,000	
Taxes payable	350,000	1,700,000
Proceeds available to general creditors		$ 400,000

Now that the claims on the proceeds from liquidation have been met, general creditors receive the balance on a pro rata basis. The distribution of the $400,000 follows:

General Creditor	Amount	Pro Rata Allocation for Balance to Be Paid
Second-mortgage balance ($1,100,000 − $300,000)	$ 800,000	$124,031
Accounts payable	180,000	27,907
Bank loan payable	900,000	248,062[a]
Subordinated debentures	700,000	0
Total	$2,580,000	$400,000

[a]Since the debentures are subordinated, the bank loan payable must be satisfied in full before any amount can go to the subordinated debentures. The subordinated debenture holders therefore receive nothing.

EXAMPLE 18.9 Nolan Company is having severe financial problems. Jefferson Bank holds a first mortgage on the plant and has an $800,000 unsecured loan that is already delinquent. The Alto Insurance Company holds $4.7 million of the company's subordinated debentures to the notes payable. Nolan is deciding whether to reorganize the business or declare bankruptcy.

Another company is considering acquiring Nolan Company by offering to take over the mortgage of $7.5 million, pay the past due taxes, and pay $4.38 million for the firm.

Nolan's balance sheet follows:

ASSETS	
Current assets	$ 2,800,000
Plant assets	11,700,000
Other assets	3,000,000
Total assets	$17,500,000

**LIABILITIES AND
STOCKHOLDERS' EQUITY**

Current liabilities		
Accounts payable	$ 1,800,000	
Taxes payable	170,000	
Bank note payable	260,000	
Other current liabilities	1,400,000	
Total current liabilities		$ 3,630,000
Noncurrent liabilities		
Mortgage payable	$ 7,500,000	
Subordinated debentures	5,300,000	
Total noncurrent liabilities		12,800,000
Total liabilities		$16,430,000
Stockholders' equity		
Common stock	$ 1,000,000	
Premium on common stock	2,300,000	
Retained earnings	(2,230,000)	
Total stockholders' equity		1,070,000
Total liabilities and stockholders' equity		$17,500,000

The impact of the proposed reorganization on creditor claims is indicated below.

Outstanding obligations		$16,430,000
Claims met through the reorganization		
Mortgage payable	$ 7,500,000	
Taxes payable	170,000	
Total		7,670,000
Balance of claims		$ 8,760,000

The cash arising from reorganization is given as $4.38 million, which is 50 percent ($4,380,000/$8,760,000) of the unsatisfied claims.

The distribution to general creditors follows:

General Creditor	Liability Due	50%	Adjusted for Subordination
Bank note payable	$ 260,000	$ 130,000	$ 260,000[a]
Subordinated debenture	5,300,000	2,650,000	2,520,000
Other creditors (accounts payable + other current liabilities)	3,200,000	1,600,000	1,600,000
Total	$8,760,000	$4,380,000	$4,380,000

[a]The bank note payable is paid in full before the subordinated debenture.

18.5   THE Z SCORE MODEL: FORECASTING BUSINESS FAILURES

The Z score is a quantitative model that Edward Altman developed in an effort to predict bankruptcy (financial distress) of a business, using a blend of the traditional financial ratios and a statistical method known as *multiple discriminant analysis* (MDA).

The *Z* score is known to be about 90 percent accurate in forecasting business failure one year in the future and about 80 percent accurate in forecasting it 2 years in the future. The model is

$$Z = 1.2*X_1 + 1.4*X_2 + 3.3*X_3 + 0.6*X_4 + 0.999*X_5$$

where X_1 = Working capital/Total assets
  X_2 = Retained earnings/Total assets
  X_3 = Earnings before interest and taxes (EBIT)/Total assets
  X_4 = Market value of equity/Book value of debt
  X_5 = Sales/Total assets

Altman also established the following guidelines for classifying firms:

Z score	Probability of failure
1.8 or less	Very high
1.81–2.99	Not sure
3.0 or higher	Unlikely

EXAMPLE 18.10 Davidson Company has the following financial data selected from its financial statements:

> Total assets = $2,000
> Retained earnings = $750
> EBIT = $266
> Sales = $3,000
> Market value of common and preferred stock = $1,425
> Book value of debt = $1,100

The calculation of Davidson's *Z* score is shown below:

$$
\begin{aligned}
X_1 &= && 400/2{,}000 \times 1.2 && = 0.240 \\
X_2 &= && 750/2{,}000 \times 1.4 && = 0.525 \\
X_3 &= && 266/2{,}000 \times 3.3 && = 0.439 \\
X_4 &= && 1{,}425/1{,}100 \times 0.6 && = 0.777 \\
X_5 &= && 3{,}000/2{,}000 \times 0.999 && = \underline{1.499} \\
& && && Z = 3.480
\end{aligned}
$$

Since Davidson's *Z* score of 3.480 is well into the "unlikely" zone, there is virtually no chance that Davidson will go bankrupt within the next 2 years.

Review Questions

1. _____ means that the company is unable to meet current debt when due.

2. If a company's liabilities exceed the fair market value of its assets, it is _____ .

3. In the case of a(n) _____ , creditors receive the balances owed them over an extended time period.

4. A voluntary reduction of the amount the debtor owes the creditor is referred to as a(n) _____ .

5. A bankruptcy proceeding may either _____ or _____ the business.

6. _____ of the Bankruptcy Reform Act of 1978 outlines the procedures to be followed in liquidation.

7. Liquidation is called for when the _____ value is greater than the _____ value of the business.

8. _____ is the process of exchanging liabilities for other types of liabilities or equity securities.

9. _____ creditors have a higher priority in bankruptcy than unsecured creditors.

10. In bankruptcy, unsecured salaries are limited to $_____ per individual.

11. In bankruptcy, _____ are paid last.

12. A(n) _____ means that the court releases the business from legitimate debts in bankruptcy.

13. The _____ is an effort to predict bankruptcy (financial distress) of a business, using a blend of the traditional financial ratios and multiple discriminant analysis (MDA).

Answers: (1) Technical insolvency; (2) bankrupt; (3) extension; (4) composition; (5) reorganize, liquidate; (6) Chapter 7; (7) liquidation, continuity; (8) Recapitalization; (9) Secured; (10) 2,000; (11) common stockholders; (12) discharge; (13) Z score model.

Solved Problems

18.1 Going-Concern Value. There was a petition for reorganization of Hazel Corporation filed under Chapter 11. It was determined by the trustee that the firm's liquidation value, after considering expenses, was $5.3 million. The trustee predicts that the reorganized business will derive $500,000 in annual profit. The cost of capital rate is 10 percent. Assume profits will continue indefinitely. Is reorganization or liquidation recommended?

SOLUTION

The value of the business as a going concern equals:

$$\$500,000 \times \frac{1}{0.10} = \$5,000,000$$

Since the value of the company as a going concern ($5 million) is less than its value in liquidation ($5.3 million), the business should be liquidated.

18.2 Debt/Equity Ratio. The present capital structure of Jones Corporation is shown below.

Debentures	$1,200,000
Collateral bonds	2,800,000
Preferred stock	700,000
Common stock	2,600,000
Total	$7,300,000

There is a high financial leverage position:

$$\frac{\text{Debt}}{\text{Equity}} = \frac{\$4,000,000}{\$3,300,000} = 1.21$$

The business is worth $4.7 million as a going concern. The trustee has formulated a less leveraged capital structure having a total capital of $4.7 million as follows:

Debentures	$ 800,000
Collateral bonds	1,500,000
Income bonds	1,300,000
Preferred stock	400,000
Common stock	700,000
Total	$4,700,000

What is the new debt/equity ratio?

SOLUTION

The income bond of $1.3 million is similar to equity in evaluating financial leverage because interest is not paid unless income exists. The new debt/equity ratio is lower at:

$$\frac{\text{Debt} + \text{collateral bonds}}{\text{Income bonds} + \text{preferred stock} + \text{common stock}} = \frac{\$2,300,000}{\$2,400,000} = 0.96$$

18.3 Reorganization or Liquidation. The balance sheet of Morris Corporation for the year ended December 31, 19X3, follows:

Balance Sheet

Current assets	$ 500,000	Current liabilities	$ 550,000
Fixed assets	520,000	Long-term liabilities	300,000
		Common stock	250,000
		Retained earnings	(80,000)
		Total liabilities and	
Total assets	$1,020,000	stockholders' equity	$1,020,000

The firm's liquidation value is $700,000. Instead of liquidating, there could be a reorganization with an investment of an additional $400,000. The reorganization is anticipated to provide earnings of $150,000 a year. A multiplier of 8 is appropriate. If the $400,000 is obtained, long-term debt holders will receive 35 percent of the common stock in the reorganized firm in substitution for their current claims. Is reorganization or liquidation recommended?

SOLUTION

Assuming the $400,000 of further investment is made, the company's going-concern value is $1.2 million ($8 \times \$150,000$). The liquidation value is stated at $700,000. Because the reorganized value is greater than the liquidation value, reorganization is recommended.

18.4 Secured Creditors. Plant and equipment with a book value of $2.3 million was sold for $2 million. The mortgage bonds on the plant and equipment are $2.6 million. How will the mortgage bondholders be treated in liquidation?

SOLUTION

The proceeds from the collateral sale are not enough to meet the secured claim. The unsatisfied portion of $600,000 of the claim becomes a general creditor claim.

18.5 Secured Creditors. Plant and equipment having a book value of $800,000 was sold for $600,000. Mortgage bonds on the plant and equipment are $500,000. How will the mortgage bondholders be treated in liquidation?

SOLUTION

The mortgage bondholders will be fully satisfied in liquidation. The surplus of $100,000 will be returned to the trustee to pay other creditors.

18.6 Distribution in Bankruptcy. Blake Corporation is bankrupt. The book and liquidation values of its assets follow.

	Book Value	Liquidation Value
Cash	$ 500,000	$ 500,000
Accounts receivable	1,700,000	1,400,000
Inventory	3,400,000	2,200,000
Land	4,700,000	3,500,000
Building	8,000,000	5,600,000
Equipment	7,000,000	3,000,000
Total assets	$25,300,000	$16,200,000

The liabilities and stockholders' equity at the liquidation date follow.

Current liabilities		
Accounts payable	$2,000,000	
Notes payable	1,000,000	
Accrued taxes	700,000	
Accrued salaries	400,000[a]	
Total current liabilities		$ 4,100,000
Long-term liabilities		
Mortgage on land	$3,500,000	
First mortgage—building	4,000,000	
Second mortgage—building	1,600,000	
Subordinated debentures	4,500,000	
Total long-term liabilities		13,600,000
Total liabilities		$17,700,000
Stockholders' equity		
Preferred stock	$4,500,000	
Common stock	6,500,000	
Retained earnings	(3,400,000)	
Total stockholders' equity		7,500,000
Total liabilities and stockholders' equity		$25,300,000

---

[a]The salary owed to each worker is below $2,000 and was incurred within 90 days of the bankruptcy petition.

Expenses associated with the bankruptcy administration were 12 percent of the proceeds. The debentures are subordinated only to the two first-mortgage bonds.

Determine the distribution of the proceeds.

SOLUTION

The distribution of the proceeds follows.

Proceeds		$16,200,000
Mortgage on land	$3,500,000	
First mortgage—building	4,000,000	
Second mortgage—building	1,600,000	
Liquidation expenses (12% × $16,200,000)	1,944,000	
Accrued salaries	400,000	
Accrued taxes	700,000	
Total		12,144,000
Balance		$ 4,056,000

The percent to be paid to general creditors is:

$$\frac{\text{Proceeds balance}}{\text{Total owed}} = \frac{\$4,056,000}{\$7,500,000} = 0.5408$$

General Creditor	Owed	Paid
Accounts payable	$2,000,000	$1,081,600
Notes payable	1,000,000	540,800
Subordinated debentures	4,500,000	2,433,600
Total	$7,500,000	$4,056,000

18.7   Distribution in Bankruptcy. The balance sheet of Larkin Corporation is shown below.

ASSETS

Current assets		
Cash	$ 7,000	
Marketable securities	5,000	
Receivables	1,000,000	
Inventory	2,800,000	
Prepaid expenses	3,500	
Total current assets		$3,815,500
Noncurrent assets		
Land	$1,700,000	
Fixed assets	2,200,000	
Total noncurrent assets		3,900,000
Total assets		$7,715,500

**LIABILITIES AND
STOCKHOLDERS' EQUITY**

Current liabilities

Accounts payable	$ 200,000	
Bank loan payable	950,000	
Accrued salaries	250,000[a]	
Employee benefits payable	80,000[b]	
Customer claims—unsecured	70,000[c]	
Taxes payable	300,000	
Total current liabilities		$1,850,000

Noncurrent liabilities

First-mortgage payable	$1,700,000	
Second-mortgage payable	1,200,000	
Subordinated debentures	600,000	
Total noncurrent liabilities		3,500,000
Total liabilities		$5,350,000

Stockholders' equity

Preferred stock	$ 400,000	
Common stock	490,000	
Paid-in capital	1,400,000	
Retained earnings	75,500	
Total stockholders' equity		2,365,500
Total liabilities and stockholders' equity		$7,715,500

[a] The salary owed to each worker is below $2,000 and was incurred within 90 days of the bankruptcy petition.

[b] Employee benefits payable have the same limitations as unsecured wages and satisfy for eligibility in bankruptcy distribution.

[c] No customer claim is greater than $900.

Additional data are as follows:

1. The mortgages relate to the firm's total noncurrent assets.
2. The subordinated debentures are subordinated to the bank loan payable.
3. The trustee has sold the current assets for $2 million and the noncurrent assets for $1.8 million.
4. The administration expense related to bankruptcy proceedings was $700,000.

Determine the distribution of the proceeds.

SOLUTION

Proceeds		$3,800,000
First mortgage—payable from $1,800,000 proceeds of noncurrent assets	$1,700,000	
Second mortgage—payable from $1,800,000 proceeds of noncurrent assets	100,000	1,800,000
Balance after secured creditors		$2,000,000
Next priority		
Administration expenses	$ 700,000	
Accrued salaries	250,000	
Employee benefits payable	80,000	
Customer claims—unsecured	70,000	
Taxes payable	300,000	1,400,000
Proceeds available to general creditors		$ 600,000

The distribution of the $600,000 to general creditors follows:

General Creditor	Amount	Pro Rata Allocation for Balance to Be Paid
Second-mortgage balance ($1,200,000 − $100,000)	$1,100,000	$231,579
Accounts payable	200,000	42,105
Bank loan payable	950,000	326,316[a]
Subordinated debentures	600,000	0
Total	$2,850,000	$600,000

[a] Since the debentures are subordinated, the bank loan payable must be met in full before any amount can go to the subordinated debentures. Thus, subordinated debenture holders receive nothing.

The holders of preferred and common stock receive nothing, since the unsecured creditors themselves have not been fully paid.

18.8   Distribution in Bankruptcy. Hover Company's balance sheet follows:

ASSETS

Current assets	$1,200,000
Land	3,000,000
Plant and equipment	2,400,000
Total assets	$6,600,000

**LIABILITIES AND
STOCKHOLDERS' EQUITY**

Current liabilities

Accounts payable	$ 500,000	
Notes payable	1,200,000	
Accrued taxes	300,000	
Total current liabilities		$2,000,000

Noncurrent liabilities

Mortgage bonds	$1,800,000[a]	
Debentures	1,000,000	
Total noncurrent liabilities		2,800,000
Total liabilities		$4,800,000

Stockholders' equity

Preferred stock	$ 500,000	
Common stock	1,300,000	
Total stockholders' equity		1,800,000
Total liabilities and stockholders' equity		$6,600,000

[a]Mortgage bonds are secured against plant and equipment.

The liquidation value for the total assets is $4 million, $1.2 million of which was received for plant and equipment. Bankruptcy costs were $150,000. Determine the distribution of the proceeds.

SOLUTION

Proceeds		$4,000,000
Mortgage bonds—secured against plant and equipment	$1,200,000	
Bankruptcy costs	150,000	
Accrued taxes	300,000	1,650,000
Balance available to general creditors		$2,350,000

The distribution to general creditors follows:

General Creditor	Owed	Pro Rata Distribution
Mortgage bonds ($1,800,000 − $1,200,000)	$ 600,000	$ 427,273
Accounts payable	500,000	356,050
Notes payable	1,200,000	854,545
Debentures	1,000,000	712,122
Total	$3,300,000	$2,350,000

Holders of preferred and common stock will receive nothing.

18.9 Z Score Model. Compute and interpret the Z scores for companies A and B below.

Company	Variables				
	X_1	X_2	X_3	X_4	X_5
A	0.4	0.35	0.3	1.75	1
B	0.15	0.12	0.1	0.5	0.5

SOLUTION

For A:
$$Z = 1.2(.4) + 1.4(.35) + 3.3(.3) + 0.6(1.75) + 0.999(1)$$
$$= 4.01$$

For B:
$$Z = 1.2(.15) + 1.4(.12) + 3.3(.1) + 0.6(.5) + 0.999(.5)$$
$$= 1.47$$

A's Z score is $4.01 > 2.99$, no concern of bankruptcy, while Company B has a Z score of 1.47, well below 1.81 and is a likely candidate for failure.

Chapter 19

Multinational Finance

Many companies are multinational corporations (MNCs) that have significant foreign operations deriving a high percentage of their sales overseas. Financial managers of MNCs require an understanding of the complexities of international finance to make sound financial and investment decisions. International finance involves consideration of managing working capital, financing the business, control of foreign exchange and political risks, and foreign direct investments. Most importantly, the financial manager has to consider the value of the US dollar relative to the value of the currency of the foreign country in which business activities are being conducted. Currency exchange rates may materially affect receivables and payables, and imports and exports of the US company in its multinational operations. The effect is more pronounced with increasing activities abroad.

19.1 SPECIAL FEATURES OF A MULTINATIONAL CORPORATION (MNC)

Multiple-currency problem. Sales revenues may be collected in one currency, assets denominated in another, and profits measured in a third.

Various legal, institutional, and economic constraints. There are variations in such things as tax laws, labor practices, balance-of-payment policies, and government controls with respect to the types and sizes of investments, types and amount of capital raised, and repatriation of profits.

Internal control problem. When the parent office of an MNC and its affiliates are widely located, internal organizational difficulties arise.

19.2 FINANCIAL GOALS OF MNCs

A survey made on financial managers of MNCs lists the financial goals of MNCs in the following order of importance:

1. Maximize growth in corporate earnings, whether total earnings, earnings before interest and taxes (EBIT), or earnings per share (EPS).

2. Maximize return on equity.

3. Guarantee that funds are always available when needed.

19.3 TYPES OF FOREIGN OPERATIONS

Companies involved in multinational business may structure their activities in the following three ways:

Wholly owned subsidiaries. A large, well-established company with much international experience may eventually have wholly owned subsidiaries.

Import/export activities. A small company with limited foreign experience operating in "risky areas" may be restricted to export and import activity.

If the company's sales force has minimal experience in export sales, it is advisable to use foreign brokers when specialized knowledge of foreign markets is needed. When sufficient volume exists, the company may establish a foreign branch sales office, including sales people and technical service staff. As the operation matures, production facilities may be located in the foreign market. However, some foreign countries require licensing before foreign sales and production can take place. In this case, a foreign licensee sells and produces the product. A problem with this is that confidential information and knowledge are passed on to the licensees who can then become a competitor at the expiration of the agreement.

451

Joint ventures. A joint venture with a foreign company is another way to proceed internationally and share the risk. Some foreign governments require this to be the path to follow to operate in their countries. The foreign company may have local goodwill to assure success. A drawback is less control over activities and a conflict of interest.

19.4   FUNCTIONS OF AN MNC's FINANCIAL MANAGER

In evaluating the impact that foreign operations have on the entity's financial health, the financial manager of an MNC should consider the extent of intercountry transactions, foreign restrictions and laws, tax structure of the foreign country, and the economic and political stability of the country. If a subsidiary is operating in a high-tax country with a double-tax agreement, dividend payments are not subject to further US taxes. One way to transfer income from high tax areas to low tax areas is to levy royalties or management fees on the subsidiaries.

19.5   THE FOREIGN EXCHANGE MARKET

Except in a few European centers, there is no central marketplace for the foreign exchange market. Rather, business is carried out over telephone or telex. The major dealers are large banks. A company that wants to buy or sell currency typically uses a commercial bank. International transactions and investments involve more than one currency. For example, when a US company sells merchandise to a Japanese firm, the former wants to be paid in dollars but the Japanese company typically expects to receive yen. Due to the foreign exchange market, the buyer may pay in one currency while the seller can receive payment in another currency.

19.6   SPOT AND FORWARD FOREIGN EXCHANGE RATES

An exchange rate is the ratio of one unit of currency to another. An exchange rate is established between the different currencies. The conversion rate between currencies depends on the demand/supply relationship. Because of the change in exchange rates, companies are susceptible to exchange rate fluctuation risks because of a net asset or net liability position in a foreign currency.

Exchange rates may be in terms of dollars per foreign currency unit (called a *direct quote*) or units of foreign currency per dollar (called an *indirect quote*). Therefore, an indirect quote is the reciprocal of a direct quote and vice versa.

$$\text{An indirect quote} = 1/\text{direct quote}$$

$$\text{Pound/\$} = 1/(\text{\$/pound})$$

Table 19-1 presents a sample of indirect and direct quotes for selected currencies.

EXAMPLE 19.1   A rate of 1.617/British pound means each pound costs the US company \$1.735. In other words, the US company gets $1/1.617 = £0.6184$ for each dollar.

The spot rate is the exchange rate for immediate delivery of currencies exchanged, while the forward rate is the exchange rate for later delivery of currencies exchanged. For example, there may be a 90-day exchange rate. The forward exchange rate of a currency will be slightly different from the spot rate at the current date because of future expectations and uncertainties.

Forward rates may be greater than the current spot rate (premium) or less than the current spot rate (discount).

Cross Rates

A cross rate is the indirect calculation of the exchange rate of one currency from the exchange rates of two other currencies.

Table 19-1.   Foreign Exchange Rates (May 3, 19X8)

Country	Contract	US Dollar Equivalent	Currency per US$
Britain	Spot	1.6170	0.6184
(Pound)	30-day future	1.6153	0.6191
	90-day future	1.6130	0.6200
	180-day future	1.6089	0.6215
Germany	Spot	0.7282	1.3733
(Mark)	30-day future	0.7290	1.3716
	90-day future	0.7311	1.3677
	180-day future	0.7342	1.3620
Japan	Spot	0.011955	83.65
(Yen)	30-day future	0.012003	83.31
	90-day future	0.012100	82.64
	180-day future	0.012247	81.65

EXAMPLE 19.2   The dollar per pound and the yen per dollar rates are given in Table 19-2. From this information, you could determine the yen per pound (or pound per yen) exchanges rates. For example, you see that

$$(\$/\text{pound}) \times (\text{yen}/\$) = (\text{yen}/£)$$
$$1.6170 \times 83.65 = 135.26 \text{ yen}/£$$

Thus, the pound per yen exchange rate is

$$1/135.26 = 0.00739 \text{ pound per yen}$$

Table 19-2 displays the cross rates among key currencies.

Table 19-2. Key Currency Cross Rates (May 3, 19X8)

	British	Germany	Japan	US
British	–	0.45032	0.00739	0.61843
Germany	2.2206	–	0.01642	1.3733
Japan	135.26	60.912	–	83.65
US	1.6170	0.72817	0.01195	–

EXAMPLE 19.3   On February 1, 19X8, forward rates on the British pound were at a premium in relation to the spot rate, while the forward rates for the Japanese yen were at a discount from the spot rate. This means that participants in the foreign exchange market anticipated that the British pound would appreciate relative to the US dollar in the future but the Japanese yen would depreciate against the dollar.

The percentage premium (P) or discount (D) is computed as follows.

$$P \text{ (or } D) = \frac{F - S}{S} \times \frac{12 \text{ months}}{n} \times 100$$

where P, S = the forward and spot rates and n = length of the forward contract in months.

If $P > S$, the result is the annualized premium in percent; otherwise, it is the annualized discount in percent.

EXAMPLE 19.4 On May 3, 1995, a 30-day forward contract in Japanese yen was selling at a 4.8 percent discount:

$$\frac{0.012003 - 0.011955}{0.011955} \times \frac{12 \text{ months}}{1 \text{ month}} \times 100 = 4.82\%$$

19.7 CURRENCY RISK MANAGEMENT

Foreign exchange rate risk exists when the contract is written in terms of the foreign currency or denominated in the foreign currency. The exchange rate fluctuations increase the riskiness of the investment and incur cash losses. The financial manager must not only seek the highest return on temporary investments but must also be concerned about changing values of the currencies invested. You do not necessarily eliminate foreign exchange risk. You may only try to contain it.

Financial Strategies

In countries where currency values are likely to drop, financial managers of the subsidiaries should:

- Avoid paying advances on purchase orders unless the seller pays interest on the advances sufficient to cover the loss of purchasing power.

- Not have excess idle cash. Excess cash can be used to buy inventory or other real assets.

- Buy materials and supplies on credit in the country in which the foreign subsidiary is operating, extending the final payment date as long as possible.

- Avoid giving excessive trade credit. If accounts receivable balances are outstanding for an extended time period, interest should be charged to absorb the loss in purchasing power.

- Borrow local currency funds when the interest rate charged does not exceed US rates after taking into account expected devaluation in the foreign country.

Types of Foreign Exchange Exposure

MNCs' financial managers are faced with the dilemma of three different types of foreign exchange risk. They are:

Translation exposure, often called *accounting exposure*, measures the impact of an exchange rate change on the firm's financial statements. An example would be the impact of a French franc devaluation on a US firm's reported income statement and balance sheet.

Transaction exposure measures potential gains or losses on the future settlement of outstanding obligations that are denominated in a foreign currency. An example would be a US dollar loss after the franc devalues, on payments received for an export invoiced in francs before that devaluation.

Operating exposure, often called *economic exposure*, is the potential for the change in the present value of future cash flows due to an unexpected change in the exchange rate.

Translation Exposure

A major purpose of translation is to provide data of expected impacts of rate changes on cash flow and equity. In the translation of the foreign subsidiaries' financial statements into the US parent's financial statements, the following steps are involved:

1. The foreign financial statements are put into US generally accepted accounting principles.

2. The foreign currency is translated into US dollars. Balance sheet accounts are translated using the current exchange rate at the balance sheet date. If a current exchange rate is not available at the balance sheet date, use the first exchange rate available after that date. Income statement accounts are translated using the weighted-average exchange rate for the period.

Current FASB rules require translation by the *current rate* method. Under the current rate method

- All balance sheet assets and liabilities are translated at the current rate of exchange in effect on the balance sheet date.

- Income statement items are usually translated at an average exchange rate for the reporting period.

- All equity accounts are translated at the historical exchange rates that were in effect at the time the accounts first entered the balance sheet.

- Translation gains and losses are reported as a separate item in the stockholders' equity section of the balance sheet.

Translation gains and losses are only included in net income when there is a sale or liquidation of the entire investment in a foreign entity.

Transaction Exposure

Foreign currency transactions may result in receivables or payables fixed in terms of the amount of foreign currency to be received or paid. Transaction gains and losses are reported in the income statement.

Foreign currency transactions are those transactions whose terms are denominated in a currency other than the entity's functional currency. Foreign currency transactions take place when a business:

- Buys or sells on credit goods or services the prices of which are denominated in foreign currencies.

- Borrows or lends funds, and the amounts payable or receivable are denominated in a foreign currency.

- Is a party to an unperformed forward exchange contract.

- Acquires or disposes of assets, or incurs or settles liabilities denominated in foreign currencies.

EXAMPLE 19.5 Monblanc Trading Company imports French cheeses for distribution in the US. On July 1, the company purchased cheese costing 100,000 francs. Payment is due in francs on October 1. The spot rate on July 1 was $0.20 per franc, and on October 1, it was $0.25 per franc. The exchange loss would be:

Liability in dollars, October 1	$20,000 (100,000 × $0.20)
Paid in dollars, October 1	25,000 (100,000 × $0.25)
Exchange loss	$ 5,000

Note that transaction losses differ from translation losses, which do not influence taxable income.

Long Versus Short Position

When there is a devaluation of the dollar, foreign assets and income in strong currency countries are worth more dollars as long as foreign liabilities do not offset this beneficial effect.

Foreign exchange risk may be analyzed by examining expected receipts or obligations in foreign currency units. A company expecting receipts in foreign currency units ("long" position in the foreign currency units) has the risk that the value of the foreign currency units will drop. This results in devaluing the foreign currency relative to the dollar. If a company is expecting to have obligations in foreign currency units ("short" position in the foreign currency units), there is risk that the value of the foreign currency will rise and it will need to buy the currency at a higher price.

If net claims are greater than liabilities in a foreign currency, the company has a "long" position, since it will benefit if the value of the foreign currency rises. If net liabilities exceed claims with respect to foreign currencies, the company is in a "short" position because it will gain if the foreign currency drops in value.

Monetary Position

Monetary balance is avoiding either a net receivable or a net payable position. Monetary assets and liabilities do not change in value with devaluation or revaluation in foreign currencies.

A company with a long position in a foreign currency will be receiving more funds in the foreign currency. It will have a net monetary asset position (monetary assets exceed monetary liabilities) in that currency.

A company with net receipts is a net monetary creditor. Its foreign exchange rate risk exposure has a net receipts position in a foreign currency that is susceptible to a drop in value.

A company with a future net obligation in foreign currency has a net monetary debtor position. It faces a foreign exchange risk of the possibility of an increase in the value of the foreign currency.

Ways to Neutralize Foreign Exchange Risk

Foreign exchange risk can be neutralized or hedged by a change in the asset and liability position in the foreign currency. Here are some ways to control exchange risk.

Entering a money-market hedge. Here the exposed position in a foreign currency is offset by borrowing or lending in the money market.

EXAMPLE 19.6   XYZ, an American importer, enters into a contract with a British supplier to buy merchandise for £4,000. The amount is payable on the delivery of the good, 30 days from today. The company knows the exact amount of its pound liability in 30 days. However, it does not know the payable in dollars. Assume that the 30-day money-market rates for both lending and borrowing in the US and UK are 0.5% and 1%, respectively. Assume further that today's foreign exchange rate is $1.50 per pound.

In a money-market hedge, XYZ can take the following steps:

Step 1.   Buy a 1-month UK money market security, worth of 4,000/(1 + 0.005) = £3,980. This investment will compound to exactly £4,000 in 1 month.

Step 2.   Exchange dollars on today's spot (cash) market to obtain the £3,980. The dollar amount needed today is

$$£3,980 \times \$1.7350 \text{ per pound} = \$6,905.30.$$

Step 3.   If XYZ does not have this amount, it can borrow it from the US money market at the going rate of 1%. In 30 days XYZ will need to repay $6,905.30 × (1 + 0.1) = $7,595.83. *Note:* XYZ need not wait for the future exchange rate to be available. On today's date, the future dollar amount of the contract is known with certainty. The British supplier will receive £4,000, and the cost of XYZ to make the payment is $7,595.83.

Hedging by purchasing forward (or futures) exchange contracts. Forward exchange contracts is a commitment to buy or sell, at a specified future date, one currency for a specified amount of another currency (at a specified exchange rate). This can be a hedge against changes in exchange rates during a period of contract or exposure to risk from such changes. More specifically, you do the following: (1) Buy foreign exchange forward contracts to cover payables denominated in a foreign currency and (2) sell foreign exchange forward contracts to cover receivables denominated in a foreign currency. This way, any gain or loss on the foreign receivables or payables due to changes in exchange rates is offset by the gain or loss on the forward exchange contract.

EXAMPLE 19.7   In the previous example, assume that the 30-day forward exchange rate is $1.6153. XYZ may take the following steps to cover its payable.

Step 1.   Buy a forward contract today to purchase £4,000 in 30 days.

Step 2.   On the 30th day pay the foreign exchange dealer £4,000 × $1.6153 per pound = $6,461.20 and collect £4,000. Pay this amount to the British supplier.

Note: using the forward contract XYZ knows the exact worth of the future payment in dollars ($6,461.20).

Note: the basic difference between futures contracts and forward contracts is that futures contracts are for specified amounts and maturities, whereas forward contracts are for any size and maturity desired.

Hedging by foreign currency options. Foreign currency options can be purchased or sold in three different types of markets: (*a*) Options on the physical currency, purchased on the over-the-counter (interbank) market; (*b*) options on the physical currency, on organized exchanges such as the Philadelphia Stock Exchange and the Chicago Mercantile Exchange; and (*c*) options on futures contracts, purchased on the International Monetary Market (IMM) of the Chicago Mercantile Exchange. *Note:* The difference between using a futures contract and using an option on a futures contract is that, with a futures contract, the company must deliver one currency against another, or reverse the contract on the exchange, while with an option the company may abandon the option and use the spot (cash) market if that is more advantageous.

Repositioning cash by *leading* and *lagging* the time at which an MNC makes operational or financial payments. Often, money- and forward-market hedges are not available to eliminate exchange risk. Under such circumstances, leading (accelerating) and lagging (decelerating) may be used to *reduce* risk. *Note:* a net asset position (i.e., assets minus liabilities) is not desirable in a weak or potentially depreciating currency. In this case, you should expedite the disposal of the asset. By the same token, you should lag or delay the collection against a net asset position in a strong currency.

Maintaining balance between receivables and payables denominated in a foreign currency. MNCs typically set up "multilateral netting centers" as a special department to settle the outstanding balances of affiliates of an MNC with each other on a net basis. It is the development of a "clearing house" for payments by the firm's affiliates. If there are amounts due among affiliates they are offset insofar as possible. The net amount would be paid in the currency of the transaction. The total amounts owed need not be paid in the currency of the transaction; thus, a much lower quantity of the currency must be acquired. *Note:* The major advantage of the system is a reduction of the costs associated with a large number of separate foreign exchange transactions.

Positioning of funds through transfer pricing. A transfer price is the price at which an MNC sells goods and services to its foreign affiliates or, alternatively, the price at which an affiliate sells to the parent. For example, a parent that wishes to transfer funds from an affiliate in a depreciating-currency country may charge a higher price on the goods and services sold to this affiliate by the parent or by affiliates from strong-currency countries. Transfer pricing affects not only transfer of funds from one entity to another but also the income taxes paid by both entities.

Operating Exposure

Operating (economic) exposure is the possibility that an unexpected change in exchange rates will cause a change in the future cash flows of a firm and its market value. It differs from translation and transaction exposures in that it is subjective and thus not easily quantified. *Note:* the best strategy to control operation exposure is to diversify operations and financing internationally.

Key Questions to Ask That Help to Identify Foreign Exchange Risk

A systematic approach to identifying an MNC's exposure to foreign exchange risk is to ask a series of questions regarding the net effects on profits of changes in foreign currency revenues and costs. The questions are:

- Where is the MNC selling? (Domestic versus foreign sales share)
- Who are the firm's major competitors? (Domestic versus foreign)
- Where is the firm producing? (Domestic versus foreign)
- Where are the firm's inputs coming from? (Domestic versus foreign)
- How sensitive is quantity demanded to price? (Elastic versus inelastic)
- How are the firm's inputs or outputs priced? (Priced in a domestic market or a global market; the currency of denomination)

Impacts of Changes in Foreign Exchange Rates

Table 19-3 summarizes the impacts of changes in foreign exchange rates on the company's products and financial transactions.

Table 19-3. The Impact of Changes in Foreign Exchange Rates

	Weak Currency (Depreciation)	Strong Currency (Appreciation)
Imports	More expensive	Cheaper
Exports	Cheaper	More expensive
Payables	More expensive	Cheaper
Receivables	Cheaper	More expensive

19.8 FORECASTING FOREIGN EXCHANGE RATES

The forecasting of foreign exchange rates is a formidable task. Most MNCs rely primarily on bank and bank services for assistance and information in preparing exchange rate projections. The following economic indicators are considered to be the most important for the forecasting process:

- Recent rate movements
- Relative inflation rates
- Balance of payments and trade
- Money supply growth
- Interest rate differentials

Interest rates

Interest rates have an important influence on exchange rates. In fact, there is an important economic relationship between any two nations' spot rates, forward rates, and interest rates. This relationship is called the *interest rate parity theorem* (IRPT). The IRPT states that the ratio of the forward and spot rates is directly related to the two interest rates. Specifically, the premium or discount should be:

$$P \text{ (or } D) = \frac{r_f - r_d}{1 + r_f}$$

where r_f and r_d = foreign and domestic interest rates.

(When interest rates are relatively low, this equation can be approximated by: P (or $D) = -(r_f - r_d)$.)

The IRPT implies that the P (or D) calculated by the equation should be the same as the P (or D) calculated by:

$$P \text{ (or } D) = \frac{F - S}{S} \times \frac{12 \text{ months}}{n} \times 100$$

EXAMPLE 19.8 On May 3, 1995, a 30-day forward contract in Japanese yens was selling at a 4.82 percent premium:

$$\frac{0.012003 - 0.011955}{0.011955} \times \frac{12 \text{ months}}{1 \text{ month}} \times 100 = 4.82\%$$

The 30-day US T-bill rate is 8% annualized. What is the 30-day Japanese rate?

Using the equation:

$$P \text{ (or } D) = \frac{r_f - r_d}{1 + r_f}$$

$$0.0482 = \frac{0.08 - r_f}{1 + r_f}$$

$$-0.0318 = -1.0482 r_f$$

$$r_f = 0.0303 = 3.03\%$$

The 30-day Japanese rate should be 3.03%.

Inflation

Inflation, which is a change in price levels, also affects future exchange rates. The mathematical relationship that links changes in exchange rates and changes in price level is called the *purchasing power parity theorem* (PPPT). The PPPT states that the ratio of the forward and spot rates is directly related to the two inflation rates:

$$\frac{F}{S} = \frac{1 + P_d}{1 + P_f}$$

where F = forward exchange rate (e.g., \$/foreign currency)
   S = spot exchange rate (e.g., \$/foreign currency)
   P_d = domestic inflation rate
   P_f = foreign inflation rate

EXAMPLE 19.9   Assume the following data for US and France:

Expected US inflation rate = 5%
Expected French inflation rate = 10%
S = \$0.220/FR

Then,

$$\frac{F}{0.220} = \frac{1.05}{1.10}$$

So

$$F = \$0.210/FR$$

Note: if France has the higher inflation rate, then the purchasing power of the franc is declining faster than that of the dollar. This will lead to a forward discount on the franc relative to the dollar.

19.9   ANALYSIS OF FOREIGN INVESTMENTS

Foreign investment decisions are basically capital budgeting decisions at the international level. The decision requires three major components:

The estimation of the relevant future cash flows. Cash flows are the dividends and possible future sales price of the investment. The estimation depends on the sales forecast, the effects on exchange rate changes, the risk in cash flows, and the actions of foreign governments.

The choice of the proper discount rate (cost of capital). The cost of capital in foreign investment projects is higher due to the increased risks of:

- Currency risk (or foreign exchange risk) – changes in exchange rates. This risk may adversely affect sales by making competing imported goods cheaper.
- Political risk (or sovereignty risk) – possibility of nationalization or other restrictions with net losses to the parent company.

Examples of Political Risks

- Expropriation of plants and equipment without compensation or with minimal compensation that is below actual market value.

- Nonconvertibility of the affiliate's foreign earnings into the parent's currency – the problem of "blocked funds."

- Substantial changes in the laws governing taxation.

- Government controls in the host country regarding wages, compensation to the personnel, hiring of personnel, the sales price of the product, making of transfer payments to the parent, and local borrowing.

Methods for Dealing with Political Risk

To the extent that forecasting political risks is a formidable task, what can an MNC do to cope with them? There are several methods suggested. They are:

- *Avoidance* Try to avoid political risk by minimizing activities in or with countries that are considered to be of high risk and by using a higher discount rate for projects in riskier countries.

- *Adaptation* Try to reduce such risk by adapting the activities (for example, by using hedging techniques discussed previously).

- *Diversification* Diversity across national borders, so that problems in one country do not risk the company.

- *Risk transfer* Buy insurance policies for political risks.

Most developed nations offer insurance for political risk to their exporters. Examples are:

In the US, the *Eximbank* offers policies to exporters that cover such political risks as war, currency inconvertibility, and civil unrest. Furthermore, the *Overseas Private Investment Corporation (OPIC)* offers policies to US foreign investors to cover such risks as currency inconvertibility, civil or foreign war damages, or expropriation.

In the UK, similar policies are offered by the *Export Credit Guarantee Department (ECGD)*; in Canada, by the *Export Development Council (EDC)*; and in Germany, by an agency called *Hermes*.

19.10 INTERNATIONAL SOURCES OF FINANCING

A company may finance its activities abroad, especially in countries it is operating in. A successful company in domestic markets is more likely to be able to attract financing for international expansion.

The most important international sources of funds are the Eurocurrency market and the Eurobond market. Also, MNCs often have access to national capital markets in which their subsidiaries are located.

The Eurocurrency market is a largely short-term (usually less than 1 year of maturity) market for bank deposits and loans denominated in any currency except the currency of the country where the market is located. For example, in London, the Eurocurrency market is a market for bank deposits and loans denominated in dollars, yens, francs, marks, and any other currency except British pounds. The main instruments used in this market are CDs and time deposits, and bank loans. *Note:* the term "market" in this context is not a physical market place, but a set of bank deposits and loans.

The Eurobond market is a long-term market for bonds denominated in any currency except the currency of the country where the market is located. Eurobonds may be of different types such as straight, convertible, and with warrants. While most Eurobonds are fixed rate, variable rate bonds also exist. Maturities vary, but 10–12 years is typical.

Although Eurobonds are issued in many currencies, you wish to select a stable, fully convertible, and actively traded currency. In some cases, if a Eurobond is denominated in a weak currency the holder has the option of requesting payment in another currency.

Sometimes, large MNCs establish wholly owned offshore finance subsidiaries. These subsidiaries issue Eurobond debt and the proceeds are given to the parent or to overseas operating subsidiaries. Debt service goes back to bondholders through the finance subsidiaries.

If the Eurobond was issued by the parent directly, the US would require a withholding tax on interest. There may also be an estate tax when the bondholder dies. These tax problems do not arise when a bond is issued by a finance subsidiary incorporated in a tax haven. Hence, the subsidiary may borrow at less cost than the parent.

In summary, the Euromarkets offer borrowers and investors in one country the opportunity to deal with borrowers and investors from many other countries, buying and selling bank deposits, bonds, and loans denominated in many currencies.

Review Questions

1. The rate at which a foreign currency can be exchanged for the domestic currency is the _____ .

2. A gain on the exchange of one currency for another due to appreciation in the home currency is a(n) _____ .

3. _____ refers to the possibility that future cash transactions will be affected by changing exchange rates.

4. The exchange rate of one currency for another for immediate delivery is the _____ .

5. _____ is one way of insuring against gains and losses on foreign exchange.

6. An agreement that requires the buyer to exchange a specified amount of a currency at a specified rate on a specified future date is a(n) _____ .

7. A(n) _____ is a corporation for which a significant amount of business is done in more than one country.

8. A weaker dollar makes US _____ relatively more expensive to consumers.

9. The gain or loss that results from restating foreign subsidiaries' financial statements in the home currency is an example of _____ .

10. _____ refers to the possibility that a company's present value of future cash inflows can be affected by exchange rate fluctuations.

11. The mathematical relationship that links changes in exchange rates and changes in price level is called the _____ .

12. The interest rate parity theorem (IRPT) states that the ratio of the forward and spot rates is directly related to the two _____ .

13. A dollar deposited in a non-US bank is often called a(n) _____ .

Answers: (1) exchange rate; (2) exchange gain; (3) Transaction risk; (4) spot rate; (5) Hedging; (6) forward contract; (7) multinational corporation (MNC); (8) imports; (9) translation risk; (10) Operating (or Economic) risk; (11) purchasing power parity theorem (PPPT); (12) interest rates; (13) Eurodollar.

Solved Problems

19.1 Spot Rates. On June 1, Johnson, Inc. received an order from a Japanese customer for 2,500,000 yen to be paid upon receipt of the goods, scheduled for August 1. The rates for $1 US are as follows:

	Exchange Rates for $1 for Yen
Spot rate, June 1	83
Forward rate, August 1	82
Spot rate, August 1	81

(a) Calculate what Johnson would receive from the Japanese customer in US dollars using the spot rate at the time of the order.

(b) Calculate what Johnson would receive from the Japanese customer in US dollars using the spot rate at the time of payment.

SOLUTION

(a) $30,120.48 (2,500,000 yen/83 yen per $)

(b) $30,864.20 (2,500,000 yen/81)

19.2 Forward Rates. Using the same data in Problem 19.1:

(a) Calculate Johnson's exchange gain or loss, if Johnson receives payment from the Japanese customer using the spot rate at the time of payment.

(b) Calculate the amount that Johnson expects to receive on August 1 if Johnson's policy is to hedge foreign currency transactions.

SOLUTION

(a) Loss of $743.72 ($30,864.20 − $30,120.48)

(b) $30,487.80 (2,500,000 yen/82)

19.3 Exchange Gain or Loss. Bonjur, Inc. imports French cheeses for distribution in the US. On April 1, the company purchased cheese costing 400,000 francs. Payment is due in francs on July 1. The spot rate on April 1 was $0.20 per franc, and on July 1, it was $0.25 per franc.

(a) How much would Bonjur have to pay in dollars for the purchase if it paid on April 1?

(b) How much would Bonjur have to pay in dollars for the purchase if it paid on July 1?

(c) If Bonjur paid for the purchase using the July 1 spot rate, what would be the exchange gain or loss?

SOLUTION

(a) 400,000 francs × $0.20 per franc = $ 80,000

(b) 400,000 francs × $0.25 per franc = $100,000

(c)   Liability in dollars, April 1 $ 80,000

     Paid in dollars, July 1   100,000

        Exchange loss $ 20,000

19.4   Spot Rates. On August 1, Kidd Trading received an order from a British customer for £1,000,000 to be paid on receipt of the goods, scheduled for November 1.

     The rates for $1 US are as follows:

	Exchange Rates for $1 for British £
Spot rate, June 1	1.617
Forward rate, August 1	1.615
Spot rate, August 1	1.616

(a)   How much does Kidd expect to receive from the British customer in dollars using the spot rate at the time of the order?

(b)   How much does Kidd expect to receive from the British customer in dollars using the spot rate at the time of payment?

SOLUTION

(a) $618,429.19 (£1,000,000/1.617)

(b) $618,811.81 (£1,000,000/1.616)

19.5   Exchange Gain or Loss and Hedging. Using the same data in Problem 19.4:

(a)   Calculate Kidd's exchange gain or loss if Kidd receives payment from the British customer using the spot rate at the time of payment.

(b)   Calculate the amount Kidd expects to receive on November 1 in dollars, if Kidd's policy is to hedge foreign currency transactions.

SOLUTION

(a)   Receivables in dollars, August 1 $618,811.81

     Received in dollars, November 1   618,429.19

        Exchange gain $ 382.62

(b) $619,195.05 (£1,000,000/1.615)

19.6   Arbitrage and Exchange Gain or Loss. You own $10,000. The dollar rate on the DM is 1.380 marks.

Country	Contract	US Dollar Equivalent (Direct)	Currency per US$ (Indirect)
Germany	Spot	0.7282	1.3733
(Mark)	30-day future	0.7290	1.3716
	90-day future	0.7311	1.3677

Based on the table above, are arbitrage profits possible? What is the gain (loss) in dollars?

SOLUTION

The dollar rate on the DM is 1.380 marks, while the table (indirect New York rate) shows 1.3773 (1/0.7282) marks. Note that the rates between Germany and New York are out of line. Thus, arbitrage profits are possible. Since the DM is cheaper in Germany, buy $10,000 worth of marks in Germany. The number of marks purchased would be 13,800 ($10,000 × 1.380) marks. Simultaneously sell the marks in New York at the prevailing rate. The amount received upon sale of the marks would be $10,049.16 (13,800 marks × $0.7282/DM) = $10,049.16. The net gain is $49.16, barring transactions costs.

19.7   Interest-Rate Parity. If the interest rates on the 30-day instruments in the US and Germany are 12 and 10 percent (annualized), respectively, what is the correct price of the 30-day forward DM? (Use the table in Problem 19.6.)

SOLUTION

First, compute the premium (discount) on the forward rate using:

$$P \text{ (or } D) = \frac{r_f - r_d}{1 + r_f}$$

Thus,

$$\frac{0.10 - 0.12}{1 + 0.10} = 0.0182$$

Compute the forward rate using the equation:

$$P \text{ (or } D) = \frac{F - S}{S} \times \frac{12 \text{ months}}{n} \times 100$$

$$0.0182 = \frac{F - 0.7282}{0.7282} \times \frac{12}{1} \times 100$$

Solving this equation for F yields: 0.7293

19.8   Interest-Rate Parity. Almond Shoe, Inc. sells to a wholesaler in Germany. The purchase price of a shipment is 50,000 DM with terms of 90 days. Upon payment, Almond will convert the DM to dollars.

Country	Contract	US Dollar Equivalent	Currency per US$
Germany	Spot	0.730	1.37
(Mark)	90-day future	0.735	1.36

(a)   If Almond's policy is to hedge its foreign exchange risk, what would it do?

(b)   Is the DM at a premium or at a discount?

(c)   What is the implied differential in interest rates between the two nations, using the interest-rate parity theory?

SOLUTION

(a)   Almond would hedge by selling DMs forward 90 days. Upon delivery of 50,000 marks in 90 days, it would receive $36,764.71 (50,000 DMs/1.36). It were to receive payment today. It would get only $36,496.35 (50,000 DMs/1.37).

(b)   The DM is at a premium because the 90-day forward rate of DM per dollar is less than the current spot rate. The DM is expected to strengthen (fewer DM to buy a dollar).

(c) The differential in interest rates is -2.96 percent, as shown below.

$$P \text{ (or } D) = \frac{F - S}{S} \times \frac{12 \text{ months}}{n} \times 100$$

$$\frac{(7.35 - 7.30)}{7.30} \times \frac{12}{3} \times 100 = -(r_f - r_d) = 2.73\%$$

This means that if the interest parity theory holds, interest rates in the US should be 2.73 percent higher than those in Germany.

19.9 Interest-Rate Parity.

Country	Contract	US Dollar Equivalent	Currency per US$
Japan	Spot	0.011955	83.65
(Yen)	90-day future	0.012100	82.64

The interest rate in Japan on 90-day government securities is 4 percent; it is 8 percent in the US. If the interest-rate parity theory holds, what is the implied 90-day forward exchange rate in yen per dollar?

SOLUTION

First, compute the premium (discount) on the forward rate using:

$$P \text{ (or } D) = \frac{r_f - r_d}{1 + r_f}$$

Thus,

$$\frac{0.04 - 0.08}{1 + 0.04} = 0.0385$$

Compute the forward rate using the equation:

$$P \text{ (or } D) = \frac{F - S}{S} \times \frac{12 \text{ months}}{n} \times 100$$

$$0.0385 = \frac{F - 0.011955}{0.011955} \times \frac{12}{3} \times 100$$

Solving this equation for F yields: 0.012070

Examination IV

Chapters 16–19

1. A warrant for Jack Corporation permits the holder to buy five shares of common stock at $25 a share. The market price of the stock is $37. What is the value of the warrant?

2. Smith Corporation issued a $1,000 bond at par. The common stock has a market price of $34. The conversion price is $40. (*a*) Into how many shares may the bond be converted? (*b*) What is the conversion value of the bond? (*c*) What is the conversion premium?

3. Tunick Corporation's convertible bond has a conversion price of $80. The conversion ratio is 12. The market price of the stock is $115. The call price is $1,200. Would the bondholder rather convert to common stock or receive the call price?

4. The following data are provided:

	Company A	Company B
Net income	$40,000	$60,000
Shares outstanding	8,000	20,000
Earnings per share	$5.00	$3.00
P/E ratio	9	15
Market price	$45	$45

Company B is the acquiring company, exchanging on a one-for-one basis its shares for the shares of company A. The exchange ratio is based on the market prices of A and B. (*a*) What will the EPS be after the merger? (*b*) What is the change in EPS for the stockholders of companies A and B?

5. The following data are provided:

Market Price per Share of Acquiring Company	Market Price per Share of Acquired Company	Price per Share Offered
$75	$25	$35

What is the exchange ratio in: (*a*) shares? (*b*) market price?

6. Jones Company wishes to acquire Masters Company. Relevant data follow:

	Jones	Masters
Net income	$60,000	$45,000
Shares outstanding	30,000	5,000

Jones Company issues its shares to make the acquisition. The ratio of exchange is 3.0 (*a*) What is the EPS of the merged company based on the original shares of each firm? (*b*) What is the EPS of Jones? (*c*) What is the EPS of Masters?

7. Glory Corporation wishes to acquire Jerry Corporation by exchanging 1.5 shares of its stock for each share of Jerry. Glory expects to have the same P/E ratio after the merger as before it. The following data are given:

	Glory	Jerry
Net income	$600,000	$200,000
Shares	200,000	25,000
Market price per share	$50	$40

(a) What is the exchange ratio of market prices? (b) What are the EPS and P/E ratios for each firm? (c) What was the P/E ratio used to obtain Jerry? (d) What is the EPS of Glory after the acquisition? (e) What is the anticipated market price per share of the merged company?

8. Brother Corporation is considering acquiring Davis Company for $190,000 in cash. Brother's current cost of capital is 12 percent. Davis has an estimated cost of capital of 10 percent after the acquisition. Anticipated cash inflows from years 1 to 12 are $20,000. Should the acquisition be made?

9. Company T wants to acquire company Z. Company T's stock sells for $90 per share. Company Z's stock sells for $35 per share. Because of merger negotiations, company T offers $45 a share. The acquisition is accomplished by an exchange of securities. What is the exchange ratio?

10. The balance sheet of Jason Corporation for the year ended December 31, 19X4, follows:

Balance Sheet

Current assets	$ 800,000	Current liabilities	$ 600,000
Noncurrent assets	300,000	Long-term liabilities	250,000
		Common stock	300,000
		Retained earnings	(50,000)
		Total liabilities and	
Total assets	$1,100,000	stockholders' equity	$1,100,000

The company's liquidation value is $800,000. Rather than liquidating, a reorganization could occur with an investment of another $350,000. The reorganization is expected to generate earnings of $120,000 a year. A multiplier of 6 is appropriate. If the $350,000 is obtained, long-term debt holders will receive 40 percent of the common stock in the reorganized business in substitution for their current claims. Is reorganization or liquidation recommended?

11. Calcot Corporation is bankrupt. The book and liquidation values of its assets follow.

	Book Value	Liquidation Value
Cash	$ 400,000	$ 400,000
Accounts receivable	1,600,000	1,300,000
Inventory	3,200,000	2,000,000
Land	5,000,000	3,800,000
Building	10,000,000	6,000,000
Equipment	8,000,000	4,000,000
Total assets	$28,200,000	$17,500,000

The liabilities and stockholders' equity at the liquidation date follow.

Current liabilities		
Accounts payable	$3,000,000	
Notes payable	1,500,000	
Accrued taxes	800,000	
Accrued salaries	300,000[a]	
Total current liabilities		$ 5,600,000
Long-term liabilities		
Mortgage on land	$3,800,000	
First mortgage—building	4,000,000	
Second mortgage—building	2,000,000	
Subordinated debentures	4,200,000	
Total long-term liabilities		14,000,000
Total liabilities		$19,600,000
Stockholders' equity		
Preferred stock	$3,500,000	
Common stock	7,000,000	
Retained earnings	(1,900,000)	
Total stockholders' equity		8,600,000
Total liabilities and stockholders' equity		$28,200,000

[a] The salary owed to each worker is less than $2,000 and was incurred within 90 days of the bankruptcy petition.

Expenses applicable to the bankruptcy administration were 15 percent of the proceeds. The debentures are subordinated only with regard to the two first-mortgage bonds. What is the distribution of the proceeds?

12. Michael Corporation's balance sheet is presented below.

ASSETS		
Current assets	$1,400,000	
Land	3,500,000	
Plant and equipment	2,500,000	
Total assets		$7,400,000
LIABILITIES AND STOCKHOLDERS' EQUITY		
Current liabilities		
Accounts payable	$ 400,000	
Notes payable	1,000,000	
Accrued taxes	200,000	
Total current liabilities		$1,600,000
Noncurrent liabilities		
Mortgage bonds	$2,000,000[a]	
Debentures	1,200,000	
Total noncurrent liabilities		3,200,000
Total liabilities		$4,800,000
Stockholders' equity		
Preferred stock	$ 800,000	
Common stock	1,800,000	
Total stockholders' equity		2,600,000
Total liabilities and stockholders' equity		$7,400,000

[a] Mortgage bonds are secured against plant and equipment.

The liquidation value of the total assets was $4.6 million, $1.4 million of which was received for plant and equipment. Bankruptcy costs were $120,000.

What is the distribution of the proceeds?

Answers to Examination IV

1.
$$($37 - $25) \times 5 = $60$$

2. (a)
$$\frac{$1,000}{40} = 25 \text{ shares}$$

(b)
$$\text{Conversion value} = \text{common stock price} \times \text{conversion ratio} = $34 \times 25 = $850$$

(c)
$$$1,000 - $850 = $150$$

3. The market value of common stock received upon conversion is:

$$$115 \times 12 = $1,380$$

The call price is $1,200. The bondholder would rather convert, since he or she receives a benefit of $180.

4. (a)

	B Shares Owned after Merger	EPS before Merger	EPS after Merger
A stockholders	8,000	$5.00	$3.57[a]
B stockholders	20,000	$3.00	$3.57[a]
Total	28,000		

[a]The new EPS is calculated as follows:

8,000 shares × $5	$ 40,000
20,000 shares × $3	60,000
Total net income	$100,000

$$\text{EPS} = \frac{\text{total net income}}{\text{total shares}} = \frac{$100,000}{28,000} = $3.57$$

(b) EPS is lower by $1.43 for A stockholders but rises by $0.57 for B stockholders.

5. (a)
$$\frac{$35}{$75} = 0.467$$

(b)
$$\frac{$35}{$25} = 1.4$$

6. (a)
$$\frac{\text{Combined net income}}{\text{Total shares}} = \frac{$105,000}{30,000 + (5,000 \times 3)} = \frac{$105,000}{45,000} = $2.33$$

(b) $2.33

(c) $2.33 × 3 = $6.99

7. (a) $\dfrac{\text{Price per share offered}}{\text{Market price of Jerry}} = \dfrac{\$50 \times 1.5}{\$40} = \dfrac{\$75}{\$40} = 1.875$

(b)

	Glory	**Jerry**
EPS (net income/number of shares)	3.0	8.0
P/E	16.67	5

(c) $1.5 \times \$50 = \$75$

$$\dfrac{\$75}{\$8} = 9.4 \text{ times}$$

(d) Total net income is:

200,000 shares $\times$ \$3	\$600,000
25,000 shares $\times$ \$8	200,000
Total net income	\$800,000

Net EPS is:

$$\dfrac{\text{Total net income}}{\text{Total shares}} = \dfrac{\$800,000}{237,500} = \$3.37$$

(e)   Anticipated market price = P/E $\times$ new EPS 16.67 $\times$ \$3.37 = \$56.18 (rounded)

8.

Year	Calculations	Present Value
0	$-\$190,000 \times 1$	$-\$190,000$
1–12	$+\$20,000 \times 6.814$	$+136,280^a$
		$-\$\ 53,720$

^{a}Using 10 percent as the discount rate.

The net present value is $-\$53,720$. Since it is negative the acquisition should not be made.

9. $\dfrac{\text{Amount paid per share of the acquired company}}{\text{Market price of the acquiring company's shares}} = \dfrac{\$45}{\$90} = 0.5$

10. Assuming the \$350,000 of further investment is made, the company's going concern value is \$720,000 ($6 \times \$120,000$). The liquidation value is given as \$800,000. Since the liquidation value exceeds the going concern value, liquidation is called for.

11. The distribution of the proceeds follows:

Proceeds		\$17,500,000
Mortgage on land	\$3,800,000	
First mortgage—building	4,000,000	
Second mortgage—building	2,000,000	
Liquidation expenses (15% $\times$ \$17,500,000)	2,625,000	
Accrued taxes	800,000	
Accrued salaries	300,000	
Total		13,525,000
Balance		\$ 3,975,000

Percent to be paid to general creditors:

$$\frac{\text{Proceeds balance}}{\text{Total owed}} = \frac{\$3,975,000}{\$8,700,000} = 0.4568965$$

General Creditor	Owed	Paid
Accounts payable	$3,000,000	$1,370,690
Notes payable	1,500,000	685,345
Subordinated debentures	4,200,000	1,918,965
Total	$8,700,000	$3,975,000

12.

Proceeds		$4,600,000
Mortgage bonds—secured against plant and equipment	$1,400,000	
Bankruptcy costs	120,000	
Accrued taxes	200,000	1,720,000
Balance available to general creditors		$2,880,000

The distribution to general creditors follows:

General Creditor	Owed	Pro Rata Distribution
Mortgage bonds ($2,000,000 − $1,400,000)	$ 600,000	$ 540,000
Accounts payable	400,000	360,000
Notes payable	1,000,000	900,000
Debentures	1,200,000	1,080,000
Total	$3,200,000	$2,880,000

Preferred stock and common stockholders will receive nothing.

Future Value of $1: FVIF$_{i,n}$

Period	1%	2%	3%	4%	5%	6%	7%	8%	9%	10%	12%	14%	15%	16%	18%	20%	24%	28%	32%	36%
1	1.0100	1.0200	1.0300	1.0400	1.0500	1.0600	1.0700	1.0800	1.0900	1.1000	1.1200	1.1400	1.1500	1.1600	1.1800	1.2000	1.2400	1.2800	1.3200	1.3600
2	1.0201	1.0404	1.0609	1.0816	1.1025	1.1236	1.1449	1.1664	1.1881	1.2100	1.2544	1.2996	1.3225	1.3456	1.3924	1.4400	1.5376	1.6384	1.7424	1.8496
3	1.0303	1.0612	1.0927	1.1249	1.1576	1.1910	1.2250	1.2597	1.2950	1.3310	1.4049	1.4815	1.5209	1.5609	1.6430	1.7280	1.9066	2.0972	2.3000	2.5155
4	1.0406	1.0824	1.1255	1.1699	1.2155	1.2625	1.3108	1.3605	1.4116	1.4641	1.5735	1.6890	1.7490	1.8106	1.9388	2.0736	2.3642	2.6844	3.0360	3.4210
5	1.0510	1.1041	1.1593	1.2167	1.2763	1.3382	1.4026	1.4693	1.5386	1.6105	1.7623	1.9254	2.0114	2.1003	2.2878	2.4883	2.9316	3.4360	4.0075	4.6526
6	1.0615	1.1262	1.1941	1.2653	1.3401	1.4185	1.5007	1.5869	1.6771	1.7716	1.9738	2.1950	2.3131	2.4364	2.6996	2.9860	3.6352	4.3980	5.2899	6.3275
7	1.0721	1.1487	1.2299	1.3159	1.4071	1.5036	1.6058	1.7138	1.8280	1.9487	2.2107	2.5023	2.6600	2.8262	3.1855	3.5832	4.5077	5.6295	6.9826	8.6054
8	1.0829	1.1717	1.2668	1.3686	1.4775	1.5938	1.7182	1.8509	1.9926	2.1436	2.4760	2.8526	3.0590	3.2784	3.7589	4.2998	5.5895	7.2058	9.2170	11.703
9	1.0937	1.1951	1.3048	1.4233	1.5513	1.6895	1.8385	1.9990	2.1719	2.3579	2.7731	3.2519	3.5179	3.8030	4.4355	5.1598	6.9310	9.2234	12.166	15.916
10	1.1046	1.2190	1.3439	1.4802	1.6289	1.7908	1.9672	2.1589	2.3674	2.5937	3.1058	3.7072	4.0456	4.4114	5.2338	6.1917	8.5944	11.805	16.059	21.646
11	1.1157	1.2434	1.3842	1.5395	1.7103	1.8983	2.1049	2.3316	2.5804	2.8531	3.4785	4.2262	4.6524	5.1173	6.1759	7.4301	10.657	15.111	21.198	29.439
12	1.1268	1.2682	1.4258	1.6010	1.7959	2.0122	2.2522	2.5182	2.8127	3.1384	3.8960	4.8179	5.3502	5.9360	7.2876	8.9161	13.214	19.342	27.982	40.037
13	1.1381	1.2936	1.4685	1.6651	1.8856	2.1329	2.4098	2.7196	3.0658	3.4523	4.3635	5.4924	6.1528	6.8858	8.5994	10.699	16.386	24.748	36.937	54.451
14	1.1495	1.3195	1.5126	1.7317	1.9799	2.2609	2.5785	2.9372	3.3417	3.7975	4.8871	6.2613	7.0757	7.9875	10.147	12.839	20.319	31.691	48.756	74.053
15	1.1610	1.3459	1.5580	1.8009	2.0789	2.3966	2.7590	3.1722	3.6425	4.1772	5.4736	7.1379	8.1371	9.2655	11.973	15.407	25.195	40.564	64.359	100.71
16	1.1726	1.3728	1.6047	1.8730	2.1829	2.5404	2.9522	3.4259	3.9703	4.5950	6.1304	8.1372	9.3576	10.748	14.129	18.488	31.242	51.923	84.953	136.96
17	1.1843	1.4002	1.6528	1.9479	2.2920	2.6928	3.1588	3.7000	4.3276	5.0545	6.8660	9.2765	10.761	12.467	16.672	22.186	38.740	66.461	112.13	186.27
18	1.1961	1.4282	1.7024	2.0258	2.4066	2.8543	3.3799	3.9960	4.7171	5.5599	7.6900	10.575	12.375	14.462	19.673	26.623	48.038	85.070	148.02	253.33
19	1.2081	1.4568	1.7535	2.1068	2.5270	3.0256	3.6165	4.3157	5.1417	6.1159	8.6129	12.055	14.231	16.776	23.214	31.948	59.567	108.89	195.39	344.53
20	1.2202	1.4859	1.8061	2.1911	2.6533	3.2071	3.8697	4.6610	5.6044	6.7275	9.6463	13.743	16.366	19.460	27.393	38.337	73.864	139.37	257.91	468.57
21	1.2324	1.5157	1.8603	2.2788	2.7860	3.3996	4.1406	5.0338	6.1088	7.4002	10.803	15.667	18.821	22.574	32.323	46.005	91.591	178.40	340.44	637.26
22	1.2447	1.5460	1.9161	2.3699	2.9253	3.6035	4.4304	5.4365	6.6586	8.1403	12.100	17.861	21.644	26.186	38.142	55.206	113.57	228.35	449.39	866.67
23	1.2572	1.5769	1.9736	2.4647	3.0715	3.8197	4.7405	5.8715	7.2579	8.9543	13.552	20.361	24.891	30.376	45.007	66.247	140.83	292.30	593.19	1178.6
24	1.2697	1.6084	2.0328	2.5633	3.2251	4.0489	5.0724	6.3412	7.9111	9.8497	15.178	23.212	28.625	35.236	53.108	79.496	174.63	374.14	783.02	1602.9
25	1.2824	1.6406	2.0938	2.6658	3.3864	4.2919	5.4274	6.8485	8.6231	10.834	17.000	26.461	32.918	40.874	62.668	95.396	216.54	478.90	1033.5	2180.0
26	1.2953	1.6734	2.1566	2.7725	3.5557	4.5494	5.8074	7.3964	9.3992	11.918	19.040	30.166	37.856	47.414	73.948	114.47	268.51	612.99	1364.3	2964.9
27	1.3082	1.7069	2.2213	2.8834	3.7335	4.8223	6.2139	7.9881	10.245	13.110	21.324	34.389	43.535	55.000	87.259	137.37	332.95	784.63	1800.9	4032.2
28	1.3213	1.7410	2.2879	2.9987	3.9201	5.1117	6.6488	8.6271	11.167	14.421	23.883	39.204	50.065	63.800	102.96	164.84	412.86	1004.3	2377.2	5483.8
29	1.3345	1.7758	2.3566	3.1187	4.1161	5.4184	7.1143	9.3173	12.172	15.863	26.749	44.693	57.575	74.008	121.50	197.81	511.95	1285.5	3137.9	7458.0
30	1.3478	1.8114	2.4273	3.2434	4.3219	5.7435	7.6123	10.062	13.267	17.449	29.959	50.950	66.211	85.849	143.37	237.37	634.81	1645.5	4142.0	10143.
40	1.4889	2.2080	3.2620	4.8010	7.0400	10.285	14.974	21.724	31.409	45.259	93.050	188.88	267.86	378.72	750.37	1469.7	5455.9	19426	66520	*
50	1.6446	2.6916	4.3839	7.1067	11.467	18.420	29.457	46.901	74.357	117.39	289.00	700.23	1083.6	1670.7	3927.3	9100.4	46890	*	*	*
60	1.8167	3.2810	5.8916	10.519	18.679	32.987	57.946	101.25	176.03	304.48	897.59	2595.9	4383.9	7370.1	20555	56347	*	*	*	*

*FVIF > 99,999

Sum of an Annuity of $1: FVIFA$_{r,n}$

Number of Periods	1%	2%	3%	4%	5%	6%	7%	8%	9%	10%	12%	14%	15%	16%	18%	20%	24%	28%	32%	36%
1	1.0000	1.0000	1.0000	1.0000	1.0000	1.0000	1.0000	1.0000	1.0000	1.0000	1.0000	1.0000	1.0000	1.0000	1.0000	1.0000	1.0000	1.0000	1.0000	1.0000
2	2.0100	2.0200	2.0300	2.0400	2.0500	2.0600	2.0700	2.0800	2.0900	2.1000	2.1200	2.1400	2.1500	2.1600	2.1800	2.2000	2.2400	2.2800	2.3200	2.3600
3	3.0301	3.0604	3.0909	3.1216	3.1525	3.1836	3.2149	3.2464	3.2781	3.3100	3.3744	3.4396	3.4725	3.5056	3.5724	3.6400	3.7776	3.9184	4.0624	4.2096
4	4.0604	4.1216	4.1836	4.2465	4.3101	4.3746	4.4399	4.5061	4.5731	4.6410	4.7793	4.9211	4.9934	5.0665	5.2154	5.3680	5.6842	6.0156	6.3624	6.7251
5	5.1010	5.2040	5.3091	5.4163	5.5256	5.6371	5.7507	5.8666	5.9847	6.1051	6.3528	6.6101	6.7424	6.8771	7.1542	7.4416	8.0484	8.6999	9.3983	10.146
6	6.1520	6.3081	6.4684	6.6330	6.8019	6.9753	7.1533	7.3359	7.5233	7.7156	8.1152	8.5355	8.7537	8.9775	9.4420	9.9299	10.980	12.135	13.405	14.798
7	7.2135	7.4343	7.6625	7.8983	8.1420	8.3938	8.6540	8.9228	9.2004	9.4872	10.089	10.730	11.066	11.413	12.141	12.915	14.615	16.533	18.695	21.126
8	8.2857	8.5830	8.8923	9.2142	9.5491	9.8975	10.259	10.636	11.028	11.435	12.299	13.232	13.726	14.240	15.327	16.499	19.122	22.163	25.678	29.731
9	9.3685	9.7546	10.159	10.582	11.026	11.491	11.978	12.487	13.021	13.579	14.775	16.085	16.785	17.518	19.085	20.798	24.712	29.369	34.895	41.435
10	10.462	10.949	11.463	12.006	12.577	13.180	13.816	14.486	15.192	15.937	17.548	19.337	20.303	21.321	23.521	25.958	31.643	38.592	47.061	57.351
11	11.566	12.168	12.807	13.486	14.206	14.971	15.783	16.645	17.560	18.531	20.654	23.044	24.349	25.732	28.755	32.150	40.237	50.398	63.121	78.998
12	12.682	13.412	14.192	15.025	15.917	16.869	17.888	18.977	20.140	21.384	24.133	27.270	29.001	30.850	34.931	39.580	50.894	65.510	84.320	108.43
13	13.809	14.680	15.617	16.626	17.713	18.882	20.140	21.495	22.953	24.522	28.029	32.088	34.351	36.786	42.218	48.496	64.109	84.852	112.30	148.47
14	14.947	15.973	17.086	18.291	19.598	21.015	22.550	24.214	26.019	27.975	32.392	37.581	40.504	43.672	50.818	59.195	80.496	109.61	149.23	202.92
15	16.096	17.293	18.598	20.023	21.578	23.276	25.129	27.152	29.360	31.772	37.279	43.842	47.580	51.659	60.965	72.035	100.81	141.30	197.99	276.97
16	17.257	18.639	20.156	21.824	23.657	25.672	27.888	30.324	33.003	35.949	42.753	50.980	55.717	60.925	72.939	87.442	126.01	181.86	262.35	377.69
17	18.430	20.012	21.761	23.697	25.840	28.212	30.840	33.750	36.973	40.544	48.883	59.117	65.075	71.673	87.068	105.93	157.25	233.79	347.30	514.66
18	19.614	21.412	23.414	25.645	28.132	30.905	33.999	37.450	41.301	45.599	55.749	68.394	75.836	84.140	103.74	128.11	195.99	300.25	459.44	700.93
19	20.810	22.840	25.116	27.671	30.539	33.760	37.379	41.446	46.018	51.159	63.439	78.969	88.211	98.603	123.41	154.74	244.03	385.32	607.47	954.27
20	22.019	24.297	26.870	29.778	33.066	36.785	40.995	45.762	51.160	57.275	72.052	91.024	102.44	115.37	146.62	186.68	303.60	494.21	802.86	1298.8
21	23.239	25.783	28.676	31.969	35.719	39.992	44.865	50.442	56.764	64.002	81.698	104.76	118.81	134.84	174.02	225.02	377.46	633.59	1060.7	1767.3
22	24.471	27.299	30.536	34.248	38.505	43.392	49.005	55.456	62.873	71.402	92.502	120.43	137.63	157.41	206.34	271.03	469.05	811.99	1401.2	2404.6
23	25.716	28.845	32.452	36.617	41.430	46.995	53.436	60.893	69.531	79.543	104.60	138.29	159.27	183.60	244.48	326.23	582.62	1040.3	1850.6	3271.3
24	26.973	30.421	34.426	39.082	44.502	50.815	58.176	66.764	76.789	88.497	118.15	158.65	184.16	213.97	289.49	392.48	723.46	1332.6	2443.8	4449.9
25	28.243	32.030	36.459	41.645	47.727	54.864	63.249	73.105	84.700	98.347	133.33	181.87	212.79	249.21	342.60	471.98	898.09	1706.8	3226.8	6052.9
26	29.525	33.670	38.553	44.311	51.113	59.156	68.676	79.954	93.323	109.18	150.33	208.33	245.71	290.08	405.27	567.37	1114.6	2185.7	4260.4	8233.0
27	30.820	35.344	40.709	47.084	54.669	63.705	74.483	87.350	102.72	121.09	169.37	238.49	283.56	337.50	479.22	681.85	1383.1	2798.7	5624.7	11197.9
28	32.129	37.051	42.930	49.967	58.402	68.528	80.697	95.338	112.96	134.20	190.69	272.88	327.10	392.50	566.48	819.22	1716.0	3583.3	7425.6	15230.2
29	32.450	38.792	45.218	52.966	62.322	73.689	87.346	103.96	124.13	148.63	214.58	312.09	377.16	456.30	669.44	984.06	2128.9	4587.6	9802.9	20714.1
30	34.784	40.568	47.576	56.084	66.438	79.058	94.460	113.28	136.30	164.49	241.33	356.78	434.74	530.31	790.94	1181.8	2640.9	5873.2	12940	28172.2
40	48.886	60.402	75.401	95.025	120.79	154.76	199.63	259.05	337.88	442.59	767.09	1342.0	1779.0	2360.7	4163.2	7343.8	22728	63977	*	*
50	64.463	84.579	112.79	152.66	209.34	290.33	406.52	573.76	815.08	1163.9	2400.0	4994.5	7217.7	10435	21813	45497	*	*	*	*
60	81.669	114.05	163.05	237.90	353.58	533.12	813.52	1253.2	1944.7	3034.8	7471.6	18535	29219	46057	*	*	*	*	*	*

*FVIFA > 99,999

Present Value of $1: PVIF$_{i,n}$

Period	1%	2%	3%	4%	5%	6%	7%	8%	9%	10%	12%	14%	15%	16%	18%	20%	24%	28%	32%	36%
1	.9901	.9804	.9709	.9615	.9524	.9434	.9346	.9259	.9174	.9091	.8929	.8772	.8696	.8621	.8475	.8333	.8065	.7813	.7576	.7353
2	.9803	.9612	.9426	.9246	.9070	.8900	.8734	.8573	.8417	.8264	.7972	.7695	.7561	.7432	.7182	.6944	.6504	.6104	.5739	.5407
3	.9706	.9423	.9151	.8890	.8638	.8396	.8163	.7938	.7722	.7513	.7118	.6750	.6575	.6407	.6086	.5787	.5245	.4768	.4348	.3975
4	.9610	.9238	.8885	.8548	.8227	.7921	.7629	.7350	.7084	.6830	.6355	.5921	.5718	.5523	.5158	.4823	.4230	.3725	.3294	.2923
5	.9515	.9057	.8626	.8219	.7835	.7473	.7130	.6806	.6499	.6209	.5674	.5194	.4972	.4761	.4371	.4019	.3411	.2910	.2495	.2149
6	.9420	.8880	.8375	.7903	.7462	.7050	.6663	.6302	.5963	.5645	.5066	.4556	.4323	.4104	.3704	.3349	.2751	.2274	.1890	.1580
7	.9327	.8706	.8131	.7599	.7107	.6651	.6227	.5835	.5470	.5132	.4523	.3996	.3759	.3538	.3139	.2791	.2218	.1776	.1432	.1162
8	.9235	.8535	.7894	.7307	.6768	.6274	.5820	.5403	.5019	.4665	.4039	.3506	.3269	.3050	.2660	.2326	.1789	.1388	.1085	.0854
9	.9143	.8368	.7664	.7026	.6446	.5919	.5439	.5002	.4604	.4241	.3606	.3075	.2843	.2630	.2255	.1938	.1443	.1084	.0822	.0628
10	.9053	.8203	.7441	.6756	.6139	.5584	.5083	.4632	.4224	.3855	.3220	.2697	.2472	.2267	.1911	.1615	.1164	.0847	.0623	.0462
11	.8963	.8043	.7224	.6494	.5847	.5268	.4751	.4289	.3875	.3505	.2875	.2366	.2149	.1954	.1619	.1346	.0938	.0662	.0472	.0340
12	.8874	.7885	.7014	.6246	.5568	.4970	.4440	.3971	.3555	.3186	.2567	.2076	.1869	.1685	.1372	.1122	.0757	.0517	.0357	.0250
13	.8787	.7730	.6810	.6006	.5303	.4688	.4150	.3677	.3262	.2897	.2292	.1821	.1625	.1452	.1163	.0935	.0610	.0404	.0271	.0184
14	.8700	.7579	.6611	.5775	.5051	.4423	.3878	.3405	.2992	.2633	.2046	.1597	.1413	.1252	.0985	.0779	.0492	.0316	.0205	.0135
15	.8613	.7430	.6419	.5553	.4810	.4173	.3624	.3152	.2745	.2394	.1827	.1401	.1229	.1079	.0835	.0649	.0397	.0247	.0155	.0099
16	.8528	.7284	.6232	.5339	.4581	.3936	.3387	.2919	.2519	.2176	.1631	.1229	.1069	.0930	.0708	.0541	.0320	.0193	.0118	.0073
17	.8444	.7142	.6050	.5134	.4363	.3714	.3166	.2703	.2311	.1978	.1456	.1078	.0929	.0802	.0600	.0451	.0258	.0150	.0089	.0054
18	.8360	.7002	.5874	.4936	.4155	.3503	.2959	.2502	.2120	.1799	.1300	.0946	.0808	.0691	.0508	.0376	.0208	.0118	.0068	.0038
19	.8277	.6864	.5703	.4746	.3957	.3305	.2765	.2317	.1945	.1635	.1161	.0829	.0703	.0596	.0431	.0313	.0168	.0092	.0051	.0029
20	.8195	.6730	.5537	.4564	.3769	.3118	.2584	.2145	.1784	.1486	.1037	.0728	.0611	.0514	.0365	.0261	.0135	.0072	.0039	.0021
25	.7798	.6095	.4776	.3751	.2953	.2330	.1842	.1460	.1160	.0923	.0588	.0378	.0304	.0245	.0160	.0105	.0046	.0021	.0010	.0005
30	.7419	.5521	.4120	.3083	.2314	.1741	.1314	.0994	.0754	.0573	.0334	.0196	.0151	.0116	.0070	.0042	.0016	.0006	.0002	.0001
40	.6717	.4529	.3066	.2083	.1420	.0972	.0668	.0460	.0318	.0221	.0107	.0053	.0037	.0026	.0013	.0007	.0002	.0001	*	*
50	.6080	.3715	.2281	.1407	.0872	.0543	.0339	.0213	.0132	.0085	.0035	.0014	.0009	.0006	.0003	.0001	*	*	*	*
60	.5504	.3048	.1697	.0951	.0535	.0303	.0173	.0099	.0057	.0033	.0011	.0004	.0002	.0001	*	*	*	*	*	*

*The factor is zero to four decimal places.

Appendix D

Present Value of an Annuity of $1: PVIFA$_{i,n}$

Number of payments	1%	2%	3%	4%	5%	6%	7%	8%	9%	10%	12%	14%	15%	16%	18%	20%	24%	28%	32%
1	0.9901	0.9804	0.9709	0.9615	0.9524	0.9434	0.9346	0.9259	0.9174	0.9091	0.8929	0.8772	0.8696	0.8621	0.8475	0.8333	0.8065	0.7813	0.7576
2	1.9704	1.9415	1.9135	1.8861	1.8594	1.8334	1.8080	1.7833	1.7591	1.7355	1.6901	1.6467	1.6257	1.6052	1.5656	1.5278	1.4568	1.3916	1.3315
3	2.9410	2.8839	2.8286	2.7751	2.7232	2.6730	2.6243	2.5771	2.5313	2.4869	2.4018	2.3216	2.2832	2.2459	2.1743	2.1065	1.9813	1.8684	1.7663
4	3.9020	3.8077	3.7171	3.6299	3.5460	3.4651	3.3872	3.3121	3.2397	3.1699	3.0373	2.9137	2.8550	2.7982	2.6901	2.5887	2.4043	2.2410	2.0957
5	4.8534	4.7135	4.5797	4.4518	4.3295	4.2124	4.1002	3.9927	3.8897	3.7908	3.6048	3.4331	3.3522	3.2743	3.1272	2.9906	2.7454	2.5320	2.3452
6	5.7955	5.6014	5.4172	5.2421	5.0757	4.9173	4.7665	4.6229	4.4859	4.3553	4.1114	3.8887	3.7845	3.6847	3.4976	3.3255	3.0205	2.7594	2.5342
7	6.7282	6.4720	6.2303	6.0021	5.7864	5.5824	5.3893	5.2064	5.0330	4.8684	4.5638	4.2883	4.1604	4.0386	3.8115	3.6046	3.2423	2.9370	2.6775
8	7.6517	7.3255	7.0197	6.7327	6.4632	6.2098	5.9713	5.7466	5.5348	5.3349	4.9676	4.6389	4.4873	4.3436	4.0776	3.8372	3.4212	3.0758	2.7860
9	8.5660	8.1622	7.7861	7.4353	7.1078	6.8017	6.5152	6.2469	5.9952	5.7590	5.3282	4.9464	4.7716	4.6065	4.3030	4.0310	3.5655	3.1842	2.8681
10	9.4713	8.9826	8.5302	8.1109	7.7217	7.3601	7.0236	6.7101	6.4177	6.1446	5.6502	5.2161	5.0188	4.8332	4.4941	4.1925	3.6819	3.2689	2.9304
11	10.3676	9.7858	9.2526	8.7605	8.3064	7.8869	7.4987	7.1390	6.8052	6.4951	5.9377	5.4527	5.2337	5.0286	4.6560	4.3271	3.7757	3.3351	2.9776
12	11.2551	10.5753	9.9540	9.3851	8.8633	8.3838	7.9427	7.5361	7.1607	6.8137	6.1944	5.6603	5.4206	5.1971	4.7932	4.4392	3.8514	3.3868	3.0133
13	12.1337	11.3484	10.6350	9.9856	9.3936	8.8527	8.3577	7.9038	7.4889	7.1034	6.4235	5.8424	5.5831	5.3423	4.9095	4.5327	3.9124	3.4272	3.0404
14	13.0037	12.1062	11.2961	10.5631	9.8986	9.2950	8.7455	8.2442	7.7862	7.3667	6.6282	6.0021	5.7245	5.4675	5.0081	4.6106	3.9616	3.4587	3.0609
15	13.8651	12.8493	11.9379	11.1184	10.3797	9.7122	9.1079	8.5595	8.0607	7.6061	6.8109	6.1422	5.8474	5.5755	5.0916	4.6755	4.0013	3.4834	3.0764
16	14.7179	13.5777	12.5611	11.6523	10.8378	10.1059	9.4466	8.8514	8.3126	7.8237	6.9740	6.2651	5.9542	5.6685	5.1724	4.7296	4.0333	3.5026	3.0882
17	15.5623	14.2919	13.1661	12.1657	11.2741	10.4773	9.7632	9.1216	8.5436	8.0216	7.1196	6.3729	6.0472	5.7487	5.2223	4.7746	4.0591	3.5177	3.0971
18	16.3983	14.9920	13.7535	12.6593	11.6896	10.8276	10.0591	9.3719	8.7556	8.2014	7.2497	6.4674	6.1280	5.8178	5.2732	4.8122	4.0799	3.5294	3.1039
19	17.2260	15.6785	14.3238	13.1339	12.0853	11.1581	10.3356	9.6036	8.9501	8.3649	7.3658	6.5504	6.1982	5.8775	5.3162	4.8435	4.0967	3.5386	3.1090
20	18.0456	16.3514	14.8775	13.5903	12.4622	11.4699	10.5940	9.8181	9.1285	8.5436	7.4694	6.6231	6.2593	5.9288	5.3527	4.8696	4.1103	3.5458	3.1129
25	22.0232	19.5235	17.4131	15.6221	14.0939	12.7834	11.6536	10.6748	9.8226	9.0770	7.8431	6.8729	6.4641	6.0971	5.4669	4.9476	4.1474	3.5640	3.1220
30	25.8077	22.3965	19.6004	17.2920	15.3725	13.7648	12.4090	11.2578	10.2737	9.4269	8.0552	7.0072	6.5660	6.1772	5.5168	4.9789	4.1601	3.5693	3.1242
40	32.8347	27.3555	23.1148	19.7928	17.1591	15.0463	13.3317	11.9246	10.7574	9.7791	8.2438	7.1050	6.6418	6.2335	5.5482	4.9966	4.1659	3.5712	3.1250
50	39.1961	31.4236	25.7298	21.4822	18.2559	15.7619	13.8007	12.2335	10.9617	9.9148	8.3045	7.1327	6.6605	6.2463	5.5541	4.9995	4.1666	3.5714	3.1250
60	44.9550	34.7609	27.8756	22.6235	18.9293	16.1614	14.0392	12.3766	11.0480	9.9672	8.3240	7.1401	6.6651	6.2492	5.5553	4.9999	4.1667	3.5714	3.1250

Appendix E

Normal Probability Distribution Table

Area of normal distribution that is z standard deviations to the left or right of the mean

Number of Standard Deviations from Mean (z)	Area to the Left or Right (One tail)	Number of Standard Deviations from Mean (z)	Area to the Left or Right (One tail)
0.00	.5000	1.55	.0606
0.05	.4801	1.60	.0548
0.10	.4602	1.65	.0495
0.15	.4404	1.70	.0446
0.20	.4207	1.75	.0401
0.25	.4013	1.80	.0359
0.30	.3821	1.85	.0322
0.35	.3632	1.90	.0287
0.40	.3446	1.95	.0256
0.45	.3264	2.00	.0228
0.50	.3085	2.05	.0202
0.55	.2912	2.10	.0179
0.60	.2743	2.15	.0158
0.65	.2578	2.20	.0139
0.70	.2420	2.25	.0122
0.75	.2264	2.30	.0107
0.80	.2119	2.35	.0094
0.85	.1977	2.40	.0082
0.90	.1841	2.45	.0071
0.95	.1711	2.50	.0062
1.00	.1577	2.55	.0054
1.05	.1469	2.60	.0047
1.10	.1357	2.65	.0040
1.15	.1251	2.70	.0035
1.20	.1151	2.75	.0030
1.25	.1056	2.80	.0026
1.30	.0968	2.85	.0022
1.35	.0885	2.90	.0019
1.40	.0808	2.95	.0016
1.45	.0735	3.00	.0013
1.50	.0668		

Index

477